Take the Next Step in Your IT Career

T0188720

Save 10%

on Exam Vouchers*

(up to a $35 value)

*Some restrictions apply. See web page for details.

CompTIA.

 SYBEX®

CompTIA®
Network+®
Study Guide
Sixth Edition

CompTIA®
Network+®
Study Guide
Exam N10-009
Sixth Edition

Todd Lammle

Jon Buhagiar

SYBEX®
A Wiley Brand

Acknowledgments

First and foremost, I want to thank Kenyon Brown (the acquisitions editor for this book) for helping me put this book together, helping with the timeline, and following up with any needs and requests. This book would not have been possible without him.

I want to thank Jon Buhagiar for his enormous contribution to this book and project. This CompTIA series is a difficult mountain to climb, and Jon was there with me every step of the way. He took away an enormous pressure on me so that I could concentrate on the meat of the chapters where I was needed most. Thank you, Jon!

Kim Wimpsett has been the development editor of this Sybex CompTIA series and the last four books. Thank you, Kim, for your patience and kindness and for working so hard on this book with me again, and I look forward to any book with you on the editorial board. For this edition, Kim filled the role of copy editor instead.

Caroline Define was the development editor of this edition of Sybex's CompTIA Network+ books. This was my first time working with Caroline, and she made it drama-free and easy!

Kim and Caroline demonstrated patience, kindness, and dedication to quality, and I'm glad to continue working with them.

Pete Gaughan was the managing editor, and Saravanan Dakshinamurthy and Magesh Elangovan were the production specialists. My thanks to you!

Todd Montgomery really came through when I was in a tight spot and helped me put some final touches on Chapters 16 and 17. Thank you, Todd—you're a lifesaver!

Chris Crayton tech edited and reviewed each topic in this guide, scrutinizing the material until we both agreed it was verifiably solid. Thank you, Chris!

—Todd Lammle

About the Authors

Todd Lammle is *the* authority on Cisco certification and internetworking and is Cisco certified in most Cisco certification categories. He is a world-renowned author, speaker, trainer, and consultant. Todd has three decades of experience working with LANs, WANs, and large enterprise licensed and unlicensed wireless networks. Lately, he's been implementing large Cisco security networks using Firepower/FTD, Thousand Eyes, CDO, and ISE, as well as Cloudflare Zero Trust networks.

His years of real-world experience are evident in his writing; he is not just an author but an experienced networking engineer with very practical experience from working on the largest networks in the world at such companies as Xerox, Hughes Aircraft, Texaco, AAA, Cisco, and Toshiba, among many others.

Todd has published more than 130 books, including the very popular *CCNA: Cisco Certified Network Associate Study Guide*, *CCNA Wireless Study Guide*, *CCNA Data Center Study Guide*, and *CCNP Security*—all from Sybex. He runs an international consulting and training company based in northern Idaho where he spends his free time in the mountains playing with his golden retrievers.

You can reach Todd through his website at www.lammle.com.

Jon Buhagiar is an information technology professional with more than two decades of experience in higher education. During the past 24 years, he has been responsible for network operations at a college in western Pennsylvania and has led several projects, such as virtualization (server and desktop), VoIP, Microsoft 365, Azure, and many other projects supporting the quality of education at the college. He has achieved several certifications from Cisco, CompTIA, and Microsoft, and has taught many of the certification paths. He is the author of several books, including Sybex's *CompTIA A+ Complete Study Guide: Exam 220-1101 and Exam 220-1102*, *CompTIA Network+ Review Guide: Exam N10-008*, and *CCNA Certification Practice Tests: Exam 200-301*.

About the Technical Editor

Chris Crayton, MCSE, CISSP, CASP+, CySA+, Cloud+, S+, N+, A+, ITF+, is a technical consultant, trainer, author, and industry-leading technical editor. He has worked as a computer technology and networking instructor, information security director, network administrator, network engineer, and PC specialist. Chris has served as technical editor and content contributor on numerous technical titles for several of the leading publishing companies. He has also been recognized with many professional and teaching awards.

Contents at a Glance

Introduction   *xxxv*

Assessment Test   *xlvi*

Chapter 1   Introduction to Networks   1

Chapter 2   The Open Systems Interconnection (OSI)
                   Reference Model   35

Chapter 3   Networking Connectors and Wiring Standards   61

Chapter 4   The Current Ethernet Specifications   101

Chapter 5   Networking Devices   133

Chapter 6   Introduction to the Internet Protocol   193

Chapter **7**   IP Addressing   241

Chapter 8   IP Subnetting, Troubleshooting IP,
                   and Introduction to NAT   271

Chapter 9   Introduction to IP Routing   319

Chapter 10   Routing Protocols   341

Chapter 11   Switching and Virtual LANs   379

Chapter 12   Wireless Networking   431

Chapter 13   Remote Network Access   489

Chapter 14   Using Statistics and Sensors to Ensure
                   Network Availability   509

Chapter 15   Organizational Documents and Policies   537

Chapter 16   High Availability and Disaster Recovery   575

Chapter 17   Data Center Architecture and Cloud Concepts   609

Chapter 18   Network Troubleshooting Methodology   643

Chapter 19   Network Software Tools and Commands   705

Chapter 20   Network Security Concepts   775

Chapter 21   Common Types of Attacks   813

Appendix A   Answers to Written Labs   859

Appendix B   Answers to Review Questions   873

Appendix C   Subnetting Class A   927

Index   935

Contents

Introduction   *xxxv*

Assessment Test   *xlvi*

Chapter 1   Introduction to Networks   1

First Things First: What's a Network?   2
    The Local Area Network   3
    Common Network Components   5
    Network Types   8
    Network Architecture: Peer-to-Peer or Client-Server?   12
Physical Network Topologies   14
    Bus Topology   15
    Star Topology   16
    Ring Topology   17
    Mesh Topology   18
    Point-to-Point Topology   19
    Point-to-Multipoint Topology   20
    Hybrid Topology   22
Topology Selection, Backbones, and Segments   22
    Selecting the Right Topology   23
    The Network Backbone   24
    Network Segments   25
    Service-Related Entry Points   25
    Service Provider Links   25
    Virtual Networking   25
    Three-Tiered Model   26
    Spine and Leaf   27
    Traffic Flow   28
Summary   29
Exam Essentials   29
Written Lab   30
Review Questions   31

**Chapter 2   The Open Systems Interconnection (OSI)
Reference Model   35**

Internetworking Models   36
    The Layered Approach   37
    Advantages of Reference Models   37

The Application Layer 40

The Presentation Layer 41

The Session Layer 41

The Transport Layer 41

The Network Layer 48

The Data Link Layer 50

The Physical Layer 52

Introduction to Encapsulation 53

Modulation Techniques 54

Summary 55

Exam Essentials 56

Written Lab 56

Review Questions 57

Chapter   3   Networking Connectors and Wiring Standards   61

Physical Media 63

Coaxial Cable 64

Twisted-Pair Cable 66

Twinaxial Cable 66

Fiber-Optic Cable 71

Transceivers 77

Media Converters 78

Serial Cables 80

Cable Properties 82

Transmission Speeds 82

Distance 82

Duplex 83

Noise Immunity (Security, EMI) 83

Frequency 83

Wiring Standards 84

T568A vs. T568B 85

Straight-Through Cable 86

Crossover Cable 87

Rolled/Rollover Cable 89

T1 Crossover Cable 89

Installing Wiring Distributions 92

MDF/IDF 92

Summary 94

Exam Essentials 95

Written Lab 95

Review Questions 97

Chapter	**4**	**The Current Ethernet Specifications**	**101**
		Network Basics	102
		Ethernet Basics	104
		Collision Domain	104
		Broadcast Domain	104
		CSMA/CD	105
		Broadband/Baseband	106
		Bit Rates vs. Baud Rate	107
		Wavelength	107
		Half- and Full-Duplex Ethernet	107
		Ethernet at the Data Link Layer	110
		Binary to Decimal and Hexadecimal Conversion	110
		Ethernet Addressing	114
		Ethernet Frames	114
		Ethernet at the Physical Layer	117
		Ethernet over Other Standards (IEEE 1905.1-2013)	123
		Ethernet over Power Line	124
		Ethernet over HDMI	125
		Summary	127
		Exam Essentials	127
		Written Lab	127
		Review Questions	129
Chapter	**5**	**Networking Devices**	**133**
		Common Network Connectivity Devices	135
		Network Interface Card	136
		Hub	138
		Bridge	138
		Switch	139
		Router	140
		Firewall	144
		IDS/IPS	145
		HIDS	145
		Access Point	146
		Wireless Range Extender	147
		Wireless LAN Controller	147
		Load Balancer	147
		Contention Methods	148
		Dynamic Host Configuration Protocol Server	150
		IPAM	156
		Other Specialized Devices	157
		Multilayer Switch	157
		Domain Name System Server	157

Network Time Protocols   166
Proxy Server   167
Encryption and Content Filtering   168
Analog Modem   169
Packet Shaper   170
VPN Concentrator/Headend   171
Media Converter   172
VoIP PBX   172
VoIP Endpoint   172
NGFW/Layer 7 Firewall   173
VoIP Gateway   173
Cable Modem   173
DSL Modem   173
Networked Devices   174
VoIP Phones   174
Printers   174
Physical Access Control Devices   174
Cameras   174
Heating Ventilation, and Air Conditioning
    (HVAC) Sensors   174
Internet of Things (IoT)   175
Industrial Control Systems   175
Planning and Implementing a Basic SOHO Network
Using Network Segmentation   175
Determining Requirements   176
Switches and Bridges at the Data Link Layer   183
Hubs at the Physical Layer   184
Environmental Considerations   185
Summary   186
Exam Essentials   186
Written Lab   187
Review Questions   189

Chapter   6   Introduction to the Internet Protocol   193

Introducing TCP/IP   195
A Brief History of TCP/IP   195
The DoD Model and TCP/IP   196
The Process/Application Layer Protocols   198
The Host-to-Host Layer Protocols   213
The Internet Layer Protocols   220
Data Encapsulation   230
Summary   234
Exam Essentials   235
Written Lab   236
Review Questions   237

Chapter   7   IP Addressing   241

IP Terminology   243
The Hierarchical IP Addressing Scheme   244
    Network Addressing   245
    Private IP Addresses (RFC 1918)   249
IPv4 Address Types   251
    Layer 2 Broadcasts   252
    Layer 3 Broadcasts   252
    Unicast Address   252
    Multicast Address (Class D)   252
Internet Protocol Version 6 (IPv6)   253
    Why Do We Need IPv6?   253
    The Benefits of and Uses for IPv6   254
    IPv6 Addressing and Expressions   255
    Shortened Expression   256
    Address Types   257
    Special Addresses   258
    Stateless Address Autoconfiguration (SLAAC)   259
    DHCPv6 (Stateful)   260
    Migrating to IPv6   260
Summary   263
Exam Essentials   264
Written Labs   265
    Written Lab 7.1   265
    Written Lab 7.2   266
Review Questions   267

Chapter   8   IP Subnetting, Troubleshooting IP, and Introduction to NAT   271

Subnetting Basics   273
    How to Create Subnets   274
    Subnet Masks   276
    Classless Inter-Domain Routing (CIDR)   276
    Subnetting Class C Addresses   279
    Subnetting Class B Addresses   289
Troubleshooting IP Addressing   296
    Determining IP Address Problems   299
Introduction to Network Address Translation (NAT)   304
    Types of Network Address Translation   306
    NAT Names   306
    How NAT Works   307
Summary   309
Exam Essentials   309
Written Lab   310
Review Questions   311

Chapter   9   Introduction to IP Routing   319

Routing Basics   320
The IP Routing Process   323
Testing Your IP Routing Understanding   329
Static and Dynamic Routing   331
Summary   334
Exam Essentials   334
Written Lab   335
Review Questions   336

Chapter   10   Routing Protocols   341

Routing Protocol Basics   343
    Administrative Distances   344
    Classes of Routing Protocols   346
Distance-Vector Routing Protocols   347
    Routing Information Protocol (RIP)   349
    RIP Version 2 (RIPv2)   349
    VLSMs and Discontiguous Networks   350
    EIGRP   353
    Border Gateway Protocol (BGP)   355
Link-State Routing Protocols   357
    Open Shortest Path First (OSPF)   357
    Intermediate System-to-Intermediate System (IS-IS)   360
High Available Routes   362
Advanced IPv6 Concepts   363
    Router Advertisement   363
    Neighbor Discovery Protocol   365
    Tunneling   366
    Dual Stack   369
IPv6 Routing Protocols   370
    RIPng   370
    EIGRPv6   371
    OSPFv3   371
Summary   371
Exam Essentials   372
Written Lab   372
Review Questions   375

Chapter   11   Switching and Virtual LANs   379

Networking Before Layer 2 Switching   381
Switching Services   385
    Limitations of Layer 2 Switching   386

Bridging vs. LAN Switching 386
Three Switch Functions at Layer 2 387
Distributed Switching 392
Spanning Tree Protocol 392
Spanning Tree Port States 394
STP Convergence 395
Rapid Spanning Tree Protocol 802.1w 396
Virtual LANs 397
VLAN Basics 398
Quality of Service 401
VLAN Memberships 402
Static VLANs 402
Dynamic VLANs 403
Identifying VLANs 403
VLAN Identification Methods 405
Routing Between VLANs 407
VLAN Trunking Protocol 409
VTP Modes of Operation 410
Do We Really Need to Put an IP Address on a Switch? 411
Switch Port Protection 414
Port Bonding 417
Device Hardening 418
Advanced Features of Switches 419
Power over Ethernet (802.3af, 802.3at) 419
Port Mirroring/Spanning (SPAN/RSPAN) 421
Jumbo Frames 424
Summary 424
Exam Essentials 424
Written Lab 425
Review Questions 426

Chapter 12 **Wireless Networking** **431**

Introduction to Wireless Technology 433
Cellular Technologies 436
The 802.11 Standards (Regulatory Impacts) 438
2.4 GHz (802.11b) 439
2.4 GHz (802.11g) 440
5 GHz (802.11a) 441
5 GHz (802.11h) 442
2.4 GHz/5 GHz (802.11n) 443
5 GHz (802.11ac) 444
Wi-Fi 6 (802.11ax) 444

Comparing 802.11 Standards   445
    Range and Speed Comparisons   446
Wireless Network Components   447
    Wireless Access Points   447
    Wireless Network Interface Card   448
    Wireless Antennas   448
Installing a Wireless Network   450
    Ad Hoc Mode: Independent Basic Service Set   451
    Infrastructure Mode: Basic Service Set identifier (BSSID)   452
    Wireless Controllers   453
    Guest Networks   455
    Captive Portals   456
    Mobile Hot Spots   456
    Signal Degradation   457
    Technologies That Facilitate the Internet of Things (IoT)   460
    Installing and Configuring WLAN Hardware   460
Site Survey   466
    Providing Capacity   468
    Multiple Floors   469
    Location-Based WLAN   470
    Site Survey Tools   470
Wireless Security   471
    Wireless Threats   471
    Open Access   475
    Service Set Identifiers, Wired Equivalent Privacy, and
        Media Access Control Address Authentication   476
    Geofencing   477
    Remote Authentication Dial-In User Service (802.1X)   477
    Temporal Key Integrity Protocol   478
    Wi-Fi Protected Access or WPA2 Pre-Shared Key   479
Summary   482
Exam Essentials   483
Written Lab   484
Review Questions   485

Chapter   13   Remote Network Access   489

Site-to-Site VPN   490
Client-to-Site VPN   491
    Clientless VPN   491
    Split Tunnel vs. Full Tunnel   491
Remote Desktop Connection   493
    Remote Desktop Protocol   493
    RDP Gateway   495

Virtual Network Computing 495
Virtual Desktop 496
Connection Methods 496
Secure Shell 496
Graphical User Interface 497
Application Programming Interface 498
Console/Rolled Serial Cable 499
Jump Box/Host 501
Where Should You Implement a Jump Box/Host? 501
In-Band vs. Out-of-Band Management 502
Summary 502
Exam Essentials 502
Written Lab 503
Review Questions 504

Chapter	14	**Using Statistics and Sensors to Ensure Network Availability**	**509**

Performance Monitoring/Metrics/Sensors 511
Device/Chassis 511
Network Metrics 513
Additional Monitoring Solutions 515
Baseline Metrics 515
Traffic Analysis 515
Performance Monitoring 516
Availability Monitoring 516
Configuration Monitoring 517
SNMP 518
Agent 518
NMS 519
Commands 519
Community Name 521
Versions 521
OIDs and the MIB 522
Authentication 522
Application Programming Interface Integration 523
Protocol Analyzer/Packet Capture 524
Port Mirroring 524
Flow Data 525
Log Aggregation 526
Network Device Logs 526
Log Reviews 527
Syslog 528
SIEM 531

Summary	532
Exam Essentials	532
Written Lab	532
Review Questions	534

Chapter   15   Organizational Documents and Policies   537

Plans and Procedures	539
Change Management	540
Incident Response Plan	542
Disaster Recovery Plan	542
Business Continuity Plan	543
Inventory Management	543
System Life Cycle	544
Standard Operating Procedures	544
Hardening and Security Policies	545
Acceptable Use Policy	545
Password Policy	546
Bring Your Own Device Policy	547
Remote Access Policy	547
Onboarding and Offboarding Policy	547
Patch Management	548
Driver/Firmware Updates	548
Security Policy	548
Data Loss Prevention	553
Common Documentation	554
Physical Network Diagram	554
Logical Network Diagram	560
Wiring Diagram	560
Layered Network Diagram	562
Site Survey Report	562
Audit and Assessment Report	563
Baseline Configurations	565
IP Address Management	566
Common Agreements	566
Nondisclosure Agreement	566
Service-Level Agreement	567
Memorandum of Understanding	567
Summary	568
Exam Essentials	568
Written Lab	568
Review Questions	570

Chapter	**16**	**High Availability and Disaster Recovery**	**575**
		Load Balancing	576
		Multipathing	577
		Network Interface Card (NIC) Teaming	578
		Redundant Hardware/Clusters	579
		Switches	579
		Routers	581
		Firewalls	583
		Servers	583
		Clusters	586
		Mean Time to Repair	586
		Mean Time Between Failure	587
		Facilities and Infrastructure Support	587
		Uninterruptible Power Supply	587
		Power Distribution Units	588
		Generator	588
		HVAC	589
		Fire Suppression	590
		Redundancy and High Availability Concepts	591
		Disaster Recovery Sites	592
		Active/Active vs. Active/Passive	593
		Backups	600
		Network Device Backup/Restore	601
		Recovery	601
		Testing	602
		Tabletop Exercises	602
		Validation Tests	602
		Summary	603
		Exam Essentials	603
		Written Lab	604
		Review Questions	605
Chapter	**17**	**Data Center Architecture and Cloud Concepts**	**609**
		Cloud Computing	611
		Characteristics of a Cloud	612
		Cloud Delivery Models	613
		Types of Services	616
		Network Function Virtualization	618
		Virtual Private Cloud	619
		Connectivity Options	620
		Cloud Gateways	621
		Multitenancy	622

Elasticity   622
Scalability   623
Network Security Groups   623
Network Security Lists   623
Security Implications/Considerations   623
Relationship Between Local and Cloud Resources   624
Infrastructure as Code   625
Automation/Orchestration   625
Source Control   627
Software-Defined Networking   628
Benefits of Software-Defined Networking   628
Components of Software-Defined Networking   629
Virtual Extensible Local Area Network   633
Layer 2 Encapsulation Limitations Addressed by VXLAN   633
Data Center Interconnect   633
Zero Trust Architecture   633
Policy-Based Authentication   634
Authorization   634
Least Privilege Access   634
Secure Access Secure Edge/Security Service Edge   634
SASE   634
SSE   635
Summary   635
Exam Essentials   636
Written Lab   636
Review Questions   638

Chapter   18   **Network Troubleshooting Methodology**   **643**

Narrowing Down the Problem   646
Did You Check the Super Simple Stuff?   647
Is Hardware or Software Causing the Problem?   651
Is It a Workstation or a Server Problem?   651
Which Segments of the Network Are Affected?   652
Is It Bad Cabling?   652
Cable Considerations   653
Cable Application   654
Troubleshooting Steps   666
Step 1: Identify the Problem   667
Step 2: Establish a Theory of Probable Cause   671
Step 3: Test the Theory to Determine the Cause   686
Step 4: Establish a Plan of Action to Resolve
    the Problem and Identify Potential Effects   689
Step 5: Implement the Solution or Escalate as Necessary   691

Step 6: Verify Full System Functionality and
Implement Preventative Measures if Applicable 694
Step 7: Document Findings, Actions, Outcomes,
and Lessons Learned Throughout the Process 694
Troubleshooting Tips 695
Don't Overlook the Small Stuff 695
Prioritize Your Problems 695
Check the Software Configuration 696
Don't Overlook Physical Conditions 697
Don't Overlook Cable Problems 698
Check for Viruses 698
Summary 699
Exam Essentials 699
Written Lab 700
Review Questions 701

Chapter   19   Network Software Tools and Commands   705

Software Tools 707
Protocol Analyzer/Packet Capture 707
Bandwidth Speed Testers 708
Port Scanners 710
NetFlow Analyzers 710
Trivial File Transfer Protocol Server 711
Connectivity Software 711
IP Scanner 712
Using *traceroute* 712
Using *ipconfig*, *ifconfig*, and *ip* 715
Using the *ipconfig* Utility 716
Using the *ifconfig* Utility 720
Using the *ip* Utility 720
Using the *iptables* Utility 721
Examples of *iptables* 721
Using the *ping* Utility 722
The Address Resolution Protocol 725
The Windows ARP Table 725
Using the *arp* Utility 726
Using the *nslookup* Utility 729
Resolving Names with the Hosts File 731
Using the *mtr* Command *(pathping)* 732
Using the Nmap Utility 734
Using the *route* Command 735
Using the *route* Command Options 736
Some Examples of the *route* Command 738

Using the *netstat* Utility   738
   The *–e* Switch   742
   The *–r* Switch   743
   The *–s* Switch   743
   The *–p* Switch   743
   The *–n* Switch   745
Using *tcpdump*   747
   Examples of Using *tcpdump*   747
Basic Networking Device Commands   748
   show running-config (Show Run)   748
   show config   749
   Cisco Discovery Protocol   749
   show ip route (route Command in Windows) 752
   show version   753
   show inventory   754
   show switch   755
   show mac-address-table   756
   show interface   756
   show arp   760
   show vlan   760
   show power   762
Hardware Tools   762
   Toner/Toner Probe   763
   Cable Tester   764
   Taps   765
   Wi-Fi Analyzers   765
   Visual Fault Locator   766
Summary   766
Exam Essentials   767
Written Lab   768
Review Questions   769

Chapter 20   Network Security Concepts   775

Common Security Terminology   777
   Threats and Risk   778
   Vulnerability   779
   Exploit   781
   Confidentiality, Integrity, and Availability 782
   Encryption   783
   Certificates   785
AAA Model   790
   Authentication   790

Authorization 798

Accounting 800

Regulatory Compliance 801

Policies, Processes, and Procedures 804

Audit 805

Summary 805

Exam Essentials 806

Written Lab 807

Review Questions 808

Chapter   21   Common Types of Attacks   813

Technology-Based Attacks 817

Denial of Service/Distributed Denial of Service 817

DNS Poisoning/Spoofing 820

VLAN Hopping 821

ARP Spoofing/Poisoning 821

Rogue Devices and Services 822

Password Attacks 824

MAC Spoofing 825

IP Spoofing 826

MAC Flooding 826

Malware 826

Human and Environmental 829

Social Engineering 829

Phishing 830

Environmental 830

Hardening Security 831

Device Gardening 832

Key Management 834

Access Control Lists 835

Content Filtering 837

Implementing Network Segmentation 837

Network Segmentation Enforcement 837

Screened Subnet 838

802.1X 840

NAC 840

MAC Filtering 841

Port Security 842

Internet of Things 843

Industrial Control Systems/Supervisory Control
and Data Acquisition 844

Separate Private/Public Networks   846
Honeypot/Honeynet   846
Bring Your Own Device   846
Guest Network Isolation   847
Physical Security Concepts   847
Video Surveillance   847
Door Locks   849
Equipment Locks   850
Summary   851
Exam Essentials   852
Written Lab   853
Review Questions   854

Appendix   A   Answers to Written Labs   859

Chapter 1: Introduction to Networks   860
Chapter 2: The Open Systems Interconnection (OSI)
   Reference Model   860
Chapter 3: Networking Connectors and Wiring Standards 860
Chapter 4: The Current Ethernet Specifications   861
Chapter 5: Networking Devices   862
Chapter 6: Introduction to the Internet Protocol   862
Chapter 7: IP Addressing   863
Chapter 8: IP Subnetting, Troubleshooting IP,
   and Introduction to NAT   864
Chapter 9: Introduction to IP Routing   865
Chapter 10: Routing Protocols   865
Chapter 11: Switching and Virtual LANs   867
Chapter 12: Wireless Networking   867
Chapter 13: Remote Network Access   868
Chapter 14: Using Statistics and Sensors to Ensure
   Network Availability   868
Chapter 15: Organizational Documents and Policies   869
Chapter 16: High Availability and Disaster Recovery 870
Chapter 17: Data Center Architecture and Cloud Concepts 870
Chapter 18: Network Troubleshooting Methodology   871
Chapter 19: Network Software Tools and Commands   871
Chapter 20: Network Security Concepts   872
Chapter 21: Common Types of Attacks   872

Appendix   B   Answers to Review Questions   873

Chapter 1: Introduction to Networks   874
Chapter 2: The Open Systems Interconnection (OSI)
   Reference Model   876

Chapter 3: Networking Connectors and Wiring Standards   878
Chapter 4: The Current Ethernet Specifications   881
Chapter 5: Networking Devices   883
Chapter 6: Introduction to the Internet Protocol   885
Chapter 7: IP Addressing   888
Chapter 8: IP Subnetting, Troubleshooting IP, and
  Introduction to NAT   890
Chapter 9: Introduction to IP Routing   892
Chapter 10: Routing Protocols   895
Chapter 11: Switching and Virtual LANs   897
Chapter 12: Wireless Networking   900
Chapter 13: Remote Network Access   902
Chapter 14: Using Statistics and Sensors to Ensure
  Network Availability   905
Chapter 15: Organizational Documents and Policies   907
Chapter 16: High Availability and Disaster Recovery   910
Chapter 17: Data Center Architecture and Cloud Concepts   912
Chapter 18: Network Troubleshooting Methodology   915
Chapter 19: Network Software Tools and Commands   917
Chapter 20: Network Security Concepts   920
Chapter 21: Common Types of Attacks   922

Appendix   C   Subnetting Class A   927

Subnetting Practice Examples: Class A Addresses   928
  Practice Example #1A: 255.255.0.0 (/16)   929
  Practice Example #2A: 255.255.240.0 (/20)   929
  Practice Example #3A: 255.255.255.192 (/26)   930
Subnetting in Your Head: Class A Addresses   930
Written Lab C.1   931
Written Lab C.2   932
Answers to Written Lab C.1   932
Answers to Written Lab C.2   933

Index   935

Table of Exercises

Exercise **1.1** Identifying Common Network Components 14

Exercise **2.1** Investigating the Applications and the OSI Model 53

Exercise **3.1** Investigating Computer Connections. 84

Exercise **3.2** Investigating Ethernet Cables. 92

Exercise **4.1** Converting Binary, Decimal, and Hexadecimal. 117

Exercise **4.2** Exploring Ethernet Standards 126

Exercise **5.1** Experimenting with DHCP 155

Exercise **5.2** Examining DNS Entries. 164

Exercise **6.1** Examining Port Numbers 234

Exercise **7.1** Identifying IP Addresses 263

Exercise **8.1** Examining IP Address and Subnet Masks. 278

Exercise **9.1** Examining the ARP Cache. 329

Exercise **10.1** Examining OS Routing 361

Exercise **11.1** Understanding Switch Functions. 397

Exercise **12.1** Examining Wireless Settings 466

Exercise **12.2** Performing a Simple Site Survey. 467

Exercise **13.1** Experimenting with RDP. 494

Exercise **14.1** Working with Performance Monitor. 517

Exercise **15.1** Creating Standard Operating Procedures 545

Exercise **15.2** Documenting Your Network 562

Exercise **16.1** Designing Facilities and Infrastructure 591

Exercise **17.1** Exploring Cloud Services 624

Exercise **18.1** Examining IP Configuration 697

Exercise **19.1** Examining DNS with *nslookup*. 731

Exercise **19.2** Examining Connections with *netstat*. 747

Exercise **20.1** Identifying Vulnerabilities 780

Exercise **20.2** Examining Self-Signed Certificates 789

Exercise **21.1** Testing Your Antimalware 829

Exercise **21.2** Experimenting with Social Engineering 831

Exercise **21.3** Planning Video Surveillance. 849

Introduction

If you're like most of us in the networking community, you probably have one or more network certifications. If that's you, you're very wise in choosing a CompTIA Network+ (N10-009) certification to proudly add to your repertoire because that achievement will make you all the more valuable as an employee.

In these challenging economic times, keeping ahead of the competition—even standing out among your present colleagues—could make a big difference in whether you gain a promotion or possibly keep your job instead of being the one who gets laid off! Or maybe this is your first attempt at certification because you've decided to venture into a new career in information technology (IT). You've realized that getting into the IT sector is a good way to go because as the Information Age marches on, the demand for knowledgeable professionals in this dynamic field will only intensify dramatically.

Either way, certification is one of the best things you can do for your career if you are working in, or want to break into, the networking profession because it proves that you know what you're talking about regarding the subjects in which you're certified. It also powerfully endorses you as a professional in a way that's very similar to a physician being board certified in a certain area of expertise.

In this book, you'll find out what the CompTIA Network+ exam is all about because each chapter covers part of the exam. I've included some great review questions at the end of each chapter to help crystallize the information you learned and solidly prepare you to ace the exam.

A really cool thing about working in IT is that it's constantly evolving, so there are always new things to learn and fresh challenges to master. Once you obtain your Network+ certification and discover that you're interested in taking it further by getting into more complex networking (and making more money), the Cisco CCNA certification is definitely your next step; you can get the skinny on that and even more in-depth certifications on my blog at www.lammle.com.

For Network+ training with Todd Lammle, both instructor-led and online, please see www.lammle.com.

What Is the Network+ Certification?

Network+ is a certification developed by the Computing Technology Industry Association (CompTIA) that exists to provide resources and education for the computer and technology community. This is the same body that developed the A+ exam for PC technicians.

The Network+ exam was designed to test the skills of network technicians with 9 to 12 months of experience in the IT networking field. It tests areas of networking technologies, such as the definition of a protocol, the Open Systems Interconnection (OSI) model and its layers, and the concepts of network design and implementation—the minimum knowledge required for working on a network and some integral prerequisites for network design and implementation.

Why Become Network+ Certified?

Because CompTIA is a well-respected developer of vendor-neutral industry certifications, becoming Network+ certified proves you're competent in the specific areas covered by the Network+ exam objectives.

Four major benefits are associated with becoming Network+ certified:

Proof of Professional Achievement   Networking professionals are pretty competitive when it comes to collecting more certifications than their peers. And because the Network+ certification broadly covers the entire field of networking, technicians want this certification a lot more than they want just Microsoft certifications—Network+ is a lot more prestigious and valuable. Because it's rare to gain something that's worth a lot with little effort, I'll be honest—preparing for the Network+ exam isn't exactly a lazy day at the beach. (However, beaches do happen to be really high on my personal list of great places to study!) And people in IT know that it isn't all that easy to pass the Network+ exam, so they'll definitely respect you more and know that you've achieved a certain level of expertise about vendor-independent, networking-related subjects.

Opportunity for Advancement   We all like to get ahead in our careers—advancement results in more responsibility and prestige, and it usually means a fatter paycheck, greater opportunities, and additional options. In the IT sector, a great way to make sure all that good stuff happens is by earning a lot of technology certifications, including Network+.

Fulfillment of Training Requirements   Network+, because of its wide-reaching industry support, is recognized as a baseline of networking information. Some companies actually specify the possession of a Network+ certification as a job requirement before they'll even consider hiring you, or it may be specified as a goal to be met before your next on the job review.

Customer Confidence   As companies discover the CompTIA advantage, they will undoubtedly require qualified staff to achieve these certifications. Many companies outsource their work to consulting firms with experience working with security. Firms that have certified staff have a definite advantage over firms that don't.

How to Become Network+ Certified

As this book goes to press, Pearson VUE is the sole Network+ exam provider. The following is the necessary contact information and exam-specific details for registering. Exam pricing might vary by country or by CompTIA membership.

Vendor	Website	Phone Number
Pearson VUE	`www.pearsonvue.com/comptia`	US and Canada: 877-551-PLUS (7587)

When you schedule the exam, you'll receive instructions regarding appointment and cancellation procedures, ID requirements, and information about the testing center location. In addition, you'll receive a registration and payment confirmation letter. Exams can be scheduled up to six weeks out or as soon as the next day (or, in some cases, even the same day).

 Exam prices and codes may vary based on the country in which the exam is administered. For detailed pricing and exam registration procedures, refer to CompTIA's website at www.comptia.org.

After you've successfully passed your Network+ exam, CompTIA will award you a certification. Within four to six weeks of passing the exam, you'll receive your official CompTIA Network+ certificate and ID card. (If you don't receive these within eight weeks of taking the test, contact CompTIA directly using the information found in your registration packet.)

Tips for Taking the Network+ Exam

Here are some general tips for taking your exam successfully:

- Bring two forms of ID with you. One must be a photo ID, such as a driver's license. The other can be a major credit card or a passport. Both forms must include a signature.

- Arrive early at the exam center so you can relax and review your study materials, particularly tables and lists of exam-related information. After you are ready to enter the testing room, you will need to leave everything outside; you won't be able to bring any materials into the testing area.

- Read the questions very carefully. Don't be tempted to jump to an early conclusion. Make sure you know exactly what each question is asking.

- Don't leave any unanswered questions. Unanswered questions are scored against you. There will be questions with multiple correct responses. When there is more than one correct answer, a message at the bottom of the screen will prompt you to either "choose two" or "choose all that apply." Be sure to read the messages displayed to know how many correct answers you must choose.

- When answering multiple-choice questions, you're not sure about, use a process of elimination to get rid of the obviously incorrect answers first. Doing so will improve your odds if you need to make an educated guess.

- On form-based tests (nonadaptive) because the hard questions will take the most time, save them for last. You can move forward and backward through the exam.

Who Should Read This Book?

You—if want to pass the Network+ exam, and pass it confidently! This book is chock-full of the exact information you need and directly maps to Network+ exam objectives, so if you use it to study for the exam, your odds of passing shoot way up.

And in addition to including every bit of knowledge you need to learn to pass the exam, I've included some really great tips and solid wisdom to equip you even further to successfully work in the real IT world.

What Does This Book Cover?

This book covers everything you need to know to pass the CompTIA Network+ exam. But in addition to studying the book, it's a good idea to practice on an actual network if you can.

Here's a list of the 21 chapters in this book:

Chapter 1, "Introduction to Networks" This chapter includes an introduction to networks and an overview of the most common physical network topologies in today's networks.

Chapter 2, "The Open Systems Interconnection (OSI) Reference Model" This chapter covers the OSI model, what it is, what happens at each of its layers, and how each layer works.

Chapter 3, "Networking Connectors and Wiring Standards" This chapter covers the various networking media and topologies, plus the cable types and properties used in today's networks.

Chapter 4, "The Current Ethernet Specifications" This chapter covers how a basic Ethernet LAN works and describes and categorizes the different Ethernet specifications.

Chapter 5, "Networking Devices" You need to understand all the various devices used in today's networks, and this chapter will describe how hubs, routers, and switches and some other devices work within a network.

Chapter 6, "Introduction to the Internet Protocol"   This is your introduction to the all-important IP protocol stack.

Chapter 7, "IP Addressing"   This chapter will take up from where Chapter 6 left off and move into IP addressing. It also contains information about public versus private addressing and DHCP.

Chapter 8, "IP Subnetting, Troubleshooting IP, and Introduction to NAT"   Beginning where Chapter 7 ends, we'll be tackling IP subnetting in this one. But no worries here—I've worked hard to make this not-so-popular-yet-vital topic as painless as possible.

Chapter 9, "Introduction to IP Routing"   This introduction to routing basically covers what routers do and how they do it. This chapter, along with Chapters 10 and 11, covers routing and switching in much more detail than necessary to meet the CompTIA Network+ objectives because this knowledge is so critical to grasp when working with today's networks.

Chapter 10, "Routing Protocols"   This chapter describes the protocols that run on routers and how they update routing tables to create a working network map.

Chapter 11, "Switching and Virtual LANs"   This chapter covers layer 2 switching, the Spanning Tree Protocol (STP), and virtual LANs (vLANS). I went deeper than needed for the exam with the routing chapters, and I'll cover switching and virtual LANs (which are also vital in today's corporate networks) more thoroughly.

Chapter 12, "Wireless Networking"   Because wireless is so essential for both home and business networks today, this chapter is loaded with all the information you need to be successful at wireless networking at home and work.

Chapter 13, "Remote Network Access"   In this chapter you'll learn the importance of providing both fault tolerance and high availability. You'll also learn about VPN architectures. These include site-to-site VPNs, client-to-site VPNs, clientless VPNs, split tunnel versus complete VPN, and SSH VPNs.

Chapter 14, "Using Statistics and Sensors to Ensure Network Availability"   In this chapter, you'll learn what sort of data you should be monitoring and some of the ways to do so.

Chapter 15, "Organizational Documents and Policies"   In this chapter, you'll learn that plans and procedures should be developed to manage operational issues such as change management, incident response, disaster recovery, business continuity, and the system life cycle. You'll also learn the standard operating procedures that should be developed to guide each of these processes.

Chapter 16, "High Availability and Disaster Recovery"   In this chapter, you will learn about redundancy concepts, fault tolerance, and the disaster recovery process.

Chapter 17, "Data Center Architecture and Cloud Concepts"   In this chapter, I'll talk a lot about the documentation aspects of network administration. The chapter will start off discussing physical diagrams and schematics and move on to the logical form as well as configuration-management documentation. You'll learn about the importance of these diagrams, the simple to complex forms they can take, and the tools used to create them—from pencil and paper to high-tech AutoCAD schematics. You'll also find out a great deal about creating performance baselines.

Chapter 18, "Network Troubleshooting Methodology"   In this chapter, you'll learn about all things troubleshooting, such as how to sleuth out and solve a lot of network problems.

Chapter 19, "Network Software Tools and Commands"   This chapter introduces the network tools you will use to help you run your networks. Specialized tasks require specialized tools, and installing network components is no exception. We use some of these tools, such as network scanners, every day.

Chapter 20, "Network Security Concepts"   In this chapter, you will learn the basic concepts, terms, and principles that all network professionals should understand to secure an enterprise network.

Chapter 21, "Common Types of Attacks"   In this chapter you will learn the common types of attacks that all network professionals should understand to secure an enterprise network.

What's Included in the Book

I've included several study tools throughout the book:

Assessment Test   At the end of this introduction is an assessment test that you can use to check your readiness for the exam. Take this test before reading the book; it will help you determine the areas you might need to brush up on. The answers to the assessment test questions appear on a separate page after the last question of the test. Each answer includes an explanation in which the material appears.

Objective Map and Opening List of Objectives   Later in this introduction is an objective map showing you where each exam objective is covered in this book. In addition, each chapter opens with a list of its exam objectives. Use these to see exactly where each of the exam topics is covered.

Exam Essentials   Each chapter includes several exam essentials. These are the key topics you should take from the chapter regarding areas to focus on when preparing for the exam.

Written Lab   Each chapter includes a written lab. These are short exercises that map to the exam objectives. Answers to these can be found in Appendix A.

Chapter Review Questions   To test your knowledge as you progress through the book, review questions are at the end of each chapter. As you finish each chapter, answer the review questions, and then check your answers—the correct answers and explanations are in Appendix B. You can reread the section that deals with each question you got wrong to ensure that you answer correctly the next time you're tested on the material.

Interactive Online Learning Environment and Test Bank

The interactive online learning environment that accompanies *CompTIA Network+ Study Guide: Exam N10-009* 6th edition provides a test bank with study tools to help you prepare for the certification exam—and increase your chances of passing it the first time! The test bank includes the following tools:

Sample Tests   All of the questions in this book are provided, including the assessment test, which you'll find at the end of this introduction, and the chapter tests, which include the review questions at the end of each chapter. In addition, there are two practice exams. Use these questions to test your knowledge of the study guide material. The online test bank runs on multiple devices.

Flashcards   Approximately 200 questions are provided in digital flashcard format (a question followed by a single correct answer). You can use the flashcards to reinforce your learning and provide last-minute test prep before the exam.

Glossary   A glossary of key terms from this book and their definitions is available as a fully searchable PDF.

Go to www.wiley.com/go/netplustestprep to register and gain access to this interactive online learning environment and test bank with study tools.

Like all exams, the Network+ certification from CompTIA is updated periodically and may eventually be retired or replaced. At some point after CompTIA is no longer offering this exam, the old editions of our books and online tools will be retired. If you have purchased this book after the exam was retired, or are attempting to register in the Sybex online learning environment after the exam was retired, please know that we make no guarantees that this exam's online Sybex tools will be available once the exam is no longer available.

How to Use This Book

If you want a solid foundation for the serious effort of preparing for the Network+ exam, then look no further because I've spent countless hours putting together this book with the sole intention of helping you pass it!

This book is loaded with valuable information, and you will get the most out of your study time if you understand how I put the book together. Here's a list that describes how to approach studying:

1. Take the assessment test immediately following this introduction. (The answers are at the end of the test, but no peeking!) It's okay if you don't know any of the answers—that's what this book is for. Carefully read over the explanation for any question you get wrong and make note of the chapter where that material is covered.

2. Study each chapter carefully, making sure you fully understand the information and the exam objectives listed at the beginning of each one. Again, pay extra-close attention to any chapter that includes material covered in questions you missed on the assessment test.

3. Complete the written lab at the end of each chapter. Do *not* skip these written exercises because they directly map to the CompTIA objectives and what you've got to have nailed down to meet them.

4. Answer all the review questions related to each chapter. Specifically note any questions that confuse you, and study the corresponding sections of the book again. And don't just skim these questions—make sure you understand each answer completely.

5. Try your hand at the practice exams. Before you take your test, be sure to visit my website for questions, videos, audios, and other useful information.

6. Test yourself using all the electronic flashcards. This is a brand-new and updated flashcard program to help you prepare for the latest CompTIA Network+ exam, and it is a really great study tool.

I tell you no lies—learning every bit of the material in this book is going to require applying yourself with a good measure of discipline. So try to set aside the same time period every day to study, and select a comfortable and quiet place to do so. If you work hard, you will be surprised at how quickly you learn this material.

If you follow the steps listed here and study with the review questions, practice exams, electronic flashcards, and all the written labs, you would almost have to try to fail the CompTIA Network+ exam. However, studying for the Network+ exam is like training for a marathon—if you don't go for a good run every day, you're not likely to finish very well.

N10-009 Exam Objectives

Speaking of objectives, you're probably pretty curious about those, right? CompTIA asked groups of IT professionals to fill out a survey rating the skills they felt were important in their jobs, and the results were grouped into objectives for the exam and divided into five domains.

This table gives you the extent by percentage that each domain is represented on the actual examination.

Objective	Percentage of Exam
1.0 Networking Concepts	23%
2.0 Network Implementation	20%
3.0 Network Operations	19%
4.0 Network Security	14%
5.0 Network Troubleshooting	24%

Objective Map

The following table shows where each objective is covered in the book.

Objective Number	Objective	Chapter
1.0	**Networking Concepts**	
	1.1 Explain concepts related to the Open Systems Interconnection (OSI) reference model.	Chapter 2, Chapter 6
	1.2 Compare and contrast networking appliances, applications, and functions.	Chapter 10
	1.3 Summarize cloud concepts and connectivity options.	Chapter 17
	1.4 Explain common networking ports, protocols, services, and traffic types.	Chapter 6, Chapter 8
	1.5 Compare and contrast transmission media and transceivers.	Chapter 3, Chapter 4, Chapter 12
	1.6 Compare and contrast network topologies, architectures, and types.	Chapter 1
	1.7 Given a scenario, use appropriate 1Pv4 network addressing.	Chapter 7, Chapter 8
	1.8 Summarize evolving use cases for modern network environments.	Chapter 7, Chapter 10, Chapter 17
2.0	**Network Implementation**	
	2.1 Explain characteristics of routing technologies.	Chapter 8, Chapter 9, Chapter 10

Objective Number	Objective	Chapter
	2.2 Given a scenario, configure switching technologies and features.	Chapter 11
	2.3 Given a scenario, select and configure wireless devices and technologies.	Chapter 5, Chapter 12
	2.4 Explain important factors of physical installations.	Chapter 16
3.0	**Network Operations**	
	3.1 Explain the purpose of organizational processes and procedures.	Chapter 15
	3.2 Given a scenario, use network monitoring technologies.	Chapter 14
	3.3 Explain disaster recovery (DR) concepts.	Chapter 16
	3.4 Given a scenario, implement IPv4 and IPv6 network services.	Chapter 5, Chapter 7
	3.5 Compare and contrast network access and management methods.	Chapter 13
4.0	**Network Security**	
	4.1 Explain the importance of basic network security concepts.	Chapter 20, Chapter 21
	4.2 Summarize various types of attacks and their impact to the network.	Chapter 21
	4.3 Given a scenario, apply network security features, defense techniques, and solutions.	Chapter 21
5.0	**Network Troubleshooting**	
	5.1 Explain the troubleshooting methodology.	Chapter 18
	5.2 Given a scenario, troubleshoot common cabling and physical interface issues.	Chapter 3, Chapter 18
	5.3 Given a scenario, troubleshoot common issues with network services.	Chapter 11, Chapter 18
	5.4 Given a scenario, troubleshoot common performance issues.	Chapter 11, Chapter 18
	5.5 Given a scenario, use the appropriate tool or protocol to solve networking issues.	Chapter 19

How to Contact the Publisher

If you believe you have found a mistake in this book, please bring it to our attention. At John Wiley & Sons, we understand how important it is to provide our customers with accurate content, but even with our best efforts an error may occur.

In order to submit your possible errata, please email it to our Customer Service Team at wileysupport@wiley.com with the subject line "Possible Book Errata Submission."

Assessment Test

1. Which network architecture defines a strict access method for various hosts?
   A. Peer-to-peer
   B. Client-server
   C. LAN
   D. Hybrid topology

2. You need to select a topology to connect two office locations, and you do not expect to add locations in the future. Which topology should you select?
   A. Point-to-point
   B. Point-to-multipoint
   C. Ring
   D. Bus

3. Which protocol data unit (PDU) is used to describe the type of data being transmitted at the Presentation layer?
   A. Bits
   B. User datagrams
   C. Frames
   D. Segments

4. Which layer is responsible for encryption and decryption?
   A. Application layer
   B. Physical layer
   C. Session layer
   D. Presentation layer

5. You need to run a UTP cable for 10 Gbps speeds with a distance of 40 meters. Which minimum cable category rating should you use?
   A. Category 5
   B. Category 5e
   C. Category 6
   D. Category 3

6. Which term describes the path of signaling on a network cable?
   A. Attenuation
   B. Duplex
   C. Demarcation
   D. EMI

7. You are working with a contractor as they are pulling and terminating fiber-optic lines. The fiber-optic lines will be located in the center of your production line. Which cable ends should you recommend that will reduce the chances of cables becoming loose from vibration on the production floor?

A. SC connectors

B. ST connectors

C. LC connectors

D. MTRJ connectors

8. Which is NOT a common cause for LAN congestion?

A. Broadcasts

B. Multicasts

C. Adding switches for connectivity

D. Multiple hubs for connectivity

9. The receiving computer checked the checksum of a frame. It had been damaged during transfer, so it is discarded. At which layer of the OSI did this occur?

A. Physical

B. Data Link

C. Network

D. Session

10. What is a reason a network administrator would segment a network with a switch?

A. Create more broadcast domains

B. Create isolation of ARP messages

C. Create fewer collision domains

D. Isolate traffic between segments

11. According to best practices, what is the proper placement of a firewall?

A. Only between the internal network and the Internet

B. At key security boundaries

C. In the DMZ

D. Only between the DMZ and the Internet

12. Which is the contention method 802.11 wireless uses?

A. CSMA/CA

B. CSMA/CD

C. DSSS

D. OFDM

13. What form of communication does a DHCP client use to initially acquire an IP address?

   A. Layer 3 broadcast

   B. Layer 3 multicast

   C. Layer 3 802.1Q

   D. Layer 3 unicast

14. Which management access method should be configured on network devices for encryption of a session?

   A. RADIUS

   B. HTTP

   C. SSH

   D. SFTP

15. Which Microsoft remote access protocol allows for local drives to be presented to the remote system?

   A. VNC

   B. RDP

   C. SSH

   D. Telnet

16. Which protocol and port number does Syslog use?

   A. UDP/161

   B. TCP/162

   C. UDP/162

   D. UDP/514

17. Which of the following is the Class B network IP range?

   A. 1–126

   B. 1–127

   C. 128–191

   D. 192–224

18. Which is true of the IP address 135.20.255.255?

   A. It is a Class A address.

   B. It is a broadcast address.

   C. It is the default gateway address.

   D. It has a default mask of 255.0.0.0.

19. What is a major reason to use private IP addressing?

   A. It allows for the conservation of public IP addresses.

   B. Since private IP addresses are non-routable on the Internet, they are secure.

   C. It keeps communications private.

   D. It allows easier setup than public IP addresses.

20. What is required when using private IP addresses to communicate with Internet hosts?

   A. Internet router

   B. IPv4 tunnel

   C. VPN tunnel

   D. Network Address Translation

21. Which routing protocol is a true link-state protocol?

   A. RIP

   B. OSPF

   C. RIPv2

   D. EIGRP

22. Why are there dashes in the age field of the following output?

```
Lab_A#sh ip arp
Protocol  Address       Age(min) Hardware Addr   Type  Interface
Internet  172.16.20.1   -        00d0.58ad.05f4  ARPA  Ethernet1
Internet  172.16.20.2   3        0030.9492.a5dd  ARPA  Ethernet1
Internet  172.16.10.1   -        0015.0506.31b0  ARPA  Ethernet0
```

   A. The ARP entry is stale.

   B. The ARP entry is invalid.

   C. These are physical interfaces.

   D. There are virtual interfaces.

23. What is the definition of route statement AD?

   A. The AD is a metric that routing protocols use to select the best route.

   B. The AD is a value assigned by network administrators for route selection.

   C. The AD is a rating of trust when multiple routes exist to the same destination.

   D. The AD is a value associated with the cost to the destination.

24. You perform a `show ip route` on the router and see several routes with an AD of 90. Which routing protocol has generated these route statements?

   A. IGRP

   B. OSPF

   C. EIGRP

   D. RIP

25. Which routing protocol uses path-vector metrics?

 A. BGP

 B. RIP

 C. OSPF

 D. EIGRP

26. Which protocol replaces ARP in IPv6?

 A. NDP

 B. ARPv6

 C. GRE

 D. RA

27. Which VTP mode will not allow the switch to participate in VTP traffic but will forward VTP traffic?

 A. Server mode

 B. Transparent mode

 C. Proxy mode

 D. Client mode

28. Which protocol is a Cisco proprietary protocol used for trunking switches?

 A. ISL

 B. 802.1Q

 C. VTP

 D. CDP

29. Which technology will give selective access to the network based upon authentication?

 A. 802.1Q

 B. ACLs

 C. 802.1X

 D. Firewall

30. How many non-overlapping channels are available with 802.11a?

 A. 3

 B. 12

 C. 23

 D. 40

31. What is the maximum data rate for the 802.11a standard?

 A. 6 Mbps

 B. 11 Mbps

 C. 22 Mbps

 D. 54 Mbps

32. What is a benefit of site-to-site IPsec VPNs?

    A. Lower bandwidth requirements

    B. Lower latency

    C. Scalability

    D. Support for multicast

33. Which cable should you use to connect to a serial port on a router?

    A. Cat 5e

    B. Rolled cable

    C. PuTTY cable

    D. SMF

34. What type of SNMP message is sent from the NMS to the agent to request information?

    A. Get-request message

    B. Get-response message

    C. Set-request message

    D. Trap message

35. What protocol provides detailed information on traffic flows between endpoints?

    A. Syslog

    B. SNMP

    C. NetFlow

    D. SPAN

36. You are contracting with a new service provider and are reviewing their service level agreement (SLA). The SLA states that their commitment to uptime is 99%. What is the expected downtime per year?

    A. 3.65 days

    B. 8.76 hours

    C. 52.56 minutes

    D. 5.29 minutes

37. You need to make sure that users do not reuse passwords when their password expires and they are required to change it? In which of the following would you require the change?

    A. BYOD

    B. Password policy

    C. DLP

    D. AUP

38. Which of the following is a measure of how long it will take to restore your data before the deletion or failure?

   A. RTO

   B. MTBF

   C. RPO

   D. MTTR

39. A recovery from tape will take 4 hours; what is this an example of?

   A. The recovery point objective (RPO)

   B. The recovery time objective (RTO)

   C. GFS rotation

   D. Backup window

40. Which cloud service is likely to be used for software development?

   A. SaaS

   B. IaaS

   C. PaaS

   D. DRaaS

41. On which network plane would a routing protocol perform?

   A. Data plane

   B. Control plane

   C. Management plane

   D. Routing plane

42. What is the next step in problem solving once a theory is confirmed?

   A. Create a hypothesis.

   B. Consider multiple approaches.

   C. Establish a plan of action.

   D. Approach multiple problems individually.

43. What is the final step in resolving a problem in the troubleshooting methodology?

   A. Implement a solution.

   B. Validate a theory.

   C. Establish a plan of action.

   D. Document.

44. Which software tool will allow you to check if a web application running on a server is online?

   A. `ping`

   B. `nslookup`

   C. `tracert/traceroute`

   D. Port scanner

45. You need to check the configured maximum transmission unit (MTU) on the interface of a Linux host; which command should you use?

    A. `ipconfig`

    B. `ifconfig`

    C. `mtuconfig`

    D. `iptables`

46. Which tool allows examination at the packet level for traffic from an application?

    A. Protocol analyzer

    B. `dig`

    C. Spectrum analyzer

    D. `nslookup`

47. Which protocol combines both the authentication and accounting into one TCP packet on port 49?

    A. TACACS+

    B. RADIUS

    C. TLS

    D. LDAP

48. Which factor of authentication requires you to present something that you have?

    A. Password

    B. Signature

    C. Fingerprint

    D. Token

49. A junior administrator comes to you in a panic. After looking at the log files, he has become convinced that an attacker is attempting to use a legitimate IP address to disrupt access elsewhere on the network. Which type of attack is this?

    A. Spoofing

    B. Social engineering

    C. Worm

    D. Password

50. You're the administrator for a large bottling company. At the end of each month, you routinely view all logs and look for discrepancies. This month, your email system error log reports a large number of unsuccessful attempts to log in. It's apparent that the email server is being targeted. Which type of attack is most likely occurring?

    A. Brute-force

    B. Backdoor

    C. Worm

    D. IP spoofing

Answers to Assessment Test

1. **B.** The client-server network architecture strictly defines hosts; clients access the information, and servers share the information. Peer-to-peer is a network architecture that allows the same host to both access and share resources in a network. Local area network (LAN) is a network type and not related to sharing information. Hybrid topology describes a topology that incorporates two or more topologies.

2. **A.** A point-to-point connection is typically used to connect two offices where expansion of locations is not a concern. A point-to-multipoint topology should be selected if an office needs to connect with several other office locations. Ring and bus are topologies and not used to describe WAN connectivity methods.

3. **B.** User datagrams are the protocol data units (PDUs) that describe data at the Presentation layer. Bits describe the data at the Physical layer. Frames describe the data at the Data Link layer. Segments describe the data at the Transport layer.

4. **D.** The Presentation layer is responsible for encryption and decryption, as well as compression and decompression. The Application layer is responsible for application programming interface (API) access and beginning the network communication process. The Physical layer is responsible for transmitting data over light, electricity, and air waves. The Session layer is responsible for setting up the dialogue between two hosts.

5. **C.** Category 6 is capable of 10 Gbps up to a maximum distance of 55 meters. Category 5 is capable of speeds of 100 Mbps at a distance of 100 meters. Category 5e is capable of 1 Gbps at a distance of 100 meters. Category 3 is only capable of a maximum speed of 10 Mbps.

6. **B.** Duplex refers to the path of signaling on a network cable. Attenuation is the degrading of signal as the cable length increased. Demarcation, or demarc, refers to the point of responsibility for a network provider. Electromagnetic interference (EMI) is interference that is induced into a network cable from an external source.

7. **B.** The straight-tip (ST) connector is the best choice for an installation near vibration sources. The SC connector is a square connector often used for multimode cable. The ST connector has a spring-loaded detent that resists vibrations and positively locks. Although LC and MTRJ connectors have detent mechanisms, the ST has a spring-loaded detent to ensure that it does not come loose.

8. **C.** Broadcasts, multicasts, and multiple hubs for connectivity are all common causes of LAN congestion. Adding switches for connectivity has no direct relationship to LAN congestion, since switches create collision domains and raise effective bandwidth.

9. **B.** The Data Link layer is responsible for checking the frame check sequence (FCS), which is a checksum of the frame. The Physical layer is responsible for transmitting data through electricity, light, or air. The Network layer is responsible for logical addressing and routing of data. The Session layer is responsible for dialogue control.

10. D. A switch creates micro-segmentation, which in turn isolates traffic between two talking computers from other computers that are not part of the communications. This in turn increases bandwidth for the computers that are not part of the communications between the two talking computers. The creation of broadcast domains can only be achieved with the addition of VLANs and a router. The isolation of address resolution protocol (ARP) messages can be achieved only by the creation of broadcast domains. Segmentation with a switch will create more collision domains, not fewer collision domains.

11. B. Firewalls should always be placed at key security boundaries, which can be the Internet and your internal network. However, proper placement is not exclusive to the boundaries of the Internet and internal networks. For example, it could be placed between two internal networks, such as R&D and guest networks. The demilitarized zone (DMZ), now also referred to as a screened subnet, is a segment of a firewall where Internet-facing services are placed. Firewalls are normally not placed only between the DMZ and the Internet because most networks have an internal network.

12. A. 802.11 uses a contention method of Carrier Sense Multiple Access/Collision Avoidance (CSMA/CA). 802.11 implements a Request-to-Send/Clear-to-Send mechanism that avoids collisions. Ethernet uses a contention method of Carrier Sense Multiple Access/Collision Detection (CSMA/CD). Both Direct-Sequence Spread Spectrum (DSSS) and Orthogonal Frequency Division Multiplexing (OFDM) are wireless modulations used to transmit data.

13. A. DHCP uses layer 3 broadcasts by sending packets to 255.255.255.255 for initial DHCP discovery. Layer 3 multicast is not used for DHCP clients. Layer 3 802.1Q is an incorrect answer because 802.1Q is used for switch trunks. Layer 3 unicasts are the form of communication clients use after obtaining an IP address.

14. C. Secure Shell (SSH) is a secure console emulation method for the administration of network devices. It allows for both the sender and receiver to create an encrypted session so data cannot be intercepted. Remote Authentication Dial-In User Service (RADIUS) is a protocol that authenticates users, and it does not provide encryption. Hypertext Transfer Protocol (HTTP) is a method for relaying Hypertext Markup Language (HTML) from a server to a requesting host; it does not provide encryption. SSH File Transfer Protocol (SFTP) is a protocol that provides encryption for file transfers, but it does not provide management access.

15. B. Remote Desktop Protocol (RDP) allows for local drives to be available to the remote machine when an RDP session is initiated. Virtual Network Computing (VNC), Secure Shell (SSH), and Telnet are not capable of redirecting drives.

16. D. The router or switch sends Syslog messages to the Syslog server on port 514 with UDP. SNMP agents listen on UDP/161. SNMP does not use TCP for messaging. SNMP sends traps on UDP/162.

17. C. The IP range for a Class B network is 128–191. Class B addressing provides 16 bits of network addressing and 16 bits of host addressing by default.

18. B. The IP address 135.20.255.255 is a Class B broadcast address. It is not a Class A address, nor is it the default gateway address. The default mask of a Class B address is 255.255.0.0.

19. A. The private IP address space was created to preserve the number of public IP addresses. Private IP addresses are non-routable on the Internet, but this does not make them secure. Private IP addresses do not keep communications private, as their name implies. Private IP addresses are not publicly addressable for communications. Private IP addresses do not allow for an easier setup than public IP addresses.

20. D. Network Address Translation (NAT) is required to communicate over the public Internet with private IP addresses. Although Internet routers are required for routing, by default they will not route private IP addresses to public IP addresses. An IPv4 tunnel or VPN tunnel is not required for communications on the Internet with private IP addresses.

21. B. Open Shortest Path First (OSPF) is a true link-state protocol. Routing Information Protocol (RIP) and RIPv2 are both distance vector protocols. Enhanced Interior Gateway Routing Protocol (EIGRP) is a hybrid routing protocol that combines the best of distance vector and link-state attributes.

22. C. Each Address Resolution Protocol (ARP) entry has a defined time-to-live in the ARP cache. However, physical interfaces are permanently added to the ARP cache, and they are signified with a dash under the age column. When ARP entries are stale, the entry will be removed from the ARP cache. If an ARP entry is invalid, it will be removed from the ARP cache.

23. C. The administrative distance (AD) is a rating of trust between different routing protocols and route methods. This trust scale is important when multiple routes exist to the same destination. Directly connected routes have administrative distances (ADs) with the highest level of trust. Route statements populated by the same dynamic routing protocol will be calculated for the best route upon their metric and not their administrative distance. The administrative distance is not assigned by the administrator for route selection. The administrative distance value is not associated with the cost to the destination, only the trust of a route statement.

24. C. The administrative distance (AD) of Enhanced Interior Gateway Routing Protocol (EIGRP) is 90. The most common ADs are 90 for EIGRP, 100 for IGRP, 110 for OSPF, and 120 for RIP. The mnemonic of 90 Exotic Indian Oval Rubies will help you remember the order; then starting with EIGRP with a value of 90, increment the following values by 10.

25. A. Border Gateway Protocol (BGP) is a path-vector routing protocol. Routing Information Protocol (RIP) is a distance-vector routing protocol. Open Shortest First Path (OSPF) is a link-state protocol. Enhanced Interior Gateway Routing Protocol (EIGRP) is considered a hybrid protocol, incorporating both distance-vector and link-state mechanisms.

26. A. The Address Resolution Protocol (ARP) in IPv6 has been replaced with Network Discovery Protocol (NDP). The NDP protocol uses neighbor solicitation (NS) and neighbor advertisements (NA) to learn neighbors in lieu of ARP broadcasts. ARPv6 is not a real protocol and therefore an invalid answer. Generic Router Encapsulation (GRE) is a tunneling protocol for other network protocols. A router advertisement (RA) packet is returned from the gateway so the host learns the gateway address.

27. B. A switch in VTP transparent mode will not participate in VTP. However, if the VTP is v2, the switch will forward and receive VTP advertisements. The VTP server mode allows the switch to act as a master for the VTP domain. VTP proxy mode is not a real mode; therefore, it is incorrect. The VTP client mode allows the switch to act as a slave to the master server.

28. A. Inter-Switch Link (ISL) is a proprietary protocol used for the trunking of switches. If you need to connect non-Cisco switches to a Cisco switch, you must use 802.1Q, the IEEE standard. VTP is not a trunking protocol; it assists in populating VLANs across Cisco switches for conformity and ease of configuration. Cisco Discovery Protocol (CDP) is not a trunking protocol either; it negotiates power by communicating its capabilities with neighboring devices. It also allows for neighbor discovery, but CDP is proprietary to Cisco, so only Cisco devices can communicate.

29. C. 802.1X allows selective access to a network at layer 2. It allows this on the switch because the switch acts as an authenticator to an AAA server, only allowing access after the user or device has been authenticated. 802.1Q is a trunking protocol used for transporting multiple VLANs over a layer 2 connection, and it does not provide authentication. An access control list (ACL) is a condition and action statement used to allow, deny, or log traffic. Firewalls contain ACLs and policies to allow, deny, and log traffic, but normally firewalls will not authenticate traffic.

30. B. The IEEE 802.11a standard provides up to 12 non-overlapping channels, or up to 23 if you add the 802.11h standard. All other answers are incorrect.

31. D. The IEEE 802.11a standard provides a maximum data rate of up to 54 Mbps. All other answers are incorrect.

32. C. Site-to-site IPsec VPNs offer scalability as a benefit. This is because each remote office only needs an Internet connection to create a VPN tunnel back to the main office. There is a certain overhead when using a VPN; therefore, higher bandwidth requirements may exist after deploying site-to-site IPsec VPNs. Latency is affected and will be higher due to the level of encryption each packet must undergo as it passes through the site-to-site VPN. Support for multicast is not a common benefit of site-to-site IPsec VPNs.

33. B. A rolled cable is used to create a serial connection from the PC to the router for configuration. A Cat 5e cable is used for Ethernet connectivity. There is no such thing as a PuTTY cable, but PuTTY is a terminal emulation program used with a serial cable. Single-mode fiber (SMF) is a type of fiber-optic cable that can span long distances.

34. A. The get-request message is used by a network management station (NMS) to request information from an SNMP agent. The get-response message is the message sent back from the client to the NMS after a get-request message is received. The set-request message is sent by the NMS to the SNMP client requesting a specific writable counter be set to the specified value. Trap messages are sent from the network device to the SNMP network management station when an event has triggered over a set threshold on the device.

35. C. The NetFlow standard provides session information including the source and destination addresses, applications, and traffic volume. Syslog is a method of collecting system messages to identify problems or it can be used for post-mortem analysis. Simple Network Management Protocol (SNMP) is a protocol used to capture performance statistics of servers, applications, and network devices. Switched Port Analyzer (SPAN) is used to mirror port traffic.

36. A. An SLA of two nines is 3.65 days per year of expected downtime. This equates to 7.2 hours per month that the service can be down. All other answers are incorrect.

37. B. A password policy defines the life, complexity, history, and complexity of passwords in the organization. A bring-your-own-device (BYOD) policy defines how personal devices can be used in the organization. Data loss prevention (DLP) software attempts to prevent data leakage. It does this by maintaining awareness of actions that can and cannot be taken with respect to a document. An acceptable use policy (AUP) defines the acceptable use of organizational resources.

38. A. The recovery time objective (RTO) is how long it takes to recover your data back to the recovery point objective (RPO). The RPO is a measurement of time from a failure, disaster, or comparable loss-causing event. RPOs measure back in time to when your data was preserved in a usable format, usually to the most recent backup. The mean time between failures (MTBF) is an average time between failures. The mean time to repair (MTTR) is the average time it takes for a vendor to repair a failure.

39. B. The recovery time objective (RTO) is a measurement of how quickly you can recover from data loss using backup. The recovery point objective (RPO) is the point in time to which you can recover in the event of a disaster. The grandfather, father, son (GFS) rotation is a systematic way to archive backup media. The backup window is the window of time in which a backup can be performed.

40. C. Platform as a service (PaaS) is commonly used by software developers. It provides a development platform that the software developer can use to create applications. An example of this is a web server with PHP and MySQL, which is hosted in the cloud. Software as a service (SaaS) is a software product similar to email or social networking software in which you use the software provided as a service. Infrastructure as a service (IaaS) allows you to rent infrastructure such as virtual machines (VMs), virtual networks, or even DNS, just to name a few. Disaster recovery as a service (DRaaS) is another popular service; you can rent storage and compute power to facilitate a disaster recovery site.

41. B. Routing protocols such as OSPF and EIGRP would perform their function on the control plane since they are controlling the routing of the data plane. The data plane is responsible for switching and routing data. Any data that is destined for endpoints is switched or routed on the data plane. The management plane is any mechanism that helps in the management of a router or switch. *Routing plane* is not a term normally used to describe data types; therefore, option D is an invalid answer.

42. C. After a theory or hypothesis is confirmed, you should establish a plan of action to resolve the problem. The creation of a hypothesis is a step in the establishment of a probable cause. Considering multiple approaches is done during the establishment of a theory. Approaching multiple problems individually is done in the initial identification of the problem in the troubleshooting methodology.

43. D. The documentation of the finding, actions, and outcomes, and lessons learned throughout the process is the final step in the resolution of a problem in the troubleshooting methodology. It allows us to solve future problems more quickly. Implementing a solution, validating a theory, and establishing a plan of action all precede the final steps in resolving a problem.

44. D. A port scanner, such as the Nmap utility, will allow you to check if an application is accepting connections. The port will return an open status, and most port scanners will check for an HTTP response. The ping utility will check only if the server is online. The nslookup utility will allow you to resolve a domain name to an IP address and vice versa. The tracert/traceroute command will allow you to watch a packet as it traverses a network path to its destination.

45. B. The ifconfig command will allow you to inspect the MTU on the interface of a Linux host. It will also allow you to change the MTU temporarily. The ipconfig command is a Windows operating system command. The command of mtuconfig is not a real command. The iptables command is an incorrect answer for this question.

46. A. A protocol analyzer will allow us to inspect packet levels of traffic that is captured from an application. The dig and nslookup commands are used to perform DNS name resolution. A spectrum analyzer is used to view the radio frequency (RF) spectrum and is not a valid answer.

47. A. TACACS+ combines both authentication and accounting into one TCP packet on port 49. RADIUS uses UDP port 1812 for authentication and port 1813 for accounting. Transport Layer Security (TLS) uses TCP port 443 but does not provide authentication or authorization. LDAP queries Active Directory on TCP port 389, but Kerberos is what authenticates users.

48. D. Token-based authentication requires you to have a hardware or software token to authenticate. A password is something that you know. A signature is something that you do. Your fingerprint is an example of something that you are, because it is unique to you.

49. A. A spoofing attack is an attempt by someone or something to masquerade as someone else (IP address) and is often used to disrupt access. Social engineering is a process in which an attacker attempts to acquire information about your network and system by social means, such as talking to people in the organization. Worms reproduce and move throughout the network to infect other systems. Password attacks are used in an attempt to guess passwords.

50. A. A brute-force attack is a type of password attack in which a password is guessed over and over until the right password is guessed. A backdoor attack is an embedded account that allows unauthorized access through an unpatched coding hole. A worm is different from a virus in that it can reproduce itself, is self-contained, and doesn't need a host application to be transported. IP spoofing is an attack where the threat actor impersonates an IP address to attack a victim.

Chapter

1

Introduction to Networks

THE FOLLOWING COMPTIA NETWORK+ EXAM OBJECTIVES ARE COVERED IN THIS CHAPTER:

✓ **Domain 1.0 Networking Concepts**

✓ **1.6 Compare and contrast network topologies, architectures, and types.**

- Mesh
- Hybrid
- Star/hub and spoke
- Spine and leaf
- Point to point
- Three-tier hierarchical model
  - Core
  - Distribution
  - Access
- Traffic flows
  - North-south
  - East-west

You'd have to work pretty hard these days to find someone who would argue when we say that our computers have become invaluable to us personally and professionally. Our society has become highly dependent on the resources they offer and on sharing them with each other. The ability to communicate with others—whether they're in the same building or in some faraway land—completely hinges on our capacity to create and maintain solid, dependable networks.

And those vitally important networks come in all shapes and sizes—ranging from small and simple to humongous and super complicated. But whatever their flavor, they all need to be maintained properly, and to do that well, you have to understand networking basics. The various types of devices and technologies that are used to create networks, as well as how they work together, is what this book is about, and I'll go through this critical information one step at a time with you. Understanding all of this will not only equip you with a rock-solid base to build on as you gain IT knowledge and grow in your career, it will also arm you with what you'll need to ace the Network+ certification exam!

To find Todd Lammle CompTIA videos and practice questions, please see www.lammle.com.

First Things First: What's a Network?

The dictionary defines the word *network* as "a group or system of interconnected people or things." Similarly, in the computer world, the term *network* means two or more connected computers that can share resources such as data and applications, office machines, an Internet connection, or some combination of these, as shown in Figure 1.1.

Figure 1.1 shows a really basic network made up of only two host computers connected; they share resources such as files and even a printer hooked up to one of the hosts. These two hosts "talk" to each other using a computer language called *binary code*, which consists of lots of 1s and 0s in a specific order that describes exactly what they want to "say."

Next, I'm going to tell you about local area networks, how they work, and even how we can connect local area networks together. Then, later in this chapter, I'll describe how to connect remote local area networks together through something known as a wide area network.

FIGURE 1.1   A basic network

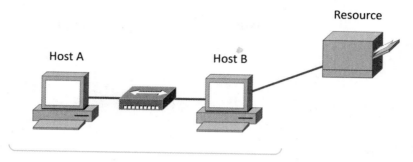

Network segment

The Local Area Network

Just as the name implies, a *local area network (LAN)* is usually restricted to spanning a particular geographic location such as an office building, a single department within a corporate office, or even a home office.

Back in the day, you couldn't put more than 30 workstations on a LAN, and you had to cope with strict limitations on how far those machines could actually be from each other. Because of technological advances, all that's changed now, and we're not nearly as restricted in regard to both a LAN's size and the distance a LAN can span. Even so, it's still best to split a big LAN into smaller logical zones known as *workgroups* to make administration easier.

> The meaning of the term *workgroup* in this context is slightly different than when the term is used in contrast to domains. In that context, a workgroup is a set of devices with no security association with one another (whereas in a domain they do have that association). In this context, we simply mean they physically are in the same network segment.

In a typical business environment, it's a good idea to arrange your LAN's workgroups along department divisions; for instance, you would create a workgroup for Accounting, another one for Sales, and maybe another for Marketing—you get the idea. Figure 1.2 shows two separate LANs, each as its own workgroup.

First, don't stress about the devices labeled *hub* and *switch*—these are just connectivity devices that allow hosts to physically connect to resources on an LAN. Trust me; I'll describe them to you in much more detail in Chapter 5, "Networking Devices."

Anyway, back to the figure. Notice that there's a Marketing workgroup and a Sales workgroup. These are LANs in their most basic form. Any device that connects to the Marketing LAN can access the resources of the Marketing LAN—in this case, the servers and printer.

FIGURE 1.2   Two separate LANs (workgroups)

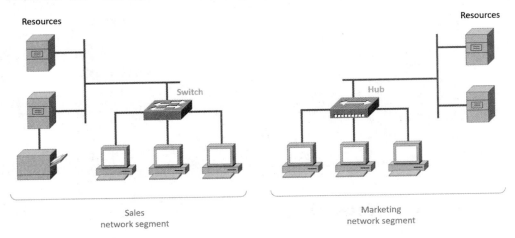

There are two problems with this:

- You must be physically connected to a workgroup's LAN to get the resources from it.
- You can't get from one LAN to the other LAN and use the server data and printing resources remotely.

This is a typical network issue that's easily resolved by using a cool device called a *router* to connect the two LANs, as shown in Figure 1.3.

FIGURE 1.3   A router connects LANs

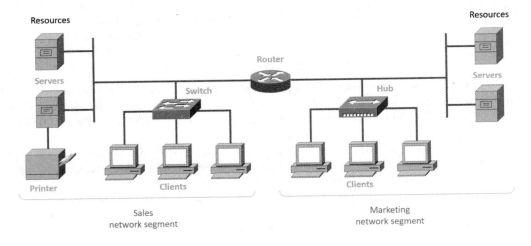

Nice—problem solved! Even though you can use routers for more than just connecting LANs, the router shown in Figure 1.3 is a great solution because the host computers from the Sales LAN can get to the resources (server data and printers) of the Marketing LAN, and vice versa.

Now, you might be thinking that we really don't need the router—that we could just physically connect the two workgroups with a type of cable that would allow the Marketing and Sales workgroups to hook up somehow. Well, we could do that, but if we did, we would have only one big, cumbersome workgroup instead of separate workgroups for Marketing and Sales, and that kind of arrangement just isn't practical for today's networks.

This is because with smaller, individual-yet-connected groups, the users on each LAN enjoy much faster response times when accessing resources, and administrative tasks are a lot easier too. Larger workgroups run more slowly because there's a legion of hosts within them that are all trying to get to the same resources simultaneously. So the router shown in Figure 1.3, which separates the workgroups while still allowing access between them, is a really great solution!

 Don't focus too much on the network connectivity devices like the hubs, routers, and switches I've mentioned so far in this chapter yet. We'll thoroughly cover them all later, in Chapter 5. Right now, I really want you to prioritize your understanding of the concepts that I'm presenting here, so at this point, all you need to know is that hubs and switches are devices that connect other devices together into a network, and routers connect networks together.

So let me define the other terms I've used so far: *workstations*, *servers*, and *hosts*.

Common Network Components

There are a lot of different machines, devices, and media that make up our networks. Let's talk about three of the most common:

- Workstations
- Servers
- Hosts

Workstations

Workstations are often seriously powerful computers that run more than one central processing unit (CPU) and whose resources are available to other users on the network to access when needed. With this much power, you might think I am describing a server—not quite, because there is an important difference between these devices that I'll cover in the next section. Workstations are often employed as systems that end users use on a daily basis. Don't confuse workstations with client machines, which can be workstations but not always. People often use the terms *workstation* and *client* interchangeably. In colloquial terms, this isn't a big deal; we all do it. But technically speaking, they are different. A *client machine* is any device on the network that can ask for access to resources like a printer or other hosts from a server or powerful workstation.

> The terms *workstation, client,* and *host* can sometimes be used inter-changeably. Computers have become more and more powerful, and the terms have become somewhat fuzzy because hosts can be clients, workstations, servers, and more! The term *host* is used to describe pretty much anything that takes an IP address.

Servers

Servers are also powerful computers. They get their name because they truly are "at the service" of the network and run specialized software known as the network operating system to maintain and control the network.

In a good design that optimizes the network's performance, servers are highly specialized and are there to handle one important labor-intensive job. This is not to say that a single server can't do many jobs, but more often than not, you'll get better performance if you dedicate a server to a single task. Here's a list of common dedicated servers:

File Server   Stores and dispenses files

Mail Server   The network's post office; handles email functions

Print Server   Manages printers on the network

Web Server   Manages web-based activities by running Hypertext Transfer Protocol Secure (HTTPS) for storing web content and accessing web pages

Fax Server   The "memo maker" that sends and receives paperless faxes over the network

Application Server   Manages network applications

Telephony Server   Handles the call center and call routing and can be thought of as a sophisticated network answering machine

Proxy Server   Handles tasks in the place of other machines on the network, particularly an Internet connection

> See how the name of each kind of server indicates what it actually does—how it serves the network? This is an excellent way to remember them.

As I said, servers are usually dedicated to doing one specific important thing within the network. Not always, though—sometimes they have more than one job. But whether servers are designated for one job or are network multitaskers, they can maintain the network's data integrity by backing up the network's software and providing redundant hardware (for fault tolerance). And no matter what, they all serve a number of client machines.

Back in Figure 1.2, I showed you an example of two really simple LAN networks. I want to make sure you know that servers must have considerably superior CPUs, hard-drive space, and memory—a lot more than a simple client's capacity—because they serve many client machines and provide any resources they require. Because they're so important, you should always put your servers in a very secure area. My company's servers are in a locked server room because not only are they really pricey workhorses, they also store huge amounts of important and sensitive company data, so they need to be kept safe from any unauthorized access.

In Figure 1.4, you can see a network populated with both workstations and servers. Also notice that the hosts can access the servers across the network, which is pretty much the general idea of having a network in the first place!

FIGURE 1.4 A network populated with servers and workstations

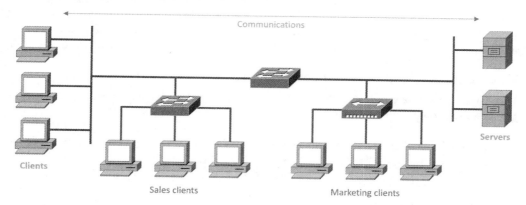

You probably picked up on the fact that there are more workstations here than servers, right? Think of why that is. If you answered that it's because one server can provide resources to what can sometimes be a huge number of individual users at the same time but workstations don't, you nailed it!

Hosts

This can be kind of confusing because when people refer to hosts, they really can be referring to almost any type of networking devices—including workstations and servers. But if you dig a bit deeper, you'll find that usually this term comes up when people are talking about resources and jobs that have to do with Transmission Control Protocol/Internet Protocol (TCP/IP). The scope of possible machines and devices is so broad because, in TCP/IP-speak, *host* means any network device with an IP address. Yes, you'll hear IT professionals throw this term around pretty loosely; for the Network+ exam, stick to the definition being network devices, including workstations and servers, with IP addresses.

Here's a bit of background: The name *host* harks back to the Jurassic period of networking when those dinosaurs known as *mainframes* were the only intelligent devices able to roam the network. These were called *hosts* whether they had TCP/IP functionality or not. In that bygone age, everything else in the network-scape was referred to as *dumb terminals* because only mainframes—hosts—were given IP addresses. Another fossilized term from way back then is *gateways*, which was used to talk about any layer 3 machines like routers. We still use these terms today, but they've evolved a bit to refer to the many intelligent devices populating our present-day networks, each of which has an IP address. This is exactly the reason you hear *host* used so broadly.

Network Types

When we refer to parts of our network, we classify the sections of the network with a type. This designation of a particular type helps us generalize its use and function. Some of these designation types can use various technologies for connectivity, and some use specific technologies. In the following sections are several different network types that you may see as a network professional.

Metropolitan Area Network

A *metropolitan area network (MAN)* is just as it sounds, a network covering a metropolitan area used to interconnect various buildings and facilities usually over a carrier provider network. Think of a MAN as a concentrated WAN and you've got it. MANs typically offer high-speed interconnections using in-ground fiber optics and can be very cost effective for high-speed interconnects.

> A carrier provider network is typically a leased network connection. These providers will lease lines between two or more networks to provide connectivity.

Wide Area Network

There are legions of people who, if asked to define a *wide area network (WAN)*, just couldn't do it. Yet most of them use the big dog of all WANs—the Internet—every day! With that in mind, you can imagine that WAN networks are what we use to span large geographic areas and truly go the distance. Like the Internet, WANs usually employ both routers and public links, so that's generally the criteria used to define them.

Here are some of the important ways that WANs are different from LANs:

- WANs usually need a router port or ports.
- WANs span larger geographic areas and/or can link disparate locations.
- WANs are usually slower.

- We can choose when and how long we connect to a WAN. A LAN is all or nothing—our workstation is connected to it either permanently or not at all, although most of us have dedicated WAN links now.

- WANs can utilize either private or public data transport media such as phone lines.

We get the word *Internet* from the term *internetwork*. An internetwork is a type of LAN and/or WAN that connects a bunch of networks, or *intranets*. In an internetwork, hosts still use hardware addresses to communicate with other hosts on the LAN. However, they use logical addresses (IP addresses) to communicate with hosts on a different LAN (other side of the router).

And *routers* are the devices that make this possible. Each connection into a router is a different logical network. Figure 1.5 demonstrates how routers are employed to create an internetwork and how they enable our LANs to access WAN resources.

FIGURE 1.5   An internetwork

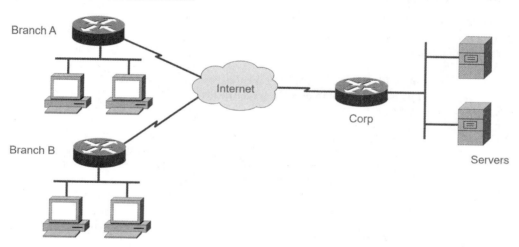

The Internet is a prime example of what's known as a *distributed WAN*—an internetwork that's made up of a lot of interconnected computers located in a lot of different places. There's another kind of WAN, referred to as *centralized*, that's composed of a main, centrally located computer or location that remote computers and devices can connect to. A good example is remote offices that connect to a main corporate office, as shown in Figure 1.5.

Personal Area Network

For close proximity connections there are *PANs*, or *personal area networks*. These are seen with smartphones and laptops in a conference room where local connections are used to collaborate and send data between devices. While a PAN can use a wired connection such as Ethernet or USB, it is more common that short distance wireless connections are used such as Bluetooth, infrared, or ZigBee.

PANs are intended for close proximity between devices such as connecting to a projector, printer, or a co-worker's computer and extend usually only a few meters.

Campus Area Network

A *CAN*, or *campus area network*, covers a limited geographical network such as a college or corporate campus. The CAN typically interconnects LANs in various buildings and offers a Wi-Fi component for roaming users.

A campus area network is between a LAN and WAN in scope. They are larger than a local area network but smaller than a metropolitan area network or wide area network.

Most CANs offer Internet connectivity as well as access to data center resources.

Storage Area Network

A *storage area network (SAN)* is designed for, and used exclusively by, storage systems. SANs interconnect servers to storage arrays containing centralized banks of hard drive or similar storage media. SANs are usually found only in data centers and do not mix traffic with other LANs. The protocols are designed specifically for storage, with Fibre Channel being the most prevalent along with iSCSI. The network hardware is different from LAN switches and routers and is designed specifically to carry storage traffic.

Fibre Channel over Ethernet (FCoE) is a technology that encapsulates Fibre Channel over Ethernet. The protocol is typically used as a transitional technology until the next generation of equipment can support iSCSI. The sweet spot to FCoE is that you can use existing Ethernet infrastructure.

Software-Defined Wide Area Network

A *software-defined wide area network (SDWAN)* is a virtual WAN architecture that uses software to manage connectivity, devices, and services and can make changes in the network based on current operations.

SDWANs integrate any type of transport architectures such as MPLS, LTE, and broadband Internet services to securely connect users to applications. The SDWAN controller can make changes in real time to add or remove bandwidth or route around failed circuits. SDWANs can simplify wide area networking management and operations by decoupling the networking hardware from its control mechanism.

Multiprotocol Label Switching

The term *Multiprotocol Label Switching (MPLS)*, as used in this chapter, will define the actual layout of what is one of the most popular WAN protocols in use today. MPLS has become one of the most innovative and flexible networking technologies on the market, and it has some key advantages over other WAN technologies:

- Physical layout flexibility
- Prioritizing of data
- Redundancy in case of link failure
- One-to-many connection

MPLS is a switching mechanism that imposes labels (numbers) to data and then uses those labels to forward data when it arrives at the MPLS network, as shown in Figure 1.6.

FIGURE 1.6   Multiprotocol Label Switching layout

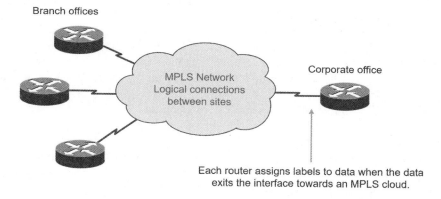

The labels are assigned on the edge of the MPLS network, and forwarding inside the MPLS network (cloud) is done solely based on labels through virtual links instead of physical links. Prioritizing data is a huge advantage; for example, voice data could have priority over basic data based on the labels. And since there are multiple paths for the data to be forwarded through the MPLS cloud, there's even some redundancy provided as well.

Multipoint Generic Routing Encapsulation

The *Multipoint Generic Routing Encapsulation (mGRE)* protocol refers to a carrier or service provider offering that dynamically creates and terminates connections to nodes on a network. mGRE is used in Dynamic Multipoint VPN deployments. The protocol enables dynamic connections without having to pre-configure static tunnel endpoints.

The protocol encapsulates user data, creates a VPN connection to one or many nodes, and, when completed, tears down the connection.

Network Architecture: Peer-to-Peer or Client-Server?

We've developed networking as a way to share resources and information, and how that's achieved directly maps to the particular architecture of the network operating system software. There are two main network types you need to know about: peer-to-peer and client-server. And by the way, it's really tough to tell the difference just by looking at a diagram or even by checking out a live video of the network humming along. However, the differences between peer-to-peer and client-server architectures are pretty major. They're not just physical; they're logical differences. You'll see what I mean in a bit.

Peer-to-Peer Networks

Computers connected in *peer-to-peer networks* do not have any central or special authority—they're all *peers*, meaning that when it comes to authority, they're all equals. The authority to perform a security check for proper access rights lies with the computer that has the desired resource being requested from it.

It also means that the computers coexisting in a peer-to-peer network can be client machines that access resources and server machines and provide those resources to other computers. This actually works pretty well as long as there isn't a huge number of users on the network, if each user backs things up locally, and if your network doesn't require much security.

If your network is running Windows, macOS, or Linux in a local LAN workgroup, you have a peer-to-peer network. Figure 1.7 gives you a snapshot of a typical peer-to-peer network. Keep in mind that peer-to-peer networks definitely present security-oriented challenges; for instance, just backing up company data can get pretty sketchy!

FIGURE 1.7 A peer-to-peer network

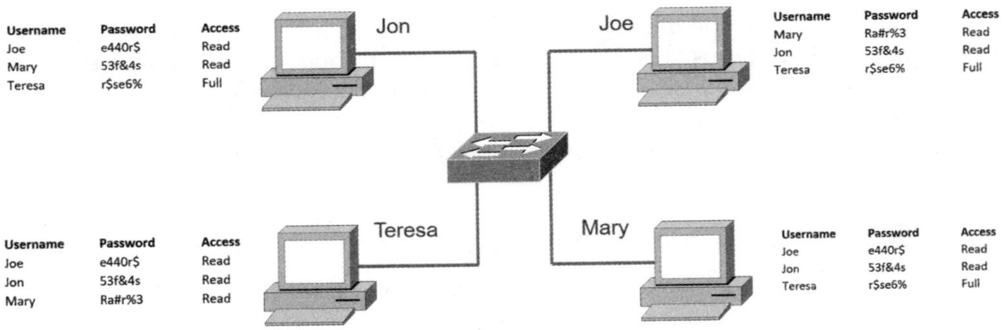

Since it should be clear by now that peer-to-peer networks aren't all sunshine, backing up all your critical data may be tough, but it's vital! Haven't all of us forgotten where we've put an important file? And then there's that glaring security issue to tangle with. Because security is not centrally governed, each and every user has to remember and maintain a list of users and passwords on each and every machine. Worse, some of those all-important passwords for the same users change on different machines—even for accessing different resources. What a mess!

Client-Server Networks

Client-server networks are pretty much the polar opposite of peer-to-peer networks because in them, a single server uses a network operating system for managing the whole network. Here's how it works: A client machine's request for a resource goes to the main server, which responds by handling security and directing the client to the desired resource. This happens instead of the request going directly to the machine with the desired resource, and it has some serious advantages. First, because the network is much better organized and doesn't depend on users remembering where needed resources are, it's a whole lot easier to find the files you need because everything is stored in one spot—on that special server. Your security also gets a lot tighter because all usernames and passwords are on that specific server, which is never ever used as a workstation. You even gain scalability because client-server networks can have legions of workstations on them. And surprisingly, with all those demands, the network's performance is actually optimized—nice!

Check out Figure 1.8, which shows a client-server network with a server that has a database of access rights, user accounts, and passwords.

FIGURE 1.8   A client-server network

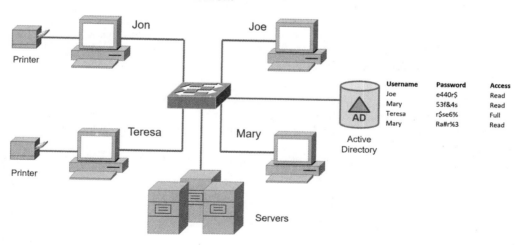

Many of today's networks are ideally a healthy blend of peer-to-peer and client-server architectures, with carefully specified servers that permit the simultaneous sharing of resources from devices running workstation operating systems. Even though the supporting machines can't handle as many inbound connections at a time, they still run the server service reasonably well. And if this type of mixed environment is designed well, most networks benefit greatly by having the capacity to take advantage of the positive aspects of both worlds.

EXERCISE 1.1

Identifying Common Network Components

This exercise will help you identify common network components in your daily life. You will list all of the servers, clients, and how they are accessed in three columns.

1. Using the knowledge in this section, list all of the possible servers that you communicate with daily.

2. Next to each of the servers, list the client application that accesses each of the servers.

3. Next to each client application, list the client (device) that runs the client application (cell phone, workstation, etc.).

4. Next list all of the connectivity methods used to connect the clients (devices) to the servers.

The list you compiled should give you a good understanding of the various clients, servers, and connectivity methods in your day-to-day life.

Physical Network Topologies

Just as a topographical map is a type of map that shows the shape of the terrain, the *physical topology* of a network is also a type of map. It defines the specific characteristics of a network, such as where all the workstations and other devices are located and the precise arrangement of all the physical media such as cables. Now, even though these two topologies are usually a lot alike, a particular network can actually have physical and logical topologies that are very different. Basically, what you want to remember is that a network's physical topology gives you the lay of the land, and the logical topology shows how a digital signal or data navigates through that layout.

Here are the topologies you're most likely to run into these days:

- Bus
- Star/hub-and-spoke
- Ring
- Mesh
- Point-to-point
- Point-to-multipoint
- Hybrid

Bus Topology

This type of topology is the most basic one of the bunch, and it really does sort of resemble a bus, but more like one that's been in a wreck! Anyway, the *bus topology* consists of two distinct and terminated ends, with each of its computers connecting to one unbroken cable running its entire length. Back in the day, we used to attach computers to that main cable with wire taps, but this didn't work all that well so we began using drop cables in their place. If we were dealing with 10Base2 Ethernet, we would slip a connector called a "T" into the main cable anywhere we wanted to connect a device to it instead of using drop cables.

Figure 1.9 depicts what a typical bus network's physical topology looks like.

FIGURE 1.9   A typical bus network's physical topology

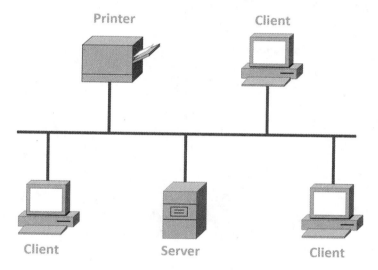

Even though all the computers on this kind of network see all the data flowing through the cable, only the one computer, which the data is specifically addressed to, actually *gets* the data. Some of the benefits of using a bus topology are that it's easy to install, and it's not very expensive, partly because it doesn't require as much cable as the other types of physical topologies. But it also has some drawbacks: For instance, it's hard to troubleshoot, change, or move, and it really doesn't offer much in the way of fault tolerance because everything is connected to that single cable. This means that any fault in the cable would basically bring down the whole network!

By the way, *fault tolerance* is the capability of a computer or a network system to respond to a condition automatically, often resolving it, which reduces the impact on the system. If fault-tolerance measures have been implemented correctly on a network, it's highly unlikely that any of that network's users will know that a problem ever existed at all.

Star Topology

A star (*hub-and-spoke*) topology's computers are connected to a central point with their own individual cables or wireless connections. You'll often find that central spot inhabited by a device like a hub, a switch, or an access point.

Star topology offers lots of advantages over bus topology, making it more widely used even though it obviously requires more physical media. One of its best features is that because each computer or network segment is connected to the central device individually, if the cable fails, it brings down only the machine or network segment related to the point of failure. This makes the network much more fault-tolerant as well as a lot easier to trouble-shoot. Another great thing about a star topology is that it's a lot more scalable—all you have to do if you want to add to it is run a new cable and connect to the machine at the core of the star. In Figure 1.10, you'll find a great example of a typical star topology.

FIGURE 1.10   Typical star topology with a switch

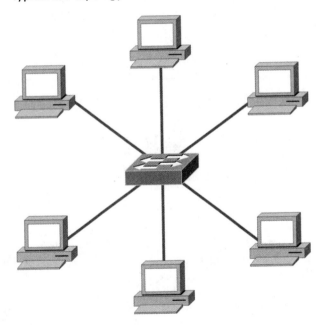

Although it is called a *star* (hub-and-spoke) topology, it also looks a lot like a bike wheel with spokes connecting to the hub in the middle of the wheel and extending outward to connect to the rim. And just as with that bike wheel, it's the hub device, actually more often a switch today, at the center of a star topology network that can give you the most grief if something goes wrong with it. If that central hub or switch happens to fail, down comes the whole network, so it's a very good thing hubs/switches don't fail often!

Just as it is with pretty much everything, a star topology has its pros and cons. But the good news far outweighs the bad, which is why people often opt for star topology. And here's a list of benefits you gain by going with it:

- New stations can be added or moved easily and quickly.
- A single cable failure won't bring down the entire network.
- It's relatively easy to troubleshoot.

And here are the disadvantages to using a star topology:

- The total installation cost can be higher because of the larger number of cables, even though prices have become more competitive.
- It has a single point of failure—the hub or other central device such as a switch.

There are two more sophisticated implementations of a star topology. The first is called a *point-to-point link*, where you have not only the device in the center of the spoke acting as a hub but also the device on the other end, which extends the network. This is still a star-wired topology, but as I'm sure you can imagine, it gives you a lot more scalability!

Another refined version is the wireless version, but to understand this variety well, you've got to have a solid grasp of all the capabilities and features of any devices populating the wireless star topology. No worries, though—I'll be covering wireless access points later in Chapter 12, "Wireless Networking." For now, it's good enough for you to know that access points are pretty much just wireless hubs or switches that behave like their wired counterparts. They create a point-by-point connection to endpoints and other wireless access points.

Ring Topology

In this type of topology, each computer is directly connected to other computers within the same network. Looking at Figure 1.11, you can see that the network's data flows from computer to computer back to the source, with the network's primary cable forming a ring. The problem is, the *ring topology* has a lot in common with the bus topology because if you want to add to the network, you have no choice but to break the cable ring, which is likely to bring down the entire network!

This is one big reason that ring topology isn't very popular—you just won't run into it a lot as I did in the 1980s and early 1990s. It's also pricey because you need several cables to connect each computer, it's really hard to reconfigure, and as you've probably guessed, it's not fault-tolerant.

But even with all that being said, if you work at an Internet service provider (ISP), you may still find a physical ring topology in use for a technology called SONET or some other WAN technology. However, you won't find any LANs in physical rings anymore.

      Although the ring topology is not used in LANs today, you will see the ring topology implemented with WAN providers.

FIGURE 1.11   A typical ring topology

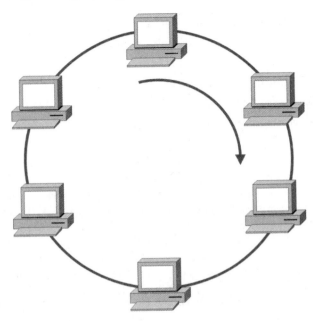

Mesh Topology

In this type of topology, you'll find that there's a path from every machine to every other one in the network. That's a lot of connections—in fact, the *mesh topology* wins the prize for "most physical connections per device"! You won't find it used in LANs very often, if ever, these days, but you will find a modified version of it known as a *hybrid mesh* used in a restrained manner on WANs, including the Internet.

Often, hybrid mesh topology networks will have quite a few connections between certain places to create redundancy (backup). And other types of topologies can sometimes be found in the mix too, which is another reason it's dubbed *hybrid*. Just remember that it isn't a full-on mesh topology if there isn't a connection between all devices in the network. And understand that it's fairly complicated. Figure 1.12 gives you a great picture of how much only four connections can complicate things!

You can clearly see that everything gets more and more complex as both the wiring and the connections multiply. For each *n* locations or hosts, you end up with $n(n-1)/2$ connections. This means that in a network consisting of only four computers, you have $4(4-1)/2$, or 6 connections. And if that little network grows to, say, a population of 10 computers, you'll then have a whopping 45 connections to cope with! That's a huge amount of overhead, so only small networks can really use this topology and manage it well. On the bright side, you get a really nice level of fault tolerance, but mesh still isn't used in corporate LANs anymore because it is so complicated to manage.

FIGURE 1.12   A typical mesh topology

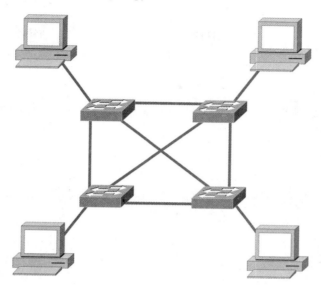

 A full mesh physical topology is least likely to have a collision, which happens when the data from two hosts trying to communicate simultaneously "collides" and gets lost.

This is also the reason you'll usually find the hybrid version in today's WANs. In fact, the mesh topology is actually pretty rare now, but it's still used because of the robust fault tolerance it offers. Because you have a multitude of connections, if one goes on the blink, computers and other network devices can simply switch to one of the many redundant connections that are up and running. And clearly, all that cabling in the mesh topology makes it a very pricey implementation. Plus, you can make your network management much less insane than it is with mesh by using what's known as a *partial mesh topology* solution instead, so why not go that way? You may lose a little fault tolerance, but if you go the partial mesh route, you still get to use the same technology between all the network's devices. Just remember that with partial mesh, not all devices will be interconnected, so it's important to choose the ones that will be wisely.

Point-to-Point Topology

As its name implies, in a *point-to-point* topology you have a direct connection between two routers or switches, giving you one communication path. The routers in a point-to-point topology can be linked by a serial cable, making it a physical network, or if they're located far apart and connected only via a circuit within a Frame Relay or MPLS network, it's a logical network instead.

Figure 1.13 illustrates three examples of a typical T1, or WAN, point-to-point connection.

FIGURE 1.13   Three point-to-point connections

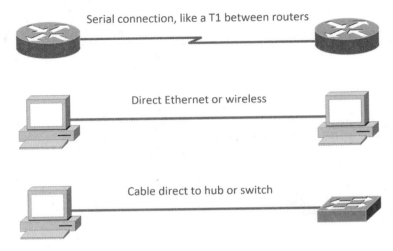

What you see here is a lightning bolt and a couple of round things with a bunch of arrows projecting from them, right? Well, the two round things radiating arrows represent our network's two routers, and that lightning bolt represents a WAN link. These symbols are industry standard, and I'll be using them throughout this book, so it's a good idea to get used to them!

So, the second part of the diagram shows two computers connected by a cable—a point-to-point link. By the way, this should remind you of something we just went over. Remember peer-to-peer networks? Good! I hope you also remember that a big drawback to peer-to-peer network sharing is that it's not very scalable. With this in mind, you probably won't be all that surprised that even if both machines have a wireless point-to-point connection, this network still won't be very scalable.

You'll usually find point-to-point networks within many of today's WANs, and as you can see in the third part of Figure 1.13, a link from a computer to a hub or switch is also a valid point-to-point connection. A common version of this setup consists of a direct wireless link between two wireless bridges that's used to connect computers in two different buildings together.

Point-to-Multipoint Topology

Again as the name suggests, a *point-to-multipoint* topology consists of a succession of connections between an interface on one router and multiple destination routers—one point of connection to multiple points of connection. Each of the routers and every one of their interfaces involved in the point-to-multipoint connection are part of the same network.

Figure 1.14 shows a WAN and demonstrates a point-to-multipoint network. You can clearly see a single, corporate router connecting to multiple branches.

FIGURE 1.14   A point-to-multipoint network, example 1

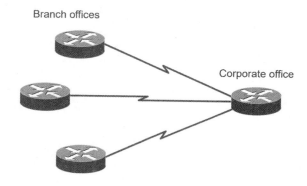

Figure 1.15 shows another prime example of a point-to-multipoint network: a college or corporate campus.

FIGURE 1.15   A point-to-multipoint network, example 2

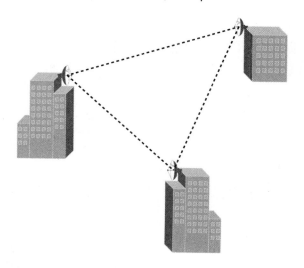

Hybrid Topology

I know I just talked about the hybrid network topology in the section about mesh topology, but I didn't give you a mental picture of it in the form of a figure. I also want to point out that *hybrid topology* means just that—a combination of two or more types of physical or logical network topologies working together within the same network.

Figure 1.16 depicts a hybrid network topology; it shows a few LANs connected by switches in a star topology configuration. The LANs are connected in a full mesh, which is connected to a router and a WAN link on a counter-rotating ring network.

FIGURE 1.16   A hybrid network

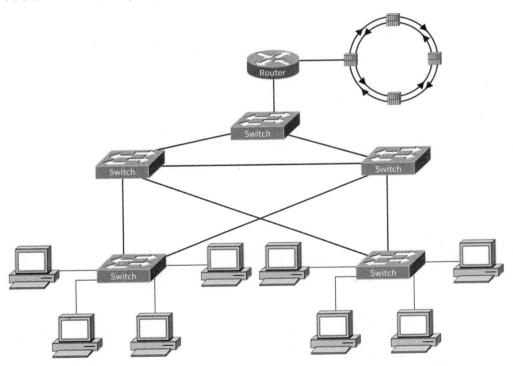

Topology Selection, Backbones, and Segments

Now that you're familiar with many different types of network topologies, you're ready for some tips on selecting the right one for your particular network. You also need to know about backbones and segments, which I'll cover in the very last part of this chapter.

🌐 **Real World Scenario**

They're Just Cables, Right?

Wrong! Regardless of the type of network you build, you need to start thinking about quality at the bottom and work up.

Think of it as if you were at an electronics store buying the cables for your home theater system. You've already spent a bunch of time and money getting the right components to meet your needs. Because you've probably parted with a hefty chunk of change, you might be tempted to cut corners, but why would you stop now and connect all your high-quality devices together with the cable equivalent of twine? No, you're smarter than that—you know that the exact cables that will maximize the sound and picture quality of your specific components can also protect them!

It's the same thing when you're faced with selecting the physical media for a specific network. You just don't want to cut corners here because this is the backbone of the network and you definitely don't want to be faced with going through the costly pain of replacing this infrastructure once it's been installed. Doing that will cost you a lot more than taking the time to wisely choose the right cables and spending the money it takes to get them in the first place. The network downtime alone can cost a company a bundle! Another reason for choosing the network's physical media well is that it will be there for a good 5 to 10 years. This means two things: It better be solid quality, and it better be scalable because that network will grow and change over the years.

Selecting the Right Topology

As you now know, not only do you have a buffet of network topologies to choose from, but each one also has pros and cons to implementing it. But it really comes down to that well-known adage "Ask the right questions." First, how much cash do you have? How much fault tolerance and security do you really need? Also, is this network likely to grow like a weed—will you need to quickly and easily reconfigure it often? In other words, how scalable does your network need to be?

For instance, if your challenge is to design a nice, cost-effective solution that involves only a few computers in a room, getting a wireless access point and some wireless network cards is definitely your best way to go because you won't need to part with the cash for a bunch of cabling and it's super easy to set up. Alternatively, suppose you're faced with coming up with a solid design for a growing company's already-large network. In that case, you're probably good to go with using a wired star topology because it will nicely allow for future changes. Remember, a star topology really shines when it comes to making additions to the network, moving things around, and making any changes happen quickly, efficiently, and cost-effectively.

If, say, you're hired to design a network for an ISP that needs to be up and running 99.9% of the time with no more than eight hours a year allowed downtime, well, you need Godzilla-strength fault tolerance. Do you remember which topology gives that up the best? (Hint: Internet.) Your primo solution is to go with either a hybrid or a partial mesh topology. Remember that partial mesh leaves you with a subset of $n(n-1)/2$ connections to maintain—a number that could very well blow a big hole in your maintenance budget!

Here's a list of things to keep in mind when you're faced with coming up with the right topology for the right network:

▪ Cost

▪ Ease of installation

▪ Ease of maintenance

▪ Fault-tolerance requirement

▪ Security requirement

The Network Backbone

Today's networks can get pretty complicated, so we need to have a standard way of communicating with each other intelligibly about exactly which part of the network we're referencing. This is the reason we divide networks into different parts called *backbones* and *segments*.

Figure 1.17 illustrates a network and shows which part is the backbone and which parts are segments.

FIGURE 1.17   Backbone and segments on a network

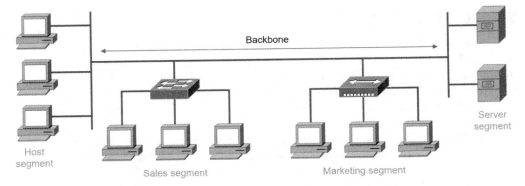

You can see that the network backbone is actually kind of like our own human backbone. It's what all the network segments and servers connect to and what gives the network its structure. As you can imagine, being such an important nerve center, the backbone must use some kind of seriously fast, robust technology—often Gigabit Ethernet or faster. And to optimize network performance—its speed and efficiency—it follows that you would want to connect all of the network's servers and segments directly to the network's backbone.

Network Segments

When we refer to a segment, we can mean any small section of the network that may be connected to, but isn't actually a piece of, the backbone. The network's workstations and servers organized into segments connect to the network backbone, which is the common connecting point for all segments; you can see this by taking another look at Figure 1.17, which displays four segments.

Service-Related Entry Points

In the networking world, clearly defined boundaries exist where one entity hands off a connection to another. These are common when connecting to a service provider's or carrier's WAN circuit.

The service entry point defines the point of responsibility. The common term used is the *demarcation point*, or *demarc* for short. A carrier will usually terminate with a piece of equipment called a *smart jack* that allows them to run diagnostics up to the physical point where the customer's network connects.

Service Provider Links

Service providers are ISPs and cable and telephone companies that provide networking services. There are many different technologies used to provide these services such as satellite links for earth station to satellite connections.

Traditional telephone companies may have extensive copper connections to homes and businesses that use digital subscriber lines (DSL) to provide last-hop, high-speed digital services. DSL used to be a popular method to connect to the Internet and a solid alternative to cable or fiber connections.

Cable companies now offer data and Internet services over their hybrid fiber/coax networks in addition to their traditional video offerings. A cable modem is installed at the customer's site and provides data, video, and voice services off the cable network.

Another common link is the *leased line*. When the provider installs a leased line, it is either a copper or fiber termination that interconnects two endpoints and is exclusive to the customer; there is no shared bandwidth, and leased lines are very secure as they are dedicated for the customer's use.

Virtual Networking

Just as the server world has been moving to virtualized processes, so has the network world. It is now common to provide networking services without deploying a hardware switch or router; it is all done in software! Companies such as VMware offer *virtual switch (vSwitch,* technology that provides the Ethernet switched and routing functions on the hypervisor, eliminating the need for external networking hardware. A vSwitch can operate and be configured the same as an external hardware appliance; just remember, a vSwitch is similar to software virtualization.

Virtualized servers do not have the means for inserting a hardware network interface card since they exist only in software. A *virtual network interface card (vNIC)* is installed to connect the virtual device to the hypervisor and, from there, out to the LAN.

Network function virtualization (NFV) is the process of taking networking functions such as routers, switches, firewalls, load balancers, and controllers and virtualizing them. This process allows all of these functions to run on a single device.

The magic behind all of the virtual networking popularity is the hypervisor. The hypervisor is software that is installed directly on a bare-metal server and allows for many virtual machines (VMs) to run, thinking they are using the server's hardware directly. This allows for many servers and virtual network devices to run on a single piece of computing hardware.

We will cover network virtualization in Chapter 17, "Data Center Architecture and Cloud Concepts."

Three-Tiered Model

The three-tiered networking model was introduced more than 20 years ago by Cisco, and it's been the gold-standard for network design. Even though it was introduced so long ago, it is still very much valid today for any hardware vendor. However, in today's small to midsize network designs, the collapsed-core model has been adopted to save the expense of additional network switching, as shown in Figure 1.18. The elements of both models are similar in function.

FIGURE 1.18   Three-tier versus collapsed-core model

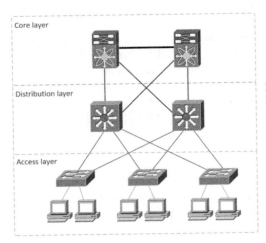
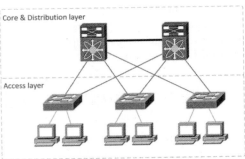

Core Layer   The core layer is also considered the backbone of the network. It is where you will find connectivity between geographic areas with WAN lines. It should be designed for high availability and only provides routing and switching of the entire network. Nothing should be done at the core layer to slow it down!

Distribution Layer   The distribution layer is often referred to as the workgroup layer or the aggregation layer because it allows for connectivity to multiple access layer switches. The distribution layer is where the control plane is located and is where packet filtering, security policies, routing between VLANs, and defining of broadcast domains are performed. You can think of it as the distribution of switching from the core to the access layer.

Access Layer   The access layer is often referred to as the edge switching layer, and it connects the end-user hosts. The access layer provides local switching and the creation of collision domains. It is simply designed for access to the network and it is where support begins for quality of service (QoS), power over Ethernet (PoE), and security.

The collapsed-core model was adopted to save cost and complexity in networks. With the powerful switching of today, we can support both the core layer and the distribution layer on the same piece of network switching equipment. It still performs the same functions as the core and distribution layer; it is just collapsed into one piece of switching equipment.

Spine and Leaf

The concept of spine-leaf switching is often referred to as a CLOS network, named after Charles Clos, who formalized the concept in 1938 of multistage circuit-switching. Spine-leaf switching creates a two-tier circuit-switched network.

With the expansion of both private and public data centers and the adoption of virtualization, a switching technology was needed that didn't fit the classic three-tier model. When we talk about virtualization, we should be open-minded that it could mean the virtualization of servers, clients, storage, applications, and just about anything you can think of that can be partitioned over many hosts. The classic three-tier and collapsed-core models work well in physical campus networks and enterprise networks; access switches provide a star topology to connect hosts on a one-to-one computer to port basis (sometimes two-to-one, if you employ VoIP phones, but I digress). This classic model does not do well in the data center.

Spine and leaf switching provides extremely fast networking switching, and it is almost exclusively used in data center network architecture. The concept is simple: Create a very fast and redundant backbone (spline) that is used only to connect leaf switches. The leaf switches in turn connect the hosts (servers) in the data center. A leaf switch will never directly talk to another leaf switch; it will always need to talk through the backbone or spine of the network. Servers will never be connected to the spine of the network directly. Servers are always connected through a leaf switch. Figure 1.19 shows a typical spine-leaf network.

FIGURE 1.19   A typical spine-leaf network

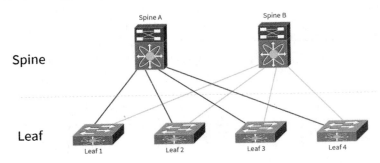

As you can see in Figure 1.19, the Spine A switch is connected to every leaf switch, and the Spine B switch is connected to every leaf switch. This allows extremely fast switching between Leaf 1 and Leaf 4 as well as any other leaf switch. Switching between two leaf switches is always two hops away no matter where they are in the network. It will traverse to the spine switch and then to the destination leaf switch.

Traffic Flow

Understanding traffic flow through your networks is important. But why? Why would you need to understand which type and direction the traffic flows through your network?

There are many reasons, but the most important, and the one we'll concentrate on here, is security.

Figure 1.20 shows the two essential points in your network to verify traffic flow, and both flows are important to understand so you know where you'll secure your data. The locations are north-south traffic flow and east-west traffic flow.

At first, the most important point for security will be the north-south traffic because data is flowing to and from your enterprise network to the outside Internet. However, this doesn't mean you should not take east-west traffic security seriously.

Let's define these two areas:

North-South   Looking at Figure 1.20, we can see the traffic found here entering and leaving your internal network. Tight security in this location is essential. The southbound traffic enters through a firewall and routers. Northbound traffic is routed from your internal network to the Internet.

East-West   East-west traffic is still important to understand that many types of attacks, particularly from the inside, must be taken seriously. You need to inspect the lateral traffic coming between server farms and data centers. There is a large amount of traffic here, and some examples of east-west data transfer are database replication, file transfers, and inter-process communication.

FIGURE 1.20   Understanding traffic flow in your network

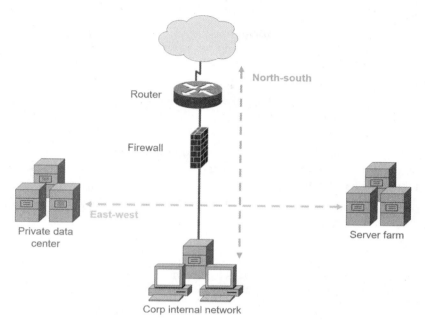

Summary

This chapter created a solid foundation for you to build your networking knowledge on as you go through this book.

You also learned that the components required to build a network aren't all you need. Understanding the various types of network connection methods, such as peer-to-peer and client-server, is also vital.

Further, you learned about the various types of logical and physical network topologies and the features and drawbacks of each. I wrapped up the chapter with a discussion about network virtualization and equipped you with the right questions to ask yourself to ensure that you come up with the right network topology for your networking needs.

Exam Essentials

Know your network topologies.   Know the names and descriptions of the topologies. Be aware of the difference between physical networks (what humans see) and logical networks (what the equipment "sees").

Know the advantages and disadvantages of the topologies.   It is essential to know what each topology brings to the table. Knowing the various characteristics of each topology comes in handy during troubleshooting.

Understand the terms *LAN* and *WAN*.   You need to understand when you would use a LAN and when you would use a WAN. A LAN is used to connect a group of hosts, and a WAN is used to connect various LANs.

Know the three-tiered model and collapsed core.   Know what the core, distribution, and access layer provide in the three-tier model. The collapsed core is used to reduce costs by collapsing the core and distribution tiers into one tier.

Understand the differences between north-south traffic and east-west traffic.   North-south traffic typically leaves the network through a routed connection. East-west traffic typically resides in the immediate network.

Written Lab

You can find the answers to the written labs in Appendix A. Fill in in the blank with the term that best fits the statement.

1. A _____ is a network typically found in your home or workplace.
2. A _____ connection connects your home or workplace to the Internet.
3. A _____ topology is also known as a hub-and-spoke topology.
4. The term _____ is used to describe the service-related entry point for a provider.
5. The _____ _____ model is used to condense the core and distribution layers into one layer.
6. A _____ is a virtualized piece of hardware that connects the virtual machine operating system to the network.
7. Fibre Channel is typically found inside a _____.
8. The term used to reference the smallest piece of the network is _____ _____.
9. The _____ technology uses labels to switch traffic.
10. The _____ _____ architecture is found in data centers to provide low-latency connectivity to servers.

Review Questions

You can find the answers to the review questions in Appendix B.

1. Which network type is locally owned and managed by an organization and used to connect the organization's LAN together?
   A. MAN
   B. CAN
   C. WAN
   D. PAN

2. Which network topology design has a centralized switch connecting all of the devices?
   A. Star topology
   B. Full mesh topology
   C. Partial mesh topology
   D. Hybrid topology

3. Which protocol can be typically found inside a PAN?
   A. Bluetooth
   B. MPLS
   C. SDWAN
   D. vNIC

4. When computers are logically grouped on a LAN based upon a functional department in the organization, what is the group called?
   A. Backbone
   B. CAN
   C. PAN
   D. Workgroup

5. Which is the primary benefit to using a star topology?
   A. Equal access
   B. Simplicity
   C. Easy to troubleshoot
   D. Redundancy

6. What type of logical connection does MPLS create to connect networks together?
   A. Peer-to-peer
   B. Client-server
   C. East-west
   D. Circuit

7. Which type of network is used exclusively for storage traffic?

   A. CAN

   B. SAN

   C. MAN

   D. LAN

8. Which type of traffic flow is routed from your internal network to the Internet?

   A. North-south

   B. East-west

   C. WAN

   D. MAN

9. Which topology incorporates some redundancy of equipment and connections to provide fault tolerance but is not completely fault-tolerant?

   A. Bus

   B. Mesh

   C. Ring

   D. Hybrid

10. Which topology should be selected if you have a central office that needs to communicate with several branch offices for WAN connectivity?

   A. Point-to-point

   B. Point-to-multipoint

   C. Mesh

   D. Bus

11. Which network architecture allows for access or sharing of resources in a network by the same host?

   A. Peer-to-peer

   B. Client-server

   C. LAN

   D. Hybrid topology

12. Which is the major advantage of client-server network architecture?

   A. Distributed security

   B. Centralized management

   C. Flexibility

   D. Equal access

13. You are setting up a network connection that requires redundancy in the event a switch or single link fails. Which topology should you select?

    A. Bus

    B. Ring

    C. Star

    D. Mesh

14. Where is the full mesh topology commonly seen in the three-tier design model?

    A. Core layer

    B. Distribution layer

    C. Access layer

    D. Routing layer

15. Which connectivity method is used within a small geographic area to connect an organization together?

    A. MAN

    B. LAN

    C. SAN

    D. PAN

16. Which virtual network element connects multiple VMs together?

    A. Hypervisor

    B. vSwitch

    C. Load balancer

    D. NFV

17. When you tether a cell phone to your laptops using wireless, what is this an example of?

    A. SAN

    B. MAN

    C. CAN

    D. PAN

18. What is the term used to describe the common network used to connect multiple network segments at high speed?

    A. Backbone

    B. WAN

    C. PAN

    D. Workgroup

19. What is a smart jack as it relates to WAN connectivity?

    A. Demarc

    B. NFV

    C. Load balancer

    D. Router

20. Which protocol is used with dynamic multipoint VPN deployments?

    A. mGRE

    B. MPLS

    C. SDWAN

    D. vNIC

Chapter

2

The Open Systems Interconnection (OSI) Reference Model

THE FOLLOWING COMPTIA NETWORK+ EXAM OBJECTIVES ARE COVERED IN THIS CHAPTER:

✓ **Domain 1.0 Networking Concepts**

✓ **1.1 Explain concepts related to the Open Systems Interconnection (OSI) reference model.**

- Layer 1 - Physical
- Layer 2 - Data link
- Layer 3 - Network
- Layer 4 - Transport
- Layer 5 - Session
- Layer 6 - Presentation
- Layer 7 - Application

In this chapter, we're going to analyze the Open Systems Interconnection model. I'll thoroughly describe each part to you in detail because it's imperative for you to grasp the OSI model's key concepts. Once solidly equipped with this vital foundation, you'll be set to move on and build your storehouse of networking knowledge.

The OSI model has seven hierarchical layers that were developed to enable different networks to communicate reliably between disparate systems.

Because this book is centering upon all things Network+, it's crucial for you to understand the OSI model as CompTIA sees it, so I'll present each of its seven layers in that light.

I'll also introduce *encapsulation*, which is the process of encoding data as it goes down the OSI model layers.

To find Todd Lammle CompTIA videos and questions, please see www.lammle.com.

Internetworking Models

In the very first networks, the computers could communicate only with other computers made by the same manufacturer. For example, companies ran either a complete DECnet solution or an IBM solution—not both together. In the late 1970s, the *Open Systems Interconnection (OSI) reference model* was created by the International Organization for Standardization (ISO) to break through this barrier.

The OSI model was meant to help vendors create interoperable network devices and software in the form of protocols, or standards, so that different vendors' networks could become compatible and work together. Like world peace, it'll probably never happen completely, but it's still a great goal.

The OSI model is the primary architectural model for networks. It describes how data and network information are communicated from an application on one computer through the network media to an application on another computer. The OSI reference model breaks this approach into layers.

Let's explore this layered approach as well as how you can utilize its key concepts to troubleshoot internetworks.

The Layered Approach

Basically, a *reference model* is a conceptual blueprint of how communications should take place. It addresses all the processes required for effective communication and divides these processes into logical groupings called *layers*. When a communication system is designed in this manner, it's known as a *layered architecture*.

Think of it like this: Say you and some friends want to start a company. One of the first things you'll do is sit down and think through what tasks must be done, who will do them, the order in which they will be done, and how they relate to each other. Ultimately, you might group these tasks into departments. Let's say you decide to have a customer service department, an inventory department, and a shipping department. Each of your departments has its own unique tasks, keeping its staff members busy and requiring them to focus only on their own duties.

In this scenario, I'm using departments as a metaphor for the layers in a communication system. For things to run smoothly, the staff of each department has to trust and rely heavily on the others to do their jobs and competently handle their unique responsibilities. During your planning sessions, you'll probably take notes, recording the entire process to facilitate later discussions about standards of operation that will serve as your business blueprint or reference model.

Once your business is launched, each department leader will need to develop practical methods to implement their assigned tasks using the specific part of the business model's blueprint that relates to their branch. These practical methods, or protocols, must be compiled into a standard operating procedures manual and followed closely. The procedures in your manual will have been included for different reasons and have varying degrees of importance and implementation. If you form a partnership or acquire another company, it will be crucial for its business protocols to either match or be compatible with yours.

Similarly, software developers can use a reference model to understand computer communication processes and see exactly what must be accomplished on any one layer and how. In other words, if I need to develop a protocol for a certain layer, I need to focus only on that specific layer's functions. I don't need to be concerned with those of any other layer because different protocols will be in place to meet the different layers' needs. The technical term for this idea is *binding*. The communication processes that are related to each other are bound, or grouped together, at a particular layer.

Advantages of Reference Models

The OSI model is hierarchical, and I'd like to point out that the same beneficial characteristics can actually apply to any layered model, such as the TCP/IP model. Understand that the central purpose of the OSI model, and all networking models, is to allow different vendors' networks to interoperate smoothly.

The Transmission Control Protocol/Internet Protocol (TCP/IP) suite was created by the Department of Defense (DoD) and will be covered in Chapter 6, "Introduction to the Internet Protocol."

These are some of the most important advantages we gain by using the OSI layered model:

- The OSI model divides network communication processes into smaller and simpler components, thus aiding component development, design, and troubleshooting.
- It allows multiple-vendor development through the standardization of network components.
- It encourages industry standardization by defining the specific functions that occur at each layer of the model.
- It allows various types of network hardware and software to communicate.
- It prevents changes in one layer from affecting other layers, facilitating development and making application programming much easier.

One of the greatest functions of the OSI specifications is to assist in data transfer between disparate hosts regardless of whether they're UNIX/Linux, Windows, or macOS-based.

But keep in mind that the OSI model isn't a physical model; it's a conceptual and comprehensive yet fluid set of guidelines, which application developers utilize to create and implement applications that run on a network. It also provides a framework for creating and implementing networking standards, devices, and internetworking schemes. The OSI model has seven layers:

- Application (layer 7)
- Presentation (layer 6)
- Session (layer 5)
- Transport (layer 4)
- Network (layer 3)
- Data Link (layer 2)
- Physical (layer 1)

Figure 2.1 summarizes the functions that occur at each layer of the OSI model. With this in mind, you're ready to delve into what takes place at each layer in detail.

Some people like to use the mnemonic Please Do Not Throw Sausage Pizza Away to remember the seven layers (starting at layer 1 and moving up to layer 7). I didn't make that up!

FIGURE 2.1   Layer functions

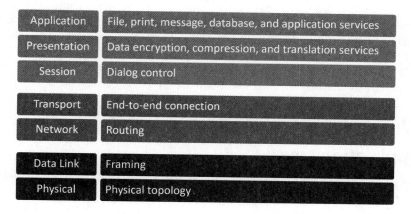

Application	File, print, message, database, and application services
Presentation	Data encryption, compression, and translation services
Session	Dialog control
Transport	End-to-end connection
Network	Routing
Data Link	Framing
Physical	Physical topology

The OSI's seven layers are divided into two groups. The top three layers define the rules of how the applications working within host machines communicate with each other as well as with end users. The bottom four layers define how the actual data is transmitted from end to end. Figure 2.2 shows the top three layers and their functions, and Figure 2.3 shows the four lower layers and their functions.

FIGURE 2.2   The upper layers

Application	Provides a user interface
Presentation	Presents data Handles processing such as encryption
Session	Keeps different applications' data separate

FIGURE 2.3   The lower layers

Transport	Provides reliable or unreliable delivery Performs error correction before retransmit
Network	Provides logical addressing, which router user for path determination
Data Link	Combines packets into bytes and bytes into frames Provides access to media using MAC address Performed error detection, not correction
Physical	Move bits between devices Specifies voltage, wire speed, and pin-out of cables

Looking at Figure 2.2, it's clear that actual users interact with the computer at the Application layer. It's also apparent that the upper layers are responsible for applications communicating between hosts. Remember that none of the upper layers "knows" anything about networking or network addresses. That's the responsibility of the four bottom layers.

Figure 2.3 illustrates that the four bottom layers define how data is transferred through physical media, switches, and routers. These bottom layers also determine how to rebuild a data stream from a transmitting host to a destination host's application.

So, let's start at the Application layer and work our way down the stack.

The Application Layer

The *Application layer* of the OSI model marks the spot where users actually communicate or interact with the computer. Technically, users communicate with the network stack through application processes, interfaces, or application programming interfaces (APIs) that connect the application in use to the operating system of the computer. The Application layer chooses and determines the availability of communicating partners along with the resources necessary to make their required connections. It coordinates partnering applications and forms a consensus on procedures for controlling data integrity and error recovery. The Application layer comes into play only when it's apparent that access to the network will be needed soon. Take the case of Google Chrome or Mozilla Firefox. You could uninstall every trace of networking components from a system, such as TCP/IP, the network card, and so on, and you could still use Chrome to view a local HTML document without a problem. But things would definitely get messy if you tried to do something like view an HTML document that had to be retrieved using HTTPS or nab a file with FTP or TFTP because Chrome or Firefox responds to requests like those by attempting to access the Application layer. So, what's happening is that the Application layer acts as an interface between the application program—which isn't part of the layered structure—and the next layer down by providing ways for the application to send information down through the protocol stack. In other words, browsers don't reside within the Application layer—they interface with Application layer protocols when they need to deal with remote resources.

The Application layer is also responsible for identifying and establishing the availability of the intended communication partner and determining whether sufficient resources for the requested communication exist.

These tasks are important because computer applications sometimes require more than just desktop resources. Often, they unite communicating components from more than one network application. Prime examples are file transfers and email as well as enabling remote access, network-management activities, and client-server processes like printing and information location. Many network applications provide services for communication over enterprise networks, but for present and future internetworking, the need is fast developing to reach beyond the limitations of current physical networking.

It's important to remember that the Application layer acts as an interface between application programs. For instance, Microsoft Word doesn't *reside* at the Application layer; it *interfaces* with the Application layer protocols. Later, in Chapter 6, "Introduction to the Internet Protocol," I'll tell you all about key programs or processes that do reside at the Application layer, like SFTP and TFTP.

The Presentation Layer

The *Presentation layer* gets its name from its purpose: It presents data to the Application layer and is responsible for data translation and code formatting.

A successful data-transfer technique is to adapt the data into a standard format before transmission. Computers are configured to receive this generically formatted data and then convert it into its native format for reading—for example, from EBCDIC to ASCII or from Unicode to ASCII, just to name a few. By providing translation services, the Presentation layer ensures that the data transferred from one system's Application layer can be read and understood by the Application layer on another system.

The OSI has protocol standards that define how standard data should be formatted. Tasks like data compression, decompression, encryption, and decryption are all associated with this layer. Some Presentation layer standards are even involved in multimedia operations.

The Session Layer

The *Session layer* is responsible for setting up, managing, and then tearing down sessions between Presentation layer entities. This layer also provides dialogue control between devices, or nodes. It coordinates communication between systems and serves to organize their communication by offering three different modes: one direction (*simplex*); both directions, but only one direction at a time (*half-duplex*); and bidirectional (*full-duplex*). To sum up, the Session layer basically keeps an application's data separate from other applications' data. For a good example, the Session layer allows multiple web browser sessions on your desktop at the same time.

The Transport Layer

The *Transport layer* segments and reassembles data into a data stream. Services located in the Transport layer handle data from upper-layer applications and unite it into the same data stream. They provide end-to-end data transport services and can establish a logical connection between the sending host and destination host on the internetwork.

The Transport layer provides the mechanisms for multiplexing upper-layer applications, establishing virtual connections, and tearing down virtual circuits. It also hides the many and sundry details of any network-dependent information from the higher layers, facilitating data transfer.

We'll cover Transmission Control Protocol (TCP) and User Datagram Protocol (UDP) thoroughly in Chapter 6, "Introduction to the Internet Protocol." Still, if you're already familiar with them, you know that they both work at the Transport layer. You also know that TCP is a reliable service and UDP is not. These two protocols give application developers more options because they have a choice between them when they're working with TCP/IP protocols.

> The term *reliable networking* relates to the Transport layer and means that acknowledgments, sequencing, and flow control will be used.

The Transport layer can be connectionless or connection-oriented, but it's especially important for you to really understand the connection-oriented portion of the Transport layer. So, let's take some time to delve into the connection-oriented (reliable) protocol of the Transport layer now.

Connection-Oriented Communication

Before a transmitting host starts to send segments down the OSI layered model, the sender's TCP process contacts the destination's TCP process to establish a connection. The resulting creation is known as a *virtual circuit*. This type of communication is called *connection-oriented*. During this initial *handshake*, the two TCP processes also agree on the amount of information that will be sent in either direction before the respective recipient's TCP sends back an acknowledgment. With everything agreed on in advance, the path is paved for reliable communication to take place.

Figure 2.4 depicts a typical reliable session taking place between sending and receiving systems. Both of the hosts' application programs begin by notifying their individual operating systems that a connection is about to be initiated.

FIGURE 2.4   Establishing a connection-oriented session

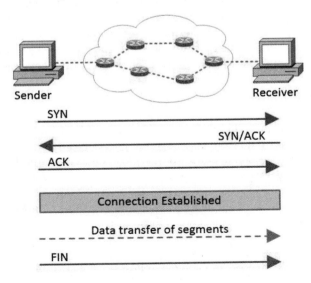

The two operating systems communicate by sending messages over the network confirming that the transfer is approved and that both sides are ready for it to take place. After all of this required synchronization occurs, a connection is fully established, and the data transfer begins. This virtual circuit setup is called *overhead*.

While the information is being transferred between hosts, the two machines periodically check in with each other, communicating through their protocol software to ensure that all is going well and that data is being received properly.

Let me sum up the steps in the connection-oriented session—the TCP three-way handshake—pictured in Figure 2.4:

1. The first "connection agreement" segment is a request for synchronization.

2. The next segments acknowledge the request and establish connection parameters—the rules—between hosts. These segments request that the receiver's sequencing is synchronized here as well so that a bidirectional connection is formed.

3. The final segment is also an acknowledgment. It notifies the destination host that the connection agreement has been accepted and that the connection has been established. Data transfer can now begin.

I know I went into a lot of detail about this connection setup, and I did that so you would have a really clear picture of how it works. You can refer to this entire process as the "TCP three-way handshake" I already mentioned, known as SYN, SYN/ACK, ACK or synchronize, synchronize-acknowledgment, acknowledgment.

That sounds pretty simple, but things don't always flow so well. Sometimes congestion can occur during a transfer because a high-speed computer is generating data traffic a lot faster than the network can handle transferring it. A bunch of computers simultaneously sending datagrams through a single gateway or to a destination can also clog things up. In the latter case, a gateway or destination can become congested even though no single source caused the problem. Either way, the problem is like a freeway bottleneck—too much traffic for too small a capacity. It's not usually one car that's the problem; it's that there are just too many cars on that particular route.

Flow Control

Data integrity is ensured at the Transport layer by maintaining *flow control* and by allowing users to request reliable data transport between systems. Flow control provides a means for the receiver to govern the amount of data sent by the sender. It prevents a sending host on one side of the connection from overflowing the buffers in the receiving host—an event that can result in lost data. Reliable data transport employs a connection-oriented communications session between systems, and the protocols involved ensure that the following will be achieved:

1. The segments delivered are acknowledged back to the sender upon their reception.

2. Any segments not acknowledged are retransmitted.

3. Segments are sequenced back into their proper order upon arrival at their destination.

4. A manageable data flow is maintained in order to avoid congestion, overloading, and data loss.

So what happens when a machine receives a flood of datagrams too quickly for it to process? It stores them in a memory section called a *buffer*. But this buffering tactic can solve the problem only if the datagrams are part of a small burst. If not and if the datagram deluge continues, a device's memory will eventually be exhausted, its flood capacity will be exceeded, and it will react by discarding any additional datagrams that arrive like a dam spilling over!

This sounds pretty bad, and it would be if it weren't for the transport function of network flood control that actually works well. But how? Instead of just dumping resources and allowing data to be lost, the transport can issue a "not ready" or "Stop" indicator to the sender, or source, of the flood, as shown in Figure 2.5.

FIGURE 2.5   Transmitting segments with flow control

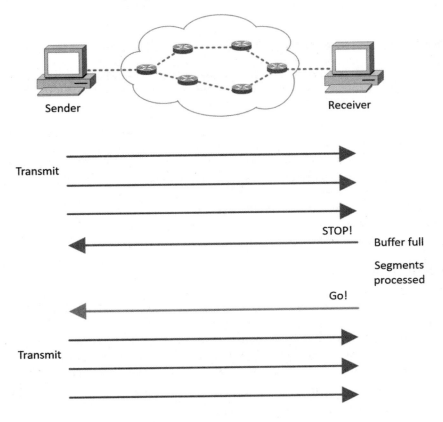

This mechanism works kind of like a stoplight, signaling the sending device to stop transmitting segment traffic to its overwhelmed peer. After the peer machine's receiver processes the segments abounding in its memory reservoir (its buffer), it sends out a "ready" transport indicator. When the machine waiting to transmit the rest of its datagrams receives this "go" indictor, it resumes its transmission.

During fundamental, reliable, connection-oriented data transfer, datagrams are delivered to the receiving host in exactly the same sequence they're transmitted. So if any data segments are lost, duplicated, or damaged along the way, a failure notice is transmitted. This error is corrected by making sure the receiving host acknowledges it has received each and every data segment, and in the correct order.

To summarize, a service is considered connection-oriented if it has the following characteristics:

- A virtual circuit is set up (such as a three-way handshake).
- It uses sequencing.
- It uses acknowledgments.
- It uses flow control.

Windowing

Ideally, data throughput happens quickly and efficiently. And as you can imagine, it would be slow if the transmitting machine had to wait for an acknowledgment after sending each segment. But because time is available *after* the sender transmits the data segment and *before* it finishes processing acknowledgments from the receiving machine, the sender uses the break as an opportunity to transmit more data. The quantity of data segments (measured in bytes) that the transmitting machine is allowed to send without receiving an acknowledgment is represented by something called a *window*.

 Windows are used to control the amount of outstanding, unacknowledged data segments.

It's important to understand that the size of the window controls how much information is transferred from one end to the other. Although some protocols quantify information by observing the number of packets, TCP/IP measures it by counting the number of bytes.

Figure 2.6 illustrates two window sizes—one set to 1 on the receiver and one set to 3 on the sender. In this simplified example, both the sending and receiving machines are workstations.

When you've configured a window size of 1, the sending machine waits for an acknowledgment for each data segment it transmits before transmitting another. If you've configured a window size of 3, the sending machine is allowed to transmit three data segments before an acknowledgment is received. In reality, the window size actually delimits the number of bytes that can be sent at a time.

FIGURE 2.6   Windowing

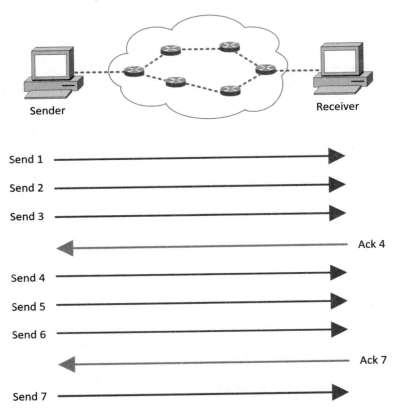

    If a receiving host fails to receive all the segments that it should acknowledge, the host can improve the communication session by decreasing the window size.

Acknowledgments

Reliable data delivery ensures the integrity of a data stream being sent from one machine to the other through a fully functional data link. It guarantees that the data won't be duplicated or lost. This is achieved through something called *positive acknowledgment with retransmission*—a technique that requires a receiving machine to communicate with the transmitting source by sending an acknowledgment message back to the sender when it receives data. The sender documents each segment it sends and waits for this acknowledgment before sending the next segment. When it sends a segment, the transmitting machine starts a timer and retransmits if it expires before an acknowledgment is returned from the receiving end.

In Figure 2.7, the sending machine transmits segments 1, 2, and 3. The receiving node acknowledges it has received them by requesting segment 4. When it receives the acknowledgment, the sender then transmits segments 4, 5, and 6. If segment 5 doesn't make it to the destination, the receiving node acknowledges that event with a request for the segment to be re-sent. The sending machine will then re-send the lost segment and wait for an acknowledgment, which it must receive in order to move on to the transmission of segment 7.

FIGURE 2.7   Transport layer reliable delivery

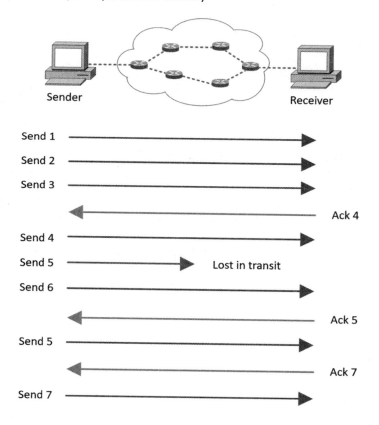

The Transport layer doesn't need to use a connection-oriented service. That choice is up to the application developer. It's safe to say that if you're connection-oriented, meaning that you've created a virtual circuit, you're using TCP. If you aren't setting up a virtual circuit, then you're using UDP and are considered connectionless.

The Network Layer

The *Network layer* manages logical device addressing, tracks the location of devices on the network, and determines the best way to move data. This means that the Network layer must transport traffic between devices that aren't locally attached. Routers are layer 3 devices that are specified at the Network layer and provide the routing services within an internetwork.

It happens like this: First, when a packet is received on a router interface, the destination IP address is checked. If the packet isn't destined for that particular router, the router looks up the destination network address in the routing table. Once the router chooses an exit interface, the packet is sent to that interface to be framed and sent out on the local network. If the router can't find an entry for the packet's destination network in the routing table, the router drops the packet.

Two types of packets are used at the Network layer:

Data Packets   These are used to transport user data through the internetwork. Protocols used to support data traffic are called *routed protocols*. Two examples of routed protocols are Internet Protocol (IP) and Internet Protocol version 6 (IPv6), which you'll learn all about coming up in Chapter 7, "IP Addressing."

Route-Update Packets   These are used to update neighboring routers about the networks connected to all routers within the internetwork. Protocols that send route-update packets are called routing protocols, and some common ones are Routing Information Protocol (RIP), RIPv2, Enhanced Interior Gateway Routing Protocol (EIGRP), and Open Shortest Path First (OSPF). Route-update packets are used to help build and maintain routing tables on each router.

Figure 2.8 pictures a routing table. The routing table used by a router includes the following information:

FIGURE 2.8   Routing table used in a router

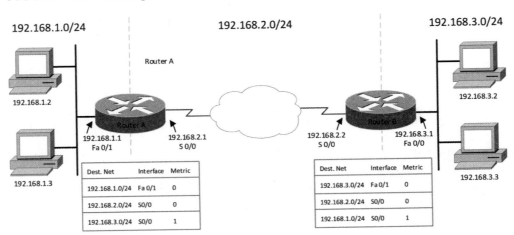

Network Addresses   These are protocol-specific network addresses. A router must maintain a routing table for individual routing protocols because each routing protocol keeps track of a network that includes different addressing schemes, like IP and IPv6. Think of it as a street sign in each of the different languages spoken by the residents who live on a particular street. If there were American, Spanish, and French folks on a street named Cat, the sign would read Cat/Gato/Chat.

Interface   This is the exit interface a packet will take when destined for a specific network.

Metric   This value equals the distance to the remote network. Different routing protocols use different ways of computing this distance. I'll cover routing protocols in Chapter 9, "Introduction to IP Routing." For now, know that some routing protocols, namely, RIP, use a *hop count*—the number of routers a packet passes through en route to a remote network. Other routing protocols alternatively use bandwidth, delay of the line, and even something known as a tick count, which equals 1/18 of a second, to make routing decisions.

Routers break up broadcast domains, which means that by default, broadcasts aren't forwarded through a router. This is a good thing because it reduces traffic on the network. Routers also break up collision domains, but this can be accomplished using layer 2 (Data Link layer) switches as well.

> Broadcast and collision domains will be covered in detail in Chapter 5, "Networking Devices." For now, remember that routers break up broadcast domains, and switches break up collision domains.

Because each interface in a router represents a separate network, it must be assigned unique network identification numbers, and each host on the network connected to that router must use the same network number.

Figure 2.9 demonstrates how a router works within an internetwork.

FIGURE 2.9   A router in an internetwork

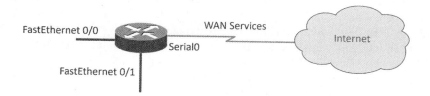

Each router interface is a broadcast domain.
Routers break up broadcast domains by
default and provide WAN services.

Here are some key points about routers that you really should commit to memory:

- Routers, by default, won't forward any broadcast or multicast packets.

- Routers use the logical address in a Network layer header to determine the next-hop router to forward the packet to.

- Routers can use access lists, created by an administrator, to control security on the types of packets that are allowed to enter or exit an interface.

- Routers can provide layer 2 bridging functions if needed and can simultaneously route through the same interface.

- Layer 3 devices (routers, in this case) provide connections between virtual LANs (VLANs).

- Routers can provide quality of service (QoS) for specific types of network traffic.

A router can also be referred to as a layer 3 switch. These terms are interchangeable.

The Data Link Layer

The *Data Link layer* provides the physical transmission of the data and handles error notification, network topology, and flow control. This means the Data Link layer ensures that messages are delivered to the proper device on an LAN using hardware (MAC) addresses and translates messages from the Network layer into bits for the Physical layer to transmit.

The Data Link layer formats the message into pieces, each called a *data frame*, and adds a customized header containing the destination and source hardware addresses. This added information forms a sort of capsule that surrounds the original message in much the same way that engines, navigational devices, and other tools were attached to the lunar modules of the Apollo project. These various pieces of equipment were useful only during certain stages of flight and were stripped off the module and discarded when their designated stage was complete. This is a great analogy for data traveling through networks because it works similarly.

It's important for you to understand that routers, which work at the Network layer, don't care about where a particular host is located. They're concerned only about where networks are located and the best way to reach them—including remote ones. Routers are totally obsessive when it comes to networks, and in this instance, obsession is a good thing! The Data Link layer is responsible for the unique identification of each device that resides on a local network.

For a host to send packets to individual hosts on a local network as well as transmit packets between routers, the Data Link layer uses hardware addressing, specifically MAC addresses. Each time a packet is sent between routers, it's framed with control information at the Data Link layer. However, that information is stripped off at the receiving router, and only the original packet is left completely intact. This framing of the packet continues for each hop until the packet is finally delivered to the correct receiving host. It's important to understand that the packet itself is never altered along the route; it's only encapsulated with the type of control information required for it to be properly passed on to the different media types.

Figure 2.10 shows the Data Link layer with the Ethernet and Institute of Electrical and Electronics Engineers (IEEE) specifications.

FIGURE 2.10   Data Link layer

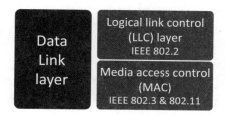

When you check it out, notice that the IEEE 802.2 standard is not only used in conjunction with the other IEEE standards, but it also adds functionality to those standards.

The IEEE Ethernet Data Link layer has two sublayers:

Media Access Control (MAC)   Defines how packets are placed on the media. Contention media access is "first come, first served" access, where everyone shares the same bandwidth. Physical addressing is defined here, as are logical topologies. What's a logical topology? It's the signal path through a physical topology. Line discipline, error notification (not correction), ordered delivery of frames, and optional flow control can also be used at this sublayer.

Logical Link Control (LLC)   Responsible for identifying Network layer protocols and then encapsulating them, an LLC header tells the Data Link layer what to do with a packet once a frame is received. It works like this: A host receives a frame and looks in the LLC header to find out where the packet is destined—say, the IP protocol at the Network layer. The LLC can also provide flow control and sequencing of control bits.

Project 802

One of the major components of the Data Link layer is the result of the IEEE's 802 subcommittees and their work on standards for local area and metropolitan area networks (LANs/MANs). The committee met in February 1980, so they used the 80 from 1980 and the 2 from the second month to create the name Project 802. The designation for an 802 standard always includes a dot (.) followed by either a single or a double digit. These numeric digits specify particular categories within the 802 standard. These standards are listed in the following table:

Standard	Topic
802.1	LAN/MAN Management (and Media Access Control Bridges)
802.2	Logical Link Control
802.3	CSMA/CD (Ethernet)
802.4	Token Passing Bus
802.5	Token Passing Ring
802.6	Distributed Queue Dual Bus (DQDB) Metropolitan Area Network (MAN)
802.7	Broadband Local Area Networks
802.8	Fiber-Optic LANs and MANs
802.9	Isochronous LANs
802.10	LAN/MAN Security
802.11	Wireless LAN
802.12	Demand Priority Access Method
802.15	Wireless Personal Area Network
802.16	Wireless Metropolitan Area Network (also called WiMAX)
802.17	Resilient Packet Ring

Note that 802.1, 802.3, 802.11, and 802.15 are the only Active 802 standards. The others are either Disbanded or Hibernating.

The takeaway is to remember that 802.3 calls out anything having to do with Ethernet, and 802.11 is anything wireless.

The Physical Layer

Finally, we're hitting bottom. Well, not in a bad way—we've now arrived at the *Physical layer*, which does two important things: It sends bits and receives bits. Bits come only in values of 1 or 0—a Morse code with numerical values. The Physical layer communicates directly with the various types of actual communication media. Different kinds of media represent these bit values in different ways. Some use audio tones, and others employ *state transitions*—changes in voltage from high to low and low to high. Specific protocols are needed for each type of media to describe the proper bit patterns to be used, how data is encoded into media signals, and the various qualities of the physical media's attachment interface.

The Physical layer specifies the electrical, mechanical, procedural, and functional requirements for activating, maintaining, and deactivating a physical link between end systems. This layer is also where you identify the interface between the *data terminal equipment (DTE)* and the *data communication equipment (DCE)*. (Some older phone company employees still call DCE data circuit-terminating equipment.) The DCE is usually located at the customer, whereas the DTE is the attached device. The services available to the DTE are most often accessed via the DCE device, which is a modem or *channel service unit/data service unit (CSU/DSU)*.

The Physical layer's connectors and different physical topologies are defined by the standards, allowing disparate systems to communicate.

Finally, the Physical layer specifies the layout of the transmission media, otherwise known as its topology. A physical topology describes the way the cabling is physically laid out, as opposed to the logical topology that we just talked about in the section "The Data Link Layer." The various physical topologies include bus, star, ring, and mesh and were described in Chapter 1, "Introduction to Networks."

EXERCISE 2.1

Investigating the Applications and the OSI Model

This exercise will help you investigate the OSI model and understand the various layers. Find an application on your computer that interacts with the network. Answer the following questions:

1. How do you interact with the application?
2. Does the application support compression/decompression or encryption/decryption?
3. How does the application communicate (half-duplex, full-duplex, simplex)?
4. Which Transport layer protocol does it use to communicate?
5. What is the IP address of your computer?
6. What method of connectivity do you have to the network?
7. Is it connected with wired or wireless?

As you answer these questions, you will notice you are learning how the application operates with the various layers from Application to Physical.

Introduction to Encapsulation

When a host transmits data across a network to another device, the data goes through *encapsulation*: It's wrapped with protocol information at each layer of the OSI model. Each layer communicates only with its peer layer on the receiving device.

To communicate and exchange information, each layer uses *protocol data units (PDUs)*. These hold the control information attached to the data at each layer of the model. They're usually attached to the header in front of the data field but can also be in the trailer, or end, of it.

At a transmitting device, the data-encapsulation method works like this:

1. User information is converted to data for transmission on the network.

2. Data is converted to segments, and a reliable connection is set up between the transmitting and receiving hosts.

3. Segments are converted to packets or datagrams, and a logical address is placed in the header so each packet can be routed through an internetwork. A packet carries a segment of data.

4. Packets or datagrams are converted to frames for transmission on the local network. Hardware (Ethernet) addresses are used to uniquely identify hosts on a local network segment. Frames carry packets.

5. Frames are converted to bits, and a digital encoding and clocking scheme is used.

Figure 2.11 shows how user data is encapsulated at a transmitting host.

FIGURE 2.11   Data encapsulation

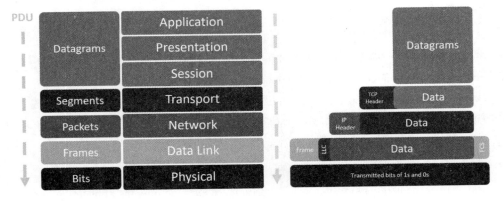

Before we move onto the next chapter, how does step 5 work when frames are converted to bits and an encoding and clocking scheme is used? This is a modulation technique, and we'll end the chapter by discussing it.

Modulation Techniques

In networks, modulation is the process of varying one or more waveform properties, called the *carrier signal*, with a signal that typically contains information to be transmitted.

Modulation of a waveform transforms a baseband (Ethernet or wireless) message signal into a passband signal. (A passband, also known as a bandpass filtered signal, is the range of frequencies or wavelengths that can pass through a filter without attenuation.) In current networks, modulation takes a digital or analog signal and puts it in another signal that can be physically transmitted.

A modulator is a device that performs modulation of a signal, and a demodulator is a device that performs demodulation, the inverse of modulation. We typically call these modems (from modulator–demodulator), which can perform both operations.

The purpose of digital modulation is to transfer a digital bit stream over an analog bandpass channel. (A good example would be data transmitting over the public switched telephone network, where a bandpass filter limits the frequency range to 300–3400 Hz, or over a limited radio frequency band.) The purpose of an analog modulation is to transfer an analog baseband (or lowpass) signal (for example, an audio signal, wireless network, or TV signal) over an analog bandpass channel at a different frequency.

Analog and digital modulation use something called frequency-division multiplexing (FDM), where several low-pass information signals are transferred simultaneously over the same shared physical network using separate passband channels (several different frequencies).

The digital baseband modulation methods found in our Ethernet networks, also known as line coding, are used to transfer a digital bit stream over a baseband channel. Baseband means that the signal being modulated uses the complete available bandwidth.

Time-division multiplexing (TDM) is a method of transmitting and receiving many independent signals over a common signal path using synchronized network devices at each end of the transmission line so that each signal appears on the line only a fraction of the time in an alternating pattern. The receiving end demultiplexes the signal back to its original form.

After you learn more foundational material about networking in the next few chapters, I'll return to the encapsulation method in Chapter 6.

Summary

You're now armed with a ton of fundamental information. You're set to build on it and are well on your way to certification.

Let's take a minute to go over what you've learned in this chapter. We started by discussing internetworking models and the advantages of having them. I then discussed the OSI model—the seven-layer model used to help application developers design applications that can run on any type of system or network. Each layer has its special jobs and select responsibilities within the model to ensure that solid, effective communications do, in fact, occur. I provided you with complete details of each layer and discussed how you need to view the specifications of the OSI model.

I also discussed the encapsulation method used in networking. Encapsulation is a highly important concept to understand, and I'll continue to discuss it throughout this book.

This chapter finished with a brief introduction to modulation of digital and analog signals.

Exam Essentials

Memorize and understand the OSI layers.   You must remember and understand the seven layers of the OSI model and what function each layer provides. The Application, Presentation, and Session layers are the upper layers responsible for communicating from a user interface to an application. The Transport layer provides segmentation, sequencing, and virtual circuits. The Network layer provides logical network addressing and routing through the internetwork. The Data Link layer frames and places data on the network medium. The Physical layer is responsible for taking 1s and 0s and encoding them into a digital signal for transmission on the network segment.

Know the sublayers of the Data Link layer.   In addition to the OSI layers, knowing that the Data Link layer is the only layer that has sublayers and the functions of those sublayers is extremely important. The Data Link layer has two sublayers: LLC and MAC. The LLC sublayer is responsible primarily for the multiplexing of Network layer protocols. The MAC sublayer is responsible for physical addressing and determining the appropriate time to place data on the network.

Written Lab

You can find the answers to the written labs in Appendix A. Fill in the OSI layers in order, from layer 7 to layer 1.

Layer 7

Layer 6

Layer 5

Layer 4

Layer 3

Layer 2

Layer 1

Review Questions

You can find the answers to the review questions in Appendix B.

1. Flow control can be found at which layer of the OSI?

    A. Transport layer

    B. Network layer

    C. Data Link layer

    D. Session layer

2. What is required before TCP can begin sending segments?

    A. Three-way handshake

    B. Port agreement

    C. Sequencing of segments

    D. Acknowledgment of segments

3. Which layer of the OSI is responsible for dialogue control of applications?

    A. Application layer

    B. Physical layer

    C. Session layer

    D. Network layer

4. Which layer is responsible for compression and decompression?

    A. Application layer

    B. Physical layer

    C. Session layer

    D. Presentation layer

5. Which OSI layer is responsible for logical addressing?

    A. Transport layer

    B. Network layer

    C. Application layer

    D. Data Link layer

6. As information travels down the network stack from the Application layer to the Physical layer, what happens?

    A. Datagrams

    B. PDUs

    C. Encapsulation

    D. Decapsulation

7. Which sublayer of the Data Link OSI layer is responsible for identifying Network layer protocols and encapsulating them?

   A. MAC

   B. LLC

   C. Data Link

   D. Session

8. Which is *not* a benefit to the OSI model?

   A. Multivendor development with a standardized model

   B. Prevents a change in one layer from affecting other layers

   C. Allows various network hardware and software to communicate

   D. Allows software to run at network speeds

9. Which three upper layers operate together?

   A. Application, Presentation, and Session

   B. Presentation, Session, and Transport

   C. Transport, Session, and Application

   D. Network, Data Link, and Physical

10. Which 802 working group defines the LLC sublayer of the Data Link layer?

   A. 802.2

   B. 802.3

   C. 802.15

   D. 802.11

11. Which concept describes transmitting multiple segments before the receiving host acknowledges the data?

   A. Sequencing

   B. Compression

   C. Windowing

   D. Encryption

12. Which device will stop broadcasts from propagating the network?

   A. Router

   B. Switch

   C. Hub

   D. WAP

13. Which is used to determine the best path to a destination network?
    A. Acknowledgment
    B. Network address
    C. Interface
    D. Metric

14. Which protocol data unit (PDU) is used to describe data at the Physical layer?
    A. Datagrams
    B. Bits
    C. Frames
    D. Segments

15. Which OSI layers are responsible for framing data and transmitting the data?
    A. LLC and Physical layers
    B. Data Link and Physical layers
    C. Network and Transport layers
    D. Session and Transport layers

16. Which layer is responsible for creating a virtual circuit?
    A. Presentation
    B. Session
    C. Transport
    D. Network

17. TCP and UDP reside at which layer of the OSI model?
    A. Physical
    B. Session
    C. Network
    D. Transport

18. What is the proper order of data encapsulation?
    A. Datagram, segment, packet, frame, bits
    B. Bits, frame, packet, segment, datagram
    C. Segment, datagram, packet, frame, bits
    D. Datagram, packet, segment, frame, bits

19. Which layer is responsible for routing data packets?

   A. Physical

   B. Data Link

   C. Transport

   D. Network

20. Which IEEE standard specifies the protocol for CSMA/CD?

   A. 802.2

   B. 802.3

   C. 802.5

   D. 802.11

Chapter

3

Networking Connectors and Wiring Standards

THE FOLLOWING COMPTIA NETWORK+ EXAM OBJECTIVES ARE COVERED IN THIS CHAPTER:

✓ **Domain 1.0 Networking Concepts**

✓ **1.5 Compare and contrast transmission media and transceivers.**

- Wired
    - Single-mode vs. multimode fiber
    - Direct attach copper
    - (DAC) cable
    - Twinaxial cable
    - Coaxial cable
    - Cable speeds
    - Plenum vs. non-plenum cable
- Transceivers
    - Protocol
    - Ethernet
    - Fibre Channel (FC)
    - Form factors
    - Small form-factor pluggable (SFP)
    - Quad small form-factor pluggable (QSFP)

- Connector types
  - Subscriber connector (SC)
  - Local connector (LC)
  - Straight tip (ST)
  - Multi-fiber push on (MPO)
  - Registered jack (RJ)11
  - RJ45
  - F-type
  - Bayonet Neill–Concelman (BNC)
  - Domain 5.0

✓ **5.2 Given a scenario, troubleshoot common cabling and physical interface issues.**

- Cable issues
  - Incorrect cable
  - Single mode vs. multimode
  - Category 5/6/7/8
  - Shielded twisted pair (STP)
  - vs. unshielded twisted pair
  - (UTP)

The idea of connecting a bunch of computers together hasn't changed a whole lot since the mid-1980s, but how we go about doing that certainly has. Like everything else, the technologies and devices we create our networks with have evolved dramatically and will continue to do so in order to keep up with the ever-quickening pace of life and the way we do business.

When you connect computers to form a network, you want error-free, blazingly fast communication, right? Although "error-free" and reality don't exactly walk hand in hand, keeping lapses in communication to a minimum and making that communication happen really fast are definitely possible. But it isn't easy, and understanding the types of media and network topologies used in networking today will go far in equipping you to reach these goals; so will being really knowledgeable about the array of components and devices used to control network traffic.

All of these networking ingredients are going to be the focus of this chapter. In it, I'll cover different types of networking media, and devices, and compare the features that they all bring into designing a solid network that's as problem free and turbocharged as possible.

To find Todd Lammle CompTIA videos and practice questions, please see www.lammle.com.

Physical Media

Most of us rely on wireless networking methods that work using technologies such as Wi-Fi, radio frequency, and infrared, but even wireless depends on a physical media backbone in place somewhere. And the majority of installed local area networks (LANs) today communicate via some kind of cabling, so let's take a look at the three types of popular cables used in modern networking designs:

- Coaxial
- Twisted-pair
- Fiber optic

Coaxial Cable

Coaxial cable, referred to as *coax*, contains a center conductor made of copper that's surrounded by a plastic jacket with a braided shield over it. A type of plastic such as polyvinyl chloride (PVC) or fluoroethylene propylene (FEP, commonly known as Teflon) covers this metal shield. The Teflon-type covering is frequently referred to as a *plenum-rated coating*, and it's definitely expensive but often mandated by local or municipal fire code when cable is hidden in walls and ceilings. Plenum rating applies to all types of cabling and is an approved replacement for all other compositions of cable sheathing and insulation like PVC-based assemblies.

The difference between plenum and non-plenum cable comes down to how each is constructed and where you can use it. Many large multistory buildings are designed to circulate air through the spaces between the ceiling of one story and the floor of the next; this space between floors is referred to as the *plenum*. And it just happens to be a perfect spot to run all the cables that connect the legions of computers that live in the building. Unless there's a fire—if that happens, the non-plenum cable becomes a serious hazard because its insulation gives off poisonous smoke that gets circulated throughout the whole building. Plus, non-plenum cables can actually become "wicks" for the fire, helping it quickly spread from room to room and floor to floor—yikes!

Because it's a great goal to prevent towering infernos, the National Fire Protection Association (NFPA) demands that cables run within the plenum have been tested and guaranteed as safe. They must be fire retardant and create little or no smoke and poisonous gas when burned. This means you absolutely can't use a non-plenum-type cable in the plenum, but it doesn't mean you can't use it in other places where it's safe. And because it's a lot cheaper, you want to use it where you can.

Thin Ethernet, or *thinnet* or 10Base2, is a thin coaxial cable. It is the same as thick coaxial cable, except it's only about 5 mm, or 2/10″, diameter coaxial cable. Thin Ethernet coaxial cable is Radio Grade 58, or just RG-58. Figure 3.1 shows an example of a thinnet. This connector resembles the coaxial connector used for cable TV, an *F-type connector*.

FIGURE 3.1   A stripped-back thinnet cable

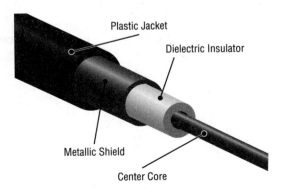

Plastic Jacket

Dielectric Insulator

Metallic Shield

Center Core

Oh, by the way, if you use thinnet cable, you've got to use Bayonet Neill–Concelman (BNC) connectors to attach stations to the network, as shown in Figure 3.2, and you have to use 50 ohm terminating resistors at each end of the cable to achieve the proper performance. In the 1980s, I remember the term British Naval Connector was also used for the BNC connector.

FIGURE 3.2 Male and female BNC connectors

You don't have to know much about most coax cable types in networks anymore, especially the thinnet and thicknet types of coaxial cable. Thicknet was known as RG-8 and was about 1/2" in diameter, also requiring 50 ohm terminating resistors on each end of the cable. Nowadays, we use 75-ohm coax for cable TV; using coax in the Ethernet LAN world is pretty much a thing of the past, but we do use them for high-bandwidth runs in our data centers. RG-6, or CATV coax, is used in our broadband world.

You can attach a BNC connector to the cable with a crimper that looks like a weird pair of pliers and has a die to crimp the connector. A simple squeeze crimps the connector to the cable. You can also use a screw-on connector, but I avoid doing that because it's not very reliable.

You can use a BNC coupler to connect two male connectors together or two female connectors together.

Table 3.1 lists some specifications for the different types of coaxial cable, but understand that we use only RG-59 and RG-6 in today's world.

TABLE 3.1   Coaxial cable specifications

RG Rating	Popular Name	Ethernet Implementation	Type of Cable
RG-58 U	N/A	None	Solid copper
RG-58 A/U	Thinnet	10Base2	Stranded copper
RG-8	Thicknet	10Base5	Solid copper
RG-59	Cable television Low cost, short distance	N/A	Solid copper
RG-6	Cable television, cable modems Longer distances than RG-59; some power implementations	N/A	Solid copper

F-type

The F connector, or F-type connector, is a form of coaxial connector that is used for cable TV. It has an end that screws to tighten the connector to the interface. It resembles the RG-58 mentioned earlier in this section.

 An advantage of using coax cable is the braided shielding that provides resistance to electronic pollution like *electromagnetic interference (EMI)*, *radio frequency interference (RFI)*, and other types of stray electronic signals that can make their way onto a network cable and cause communication problems.

Twisted-Pair Cable

Twisted-pair cable consists of multiple individually insulated wires that are twisted together in pairs. Sometimes a metallic shield is placed around them, which is why it's called *shielded twisted-pair (STP)*. Cable without outer shielding is called *unshielded twisted-pair (UTP)*, and it's used in twisted-pair Ethernet (10BaseT, 100BaseTX, 1000BaseTX, 10GBaseT, and 40GBaseT) networks.

Twinaxial Cable

Twinaxial cabling is used for short-distance high-speed connections such as 10 and 40G Ethernet connections in a data center. Twinaxial is also known as *twinax*. The advantage of using twinaxial cable is that there are significant cost savings over fiber-optic cabling since twinaxial cables are copper-based. If your distance is 10 meters or less, using these cables can be a considerable cost savings.

Also in the twinaxial family is direct attach copper (DAC) cable. DAC has connectors at either end of a fixed-length ~26-28 AWG twinaxial copper cable that allows direct communication between devices over copper wire. Like shielded twisted pair (SSTP), DAC uses electromagnetic shielding around the copper cable to increase speeds and to keep communication reliable.

Ethernet Cable Descriptions

Ethernet cable types are described using a code that follows this format: *N <Signaling> X*. The *N* refers to the signaling rate in megabits per second. *<Signaling>* stands for the signaling type—either baseband or broadband—and the *X* is a unique identifier for a specific Ethernet cabling scheme.

Here's a common example: 100Base*X*. The 100 tells us that the transmission speed is 100 Mb, or 100 megabits. The *X* value can mean several different things; for example, a *T* is short for *twisted-pair*. This is the standard for running 100-megabit Ethernet over two pairs (four wires) of Category 5, 5e, 6, 6a, 7, and 8 UTP.

So why are the wires in this cable type twisted? Because when electromagnetic signals are conducted on copper wires in close proximity—like inside a cable—it causes interference called *crosstalk*. Twisting two wires together as a pair minimizes interference and even protects against interference from outside sources. This cable type is the most common today for the following reasons:

- It's cheaper than other types of cabling.
- It's easy to work with.
- It allows transmission rates that were impossible 10 years ago.

UTP cable is rated in these categories:

Category 1   Two twisted wire pairs (four wires). It's the oldest type and is only voice grade—it isn't rated for data communication. People refer to it as plain old telephone service (POTS). Before 1983, this was the standard cable used throughout the North American telephone system. POTS cable still exists in parts of the public switched telephone network (PSTN) and supports signals limited to the 1 MHz frequency range.

Category is often shortened to *Cat*. Today, any cable installed should be a minimum of Cat 5e because some cable is now certified to carry bandwidth signals of 350 MHz or beyond. This allows unshielded twisted-pair cables to exceed speeds of 1 Gbps—fast enough to carry broadcast-quality video over a network.

Category 2   Four twisted wire pairs (eight wires). It handles up to 4 Mbps, with a frequency limitation of 10 MHz, and is now obsolete.

Category 3   Four twisted wire pairs (eight wires) with three twists per foot. This type can handle transmissions up to 16 MHz. It was popular in the mid-1980s for up to 10 Mbps Ethernet, but it's now limited to telecommunication equipment and, again, is obsolete for networks.

Category 4   Four twisted wire pairs (eight wires), rated for 20 MHz; also obsolete.

Category 5   Four twisted wire pairs (eight wires), used for 100BaseTX (two pair wiring) and rated for 100 MHz. But why use Cat 5 when you can use Cat 5e for the same price? I am not sure you can even buy plain Cat 5 anymore! Using Cat 6 is an option, but it's slightly harder to install due to its size compared to 5e.

Category 5e (Enhanced)   Four twisted wire pairs (eight wires), recommended for 1000BaseT (four pair wiring) and rated for 100 MHz but capable of handling the disturbance on each pair that's caused by transmitting on all four pairs at the same time—a feature that's needed for Gigabit Ethernet. Any category below 5e shouldn't be used in today's network environments.

Figure 3.3 shows a basic Cat 5e cable with the four wire pairs twisted to reduce crosstalk.

FIGURE 3.3   Cat 5e UTP cable

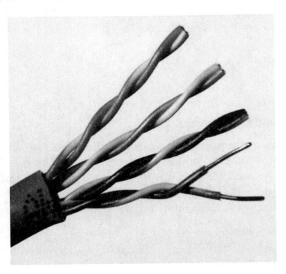

Category 6   Four twisted wire pairs (eight wires), used for 1000BaseTX (two pair wiring) and rated for 250 MHz. Cat 6 became a standard in June 2002. You would usually use it as riser cable to connect floors. If you're installing a new network in a new building, there's no reason to use anything but Category 6 UTP cabling and running fiber runs between floors.

Category 6A (Augmented)   Characterized to 500 MHz with improved crosstalk characteristics, which allows 10GBaseT to be run for up to 100 meters (basic Cat 6 cable has a reduced maximum length when used for 10GBaseT). The most important point is a performance difference between Electronic Industries Alliance and Telecommunications Industry Association (EIA/TIA) component specifications for the NEXT (near-end crosstalk) transmission parameter. Running at a frequency of 500 MHz, an ISO/IEC Cat 6A connector provides double the power (3db) of a Cat 6A connector that conforms with the EIA/TIA specification. Note that 3 dB equals a 100 percent increase of a near-end crosstalk noise reduction.

Category 7   Allows 10 Gigabit Ethernet over 100 meters of copper cabling. The cable contains four twisted copper wire pairs, just like the earlier standards.

Category 8   Developed to address the ever-increasing speed of Ethernet and added support for 25G and 40G transmission with a distance of 30 meters, which is perfect for data center deployments.

Connecting UTP

BNC connectors won't fit very well on UTP cable, so you need to use a *registered jack (RJ)* connector, which you're familiar with because most telephones connect with them. The connector used with UTP cable is called RJ-11 for phones that use four wires; RJ-45 has four pairs (eight wires), as shown in Figure 3.4.

FIGURE 3.4   RJ-11 and RJ-45 connectors

RJ-11

RJ-45

Figure 3.5 shows the pin-outs used in a typical RJ-45 connector.

Most of the time, UTP uses RJ connectors, and you use a crimper to attach them to a cable, just as you would with BNC connectors. The only difference is that the die that holds the connector is a different shape. Higher-quality crimping tools have interchangeable dies for both types of cables. We don't use RJ-11 for LANs, but we do use them for our home Digital Subscriber Line (DSL) connections.

FIGURE 3.5   The pin-outs in an RJ-45 connector, T568B standard

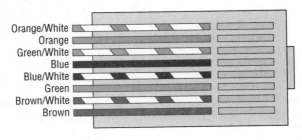

   RJ-11 uses two wire pairs, and RJ-45 uses four wire pairs.

There's one other type of copper connector, called the RJ-48c, which looks exactly like an RJ-45 connector. This plug is similar to the RJ-45 in that it has four wire pairs, but they are wired differently and used for different circumstances.

RJ-45 is mainly used in LANs with short distances (typically up to 100 meters), where the RJ-48c wiring type would be used with a T1 connection, which is a long-distance wide area network (WAN). In addition, to protect the signal in an RJ-48c, the wires are typically shielded, whereas the RJ-45 uses unshielded wiring.

 Real World Scenario

Category Cabling Tips

Since you want data rates faster than 100 Mbps over UTP, ensure that all components are rated to deliver this and be really careful when handling all components. If you yank on Cat 5e cable, it will stretch the number of twists inside the jacket, rendering the Cat 5e label on the outside of the cable invalid. Cat 6 cabling has a plastic spine to prevent stretching issues. Newer standards like 7 and 8 have metal shielding in the cable to prevent these problems.

Also, be certain to connect and test all four pairs of wire. Although today's wiring usually uses only two pairs (four wires), the standard for Gigabit Ethernet over UTP requires that all four pairs (eight wires) be in good condition.

Also be aware that a true Cat 5e/6/7/8 cabling system uses rated components from end to end, patch cables from workstation to wall panel, cable from wall panel to patch panel, and patch cables from patch panel to hub. So if any components are missing or if the lengths don't match the Category 5e/6/7/8 specification, you just don't have a Category 5e/6/7/8 cabling installation. And certify that the entire installation is Category 5e/6/7/8-compliant. I've got to warn you that doing this requires some pretty pricey test equipment to make the appropriate measurements!

Fiber-Optic Cable

Because fiber-optic cable transmits digital signals using light impulses rather than electricity, it's immune to EMI and RFI. Anyone who's seen a network's UTP cable run down an elevator shaft would definitely appreciate this fiber feature. Fiber cable allows light impulses to be carried on either a glass or a plastic core. Glass can carry the signal a greater distance, but plastic costs less. Whichever the type of core, it's surrounded by a glass or plastic cladding with a different refraction index that reflects the light back into the core. Around this is a layer of flexible plastic buffer that can be wrapped in an armor coating that's usually Kevlar, which is then sheathed in PVC or plenum.

The cable itself comes in either single-mode fiber or multimode fiber; the difference between them is in the number of light rays (the number of signals) they can carry. Multimode fiber is most often used for shorter-distance applications and single-mode fiber for spanning longer distances.

Although fiber-optic cable may sound like the solution to many problems, it has its pros and cons just like the other cable types.

Here are the pros of fiber-optic cable:

- It's completely immune to EMI and RFI.

- It can transmit up to 40 kilometers (about 25 miles).

And here are the cons of fiber-optic cable:

- It's difficult to install.

- It's more expensive than twisted-pair.

- Troubleshooting equipment is more expensive than twisted-pair test equipment.

- It's harder to troubleshoot.

Single-Mode Fiber

Single-mode fiber-optic cable (SMF) is a very high-speed, long-distance media that consists of a single strand—sometimes two strands—of glass fiber that carries the signals. Light-emitting diodes (LEDs) and laser are the light sources used with SMF. The light source is transmitted from end to end and pulsed to create communication. This is the type of fiber cable employed to span really long distances because it can transmit data up to 90 times farther than multimode fiber at a faster rate. That is 40 to 80 kilometers depending on the transceiver being used!

Clearly, because the transmission media is glass, the installation of SMF can be a bit tricky. Yes, there are outer layers protecting the glass core, but the cable still shouldn't be crimped or pinched around any tight corners.

Multimode Fiber

Multimode fiber-optic cable (MMF) also uses light to communicate a signal, but with it, the light is dispersed on numerous paths as it travels through the core and is reflected back. A special material called *cladding* is used to line the core and focus the light back onto it. MMF provides high bandwidth at high speeds over medium distances (up to about 3,000 feet), but beyond that it can be really inconsistent. This is why MMF is most often used within a smaller area of one building; SMF can be used between buildings.

MMF is available in glass or in a plastic version that makes installation a lot easier and increases the installation's flexibility. Fiber specifications are covered in great detail in Chapter 4, "The Current Ethernet Specifications."

Fiber Connectors

There are several different fiber connectors to use in a fiber-optic installation. I will cover the most common fiber connectors used in networks today. Each fiber connector has a benefit or purpose in a fiber-optic installation. It is important to know the visual differences between the fiber connectors and their respective names.

Straight Tip (ST)

The *straight tip (ST)* connector, shown in Figure 3.6, was originally designed by AT&T for fiber-optic cables. It is commonly used with single-mode fiber, discussed earlier. The connector is one of the most popular connectors to date with fiber optics for WAN connectivity on SMF. The cable connector can be found in both SMF and MMF cable installations. The cable operates similar to a BNC connector; it is a bayonet-style mechanism that you twist and lock into position. The benefit to this cable is that it will not come loose over time because of the positive locking mechanism.

FIGURE 3.6 An ST connector

> **NOTE**
>
> Another type of connector I want to mention is the FC connector (although not covered in the Network+ exam objectives, it's important to know for foundation), or field assembly connector, also called the ferrule connector, which isn't very popular. It's still used in telecommunications and measurement equipment with single-mode lasers. It looks identical to ST connectors but has a screw mechanism in lieu of a BNC connector.

Subscriber Connector (SC)

The *subscriber (or square) connector (SC)* is a square connector with a floating ferrule that contains the fiber-optic cable, as shown in Figure 3.7. The cable comes with a plastic clip that holds the transmit and receive cables secure for insertion. These clips generally allow you to disassemble the cable ends so transmit and receive can be swapped. The SC connector is often referred to by installers as "Square Charlie," and it's the way I've remembered the shape throughout the years. It can be found in SMF and MMF installations, but it is most popular with MMF installations. The SC connector is larger than most modern connectors, so it is starting to be replaced in new installations. The cable operates with a push-on/pull-off mating mechanism.

FIGURE 3.7   An SC connector

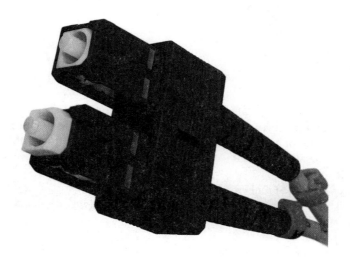

Small Form Factor Fiber-Optic Connectors

Another fiber-optic connector is the *small form factor (SFF)* style of connector, which allows more fiber-optic terminations in the same amount of space than its standard-sized counterparts. The three most popular versions are the *mechanical transfer registered jack (MT-RJ or MTRJ)*, designed by AMP, the *local connector (LC)*, designed by Lucent, and the *multi-fiber push on (MPO)* developed and licensed by NTT Group.

The MT-RJ fiber-optic connector was the first small form factor fiber-optic connector to be widely used, and it's only one-third the size of the SC and ST connectors it most often replaces. It offers these benefits:

- Small size

- TX and RX strands in one connector

- Keyed for single polarity

- Pre-terminated ends that require no polishing or epoxy

- Easy to use

Figure 3.8 shows an example of an MT-RJ fiber-optic connector.

FIGURE 3.8 A sample MT-RJ fiber-optic connector

The local connector (LC) resembles an RJ-style connector; it has a spring-loaded detent similar to the RJ connector that allows it to be held in place. The LC connector has become a popular cable connector because of its size; this allows greater density of ports on a switch. The connector is commonly found on MMF and SMF optic cables. The cable cannot be disassembled like the SC connector (see Figure 3.7), so transmit and receive fiber lines cannot be swapped side to side.

LC is a newer style of SFF fiber-optic connector that's pulling ahead of the MT-RJ. It's especially popular for use with Fibre Channel adapters (FCs) and is a standard used for fast storage area networks and Gigabit Ethernet adapters.

Since I just brought up Fibre Channel (FC), let's stop and define it: FC is a very high-speed data transfer protocol (usually running at 2 Gbps, 4 Gbps, 8 Gbps, 16 Gbps, and 32 Gbps) that is different than any other type of storage transfer protocol. FC delivers what is called raw black date, in order and lossless. FC connects data storage called storage area networks (SANs).

The Fibre Channel protocol, in the past, was mostly used for supercomputers, but now it is a common connection type in an enterprise's SAN.

What is interesting about Fibre Channel networks is that the FC switches create a large, switched fabric, and the switches in an FC network operate in unison as one big switch.

FC transceivers and Ethernet optical modules use different protocols. The FC transceiver belongs to the Fibre Channel protocol, which does not follow the OSI model. Ethernet optical modules use the IEEE 802.3 standard for packet-based physical communication in an LAN.

Figure 3.9 depicts an example of the LC connector.

FIGURE 3.9   A sample LC fiber-optic connector

The LC fiber-optic connector has similar advantages to MT-RJ and other SFF-type connectors, but it's easier to terminate. It uses a ceramic insert just as standard-sized fiber-optic connectors do.

The multi-fiber push on connector is yet another SFF high-density fiber-optic connector that provides 2, 8, 12, or 24 fiber-optic connections in a single connector, as shown in Figure 3.10. The MPO connector typically fans out from a single connector to multiple LC connectors to provide 10 Gbps to 100 Gbps for each connection. This provides a single interface from a fiber distribution panel to multiple transceivers in a network switch.

FIGURE 3.10   An MPO connector

APC vs. UPC

The *angled physical contact (APC)* and *ultra physical contact (UPC)* is a not a connector; it is a finish on the end of the connector to curtain optical decibel loss. The choice between APC and UPC can make a pretty big difference on how your network will perform.

The ultra-polished connector looks like what you'd expect to find in a fiber-optic end. The cut is perfectly straight, as shown on the bottom of Figure 3.11.

FIGURE 3.11   APC and UPC connectors

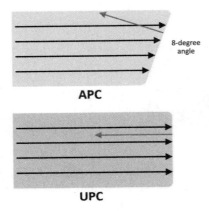

The angle-polished connector looks like the one on the top in Figure 3.11. Notice the perfectly cut angle, which seems odd, but there is a reason for this, and it's a good one!

With the UPC, the light is reflected back down to the core of the fiber cable, which causes a loss of decibels called a return loss because the angled connector causes the light to reflect into the cladding—the thick sides of the glass instead of the core. But the APC doesn't cause nearly as much decibel loss when using this type of connector. Very cool design indeed!

You can tell the difference between an APC and UPC connector finish by looking at the color of the plastic that composes the connector. A green connector has an APC finish on the connector end, and a blue connector has a UPC finish on the connector end.

 **Real World Scenario**

Should I Use Copper or Fiber?

If your data runs are measured in miles, fiber optic is your cable of choice because copper can't give you more than about 1,500 feet without electronics regenerating the signal. The standards limit UTP to a pathetic 328 feet.

Another good reason to opt for fiber is if you require high security because it doesn't create a readable magnetic field. Although fiber-optic technology was initially super expensive and nasty to work with, it's now commonly used for Gigabit, 10 or 40 GB Internet backbones.

Ethernet running at 10 Mbps over fiber-optic cable to the desktop is designated 10BaseFL; the 100 Mbps version of this implementation is 100BaseFX. The *L* in the 10 Mbps version stands for *link*. Other designations are *B* for *backbone* and *P* for *passive*.

Fiber Distribution Panel

Fiber distribution panels (FDPs) are termination and distribution systems for fiber-optic cable facilities. They consist of a cable management tray and a splice drawer. They are designed for central offices, remote offices, and LANs using fiber-optic facilities.

Fiber-Optic Transceivers

Fiber-optic transceivers can be either unidirectional (simplex) or bidirectional (duplex).

Unidirectional An optic fiber cable is unidirectional when it can only transmit data in one direction, either from the source to the destination or vice versa.

Bidirectional Bidirectional optic fiber cable is capable of transmitting data in both directions simultaneously. Bidirectional communication is possible if the cable used is following the EEE 802.3ah 1000BASE-BX10-D and 1000BASE-BX10-U standards. The communication over a single strand of fiber is achieved by separating the transmission wavelength of the two devices, as depicted in Figure 3.12.

FIGURE 3.12   Bidirectional communication

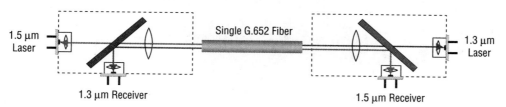

Transceivers

A transceiver is a device made up of both a transmitter and a receiver, which are combined and share common circuitry or a single housing. The term applies to wireless communications devices such as cellular telephones, cordless telephone sets, handheld two-way radios, and mobile two-way radios. Occasionally, the term is used in reference to transmitter and receiver devices in cable or optical fiber systems.

SFP+   The *small form-factor pluggable (SFP)* is a compact pluggable optical module transceiver used for both telecommunication and data communications applications. The *enhanced small form-factor pluggable (SFP+)* transceiver is an enhanced version of the SFP that supports data rates up to 16 Gbit/s.

QSFP   The *quad small form-factor pluggable (QSFP)* is another compact, hot-pluggable transceiver used for data communications applications. It interfaces networking hardware (such as servers and switches) to a fiber-optic cable or active or passive electrical copper connection. It allows data rates from 4x1 Gbps for QSFP and 4x10 Gbit/s for QSFP+ to the highest rate of 4x28 Gbit/s known as QSFP28 used for 100 Gbit/s links.

Media Converters

Sometimes, you'll need to convert from one media type to another. Maybe you need to go from one mode of fiber to another mode, or in an even more extreme case, you need to go from fiber to Ethernet. If you're faced with situations like these, you'll need to be familiar with some of the more common media converters:

Single-Mode Fiber to Ethernet   These devices accept a fiber connector and an Ethernet connector and convert the signal from Ethernet and single-mode fiber (see Figure 3.13).

FIGURE 3.13   Single-mode fiber to Ethernet

Multimode Fiber to Ethernet   These devices accept a fiber connector and an Ethernet connector and convert the signal from Ethernet and multimode fiber (see Figure 3.14).

FIGURE 3.14   Multimode fiber to Ethernet

Fiber to Coaxial   These devices accept a fiber connector and a coaxial connector and convert digital signals from optical to coax (see Figure 3.15).

FIGURE 3.15   Fiber to coaxial

Front

Back

Single-Mode to Multimode Fiber   These devices accept a single-mode fiber connector and a multimode fiber connector and convert the signals between the two (see Figure 3.16).

FIGURE 3.16   Single-mode to multimode fiber

FIGURE 3.16   Single-mode to multimode fiber

Serial Cables

Except for multimode fiber, all the cable varieties I've talked about so far are considered serial cable types. In network communications, *serial* means that one bit after another is sent out onto the wire or fiber and interpreted by a network card or other type of interface on the other end.

Each 1 or 0 is read separately and then combined with others to form data. This is very different from parallel communication, where bits are sent in groups and have to be read together to make sense of the message they represent. A good example of a parallel cable is an older Centronics printer cable—which has been mostly replaced by USB, as I'll get to in a minute.

RS-232

Recommended Standard 232 (RS-232) was a cable standard commonly used for serial data signals connecting the data Terminal Equipment (DTE) and the Data Communications Equipment (DCE), such as a computer's serial port to an external modem.

Figure 3.17 shows an example of one of the many types of RS-232 cables. These cables normally connect to a connector on the device called a *DB-9*.

FIGURE 3.17   RS-232 cable ends

Because laptops don't even come with these types of connectors anymore, they've pretty much been replaced by things like USB and USB-C.

DB-25

Now here's a connector that has been around for a while! The D series of connectors was invented by ITT Cannon in 1952, and the *D* was followed by *A*, *B*, *C*, *D*, or *E*, which described the shell size, and then the numbers of pins or sockets. DB-25 tells us we have 25 pins in a "B" size shell. RS-232 devices usually used the DB-25 connector, but today we don't use RS-232 or DB-25, and we rarely use a DB-9, which used to be used for Cisco console cables but has mostly been replaced by USB.

Universal Serial Bus

Universal Serial Bus (USB) is now the built-in serial bus du jour of most motherboards. You usually get a maximum of 4 external USB interfaces, but add-on adapters can take that up to as many as 16 serial interfaces. USB can actually connect a maximum of 127 external devices, and it's a much more flexible peripheral bus than either serial or parallel.

We use USB to connect printers, scanners, and a host of other input devices such as keyboards, joysticks, and mice. When connecting USB peripherals, you've got to connect them either directly to one of the USB ports on the PC or to a USB hub that is connected to one of those USB ports. You can see a picture of this in Figure 3.18.

FIGURE 3.18   A USB port

Hubs can be chained together to provide multiple USB connections, but even though you can connect up to 127 devices, it's really not practical to go there. Each device has a USB plug, as shown in Figure 3.19.

FIGURE 3.19   A USB plug

Cable Properties

We use so many different types of cables in a network because each type has its own properties that specifically make it the best to use for a particular area or purpose. Different types vary in transmission speeds, distance, duplex, noise immunity, and frequency; I'll cover each next.

Transmission Speeds

Based on the type of cable or fiber you choose and the network that it's installed in, network administrators can control the speed of a network to meet the network's traffic demands. Admins usually permit, or would like to have, transmission speeds of up to 10 Gbps or higher on the core areas of their networks that connect various network segments. In the distribution and access areas, where users connect to switches, it's typically 100/1000 Mbps per connection, but transmission speeds are creeping up because the traffic demand is getting higher.

Distance

Deciding factors used in choosing what cable type to use often come down to the topology of a network and the distance between its components. Some network technologies can run much farther than others without communication errors, but all network communication technologies are prone to *attenuation*—the degradation of a signal due to the medium itself and the distance signals have to travel. Some cable types suffer from attenuation more than others. For instance, any network using twisted-pair cable should have a maximum segment length of only 328 feet (100 meters).

Duplex

All communications are either half-duplex or full-duplex. The difference is whether the communicating devices can "talk" and "listen" at the same time.

During half-duplex communication, a device can either send communication or receive communication, but not both at the same time. Think walkie-talkie—when you press the button on the walkie-talkie, you turn the speaker off and you can't hear anything the other side is saying.

In full-duplex communication, both devices can send and receive communication at the same time. This means that the effective throughput is doubled and communication is much more efficient. Full duplex is typical in most of today's switched networks. I'll discuss both full- and half-duplex in more detail in Chapter 4, "The Current Ethernet Specifications."

Noise Immunity (Security, EMI)

Anytime electrons are pushed through two wires next to each other, a magnetic current is created. And we can create a current in the wires. This is good because without *magnetic flux*, we wouldn't be using computers—the power that surges through them is a result of it. The bad news is that it also creates two communications issues.

First, because the wire is creating a current based on the 1s and 0s coursing through it, with the right tools in hand, people can read the message in the wire without cutting it or even removing the insulation. You've heard of this—it's called *tapping* the wire, and it's clearly a valid security concern. In ancient history, high-security installations like the Pentagon actually encased communication wires in lead shielding to prevent them from being tapped. STP wires make tapping a little harder, but not hard enough.

The best way to solve the magnetic-flux problem caused by electricity is to not use these wires at all. As I said, fiber-optic cables carry the signal as light on a glass or a really pure plastic strand, and light is not susceptible to magnetic flux, making fiber optics a whole lot harder to tap. It's still not impossible—you can do it at the equipment level, but you have to actually cut and then repair the cable to do that, which isn't likely to go unnoticed.

The second magnetic-flux issue comes from the outside in instead of from the inside out. Because wires can take on additional current if they're near any source of magnetism, you've got to be really careful where you run your cables. You can avoid EMI by keeping copper cables away from all powerful magnetic sources like electric motors, speakers, amplifiers, fluorescent light ballasts, and so on. Just keep them away from anything that can generate a magnetic field!

Frequency

Each cable type has a specified maximum frequency that gives you the transmission bandwidth it can handle. Cat 5e cable is tested to 100 MHz maximum frequency and can run 1 Gbps signals for relatively short distances. That's maxing it out, but it's still good for connecting desktop hosts at high speeds. On the other hand, Cat 6 is a 250 MHz cable that can handle 1 Gbps data flow all day long with ease. Cat 6 has a lot more twists and thicker cables, so it's best used when connecting floors of a building; however, be sure to check out Cat 7 and 8, which is more of our future cabling.

EXERCISE 3.1

Investigating Computer Connections

This exercise is to help you investigate the various computer connections in your workplace or home. Answer the following questions after inspecting the back of your computer and your Internet connection:

1. Which ports can you identify (DB-9, USB, RJ-45, just to name a few)?

2. How is your computer connected to the network?

3. What type of connections does your router have?

As you answer these questions you will probably have other questions, such as speed, distance, noise immunity, and many others. Try to investigate your provider and their connection to your home or business.

    Although a signal is measured as bandwidth, the capacity to carry the signal in a cable is measured as frequency.

Wiring Standards

Ethernet cabling is an important thing to understand, especially if you're planning to work on any LAN. There are different types of wiring standards available:

- T568A
- T568B
- Straight-through
- Crossover
- Rolled/rollover

We will look into each of these, and then I'll end this discussion with some examples.

T568A vs. T568B

If you look inside a network cable, you'll find four pairs of wires twisted together to prevent crosstalk; they're also twisted like this to help prevent EMI and tapping. The same pins have to be used on the same colors throughout a network to receive and transmit, but how do you decide which color wire goes with which pin? The good news is that you don't have to decide—at least not completely.

Two wiring standards have surfaced that have been agreed on by more than 60 vendors, including AT&T, 3Com (acquired by HP), and Cisco, although there isn't 100% agreement. In other words, over the years, some network jacks have been pinned with the T568A standard, and some have used the T568B standard, which can cause a bit of confusion if you don't know what you're looking at in your network.

T568A By looking at Figure 3.20, you can see that the green pair is used for pins 1 and 2 but the orange pair is split to pins 3 and 6, separated by the blue pair.

FIGURE 3.20 T568A wired standard

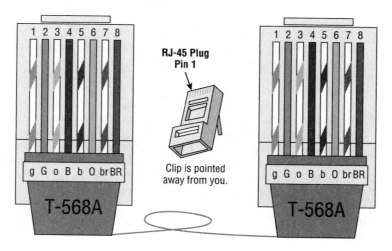

T568B Now take a look at Figure 3.21. The orange pair is pins 1 and 2, and the green pair is pins 3 and 6, again separated by the blue pair.

 Note that the only difference between T568A and T568B is that pairs 2 and 3 (orange and green) are swapped. Also, you can use a UTP coupler to connect two RJ-45 connectors together to lengthen a cable or to make a straight-through cable into a crossover, and vice versa.

FIGURE 3.21 T568B wired standard

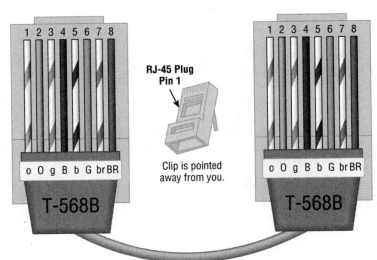

If you're thinking, "What's the difference, and why does it matter?" the answer is the position of four wires on one side of the cable—that's it!

 If you're installing new cabling to each cubicle and/or office, you need to make sure to connect all eight pins—and use Cat 5e through 8. Voice over IP (VoIP) uses all eight pins, and it's really common to have voice and data on the same wire at the same time in today's networks. Pins 4, 5, 7, and 8 are used in both standards. They are needed for 1000BaseT, Power over Ethernet (PoE), and specialized versions of 100 Mbps networks. We will cover PoE in Chapter 11, "Switching and Virtual LANs."

This only leaves the wire pairs to connect to pins 1, 2, 3, and 6 for data. Remember, if we connect the green-white, green, orange-white, and orange wires to pins 1, 2, 3, and 6, respectively, on both sides of the cable, we're using the T568A standard and creating the kind of straight-through cable that's regularly implemented as a regular *patch cable* for most networks. On the other hand, if we switch from pin 1 to pin 3 and from pin 2 to pin 6 on one side only, we've created a *crossover cable* for most networks. Let's take a look.

Straight-Through Cable

The straight-through cable is used to connect a host to a switch or hub or a router to a switch or hub.

NOTE   No worries—I'll tell you all about devices like switches, hubs, and routers in detail in Chapter 5, "Networking Devices."

Four wires are used in straight-through cable to connect 10/100 Ethernet devices. It's really pretty simple to do this; Figure 3.22 depicts the four wires used in a straight-through Ethernet cable.

FIGURE 3.22   Straight-through Ethernet cable

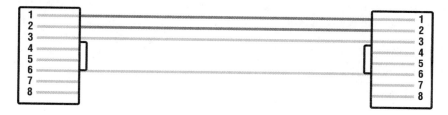

Notice that only pins 1, 2, 3, and 6 are used. Connect 1 to 1, 2 to 2, 3 to 3, and 6 to 6 and you'll be up and networking in no time. Just remember that this would be a 10/100 Ethernet-only cable, so it wouldn't work with 1000 Mbps or greater Ethernet.

Crossover Cable

The same four wires are used in this cable, and just as with the straight-through cable, you simply connect the different pins together. Crossover cables can be used to connect these devices:

- Switch to switch
- Hub to hub
- Host to host
- Hub to switch
- Router direct to host

Take a look at Figure 3.23, which demonstrates how each of the four wires is used in a crossover Ethernet cable.

Okay, did you notice that instead of connecting 1 to 1, 2 to 2, and so on, we connected pins 1 to 3 and 2 to 6 on each side of the cable? A crossover cable is typically used to connect two switches, but it can also be used to test communications between two workstations directly, bypassing the switch.

A crossover cable is used only in Ethernet UTP installations. You can connect two workstation NICs or a workstation and a server NIC directly with it.

FIGURE 3.23   Crossover Ethernet cable

If you are trying to match the straight-through and crossover cables with the T568A and T568B standard, here is how it would look:

T568A+T568A = straight-through

T568B+T568B = straight-through

T568A+T568B = crossover

You're going to find out a lot more about how important it is to label basically everything. But for now, make sure to label a crossover cable as what it is so that no one tries to use it as a workstation patch cable. If they do that, the workstation won't be able to communicate with the hub and the rest of the network!

It's really cool that you can carry a crossover cable with you in your tool bag along with your laptop—then, if you want to ensure that a server's NIC is functioning correctly, you can just connect your laptop directly to the server's NIC using your handy crossover cable. You should be able to log in to the server if both NICs are configured correctly.

Use a cable tester to make sure that what you're dealing with is in fact a crossover cable. The tester can also tell you if there's a problem with the cable. Figure 3.24 shows an inexpensive cable tester for UTP.

This cost-effective little tool will tell you beyond a shadow of a doubt if you have a straight-through or crossover cable—or even if there's a problem with the cable.

UTP Gigabit Wiring (1000BaseT)

In the previous examples of 10BaseT and 100BaseT UTP wiring, only two wire pairs were used, but that's just not good enough for Gigabit UTP transmission.

1000BaseT UTP wiring (Figure 3.25) requires four wire pairs and uses more advanced electronics so that every pair in the cable can transmit simultaneously. Even so, Gigabit wiring is almost identical to my earlier 10/100 example, except that we'll use the other two pairs in the cable.

For a straight-through cable it's still 1 to 1, 2 to 2, and so on up to pin 8.

FIGURE 3.24   An inexpensive cable tester

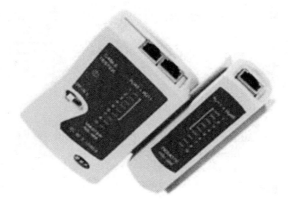

FIGURE 3.25   UTP gigabit crossover Ethernet cable

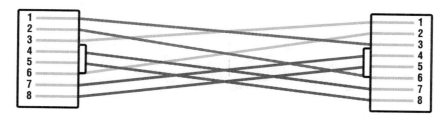

Rolled/Rollover Cable

Although *rolled cable* isn't used to connect any Ethernet connections together, you can use a rolled Ethernet cable to connect a host EIA-TIA 232 interface to a router console serial communication (COM) port.

If you have a Cisco router or switch, you would use this cable to connect your PC, Mac, or a device like a tablet to the Cisco hardware. Eight wires are used in this cable to connect serial devices, although not all eight are used to send information, just as in Ethernet networking. Figure 3.26 shows the eight wires used in a rolled cable.

These are probably the easiest cables to make because you just cut the end off on one side of a straight-through cable, turn it over, and put it back on—with a new connector, of course!

T1 Crossover Cable

There is an older device called a CSU/DSU, which used to be all-so-important. This old device may still be your connection to the Internet for the enterprise if you have serial

FIGURE 3.26   Rolled Ethernet cable

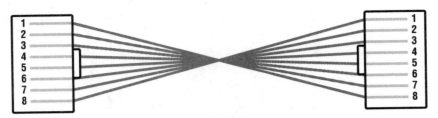

WANs. The type of cable you use to connect to this device from your router depends on the interface types that are available on the router.

The router may connect with several types of serial cables if a T1 connection is not built into it. If a T1 connection is built into the router, you will use an Ethernet cable. Figure 3.27 shows a T1 crossover cable connected to an RJ-45 connector.

FIGURE 3.27   AT1 crossover cable

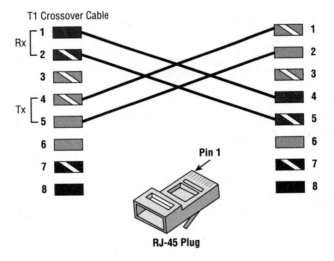

In rare instances you may need to run a cable between two CSU/DSUs. In that case you would need a T1 crossover cable. A T1 cable uses pairs 1 and 2, so connecting two T1 CSU/DSU devices back-to-back requires a crossover cable that swaps these pairs. Specifically, pins 1, 2, 4, and 5 are connected to 4, 5, 1, and 2, respectively.

Test Your Cable Understanding

You've taken a look at the various RJ-45 UTP cables. With that in mind, what cable is used between the switches in the following image?

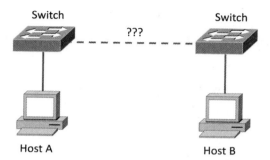

For host A to ping host B, you need a crossover cable to connect the two switches. But what types of cables are used in the network shown in the following image?

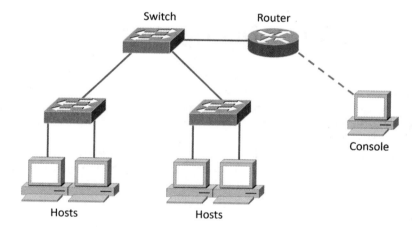

In the second example, there are a variety of cables in use. For the connection between the switches, we'd clearly use a crossover cable like the one you saw in the earlier example. The trouble is, here we have a console connection that uses a rolled cable. Plus, the connection from the router to the switch is a straight-through cable, which is also what's running between the hosts to the switches.

EXERCISE 3.2

Investigating Ethernet Cables

This exercise will help you investigate the wiring for the Ethernet cables you have or use on a daily basis.

1. Locate a cable that you can disconnect or see if you have a spare cable.

2. Inspect the ends next to each other and write their color codes down from left to right.

Answer the following questions after inspecting the network cabling:

1. What type of cable is it, and what EIA/TIA 568 wiring code does it use?

2. Is the cable a straight-through or crossover cable?

3. What was the cable connecting?

As you investigate the network cable, you will have an applied knowledge of how cables are made with the EIA/TIA 568 wiring standards and the application of the cable.

Installing Wiring Distributions

By now, you're probably getting the idea that there are a lot more components in the average computer networks than meets the eye, right? If this isn't exactly a news bulletin to you, then you either already are or have been involved in the initial installation of a network. If this describes you, you probably will be, or already are, involved in the purchase and installation of the components that will connect the computers throughout your organization's building. And it may also be up to you to verify that all of the network components have been installed properly and tested. So, let's go over each of these components and the process of verifying their proper installation.

MDF/IDF

The *main distribution frame (MDF)* is a wiring point that's generally used as a reference point for telephone lines. It's also considered the WAN termination point. It's installed in the building as part of the prewiring, and the internal lines are connected to it. After that, all that's left is to connect the external (telephone company) lines to the other side to complete the circuit. Often, another wire frame called an *intermediate distribution frame (IDF)* is located in an equipment or telecommunications room. It's connected to the MDF and is used to provide greater flexibility for the distribution of all the communications lines to the building. It's typically a sturdy metal rack designed to hold the bulk of cables coming from all over the building!

25 Pair

A *25-pair cable* consists of 25 individual pairs of wires all inside one common insulating jacket. It's not generally used for data cabling, just for telephone cabling, and especially for backbone and cross-connect cables because it reduces the cable clutter significantly. This type of cable is often referred to as a *feeder cable* because it supplies signal to many connected pairs.

66 Block

If you know what a *66 block* is, either you're really old or you work in an old building since they came out in 1962 and can really only be used for old analog telephone connections. This uses the 25-pair cable I just mentioned and is a standard termination block containing 50 rows, which created an industry standard for easy termination of voice cabling.

110 Block

A newer type of wiring distribution point called a *110 block* has replaced most telephone wire installations and is also used for computer networking. On one side, wires are punched down; the other side has RJ-11 (for phone) or RJ-45 (for network) connections.

You'll find 110 blocks in sizes from 25 to more than 500 wire pairs, and some can carry 1 Gbps connections when used with Category 6 or greater cables. The hitch is that using Cat 6 with the 110 block is really difficult because of the size of the Cat 6 wiring. Figure 3.28 shows a 110 block and describes each section used in the 110 block.

There is a proprietary European variant of the 110 block called a Krone block. The *Krone* block is compatible with the 110 block and can be used interchangeably.

FIGURE 3.28   A 110 block

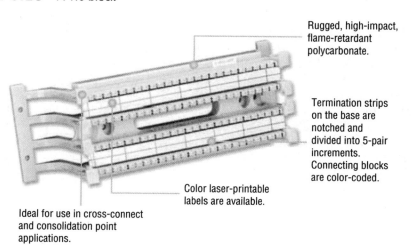

Rugged, high-impact, flame-retardant polycarbonate.

Termination strips on the base are notched and divided into 5-pair increments. Connecting blocks are color-coded.

Color laser-printable labels are available.

Ideal for use in cross-connect and consolidation point applications.

BIX Block

Another type of punch-down block is the *BIX* block. A BIX block can terminate up to 25 cable pairs and have a slip-in fitting that does not require pre-stripped wires.

Demarc/Demarc Extension

The *demarc* (short for demarcation) is the last point of responsibility for the service provider. It's often at the MDF in your building connection, especially if your building is large, but it's usually just an RJ-45 jack that your channel service unit/data service unit (CSU/DSU) connects from your router to WAN connections.

Network admins often test for connectivity on both sides of the demarc when troubleshooting to determine whether the problem is internal or external. The length of copper or fiber that begins after the demarc but still doesn't reach up to your office is referred to as a *demarc extension.*

Smart Jack

A *smart jack*, also called a network interface device (NID) or network interface unit (NIU), is owned by the PSTN and is a special network interface that's often used between the service provider's network and the internal network. You can't physically test to an actual demarc because it's just an RJ-45 jack, but the service provider may install an NID that has power and can be looped for testing purposes.

The smart jack device may also provide for code and protocol conversion, making the signal from the service provider usable by the devices on the internal network like the CSU/DSU.

Summary

I know getting through this chapter probably wasn't the most fun you've had recently. But understanding all those types of wires and cabling, along with their unique capacities, their associated standards, and the right connectors to use with them plus where to place them, is integral to having a solid, foundational understanding of the things that make a great network run quickly and reliably.

It's critical for you to grasp the basics of networking. Having the facts about how a good network is designed and implemented and what goes into that process will make you an effective and efficient technician—and maybe, someday, a highly paid network administrator.

Exam Essentials

Know the various types of cables used in today's networks.   Coaxial (other than for cable modems) is rarely used, but twisted-pair cable and fiber-optic cable are very common in today's networks.

Know the various types of ends that are used on each type of cable.   Coax uses BNC; twisted-pair uses RJ-11 for voice and RJ-45 for data; and fiber uses various ends, depending on its use. Know how to identify each type of connector.

Describe the various types of media converters that are available.   These include single-mode fiber to Ethernet, multimode fiber to Ethernet, fiber to coaxial, and single-mode to multimode fiber.

Understand what a T568A to T568A cable is.   A T568A to T568A cable is also known as an Ethernet straight-through cable and is used to connect hosts to switches, for example.

Understand what a T568A to T568B cable is.   A T568A to T568B cable is also known as an Ethernet crossover cable and is used to connect switches to switches, for example.

Define the function of a T1 crossover cable.   In rare instances, you may have the need to run a cable between two CSU/DSUs.

Know the various transceivers in use.   You should know how to identify the SFP, QSFP, FC, and Ethernet transceivers. In addition, you should know the benefits of each of the transceivers.

Written Lab

You can find the answers to the written labs in Appendix A. Fill out the respective EIA/TIA 568A and B wiring standard.
EIA/TIA 568A

Pin 1

Pin 2

Pin 3

Pin 4

Pin 5

Pin 6

Pin 7

Pin 8

EIA/TIA 568B

Pin 1

Pin 2

Pin 3

Pin 4

Pin 5

Pin 6

Pin 7

Pin 8

Review Questions

You can find the answers to the review questions in Appendix B.

1. You are planning to run fiber-optic cable between two buildings that are 6,000 feet apart. Which is the best solution to complete this project?

   A. SMF

   B. MMF

   C. MDF

   D. IDF

2. You need to connect a switch to another switch. Which type of cable should you use to properly create the connection between the two switches?

   A. Straight-through cable

   B. Rolled cable

   C. Crossover cable

   D. T1 crossover cable

3. You are designing a network in a building that has arc welders. Which cable should be used to eliminate EMI?

   A. Category 5e

   B. UTP

   C. Twinaxial

   D. Fiber optic

4. Which connector type is typically found on a Category 6 cable?

   A. RJ-45

   B. RJ-11

   C. BNC

   D. APC

5. You need to make a Category 5e crossover cable. Which wiring standard will you use on both ends?

   A. 568A-to-568A

   B. 568B-to-568A

   C. 568B-to-568B

   D. APC-to-UPC

6. You need to install cabling in an office space and want to be assured that toxic vapors will not be created in the event of a fire. Which cable type should you choose?

   A. PVC

   B. FEP

   C. Non-plenum

   D. Plenum

7. Which serial connection method is typically used for connecting peripherals to a PC?

   A. DB-9

   B. USB

   C. Category 3

   D. Rolled cable

8. You need to run a UTP cable for 10 Gbps speeds with a distance of 100 meters. Which minimum cable category rating should you use?

   A. Category 5

   B. Category 5e

   C. Category 6

   D. Category 6A

9. Which is an incorrect statement about smart jacks?

   A. A smart jack is a demarcation point.

   B. A smart jack can be remotely put into a loopback mode.

   C. A smart jack can report trouble in a circuit.

   D. A smart jack is also called a network interface device (NID).

10. Which term describes what happens to the signal in a network cable as you make the cable's distance greater?

    A. Attenuation

    B. Duplex

    C. Demarcation

    D. EMI

11. Which cable has no metallic shielding?

    A. STP

    B. UTP

    C. Coaxial

    D. Twinaxial

12. Which connector is typically used on the end of a coaxial cable?

   A. RJ-45

   B. RJ-11

   C. SC

   D. F-type

13. Which fiber-optic connector uses a BNC style mechanism to lock the cable in place?

   A. ST

   B. SC

   C. LC

   D. MT-RJ

14. Which technique is used to prevent crosstalk on network cables?

   A. T-568A/B wiring standard

   B. Use of STP cables

   C. Rolling the cable

   D. Short distance installations

15. Which transceiver will support up to 40 Gbps links?

   A. SFP+

   B. QSFP

   C. QSFP+

   D. QSFP28

16. Which connector will you find on a rolled cable?

   A. RJ-11

   B. RJ-45

   C. BNC

   D. SC

17. What is the main difference between single-mode fiber (SMF) and multimode fiber (MMF)?

   A. Electrical signals.

   B. Number of light rays.

   C. Category rating.

   D. That signal-mode can be run a shorter distance.

18. Which fiber-optic connector has a very small footprint for high-density installations?

   A. SC

   B. ST

   C. LC

   D. FC

19. You need to connect a switch that only supports multimode fiber to an existing single-mode fiber-optic line. What should you use to create a connection?

A. APC connector

B. UPC connector

C. SFP+ transceiver

D. Media converter

20. Which cable type is considered a patch cable?

A. Straight-through cable

B. Rolled cable

C. Crossover cable

D. STP

Chapter

4

The Current Ethernet Specifications

THE FOLLOWING COMPTIA NETWORK+ EXAM OBJECTIVES ARE COVERED IN THIS CHAPTER:

✓ **Domain 1.0 Networking Concepts**

✓ **1.5 Compare and contrast transmission media and transceivers.**

- ▪ Wired

    - ▪ 802.3 standards

    - ▪ Coaxial cable

Before we dive into the complex worlds of networking devices, the TCP/IP and DoD models, IP addressing, subnetting, and routing in the upcoming chapters, you have to understand the big picture of LANs and learn the answer to these key questions: How is Ethernet used in today's networks? What are Media Access Control (MAC) addresses, and how are these identifiers utilized in networking?

This chapter will answer those questions and more. I'll not only discuss the basics of Ethernet and the way MAC addresses are used on an Ethernet LAN, I'll also cover the protocols used with Ethernet at the Data Link layer. You'll also learn about the various Ethernet specifications.

So now, let's get started with the fundamentals of connecting two hosts together.

To find Todd Lammle CompTIA videos and questions, please see www.lammle.com.

Network Basics

Networks and networking have grown exponentially over the last 20 years—understandably so. They've had to evolve at light speed to keep up with huge increases in basic mission-critical user needs ranging from sharing data and printers to more advanced demands like videoconferencing. Unless everyone who needs to share network resources is located in the same office area (an increasingly uncommon situation), the challenge is to connect the sometimes large number of relevant networks so all users can share the networks' wealth.

Let's take a look at how communication happens on a basic local area network (LAN), which I started to discuss in Chapter 1, "Introduction to Networks." Starting with Figure 4.1, you get a picture of a primary LAN network that's connected using an Ethernet connection to a hub. This network is actually one collision domain and one broadcast domain, but don't stress if you have no idea what this means, as I'll start to cover those terms in this chapter; however, I'm going to talk about both collision and broadcast domains in depth in Chapter 5, "Networking Devices."

About Figure 4.1: How would you say the PC named Bob communicates with the PC named Sally? Well, they're both on the same LAN connected with a multiport repeater (a hub). So does Bob send out the data message "Hey, Sally, you there?" or does Bob use Sally's IP address and put things more like "Hey, 192.168.0.3, are you there?" I hope you picked the IP address option, but even if you did, the news is still bad—both answers are wrong! Why? Because Bob is actually going to use Sally's MAC address (known as a *hardware address*), which is burned right into the network card of Sally's PC, to get hold of her.

FIGURE 4.1   The basic network

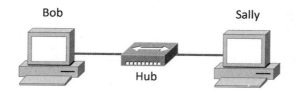

This is all good, but how does Bob get Sally's MAC address when Bob knows only Sally's name and doesn't even have her IP address? Bob is going to start by using name resolution (hostname–to–IP address resolution), something that's usually accomplished using the Domain Name System (DNS). And note that if these two hosts are on the same LAN, Bob can just broadcast to Sally asking her for the information (no DNS needed)—welcome to Microsoft Windows!

Here's the output from a network analyzer depicting a simple name-resolution process from Bob to Sally:

```
Time        Source    Destination    Protocol   Info
53.892794 192.168.0.2 192.168.0.255 NBNS     Name query NB SALLY<00>
```

As I already mentioned, because the two hosts are on a local LAN, Windows (Bob) will broadcast to resolve the name Sally (notice the destination 192.168.0.255 is a broadcast address). Let's take a look at the rest of the information:

```
EthernetII,Src:192.168.0.2(00:14:22:be:18:3b),Dst:Broadcast(ff:ff:ff:ff:ff:ff)
```

This output shows that Bob knows his own MAC address and source IP address but not Sally's IP address or MAC address. So, Bob sent a Data Link layer broadcast address of all Fs and an IP LAN broadcast to 192.168.0.255. Again, no worries—you're going to learn all about broadcasts in Chapter 6, "Introduction to the Internet Protocol."

After the name is resolved, the next thing Bob has to do is broadcast on the LAN to get Sally's MAC address so he can communicate to her PC:

```
Time    Source     Destination Protocol Info
5.153054 192.168.0.2 Broadcast  ARP Who has 192.168.0.3? Tell 192.168.0.2
```

Next, check out Sally's response:

```
Time     Source     Destination Protocol Info
5.153403  192.168.0.3 192.168.0.2 ARP 192.168.0.3 is 00:0b:db:99:d3:5e
5.53.89317 192.168.0.3 192.168.0.2 NBNS Name query response NB 192.168.0.3
```

Sweet—Bob now has both Sally's IP address and her MAC address (00:0b:db:99:d3:5e). These are both listed as the source address at this point because this information was sent from Sally back to Bob. So, *finally*, Bob has all the goods he needs to communicate with Sally. And just so you know, a little later I'm also going to tell you all about Address Resolution Protocol (ARP) and show you exactly how Sally's IP address was resolved to a MAC address, in Chapter 6.

Importantly, I want you to understand that Sally still had to go through the same resolution processes to communicate back to Bob—sounds crazy, huh? Consider this a welcome to IPv4 and basic networking with Windows—and we haven't even added a router yet!

Ethernet Basics

Ethernet is a contention media-access method that allows all hosts on a network to share the same bandwidth of a link. Ethernet is popular because it's readily scalable, meaning that it's comparatively easy to integrate new technologies, such as Fast Ethernet and Gigabit Ethernet, into an existing network infrastructure. It's also relatively simple to implement in the first place, and with it, troubleshooting is reasonably straightforward.

Ethernet uses both Data Link and Physical layer specifications, and this part of the chapter will give you both the Data Link layer and Physical layer information you need to effectively implement, troubleshoot, and maintain an Ethernet network.

In the following sections, I'll also cover some basic terms used in networking with Ethernet technologies. Let's start with collision domains.

Collision Domain

The term *collision domain* is an Ethernet term that refers to a particular network scenario wherein one device sends a packet out on a network segment and thereby forces every other device on that same physical network segment to pay attention to it. This is bad because if two devices on one physical segment transmit at the same time, a *collision event*—a situation where each device's digital signals interfere with another on the wire—occurs and forces the devices to retransmit later. Collisions have a dramatically negative effect on network performance, so they're definitely something we want to avoid!

The situation I just described is typically found in a hub environment where each host segment connects to a hub that represents only one collision domain and one broadcast domain. This begs the question, "What's a broadcast domain?"

Broadcast Domain

Here's that answer: A *broadcast domain* refers to the set of all devices on a network segment that hear all the broadcasts sent on that segment.

Even though a broadcast domain is typically a boundary delimited by physical media like switches and repeaters, it can also reference a logical division of a network segment where all hosts can reach each other via a Data Link layer (hardware address) broadcast.

That's the basic story, but rest assured, I'll be delving deeper into the skinny on collision and broadcast domains a bit later in Chapter 6.

CSMA/CD

Ethernet networking uses *carrier sense multiple access with collision detection (CSMA/CD)*, a media access control contention method that helps devices share the bandwidth evenly without having two devices transmit at the same time on the network medium. CSMA/CD was created to overcome the problem of those collisions that occur when packets are transmitted simultaneously from different hosts. And trust me—good collision management is crucial because when a host transmits in a CSMA/CD network, all the other hosts on the network receive and examine that transmission. Only bridges, switches, and routers, but not hubs, can effectively prevent a transmission from propagating throughout the entire network.

So, how does the CSMA/CD protocol work? Let's start by taking a look at Figure 4.2, where a collision has occurred in the network.

When a host wants to transmit over the network, it first checks for the presence of a digital signal on the wire. If all is clear, meaning that no other host is transmitting, the host will then proceed with its transmission. But it doesn't stop there. The transmitting host constantly monitors the wire to make sure no other hosts begin transmitting. If the host detects another signal on the wire, it sends out an extended jam signal that causes all hosts on the segment to stop sending data (think busy signal). The hosts respond to that jam signal by waiting a while before attempting to transmit again. Backoff algorithms, represented by the clocks counting down on either side of the jammed devices, determine when the colliding stations can retransmit. If collisions keep occurring after 15 tries, the hosts attempting to transmit will then time out. Pretty clean!

When a collision occurs on an Ethernet LAN, the following things happen:

1. A jam signal informs all devices that a collision occurred.

2. The collision invokes a random backoff algorithm.

3. Each device on the Ethernet segment stops transmitting for a short time until the timers expire.

4. All hosts have equal priority to transmit after the timers have expired.

The following are the effects of having a CSMA/CD network that has sustained heavy collisions:

- Delay

- Low throughput

- Congestion

FIGURE 4.2   CSMA/CD

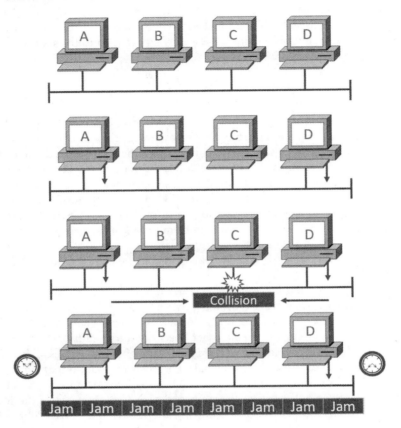

Backoff on an 802.3 Ethernet network is the retransmission delay that's enforced when a collision occurs. When a collision occurs, a host will resume transmission after the forced time delay has expired. After this backoff delay period has expired, all stations have equal priority to transmit data.

Broadband/Baseband

We have two ways to send analog and digital signals down a wire: broadband and baseband.

We hear the term *broadband* used a lot these days because that is pretty much what everyone uses at home. It allows us to have both our analog voice and digital data carried on the same network cable or physical medium. Broadband allows us to send multiple frequencies of different signals down the same wire at the same time (called frequency-division multiplexing) and to send both analog and digital signals.

Baseband is what all LANs use. This is where all the bandwidth of the physical media is used by only one signal. For example, Ethernet uses only one digital signal at a time, and it requires all the available bandwidth. If multiple signals are sent from different hosts at the same time, we get collisions; same with wireless, except that uses only analog signaling via radio waves.

Bit Rates vs. Baud Rate

Bit rate is a measure of the number of data bits (0s and 1s) transmitted in one second in either a digital or analog signal. A figure of 56,000 bits per second (bps) means 56,000 0s or 1s can be transmitted in one second, which we simply refer to as bps.

In the 1970s and 1980s, we used the term *baud rate* a lot, but that was replaced by *bps* because it was more accurate. *Baud* was a term of measurement named after a French engineer, Jean-Maurice-Émile Baudot, because he used it to measure the speed of telegraph transmissions.

One baud is one electronic state change per second—for example, from 0.2 volts to 3 volts or from binary 0 to 1. However, since a single state change can involve more than a single bit of data, the bps unit of measurement has replaced it as a more accurate definition of how much data you're transmitting or receiving.

Wavelength

Has anyone ever told you that they were on the same wavelength as you? That means they thought you were basically thinking the same way they were. The same is true of the inverse—if they say, "You're not on the same wavelength." With electromagnetic radiation, radio waves, light waves, or even infrared (heat) waves make characteristic patterns as they travel through space. Some patterns can be the same, and some can be different, as shown in Figure 4.3.

Each wave pattern has a certain shape and length. The distance between peaks (high points) is called *wavelength*. If two wave patterns are different, we would say they're not on the same wavelength, and that is the way we tell different kinds of electromagnetic energy apart. We can use this to our advantage in electronics by sending traffic on different wavelengths at the same time.

In the following sections, I'm going to cover Ethernet in detail at both the Data Link layer (layer 2) and the Physical layer (layer 1).

Half- and Full-Duplex Ethernet

Just so you know, half-duplex Ethernet is defined in the original 802.3 Ethernet specification. Basically, when you run half-duplex, you're using only one wire pair with a digital signal either transmitting or receiving. This really isn't all that different from full-duplex because you can both transmit and receive—you just don't get to do that at the same time running half-duplex as you can if you're running full-duplex.

FIGURE 4.3 Shorter and longer wavelengths

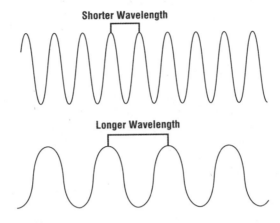

Here's how it works: If a host hears a digital signal, it uses the CSMA/CD protocol to help prevent collisions and to permit retransmitting if a collision does occur. Half-duplex Ethernet—typically 10BaseT—is only about 30 to 40% efficient because a large 10BaseT network will usually provide only 3 Mbps to 4 Mbps at most. Although it's true that 100 Mbps Ethernet can and sometimes does run half-duplex, it's just not very common to find that happening anymore.

In contrast, full-duplex Ethernet uses two pairs of wires at the same time instead of one measly wire pair like half-duplex employs. Plus, full-duplex uses a point-to-point connection between the transmitter of the sending device and the receiver of the receiving device (in most cases the switch). This means that with full-duplex data transfer, you not only get faster data-transfer speeds, but you get collision prevention too—sweet!

You don't need to worry about collisions because now it's like a freeway with multiple lanes instead of the single-lane road provided by half-duplex. Full-duplex Ethernet is supposed to offer 100% efficiency in both directions—for example, you can get 20 Mbps with a 10 Mbps Ethernet running full-duplex, 200 Mbps for Fast Ethernet, or even 2000 Mbps for Gigabit Ethernet. But this rate is something known as an *aggregate rate*, which translates as "you're supposed to get" 100% efficiency. No guarantees, in networking as in life.

Full-duplex Ethernet can be used in many situations; here are some examples:

▪ With a connection from a switch to a host

▪ With a connection from a switch to a switch

▪ With a connection from a host to a host using a crossover cable

You can run full-duplex with just about any device except a hub.

You may be wondering: If it's capable of all that speed, why wouldn't it deliver? Well, when a full-duplex Ethernet port is powered on, it first connects to the remote end and then negotiates with the other end of the Fast Ethernet link. This is called an *auto-detect mechanism*. This mechanism first decides on the exchange capability, which means it checks to see if it can run at 10, 100, or even 1000 Mbps. It then checks to see if it can run full-duplex, and if it can't, it will run half-duplex instead.

Hosts usually auto-detect both the Mbps and the duplex type available (the default setting), but you can manually set both the speed and duplex type on the network interface card (NIC), as shown here in the Network Connection Properties for a network adapter.

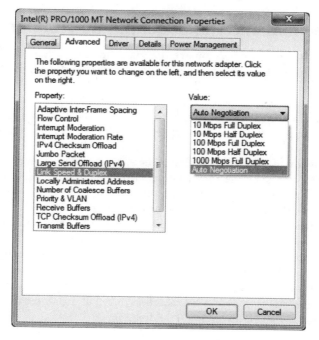

Today, it's pretty rare to go into a NIC configuration on a host and change these settings, but this example demonstrates that you can do that if you want.

Remember that half-duplex Ethernet shares a collision domain and provides a lower effective throughput than full-duplex Ethernet, which typically has a private collision domain and a higher effective throughput.

Lastly, remember these important points:

- There are no collisions in full-duplex mode.
- A dedicated switch port is required for each full-duplex host.
- The host network card and the switch port must be capable of operating in full-duplex mode.

Now let's take a look at how Ethernet works at the Data Link layer.

Ethernet at the Data Link Layer

Ethernet at the Data Link layer is responsible for Ethernet addressing, commonly referred to as *hardware addressing* or *MAC addressing*. Ethernet is also responsible for framing packets received from the Network layer and preparing them for transmission on the local network.

Ethernet MAC addresses are made up of hexadecimal addresses. So, before I discuss MAC addresses, let's start by talking about binary, decimal, and hexadecimal addresses and how to convert one to another.

Binary to Decimal and Hexadecimal Conversion

Understanding the differences between binary, decimal, and hexadecimal numbers and how to convert one format into the other is very important before we discuss the TCP/IP protocol stack and IP addressing in Chapters 6 and 7, "IP Addressing."

So, let's get started with binary numbering. It's pretty simple, really. Each digit used is limited to being either a 1 (one) or a 0 (zero), and each digit is called 1 bit (short for *bi*nary digi*t*). Typically, you count either 4 or 8 bits together, with these being referred to as a *nibble* and a *byte*, respectively.

What's interesting about binary numbering is the value represented in a decimal format— the typical decimal format being the base-10 number scheme that we've all used since kindergarten. The binary numbers are placed in a value spot, starting at the right and moving left, with each spot having double the value of the previous spot.

Table 4.1 shows the decimal values of each bit location in a nibble and a byte. Remember, a nibble is four bits, and a byte is eight bits. In network addressing, we often refer to a byte as an *octet*. Mathematically, octal addressing actually refers to base 8, which is completely different from the base 10 we are familiar with. So, technically speaking we are using the term incorrectly, but it's the common usage anyway. When we get to subnetting in Chapter 8, "IP Subnetting, Troubleshooting IP, and Introduction to NAT," you'll see that I'll use *byte* and *octet* interchangeably when discussing IP addressing.

TABLE 4.1   Binary values

Nibble Values	Byte Values
8 4 2 1	128 64 32 16 8 4 2 1

What all this means is that if a one digit (1) is placed in a value spot, then the nibble or byte takes on that decimal value and adds it to any other value spots that have a 1. And if a zero (0) is placed in a bit spot, you don't count that value.

Let me clarify things for you—if we have a 1 placed in each spot of our nibble, we then add up 8 + 4 + 2 + 1 to give us a maximum value of 15. Another example for our nibble values is 1010, which means that the 8 bit and the 2 bit are turned on and equal a decimal value of 10. If we have a nibble binary value of 0110, then our decimal value is 6 because the 4 and 2 bits are turned on.

But the byte values can add up to a value that's significantly higher than 15. This is how—if we count every bit as a one (1), then the byte binary value looks like this (remember, 8 bits equal a byte):

11111111

We then count up every bit spot because each is turned on. It looks like this, which demonstrates the maximum value of a byte:

128 + 64 + 32 + 16 + 8 + 4 + 2 + 1 = 255

A binary number can equal plenty of other decimal values. Let's work through a few examples:

10010110

Which bits are on? The 128, 16, 4, and 2 bits are on, so we'll just add them up: 128 + 16 + 4 + 2 = 150.

01101100

Which bits are on? The 64, 32, 8, and 4 bits are on, so we add them up: 64 + 32 + 8 + 4 = 108.

11101000

Which bits are on? The 128, 64, 32, and 8 bits are on, so we add the values:

128 + 64 + 32 + 8 = 232.

You should memorize Table 4.2 before braving the IP sections in Chapters 6 and 7 since this lists all available subnet masks.

TABLE 4.2 Binary-to-decimal memorization chart

Binary Value	Decimal Value
10000000	128
11000000	192
11100000	224
11110000	240
11111000	248

TABLE 4.2   Binary-to-decimal memorization chart *(continued)*

Binary Value	Decimal Value
11111100	252
11111110	254
11111111	255

Hexadecimal addressing is completely different than binary or decimal—it's converted by reading nibbles, not bytes. We can convert these bits to hex pretty simply by using a nibble. First, understand that the hexadecimal addressing scheme uses only 0 through 9. And because the numbers 10, 11, 12, and so on can't be used (because they are two-digit numbers), the letters *A*, *B*, *C*, *D*, *E*, and *F* are used to represent 10, 11, 12, 13, 14, and 15, respectively.

Table 4.3 shows the binary and decimal values for each hexadecimal digit.

TABLE 4.3   Hex-to-binary-to-decimal chart

Hexadecimal Value	Binary Value	Decimal Value
0	0000	0
1	0001	1
2	0010	2
3	0011	3
4	0100	4
5	0101	5
6	0110	6
7	0111	7
8	1000	8
9	1001	9
A	1010	10

Hexadecimal Value	Binary Value	Decimal Value
B	1011	11
C	1100	12
D	1101	13
E	1110	14
F	1111	15

Did you notice that the first 10 hexadecimal digits (0–9) are the same values as the decimal values? If not, look again. This handy fact makes those values super easy to convert.

So suppose you have something like this: 0x6A. (Some manufacturers put *0x* in front of characters so you know that they're a hex value, while others give you an *h*. It doesn't have any other special meaning.) What are the binary and decimal values? To correctly answer that question, all you have to remember is that each hex character is one nibble and two hex characters together make a byte. To figure out the binary value, first put the hex characters into two nibbles and then put them together into a byte. 6 = 0110 and A (which is 10 in decimal) = 1010, so the complete byte is 01101010.

To convert from binary to hex, just break the byte into nibbles.

Here's how you do that: Say you have the binary number 01010101. First, break it into nibbles—0101 and 0101—with the value of each nibble being 5 because the 1 and 4 bits are on. This makes the hex answer 0x55. And in decimal format, the binary number is 01010101, which converts to 64 + 16 + 4 + 1 = 85.

Now try another binary number:

11001100

Our answer is 1100 = 12 and 1100 = 12 (therefore, it's converted to CC in hex). The decimal conversion answer is 128 + 64 + 8 + 4 = 204.

One more example, and then we need to get working on the Physical layer. Suppose we're given the following binary number:

10110101

The hex answer is 0xB5 because 1011 converts to B and 0101 converts to 5 in hex value. The decimal equivalent is 128 + 32 + 16 + 4 + 1 = 181.

See the written lab at the end of this chapter for more practice with binary/hex/decimal conversion.

Ethernet Addressing

Now that you've got binary-to-decimal and hexadecimal address conversion down, we can get into how Ethernet addressing works. It uses the *Media Access Control (MAC) address* burned into each and every Ethernet NIC. The MAC, or hardware, address is a 48-bit (6-byte) address written in a hexadecimal format.

Figure 4.4 shows the 48-bit MAC addresses and how the bits are divided.

FIGURE 4.4   Ethernet addressing using MAC addresses

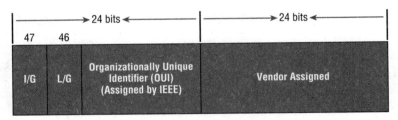

The *organizationally unique identifier (OUI)* is assigned by the Institute of Electrical and Electronics Engineers (IEEE) to an organization. It's composed of 24 bits, or 3 bytes. The organization, in turn, assigns a globally administered address (24 bits, or 3 bytes) that is unique to every adapter it manufactures. Look closely at the figure. The Individual/Group (I/G) address bit is used to signify if the destination MAC address is a unicast or a multicast/broadcast layer 2 address. If the bit is set to 0, then it is an Individual MAC address and is a unicast address. If the bit is set to 1, it is a Group address and is a multicast/broadcast address.

The next bit is the Local/Global bit (L/G). This bit is used to tell if the MAC address is the burned-in-address (BIA) or a MAC address that has been changed locally. You'll see this happen when we get to IPv6 addressing. The low-order 24 bits of an Ethernet address represent a locally administered or manufacturer-assigned code. This portion commonly starts with 24 0s for the first card made and continues in order until there are 24 1s for the last (16,777,216th) card made. You'll find that many manufacturers use these same six hex digits as the last six characters of their serial number on the same card.

Ethernet Frames

The Data Link layer is responsible for combining bits into bytes and bytes into frames. Frames are used at the Data Link layer to encapsulate packets handed down from the Network layer for transmission on a type of physical media access.

The function of Ethernet stations is to pass data frames between each other using a group of bits known as a MAC frame format. This provides error detection from a cyclic redundancy check (CRC). But remember—this is error detection, not error correction. Figure 4.5 depicts the 802.3 frames and Ethernet frame.

FIGURE 4.5   802.3 and Ethernet frame formats in bytes

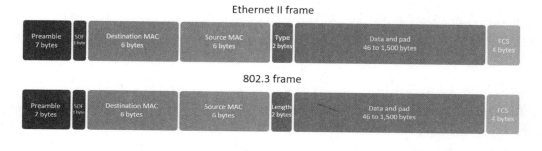

Ethernet II frame

| Preamble 7 bytes | SOF 1 byte | Destination MAC 6 bytes | Source MAC 6 bytes | Type 2 bytes | Data and pad 46 to 1,500 bytes | FCS 4 bytes |

802.3 frame

| Preamble 7 bytes | SOF 1 byte | Destination MAC 6 bytes | Source MAC 6 bytes | Length 2 bytes | Data and pad 46 to 1,500 bytes | FCS 4 bytes |

Encapsulating a frame within a different type of frame is called *tunneling*.

The following information regarding frame headings and the various types of Ethernet frames are beyond the scope of the CompTIA Network+ objectives. Throughout the rest of this book, I'll show you screenshots from a network analyzer. It's always good to understand what you are looking at, so I include this information to help you understand a frame structure.

Following are the details of the different fields in the 802.3 and Ethernet frame types:

Preamble   An alternating 1,0 pattern provides a clock at the start of each packet, which allows the receiving devices to lock the incoming bit stream.

Start of Frame Delimiter (SOF)/Synch   The preamble is seven octets, and the start of a frame (SOF) is one octet (synch). The SOF is 10101011, where the last pair of 1s allows the receiver to come into the alternating 1,0 pattern somewhere in the middle and still sync up and detect the beginning of the data.

Destination Address (DA)   This transmits a 48-bit value using the least significant bit (LSB) first. The DA is used by receiving stations to determine whether an incoming packet is addressed to a particular host and can be an individual address or a broadcast or multicast MAC address. Remember that a broadcast is all 1s (or Fs in hex) and is sent to all devices, but a multicast is sent only to a similar subset of hosts on a network.

Source Address (SA)   The SA is a 48-bit MAC address used to identify the transmitting device, and it uses the LSB first. Broadcast and multicast address formats are illegal within the SA field.

Length or Type   802.3 uses a Length field, but the Ethernet frame uses a Type field to identify the Network layer protocol. 802.3 by itself cannot identify the upper-layer routed protocol and must be used with an LAN protocol.

Data   This is a packet sent down to the Data Link layer from the Network layer. The size can vary from 64 to 1,500 bytes.

Frame Check Sequence (FCS)   FCS is a field that is at the end of the frame and is used to store the CRC.

Now let's take a minute to look at some frames caught on our trusty network analyzer. You can see that the following frame has only three fields: Destination, Source, and Type, displayed as Protocol Type on this analyzer:

```
Destination:  00:60:f5:00:1f:27
Source:     00:60:f5:00:1f:2c
Protocol Type: 08-00 IP
```

This is an Ethernet_II frame. Notice that the Type field is IP, or 08-00 (mostly just referred to as 0x800) in hexadecimal.

The next frame has the same fields, so it must be an Ethernet_II frame too:

```
Destination:  ff:ff:ff:ff:ff:ff Ethernet Broadcast
Source:     02:07:01:22:de:a4
Protocol Type: 08-00 IP
```

Did you notice that this frame was a broadcast? You can tell because the destination hardware address is all 1s in binary, or all *F*s in hexadecimal.

Let's take a look at one more Ethernet_II frame. You can see that the Ethernet frame is the same Ethernet_II frame we use with the IPv4 routed protocol. The difference is that the Type field has 0x86dd when we are carrying IPv6 data, and when we have IPv4 data, we use 0x0800 in the Protocol field:

```
Destination: IPv6-Neighbor-Discovery_00:01:00:03 (33:33:00:01:00:03)
Source: Aopen_3e:7f:dd (00:01:80:3e:7f:dd)
Type: IPv6 (0x86dd)
```

This is the beauty of the Ethernet_II frame. Because of the Protocol field, we can run any Network layer–routed protocol, and it will carry the data because it can identify that particular Network layer protocol!

EXERCISE 4.1

Converting Binary, Decimal, and Hexadecimal

This exercise is to help you investigate the binary, decimal, and hexadecimal used in your computer.

1. Open the command prompt by clicking Start and then type **cmd** and press Enter.

2. In the open command prompt, type **ipconfig /all**.

3. Examine the output and find your current active adapter.

4. Look at the IP address and take each octet (decimal number) between the dots and convert it to binary using the technique described earlier.

5. Now open the Microsoft calculator and select Programming mode.

6. Select Bin on the menu; then start typing the binary number and select Dec on the menu to convert the number. The leading zeros will not show up as you are typing as they have no value.

    If you've done this correctly, you should get the same decimal number you started with. You can also use this method for hexadecimal conversion. Try it with each digit in the MAC address of your adapter. Keep in mind that leading zeros will not display, since they have no value, like writing you have $010.00. It makes no sense to us, but the computer needs the zeros, so we have to add the padding.

Ethernet at the Physical Layer

Ethernet was first implemented by a group called DIX (Digital, Intel, and Xerox). DIX created and implemented the first Ethernet LAN specification, which the IEEE used to create the IEEE 802.3 Committee. This was a 10 Mbps network that ran on coax, then on twisted-pair, and finally on fiber physical media.

The IEEE extended the 802.3 Committee to three new committees known as 802.3u (Fast Ethernet), 802.3ab (Gigabit Ethernet on Category 5+), and then finally 802.3ae (10 Gbps over fiber and coax).

Figure 4.6 shows the IEEE 802.3 and original Ethernet Physical layer specifications.

When designing your LAN, it's really important to understand the different types of Ethernet media available to you. Sure, it would be great to run Gigabit Ethernet to each desktop and 10 Gbps or 40 Gbps between switches, as well as to servers. Although this is starting to happen, justifying the cost of that network today for most companies would be a pretty hard sell. But if you mix and match the different types of Ethernet media methods currently available instead, you can come up with a cost-effective network solution that works great!

FIGURE 4.6   Ethernet Physical layer specifications

							802.2 LLC				
Data Link							802.3 MAC				
Physical	Ethernet	10Base-T	100Base-TX	100Base-FX	1000Base-CX	1000Base-T	1000Base-SX	1000Base-LX	1000Base-ZX	10GBase-T	

The Electronic Industries Association and the newer Telecommunications Industry Alliance (EIA/TIA) together form the standards body that creates the Physical layer specifications for Ethernet. The EIA/TIA specifies that Ethernet use a *registered jack (RJ) connector* on *unshielded twisted-pair (UTP)* cabling (RJ-45). However, the industry is calling this just an 8-pin modular connector.

Each Ethernet cable type that is specified by the EIA/TIA has something known as *inherent attenuation*, which is defined as the loss of signal strength as it travels the length of a cable and is measured in decibels (dB). The cabling used in corporate and home markets is measured in categories. A higher-quality cable will have a higher-rated category and lower attenuation. For example, Category 5 is better than Category 3 because Category 5 cables have more wire twists per foot and therefore less crosstalk. *Crosstalk* is the unwanted signal interference from adjacent pairs in the cable.

Here are the original IEEE 802.3 standards:

10Base2   This is also known as *thinnet* and can support up to 30 workstations on a single segment. It uses 10 Mbps of baseband technology, coax up to 185 meters in length, and a physical and logical bus with Attachment Unit Interface (AUI) connectors. The 10 means 10 Mbps, and *Base* means baseband technology—a signaling method for communication on the network—and the 2 means almost 200 meters. 10Base2 Ethernet cards use BNC (British Naval Connector, Bayonet Neill-Concelman, or Bayonet Nut Connector) and T-connectors to connect to a network.

10Base5   Also known as *thicknet*, 10Base5 uses a physical and logical bus with AUI connectors, 10 Mbps baseband technology, and coax up to 500 meters in length. You can go up to 2,500 meters with repeaters and 1,024 users for all segments.

Ideally, you will never need to deal with 10Base2 or 10Base5 in your professional career. These technologies have not been used in the past 20 years, but they serve as a reference.

You may find 10Base2 cabling still in the ceilings and walls of older installations, but I hope not! Also, if you ever move a ceiling tile and see a cable in the ceiling that looks like a small yellow garden host with green stripes, you just found 10Base5 cabling.

10BaseT   This is 10 Mbps using Category 3 UTP wiring. Unlike on 10Base2 and 10Base5 networks, each device must connect into a hub or switch, and you can have only one host per segment or wire. It uses an RJ-45 connector (eight-pin modular connector) with a physical star topology and a logical bus.

Each of the 802.3 standards defines an AUI, which allows a one-bit-at-a-time transfer to the Physical layer from the Data Link media-access method. This allows the MAC address to remain constant but means the Physical layer can support both existing and new technologies. The original AUI interface was a 15-pin connector, which allowed a transceiver (transmitter/receiver) that provided a 15-pin-to-twisted-pair conversion.

There's an issue, though—the AUI interface can't support 100 Mbps Ethernet because of the high frequencies involved. So basically, 100BaseT needed a new interface, and the 802.3u specifications created one called the Media Independent Interface (MII) that provides 100 Mbps throughput. The MII uses a nibble, which you of course remember is defined as 4 bits. Gigabit Ethernet uses a Gigabit Media Independent Interface (GMII) and transmits 8 bits at a time.

802.3u (Fast Ethernet) is compatible with 802.3 Ethernet because they share the same physical characteristics. Fast Ethernet and Ethernet use the same maximum transmission unit (MTU) and the same MAC mechanisms, and they both preserve the frame format that is used by 10BaseT Ethernet. Basically, Fast Ethernet is just based on an extension to the IEEE 802.3 specification, and because of that, it offers us a speed increase of 10 times 10BaseT.

Here are the expanded IEEE Ethernet 802.3 standards, starting with Fast Ethernet:

100BaseTX (IEEE 802.3u)   100BaseTX, most commonly known as Fast Ethernet, uses EIA/TIA Category 5 or 5e or 6 and UTP two-pair wiring. It allows for one user per segment up to 100 meters long (328 feet) and uses an RJ-45 connector with a physical star topology and a logical bus.

100BaseT and 100BaseTX: What's the difference? 100BaseT is the name of a group of standards for Fast Ethernet that includes 100BaseTX. Also included are 100BaseT4 and 100BaseT2. The same can be said about 1000BaseT and 1000BaseX.

100BaseFX (IEEE 802.3u)   This uses 62.5/125-micron multimode fiber cabling up to 412 meters long and point-to-point topology. It uses ST and SC connectors, which are media-interface connectors.

Ethernet's implementation over fiber can sometimes be referred to as 100BaseTF even though this isn't an actual standard. It just means that Ethernet technologies are being run over fiber cable.

1000BaseCX (IEEE 802.3z)   This is copper twisted-pair called twinax (a balanced coaxial pair) that can run only up to 25 meters and uses a special nine-pin connector known as the High-Speed Serial Data Connector (HSSDC).

1000BaseT (IEEE 802.3ab)   1000BaseT uses Category 5, four-pair UTP wiring, and up to 100 meters long (328 feet).

1000BaseTX   1000BaseTX uses Category 5 and two-pair UTP wiring up to 100 meters long (328 feet). 1000BaseTX has been replaced by Category 6 cabling.

1000BaseSX (IEEE 802.3z)   The implementation of Gigabit Ethernet runs over multi-mode fiber-optic cable instead of copper twisted-pair cable and uses short wavelength laser. Multimode fiber (MMF), using a 62.5- and 50-micron core, utilizes an 850 nanometer (nm) laser and can go up to 220 meters with 62.5-micron; 550 meters with 50-micron.

1000BaseLX (IEEE 802.3z)   This is single-mode fiber that uses a 9-micron core, 1,300 nm laser, and can go from 3 km up to 10 km.

10GBaseT   10GBaseT is a standard created by the IEEE 802.3an committee to provide 10 Gbps connections over conventional UTP cables (Category 5e, 6, 6A, or 7 cables). 10GBaseT allows the conventional RJ-45 used for Ethernet LANs. It can support signal transmission at the full 100-meter distance specified for LAN wiring. If you need to implement a 10 Gbps link, this is the most economical way to go!

10GBaseSR   This implementation of 10 Gigabit Ethernet uses short-wavelength lasers at 850 nm over multimode fiber. It has a maximum transmission distance of between 2 and 300 meters (990 feet), depending on the size and quality of the fiber.

10GBaseLR   This implementation of 10 Gigabit Ethernet uses long-wavelength lasers at 1,310 nm over single-mode fiber. It also has a maximum transmission distance between 2 meters and 10 km, or 6 miles, depending on the size and quality of the fiber.

10GBaseER   This implementation of 10 Gigabit Ethernet running over single-mode fiber uses extra-long-wavelength lasers at 1,550 nm. It has the longest transmission distances possible of all the 10 Gigabit technologies: anywhere from 2 meters up to 40 km, again depending on the size and quality of the fiber used.

10GBaseSW   10GBaseSW, as defined by IEEE 802.3ae, is a mode of 10GBaseS for MMF with an 850 nm laser transceiver and a bandwidth of 10 Gbps. It can support up to 300 meters of cable length. This media type is designed to connect to SONET equipment.

10GBaseLW   10GBaseLW is a mode of 10GBaseL supporting a link length of 10 km on standard single-mode fiber (SMF) (G.652). This media type is also designed to connect to SONET equipment.

10GBaseEW   10GBaseEW is a mode of 10GBaseE supporting a link length of up to 40 km on SMF based on G.652 using optical-wavelength 1,550 nm. This is another media type designed to connect to SONET equipment.

40GBaseT 40GBaseT is a standard created by the IEEE 802.3bq committee and supports Ethernet speeds up to 40 Gbps and is also used for 25 Gbps Ethernet connections commonly found in server NICs. There is less distance than the slower Ethernet types with 40GBase T limited to 30 meters. This is usually sufficient for data center cabling. Category 8 cabling is required to support the high data rates of 25GBaseT and 40GBaseT.

Suppose you want to implement a network medium that is not suscep-tible to electromagnetic interference (EMI). In that case, fiber-optic cable provides a more secure, long-distance cable that is not susceptible to EMI at high speeds like UTP is.

Table 4.4 summarizes the cable types.

TABLE 4.4 Common Ethernet cable types

Ethernet Name	Cable Type	Maximum Speed	Maximum Transmission Distance	Notes
10BaseT	UTP	10 Mbps	100 meters per segment	One of the most popular network cabling schemes.
100BaseTX	UTP, STP	100 Mbps	100 meters per segment	Two pairs of Category 5 UTP.
10BaseFL	Fiber	10 Mbps	Varies (ranges from 500 meters to 2,000 meters)	Ethernet over fiber optics to the desktop.
100BaseFX	MMF	100 Mbps	2,000 meters	100 Mbps Ethernet over fiber optics.
1000BaseT	UTP	1000 Mbps	100 meters	Four pairs of Category 5 or higher.
1000BaseTX	UTP	1000 Mbps	100 meters	Two pairs of Category 6 or higher.
1000BaseSX	MMF	1000 Mbps	550 meters	Uses SC fiber connectors. Max length depends on fiber size.
1000BaseCX	Balanced, shielded copper	1000 Mbps	25 meters	Uses a special connector, the HSSDC.

TABLE 4.4   Common Ethernet cable types *(continued)*

Ethernet Name	Cable Type	Maximum Speed	Maximum Transmission Distance	Notes
1000BaseLX	MMF and SMF	1000 Mbps	550 meters multimode/ 2,000 meters single mode	Uses longer wavelength laser than 1000BaseSX. Uses SC and LC connectors.
10GBaseT	UTP	10 Gbps	100 meters	Connects to the network like a Fast Ethernet link using UTP.
10GBaseSR	MMF	10 Gbps	300 meters	850 nm laser. Max length depends on fiber size and quality.
10GBaseLR	SMF	10 Gbps	10 kilometers	1,310 nm laser. Max length depends on fiber size and quality.
10GBaseER	SMF	10 Gbps	40 kilometers	1,550 nm laser. Max length depends on fiber size and quality.
10GBaseSW	MMF	10 Gbps	400 meters	850 nm laser transceiver.
10GBaseLW	SMF	10 Gbps	10 kilometers	Typically used with SONET.
10GBaseEW	SMF	10 Gbps	40 kilometers	1,550 nm optical wavelength.
40GBaseT	UTP Category 8	40 Gbps	30 Meters	Connects to the network like a Fast Ethernet link using UTP.

    An advantage of 100BaseFX over 100BaseTX is longer cable runs, but 100BaseTX is easier to install.

I know there's a lot of information to remember about the various Ethernet and fiber types used in today's networks, but for the CompTIA Network+ exam, you really need to know them. Trust me, I haven't inundated you with unnecessary information!

🌐 Real World Scenario

Deploy the Appropriate Wired Connectivity Standard

You have been tasked with installing wiring to handle the new networking technologies of 1000 Mbps to the desktop and Voice over IP (VoIP), with 10 Gbps between the access switches and the core switches. What cabling do you consider installing to accomplish this in a cost-effective manner?

First, you need to verify your distances. Since this will not include any wireless stations, you need to double-check the distances to each station and make sure the phone is within 100 meters (or closer) for connectivity to your access switches.

Once you have your distances verified at 100 meters or less, you can use UTP wiring to the stations and phones and possibly even connect the stations into the back of the phones. Most phones have switches included, so this means you need to run only one Category 5 or better 1000BaseT four-pair cable to each cubicle or office.

For your connections from your access switches to your core switches, you can use 10GBaseT if your runs are 100 meters or less, or you can use 10GBaseSR, which allows runs up to 400 meters using multimode fiber.

Ethernet over Other Standards (IEEE 1905.1-2013)

IEEE 1905.1-2013 is an IEEE standard that defines a convergent digital home network for both wireless and wireline technologies. The technologies include IEEE 802.11 (Wi-Fi), IEEE 1901 (HomePlug, HD-PLC) powerline networking, IEEE 802.3 Ethernet, and Multimedia over Coax (MoCA). The 1905.1-2013 was published in April 2013. The IEEE 1905.1 Standard Working Group is sponsored by the IEEE Power Line Communication Standards Committee (PLCSC). The idea behind the 1905.1 technology standards is simple setup, configuration, and operation of home networking devices using both wired and wireless technologies. This will take advantage of the performance, coverage, and mobility benefits of multiple interfaces (Ethernet, Wi-Fi, Powerline, and MoCA), which enables better coverage and throughput in every room for both wireless and fixed devices.

We'll discuss the following:

- Ethernet over Power Line
- Ethernet over HDMI

Ethernet over Power Line

In February 2011, the IEEE finally published a standard for Broadband over Power Line (BPL) called IEEE 1901, also referred to as Power Line Communication (PLC) or even Power Line Digital Subscriber Line (PDSL). Although this technology has been available for decades in theory, without an IEEE standard it was just not adopted as an alternative to other high-speed media.

Recently this technology has gained traction, especially from the power companies that gather data from the power meter installed in your house. It relays this information to the power company and specifically reports how much power is being used by your residence.

In the future, BPL will allow you to just plug a computer into a wall power socket and have more than 500 Mbps for up to 1,500 meters.

Near my home in Boulder, Colorado, Xcel Energy is using BPL in combination with radio links for its SmartGridCity pilot project, which will send data from power meters, hot water heaters, thermostats, and more.

Figure 4.7 shows an example of an adapter.

FIGURE 4.7   Powerline adapter sets

This technology can be used to deliver Internet access to the home as well. For a computer (or any other device), you would simply need to plug a BPL modem into any outlet in an equipped building to have high-speed Internet access. Figure 4.8 shows the basic BPL installation.

FIGURE 4.8   Basic BPL installation

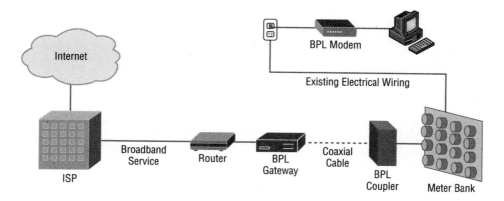

After the gateway is connected through the coupler to the meter bank for the building, any electrical outlet can be used with the BPL modem to receive the ISP connection to the Internet. The following challenges still exist:

- The fact that power lines are typically noisy.
- The frequency at which the information is transmitted is used by shortwave, and the unshielded power lines can act as antennas, thereby interfering with shortwave communications.

Ethernet over HDMI

HDMI Ethernet Channel technology consolidates video, audio, and data streams into a single HDMI cable, combining the signal quality of HDMI connectivity with the power and flexibility of home entertainment networking.

Figure 4.9 shows how a possible home entertainment network will look before and after Ethernet over HDMI is implemented.

It incorporates a dedicated data channel into the HDMI link, enabling high-speed, bidirectional networking at up to 100 Mbps.

Armed with the basics covered in the chapter, you're equipped to go to the next level and put Ethernet to work using various network devices. But to ensure that you're really ready, read the summary, go over the exam essentials, and do the written lab and review questions for this chapter!

FIGURE 4.9 Ethernet over HDMI

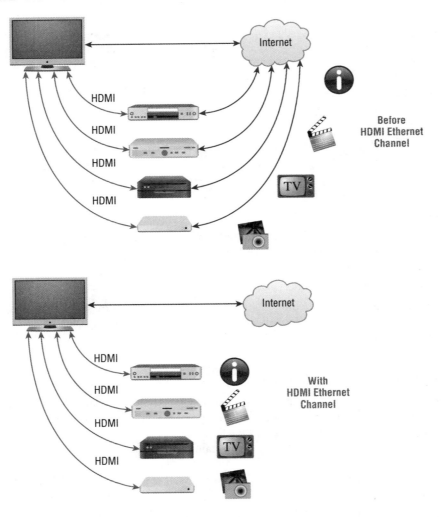

Exploring Ethernet Standards

This exercise is to help you to explore the various Ethernet standards you use every day. Examine your physical network connections on your computer, switch, router, firewall, and Internet connection. Then answer the following questions:

1. What is the connection being used for (computer to switch, switch to router, etc.)?

2. Which Ethernet specification is the connection using?

3. What is the maximum speed of the connection?

4. What is the maximum distance?

5. What media does the connection use?

This is a great exercise to do at your workplace. However, it is also nice to review your wired Ethernet connections at home. You can identify bottlenecks and restrictions and plan for future upgrades.

Summary

In this chapter, you learned the fundamentals of Ethernet networking, how hosts communicate on a network, and how CSMA/CD works in an Ethernet half-duplex network.

I also showed you the differences between half- and full-duplex modes.

I finished the chapter with a description of the common Ethernet cable types and standards used in today's networks. And by the way, you'd be wise to study that section really well!

Exam Essentials

Understand basic Ethernet communication.   Know how hosts use hardware addresses to communicate on an Ethernet LAN.

Understand Ethernet addressing.   Know the hexadecimal addressing scheme used to create an Ethernet address.

Understand binary, decimal, and hexadecimal addressing.   Know the different addressing types, and also use the written lab to practice your conversions.

Know the various Ethernet standards.   This includes understanding the various copper and fiber-based standards.

Written Lab

You can find the answers to the written labs in Appendix A. Fill in the blank with the answer to conversion of decimal, binary, and hexadecimal statements.

1. The decimal value of _____ is equal to the 0xF in hexadecimal.

2. The decimal value of 5 equals _____ in binary.

3. The decimal value of 14 equals _____ in hexadecimal.

4. The binary value of 0111 equals _____ in decimal.

5. The binary value of _____ equals 28 in decimal.

6. The hexadecimal value of _____ equals 16 in decimal.

7. The decimal value of _____ equals 0xb in hexadecimal.

8. The hexadecimal value of 0xE equals _____ in binary.

9. The decimal value of 177 equals _____ in binary.

10. The decimal value of 208 equals _____ in hexadecimal.

Review Questions

You can find the answers to the review questions in Appendix B.

1. Which contention method does 802.3 Ethernet use for collisions?
   - **A.** CSMA/CD
   - **B.** CSMA/CA
   - **C.** Half-duplex
   - **D.** Full-duplex

2. Which field in an Ethernet frame is used to check the integrity of the frame?
   - **A.** SOF
   - **B.** Preamble
   - **C.** DA
   - **D.** FCS

3. What is the significance of the preamble?
   - **A.** The preamble allows the switch to allocate a buffer.
   - **B.** The preamble allows the switch to sense collisions before data is transmitted.
   - **C.** The preamble allows the switch to sync timing for the receipt of information to follow.
   - **D.** The preamble allows the switch to read the sequence and acknowledge receipt of the frame.

4. In a layer 2 frame, where is the destination MAC address?
   - **A.** The destination MAC address is the first 6 bytes after the preamble.
   - **B.** The destination MAC address is the second 6 bytes after the preamble.
   - **C.** The destination MAC address is the payload data.
   - **D.** The destination MAC address is found in the preamble.

5. How many bits is the OUI assigned by the IEEE?
   - **A.** 6 bits
   - **B.** 22 bits
   - **C.** 24 bits
   - **D.** 48 bits

6. If the I/G or Individual/Group bit is set to 1 in the OUI portion of the MAC address, which statement is true?
   - **A.** The MAC address is a unique individual computer by the IEEE.
   - **B.** The MAC address is locally governed.
   - **C.** The MAC address is a broadcast or multicast.
   - **D.** The MAC address should always be broadcast.

7. If the L/G or Local/Group bit is set to 1 in the OUI portion of the MAC address, which statement is true?

   A. The MAC address is a unique individual computer by the IEEE.

   B. The MAC address is locally governed.

   C. The MAC address is a broadcast or multicast.

   D. The MAC address should always be broadcast.

8. Which is a reason that the Ethernet protocol uses physical addresses?

   A. It creates a differentiation between layer 2 and layer 3 communications.

   B. It defines a logical address scheme for devices.

   C. It uniquely identifies devices at layer 2.

   D. It allows the node to decide if the device is remote or local.

9. What is the 2-byte type field used for in an Ethernet frame?

   A. It defines the data type contained within the frame.

   B. It identifies the upper-layer protocol for the data contained within the frame.

   C. It is a calculation with the FCS to provide error detection.

   D. It describes the length of data contained within the frame.

10. What is the purpose of the State of Frame delimiter byte in a frame?

   A. It provides physical timing for the frame that follows.

   B. It divides the data and the physical timing portion of the frame.

   C. It provides a means for the receiving node to know when data begins.

   D. It delimits the destination and source MAC address.

11. How many bits are in a nibble?

   A. 1

   B. 4

   C. 8

   D. 16

12. How many bits are in a MAC address?

   A. 8

   B. 24

   C. 48

   D. 64

13. You need to connect a fiber-optic line between two floors of a building that are 200 meters apart. Which Ethernet technology is the most cost effective that will accomplish the task?

A. 10GBaseER

B. 10GBaseT

C. 10GBaseSR

D. 10GBaseLR

14. Which technology provides Internet connectivity over power lines?

A. BPL

B. MoCA

C. HDMI

D. HomePlug

15. Which statement is true when a collision is detected on the network?

A. The sender on the segment has the right of way.

B. A jam signal is sent to all hosts on the segment.

C. The receiver on the segment acknowledges the collision.

D. Once the collision clears, all hosts have equal access on the segment.

16. How many bits are used to represent the hexadecimal value of 0x0020?

A. 2

B. 4

C. 8

D. 16

17. Which 3 bytes of the Media Access Control (MAC) address F3-B2-CD-E4-F4-42 designate the unique station identifier?

A. F3-B2-CD

B. B2-CD-E4

C. E4-F4-42

D. CD-E4-F4

18. Which protocol does a host use to find the hardware address of a neighbor host by using the destination IP address?

A. TCP

B. UDP

C. ARP

D. DNS

19. What are the speed, maximum distance, and media of 10GBaseT?

    A. 10 Mb/s, 100 meters, and fiber optic

    B. 10 Gb/s, 100 meters, and fiber optic

    C. 10 Gb/s, 100 meters, and copper

    D. 10 Gb/s, 300 meters, and copper

20. How many wire pairs are used with 1000BaseTX?

    A. Two

    B. One

    C. Four

    D. Eight

Chapter

5

Networking Devices

THE FOLLOWING COMPTIA NETWORK+ EXAM OBJECTIVES ARE COVERED IN THIS CHAPTER:

✓ **Domain 2.0 Network Implementation**

✓ **2.3 Given a scenario, select and configure wireless devices and technologies**

    ▪ Autonomous vs. lightweight access point

✓ **Domain 3.0 Network Operations**

✓ **3.4 Given a scenario, implement IPv4 and IPv6 network services.**

    ▪ Dynamic addressing

        ▪ DHCP

        ▪ Reservations

        ▪ Scope

        ▪ Lease time

        ▪ Options

        ▪ Relay/IP helper

        ▪ Exclusions

    ▪ Name resolution

        ▪ DNS

        ▪ Domain Name Security

    ▪ Extensions (DNSSEC)

        ▪ DNS over HTTPS (DoH) and DNS over TLS (DoT)

    ▪ Record types

        ▪ Address (A)

        ▪ AAAA

       ▪ Canonical name (CNAME)

- Mail exchange (MX)
- Text
- Nameserver (NS)
- Pointer
- Zone types
  - Forward
  - Reverse
- Authoritative vs. non-authoritative
- Primary vs. secondary
- Recursive
  - Hosts file
- Time protocols
  - NTP
  - Precision Time Protocol (PTP)
  - Network Time Security (NTS)

In this chapter, I'll tell you all about the networking devices I've introduced so far. I'll go into much greater detail about each device, and yes—I'm going to present even more of them to you! Because all the components that you'll learn about shortly are typically found in today's networks and internetworks, it's very important that you be familiar with them.

We'll start by covering the more common network devices that you would be most likely to come across and then move on to discuss some of the more specialized devices that you may or may not always find running in a network.

I'll finish the chapter by using examples to discuss how routers, hubs, and switches work within internetworks today.

To find Todd Lammle CompTIA videos and practice questions, please see www.lammle.com.

Common Network Connectivity Devices

By now, you should be fairly savvy regarding the various types of network media and connections, so it's time to learn about some of the devices they hook up to that are commonly found on today's networks.

First, I'll define the basic terms; then, later in this chapter, I'll show you how these devices actually work within a network. At that time, I'll give you more detailed descriptions of these devices and the terminology associated with them.

Because these devices connect network entities, they're known as *connectivity devices*. Here's a list of the devices and related concepts I'll be covering in this chapter:

- Network interface card
- Hub
- Bridge
- Basic switch
- Basic router
- Basic firewall
- IDS/IPS/HIDS
- Access point

- Wireless range extender
- Contention methods
- Dynamic Host Configuration Protocol server
- Load balancer
- Proxy server
- Cable modem
- DSL modem
- Repeater
- Voice gateway
- Media converter
- VPN headend
- Voice over Internet Protocol phone
- Printer
- Physical access control devices
- Cameras
- Heating, ventilation, and air conditioning sensors
- Internet of Things
- Refrigerator
- Smart speakers
- Smart thermostats
- Smart doorbells
- Industrial control systems/supervisory control and data acquisition

Network Interface Card

Those of you who aren't familiar with NICs probably want to be, at this point, so here goes: A *network interface card (NIC)* is installed in your computer to connect, or interface, your computer to the network. It provides the physical, electrical, and electronic connections to the network media. The NIC is called a layer 2 device because the information it uses for communication, the MAC address, resides on the Data Link layer of the Open Systems Interconnection (OSI) model.

A NIC either is an expansion card or is built right into the computer's motherboard. Today, almost all NICs are built into the computer motherboard, providing 10, 100, and 1,000 mega-bits per second (Mbps), but there was a time when all NICs were expansion cards that plugged into motherboard expansion slots. In some notebook computers, NIC adapters can be connected to the USB port or through a PC card slot. Ethernet speeds have been steadily increasing, especially in server chassis with 25, 40, and 100 Gbps NICs now quite common.

Figure 5.1 shows a typical 1 Gbps Ethernet NIC.

FIGURE 5.1   Network interface card

Nowadays, most PCs and laptops of all types come with an Ethernet and wireless connector built into the motherboard, so you usually don't need a separate card. It's rare to find a laptop today without a built-in wireless network card, but you can buy external wireless cards for desktops and laptops if you've got legacy equipment that needs them.

NICs today usually have one, two, or more LEDs; one, usually green, is called a link light, indicating that an Ethernet connection has been established with the device on the other end of the cable, and it flickers when traffic is being passed back or forth. The other, or others, usually indicates the speed of the connection: 10, 100, or 1,000 Mbps. There's no universal standard for NIC LEDs, so check the manual to familiarize yourself with the ones you are working with. But it's not always that cut-and-dried that a blinking LED can mean the NIC is receiving a proper signal from the hub or switch; it can also indicate connectivity to and detection of a carrier on a segment. Another possibility is that it's found connectivity with a router or other end device using a crossover cable.

The other LED is aptly named the activity LED, and it tends to flicker constantly. That activity indicates the intermittent transmission and reception of frames arriving at the network or leaving it.

The first LED you should verify is the link LED because if it's not illuminated, the activity LED simply cannot illuminate.

Hub

As you learned earlier, a *hub* is the device that connects all the segments of the network together in a star topology Ethernet network. As a hub has no intelligence, it is a layer 1 (Physical layer) device. Each device in the network connects directly to the hub through a single cable and is used to connect multiple devices without segmenting a network. Any transmission received on one port will be sent out to all the other ports in the hub, including the receiving pair for the transmitting device, so that Carrier Sense Multiple Access with Collision Detection (CSMA/CD) on the transmitter can monitor for collisions.

Basically, this means that if one station sends a broadcast, all the others will receive it; yet based on the addressing found in the Ethernet frame, only the intended recipient will actually listen and process it. This arrangement simulates the physical bus that the CSMA/CD standard was based on, and it's why we call the use of a hub in an Ethernet environment a physical star/logical bus topology.

Figure 5.2 depicts a typical hub as you might find it employed within a small network. Since there are only two users, there isn't a problem in using a hub here. However, if there were 20 users, everyone would see Bob's request to send a packet to Sally. Most of the time, hubs really aren't recommended for corporate networks because of their limitations.

FIGURE 5.2   A typical hub

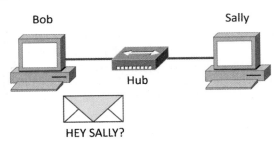

It's important to note that hubs are nothing more than glorified repeaters that are incapable of recognizing frames and data structures—the reason they act with such a lack of intelligence. A broadcast sent out by any device on the hub will be propagated to all devices connected to it. And just as in a physical bus topology configuration, any two or more of those connected devices have the potential of causing a collision with each other, which means that this hardware device will create a LAN with the most network traffic collisions. Hubs are not suggested for use in today's corporate network for this reason.

Bridge

A *bridge*—specifically, a transparent bridge—is a network device that connects two similar network segments together. Its primary function is to keep traffic separated on either side of the bridge, breaking up collision domains, as pictured in Figure 5.3.

FIGURE 5.3   Bridges break up collision domains.

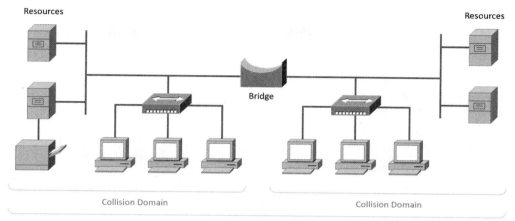

What we can see here is that traffic is allowed to pass through the bridge only if the transmission is intended for a station on the opposite side. The main reasons you would place a bridge in your network would be to connect two segments together or to divide a busy network into two segments. As bridges use MAC addresses to make forwarding decisions, they are considered layer 2 devices.

Bridges are software-based, so, interestingly, you can think of a switch as a hardware-based, multiport bridge. In fact, the terms *bridge* and *switch* are often used interchangeably because the two devices used basically the same bridging technologies. The past tense is there for a reason—you'd be hard-pressed to buy a bridge today.

Switch

Switches connect multiple segments of a network together much like hubs do, but with three significant differences—a switch recognizes frames and pays attention to the source and destination MAC address of the incoming frame as well as the port on which it was received. A switch makes each of its ports a unique, singular collision domain. Hubs don't do those things. They simply send anything they receive on one port out to all the others. As switches use MAC addresses to make forwarding decisions, they are considered layer 2 devices.

So, if a switch determines that a frame's final destination happens to be on a segment that's connected via a different port than the one on which the frame was received, the switch will only forward the frame out from the specific port on which its destination is located. If the switch can't figure out the location of the frame's destination, it will flood the frame out every port except the one on which the frame port was received.

Figure 5.4 shows a typical low-cost Ethernet switch. It looks a lot like a hub. However, switches can come in very large, expensive sizes. Switches that can perform the basic switching process and do not allow you to configure more advanced features—like adding an IP address for connecting to the device or adding VLANs—are called unmanaged switches. Others, like Cisco switches that do allow an IP address to be configured for management with such applications as simple network management protocol (SNMP) and do allow special ports to be configured (as in VoIP), are called managed switches.

FIGURE 5.4   Typical Ethernet switch

That's as far as we're going with switches right now. I'll bring them up later on in this chapter and cover them in much greater detail in Chapter 11, "Switching and Virtual LANs." For now, you can think of a switch as a faster, smarter bridge that has more ports.

Switches are layer 2 devices, which means they segment the network with MAC addresses. If you see the term *layer 3 switch*, that means you are talking about a router, not a layer 2 switch. The terms *router* and *layer 3 switch* are interchangeable.

Router

A *router* is a network device used to connect many, sometimes disparate, network segments together, combining them into what we call an *internetwork*. A well-configured router can make intelligent decisions about the best way to get network data to its destination. It gathers the information it needs to make these decisions based on a network's particular performance data. As routers use IP addresses to make forwarding decisions, they are considered layer 3 devices.

Figure 5.5 shows a small office, home office (SOHO) router that provides wired and wireless access for hosts and connects them to the Internet without any necessary configuration. But know that I certainly don't recommend leaving a router with the default configuration! No worries, though—I'll go over the configuration process with you in Chapter 10, "Routing Protocols."

Routers can be multifaceted devices that behave like computers unto themselves with their own complex operating systems—for example, Cisco's IOS. You can even think of them as CPUs that are totally dedicated to the process of routing packets. And because of their complexity and flexibility, you can configure them to actually perform the functions of other types of network devices (like firewalls, for example) by simply implementing a specific feature within the router's software.

FIGURE 5.5   Router connected to the Internet, providing access for multiple hosts

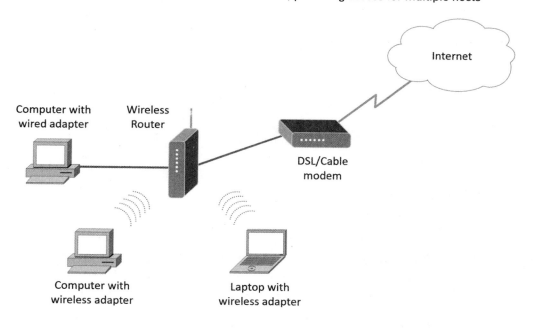

Computer with wired adapter

Wireless Router

DSL/Cable modem

Internet

Computer with wireless adapter

Laptop with wireless adapter

Routers can have many different names: *layer 3 switch* and *multilayer switch* are the most common, besides the name *router*, of course. Remember, if you hear just the word *switch*, that means a layer 2 device. Routers, layer 3 switches, and multilayer switches are all layer 3 devices.

Interface Configurations

When configuring interfaces on a router or switch, unless you're doing complex configurations such as connecting up a Voice over IP (VoIP) network, the interface configurations are pretty straightforward.

There is a major difference between a router interface and a switch interface configuration, however. On a switch, you do not add an IP address since they read only to layer 2, and most of the time, you never even need to configure a switch interface. First, they are enabled by default, and second, they are very good at auto-detecting the speed, duplex, and, in newer switches, even the Ethernet cable type (crossover or straight-through). A router is much different, and an IP address is expected on each interface; they are not enabled by default, and a good layer 3 network design must be considered before installing a router.

Let's start by taking a look at a basic Cisco switch configuration. First, notice by the output shown that there is no configuration on the interfaces, yet you can plug this switch into your network and it would work. This is because all ports are enabled and there are some very basic configurations that allow the switch to run without any configuration—they can be considered plug-and-play in a small or home network:

```
Switch#sh running-config
[output cut]
!
interface FastEthernet0/1
!
interface FastEthernet0/2
!
interface FastEthernet0/3
!
interface FastEthernet0/4
!
interface FastEthernet0/5
!
interface FastEthernet0/6
!
interface FastEthernet0/7
!
interface FastEthernet0/8
!
```

Let's take a look at a configuration of a simple switch interface. First, we'll notice the duplex options:

```
Switch(config-if)#duplex ?
  auto  Enable AUTO duplex configuration
  full  Force full duplex operation
  half  Force half-duplex operation
```

All switch ports are set to duplex auto by default, and usually you can just leave this configuration alone. However, be aware that if your network interface card is set to half-duplex and the switch port is configured for full-duplex, the port will receive errors and you'll eventually get a call from the user. This is why it is advised to just leave the defaults on your hosts and switch ports, but it is a troubleshooting spot to check when a problem is reported from a single user.

The next configuration and/or troubleshooting spot you may need to consider is the speed of the port:

```
Switch(config-if)#speed ?
  10    Force 10 Mbps operation
  100   Force 100 Mbps operation
  1000   Force 1000 Mbps operation
  auto  Enable AUTO speed configuration
```

Again, this is set to auto, but you may want to force the port to be 1000 and full-duplex. Typically, the NIC will run this without a problem and you'll be sure you're getting the most bang for your buck on your switch port.

Let's take a look at a router interface. We're pretty much going to configure (or not configure) the same parameters. However, you should be very aware that a router interface and a switch interface perform different functions. A router interface will break up collision domains just as a switch interface does, but the purpose of a router interface is to create and maintain broadcast domains and the connectivity of WAN services. Basic layer 2 switches cannot provide these services. As I mentioned, you must have a layer 3 design before you can implement a router, meaning you must have your subnet design laid out on your network diagram, and your IP addressing scheme must be completely understood. You cannot start configuring router interfaces randomly; there must be a design, and it needs to be correct.

Unlike switches, router interfaces do not just work when you plug them into the network—they must be configured and enabled. All ports are shut down by default, and why shouldn't they be? Unless you have a network design and understand IP addressing, what good is a router to your network?

Let's take a look:

```
Router(config-if)#duplex ?
  auto  Enable AUTO duplex configuration
  full  Force full duplex operation
  half  Force half-duplex operation
```

```
Router(config-if)#speed ?
  10    Force 10 Mbps operation
  100   Force 100 Mbps operation
  1000   Force 1000 Mbps operation
  auto  Enable AUTO speed configuration
```

```
Router(config-if)#ip address ?
  A.B.C.D  IP address
  dhcp     IP Address negotiated via DHCP
  pool     IP Address autoconfigured from a local DHCP pool
```

First, we can see that the basics are there, duplex and speed, but also, to make a router interface useful at all we must add an IP address. Notice that the options allow you to configure a specific IP address or allow the interface to receive the address from a DHCP server. You would use this option only if you had an IP address reservation for the router interface on your DHCP server since having your router get a random IP address from a DHCP server would be hard to manage. Let's finish the basics:

```
Router(config-if)#ip address 1.1.1.1 255.0.0.0
Router(config-if)#no shutdown
Router(config-if)#
*Oct  5 17:26:46.522: %LINK-3-UPDOWN: Interface FastEthernet0/0,
changed state to up
*Oct  5 17:26:47.522: %LINEPROTO-5-UPDOWN: Line protocol on
Interface FastEthernet0/0, changed state to up
```

The interface can now be connected to a layer 2 switch, and the hosts connected to the same broadcast domain must set their default gateway address to 1.1.1.1, and *voilà*, they can now send packets to the router.

Firewall

So what, exactly, is a *firewall*? Basically, firewalls are your network's security guards, and to be real, they're probably the most important thing to implement on your network. That's because today's networks are almost always connected to the Internet—a situation that makes security crucial! A firewall protects your LAN resources from invaders that prowl the Internet for unprotected networks while simultaneously preventing all or some of your LAN's computers from accessing certain services on the Internet. You can employ them to filter packets based on rules that you or the network administrator create and configure to strictly delimit the type of information allowed to flow in and out of the network's Internet connection. Firewalls operate at multiple layers of the OSI model. Some firewalls can operate up to the Application layer.

A firewall can be either a stand-alone "black box" or a software implementation placed on a server or router. Either way, the firewall will have at least two network connections: one to the Internet (known as the *public* side) and one to the network (known as the *private* side). Sometimes, there is a second firewall, as shown in Figure 5.6. This firewall is used to connect servers and equipment that can be considered both public and private (like web and email servers). This intermediary network is known as a screened subnet or, as it is often called, a *demilitarized zone (DMZ)*.

Firewalls are the first line of defense for an Internet-connected network. Without them in place, any network that's connected to the Internet is essentially wide open to anyone with a little technical savvy who seeks to exploit LAN resources and/or access your network's sensitive information.

FIGURE 5.6   Example of firewalls with a screened subnet or DMZ

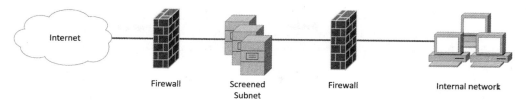

In network security, a *screened subnet* refers to the use of one or more logical screening routers as a first defense on your network.

A typical firewall design can define three separate networks, or zones, to separate the external (untrusted) zone to a trusted (internal and DMZ) zone, also referred to as a perimeter network. Now, CompTIA likes to call this perimeter network a screened subnet or DMZ, where your DNS server and possibly HTTPS web servers are located.

IDS/IPS

Intrusion detection systems (IDSs) and *intrusion prevention systems (IPSs)* are very important in today's networks. They are network security appliances that monitor networks and packets for malicious activity. An IDS is considered monitor mode and just records and tells you about problems, whereas an IPS can work in real time to stop threats as they occur.

The main difference between them is that an IPS works inline to actively prevent and block intrusions that are detected based on the rules you set up. IPSs can send an alarm, create correlation rules and remediation, drop malicious packets, provide malware protection, and reset the connection of offending source hosts.

HIDS

In a *host-based IDS (HIDS)*, software runs on one computer to detect abnormalities on that system alone by monitoring applications, system logs, and event logs—not by directly monitoring network traffic.

Systems like these are typically implemented on servers because they're a bear to manage if spread across several client computers on a network. Plus, if the IDS database is on the local computer and its data becomes compromised by an attack, the IDS data could be corrupted, too.

Other types of IDSs are protocol-based (PIDS), which monitor traffic for one protocol on one server, and application protocol-based (APIDS), which monitor traffic for a group of servers running the same application (such as SQL).

Access Point

I'll be covering access points (APs) also known as wireless access points (WAPs) in depth in Chapter 12, "Wireless Networking," but I'll introduce them here. Understand that an AP is just a hub that accepts wireless clients via an analog wireless signal. APs operate at layer 2.

It's no secret that wireless is the key to all networks in the world today. Wireless networks are even more important, now more than ever connecting all of our home appliances so they can communicate to apps we control and the Internet. The ease of communicating on a network using an AP instead of having to use an Ethernet cable has changed our world forever.

Figure 5.7 shows how an AP would look in a small network, such as a home.

FIGURE 5.7   Example of an AP in a network

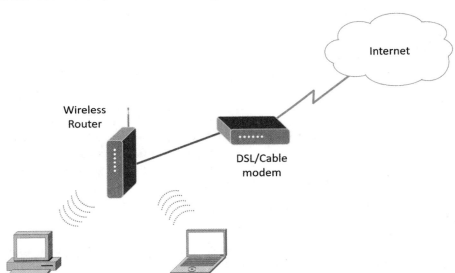

The wireless client modulates a digital signal to an analog signal, which the AP can read and demodulate back to a digital signal. The type of AP described in Figure 5.7 is known as an autonomous AP because it manages the wireless area with no controller or manager.

The AP creates one collision domain and can run only half-duplex, which is why you can describe an AP as being like a hub. However, even though some standards provide some full-duplex-type connectivity, a wireless host will never achieve the same type of throughput, security, and consistency that a wired Ethernet network would, but does that matter? Like rock 'n' roll, wireless is here to stay.

Wireless Range Extender

In some cases you need the WLAN to extend further than the technology in use is designed to deliver. In that case, you can deploy an extender. These are radios and antennas that operate in the same frequency or channel and receive the signal as a station would and then transmit it in the direction you desire to clients that are out of reach of the original AP.

These devices should be placed so there is at least 15% overlap of the coverage areas of the AP and the extender.

Wireless LAN Controller

In larger wireless networks, managing dozens, hundreds, or even thousands of wireless access points becomes an administrative burden. This led to the design and deployment of a centralized Wi-Fi configuration controller known as a WLC, or *wireless LAN controller*. The WLC lets you configure the complete network on a single device and push the configurations out to the Wi-Fi access points, referred to as lightweight access points, because the controller does the heavy lifting. The access points also tunnel the user data back to the controller, forwarding the traffic onto the LAN.

WLCs greatly reduce the amount of administrative overhead required to manage large enterprise wireless networks.

Load Balancer

Your average router just sends incoming packets to their specified, correlative IP address on the network, but a *load balancer* can send incoming packets to multiple machines hidden behind one IP address—cool, right?

In large and busy networks, often a single server does not have the capabilities to serve all requested traffic. For example, a very busy website on the Internet could have hundreds of thousands of incoming requests every second. This is often too large for a single server to accommodate. Also, if that server were to fail, the whole website could go offline.

Load balancers solve this problem by publishing a virtual IP address to a domain to receive incoming traffic. The load balancer then has a pool of real servers that it distributes the connections to. The distribution can be based on round robin, least number of connections, response time, a weighted percentage, or other metrics to evenly distribute the workload to the servers.

Health checks are performed to make sure that the servers are operational. If one does not respond, it can be automatically taken offline with the site still operating on the remaining servers.

Capacity can be dynamically added or removed using load balancers by using either manual or automatic scaling based on the current servers' workloads. New servers can dynamically be added and removed from the pool to scale the service up or down.

Today's load-balancing routers follow various rules to determine specifically how they will route network traffic. Depending on your needs, you can set rules based on the least load, fault tolerance, the fastest response times, or just dividing up (balancing) outbound requests for smooth network operations.

In fact, the fault tolerance, or redundancy, as well as the scalability so vital to large networking environments and e-commerce are some of the great benefits we gain using load balancers.

Think about this scenario: Say you have a website where people are placing orders for the stuff you're selling. Obviously, the orders placed vary in size, and the rate at which they come in varies; you definitely wouldn't want your servers becoming so overloaded that they hose up and crash your site, causing you to lose lots of money, now would you? That's where balancing the load of traffic between a group of servers comes to the rescue, because even if one of them freezes, your customers will still be able to access your site and place orders.

Contention Methods

In both wireless and wired environments that are shared mediums, meaning devices share a collision domain, such as when connected to a hub or when connected to a wireless access point, there is potential for frames from multiple devices colliding, destroying both packets. Both wired and wireless environments use a *contention method* to arbitrate access to the medium to help prevent collisions or at the least to recover from them when they occur. In the following sections, we'll look at the method used in each environment.

CSMA/CA

When the device sending the frame is transmitting onto a wireless network, the *Carrier Sense Multiple Access with Collision Avoidance (CSMA/CA)* contention method is used. The method starts with a check of the medium (in this case, a check of the radio frequency) for activity called *physical carrier sense*.

The frame will go to the AP. The AP will acknowledge reception of the frame. If the frame is destined for another wireless station located on this wireless LAN, the frame will be forwarded to it by the AP. When this occurs, the AP will follow the same CSMA/CA contention method to get the frame onto the wireless medium.

If the frame is destined for a station on the wired LAN, the AP will drop the 802.11 MAC header (which is structured differently from an Ethernet MAC header) and build a new Ethernet MAC header by using its MAC address as the source address and the MAC address of the default gateway as the destination. The LAN router will receive the frame, and normal LAN routing to the destination will continue from there, using the CSMA/CD contention mechanism (covered a bit later) to place the frame in the wire at each step. If frames are returned to the station, the AP will receive them, drop the Ethernet MAC header, build an 802.11 MAC header, and return the frame to the wireless station. When this occurs, the AP will follow the same CSMA/CA contention method to get the frame onto the wireless medium.

Describing CSMA/CA Operation

Because it is impossible for wireless stations to detect collisions, the CSMA/CA contention method is required to arbitrate access to the network. It requires a more involved process of checking for existing wireless traffic before a frame can be transmitted wirelessly. The stations (including the AP) must also acknowledge all frames. The steps in the process are as follows:

1. Laptop A has a frame to send to laptop B. Before sending, laptop A must check for traffic in two ways. First, it performs carrier sense, which means it listens to see whether any radio waves are being received on its transmitter.

2. If the channel is *not* clear (traffic is being transmitted), laptop A will decrement an internal countdown mechanism called the *random back-off algorithm*. This counter will have started counting down after the last time this station was allowed to transmit. All stations will be counting down their own individual timers. When a station's timer expires, it is allowed to send.

3. If laptop A checks for carrier sense and there is no traffic and its timer hits zero, it will send the frame.

4. The frame goes to the AP.

5. The AP sends an acknowledgment back to laptop A. Until that acknowledgment is received by laptop A, all other stations must remain silent. The AP will cache the frame, where it already may have other cached frames that need to be relayed to other stations. Each frame that the AP needs to relay must wait its turn to send the frame using the same mechanism as the stations.

6. When the frame's turn comes up in the cache queue, the frame from laptop A will be relayed to laptop B.

7. Laptop B sends an acknowledgment back to the AP. Until that acknowledgment is received by the AP, all other stations must remain silent.

When you consider that this process has to occur for every single frame and that there are many other frame types used by the AP to manage other functions of the network that also create competition for air time, it is no wonder that actual throughput on a wireless LAN is at best about half the advertised rate.

For example, if two wireless stations were the only wireless clients and they were using 802.11g, which is capable of 54 Mbps, the *very best* throughput experienced would be about 25 to 28 Mbps. Moreover, as soon as a third station arrives, throughput will go down again because the stations are dividing the air time by 3 instead of 2. Add a fourth, and it gets even worse! Such is the challenge of achieving throughput on a wireless LAN.

CSMA/CD

When the device sending the frame is transmitting onto a wired network, the *Carrier Sense Multiple Access with Collision Detection (CSMA/CD)* contention method is used. This method is somewhat more efficient because it is possible for wired computers to detect collisions while wireless stations cannot. When a host's or router's interface needs to send a frame, it checks the wire, and if no traffic is detected, it sends without checking a random back-off timer.

However, it continues to listen, and if it detects that a collision has occurred, it sends out a jam signal that requires all stations to stop transmitting. Then the two computers that were involved in the collision will both wait a random amount of time (that each arrives at independently) and will resend. So instead of using a random break-off algorithm every time a transmission occurs, Ethernet uses its ability to detect collisions and uses this timer only when required, which makes the process more efficient.

Describing CSMA/CD Operation

CSMA/CD has mechanisms that help minimize but not eliminate collisions. Its operation is as follows:

1. When a device needs to transmit, it checks the wire. If a transmission is already underway, the device can tell. This is called *carrier sense*.

2. If the wire is clear, the device will transmit. Even as it is transmitting, it is performing carrier sense.

3. If another host is sending simultaneously, there will be a collision. The collision is detected by both devices through carrier sense.

4. Both devices will issue a jam signal to all the other devices, which indicates to them to *not* transmit.

5. Then both devices will increment a retransmission counter. This is a cumulative total of the number of times this frame has been transmitted and a collision has occurred. There is a maximum number at which the device aborts the transmission of the frame.

6. Both devices will calculate a random amount of time and will wait that amount of time before transmitting again. This calculation is called a *random back-off*.

7. In most cases, because both devices choose random amounts of time to wait, another collision will not occur.

Dynamic Host Configuration Protocol Server

Even though I'm going to get into the finer points of DHCP soon, in Chapter 6, "Introduction to the Internet Protocol," I want to give you some basic insight into this server service here.

In essence, DHCP servers assign IP addresses to hosts. This protocol gives us a much easier way to administer—by automatically providing IP information—than the alternative and tedious method known as static IP addressing or *static assignment*, where we have to address each host manually. It works well in any network environment, from tiny to huge, and allows all types of hardware to be employed as a DHCP server, including routers.

It works like this: A DHCP server receives a request for IP information from a DHCP client using a broadcast (as Chapter 6 will show you in detail). The DHCP server is configured by the administrator with what is called a pool of addresses that it uses for this purpose. When the administrator configures this pool, they can also set some addresses in the pool as "off limits." These are called IP exclusions or *exclusion ranges*. It means that these addresses cannot be assigned. An example might be the address of the router interface.

The only hitch is that if the DHCP server isn't on the same segment as the DHCP client, the broadcast won't be received by the server because, by default, routers won't forward broadcasts, as shown in Figure 5.8.

FIGURE 5.8   DHCP client sends broadcasts looking for a DHCP server.

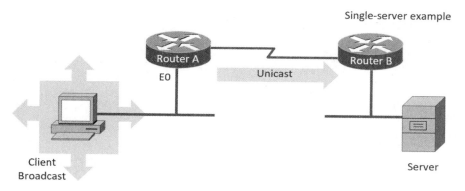

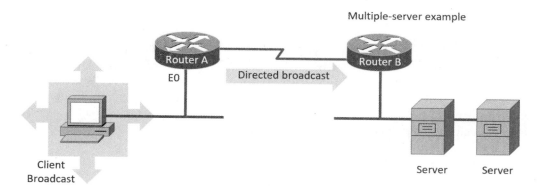

In Figure 5.8, Router A is configured with the IP helper address command on interface E0 of the router. Whenever interface E0 receives a broadcast request, Router A will forward that request as a unicast (meaning instead of a broadcast, the packet now has the destination IP address of the DHCP server).

So, as shown in the figure, you can configure Router A to forward these requests and even use multiple DHCP servers for redundancy, if needed. This works because the router has been configured to forward the request to a single server using a unicast or by sending the request to multiple servers via a directed broadcast.

Personally, most of the time I use a Windows server to act as the DHCP server for my entire internetwork and have my routers forward client requests. It is possible to have a DHCP server on every network segment, but that is not necessary because of the routers' forwarding ability.

Figure 5.9 shows a Windows server with something called scope options.

FIGURE 5.9   A Windows DHCP server's scope options

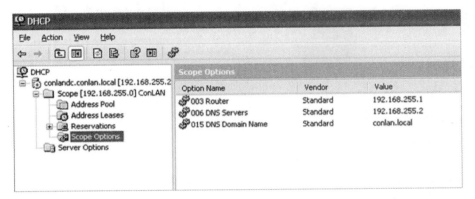

Scope options provide IP configuration for hosts on a specific subnet. Below Scope Options, you'll find Server Options; these options provide IP information for all scopes configured on the server. If I had just one Domain Name System (DNS) server for the entire network, I'd configure the server options with my DNS server information; that DNS server information would then show up automatically in all scopes configured on my server.

So, what exactly does a DHCP client ask for, and what does a DHCP server provide? Is it just an IP address, a mask, and a default gateway? No, it is much more than that. Scope options comprise the informational elements that the DHCP server can provide to the DHCP clients. Here are some examples of these options:

- TTL (provides the default TCP TTL value for TCP packets sent by the client)

- DNS server

- TFTP server (especially important for IP phones that need to get a configuration for a TFTP server)

Let's take a look at a DHCP client request on an analyzer. Figure 5.10 shows the options that the client is requesting from the DHCP server.

First, you can see that the DHCP service runs on top of the BootP protocol (port 68) and that the DHCP client is looking for a BootP server (port 67). The client IP address is 0.0.0.0, and the client doesn't know the DHCP server address either because this is a broadcast to 255.255.255.255 (the Data Link layer broadcast shows ff:ff:ff:ff:ff:ff). Basically, all the

DHCP client knows for sure is its own MAC address. The client is "requesting" a certain IP address because this is the IP address it received from the server the last time it requested an IP address.

FIGURE 5.10   DHCP client request to a DHCP server

```
⊞ Frame 33 (344 bytes on wire, 344 bytes captured)
⊞ Ethernet II, Src: Usi_d0:e9:35 (00:1e:37:d0:e9:35), Dst: Broadcast (ff:ff:ff:ff:ff:ff)
⊞ Internet Protocol, Src: 0.0.0.0 (0.0.0.0), Dst: 255.255.255.255 (255.255.255.255)
⊞ User Datagram Protocol, Src Port: bootpc (68), Dst Port: bootps (67)
⊟ Bootstrap Protocol
    Message type: Boot Request (1)
    Hardware type: Ethernet
    Hardware address length: 6
    Hops: 0
    Transaction ID: 0xb16f1532
    Seconds elapsed: 0
  ⊞ Bootp flags: 0x8000 (Broadcast)
    Client IP address: 0.0.0.0 (0.0.0.0)
    Your (client) IP address: 0.0.0.0 (0.0.0.0)
    Next server IP address: 0.0.0.0 (0.0.0.0)
    Relay agent IP address: 0.0.0.0 (0.0.0.0)
    Client MAC address: Usi_d0:e9:35 (00:1e:37:d0:e9:35)
    Server host name not given
    Boot file name not given
    Magic cookie: (OK)
  ⊞ Option: (t=53,l=1) DHCP Message Type = DHCP Discover
  ⊞ Option: (t=116,l=1) DHCP Auto-Configuration
  ⊞ Option: (t=61,l=7) Client identifier
  ⊞ Option: (t=50,l=4) Requested IP Address = 10.100.36.38
  ⊞ Option: (t=12,l=14) Host Name = "globalnet-todd"
  ⊞ Option: (t=60,l=8) Vendor class identifier = "MSFT 5.0"
  ⊞ Option: (t=55,l=12) Parameter Request List
    End Option
```

The DHCP client Parameter Request List option shown at the bottom of Figure 5.10 has been expanded and is shown in Figure 5.11. Notice all the parameter information that can be sent to a DHCP client from the server.

FIGURE 5.11   DHCP client parameter request list

```
⊟ Option: (t=55,l=12) Parameter Request List
    Option: (55) Parameter Request List
    Length: 12
    Value: 010F03062C2E2F1F2179F92B
    1 = Subnet Mask
    15 = Domain Name
    3 = Router
    6 = Domain Name Server
    44 = NetBIOS over TCP/IP Name Server
    46 = NetBIOS over TCP/IP Node Type
    47 = NetBIOS over TCP/IP Scope
    31 = Perform Router Discover
    33 = Static Route
    121 = Classless Static Route
    249 = Classless Static Route (Microsoft)
    43 = Vendor-Specific Information
    End Option
```

That is quite a request list! The DHCP server will respond with the options that it has configured and are available to provide to a DHCP client. Let's take a look and see what the server responds with. Figure 5.12 shows the DHCP server response.

FIGURE 5.12 DHCP server response

```
□ Frame 34 (359 bytes on wire, 359 bytes captured)
⊞ Ethernet II, Src: Cisco_90:ed:80 (00:0b:5f:90:ed:80), Dst: Broadcast (ff:ff:ff:ff:ff:ff)
⊞ Internet Protocol, Src: 10.100.36.33 (10.100.36.33), Dst: 255.255.255.255 (255.255.255.255)
⊞ User Datagram Protocol, Src Port: bootps (67), Dst Port: bootpc (68)
□ Bootstrap Protocol
    Message type: Boot Reply (2)
    Hardware type: Ethernet
    Hardware address length: 6
    Hops: 0
    Transaction ID: 0xb16f1532
    Seconds elapsed: 0
  ⊞ Bootp flags: 0x8000 (Broadcast)
    Client IP address: 0.0.0.0 (0.0.0.0)
    Your (client) IP address: 10.100.36.38 (10.100.36.38)
    Next server IP address: 10.100.36.12 (10.100.36.12)
    Relay agent IP address: 10.100.36.33 (10.100.36.33)
    Client MAC address: Usi_d0:e9:35 (00:1e:37:d0:e9:35)
    Server host name not given
    Boot file name not given
    Magic cookie: (OK)
  ⊞ Option: (t=53,l=1) DHCP Message Type = DHCP Offer
  ⊞ Option: (t=1,l=4) Subnet Mask = 255.255.255.224
  ⊞ Option: (t=58,l=4) Renewal Time Value = 11 hours, 30 minutes
  ⊞ Option: (t=59,l=4) Rebinding Time Value = 20 hours, 7 minutes, 30 seconds
  ⊞ Option: (t=51,l=4) IP Address Lease Time = 23 hours
  ⊞ Option: (t=54,l=4) Server Identifier = 10.100.36.12
  ⊞ Option: (t=15,l=16) Domain Name = "globalnet.local"
  ⊞ Option: (t=3,l=4) Router = 10.100.36.33
  ⊞ Option: (t=6,l=8) Domain Name Server
  ⊞ Option: (t=44,l=4) NetBIOS over TCP/IP Name Server = 10.100.36.13
  ⊞ Option: (t=46,l=1) NetBIOS over TCP/IP Node Type = H-node
    End Option
```

The client is going to get the IP address that it asked for (10.100.36.38), a subnet mask of 255.255.255.224, a lease time of 23 hours (the amount of time before the IP address and other DHCP information expires on the client), the IP address of the DHCP server, the default gateway (router), the DNS server IP address (it gets two), the domain name used by DNS, and some NetBIOS information (used by Windows for name resolution).

The *lease time* is important and can even be used to tell you if you have a DHCP problem or, more specifically, that the DHCP server is no longer handing out IP addresses to hosts. If hosts start failing to get onto the network one at a time as they try to get a new IP address as their lease time expires, you need to check your server settings.

Here is another example of a possible DHCP problem: You arrive at work after a weekend and find that some hosts were left on and some were shut down. The hosts that were left running and not shut down are still working, but the hosts that were shut down and were restarted on Monday morning do not get a new IP address. This is a good indication that you need to head over to your DHCP server and take a look at what is going on.

A DHCP server can also be configured with a reservation list so that a host always receives the same IP address. When this is done, the reservation is made on the basis of the router interface MAC address. Therefore, it is sometimes called a MAC reservation. You would use this reservation list for routers or servers if they were not statically assigned. However, you can use reservation lists for any host on your network as well.

DHCP is an Application layer protocol. While the DORA (Discover, Offer, Request, Acknowledgment) components operate at layer 2, the protocol is managed and responds to the Application layer. DHCP uses UDP ports 67 and 68.

EXERCISE 5.1

Experimenting with DHCP

In this exercise you will experiment with DHCP on your computer. You will release the IP address and renew the IP address. This may result in a new IP address or new lease time. Be aware that you will loose connectivity while performing this exercise.

1. Open the command prompt by clicking Start, typing **cmd**, and pressing Enter.

2. In the command prompt, type **ipconfig /all** and make note of the IP address and the Lease Obtained date/time.

3. Type **ipconfig /release**.

4. Type **ipconfig /renew**.

5. Type **ipconfig /all** and examine the IP address and Lease Obtained date/time.

You should have the same IP address, depending on how busy your network is. However, the Lease Obtained date/time should change since you relinquished the IP lease and obtained a new one.

DHCP Relay

If you need to provide addresses from a DHCP server to hosts that aren't on the same LAN as the DHCP server, you can configure your router interface to relay or forward the DHCP client requests, as shown in Figure 5.13. This is referred to as a *DHCP relay*. If we don't provide this service, our router would receive the DHCP client broadcast, promptly discard it, and the remote host would never receive an address—unless we added a DHCP server on every broadcast domain! Let's take a look at how we would typically configure DHCP service in today's networks.

FIGURE 5.13 Configuring a DHCP relay

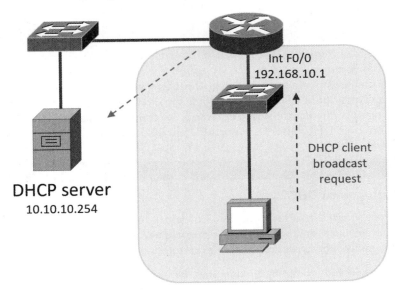

So we know that because the hosts off the router don't have access to a DHCP server, the router will simply drop their client request broadcast messages by default. To solve this problem, we can configure the F0/0 interface of the router to accept the DHCP client requests and forward them to the DHCP server like this:

```
Router#config t
Router(config)#interface fa0/0
Router(config-if)#ip helper-address 10.10.10.254
```

Now I know that was a pretty simple example, and there are definitely other ways to configure the relay, but rest assured that I've covered the objectives for you. Also, I want you to know that ip helper-address forwards more than just DHCP client requests, so be sure to research this command before you implement it!

IPAM

IP address management (IPAM) tools are software products that integrate the management of DHCP and DNS. They are used to plan, track, and manage the IP addresses.

With the integration of DNS and DHCP, each process is kept abreast of changes made to the other service. Many products offer additional functionality, such as tracking IP addresses in use and the devices an IP is assigned to, as well as at what time and to which user an IP address was assigned.

Other Specialized Devices

In addition to the network connectivity devices I've discussed with you, several devices, while not directly connected to a network, do actively participate in moving network data. Here's a list of them:

- Multilayer switch
- DNS server
- Network Time Protocol
- Proxy server
- Encryption devices
- Analog modem
- Packet shaper
- VPN concentrator headend
- Media converter
- VoIP PBX
- VoIP endpoint
- NGFW/layer 7 firewall
- VoIP gateway
- Cable modem
- DSL modem

Multilayer Switch

A *multilayer switch (MLS)* is a computer networking device that switches on OSI layer 2 like an ordinary network switch but provides routing. A 24-port MLS gives you the best of both worlds. It operates at layer 3 (routing) while still providing 24 collision domains, which a router could not do.

The major difference between the packet-switching operation of a router and that of a layer 3 or multilayer switch lies in the physical implementation. In routers, packet switching takes place using a microprocessor, whereas a layer 3 switch handles this by using application-specific integrated circuit (ASIC) hardware. I'd show you a picture of a layer 3 switch, but they look just like regular layer 2 switches, and you already know what those look like. The differences are the hardware inside and the operating system.

Domain Name System Server

A *Domain Name System (DNS) server* is one of the most important servers in your network and on the Internet as well. Why? Because without a DNS server, you would have to type https://206.123.114.186 instead of simply entering www.lammle.com. So it follows that you can pretty much think of the DNS system as the phone book of the Internet.

A hostname is typically the name of a device that has a specific IP address; on the Internet, it is part of what is known as a fully qualified domain name (FQDN). An FQDN consists of a hostname and a domain name.

The process of finding the IP address for any given hostname is known as *name resolution*, and it can be performed in several ways: a hosts file (meaning you statically type in all names and IP addresses on each and every host), a request broadcast on the local network, or DNS. DNS is the most popular today and is the resolution method you really need to know.

On the Internet, domains are arranged in a hierarchical tree structure. The following list includes some of the root or top-level domains currently in use:

.com   A commercial organization. Most companies end up as part of this domain.

.edu   An educational establishment, such as a university.

.gov   A branch of the US government.

.int   An international organization, such as NATO or the United Nations.

.mil   A branch of the US military.

.net   A network organization.

.org   A nonprofit organization.

Your local ISP is probably a member of the .net domain, and your company is probably part of the .com domain. The .gov and .mil domains are reserved strictly for use by the government and the military within the United States. In other parts of the world, the final part of a domain name represents the country in which the server is located (.ca for Canada, .jp for Japan, .uk for Great Britain, and .ru for Russia, for example). Well over 130 countries are represented on the Internet.

The .com domain is by far the largest, followed by the .edu domain. Some new domain names are becoming popular, however, because of the increasing number of domain-name requests. These include .firm for businesses and companies, .store for businesses selling goods rather than services, .arts for cultural and entertainment organizations, and .info for informational services. The domains .cc, .biz, .travel, and .post are also in use on the Internet.

Figure 5.14 shows how, when you type in a domain name, the DNS server resolves it, allowing the host to send the HTTPS packets to the server.

This Command Prompt screen shows how the DNS server can resolve the human name to the IP address of the Lammle.com server when I ping the server by the name instead of the IP address.

It should be easy to imagine how hard life would be without DNS translating human names to IP addresses, routing your packet through the Internet or internetwork to get to your servers. Figure 5.15 gives you an example of a Windows server configured as a DNS server.

FIGURE 5.14   DNS resolution example

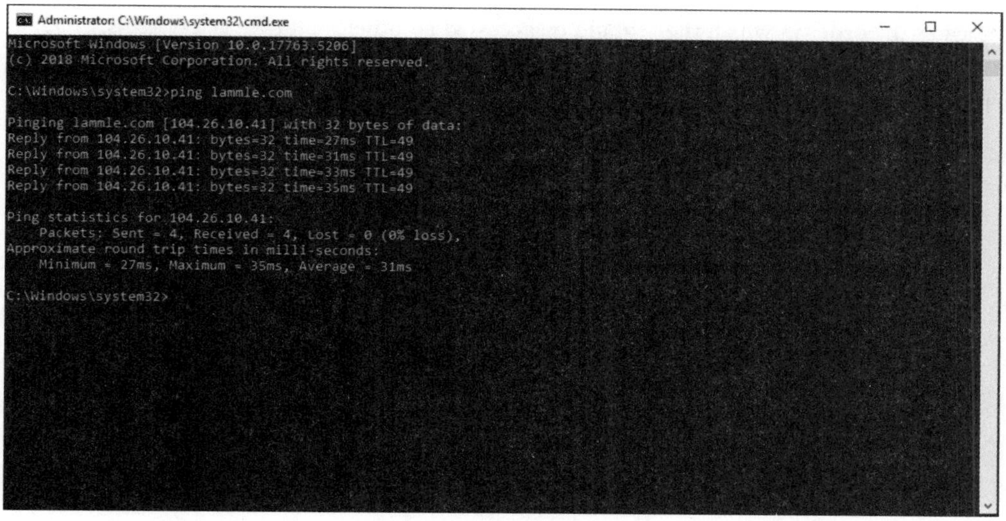

To complete unqualified DNS names that will be used to search and submit DNS queries at the client for resolution, you must have a list of DNS suffixes that can be appended to these DNS names. For DHCP clients, this can be set by assigning the DNS domain name option (option 15) and providing a single DNS suffix for the client to append and use in searches. For example, if you just wanted to ping todd instead of pinging todd.lammle.com, you can configure the DHCP server option 15 to provide the suffix for you.

Now the hosts can receive the IP address of this DNS server, and then this server will resolve hostnames to correct IP addresses. This is a mission-critical service in today's networks, don't you think? As shown in Figure 5.15, if I ping from a host to conlanpc1, the host will send the name-resolution request to the DNS server and translate this name to IP address 192.168.255.8.

Host (A) is called an A record or *address (A)* record and is what gives you the IP address of a domain or host. In IPv6, it's called a quad-A or AAAA record. In Figure 5.15, you can see that each name has an A record, which is associated to an IP address. So, A records resolve hostnames to IP addresses, but what happens if you know the IP address and want to know the hostname? There is a record for this, too! It's called the *pointer record (PTR)*.

Another typical type of record found on DNS servers is the *mail exchanger (MX) record*, which is used to translate mail records. The MX record points to the mail exchanger for a particular host. DNS is structured so that you can actually specify several mail exchangers for one host. This feature provides a higher probability that email will arrive at its intended destination. The mail exchangers are listed in order in the record, with a priority code that indicates the order in which they should be accessed by other mail-delivery systems.

FIGURE 5.15   A Windows DNS server

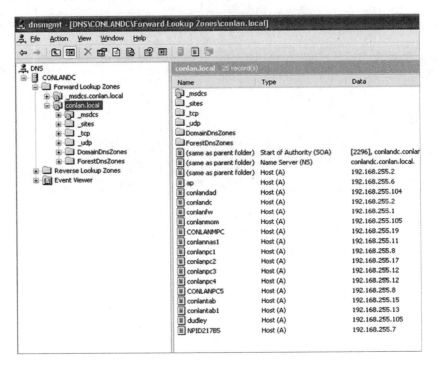

There are many types of records the DNS server keeps as, shown in Table 5.1.

TABLE 5.1   Additional DNS record types

Record Type	Explanation
A	Address record returns the IP address of the domain.
AAAA	Used to map hostnames to an IPv6 address of the host.
TXT (SPF)	The text record specifies a list of authorized hostnames/IP addresses that mail can originate from for a given domain name.

Record Type	Explanation
TXT (DKIM)	Domain Keys Identified Mail, used to provide authentication of mail sent and received by the same email system and is used to prevent spam.
SRV	DNS service or generalized service location record. Specifies a port number in addition to the IP address.
CAA	Certificate Authority Authorization, allows domain name owners to specify authorized certificate authorities.
CNAME	Canonical name records are used to alias one domain name to another such as toddlammle.com to Lammle.com.
SOA	Start of authority, provides administrative information about the domain or zone such as the email of the administrator, when the domain was last updated, and time intervals such as refresh and time to live.
PTR	The pointer record used for reverse DNS lookup. which returns the domain name when given the IP address.
MX	Mail exchanger record specifies how email messages should be routed.
NS	Name server, represents the authoritative DNS server for the domain. Authoritative servers store and manage the official DNS records for domains, which in turn provide accurate and up-to-date information. Non-authoritative servers act as intermediaries, forwarding and caching DNS queries. This helps to improve performance and reduce latency.

If the first-priority mail exchanger doesn't respond in a given amount of time, the mail-delivery system tries the second one, and so on. Here are some sample mail-exchange records:

```
hostname.company.com.    IN    MX    10 mail.company.com.
hostname.company.com.    IN    MX    20 mail2.company.com.
hostname.company.com.    IN    MX    30 mail3.company.com.
```

In this example, if the first mail exchanger, mail.company.com, does not respond, the second one, mail2.company.com, is tried, and so on.

Another important record type on a DNS server is the *canonical name (CNAME) record*. This is also commonly known as the *alias record*, and it allows hosts to have more than one name. For example, suppose your web server has the hostname www and you want that machine to also have the name ftp so that users can use FTP to access a different portion of the file system as an FTP root. You can accomplish this with a CNAME record. Given that you already have an address record established for the hostname **www**, a CNAME record that adds `ftp` as a hostname would look something like this:

```
www.company.com.        IN    A       204.176.47.2
ftp.company.com.        IN    CNAME   www.company.com.
```

When you put all these record types together in a zone file, or DNS table, it might look like this:

```
mail.company.com.       IN    A       204.176.47.9
mail2.company.com.      IN    A       204.176.47.21
mail3.company.com.      IN    A       204.176.47.89
yourhost.company.com.   IN    MX      10 mail.company.com.
yourhost.company.com.   IN    MX      20 mail2.company.com.
yourhost.company.com.   IN    MX      30 mail3.company.com.
www.company.com.        IN    A       204.176.47.2
ftp.company.com.        IN    CNAME   www.company.com.
```

DNS uses zone transfers from the primary DNS server for a zone to update standby servers; this allows us to have some redundancy in our DNS deployments and distribute the workload across multiple DNS servers. Primary DNS servers host controlling zone files, while secondary DNS servers provide reliability and redundancy for the DNS primary server.

There are two types of zones: Forward and Reverse. Forward lookup zones resolve names to IP addresses, and Reverse lookup zones resolve IP addresses to names. Forwarders are used on your DNS server to forward requests if your DNS server does not have an authoritative answer.

When a client gets a DNS reply from a query, it will store it locally (cached) for a period of time to reduce the number of lookups on the DNS servers. In each DNS reply there is a field called TTL, or time to live. This instructs the client how long to store the replay before requesting again. This allows us to reduce the network workload and keep the DNS data fresh on the client. All devices use a cache system that stores the requests locally for a period of time, and the *time to live (TTL)* value tells the client how long that should be.

What if you know the IP address but want to know what the domain name is? DNS can perform reverse lookup to query the server with the IP address, and it will return the domain name. Other lookup types include recursive and iterative. When a DNS system uses a recursive lookup, one DNS server will query other DNS servers instead of the client performing all of the operations. The other option is to have the client communicate with multiple DNS servers during the name resolution process, which is referred to as an iterative DNS query.

Finally, there are other record types you should know about such as AAAA (for authentication IPV6 host addresses), PTR (pointer) records, and SOA (start of authority) records. PTR records are IP address–to–name mapping records rather than name–to–IP address mapping records. They reside in what is called a *reverse lookup zone* (or table) in the server and are used when an IP address is known but not a name. The start of authority, or SOA, record stores information about the DNS domain or zone such as how to contact the administrator, when the domain was last updated, and how long the server should wait between refreshes.

Let's take a look a tad deeper for a minute into how resolution takes place between a host and a DNS server. Figure 5.16 shows a DNS query from my host to `www.lammle.com` from a browser.

FIGURE 5.16   A DNS query to `www.lammle.com`

```
⊞ Frame 775: 74 bytes on wire (592 bits), 74 bytes captured (592 bits) on interface 0
⊞ Ethernet II, Src: Vmware_3e:06:c4 (00:0c:29:3e:06:c4), Dst: Vmware_fb:70:bb (00:50:56:fb:70:bb)
⊞ Internet Protocol Version 4, Src: 192.168.133.147 (192.168.133.147), Dst: 192.168.133.2 (192.168.133.2)
⊞ User Datagram Protocol, Src Port: 53870 (53870), Dst Port: domain (53)
⊟ Domain Name System (query)
    [Response In: 826]
    Transaction ID: 0xb8e0
  ⊞ Flags: 0x0100 Standard query
    Questions: 1
    Answer RRs: 0
    Authority RRs: 0
    Additional RRs: 0
  ⊟ Queries
    ⊟ www.lammle.com: type A, class IN
        Name: www.lammle.com
        Type: A (Host address)
        Class: IN (0x0001)
```

This figure shows that DNS uses User Datagram Protocol (UDP) at the Transport layer (it uses Transport Control Protocol [TCP] if it is updating its phone book pages—we call these *zone updates*), and this query is asking destination port 53 (the DNS service) on host 192.168.133.2 who the heck `www.lammle.com` is.

Let's take a look at the server's response. Figure 5.17 shows the DNS answer to our query for `www.lammle.com`.

FIGURE 5.17   The DNS answer to our query

```
⊟ Frame 826: 104 bytes on wire (832 bits), 104 bytes captured (832 bits) on interface 0
⊞ Ethernet II, Src: Vmware_fb:70:bb (00:50:56:fb:70:bb), Dst: Vmware_3e:06:c4 (00:0c:29:3e:06:c4)
⊞ Internet Protocol Version 4, Src: 192.168.133.2 (192.168.133.2), Dst: 192.168.133.147 (192.168.133.147)
⊞ User Datagram Protocol, Src Port: domain (53), Dst Port: 53870 (53870)
⊟ Domain Name System (response)
    [Request In: 775]
    [Time: 0.916685000 seconds]
    Transaction ID: 0xb8e0
  ⊞ Flags: 0x8180 Standard query response, No error
    Questions: 1
    Answer RRs: 2
    Authority RRs: 0
    Additional RRs: 0
  ⊟ Queries
    ⊟ www.lammle.com: type A, class IN
        Name: www.lammle.com
        Type: A (Host address)
        Class: IN (0x0001)
  ⊟ Answers
    ⊟ www.lammle.com: type CNAME, class IN, cname lammle.com
        Name: www.lammle.com
        Type: CNAME (Canonical name for an alias)
        Class: IN (0x0001)
        Time to live: 5 seconds
        Data length: 2
        Primaryname: lammle.com
    ⊟ lammle.com: type A, class IN, addr 184.172.53.52
        Name: lammle.com
        Type: A (Host address)
        Class: IN (0x0001)
        Time to live: 5 seconds
        Data length: 4
        Addr: 184.172.53.52 (184.172.53.52)
```

Port 53 answered from server 192.168.133.147 with a CNAME and an A record with the IP address of 184.172.53.52. My host can now go to that server requesting HTTP pages using the IP address.

DNS is an Application layer protocol. DNS queries are made on UDP port 53.

EXERCISE 5.2

Examining DNS Entries

In this exercise, you will explore several different types of DNS entries. This will help you apply the knowledge learned to give you a better understanding of DNS.

1.   Open the command prompt by clicking Start, typing **cmd**, and then pressing Enter.

2.   In the open command prompt, type **nslookup www.wiley.com** and examine the result.

The result by default is the A record for the query.

3.   On a new line in the command prompt, type **nslookup -q=cname www.wiley.com** and examine the result.

By modifying the query with the -q=cname switch, the CName is returned for www.wiley.com.

4.   On a new line in the command prompt, type **nslookup -q=mx wiley.com** and examine the result.

By modifying the query with the -q=mx switch and submitting only the domain name, the MX records are returned for wiley.com.

Adapt these steps to a random site. Be aware that the results will be different depending on the records being used. In the previous example, an A, CName, and MX record were configured.

Dynamic DNS

At one time all DNS records had to be manually entered into the DNS server and edited manually when changes occurred. Today, DNS is dynamic. It uses *dynamic assignment* and works in concert with the DHCP function. Hosts register their names with the DNS server as they receive their IP address configuration from the DHCP server. Some older operating systems are not capable of self-registration, but the DHCP server can even be configured to perform registration on behalf of these clients with the DNS server.

This doesn't mean that manual records cannot be created if desired. In fact, some of the record types we have discussed can only be created manually. These include MX and CNAME records.

Internal and External DNS

DNS servers can be located in the screened subnet (or DMZ) or inside the intranet, as shown in Figure 5.18.

FIGURE 5.18 Internal and external DNS

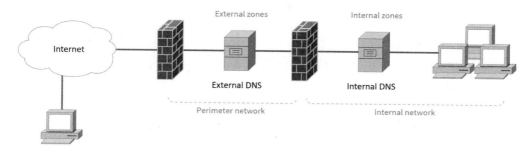

When located in the DMZ, the DNS server should only contain the records of the devices that are placed in the DMZ. Implementing separate internal and external DNS servers might require you to include external resource records in the internal DNS zone. You need to do this when the Active Directory forest root uses the same DNS domain name as the external network or when you want to reference the externally accessible resources by their true IP addresses in the perimeter network rather than using the addresses published to the Internet by the firewall protecting the perimeter network.

Third-Party/Cloud-Hosted DNS

Some smaller organizations find that it makes more sense to outsource the DNS function. Rather than hire and train staff to set up, configure, and maintain the infrastructure required to keep name resolution up and secure, they might find it more cost effective to utilize a third party who makes it their business to provide this service. There is no shortage of cloud providers falling all over themselves to provide you with cloud-based storage, and these same vendors stand ready to provide you with DNS as a service, and they'll probably do a better job at it than you will.

Domain Name System Security Extensions (DNSSEC)

DNSSEC is not a single protocol but a suite of new extensions created by Extension Mechanisms for DNS (EDNS). EDNS was created to expand the size of various parameters of the DNS protocol, which was originally created too small and had size restrictions that engineers found too limited in today's Internet.

Because of this expansion, new security specifications were created by the Internet Engineering Task Force (IETF) to secure data that is exchanged in the DNS protocol, and this was named DNSSEC. This protocol provides cryptographic authentication of data, authenticated denial of existence, and data integrity.

DNS over HTTPS (DoH) and DNS over TLS (DoT)

These two protocols are a great addition to the DNS protocol unless you are a cyber security expert trying to find DNS data for Next Generation Firewall (NGFW) tuning since the DNS queries are encrypted. This means you cannot see the URL, URL reputation, or the URL category or these queries. All these are necessary when tuning a Snort process (IPS) with URL filtering.

DNS over HTTPS   DoH is an Internet security protocol that communicates encrypted DNS information over HTTPS connections. DNS queries, as well as responses, are encrypted with DoH, which means that would-be attackers cannot forge or even alter DNS traffic. This also means that DoH looks like any other HTTPS traffic. DoH is used by Firefox by default. However, other browsers can support DoH; they just are not enabled by default.

DNS over TLS   Like DoH, DoT is a standard that encrypts DNS queries, which provides the security and privacy that users look for. Like DoH, DoT uses TLS (used to be called SSL) to encrypt and authenticate DNS communications. DoH uses TCP, but DoT uses UDP for DNS queries.

The DoH and DoT standards were developed separately, which means that each ended up with its own RFC documentation. It's important to distinguish that DoT uses TCP port 853 as well as UDP port 8853, while DoH uses port TCP 443, and because DoH uses the same TCP 443 port used by other HTTPS traffic, identifying the DoH from other HTTPS traffic is difficult.

You'll also see a protocol called DNS over QUIC (DoQ) created by Google and used by Chrome. This is a transport layer encryption and not the query encryption that DoH and DoT use. DoQ basically does the same thing as both DoH and DoT, meaning that the connection to the configured DNS server is encrypted; however, DoQ uses UDP port 443 instead of TCP 443.

Network Time Protocols

The *Network Time Protocol (NTP)* provides the time synchronization of the clocks on networking devices and computers on a network. This is used for distributed tasks that require accurate time to make sure tasks are processed in the correct sequence and recorded properly. NTP is needed for security and log tracking across many devices to correlate and trace events based on time. Many network management applications rely on timestamps for performance measurements and troubleshooting. If all of the devices in a network did not have the same time provided by syncing to a master clock using NTP, these would not be possible. The NTP protocol operates on UDP port 123.

Stratum   *Stratum* levels are how accurate the time source is. If the primary reference clock is a master time source such as a nuclear clock or a satellite navigation array, it is considered to be stratum level 0. Stratum 1 takes its time source from a stratum 0 clock, stratum 2 syncs from stratum 1, and so on. The accuracy is less the further you are from a stratum 0 time source.

Clients   Clients use the NTP protocol to query NTP servers to set their clocks. If every device in a network uses NTP, then all the clocks will be synchronized.

Once a client has synchronized its clock from an NTP time server, it will generally check every 10 minutes to keep its time updated.

Servers   NTP servers can be specialized hardware on your network that sync to stratum 0 devices or on the Internet. The site at `https://tf.nist.gov/tf-cgi/servers.cgi` lists servers available for public use.

Network Time Security (NTS)

NTP is a great tool to provide exact time to your network devices. However, it's possible that you may receive time from an unauthorized server without knowing it.

As the name suggests, Network Time Security (NTS) provides cryptographic security for the client-server mode of NTP. Users can now get time for their network devices in an authenticated manner. By using NTS, you can be sure your devices are receiving accurate time from a reliable source.

NTS keeps the encryption process separate from the low-latency time synchronization. This process allows you to introduce encryption into the time distribution system without increasing latency and affecting the accuracy of the time received.

Proxy Server

A *proxy server* is basically a type of server that handles its client-machine requests by forwarding them to other servers while allowing granular control over the traffic between the local LAN and the Internet. When it receives a request, the proxy will then connect to the specific server that can fulfill the request for the client that wants it. A proxy server operates at the Application layer of the OSI model.

Sometimes the proxy modifies the client's request or a server's response to it—or even handles the client's request itself. It will actually cache, or "remember," the specific server that would have normally been contacted for the request in case it's needed another time. This behavior really speeds up the network's function, thereby optimizing its performance. However, proxy servers can also limit the availability of the types of sites that users on a LAN have access to, which is a benefit for an administrator of the network if users are constantly connected to non-work or prohibited sites and using all the WAN bandwidth.

Figure 5.19 shows where a proxy server would be typically found in a small-to-medium network.

FIGURE 5.19   A proxy server

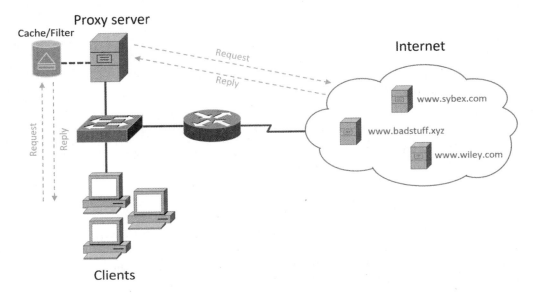

There are two main types of proxy servers you'll typically find working in present-day networks:

Web Proxy Server   A web proxy server is usually used to create a web cache. You experience this when you google a site you've visited before. The web proxy "remembers" you, and the site not only loads faster but sometimes even recalls your personal information by automatically filling in your username—or even your billing/shipping information when you place another order.

Caching Proxy Server   A caching proxy server speeds up the network's service requests by recovering information from a client's earlier request. Caching proxies keep local copies of the resources requested often, which really helps minimize the upstream use of bandwidth. These servers can greatly enhance network performance.

I want to mention one more thing before we move on from proxies, and that is reverse proxies. Unlike a forward proxy, a reverse proxy takes requests from the Internet and forwards them to servers in an internal network, whereas the forward proxy we discussed in this section takes client requests and sends them to the Internet.

Encryption and Content Filtering

Although a number of the devices we have discussed can perform encryption services, there are dedicated appliances that can perform encryption as well. The advantage of using these devices is that they normally provide more choice of encryption methods and stronger encryption options. They also offload the process from other devices like routers and servers, which is a good thing since the encryption/decryption process is very processor intensive and interferes with other functions that those routers and servers might be performing.

Sometimes these devices are called encryption gateways. They can either sit in line with a server or a local network, encrypting and decrypting all traffic, or function as an application server, encrypting any file sent to them within a network. Figure 5.20 shows examples of encryption appliances.

FIGURE 5.20   Encryption appliances

While an encryption appliance is dedicated to encryption, a content filtering appliance scans the content of what goes through it and filters out specific content or content types. Dedicating a device to this process offloads the work from servers or routers that could do this but at a cost of greatly slowing the devices. Also, there is usually more functionality and granular control available with a dedicated appliance.

Email is a good example of what you might run through one of these devices to filter out spam and objectionable content before the email is delivered. Another example of the use of a content filter might be to block websites based on the content of the web pages rather than on the basis of the URL or IP address. Figure 5.21 shows an example of a dedicated content/URL filtering appliance from SecPoint.

Analog Modem

A modem (modulator-demodulator) is a device that modulates an analog carrier signal to encode digital information and demodulates the signal to decode the transmitted information. I gave you an example of this when I explained APs earlier in the chapter because an AP modulates and demodulates a signal just like a modem.

FIGURE 5.21   Content filtering appliance

Figure 5.22 shows a current analog modem that can be used in today's networks, albeit with slow throughput.

FIGURE 5.22   Analog modem

The goal is to produce a signal that can be transmitted easily and decoded to reproduce the original digital data. These signals are transmitted over telephone lines and demodulated by another modem at the receiver side in order to read the digital data.

Because modems connect to phone lines, the location and installation of these devices is fairly cut-and-dried. It will have to be near a phone line, with one end connected to the phone line and another to a computer or modem bank. The analog modem operates at layer 1, like a repeater.

Packet Shaper

Packet shaping (also known as traffic shaping, it's a form of rate limiting) is an Internet-working traffic management technique that delays some or all packets to bring them into compliance with your or your company's traffic profile. Figure 5.23 shows a dedicated packet shaper appliance from Blue Coat.

FIGURE 5.23   Packet shaper

    This process is used to optimize or guarantee performance, improve latency, and/or increase usable bandwidth for some kinds of packets by delaying other kinds, decided on by you.

VPN Concentrator/Headend

A VPN concentrator, or as it is often called, a headend, is a device that accepts multiple VPN connections from remote locations. Although this function can be performed by a router or server, as with the encryption gateways and content filtering devices discussed earlier, the same performance benefits can be derived from dedicating a device to this. Moreover, additional functionality usually comes with these devices, one of which is shown in Figure 5.24.

FIGURE 5.24   VPN headend

    A headend device is a central control device required by some networks (for example, LANs or MANs). A headend device can also refer to a central control device within CATV systems that provides centralized functions such as re-modulation.

Media Converter

Media converters are used when you need to convert from one type of cabling to another type. This might be required to convert from one type of fiber to another or from Ethernet to fiber, for example. Figure 5.25 shows an Ethernet-to-fiber conversion box. Obviously, the location of these devices depends on where the conversion needs to take place. Media converters operate at layer 1.

FIGURE 5.25   Media converter

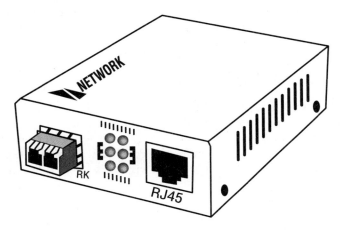

VoIP PBX

A private branch exchange (PBX) is a private telephone switch that resides on the customer premises. It has a direct connection to the telecommunication provider's switch. It performs call routing within the internal phone system. This is how a company can have two "outside" lines but 50 internal phones. The call comes in on one of the two outside lines, and the PBX routes it to the proper extension. Sometimes the system converts analog to digital but not always.

A VoIP PBX is one that switches calls between VoIP users on local lines while allowing all users to share a certain number of external phone lines. The typical IP PBX can also switch calls between a VoIP user and a traditional telephone user or between two traditional telephone users in the same way that a conventional PBX does.

VoIP Endpoint

VoIP endpoints are desktop phone systems or wireless phone systems that are part of the converged networks where data and voice traffic are now combined in today's networks.

These endpoints may also be implemented as conferencing systems in meeting rooms. There is more flexibility and freedom in the location and installation of these systems as more wireless modes of connectivity are introduced for these devices.

NGFW/Layer 7 Firewall

Next-generation firewalls (NGFWs) are a category of devices that attempt to address traffic inspection and application awareness shortcomings of a traditional stateful firewall without hampering the performance. Although unified threat management (UTM) devices also attempt to address these issues, they tend to use separate internal engines to perform individual security functions. This means a packet may be examined several times by different engines to determine whether it should be allowed into the network.

NGFWs are application aware, which means they can distinguish between specific applications instead of allowing all traffic coming in via typical web ports. Moreover, they examine packets only once during the deep packet inspection phase (which is required to detect malware and anomalies).

VoIP Gateway

A VoIP gateway is a network device that helps to convert voice and fax calls between an IP network and a public switched telephone network (PSTN) in real time. A VoIP gateway can typically support at least two T1/E1 digital channels. Most VoIP gateways feature at least one Ethernet and telephone port. Various protocols, such as Media Gateway Control Protocol (MGCP), Session Initiation Protocol (SIP), and Lightweight Telephony Protocol (LTP), can help to control a gateway.

Cable Modem

A cable modem allows for voice, video, and data (usually Internet) to connect from a home or small business to a cable provider's network. The cable modem is installed at the customer site and connects to the coax (coaxial) cable network. The Data Over Cable Service Interface Specifications (DOCSIS) standard allows both voice and data to share the cable with the standard video TV offerings provided by the local cable company.

DSL Modem

Digital Subscriber Line (DSL) modems are commonly deployed by traditional phone companies that have twisted-pair copper as the local connection to homes and businesses. DSL modems allow for voice, video, and data (usually Internet) to piggyback on the local copper line as a high-frequency carrier above the standard voice frequencies.

Networked Devices

The field of networking is constantly evolving. In the good old days networks usually only connected desktop computers to servers and printers. In today's world, almost everything is being networked. As a network engineer, you must be aware of these devices and their requirements.

VoIP Phones

As you learned earlier in this chapter, phones have migrated from the older analog style to digital Ethernet. While they tend to be low bandwidth, they are sensitive to delay and jitter so some form of quality of service (QoS) is usually required on the network to make sure the voice quality is acceptable.

Printers

Instead of having a printer connected to each desktop, they can be shared on the network with NIC cards installed directly in the printer or by using a print server that connects to the Ethernet network and to the printer using a serial or parallel connection.

Physical Access Control Devices

In modern office buildings and industrial sites, access control systems are installed at key points such as a door or a gate. These devices are connected to an authorization server on the network, which can connect back to directory services such as Microsoft Active Directory. When a user scans their badge, a lookup is performed by the server and a response is sent back to the access control device to either unlock the door or prevent the person from entering.

Cameras

Cameras have moved from the analog world to digital and are now very common in today's networks. They operate off TCP/IP and send video feeds back to a central server for processing and recording. Advanced features may include Pan/Tilt/Zoom (PTZ) to remotely control the camera, and detection capabilities such as facial recognition are now common. Some cameras have heat and metal sensing capabilities.

Heating Ventilation, and Air Conditioning (HVAC) Sensors

Modern office buildings and industrial sites have intelligent HVAC systems that use sensors to monitor and control air conditioning and heating systems. This allows them to either manually or automatically adjust the environmental controls and has the added advantage of cost saving by changing the temperature values after hours when no one is in the facility.

Internet of Things (IoT)

The number of devices connected to the Internet has exploded in the past few years and only shows signs of increasing to billions of devices.

Wearable devices such as watches, fitness analyzers, and medical sensors are driving this growth. At home we now have digital assistants such as Siri and Alexa that connect to digital smart devices such as doorbells, refrigerators, thermostats, lights, cameras, televisions, and speakers.

This is collectively known as the *Internet of Things (IoT)*, and the number and types of things is constantly increasing as new products and applications are introduced.

We see IoT devices everywhere, including weather monitoring stations, traffic control devices, security devices, and devices for an almost infinite number of other uses. They connect to the network using what connectivity options are available at their locations. Common network connections include Ethernet, Wi-Fi, Bluetooth, and cellular. IoT devices connect to centralized server applications and usually consume very little network bandwidth. However, if there are a very large number of IoT devices, the additive bandwidth may become significant.

Industrial Control Systems

The *industrial control systems (ICS)* technology space uses sensors for monitoring and controlling everything from power grids to machines on the factory floor. By monitoring machinery, companies can proactively detect problems and flag the device for maintenance, potentially saving money on repairs and downtime. Other uses are to monitor assembly line workflows and dynamically change them based on workload.

The *supervisory control and data acquisition (SCADA)* architecture is an industry standard for monitoring and collecting industrial data such as a power grid or water utility.

SCADA systems consist of an architecture that includes computers, sensors, and networks that collect and display the status of the monitored systems in a graphical format. SCADA systems are used to monitor electrical or water systems, industrial plants, and machinery. The monitored systems use programmable logic controllers (PLCs) or other types of sensors such as flow or electrical meters to interface with the machinery or systems.

Planning and Implementing a Basic SOHO Network Using Network Segmentation

It's likely that at some point you'll have to break up one large network into a bunch of smaller ones because user response will have dwindled to a slow crawl as the network grew and grew. With all that growth, your LAN's traffic congestion will have reached epic proportions.

Determining Requirements

When implementing a SOHO network, the first thing to be done is to identify the requirements of the network and the constraints around which you must operate. This should drive your design and device choices. An example set of requirements and constraints might be as follows:

- A small number of computers are needed.

- There is a high need for Internet access.

- Resources need to be shared.

- Wired hosts and wireless hosts will need to communicate with each other.

- Security is very important.

With these constraints in mind, you might find that you'll need more than just a switch and some Ethernet cabling for this project. There is a need for a router, an AP, and a firewall in this case. In addition, you need to think about compatibility between equipment and the types and brands of equipment to buy as well as environmental issues or limitations.

One of the most important considerations you must take very seriously when building a basic network is LAN traffic congestion, which can be lessened with network segmentation and is directly related to device types and compatibility requirements as well as equipment limitations. Let's look at how to use the segmentation devices I have defined so far in this chapter.

Here's a list of some of the nasty things that commonly cause LAN traffic congestion:

- Too many hosts in a broadcast domain

- Broadcast storms

- Multicasting

- Low bandwidth

- Adding hubs for connectivity to the network

The answer to fixing a huge but slow network is to break it up into a number of smaller networks—something called *network segmentation*. You do this by using devices like routers and switches, which are sometimes still referred to as bridges because switches still use bridging technologies. Figure 5.26 displays a network that's been segmented with a switch so each network segment connected to the switch is now a separate collision domain. But make note of the fact that this network is actually still one *broadcast domain*—the set of all devices on a network segment that hear all the broadcasts sent on that segment.

And keep in mind that the hub used in Figure 5.26 just extended the one collision domain from the switch port.

Routers are used to connect networks together and route packets of data from one network to another. (Cisco has become the de facto standard for routers because of its high-quality router products, great selection, and fantastic service.) Routers, by default, break up a broadcast domain. Figure 5.27 shows a router in our little network that creates an internetwork and breaks up broadcast domains.

FIGURE 5.26   A switch can replace the hub, breaking up collision domains.

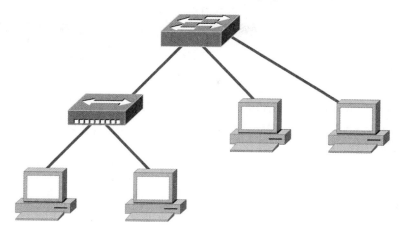

FIGURE 5.27   Routers create an internetwork.

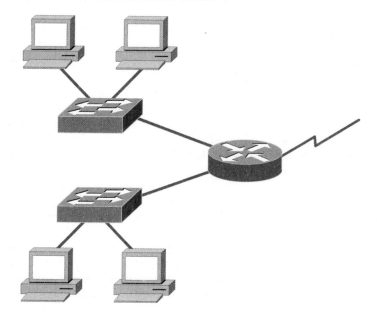

The network in Figure 5.27 is pretty cool. Each host is connected to its own collision domain, and the router has created two broadcast domains. And don't forget that the router provides connections to WAN services as well. The router uses something called a serial interface for WAN connections: specifically, a V.35 physical interface.

Breaking up a broadcast domain is important because when a host or server sends a network broadcast, every device on the network must read and process that broadcast—unless you've got a router. When the router's interface receives this broadcast, it can respond by basically saying, "Thanks, but no thanks," and discard the broadcast without forwarding it on to other networks. Even though routers are known for breaking up broadcast domains by default, it's important to remember that they break up collision domains as well.

There are two advantages of using routers in your network:

- They don't forward broadcasts by default.
- They can filter the network based on layer 3 (Network layer) information (such as an IP address).

Four router functions in your network are as follows:

- Packet switching
- Packet filtering
- Internetwork communication
- Path selection

Remember that routers are really switches; they're actually what we call layer 3 switches. Unlike layer 2 switches, which forward or filter frames, routers (layer 3 switches) use logical addressing and provide what is called *packet switching*. Routers can also provide packet filtering by using access lists, and when routers connect two or more networks together and use logical addressing (IP or IPv6), this is called an *internetwork*. Last, routers use a *routing table* (map of the internetwork) to make path selections and to forward packets to remote networks.

Conversely, switches aren't used to create internetworks (they do not break up broadcast domains by default); they're employed to add functionality to a network LAN. The main purpose of a switch is to make a LAN work better—to optimize its performance—providing more bandwidth for the LAN's users. And switches don't forward packets to other networks as routers do. Instead, they only "switch" frames from one port to another within the switched network.

By default, switches break up collision domains, as mentioned in Chapter 4, "The Current Ethernet Specifications." *Collision domain* is an Ethernet term used to describe a network scenario wherein one particular device sends a packet on a network segment, forcing every other device on that same segment to pay attention to it. At the same time, a different device tries to transmit, leading to a collision, after which both devices must retransmit, one at a time. Not very efficient! This situation is typically found in a hub environment where each host segment connects to a hub that represents only one collision domain and only one broadcast domain. By contrast, every port on a switch represents its own collision domain.

    Switches create separate collision domains but a single broadcast domain. Routers provide a separate broadcast domain for each interface.

The term *bridging* was introduced before routers and hubs were implemented, so it's pretty common to hear people referring to bridges as switches. That's because bridges and switches basically do the same thing—break up collision domains on a LAN. (In reality, you cannot buy a physical bridge these days, only LAN switches, but these switches use bridging technologies.)

So this means a switch is basically just a multiple-port bridge with more brainpower, right? Well, pretty much, but there are differences. Switches do provide this function, but they do so with greatly enhanced management ability and features. Plus, most of the time, bridges had only two or four ports. Yes, you could get your hands on a bridge with up to 16 ports, but that's nothing compared to the hundreds available on some switches.

You would use a bridge in a network to reduce collisions within broadcast domains and to increase the number of collision domains in your network. Doing this provides more bandwidth for users. And keep in mind that using hubs in your network can contribute to congestion on your Ethernet network. As always, plan your network design carefully!

Figure 5.28 shows how a network would look with all these internetwork devices in place. Remember that the router will not only break up broadcast domains for every LAN interface but also break up collision domains.

When you look at Figure 5.28, do you see the router at center stage and see how it connects each physical network together? We have to use this layout because of the older technologies involved—bridges and hubs.

On the top internetwork in Figure 5.28, you'll notice that a bridge is used to connect the hubs to a router. The bridge breaks up collision domains, but all the hosts connected to both hubs are still crammed into the same broadcast domain. Also, the bridge creates only two collision domains, so each device connected to a hub is in the same collision domain as every other device connected to that same hub. This is actually pretty lame, but it's still better than having one collision domain for all hosts.

Notice something else: The three hubs at the bottom that are connected also connect to the router, creating one collision domain and one broadcast domain. This makes the bridged network look much better indeed.

Although bridges/switches are used to segment networks, they will not isolate broadcast or multicast packets.

The best network connected to the router is the LAN switch network on the left. Why? Because each port on that switch breaks up collision domains. But it's not all good—all devices are still in the same broadcast domain. Do you remember why this can be a really bad thing? Because all devices must listen to all broadcasts transmitted, that's why. And if your broadcast domains are too large, the users have less bandwidth and are required to process more broadcasts, and network response time will slow to a level that could cause office riots.

FIGURE 5.28 Internetworking devices

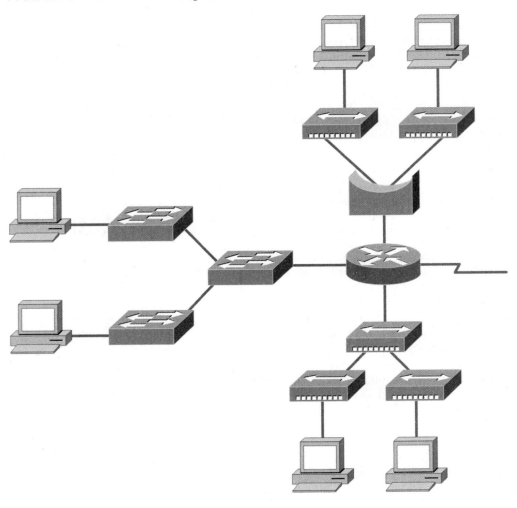

Once we have only switches in our network, things change a lot. Figure 5.29 shows the network that is typically found today.

Here I've placed the LAN switches at the center of the network world so the router is connecting only logical networks together. If I implement this kind of setup, I've created virtual LANs (VLANs), something I'm going to tell you about in Chapter 11. So don't stress. But it is really important to understand that even though you have a switched network, you still need a router to provide your inter-VLAN communication, or internetworking. Don't forget that.

FIGURE 5.29 Switched networks creating an internetwork

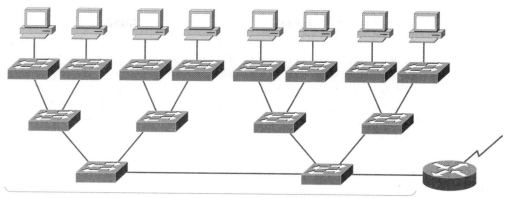

Broadcast Domain

Obviously, the best network is one that's correctly configured to meet the business requirements of the company it serves. LAN switches with routers, correctly placed in the network, are the best network design. This book will help you understand the basics of routers and switches so you can make informed decisions on a case-by-case basis.

Let's go back to Figure 5.28 again. Looking at the figure, how many collision domains and broadcast domains are in this internetwork? I hope you answered nine collision domains and three broadcast domains.

The broadcast domains are definitely the easiest to see because only routers break up broadcast domains by default. And because there are three connections, that gives you three broadcast domains. But do you see the nine collision domains? Just in case that's a no, I'll explain. The all-hub network is one collision domain; the bridge network equals three collision domains. Add in the switch network of five collision domains—one for each switch port—and you've got a total of nine.

Now, in Figure 5.29, each port on the switch is a separate collision domain, and each VLAN is a separate broadcast domain. But you still need a router for routing between VLANs. How many collision domains do you see here? I'm counting 10—remember that connections between the switches are considered collision domains.

 Real World Scenario

Should I Replace All My Hubs with Switches?

You're a network administrator at a large company in San Jose. The boss comes to you and says that he got your requisition to buy a switch and is not sure about approving the expense; do you really need it?

Well, if you can have it, sure—why not? Switches really add a lot of functionality to a network that hubs just don't have. But most of us don't have an unlimited budget. Hubs still can create a nice network—that is, of course, if you design and implement the network correctly.

Let's say that you have 40 users plugged into four hubs, 10 users each. At this point, the hubs are all connected together so that you have one large collision domain and one large broadcast domain. If you can afford to buy just one switch and plug each hub into a switch port, as well as plug the servers into the switch, then you now have four collision domains and one broadcast domain. Not great; but for the price of one switch, your network is a much better thing. So, go ahead! Put that requisition in to buy all new switches. What do you have to lose?

Now that you've gotten an introduction to internetworking and the various devices that live in an internetwork, it's time to head into internetworking models.

As I mentioned earlier, routers break up broadcast domains, which means that by default, broadcasts aren't forwarded through a router. Do you remember why this is a good thing? Routers break up collision domains, but you can also do that using layer 2 (Data Link layer) switches. Because each interface in a router represents a separate network, it must be assigned unique network identification numbers, and each host on the network connected to that router must use the same network number. Figure 5.30 shows how a router works in an internetwork.

FIGURE 5.30   A router in an internetwork

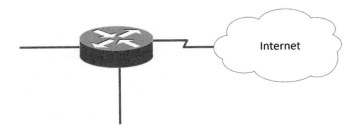

Here are some points about routers that you should commit to memory:

- Routers, by default, will not forward any broadcast or multicast packets.

- Routers use the logical address in a Network layer header to determine the next hop router to forward the packet to.

- Routers can use access lists, created by an administrator, to control security on the types of packets that are allowed to enter or exit an interface.

- Routers can provide layer 2 bridging functions if needed and can simultaneously route through the same interface.

- Layer 3 devices (routers, in this case) provide connections between virtual LANs (VLANs).

- Routers can provide quality of service (QoS) for specific types of network traffic.

 Switching and VLANs are covered in Chapter 11.

Switches and Bridges at the Data Link Layer

Layer 2 switching is considered hardware-based bridging because it uses specialized hardware called an *application-specific integrated circuit (ASIC)*. ASICs can run up to multigigabit speeds with very low latency rates.

 Latency is the time measured from when a frame enters a port to when it exits.

Bridges and switches read each frame as it passes through the network. The layer 2 device then puts the source hardware address in a filter table and keeps track of which port the frame was received on. This information (logged in the bridge's or switch's filter table) is what helps the machine determine the location of the specific sending device. Figure 5.31 shows a switch in an internetwork.

FIGURE 5.31 A switch in an internetwork

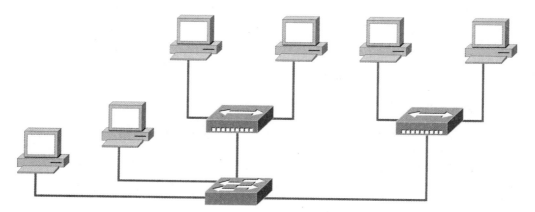

The real estate business is all about location, location, location, and it's the same way for both layer 2 and layer 3 devices. Although both need to be able to negotiate the network, it's crucial to remember that they're concerned with very different parts of it. Primarily, layer

3 machines (such as routers) need to locate specific networks, whereas layer 2 machines (switches and bridges) need to eventually locate specific devices. So, networks are to routers as individual devices are to switches and bridges. And routing tables that "map" the inter-network are for routers, as filter tables that "map" individual devices are for switches and bridges.

After a filter table is built on the layer 2 device, it will forward frames only to the segment where the destination hardware address is located. If the destination device is on the same segment as the frame, the layer 2 device will block the frame from going to any other seg-ments. If the destination is on a different segment, the frame can be transmitted only to that segment. This is called *transparent bridging*.

When a switch interface receives a frame with a destination hardware address that isn't found in the device's filter table, it will forward the frame to all connected segments. If the unknown device that was sent the "mystery frame" replies to this forwarding action, the switch updates its filter table regarding that device's location. But in the event that the desti-nation address of the transmitting frame is a broadcast address, the switch will forward all broadcasts to every connected segment by default.

All devices that the broadcast is forwarded to are considered to be in the same broadcast domain. This can be a problem; Layer 2 devices propagate layer 2 broadcast storms that choke performance, and the only way to stop a broadcast storm from propagating through an internetwork is with a layer 3 device—a router.

The biggest benefit of using switches instead of hubs in your internetwork is that each switch port is actually its own collision domain. (Conversely, a hub creates one large collision domain.) But even armed with a switch, you still can't break up broadcast domains. Neither switches nor bridges will do that. They'll typically simply forward all broadcasts instead.

Another benefit of LAN switching over hub-centered implementations is that each device on every segment plugged into a switch can transmit simultaneously—at least they can as long as there is only one host on each port and a hub isn't plugged into a switch port. As you might have guessed, hubs allow only one device per network segment to communicate at a time.

Hubs at the Physical Layer

As you know, a hub is really a multiple-port repeater. A repeater receives a digital signal, reamplifies or regenerates that signal, and then forwards the digital signal out all active ports without looking at any data. An active hub does the same thing. Any digital signal received from a segment on a hub port is regenerated or reamplified and transmitted out all ports on the hub. This means all devices plugged into a hub are in the same collision domain as well as in the same broadcast domain. Figure 5.32 shows a hub in a network.

Hubs, like repeaters, don't examine any of the traffic as it enters and is then transmitted out to the other parts of the physical media. Every device connected to the hub, or hubs, must listen if a device transmits. A physical star (hub and spoke) network—where the hub is a central device and cables extend in all directions out from it—is the type of topology a hub creates. Visually, the design really does resemble a star, whereas Ethernet networks run a logical bus topology, meaning that the signal has to run through the network from end to end.

FIGURE 5.32   A hub in a network

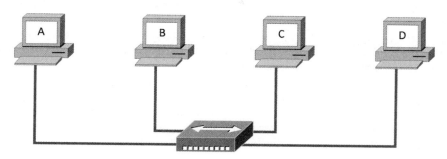

 Hubs and repeaters can be used to enlarge the area covered by a single LAN segment, although I do not recommend this. LAN switches and/or wireless APs are affordable for almost every situation.

Environmental Considerations

All of the equipment discussed in this chapter—switches, routers, hubs, and so on—require proper environmental conditions to operate correctly. These devices have the same needs as any computing device. The environmental concerns can be categorized thusly:

Temperature   Like any device with a CPU, infrastructure devices such as routers, switches, and specialty appliances must have a cool area to operate. When temperatures rise, servers start rebooting, and appliance CPUs start overworking as well. The rooms where these devices are located should be provided with heavy-duty HVAC systems and ample ventilation. It may even be advisable to dedicate a suite for this purpose and put the entire system on a UPS with a backup generator in the case of total loss of power.

Modern data centers use the architecture of hot and cold aisles. This maximizes the cooling of the equipment racks by forcing cold air in one row of racks and the exhaust of the hot air exiting into the next row.

Humidity   The air around these systems can be neither too damp nor too dry; it must be "just right." If it is too dry, static electricity will build up in the air, making the situation ripe for damaging a system. It takes very little static electricity to fry some electrical components. If it is too damp, connections start corroding, and shorts begin to occur. A humidifying system should be used to maintain the level above 50 percent. The air conditioning should keep it within acceptable levels on the upper end.

Summary

Whew, this chapter covered quite a bit of information. You learned the difference between a router, a switch (bridge), and a hub and when to use each one. I also covered some devices that you might find in a network today, but not as often, such as VPN concentrators and content filters.

The information I discussed about DNS and DHCP is critical to your success on the Network+ exam, and I highly suggest that you reread those sections. I covered how both the DNS and DHCP services work on a network.

In addition to the most common devices, I discussed the specialized network devices mentioned in the Network+ objectives. I finished the chapter by discussing environmental conditions.

All of the information in this chapter is fundamental, and you must understand it before moving on to the other chapters in this book.

Exam Essentials

Understand how DHCP works and its purpose.   Dynamic Host Configuration Protocol (DHCP) provides IP configuration information to hosts. It is important to know how a DHCP client requests information from a server, how a server receives this information, and also how the server responds to the client and with what type of information.

Understand how DNS works and its purpose.   The Domain Name System (DNS) is used to resolve human names to IP addresses. Understanding how DNS resolves these names is critical, as is understanding how a DNS query is sent and how a DNS server responds. Know the different types of DNS records and what they are used for.

Understand the difference between a hub, a switch (bridge), and a router.   A hub just connects network segments together. A switch/bridge segments the network using MAC addresses, and a router segments the network using logical addressing (IP and IPv6). Switches break up collision domains, and routers break up broadcast domains by default.

Remember the different names for a router.   A router is a layer 3 hardware device, but it can also be called a layer 3 switch or a multilayer switch.

Remember the various devices used on networks today and when you would use each one and how.   Understand the differences and how each device works: routers, switches, hubs, DNS servers, and DHCP servers.

Identify the purpose, benefits, and characteristics of using a proxy service.   A proxy server keeps a LAN somewhat separated from the Internet. Doing so increases security and filtering control and has the tendency to speed up Internet access through caching of recently used web pages.

Describe the proper use of network segmentation when planning and implementing a basic SOHO network.   Understand and apply the concepts of proper network segmentation when planning the use of various devices in the design of a SOHO network.

Describe the benefits of using a network load balancer.   Network load balancers allow incoming connections to be spread out across multiple servers for scalability and resiliency. Understand the architecture of how load balancers are inserted into a network.

Describe the benefits of using dedicated appliances for certain services.   Using appliances to offload functions such as encryption, content filtering, and VPN concentrators can decrease the workload of other systems and add functionality that may be present in these dedicated devices.

Also, wireless LAN controllers let you configure the complete network on a single device and push the configurations out to the Wi-Fi access points. The access points also tunnel the user data back to the controller, which then forwards the traffic onto the local area network (LAN).

Lastly, NTP servers provide accurate date and time information to servers and networking equipment.

Identify the environmental requirements of infrastructure devices.   A cool temperature, ample ventilation, and the proper humidity level are all keys to maintaining the operation of devices such as routers, switches, and appliances.

Written Lab

Complete the table by filling in the appropriate layer of the OSI or hub, switch, or router device. You can find the answers in Appendix A.

Description	Device or OSI layer
This device sends and receives information about the Network layer.	
This layer creates a virtual circuit before transmitting between two end stations.	
A layer 3 switch or multilayer switch.	
This device uses hardware addresses to filter a network.	
Ethernet is defined at these layers.	
This layer supports flow control and sequencing.	
This device can measure the distance to a remote network.	
Logical addressing is used at this layer.	

Description	Device or OSI layer
Hardware addresses are defined at this layer.	
This device creates one big collision domain and one large broadcast domain.	
This device creates many smaller collision domains, but the network is still one large broadcast domain.	
This device can never run full-duplex.	
This device breaks up collision domains and broadcast domains.	

Review Questions

You can find the answers to the review questions in Appendix B.

1. You have been asked to change the IP address in external DNS for a mail server in your organization. Which record can be changed with the least amount of effort?

    A.   A record

    B.   MX record

    C.   PTR record

    D.   TXT record

2. Which is a valid reason to implement a wireless LAN controller?

    A.   Centralized provisioning

    B.   The use of autonomous WAPs

    C.   Multiple SSIDs

    D.   Multiple VLANs

3. What is the benefit of network segmentation?

    A.   Decreased broadcast domains

    B.   Increased broadcast domains

    C.   Decreased collision domains

    D.   Increased collision domains

4. Which protocol and port do you need to configure on the inbound host-based firewall for a DHCP server?

    A.   UDP/67

    B.   TCP/67

    C.   UDP/68

    D.   TCP/68

5. Which type of device will detect but not prevent unauthorized access?

    A.   Firewall

    B.   IPS

    C.   IDS

    D.   Honeypots

6. Your organization expects a considerable amount of traffic to your web server, so you plan to install several web servers. How can you maintain one FQDN and allow customers to be directed to the next free web servers?

   A. Router

   B. Firewall

   C. Load balancer

   D. Proxy

7. Your organization has deployed several autonomous WAPs. Users complain that they consistently drop the wireless connection when roaming. What should you recommend to resolve this issue?

   A. Wireless range extenders

   B. More autonomous WAPs

   C. Switching the channels the WAPs are using

   D. Wireless LAN controller

8. You need to make sure that a printer is configured with the same IP address every time it is turned on. However, the printer is too troublesome to configure a static IP address. What can be done to achieve the goal?

   A. Configure an A record for the printer in DNS.

   B. Configure a DHCP exclusion for the printer.

   C. Configure a DHCP reservation for the printer.

   D. Configure a PTR record for the printer in DNS.

9. Which record type is used for an IPv4 address mapping to FQDN for DNS queries?

   A. The A record

   B. The CName record

   C. The PTR record

   D. The AAAA record

10. Which device will act as a multiport repeater in the network?

    A. Hub

    B. Switch

    C. Bridge

    D. WAP

11. Which is a correct statement when hubs are replaced with switches?

    A. The replacement increases collision domains.

    B. The replacement decreases collision domains.

    C. The replacement increases broadcast domains.

    D. The replacement decreases broadcast domains.

12. When firewalls are placed in a network, which zone contains Internet-facing services?

    A. Outside zone

    B. Enterprise network zone

    C. Demilitarized zone

    D. Inside zone

13. Which is a false statement about firewalls?

    A. Firewalls can protect a network from external attacks.

    B. Firewalls are commonly deployed to protect a network from internal attacks.

    C. Firewalls can provide stateful packet inspection.

    D. Firewalls can control application traffic.

14. Which statement is correct about reverse lookups?

    A. A reverse lookup is when the request needs to be reversed to another DNS server.

    B. A reverse lookup is the resolution of an IP address to FQDN.

    C. A reverse lookup is when the DNS queried can answer the request without asking another DNS server.

    D. A reverse lookup is the resolution of an FQDN to an IP address.

15. What gets appended to hostname queries for DNS resolution?

    A. The DNS suffix

    B. The DNS zone

    C. The host header

    D. The hostname PTR record

16. Which type of DNS record holds the IPv4 IP address for a hostname?

    A. The A record

    B. The CName record

    C. The PTR record

    D. The AAAA record

17. Which of the following devices can work at both layers 2 and 3 of the OSI model?

    A. Hub

    B. Switch

    C. Multilayer switch

    D. Bridge

18. What is an advantage of using DHCP in a network environment?

    A. More difficult administration of the network

    B. Static IP addressing

    C. Can send an operating system for the PC to boot from

    D. Automatically assigns IP addresses to hosts

19. What is a benefit to installing a proxy server?

    A. Web caching

    B. Throughput increase

    C. DHCP services

    D. Support for user authentication

20. Which protocol and port number does DNS use for direct queries?

    A. UDP/53

    B. TCP/53

    C. UDP/55

    D. UDP/68

Chapter

6

Introduction to the Internet Protocol

THE FOLLOWING COMPTIA NETWORK+ EXAM OBJECTIVES ARE COVERED IN THIS CHAPTER:

✓ **Domain 1.0 Networking Concepts**

✓ **1.1 Explain concepts related to the Open Systems Interconnection (OSI) reference model.**

- ▪ Layer 1 - Physical
- ▪ Layer 2 - Data link
- ▪ Layer 3 - Network
- ▪ Layer 4 - Transport
- ▪ Layer 5 - Session
- ▪ Layer 6 - Presentation
- ▪ Layer 7 - Application

✓ **1.4 Explain common networking ports, protocols, services, and traffic types.**

✓ **Protocols Ports**

- ▪ File Transfer Protocol (FTP)   20/21
- ▪ Secure File Transfer Protocol (SFTP)   22
- ▪ Secure Shell (SSH)   22
- ▪ Telnet   23
- ▪ Simple Mail Transfer Protocol (SMTP)   25
- ▪ Domain Name System (DNS)   53
- ▪ Dynamic Host Configuration Protocol (DHCP)   67/68
- ▪ Trivial File Transfer Protocol (TFTP)   69
- ▪ Hypertext Transfer Protocol (HTTP)   80

- Network Time Protocol (NTP)   123
- Simple Network Management Protocol (SNMP)   161/162
- Lightweight Directory Access Protocol (LDAP)   389
- Hypertext Transfer Protocol Secure (HTTPS)   443
- Server Message Block (SMB)   445
- Syslog   514
- Simple Mail Transfer Protocol Secure (SMTPS)   587
- Lightweight Directory Access Protocol over SSL (LDAPS)   636
- Structured Query Language (SQL) Server   1433
- Remote Desktop Protocol (RDP)   3389
- Session Initiation Protocol (SIP)   5060/5061

✓ Internet Protocol (IP) types

- Internet Control Message Protocol (ICMP)
- Transmission Control Protocol (TCP)
- User Datagram Protocol (UDP)
- Generic Routing Encapsulation (GRE)
- Internet Protocol Security (IPSec)
    - Authentication Header (AH)
    - Encapsulating Security Payload (ESP)
    - Internet Key Exchange (IKE)

The Transmission Control Protocol/Internet Protocol (TCP/IP) suite was created by the Department of Defense (DoD) to ensure and preserve data integrity as well as to maintain communications in the event of catastrophic war.

So it follows that if designed and implemented correctly, a TCP/IP network can truly be a solid, dependable, and resilient network solution. In this chapter, I'll cover the protocols of TCP/IP.

I'll begin by covering the DoD's version of TCP/IP and then compare this version and its protocols with the OSI reference model discussed in Chapter 2, "The Open Systems Interconnection (OSI) Reference Model."

After going over the various protocols found at each layer of the DoD model, I'll finish the chapter by adding more detail to the explanation of data encapsulation that I started in Chapter 2.

To find Todd Lammle CompTIA videos and practice questions, please see www.lammle.com.

Introducing TCP/IP

Because TCP/IP is so central to working with the Internet and intranets, it's essential for you to understand it in detail. I'll begin by giving you some background on TCP/IP and how it came about and then move on to describe the important technical goals defined by the original designers. After that, you'll find out how TCP/IP compares to a theoretical model—the Open Systems Interconnection (OSI) model.

A Brief History of TCP/IP

The very first request for comments (RFC) was published in April 1969, which paved the way for today's Internet and its protocols. Each of these protocols is specified in the multitude of RFCs, which are observed, maintained, sanctioned, filed, and stored by the Internet Engineering Task Force (IETF).

TCP first came on the scene in 1974. In 1978, it was divided into two distinct protocols, TCP and IP, and finally documented into an RFC in 1980. Then, in 1983, TCP/IP replaced the Network Control Protocol (NCP) and was authorized as the official data transport means for anything connecting to ARPAnet. ARPAnet was the Internet's ancestor, created by ARPA, the DoD's Advanced Research Projects Agency, again, way back in 1969 in reaction to the Soviets' launching of *Sputnik*. ARPA was soon redubbed DARPA, and it was divided into ARPAnet and MILNET (also in 1983); both were finally dissolved in 1990.

But contrary to what you might think, most of the development work on TCP/IP happened at UC Berkeley in Northern California, where a group of scientists were simultaneously working on the Berkeley version of UNIX, which soon became known as the BSD, or the Berkeley Software Distribution series of UNIX versions. Of course, because TCP/IP worked so well, it was packaged into subsequent releases of BSD UNIX and offered to other universities and institutions if they bought the distribution tape. Basically, BSD UNIX bundled with TCP/IP began as shareware in the world of academia and, as a result, became the basis of the huge success and exponential growth of today's Internet as well as smaller private and corporate intranets.

As usual, what may have started as a small group of TCP/IP aficionados evolved, and as it did, the US government created a program to test any new published standards and ensure they passed certain criteria. This was to protect TCP/IP's integrity and to ensure that no developer changed anything too dramatically or added any proprietary features. It's this very quality—this open-systems approach to the TCP/IP family of protocols—that pretty much sealed its popularity because it guarantees a solid connection between myriad hardware and software platforms with no strings attached.

The DoD Model and TCP/IP

The DoD model is basically a condensed version of the OSI model; it's composed of four, instead of seven, layers:

- Process/Application layer
- Host-to-Host layer
- Internet layer
- Network Access layer

Figure 6.1 shows a comparison of the DoD model and the OSI reference model. As you can see, the two are similar in concept, but each has a different number of layers with different names.

FIGURE 6.1 The DoD model and OSI model

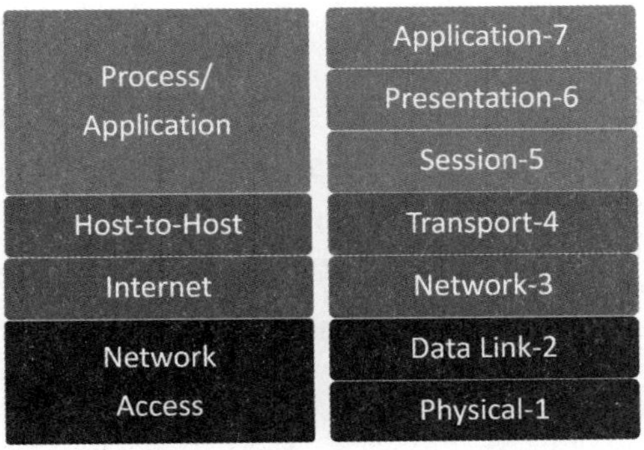

When the different protocols in the IP stack are discussed, two layers of the OSI and DoD models are interchangeable. In other words, the Internet layer and the Network layer describe the same thing, as do the Host-to-Host layer and the Transport layer. The other two layers of the DoD model, Process/Application and Network Access, are composed of multiple layers of the OSI model.

A vast array of protocols operate at the DoD model's *Process/Application layer* to integrate the various activities and duties spanning the focus of the OSI's corresponding top three layers (Application, Presentation, and Session). We'll be looking closely at those protocols in the next part of this chapter. The Process/Application layer defines protocols for node-to-node application communication and also controls user-interface specifications.

The *Host-to-Host layer* parallels the functions of the OSI's Transport layer, defining protocols for setting up the level of transmission service for applications. It tackles issues such as creating reliable end-to-end communication and ensuring the error-free delivery of data. It handles packet sequencing and maintains data integrity.

The *Internet layer* corresponds to the OSI's Network layer, designating the protocols relating to the logical transmission of packets over the entire network. It takes care of the logical addressing of hosts by giving them an IP address, and it handles the routing of packets among multiple networks.

At the bottom of the DoD model, the *Network Access layer* monitors the data exchange between the host and the network. The equivalent of the Data Link and Physical layers of the OSI model, the Network Access layer oversees hardware addressing and defines protocols for the physical transmission of data.

The DoD and OSI models are alike in design and concept and have similar functions in similar layers. Figure 6.2 shows the TCP/IP protocol suite and how its protocols relate to the DoD model layers.

FIGURE 6.2   The TCP/IP protocol suite

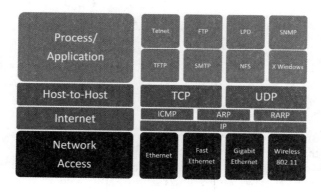

We'll now look at the different protocols in more detail, starting with the Process/Application layer protocols.

The Process/Application Layer Protocols

In the following sections, I'll describe the different applications and services typically used in IP networks and list their associated port numbers as well, which are discussed in detail in this chapter.

File Transfer Protocol (TCP 20, 21)

File Transfer Protocol (FTP) is the protocol that actually lets you transfer files across an IP network, and it can accomplish this between any two machines that are using it. But FTP isn't just a protocol; it's also a program. Operating as a protocol, FTP is used by applications. As a program, it's employed by users to perform file tasks by hand. FTP also allows for access to both directories and files and can accomplish certain types of directory operations, such as relocating files into different directories. Figure 6.3 shows an FTP example.

FIGURE 6.3   File Transfer Protocol

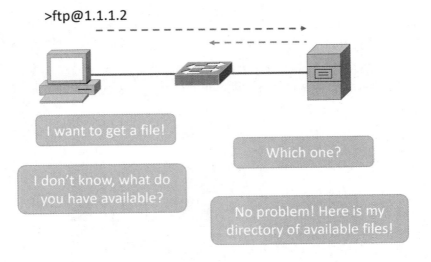

Accessing a host through FTP is only the first step, though. Users must then be subjected to an authentication login that's probably secured with passwords and usernames implemented by system administrators to restrict access. You can get around this somewhat by adopting the username *anonymous*—although what you'll gain access to will be limited.

Even when employed by users manually as a program, FTP's functions are limited to listing and manipulating directories, typing file contents, and copying files between hosts. It can't execute remote files as programs. The problem with FTP is that all data is sent in clear text, just as with Telnet. If you need to make sure your FTP transfers are secure, then you'll use SFTP, which is covered after the next section.

Secure Shell (TCP 22)

The *Secure Shell (SSH)* protocol sets up a secure Telnet session over a standard TCP/IP connection and is employed for doing things like logging into other systems, running programs on remote systems, and moving files from one system to another. Figure 6.4 shows an SSH example.

FIGURE 6.4   SSH

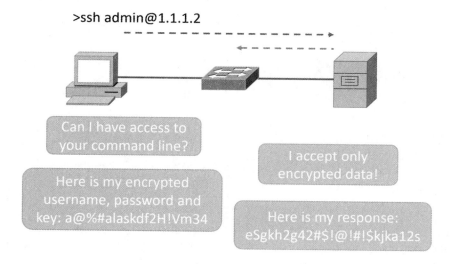

And it does all of this while maintaining a nice, strong, encrypted connection. You can think of it as the new-generation protocol that's now used in place of rsh and rlogin—even Telnet.

Secure File Transfer Protocol (TCP 22)

Secure File Transfer Protocol (SFTP) is used when transferring files over an encrypted connection. It uses an SSH session (which was previously covered), which encrypts the connection, and SSH uses port 22, hence the port 22 for SFTP.

Apart from the secure part, it's used just as FTP is—for transferring files between computers on an IP network, such as the Internet.

Telnet (TCP 23)

Telnet is the chameleon of protocols—its specialty is terminal emulation. It allows a user on a remote client machine, called the Telnet client, to access the resources of another machine, the Telnet server. Telnet achieves this by pulling a fast one on the Telnet server and making the client machine appear as though it were a terminal directly attached to the local network. This projection is actually a software shell—a virtual terminal that can interact with the chosen remote host. Figure 6.5 shows a Telnet example.

FIGURE 6.5   Telnet

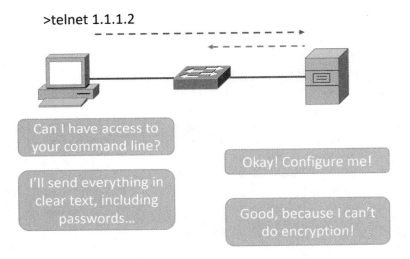

These emulated terminals are of the text-mode type and can execute refined procedures such as displaying menus that give users the opportunity to choose options and access the applications on the duped server. Users begin a Telnet session by running the Telnet client software and then logging into the Telnet server.

Telnet offers no security or encryption and is replaced by Secure Shell (SSH) when security across the remote-configuration session is needed or desired.

Simple Mail Transfer Protocol (TCP 25)

Simple Mail Transfer Protocol (SMTP), answering our ubiquitous call to email, uses a spooled, or queued, method of mail delivery. Once a message has been sent to a destination, the message is spooled to a device—usually a disk. The server software at the destination posts a vigil, regularly checking the queue for messages. When it detects them, it proceeds to deliver them to their destination. SMTP is used to send mail; POP3 is used to receive mail.

Domain Name System (TCP and UDP 53)

Domain Name System (DNS) resolves hostnames—specifically, Internet names, such as www.lammle.com—to their corresponding IP addresses.

You don't have to use DNS; you can just type in the IP address of any device you want to communicate with. An IP address identifies hosts on a network and the Internet as well. However, DNS was designed to make our lives easier. Think about this: What would happen if you wanted to move your web page to a different service provider? The IP address would change, and no one would know what the new one was. DNS allows you to use a domain name to specify an IP address. You can change the IP address as often as you want and no one will know the difference. Figure 6.6 shows a DNS example.

FIGURE 6.6 Domain Name System

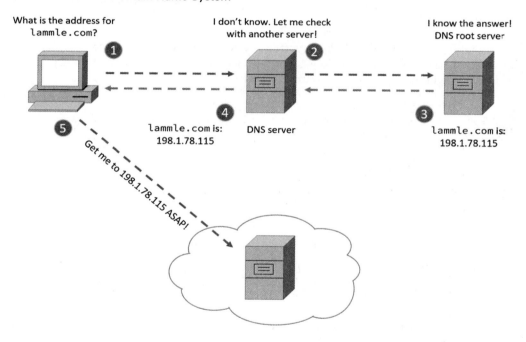

DNS is used to resolve a *fully qualified domain name (FQDN)*—for example, www.lammle.com or todd.lammle.com—to an IP address. An FQDN, or DNS namespace, is a hierarchy that can logically locate a system based on its domain identifier.

If you want to resolve the name *todd*, you must either type in the FQDN of todd.lammle.com or have a device, such as a PC or router, add the suffix for you. For example, on a Cisco router, you can use the command ip domain-name lammle.com to append each request with the lammle.com domain. If you don't do that, you'll have to type in the FQDN to get DNS to resolve the name.

An important thing to remember about DNS is that if you can ping a device with an IP address but can't use its FQDN, you might have some type of DNS configuration failure.

Dynamic Host Configuration Protocol/Bootstrap Protocol (UDP 67/68)

Dynamic Host Configuration Protocol (DHCP) assigns IP addresses to hosts with information provided by a server. It allows easier administration and works well in small to even very large network environments. Many types of hardware can be used as a DHCP server, including routers.

DHCP differs from Bootstrap Protocol (BootP) in that BootP assigns an IP address to a host but the host's hardware address must be entered manually in a BootP table. You can think of DHCP as a dynamic BootP. But remember that BootP is also used to send an operating system that a host can boot from. DHCP can't do that.

Please also read the sections on DHCP and DNS servers in Chapter 5, "Networking Devices," if you have not done so; both figure largely in the exam objectives.

But there is a lot of information a DHCP server can provide to a host when the host is requesting an IP address from the DHCP server. Here's a partial list of the information a DHCP server can provide:

- IP address
- Subnet mask
- Domain name
- Default gateway (routers)
- DNS

A DHCP server can give even more information than this, but the items in the list are the most common.

A client that sends out a DHCP Discover message in order to receive an IP address sends out a broadcast at both layer 2 and layer 3. The layer 2 broadcast is all *F*s in hex, which looks like this: FF:FF:FF:FF:FF:FF. The Layer 3 broadcast is 255.255.255.255, which means all networks and all hosts. DHCP is connectionless, which means it uses User Datagram Protocol (UDP) at the Transport layer, also known as the Host-to-Host layer, which we'll discuss later in this chapter.

In case you don't believe me, here's an example of output from my trusty analyzer:

```
Ethernet II,Src:192.168.0.3(00:0b:db:99:d3:5e),Dst:Broadcast(ff:ff:ff
:ff:ff:ff)
Internet Protocol,Src:0.0.0.0(0.0.0.0),Dst:255.255.255.255(255.255.255.255).
```

The Data Link and Network layers are both sending out "all hands" broadcasts saying, "Help—I don't know my IP address!"

Figure 6.7 shows the process of a client-server relationship using a DHCP connection.

FIGURE 6.7   DHCP client four-step process

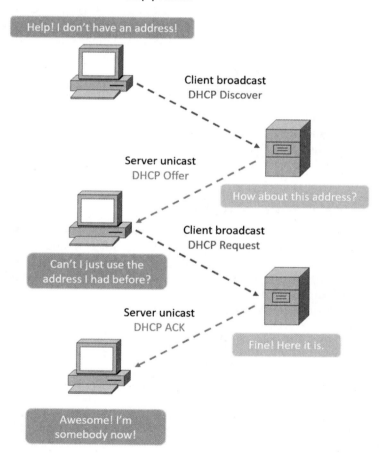

The following is the four-step process (sometimes known as the DORA process) a client takes to receive an IP address from a DHCP server:

1. The DHCP client broadcasts a DHCP Discover message looking for a DHCP server (port 67).

2. The DHCP server that received the DHCP Discover message sends a unicast DHCP Offer message back to the host.

3. The client then broadcasts to the server a DHCP Request message asking for the offered IP address and possibly other information.

4. The server finalizes the exchange with a unicast DHCP Acknowledgment message.

What happens if you have a few hosts connected together with a switch or hub and you don't have a DHCP server? You can add IP information by hand (this is called *static IP addressing*), or Windows provides what is called Automatic Private IP Addressing (APIPA), a feature of later Windows operating systems. With APIPA, clients can automatically self-configure an IP address and subnet mask (basic IP information that hosts use to communicate, which is covered in detail in Chapter 7, "IP Addressing," and Chapter 8, "IP Subnetting, Troubleshooting IP, and Introduction to NAT") when a DHCP server isn't available. The IP address range for APIPA is 169.254.0.1 through 169.254.255.254. The client also configures itself with a default Class B subnet mask of 255.255.0.0. If you have a DHCP server and your host is using this IP address, this means your DHCP client on your host is not working or the server is down or can't be reached because of a network issue.

Trivial File Transfer Protocol (UDP 69)

Trivial File Transfer Protocol (TFTP) is the stripped-down, stock version of FTP, but it's the protocol of choice if you know exactly what you want and where to find it—plus it's easy to use, and it's fast, too! It doesn't give you the abundance of functions that FTP does, though. TFTP has no directory-browsing abilities; it can do nothing but send and receive files. Figure 6.8 shows a TFTP example.

This compact little protocol also skimps in the data department, sending much smaller blocks of data than FTP, and there's no authentication as with FTP, so it's insecure. Few sites support it because of the inherent security risks.

FIGURE 6.8   Trivial FTP

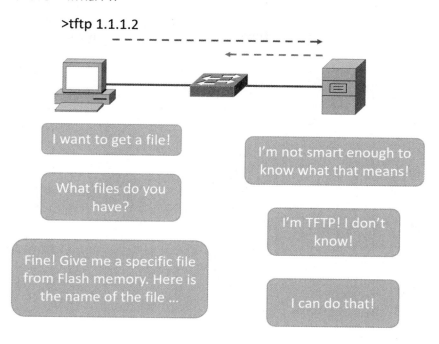

Real World Scenario

When Should You Use FTP?

The folks at your San Francisco office need a 50 MB file emailed to them right away. What do you do? Most email servers would reject the email because they have size limits. Even if there's no size limit on the server, it would still take a while to send this big file. FTP to the rescue! Most ISPs don't allow files larger than 10 MB to be emailed, so FTP is an option you should consider if you need to send and receive.

If you need to give someone a large file or you need to get a large file from someone, FTP is a nice choice. Smaller files (smaller than 10 MB) can be sent via email if you have the bandwidth (who doesn't these days?), even if they're compressed. To use FTP, you'll need to set up an FTP server on the Internet so that the files can be shared.

Besides, FTP is faster than email, which is another reason to use FTP for sending or receiving large files. In addition, because it uses TCP and is connection-oriented, if the session dies, FTP can sometimes start up where it left off. Try that with your email client!

Hypertext Transfer Protocol (TCP 80)

All those snappy websites comprising a mélange of graphics, text, links, and so on—the *Hypertext Transfer Protocol (HTTP)* is making it all possible. Figure 6.9 shows an HTTP example.

FIGURE 6.9   HTTP

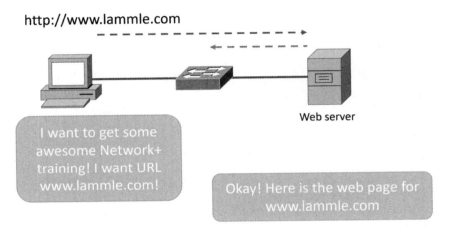

It's used to manage communications between web browsers and web servers, and it opens the right resource when you click a link, wherever that resource may actually reside. See the "Hypertext Transfer Protocol Secure (TCP 443)" section for what we normally use today for this type of data transfer because HTTP does not encrypt data during client-to-server communication.

Post Office Protocol v3 (TCP 110)

Post Office Protocol (POP) gives us a storage facility for incoming mail, and the latest version is called POP3 (sound familiar?). Basically, how this protocol works is when a client device connects to a POP3 server, messages addressed to that client are released for downloading. It doesn't allow messages to be downloaded selectively, but once they are, the client-server interaction ends, and you can delete and tweak your messages locally at will. A newer standard, IMAP, is being used more and more in place of POP3 because of its flexibility and security.

Network Time Protocol (UDP 123)

Kudos to Professor David Mills of the University of Delaware for coming up with this handy protocol that's used to synchronize the clocks on our computers to one standard time source (typically, an atomic clock). *Network Time Protocol (NTP)* works in conjunction with other synchronization utilities to ensure that all computers on a given network agree on the time. See Figure 6.10.

FIGURE 6.10   Network Time Protocol

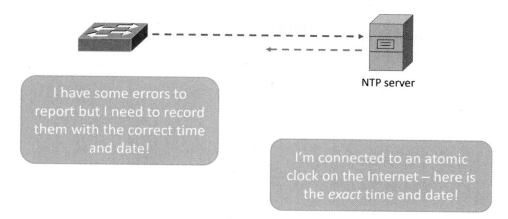

NTP server

I have some errors to report but I need to record them with the correct time and date!

I'm connected to an atomic clock on the Internet — here is the *exact* time and date!

This may sound pretty simple, but it's very important because so many of the transactions done today are time- and date-stamped. Think about your precious databases, for one. It can mess up a server pretty badly if it's out of sync with the machines connected to it, even by mere seconds (think crash!). You can't have a transaction entered by a machine at, say, 1:50 a.m. when the server records that transaction as having occurred at 1:45 a.m. So basically, NTP works to prevent "back to the future sans DeLorean" from bringing down the network—very important indeed!

Internet Message Access Protocol (TCP 143)

Because *Internet Message Access Protocol (IMAP)* makes it so you get control over how you download your mail, with it, you also gain some much-needed security. It lets you peek at the message header or download just a part of a message—you can now just nibble at the bait instead of swallowing it whole and then choking on the hook hidden inside!

With it, you can choose to store messages on the email server hierarchically and link to documents and user groups too. IMAP even gives you search commands to use to hunt for messages based on their subject, header, or content. As you can imagine, it has some serious authentication features—it actually supports the Kerberos authentication scheme that MIT developed. And yes, IMAP4 is the current version.

Simple Network Management Protocol (UDP 161/162)

Simple Network Management Protocol (SNMP) collects and manipulates valuable network information. It gathers data by polling the devices on the network from a management station at fixed or random intervals, requiring them to disclose certain information. When all is well, SNMP receives something called a *baseline*—a report delimiting the operational traits of a healthy network. This protocol can also stand as a watchdog over the network, quickly notifying managers of any sudden turn of events. The network watchdogs are called *agents*, and when aberrations occur, agents send an alert called a *trap* to the management station. The Network Management System (NMS) polls the agents through a Management Information Base (MIB). The MIB is basically a database with a set of predefined questions the NMS can ask the agents regarding the health of the device or network. Figure 6.11 shows an NMS station at work.

FIGURE 6.11 Network Management Station

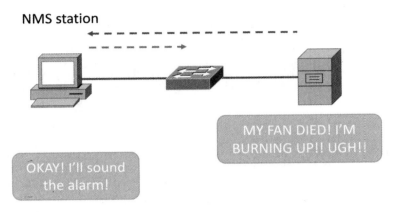

In addition, SNMP can help simplify the process of setting up a network as well as the administration of your entire internetwork.

SNMP Versions 1, 2, and 3

SNMP versions 1 and 2 are pretty much obsolete. This doesn't mean you won't see them in a network at some time, but v1 is super old and, well, outdated. SNMPv2 provided improvements, especially in performance. But one of the best additions was what was called GETBULK, which allowed a host to retrieve a large amount of data at once. However, v2 never really caught on in the networking world. SNMPv3 is now the standard and uses both TCP and UDP, unlike v1, which used only UDP. Version 3 added even more security and message integrity, authentication, and encryption. So, be careful when running SNMPv1 and v2 because they are susceptible to a packet sniffer reading the data.

Lightweight Directory Access Protocol (TCP 389)

If you're the system administrator of any decent-sized network, odds are you have a type of directory in place that keeps track of all your network resources, such as devices and users. But how do you access those directories? Through the *Lightweight Directory Access*

Protocol (LDAP), that's how. LDAP is a protocol used to access and query directory services systems such as Microsoft Active Directory. And there is a secure version of LDAP called LDAPS that uses port 636, which I'll cover a bit later.

This protocol standardizes how you access directories, and its first and second inceptions are described in RFCs 1487 and 1777, respectively. There were a few glitches in those two earlier versions, so a third version—the one most commonly used today—was created to address those issues and is described in RFC 3377.

Hypertext Transfer Protocol Secure (TCP 443)

Hypertext Transfer Protocol Secure (HTTPS) is a secure version of HTTP that arms you with a whole bunch of security tools for keeping transactions between a web browser and a server secure. It's what your browser needs to fill out forms, sign in, authenticate, and encrypt an HTTP message when you make a reservation or buy something online. The Chromium browser actually requires HTTPS encryption or it will notify you that there is no privacy.

> Both SSH (port 22) and HTTPS (port 443) are used to encrypt packets over your intranet and the Internet.

Transport Layer Security/Secure Sockets Layer (TCP 995/465)

Both *Transport Layer Security (TLS)* and its forerunner, *Secure Sockets Layer (SSL)*, are cryptographic protocols that come in really handy for enabling secure online data-transfer activities like browsing the web, instant messaging, Internet faxing, and so on. They're so similar that it's not within the scope of this book to detail the differences between them. They both use X.509 certificates and asymmetric cryptography to authenticate to the host they are communicating with and to exchange a key. This key is then used to encrypt data flowing between the hosts. This allows for data/message confidentiality, message integrity, and message authentication.

Even though I listed TLS/SSL as using ports 995 and 465, which is true if you're using Gmail, TLS/SSL isn't tied down to any certain ports and can use various different ones.

Server Message Block (TCP 445)

Server Message Block (SMB) is used for sharing access to files and printers and other communications between hosts on a Microsoft Windows network. SMB runs mostly on TCP port 445 now, but SMB can also run on UDP port 137 and 138 and on TCP port 137 and 139 using NetBIOS.

Syslog (UDP 514)

Reading system messages from a switch's or router's internal buffer is the most popular and efficient method of seeing what's going on with your network at a particular time. But the best way is to log messages to a *syslog* server, which stores messages from you and can even time-stamp and sequence them for you, and it's easy to set up and configure!

Syslog allows you to display, sort, and even search messages, all of which makes it a really great troubleshooting tool. The search feature is especially powerful because you can use keywords and even severity levels. Plus, the server can email admins based on the severity level of the message.

Network devices can be configured to generate a syslog message and forward it to various destinations. These four examples are popular ways to gather messages from Cisco devices:

- Logging buffer (on by default)
- Console line (on by default)
- Terminal lines (using the terminal monitor command)
- Syslog server

The severity levels, from the most severe level to the least severe, are explained in Table 6.1. Informational is the default and will result in all messages being sent to the buffers and console.

TABLE 6.1   Severity levels

Severity Level	Explanation
Emergency (severity 0)	System is unusable.
Alert (severity 1)	Immediate action is needed.
Critical (severity 2)	Critical condition.
Error (severity 3)	Error condition.
Warning (severity 4)	Warning condition.
Notification (severity 5)	Normal but significant condition.
Information (severity 6)	Normal information message.
Debugging (severity 7)	Debugging message.

SMTPS (TCP 587)

As discussed previously, Simple Mail Transfer Protocol (SMTP), answering our ubiquitous call to email, uses a spooled, or queued, method of mail delivery using TCP port 25. However, this email is sent in clear text, and some email servers can still use this.

SMTPS encrypts email when it is sent, and most email servers use or can use port 587 to send email now; some even demand it. This port, coupled with TLS encryption, will ensure that email is securely sent, following the guidelines set out by the IETF of course.

Lightweight Directory Access Protocol over SSL (TCP 636)

Taking off from our discussion earlier on TCP 389 LDAP, understand that this traffic is transmitted unsecured. Bring in LDAP over SSL TCP 636, which is the suggested use of LDAP in today's networks. To make this function correctly, you need to install a proper certificate from a Microsoft certification authority (CA) or other type of CA.

IMAP over SSL (TCP 993)

Because Internet Message Access Protocol (IMAP) makes it so you get control over how you download your mail, with it, you also gain some much-needed security. However, IMAP over SSL means that IMAP traffic travels over a security socket to a security port, using TCP port 993 usually.

POP3 over SSL (TCP 995)

As discussed previously. Post Office Protocol (POP) gives us a storage facility for incoming mail, and the latest version of POP is called POP3. This email is probably downloaded in clear text. Either POP3 over SSL or IMAP over SSL is more commonly used to encrypt emails being downloaded from servers today.

Structured Query Language (SQL) Server (TCP 1433)

Microsoft SQL Server has grown from a simple relational database engine to a multipurpose enterprise-level data platform. TCP port 1433 is the default port for SQL Server, and it's also the official Internet Assigned Number Authority (IANA) socket number for SQL Server. Client systems use TCP 1433 to connect to the database engine.

SQLnet (TCP 1521)

SQLnet (also referred to as SQL*Net and Net8) is Oracle's networking software that allows remote data access between programs using Oracle Database. Applications and databases are shared with different machines and continue communicating as if they were local.

SQLnet is based on Oracle's Transparent Network Substrate (TNS), a network technology that provides a generic interface to all network protocols; however, this is no longer needed today since we have TCP/IP.

SQL*Net is used by both client and server to communicate with one another. Without the Net8 layer acting as the interpreter, the client and server processes cannot interconnect (notice how I used all three names in this section—and all define the same thing).

MySQL (TCP 3306)

MySQL is a relational database management system based on SQL, or Structured Query Language. This is used within companies for data warehousing, e-commerce, logging applications, and more. The most common use for MySQL is for the purpose of a cloud-based database.

Remote Desktop Protocol (TCP 3389)

Remote Desktop Protocol (RDP) is a proprietary protocol developed by Microsoft. It allows you to connect to another computer and run programs. RDP operates like Telnet, except instead of getting a command-line prompt as you do with Telnet, you get the actual graphical user interface (GUI) of the remote computer. Clients exist for most versions of Windows, and Macs now come with a preinstalled RDP client.

Microsoft currently calls its official RDP server software Remote Desktop Services; it was called Terminal Services for a while. Microsoft's official client software is called Remote Desktop Connection (RDC), which was called Terminal Services Client in the past.

RDP is an excellent tool for remote clients, allowing users to connect to their work computer from home, for example, and get their email or perform work on other applications without running or installing any of the software on their home computer.

SIP (VoIP) (TCP or UDP 5060/TCP 5061)

Session Initiation Protocol (SIP) is a hugely popular signaling protocol used to construct and deconstruct multimedia communication sessions for many things like voice and video calls, videoconferencing, streaming multimedia distributions, instant messaging, presence information, and online games over the Internet. SIP commonly works in conjunction with RTP (VoIP) streams to set up the connection between endpoints.

RTP (VoIP) (UDP 5004/TCP 5005)

Real-time Transport Protocol (RTP) describes a packet-formatting standard for delivering audio and video over the Internet. Although initially designed as a multicast protocol, it's now used for unicast applications too. It's commonly employed for streaming media, videoconferencing, and push-to-talk systems—all things that make it a de facto standard in Voice over IP (VoIP) industries.

MGCP (Multimedia) (TCP 2427/2727)

Media Gateway Control Protocol (MGCP) is a standard protocol for handling the signaling and session management needed during a multimedia conference.

The protocol defines a means of communication between a media gateway, which converts data from the format required for a circuit-switched network to that required for a packet-switched network, and the media gateway controller.

MGCP can be used to set up, maintain, and terminate calls between multiple endpoints.

H.323 (Video) (TCP 1720)

H.323 is a protocol that provides a standard for video on an IP network that defines how real-time audio, video, and data information is transmitted. This standard provides signaling, multimedia, and bandwidth control mechanisms. H.323 uses the RTP standard for communication.

Internet Group Management Protocol

Internet Group Management Protocol (IGMP) is the TCP/IP protocol used for managing IP multicast sessions. It accomplishes this by sending out unique IGMP messages over the network to reveal the multicast-group landscape and to find out which hosts belong to which multicast group. The host machines in an IP network also use IGMP messages to become members of a group and to quit the group too. IGMP messages come in seriously handy for tracking group memberships as well as active multicast streams. IGMP works at the Network layer and doesn't use port numbers.

NetBIOS (TCP and UDP 137–139)

Network Basic Input/Output System works only in the upper layers of the OSI model and allows for an interface on separate computers to communicate over a network.

It was first created in the early 1980s to work on an IBM LAN and was proprietary. Microsoft and Novell both created a NetBIOS implementation to allows their hosts to communicate to their servers, but Microsoft's version became the de facto version.

The Host-to-Host Layer Protocols

The main purpose of the Host-to-Host layer is to shield the upper-layer applications from the complexities of the network. This layer says to the upper layer, "Just give me your data stream, with any instructions, and I'll begin the process of getting your information ready to send."

The following sections describe the two protocols at this layer:

- Transmission Control Protocol (TCP)
- User Datagram Protocol (UDP)

In addition, we'll look at some of the key host-to-host protocol concepts as well as the port numbers.

Transmission Control Protocol

Transmission Control Protocol (TCP) takes large blocks of information from an application and breaks them into segments. It numbers and sequences each segment so that the destination's TCP process can put the segments back into the order the application intended. After these segments are sent, TCP (on the transmitting host) waits for an acknowledgment from the receiving end's TCP process, retransmitting those segments that aren't acknowledged.

Remember that in a reliable transport operation, a device that wants to transmit sets up a connection-oriented communication with a remote device by creating a session. The transmitting device first establishes a connection-oriented session with its peer system; that session is called a *call setup* or a *three-way handshake*. Data is then transferred, and when the transfer is complete, a call termination takes place to tear down the virtual circuit.

Because the upper layers send a data stream to the protocols in the Transport layer, I'll demonstrate how TCP segments a data stream and prepares it for the Internet layer.

When the Internet layer receives the data stream, it routes the segments as packets through an internetwork. The segments are handed to the receiving host's Host-to-Host layer protocol, which rebuilds the data stream to hand to the upper-layer protocols.

TCP is a full-duplex, connection-oriented, reliable, and accurate protocol, but establishing all these terms and conditions, in addition to error checking, is no small task. TCP is very complicated, and so not surprisingly, it's costly in terms of network overhead. And since today's networks are much more reliable than those of yore, this added reliability is often unnecessary. Most programmers use TCP because it removes a lot of programming work, but for real-time video and VoIP, *User Datagram Protocol (UDP)* is often better because using it results in less overhead.

TCP Segment Format

Since the upper layers send a data stream to the protocols in the Transport layers, I'll use Figure 6.12 to demonstrate how TCP segments a data stream and prepares it for the Internet layer. When the Internet layer receives the data stream, it routes the segments as packets through an internetwork. The segments are handed to the receiving host's Host-to-Host layer protocol, which rebuilds the data stream for the upper-layer applications or protocols.

The TCP header is 24 bytes long, or up to 60 bytes with options. Figure 6.12 shows the TCP segment format and the different fields within the TCP header.

FIGURE 6.12   TCP segment format

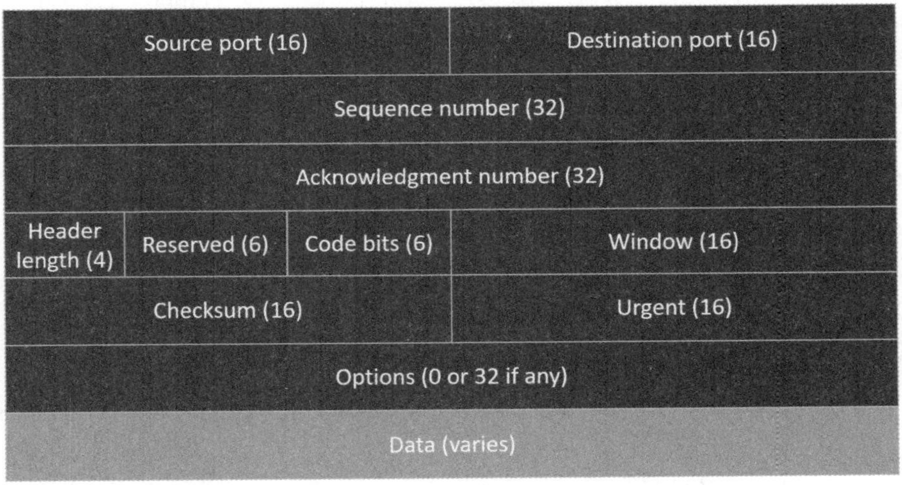

Again, it's good to understand what each field in the TCP segment is in order to build a strong educational foundation:

Source Port   This is the port number of the application on the host sending the data.

Destination Port   This is the port number of the application requested on the destination host.

Sequence Number   A number used by TCP that puts the data back in the correct order or retransmits missing or damaged data during a process called sequencing.

Acknowledgment Number   The value is the TCP octet that is expected next.

Header Length   The number of 32-bit words in the TCP header, which indicates where the data begins. The TCP header (even one including options) is an integral number of 32 bits in length.

Reserved   Always set to zero.

Code Bits/TCP Flags   Controls functions used to set up and terminate a session.

Window   The window size the sender is willing to accept, in octets.

Checksum   The cyclic redundancy check (CRC), used because TCP doesn't trust the lower layers and checks everything. The CRC checks the header and data fields.

Urgent   A valid field only if the Urgent pointer in the code bits is set. If so, this value indicates the offset from the current sequence number, in octets, where the segment of non-urgent data begins.

Options   May be 0, meaning that no options have to be present, or a multiple of 32 bits. However, if any options are used that do not cause the option field to total a multiple of 32 bits, padding of 0s must be used to make sure the data begins on a 32-bit boundary. These boundaries are known as words.

Payload (Data)   Handed down to the TCP protocol at the Transport layer, which includes the upper-layer headers.

Let's take a look at a TCP segment copied from a network analyzer. In the following output, I have bolded the Payload (data) area that the packet is carrying to the destination host:

```
TCP - Transport Control Protocol
Source Port: 5973
Destination Port: 23
Sequence Number: 1456389907
Ack Number: 1242056456
Offset: 5
Reserved: %000000
Code: %011000
Ack is valid
Push Request
Window: 61320
```

```
Checksum: 0x61a6
Urgent Pointer: 0
No TCP Options
```
TCP Data Area:
vL.5.+.5.+.5.+.5 76 4c 19 35 11 2b 19 35 11 2b 19 35 11
2b 19 35 +. 11 2b 19
```
Frame Check Sequence: 0x0d00000f
```

Did you notice that everything I talked about earlier is in the segment? As you can see from the number of fields in the header, TCP creates a lot of overhead. Again, this is why application developers may opt for efficiency over reliability to save overhead and go with UDP instead. It's also defined at the Transport layer as an alternative to TCP.

User Datagram Protocol

If you were to compare *User Datagram Protocol (UDP)* with TCP, the former is basically the scaled-down economy model that's sometimes referred to as a *thin protocol*. Like a thin person on a park bench, a thin protocol doesn't take up a lot of room—or in this case, much bandwidth on a network.

UDP doesn't offer all the bells and whistles of TCP either, but it does do a fabulous job of transporting information that doesn't require reliable delivery—and it does so using far fewer network resources.

There are some situations in which it would definitely be wise for developers to opt for UDP rather than TCP. Remember the watchdog SNMP up there at the Process/Application layer? SNMP monitors the network, sending intermittent messages and a fairly steady flow of status updates and alerts, especially when running on a large network. The cost in overhead to establish, maintain, and close a TCP connection for each one of those little messages would reduce what would be an otherwise healthy, efficient network to a dammed-up bog in no time!

Another circumstance calling for UDP over TCP is when reliability is already handled at the Process/Application layer. DNS handles its own reliability issues, making the use of TCP both impractical and redundant. But ultimately, it's up to the application developer to decide whether to use UDP or TCP, not the user who wants to transfer data faster.

UDP does *not* sequence the segments and doesn't care in which order the segments arrive at the destination. But after that, UDP sends the segments off and forgets about them. It doesn't follow through, check up on them, or even allow for an acknowledgment of safe arrival—complete abandonment. Because of this, it's referred to as an *unreliable* protocol. This doesn't mean that UDP is ineffective, only that it doesn't handle issues of reliability. Because UDP assumes that the application will use its own reliability method, it doesn't use any. This gives an application developer a choice when running the IP stack: TCP for reliability or UDP for faster transfers.

Further, UDP doesn't create a virtual circuit, nor does it contact the destination before delivering information to it. Because of this, it's also considered a *connectionless* protocol.

Figure 6.13 clearly illustrates UDP's markedly low overhead as compared to TCP's hungry usage. Look at the figure carefully—can you see that UDP doesn't use windowing or provide for acknowledgments in the UDP header?

FIGURE 6.13   UDP segment

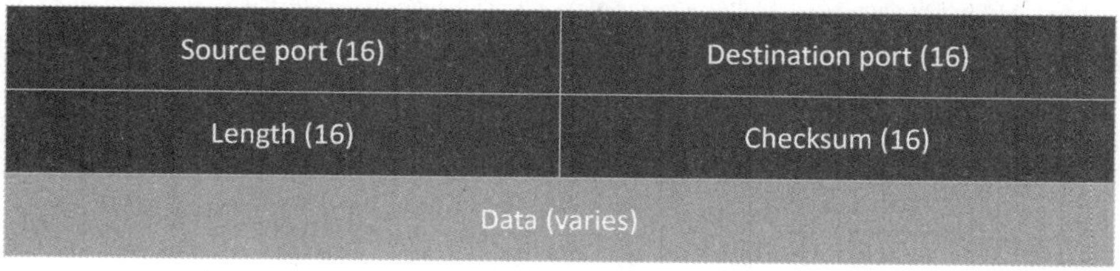

Source port (16)	Destination port (16)
Length (16)	Checksum (16)
Data (varies)	

For more detailed information regarding the UDP header, which is beyond the scope of the CompTIA Network+ exam objectives, please see my book *CCNA: Cisco Certified Network Associate Study Guide* (Sybex, 2019).

Key Concepts of Host-to-Host Protocols

Now that you've seen both a connection-oriented (TCP) and connectionless (UDP) protocol in action, it would be good to summarize the two here. Table 6.2 highlights some of the key concepts that you should keep in mind regarding these two protocols. You should memorize this table.

TABLE 6.2   Key features of TCP and UDP

TCP	UDP
Sequenced	Unsequenced
Reliable	Unreliable
Connection-oriented	Connectionless
Virtual circuit	Low overhead
Acknowledgments	No acknowledgment
Windowing flow control	No windowing or flow control of any type

A telephone analogy could help you understand how TCP works. Most of us know that before you speak to someone on the phone, you must first establish a connection with that person—wherever they are. This is like a virtual circuit with TCP. If you were giving someone important information during your conversation, you might say, "You know?" or ask, "Did you get that?" Saying something like this is a lot like a TCP acknowledgment—it's designed to get your verification. From time to time (especially on cell phones), people also ask, "Are you still there?" They end their conversations with a "Goodbye" of some kind, putting closure on the phone call. TCP also performs these types of functions.

Alternatively, using UDP is like sending a postcard. To do that, you don't need to contact the other party first. You write your message, address the postcard, and mail it. This is analogous to UDP's connectionless orientation. Because the message on the postcard is probably not a matter of life or death, you don't need an acknowledgment of its receipt. Similarly, UDP doesn't involve acknowledgments.

Port Numbers

TCP and UDP must use *port numbers* to communicate with the upper layers because they're what keep track of different simultaneous conversations originated by or accepted by the local host. Originating source port numbers are dynamically assigned by the source host and will usually have a value of 1024 or higher. Ports 1023 and below are defined in RFC 3232, which discusses what are called *well-known port numbers*.

Virtual circuits that don't use an application with a well-known port number are assigned port numbers randomly from a specific range instead. These port numbers identify the source and destination application or process in the TCP segment.

Figure 6.14 illustrates how both TCP and UDP use port numbers.

FIGURE 6.14   Port numbers for TCP and UDP

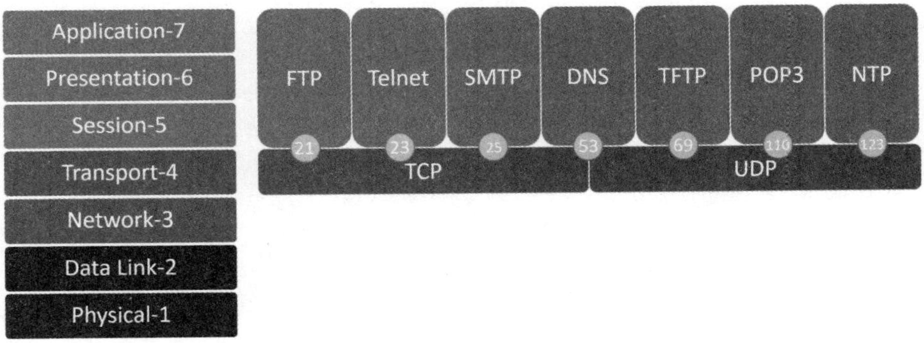

You just need to remember that numbers below 1024 are considered well-known port numbers and are defined in RFC 3232. Numbers 1024 and above are used by the upper layers to set up sessions with other hosts and by TCP as source and destination identifiers in the TCP segment.

Table 6.3 gives you a list of the typical applications used in the TCP/IP suite, their well-known port numbers, and the Transport layer protocols used by each application or process. It's important that you study and memorize this table for the CompTIA Network+ exam.

TABLE 6.3 Key protocols that use TCP and UDP

TCP	UDP
Telnet 23	SNMPv1/2 161
SMTP 25	TFTP 69
HTTP 80	DNS 53
FTP 20, 21	BOOTPS/DHCP 67,68
SFTP 22	NTP 123
DNS 53	Syslog 514
HTTPS 443	SIP 5060/5061
SSH 22	
SMB 445	
POP3 110	
IMAP4 143	
RDP 3389	
SNMPv3 161	
LDAP 389	
SMTPS 587	
LDAPS 636	
SQL 1433	
SIP 5060/5061	

Notice that DNS uses both TCP and UDP. Whether it opts for one or the other depends on what it's trying to do. Even though it's not the only application that can use both protocols, it's certainly one that you should remember in your studies.

The Internet Layer Protocols

In the DoD model, there are two main reasons for the Internet layer's existence: routing and providing a single network interface to the upper layers.

None of the other upper- or lower-layer protocols have any functions relating to routing—that complex and important task belongs entirely to the Internet layer. The Internet layer's second duty is to provide a single network interface to the upper-layer protocols. Without this layer, application programmers would need to write what are called *hooks* into every one of their applications for each different Network Access protocol. This would not only be a pain in the neck, but it would also lead to different versions of each application— one for wired Ethernet, another one for wireless Ethernet, and so on. To prevent this, IP provides one single network interface for the upper-layer protocols. That accomplished, it's then the job of IP and the various Network Access protocols to get along and work together.

All network roads don't lead to Rome—they lead to IP. And all the other protocols at this layer, as well as all those at the upper layers, use it. Never forget that. All paths through the DoD model go through IP. The following sections describe the protocols at the Internet layer:

- Internet Protocol
- Internet Control Message Protocol
- Address Resolution Protocol
- Reverse Address Resolution Protocol
- Generic Router Encapsulation
- IP Security

Internet Protocol

Internet Protocol (IP) is essentially the Internet layer. The other protocols found here merely exist to support it. IP holds the big picture and could be said to "see all" in that it's aware of all the interconnected networks. It can do this because all the machines on the network have a software, or logical, address called an IP address, which I'll cover more thoroughly in the next chapter.

IP looks at each packet's destination address. Then, using a routing table, it decides where a packet is to be sent next, choosing the best path. The protocols of the Network Access layer at the bottom of the DoD model don't possess IP's enlightened scope of the entire network; they deal only with physical links (local networks).

Identifying devices on networks requires answering these two questions: Which network is it on? And what is its ID on that network? The answer to the first question is the *software address*, or *logical address* (the correct street). The answer to the second question is the *hardware address* (the correct mailbox). All hosts on a network have a logical ID called an IP address. This is the software, or logical, address and contains valuable encoded information, greatly simplifying the complex task of routing. (IP is discussed in RFC 791.)

IP receives segments from the Host-to-Host layer and fragments them into packets if necessary. IP then reassembles packets back into segments on the receiving side. Each packet is assigned the IP address of the sender and of the recipient. Each router (Layer 3 device) that receives a packet makes routing decisions based on the packet's destination IP address.

Figure 6.15 shows an IPv4 header. This will give you an idea of what IP has to go through every time user data is sent from the upper layers to a remote network.

FIGURE 6.15   IPv4 header

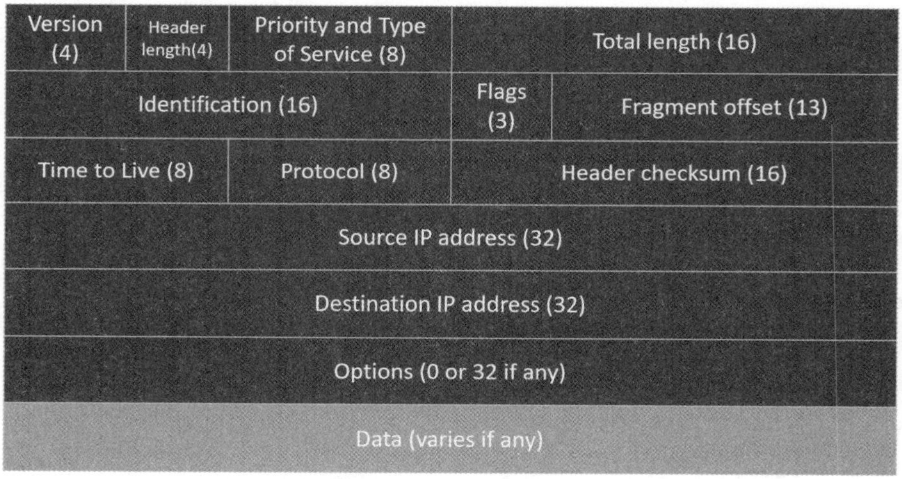

Version (4)	Header length(4)	Priority and Type of Service (8)	Total length (16)		
Identification (16)			Flags (3)	Fragment offset (13)	
Time to Live (8)		Protocol (8)	Header checksum (16)		
Source IP address (32)					
Destination IP address (32)					
Options (0 or 32 if any)					
Data (varies if any)					

The following fields make up the IP header:

Version   IP version number.

Header Length   Header length (HLEN) in 32-bit words.

Priority and Type of Service   Type of Service tells how the datagram should be handled. The first 3 bits are the priority bits, now called the differentiated services bits.

Total Length   Length of the packet, including header and data.

Identification   Unique IP-packet value used to differentiate fragmented packets from different datagrams.

Flags   Specifies whether fragmentation of the packet should occur.

Fragment Offset   Provides fragmentation and reassembly if the packet is too large to put in a frame. It also allows different maximum transmission units (MTUs define the size of packets) on the Internet.

Time To Live   Set into a packet when it is originally generated. If it doesn't get to where it's supposed to go before the TTL expires, boom—it's gone. This stops IP packets from continuously circling the network looking for a home.

Protocol   Port of upper-layer protocol; for example, TCP is port 6 or UDP is port 17. Also supports Network layer protocols, like ARP and ICMP, and can be referred to as the Type field in some analyzers. We'll talk about this field more in a minute.

Header Checksum   Cyclic redundancy check (CRC) on header only.

Source IP Address   32-bit IP address of sending station.

Destination IP Address   32-bit IP address of the station this packet is destined for.

Options   Used for network testing, debugging, security, and more.

Data   After the IP option field, will be the upper-layer data.

Here's a snapshot of an IP packet caught on a network analyzer. Notice that all the header information discussed previously appears here:

```
IP Header - Internet Protocol Datagram
Version: 4
Header Length: 5
Precedence: 0
Type of Service: %000
Unused: %00
Total Length: 187
Identifier: 22486
Fragmentation Flags: %010 Do Not Fragment
Fragment Offset: 0
Time To Live: 60
IP Type: 0x06 TCP
Header Checksum: 0xd031
Source IP Address: 10.7.1.30
Dest. IP Address: 10.7.1.10
No Internet Datagram Options
```

The Type field is typically a Protocol field, but this analyzer sees it as an IP Type field. This is important. If the header didn't carry the protocol information for the next layer, IP wouldn't know what to do with the data carried in the packet. The preceding example clearly tells IP to hand the segment to TCP.

Figure 6.16 demonstrates how the Network layer sees the protocols at the Transport layer when it needs to hand a packet up to the upper-layer protocols.

FIGURE 6.16   The Protocol field in an IP header

In this example, the Protocol field tells IP to send the data to either TCP port 6 or UDP port 17. But it will be UDP or TCP only if the data is part of a data stream headed for an upper-layer service or application. It could just as easily be destined for Internet Control Message Protocol (ICMP), Address Resolution Protocol (ARP), or some other type of Network layer protocol.

Table 6.4 lists some other popular protocols that can be specified in the Protocol field.

TABLE 6.4   Possible protocols found in the Protocol field of an IP header

Protocol	Protocol Number
ICMP	1
IP in IP (tunneling)	4
TCP	6
UDP	17
EIGRP	88
OSPF	89
IPv6	41
GRE	47
Layer 2 tunnel (L2TP)	115

You can find a complete list of Protocol field numbers at www.iana.org/ assignments/protocol-numbers.

Internet Control Message Protocol

Internet Control Message Protocol (ICMP) works at the Network layer and is used by IP for many different services. ICMP is a management protocol and messaging service provider for IP. Its messages are carried as IP packets.

ICMP packets have the following characteristics:

- They can provide hosts with information about network problems.
- They are encapsulated within IP datagrams.

The following are some common events and messages that ICMP relates to, and the two most popular programs that use ICMP:

Destination Unreachable   If a router can't send an IP datagram any further, it uses ICMP to send a message back to the sender, advising it of the situation. For example, take a look at Figure 6.17, which shows that the Ethernet interface of the Lab B router is down.

FIGURE 6.17   An ICMP error message is sent to the sending host from the remote router.

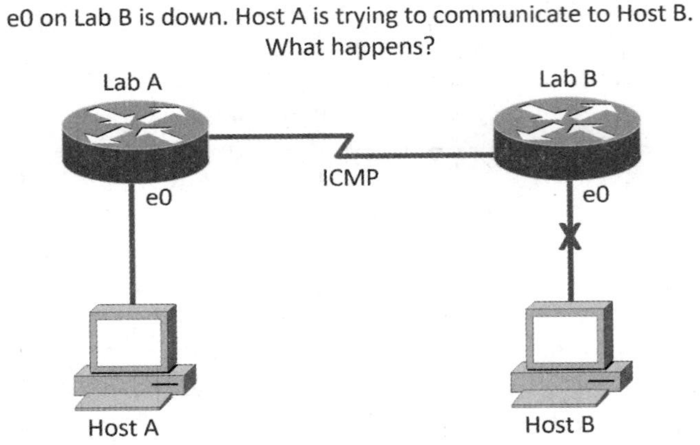

e0 on Lab B is down. Host A is trying to communicate to Host B.
What happens?

When Host A sends a packet destined for Host B, the Lab B router will send an ICMP Destination Unreachable message back to the sending device (directly to Host A, in this example).

Buffer Full   If a router's memory buffer for receiving incoming datagrams is full, it will use ICMP to send out this message until the congestion abates.

Hops   Each IP datagram is allotted a certain number of routers, called *hops*, to pass through. If a datagram reaches its limit of hops before arriving at its destination, the last router to receive it deletes it. The executioner router then uses ICMP to send an obituary message, informing the sending machine of the demise of its datagram.

Ping   Ping uses ICMP echo request and reply messages to check the physical and logical connectivity of machines on an internetwork.

Traceroute   Traceroute uses IP packet time to live time-outs to discover the path a packet takes as it traverses an internetwork.

Both Ping and Traceroute (also just called Trace, and Microsoft Windows uses `tracert`) allow you to verify address configurations in your internetwork.

Address Resolution Protocol

Address Resolution Protocol (ARP) finds the hardware address of a host from a known IP address. Here's how it works: When IP has a datagram to send, it must inform a Network Access protocol, such as Ethernet or wireless, of the destination's hardware address on the local network. (It has already been informed by upper-layer protocols of the destination's IP address.) If IP doesn't find the destination host's hardware address in the ARP cache, it uses ARP to find this information.

As IP's detective, ARP interrogates the local network by sending out a broadcast asking the machine with the specified IP address to reply with its hardware address. So basically, ARP translates the software (IP) address into a hardware address—for example, the destination machine's Ethernet address. Figure 6.18 shows how an ARP broadcast looks to a local network.

FIGURE 6.18   Local ARP broadcast

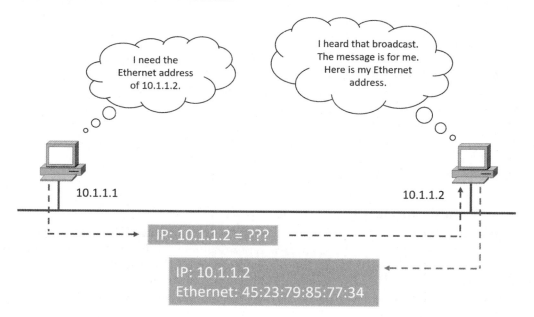

ARP resolves IP addresses to Ethernet (MAC) addresses.

The following trace shows an ARP broadcast—notice that the destination hardware address is unknown and is all 0s in the ARP header. In the Ethernet header, a destination of all *F*s in hex (all 1s in binary), a hardware-address broadcast, is used to make sure all devices on the local link receive the ARP request:

```
Flags:          0x00
Status:         0x00
Packet Length: 64
Timestamp:      09:17:29.574000 12/06/21
Ethernet Header
 Destination:    FF:FF:FF:FF:FF:FF Ethernet Broadcast
 Source:         00:A0:24:48:60:A5
 Protocol Type: 0x0806 IP ARP
ARP - Address Resolution Protocol
 Hardware:               1 Ethernet (10Mb)
 Protocol:               0x0800 IP
 Hardware Address Length: 6
 Protocol Address Length: 4
 Operation:              1 ARP Request
 Sender Hardware Address: 00:A0:24:48:60:A5
 Sender Internet Address: 172.16.10.3
 Target Hardware Address: 00:00:00:00:00:00 (ignored)
 Target Internet Address: 172.16.10.10
Extra bytes (Padding):
 ............... 0A 0A 0A 0A 0A 0A 0A 0A 0A 0A 0A 0A 0A
  0A 0A 0A 0A 0A
Frame Check Sequence: 0x00000000
```

Reverse Address Resolution Protocol (RARP)

When an IP machine happens to be a diskless machine, it has no way of initially knowing its IP address. But it does know its MAC address. *Reverse Address Resolution Protocol (RARP)* discovers the identity of the IP address for diskless machines by sending out a packet that includes its MAC address and a request for the IP address assigned to that MAC address. A designated machine, called a *RARP server*, responds with the answer, and the identity crisis is over. RARP uses the information it does know about the machine's MAC address to learn its IP address and complete the machine's ID portrait.

Figure 6.19 shows a diskless workstation asking for its IP address with a RARP broadcast.

FIGURE 6.19   RARP broadcast example

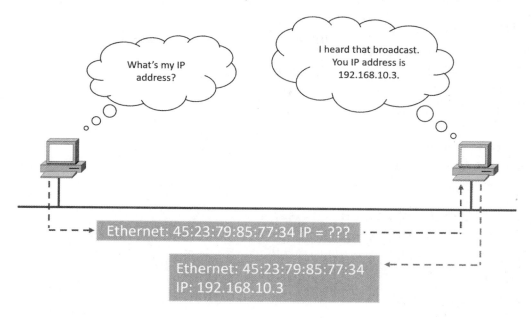

Generic Routing Encapsulation (GRE)

Generic Routing Encapsulation (GRE) is a tunneling protocol that can encapsulate many protocols inside IP tunnels. Some examples would be routing protocols such as EIGRP and OSPF and the routed protocol IPv6. Figure 6.20 shows the different pieces of a GRE header.

FIGURE 6.20   Generic Routing Encapsulation (GRE) tunnel structure

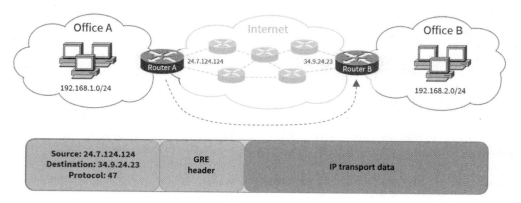

A GRE tunnel interface supports a header for each of the following:

- A passenger protocol or encapsulated protocols like IP or IPv6, which is the protocol being encapsulated by GRE
- GRE encapsulation protocol
- A transport delivery protocol, typically IP

GRE tunnels have the following characteristics:

- GRE uses a protocol-type field in the GRE header, so any layer 3 protocol can be used through the tunnel.
- GRE is stateless and has no flow control.
- GRE offers no security.
- GRE creates additional overhead for tunneled packets—at least 24 bytes.

Internet Protocol Security (IPSec)

As I just mentioned, GRE by itself provides no security—no form of payload confidentiality or encryption. If the packets are sniffed over the public networks, their contents are in plain-text, and although IPSec provides a secure method for tunneling data across an IP network, it has limitations.

IPSec does not support IP broadcast or IP multicast, preventing the use of protocols that need them, like routing protocols. IPSec also does not support the use of the multiprotocol traffic. GRE is a protocol that can be used to "carry" other passenger protocols like IP broadcast or IP multicast, as well as non-IP protocols. So using GRE tunnels with IPSec allows you to run a routing protocol, IP multicast, and multiprotocol traffic across your network.

With a generic hub-and-spoke topology (Corp to Branch, for example), you can implement static tunnels, typically GRE over IPSec, between the corporate office and branch offices. When you want to add a new spoke to the network, all you need to do is configure it on the hub router. The traffic between spokes has to traverse the hub, where it must exit one tunnel and enter another. Static tunnels can be an appropriate solution for small networks, but this solution actually becomes an unacceptable problem as the number of spokes grows larger and larger!

The two primary security protocols used by IPSec are *Authentication Header (AH)* and *Encapsulating Security Payload (ESP)*.

Authentication Header (AH)

The AH protocol provides authentication for the data and the IP header of a packet using a one-way hash for packet authentication. It works like this: The sender generates a one-way hash; then the receiver generates the same one-way hash. If the packet has changed in any way, it won't be authenticated and will be dropped. So basically, IPSec relies upon AH to guarantee authenticity. AH checks the entire packet, but it doesn't offer any encryption services.

This is unlike ESP, which provides an integrity check only on the data of a packet.

Encapsulating Security Payload (ESP)

It won't tell you when or how the NASDAQ is going to bounce up and down like a super-ball, but ESP will provide confidentiality, data origin authentication, connectionless integrity, anti-replay service, and limited traffic-flow confidentiality by defeating traffic flow analysis—which is almost as good! Anyway, there are five components of ESP:

Confidentiality (Encryption)   This allows the sending device to encrypt the packets before transmitting in order to prevent eavesdropping. Confidentiality is provided through the use of symmetric encryption algorithms. Confidentiality can be selected separately from all other services, but the confidentiality selected must be the same on both endpoints of your VPN. The following cryptographic algorithms are defined for use with IPSec:

- HMAC-SHA1/SHA2 for integrity protection and authenticity
- TripleDES-CBC for confidentiality
- AES-CBC and AES-CBC for confidentiality
- AES-GCM AND ChaCha20-Poly1305 providing confidentiality and authentication together efficiently

Data Integrity   Data integrity allows the receiver to verify that the data received was not altered in any way along the way. IPSec uses checksums as a simple check of the data.

Authentication   Authentication ensures that the connection is made with the correct partner. The receiver can authenticate the source of the packet by guaranteeing and certifying the source of the information.

Anti-Replay Service   Anti-replay election is based upon the receiver, meaning the service is effective only if the receiver checks the sequence number. In case you were wondering, a replay attack is when a hacker nicks a copy of an authenticated packet and later transmits it to the intended destination. When the duplicate, authenticated IP packet gets to the destination, it can disrupt services and generally wreak havoc. The *Sequence Number* field is designed to foil this type of attack.

Traffic Flow   For traffic flow confidentiality to work, you need to have at least tunnel mode selected. It's most effective if it's implemented at a security gateway where tons of traffic amasses because it's precisely the kind of environment that can mask the true source-destination patterns to bad guys who are trying to breach your network's security.

Internet Key Exchange (IKE)

Internet Key Exchange (IKE) is a management protocol that is used to negotiate security associations (SA) between endpoints. A security association will define the authentication, encryption, and IPSec protocols used for establishing the IPSec connection.

IKE will use the Internet Security Association and Key Management Protocol (ISAKMP) to manage the two phases for the connection:

Phase 1 (Main mode)   Phase 1 is where the parameters (policies) are agreed upon by the endpoints. The hash, authentication, group, lifetime, and encryption to be used, known as the HAGLE, will be agreed upon by the endpoints to establish a shared set of policies. Once it is agreed upon, both parties will authenticate and calculate a shared secret symmetrical encryption key. Upon successful authentication, the initial encryption tunnel will be created between the endpoints, and this will pave the way for phase 2.

Phase 2 (Quick mode)   Phase 2 is the negotiation and connection of IPSec. The initial encryption tunnel created via phase 1 is used to encrypt the negotiation of protocols and algorithms for phase 2 of the IKE process. This negotiation is called the IPSec transform set, and it contains details about the AH and ESP protocols to be used between endpoints. It will also contain details about the encryption, hashing, and mode that the IPSec tunnel will operate in.

The various configuration and details for IKE and ISAKMP protocol are above and beyond the objective for this book. The key takeaway should be that IKE is used to negotiate the IPSec tunnel, and this is done in two phases. For more detailed information about IKE, please visit `https://docs.paloaltonetworks.com /network-security/ipsec-vpn/administration/ ipsec-vpn-basics/internet-key-exchange-ike-for-vpn`.

Data Encapsulation

I started to discuss data encapsulation in Chapter 2, but I could provide only an overview at that point in the book because you needed to have a firm understanding of how ports work in a virtual circuit. Having read the last five chapters of foundational material, you're ready to get more into the details of encapsulation.

When a host transmits data across a network to another device, the data goes through *encapsulation*: It's wrapped with protocol information at each layer of the OSI model. Each layer communicates only with its peer layer on the receiving device.

To communicate and exchange information, each layer uses *protocol data units (PDUs)*. These hold the control information attached to the data at each layer of the model. They're usually attached to the header in front of the data field but can also be in the trailer, or end, of it.

Each PDU attaches to the data by encapsulating it at each layer of the OSI model, and each has a specific name depending on the information provided in each header. This PDU information is read only by the peer layer on the receiving device. After it's read, it's stripped off, and the data is then handed to the next layer up.

Figure 6.21 shows the PDUs and how they attach control information to each layer. This figure demonstrates how the upper-layer user data is converted for transmission on the network.

FIGURE 6.21   Data encapsulation

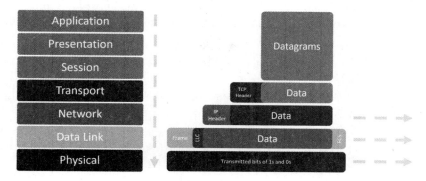

The data stream is then handed down to the Transport layer, which sets up a virtual circuit to the receiving device by sending over a sync packet. Next, the data stream is broken up into smaller pieces, and a Transport layer header (a PDU) is created and attached to the header of the data field; now the piece of data is called a *segment*. Each segment is sequenced so the data stream can be put back together on the receiving side exactly as it was transmitted.

Each segment is then handed to the Network layer for network addressing and routing through the internetwork. Logical addressing (for example, IP) is used to get each segment to the correct network. The Network layer protocol adds a control header to the segment handed down from the Transport layer, and what we have now is called a *packet* or *datagram*. Remember that the Transport and Network layers work together to rebuild a data stream on a receiving host, but it's not part of their work to place their PDUs on a local network segment—which is the only way to get the information to a router or host.

It's the Data Link layer that's responsible for taking packets from the Network layer and placing them on the network medium (cable or wireless). The Data Link layer encapsulates each packet in a *frame*, and the frame's header carries the hardware address of the source and destination hosts. If the destination device is on a remote network, then the frame is sent to a router to be routed through an internetwork. Once it gets to the destination network, a new frame is used to get the packet to the destination host.

To put this frame on the network, it must first be put into a digital signal. Because a frame is really a logical group of 1s and 0s, the Physical layer is responsible for encoding these digits into a digital signal, which is read by devices on the same local network. The receiving devices will synchronize on the digital signal and extract (decode) the 1s and 0s from the digital signal. At this point, the devices build the frames, run a cyclic redundancy check (CRC), and then check their answer against the answer in the frame's Frame Check Sequence (FCS) field. If it matches, the packet is pulled from the frame, and what's left of the frame is discarded. This process is called *de-encapsulation*. The packet is handed to the Network layer, where the address is checked. If the address matches, the segment is pulled from the packet, and what's left of the packet is discarded. The segment is processed at the Transport layer, which rebuilds the data stream and acknowledges to the transmitting station that it received each piece. It then happily hands the data stream to the upper-layer application.

In summary, at a transmitting device, the data-encapsulation method works like this:

1. User information is converted to data for transmission on the network.

2. Data is converted to segments, and a reliable connection is set up between the transmitting and receiving hosts.

3. Segments are converted to packets or datagrams, and a logical address is placed in the header so each packet can be routed through an internetwork.

4. Packets or datagrams are converted to frames for transmission on the local network. Hardware (Ethernet) addresses are used to uniquely identify hosts on a local network segment.

5. Frames are converted to bits, and a digital encoding and clocking scheme is used.

To explain this in more detail using the layer addressing, I'll use Figure 6.22.

FIGURE 6.22   PDU and layer addressing

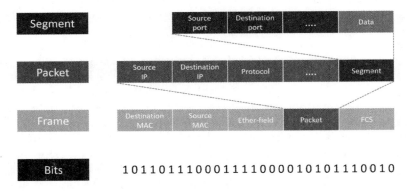

Remember that a data stream is handed down from the upper layer to the Transport layer. As technicians, we really don't care who the data stream comes from because that's a programmer's problem. Our job is to rebuild the data stream reliably and hand it to the upper layers on the receiving device.

Before we go further in our discussion of Figure 6.22, let's review port numbers and make sure you understand them. The Transport layer uses port numbers to define both the virtual circuit and the upper-layer process, as you can see from Figure 6.23.

The Transport layer takes the data stream, makes segments out of it, and establishes a reliable session by creating a virtual circuit. It then sequences (numbers) each segment and uses acknowledgments and flow control. If you're using TCP, the virtual circuit is defined by the source port number. Remember, the host just makes this up starting at port number 1024 (0 through 1023 are reserved for well-known port numbers). The destination port number defines the upper-layer process (application) that the data stream is handed to when the data stream is reliably rebuilt on the receiving host.

FIGURE 6.23   Port numbers at the Transport layer

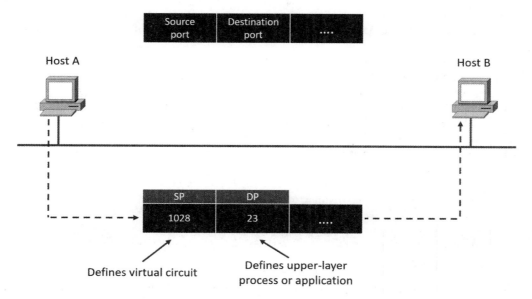

Now that you understand port numbers and how they're used at the Transport layer, let's go back to Figure 6.22. Once the Transport layer header information is added to the piece of data, it becomes a segment and is handed down to the Network layer along with the destination IP address. (The destination IP address was handed down from the upper layers to the Transport layer with the data stream, and it was discovered through a name resolution method at the upper layers—probably DNS.)

The Network layer adds a header, and adds the logical addressing (IP addresses), to the front of each segment. Once the header is added to the segment, the PDU is called a *packet*. The packet has a protocol field that describes where the segment came from (either UDP or TCP) so it can hand the segment to the correct protocol at the Transport layer when it reaches the receiving host.

The Network layer is responsible for finding the destination hardware address that dictates where the packet should be sent on the local network. It does this by using ARP. IP at the Network layer looks at the destination IP address and compares that address to its own source IP address and subnet mask. If it turns out to be a local network request, the hardware address of the local host is requested via an ARP request. Suppose the packet is destined for a remote host. In that case, IP will get the IP address of the default gateway from its configuration information and then ARP for the hardware address of the default gateway (router) instead.

The packet, along with the destination hardware address of either the local host or the default gateway, is then handed down to the Data Link layer. The Data Link layer will add a header to the front of the packet, and the piece of data then becomes a *frame*. (We call it a frame because both a header and a trailer are added to the packet, which makes the data resemble bookends or a frame, if you will.) This is shown in Figure 6.22. The frame uses an Ether-Type field to describe which protocol the packet came from at the Network layer. Now a CRC is run on the frame, and the answer to the CRC is placed in the FCS field found in the trailer of the frame.

The frame is now ready to be handed down, one bit at a time, to the Physical layer, which will use bit-timing rules to encode the data into a digital signal. Every device on the network segment will synchronize with the clock, extract the 1s and 0s from the digital signal, and build a frame. After the frame is rebuilt, a CRC is run to make sure the frame is okay. If everything turns out to be good, the hosts will check the destination address to see if the frame is for them.

If all this is making your eyes cross and your brain freeze, don't freak—things will become much clearer as we go through the book—really! Soon, I'll be going over exactly how data is encapsulated and routed through an internetwork in even more detail, in an easy-to-understand, step-by-step manner, in Chapter 9, "Introduction to IP Routing."

EXERCISE 6.1

Examining Port Numbers

In this exercise you will examine the port numbers in use on your computer.

1. Open the command prompt by clicking Start; then type **cmd**, right-click, and select Run As Administrator.

2. In the command prompt, type **netstat –nab** and press Enter.

3. Examine the various connections for each of the applications.

You will notice in the output of the command that the switches group the connections for each application. The source and destination IP address and the source and destination ports are in the output. All of the established connections are virtual circuits the operating system has currently open.

Summary

Protocols, protocols everywhere—so many different reasons for them, and so many jobs they do for us! And sometimes they even work in conjunction with each other. This can seem like way too much information, but no worries—as you become familiar with the various layers and their functions, I promise it will soon become clear that this hierarchical structure is a seriously tight, robust networking foundation.

Similarly, as you understand the TCP/IP big picture, the reason why all those protocols exist and are necessary will also become much easier to understand. They're really like a team that works jointly, from layer to layer, to make our TCP/IP networks the wonderful, great tools they are.

Exam Essentials

Remember the Process/Application layer protocols. Telnet is a terminal-emulation program that allows you to log into a remote host and run programs. File Transfer Protocol (FTP) is a connection-oriented service that allows you to transfer files. Trivial FTP (TFTP) is a connectionless file transfer program. Review the other various applications discussed in this chapter.

Understand data encapsulation and decapsulation within the OSI model context. This includes Ethernet header, the Internet Protocol (IP) header, Transmission Control Protocol (TCP)/User Datagram Protocol (UDP) headers, TCP flags, Payload, and Maximum transmission unit (MTU).

Be able to explain common ports and protocols, their application, and encrypted alternatives. Know all the protocols and ports listed in the CompTIA N+ objectives for FTP, SSH, SFTP, and many more.

Be able to identify and define protocol types. This includes Internet Control Message Protocol (ICMP), TCP, UDP, Generic Routing Encapsulation (GRE), Internet Protocol Security (IPSec), Authentication Header (AH)/Encapsulating Security Payload (ESP), and Internet Key Exchange (IKE).

Remember the Host-to-Host layer protocols. Transmission Control Protocol (TCP) is a connection-oriented protocol that provides reliable network service by using acknowledgments and flow control. User Datagram Protocol (UDP) is a connectionless protocol that provides low overhead and is considered unreliable.

Remember the Internet layer protocols. Internet Protocol (IP) is a connectionless protocol that provides logical network addressing and routing through the internetwork. Address Resolution Protocol (ARP) finds a hardware address from a known IP address. Internet Control Message Protocol (ICMP) provides diagnostics and Destination Unreachable messages.

Written Lab

You can find the answers to the written labs in Appendix A. Fill in accompanying Transport layer protocol and the port number.

Service protocol	Transport protocol	Port number
SFTP		
Telnet		
SMTP		
NTP		
LDAP		
TFTP		
RDP		
Syslog		
SMB		
IMAP		
HTTP		
HTTPS		
LDAPS		
SMTPS		
SSH		
SQL		

Review Questions

You can find the answers to the review questions in Appendix B.

1. Which is a correct statement about the Transmission Control Protocol (TCP)?
   A. TCP is a connectionless protocol.
   B. TCP allows for error correction.
   C. TCP is faster than UDP.
   D. TCP allows for retransmission of lost segments.

2. How does TCP guarantee delivery of segments to the receiver?
   A. Via the destination port
   B. TCP checksums
   C. Window size
   D. Sequence and acknowledgment numbers

3. When a programmer decides to use UDP as a transport protocol, what is a decision factor?
   A. Redundancy of acknowledgment is not needed.
   B. Guaranteed delivery of segments is required.
   C. Windowing flow control is required.
   D. A virtual circuit is required.

4. Which mechanism allows for the Transport layer to communicate with the Session layer?
   A. Headers
   B. Port numbers
   C. MAC address
   D. Checksums

5. Why does DNS use UDP for queries?
   A. DNS requires acknowledgment of the request for auditing.
   B. The requests require flow control of UDP.
   C. DNS requests are usually small and do not require connections setup.
   D. DNS requires a temporary virtual circuit.

6. Which protocol requires the programmer to deal with lost segments?
   A. SSL
   B. TCP
   C. UDP
   D. NMS

7. Which protocol can encapsulate many different protocols inside an IP tunnel?

  A. GRE

  B. RARP

  C. ARP

  D. ICMP

8. Which protocol provides confidentiality?

  A. AH

  B. ESP

  C. GRE

  D. PDU

9. Which protocol is used for configuration access to network appliances but is *not* encrypted?

  A. SSH

  B. HTTPS

  C. Telnet

  D. RDP

10. Which protocol is used by applications that need low overhead at the Transport layer?

  A. TCP

  B. IP

  C. ARP

  D. UDP

11. Which layer in the DoD model is directly related to the Transport layer of the OSI model?

  A. Process/Application layer

  B. Host-to-Host layer

  C. Internet layer

  D. Network Access layer

12. Which element is used with TCP to provide a virtual circuit?

  A. Sequence numbers

  B. Acknowledgment numbers

  C. Protocol numbers

  D. Port numbers

13. Which protocol uses UDP/123?

  A. TFTP

  B. NTP

  C. HTTPS

  D. DNS

14. Which DoD layer allows for the logical addressing of hosts?

   A. Process/Application layer

   B. Host-to-Host layer

   C. Internet layer

   D. Network Access layer

15. What is the process called when data moves up the OSI model?

   A. Encapsulation

   B. Decapsulation

   C. FCS

   D. PDU

16. Which protocol provides an IP address from a physical address?

   A. ICMP

   B. TCP

   C. ARP

   D. RARP

17. What protocol from the Internet Protocol (IP) stack is used for diagnostics and error messages?

   A. TCP

   B. ICMP

   C. ARP

   D. UDP

18. Which IP service uses the UDP protocol?

   A. DHCP

   B. SMTP

   C. FTP

   D. HTTP

19. You need to make sure that the time is consistent across all your network devices. What protocol do you need to run on your network?

   A. FTP

   B. SFTP

   C. NTP

   D. SSH

20. Which of the following allows a server to distinguish among different simultaneous requests from the same host?

   A. They use different port numbers.

   B. The IP address that the request originates from.

   C. A server is unable to accept multiple simultaneous sessions from the same host. One session must end before another can begin.

   D. Each request uses a different sequence and acknowledgment number.

Chapter

7

IP Addressing

THE FOLLOWING COMPTIA NETWORK+ EXAM OBJECTIVES ARE COVERED IN THIS CHAPTER:

✓ **Domain 1.0 Networking Concepts**

✓ **1.7 Given a scenario, use appropriate IPv4 network addressing.**

- Public vs. private
  - Automatic Private IP Addressing (APIPA)
  - RFC1918
  - Loopback/localhost
- Subnetting
  - Variable Length Subnet Mask (VLSM)
  - Classless Inter-domain Routing (CIDR)
- IPv4 address classes
  - Class A
  - Class B
  - Class C
  - Class D
  - Class E

✓ **1.8 Summarize evolving use cases for modern network environments.**

- IPv6 addressing
  - Mitigating address exhaustion
  - Compatibility requirements
    - Tunneling
    - Dual stack
    - NAT64

✓ **Domain 3.0 Network Operations**

✓ **3.4 Given a scenario, implement IPv4 and IPv6 network services.**

  ▪ Stateless address autoconfiguration (SLAAC)

One of the most important topics in any discussion of TCP/IP is IP addressing. An IP address is a numeric identifier assigned to each machine on an IP network. It designates the specific location of a device on the network.

An IP address is a logical address, not a hardware address—the latter is hard-coded on a network interface card (NIC) and used for finding hosts on a local network. IP addressing was designed to allow hosts on one network to communicate with a host on a different network regardless of the type of LANs the hosts are participating in.

Before we get into the more complicated aspects of IP addressing, you need to understand some of the basics. First I'm going to explain some of the fundamentals of IP addressing and its terminology. Then you'll learn about the hierarchical IP addressing scheme and private IP addresses.

I'll define unicast, multicast, and broadcast addresses and then finish the chapter with a discussion on IPv6. And I promise to make it all as painless as possible.

The reason that we would even discuss IPv6 (besides to cover the Network+ exam objectives, of course) is the lack of IPv4 addresses available for use in future networks, which we need to keep our corporate and private networks and even the Internet running. Basically, we're running out of IP addresses for all our new hosts! IPv6 will fix this for us.

To find Todd Lammle CompTIA videos and practice questions, please see www.lammle.com.

IP Terminology

Throughout this chapter, you'll learn several important terms vital to your understanding of the Internet Protocol. Here are a few to get you started:

Bit   A *bit* is one binary digit, either a 1 or a 0.

Byte   A *byte* is 7 or 8 bits, depending on whether parity is used. For the rest of this chapter, always assume a byte is 8 bits.

Octet   An octet, made up of 8 bits, is just an ordinary 8-bit binary number. In this chapter, the terms *byte* and *octet* are completely interchangeable, and they are typically displayed in decimal up to 255.

Network Address   This is the designation used in routing to send packets to a remote network—for example, 10.0.0.0, 172.16.0.0, and 192.168.10.0.

IP Address   A logical address used to define a single host; however, IP addresses can be used to reference many or all hosts as well. If you see something written as just IP, it is referring to IPv4. IPv6 will always be written as IPv6.

Broadcast Address   The *broadcast address* is used by applications and hosts to send information to all hosts on a network. Examples include 255.255.255.255, which designates all networks and all hosts; 172.16.255.255, which specifies all subnets and hosts on network 172.16.0.0; and 10.255.255.255, which broadcasts to all subnets and hosts on network 10.0.0.0.

The Hierarchical IP Addressing Scheme

An IP address consists of 32 bits of information. These bits are divided into four sections, referred to as octets or bytes, and four octets sum up to 32 bits (8 × 4 = 32). You can depict an IP address using one of three methods:

- Dotted-decimal, as in 172.16.30.56

- Binary, as in 10101100.00010000.00011110.00111000

- Hexadecimal, as in AC.10.1E.38

Each of these examples validly represents the same IP address. Hexadecimal is used with IPv6, and IP addressing uses dotted-decimal or binary, but you still might find an IP address stored in hexadecimal in some programs. Windows is a good example of a program that stores a machine's IP address in hex. Windows 11 (and all other Windows versions) stores the IP addresses in hexadecimal subkeys in HKEY_LOCAL_MACHINE\SYSTEM\CurrentControlSet\ Services\ Tcpip\Parameters\Interfaces.

The 32-bit IP address is known as a structured, or hierarchical, address as opposed to a flat, or nonhierarchical, address. Although either type of addressing scheme can be used, *hierarchical addressing* has been chosen for a very important reason. The major advantage of this scheme is that it can handle a large number of addresses, namely, 4.3 billion (a 32-bit address space with two possible values for each position—either 0 or 1—gives you 2^{32}, or 4,294,967,296). The disadvantage of the flat-addressing scheme, and the reason it's not used for IP addressing, relates to routing. If every address were unique, all routers on the Internet would need to store the address of each and every machine on the Internet. This would make efficient routing impossible, even if only a fraction of all possible addresses were used.

The solution to this problem is to use a two- or three-level hierarchical addressing scheme that is structured by network and host or by network, subnet, and host.

This two- or three-level scheme is comparable to a telephone number. The first section, the area code, designates a very large area. The second section, the prefix, narrows the scope to a local calling area. The final segment, the customer number, zooms in on the specific connection. IP addresses use the same type of layered structure. Rather than all 32 bits being treated as a unique identifier, as in flat addressing, a part of the address is designated as the network address and the other part is designated as either the subnet and host or just the host address.

Next, I'm going to cover IP network addressing and the different classes of addresses used for our networks.

Network Addressing

The *network address*—also called the network number—uniquely identifies each network. Every machine on the same network shares that network address as part of its IP address. In the IP address 172.16.30.56, for example, 172.16 is the network address (and in just a minute I'll show you how this is true).

The *host address* is assigned to, and uniquely identifies, each machine on a network. This part of the address must be unique because it identifies a particular machine—an individual—as opposed to a network, which is a group. So in the sample IP address 172.16.30.56, the 30.56 is the host address.

The designers of the Internet decided to create classes of networks based on network size. For the small number of networks possessing a very large number of hosts, they created the rank *Class A network*. At the other extreme is the *Class C network*, which is reserved for the numerous networks with a small number of hosts. The class distinction for networks between very large and very small is predictably the *Class B network*.

Subdividing an IP address into a network and host address is determined by the class designation of your network. Figure 7.1 summarizes the classes of networks—a subject I'll explain in much greater detail throughout this chapter.

FIGURE 7.1   Summary of the three classes of networks

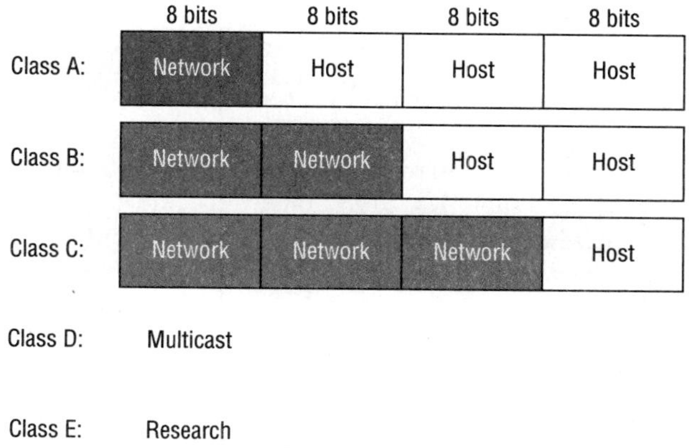

	8 bits	8 bits	8 bits	8 bits
Class A:	Network	Host	Host	Host
Class B:	Network	Network	Host	Host
Class C:	Network	Network	Network	Host
Class D:	Multicast			
Class E:	Research			

To ensure efficient routing, Internet designers defined a mandate for the leading-bits section of the address for each different network class. For example, since a router knows that a Class A network address always starts with a 0, the router might be able to speed a packet on its way after reading only the first bit of its address. This is where the address schemes define the difference between a Class A, a Class B, and a Class C address. Coming up, I'll discuss the differences between these three classes followed by a discussion of the Class D and Class E addresses. For now, know that Classes A, B, and C are the only ranges that are used to address hosts in our networks.

Class A Addresses

In a Class A network address, the first byte is assigned to the network address, and the three remaining bytes are used for the host addresses. The Class A format is as follows:

`network.host.host.host`

For example, in the IP address 49.22.102.70, the 49 is the network address and 22.102.70 is the host address. Every machine on this particular network would begin with the distinctive network address of 49.

Class A network addresses are 1 byte long, with the first bit of that byte reserved and the 7 remaining bits available for manipulation or addressing. As a result, the theoretical maximum number of Class A networks that can be created is 128. Why? Well, each of the 7-bit positions can be either a 0 or a 1 and 2^7 gives you 128.

The designers of the IP address scheme said that the first bit of the first byte in a Class A network address must always be off, or 0. This means a Class A address must be between 0 and 127 in the first byte, inclusive.

Consider the following network address:

`0xxxxxxx`

If we turn the other 7 bits all off and then turn them all on, we'll find the Class A range of network addresses:

```
00000000 = 0
01111111 = 127
```

So, a Class A network is defined in the first octet between 0 and 127, and it can't be less or more.

To complicate matters further, the network address of all 0s (0000 0000) is reserved to designate the default route (see Table 7.1). Additionally, the address 127, which is reserved for diagnostics, can't be used either, which means you can really only use the numbers 1 to 126 to designate Class A network addresses. This means the actual number of usable Class A network addresses is 128 minus 2, or 126.

Each Class A address has 3 bytes (24 bit positions) for the host address of a machine. This means there are 2^{24}—or 16,777,216—unique combinations and, therefore, precisely that many potential unique host addresses for each Class A network. Because host addresses with the two patterns of all 0s and all 1s are reserved, the actual maximum usable number of hosts for a Class A network is 2^{24} minus 2, which equals 16,777,214. Either way, you can see that's a seriously huge number of hosts to have on a network segment!

TABLE 7.1   Reserved IP addresses

Address	Function
Network address of all 0s	Interpreted to mean "this network or segment."
Network address of all 1s	Interpreted to mean "all networks."
Network 127.0.0.1	Reserved for loopback tests. Designates the local host and allows that host to send a test packet to itself without generating network traffic.
Host address of all 0s	Interpreted to mean "network address" or any host on specified network.
Host address of all 1s	Interpreted to mean "all hosts" on the specified network; for example, 126.255.255.255 means "all hosts" on network 126 (Class A address).
Entire IP address set to all 0s	Used by Cisco routers to designate the default route. Could also mean "any network."
Entire IP address set to all 1s (same as 255.255.255.255)	Broadcast to all hosts on the current network; sometimes called an "all 1s broadcast" or limited broadcast.

Here's an example of how to figure out the valid host IDs in a Class A network address:

- All host bits off is the network address: 10.0.0.0.
- All host bits on is the broadcast address: 10.255.255.255.

The valid hosts are the numbers in between the network address and the broadcast address: 10.0.0.1 through 10.255.255.254. Notice that 0s and 255s can be valid host IDs. All you need to remember when trying to find valid host addresses is that the host bits can't ever be all turned off or all turned on at the same time.

Class B Addresses

In a Class B network address, the first 2 bytes are assigned to the network address, and the remaining 2 bytes are used for host addresses. The format is as follows:

network.network.host.host

For example, in the IP address 172.16.30.56, the network address is 172.16, and the host address is 30.56.

With a network address being 2 bytes (8 bits each), we're left with 2^{16} unique combinations. But the Internet designers decided that all Class B network addresses should start with the binary digit 1, then 0. This leaves 14 bit positions available to manipulate, so in reality, we get 16,384 (that is, 2^{14}) unique Class B network addresses.

In a Class B network, the request or comments (RFCs) state that the first bit of the first byte must always be turned on, but the second bit must always be turned off. If we turn the other 6 bits all off and then all on, we will find the range for a Class B network:

```
10000000 = 128
10111111 = 191
```

As you can see, a Class B network is defined when the first byte is configured from 128 to 191.

A Class B address uses 2 bytes for host addresses. This is 2^{16} minus the two reserved patterns (all 0s and all 1s), for a total of 65,534 possible host addresses for each Class B network.

Here's an example of how to find the valid hosts in a Class B network:

- **All host bits turned off is the network address:** 172.16.0.0.

- **All host bits turned on is the broadcast address:** 172.16.255.255.

The valid hosts would be the numbers in between the network address and the broadcast address: 172.16.0.1 through 172.16.255.254.

Class C Addresses

The first 3 bytes of a Class C network address are dedicated to the network portion of the address, with only 1 measly byte remaining for the host address. Here's the format:

network.network.network.host

Using the example IP address 192.168.100.102, the network address is 192.168.100, and the host address is 102.

In a Class C network address, the first 3 bit positions are always the binary 110. The calculation is as follows: 3 bytes, or 24 bits, minus 3 reserved positions leaves 21 positions. Hence, there are 2^{21}, or 2,097,152, possible Class C networks.

For Class C networks, the RFCs define the first 2 bits of the first octet as always turned on, but the third bit can never be on. Following the same process as the previous classes, convert from binary to decimal to find the range. Here's the range for a Class C network:

```
11000000 = 192
11011111 = 223
```

So, if you see an IP address with a range from 192 up to 223, you'll know it's a Class C IP address.

Each unique Class C network has 1 byte to use for host addresses. This gets us to 2^8, or 256, minus the two reserved patterns of all 0s and all 1s for a total of 254 available host addresses for each Class C network.

Here's an example of how to find a valid host ID in a Class C network:

- **All host bits turned off is the network ID:** 192.168.100.0.

- **All host bits turned on is the broadcast address:** 192.168.100.255.

The valid hosts would be the numbers in between the network address and the broadcast address: 192.168.100.1 through 192.168.100.254.

Class D and E Addresses

Addresses with the first octet of 224 to 255 are reserved for Class D and E networks. Class D (224–239) is used for multicast addresses and Class E (240–255) for scientific purposes. You do need to remember that the multicast range is from 224.0.0.0 through 239.255.255.255. Multicasts will be covered later in this chapter.

Special Purposes of Network Addresses

Some IP addresses are reserved for special purposes, so network administrators can't ever assign them to hosts. Table 7.1 listed the members of this exclusive little club and the reasons they're included in it.

Private IP Addresses (RFC 1918)

The people who created the IP addressing scheme also created what we call *private IP addresses*. These addresses can be used on a private network, but they're not routable through the Internet. This is designed for the purpose of creating a measure of much-needed security, but it also conveniently saves valuable IP address space.

If every host on every network had to have real routable IP addresses, we would have run out of available IP addresses to hand out years ago. But by using private IP addresses, ISPs, corporations, and home users need only a relatively tiny group of bona fide IP addresses to connect their networks to the Internet. This is economical because they can use private IP addresses on their inside networks and get along just fine.

To accomplish this task, the ISP and the corporation—the end users, no matter who they are—need to use something called network address translation (NAT), which basically takes a private IP address and converts it for use on the Internet. NAT provides security in that these IP addresses cannot be seen by external users. External users will only be able to see the public IP address to which the private IP address has been mapped. Moreover, multiple devices in the same private network can use the same, real IP address to transmit out onto the Internet. Doing things this way saves megatons of address space—a very good thing for us all!

Table 7.2 lists the RFC 1918 reserved private addresses.

TABLE 7.2   Reserved RFC 1918 IP address space

Address Class	Reserved Address Space
Class A	10.0.0.0 through 10.255.255.255 (prefix /8)
Class B	172.16.0.0 through 172.31.255.255 (prefix /12)
Class C	192.168.0.0 through 192.168.255.255 (prefix /16)

🌐 Real World Scenario

So, What Private IP Address Should I Use?

That's a really great question: Should you use Class A, Class B, or even Class C private addressing when setting up your network? Let's take Acme Corporation in San Francisco as an example. This company is moving into a new building and needs a whole new network (what a treat this is!). It has 14 departments, with about 70 users in each. You could probably squeeze three or four Class C addresses to use, or maybe you could use a Class B, or even a Class A just for fun.

The rule of thumb in the consulting world is, when you're setting up a corporate network—regardless of how small it is—you should use a Class A network address because it gives you the most flexibility and growth options. For example, if you used the 10.0.0.0 network address with a /24 mask, then you'd have 65,536 networks, each with 254 hosts. Lots of room for growth with this network design! You would then subnet this network address space using Classless Inter-Domain Routing (CIDR, also referred to as variable-length sub-net mask, or VLSM), which provides only the needed number of hosts to each department or building without wasting IP addresses. (A /24 tells you that a subnet mask has 24 bits out of 32 bits turned on for subnetting a network. This will be covered, as well as CIDR, in more detail in Chapter 8, "IP Subnetting, Troubleshooting IP, and Introduction to NAT.")

But if you're setting up a home network, you'd opt for a Class C address because it is the easiest for people to understand and configure. Using the default Class C mask gives you one network with 254 hosts—plenty for a home network.

With the Acme Corporation, a nice 10.1.*x*.0 with a /24 mask (the *x* is the subnet for each department) makes this easy to design, install, and troubleshoot.

Virtual IP (VIP)

When a public IP address is substituted for the actual private IP address that has been assigned to the network interface of the device, the public IP address becomes an example of what is called a *virtual IP address*. This means it doesn't correspond to an actual physical network interface. A well-used example is a subinterface configured on a physical router interface, which allows you to create multiple IPs or subnets on one interface.

There are other examples of such virtual IP addresses. For example, when a web proxy server substitutes its IP address for the sender's IP address before sending a packet to the Internet, it is another example of creating a virtual IP address.

APIPA

I discussed this in Chapter 6, "Introduction to the Internet Protocol," but it is worth repeating here. What happens if you have a few hosts connected together with a switch or hub and you don't have a DHCP server? You can add static IP information to a host, or you can use what is called Automatic Private IP Addressing (APIPA). I don't recommend this, but APIPA is a "feature," so you do need to remember it, which is why I'm mentioning it two chapters in a row!

With APIPA, clients can automatically self-configure an IP address and subnet mask, which is the minimum information needed for hosts to communicate when a DHCP server isn't available. In this way, it could be thought of as a DHCP failover scheme. If all of the hosts set themselves with an APIPA address, they could communicate with one another but unfortunately not with any addresses that were statically configured, such as default gateways!

The IP address range for APIPA is 169.254.0.1 through 169.254.255.254. The client also configures itself with a default Class B subnet mask of 255.255.0.0.

However, when you're in your corporate network and you're running a DHCP server, and your host displays that it is using this IP address range, this means that either your DHCP client on the host is not working, or the DHCP server is down or can't be reached because of a network issue. For example, if you plug a DHCP client into a port that is disabled, the host will receive an APIPA address. I don't know anyone who has seen a host in the APIPA address range and been happy about it! If users cannot connect to the Internet and their IP addresses fall into the APIPA address range, the DHCP server is most likely the problem.

IPv4 Address Types

Most people use *broadcast* as a generic term, and most of the time, we understand what they mean. But not always. For example, you might say, "The host broadcasted through a router to a DHCP server," but, well, it's pretty unlikely that this would ever really happen. What you probably mean—using the correct technical jargon—is, "The DHCP client broadcasted for an IP address; a router then forwarded this as a unicast packet to the DHCP server." Oh, and remember that with IPv4, broadcasts are pretty important, but with IPv6, there aren't any broadcasts sent at all—as you'll see in a bit!

Okay, I've referred to broadcast addresses throughout earlier chapters, and even showed you some examples of various IP addresses. But I really haven't gone into the different terms and uses associated with them yet, and it's about time I did. So here are the four IPv4 address types that I'd like to define for you:

Layer 2 Broadcasts   These are sent to all nodes on a LAN.

Broadcasts (Layer 3)   These are sent to all nodes on the network.

Unicast   This is an address for a single interface, and these are used to send packets to a single destination host.

Multicast   These are packets sent from a single source and transmitted to many devices on different networks. Referred to as *one-to-many*.

Layer 2 Broadcasts

First, understand that layer 2 broadcasts are also known as hardware broadcasts—they only go out on a LAN, and they don't go past the LAN boundary (router).

The typical hardware address is 6 bytes (48 bits) and looks something like 0c.43.a4.f3.12.c2. The broadcast would be all 1s in binary, which would be all *F*s in hexadecimal, as in FF.FF .FF.FF.FF.FF.

Layer 3 Broadcasts

Then there are the plain old broadcast addresses at layer 3. Broadcast messages are meant to reach all hosts on a broadcast domain. These are the network broadcasts that have all host bits on.

Here's an example that you're already familiar with: The network address of 172.16.0.0 would have a broadcast address of 172.16.255.255—all host bits on. Broadcasts can also be "any network and all hosts," as indicated by 255.255.255.255.

A good example of a broadcast message is an Address Resolution Protocol (ARP) request. When a host has a packet, it knows the logical address (IP) of the destination. To get the packet to the destination, the host needs to forward the packet to a default gateway if the destination resides on a different IP network. If the destination is on the local network, the source will forward the packet directly to the destination. Because the source doesn't have the MAC address to which it needs to forward the frame, it sends out a broadcast, something that every device in the local broadcast domain will listen to. This broadcast says, in essence, "If you are the owner of IP address 192.168.2.3, please forward your MAC address to me," with the source giving the appropriate information.

Unicast Address

A unicast address is assigned to a single interface, and this term is used in both IPv4 and IPv6 to describe your host interface IP address.

Multicast Address (Class D)

Multicast is a different beast entirely. At first glance, it appears to be a hybrid of unicast and broadcast communication, but that isn't quite the case. Multicast does allow point-to-multipoint communication, which is similar to broadcasts, but it happens in a different manner. The crux of *multicast* is that it enables multiple recipients to receive messages without flooding the messages to all hosts on a broadcast domain. However, this is not the default behavior—it's what we can do with multicasting if it's configured correctly!

Multicast works by sending messages or data to IP multicast group addresses. Routers then forward copies (unlike broadcasts, which are not forwarded) of the packet out every interface that has hosts subscribed to a particular group address. This is where multicast differs from broadcast messages—with multicast communication, copies of packets, in theory, are sent only to subscribed hosts. When I say in theory, this means the hosts will receive, for example, a multicast packet destined for 224.0.0.10 (this is an EIGRP packet, and only a router running the EIGRP protocol will read it). All hosts on the broadcast LAN (Ethernet is a broadcast multi-access LAN technology) will pick up the frame, read the destination address, and immediately discard the frame, unless they are in the multicast group. This saves PC processing, not LAN bandwidth. Multicasting can cause severe LAN congestion, in some instances, if not implemented carefully.

There are several different groups that users or applications can subscribe to. The range of multicast addresses starts with 224.0.0.0 and goes through 239.255.255.255. As you can see, this range of addresses falls within IP Class D address space based on classful IP assignment.

Internet Protocol Version 6 (IPv6)

People refer to IPv6 as "the next-generation Internet protocol," and it was originally created as the answer to IPv4's inevitable, looming address-exhaustion crisis. Though you've probably heard a thing or two about IPv6 already, it has been improved even further in the quest to bring us the flexibility, efficiency, capability, and optimized functionality that can truly meet our ever-increasing needs. The capacity of its predecessor, IPv4, pales in comparison—and that's the reason it will eventually fade into history completely.

The IPv6 header and address structure has been completely overhauled, and many of the features that were basically just afterthoughts and addendums in IPv4 are now included as full-blown standards in IPv6. It's well-equipped, poised, and ready to manage the mind-blowing demands of the Internet to come.

Why Do We Need IPv6?

Well, the short answer is because we need to communicate and our current system isn't really cutting it anymore—kind of like how the Pony Express couldn't compete with airmail. Just look at how much time and effort we've invested in coming up with slick new ways to conserve bandwidth and IP addresses.

It's reality is that the number of people and devices that connect to networks increases each and every day. That's not a bad thing at all—we're finding new and exciting ways to communicate with more people all the time, something that's become integral to our culture today. In fact, it's now pretty much a basic human need. But the forecast isn't exactly blue skies and sunshine because, as I alluded to in this chapter's introduction, IPv4, upon which our ability to communicate is presently dependent, is going to run out of addresses for us to use. IPv4 has only about 4.3 billion addresses available—in theory—and we know that we don't even get to use all of those. There really are only about 250 million addresses that can be assigned to devices. Sure, the use of Classless Inter-Domain Routing (CIDR, also referred to as variable-length subnet mask, or VLSM) and NAT/PAT has helped to delay the inevitable dearth of addresses, but the truth is we will run out of them, and it's going to happen within a few years. China is barely online, and we know a huge population of people and corporations there surely want to be. There are a lot of reports that give us all kinds of numbers, but all you really need to think about to convince yourself that I'm not just being an alarmist is the fact that there are about 7.8 billion people in the world today, and it's estimated that just over 59 percent of that population is connected to the Internet—wow! IPv6 to the rescue!

That statistic is basically screaming at us the ugly truth that, based on IPv4's capacity, every person can't have a single computer with an IP address—let alone all the other devices we use with them. I have more than one computer, and it's pretty likely you do, too. And I'm not even including in the mix phones, laptops, game consoles, fax machines, routers, switches, and a mother lode of other devices we use every day! So I think I've made it pretty clear that we've got to do something before we run out of addresses and lose the ability to connect with each other as we know it. And that "something" just happens to be implementing IPv6.

- Refrigerator

- Smart speakers

- Smart thermostats

- Smart doorbells

- Industrial control systems/supervisory control and data acquisition (SCADA)

The Benefits of and Uses for IPv6

What's so fabulous about IPv6? Is it really the answer to our coming dilemma? Is it really worth it to upgrade from IPv4? All good questions—you may even think of a few more. Of course, there's going to be that group of people with the time-tested and well-known "resistance-to-change syndrome," but don't listen to them. If we had done that years ago, we'd still be waiting weeks, even months, for our mail to arrive via horseback. Instead, just know that the answer is a resounding YES! Not only does IPv6 give us lots of addresses (3.4×10^{38} = definitely enough), but there are many other features built into this version that make it well worth the cost, time, and effort required to migrate to it.

Today's networks, as well as the Internet, have a ton of unforeseen requirements that simply were not considerations when IPv4 was created. We've tried to compensate with a collection of add-ons that can actually make implementing them more difficult than mandating them by a standard. By default, IPv6 has improved upon and included many of those features as standard and mandatory. One of these sweet new standards is IPSec—a feature that provides end-to-end security. Another little beauty is known as *mobility*, and as its name suggests, it allows a device to roam from one network to another without dropping connections.

But it's the efficiency features that are really going to rock the house! For starters, the header in an IPv6 packet has half the fields, and they are aligned to 64 bits, which gives us some seriously souped-up processing speed—compared to IPv4, lookups happen at light speed. Most of the information that used to be bound into the IPv4 header was taken out, and now you can choose to put it, or parts of it, back into the header in the form of optional extension headers that follow the basic header fields.

And of course there's that whole new universe of addresses (3.4×10^{38}) we talked about already. But where did we get them? Did that *Criss Angel Mindfreak* dude just show up and, blammo, they all materialized? The obvious answer is no, but that huge proliferation of addresses had to come from somewhere, right? Well, it just so happens that IPv6 gives us a substantially larger address space, meaning the address is a whole lot bigger—four times bigger, as a matter of fact! An IPv6 address is actually 128 bits in length, and no worries—I'm going to break down the address piece by piece and show you exactly what it looks like coming up in the next section, "IPv6 Addressing and Expressions." For now, let me just say that all that additional room permits more levels of hierarchy inside the address space and a more flexible address architecture. It also makes routing much more efficient and scalable because the addresses can be aggregated a lot more effectively. And IPv6 also allows multiple addresses for hosts and networks. Plus, the new version of IP now includes an expanded use of multicast communication (one device sending to many hosts or to a select group), which will also join in to boost efficiency on networks because communications will be more specific.

IPv4 uses broadcasts very prolifically, causing a bunch of problems, the worst of which is of course the dreaded broadcast storm—an uncontrolled deluge of forwarded broadcast traffic that can bring an entire network to its knees and devour every last bit of bandwidth. Another nasty thing about broadcast traffic is that it interrupts each and every device on the network. When a broadcast is sent out, every machine has to stop what it's doing and analyze the traffic, whether the broadcast is meant for it or not.

But smile, everyone: There is no such thing as a broadcast in IPv6 because it uses multicast traffic instead. And there are two other types of communication as well: unicast, which is the same as it is in IPv4, and a new type called *anycast*. Anycast communication allows the same address to be placed on more than one device so that when traffic is sent to one device addressed in this way, it is routed to the nearest host that shares the same address. This is just the beginning—we'll get more into the various types of communication later in this chapter in the section "Address Types."

IPv6 Addressing and Expressions

Just as understanding how IP addresses are structured and used is critical with IPv4 addressing, it's also vital when it comes to IPv6. You've already read about the fact that at 128 bits, an IPv6 address is much larger than a 32-bit IPv4 address. Because of this, as well as because of the new ways the addresses can be used, you've probably guessed that IPv6 will be more complicated to manage. But no worries! As I said, I'll break it down into the basics and show you what the address looks like, how you can write it, and what many of its common uses are. It's going to be a little weird at first, but before you know it, you'll have it nailed.

So let's take a look at Figure 7.2, which has a sample IPv6 address broken down into sections.

As you can now see, the address is truly much larger—but what else is different? Well, first, notice that it has eight groups of numbers instead of four and also that those groups are separated by colons instead of periods. And hey, wait a second . . . there are letters in that address! Yep, the address is expressed in hexadecimal just like a MAC address is, so you could say this address has eight 16-bit hexadecimal colon-delimited blocks. That's already quite a mouthful, and you probably haven't even tried to say the address out loud yet.

FIGURE 7.2   IPv6 address example

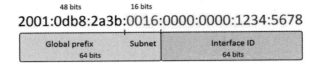

One other thing I want to point out is for when you set up your test network to play with IPv6, because I know you're going to want to do that. When you use a web browser to make an HTTPS connection to an IPv6 device, you have to type the address into the browser with brackets around the literal address. Why? Well, a colon is already being used by the browser for specifying a port number. So basically, if you don't enclose the address in brackets, the browser will have no way to identify the information.

Here's an example of how this looks:

```
https://[2001:0db8:3c4d:0012:0000:0000:1234:56ab]/default.html
```

Now obviously, if you could, you would rather use names to specify a destination (like www.lammle.com); but even though it's definitely going to be a pain in the rear, you just have to accept the fact that sometimes you have to bite the bullet and type in the address number. It should be pretty clear that DNS is extremely important when implementing IPv6.

Shortened Expression

The good news is, there are a few tricks to help rescue you when you're writing these monster addresses. For one thing, you can actually leave out parts of the address to abbreviate it, but to get away with doing that you have to follow a couple of rules. First, you can drop any leading zeros in each of the individual blocks. After you do that, the sample address from earlier would then look like this:

```
2001:db8:3c4d:12:0:0:1234:56ab
```

That's a definite improvement—at least you don't have to write all of those extra zeros! But what about whole blocks that don't have anything in them except zeros? Well, you can kind of lose those, too—at least some of them. Again referring to our sample address, you can remove the two blocks of zeros by replacing them with double colons, like this:

```
2001:db8:3c4d:12::1234:56ab
```

Cool—you replaced the blocks of all zeros with double colons. The rule you have to follow to get away with this is that you can replace only one contiguous block of zeros in an address. So if my address has four blocks of zeros and each of them is separated, I don't get to replace them all. Check out this example:

```
2001:0000:0000:0012:0000:0000:1234:56ab
```

And just know that you *can't* use double colons twice, like this:

`2001::12::1234:56ab`

Instead, this is the best that you can do:

`2001::12:0:0:1234:56ab`

The reason why this example is your best shot is that if you remove two sets of zeros, the device looking at the address will have no way of knowing where the zeros go back in. Basically, the router would look at the incorrect address and say, "Well, do I place two blocks into the first set of double colons and two into the second set, or do I place three blocks into the first set and one block into the second set?" And on and on it would go because the information the router needs just isn't there.

Address Types

We're all familiar with IPv4's unicast, broadcast, and multicast addresses, which basically define who or at least how many other devices we're talking to. But as I mentioned, IPv6 introduces the anycast address type. Broadcasts, as we know them, have been eliminated in IPv6 because of their cumbersome inefficiency.

Since a single interface can have multiple types of IPv6 addresses assigned for various purposes, let's find out what each of these types of IPv6 addresses are and the communication methods of each:

Unicast   Packets addressed to a unicast address are delivered to a single interface, same as in IPv4. For load balancing, multiple interfaces can use the same address.

Global Unicast Addresses   These are your typical publicly routable addresses, and they're used the same way globally unique addresses are in IPv4.

Link-Local Addresses   These are like the APIPA addresses in IPv4 in that they're not meant to be routed and are unique for each link (LAN). Think of them as a handy tool that gives you the ability to throw a temporary LAN together for meetings or for creating a small LAN that's not going to be routed but still needs to share and access files and services locally. However, link-local is used on every LAN that connects to a router interface as well. The link local address will be an FE80::/10 address.

Unique Local Addresses   These addresses are also intended for nonrouting purposes, but they are nearly globally unique, so it's unlikely you'll ever have one of them overlap with any other address. Unique local addresses were designed to replace site-local addresses, so they basically do almost exactly what IPv4 private addresses do—allow communication throughout a site while being routable to multiple local networks. The difference between link-local and unique local is that unique local can be routed within your organization or company.

Multicast   Again, as in IPv4, packets addressed to a multicast address are delivered to all interfaces identified by the multicast address. Sometimes people call them *one-to-many addresses*. It's really easy to spot multicast addresses in IPv6 because they always start with *FF*.

Anycast Like multicast addresses, an anycast address identifies multiple interfaces, but there's a big difference: The anycast packet is delivered to only one address—actually, to the first IPv6 address it finds defined in terms of routing distance. And again, this address is special because you can apply a single address to more than one interface. You could call them one-to-one-of-many addresses, but just saying anycast is a lot easier. This is also referred to as one-to-nearest addressing.

You're probably wondering if there are any special, reserved addresses in IPv6 because you know they're there in IPv4. Well, there are—plenty of them! Let's go over them now.

Special Addresses

I'm going to list some of the addresses and address ranges that you should definitely make a point to remember in Table 7.3 because you'll eventually use them. They're all special or reserved for specific use, but unlike IPv4, IPv6 gives us a galaxy of addresses, so reserving a few here and there doesn't hurt a thing.

TABLE 7.3   Special IPv6 addresses

Address	Meaning
0:0:0:0:0:0:0:0	Equals ::. This is the equivalent of IPv4's 0.0.0.0 and is typically the source address of a host before the host receives an IP address when you're using DHCP-driven stateful configuration.
0:0:0:0:0:0:0:1	Equals ::1. The equivalent of 127.0.0.1 in IPv4.
0::FFFF:192.168.100.1	This is how an IPv4 address would be written in a mixed IPv6/IPv4 network environment.
2000::/3	The global unicast address range allocated for Internet access.
FC00::/7	The unique local unicast range.
FE80::/10	The link-local unicast range.
FF00::/8	The multicast range.
3FFF:FFFF::/32	Reserved for examples and documentation.
2001:0DB8::/32	Also reserved for examples and documentation.
2002::/16	Used with 6to4 tunneling, which is an IPv4-to-IPv6 transition system. The structure allows IPv6 packets to be transmitted over an IPv4 network without the need to configure explicit tunnels.

Stateless Address Autoconfiguration (SLAAC)

Autoconfiguration is an especially useful solution because it allows devices on a network to address themselves with a link-local unicast address as well as with a global unicast address. This process happens through first learning the prefix information from the router and then appending the device's own interface address as the interface ID. But where does it get that interface ID? Well, you know every device on an Ethernet network has a physical MAC address, which is exactly what's used for the interface ID. But since the interface ID in an IPv6 address is 64 bits in length and a MAC address is only 48 bits, where do the extra 16 bits come from? The MAC address is padded in the middle with the extra bits—it's padded with FF:FE.

For example, let's say I have a device with a MAC address that looks like this: 0060:d673:1987. After it's been padded, it would look like this: 0260:d6FF:FE73:1987. Figure 7.3 illustrates what an Extended Unique Identifier (EUI-64) address looks like.

FIGURE 7.3   EUI-64 interface ID assignment

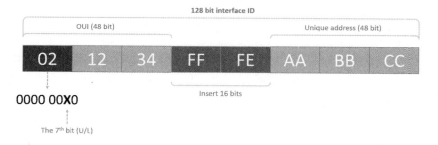

So where did that 2 in the beginning of the address come from? Another good question. You see that part of the process of padding, called modified EUI-64 format, changes the Universal/Local (U/L) bit to specify if the address is locally unique or globally unique. And the bit that gets changed is the 7th bit in the address.

The reason for modifying the U/L bit is that, when using manually assigned addresses on an interface, you can simply assign the address 2001:db8:1:9::1/64 instead of the much longer 2001:db8:1:9:0200::1/64. Also, if you are going to manually assign link-local addresses, you can assign the short address fe80::1 instead of the long fe80::0200:0:0:1 or fe80:0:0:0:0200::1. So, even though at first glance it seems the IETF made this harder for you to simply understand IPv6 addressing by flipping the 7th bit, in reality this made addressing much simpler. Also, since most people don't typically override the burned-in address, the U/L bit is by default a 0, which means that you'll see this inverted to a 1 most of the time. But because you're studying the exam objectives, you'll need to look at inverting it both ways.

Here are a few examples:

- MAC address 0090:2716:fd0f
- IPv6 EUI-64 address: 2001:0db8:0:1:0290:27ff:fe16:fd0f

That one was easy! Too easy for the exam objectives, so let's do another:

- MAC address aa12:bcbc:1234
- IPv6 EUI-64 address: 2001:0db8:0:1:a812:bcff:febc:1234

10101010 represents the first 8 bits of the MAC address (aa), which when inverting the 7th bit becomes 10101000. The answer becomes a8. I can't tell you how important this is for you to understand, so bear with me and work through a couple more!

- MAC address 0c0c:dede:1234
- IPv6 EUI-64 address: 2001:0db8:0:1:0e0c:deff:fede:1234

0c is 00001100 in the first 8 bits of the MAC address, which then becomes 00001110 when flipping the 7th bit. The answer is then 0e. Let's practice one more:

- MAC address 0b34:ba12:1234
- IPv6 EUI-64 address: 2001:0db8:0:1:0934:baff:fe12:1234

0b in binary is 00001011, the first 8 bits of the MAC address, which then becomes 00001001. The answer is 09.

    Pay extra-special attention to this EUI-64 address assignment and be able to convert the 7th bit based on the EUI-64 rules!

DHCPv6 (Stateful)

DHCPv6 works pretty much the same way DHCP does in v4, with the obvious difference that it supports IPv6's new addressing scheme. And it might come as a surprise, but there are a couple of other options that DHCP still provides for us that autoconfiguration doesn't. And no, I'm not kidding—in autoconfiguration, there's absolutely no mention of DNS servers, domain names, or many of the other options that DHCP has always generously provided for us via IPv4. This is a big reason that the odds favor DHCP's continued use in IPv6 into the future at least partially—maybe even most of the time!

This means that you're definitely going to need another server around to supply and dispense all the additional, required information—maybe to even manage the address assignment, if needed!

Migrating to IPv6

We certainly have talked a lot about how IPv6 works and how we can configure it to work on our networks, but what is doing that going to cost us? And how much work is it really going to take? Good questions for sure, but the answers to them won't be the same for everyone. This is because how much you are going to end up having to pony up is highly dependent upon what you've got going on already in terms of your infrastructure. Obviously, if you've been making your really old routers and switches "last" and therefore have to upgrade every one of them so that they're IPv6-compliant, that could very well turn out to be a good-sized chunk of change! Oh, and that sum doesn't even include server and computer operating systems (OSs) and the blood, sweat, and maybe even tears spent on making all your applications compliant. So, my friend, it could cost you quite a bit! The good news is that unless you've really let things go, many OSs and network devices have been IPv6-compliant for a few years—we just haven't been using all their features until now.

Then there's that other question about the amount of work and time. Straight up—this one could still be pretty intense. No matter what, it's going to take you some time to get all of your systems moved over and make sure that things are working correctly. And if you're talking about a huge network with tons of devices, well, it could take a really long time! But don't panic—that's why migration strategies have been created, to allow for a gradual integration. I'm going to show you three of the primary transition strategies available to us. The first is called dual stacking, which allows a device to have both the IPv4 and IPv6 protocol stacks running so it's capable of continuing on with its existing communications and simultaneously running newer IPv6 communications as they're implemented. The next strategy is the 6to4 tunneling approach; this is your choice if you have an all-IPv6 network that must communicate over an IPv4 network to reach another IPv6 network. I'll surprise you with the third one just for fun!

Dual Stacking

This is the most common type of migration strategy because, well, it's the easiest on us—it allows our devices to communicate using either IPv4 or IPv6. Dual stacking lets you upgrade your devices and applications on the network one at a time. As more and more hosts and devices on the network are upgraded, more of your communication will happen over IPv6, and after you've arrived—everything's running on IPv6 and you get to remove all the old IPv4 protocol stacks you no longer need.

6to4 Tunneling

6to4 tunneling is really useful for carrying IPv6 packets over a network that's still running IPv4. It's quite possible that you'll have IPv6 subnets or other portions of your network that are all IPv6, and those networks will have to communicate with each other. Not so complicated, but when you consider that you might find this happening over a WAN or some other network that you don't control, well, that could be a bit ugly. So what do we do about this if we don't control the whole tamale? Create a tunnel that will carry the IPv6 traffic for us across the IPv4 network, that's what.

The whole idea of tunneling isn't a difficult concept, and creating tunnels really isn't as hard as you might think. All it really comes down to is snatching the IPv6 packet that's happily traveling across the network and sticking an IPv4 header onto the front of it. Kind of like catch-and-release fishing, except that the fish doesn't get something plastered on its face before being thrown back into the stream.

To get a picture of this, take a look at Figure 7.4.

FIGURE 7.4   A 6to4 tunnel

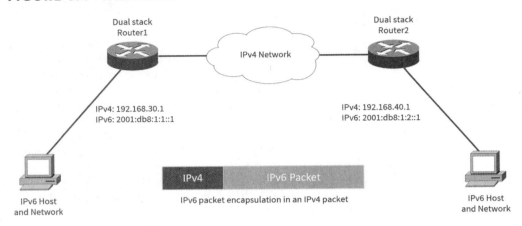

Nice—but to make this happen, we're going to need a couple of dual-stacked routers, which I just demonstrated for you, so you should be good to go. Now we have to add a little configuration to place a tunnel between those routers. Tunnels are pretty simple—we just have to tell each router where the tunnel begins and where we want it to end up. The opposite of this would be a *4to6 tunnel*, which is rare to find because this means your whole business network is IPv4 (okay, this sounds normal so far), but you're traversing an IPv6-only Internet to get to another IPv4 network. Not so common at the time of this writing.

One important note here—if the IPv4 network that you're traversing in this 6to4 situation has a NAT translation point, it would absolutely break the tunnel encapsulation we've just created! Over the years, NAT/PAT has been upgraded a lot so that it can handle specific protocols and dynamic connections, and without one of these upgrades, NAT likes to demolish most connections. And since this transition strategy isn't present in most NAT implementations, that means trouble.

But there is a way around this little problem (the third strategy I told you about), and it's called *Teredo*, which allows all your tunnel traffic to be placed in UDP packets. NAT doesn't blast away at UDP packets, so they won't get broken as other protocol packets do. So with Teredo in place and your packets disguised under their UDP cloak, the packets will easily slip by NAT alive and well!

Miredo is a tunneling technique used on native IPv6 Linux and BSD UNIX machines to communicate on the IPv4 Internet directly without a dual-stack router or 6to4 tunnel. This is rarely used.

EXERCISE 7.1

Identifying IP Addresses

In this exercise, you will identify the various IP addresses you currently use.

1. Open the command prompt by clicking Start, typing **cmd**, and pressing Enter.

2. In the command prompt, type **ipconfig /all** and make note of the IP address.

3. Make note of the addresses present on your computer.

4. Open a web browser and go to whatismyipaddress.com or a similar site.

5. Make a note of the address that shows as your public IP address.

What type of IP addresses are present on your computer? Identify the version, class, and type of IP addresses in use. Are the IP addresses public or private? What type of IP addresses are in use on your Internet connection? Identify the version and class of IP addresses.

Summary

In this chapter, I covered the very basics of both IPv4 and IPv6 and how they work in an internetwork (remember that if the acronym *IP* is used alone, it is referring to just IPv4). As you now know by reading this chapter, even when discussing and configuring the basics, there is a lot to understand—and we just scratched the surface. We also covered RFC 1918, APIPA addresses, address Classes A-D, NAT, EUI-64, tunneling, dual-stack and virtual IP addressing. But trust me when I say this—you now know more than you'll need to meet the Network+ objectives.

I discussed in detail the difference between each class of address and how to find a network address, broadcast address, and valid host range.

I explained why we need IPv6 and the benefits associated with it. I followed that up by covering addressing with IPv6 as well as how to use the shortened expressions. And during the discussion on addressing with IPv6, I showed you the different address types, plus the special addresses reserved in IPv6.

The next chapter is very important, but it's one that some people find rather challenging, so take a break and get ready for a really fun but long chapter on IP subnetting. I promise not to torture you too much!

Exam Essentials

Remember the Class A range.   The IP range for a Class A network is 1 through 126. This provides 8 bits of network addressing and 24 bits of host addressing by default.

Remember the Class B range.   The IP range for a Class B network is 128 through 191. Class B addressing provides 16 bits of network addressing and 16 bits of host addressing by default.

Remember the Class C range.   The IP range for a Class C network is 192 through 223. Class C addressing provides 24 bits of network addressing and 8 bits of host addressing by default.

Remember the private IP ranges.   The Class A private address range is 10.0.0.0 through 10.255.255.255. The Class B private address range is 172.16.0.0 through 172.31.255.255. The Class C private address range is 192.168.0.0 through 192.168.255.255.

Remember the APIPA range.   The IP address range for APIPA is 169.254.0.1 through 169.254.255.254. The client also configures itself with a default Class B subnet mask of 255.255.0.0.

Understand why we need IPv6.   Without IPv6, the world would soon be depleted of IP addresses.

Understand link-local.   Link-local addresses are like an IPv4 APIPA IP address, but they can't be routed at all, not even in your organization.

Understand unique local.   This, like link-local, is like a private IP address in IPv4 and cannot be routed to the Internet. However, the difference between link-local and unique local is that unique local can be routed within your organization or company.

Remember IPv6 addressing.   IPv6 addressing is not like IPv4 addressing. IPv6 addressing has much more address space and the address is 128 bits long, represented in hexadecimal, unlike an IPv4 address, which is only 32 bits long and represented in decimal.

Understand and be able to read an EUI-64 address with the 7th bit inverted.   Hosts can use autoconfiguration to obtain an IPv6 address, and one of the ways is through what is called EUI-64. This takes the unique MAC address of a host and inserts FF:FE in the middle of the address to change a 48-bit MAC address to a 64-bit interface ID. In addition to the 16 bits being inserted into the interface ID, the 7th bit of the first byte is inverted, typically from a 0 to a 1.

Written Labs

You can find the answers to the written labs in Appendix A.

Written Lab 7.1

Provide the answers to the following questions:

1. What is the valid range used for a Class C private IP address?
2. Name some of the benefits of IPv6 over IPv4.
3. What is the term for the autoconfiguration technology responsible for addresses that start with 169.254?
4. What defines a unicast address?
5. What defines a multicast address?
6. What is the name for a 48-bit (6-byte) numerical address physically assigned to a network interface, such as a NIC?
7. IPv6 has how many more bits, compared to addresses in IPv4?
8. What is the private address range for Class B networks?
9. What is the Class C range of values for the first octet in decimal and in binary?
10. What is the 127.0.0.1 address used for?

Written Lab 7.2

In this lab, write the answers to the following IPv6 questions:

1. Which type of packet is addressed and delivered to only a single interface?
2. Which type of address is used just like a regular public routable address in IPv4?
3. Which type of address is not meant to be routed?
4. Which type of address is not meant to be routed to the Internet but is still globally unique?
5. Which type of address is meant to be delivered to multiple interfaces?
6. Which type of address identifies multiple interfaces, but packets are delivered only to the first address it finds?
7. Which addressing type is also referred to as one-to-nearest?
8. IPv4 had a loopback address of 127.0.0.1. What is the IPv6 loopback address?
9. What does a link-local address always start with?
10. What does a unique local unicast range start with?

Review Questions

You can find the answers to the review questions in Appendix B.

1. Which of the following addresses is not allowed on the Internet?
    A. 191.192.168.1
    B. 191.168.169.254
    C. 172.32.255.0
    D. 172.31.12.251

2. A host automatically configured with an address from which of the following ranges indicates an inability to contact a DHCP server?
    A. 169.254.0.x with a mask of 255.255.255.0
    B. 169.254.x.x with a mask of 255.255.0.0
    C. 169.254.x.x with a mask of 255.255.255.0
    D. 169.255.x.x with a mask of 255.255.0.0

3. Which statement regarding private IP addresses is most accurate?
    A. Private addresses cannot be used in intranets that require routing.
    B. Private addresses must be assigned by a registrar or ISP.
    C. A remote host across the Internet cannot ping your host if it has a private address.
    D. Private addresses can be used only by a single administrative domain.

4. Which of the following is a valid Class A address?
    A. 191.10.0.1
    B. 127.10.0.1
    C. 128.10.0.1
    D. 126.10.0.1

5. Which of the following is a valid Class B address?
    A. 10.1.1.1
    B. 126.1.1.1
    C. 129.1.1.1
    D. 192.168.1.1

6. Which of the following describes a broadcast address?
    A. All network bits are on (1s).
    B. All host bits are on (1s).
    C. All network bits are off (0s).
    D. All host bits are off (0s).

7. Which of the following is a layer 2 broadcast?

   A. FF.FF.FF.EE.EE.EE

   B. FF.FF.FF.FF.FF.FF

   C. 255.255.255.255

   D. 255.0.0.0

8. In a Class C IP address, how long is the network address?

   A. 8 bits

   B. 16 bits

   C. 24 bits

   D. 32 bits

9. Which of the following is true when describing a unicast address?

   A. Packets addressed to a unicast address are delivered to a single interface.

   B. These are your typical publicly routable addresses, just like regular publicly routable addresses in IPv4.

   C. These are like private addresses in IPv4 in that they are not meant to be routed.

   D. These addresses are meant for nonrouting purposes, but they are almost globally unique, so it is unlikely they will have an address overlap.

10. A host is rebooted, and you view the IP address that it was assigned. The address is 169.123.13.34. Which of the following happened?

   A. The host received an APIPA address.

   B. The host received a multicast address.

   C. The host received a public address.

   D. The host received a private address.

11. An IPv4 address uses 32 bits. How many bits is an IPv6 address?

   A. 64

   B. 128

   C. 192

   D. 255

12. Which of the following is true when describing a multicast address?

   A. Packets addressed to a unicast address from a multicast address are delivered to a single interface.

   B. Packets are delivered to all interfaces identified by the address. This is also called a one-to-many address.

   C. It identifies multiple interfaces and is delivered to only one address. This address can also be called one-to-one-of-many.

   D. These addresses are meant for nonrouting purposes, but they are almost globally unique so it is unlikely they will have an address overlap.

13. Which of the following is true when describing an anycast address?

  A. Packets addressed to a unicast address from an anycast address are delivered to a single interface.

  B. Packets are delivered to all interfaces identified by the address. This is also called a one-to-many address.

  C. This address identifies multiple interfaces, and the anycast packet is delivered to only one address: the closest one. This address can also be called one-to-nearest.

  D. These addresses are meant for nonrouting purposes, but they are almost globally unique so it is unlikely they will have an address overlap.

14. You want to ping the loopback address of your local host. Which two options could you type? (Choose two.)

  A. `ping 127.0.0.1`

  B. `ping 0.0.0.0`

  C. `ping ::1`

  D. `trace 0.0.::1`

15. What two statements about IPv6 addresses are true? (Choose two.)

  A. Leading zeros are required.

  B. Two colons (::) are used to represent successive hexadecimal fields of zeros.

  C. Two colons (::) are used to separate fields.

  D. A single interface will have multiple IPv6 addresses of different types.

16. What two statements about IPv4 and IPv6 addresses are true? (Choose two.)

  A. An IPv6 address is 32 bits long, represented in hexadecimal.

  B. An IPv6 address is 128 bits long, represented in decimal.

  C. An IPv4 address is 32 bits long, represented in decimal.

  D. An IPv6 address is 128 bits long, represented in hexadecimal.

17. Which of the following is a Class C network address?

  A. 10.10.10.0

  B. 127.0.0.1

  C. 128.0.0.0

  D. 192.255.254.0

18. Which of the following are private IP addresses? (Choose two.)

  A. 12.0.0.1

  B. 168.172.19.39

  C. 172.20.14.36

  D. 172.33.194.30

  E. 192.168.24.43

19. IPv6 unicast routing is running on the Corp router. Which of the following addresses would be used as the EUI-64 address?

```
Corp#sh int f0/0
FastEthernet0/0 is up, line protocol is up
Hardware is AmdFE, address is 000d.bd3b.0d80 (bia 000d.bd3b.0d80)
[output cut]
```

    A. FF02::3c3d:0d:bdff:fe3b:0d80

    B. FE80::3c3d:2d:bdff:fe3b:0d80

    C. FE80::3c3d:0d:bdff:fe3b:0d80

    D. FE80::3c3d:2d:ffbd:3bfe:0d80

20. Which of the following is an invalid IP address for a host?

    A. 10.0.0.1

    B. 128.0.0.1

    C. 224.0.0.1

    D. 172.0.0.1

Chapter

8

IP Subnetting, Troubleshooting IP, and Introduction to NAT

THE FOLLOWING COMPTIA NETWORK+ EXAM OBJECTIVES ARE COVERED IN THIS CHAPTER:

✓ **Domain 1.0 Networking Concepts**

✓ **1.4 Explain common networking ports, protocols, services, and traffic types.**

- Traffic types
    - Unicast
    - Multicast
    - Anycast
    - Broadcast

✓ **1.7 Given a scenario, use appropriate IPv4 network addressing.**

- Public vs. private
    - Automatic Private IP Addressing (APIPA)
    - RFC1918
    - Loopback/localhost
- Subnetting
    - Variable Length Subnet Mask (VLSM)
    - Classless Inter-domain Routing (CIDR)

- IPv4 address classes
  - Class A
  - Class B
  - Class C
  - Class D
  - Class E

✓ Domain 2.0 Network Implementation

✓ 2.1 Explain characteristics of routing technologies.

- Address translation
  - NAT
  - Port address translation (PAT)

This chapter's focus will really zoom in on IP addressing to ensure that you have it nailed down tight. This is an integral aspect of networking, and it's important to your success on the exams and as a professional, too!

We'll start with subnetting an IP network. You're going to have to really apply yourself because it takes time and practice to do subnetting correctly and quickly. So, be patient and do whatever it takes to get this stuff dialed in. This chapter truly is important—possibly the most important chapter in this book for you to understand. Make it part of you!

I'll thoroughly cover IP subnetting from the very beginning. I know this might sound weird to you, but I think you'll be much better off if you can try to forget everything you've learned about subnetting before reading this chapter—especially if you've been to a Microsoft class!

I'll also take you through IP address troubleshooting and walk you through each of the steps recommended when you're faced with troubleshooting an IP network. Finally, I'll finish up with an introduction to network address translation (NAT)—there are various types of NAT, and you need to know when you would use each one.

So get psyched—you're about to go for quite a ride! This chapter will truly help you understand IP addressing and networking, so don't get discouraged or give up. If you stick with it, I promise that one day you'll look back on this and be really glad you decided to stay the course. It's one of those things that after you understand it, you'll laugh at that time, way back when, when you thought this was hard. So, are you ready now? Let's go!

To find Todd Lammle CompTIA videos and practice questions, please see www.lammle.com.

Subnetting Basics

In Chapter 7, "IP Addressing," you learned how to define and find the valid host ranges used in a Class A, Class B, or Class C network address by turning the host bits all off and then all on. This is very good, but here's the catch: You were defining only one network. What would happen if you wanted to take one network address range and create six networks from it? You would have to do something called *subnetting*, because that's what allows you to take one larger network and break it into a bunch of smaller networks.

There are loads of reasons in favor of subnetting, including the following benefits:

Reduced Network Traffic   We all appreciate less traffic of any kind. With networks, it's no different. Without trusty routers, packet traffic could grind the entire network down to a near standstill. With routers, most traffic will stay on the local network; only packets destined for other networks will pass through the router. Routers create broadcast domains. The more broadcast domains you create, the smaller the broadcast domains and the less network traffic on each network segment.

Optimized Network Performance   This is the very cool reward you get when you reduce network traffic!

Simplified Management   It's easier to identify and isolate network problems in a group of smaller connected networks than within one gigantic network.

Facilitated Spanning of Large Geographical Distances   Because WAN links are considerably slower and more expensive than LAN links, a single large network that spans long distances can create problems in every area previously listed. Connecting multiple smaller networks makes the system more efficient.

Next, we're going to move on to subnetting a network address. This is the good part—ready?

How to Create Subnets

To create subnetworks, you take bits from the host portion of the IP address and reserve them to define the subnet address. This means fewer bits for hosts, so the more subnets, the fewer bits are left available for defining hosts.

Soon, I'll show you how to create subnets, starting with Class C addresses. But before you actually implement subnetting, you really need to determine your current requirements as well as plan for future conditions.

Follow these steps—they're your recipe for solid design:

1. Determine the number of required network IDs:
   - One for each subnet
   - One for each wide area network (WAN) connection

2. Determine the number of required host IDs per subnet:
   - One for each TCP/IP host
   - One for each router interface

3. Based on the previous requirements, create the following:
   - One subnet mask for your entire network
   - A unique subnet ID for each physical segment
   - A range of host IDs for each subnet

Understanding the Powers of 2

By the way, powers of 2 are really important to memorize for use with IP subnetting. To review powers of 2, remember that when you see a number with another number to its upper right (an exponent), this means you should multiply the number by itself as many times as the upper number specifies. For example, 2^3 is $2 \times 2 \times 2$, which equals 8. Here's a list of powers of 2 that you should commit to memory:

$2^1 = 2$

$2^2 = 4$

$2^3 = 8$

$2^4 = 16$

$2^5 = 32$

$2^6 = 64$

$2^7 = 128$

$2^8 = 256$

$2^9 = 512$

$2^{10} = 1,024$

$2^{11} = 2,048$

$2^{12} = 4,096$

$2^{13} = 8,192$

$2^{14} = 16,384$

If you hate math, don't get stressed out about knowing all these exponents—it's helpful to know them, but it's not absolutely necessary. Here's a little trick, because you're working with 2s: Each successive power of 2 is double the previous one.

For example, all you have to do to remember the value of 2^9 is to first know that $2^8 = 256$. Why? Because when you double 2 to the eighth power (256), you get 2^9 (or 512). To determine the value of 2^{10}, simply start at $2^8 = 256$, and then double it twice.

You can go the other way as well. If you needed to know what 2^6 is, for example, you just cut 256 in half two times: once to reach 2^7 and then one more time to reach 2^6. Not bad, right?

Subnet Masks

For the subnet address scheme to work, every machine on the network must know which part of the host address will be used as the subnet address. This is accomplished by assigning a *subnet mask* to each machine. A subnet mask is a 32-bit value that allows the recipient of IP packets to distinguish the network ID portion of the IP address from the host ID portion of the IP address.

The network administrator creates a 32-bit subnet mask composed of 1s and 0s. The 1s in the subnet mask represent the positions that refer to the network, or subnet, addresses.

Not all networks need subnets, meaning they use the default subnet mask. This is basically the same as saying that a network doesn't have a subnet address.

Table 8.1 shows the default subnet masks for Classes A, B, and C. These default masks cannot and do not change. In other words, you can't make a Class B subnet mask read 255.0.0.0. If you try, the host will read that address as invalid and usually won't even let you type it in. For a Class A network, you can't change the first byte in a subnet mask; it must read 255.0.0.0 at a minimum. Similarly, you cannot assign 255.255.255.255, because this is all 1s—a broadcast address. A Class B address must start with 255.255.0.0, and a Class C has to start with 255.255.255.0. Check out Table 8.1.

TABLE 8.1   Default subnet masks

Class	Format	Default Subnet Mask
A	network.host.host.host	255.0.0.0
B	network.network.host.host	255.255.0.0
C	network.network.network.host	255.255.255.0

In Chapter 7 we discussed the addresses with the first octet of 224 to 255 are reserved for Class D and E networks. Class D (224–239) is used for multicast addresses and Class E (240–255) for scientific purposes. But they're really beyond the scope of this book, so I'm not going to go into detail about them here. But you do need to remember that the multicast range is from 224.0.0.0 through 239.255.255.255.

Classless Inter-Domain Routing (CIDR)

Another term you need to know is *Classless Inter-Domain Routing (CIDR)*. It's basically the method that Internet service providers (ISPs) use to allocate a number of addresses to a company or a home connection. They provide addresses in a certain block size; I'll be going into that in greater detail later in this chapter. Another term for the use of different length subnet masks in the network is *variable-length subnet masking (VLSM)*.

When you receive a block of addresses from an ISP, what you get will look something like this: 192.168.10.32/28. This is telling you what your subnet mask is. The slash notation (/) means how many bits are turned on (1s). Obviously, the maximum could only be /32 because a byte is 8 bits and there are 4 bytes in an IP address: 4 × 8 = 32. But keep in mind that the largest subnet mask available (regardless of the class of address) can only be a /30 because you have to keep at least 2 bits for host bits.

Take, for example, a Class A default subnet mask, which is 255.0.0.0. This means that the first byte of the subnet mask is all ones (1s), or 11111111. When referring to a slash notation, you need to count all the 1 bits to figure out your mask. The 255.0.0.0 is considered a /8 because it has 8 bits that are 1s—that is, 8 bits that are turned on.

A Class B default mask would be 255.255.0.0, which is a /16 because 16 bits are (1s): 11111111.11111111.00000000.00000000.

Table 8.2 lists every available subnet mask and its equivalent CIDR slash notation.

TABLE 8.2 CIDR values

Subnet Mask	CIDR Value
255.0.0.0	/8
255.128.0.0	/9
255.192.0.0	/10
255.224.0.0	/11
255.240.0.0	/12
255.248.0.0	/13
255.252.0.0	/14
255.254.0.0	/15
255.255.0.0	/16
255.255.128.0	/17
255.255.192.0	/18
255.255.224.0	/19
255.255.240.0	/20
255.255.248.0	/21

TABLE 8.2   CIDR values *(continued)*

Subnet Mask	CIDR Value
255.255.252.0	/22
255.255.254.0	/23
255.255.255.0	/24
255.255.255.128	/25
255.255.255.192	/26
255.255.255.224	/27
255.255.255.240	/28
255.255.255.248	/29
255.255.255.252	/30

Although, according to RFC 1518, any device or software that claims to be CIDR-compliant will allow supernetting, meaning a traditional Class C address can be used with a /23 subnet mask, in almost all cases. The /8 through /15 can be used only with Class A network addresses; /16 through /23 can be used by Class A and B network addresses; and /24 through /30 can be used by Class A, B, and C network addresses. This is a big reason most companies use Class A network addresses. By being allowed the use of all subnet masks, they gain the valuable benefit of maximum flexibility for their network design.

Supernetting is the opposite of subnetting. Subnetting is the division of a network into subnets. Supernetting is the method of combining smaller networks in a single address.

EXERCISE 8.1

Examining IP Address and Subnet Masks

In this exercise, you will examine your IP address and subnet mask.

1. Open the command prompt by clicking Start, typing **cmd**, and then pressing Enter.

2. In the command prompt, type **ipconfig /all** and make note of the IP address and subnet mask.

3. Examine how many bits your subnet mask is using and write it down in CIDR notation.

4. Identify the network ID portion of your IP address and write it down.

5. Identify the host ID portion of the IP address and write it down.

6. Identify the class of IP address being used on your computer by examining the first octet.

After examining your IP address and subnet mask, you should have a good understanding of the subnet mask compared to the class of IP address. You should also know the network that the host belongs to and CIDR notation.

Subnetting Class C Addresses

There are many different ways to subnet a network. The right way is the way that works best for you. In a Class C address, only 8 bits are available for defining the hosts. Remember that subnet bits start at the left and go to the right, without skipping bits. This means the only Class C subnet masks can be those listed here:

Binary	Decimal	CIDR
00000000	0	/24
10000000	128	/25
11000000	192	/26
11100000	224	/27
11110000	240	/28
11111000	248	/29
11111100	252	/30

We can't use a /31 or /32 because, remember, we have to leave at least 2 host bits for assigning IP addresses to hosts.

Get ready for something special. I'm going to teach you an alternate method of subnetting that makes it a whole lot easier to subnet larger numbers in no time. Trust me, you really do need to be able to subnet fast!

Subnetting a Class C Address: The Fast Way!

When you've chosen a possible subnet mask for your network and need to determine the number of subnets, valid hosts, and broadcast addresses of a subnet that the mask provides, all you need to do is answer five simple questions:

- How many subnets does the chosen subnet mask produce?

- How many valid hosts per subnet are available?

- What are the valid subnets?

- What's the broadcast address of each subnet?

- What are the valid hosts in each subnet?

At this point, it's important that you both understand and have memorized your powers of 2. Please refer to the sidebar "Understanding the Powers of 2" earlier in this chapter if you need some help. Here's how you get the answers to those five big questions:

- *How many subnets?* 2^x = number of subnets. x is the number of masked bits, or the 1s. For example, in 11000000, the number of 1s gives us 2^2 subnets. In this example, there are four subnets.

- *How many hosts per subnet?* $2^y - 2$ = number of hosts per subnet. y is the number of unmasked bits, or the 0s. For example, in 11000000, the number of 0s gives us $2^6 - 2$ hosts. In this example, there are 62 hosts per subnet. You need to subtract 2 for the subnet address and the broadcast address, which are not valid hosts.

- *What are the valid subnets?* 256 – subnet mask = block size, or increment number. An example would be 256 – 192 = 64. The block size of a 192 mask is always 64. Start counting at zero in blocks of 64 until you reach the subnet mask value, and these are your subnets. 0, 64, 128, 192. Easy, huh?

- *What's the broadcast address for each subnet?* Now here's the really easy part. Because we counted our subnets in the last section as 0, 64, 128, and 192, the broadcast address is always the number right before the next subnet. For example, the 0 subnet has a broadcast address of 63 because the next subnet is 64. The 64 subnet has a broadcast address of 127 because the next subnet is 128. And so on. And remember, the broadcast address of the last subnet is always 255.

- *What are the valid hosts?* Valid hosts are the numbers between the subnets, omitting all the 0s and all the 1s. For example, if 64 is the subnet number and 127 is the broadcast address, then 65–126 is the valid host range—it's *always* the numbers between the subnet address and the broadcast address.

I know this can truly seem confusing. But it really isn't as hard as it seems to be at first—just hang in there! Why not try a few and see for yourself?

Subnetting Practice Examples: Class C Addresses

Here's your opportunity to practice subnetting Class C addresses using the method I just described. Exciting, isn't it? We're going to start with the first Class C subnet mask and work through every subnet that we can using a Class C address. When we're done, I'll show you how easy this is with Class B networks too!

Practice Example #1C: 255.255.255.128 (/25)

Because 128 is 10000000 in binary, there is only 1 bit for subnetting, and there are 7 bits for hosts. We're going to subnet the Class C network address 192.168.10.0.

192.168.10.0 = Network address

255.255.255.128 = Subnet mask

Now, let's answer the big five:

- *How many subnets?* Because 128 is 1 bit on (10000000), the answer is $2^1 = 2$.
- *How many hosts per subnet?* We have 7 host bits off (10000000), so the equation is $2^7 - 2 = 126$ hosts.
- *What are the valid subnets?* 256 − 128 = 128. Remember, we'll start at zero and count in our block size, so our subnets are 0, 128.
- *What's the broadcast address for each subnet?* The number right before the value of the next subnet is all host bits turned on and equals the broadcast address. For the 0 subnet, the next subnet is 128, so the broadcast address of the 0 subnet is 127.
- *What are the valid hosts?* These are the numbers between the subnet and broadcast address. The easiest way to find the hosts is to write out the subnet address and the broadcast address. This way, the valid hosts are obvious. The following table shows the 0 and 128 subnets, the valid host ranges of each, and the broadcast address of both subnets:

Subnet	0	128
First host	1	129
Last host	126	254
Broadcast	127	255

Before moving on to the next example, take a look at Figure 8.1. Okay, looking at a Class C /25, it's pretty clear there are two subnets. But so what—why is this significant? Well actually, it's not, but that's not the right question. What you really want to know is what you would do with this information!

The key to understanding subnetting is to understand the very reason you need to do it. And I'm going to demonstrate this by going through the process of building a physical network—and let's add a router. (We now have an internetwork, as I truly hope you already know!) Because we added that router, for the hosts on our internetwork to communicate, they must now have a logical network addressing scheme. We could use IPv6, but IPv4 is still the most popular, and it also just happens to be what we're studying at the moment, so that's what we're going with.

Now take a look back at Figure 8.1. By the way, the output you see after the diagram is the routing table of the router, which was displayed by executing the show ip route command on the router. There are two physical networks, so we're going to implement a logical addressing scheme that allows for two logical networks. As always, it's a really good idea to look ahead and consider any likely growth scenarios—both short and long term, but for this example, a /25 will do the trick.

FIGURE 8.1   Implementing a Class C /25 logical network

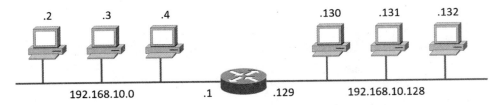

```
Router#show ip route
[output cut]
C 192.168.10.0 is directly connected to Ethernet 0
C 192.168.10.128 is directly connected to Ethernet 1
```

Practice Example #2C: 255.255.255.192 (/26)

In this second example, we're going to subnet the network address 192.168.10.0 using the subnet mask 255.255.255.192.

192.168.10.0 = Network address

255.255.255.192 = Subnet mask

It's time to answer the big five:

- *How many subnets?* Because 192 is 2 bits on (11000000), the answer is $2^2 = 4$ subnets.
- *How many hosts per subnet?* We have 6 host bits off (11000000), so the equation is $2^6 - 2 = 62$ hosts.
- *What are the valid subnets?* 256 − 192 = 64. Remember, we start at zero and count in our block size, so our subnets are 0, 64, 128, and 192.
- *What's the broadcast address for each subnet?* The number right before the value of the next subnet is all host bits turned on and equals the broadcast address. For the 0 subnet, the next subnet is 64, so the broadcast address for the 0 subnet is 63.
- *What are the valid hosts?* These are the numbers between the subnet and broadcast address. The easiest way to find the hosts is to write out the subnet address and the broadcast address. This way, the valid hosts are obvious. The following table shows the 0, 64, 128, and 192 subnets, the valid host ranges of each, and the broadcast address of each subnet:

The subnets (do this first)	0	64	128	192
Our first host (perform host addressing last)	1	65	129	193
Our last host	62	126	190	254
The broadcast address (do this second)	63	127	191	255

Again, before getting into the next example, you can see that we can now subnet a /26. And what are you going to do with this fascinating information? Implement it! We'll use Figure 8.2 to practice a /26 network implementation.

FIGURE 8.2   Implementing a Class C /26 logical network

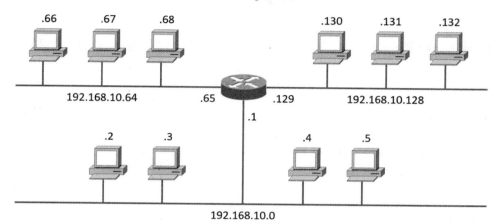

```
Router#show ip route
[output cut]
C 192.168.10.0 is directly connected to Ethernet 0
C 192.168.10.64 is directly connected to Ethernet 1
C 192.168.10.128 is directly connected to Ethernet 2
```

The /26 mask provides four subnetworks, and we need a subnet for each router interface. With this mask, in this example, we actually have room to add another router interface.

Practice Example #3C: 255.255.255.224 (/27)

This time, we'll subnet the network address 192.168.10.0 and subnet mask 255.255.255.224.

192.168.10.0 = Network address

255.255.255.224 = Subnet mask

- *How many subnets?* 224 is 11100000, so our equation is $2^3 = 8$.
- *How many hosts?* $2^5 - 2 = 30$.
- *What are the valid subnets?* 256 – 224 = 32. We just start at zero and count to the subnet mask value in blocks (increments) of 32: 0, 32, 64, 96, 128, 160, 192, and 224.

- *What's the broadcast address for each subnet (always the number right before the next subnet)?*
- *What are the valid hosts (the numbers between the subnet number and the broadcast address)?*

To answer the last two questions, first just write out the subnets, and then write out the broadcast address—the number right before the next subnet. Last, fill in the host address. The following table gives you all the subnets for the 255.255.255.224 Class C subnet mask:

The subnet address	0	32	64	96	128	160	192	224
The first valid host	1	33	65	97	129	161	193	225
The last valid host	30	62	94	126	158	190	222	254
The broadcast address	31	63	95	127	159	191	223	255

Practice Example #4C: 255.255.255.240 (/28)

Let's practice on another one:

192.168.10.0 = Network address

255.255.255.240 = Subnet mask

- *Subnets?* 240 is 11110000 in binary. $2^4 = 16$.
- *Hosts?* 4 host bits, or $2^4 - 2 = 14$.
- *Valid subnets?* 256 − 240 = 16. 0, 16, 32, 48, 64, 80, 96, 112, 128, 144, 160, 176, 192, 208, 224, 240.
- *Broadcast address for each subnet?*
- *Valid hosts?*

To answer the last two questions, check out the following table. It gives you the subnets, valid hosts, and broadcast address for each subnet. First, find the address of each subnet using the block size (increment). Second, find the broadcast address of each subnet increment (it's always the number right before the next valid subnet); then, just fill in the host address. The following table shows the available subnets, hosts, and broadcast address provided by a Class C network 255.255.255.240 mask:

Subnet	0	16	32	48	64	80	96	112	128	144	160	176	192	208	224	240
First host	1	17	33	49	65	81	97	113	129	145	161	177	193	209	225	241
Last host	14	30	46	62	78	94	110	126	142	158	174	190	206	222	238	254
Broadcast	15	31	47	63	79	95	111	127	143	159	175	191	207	223	239	255

Practice Example #5C: 255.255.255.248 (/29)

Let's keep practicing:

192.168.10.0 = Network address

255.255.255.248 = Subnet mask

- *Subnets?* 248 in binary = 11111000. 2^5 = 32.
- *Hosts?* $2^3 - 2 = 6$.
- *Valid subnets?* 256 − 248 = 8, start at zero: 0, 8, 16, 24, 32, 40, 48, 56, 64, 72, 80, 88, 96, 104, 112, 120, 128, 136, 144, 152, 160, 168, 176, 184, 192, 200, 208, 216, 224, 232, 240, and 248.
- *Broadcast address for each subnet?*
- *Valid hosts?*

Take a look at the following table. It shows some of the subnets (first four and last four only), valid hosts, and broadcast address for the Class C 255.255.255.248 mask:

Subnet	0	8	16	24	...	224	232	240	248
First host	1	9	17	25	...	225	233	241	249
Last host	6	14	22	30	...	230	238	246	254
Broadcast	7	15	23	31	...	231	239	247	255

Practice Example #6C: 255.255.255.252 (/30)

I know, I know—but just one more:

192.168.10.0 = Network address

255.255.255.252 = Subnet mask

- *Subnets?* 64.
- *Hosts?* 2.
- *Valid subnets?* 0, 4, 8, 12, and so on, all the way to 252.
- *Broadcast address for each subnet (always the number right before the next subnet)?*
- *Valid hosts (the numbers between the subnet number and the broadcast address)?*

The following table shows you the subnet, valid host, and broadcast address of the first four and last four subnets in the 255.255.255.252 Class C subnet:

Subnet	0	4	8	12	...	240	244	248	252
First host	1	5	9	13	...	241	245	249	253
Last host	2	6	10	14	...	242	246	250	254
Broadcast	3	7	11	15	...	243	247	251	255

Subnetting in Your Head: Class C Addresses

It really is possible to subnet in your head by looking at a valid IP address and subnet mask. This is extremely important for IP addressing and troubleshooting. Even if you don't believe me that you can subnet in your head, I'll show you how. And it's not all that hard either—take the following example: What is the subnet, broadcast address, and valid host range that this host IP address is a part of?

192.168.10.33 = Host address

255.255.255.224 = Subnet mask

 Real World Scenario

Should We Really Use This Mask That Provides Only Two Hosts?

Imagine you are the network administrator for Acme Corporation in San Francisco, with dozens of WAN links connecting to your corporate office. Right now your network is a classful network, which means that the same subnet mask is on each host and router interface. You've read about classless routing where you can have different size masks, but you don't know what to use on your point-to-point WAN links. Is 255.255.255.252 (/30) a helpful mask in this situation?

Yes, this is a very helpful mask in wide area networks.

If you use the 255.255.255.0 mask, then each network will have 254 hosts, but you use only two addresses with a WAN link! That is a waste of 252 hosts per subnet. If you use the 255.255.255.252 mask, then each subnet has only two hosts, and you don't waste precious addresses.

First, determine the subnet and broadcast address of this IP address. You can do this by answering question 3 of the big five questions: 256 – 224 = 32. Start at zero: 0, 32, 64. The address of 33 falls between the two subnets of 32 and 64 and must be part of the 192.168.10.32 subnet. The next subnet is 64, so the broadcast address of the 32 subnet is 63. (Remember that the broadcast address of a subnet is always the number right before the next subnet.) The valid host range is 33–62 (the numbers between the subnet and broadcast address). I told you this is easy!

Okay, let's try another one. What is the subnet, broadcast address, and valid host range that this host IP address is part of?

192.168.10.33 = Host address

255.255.255.240 = Subnet mask

256 – 240 = 16. Start at zero and count till you pass the valid host in the problem: 0, 16, 32, 48. Bingo—the host address is between the 32 and 48 subnets. The subnet is 192.168.10.32, and the broadcast address is 47 (the next subnet is 48). The valid host range is 33–46 (the numbers between the subnet number and the broadcast address).

We need to do more, just to make sure you have this down.

You have a host address of 192.168.10.174 with a mask of 255.255.255.240. What is the subnet, broadcast address, and valid host range that this host IP address is part of?

The mask is 240, so we need our block size: 256 – 240 = 16. Just keep adding 16 until we pass the host address of 174, starting at zero, of course: 0, 16, 32, 48, 64, 80, 96, 112, 128, 144, 160, 176. The host address of 174 is between 160 and 176, so the subnet is 160. The broadcast address is 175; the valid host range is 161–174. That was a tough one.

Let's do one more just for fun. This is the easiest one of all Class C subnetting:

192.168.10.17 = Host address

255.255.255.252 = Subnet mask

What subnet and broadcast address is this IP address a part of? 256 – 252 = 4. Start at zero (always start at zero unless told otherwise): 0, 4, 8, 12, 16, 20, and so on. You've got it! The host address is between the 16 and 20 subnets. The subnet is 192.168.10.16, and the broadcast address is 19. The valid host range is 17–18.

Now that you're all over Class C subnetting, let's move on to Class B subnetting. But before we do, let's do a quick review.

So What Do You Know Now?

Here's where you can really apply what you've learned so far and begin committing it all to memory. This is a very cool section that I've been using in my classes for years. It will really help you nail down subnetting!

When you see a subnet mask or slash notation (CIDR), you should know the following when working with Class C networks.

/25

What do you know about a /25?

- 128 mask
- 1 bit on and 7 bits off (10000000)
- Block size of 128
- 2 subnets, each with 126 hosts

/26

And what do you know about a /26?

- 192 mask
- 2 bits on and 6 bits off (11000000)

- Block size of 64
- 4 subnets, each with 62 hosts

/27

What about a /27?

- 224 mask
- 3 bits on and 5 bits off (11100000)
- Block size of 32
- 8 subnets, each with 30 hosts

/28

And what about a /28?

- 240 mask
- 4 bits on and 4 bits off
- Block size of 16
- 16 subnets, each with 14 hosts

/29

What do you know about a /29?

- 248 mask
- 5 bits on and 3 bits off
- Block size of 8
- 32 subnets, each with 6 hosts

/30

And last, what about a /30?

- 252 mask
- 6 bits on and 2 bits off
- Block size of 4
- 64 subnets, each with 2 hosts

Regardless of whether you have a Class A, Class B, or Class C address, the /30 mask will provide you with only two hosts, ever. This mask is suited almost exclusively for use on point-to-point links.

If you can memorize this "So What Do You Know Now?" section, you'll be much better off in your day-to-day job and in your studies. Try saying it out loud, which helps you memorize things—yes, your significant other and/or co-workers will think you've lost it, but they probably already do if you're in the networking field. And if you're not yet in the networking field but are studying all this to break into it, you might as well have people start thinking you're a little "different" now because they will eventually anyway.

It's also helpful to write these on some type of flashcards and have people test your skill. You'd be amazed at how fast you can get subnetting down if you memorize block sizes as well as this "So What Do You Know Now?" section.

Subnetting Class B Addresses

Before we dive into this, let's look at all the possible Class B subnet masks. Notice that we have a lot more possible subnet masks than we do with a Class C network address:

255.255.0.0	(/16)
255.255.128.0	(/17)
255.255.192.0	(/18)
255.255.224.0	(/19)
255.255.240.0	(/20)
255.255.248.0	(/21)
255.255.252.0	(/22)
255.255.254.0	(/23)
255.255.255.0	(/24)
255.255.255.128	(/25)
255.255.255.192	(/26)
255.255.255.224	(/27)
255.255.255.240	(/28)
255.255.255.248	(/29)
255.255.255.252	(/30)

We know the Class B network address has 16 bits available for host addressing. This means we can use up to 14 bits for subnetting (because we have to leave at least 2 bits for host addressing). Using a /16 means you are not subnetting with Class B, but it is a mask you can use.

NOTE   By the way, do you notice anything interesting about that list of subnet values—a pattern, maybe? Ah-ha! That's exactly why I had you memorize the binary-to-decimal numbers earlier in this chapter. Because subnet mask bits start on the left and move to the right and bits can't be skipped, the numbers are always the same regardless of the class of address. Memorize this pattern.

The process of subnetting a Class B network is pretty much the same as it is for a Class C, except that you have more host bits and you start in the third octet.

Use the same subnet numbers for the third octet with Class B that you used for the fourth octet with Class C, but add a 0 to the network portion and a 255 to the broadcast section in the fourth octet. The following table shows you an example host range of two subnets used in a Class B 240 (/20) subnet mask:

First Subnet	Second Subnet
16.0	32.0
31.255	47.255

Notice that these are the same numbers we used in the fourth octet with a /28 mask, but we moved them to the third octet and added a .0 and .255 at the end. Just add the valid hosts between the numbers, and you're set!

Subnetting Practice Examples: Class B Addresses

The following sections will give you an opportunity to practice subnetting Class B addresses. Again, I have to mention that this is the same as subnetting with Class C, except we start in the third octet—with the exact same numbers!

Practice Example #1B: 255.255.128.0 (/17)

Let's take a look at our first example:

172.16.0.0 = Network address

255.255.128.0 = Subnet mask

- *Subnets?* $2^1 = 2$ (same as Class C).
- *Hosts?* $2^{15} - 2 = 32,766$ (7 bits in the third octet, and 8 in the fourth).
- *Valid subnets?* 256 − 128 = 128. 0, 128. Remember that subnetting in Class B starts in the third octet, so the subnet numbers are really 0.0 and 128.0, as shown in the next table. These are the exact numbers we used with Class C; we use them in the third octet and add a 0 in the fourth octet for the network address.
- *Broadcast address for each subnet?*

The following table shows the two subnets available, the valid host range, and the broadcast address of each:

Subnet	0.0	128.0
First host	0.1	128.1
Last host	127.254	255.254
Broadcast	127.255	255.255

Notice that we just added the fourth octet's lowest and highest values and came up with the answers. And again, it's done the same way as for a Class C subnet. We just use the same numbers in the third octet and added 0 and 255 in the fourth octet—pretty simple, huh? I really can't say this enough: It's not hard. The numbers never change. We just use them in different octets!

Practice Example #2B: 255.255.192.0 (/18)

Let's take a look at a second example with Class B.

172.16.0.0 = Network address

255.255.192.0 = Subnet mask

- *Subnets?* $2^2 = 4$.
- *Hosts?* $2^{14} - 2 = 16,382$ (6 bits in the third octet, and 8 in the fourth).
- *Valid subnets?* $256 - 192 = 64$. 0, 64, 128, 192. Remember that we're in the third octet, so the subnet numbers are really 0.0, 64.0, 128.0, and 192.0, as shown in the next table.
- *Broadcast address for each subnet?*
- *Valid hosts?*

The following table shows the four subnets available, the valid host range, and the broadcast address of each:

Subnet	0.0	64.0	128.0	192.0
First host	0.1	64.1	128.1	192.1
Last host	63.254	127.254	191.254	255.254
Broadcast	63.255	127.255	191.255	255.255

Again, it's pretty much the same as it is for a Class C subnet—we just added 0 and 255 in the fourth octet for each subnet in the third octet.

Practice Example #3B: 255.255.240.0 (/20)

Let's take a look:

172.16.0.0 = Network address

255.255.240.0 = Subnet mask

- *Subnets?* $2^4 = 16$.
- *Hosts?* $2^{12} - 2 = 4,094$.
- *Valid subnets?* $256 - 240 = 16$, but we start counting from 0. 0, 16, 32, 48, and so on, up to 240. Notice that these are the same numbers as a Class C 240 mask—we just put them in the third octet and add a 0 and 255 in the fourth octet.
- *Broadcast address for each subnet?*
- *Valid hosts?*

The following table shows the first four subnets, valid hosts, and broadcast address in a Class B 255.255.240.0 mask:

Subnet	0.0	16.0	32.0	48.0
First host	0.1	16.1	32.1	48.1
Last host	15.254	31.254	47.254	63.254
Broadcast	15.255	31.255	47.255	63.255

Practice Example #4B: 255.255.254.0 (/23)

Let's take a look:

172.16.0.0 = Network address

255.255.254.0 = Subnet mask

- *Subnets? 2^7 = 128.*
- *Hosts? $2^9 - 2$ = 510.*
- *Valid subnets? 256 − 254 = 0, 2, 4, 6, 8, and so on, up to 254.*
- *Broadcast address for each subnet?*
- *Valid hosts?*

The following table shows the first five subnets, valid hosts, and broadcast address in a Class B 255.255.254.0 mask:

Subnet	0.0	2.0	4.0	6.0	8.0
First host	0.1	2.1	4.1	6.1	8.1
Last host	1.254	3.254	5.254	7.254	9.254
Broadcast	1.255	3.255	5.255	7.255	9.255

Practice Example #5B: 255.255.255.0 (/24)

Contrary to popular belief, 255.255.255.0 used with a Class B network address is not called a Class B network with a Class C subnet mask. It's amazing how many people see this mask used in a Class B network and think it's a Class C subnet mask. This is a Class B subnet mask with 8 bits of subnetting—it's considerably different from a Class C mask. Subnetting this address is fairly simple:

172.16.0.0 = Network address

255.255.255.0 = Subnet mask

- *Subnets? 2^8 = 256.*
- *Hosts? $2^8 - 2$ = 254.*

- *Valid subnets?* 256 – 255 = 1. 0, 1, 2, 3, and so on, all the way to 255.
- *Broadcast address for each subnet?*
- *Valid hosts?*

The following table shows the first four and last two subnets, the valid hosts, and the broadcast address in a Class B 255.255.255.0 mask:

Subnet	0.0	1.0	2.0	3.0	. . .	254.0	255.0
First host	0.1	1.1	2.1	3.1	. . .	254.1	255.1
Last host	0.254	1.254	2.254	3.254	. . .	254.254	255.254
Broadcast	0.255	1.255	2.255	3.255	. . .	254.255	255.255

Practice Example #6B: 255.255.255.128 (/25)

This is one of the hardest subnet masks you can play with. And worse, it actually is a really good subnet to use in production because it creates more than 500 subnets with a whopping 126 hosts for each subnet—a nice mixture. So, don't skip over it!

172.16.0.0 = Network address

255.255.255.128 = Subnet mask

- *Subnets?* $2^9 = 512$.
- *Hosts?* $2^7 - 2 = 126$.
- *Valid subnets?* Now for the tricky part. 256 – 255 = 1. 0, 1, 2, 3, and so on for the third octet. But you can't forget the one subnet bit used in the fourth octet. Remember when I showed you how to figure one subnet bit with a Class C mask? You figure this out the same way. (Now you know why I showed you the 1-bit subnet mask in the Class C section—to make this part easier.) You actually get two subnets for each third octet value, hence the 512 subnets. For example, if the third octet is showing subnet 3, the two subnets would actually be 3.0 and 3.128.
- *Broadcast address for each subnet?*
- *Valid hosts?*

The following table shows how you can create subnets, valid hosts, and broadcast addresses using the Class B 255.255.255.128 subnet mask (the first eight subnets are shown and then the last two subnets):

Subnet	0.0	0.128	1.0	1.128	2.0	2.128	3.0	3.128	. . .	255.0	255.128
First host	0.1	0.129	1.1	1.129	2.1	2.129	3.1	3.129	. . .	255.1	255.129
Last host	0.126	0.254	1.126	1.254	2.126	2.254	3.126	3.254	. . .	255.126	255.254
Broadcast	0.127	0.255	1.127	1.255	2.127	2.255	3.127	3.255	. . .	255.127	255.255

Practice Example #7B: 255.255.255.192 (/26)

Now, this is where Class B subnetting gets easy. Because the third octet has a 255 in the mask section, whatever number is listed in the third octet is a subnet number. However, now that we have a subnet number in the fourth octet, we can subnet this octet just as we did with Class C subnetting. Let's try it:

172.16.0.0 = Network address

255.255.255.192 = Subnet mask

- *Subnets?* $2^{10} = 1024$.
- *Hosts?* $2^6 - 2 = 62$.
- *Valid subnets?* $256 - 192 = 64$. The subnets are shown in the following table. Do these numbers look familiar?
- *Broadcast address for each subnet?*
- *Valid hosts?*

The following table shows the first eight subnet ranges, valid hosts, and broadcast address:

Subnet	0.0	0.64	0.128	0.192	1.0	1.64	1.128	1.192
First host	0.1	0.65	0.129	0.193	1.1	1.65	1.129	1.193
Last host	0.62	0.126	0.190	0.254	1.62	1.126	1.190	1.254
Broadcast	0.63	0.127	0.191	0.255	1.63	1.127	1.191	1.255

Notice that for each subnet value in the third octet, you get subnets 0, 64, 128, and 192 in the fourth octet.

Practice Example #8B: 255.255.255.224 (/27)

This is done the same way as the preceding subnet mask, except that we have more subnets and fewer hosts per subnet available.

172.16.0.0 = Network address

255.255.255.224 = Subnet mask

- *Subnets?* $2^{11} = 2048$.
- *Hosts?* $2^5 - 2 = 30$.
- *Valid subnets?* $256 - 224 = 32$. 0, 32, 64, 96, 128, 160, 192, 224.
- *Broadcast address for each subnet?*
- *Valid hosts?*

The following table shows the first eight subnets:

Subnet	0.0	0.32	0.64	0.96	0.128	0.160	0.192	0.224
First host	0.1	0.33	0.65	0.97	0.129	0.161	0.193	0.225
Last host	0.30	0.62	0.94	0.126	0.158	0.190	0.222	0.254
Broadcast	0.31	0.63	0.95	0.127	0.159	0.191	0.223	0.255

This next table shows the last eight subnets:

Subnet	255.0	255.32	255.64	255.96	255.128	255.160	255.192	255.224
First host	255.1	255.33	255.65	255.97	255.129	255.161	255.193	255.225
Last host	255.30	255.62	255.94	255.126	255.158	255.190	255.222	255.254
Broadcast	255.31	255.63	255.95	255.127	255.159	255.191	255.223	255.255

Subnetting in Your Head: Class B Addresses

Are you nuts? Subnet Class B addresses in our heads? It's actually easier than writing it out—I'm not kidding! Let me show you the steps:

1. What subnet and broadcast address is the IP address 172.16.10.33 255.255.255.224 (/27) a member of?

   The interesting octet is the fourth octet. 256 − 224 = 32. 32 + 32 = 64. Bingo: 33 is between 32 and 64. However, remember that the third octet is considered part of the subnet, so the answer is the 10.32 subnet. The broadcast is 10.63 because 10.64 is the next subnet. That was a pretty easy one.

2. What subnet and broadcast address is the IP address 172.16.66.10 255.255.192.0 (/18) a member of?

   The interesting octet is the third octet instead of the fourth octet. 256 − 192 = 64. 0, 64, 128. The subnet is 172.16.64.0. The broadcast must be 172.16.127.255 because 128.0 is the next subnet.

Notice in the last example I started counting at zero. This is called *ip subnet-zero*. It is a command that if executed on a router, allows us to use the zero subnet as our first subnet. This may or may not be enabled on your router. If it is not enabled, then you cannot start counting subnets at zero. Most routers, if not all routers these days, support ip subnet-zero.

3. What subnet and broadcast address is the IP address 172.16.50.10 255.255.224.0 (/19) a member of?

    256 − 224 = 0, 32, 64 (remember, we always start counting at zero). The subnet is 172.16.32.0, and the broadcast must be 172.16.63.255 because 64.0 is the next subnet.

4. What subnet and broadcast address is the IP address 172.16.46.255 255.255.240.0 (/20) a member of?

    256 − 240 = 16. The third octet is interesting to us. 0, 16, 32, 48. This subnet address must be in the 172.16.32.0 subnet, and the broadcast must be 172.16.47.255 because 48.0 is the next subnet. So, yes, 172.16.46.255 is a valid host.

5. What subnet and broadcast address is the IP address 172.16.45.14 255.255.255.252 (/30) a member of?

    Where is the interesting octet? 256 − 252 = 0, 4, 8, 12, 16 (in the fourth octet). The subnet is 172.16.45.12, with a broadcast of 172.16.45.15 because the next subnet is 172.16.45.16.

6. What is the subnet and broadcast address of the host 172.16.88.255/20?

    What is a /20? If you can't answer this, you can't answer this question, can you? A /20 is 255.255.240.0, which gives us a block size of 16 in the third octet, and because no subnet bits are on in the fourth octet, the answer is always 0 and 255 in the fourth octet. 0, 16, 32, 48, 64, 80, 96. Bingo: 88 is between 80 and 96, so the subnet is 80.0 and the broadcast address is 95.255.

7. A router receives a packet on an interface with a destination address of 172.16.46.191/26. What will the router do with this packet?

    Discard it. Do you know why? 172.16.46.191/26 is a 255.255.255.192 mask, which gives us a block size of 64. Our subnets are then 0, 64, 128, 192. 191 is the broadcast address of the 128 subnet, so a router, by default, will discard any broadcast packets.

Troubleshooting IP Addressing

Troubleshooting IP addressing is obviously an important skill because running into trouble somewhere along the way is pretty much a sure thing, and it's going to happen to you. No, I'm not a pessimist; I'm just keeping it real. Because of this nasty fact, it will be great when you can save the day because you can both figure out (diagnose) the problem and fix it on an IP network whether you're at work or at home!

Let's use Figure 8.3 as an example of your basic IP trouble—poor Sally can't log into the Windows server. Do you deal with this by calling the Microsoft team to tell them their server is a pile of junk and causing all your problems? Tempting, but probably not such a great idea—let's first double-check our network instead. Check out Figure 8.3.

FIGURE 8.3 Basic IP troubleshooting

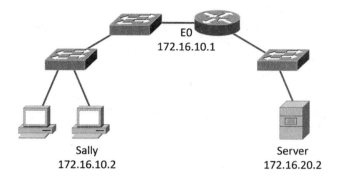

Sally
172.16.10.2

EO
172.16.10.1

Server
172.16.20.2

Let's get started by going over the basic troubleshooting steps. They're pretty simple but important nonetheless. Pretend you're at Sally's host and she's complaining that she can't communicate to a server that just happens to be on a remote network:

1. Open a command prompt window on Sally's host, and ping 127.0.0.1.

```
C:\>ping 127.0.0.1
Pinging 127.0.0.1 with 32 bytes of data:
Reply from 127.0.0.1: bytes=32 time<1ms TTL=128
Reply from 127.0.0.1: bytes=32 time<1ms TTL=128
Reply from 127.0.0.1: bytes=32 time<1ms TTL=128
Reply from 127.0.0.1: bytes=32 time<1ms TTL=128
Ping statistics for 127.0.0.1:
    Packets: Sent = 4, Received = 4, Lost = 0 (0% loss),
Approximate round trip times in milli-seconds:
    Minimum = 0ms, Maximum = 0ms, Average = 0ms
```

This is the diagnostic, or IPv4 loopback address, and if you get a successful ping, your IP stack is considered to be initialized. If it fails, then you have an IP stack failure and need to reinstall TCP/IP on the host.

 If you ping the loopback address and receive an "unable to contact IP driver, error code 2" message, you need to reinstall the TCP/IP protocol suite on the host.

2. Now, from the same command prompt window, ping the IP address of the local host.

```
C:\>ping 172.16.10.2
Pinging 172.16.10.2 with 32 bytes of data:
Reply from 172.16.10.2: bytes=32 time<1ms TTL=128
Reply from 172.16.10.2: bytes=32 time<1ms TTL=128
```

```
Reply from 172.16.10.2: bytes=32 time<1ms TTL=128
Reply from 172.16.10.2: bytes=32 time<1ms TTL=128
Ping statistics for 172.16.10.2:
    Packets: Sent = 4, Received = 4, Lost = 0 (0% loss),
Approximate round trip times in milli-seconds:
    Minimum = 0ms, Maximum = 0ms, Average = 0ms
```

If that's successful, your network interface card (NIC) is functioning. If it fails, there is a problem with the NIC. Success here doesn't mean that a cable is plugged into the NIC, only that the IP protocol stack on the host can communicate to the NIC (via the LAN driver).

3. From the command prompt window, ping the default gateway (router).

```
C:\>ping 172.16.10.1
Pinging 172.16.10.1 with 32 bytes of data:
Reply from 172.16.10.1: bytes=32 time<1ms TTL=128
Reply from 172.16.10.1: bytes=32 time<1ms TTL=128
Reply from 172.16.10.1: bytes=32 time<1ms TTL=128
Reply from 172.16.10.1: bytes=32 time<1ms TTL=128
Ping statistics for 172.16.10.1:
    Packets: Sent = 4, Received = 4, Lost = 0 (0% loss),
Approximate round trip times in milli-seconds:
    Minimum = 0ms, Maximum = 0ms, Average = 0ms
```

If the ping works, it means that the NIC is plugged into the network and can communicate on the local network. If it fails, you have a local physical network problem that could be anywhere from the NIC to the router.

4. If steps 1 through 3 were successful, try to ping the remote server.

```
C:\>ping 172.16.20.2
Pinging 172.16.20.2 with 32 bytes of data:
Reply from 172.16.20.2: bytes=32 time<1ms TTL=128
Reply from 172.16.20.2: bytes=32 time<1ms TTL=128
Reply from 172.16.20.2: bytes=32 time<1ms TTL=128
Reply from 172.16.20.2: bytes=32 time<1ms TTL=128
Ping statistics for 172.16.20.2:
    Packets: Sent = 4, Received = 4, Lost = 0 (0% loss),
Approximate round trip times in milli-seconds:
    Minimum = 0ms, Maximum = 0ms, Average = 0ms
```

If that works, then you know that you have IP communication between the local host and the remote server. You also know that the remote physical network is working.

If the user still can't communicate with the server after steps 1 through 4 are successful, you probably have some type of name resolution problem and need to check your Domain Name System (DNS) settings. But if the ping to the remote server fails, then you know you have some type of remote physical network problem and need to go to the server and work through steps 1 through 3 until you find the snag.

Before we move on to determining IP address problems and how to fix them, I just want to mention some basic yet handy command-line tools that you can use to help troubleshoot your network from both a PC and a Cisco router (the commands might do the same thing, but they are implemented differently):

Packet InterNet Groper (ping)   Uses an Internet Control Message Protocol (ICMP) echo request and replies to test if a host IP stack is initialized and alive on the network.

Traceroute   Displays the list of routers on a path to a network destination by using time to live (TTL) time-outs and ICMP error messages. This command will work on a router, MAC, or Linux box, but not from a Windows command prompt.

Tracert   Same command as `traceroute`, but it's a Microsoft Windows command and will not work on other devices, like a Cisco router or macOS or Linux box.

arp -a   Displays IP–to–MAC-address mappings on a Windows PC.

ipconfig /all   Used only from a command prompt. Shows you the PC network configuration.

Once you've gone through all these steps and used the appropriate command-line tools, if necessary, what do you do if you find a problem? How do you go about fixing an IP address configuration error? That's exactly what you're going to learn about next—how to determine specific IP address problems and what you can do to fix them.

Determining IP Address Problems

It's common for a host, router, or other network device to be configured with the wrong IP address, subnet mask, or default gateway. Because this happens way too often, I'm going to teach you how to both determine and fix IP address configuration errors.

Once you've worked through the four basic steps of troubleshooting and determined there's a problem, you obviously then need to find and fix it. It really helps to draw out the network and IP addressing scheme. If it's already done, consider yourself lucky and go buy a lottery ticket because although it should be done, it rarely is. And if it is, it's usually outdated or inaccurate anyway. Typically it is not done, and you'll probably just have to bite the bullet and start from scratch.

Once you have your network accurately drawn out, including the IP addressing scheme, you need to verify each host's IP address, mask, and default gateway address to determine the problem. (I'm assuming that you don't have a physical problem or that if you did, you've already fixed it.)

Let's check out the example illustrated in Figure 8.4. A user in the sales department calls and tells you that she can't get to ServerA in the marketing department. You ask her if she can get to ServerB in the marketing department, but she doesn't know because she doesn't have rights to log onto that server. What do you do?

FIGURE 8.4   IP address problem 1

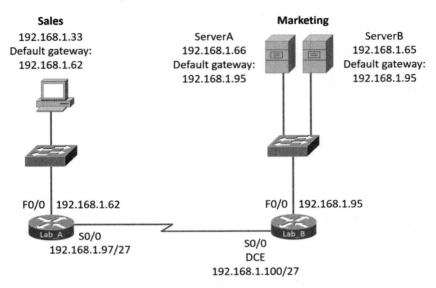

You ask the client to go through the four troubleshooting steps that you learned about in the preceding section. Steps 1 through 3 work, but step 4 fails. By looking at the figure, can you determine the problem? Look for clues in the network drawing. First, the WAN link between the Lab_A router and the Lab_B router shows the mask as a /27. You should already know that this mask is 255.255.255.224 and then determine that all networks are using this mask. The network address is 192.168.1.0. What are our valid subnets and hosts? 256 − 224 = 32, so this makes our subnets 0, 32, 64, 96, 128, and so on. So, by looking at the figure, you can see that subnet 32 is being used by the sales department, the WAN link is using subnet 96, and the marketing department is using subnet 64.

Now you have to determine what the valid host ranges are for each subnet. From what you learned at the beginning of this chapter, you should now be able to easily determine the subnet address, broadcast addresses, and valid host ranges. The valid hosts for the Sales LAN are 33 through 62—the broadcast address is 63 because the next subnet is 64, right? For the Marketing LAN, the valid hosts are 65 through 94 (broadcast 95), and for the WAN link, 97 through 126 (broadcast 127).

By looking at the figure, you can determine that the default gateway on the Lab_B router is incorrect. That address is the broadcast address of the 64 subnet, so there's no way it could be a valid host.

Did you get all that? Maybe we should try another one, just to make sure. Figure 8.5 shows a network problem. A user in the Sales LAN can't get to ServerB. You have the user run through the four basic troubleshooting steps and find that the host can communicate to the local network but not to the remote network. Find and define the IP addressing problem.

FIGURE 8.5   IP address problem 2

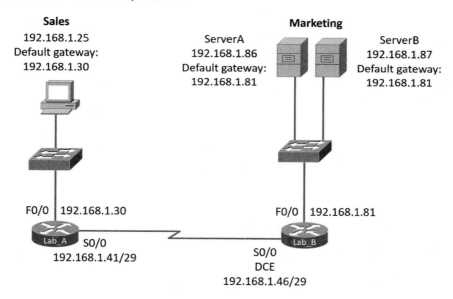

If you use the same steps used to solve the last problem, you can see first that the WAN link again provides the subnet mask to use—/29, or 255.255.255.248. You need to determine what the valid subnets, broadcast addresses, and valid host ranges are to solve this problem.

The 248 mask is a block size of 8 (256 – 248 = 8), so the subnets both start and increment in multiples of 8. By looking at the figure, you see that the Sales LAN is in the 24 subnet, the WAN is in the 40 subnet, and the Marketing LAN is in the 80 subnet. Can you see the problem yet? The valid host range for the Sales LAN is 25–30, and the configuration appears correct. The valid host range for the WAN link is 41–46, and this also appears correct. The valid host range for the 80 subnet is 81–86, with a broadcast address of 87 because the next subnet is 88. ServerB has been configured with the broadcast address of the subnet.

Now that you can figure out misconfigured IP addresses on hosts, what do you do if a host doesn't have an IP address and you need to assign one? What you need to do is look at other hosts on the LAN and figure out the network, mask, and default gateway. Let's take a look at a couple of examples of how to find and apply valid IP addresses to hosts.

You need to assign a server and router IP addresses on a LAN. The subnet assigned on that segment is 192.168.20.24/29, and the router needs to be assigned the first usable address and the server the last valid host ID. What are the IP address, mask, and default gateway assigned to the server?

To answer this, you must know that a /29 is a 255.255.255.248 mask, which provides a block size of 8. The subnet is known as 24, the next subnet in a block of 8 is 32, so the broadcast address of the 24 subnet is 31, which makes the valid host range 25–30:

Server IP address: 192.168.20.30

Server mask: 255.255.255.248

Default gateway: 192.168.20.25 (router's IP address)

As another example, let's take a look at Figure 8.6 and solve this problem.

FIGURE 8.6   Find the valid host

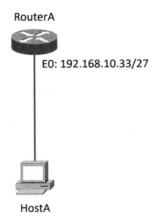

RouterA

E0: 192.168.10.33/27

HostA

Look at the router's IP address on Ethernet0. What IP address, subnet mask, and valid host range could be assigned to the host?

The IP address of the router's Ethernet0 is 192.168.10.33/27. As you already know, a /27 is a 224 mask with a block size of 32. The router's interface is in the 32 subnet. The next subnet is 64, so that makes the broadcast address of the 32 subnet 63 and the valid host range 33–62:

Host IP address: 192.168.10.34–62 (any address in the range except for 33, which is assigned to the router)

Mask: 255.255.255.224

Default gateway: 192.168.10.33

Figure 8.7 shows two routers with Ethernet configurations already assigned. What are the host addresses and subnet masks of hosts A and B?

FIGURE 8.7   Find the valid host #2.

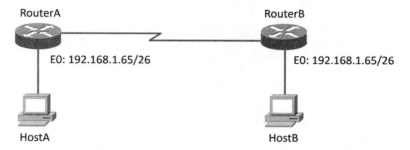

RouterA has an IP address of 192.168.10.65/26 and RouterB has an IP address of 192.168.10.33/28. What are the host configurations? RouterA Ethernet0 is in the 192.168.10.64 subnet, and RouterB Ethernet0 is in the 192.168.10.32 network:

HostA IP address: 192.168.10.66–126

HostA mask: 255.255.255.192

HostA default gateway: 192.168.10.65

HostB IP address: 192.168.10.34–46

HostB mask: 255.255.255.240

HostB default gateway: 192.168.10.33

Just a couple more examples, and then this section is history. Hang in there!

Figure 8.8 shows two routers; you need to configure the S0/0 interface on RouterA. The network assigned to the serial link is 172.16.16.0/22. What IP address can be assigned?

FIGURE 8.8   Find the valid host address #3.

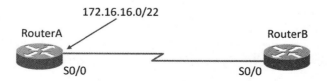

First, you must know that a /22 CIDR is 255.255.252.0, which makes a block size of 4 in the third octet. Because 16 is listed, the available range is 16.1 through 19.254; so, for example, the IP address S0/0 could be 172.16.18.255 because that's within the range.

Okay, last one! You have one Class C network ID, and you need to provide one usable subnet per city while allowing enough usable host addresses for each city specified in Figure 8.9. What is your mask?

FIGURE 8.9   Find the valid subnet mask.

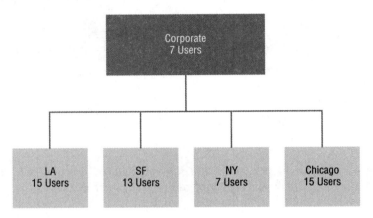

Actually, this is probably the easiest thing you've done all day! I count 5 subnets needed, and the Chicago office needs 15 users (always look for the network that needs the most hosts). What block size is needed for the Chicago office? 32. (Remember, you cannot use a block size of 16 because you always have to subtract 2!) What mask provides you with a block size of 32? 224. Bingo! This provides 8 subnets, each with 30 hosts.

Introduction to Network Address Translation (NAT)

Similar to Classless Inter-Domain Routing (CIDR), the original intention for NAT was to slow the depletion of available IP address space by allowing many private IP addresses to be represented by some smaller number of public IP addresses.

Since then, it's been discovered that NAT is also a useful tool for network migrations and mergers, server load sharing, and creating "virtual servers." So I'm going to describe the basics of NAT functionality and the terminology common to NAT.

At times, NAT really decreases the overwhelming amount of public IP addresses required in your networking environment. And NAT comes in very handy when two companies that have duplicate internal addressing schemes merge. NAT is also great to have around when an organization changes its ISP and the networking manager doesn't want the hassle of changing the internal address scheme.

Here's a list of situations when it's best to have NAT on your side:

- You need to connect to the Internet and your hosts don't have globally unique IP addresses.

- You change to a new ISP that requires you to renumber your network.

- You need to merge two intranets with duplicate addresses.

You typically use NAT on a border router. For an illustration of this, see Figure 8.10, where NAT would be configured on the Corporate router.

FIGURE 8.10 Where to configure NAT

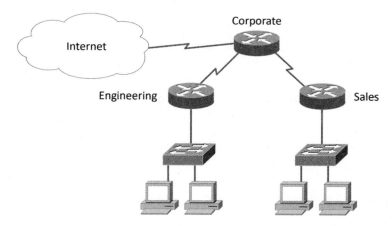

Now you may be thinking, "NAT is totally cool. It's the grooviest, greatest network gadget, and I just gotta have it." Well, hang on a minute. There are truly some serious snags related to NAT use. Oh, don't get me wrong: It really can save you sometimes, but there's a dark side you need to know about too. For a visual of the pros and cons linked to using NAT, check out Table 8.3.

TABLE 8.3   Advantages and disadvantages of implementing NAT

Advantages	Disadvantages
Conserves legally registered addresses	Translation introduces switching path delays.
Reduces address overlap occurrences	Loss of end-to-end IP traceability.
Increases flexibility when connecting to the Internet	Certain applications will not function with NAT enabled.
Eliminates address renumbering as the network changes	

Types of Network Address Translation

In this section, I'm going to go over the three types of NAT with you:

Static NAT (SNAT)   This type of NAT is designed to allow one-to-one mapping between local and global addresses. Keep in mind that the static version requires you to have one real Internet IP address for every host on your network.

Dynamic NAT (DNAT)   This version gives you the ability to map an unregistered IP address to a registered IP address from a pool of registered IP addresses. You don't have to statically configure your router to map an-inside-to-an-outside address as you would using static NAT, but you do have to have enough real, bona fide IP addresses for everyone who's going to be sending packets to and receiving them from the Internet.

Overloading   This is the most popular type of NAT configuration. Understand that overloading really is a form of dynamic NAT that maps multiple unregistered IP addresses to a single registered IP address—many-to-one—by using different ports. Now, why is this so special? Well, because it's also known as port address translation (PAT). And by using PAT (NAT Overload), you get to have thousands of users connect to the Internet using only one real global IP address—pretty slick, yeah? Seriously, NAT Overload is the real reason we haven't run out of valid IP addresses on the Internet. Really, I'm not joking.

NAT Names

The names we use to describe the addresses used with NAT are pretty simple. Addresses used after NAT translations are called *global* addresses. These are usually the public addresses used on the Internet, but remember, you don't need public addresses if you aren't going on the Internet.

   Local addresses are the ones we use before network translation. So, the inside local address is actually the private address of the sending host that's trying to get to the Internet, while the outside local address is the address of the destination host. The latter is usually a public address (web address, mail server, and so on) and is how the packet begins its journey.

After translation, the inside local address is then called the *inside global address*, and the outside global address then becomes the name of the destination host. Check out Table 8.4, which lists all this terminology, for a clear picture of the various names used with NAT.

TABLE 8.4 NAT terms

Name	Meaning
Inside local	Name of the inside source address before translation
Outside local	Name of the destination host before translation
Inside global	Name of the inside host after translation
Outside global	Name of the outside destination host after translation

How NAT Works

Now it's time to look at how this whole NAT thing works. I'm going to start by using Figure 8.11 to describe the basic translation of NAT.

In the example shown in Figure 8.11, host 10.1.1.1 sends an outbound packet to the border router configured with NAT. The router identifies the IP address as an inside local IP address destined for an outside network, translates the address, and documents the translation in the NAT table.

The packet is sent to the outside interface with the new translated source address. The external host returns the packet to the destination host, and the NAT router translates the inside global IP address back to the inside local IP address using the NAT table. This is as simple as it gets.

Let's take a look at a more complex configuration using overloading, or what is also referred to as PAT. I'll use Figure 8.12 to demonstrate how PAT works.

With overloading, all inside hosts get translated to one single IP address, which is why it's called *overloading*. Again, the reason we have not run out of available IP addresses on the Internet is because of overloading port address translation.

Take a look at the NAT table in Figure 8.12 again. In addition to the inside local IP address and outside global IP address, we now have port numbers. These port numbers help the router identify which host should receive the return traffic.

FIGURE 8.11   Basic NAT translation

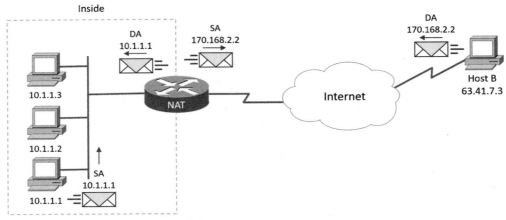

NAT Table

Inside Local IP Addresses	Inside Global IP Addresses
10.1.1.3	170.168.2.4
10.1.1.2	170.168.2.3
10.1.1.1	170.168.2.2

FIGURE 8.12   NAT overloading example (PAT)

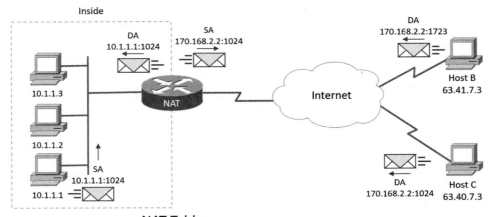

NAT Table

Protocol	Inside Local IP Addresses	Inside Global IP Addresses: Port	Outside Global IP Address: Port
TCP	10.1.1.3:1492	170.168.2.2:1492	63.41.7.3:23
TCP	10.1.1.2:1723	170.168.2.2:1723	63.41.7.3:23
TCP	10.1.1.1:1024	170.168.2.2:1024	63.40.7.3:23

Port numbers are used at the Transport layer to identify the local host in this example. If we had to use IP addresses to identify the source hosts, that would be called *static NAT*, and we would run out of addresses. PAT allows us to use the Transport layer to identify the hosts, which in turn allows us to use (theoretically) up to 65,000 hosts with one real IP address.

One last thing: We've been discussing translating IP addresses using some type of network address translation. However, using a router or firewall, you can also perform port forwarding, which is translating the port number of a packet to a new destination. The destination may be a predetermined network port (using any IP protocol, but typically TCP or UDP ports) on a host within a private network behind a NAT router. Based on the received port number, a remote host can communicate to servers behind the NAT gateway to the local network.

You're done, the diva has sung, the chicken has crossed the road. . .whew! Take a good break, and then come back and go through the written lab and review questions.

Summary

Did you read Chapter 7 and this chapter and understand everything on the first pass? If so, that is fantastic—congratulations! The thing is, you probably got lost a couple of times, and as I told you, that's what usually happens, so don't stress. Don't feel bad if you have to read each chapter more than once, or even 10 times, before you're truly good to go.

This chapter provided you with an important understanding of IP subnetting. After reading this chapter, you should be able to subnet IP addresses in your head.

You should also understand the basic troubleshooting methods. You must remember the four steps you take when trying to narrow down exactly where a network/IP addressing problem is and then know how to proceed systematically in order to fix it. In addition, you should be able to find valid IP addresses and subnet masks by looking at a network diagram.

I finished this chapter with an introduction to network address translation. I discussed the difference between static and dynamic NAT and NAT overloading (PAT).

Exam Essentials

Remember the steps to subnet in your head.   Understand how IP addressing and subnetting work. First, determine your block size by using the 256-subnet mask math. Then, count your subnets and determine the broadcast address of each subnet—it is always the number right before the next subnet. Your valid hosts are the numbers between the subnet address and the broadcast address.

Understand the various block sizes.   This is an important part of understanding IP addressing and subnetting. The valid block sizes are always 4, 8, 16, 32, 64, 128, and so on. You can determine your block size by using the 256-subnet mask math.

Remember the four diagnostic steps. The four simple steps for troubleshooting are ping the loopback address, ping the NIC, ping the default gateway, and ping the remote device.

You must be able to find and fix an IP addressing problem. Once you go through the four troubleshooting steps, you should be able to determine the IP addressing problem by drawing out the network and finding the valid and invalid hosts addressed in your network.

Understand basic NAT terminology. You want to know the difference between inside local and inside global. Inside local is before translation, and inside global is after translation. Inside global is a registered address representing an inside host to an outside network. You should also understand PAT and how it works by using different port numbers to map multiple private IP addresses to a single registered IP address.

Written Lab

You can find the answers to the written labs in Appendix A. This lab will help you get familiar with the CIDR subnet mask. Fill in the blanks in the table.

CIDR	Subnet mask
/13	
	255.0.0.0
	255.254.0.0
/30	
/22	
	255.255.255.192
/28	
	240.0.0.0
/18	
/27	
/29	
	255.255.248.0
	255.224.0.0
/25	
	255.192.0.0

Review Questions

You can find the answers to the review questions in Appendix B.

1. Which is true of the IP address 135.20.255.255?

   A. It is a Class A address.

   B. It is a broadcast address.

   C. It is the default gateway address.

   D. It has a default mask of 255.0.0.0.

2. You have been given an IP address network of 203.23.23.0. You are asked to subnet it for two hosts per network. What is the subnet mask you will need to use to maximize networks?

   A. 255.255.255.252

   B. 255.255.255.248

   C. 255.255.255.240

   D. 255.255.255.224

3. You require the subnetting of the network address 192.168.1.0 to allow for 10 hosts per subnet while maintaining the maximum number of subnets. What should the subnet mask be?

   A. 255.255.255.192

   B. 255.255.255.224

   C. 255.255.255.240

   D. 255.255.255.248

4. You have been assigned a network ID of 131.44.0.0/16 by your ISP. Your organization needs to use this network ID over four campuses. What mask should be used to subnet it to achieve the goal while maximizing host IP addresses?

   A. 255.255.128.0

   B. 255.255.192.0

   C. 255.255.252.0

   D. 255.255.255.0

5. What is the CIDR notation for a subnet mask of 255.255.240.0?

   A. /19

   B. /20

   C. /22

   D. /28

6. You have been given an IP address network of 213.43.53.0. You are asked to subnet it for 22 hosts per network. What is the subnet mask you will need to use to maximize networks?

    A. 255.255.255.252

    B. 255.255.255.248

    C. 255.255.255.240

    D. 255.255.255.224

7. Which valid IP is in the same network as 192.168.32.61/26?

    A. 192.168.32.59

    B. 192.168.32.63

    C. 192.168.32.64

    D. 192.168.32.72

8. You are setting up a network in which you need 15 subnetworks. You have been given a network address of 153.20.0.0, and you need to maximize the number of hosts in each network. Which subnet mask will you use?

    A. 255.255.224.0

    B. 255.255.240.0

    C. 255.255.248.0

    D. 255.255.252.0

9. An ISP gives you an IP address of 209.183.160.45/30 to configure your end of the serial connection. Which IP address will be on the ISP side?

    A. 209.183.160.43/30

    B. 209.183.160.44/30

    C. 209.183.160.46/30

    D. 209.183.160.47/30

10. In the following exhibit, what needs to be changed for Computer A to successfully communicate with Computer B (assume the least amount of effort to fix the problem)?

    A. Computer A needs to have its IP address changed.

    B. Computer B needs to have its IP address changed.

    C. The default gateway IP address for Computer A needs to be changed.

    D. The default gateway IP address for Computer B needs to be changed.

11. In the following exhibit, what needs to be changed for Computer A to successfully communicate with Computer B (assume the least amount of effort to fix the problem)?

Computer A   192.168.1.30/27 192.168.1.66/27   Computer B

192.168.1.33/27   192.168.1.67/27

- **A.** Computer A needs to have its IP address changed.
- **B.** Computer B needs to have its IP address changed.
- **C.** The default gateway IP address for Computer A needs to be changed.
- **D.** The default gateway IP address for Computer B needs to be changed.

12. Which subnet does host 131.50.39.23/21 belong to?
- **A.** 131.50.39.0/21
- **B.** 131.50.32.0/21
- **C.** 131.50.16.0/21
- **D.** 131.50.8.0/21

13. A computer has an IP address of 145.50.23.1/22. What is the broadcast address for that computer?
- **A.** 145.50.254.255
- **B.** 145.50.255.255
- **C.** 145.50.22.255
- **D.** 145.50.23.255

14. Which method will allow you to use RFC 1918 addresses for Internet requests?
- **A.** CIDR
- **B.** Classful addressing
- **C.** NAT
- **D.** VPN

15. In the following exhibit, what is the inside local IP address?

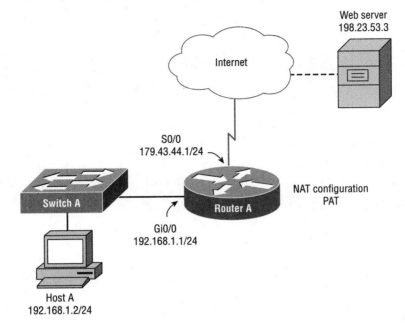

A. 192.168.1.2 Host A

B. 192.168.1.1 Router A Gi0/0

C. 179.43.44.1 Router A S0/0

D. 198.23.53.3 web server

16. In the following exhibit, what is the inside global IP address?

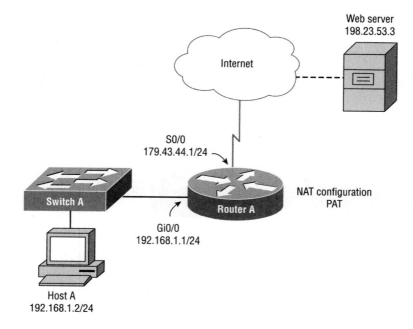

A. 192.168.1.2 Host A

B. 192.168.1.1 Router A Gi0/0

C. 179.43.44.1 Router A S0/0

D. 198.23.53.3 web server

17. In the following exhibit, what is the outside global IP address?

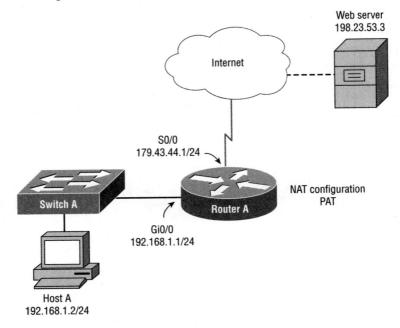

A. 192.168.1.2 Host A

B. 192.168.1.1 Router A Gi0/0

C. 179.43.44.1 Router A S0/0

D. 198.23.53.3 web server

18. What is the maximum number of IP addresses that can be assigned to hosts on a local subnet that uses the 255.255.255.248 subnet mask?

    A. 6

    B. 15

    C. 16

    D. 30

    E. 31

    F. 62

19. If a host on a network has the address 172.16.45.14/30, what is the subnetwork this host belongs to?

    A. 172.16.45.0

    B. 172.16.45.4

    C. 172.16.45.8

    D. 172.16.45.12

    E. 172.16.45.16

20. On which of the following devices are you typically able to implement NAT?

    A. Hub

    B. Ethernet switch

    C. Router

    D. Bridge

Chapter

9

Introduction to IP Routing

THE FOLLOWING COMPTIA NETWORK+ EXAM OBJECTIVES ARE COVERED IN THIS CHAPTER:

✓ **Domain 2.0 Network Implementation**

✓ **2.1 Explain characteristics of routing technologies.**

- Static routing
- Dynamic routing
    - Border Gateway Protocol (BGP)
    - Enhanced Interior Gateway Routing Protocol (EIGRP)
    - Open Shortest Path First (OSPF)
- Route selection
    - Administrative distance
    - Prefix length
    - Metric

IP routing is the process of moving packets from one network to another network using routers. The IP routing process is a super-important subject to understand because it pertains to all routers and configurations that use IP.

Before you read this chapter, you need to understand the difference between a routing protocol and a routed protocol. A *routing protocol* is a tool used by routers to dynamically find all the networks in the internetwork as well as to ensure that all routers have the same routing table. Basically, a routing protocol determines the path of a packet through an internetwork. Examples of routing protocols are Routing Information Protocol (RIP), Routing Information Protocol version 2 (RIPv2), Enhanced Interior Gateway Routing Protocol (EIGRP), Open Shortest Path First (OSPF), and Border Gateway Protocol (BGP).

Once all routers know about all networks, a *routed protocol* can be used to send user data (packets) through the established internetwork. Routed protocols are assigned to an interface and determine the method of packet delivery. Examples of routed protocols are Internet Protocol (IP) and Internet Protocol version 6 (IPv6).

In this chapter, I'm going to describe IP routing with routers. I will explain, in a step-by-step fashion, the IP routing process. I will also explain static and dynamic routing on a conceptual level, with more details about dynamic routing in Chapter 10, "Routing Protocols."

To find Todd Lammle CompTIA videos and practice questions, please see www.lammle.com.

Routing Basics

Once you create an internetwork by connecting your wide area networks (WANs) and local area networks (LANs) to a router, you need to configure logical network addresses, such as IP addresses, to all hosts on the internetwork so that they can communicate via routers across that internetwork.

In IT, routing essentially refers to the process of taking a packet from one device and sending it through the network to another device on a different network. Routers don't really care about hosts—they care only about networks and the best path to each network. The logical network address of the destination host is used to get packets to a network through a routed network, and then the hardware address of the host is used to deliver the packet from a router to the correct destination host.

If your network has no routers, then it should be apparent that, well, you are not routing. But if you do have them, they're there to route traffic to all the networks in your internetwork. To be capable of routing packets, a router must know at least the following information:

- Destination network address
- Neighbor routers from which it can learn about remote networks
- Possible routes to all remote networks
- The best route to each remote network
- How to maintain and verify routing information

The router learns about remote networks from neighbor routers or from an administrator. The router then builds a *routing table* (a map of the internetwork) that describes how to find the remote networks. If a network is directly connected, then the router already knows how to get to it.

If a network isn't directly connected to the router, the router must use one of two ways to learn how to get to it. One way is called *static routing*, which can be a ton of work because it requires someone to type all network locations into the routing table. The other way is dynamic routing.

In *dynamic routing*, a protocol on one router communicates with the same protocol running on neighbor routers. The routers then update each other about all the networks they know about and place this information into the routing table. If a change occurs in the network, the dynamic routing protocols automatically inform all routers about the event. If static routing is used, the administrator is responsible for updating all changes by hand into all routers. Understandably, in a large network, it's common to find that a combination of both dynamic and static routing is being used.

Before we jump into the IP routing process, let's take a look at a simple example that demonstrates how a router uses the routing table to route packets out of an interface. We'll be going into a more detailed study of this process in a minute.

Figure 9.1 shows a simple two-router network. Lab_A has one serial interface and three LAN interfaces.

Looking at Figure 9.1, can you figure out which interface Lab_A will use to forward an IP datagram to a host with an IP address of 10.10.10.10?

By using the Cisco IOS command show ip route, we can see the routing table (map of the internetwork) that router Lab_A will use to make all forwarding decisions:

```
Router_A#show ip route
[output cut]
Gateway of last resort is not set
C       10.10.10.0/24 is directly connected, FastEthernet0/0
C       10.10.20.0/24 is directly connected, FastEthernet0/1
C       10.10.30.0/24 is directly connected, FastEthernet0/2
C       10.10.40.0/24 is directly connected, Serial 0/0
```

FIGURE 9.1 A simple routing example

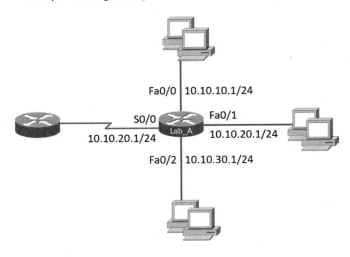

The C in the routing table output means that the networks listed are "directly connected," and until we add a routing protocol—something like RIP, EIGRP, and so on—to the routers in our internetwork, or use static routes, we'll have only directly connected networks in our routing table.

So, let's get back to the original question: By looking at the figure and the output of the routing table, can you tell what Lab_A will do with a received packet that has a destination IP address of 10.10.10.10? If you answered, "The router will packet-switch the packet to interface FastEthernet 0/0, and this interface will then frame the packet and send it out on the network segment," you're right.

Just because we can, let's look at a different example. Based on the output of the next routing table, which interface will a packet with a destination address of 10.10.10.14 be forwarded to?

```
Router_A#sh ip route
[output cut]
Gateway of last resort is not set
C       10.10.10.16/28 is directly connected, FastEthernet0/0
C       10.10.10.8/29 is directly connected, FastEthernet0/1
C       10.10.10.4/30 is directly connected, FastEthernet0/2
C       10.10.10.0/30 is directly connected, Serial 0/0
```

First, you can see that the network is subnetted and that each interface has a different mask. And I have to tell you, you positively can't answer this question if you can't subnet—no way! Here's the answer: 10.10.10.14 would be a host in the 10.10.10.8/29 subnet connected to the FastEthernet 0/1 interface. Don't freak if this one left you staring vacantly. Instead, if you're struggling, go back and reread Chapter 8, "IP Subnetting, Troubleshooting IP, and Introduction to NAT," until you get it. This should then make perfect sense to you.

When the routing tables of all routers in the network are complete (because they include information about all the networks in the inter-network), they are considered *converged*, or in a steady state. This is covered in more detail in Chapter 10.

Now, let's get into this process in more detail.

The IP Routing Process

The IP routing process is actually pretty simple, and it doesn't change, regardless of the size of your network. I'm going to use Figure 9.2 to give you a picture of this step-by-step process. The question I'm asking is this: What happens when Host_A wants to communicate with Host_B on a different network? I'll go through how to answer that question by breaking down the process with headings to make it easier to understand. First, check out Figure 9.2.

FIGURE 9.2   IP routing example using two hosts and one router

Suppose that a user on Host_A pings Host_B's IP address. Routing doesn't get any simpler than this, but it still involves a lot of steps. Let's work through them.

A packet is created on the host:

1. Internet Control Message Protocol (ICMP) creates an echo request payload (which is just the alphabet in the data field).

2. ICMP hands that payload to IP, which then creates a packet. At a minimum, this packet contains an IP source address, an IP destination address, and a Protocol field with 01h. (Remember that Cisco likes to use *0x* in front of hex characters, so this could look like 0x01.) All of that tells the receiving host whom it should hand the payload to when the destination is reached. In this example, it's ICMP.

The packet is forwarded:

3. After the packet is created, IP determines whether the destination IP address is on the local network or a remote one.

4. Because IP has discovered that this is a remote request, the packet needs to be sent to the default gateway so the packet can be routed to the correct remote network. The Registry in Windows is parsed to find the configured default gateway.

5. The default gateway of host 172.16.10.2 (Host_A) is configured to 172.16.10.1. For this packet to be sent to the default gateway, the hardware address of the router's inter-face Ethernet 0 (configured with the IP address of 172.16.10.1) must be known. Why? So the packet can be handed down to the Data Link layer, framed, and sent to the router's interface that's connected to the 172.16.10.0 network. Because hosts only com-municate via hardware addresses on the local LAN, it's important to recognize that for Host_A to communicate to Host_B, it has to send packets to the Media Access Control (MAC) address of the default gateway on the local network.

MAC addresses are always local on the LAN and never go through and past a router.

6. The Address Resolution Protocol (ARP) cache of the host is checked to see whether the IP address of the default gateway has already been resolved to a hardware address. If it has, the packet is then free to be handed to the Data Link layer for framing. (The hardware-destination address is also handed down with that packet.) To view the ARP cache on your host, use the following command:

```
C:\>arp -a
Interface: 172.16.10.2 --- 0x3
  Internet Address     Physical Address     Type
  172.16.10.1          00-15-05-06-31-b0    dynamic
```

If the hardware address isn't already in the ARP cache of the host, an ARP broadcast is sent out onto the local network to search for the hardware address of 172.16.10.1. The router responds to that request and provides the hardware address of Ethernet 0, and the host caches this address.

7. After the packet and destination hardware address have been handed to the Data Link layer, the LAN driver is used to provide media access via the type of LAN being used (in this example, it's Ethernet). A frame is then generated, encapsulating the packet with control information. Within that frame are the hardware-destination and source addresses plus, in this case, an Ether-Type field that describes the Network layer pro-tocol that handed the packet to the Data Link layer—in this instance, IP. At the end of the frame is something called a Frame Check Sequence (FCS) field that houses the result of the cyclic redundancy check (CRC). The frame would look something like what I've detailed in Figure 9.3. It contains Host_A's hardware (MAC) address and the hardware-destination address of the default gateway. It does not include the remote host's MAC address—remember that because it's important!

FIGURE 9.3   Frame used from Host_A to the Lab_A router when Host_B is pinged

Destination MAC (Router's E0 MAC Address)	Source MAC (Host_A MAC Address)	Ether-Type field	Packet	FCS (CRC)

8. When the frame is completed, it's handed down to the Physical layer to be placed onto the physical medium one bit at a time. In this example, the physical medium is twisted-pair wire.

   The router receives the packet:

9. Every device within the collision domain receives these bits and builds the frame. They each run a CRC and check the answer in the FCS field. If the answers don't match, the frame is discarded. But if the CRC matches, then the hardware-destination address is checked to see if it matches, too (in this example, it's the router's interface, Ethernet 0). If it's a match, then the Ether-Type field is checked to find the protocol used at the Network layer.

10. The packet is pulled from the frame, and what is left of the frame is discarded. The packet is then handed to the protocol listed in the Ether-Type field—it's given to IP.

    The router routes the packet:

11. IP receives the packet and checks the IP destination address. Because the packet's destination address doesn't match any of the addresses configured on the receiving router's interfaces, the router will look up the destination IP network address in its routing table.

12. The routing table must have an entry for the network 172.16.20.0 or the packet will be discarded immediately and an ICMP message will be sent back to the originating device with a Destination Unreachable message.

13. If the router does find an entry for the destination network in its table, the packet is switched to the exit interface—in this example, interface Ethernet 1. The following output displays the Lab_A router's routing table. The C means "directly connected." No routing protocols are needed in this network because all networks (all two of them) are directly connected:

```
Lab_A>sh ip route
Codes:C - connected,S - static,I - IGRP,R - RIP,M - mobile,B -
   BGP, D - EIGRP,EX - EIGRP external,O - OSPF,IA - OSPF inter
   area, N1 - OSPF NSSA external type 1, N2 - OSPF NSSA external
type 2, E1 - OSPF external type 1, E2 - OSPF external type 2,
E - EGP,i - IS-IS, L1 - IS-IS level-1, L2 - IS-IS level-2, ia
   - IS-IS intearea * - candidate default, U - per-user static
   route, o - ODR P - periodic downloaded static route

Gateway of last resort is not set

     172.16.0.0/24 is subnetted, 2 subnets
C       172.16.10.0 is directly connected, Ethernet0
C       172.16.20.0 is directly connected, Ethernet1
```

14. The router packet-switches the packet to the Ethernet 1 buffer.

15. Now that the packet is in the Ethernet 1 buffer, IP needs to know the hardware address of the destination host and first checks the ARP cache. If the hardware address of Host_B has already been resolved and is in the router's ARP cache, then the packet and the hardware address are handed down to the Data Link layer to be framed. Let's take a look at the ARP cache on the Lab_A router by using the show ip arp command:

```
Lab_A#sh ip arp
Protocol   Address      Age(min) Hardware Addr   Type   Interface
Internet   172.16.20.1    -        00d0.58ad.05f4  ARPA   Ethernet1
Internet   172.16.20.2    3        0030.9492.a5dd  ARPA   Ethernet1
Internet   172.16.10.1    -        0015.0506.31b0  ARPA   Ethernet0
Internet   172.16.10.2    12       0030.9492.a4ac  ARPA   Ethernet0
```

The dash (-) means that this is the physical interface on the router. From this output, we can see that the router knows the 172.16.10.2 (Host_A) and 172.16.20.2 (Host_B) hardware addresses. Cisco routers will keep an entry in the ARP table for four hours. But if the hardware address hasn't already been resolved, the router then sends an ARP request out E1 looking for the hardware address of 172.16.20.2. Host_B responds with its hardware address, and the packet and hardware-destination address are both sent to the Data Link layer for framing.

16. The Data Link layer creates a frame with the destination and source hardware address, Ether-Type field, and FCS field at the end. The frame is handed to the Physical layer to be sent out on the physical medium one bit at a time.

Finally, the remote host receives the packet:

17. Host_B receives the frame and immediately runs a CRC. If the result matches what's in the FCS field, the hardware-destination address is then checked. If the host finds a match, the Ether-Type field is then checked to determine the protocol that the packet should be handed to at the Network layer—IP, in this example.

18. At the Network layer, IP receives the packet and checks the IP destination address. Because there's finally a match made, the Protocol field is checked to find out whom the payload should be given to.

19. The payload is handed to ICMP, which understands that this is an echo request. ICMP responds to this by immediately discarding the packet and generating a new payload as an echo reply.

The destination host becomes a source host:

20. A packet is created, including the source and destination IP addresses, Protocol field, and payload. The destination device is now Host_A.

21. IP checks to see whether the destination IP address is a device on the local LAN or on a remote network. Because the destination device is on a remote network, the packet needs to be sent to the default gateway.

22. The default gateway IP address is found in the Registry of the Windows device, and the ARP cache is checked to see whether the hardware address has already been resolved from an IP address.

23. After the hardware address of the default gateway is found, the packet and destination hardware addresses are handed down to the Data Link layer for framing.

24. The Data Link layer frames the packet of information and includes the following in the header:
    - The destination and source hardware addresses
    - The Ether-Type field with 0x0800 (IP) in it
    - The FCS field with the CRC result in tow

25. The frame is now handed down to the Physical layer to be sent out over the network medium one bit at a time.

    Time for the router to route another packet:

26. The router's Ethernet 1 interface receives the bits and builds a frame. The CRC is run, and the FCS field is checked to make sure the answers match.

27. When the CRC is found to be okay, the hardware-destination address is checked. Because the router's interface is a match, the packet is pulled from the frame, and the Ether-Type field is checked to see which protocol at the Network layer the packet should be delivered to.

28. The protocol is determined to be IP, so it gets the packet. IP runs a CRC check on the IP header first and then checks the destination IP address.

> IP does not run a complete CRC the way the Data Link layer does—it only checks the header for errors.

Because the IP destination address doesn't match any of the router's interfaces, the routing table is checked to see whether it has a route to 172.16.10.0. If it doesn't have a route over to the destination network, the packet will be discarded immediately. (This is the source point of confusion for a lot of administrators—when a ping fails, most people think the packet never reached the destination host. But as we see here, that's not *always* the case. All it takes is just one of the remote routers to be lacking a route back to the originating host's network and—*poof!*—the packet is dropped on the *return trip*, not on its way to the host.)

> Just a quick note to mention that when (if) the packet is lost on the way back to the originating host, you will typically see a Request Timed Out message because it is an unknown error. If the error occurs because of a known issue, such as a route that is not in the routing table on the way to the destination device, you will see a Destination Unreachable message. This should help you determine if the problem occurred on the way to the destination or on the way back.

29. In this case, the router does know how to get to network 172.16.10.0—the exit interface is Ethernet 0—so the packet is switched to interface Ethernet 0.

30. The router checks the ARP cache to determine whether the hardware address for 172.16.10.2 has already been resolved.

31. Because the hardware address to 172.16.10.2 is already cached from the originating trip to Host_B, the hardware address and packet are handed to the Data Link layer.

32. The Data Link layer builds a frame with the destination and source hardware addresses and then puts IP in the Ether-Type field. A CRC is run on the frame, and the result is placed in the FCS field.

33. The frame is then handed to the Physical layer to be sent out onto the local network one bit at a time.

The original source host, now the destination host, receives the reply packet:

34. The destination host receives the frame, runs a CRC, checks the hardware destination address, and looks in the Ether-Type field to find out whom to hand the packet to.

35. IP is the designated receiver, and after the packet is handed to IP at the Network layer, IP checks the Protocol field for further direction. IP finds instructions to give the payload to ICMP, and ICMP determines the packet to be an ICMP echo reply.

36. ICMP acknowledges that it has received the reply by sending an exclamation point (!) to the user interface. ICMP then attempts to send four more echo requests to the destination host.

You've just been introduced to "Todd's 36 easy steps to understanding IP routing." The key point to understand here is that if you had a much larger network, the process would be the *same*. In a really big internetwork, the packet just goes through more hops before it finds the destination host.

It's super important to remember that when Host_A sends a packet to Host_B, the destination hardware address used is the default gateway's Ethernet interface. Why? Because frames can't be placed on remote networks—only local networks. So, packets destined for remote networks must go through the default gateway.

Let's take a look at Host_A's ARP cache now by using the arp -a command from the command prompt:

```
C:\ >arp -a
Interface: 172.16.10.2 --- 0x3
  Internet Address      Physical Address      Type
  172.16.10.1           00-15-05-06-31-b0     dynamic
  172.16.20.1           00-15-05-06-31-b0     dynamic
```

Did you notice that the hardware (MAC) address that Host_A uses to get to Host_B is the Lab_A E0 interface?

Hardware addresses are *always* local, and they never pass a router's interface. Understanding this process is as important to internetworking as breathing air is to you, so carve this into your memory!

Examining the ARP Cache

In this exercise, you will examine the ARP cache of your computer.

1. Open the command prompt by clicking Start, typing **cmd**, and pressing Enter.

2. In the command prompt, type **ipconfig** and make note of the IP address of the default gateway.

3. Type the command **ping www.wiley.com**, press Enter, and wait for the command to complete.

4. Type the command **arp -g** and locate the entry for the default gateway.

5. Examine other ARP entries that might exist in the ARP cache.

In the exercise you examined the ARP entry for the default gateway. The result of this exercise is obtaining the MAC address of the default gateway (router). The MAC address for the default gateway is only relevant to the local clients on the network.

Testing Your IP Routing Understanding

I want to make sure you understand IP routing because it's really that important. So, I'm going to use this section to test your understanding of the IP routing process by having you look at a couple of figures and answer some very basic IP routing questions.

Figure 9.4 shows a LAN connected to RouterA, which is, in turn, connected via a WAN link to RouterB. RouterB has a LAN connected with an HTTP server attached. Take a look.

FIGURE 9.4   IP routing example 1

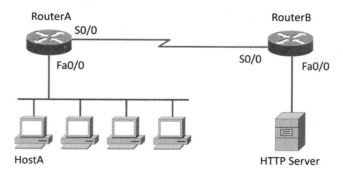

The critical information you need to glean from this figure is exactly how IP routing will occur in this example. Okay, we'll cheat a bit. I'll give you the answer, but then you should go back over the figure and see if you can answer example 2 without looking at my answers:

1. The destination address of a frame, from HostA, will be the MAC address of the Fa0/0 interface of the RouterA router.

2. The destination address of a packet will be the IP address of the network interface card (NIC) of the HTTP server.

3. The destination port number in the segment header will have a value of 80.

That example was a pretty simple one, and it was also very to the point. One thing to remember is that if multiple hosts are communicating to the server using HTTP, they must all use a different source port number. That is how the server keeps the data separated at the Transport layer.

Let's mix it up a little and add another internetworking device into the network and then see if you can find the answers. Figure 9.5 shows a network with only one router but two switches.

FIGURE 9.5 IP routing example 2

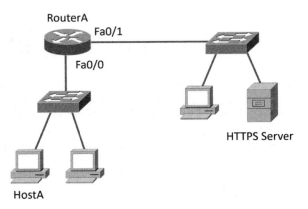

What you want to understand about the IP routing process here is what happens when HostA sends data to the HTTPS server:

1. The destination address of a frame from HostA will be the MAC address of the Fa0/0 interface of the RouterA router.

2. The destination address of a packet will be the IP address of the NIC of the HTTPS server.

3. The destination port number in the segment header will have a value of 443.

Notice that neither switch was used as either a default gateway or another destination. That's because switches have nothing to do with routing. I wonder how many of you chose the switch as the default gateway (destination) MAC address for HostA. If you did, don't feel bad—just take another look with that fact in mind. It's very important to remember that the destination MAC address will always be the router's interface—if your packets are destined for outside the LAN, as they were in these last two examples.

Static and Dynamic Routing

How does a router send packets to remote networks when the only way it can send them is by looking at the routing table to find out how to get to the remote networks? And what happens when a router receives a packet for a network that isn't listed in the routing table? It doesn't send a broadcast looking for the remote network—the router just discards the packet.

There are several ways to configure the routing tables to include all the networks so that packets will be forwarded. Understand that what's best for one network isn't necessarily what's best for another. Knowing about and being able to recognize the different types of routing will really help you come up with the best solution for your specific environment and business requirements.

> Routing convergence is the time required by the routing protocols to update the routing tables (forwarding tables) on all routers in the network.

Looking at Figure 9.6, you can see that we can configure a router with either static or dynamic routing. If we choose static routing, then we have to go to each router and type in each network and the path that IP will use to send packets. However, static routing does not scale well in large networks, but dynamic routing does because network routes are automatically added to the routing table via the routing protocol.

FIGURE 9.6   Routing options

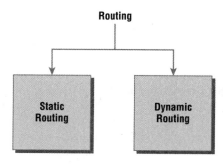

Dynamic routing protocols break up into many different categories or types of protocols, as shown in Figure 9.7. The first split in the dynamic protocol branch is the division of interior gateway protocols (IGPs) and exterior gateway protocols (EGPs). We are going to talk about each protocol and category, but for now the difference between IGP and EGP is interior or exterior routing of an autonomous system (AS).

FIGURE 9.7   Dynamic routing options

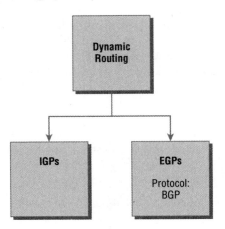

An *autonomous system* is a collection of networks or subnets that are in the same administrative domain. This is another way of saying an administrative domain is within your company's network, and you control or administer all the subnets that are within it. You control and set the policy for what happens in the network or autonomous system. I hope you can now see that an IGP operates and routes within an AS and an EGP works outside or between more than one AS.

The most popular protocol for an EGP is Border Gateway Protocol (BGP), which is typically used by ISPs or really large corporations. As an administrator of a small to medium network, you'll probably never use BGP. (BGP will be discussed in Chapter 10.)

Now that we have that out of the way, let's talk about all the great things that dynamic routing protocols do for us. The thing that comes to mind first is the amount of time and energy we save configuring routers. We won't have to go to every single router and define for it, with a static route, what and where every destination network is. If that were the only way to configure routing, there would probably be a lot fewer of us interested in doing this for a living. Thankfully, we have routing protocols that do much of the work for us. We still have to know what the routing protocols are going to do and how they will do it, but the protocols will take care of most of the updating and sending information to each other.

That is the end of the EGP branch of the tree, but the IGP branch continues to split out as we go down further. Looking at Figure 9.8, with the IGP split, you can see that there are two primary categories: distance-vector (DV) and link-state (LS) routing protocols.

FIGURE 9.8   DV and LS routing protocols

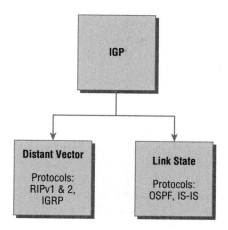

No worries—I'm going to discuss all of these types of protocols in Chapter 10, "Routing Protocols." But in the distance-vector category, for example, we have RIP and Interior Gateway Routing Protocol (IGRP). Under the link-state category are the nonproprietary OSPF and Intermediate System-to-Intermediate System (IS-IS) that were designed to work in larger internetworks.

Now, in Figure 9.9, you can see from the diagram that there is a third category: the hybrid protocol category.

FIGURE 9.9   Hybrid routing

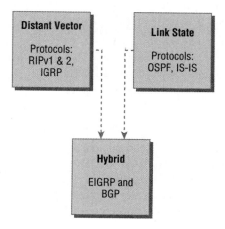

The only protocols under this category are EIGRP and BGP. EIGRP is Cisco proprietary (or used to be, but people mostly just run this with Cisco gear) and uses the features of both DV and LS. Now that we have a handle on IP routing, let's move on to Chapter 10 and discuss the IGP routing protocols introduced in this chapter.

Summary

This chapter covered the IP routing process in detail. It's extremely important that you really understand the basics we covered in this chapter because everything that's done on a router typically will have some type of IP routing configured and running.

You learned in this chapter how IP routing uses frames to transport packets between routers and to the destination host. Understanding the process of how packets and frames traverse a network is critical to your fundamental understanding of IP routing.

After I covered the basics of IP routing, I went through some examples to test your understanding and to emphasize the importance of the IP routing fundamentals that you need. I finished the chapter with an introduction to static and dynamic routing and explained IGP and EGP as well as the difference between distance-vector and link-state routing protocols. In the next chapter, we'll continue with dynamic routing by discussing the various dynamic routing protocols.

Exam Essentials

Understand the basic IP routing process.   You need to remember that the frame changes at each hop, but that the packet is never changed or manipulated in any way until it reaches the destination device.

Understand that MAC addresses are always local.   A MAC (hardware) address will be used only on a local LAN. It will never pass a router's interface.

Understand that a frame carries a packet to only two places.   A frame uses MAC (hardware) addresses to send a packet on a LAN. The frame will take the packet to either a host on the LAN or a router's interface if the packet is destined for a remote network.

Remember the difference between static and dynamic routing.   Static routing is where you, as the administrator, by hand add every route into every routing table on every router on the network. This is as much work as it sounds like, which is why we use dynamic routing protocols that do the work for us. Of course, we'll discuss dynamic routing protocols more in the next chapter, but the main job of a routing protocol is to update routing tables.

Written Lab

You can find the answers to the written labs in Appendix A. Using the following figure, fill in the pseudo route table and answer the following statements.

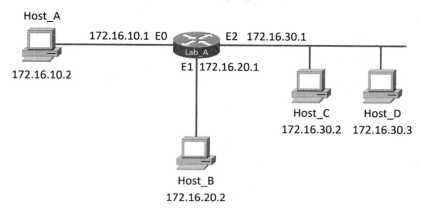

Destination network   **Exit interface**

1. When a packet is sent from Host_A to Host_C, Host_A will use ARP to determine the MAC address of ____.

2. When a packet is sent from Host_C to Host_D, Host_C will use ARP to determine the MAC address of ____.

3. When a packet is routed through Lab_A router destined for 172.16.30.3, interface ____ will send an ARP request for ____.

4. Host_A sends a packet to Host_C; after passing through the router the source IP address will be ____ and the destination IP address will be ____.

5. Host_A sends a packet to 172.16.20.2; interface ____ will send an ARP request to ____.

Review Questions

You can find the answers to the review questions in Appendix B.

1. Which is required for the successful routing of a packet through a router?
   A. Originating network of a packet
   B. Return path for the network packet
   C. Destination network of a packet
   D. Destination host of a packet

2. Which Cisco IOS command will display the route table?
   A. `show ip route`
   B. `show route`
   C. `display route`
   D. `show routing`

3. Which is true about static routes?
   A. Routes are automatically updated.
   B. New routes are learned periodically.
   C. Static routes are the best for traffic flow.
   D. All routes must be manually configured.

4. Using the following example, what does the C in the route statement mean?

   ```
   Gateway of last resort is not set
   C      192.168.1.0/24 is directly connected, FastEthernet0/0
   C      192.168.2.0/24 is directly connected, FastEthernet0/1
   ```

   A. The gateway of last resort is not set.
   B. The route is statically configured.
   C. The network is configured on the interface.
   D. The network is a continuation of another route.

5. What happens when the destination IP address of a packet is not in the same network as the host?
   A. The destination IP address is set to the default gateway.
   B. The destination MAC address is set to the default gateway.
   C. The source IP address is set to the default gateway.
   D. The source MAC address is set to the default gateway.

6. Which command can be used on a Cisco router to view the ARP cache?

   A. `show arp`

   B. `show arp-cache`

   C. `arp -g`

   D. `show ip arp`

7. What is the term used to describe the map of the internetwork inside a router?

   A. Route map

   B. Route table

   C. Dynamic route

   D. Static route

8. Which protocol is used to derive the MAC address of the default gateway?

   A. ARP

   B. ICMP

   C. RARP

   D. Dynamic routing

9. What is the Ether-Type field set to for the IPv4 protocol?

   A. 0x0806

   B. 0x86dd

   C. 0x0800

   D. 0x8035

10. You are the network administrator for a small network that has multiple locations. You expect to add more in the future and want to ensure that routing is not troublesome and will be automated. Which should you employ?

   A. Static routing

   B. Dynamic routing

   C. Dynamic Host Configuration Protocol

   D. Reverse Address Resolution Protocol

11. What will happen if the router does not have a route to the destination network for a ping packet? (Choose two.)

   A. The packet will be returned to the sender.

   B. The packet will be logged.

   C. The packet will be dropped.

   D. An ICMP packet is sent to the sender.

   E. The router will request a dynamic update.

12. What is at the end of a frame that allows the destination to verify that the frame was transmitted intact?

   A. Source MAC address

   B. Destination MAC address

   C. Ether-Type

   D. FCS

13. What is the message if an ICMP ping packet is lost along the way en route to the destination?

   A. Request timed out

   B. Unknown error

   C. Destination unreachable

   D. Problem occurred

14. Which interface will the router switch the packet to for a destination of 172.16.20.94?

```
Gateway of last resort is not set

C        172.16.20.0/27  is directly connected, FastEthernet 0/0
C        172.16.20.32/27 is directly connected, FastEthernet 0/1
C        172.16.20.64/27 is directly connected, FastEthernet 0/2
C        172.16.20.128/27 is directly connected, FastEthernet 0/3
```

   A. FastEthernet 0/0

   B. FastEthernet 0/1

   C. FastEthernet 0/2

   D. FastEthernet 0/3

15. Which of these statements best describes dynamic routing?

   A. All network IDs must be manually entered into the routing table.

   B. All host IDs must be manually entered into the routing table.

   C. Routing tables are updated automatically when changes occur in the network.

   D. Dynamic routing is the default for all routers.

16. Which of these statement regarding MAC addresses is true correct?

   A. The destination MAC address does not change through the routing process.

   B. MAC addresses are always local on the LAN and never routed.

   C. The default gateway MAC address is always the same on all interfaces.

   D. Route decisions are based on the destination MAC address.

17. What is the term used to describe the result of all routes being updated in the routing table via a dynamic routing protocol?

   A. Dynamic updates

   B. Route updates

   C. DNS resolution

   D. Convergence

18. What command would be used to view the ARP cache on your host?

   A. `show ip route`

   B. `show ip arp`

   C. `show protocols`

   D. `arp -a`

19. Where along the IP routing process does a packet get changed?

   A. Router

   B. Source host

   C. Destination host

   D. All of the above

20. What is the term used to describe a collection of networks or subnets that are in the same administrative domain?

   A. Autonomous system

   B. IGP

   C. Administrative distance

   D. EGP

Chapter

10

Routing Protocols

THE FOLLOWING COMPTIA NETWORK+ EXAM OBJECTIVES ARE COVERED IN THIS CHAPTER:

✓ **Domain 1.0 Networking Concepts**

✓ **1.2 Compare and contrast networking appliances, applications, and functions.**

- Physical and virtual appliances
  - Router

✓ **1.8 Summarize evolving use cases for modern network environments.**

- IPv6 addressing
  - Mitigating address exhaustion
  - Compatibility requirements
  - Tunneling
  - Dual stack

✓ **Domain 2.0 Network Implementation**

✓ **2.1 Explain characteristics of routing technologies.**

- Static routing
- Dynamic routing
  - Border Gateway Protocol (BGP)
  - Enhanced Interior Gateway
  - Routing Protocol (EIGRP)
  - Open Shortest Path First (OSPF)
- Route selection
  - Administrative distance
  - Prefix length
  - Metric

- First Hop Redundancy Protocol (FHRP)
- Virtual IP (VIP)
- Subinterfaces

Routing protocols are critical to a network's design. This chapter focuses on dynamic routing protocols. Dynamic routing protocols run only on routers that use them in order to discover networks and update their routing tables. Using dynamic routing is easier on you, the system administrator, than using the labor-intensive, manually achieved static routing method, but it'll cost you in terms of router CPU processes and bandwidth on the network links.

The source of the increased bandwidth usage and CPU cycles is the operation of the dynamic routing protocol itself. A router running a dynamic routing protocol shares routing information with its neighboring routers, and it requires additional CPU cycles and additional bandwidth to accomplish that.

In this chapter, I'll give you all the basic information you need to know about routing protocols so you can choose the correct one for each network you work on or design.

To find Todd Lammle CompTIA videos and practice questions, please see www.lammle.com.

Routing Protocol Basics

Because getting a solid visual can really help people learn, I'll get you started by combining the last few figures used in Chapter 9, "Introduction to IP Routing." This way, you can get the big picture and really understand how routing works. Figure 10.1 shows the complete routing tree that I broke up piece by piece at the end of Chapter 9.

As I touched on in Chapter 9, two types of routing protocols are used in internetworks: interior gateway protocols (IGPs) and exterior gateway protocols (EGPs). IGPs are used to exchange routing information with routers in the same *autonomous system (AS)*. An AS is a collection of networks under a common administrative domain, which simply means that all routers sharing the same routing table information are in the same AS. EGPs are used to communicate between multiple ASs. A nice example of an EGP would be Border Gateway Protocol (BGP).

There are a few key points about routing protocols that I think it would be a good idea to talk over before getting deeper into the specifics of each one. First on the list is something known as an administrative distance.

FIGURE 10.1   Routing flow tree

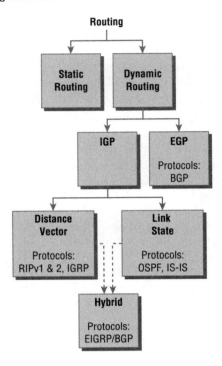

Administrative Distances

The *administrative distance (AD)* is used to rate the trustworthiness of routing information received on one router from its neighboring router. An AD is represented as an integer from 0 to 255, where 0 equals the most trusted route and 255 the least. A value of 255 essentially means, "No traffic is allowed to be passed via this route."

If a router receives two updates listing the same remote network, the first thing the router checks is the AD. If one of the advertised routes has a lower AD than the other, the route with the lower AD is the one that will get placed in the routing table.

If both advertised routes to the same network have the same AD, then routing protocol metrics like *hop count* or the amount of bandwidth on the lines will be used to find the best path to the remote network. And as it was with the AD, the advertised route with the lowest metric will be placed in the routing table. But if both advertised routes have the same AD as well as the same metrics, then the routing protocol will *load-balance* to the remote network. To perform load balancing, a router will send packets down each link to test for the best one.

Real World Scenario

Why Not Just Turn on All Routing Protocols?

Many customers have hired me because all their employees were complaining about a slow, intermittent network that had a lot of latency. Many times, I have found that the administrators did not truly understand routing protocols and just enabled them all on every router.

This may sound laughable, but it is true. When an administrator tried to disable a routing protocol, such as the Routing Information Protocol (RIP), they would receive a call that part of the network was not working. First, understand that because of default ADs, although every routing protocol was enabled, only the Enhanced Interior Gateway Routing Protocol (EIGRP) would show up in most of the routing tables. This meant that Open Shortest Path First (OSPF), Intermediate System-to-Intermediate System (IS-IS), and RIP would be running in the background but just using up bandwidth and CPU processes, slowing the routers almost to a crawl.

Disabling all the routing protocols except EIGRP (this would work only on an all-Cisco router network) improved the network at least 30%. In addition, finding the routers that were configured only for RIP and enabling EIGRP solved the calls from users complaining that the network was down when RIP was disabled on the network. Last, I replaced the core routers with better routers with more memory, enabling faster, more efficient routing, and raising the network response time to a total of 50 percent.

Table 10.1 shows the default Ads that a router uses to decide which route to take to a remote network.

TABLE 10.1   Default administrative distances

Route Source	Default AD
Connected interface	0
Static route	1
External BGP	20
Internal EIGRP	90
IGRP	100
OSPF	110

TABLE 10.1   Default administrative distances *(continued)*

Route Source	Default AD
IS-IS	115
RIPv1 and RIPv2	120
External EIGRP	170
Internal BGP	200
Unknown	255 (this route will never be used)

Understand that if a network is directly connected, the router will always use the interface connected to that network. Also good to know is that if you configure a static route, the router will believe that route to be the preferred one over any other routes it learns about dynamically. You can change the ADs of static routes, but by default, they have an AD of 1. That's only one place above zero, so you can see why a static route's default AD will always be considered the best by the router.

This means that if you have a static route, a RIP-advertised route, and an EIGRP-advertised route listing the same network, then by default, the router will always use the static route unless you change the AD of the static route.

Classes of Routing Protocols

The three classes of routing protocols introduced in Chapter 9, and shown in Figure 10.1, are as follows:

Distance Vector   The *distance-vector protocols* find the best path to a remote network by judging—you guessed it—distance. Each time a packet goes through a router, it equals something we call a *hop*, and the route with the fewest hops to the destination network will be chosen as the best path to it. The vector indicates the direction to the remote network. RIP, RIPv2, and Interior Gateway Routing Protocol (IGRP) are distance-vector routing protocols. These protocols send the entire routing table to all directly connected neighbors.

Link State   Using *link-state protocols*, also called *shortest path first protocols*, the routers each create three separate tables. One of these tables keeps track of directly attached neighbors, one determines the topology of the entire internetwork, and one is used as the actual routing table. Link-state routers know more about the internetwork than any distance-vector routing protocol. OSPF and IS-IS are IP routing protocols that are completely link state. Link-state protocols send updates containing the state of their own links to all other routers on the network.

Hybrid   A *hybrid protocol* uses aspects of both distance vector and link state, and formerly, EIGRP was the only one you needed to understand to meet the Network+ objectives. But now, BGP is also listed as a hybrid routing protocol because of its capability to work as an EGP and be used in supersized internetworks internally. When deployed in this way, it's called internal BGP, or iBGP, but understand that it's still most commonly utilized as an EGP.

I also want you to understand that there's no one set way of configuring routing protocols for use in every situation because this really needs to be done on a case-by-case basis. Even though all of this might seem a little intimidating, if you understand how each of the different routing protocols works, I promise you'll be capable of making good, solid decisions that will truly meet the individual needs of any business!

Distance-Vector Routing Protocols

Okay, the distance-vector routing algorithm passes its complete routing table contents to neighboring routers, which then combine the received routing table entries with their own routing tables to complete and update their individual routing tables. This is called *routing by rumor* because a router receiving an update from a neighbor router believes the information about remote networks without verifying for itself if the news is actually correct.

It's possible to have a network that has multiple links to the same remote network, and if that's the case, the AD of each received update is checked first. As I said, if the AD is the same, the protocol will then have to use other metrics to determine the best path to use to get to that remote network.

Distance vector uses only hop count to determine the best path to a network. If a router finds more than one link with the same hop count to the same remote network, it will automatically perform what's known as *round-robin load balancing*.

It's important to understand what a distance-vector routing protocol does when it starts up. In Figure 10.2, the four routers start off with only their directly connected networks in their routing table. After a distance-vector routing protocol is started on each router, the routing tables are then updated with all route information gathered from neighbor routers.

As you can see in Figure 10.2, each router has only the directly connected networks in its routing table. Also notice that their hop count is zero in every case. Each router sends its complete routing table, which includes the network number, exit interface, and hop count to the network, out to each active interface.

Now, in Figure 10.3, the routing tables are complete because they include information about all the networks in the internetwork. They are considered *converged*. The hop count for every directly connected network remains zero, but notice that the hop count is incremented by one each time the path completely passes through a router. So, for router 2621A, the path to the 172.16.10.0 network still has a hop count of zero, but the hop count for the path to network 172.16.20.0 is one. The hop count to networks 172.16.30.0 and 172.16.40.0 increases to two, and so on. Usually, data transmission will cease while routers are converging—a good reason in favor of fast convergence time! In fact, one of the main problems with RIP is its slow convergence time.

FIGURE 10.2   The internetwork with distance-vector routing

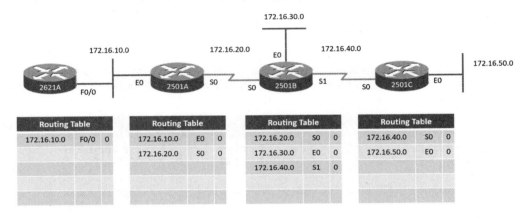

Routing Table		
172.16.10.0	F0/0	0

Routing Table		
172.16.10.0	EO	0
172.16.20.0	SO	0

Routing Table		
172.16.20.0	SO	0
172.16.30.0	EO	0
172.16.40.0	S1	0

Routing Table		
172.16.40.0	SO	0
172.16.50.0	EO	0

FIGURE 10.3   Converged routing tables

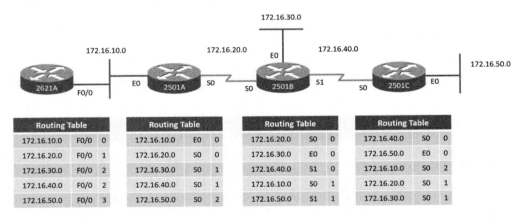

Routing Table		
172.16.10.0	F0/0	0
172.16.20.0	F0/0	1
172.16.30.0	F0/0	2
172.16.40.0	F0/0	2
172.16.50.0	F0/0	3

Routing Table		
172.16.10.0	EO	0
172.16.20.0	SO	0
172.16.30.0	SO	1
172.16.40.0	SO	1
172.16.50.0	SO	2

Routing Table		
172.16.20.0	SO	0
172.16.30.0	EO	0
172.16.40.0	S1	0
172.16.10.0	SO	1
172.16.50.0	S1	1

Routing Table		
172.16.40.0	SO	0
172.16.50.0	EO	0
172.16.10.0	SO	2
172.16.20.0	SO	1
172.16.30.0	SO	1

As you can see in Figure 10.3, once all the routers have converged, the routing table in each router keeps information about three important things:

- The remote network number
- The interface that the router will use to send packets to reach that particular network
- The hop count, or metric, to the network

Remember! Routing convergence time is the time required by protocols to update their forwarding tables after changes have occurred.

Let's start discussing dynamic routing protocols with one of the oldest routing protocols that is still in existence today.

Routing Information Protocol (RIP)

RIP is a true distance-vector routing protocol. It sends the complete routing table out to all active interfaces every 30 seconds. RIP uses only one thing to determine the best way to a remote network—the hop count. And because it has a maximum allowable hop count of 15 by default, a hop count of 16 would be deemed unreachable. This means that although RIP works fairly well in small networks, it's pretty inefficient on large networks with slow WAN links or on networks populated with a large number of routers. Worse, this dinosaur of a protocol has a bad history of creating routing loops, which were somewhat kept in check by using things like maximum hop count. This is the reason why RIP only permits going through 15 routers before it will judge that route to be invalid. If all that isn't nasty enough for you, RIP also happens to be glacially slow at converging, which can easily cause latency in your network!

RIP version 1 uses only *classful routing*, which means that all devices in the network must use the same subnet mask for each specific address class. This is because RIP version 1 doesn't send updates with subnet mask information in tow. RIP version 2 provides something called *prefix routing* and does send subnet mask information with the route updates. Doing this is called *classless routing*.

RIP Version 2 (RIPv2)

Let's spend a couple of minutes discussing RIPv2 before we move into the advanced distance-vector (also referred to as hybrid), Cisco-proprietary routing protocol EIGRP.

RIP version 2 is mostly the same as RIP version 1. Both RIPv1 and RIPv2 are distance-vector protocols, which means that each router running RIP sends its complete routing tables out to all active interfaces at periodic time intervals. Also, the timers and loop avoidance schemes are the same in both RIP versions. Both RIPv1 and RIPv2 are configured with classful addressing (but RIPv2 is considered classless because subnet information is sent with each route update), and both have the same AD (120).

But there are some important differences that make RIPv2 more scalable than RIPv1. And I've got to add a word of advice here before we move on: I'm definitely not advocating using RIP of either version in your network. But because RIP is an open standard, you can use RIP with any brand of router. You can also use OSPF because OSPF is an open standard as well.

Table 10.2 discusses the differences between RIPv1 and RIPv2.

TABLE 10.2   RIPv1 vs. RIPv2

RIPv1	RIPv2
Distance vector	Distance vector
Maximum hop count of 15	Maximum hop count of 15
Classful	Classless
Broadcast based	Uses multicast 224.0.0.9
No support for VLSM	Supports VLSM networks
No authentication	Allows for MD5 authentication
No support for discontiguous networks	Supports discontiguous networks (covered in the next section, "VLSMs and Discontiguous Networks")

RIPv2, unlike RIPv1, is a classless routing protocol (even though it is configured as classful, like RIPv1), which means that it sends subnet mask information along with the route updates. By sending the subnet mask information with the updates, RIPv2 can support variable-length subnet masks (VLSMs), which are described in the next section; in addition, network boundaries are summarized.

VLSMs and Discontiguous Networks

VLSMs allow classless routing, meaning that the routing protocol sends subnet-mask information with the route updates. The reason it's good to do this is to save address space. If we didn't use a routing protocol that supports VLSMs, then every router interface, every node (PC, printer, server, and so on), would have to use the same subnet mask.

As the name suggests, with VLSMs we can have different subnet masks for different router interfaces. Check out Figure 10.4 to see an example of why classful network designs are inefficient.

Looking at this figure, you'll notice that we have two routers, each with two LANs and connected together with a WAN serial link. In a typical classful network design example (RIP or RIPv2 routing protocol), you could subnet a network like this:

192.168.10.0 = Network

255.255.255.240 (/28) = Mask

Our subnets would be (you know this part, right?) 0, 16, 32, 48, 64, 80, and so on. This allows us to assign 16 subnets to our internetwork. But how many hosts would be available on each network? Well, as you probably know by now, each subnet provides only 14 hosts.

FIGURE 10.4   Typical classful network

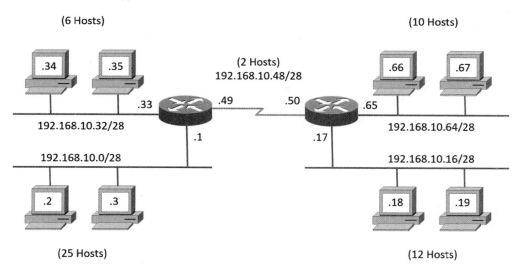

This means that with a /28 mask, each LAN can support 14 valid hosts—one LAN requires 25 addresses, so a /28 mask doesn't provide enough addresses for the hosts in that LAN! Moreover, the point-to-point WAN link also would consume 14 addresses when only 2 are required. It's too bad we can't just nick some valid hosts from that WAN link and give them to our LANs.

All hosts and router interfaces have the same subnet mask—again, this is called classful routing. And if we want this network to be more efficient, we definitely need to add different masks to each router interface.

But there's still another problem—the link between the two routers will never use more than two valid hosts! This wastes valuable IP address space, and it's the big reason I'm talking to you about VLSM networking.

Now let's take Figure 10.4 and use a classless design, which will become the new network shown in Figure 10.5. In the previous example, we wasted address space—one LAN didn't have enough addresses because every router interface and host used the same subnet mask. Not so good.

What would be good is to provide only the needed number of hosts on each router interface, meaning VLSMs. Remember that if a "classful routed network" requires that all subnet masks be the same length, then it follows that a "classless routed network" would allow us to use variable-length subnet masks (VLSMs).

So, if we use a /30 on our WAN links and a /27, /28, and /29 on our LANs, we'll get 2 hosts per WAN interface and 30, 14, and 6 hosts per LAN interface—nice! This makes a huge difference—not only can we get just the right number of hosts on each LAN, we still have room to add more WANs and LANs using this same network.

FIGURE 10.5 Classless network design

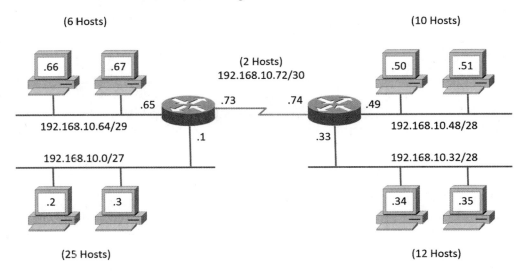

(6 Hosts)   (10 Hosts)

Remember, to implement a VLSM design on your network, you need to have a routing protocol that sends subnet-mask information with the route updates. This would be RIPv2, EIGRP, or OSPF. RIPv1 and IGRP will not work in classless networks and are considered classful routing protocols.

 By using a VLSM design, you do not necessarily make your network run better, but you can save a lot of IP addresses.

Now, what's a discontiguous network? It's one that has two or more subnetworks of a classful network connected by different classful networks. Figure 10.6 displays a typical discontiguous network.

FIGURE 10.6 A discontiguous network

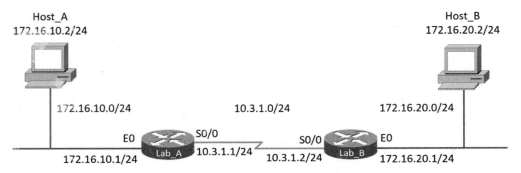

The subnets 172.16.10.0 and 172.16.20.0 are connected with a 10.3.1.0 network. By default, each router thinks it has the only 172.16.0.0 classful network.

It's important to understand that discontiguous networks just won't work with RIPv1 at all. They don't work by default on RIPv2 or EIGRP either, but discontiguous networks do work on OSPF networks by default because OSPF does not auto-summarize like RIPv2 and EIGRP.

> Route aggregation is essentially combining multiple subnets into one larger subnet, and it's also known as supernetting. You would implement this type of route summarization if you required more efficient routing tables in large networks.

EIGRP

EIGRP is a classless, enhanced distance-vector protocol that possesses a real edge over another older Cisco proprietary protocol, IGRP. That's basically why it's called Enhanced IGRP.

EIGRP uses the concept of an autonomous system to describe the set of contiguous routers that run the same routing protocol and share routing information. But unlike IGRP, EIGRP includes the subnet mask in its route updates. And as you now know, the advertisement of subnet information allows us to use VLSMs when designing our networks.

EIGRP is referred to as a *hybrid routing protocol* because it has characteristics of both distance-vector and link-state protocols. For example, EIGRP doesn't send link-state packets as OSPF does; instead, it sends traditional distance-vector updates containing information about networks plus the cost of reaching them from the perspective of the advertising router. But EIGRP has link-state characteristics as well—it synchronizes routing tables between neighbors at startup and then sends specific updates only when topology changes occur. This makes EIGRP suitable for very large networks.

There are a number of powerful features that make EIGRP a real standout from RIP, RIPv2, and other protocols. The main ones are listed here:

- Support for IP and Ipv6 (and some other useless routed protocols) via protocol-dependent modules
- Considered classless (same as RIPv2 and OSPF)
- Support for VLSM/Classless Inter-Domain Routing (CIDR)
- Support for summaries and discontiguous networks
- Efficient neighbor discovery
- Communication via Reliable Transport Protocol (RTP)
- Best path selection via Diffusing Update Algorithm (DUAL)

Another great feature of EIGRP is that it's simple to configure and turn on like a distance-vector protocol, but it keeps track of more information than a distance vector does. It creates and maintains additional tables instead of just one table as distance-vector routing protocols do. To determine the best path to each network, EIGRP uses bandwidth and delay of the line as well as sending reliability, load, and the MTU information between routers, but it uses only bandwidth and delay by default.

These tables are called the neighbor table, *topology table*, and routing table, as shown in Figure 10.7.

FIGURE 10.7   EIGRP tables

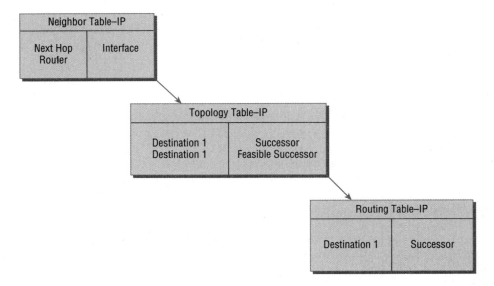

Neighbor Table   Each router keeps state information about adjacent neighbors. When a newly discovered neighbor is learned on a router interface, the address and interface of that neighbor are recorded, and the information is held in the neighbor table and stored in RAM. Sequence numbers are used to match acknowledgments with update packets. The last sequence number received from the neighbor is recorded so that out-of-order packets can be detected.

Topology Table   The topology table is populated by the neighbor table, and the best path to each remote network is found by running the diffusing update algorithm (DUAL). The topology table contains all destinations advertised by neighboring routers, holding each destination address and a list of neighbors that have advertised the destination. For each neighbor, the advertised metric, which comes only from the neighbor's routing table, is recorded. If the neighbor is advertising this destination, it must be using the route to forward packets.

Successor (Routes in a Routing Table)   A successor route (think successful!) is the best route to a remote network. A successor route is used by EIGRP to forward traffic to a destination and is stored in the routing table. It is backed up by a feasible successor route that is stored in the topology table—if one is available.

Feasible Successor (Backup Routes)   A *feasible successor* is a path considered a backup route. EIGRP will keep up to six feasible successors in the topology table. Only the one with the best metric (the successor) is copied and placed in the routing table.

By using the feasible distance and having feasible successors in the topology table as backup links, EIGRP allows the network to converge instantly, and updates to any neighbor consist only of traffic sent from EIGRP. All of these things make for a very fast, scalable, fault-tolerant routing protocol.

Route redistribution is the term used for translating from one routing protocol into another. An example would be where you have an old router running RIP but you have an EIGRP network. You can run route redistribution on one router to translate the RIP routes into EIGRP.

Border Gateway Protocol (BGP)

In a way, you can think of Border Gateway Protocol as the heavyweight of routing protocols. This is an external routing protocol (used between autonomous systems, unlike RIP or OSPF, which are internal routing protocols) that uses a sophisticated algorithm to determine the best route.

Even though BGP is an EGP by default, it can be used within an AS, which is one of the reasons the objectives are calling this a hybrid routing protocol. Another reason they call it a hybrid is because it's often known as a path-vector protocol instead of a distance-vector like RIP.

In fact, it just happens to be the core routing protocol of the Internet. And it's not exactly breaking news that the Internet has become a vital resource in so many organizations, is it? No—but this growing dependence has resulted in redundant connections to many different ISPs.

This is where BGP comes in. The sheer onslaught of multiple connections would totally overwhelm other routing protocols like OSPF, which I am going to talk about shortly. BGP is essentially an alternative to using default routes for controlling path selections. *Default routes* are configured on routers to control packets that have a destination IP address that is not found in the routing table.

Because the Internet's growth rate shows no signs of slowing, ISPs use BGP for its ability to make classless routing and summarization possible. These capabilities help to keep routing tables smaller and more efficient at the ISP core.

BGP is used for IGPs to connect ASs in larger networks, if needed, as shown in Figure 10.8.

FIGURE 10.8   Border Gateway Protocol

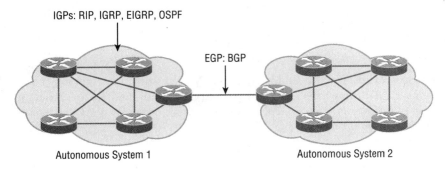

An autonomous system (AS) is a collection of networks under a common administrative domain. IGPs operate within an autonomous system, and EGPs connect different autonomous systems together.

So yes, very large private IP networks can make use of BGP. Let's say you wanted to join a number of large OSPF networks together. Because OSPF just couldn't scale up enough to handle such a huge load, you would go with BGP instead to connect the ASs. Another situation in which BGP would come in really handy would be if you wanted to multi-home a network for better redundancy, either to a multiple access point of a single ISP or to multiple ISPs.

Internal routing protocols are employed to advertise all available networks, including the metric necessary to get to each of them. BGP is a personal favorite of mine because its routers exchange path vectors that give you detailed information on the BGP AS numbers, hop by hop (called an AS path), required to reach a specific destination network. Also good to know is that BGP doesn't broadcast its entire routing table like RIP does; it updates a lot more like OSPF, which is a huge advantage. Also, the routing table with BGP is called a Routing Information Base (RIB).

And BGP also tells you about any/all networks reachable at the end of the path. These factors are the biggest differences you need to remember about BGP. Unlike IGPs that simply tell you how to get to a specific network, BGP gives you the big picture on exactly what's involved in getting to an AS, including the networks located in that AS itself.

And there's more to that "BGP big picture"—this protocol carries information like the network prefixes found in the AS and includes the IP address needed to get to the next AS (the next-hop attribute). It even gives you the history on how the networks at the end of the path were introduced into BGP in the first place, known as the origin code attribute.

All of these traits are what makes BGP so useful for constructing a graph of loop-free autonomous systems, for identifying routing policies, and for enabling us to create and enforce restrictions on routing behavior based upon the AS path—sweet!

Link-State Routing Protocols

Link-state protocols also fall into the classless category of routing protocols, and they work within packet-switched networks. OSPF and IS-IS are two examples of link-state routing protocols.

Remember, for a protocol to be a classless routing protocol, the subnet-mask information must be carried with the routing update. This enables every router to identify the best route to each and every network, even those that don't use class-defined default subnet masks (i.e. 8, 16, or 24 bits), such as VLSM networks. All neighbor routers know the cost of the network route that's being advertised. One of the biggest differences between link-state and distance-vector protocols is that link-state protocols learn and maintain much more information about the internetwork than distance-vector routing protocols do. Distance-vector routing protocols only maintain routing tables with the destination routes and vector costs (like hop counts) in them. Link-state routing protocols maintain two additional tables with more detailed information, with the first of these being the neighbor table. The neighbor table is maintained through the use of *Hello packets* that are exchanged by all routers to determine which other routers are available to exchange routing data with. All routers that can share routing data are stored in the neighbor table.

The second table maintained is the topology table, which is built and sustained through the use of link-state advertisements or packets (LSAs or LSPs). In the topology table, you'll find a listing for every destination network plus every neighbor (route) through which it can be reached. Essentially, it's a map of the entire internetwork.

Once all of that raw data is shared and each router has the data in its topology table, the routing protocol runs the Shortest Path First (SPF) algorithm to compare it all and determine the best paths to each of the destination networks.

Open Shortest Path First (OSPF)

Open Shortest Path First (OSPF) is an open-standard routing protocol that's been implemented by a wide variety of network vendors, including Cisco. OSPF works by using the *Dijkstra algorithm*. First, a shortest-path tree is constructed, and then the routing table is populated with the resulting best paths. OSPF converges quickly (although not as fast as EIGRP), and it supports multiple, equal-cost routes to the same destination. Like EIGRP, it supports both IP and Ipv6 routed protocols, but OSPF must maintain a separate database and routing table for each, meaning you're basically running two routing protocols if you are using IP and Ipv6 with OSPF.

OSPF provides the following features:

- Consists of areas and autonomous systems
- Minimizes routing update traffic
- Allows scalability
- Supports VLSM/CIDR

- Has unlimited hop count
- Allows multivendor deployment (open standard)
- Uses a loopback (logical) interface to keep the network stable

OSPF is the first link-state routing protocol that most people are introduced to, so it's good to see how it compares to more traditional distance-vector protocols like RIPv2 and RIPv1. Table 10.3 compares these three protocols.

TABLE 10.3 OSPF and RIP comparison

Characteristic	OSPF	RIPv2	RIPv1
Type of protocol	Link state	Distance vector	Distance vector
Classless support	Yes	Yes	No
VLSM support	Yes	Yes	No
Auto-summarization	No	Yes	Yes
Manual summarization	Yes	No	No
Discontiguous support	Yes	Yes	No
Route propagation	Multicast on change	Periodic multicast	Periodic broadcast
Path metric	Bandwidth	Hops	Hops
Hop-count limit	None	15	15
Convergence	Fast	Slow	Slow
Peer authentication	Yes	Yes	No
Hierarchical network	Yes (using areas)	No (flat only)	No (flat only)
Updates	Event triggered	Route table updates time intervals	Route table updates
Route computation	Dijkstra	Bellman-Ford	Bellman-Ford

OSPF has many features beyond the few I've listed in Table 10.3, and all of them contribute to a fast, scalable, and robust protocol that can be actively deployed in thousands of production networks. One of OSPF's most noteworthy features is that after a network change, such as when a link changes to up or down, OSPF converges with serious speed! In fact, it's the fastest of any of the interior routing protocols we'll be covering. Just to make sure you're clear, convergence refers to when all routers have been successfully updated with the change.

OSPF is supposed to be designed in a hierarchical fashion, which basically means that you can separate the larger internetwork into smaller internetworks called *areas*. This is definitely the best design for OSPF.

The following are reasons you really want to create OSPF in a hierarchical design:

- To decrease routing overhead

- To speed up convergence

- To confine network instability to single areas of the network

Pretty sweet benefits! But you have to earn them—OSPF is more elaborate and difficult to configure in this manner.

Figure 10.9 shows a typical OSPF simple design. Notice how each router connects to the backbone—called area 0, or the backbone area. OSPF must have an area 0, and all other areas should connect to this area. Routers that connect other areas to the backbone area within an AS are called area border routers (ABRs). Still, at least one interface of the ABR must be in area 0.

FIGURE 10.9   OSPF design example

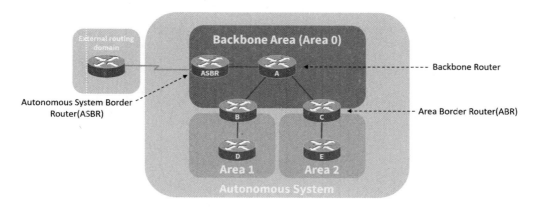

OSPF runs inside an autonomous system, but it can also connect multiple autonomous systems together. The router that connects these ASs is called an *autonomous system border router (ASBR)*. Typically, in today's networks, BGP is used to connect between ASs, not OSPF.

Ideally, you would create other areas of networks to help keep route updates to a minimum and to keep problems from propagating throughout the network. But that's beyond the scope of this chapter. Just make note of it for your future networking studies.

Intermediate System-to-Intermediate System (IS-IS)

IS-IS is an IGP, meaning that it's intended for use within an administrative domain or network, not for routing between ASs. That would be a job that an EGP (such as BGP, which we covered earlier) would handle instead.

IS-IS is a link-state routing protocol, meaning it operates by reliably flooding topology information throughout a network of routers. Each router then independently builds a picture of the network's topology, just as they do with OSPF. Packets or datagrams are forwarded based on the best topological path through the network to the destination.

Figure 10.10 shows an IS-IS network and the terminology used with IS-IS.

FIGURE 10.10   IS-IS network terminology

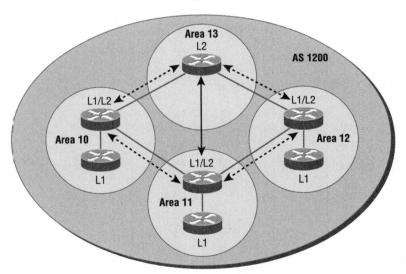

Here are the definitions for the terms used in the IS-IS network shown in Figure 10.10:

L1   Level 1 intermediate systems route within an area. When the destination is outside an area, they route toward a Level 2 system.

L2   Level 2 intermediate systems route between areas and toward other ASs.

The similarity between IS-IS and OSPF is that both employ the Dijkstra algorithm to discover the shortest path through the network to a destination network. The difference between IS-IS and OSPF is that IS-IS uses Connectionless Network Service (CLNS) to provide connectionless delivery of data packets between routers, and it also doesn't require an area 0 like OSPF does. OSPF uses IP to communicate between routers instead.

An advantage to having CLNS around is that it can easily send information about multiple routed protocols (IP and IPv6), and as I already mentioned, OSPF must maintain a completely different routing database for IP and IPv6, respectively, for it to be able to send updates for both protocols.

IS-IS supports the most important characteristics of OSPF and EIGRP because it supports VLSM and also because it converges quickly. Each of these three protocols has advantages and disadvantages, but it's these two shared features that make any of them scalable and appropriate for supporting the large-scale networks of today.

One last thing—even though it's not as common, IS-IS, although comparable to OSPF, is actually preferred by ISPs because of its ability to run IP and IPv6 without creating a separate database for each protocol as OSPF does. That single feature makes it more efficient in very large networks.

EXERCISE 10.1

Examining OS Routing

In this exercise, you will examine the local routing table in the operating system. Your operating system's internal router will not participate in dynamic routing without additional services like Routing and Remote Access Services (RRAS). However, default routing is supported out of the box by the operating system, and this can be configured with the route command.

1.   Open the command prompt by clicking Start, typing **cmd**, and pressing Enter.

2.   In the command prompt, type **route print** and take note of the network destinations, interface, and metric.

All layer 3 packet routing is performed through this internal router. You will notice several familiar networks, such as the default route 0.0.0.0/0 and the loopback 127.0.0.1/8, just to name a few. These routes are for the operating system to communicate with the external network. If you want to route between two or more interfaces, additional services such as RRAS need to be installed.

High Available Routes

Looking closer at your organization, the default gateway is the only way out of your network. If a router fails or needs to be serviced, the default gateway will become unavailable. This might not be a problem for average web surfing. However, if VoIP depends on the default gateway, you now have a bigger problem.

Since the default gateway is just an IP address configured on every host that responds to ARP requests, you can virtualize it using a *first-hop redundancy protocol (FHRP)*. You can create a highly available default gateway by letting more than one router respond to an ARP request. As you can see in Figure 10.11, all you need to do is use a virtual IP address and virtual MAC address. No one router owns the virtual IP address or the virtual MAC address. However, they all respond to ARP requests with the configured virtual MAC address. Two protocols are used for creating highly available default gateways: *Virtual Router Redundancy Protocol (VRRP)* and *Hot Standby Router Protocol (HSRP)*.

FIGURE 10.11   Typical HSRP setup

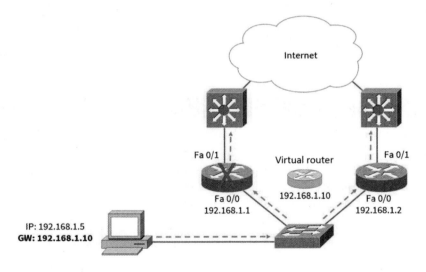

VRRP is an open standard FHRP for creating highly available routers. VRRP functions in an active/passive configuration; only the active router will answer requests for ARP requests for the virtual IP address with the associated virtual MAC address. If the active router fails, the passive router will become the new active router and start serving ARP requests for the virtual IP address and the associated virtual MAC address.

HSRP is a Cisco proprietary FHRP for creating highly available routers. HSRP also functions as an active/passive configuration, as shown in Figure 10.11. The operation of HSRP is identical to VRRP, except that all devices must be Cisco devices.

Firewalls can also be implemented for high availability using the same standard FHRPs that routers commonly use, as shown in Figure 10.12. One consideration is that the provider supports FHRPs for a redundant firewall connecting to the Internet. Although we can use FHRP for redundancy of outbound traffic, the provider would need to support FHRP for redundancy of inbound traffic. If your organization is using two different providers, then the problem becomes much more complex. Another consideration is that both firewalls have the same configuration or you risk a potential security problem.

FIGURE 10.12   FHRP and firewalls

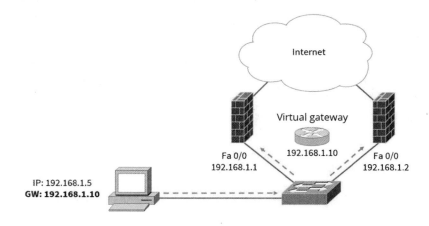

 FHRP operation, implementation, and configuration is covered in depth in Chapter 16, "High Availability and Disaster Recovery."

Advanced IPv6 Concepts

Before we jump into the coverage of IPv6 routing protocols, we need to discuss some of the operations that are performed differently in IPv6 than in IPv4, including several operations that are radically different. We'll also discuss in the following sections some of the methods that have been developed over the past few years to ease the pain of transitioning to an IPv6 environment from one that is IPv4.

Router Advertisement

A router advertisement is part of a new system configuration option in IPv6. This is a packet sent by routers to give the host a network ID (called a prefix in IPv6) so that the host can generate its own IPv6 address derived from its MAC address.

To perform autoconfiguration, a host goes through a basic three-step process:

1. First, the host needs the prefix information, similar to the network portion of an IPv4 address, to configure its interface, so it sends a router solicitation (RS) request for it. This RS is then sent out as a multicast to all routers (FF02::2). The actual information being sent is a type of ICMP message, and like everything in networking, this ICMP message has a number that identifies it. The RS message is ICMP type 133.

2. The router answers back with the required prefix information via a router advertisement (RA). An RA message also happens to be a multicast packet that's sent to the all-nodes multicast address (FF02::1) and is ICMP type 134. RA messages are sent on a periodic basis, but the host sends the RS for an immediate response so it doesn't have to wait until the next scheduled RA to get what it needs.

3. Upon receipt, the host will generate an IPv6 address. The exact process used (stateless or stateful autoconfiguration or by DHCPv6) is determined by instructions within the RA.

Figure 10.13 shows the first two steps.

FIGURE 10.13   First two steps to IPv6 autoconfiguration

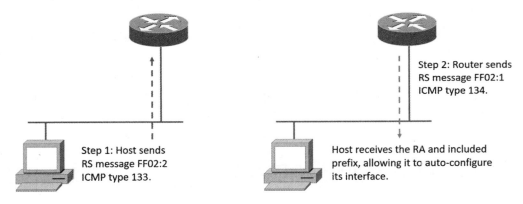

Step 2: Router sends RS message FF02:1 ICMP type 134.

Step 1: Host sends RS message FF02:2 ICMP type 133.

Host receives the RA and included prefix, allowing it to auto-configure its interface.

By the way, when the host generates an IPV6 address using the prefix and its MAC address, the process is called stateless autoconfiguration because it doesn't contact or connect to and receive any further information from the other device.

Take a look at Figure 10.14. In this figure, the Branch router needs to be configured, but I just don't feel like typing in an IPv6 address on the interface connecting to the Corp router. I also don't feel like typing in any routing commands, but I need more than a link-local address on that interface, so I'm going to have to do something! So basically, I want to have the Branch router work with IPv6 on the internetwork with the least amount of effort from me. Let's see if I can get away with that.

FIGURE 10.14   IPv6 autoconfiguration example

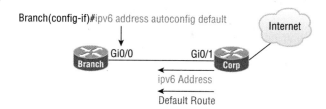

Aha—there is an easy way! I love IPv6 because it allows me to be relatively lazy when dealing with some parts of my network, yet it still works really well. When I use the command ipv6 address autoconfig, the interface will listen for RAs and then, via the EUI-64 format, assign itself a global address—sweet!

Neighbor Discovery Protocol

The Neighbor Discovery Protocol (NDP) is a protocol in the Internet protocol suite used with Internet Protocol version 6 (IPv6). It operates at the link layer of the Internet model and is responsible for gathering various information required for Internet communication, including the configuration of local connections and the domain name servers and gateways used to communicate with more distant systems.

One of the big changes in IPv6 is the discontinuation of the use of all broadcasts, including the ARP broadcast. Devices use a new process to send to one another within a subnet. They send to one another's *link-local address* rather than the MAC addresses. Even devices that have been assigned an IPv6 address manually will still generate a link-local address. These addresses are generated using the MAC address as is done in stateless auto-configuration; the prefix is *not* learned from the router. A link-local address always adopts a prefix of FE80::/64.

That means that rather than needing to learn a MAC address to send locally, the host needs to learn the link-local addresses of all of the other hosts in its subnet. This is done using a process called neighbor discovery. This is done using neighbor solicitation messages and neighbor advertisement messages. These are both sent to IPv6 multicast addresses that have been standardized for this process.

Neighbor solicitation messages are sent on the local link when a host needs the link-layer address of another node (see Figure 10.15). The source address in a neighbor solicitation message is the IPv6 address of the node sending the neighbor solicitation message. The destination address in the neighbor solicitation message is the solicited-node multicast address that corresponds to the IPv6 address of the destination node. The neighbor solicitation message also includes the link-layer address of the source node.

The destination node replies by sending a neighbor advertisement message, which has a value of 136 in the Type field of the ICMP packet header, on the local link. The data portion of the neighbor advertisement message includes the link-layer address of the node sending the neighbor advertisement message. After the source node receives the neighbor advertisement, the source node and destination node can communicate.

FIGURE 10.15 IPv6 neighbor discovery: neighbor solicitation message

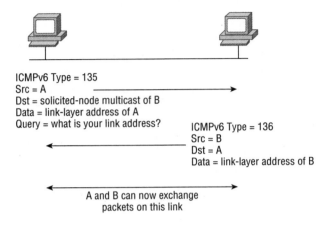

Tunneling

When tunneling is used as a transition mechanism to IPv6, it involves encapsulating one type of protocol in another type of protocol for the purpose of transmitting it across a network that supports the packet type or protocol. At the tunnel endpoint, the packet is de-encapsulated, and the contents are then processed in its native form.

Overlay tunneling encapsulates IPv6 packets in IPv4 packets for delivery across an IPv4 network. Overlay tunnels can be configured between border routers or between a border router and a host capable of supporting both IPv6 and IPv4. Cisco IOS supports the following tunnel types:

- Manual
- Routing encapsulation (GRE)
- 6to4
- ISATAP

Some of the more significant methods are covered in the following sections.

GRE Tunnels

Although not used as an IPv6 transition mechanism, Generic Routing Encapsulation (GRE) tunnels are worth discussing while talking about tunneling. GRE is a general-purpose encapsulation that allows for transporting packets from one network through another network through a VPN. One of its benefits is its ability to use a routing protocol. It also can carry non-IP traffic, and when implemented as a GRE over IPSec tunnel, it supports encryption.

When this type of tunnel is built, the GRE encapsulation will occur before the IPSec encryption process. One key thing to keep in mind is that the tunnel interfaces on either end must be in the same subnet.

6to4 Tunneling

6to4 tunneling is super useful for carrying IPv6 data over a network that is still IPv4. In some cases, you will have IPv6 subnets or portions of your network that are all IPv6, and those networks will have to communicate with each other. This could happen over a WAN or some other network that you do not control. So how do we fix this problem? By creating a tunnel that will carry the IPv6 traffic for you across the IPv4 network. Now having a tunnel is not that hard, and it isn't difficult to understand. It is really taking the IPv6 packet that would normally be traveling across the network, grabbing it up, and placing an IPv4 header on the front of it that specifies an IPv4 protocol type of 41.

When you're configuring either a manual or automatic tunnel (covered in the next two sections), three key pieces must be configured:

- The tunnel mode
- The IPv4 tunnel source
- A 6to4 IPv6 address that lies within 2002 ::/16

Manual IPv6 Tunneling

To make this happen we are going to have a couple of dual-stacked routers. We just have to add a little configuration to place a tunnel between the routers. Tunnels are very simple. We just have to tell each router where the tunnel is starting and where it has to end up. Let's take a look. The following configuration creates what is known as a manual IPv6 tunnel:

```
Router1(config)#int tunnel 0
Router1(config-if)#ipv6 address 2001:db8:1:1::1/64
Router1(config-if)#tunnel source 192.168.30.1
Router1(config-if)#tunnel destination 192.168.40.1
Router1(config-if)#tunnel mode ipv6ip

Router2(config)#int tunnel 0
Router2(config-if)#ipv6 address 2001:db8:2:2::1/64
Router2(config-if)#tunnel source 192.168.40.1
Router2(config-if)#tunnel destination 192.168.30.1
Router2(config-if)#tunnel mode ipv6ip
```

This will allow our IPv6 networks to communicate over the IPv4 network. Now this is not meant to be a permanent configuration. The end goal should be to have an all-IPv6 network end to end.

6to4 (Automatic)

The following configuration uses what is known as automatic 6to4 tunneling. This allows for the endpoints to auto-configure an IPv6 address where a site-specific /48 bit prefix is dynamically constructed by prepending the prefix 2002 to an IPv4 address assigned to the site. This means the first 2 bytes of the IPv6 address will be 0x2002, and the next 4 bytes will be the hexadecimal equivalent of the IPv4 address. Therefore, in this case 192.168.99.1 translates to 2002:c0a8:6301:: /48. Tunnel interface 0 is configured without an IPv4 or IPv6 address because the IPv4 or IPv6 addresses on Ethernet interface 0 are used to construct a tunnel source address. A tunnel destination address is not specified because the destination address is automatically constructed. It is also possible for each tunnel to have multiple destinations, which is not possible when creating a manual IPv6 tunnel.

```
Router(config)# interface ethernet 0
Router(config-if)# ip address 192.168.99.1 255.255.255.0
Router(config-if)# ipv6 address 2002:c0a8:6301::/48 eui-64
Router(config-if)# exit
Router(config)# interface tunnel 0
Router(config-if)# no ip address
Router(config-if)# ipv6 unnumbered ethernet 0
Router(config-if)# tunnel source ethernet 0
Router(config-if)# tunnel mode ipv6ip 6to4
Router(config-if)# exit
```

When using automatic 6to4 tunnels, in many cases you will need to reference the tunnel endpoint when creating the neighbor statement (for example, in BGP). When doing so, you can refer to the auto-configured address in the preceding example in three ways in the neighbor command.

```
::  c0a8:6301
::  192.168.99.1
0:0:0:0:0:0:192.168.99.1
```

To configure a static route to a network that needs to cross a 6to4 tunnel, use the `ipv6 route` command. When you do so, the least significant 32 bits of the address referenced by the command will correspond to the IPv4 address assigned to the tunnel source. For example, in the following command, the final 32 bits will be the IPv4 address of the tunnel 0 interface:

```
Ipv6 route 2002::/16 tunnel 0
```

ISATAP Tunneling

Intra-Site Automatic Tunnel Addressing Protocol is another mechanism for transmitting IPv6 packets over an IPv4 network. The word *automatic* means that once an ISATAP server/router has been set up, only the clients must be configured to connect to it. A sample configuration is shown here:

```
R1(config)#ipv6 unicast-routing
R1(config)#interface tunnel 1
R1(config-if)# tunnel source ethernet 0
R1(config-if)# tunnel mode ipv6ip isatap
R1(config-if)#  ipv6 address 2001:DB8::/64 eui-64
```

One other thing that may be noteworthy: If the IPv4 network that you are traversing in this situation has a NAT translation point, it will break the tunnel encapsulation that we have created. In the following section, a solution is discussed.

Teredo

Teredo gives full IPv6 connectivity for IPv6 hosts that are on an IPv4 network but have no direct native connection to an IPv6 network. Its distinguishing feature is that it is able to perform its function even from behind network address translation (NAT) devices such as home routers.

The Teredo protocol performs several functions:

- Diagnoses UDP over IPv4 (UDPv4) connectivity and discovers the kind of NAT present (using a simplified replacement to the STUN protocol)

- Assigns a globally routable unique IPv6 address to each host

- Encapsulates IPv6 packets inside UDPv4 datagrams for transmission over an IPv4 network (this includes NAT traversal)

- Routes traffic between Teredo hosts and native (or otherwise non-Teredo) IPv6 hosts

There are several components that can make up the Teredo infrastructure:

Teredo Client   A host that has IPv4 connectivity to the Internet from behind a NAT device and uses the Teredo tunneling protocol to access the IPv6 Internet.

Teredo Server   A well-known host that is used for initial configuration of a Teredo.

Teredo Relay   The remote end of a Teredo tunnel. A Teredo relay must forward all of the data on behalf of the Teredo clients it serves, with the exception of direct Teredo client to Teredo client exchanges.

Teredo Host-Specific Relay   A Teredo relay whose range of service is limited to the very host it runs on.

Dual Stack

This is the most common type of migration strategy. It allows the devices to communicate using either IPv4 or IPv6. This technique allows for a one-by-one upgrade of applications and devices on the network. As more and more things on the network are upgraded, more of your communication will occur over IPv6. Eventually all devices and software will be upgraded, and the IPv4 protocol stacks can be removed. The configuration of dual stacking on a Cisco router is very easy. It requires nothing more than enabling IPv6 forwarding and applying an address to the interfaces that are already configured with IPv4. It will look something like this:

```
Corp(config)#ipv6 unicast-routing
Corp(config)#interface fastethernet 0/0
Corp(config-if)#ipv6 address 2001:db8:3c4d:1::/64 eui-64
Corp(config-if)#ip address 192.168.255.1 255.255.255.0
```

IPv6 Routing Protocols

Most of the routing protocols we've already discussed have been upgraded for use in IPv6 networks. Also, many of the functions and configurations that we've already learned will be used in almost the same way as they're used now. Knowing that broadcasts have been eliminated in IPv6, it follows that any protocols that use entirely broadcast traffic will go the way of the dodo—but unlike the dodo, it'll be good to say good-bye to these bandwidth-hogging, performance-annihilating little gremlins!

The routing protocols that we'll still use in version 6 got a new name and a facelift. Let's talk about a few of them now.

First on the list is RIPng (next generation). Those of you who have been in IT for a while know that RIP has worked very well for us on smaller networks, which happens to be the reason it didn't get whacked and will still be around in IPv6. And we still have EIGRPv6 because it already had protocol-dependent modules and all we had to do was add a new one to it for the IPv6 protocol. Rounding out our group of protocol survivors is OSPFv3—that's not a typo; it really is version 3. OSPF for IPv4 was actually version 2, so when it got its upgrade to IPv6, it became OSPFv3.

RIPng

To be honest, the primary features of RIPng are the same as they were with RIPv2. It is still a distance-vector protocol, has a max hop count of 15, and still has the same loop avoidance mechanisms as well as using UDP port 521.

And it still uses multicast to send its updates too, but in IPv6, it uses FF02::9 for the transport address. This is actually kind of cool because in RIPv2, the multicast address was 224.0.0.9, so the address still has a 9 at the end in the new IPv6 multicast range. In fact, most routing protocols got to keep a little bit of their IPv4 identities like that.

But of course there are differences in the new version or it wouldn't be a new version, would it? We know that routers keep the next-hop addresses of their neighbor routers for every destination network in their routing table. The difference is that with RIPng, the router keeps track of this next-hop address using the link-local address, not a global address. So just remember that RIPng will pretty much work the same way as with IPv4.

EIGRPv6

As with RIPng, EIGRPv6 works much the same as its IPv4 predecessor does—most of the features that EIGRP provided before EIGRPv6 will still be available.

EIGRPv6 is still an advanced distance-vector protocol that has some link-state features. The neighbor-discovery process using Hellos still happens, and it still provides reliable communication with a reliable transport protocol that gives us loop-free fast convergence using DUAL.

Hello packets and updates are sent using multicast transmission, and as with RIPng, EIGRPv6's multicast address stayed almost the same. In IPv4 it was 224.0.0.10; in IPv6, it's FF02::A (A = 10 in hexadecimal notation).

Last to check out in our group is what OSPF looks like in the IPv6 routing protocol.

OSPFv3

The new version of OSPF continues the trend of the routing protocols having many similarities with their IPv4 versions.

The foundation of OSPF remains the same—it is still a link-state routing protocol that divides an entire internetwork or autonomous system into areas, making a hierarchy.

Adjacencies (neighbor routers running OSPF) and next-hop attributes now use link-local addresses, and OSPFv3 still uses multicast traffic to send its updates and acknowledgments, with the addresses FF02::5 for OSPF routers and FF02::6 for OSPF-designated routers, which provide topological updates (route information) to other routers. These new addresses are the replacements for 224.0.0.5 and 224.0.0.6, respectively, which were used in OSPFv2.

> Shortest Path Bridging (SPB), specified in the IEEE 802.1aq standard, is a computer networking technology intended to simplify the creation and configuration of networks and replace the older 802.1d/802.1w protocols while enabling multipath routing.

Summary

This chapter covered the basic routing protocols that you may find on a network today. Probably the most common routing protocols you'll run into are RIP, OSPF, and EIGRP.

I covered RIP, RIPv2, and the differences between the two RIP protocols as well as EIGRP, and BGP in the sections on distance-vector protocols. I also covered IPv6 routing protocols and some advanced IPv6 operations, including transitional mechanisms such as dual stacking and tunneling.

I finished by discussing OSPF and IS-IS and when you would possibly see each one in a network.

With all this routing information behind you, it's time to go through some review questions and then move on to learning all about switching in the next chapter.

Exam Essentials

Understand the various dynamic routing protocols including RIP, OSPF, EIGRP, and BGP.   RIP is a distance-vector routing protocol. It sends the complete routing table out to all active interfaces every 30 seconds. RIP uses hop count to determine the best path to a remote network. EIGRP is also a distant-vector protocol that uses link-state characteristics to determine the best path to a remote network. BGP is an external protocol that uses a path vector protocol between autonomous systems. OSPF is an open-standard and link-state protocol that uses the Dijkstra algorithm for best path selection.

Be able to distinguish between link state vs. distance vector vs. hybrid.   Link-state protocols use an algorithm to learn more information about the internetwork. Distance-vector protocols use a hop count to determine neighbors. Hybrid protocols will use a combination of distance vector and link state to determine the best path selection.

Know what the Neighborhood Discovery Protocol (NDP) and Router Advertisement (RA) protocol is used for.   NDP is used in an IPv6 network to discover various information from neighboring devices. Router advertisements are used to detect the gateway out of the network.

Remember the differences between RIPv1 and RIPv2.   RIPv1 sends broadcasts every 30 seconds and has an AD of 120. RIPv2 sends multicasts (224.0.0.9) every 30 seconds and also has an AD of 120. RIPv2 sends subnet mask information with the route updates, which allows it to support classless networks and discontiguous networks. RIPv2 also supports authentication between routers, and RIPv1 does not.

Compare OSPF and RIPv1.   OSPF is a link-state protocol that supports VLSM and classless routing; RIPv1 is a distance-vector protocol that does not support VLSM and supports only classful routing.

Understand the various compatibility requirements.   Know the various compatibility strategies for supporting both IPv4 and IPv6. This should include tunneling of IPv6 through an IPv4 network, Teredo, ISATAP tunneling, and dual stack.

Written Lab

You can find the answers to the written labs in Appendix A. Using the following figure, converge the respective routing table by filling in the blanks for the network ID, exit interface, and metric (hop count). The tables are prepopulated with the directly connected network IDs, exit interface, and metric.

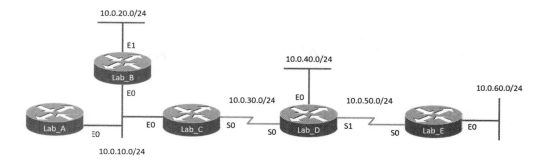

Lab_A

Network ID	Exit Interface	Metric
10.0.10.0/24	E0	0

Lab_B

Network ID	Exit Interface	Metric
10.0.10.0/24	E0	0
10.0.30.0/24	E1	0

Lab_C

Network ID	Exit Interface	Metric
10.0.10.0/24	E0	0
10.0.30.0/24	S0	0

Lab_D

Network ID	Exit Interface	Metric
10.0.30.0/24	S0	0
10.0.40.0/24	E0	0
10.0.50.0/24	S1	0

Lab_E

Network ID	Exit Interface	Metric
10.0.50.0/24	S0	0
10.0.60.0/24	E0	0

Review Questions

You can find the answers to the review questions in Appendix B.

1. Which high-availability protocol is an open standard?
   - **A.** NLB
   - **B.** HSRP
   - **C.** OSPF
   - **D.** VRRP

2. How are routers managed with interior gateway protocols?
   - **A.** Routers are grouped into autonomous systems.
   - **B.** Routing protocols are redistributed between ASs.
   - **C.** All routers use the same interior routing protocol.
   - **D.** All network IDs are advertised with the same autonomous system number.

3. What is the maximum hop count for RIP?
   - **A.** 15 hops
   - **B.** 100 hops
   - **C.** 255 hops
   - **D.** 16 hops

4. Which statement is true about RIPv2 advertisements?
   - **A.** RIPv2 allows for neighborship through hello packets.
   - **B.** RIPv2 broadcasts only updates on all active interfaces.
   - **C.** RIPv2 multicasts the full routing table every 30 seconds.
   - **D.** RIPv2 multicasts the full routing table every 60 seconds.

5. Which multicast address does RIPv2 use for advertising routes?
   - **A.** 224.0.0.5
   - **B.** 224.0.0.9
   - **C.** 224.0.0.6
   - **D.** 224.0.0.2

6. Which routing protocol will not contain a topology of the network?
   - **A.** EIGRP
   - **B.** RIP
   - **C.** OSPF
   - **D.** BGP

7. When a static route is made, what is the default AD?

    A. AD of 1

    B. AD of 0

    C. AD of 2

    D. AD of 255

8. Why are ADs used with routing tables?

    A. ADs define protocol standards.

    B. ADs define reliability of routing protocols.

    C. ADs allow for the shortest distance between routes.

    D. ADs are programmed by the administrator for path selection.

9. What is the metric for OSPF?

    A. Link

    B. Delay, bandwidth, reliability, load

    C. K metrics

    D. Bandwidth

10. You are examining a router and discover that there is a static default route configured for a next hop of 192.168.1.2. You also notice that there is a default route being populated from RIP for a next hop of 192.168.2.2. Which default route will be selected?

    A. The route with the lowest AD

    B. The route with the highest AD

    C. The route with the lowest metric

    D. The route being populated from RIP

11. Which routing protocol is a distance-vector routing protocol?

    A. OSPF

    B. RIP

    C. EIGRP

    D. BGP

12. Which statement accurately describes a routing loop?

    A. Packets are routed out one interface but come back on a different interface.

    B. Packets are transmitted within a series of routers and never reach the destination.

    C. Packets reach the expiry TTL before reaching the destination network.

    D. Packets are routed via an inefficient path.

13. What is the AD of RIP?

    A. AD of 90

    B. AD of 100

    C. AD of 110

    D. AD of 120

14. Which routing protocol is a link-state routing protocol?

    A. OSPF

    B. RIP

    C. EIGRP

    D. IGRP

15. Which routing technique requires no administrator intervention when a route goes down?

    A. Dynamic routing

    B. Directly connected routes

    C. Default routing

    D. Static routing

16. Which is an advantage of dynamic routing protocols?

    A. Resiliency when routes become unavailable

    B. Lower router RAM usage

    C. Lower router CPU usage

    D. Less bandwidth usage

17. Which routing protocol broadcasts updates for routes?

    A. RIPv1

    B. OSPF

    C. EIGRP

    D. BGP

18. What is an advantage of dynamic routing protocols?

    A. Centralized routing tables

    B. Optimized route selection

    C. Ease of configuration

    D. Lower bandwidth utilization

19. Which protocol is considered a hybrid protocol?

    A. RIP

    B. OSPF

    C. EIGRP

    D. BGP

20. What is a characteristic of distance-vector protocols?

    A. They track the status of routes learned.

    B. They re-advertise routes learned.

    C. Each router keeps its own topology database.

    D. Each router checks the routes it learns.

Chapter 11

Switching and Virtual LANs

THE FOLLOWING COMPTIA NETWORK+ EXAM OBJECTIVES ARE COVERED IN THIS CHAPTER:

✓ **Domain 2.0 Network Implementation**

✓ **2.2 Given a scenario, configure switching technologies and features.**

- ▪ Virtual Local Area Network (VLAN)
  - ▪ VLAN database
  - ▪ Switch Virtual Interface (SVI)
- ▪ Interface configuration
  - ▪ Native VLAN
  - ▪ Voice VLAN
  - ▪ 802.1Q tagging
  - ▪ Link aggregation
  - ▪ Speed
  - ▪ Duplex
- ▪ Spanning tree
- ▪ Maximum transmission unit (MTU)
  - ▪ Jumbo frames

✓ **Domain 5.0 Network Troubleshooting**

✓ **5.3 Given a scenario, troubleshoot common issues with network services.**

- Switching issues
  - STP
    - Network loops
    - Root bridge selection
    - Port roles
    - Port states

✓ **5.4 Given a scenario, troubleshoot common performance issues.**

Layer 2 switching is the process of using the hardware addresses of devices on a LAN to segment a network. Because you've got the basic ideas down, I'm now going to focus on the more in-depth particulars of layer 2 switching and how it works.

You already know that switching breaks up large collision domains into smaller ones and that a collision domain is a network segment with two or more devices sharing the same bandwidth. A hub network is a typical example of this type of technology. But because each port on a switch is actually its own collision domain, you can create a much better Ethernet LAN by simply replacing your hubs with switches!

Switches truly have changed the way networks are designed and implemented. If a pure switched design is properly implemented, it will result in a clean, cost-effective, and resilient internetwork. In this chapter, we'll survey and compare how networks were designed before and after switching technologies were introduced.

Routing protocols like Routing Information Protocol (RIP), which you learned about in Chapter 10, "Routing Protocols," employ processes for preventing network loops from occurring at the Network layer. This is all good, but if you have redundant physical links between your switches, routing protocols won't do a thing to stop loops from occurring at the Data Link layer. That's exactly the reason Spanning Tree Protocol was developed—to put a stop to loops taking place within a layer 2 switched network. The essentials of this vital protocol, as well as how it works within a switched network, are some of the important subjects that we'll cover thoroughly in this chapter.

To finish up this chapter, you're going to learn exactly what a VLAN is and how VLAN memberships are used in a switched network as well as how trunking is used to send information from all VLANs across a single link. Good stuff!

Networking Before Layer 2 Switching

Because knowing the history of something really helps with understanding why things are the way they are today, I'm going to go back in time a bit and talk about the condition of networks before switches and the part switches have played in the evolution of corporate

LANs by helping to segment them. For a visual of how a typical network design looked before LAN switching, check out the network in Figure 11.1.

FIGURE 11.1 A network before switching

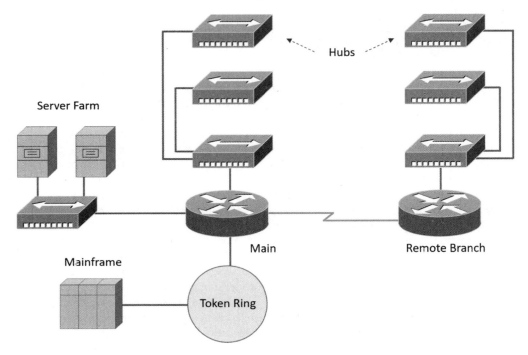

The design in Figure 11.1 was called a *collapsed backbone* because all the hosts involved had to go to the corporate backbone to reach any network services—both LAN and mainframe.

Going back even further, before networks like the one shown in Figure 11.1 had physical segmentation devices such as routers and hubs, there was the mainframe network. This type of network comprised mainframe controllers made by IBM, Honeywell, Sperry, DEC, and so on and dumb terminals that connected into the controller(s). Any remote sites were connected to the mainframe with bridges.

And then the PC began its rise to stardom, and the mainframe was connected to an Ethernet or Token Ring LAN where the servers were installed. These servers were usually OS/2 or LAN Manager because this was "pre-NT." Each floor of a building ran either coax or twisted-pair wiring to the corporate backbone, which was then connected to a router. PCs ran an emulating software program that allowed them to connect to mainframe services, giving those PCs the ability to access services from the mainframe and LAN simultaneously.

Eventually, the PC became robust enough to allow application developers to port applications more effectively than they ever could before—an advance that markedly reduced networking prices and enabled businesses to grow at a much faster rate.

Moving forward to when Novell rose to popularity in the late 1980s and early 1990s, OS/2 and LAN Manager servers were by and large replaced with NetWare servers. This made the Ethernet network even more popular because that's what Novell 3.x servers used to communicate with client-server software.

So basically, that's the story about how the network in Figure 11.1 came into being. But soon a big problem arose with this configuration. As the corporate backbone grew and grew, network services became slower and slower. A big reason for this was that at the same time this huge burst in growth was taking place, LAN services began to require even faster response times. This resulted in networks becoming totally saturated and overwhelmed. Everyone was dumping the dumb terminals used to access mainframe services in favor of those slick new PCs so they could more easily connect to the corporate backbone and network services.

And all this was taking place before the Internet's momentous popularity, so everyone in the company needed to access the corporate network's own, internal services. Without the Internet, all network services were internal, meaning that they were exclusive to the company network. As you can imagine, this situation created a screaming need to segment that single, humongous, and now plodding corporate network, which was connected together with sluggish old routers.

How was this issue addressed? Well, at first, Cisco responded by simply creating faster routers (no doubt about that), but still more segmentation was needed, especially on the Ethernet LANs. The invention of Fast Ethernet was a very good and helpful thing, yet it too fell short of solving that network segmentation need. But devices called *bridges* did provide relief, and they were first used in the networking environment to break up collision domains.

Sounds good, but only so much—bridges were sorely limited by the number of ports and other network services they could provide, and that's when layer 2 switches came to the rescue. These switches saved the day by breaking up collision domains on each and every port—like a bridge—but switches could provide hundreds of ports! This early, switched LAN looked like the network pictured in Figure 11.2.

As you can see here, each hub was placed into a switch port—an innovation that vastly improved the network. So now, instead of each building being crammed into the same collision domain, each hub became its own separate collision domain. Yet still, as is too often the case, there was a catch—switch ports were still very new and, therefore, super expensive. Because switches were so cost prohibitive, simply adding a switch into each floor of the building just wasn't going to happen—at least not yet. But thanks to whomever you choose to thank for these things, the switch price tag has dropped dramatically; now, having every one of your users plugged into a switch port is a really good solution, and cost effective too!

So there it is—if you're going to create a network design and implement it, including switching services is a must.

A typical, contemporary, and complete switched network design/implementation would look something like Figure 11.3.

FIGURE 11.2 The first switched LAN

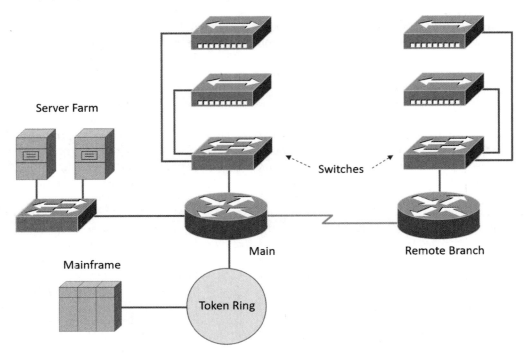

FIGURE 11.3 The typical switched network design

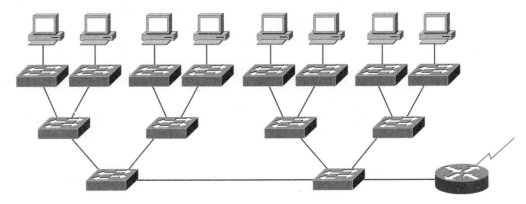

"But wait—there's still a router in there!" you say. Yes, it's not a mirage—there *is* a router in there. But its job has changed quite a bit. Instead of performing physical segmentation, it now creates and handles logical segmentation. Those logical segments are called VLANs, and no worries, I promise to explain them thoroughly throughout the rest of this chapter.

Switching Services

Bridges use software to create and manage a filter table, but switches use *application-specific integrated circuits (ASICs)* to accomplish this. Even so, it's still okay to think of a layer 2 switch as a multiport bridge because their basic reason for being is the same: to break up collision domains.

Layer 2 switches and bridges are faster than routers because they don't take up time looking at the Network layer header information. Instead, they look at the frame's hardware addresses before deciding to forward, flood, or drop the frame.

Switches create private, dedicated collision domains and provide independent bandwidth on each port, unlike hubs. Figure 11.4 shows Six hosts connected to a switch—all running 100 Mbps full duplex to the server. Unlike with a hub, each host has full-duplex, 100 Mbps of dedicated communication to the server. Common switchports today can pass traffic at 10/100/1000 Mbps depending on the connected device. By default, the switchports are set to auto-configure.

FIGURE 11.4   Switches create private domains

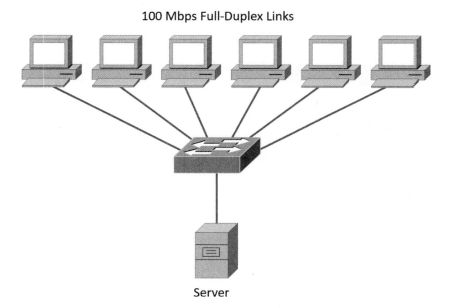

100 Mbps Full-Duplex Links

Server

Layer 2 switching provides the following benefits:

- Hardware-based bridging (ASIC)
- Wire speed
- Low latency
- Low cost

What makes layer 2 switching so efficient is that no modification to the data packet takes place. The device reads only the frame encapsulating the packet, which makes the switching process considerably faster and less error prone than routing processes.

And if you use layer 2 switching for both workgroup connectivity and network segmentation (breaking up collision domains), you can create a flatter network design with more network segments than you can with traditional routed networks.

Plus, layer 2 switching increases bandwidth for each user because, again, each connection (interface) into the switch is its own collision domain. This feature makes it possible for you to connect multiple devices to each interface—very cool.

Coming up, we'll dive deeper into the layer 2 switching technology.

Limitations of Layer 2 Switching

Because people usually toss layer 2 switching into the same category as bridged networks, we also tend to think it has the same hang-ups and issues that bridged networks do. Keep in mind that bridges are good and helpful things if we design the network correctly, keeping our devices' features as well as their limitations in mind. To end up with a solid design that includes bridges, there are two really important things to consider:

- You absolutely have to break up the collision domains properly.
- A well-oiled, functional bridged network is one whose users spend 80 percent of their time on the local segment.

So, bridged networks break up collision domains, but remember, that network is really still just one big broadcast domain. Neither layer 2 switches nor bridges break up broadcast domains by default—something that not only limits your network's size and growth potential but can also reduce its overall performance!

Broadcasts and multicasts, along with the slow convergence time of spanning trees, can give you some major grief as your network grows. These are the big reasons layer 2 switches and bridges just can't completely replace routers (layer 3 devices) in the internetwork.

Bridging vs. LAN Switching

It's true—layer 2 switches really are pretty much just bridges that give us lots more ports. But the comparison doesn't end there. Here's a list of some significant differences and similarities between bridges and switches that you need to keep in mind:

- Bridges are software-based, whereas switches are hardware-based because they use ASIC chips to help make filtering decisions.
- A switch can be viewed as a multiport bridge.
- There can be only one spanning-tree instance per bridge, whereas switches can have many. (I'm going to tell you all about spanning trees in a bit.)
- Switches have a higher number of ports than most bridges.
- Both bridges and switches forward layer 2 broadcasts.

- Bridges and switches learn MAC addresses by examining the source address of each frame received.
- Both bridges and switches make forwarding decisions based on layer 2 addresses.

Three Switch Functions at Layer 2

There are three distinct functions of layer 2 switching—you need to know these! They are as follows:

- Address learning
- Forward/filter decisions
- Loop avoidance

The next three sections cover these functions in detail.

Address Learning

Layer 2 switches and bridges are capable of *address learning*; that is, they remember the source hardware address of each frame received on an interface and enter this information into a MAC database known as a *forward/filter table*. But first things first—when a switch is initially powered on, the MAC forward/filter table is empty, as shown in Figure 11.5.

FIGURE 11.5   Empty forward/filter table on a switch

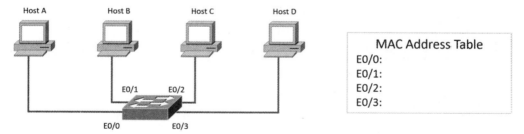

When a device transmits and an interface receives a frame, the switch places the frame's source address in the MAC forward/filter table, which allows it to remember the interface on which the sending device is located. The switch then has no choice but to flood the network with this frame out of every port except the source port because it has no idea where the destination device is actually located.

If a device answers this flooded frame and sends a frame back, then the switch will take the source address from that frame and place that MAC address in its database as well, thereby associating the newly discovered address with the interface that received the frame. Because the switch now has both of the relevant MAC addresses in its filtering table, the two devices can make a point-to-point connection. The switch doesn't need to flood the frame as it did the first time because now the frames can and will be forwarded only between the two devices recorded in the table. This is exactly the thing that makes layer 2 switches better than hubs, because in a hub network, all frames are forwarded out all ports every time—no matter what. This is because hubs just aren't equipped to collect, store, and draw upon data in a table as a switch is. Figure 11.6 shows the processes involved in building a MAC database.

FIGURE 11.6   How switches learn hosts' locations

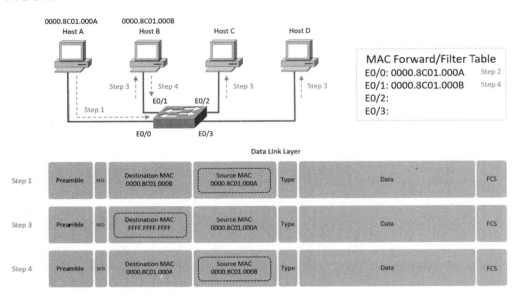

In this figure, you can see four hosts attached to a switch. When the switch is powered on, it has nothing in its MAC address forward/filter table (just as in Figure 11.5). But when the hosts start communicating, the switch places the source hardware address of each frame in the table along with the port that the frame's address corresponds to.

Let me give you a step-by-step example of how a forward/filter table becomes populated:

1. Host A sends a frame to Host B. Host A's MAC address is 0000.8c01.000A, and Host B's MAC address is 0000.8c01.000B.

2. The switch receives the frame on the E0/0 interface and places the source address in the MAC address table, associating it with the port it came in on.

3. Because the destination address is not in the MAC database, the frame is forwarded (*flooded*) out all interfaces—except the source port.

4. Host B receives the frame and responds to Host A. The switch receives this frame on interface E0/1 and places the source hardware address in the MAC database, associating it with the port it came in on.

5. Host A and Host B can now make a point-to-point connection, and only the two devices will receive the frames. Hosts C and D will not see the frames, nor are their MAC addresses found in the database, because they haven't yet sent a frame to the switch.

Oh, by the way, it's important to know that if Host A and Host B don't communicate to the switch again within a certain amount of time, the switch will flush their entries from the database to keep it as current as possible.

Forward/Filter Decisions

When a frame arrives at a switch interface, the destination hardware address is compared to the forward/filter MAC database and the switch makes a *forward/filter decision*. In other words, if the destination hardware address is known (listed in the database), the frame is sent out only the specified exit interface. The switch will not transmit the frame out any interface except the destination interface. Not transmitting the frame preserves bandwidth on the other network segments and is called *frame filtering*.

But as I mentioned earlier, if the destination hardware address isn't listed in the MAC database, then the frame is flooded out all active interfaces except the interface on which the frame was received. If a device answers the flooded frame, the MAC database is updated with the device's location—its particular interface.

So, by default, if a host or server sends a broadcast on the LAN, the switch will flood the frame out all active ports except the source port. Remember, the switch creates smaller collision domains, but it's still one large broadcast domain by default.

In Figure 11.7, you can see Host A sending a data frame to Host D. What will the switch do when it receives the frame from Host A?

FIGURE 11.7   Forward/filter table

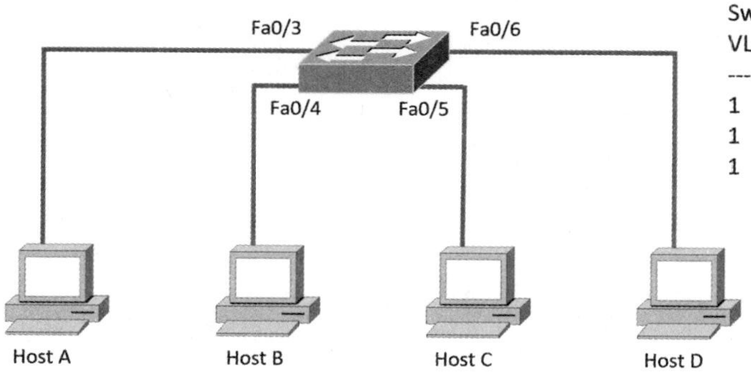

```
Switch# sh mac address-table
VLAN      MAC Address      Ports
---------  --------------------  ---------
1         0005.dccd.d74b    Fa0/4
1         000a.f467.9e80    Fa0/5
1         000a.f467.9e8b    Fa0/6
```

If you answered that because Host A's MAC address is not in the forward/filter table, the switch will add the source address and port to the MAC address table and then forward the frame to Host D, you're halfway there. If you also came back with, "If Host D's MAC address was not in the forward/filter table, the switch would have flooded the frame out all ports except for port Fa0/3," then congratulations—you nailed it!

Let's take a look at the output of a `show mac address-table` command as seen from a Cisco Catalyst switch (the MAC address table works pretty much exactly the same on all brands of switches):

```
Switch#sh mac address-table
Vlan    Mac Address      Type      Ports
---     -------------    ------    -----
  1     0005.dccb.d74b   DYNAMIC   Fa0/1
  1     000a.f467.9e80   DYNAMIC   Fa0/3
  1     000a.f467.9e8b   DYNAMIC   Fa0/4
  1     000a.f467.9e8c   DYNAMIC   Fa0/3
  1     0010.7b7f.c2b0   DYNAMIC   Fa0/3
  1     0030.80dc.460b   DYNAMIC   Fa0/3
  1     0030.9492.a5dd   DYNAMIC   Fa0/1
  1     00d0.58ad.05f4   DYNAMIC   Fa0/1
```

Now suppose the preceding switch received a frame with the following MAC addresses:

Source MAC: 0005.dccb.d74b

Destination MAC: 000a.f467.9e8c

How will the switch handle this frame? The right answer is that the destination MAC address will be found in the MAC address table and the frame will be forwarded out Fa0/3 only. Remember that if the destination MAC address is not found in the forward/filter table, it will forward the frame out all ports of the switch looking for the destination device.

Now that you can see the MAC address table and how switches add hosts' addresses to the forward filter table, how do you stop switching loops if you have multiple links between switches? Let's talk about this possible problem in more detail.

Loop Avoidance

Redundant links between switches can be a wise thing to implement because they help prevent complete network failures in the event that one link stops working.

But it seems like there's always a downside—even though redundant links can be extremely helpful, they often cause more problems than they solve. This is because frames can be flooded down all redundant links simultaneously, creating network loops as well as other evils. Here are a few of the problems you can face:

- If no loop avoidance schemes are put in place, the switches will flood broadcasts endlessly throughout the internetwork. This is sometimes referred to as a broadcast storm. (In real life, it's often referred to in less polite ways that we're not permitted to repeat in print!) Figure 11.8 illustrates how a broadcast can be propagated throughout the network. Pay special attention to how a frame is continually being flooded through the internetwork's physical network media. One way to test the loop avoidance operations of your switch network is to plug one end of a cable into one port and the other end of the same cable into another port. If loop avoidance is not operational, this should cause a big broadcast storm!

FIGURE 11.8   Broadcast storm

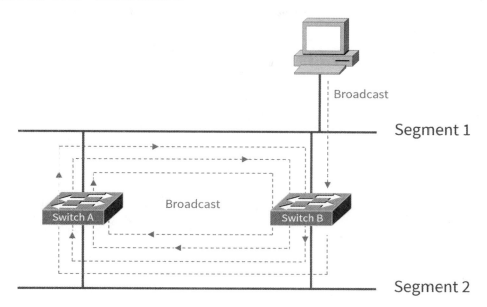

- What you see in Figure 11.8 is that a device can receive multiple copies of the same frame because that frame can arrive from different segments at the same time. Figure 11.9 demonstrates how a whole bunch of frames can arrive from multiple segments simultaneously. The server in the figure sends a unicast frame to another device connected to Segment 1. Because it's a unicast frame, Switch A receives and forwards the frame, and Switch B provides the same service—it forwards the unicast. This is bad because it means that the destination device on Segment 1 receives that unicast frame twice, causing additional overhead on the network.

- You may have thought of this one: The MAC address filter table could be totally confused about the device's location because the switch can receive the frame from more than one link. Worse, the bewildered switch could get so caught up in constantly updating the MAC filter table with source hardware address locations that it might fail to forward a frame! This is called *thrashing* the MAC table.

- One of the nastiest things that can happen is having multiple loops propagating throughout a network. This means you end up with loops occurring within other loops, and if a broadcast storm happened at the same time, the network wouldn't be able to perform frame switching at all—it's toast!

All of these problems spell disaster (or something like it) and are decidedly ugly situations that just must be avoided or at least fixed somehow. That's where the Spanning Tree Protocol comes into the game. It was developed to solve each and every one of the problems I just told you about.

FIGURE 11.9   Multiple frame copies

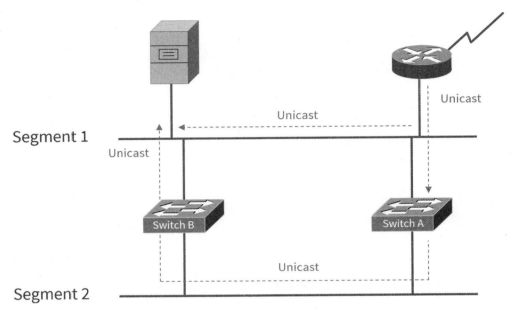

Distributed Switching

In a virtual environment such as you might find in many of today's data centers, not only are virtual servers used in the place of physical servers, but virtual switches (software-based) are used to provide connectivity between the virtual systems. These virtual servers reside on physical devices that are called hosts. The virtual switches can be connected to a physical switch to enable access to the virtual servers from the outside world.

One of the unique features of these virtual switches is the ability of the switches to span multiple physical hosts. When this is done, the switch is called a distributed switch. This provides connectivity between virtual servers that are located on different hosts, as shown in Figure 11.10.

Spanning Tree Protocol

Once upon a time, a company called Digital Equipment Corporation (DEC) was purchased and renamed Compaq. But before that happened, DEC created the original version of *Spanning Tree Protocol (STP)*. The IEEE later created its own version of STP called 802.1D. Yet again, it's not all clear skies—by default, most switches run the IEEE 802.1D version of STP, which isn't compatible with the DEC version. The good news is that there is a newer industry standard called 802.1w, which is faster but not enabled by default on any switches.

FIGURE 11.10   Distributed switching

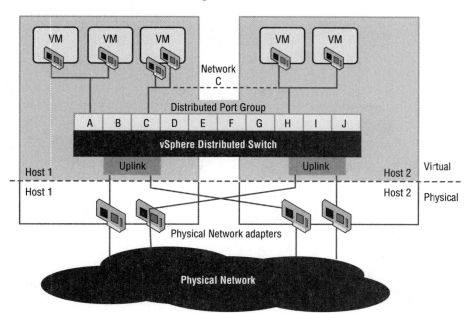

To begin with, STP's main task is to stop network loops from occurring on your layer 2 network (bridges or switches). It achieves this feat by vigilantly monitoring the network to find all links and making sure that no loops occur by shutting down any redundant ones. STP uses the *Spanning Tree Algorithm (STA)* to first create a topology database and then search out and destroy redundant links. With STP running, frames will be forwarded only on the premium, STP-picked links. Switches transmit Bridge Protocol Data Units (BPDUs) out all ports so that all links between switches can be found.

STP is a layer 2 protocol that is used to maintain a loop-free switched network.

STP is necessary in networks such as the one shown in Figure 11.11.

In Figure 11.11, you see a switched network with a redundant topology (switching loops). Without some type of layer 2 mechanism to stop network loops, we would fall victim to the problems I discussed previously: broadcast storms and multiple frame copies.

Understand that the network in Figure 11.11 would actually sort of work, albeit extremely slowly. This clearly demonstrates the danger of switching loops. And to make matters worse, it can be super hard to find this problem once it starts!

FIGURE 11.11 A switched network with switching loops

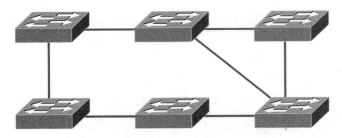

Spanning Tree Port States

The ports on a bridge or switch running STP can transition through five different states:

Blocking A blocked port won't forward frames; it just listens to BPDUs and will drop all other frames. The purpose of the blocking state is to prevent the use of looped paths. All ports are in a blocking state by default when the switch is powered up.

Listening The port listens to BPDUs to make sure no loops occur on the network before passing data frames. A port in listening state prepares to forward data frames without populating the MAC address table.

Learning The switch port listens to BPDUs and learns all the paths in the switched network. A port in learning state populates the MAC address table but doesn't forward data frames. Forward delay is the time it takes to transition a port from listening to learning mode. It's set to 15 seconds by default.

Forwarding The port sends and receives all data frames on the bridged port. If the port is still a designated or root port at the end of the learning state, it enters the forwarding state.

Disabled A port in the disabled state (administratively) does not participate in the frame forwarding or STP. A port in the disabled state is virtually nonoperational.

 Switches populate the MAC address table in learning and forwarding modes only.

Switch ports are usually in either the blocking or forwarding state. A forwarding port is one that has been determined to have the lowest (best) cost to the root bridge. But when and if the network experiences a topology change because of a failed link or when someone adds a new switch into the mix, you'll find the ports on a switch in the listening and learning states.

As I mentioned, blocking ports is a strategy for preventing network loops. Once a switch determines the best path to the root bridge, all other redundant ports will be in blocking mode. Blocked ports can still receive BPDUs—they just don't send out any frames.

If a switch determines that a blocked port should now be the designated, or root, port, say because of a topology change, the port will respond by going into listening mode and checking all the BPDUs it receives to ensure that it won't create a loop once the port goes back into forwarding mode.

STP Convergence

Convergence is what happens when all the ports on bridges and switches have transitioned to either forwarding or blocking modes. During this phase, no data will be forwarded until the convergence event is complete. Plus, before data can begin being forwarded again, all devices must be updated. Yes—you read that right: When STP is converging, all host data stops transmitting! So if you want to remain on speaking terms with your network's users (or remain employed for any length of time), you positively must make sure that your switched network is physically designed really well so that STP can converge quickly and painlessly.

Figure 11.12 demonstrates a really great way to design and implement your switched network so that STP converges efficiently.

FIGURE 11.12   An optimal hierarchical switch design

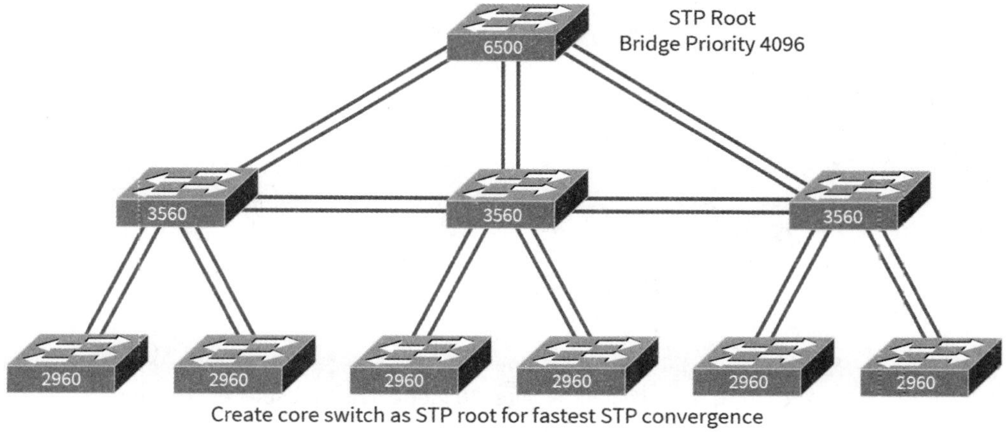

Create core switch as STP root for fastest STP convergence

Convergence is truly important because it ensures that all devices are in either the forwarding mode or the blocking mode. But as I've drilled into you, it does cost you some time. It usually takes 50 seconds to go from blocking to forwarding mode, and I don't recommend changing the default STP timers. (You can adjust those timers if you really have to.) By creating your physical switch design in a hierarchical manner, as shown in Figure 11.12, you can make your core switch the STP root. This makes everyone happy because it makes STP convergence happen fast.

Because the typical spanning-tree topology's time to convergence from blocking to forwarding on a switch port is 50 seconds, it can create time-out problems on your servers or hosts—like when you reboot them. To address this hitch, you can disable spanning tree on individual ports.

Rapid Spanning Tree Protocol 802.1w

How would you like to have a good STP configuration running on your switched network (regardless of the brand of switches) but instead of taking 50 seconds to converge, the switched network can converge in about 5 seconds, or maybe even less. How does that sound? Absolutely—yes, we want this! Well then, welcome to the world of *Rapid Spanning Tree Protocol (RSTP)*.

RSTP was not designed to be a "brand-new" protocol but more of an evolution of the 802.1D standard, with faster convergence time when a topology change occurs. Backward compatibility was a must when 802.1w was created.

The 802.1w is defined in these different port states (compared to 802.1D):

- Disabled = discarding
- Blocking = discarding
- Listening = discarding
- Learning = learning
- Forwarding = forwarding

To verify the spanning-tree type running on your Cisco switch, use the following command:

```
S1#sh spanning-tree
VLAN0001
  Spanning tree enabled protocol ieee
  Root ID    Priority    32769
             Address     000d.29bd.4b80
             Cost        3012
             Port        56 (Port-channel1)
             Hello Time   2 sec  Max Age 20 sec  Forward Delay 15 sec

  Bridge ID  Priority    49153   (priority 49152 sys-id-ext 1)
             Address     001b.2b55.7500
             Hello Time   2 sec  Max Age 20 sec  Forward Delay 15 sec
             Aging Time 15
  Uplinkfast enabled
```

```
Interface        Role Sts Cost    Prio.Nbr Type
-----------------------------------------------------
Fa0/3            Desg FWD 3100    128.3    Edge Shr
Fa0/4            Desg FWD 3019    128.4    Edge P2p
Fa0/8            Desg FWD 3019    128.8    P2p
Po1              Root FWD 3012    128.56   P2p
```

Since the type output shows Spanning tree enabled protocol ieee, we know we are running the 802.1D protocol. If the output shows RSTP, then you know your switch is running the 802.1w protocol.

EXERCISE 11.1

Understanding Switch Functions

In this exercise, you will explain the various functions of a switch.

1. Write out the main functions of a switch.

2. Explain how each function operates and the protocols involved.

After learning the three functions of a switch from this section, you should be able to articulate how each function operates.

Virtual LANs

I know I keep telling you this, but I've got to be sure you never forget it, so here I go one last time: By default, switches break up collision domains, and routers break up broadcast domains. Okay, I feel better! Now we can move on.

In contrast to the networks of yesterday, which were based on collapsed backbones, today's network design is characterized by a flatter architecture—thanks to switches. So now what? How do we break up broadcast domains in a pure switched internetwork? By creating a virtual local area network (VLAN), that's how!

A VLAN is a logical grouping of network users and resources connected to administratively defined ports on a switch. When you create VLANs, you gain the ability to create smaller broadcast domains within a layer 2 switched internetwork by assigning the various ports on the switch to different subnetworks. A VLAN is treated like its own subnet or broadcast domain, meaning that frames broadcasted onto the network are only switched between the ports logically grouped within the same VLAN.

So, does this mean we no longer need routers? Maybe yes, maybe no—it really depends on what your specific goals and needs are. By default, hosts in a specific VLAN can't communicate with hosts that are members of another VLAN, so if you want inter-VLAN communication, the answer is yes, you still need a router.

VLAN Basics

Figure 11.13 shows how layer 2 switched networks are typically designed—as flat networks. With this configuration, every broadcast packet transmitted is seen by every device on the network regardless of whether the device needs to receive that data or not.

FIGURE 11.13   Flat network structure

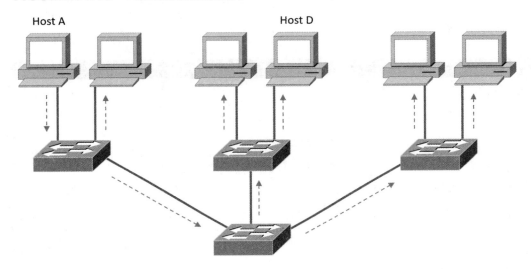

By default, routers allow broadcasts to occur only within the originating network, whereas switches forward broadcasts to all segments. Oh, and by the way, the reason it's called a *flat network* is because it's one *broadcast domain*, not because the actual design is physically flat. In Figure 11.13, you can see Host A sending out a broadcast and all ports on all switches forwarding it—all except each port that receives it.

Now check out Figure 11.14. It pictures a switched network and shows Host A sending a frame with Host D as its destination. What's important to get out of this figure is that the frame is forwarded only out of the port where Host D is located. This is a huge improvement over the old hub networks, unless having one collision domain by default is what you really want. (I'm guessing not!)

Okay, you already know that the coolest benefit you gain by having a layer 2 switched network is that it creates an individual collision domain segment for each device plugged into each port on the switch. But as is often the case, new advances bring new challenges with them. One of the biggest is that the greater the number of users and devices, the more broadcasts and packets each switch must handle.

And of course, the all-important issue of security and its demands also must be considered—while simultaneously becoming more complicated! VLANs present a security challenge because by default, within the typical layer 2 switched internetwork, all users can see all devices. And you can't stop devices from broadcasting, plus you can't stop users from trying to respond to broadcasts. This means your security options are dismally limited to placing passwords on your servers and other devices.

FIGURE 11.14   The benefit of a switched network

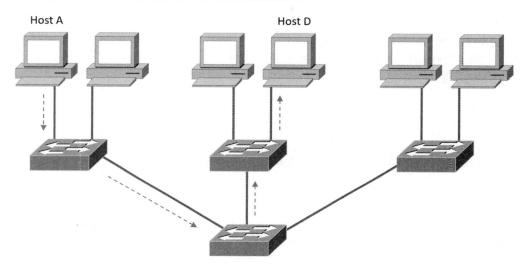

To understand how a VLAN looks to a switch, it's helpful to begin by first looking at a traditional network. Figure 11.15 shows how a network used to be created using hubs to connect physical LANs to a router.

FIGURE 11.15   Physical LANs connected to a router

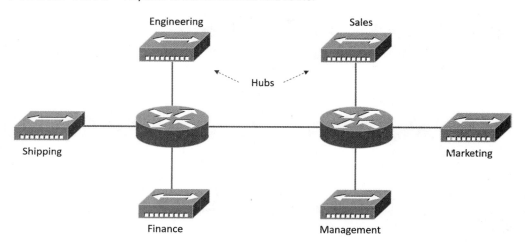

Here you can see that each network is attached with a hub port to the router (each segment also has its own logical network number, even though this isn't obvious looking at the figure). Each host attached to a particular physical network has to match that network's logical network number in order to be able to communicate on the internetwork. Notice that each department has its own LAN, so if we needed to add new users to, let's say, Sales, we would just plug them into the Sales LAN and they would automatically be part of the Sales collision and broadcast domain. This design actually did work well for many years.

But there was one major flaw: What happens if the hub for Sales is full and we need to add another user to the Sales LAN? Or, what do we do if there's no more physical space for a new employee where the Sales team is located? Hmmm, well, let's say there just happens to be plenty of room over in the Finance section of the building. That new Sales team member will just have to sit on the same side of the building as the Finance people, and we'll just plug the poor soul into the hub for Finance. Simple, right?

So wrong! Doing this obviously makes the new user part of the Finance LAN, which is very bad for many reasons. First and foremost, we now have a major security issue. Because the new Sales employee is a member of the Finance broadcast domain, the newbie can see all the same servers and access all network services that the Finance folks can. Second, for this user to access the Sales network services that they need to get their job done, they would have to go through the router to log into the Sales server—not exactly efficient.

Now, let's look at what a switch accomplishes for us. Figure 11.16 demonstrates how switches come to the rescue by removing the physical boundary to solve our problem. It also shows how six VLANs (numbered 2 through 7) are used to create a broadcast domain for each department. Each switch port is then administratively assigned a VLAN membership, depending on the host and which broadcast domain it's placed in.

FIGURE 11.16   Switches removing the physical boundary

Marketing	VLAN 2	172.16.20.0/24
Shipping	VLAN 3	172.16.30.0/24
Engineering	VLAN 4	172.16.40.0/24
Finance	VLAN 5	172.16.50.0/24
Management	VLAN 6	172.16.60.0/24
Sales	VLAN 7	172.16.70.0/24

So now if we needed to add another user to the Sales VLAN (VLAN 7), we could just assign the port to VLAN 7 regardless of where the new Sales team member is physically located—nice! This illustrates one of the sweetest advantages to designing your network with VLANs over the old collapsed backbone design. Now, cleanly and simply, each host that needs to be in the Sales VLAN is merely assigned to VLAN 7.

Notice that I started assigning VLANs with VLAN number 2. The number is irrelevant, but you might be wondering what happened to VLAN 1. Well, that VLAN is an administrative VLAN, and even though it can be used for a workgroup, Cisco recommends that you use it for administrative purposes only. You can't delete or change the name of VLAN 1, and by default, all ports on a switch are members of VLAN 1 until you actually do change them.

Now, because each VLAN is considered a broadcast domain, it's got to also have its own subnet number (refer again to Figure 11.16). And if you're also using IPv6, then each VLAN must also be assigned its own IPv6 network number. So you don't get confused, just keep thinking of VLANs as separate subnets or networks.

Let's get back to that "because of switches, we don't need routers anymore" misconception. When looking at Figure 11.16, you can see that there are seven VLANs, or broadcast domains, counting VLAN 1 (not shown in the figure). The hosts within each VLAN can communicate with each other but not with anything in a different VLAN because the hosts in any given VLAN "think" that they're actually in a collapsed backbone, illustrated in Figure 11.15.

So what handy little device do you think we need to enable the hosts in Figure 11.16 to communicate with a host or hosts on a different VLAN? You guessed it—a router! Those hosts absolutely need to go through a router, or some other layer 3 device, just as they do when they're configured for internetwork communication (as shown in Figure 11.15). It works the same way it would if we were trying to connect different physical networks. Communication between VLANs must go through a layer 3 device. So don't expect mass router extinction anytime soon!

 To provide inter-VLAN communication (communication between VLANs), you need to use a router or a layer 3 switch.

Quality of Service

Before we dive in further into VLANs, I want to make sure that you have a fundamental understanding of QoS and why it is important.

Quality of service (QoS) refers to the way the resources are controlled so that the quality of services is maintained. It's basically the ability to provide a different priority for one or more types of traffic over other levels; priority is applied to different applications, data flows, or users so that they can be guaranteed a certain performance level.

QoS methods focus on one of five problems that can affect data as it traverses network cable:

- Delay
- Dropped packets

- Error
- Jitter
- Out-of-order delivery

QoS can ensure that applications with a required bit rate receive the necessary bandwidth to work properly. Clearly, on networks with excess bandwidth, this is not a factor, but the more limited your bandwidth is, the more important a concept like this becomes.

> QoS allows administrators to predict, monitor, and control bandwidth use to ensure it is available to programs and apps that need it.

VLAN Memberships

Most of the time, VLANs are created by a system administrator who proceeds to assign switch ports to each one. VLANs of this type are known as *static VLANs*. If you don't mind doing a little more work when you begin this process, assign all the host devices' hardware addresses into a database so your switches can be configured to assign VLANs dynamically anytime you plug a host into a switch. I hate saying things like "obviously," but obviously, this type of VLAN is known as a *dynamic VLAN*. I'll be covering both static and dynamic VLANs next.

Static VLANs

Creating static VLANs is the most common way to create a VLAN, and one of the reasons for that is because static VLANs are the most secure. This security stems from the fact that any switch port you've assigned a VLAN association to will always maintain it unless you change the port assignment manually.

Static VLAN configuration is pretty easy to set up and supervise, and it works really well in a networking environment where any user movement within the network needs to be controlled. It can be helpful to use network management software to configure the ports, but you don't have to use it if you don't want to.

In Figure 11.16, each switch port was configured manually with a VLAN membership based on which VLAN the host needed to be a member of—remember, the device's actual physical location doesn't matter one bit as long as the VLAN assignments are correctly configured. Which broadcast domain your hosts become members of is purely up to you. And again, remember that each host also has to have the correct IP address information. For instance, you must configure each host in VLAN 2 into the 172.16.20.0/24 network for it to become a member of that VLAN. It's also a good idea to keep in mind that if you plug a host into a switch, you have to verify the VLAN membership of that port. If the membership is different than what's needed for that host, the host won't be able to gain access to the network services that it needs, such as a workgroup server.

Static access ports are either manually assigned to a VLAN or assigned through a RADIUS server for use with IEEE 802.1X. It's easy to set an incorrect VLAN assignment on a port, so using a RADIUS server can help in your configurations.

Dynamic VLANs

On the other hand, a dynamic VLAN determines a host's VLAN assignment automatically. Using intelligent management software, you can base VLAN assignments on hardware (MAC) addresses, protocols, or even applications that work to create dynamic VLANs.

For example, let's say MAC addresses have been entered into a centralized VLAN management application and you hook up a new host. If you attach it to an unassigned switch port, the VLAN management database can look up the hardware address and both assign and configure the switch port into the correct VLAN. Needless to say, this makes management and configuration much easier because if a user moves, the switch will simply assign them to the correct VLAN automatically. But here again, there's a catch—initially, you've got to do a lot more work setting up the database. It can be very worthwhile, though!

And here's some more good news: You can use the VLAN Management Policy Server (VMPS) service to set up a database of MAC addresses to be used for the dynamic addressing of your VLANs. The VMPS database automatically maps MAC addresses to VLANs.

Identifying VLANs

Know that switch ports are layer 2–only interfaces that are associated with a physical port. A switch port can belong to only one VLAN if it is an access port or all VLANs if it is a trunk port, as I'll explain in a minute. You can manually configure a port as an access or trunk port, or you can let the Dynamic Trunking Protocol (DTP) operate on a per-port basis to set the switch port mode. DTP does this by negotiating with the port on the other end of the link.

Switches are definitely pretty busy devices. As frames are switched throughout the network, they've got to be able to keep track of all the different port types plus understand what to do with them depending on the hardware address. And remember—frames are handled differently according to the type of link they're traversing.

There are two different types of links in a switched environment: access ports and trunk ports.

Access Ports

An access port belongs to and carries the traffic of only one VLAN. Anything arriving on an access port is simply assumed to belong to the VLAN assigned to the port. Any device attached to an *access link* is unaware of a VLAN membership—the device just assumes it's part of the same broadcast domain, but it doesn't have the big picture, so it doesn't understand the physical network topology at all.

Another good thing to know is that switches remove any VLAN information from the frame before it's forwarded out to an access-link device. Remember that access-link devices can't communicate with devices outside their VLAN unless the packet is routed. And you can only create a switch port to be either an access port or a trunk port—not both. So you've got to choose one or the other, and know that if you make it an access port, that port can be assigned to one VLAN only.

Voice Access Ports

Not to confuse you, but all that I just said about the fact that an access port can be assigned to only one VLAN is really only sort of true. Nowadays, most switches will allow you to add a second VLAN to an access port on a switch port for your voice traffic; it's called the voice VLAN. The voice VLAN used to be called the auxiliary VLAN, which allowed it to be overlaid on top of the data VLAN, enabling both types of traffic through the same port. Even though this is technically considered to be a different type of link, it's still just an access port that can be configured for both data and voice VLANs. This allows you to connect both a phone and a PC device to one switch port but still have each device in a separate VLAN. If you are configuring voice VLANs, you'll want to configure QoS on the switch ports to provide a higher precedence to voice traffic over data traffic to improve sound quality.

Suppose you plug a host into a switch port and users are unable to access any server resources. The two typical reasons this happens is because the port is configured in the wrong VLAN membership or STP has shut down the port because STP thought there was possibly a loop.

Trunk Ports

Believe it or not, the term *trunk port* was inspired by the telephone system trunks that carry multiple telephone conversations at a time. So it follows that trunk ports can similarly carry multiple VLANs at a time.

A *trunk link* is a 100 Mbps or 1000 Mbps point-to-point link between two switches, between a switch and router, or even between a switch and server, and it carries the traffic of multiple VLANs—from 1 to 4,094 VLANs at a time.

Trunking can be a real advantage because with it, you get to make a single port part of a whole bunch of different VLANs at the same time. This is a great feature because you can actually set ports up to have a server in two separate broadcast domains simultaneously so your users won't have to cross a layer 3 device (router) to log in and access it. Another benefit of trunking comes into play when you're connecting switches. Information from multiple VLANs can be carried across trunk links, but by default, if the links between your switches aren't trunked, only information from the configured VLAN will be switched across that link.

Check out Figure 11.17. It shows how the different links are used in a switched network. All hosts connected to the switches can communicate to all ports in their VLAN because of the trunk link between them. Remember, if we used an access link between the switches, this would allow only one VLAN to communicate between switches. As you can see, these hosts are using access links to connect to the switch, so they're communicating in one VLAN only. That means that without a router, no host can communicate outside its own VLAN, but the hosts can send data over trunked links to hosts on another switch configured in their same VLAN.

FIGURE 11.17   Access and trunk links in a switched network

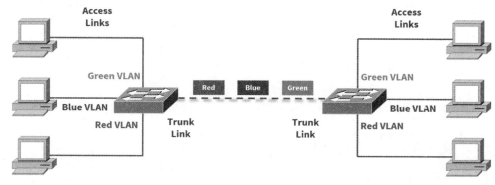

VLANs can span across multiple switches
by using trunk links, which carry traffic
for multiple VLANs.

It's finally time to tell you about the VLAN identification methods.

VLAN Identification Methods

VLAN identification is what switches use to keep track of all those frames as they're traversing a switch fabric. All of our hosts connect together via a switch fabric in our switched network topology. It's how switches identify which frames belong to which VLANs, and there's more than one trunking method: ISL and 802.1Q.

Inter-Switch Link (ISL)

Inter-Switch Link (ISL) is a way of explicitly tagging VLAN information onto an Ethernet frame. This tagging information allows VLANs to be multiplexed over a trunk link through an external encapsulation method (ISL), which allows the switch to identify the VLAN membership of a frame over the trunked link.

By running ISL, you can interconnect multiple switches and still maintain VLAN information as traffic travels between switches on trunk links. ISL functions at layer 2 by encapsulating a data frame with a new header and cyclic redundancy check (CRC).

Of note is that this is proprietary to Cisco switches, and it's used for Fast Ethernet and Gigabit Ethernet links only. *ISL routing* is pretty versatile and can be used on a switch port, on router interfaces, and on server interface cards to trunk a server.

Port Tagging/IEEE 802.1Q

Created by the IEEE as a standard method of frame tagging, IEEE 802.1Q works by inserting a field into the frame to identify the VLAN. This is one of the aspects of 802.1Q that makes it your only option if you want to trunk between a Cisco switched link and another brand of switch. In a mixed environment, you've just got to use 802.1Q for the trunk to work!

Unlike ISL, which encapsulates the frame with control information, 802.1Q inserts an 802.1Q field along with tag control information, as shown in Figure 11.18.

FIGURE 11.18   IEEE 802.1Q encapsulation with and without the 802.1Q tag

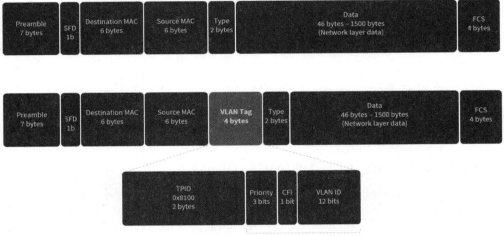

To meet the exam objectives, it's really the 12-bit VLAN ID that matters, so keep your focus on it. This field identifies the VLAN and can be 2∧12 minus 2 for the 0 and 4,095 reserved VLANs, which means an 802.1Q tagged frame can carry information for 4,094 VLANs.

It works like this: You first designate each port that's going to be a trunk with 802.1Q encapsulation. The other ports must be assigned a specific VLAN ID in order for them to communicate. VLAN 1 is the default native VLAN, and when 802.1Q is used, all traffic for a native VLAN is *untagged*. The ports that populate the same trunk create a group with this native VLAN, and each port gets tagged with an identification number reflecting that membership. Again, the default is VLAN 1. The native VLAN allows the trunks to accept information that was received without any VLAN identification or frame tag.

The basic purpose of ISL and 802.1Q frame-tagging methods is to provide inter-switch VLAN communication. Remember that any ISL or 802.1Q frame tagging is removed if a frame is forwarded out an access link— tagging is used internally and across trunk links only!

Routing Between VLANs

Hosts in a VLAN live in their own broadcast domain and can communicate freely. VLANs create network partitioning and traffic separation at layer 2 of the OSI. As I said when I told you why we still need routers, if you want hosts or any other IP-addressable device to communicate between VLANs, you must have a layer 3 device to provide routing. There are three different approaches to support VLAN routing: You can use a router that has an interface for each VLAN, a router that supports ISL or 802.1Q routing, or a layer 3 enabled switch.

What we see in Figure 11.19 is that each router interface is plugged into an access link. This means that each of the routers' interface IP addresses would then become the default gateway address for each host in each respective VLAN. This solution is not scalable, because you will run out of physical interfaces before running out of VLANs.

FIGURE 11.19   Router connecting three VLANs together for inter-VLAN communication, with one router interface for each VLAN

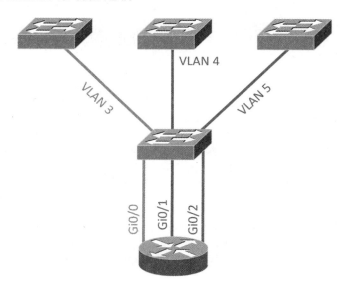

Instead of using a router interface for each VLAN, you can use one GigabitEthernet interface and run ISL or 802.1q trunking. Figure 11.20 shows how a GigabitEthernet interface on a router will look when configured with ISL or 802.1q trunking. This allows all VLANs to communicate through one interface. This is typically referred to as a router on a stick (ROAS) for Inter-VLAN routing. Here we see one physical interface divided into multiple subinterfaces, with one subnet assigned per VLAN, each subinterface being the default gateway address for each VLAN/subnet. An encapsulation identifier must be assigned to each subinterface to define the VLAN ID of that subinterface.

FIGURE 11.20   Router on a stick: single router interface connecting all three VLANs together for inter-VLAN communication

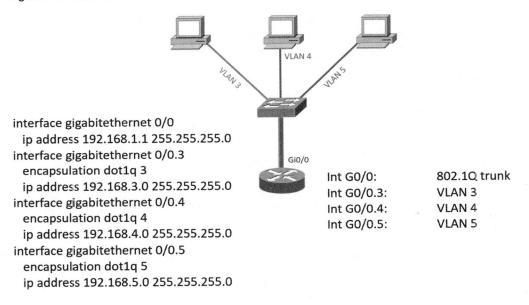

```
interface gigabitethernet 0/0
    ip address 192.168.1.1 255.255.255.0
interface gigabitethernet 0/0.3
    encapsulation dot1q 3
    ip address 192.168.3.0 255.255.255.0
interface gigabitethernet 0/0.4
    encapsulation dot1q 4
    ip address 192.168.4.0 255.255.255.0
interface gigabitethernet 0/0.5
    encapsulation dot1q 5
    ip address 192.168.5.0 255.255.255.0
```

Int G0/0:	802.1Q trunk
Int G0/0.3:	VLAN 3
Int G0/0.4:	VLAN 4
Int G0/0.5:	VLAN 5

I really want to point out that this creates a potential bottleneck, as well as a single point of failure, so your host/VLAN count is limited. To how many? Well, that depends on your traffic level. Keep in mind every packet you route to the router will need to come back through the same link to get to its respective destination. To really make things right, you'd be better off using a higher-end switch and routing on the backplane. But if you just happen to have a router sitting around, configuring this method will get you by.

But wait, there's still one more way to go about routing! Instead of using an external router interface for each VLAN, or an external router on a stick, we can configure logical interfaces on the backplane of the layer 3 switch; this is called inter-VLAN routing (IVR), and it's configured with a switched virtual interface (SVI).

Figure 11.21 shows how hosts see these virtual interfaces.

FIGURE 11.21   With IVR, routing runs on the backplane of the switch, and it appears to the hosts that a router is present.

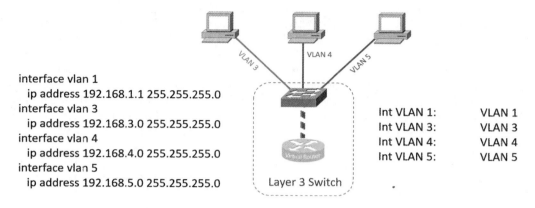

```
interface vlan 1
  ip address 192.168.1.1 255.255.255.0
interface vlan 3
  ip address 192.168.3.0 255.255.255.0
interface vlan 4
  ip address 192.168.4.0 255.255.255.0
interface vlan 5
  ip address 192.168.5.0 255.255.255.0
```

Int VLAN 1:	VLAN 1
Int VLAN 3:	VLAN 3
Int VLAN 4:	VLAN 4
Int VLAN 5:	VLAN 5

In Figure 11.21, it appears there's a router present, but there is no physical router present as there was when we used router on a stick. The IVR process takes little effort, but it's easy to implement, which makes it very cool! Plus, it's a lot more efficient for inter-VLAN routing than an external router is.

Don't worry about learning syntax for configuring routers and switches for the CompTIA Network+ exam. The fundamental design of per interface VLAN, ROAS, and IVR configured with SVI for VLAN routing is the key takeaway.

VLAN Trunking Protocol

The basic goals of *VLAN Trunking Protocol (VTP)* are to manage all configured VLANs across a switched internetwork and to maintain consistency throughout that network. VTP allows you to add, delete, and rename VLANs—and information about those actions is then propagated to all other switches in the VTP domain.

Here's a list of some of the cool features VTP has to offer:

- Consistent VLAN configuration across all switches in the network

- Accurate tracking and monitoring of VLANs

- Dynamic reporting of added VLANs to all switches in the VTP domain

- Adding VLANs using plug-and-play

Very nice, but before you can get VTP to manage your VLANs across the network, you have to create a VTP server (really, you don't need to even do that since all switches default to VTP server mode, but just make sure you have a server). All servers that need to share VLAN information must use the same domain name, and a switch can be in only one domain at a time. So basically, this means that a switch can share VTP domain information with other switches only if they're configured into the same VTP domain. You can use a VTP domain if you have more than one switch connected in a network, but if you've got all your switches in only one VLAN, you just don't need to use VTP. Do keep in mind that VTP information is sent between switches only via a trunk port.

Switches advertise VTP management domain information as well as a configuration revision number and all known VLANs with any specific parameters. But there's also something called *VTP transparent mode*. In it, you can configure switches to forward VTP information through trunk ports but not to accept information updates or update their VTP databases.

If you've got sneaky users adding switches to your VTP domain behind your back, you can include passwords, but don't forget—every switch must be set up with the same password. And as you can imagine, this little snag can be a real hassle administratively!

Switches detect any added VLANs within a VTP advertisement and then prepare to send information on their trunk ports with the newly defined VLAN in tow. Updates are sent out as revision numbers that consist of summary advertisements. Anytime a switch sees a higher revision number, it knows the information it's getting is more current, so it will overwrite the existing VLAN database with the latest information.

You should know these requirements for VTP to communicate VLAN information between switches:

- The VTP management domain name of both switches must be the same.
- One of the switches has to be configured as a VTP server.
- If a VTP is used, a password must be set.
- No router is necessary.

Now that you've got that down, we're going to delve deeper into the world of VTP with VTP modes.

VTP Modes of Operation

Figure 11.22 shows you all three different modes of operation within a VTP domain.

Server   This is the default mode for all Catalyst switches. You need at least one server in your VTP domain to propagate VLAN information throughout that domain. Also important is that the switch must be in server mode for you to be able to create, add, and delete VLANs in a VTP domain. VLAN information has to be changed in server mode, and any change made to VLANs on a switch in server mode will be advertised to the entire VTP domain. In VTP server mode, VLAN configurations are saved in NVRAM on the switch.

Client   In client mode, switches receive information from VTP servers, but they also receive and forward updates, so in this way they behave like VTP servers. The difference is that they can't create, change, or delete VLANs. Plus, none of the ports on a client switch can be added to a new VLAN before the VTP server notifies the client switch of the new VLAN and the VLAN exists in the client's VLAN database. Also good to know is that VLAN information sent from a VTP server isn't stored in NVRAM, which is important because it means that if the switch is reset or reloaded, the VLAN information will be deleted. Here's a hint: If you want a switch to become a server, first make it a client so it receives all the correct VLAN information, and then change it to a server—so much easier!

FIGURE 11.22 VTP modes

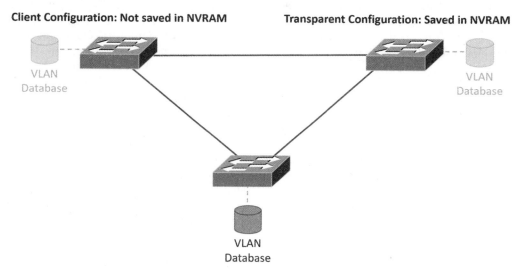

Client Configuration: Not saved in NVRAM

Transparent Configuration: Saved in NVRAM

VLAN Database

VLAN Database

VLAN Database

Server Configuration: Saved in NVRAM

Transparent Switches in transparent mode don't participate in the VTP domain or share its VLAN database, but they'll still forward VTP advertisements through any configured trunk links. An admin on a transparent switch can create, modify, and delete VLANs because they keep their own database—one they keep secret from the other switches. Despite being kept in NVRAM memory, the VLAN database in transparent mode is actually only locally significant. The whole purpose of transparent mode is to allow remote switches to receive the VLAN database from a VTP-server-configured switch through a switch that is not participating in the same VLAN assignments.

Do We Really Need to Put an IP Address on a Switch?

The answer is absolutely not! Switches have all ports enabled and ready to rock. Take the switch out of the box, plug it in, and the switch starts learning MAC addresses in the CAM. But since the switches are providing layer 2 services, why do we need an IP address? Because you still need an IP address for *in-band* management, which is used with your *virtual terminals*, that's why. Telnet, SSH, SNMP, and so on all require IP addresses to communicate with the switch, in-band, through the network. And remember, since all ports are enabled by default, you need to shut down unused ports or assign them to an unused

VLAN. Configuring a switch *out-of-band* means you're not going through the network to configure the device; you're actually using a port, such as a console port, to configure the switch instead. Most of the time, you'll use the console port upon starting up the switch. After that, all the management will be completed in-band.

So now you know that the switch needs a management IP address for in-band management purposes, but exactly where do you want to place it? Conveniently, there's something predictably called the management VLAN interface, and that's clearly your target. It's a routed interface found on every switch, and it's referred to as interface VLAN 1. Good to know that this management interface can be changed, and all manufacturers recommend changing it to a different management interface for security purposes.

Yes, you can buy switches that are *unmanaged*, but you would never ever want to do that for an enterprise network! The only environment in which doing that would make sense is in a home network, but that's about it. Anything you get for an office or larger network absolutely must be a *managed* switch!

With all that in mind, let's get down to configuring a switch now.

We'll begin our configuration by connecting into the switch via the console and setting the administrative functions. At this point, we'll also assign an IP address to each switch, but as I said, doing that isn't really necessary to make our network function. The only reason we're going to do that is so we can manage/administer it remotely—in-band—via a protocol like Telnet. Let's use a simple IP scheme like 192.168.10.16/28. And by the way, this mask should be familiar to you. Let's check out the following output:

```
Switch>enable
Switch#config t
Switch(config)#hostname S1
S1(config)#enable secret todd
S1(config)#int f0/15
S1(config-if)#description 1st connection to S3
S1(config-if)#int f0/16
S1(config-if)#description 2nd connection to S3
S1(config-if)#speed 1000
S1(config-if)#duplex full
S1(config-if)#line console 0
S1(config-line)#password console
S1(config-line)#login
S1(config-line)#line vty 0 15
S1(config-line)#password telnet
S1(config-line)#login
S1(config-line)#int vlan 1
S1(config-if)#ip address 192.168.10.17 255.255.255.240
S1(config-if)#no shut
S1(config-if)#exit
```

```
S1(config)#ip default-gateway 192.168.10.30
S1(config)#banner motd #this is my S1 switch#
S1(config)#exit
S1#copy run start
Destination filename [startup-config]? [enter]
Building configuration...
[OK]
S1#
```

In this output, the first thing to notice is that there aren't any IP addresses configured on the switch's physical interfaces. Since all ports on a switch are enabled by default, there's not really a whole lot to configure. But look again—I configured the speed and duplex of the switch to gigabit, full-on port 16. Most of the time you would just leave these as auto-detect, and I actually recommend doing that. This is not the same technology used between switches to determine the cable type, which is auto Medium Dependent Interface Crossover (MDI-X).

My next step is to set the console password for out-of-band management and then the VTY (Telnet) password for in-band management. The next task is to set the default gateway of the switch and banner. So you don't get confused, I want to clarify that the *default gateway* is used to send management (in-band) traffic to a remote network so you can manage the switch remotely. Understand this is not the default gateway for the hosts—the default gateway would be the router interface address assigned to each VLAN.

The IP address is configured under a logical interface, called a management domain or VLAN. You can use default VLAN 1 to manage a switched network just as we're doing here, or you can be smart and opt to use a different VLAN for management.

The preceding configuration demonstrates how to configure the switch for local management, meaning that the passwords to log into the switch are right there in the switch's configuration. You can also configure switches and routers to store their usernames and passwords remotely for ease of configuration using an AAA server. Doing this allows you to change the passwords at one device without having to telnet into each device separately to change passwords.

To get this done, use the following command:

```
S1(config)#aaa authentication login default
```

This tells the switch to use AAA when Telnet or SSH is used for in-band management. This next command tells the switch to use the AAA server if someone is trying to access the console of the switch:

```
S1(config)#aaa authentication login console
```

So remember, no IP addresses on physical switch interfaces, no routing protocols there either, and so on. We're performing layer 2 switching at this point, not routing!

Switch Port Protection

There are many features that are available to mitigate switch attacks. In the following sections, we'll examine some of these protections.

Port Security

Clearly, it's a bad idea to have your switches available for anyone to just plug into and play around with. Security is a big deal—even more of a concern regarding wireless security, so why wouldn't we demand switch security as much, if not more?

But just how do we actually prevent someone from simply plugging a host into one of our switch ports—or worse, adding a hub, switch, or access point into the Ethernet jack in their office? By default, MAC addresses dynamically appear in your MAC forward/filter database, but the good news is that you can stop bad guys in their tracks by using port security!

Figure 11.23 pictures two hosts connected to the single switch port Fa0/3 via either a hub or access point (AP).

FIGURE 11.23   Port security on a switch port restricts port access by MAC address.

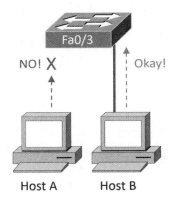

Port Fa0/3 is configured to observe and allow only certain MAC addresses to associate with the specific port, so in this example, Host A is denied access, but Host B is allowed to associate with the port.

By using port security, you can limit the number of MAC addresses that can be assigned dynamically to a port, set static MAC addresses, and—here's my favorite part—set penalties for users who abuse your policy! Personally, I like to have the port shut down when the security policy is violated. Making abusers bring me a memo from their boss explaining why they violated the security policy brings with it a certain poetic justice, which is nice. And I'll also require something like that before I'll enable their port again. Things like this really seem to help people remember to behave!

DHCP Snooping

A rogue DHCP server (one not under your control that is giving out incompatible IP addresses) can be an annoyance that causes users to be unable to connect to network resources, or it may play a part in several types of attacks. In either case, DHCP snooping is a switch feature that can help to prevent your devices from communicating with illegitimate DHCP servers.

When enabled, DHCP snooping allows responses to client requests from only DHCP servers located on trusted switch ports (which you define). When only ports where company DHCP servers are located are configured to be trusted, rogue DHCP servers will be unable to respond to client requests.

The protection doesn't stop there, however. The switch will also, over time, develop an IP address–to–MAC address table called the bindings table, derived from "snooping" on DHCP traffic to and from the legitimate DHCP server. The bindings table will alert the switch to any packets that have mappings that do not match the table. These frames will be dropped. The bindings table is also used with ARP inspection, which makes the configuration of DHCP snooping a prerequisite of ARP inspection.

ARP Inspection

Many on-path (previously known as man-in-the-middle) attacks are made possible by the attacker polluting the ARP cache of the two victims such that their cache maps each other's IP addresses to the MAC address of the attacker, thus allowing the attacker to receive all traffic in the conversation.

Dynamic ARP inspection (DAI) is a feature that, when configured, uses the DHCP snooping database of IP address–to–MAC address mappings to verify the MAC address mappings of each frame going through the switch. In this way, any frames with incorrect or altered mappings are dropped by the switch, thus breaking any attacks depending on these bogus mappings. Because it uses the DHCP snooping database, the configuration of DHCP snooping is a prerequisite to enabling DAI.

Flood Guard

Switches can undergo an attack where some malicious individual floods the switch with unknown MAC addresses. Since switches record all MAC addresses of received frames, the switch will continue to update its MAC table with these MAC addresses until it pushes all legitimate MAC addresses out of the limited space provided for the MAC table in memory. Once this occurs, all traffic received by the switch will be unknown to the switch and it will flood this traffic out of all ports, basically turning the switch into a hub. Now the attacker can connect a sniffer to his port and receive all traffic rather than only the traffic destined for that port as would normally be the case. This attack is shown in Figure 11.24.

Flood guard is a feature that can be implemented to prevent this attack. It uses two mechanisms to accomplish this: unknown unicast flood blocking (UUFB) and unknown unicast flood rate-limiting (UUFRL).

FIGURE 11.24   Flood guard process

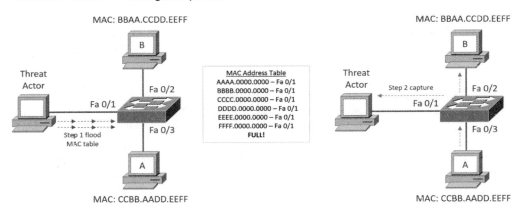

The UUFB feature blocks unknown unicast and multicast traffic flooding at a specific port, only permitting egress traffic with MAC addresses that are known to exist on the port. The UUFRL feature applies a rate limit globally to unknown unicast traffic on all VLANs.

When these two features are combined, flooding attacks can be prevented in switches that support the features.

BPDU Guard

When a switch that is unknown to you and not under your control is connected to one of your switches, it can play havoc with your STP topology and may even allow the rogue switch to become the root bridge! As you know, when a switch starts receiving STP BPDUs from a new switch, the information in the BPDU (specifically the switch priority) is used to determine if the switch might be a new root bridge (causing a new election) or if the STP topology should be changed.

To prevent this from occurring, a feature called BPDU Guard can be implemented. This feature should be enabled on all switch ports that do not connect to known switches. Since most connections between switches and from the switch to a router are trunk ports, then it is typically enabled on all access ports or ports that connect to end devices.

The effect of enabling this feature is simple but effective. The ports on which it is enabled will be shut down when a BPDU is received. While reenabling the port can be done manually, you can also configure the port to wait a period and then reenable itself automatically as well.

Root Guard

Another feature that can be used to maintain the desired STP topology is called Root Guard. This feature is like BPDU Guard in that it also prevents a new switch from altering the topology. It is applied to all interfaces on the current root bridge and prevents these ports from becoming root ports. Despite the name, root ports are present only on non-root switches and represent the best path back to the root bridge.

The feature prevents this by disabling a port if a BPDU is received that, because of its superior priority number, would cause a new root bridge election. It differs from BPDU Guard in that BPDU Guard disables a port where it is configured when *any* BPDU is received. This would be undesirable behavior on the root bridge as it needs to receive those BPDUs to maintain the topology. So, in summary, it helps to maintain the current root bridge's role as the root bridge.

Port Bonding

Know that almost all Ethernet networks today will typically have multiple links between switches because this kind of design provides redundancy and resiliency. On a physical design that includes multiple links between switches, STP will do its job and put a port or ports into blocking mode. In addition to that, routing protocols like OSPF and EIGRP could see all these redundant links as individual ones, depending on the configuration, which can mean an increase in routing overhead.

We can gain the benefits from multiple links between switches by using port channeling. EtherChannel is a port channel technology that was originally developed by Cisco as a switch-to-switch technique for grouping several Fast Ethernet or Gigabit Ethernet ports into one logical channel.

Also important to note is that once your port channel is up and working, layer 2 STP and layer 3 routing protocols will treat those bundled links as a single one, which would stop STP from performing blocking. An additional nice result is that because the routing protocols now see this as only a single link, a single adjacency across the link can be formed—elegant!

Figure 11.25 shows how a network would look if we had four connections between switches, before and after configuring port channels.

FIGURE 11.25   Before and after port channels

Now as usual there's the Cisco version and the IEEE version of port channel negotiation protocols to choose from, and you can take your pick. Cisco's version is called Port Aggregation Protocol (PAgP), and the IEEE 802.3ad standard is called Link Aggregation Control Protocol (LACP). Both versions work equally well, but the way you configure each is slightly different. Keep in mind that both PAgP and LACP are negotiation protocols and that EtherChannel can actually be statically configured without PAgP or LACP. Still, it's better to use one of these protocols to help with compatibility issues as well as to manage link additions and failures between two switches.

Cisco EtherChannel allows us to bundle up to eight active ports between switches. The links must have the same speed, duplex setting, and VLAN configuration. In other words, you can't mix interface types and configurations into the same bundle.

Here are a few things to remember:

Port Channeling/Bonding   This refers to combining two to eight Fast Ethernet or Gigabit Ethernet ports together between two switches into one aggregated logical link to achieve more bandwidth and resiliency.

EtherChannel   This is Cisco's proprietary term for port channeling.

PAgP   This is a Cisco proprietary port channel negotiation protocol that aids in the automatic creation of EtherChannel links. All links in the bundle must match the same parameters (speed, duplex, VLAN info), and when PAgP identifies matched links, it groups the links into an EtherChannel. This is then added to STP as a single bridge port. At this point, PAgP's job is to send packets every 30 seconds to manage the link for consistency, any link additions and modifications, and failures.

LACP (802.3ad)   This has the same purpose as PAgP, but it's nonproprietary, so it can work between multivendor networks.

Device Hardening

A discussion of switch security would be incomplete without discussing device hardening. Actually, this section is applicable to not only the routers and switches in your network but to all devices, including endpoints such as laptops, mobile devices, and desktops.

One of the ongoing goals of operations security is to ensure that all systems have been hardened to the extent that is possible and still provide functionality. The hardening can be accomplished both on a physical and logical basis. From a logical perspective, you can do the following:

- Remove unnecessary applications.
- Disable unnecessary services.
- Block unrequired ports.
- Tightly control the connection of external storage devices and media, if it's allowed at all.
- Keep firmware updated.

Advanced Features of Switches

Switches really expand our flexibility when we're designing our networks. The features that we need to cover for the CompTIA Network+ objectives are as follows:

- Power over Ethernet (PoE)/Power over Ethernet Plus (PoE+)
- Port mirroring/spanning (local versus remote)
- Jumbo frames

Power over Ethernet (802.3af, 802.3at)

Power over Ethernet (PoE and PoE+) technology describes a system for transmitting electrical power, along with data, to remote devices over standard twisted-pair cable in an Ethernet network. This technology is useful for powering IP telephones (Voice over IP, or VoIP), wireless LAN access points, network cameras, remote network switches, embedded computers, and other appliances—situations where it would be inconvenient, expensive, and possibly not even feasible to supply power separately. One reason for this is that the main wiring usually must be done by qualified and/or licensed electricians for legal and/or insurance mandates.

The IEEE has created a standard for PoE called 802.3af, and for PoE+ it's referred to as 802.3at. This standard describes precisely how a powered device is detected and also defines two methods of delivering Power over Ethernet to a given powered device. Keep in mind that the PoE+ standard, 802.3at, delivers more power than 802.3af, which is compatible with Gigabit Ethernet with four-wire pairs at 25.5 watts.

This process happens one of two ways: either by receiving the power from an Ethernet port on a switch (or other capable device) or via a power injector. You can't use both approaches to get the job done; this can lead to serious trouble, so be sure before connecting!

 Real World Scenario

PoE

It would be rare for me not to design a network around PoE. Most of my consulting work is wireless networking, including large outdoor wireless networks. When I design the network, I order equipment based on the amount of power needed to run it, knowing I'll have only a few electrical outlets, or even no outlets if all my equipment is outside. This means that all my switches must run PoE to my access points and wireless bridges and must do this for long distances.

For me to accomplish this, I need to order the more expensive, large-scale enterprise switches. If you have devices that need PoE but do not have long-distance connections, you can use lower-end switches, but you must verify that they provide the right amount of power. There was a customer who called me because their network access points were going up and down. The bottom line is that they had purchased less-expensive switches, and there was not enough power to run the equipment. They ended up buying all new switches. So, before you buy a PoE switch, verify that the switch provides the right power for your environment.

Figure 11.26 shows an example of a switch that requires PoE injectors to provide PoE to devices versus a switch that provides PoE to any PoE-capable device. A switch that provides PoE makes for a much simpler installation and maintenance in the future!

FIGURE 11.26   Non-PoE switch versus a PoE switch

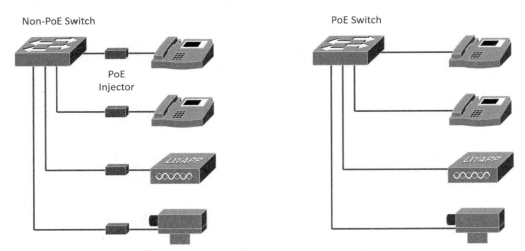

As I just said, if you don't have a switch with PoE, then you can use a power injector. Figure 11.27 shows a typical power injector physically installed in a network.

Use caution when using an external power injector! Take the time to make sure the power injector provides the voltage level for which your device was manufactured.

Because most higher-end switches provide PoE, we don't need to worry about injectors, but if you are adding a wireless bridge into an existing network that has switches without PoE, you need to add a power injector. Figure 11.28 shows a power injector used for a wireless bridge.

FIGURE 11.27   An external power injector used for PoE

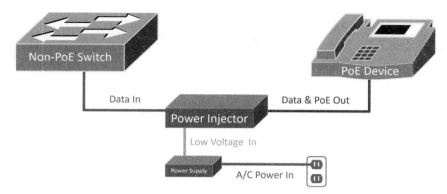

FIGURE 11.28   Wireless bridge power injector

Now, let's discuss how we would troubleshoot a network that has a switch in the LAN instead of a hub.

Port Mirroring/Spanning (SPAN/RSPAN)

Port mirroring, also called *Switch Port Analyzer (SPAN) and Remote SPAN*, allows you to sniff traffic on a network when using a switch. In Figure 11.29, you can see how a typical switch will read the forward/filter table and send traffic only out the destination port (this is the whole idea of using a switch, so this is good!).

FIGURE 11.29   Switches send frames out the destination port only.

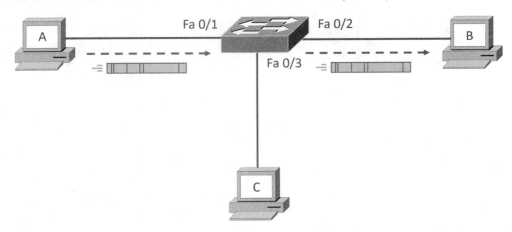

All good, but a problem with this arises when you need to sniff traffic on the network. Figure 11.29 illustrates this issue; the sniffer isn't seeing data coming from Host A to Host B. To solve this little snag, you can temporarily place a hub between Host A and Host B, as demonstrated in Figure 11.30.

FIGURE 11.30   Place a hub between two hosts to troubleshoot.

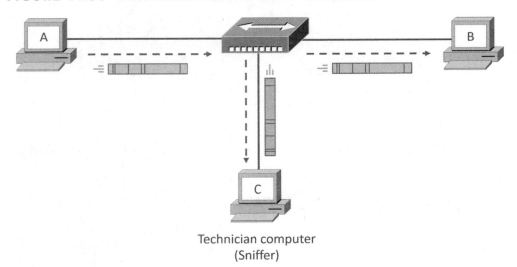

This method will allow you to see the frames sent from Host A to Host B. The bad news, however, is that by doing this, you'll bring down the network temporarily.

The port-mirroring option allows you to place a port in span mode so that every frame from Host A is captured by both Host B and the sniffer, as shown in Figure 11.31. This would also be a helpful option to take advantage of if you were connecting an IDS or IPS to the switch as well.

FIGURE 11.31 Port spanning/mirroring

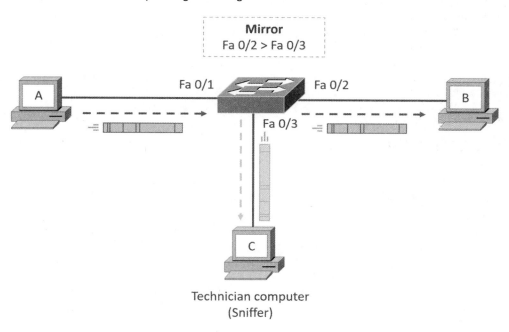

Be careful when using port mirroring because it can cause a lot of overhead on the switch and possibly crash your network. Because of this, it's a really good idea to use this feature at strategic times, and only for short periods if possible.

The last thing I want you to bear in mind is that RSPAN extends SPAN by enabling remote monitoring of multiple switches across your network. The traffic for each RSPAN session is carried over a user-specified RSPAN VLAN, which is dedicated for a specific RSPAN session in all participating switches.

Jumbo Frames

Jumbo frames are just that, bigger frames! The maximum size of an Ethernet frame is 1500 bytes, and a jumbo frame is 9000 bytes. iSCSI storage benefits from these jumbo frames. If jumbo frames are used, data is less likely to be fragmented into smaller 1500-byte frames. When packet fragmentation occurs, the higher-level protocol of IP at layer 3 must reassemble the fragments. The reassembly of these fragmented packets causes latency and higher CPU utilization. Latency is the enemy of SANs.

A caveat to jumbo frames is that all the network equipment in the switching path must support this larger framing of data, also called the maximum transmission unit (MTU). If one of the switches doesn't support the jumbo frames MTU and you turn on jumbo frames at each end (initiator and target), you could end up with a performance decrease of up to 30% or higher!

Summary

In this chapter, I talked about the differences between switches and bridges and how they both work at layer 2 and create a MAC address forward/filter table to make decisions about whether to forward or flood a frame.

I also discussed problems that can occur if you have multiple links between bridges (switches) and how to solve these problems by using the Spanning Tree Protocol (STP).

This chapter also introduced you to the world of virtual LANs and described how switches can use them. We talked about how VLANs break up broadcast domains in a switched internetwork—a very important, necessary thing because layer 2 switches only break up collision domains, and, by default, all switches make up one large broadcast domain. I also described access links and went over how trunked VLANs work across a Fast Ethernet link.

Trunking is a crucial technology to understand well when you're dealing with a network populated by multiple switches that are running several VLANs.

Exam Essentials

Remember the three switch functions.   Address learning, forward/filter decisions, and loop avoidance are the functions of a switch.

Understand the main purpose of the Spanning Tree Protocol in a switched LAN.   The main purpose of STP is to prevent switching loops in a network with redundant switched paths.

Remember the states of STP. The purpose of the blocking state is to prevent the use of looped paths. A port in the listening state prepares to forward data frames without populating the MAC address table. A port in the learning state populates the MAC address table but doesn't forward data frames. A port in the forwarding state sends and receives all data frames on the bridged port. Last, a port in the disabled state is virtually nonoperational.

Remember to check a switch port's VLAN assignment when plugging in a new host. If you plug a new host into a switch, then you must verify the VLAN membership of that port. If the membership is different than what is needed for that host, the host will not be able to reach the needed network services, such as a workgroup server.

Understand what PoE provides. Power over Ethernet was created to provide power to devices that are connected to a switch port but that are not in a place that has a power outlet—for example, an access point in a ceiling.

Understand what jumbo frames provide. Jumbo frames allow the maximum transmission unit (MTU) to be extended to 9000 bytes from the default 1500 bytes.

List features that can be used to maintain the STP topology. These include BPDU Guard, Root Guard, and flood guards.

Written Lab

You can find the answers to the written labs in Appendix A. Fill in in the blank with the term that best fits the statement.

1. A switch will flood all the interface ports on a switch, if the _____ MAC address is not in the forward/filter table.

2. Switches learn the MAC addresses by the _____ MAC address of the frame.

3. _____ _____ _____ prevents loops in switched networks.

4. _____ is an IEEE protocol used for trunk links.

5. _____ delivers 25.5 watts for PoE.

6. Hosts are typically connected to _____ links on a switch.

7. _____ is the default state for 802.1D STP ports.

8. It takes ___ _____ to converge STP from blocking to forwarding.

9. _____/_____ decisions are based on the MAC address table.

10. _____ prioritizes traffic by at the Data Link layer.

Review Questions

You can find the answers to the review questions in Appendix B.

1. Which devices provide the lowest latency and highest bandwidth for connectivity?

   A. Hubs

   B. Switches

   C. Bridges

   D. Routers

2. Which is a function of a layer 2 switch?

   A. Forwarding the data based upon logical addressing

   B. Repeating the electrical signal to all ports

   C. Learning the MAC address by examining the destination MAC addresses

   D. Determining the forwarding interfaces based upon the destination MAC address and tables

3. Which quality of service (QoS) method is used at layer 2 of the OSI?

   A. 802.1Q

   B. ToS

   C. Diffserv

   D. CoS

4. You need to trunk two switches from two different vendors together. Which trunking protocol should you use?

   A. ISL

   B. 802.1D

   C. 802.1Q

   D. 802.1w

5. When calculating Spanning Tree Protocol (STP), which switch will always become the root bridge?

   A. The switch with the highest priority

   B. The switch with the highest MAC address

   C. The switch with the lowest MAC address

   D. The switch with the lowest priority

6. You need to restrict a switch port to a maximum of two devices. What should you implement to guarantee only two devices can communicate on the switch port?

   A. Jumbo frames

   B. 802.1X

   C. ACLs

   D. Port security

7. Which is a benefit to converting a network from a flat layer 2 network to a routed layer 3 VLAN-enabled network?

   A. Increased collision domains for increased bandwidth

   B. Reduced complexity of design and operations

   C. Flexibility of user management and design

   D. Decreased number of broadcast domains for increased bandwidth

8. Which is a correct statement about frames and VLANs?

   A. Broadcast frames are sent to ports that are configured in different VLANs.

   B. Unicast frames that are not in the MAC address table are flooded to all ports in all VLANs.

   C. The ports that link switches together must be access links.

   D. Frames with a destination MAC that are not in the MAC address table are flooded to only ports in the respective VLAN.

9. Static VLANs are being used on a switch's interface. Which of the following statements is correct?

   A. Nodes use a VLAN policy server.

   B. Nodes are assigned VLANs based on their MAC address.

   C. Nodes are unaware of the VLAN in which they are configured.

   D. All nodes are in the same VLAN.

10. What is a direct benefit of adding VLANs?

    A. An increase of broadcast domains while decreasing collision domains

    B. An increase of broadcast domains while increasing collision domains

    C. A decrease of broadcast domains while decreasing collision domains

    D. A decrease of broadcast domains while increasing collisions domains

11. Which statement describes dynamic VLANs?

    A. The access port is switched into the respective VLAN based upon user credentials.

    B. The access port is switched into the respective VLAN based upon the computer's IP address.

    C. The access port is switched into the respective VLAN based upon the computer's MAC address.

    D. The access port is switched into the respective VLAN based upon security ACLs.

12. Which type of port removes the VLAN ID from the frame before it egresses the interface?

    A. Access port

    B. Trunk port

    C. Voice port

    D. Native port

13. When you are protecting an interface with port security, to which mode should you set the switch port?

    A. Access mode

    B. Dynamic mode

    C. Trunk mode

    D. Voice mode

14. Which VLAN is the default VLAN used to configure all switches from the factory?

    A. VLAN 999

    B. VLAN 1002

    C. VLAN 1005

    D. VLAN 1

15. You have been asked to segment the network for an R&D workgroup. The requirement is to allow the R&D group access to the existing servers, but no other VLANs should be able to access R&D. How can this be achieved with maximum flexibility?

    A. Create a new VLAN, configure a routed SVI interface, and apply ACLs to the VLAN.

    B. Create a new VLAN, configure a routed SVI interface, and apply extended ACLs to the R&D switch ports.

    C. Create a new VLAN, and install a new R&D server in the new VLAN.

    D. Create a new VLAN, and trunk the existing file server for both the production and R&D networks.

16. How does IEEE 802.1Q tag frames?

    A. 802.1Q adds a 32-bit header to the frame with the VLAN tagging information.

    B. 802.1Q adds a 32-bit header to the packet with the VLAN tagging information.

    C. 802.1Q inserts a 32-bit field between the source MAC address and the type field.

    D. 802.1Q inserts a 32-bit field between the destination MAC address and the type field.

17. Which of the following is a true statement about static access ports?

    A. An access port can carry VLANs via tagging.

    B. A client computer can request the VLAN to be placed in.

    C. A client computer cannot see any VLAN tagging information.

    D. A client computer can see the VLAN tagging information.

18. You want to delete VLAN 1 for security reasons. However, the switch will not let you. What is the reason you cannot delete VLAN 1?

  A. The VLAN is still configured on a port.

  B. The VLAN serves as the switch's main management IP.

  C. The VLAN is protected from deletion.

  D. The VLAN is still configured as a native VLAN on a trunk.

19. Which statement is correct about native VLANs?

  A. Any traffic tagged will be placed on the native VLAN.

  B. Any traffic that is not allowed over the trunk will be placed on the native VLAN.

  C. Any traffic not tagged will be placed on the native VLAN.

  D. Any traffic that is tagged with ISL on an 802.1Q trunk will be placed on the native VLAN.

20. What is the function of the VTP?

  A. VTP allows for dynamic trunking between links.

  B. VTP allows for propagation of the VLAN database.

  C. VTP detects trunk encapsulation and negotiates trunks.

  D. VTP allows for propagation of the trunking database.

Chapter

12

Wireless Networking

THE FOLLOWING COMPTIA NETWORK+ EXAM OBJECTIVES ARE COVERED IN THIS CHAPTER

✓ **Domain 1.0 Networking Concepts**

✓ **1.5 Compare and contrast transmission media and transceivers.**

- Wireless
    - 802.11 standards
    - Cellular
    - Satellite

✓ **Domain 2.0 Network Implementation**

✓ **2.3 Given a scenario, select and configure wireless devices and technologies.**

- Channels
    - Channel width
    - Non-overlapping channels
    - Regulatory impacts
    - 802.11h
- Frequency options
    - 2.4GHz
    - 5GHz
    - 6GHz
    - Band steering
- Service set identifier (SSID)
    - Basic service set identifier (BSSID)
    - Extended service set identifier (ESSID)

- Network types
  - Mesh networks
  - Ad hoc
  - Point to point
  - Infrastructure
- Encryption
  - Wi-Fi Protected Access 2 (WPA2)
  - WPA3
- Guest networks
  - Captive portals
- Authentication
  - Pre-shared key (PSK) vs. Enterprise
- Antennas
  - Omnidirectional vs. directional
- Autonomous vs. lightweight access point

If you want to understand the basic wireless LANs (WLANs) most commonly used today, just think 10BaseT Ethernet with hubs. What this means is that our WLANs typically run half-duplex communication—everyone is sharing the same bandwidth, and only one user is communicating at a time.

This isn't necessarily bad; it's just not good enough. Because most people rely on wireless networks today, it's critical that they evolve faster than greased lightning to keep up with our rapidly escalating needs. The good news is that this is actually happening—and it even works securely! We'll discuss these newer, faster technologies in this chapter.

The goal in this chapter is to introduce you to wireless networks and the technologies in use today. I'll also cover the various components used, the IEEE 802.11 standards, wireless installation, and, of course, wireless security.

To find Todd Lammle CompTIA videos and practice questions, please see www.lammle.com.

Introduction to Wireless Technology

Transmitting a signal using the basic 802.11 specifications works a lot like it does with a basic Ethernet hub: They're both two-way forms of communication, and they both use the same frequency to both transmit and receive, often referred to as *half-duplex* as mentioned in the chapter introduction. Wireless LANs (WLANs) use radio frequencies (RFs) that are radiated into the air from an antenna that creates radio waves. These waves can be absorbed, refracted, or reflected by walls, water, and metal surfaces, resulting in low signal strength. So because of this innate vulnerability to surrounding environmental factors, it's pretty apparent that wireless will never offer us the same robustness as a wired network can, but that still doesn't mean we're not going to run wireless. Believe me, we definitely will!

We can increase the transmitting power, and we'd be able to gain a greater transmitting distance, but doing so can create some nasty distortion, so it has to be done carefully. By using higher frequencies, we can attain higher data rates, but this is, unfortunately, at the cost of decreased transmitting distances. And if we use lower frequencies, we get to transmit greater distances but at lower data rates. This should make it pretty clear to you that understanding all the various types of WLANs you can implement is imperative to creating the LAN solution that best meets the specific requirements of the unique situation you're dealing with.

Also important to note is the fact that the 802.11 specifications were developed so that there would be no licensing required in most countries—to ensure that the user has the freedom to install and operate without any licensing or operating fees. This means that any manufacturer can create wireless networking products and sell them at a local computer store or wherever. It also means that all our computers should be able to communicate wirelessly without configuring much, if anything at all.

Various agencies have been around for a very long time to help govern the use of wireless devices, frequencies, standards, and how the frequency spectrums are used. Table 12.1 shows the current agencies that help create, maintain, and even enforce wireless standards worldwide.

TABLE 12.1   Wireless agencies and standards

Agency	Purpose	Website
Institute of Electrical and Electronics Engineers (IEEE)	Creates and maintains operational standards	www.ieee.org
Federal Communications Commission (FCC)	Regulates the use of wireless devices in the United States	www.fcc.gov
European Telecommunications Standards Institute (ETSi)	Chartered to produce common standards in Europe	www.etsi.org
Wi-Fi Alliance	Promotes and tests for WLAN interoperability	www.wi-fi.org
WLAN Association (WLANA)	Educates and raises consumer awareness regarding WLANs	www.wlana.org

Because WLANs transmit over radio frequencies, they're regulated by the same types of laws used to govern things like AM/FM radios. In the United States, it's the Federal Communications Commission (FCC) that regulates the use of wireless LAN devices, and the Institute of Electrical and Electronics Engineers (IEEE) takes it from there and creates standards based on what frequencies the FCC releases for public use.

The FCC has released three unlicensed bands for public use: 900 MHz, 2.4 GHz, and 5 GHz. The 900 MHz and 2.4 GHz bands are referred to as the Industrial, Scientific, and Medical (ISM) bands, and the 5 GHz band is known as the Unlicensed National Information Infrastructure (U-NII) band. Figure 12.1 shows where the unlicensed bands sit within the RF spectrum.

FIGURE 12.1   Unlicensed frequencies

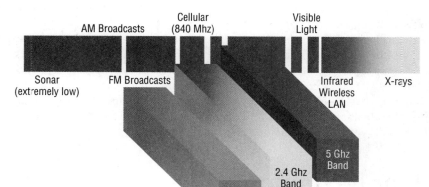

So it follows that if you opt to deploy wireless in a range outside the three public bands shown in Figure 12.1, you need to get a specific license from the FCC to do so. Once the FCC opened the three frequency ranges for public use, many manufacturers were able to start offering myriad products that flooded the market, with 802.11AC/AX being the most widely used wireless network found today.

Figure 12.2 shows the WLAN history that is important to us. Although wireless transmissions date back many, many years, the type we really care about is wireless as related to WLANs starting in the 1990s. Use of the ISM band started in early 1990, and it's deployed today in multiple environments, including outdoor links, mesh networks, office buildings, healthcare facilities, warehouses, and homes.

FIGURE 12.2   Wireless LAN history

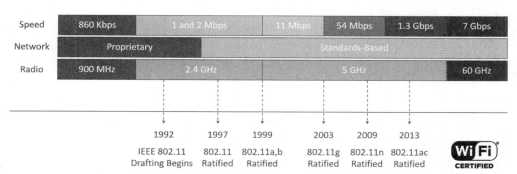

802.11ac (now referred to as Wi-Fi 5) was released in December 2013, 802.11ax (Wi-Fi 6) was released 2019, and although they are not shown in Figure 12.2, I'll discuss these in detail throughout this chapter.

The Wi-Fi Alliance grants certification for interoperability among 802.11 products offered by various vendors. This certification provides a sort of comfort zone for the users purchasing the many types of products, although in my personal experience, it's just a whole lot easier if you buy all your access points from the same manufacturer.

In the current US WLAN market, there are several accepted operational standards and drafts created and maintained by the IEEE. We'll now take a look at these standards and then talk about how the most commonly used standards work.

Cellular Technologies

As part of implementing the appropriate cellular and mobile wireless technologies and configurations, consider the following options:

GSM   The Global System for Mobile Communications (GSM) is a type of cell phone that contains a subscriber identity module (SIM) chip. These chips contain all the information about the subscriber and must be present in the phone for it to function. One of the dangers with these phones is cell phone cloning, a process where copies of the SIM chip are made, allowing another user to make calls as the original user. Secret key cryptography is used (using a common secret key) when authentication is performed between the phone and the network.

FDMA   Frequency-division multiple access (FDMA) is one of the modulation techniques used in cellular wireless networks. It divides the frequency range into bands and assigns a band to each subscriber. This was used in 1G cellular networks.

TDMA   Time-division multiple access (TDMA) increases the speed over FDMA by dividing the channels into time slots and assigning slots to calls. This also helps to prevent eavesdropping on calls.

CDMA   Code division multiple access (CDMA) assigns a unique code to each call or transmission and spreads the data across the spectrum, allowing a call to make use of all frequencies.

3G   This third generation (3G) of cellular data networks was really a game changer at 1G and 2G and allowed the basics to get smartphones working and achieving usable data speeds, sort of, but 2 Mbps was a lot of bandwidth in the 1990s and really provided us with the start of smartphone applications, which led to more research and technologies and of course the plethora of applications we now have.

2G networks handled phone calls, basic text messaging, and small amounts of data over a protocol called Multimedia Messaging Service (MMS). When 3G connectivity arrived, a number of larger data formats became much more accessible, such as HTML pages, videos, and music, and there was no going back!

4G   The term 4G stands for fourth generation of speed and connection standards for cellular data networks. The speeds really helped push smartphones to customers as it provided from 100 Mbps up to 1 Gbps, but you'd have to be in a 4G mobile hotspot to achieve the maximum speed.

LTE   Most 4G networks were called Long-Term Evolution (LTE), which was also called 4G LTE. Although 5G has taken over and 6G is probably here to stay, LTE is still prevalent in many markets, and I still see it on my phones at times. The reality is that in the 2000s your phone would display 4G, but it didn't really mean it because it just couldn't provide what the standard mandated.

When the cellular standards bodies set the minimum speeds for 4G, they could never reach those speeds, even though cell carriers spend millions trying to get them. Because of this, the regulating body decided that LTE (which really was just the pursuit of the 4G standard) could be labeled as 4G as long as it provided an improvement over the 3G technology speeds.

5G   5G, which stands for "fifth generation" of cellular technology, is a standard for mobile telecommunications service that is significantly faster than today's 4G technology, up to 100 times faster.

Since this technology has been out for years, you know you can upload or download videos and use data-intensive apps or other applications much more quickly and smoothly than what we had in the past with 3G and 4G.

This is because 5G technology utilizes a higher-frequency band of the wireless spectrum called millimeter wave that allows data to be transferred much more rapidly than the lower-frequency band dedicated to 4G.

However, the millimeter wave signals don't travel as far, so you need more antennas spaced closer together than the previous wireless 3G and 4G.

Table 12.2 compares 3G, 4G, and 5G.

TABLE 12.2   Cellular comparisons

Technology	3G	4G	5G
Deployment	1990	2000	2014
Bandwidth	2 Mbps	200 to 1000 Mbps	1 to 10 Gbps
Standards	WCDMA, CDMA-2000	CDMA, LTE, WiMAX	OFDM, MIMO, nm Waves
Technology	CDMA/IP	Unified IP, LAN/WAN	Unified IP, LAN/WAN

The 802.11 Standards (Regulatory Impacts)

Taking off from what you learned in Chapter 1, "Introduction to Networks," wireless networking has its own 802 standards group—remember, Ethernet's committee is 802.3. Wireless starts with 802.11. And even cellular networks are becoming huge players in our wireless experience. But for now, we're going to concentrate on the 802.11 standards committee and subcommittees.

IEEE 802.11 was the first, original standardized WLAN at 1 Mbps and 2 Mbps. It runs in the 2.4 GHz radio frequency. It was ratified in 1997, although we didn't see many products pop up until around 1999 when 802.11b was introduced. All the committees listed in Table 12.3 made amendments to the original 802.11 standard except for 802.11F and 802.11T, which produced stand-alone documents.

TABLE 12.3 802.11 committees and subcommittees

Committee	Purpose
IEEE 802.11a	54 Mbps, 5 GHz standard
IEEE 802.11ac	1 Gbps, 5 GHz standard (Wi-Fi 5)
IEEE 802.11ax	10 Gbps, 2.4, 5, and 6 GHz frequency range (Wi-Fi 6) published in Feb 2021
IEEE 802.11b	Enhancements to 802.11 to support 5.5 Mbps and 11 Mbps
IEEE 802.11c	Bridge operation procedures; included in the IEEE 802.1D standard
IEEE 802.11d	International roaming extensions
IEEE 802.11e	Quality of service
IEEE 802.11F	Inter-Access Point Protocol
IEEE 802.11g	54 Mbps, 2.4 GHz standard (backward compatible with 802.11b)
IEEE 802.11h	Dynamic Frequency Selection (DFS) and Transmit Power Control (TPC) at 5 GHz
IEEE 802.11i	Enhanced security
IEEE 802.11j	Extensions for Japan and US public safety

Committee	Purpose
IEEE 802.11k	Radio resource measurement enhancements
IEEE 802.11m	Maintenance of the standard; odds and ends
IEEE 802.11n	Higher throughput improvements using multiple-input, multiple-output (MIMO) antennas (Wi-Fi 4)
IEEE 802.11p	Wireless Access for the Vehicular Environment (WAVE)
IEEE 802.11r	Fast roaming
IEEE 802.11s	ESS Extended Service Set Mesh Networking
IEEE 802.11T	Wireless Performance Prediction (WPP)
IEEE 802.11u	Internetworking with non-802 networks (cellular, for example)
IEEE 802.11v	Wireless network management
IEEE 802.11w	Protected management frames
IEEE 802.11y	3650–3700 operation in the United States

 One type of wireless networking that doesn't get a whole lot of attention is infrared wireless. Infrared wireless uses the same basic transmission method as many television remote controls—that's right, infrared technology. Infrared is used primarily for short-distance, point-to-point communications, like those between a peripheral and a PC, with the most widely used for peripherals being the IrDA standard.

Now let's discuss some important specifics of the most popular 802.11 WLANs.

2.4 GHz (802.11b)

First on the menu is the 802.11b standard. It was the most widely deployed wireless standard, and it operates in the 2.4 GHz unlicensed radio band that delivers a maximum data rate of 11 Mbps. The 802.11b standard has been widely adopted by both vendors and customers who found that its 11 Mbps data rate worked pretty well for most applications. But now that 802.11b has a big brother (802.11g), no one goes out and just buys an 802.11b card or access point anymore—why would you buy a 10 Mbps Ethernet card when you can score a 10/100 Ethernet card for the same price?

An interesting thing about all 802.11 WLAN products is that they have the ability to data-rate-shift while moving. This allows the person operating at 11 Mbps to shift to 5.5 Mbps, then 2 Mbps, and finally still communicate farthest from the access point at 1 Mbps. Furthermore, this rate shifting happens without losing the connection and with no interaction from the user. Rate shifting also occurs on a transmission-by-transmission basis. This is important because it means that the access point can support multiple clients at varying speeds depending upon the location of each client.

The problem with all 802.11b communication lies in how the Data Link layer is dealt with. To solve problems in the RF spectrum, a type of Ethernet contention management was created called *carrier sense multiple access with collision avoidance (CSMA/CA)*.

CSMA/CA also has an optional implementation called a *Request to Send, Clear to Send (RTS/CTS)* because of the way that hosts must communicate with the access point (AP). For every packet sent, an RTS/CTS and acknowledgment must be received, and because of this rather cumbersome process, it's kind of hard to believe it all actually works when you use this!

To get a clear picture of this, check out Figure 12.3.

FIGURE 12.3   802.11b CSMA/CA

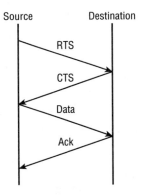

2.4 GHz (802.11g)

The 802.11g standard was ratified in June 2003 and is backward compatible to 802.11b. The 802.11g standard delivers the same 54 Mbps maximum data rate as you'll find in the 802.11a range but runs in the 2.4 GHz range—the same as 802.11b.

Because 802.11b/g operates in the same 2.4 GHz unlicensed band, migrating to 802.11g is an affordable choice for organizations with existing 802.11b wireless infrastructures. Just keep in mind that 802.11b products can't be "software upgraded" to 802.11g. This limitation is because 802.11g radios use a different chipset to deliver the higher data rate.

But still, much like Ethernet and Fast Ethernet, 802.11g products can be commingled with 802.11b products in the same network. Yet, for example, and completely unlike Ethernet, if you have four users running 802.11g cards and one user starts using an 802.11b card, everyone connected to the same access point is then forced to run the 802.11b signal modulation method—an ugly fact that really makes throughput suffer badly. So to optimize performance, it's recommended that you disable the 802.11b-only modes on all your access points.

To explain this further, 802.11b uses a *modulation technique* called *direct-sequence spread spectrum (DSSS)* that's just not as robust as the *orthogonal frequency-division multiplexing (OFDM)* modulation used by both 802.11g and 802.11a. 802.11g clients using OFDM enjoy much better performance at the same ranges as 802.11b clients do, but— and remember this—when 802.11g clients are operating at the 802.11b rates (11 Mbps, 5.5 Mbps, 2 Mbps, and 1 Mbps), they're actually using the same modulation 802.11b uses.

So, regarding the throughput of different WLAN standards, you know that 802.11b has a top throughput of 11 Mbps, and 802.11g has a top throughput of 54 Mbps. But with that said, do you really think we're actually getting that type of throughput? The answer is absolutely not! This is because in reality, about 70 percent or more of the RF bandwidth is used for management of the wireless network itself! The actual bandwidth the user experiences using an application is called goodput, even though you won't hear this term used a lot. Just remember that *goodput* refers to the actual data throughput, not the theoretical number that the standards describe.

Figure 12.4 shows the 14 different channels (each 22 MHz wide) that the FCC released in the 2.4 GHz range.

FIGURE 12.4   ISM 2.4 GHz channels

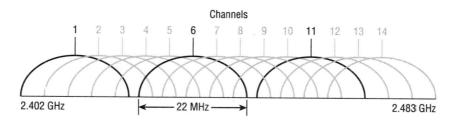

In the United States, only 11 channels are configurable, with channels 1, 6, and 11 being non-overlapping. This allows you to have three access points in the same area without experiencing interference. You must be aware of the channels when installing APs in a large environment so you do not overlap channels. If you configure one AP with channel 1, then the next AP would be configured in channel 11, the channel farthest from that configured on the first AP.

5 GHz (802.11a)

The IEEE ratified the 802.11a standard in 1999, but the first 802.11a products didn't begin appearing on the market until late 2001—and boy, were they pricey! The 802.11a standard delivers a maximum data rate of 54 Mbps with 12 non-overlapping frequency channels. Figure 12.5 shows the U-NII band.

FIGURE 12.5   U-NII 5 GHz band has 12 non-overlapping channels (US).

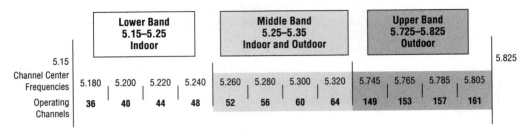

Operating in the 5 GHz radio band, 802.11a is also immune to interference from devices that operate in the 2.4 GHz band, like microwave ovens, cordless phones, and Bluetooth devices. 802.11a isn't backward compatible with 802.11b because they are different frequencies, so you don't get to "upgrade" part of your network and expect everything to work together in perfect harmony. But no worries—there are plenty of dual-radio devices that will work in both types of networks. A definite plus for 802.11a is that it can work in the same physical environment without interference from 802.11b users.

Similar to the 802.11b radios, all 802.11a products also have the ability to data-rate-shift while moving. The 802.11a products allow the person operating at 54 Mbps to shift to 48 Mbps, 36 Mbps, 24 Mbps, 18 Mbps, 12 Mbps, and 9 Mbps, and, finally, still communicate farthest from the AP at 6 Mbps.

There's also an extension to the 802.11a specification called 802.11h, which is described next.

5 GHz (802.11h)

The FCC added 11 new channels in February 2004, and in 2008, we were finally able to begin using these channels based on manufacturers' releases of more 802.11a 5 GHz products. This means that we gained access to up to 23 non-overlapping channels! And there are even two new features to the 5 GHz radio that are part of the 802.11h specification: *Dynamic Frequency Selection (DFS)* and *Transmit Power Control (TPC)*.

Dynamic Frequency Selection (DFS)   This cool feature continuously monitors a device's operating range for any radar signals that are allowed to operate in portions of the 5 GHz band as well as 802.11a before transmitting. If DFS discovers any radar signals, it'll either abandon the occupied channel or mark it as unavailable to prevent interference from occurring on the WLAN.

Transmit Power Control (TPC)   Even though it's been employed by the mobile phone industry for a long time, this technology has some handy new uses. You can set the client machine's adapter and the access point's transmit power to cover various size ranges—a feature that's useful for many reasons. For one, setting the access point's transmit power to 5 milliwatts (mW) reduces cell range, which works great if you've got a compact area with high-density usage.

Further advantages include the fact that TPC enables the client and the access point to communicate with less power. This means the client machine can fine-tune its transmit power dynamically so it uses just enough energy to preserve its connection to the access point and conserve its battery power plus reduce interference on the neighboring WLAN cells—sweet!

2.4 GHz/5 GHz (802.11n)

802.11n builds on previous 802.11 standards by adding *multiple-input, multiple-output (MIMO)*, which employs multiple transmitters and receiver antennas to increase data throughput. 802.11n can have up to eight antennas, but most of today's access points use four. These are sometimes referred to as *smart antennas*, and if you did have four of them, two would be used for transmitting simultaneously with the other two receiving simultaneously. This setup allowed for much higher data rates than 802.11a/b/g. In fact, the marketing people claim it provided about 250 Mbps, but personally, I've never really seen that level of throughput with 802.11n. Even if what they're saying is true, exactly how would that help if all you've got is a 100 Mbps DSL connection to the Internet?

 802.11n allows for communication at both the 2.4 GHz and 5 GHz frequencies by using channel bonding.

Unlike 802.11a and 802.11g, which are locked into using the 5.0 GHz and 2.4 GHz spectrums, respectively, with 802.11n you can control which of the spectrums (or both) you want to allow in your WLAN! Listed next are some additional components of 802.11n that give people reason to say 802.11n has greater reliability and predictability:

40 MHz Channels   802.11g and 802.11a use 20 MHz channels, and tones on the sides of each channel are not used to protect the main carrier, which means that 11 Mbps are unused or wasted. However, 802.11n aggregates two 40 MHz carriers to double the speed from 54 Mbps to 108 Mbps, and add the 11 Mbps that we gain from not wasting the side tones and we have 119 Mbps.

MAC Efficiency   802.11 protocols require acknowledgment of each and every frame. 802.11n can pass many packets before an acknowledgment is required, which saves you on overhead. This is called *block acknowledgment.*

So What Is Wi-Fi?

You may have seen products that are 802.11 compliant with a small sticker on them that says "Wi-Fi." You might be able to guess that this rather odd phrase stands for wireless fidelity, but you may not know what its implications are. Simply put, that sticker indicates that the product in question has passed certification testing for 802.11 interoperability by the Wi-Fi Alliance. This nonprofit group was formed to ensure that all 802.11a/b/g/n/ac/ax wireless devices would communicate seamlessly. So, Wi-Fi is a good thing.

Multiple-Input, Multiple-Output (MIMO)   Several frames are sent by several antennas over several paths and are then recombined by another set of antennas to optimize throughput and multipath resistance. This is called *spatial multiplexing*.

Multiuser Multiple-Input, Multiple-Output (MU-MIMO)   MU-MIMO is an enhancement over the original MIMO technology. It allows antennas to be spread over a multitude of independent access points. MU-MIMO does not directly affect data rates. What it does do, though, is help multiple devices like Wi-Fi routers coordinate when they communicate with one another better and faster than before. Overall, because MU-MIMO allows multiple devices to transmit at once, it makes more efficient use of channels.

5 GHz (802.11ac)

802.11ac is a Wi-Fi standard that works in the 5 GHz range and delivers up to 1 gigabit throughput that was approved by the 802.11 standards committee in January 2014. Still, just as it is with 802.11n, you won't find that the speeds described in the standard actually line up with the marketing material.

For example, for a single link, which is basically one host to AP, the best throughput you can hope to get would be 500 Mbps, which is fantastic if it actually happens! But unless you have a Gigabit Internet connection, 802.11ac won't really help so much. To be fair, in a small network, or if you're transferring files in your internal WLAN or to your internal network, this new specification could actually be useful.

At this point, you're probably wondering how these people can claim to achieve these theoretical rates, right? That's an excellent question! They get these values by increasing the RF band usage from 20 MHz wide channels with 802.11a/b/g to 40 MHz with 802.11n and up to 160 MHz wide channels with 802.11ac. But again, for typical commercial 802.11ac products, 80 MHz would be a lot more realistic. The problem with this scenario centers on the fact that if any interference is found in the 80 MHz wide channel, it drops down to 40 MHz wide channels. Worse, if interference is still found at that level, it will drop even further down to 20 MHz wide channels.

In addition to the wider channels, we can also get more MIMO spatial streams than we can with 802.11n—up to eight, where 802.11n supported only four. Furthermore, and optionally, a downlink of multiuser MIMO (MU-MIMO) supports up to four clients and, most important, a modulation of QAM-256 compared to QAM-64 with 802.11a/g.

The last thing I want to point out is the fact that 802.11n had added fields in the wireless frame to identify 802.11a and 802.11g as high throughput (HT), whereas 802.11ac adds four fields to identify the frames as very high throughput (VHT).

Wi-Fi 6 (802.11ax)

So, what is Wi-Fi 6, and is it faster than Wi-Fi 5? Well, I would hope so since it is one number greater than 5, but that is only because this is the sixth generation of Wi-Fi with enough changes to possibly give us twice the speed, but only time will tell if that is true.

To say that 802.11ax and Wi-Fi 6 are the same thing would definitely be true, and it's great marketing right now for the Wi-Fi manufacturers.

Figure 12.6 shows us the difference from 802.11ac (Wi-Fi 5), and the first thing you should notice is that ax uses both 2.4 and 5 GHz, where ac uses only 5 GHz, and ax has more OFDM symbols and a higher modulation, which provides superior data rates.

FIGURE 12.6   Comparing Wi-Fi 5 to Wi-Fi 6

TABLE 1: COMPARING Wi-Fi 5 AND Wi-Fi 6 STANDARDS		
Parameter	**Wi-Fi 5 (802.11ac)**	**Wi-Fi 6 (802.11ax)**
Frequency	5 GHz	2.4 and 5.0 GHz
Bandwidths (channels)	20, 40, 80+80,160 MHz	20, 40, 80+80,160 MHz
Access	OFDM	OFDMA
Antennas	MU-MIMO (4 x 4)	MU-MIMO (8 x 8)
Modulation	256QAM	1024QAM
Maximum data rate	3.5 Gb/s	9.6 Gb/s
Maximum users/AP	4	8

This newer Wi-Fi 6 technology includes the following benefits:

- Denser modulation using 1024 Quadrature Amplitude Modulation (QAM), enabling a more than 35 percent speed burst.
- Orthogonal frequency-division multiple access (OFDMA)-based scheduling to reduce overhead and latency.
- Robust high efficiency signaling for better operation at a significantly lower received signal strength Indicator (RSSI).
- Better scheduling and longer device battery life with Target Wake Time (TWT).

Comparing 802.11 Standards

Before I move on to wireless installations, take a look at Figure 12.7, which lists, for each of the IEEE standards in use today, the year of ratification as well as the frequency, number of non-overlapping channels, physical layer transmission technique, and data rates.

I mentioned earlier that 802.11b runs DSSS, whereas 802.11g and 802.11a both run the OFDM modulation technique (802.11ac runs up to OFDM 256-QAM).

FIGURE 12.7   Current standards for spectrums and speeds

	802.11	802.11b	802.11a	802.11g		802.11n	802.11ac
Ratified	1997	1999	1999	2003		2010	2013
Frequency Band	2.4 GHz	2.4 GHz	5 GHz	2.4 GHz		2.4 GHz–5 GHz	5 GHz
No. of Channels	3	3	Up to 23	3		Varies	Varies
Transmission	IR, FHSS, DSSS	DSSS	OFDM	DSSS	OFDM	DSSS, CCK, OFDM	OFDM
Data Rates (Mbps)	1, 2	1, 2, 5.5, 11	6, 9, 12, 18, 24, 36, 48, 54	1, 2, 5.5, 11	6, 9, 12, 18, 24, 36, 48, 54	100+	1000+

Range and Speed Comparisons

Now let's take a look at Table 12.4, which delimits the range comparisons of each 802.11 standard and shows these different ranges using an indoor open-office environment as a factor. (We'll be using the default power settings.)

TABLE 12.4   Range and speed comparisons

Standard	802.11b	802.11a	802.11g	802.11n	802.11ac	802.11ax
Speed	11 Mbps	54 Mbps	54 Mbps	300 Mbps	1 Gbps	3.5+ Gbps
Frequency	2.4 GHz	5 GHz	2.4 GHz	2.4/5 GHz	5 GHz	2.4/5/6 GHz
Range ft.	100–150	25–75	100–150	>230	>230	Unknown

You can see that to get the full 54 Mbps benefit of both 802.11a and 802.11g, you need to be between 75 feet and 150 feet (maximum) away, which will likely be even less if there happen to be any obstructions between the client and the access point. 802.11n gives more distance than all three standards shown in Figure 12.7 (up to twice the distance), and understand that 802.11ac won't give you more distance than 802.11n, but certainly more speed. However, 802.11ax (Wi-Fi 6) is the current standard with more than three times the speed of 802.11ac.

Wireless Network Components

Though it might not seem this way to you right now, wireless networks are less complex than their wired cousins because they require fewer components. To make a wireless network work properly, all you really need are two main devices: a wireless access point and a wireless NIC, the latter of which is typically built into your laptop. This also makes it a lot easier to install a wireless network because, basically, you just need an understanding of these two components to do so.

Wireless Access Points

You'll find a central component—like a hub or switch—in the vast majority of wired networks that serves to connect hosts and allow them to communicate with each other. It's the same idea with wireless networks. They also have a component that connects all wireless devices together, only that device is known as a *wireless access point (WAP)*, or just AP. Wireless access points have at least one antenna (typically two for better reception—a solution called *diversity*, and up to eight to support 802.11ac/ax) and an Ethernet port to connect them to a wired network. Figure 12.8 shows an example of a typical wireless access point.

FIGURE 12.8   A wireless access point

Linksys Holdings, Inc.

You can even think of an AP as a bridge between the wireless clients and the wired network. In fact, an AP can be used as a wireless bridge (depending on the settings) to bridge two wired network segments together.

In addition to the stand-alone AP, there is another type of AP that includes a built-in router, which you can use to connect both wired and wireless clients to the Internet (the most popular home brand being Linksys, a division of Cisco). In summation, an AP can operate as a repeater, bridge (switch), or router, depending on its hardware and its implementation.

These devices are usually known as (surprise) wireless routers. They're usually employed as network address translation (NAT) servers by using the one ISP-provided global IP address to multiplex numerous local IP addresses that are generally doled out to inside clients by the wireless router from a pool within the 192.168.*x.x* range.

Wireless Network Interface Card

Every host that wants to connect to a wireless network needs a wireless *network interface card (NIC)* to do so. Basically, a wireless NIC does the same job as a traditional NIC, but instead of having a socket to plug some cable into, the wireless NIC has a radio antenna. In addition to the different types of wireless networking (I'll talk about those in a minute), wireless NICs (like other NICs) can differ in the type of connection they use to connect to the host computer.

Figure 12.9 shows an example of a wireless NIC.

The wireless card shown in Figure 12.9 is used in a desktop PC. There are various options for laptops as well. All new laptops have wireless cards built into the motherboard.

These days, it's pretty rare to use an external wireless client card because all laptops come with them built in, and desktops can be ordered with them too. But it's good to know that you can still buy the client card shown in Figure 12.9. Typically, you would use cards like the one shown in the figure for areas of poor reception because they can have a better range—depending on the antenna you use, or because you want to upgrade the built-in card to 802.11n/ac/ax. It might be cheaper and easier to just buy a new PC these days.

Wireless Antennas

Wireless antennas act as both transmitters and receivers. There are two broad classes of antennas on the market today: *Omni directional* (or point-to-multipoint) and *directional,* or *Yagi* (point-to-point). Yagi antennas usually provide greater range than Omni antennas of equivalent gain. Why? Because Yagis focus all their power in a single direction, whereas Omnis must disperse the same amount of power in all directions at the same time. A downside to using a directional antenna is that you've got to be much more precise when aligning communication points. This is why a Yagi is really only a good choice for point-to-point bridging of access points. It's also why most APs use Omnis, because, often, clients and other APs could be located in any direction at any given moment.

FIGURE 12.9   A wireless NIC

To get a picture of this, think of the antenna on your car (if you still have one!). Yes, it's a non-networking example, but it's still a good one because it clarifies that your car's particular orientation doesn't affect the signal reception of whatever radio station you are listening to—well, most of the time, anyway. If you're in the boonies, you're out of range, something that also applies to the networking version of Omnis.

The television aerials that *some* of us are old enough to remember rotating into a specific direction for a certain channel are examples of Yagi antennas. (How many of you labeled your set-top antenna dial for the actual TV stations you could receive?) Believe it or not, they still look the same to this day!

Both Omnis and Yagis are rated according to their signal gain with respect to an actual or theoretical laboratory reference antenna. These ratings are relative indicators of the corresponding production antenna's range. Range is also affected by the bit rate of the underlying technology, with higher bit rates extending shorter distances. Remember, a Yagi will always have a longer range than an equivalently rated Omni, but as I said, the straight-line Yagi will be very limited in its coverage area.

Both antennas are also rated in units of decibel isotropic (dBi) or decibel dipole (dBd), based on the type of reference antenna (isotropic or dipole) of equivalent frequency that was initially used to rate the production antenna. A positive value for either unit of measure represents a gain in signal strength with respect to the reference antenna. *Merriam-Webster* defines *isotropic* as "exhibiting properties (as velocity of light transmission) with the same values when measured along axes in all directions." Isotropic antennas are not able to be produced in reality, but their properties can be engineered from antenna theory for reference purposes.

It's pretty much a given that antennas operating with frequencies below 1 GHz are measured in dBd, while those operating above 1 GHz are measured in dBi. But because this rule doesn't always work definitively, sometimes we have to compare the strength of one antenna measured in dBd with another measured in numerically equivalent dBi to determine which one is stronger. This is exactly why it's important to know that a particular numerical magnitude of dBd is more powerful than the same numerical magnitude of dBi.

I know this sounds pretty complicated, but because the relationship between these two values is linear, it really makes the conversion a lot easier than you might think. Here's how it works: At the same operating frequency, a dipole antenna has about 2.2 dB gain over a 0 dBi theoretical isotropic antenna, which means you can easily convert from dBd to dBi by adding 2.2 to the dBd rating. Conversely, subtract 2.2 from the dBi rating and you get the equivalent dBd rating.

Armed with what you've learned about the difference between Omni and Yagi antennas and the difference between dBd and dBi gain ratings, you should be able to compare the relative range of transmission of one antenna with respect to another based on a combination of these characteristics. For example, the following four antenna ratings are given in relative order from greatest to least range:

- 7 dBd Yagi (equivalent to a 9.2 dBi Yagi)

- 7 dBi Yagi (longer range than 7 dBi Omni)

- 4.8 dBd Omni (equivalent to a 7 dBi Omni)

- 4.8 dBi Omni (equivalent to a 2.6 dBd Omni)

 If you're having an intermittent problem with hosts connecting to the wireless network and varying signal strengths at different locations, check the location of your antennas in the office or warehouse to make sure you're getting the best coverage possible.

So now that you understand the basic components involved in a wireless network, it's time to use what you learned about the standards we use in our everyday home and corporate wireless networks and the different ways that they're actually installed.

Installing a Wireless Network

Let's say you just bought a wireless AP for your laptop to use to connect to the Internet. What's next? Well, that all depends on the type of installation you want to create with your new toys. First, it's important you understand where to place the AP. For example, you don't want to place the AP on or near a metal filing cabinet or other obstructions. Once you decide on the AP's placement, you can configure your wireless network.

There are two main installation types, ad hoc and infrastructure mode, and each 802.11 wireless network device can be installed in one of these two modes, also called *service sets*.

Ad Hoc Mode: Independent Basic Service Set

This is the easiest way to install wireless 802.11 devices. In this mode, the wireless NICs (or other devices) can communicate directly without the need for an AP. A good example of this is two laptops with wireless NICs installed. If both cards were set up to operate in ad hoc mode, they could connect and transfer files as long as the other network settings, like protocols, were set up to enable this as well. We'll also call this an *independent basic service set (IBSS)*, which is created as soon as two wireless devices communicate.

To set up a basic ad hoc wireless network, all you need are two wireless NICs and two computers. First (assuming they aren't built in), install the cards into the computers according to the manufacturer's directions. During the software installation, you'll be asked if you want to set up the NIC in ad hoc mode or infrastructure mode. For an ad hoc network, you would obviously go with the ad hoc mode setting. Once that's done, all you've got to do is bring the computers within range (90–100 m) of each other, and voilà—they'll "see" each other and be able to connect to each other.

Figure 12.10 shows an example of an ad hoc wireless network. (Note the absence of an access point.)

FIGURE 12.10   A wireless network in ad hoc mode

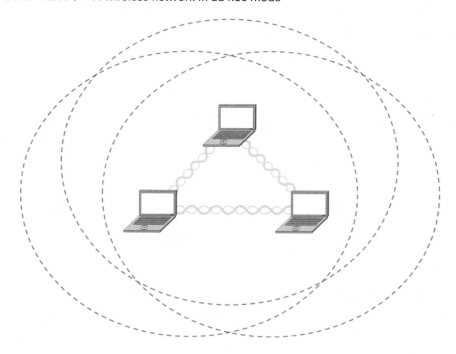

An ad hoc network would not scale well and really is not recommended due to collision and organization issues. With the low costs of APs, this type of network is just not needed today.

Infrastructure Mode: Basic Service Set identifier (BSSID)

The most common use of wireless networking equipment is to give us the wireless equivalent of a wired network. To do this, all 802.11 wireless equipment has the ability to operate in what's known as infrastructure mode, also referred to as a *basic service set identifier (BSSID)*, which is provided by an AP. The term *basic service area (BSA)* is also used at times to define the area managed by the AP, but *BSS* is the most common term used to define the cell area.

In infrastructure mode, NICs communicate only with an access point instead of directly with each other as they do when they're in ad hoc mode. All communication between hosts, plus with any wired portion of the network, must go through the access point. A really important fact to remember is that in this mode, wireless clients actually appear to the rest of the network as though they were standard, wired hosts.

Figure 12.11 shows a typical infrastructure mode wireless network. Pay special attention to the access point and the fact that it's also connected to the wired network. This connection from the access point to the wired network is called the *distribution system (DS)* and is referred to as wireless bridging.

FIGURE 12.11   A wireless network in infrastructure mode

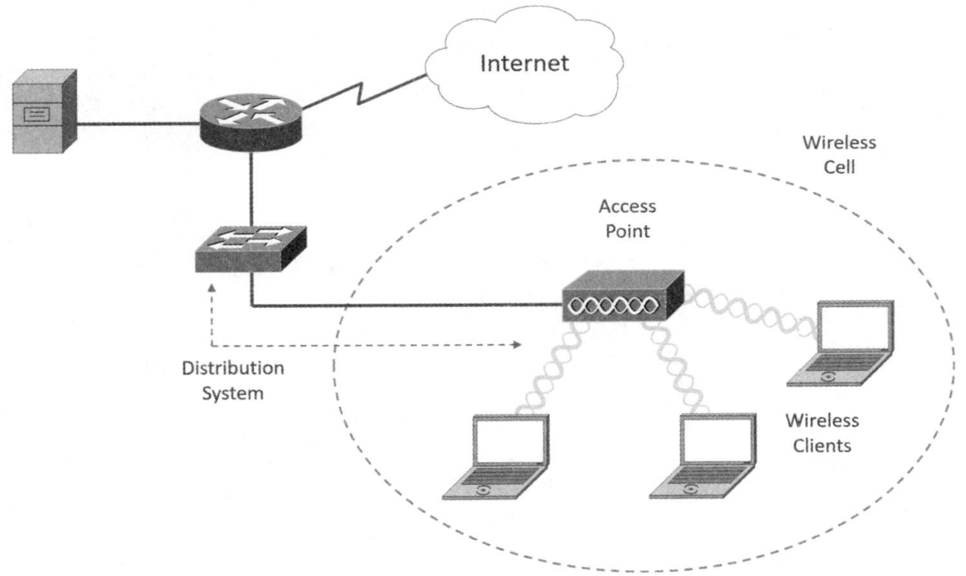

When you configure a client to operate in wireless infrastructure mode, you need to understand a couple of basic wireless concepts—namely, SSID and security. The *service set identifier (SSID)* refers to the unique 32-character identifier that represents a particular wireless network and defines the basic service set. Oh, and by the way, a lot of people use the terms *SSID* and *BSS* interchangeably, so don't let that confuse you! All devices involved in a particular wireless network must be configured with the same SSID.

Good to know is that if you set all your access points to the same SSID, mobile wireless clients can roam around freely within the same network. Doing this creates an *extended service set identifier (ESSID)* and provides more coverage than a single access point. Figure 12.12 shows two APs configured with the same SSID in an office, thereby creating the ESSID network.

FIGURE 12.12   Extended service set identifier (ESSID)

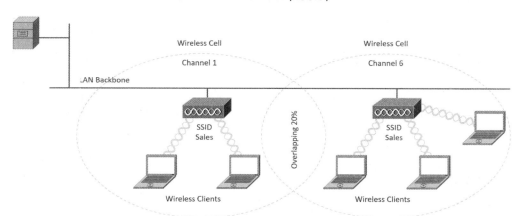

For users to be able to roam throughout the wireless network—from AP to AP without losing their connection to the network—all AP signal areas must overlap by 10 percent of their signal or more. To make this happen, be sure the channels on each AP are set differently. And remember, in an 802.11b/g network, there are only three non-overlapping channels (1, 6, 11), so careful design is super important here!

Wireless Controllers

You'd be hard-pressed to find an enterprise WLAN that doesn't use wireless controllers. In fact, every wireless enterprise manufacturer has a controller to manage the APs in the network.

Looking at Figure 12.13, you can see the difference between stand-alone, or autonomous APs, and the controller solution. In an autonomous solution, all the APs have a full operating system loaded and running, and each must be managed separately.

When we look at the traffic a wireless LAN controller facilitates, there are three main types of data: the control, data, and management planes. These terms are universal with all networking equipment, not just wireless equipment. The control plane is the data that WAPs use to control internal functions, like SSID and channel assignment. The data plane is the data that WAPs move between the wireless clients and the network. The management plane is the management data for configuration and diagnostics. In Figure 12.13, you see an autonomous access point deployment versus a WLAN controller deployment, along with the three planes of data.

FIGURE 12.13   Stand-alone and controller-based wireless networks

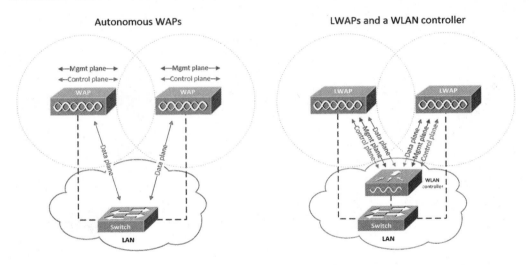

In the controller-based system, the APs are what we refer to as lightweight, meaning they do not have a full operating system running on them. The controller and AP split duties—a solution known as *split MAC*. APs running with a controller are referred to as lightweight, but you'll also hear the term *thin AP*, whereas you'll hear the term *thick* when referring to APs that run a full OS.

Take another look at Figure 12.13. You can also see that the administrator isn't managing each AP independently when using the WLAN controller solution. Instead, the administrator configures the controller, which in turn pushes out the configuration needed for each AP. Controllers allow us to design and implement larger enterprise wireless networks with less time and tedium, which is very important in today's world!

One feature that also gives controllers the ability to provide a great solution is when you're dealing with a location that's overloaded with clients because it utilizes VLAN pooling, or virtual LAN pooling. This is very cool because it allows you to partition a single large wireless broadcast domain into multiple VLANs and then either statically or randomly assign clients into a pool of VLANs. So, all clients get to keep the same SSID and stay connected to the wireless network, even when they roam. They're just in different broadcast domains.

For split MAC to work in a wireless controller network, the APs and controller run a protocol to enable them to communicate. The proprietary protocol that Cisco used was called Lightweight Access Point Protocol (LWAPP), and it's pictured in Figure 12.14.

FIGURE 12.14   LWAPP

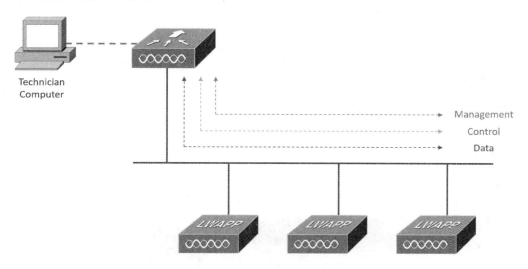

Keep in mind that LWAPP isn't used too much these days, but a newer, more secure protocol called Control and Provisioning of Wireless Access Points (CAPWAP), which also happens to be nonproprietary, has replaced it to become the standard that most controller manufacturers use today.

Guest Networks

Typically, you'll configure a WLAN for your enterprise VLANs and provide authentication and encryption, possibly even two-factor authentication. However, if contractors or guests come into your facility, you may need to provide them access to the wireless. This is not abnormal.

For example, creating a guest VLAN is needed in most circumstances, or sometimes creating a training VLAN for the training rooms is needed. This would allow access without authentication but provide security with a pre-shared key.

Captive Portals

To provide authentication and security on the guest wireless network, you can provide users with a username and password to enter in the splash screen that pops up when they connect to the VLAN. This splash screen is called a captive portal.

A captive portal is a web page that the user is presented with when connecting to a guest, or public, network for the first time. The user is required to both view and agree with the terms of use before they can access the wireless network. You'll see these at airports, hotels, and some coffee shops.

Mobile Hot Spots

Let's say you're in a location that doesn't have an AP installed, or they want to charge you for access, and you want to connect your laptop, tablet, or even play a game. What can you do?

You've got a couple of options, but they all include the cellular network as an infrastructure. Not to be an ad for AT&T, but Figure 12.15 shows a mobile hot spot device that connects your laptop, tablet, media devices, or even a gaming device to the Internet at decent speeds. Pretty much all cellular vendors sell a version of these hot spots now.

FIGURE 12.15   Mobile hot spot

But let's say you don't want to carry yet another device around with you and you just want to use your phone instead. Figure 12.16 shows how I turned my iPhone into an AP for my laptop. First I went to Settings and then chose Personal Hotspot. If that option doesn't show up for you, just give a quick shout to your carrier and have it enabled.

I pay very little to AT&T for my AP capability, but I still have to pay for my usage, so I use it only when I'm someplace like an airport and I want security without paying for access to their Internet wireless. Airport wireless hot spots are notoriously slow anyway, and you'd be dead in the water if you intend to use this type of wireless networking for something like gaming, which requires a ton of bandwidth!

FIGURE 12.16   iPhone hot spot

 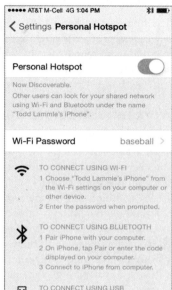

Signal Degradation

Something that's really important to consider when installing a wireless network is signal degradation. Because the 802.11 wireless protocols use radio frequencies, the signal strength varies according to many factors. The weaker the signal, the less reliable the network connection will be and so the less usable as well. (Think dropped calls!) There are several key factors that affect signal strength:

Distance   This one is definitely on the obvious side—the farther away from the WAP you get, the weaker the signal you get. Most APs have a very limited maximum range that equals less than 100 meters for most systems. You can extend this range to some degree using amplifiers or repeaters, or even by using different antennas.

Walls and Other Barriers   Also easy to imagine is the fact that the more walls and other office barriers a wireless signal has to pass through, the more attenuated (reduced) the signal becomes. Also, the thicker the wall, the more it interrupts the signal. So in an indoor office area with lots of walls, the range of your wireless network could be as low as 25 feet! You really have to be careful where you place your APs!

Protocols Used   This one isn't so apparent, but it certainly is a factor that affects, and can even determine, the range of a wireless LAN. The various wireless 802.11 protocols have different maximum ranges. As discussed earlier and illustrated in Figure 12.7, the maximum effective range varies quite a bit depending on the 802.11 protocol used. For example, if you have a client running the 802.11ac protocol but it connects to an AP running only the 802.11n protocol, you'll only get a throughput of 600 Mbps to the client.

Interference   The final factor that affects wireless performance is outside interference. Because 802.11 wireless protocols operate in the 900 MHz, 2.4 GHz, and 5 GHz ranges, interference can come from many sources. These include wireless devices like Bluetooth, cordless telephones, cell phones, other wireless LANs, and any other device that transmits RF near the frequency bands that 802.11 protocols use.

Other Network Infrastructure Implementations

We've discussed the wireless LANs created by installing APs, but there are other technologies, like personal area networks (PANs), that create wireless infrastructures too. By far, the best known is the ever-popular Bluetooth, but there are other wireless technologies we can use as well, and we'll take some time to explore these soon.

For now, it's back to Bluetooth, which happens to have a fantastic history behind it! The technology was actually named after a fabled 10th century Viking king, Harald I (Harald "Blatand" Gormsson), who was faced with the challenge of dealing with many disparate tribes; he needed to communicate with them all and they needed to get along with each other. Blatand, who it's said got his unique nickname due to sporting an unfortunately prominent blue tooth, was having a really tough time getting this to happen. However, the Viking king was a famously great diplomat possessing a wonderful way with words, and he effectively and nonviolently united ancient Norway and Denmark into a single territory via his powerful communication skills. Incidentally, *Blatand* happens to translate into *Bluetooth* in English.

Fast-forward to modern times and a Scandinavian company called Ericsson and a highly gifted technological innovator, Jim Kardach. As one of the founders of Bluetooth, Kardach's challenge was a decent, modern-day analogy of the ancient Viking king's—he was faced with making disparate phones, computers, and other devices communicate and cooperate effectively. To answer the challenge, Kardach came up with an elegant, technological wireless solution to make all these disparate devices communicate and play well with each other. To come up with an equally cool name for the brilliant innovation, he did some research, discovered the legend of the ancient Viking king, and codenamed the new technology Bluetooth. It stuck! Now all that was left was to create a super slick logo for it. Today's Bluetooth icon is actually the legendary king's initials in ancient Viking runes merged together—how cool is that?

Bluetooth 1.0 was far slower than what we have now. Data speeds capped off at 1 Mbps, and the range reached only as far as 10 meters.

When Bluetooth 2.0 came out, GFSK was taken out in favor of two newer schemes: p/4-DQPSK and 8DPSK, which used changes in the waveforms' phase to carry information, as opposed to frequency modulation. These two schemes resulted in unprecedented data speeds of 2 Mbps and 3 Mbps, respectively. Bluetooth 3.0 further improved data speeds with the addition of 802.11 for up to 24 Mbps of data transfer, although this was not a mandatory part of the 3.0 specification.

Because of the large amount of energy that was required from Bluetooth versions 1.0 to 3.0, also known as Bluetooth Classic, small devices would continue to suffer from short battery life, making early versions of Bluetooth impractical for IoT use.

Versions 4.0 and 5.0: Bluetooth Low Energy.

To meet the increasing demand for wireless connectivity between small devices, Bluetooth 4.0 was introduced to the market with a new category of Bluetooth: Bluetooth Low Energy (BLE). Geared toward applications requiring low power consumption, BLE returns to a lower data throughput of 1 Mbps using the GFSK modulation scheme. Although BLE's max data throughput of 1 Mbps may not be suitable for products that require a continuous stream of data like wireless headphones, other IoT applications only need to send small bits of data periodically. An example are fitness wearables that relay small amounts of temperature data to your smartphone only when requested (from a mobile app, perhaps). With the focus on keeping energy demands low, Bluetooth Low Energy makes many coin-cell battery-operated IoT applications (e.g. beacons) feasible.

The most recent version of the Bluetooth protocol, Bluetooth 5, is an improvement upon the previous BLE standards. It is still geared toward low-powered applications but improves upon BLE's data rate and range. Unlike version 4.0, Bluetooth 5.0 offers four different data rates to accommodate a variety of transmission ranges: 2 Mbps, 1 Mbps, 500 kbps, 125 kbps. Because an increase in transmission range requires a reduction in data rate, the lower data rate of 125 kbps was added to support applications that benefit more from improved range.

To delve a little deeper into wireless technologies, the idea of PANs is to allow personal items such as keyboards, mice, and phones to communicate to our PC/laptop/display/TV wirelessly instead of having to use any wires at all—over short distances of up to 30 feet, of course. This idea of the wireless office hasn't quite come to fruition completely yet, but you have to admit that Bluetooth really has helped us out tremendously in our offices and especially in our cars!

There are two other network infrastructure implementations in the PAN area: infrared (IR) and near-field communication (NFC).

Like Bluetooth, IR has some history behind it, but the technology's idea only goes back to about 1800 because that's when it was first said that the energy from the sun radiates to Earth in infrared. We can use IR to communicate short range with our devices, like Bluetooth-enabled ones, but it isn't really as popular as Bluetooth to use within network infrastructures. Unlike Wi-Fi and Bluetooth, the infrared wireless signals cannot penetrate walls and only work line-of-sight. Last, the rates are super slow, and most transfers are only 115 Kbps—up to 4 Mbps on a really good day!

The last implementation I want to cover is called near-field communication (NFC). For NFC to work, the actual antenna must be smaller than the wavelength on both the transmitter and receiver. For instance, if you look at a 2.4 GHz or 5 GHz antenna, they are the exact length of one wavelength for that specific frequency. With NFC, the antenna is about one-quarter the size of the wavelength, which means that the antenna can create either an electric field or a magnetic field but not an electromagnetic field.

NFC can be used for wireless communication between devices like smartphones and/or tablets, but you need to be near the device transmitting the RF to pick up the signal—really close. A solid example would be when you're swiping your phone over a QR code or contactless payment terminal.

Technologies That Facilitate the Internet of Things (IoT)

Internet of Things (IoT) is the newest buzzword in IT, and it means the introduction of all sorts of devices to the network (and Internet) that were not formerly there. Refrigerators, alarm systems, building service systems, elevators, and power systems are now equipped with networked sensors allowing us to monitor and control these systems from the Internet.

These systems depend on several technologies to facilitate their operations:

Z-Wave   Z-Wave is a wireless protocol used for home automation. It uses a mesh network using low-energy radio waves to communicate from appliance to appliance. Residential appliances and other devices, such as lighting control, security systems, thermostats, windows, locks, swimming pools, and garage door openers can use this system.

ANT+   ANT+ is another wireless protocol for monitoring sensor data such as a person's heart rate or a bicycle's tire pressure as well as for controlling systems like indoor lighting and television sets. ANT+ is designed and maintained by the ANT+ Alliance, which is owned by Garmin.

Bluetooth   Some systems use Bluetooth. Bluetooth was discussed earlier in this chapter.

NFC   Some systems use near-field communication. NFC was discussed earlier in this chapter.

IR   Some systems use infrared. Infrared (IR) was discussed earlier in this chapter.

RFID   While radio frequency identification (RFID) is mostly known for asset tracking, it can also be used in the IoT. Objects are given an RFID tag so they are uniquely identifiable. Also, an RFID tag allows the object to wirelessly communicate certain types of information.

Truly smart objects will be embedded with both an RFID tag and a sensor to measure data. The sensor may capture fluctuations in the surrounding temperature, changes in quantity, or other types of information.

802.11   Finally, 802.11 can also be used for this communication. 802.11 was discussed earlier in this chapter.

Installing and Configuring WLAN Hardware

As I said earlier, installing 802.11 equipment is actually fairly simple—remember that there are really only two main types of components in 802.11 networks: Aps and NICs. Wireless NIC installation is just like installing any other network card, but nowadays most, if not all, laptops have wireless cards preinstalled, and that's as easy as it gets! And just as with connecting an Ethernet card to a LAN switch, you need the wireless network card to connect to an access point.

The AP installation can be fairly simple as well. Take it out of the box, connect the antenna(s) if necessary, connect the power, and then place the AP where it can reach the highest number of clients. This last part is probably the trickiest, but it really just involves a little common sense and maybe a bit of trial and error. Knowing that walls obstruct the signal means that putting the AP out in the open—even indoors—works better. And you also know it should be placed away from sources of RF interference, so putting it next to the microwave or phone system is probably a really bad idea too. Near a metal filing cabinet is also not so good. So, just experiment and move your AP around to find the spot that gives you the best signal strength for all the clients that need to use it.

Now that you have the hardware installed, it's time to configure it, right? Let's get started.

No worries—configuring your AP and NIC to work together isn't as tricky as it sounds. Most wireless equipment is designed to work almost without configuration, so by default, you can pretty much turn things on and start working. The only things you need to configure are customization settings (name, network address, and so on) and security settings, and even these aren't required. But because I do highly recommend configuring them, I'll take you through that now.

NIC Configuration

Windows hosts and servers include software to automatically configure a wireless connection, and they do so automatically if you install a wireless NIC—assuming that somehow you have a Windows machine without a wireless NIC installed on the motherboard. And if you have one without a NIC installed, your Windows machine is really old!

Configuring a Windows client is pretty simple, but what do you do if you can't get it to actually work afterward? If this happens to you, searching for the solution could eat up a serious amount of your time! Following these steps could save you from that frustrating quest:

1. To find a wireless network, just go to the lower-right corner of your screen and click the icon that looks like a wireless wave. You will see the box shown here.

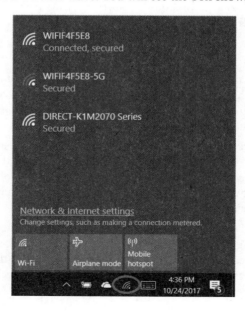

2. Double-click the network you want to join, and click Connect Anyway, even if it's an unsecured network. You'll then see a screen showing that it's trying to connect.

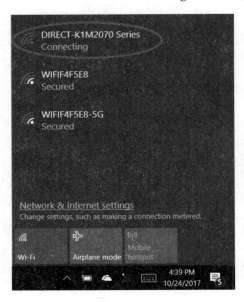

3. If you're using security, the AP will ask you for your credentials.

4. Check your TCP/IP settings to find out if you're not really connected to the Internet and troubleshoot from there.

AP Configuration

Once you've successfully configured your workstation(s), it's time to move on and configure the AP. There are literally hundreds of different APs out there, and of course, each uses a different method to configure its internal software. The good news is that for the most part, they all follow the same general patterns:

1. Out of the box, the AP should come configured with an IP address that's usually something similar to 192.168.1.1. But check the documentation that comes with the AP to be sure. You can just take the AP out of its box, plug it into a power outlet, and connect it to your network, but to manage the AP, you've got to configure its IP address scheme to match your network's.

2. You should receive a DHCP address from the AP when you connect, but if you don't get one, start by configuring a workstation on the wired network with an IP address (192.168.1.2 or similar) and subnet mask on the same subnet as the AP's. You should then be able to connect to the AP to begin the configuration process. Usually, you do this via a web browser or with a manufacturer-supplied configuration program.

3. Once you have successfully connected to the AP, you then get to configure its parameters.

The following are the minimum parameters common to APs that you should configure for your AP to work properly. (Remember, typically an AP works right out of the box, but it is unsecure too!)

SSID   As I talked about earlier, this is the name of the wireless network that your AP will advertise. If this new AP is to be part of an existing wireless network, it needs to be configured with the same SSID as the existing network. In a network with only one AP, you can think of the SSID as the "name" of the AP.

AP IP Addresses   Remember, even though most APs come preconfigured with an IP address, it may not be one that matches the wired network's IP addressing scheme. So it follows that you should configure the AP's IP addresses (including the address, subnet mask, and default gateway addresses) to match the wired network you want it connected to. An AP does not need an IP address to work in your network. The IP address of the AP is used only to manage the AP.

Operating Mode (Access Point or Bridging)   Access points can operate in one of two main modes: *Access Point mode* or *Bridging mode*. Access Point mode allows the AP to operate as a traditional access point to allow a wireless client transparent access to a wired network. Alternatively, two APs set to Bridging mode provide a wireless bridge between two wired network segments.

Password   Every access point has some kind of default password that's used to access the AP's configuration. For security reasons, it's a good idea to change this as soon as you can to connect to and configure the AP.

Wireless Channel   802.11 wireless networks can operate on different channels to avoid interference. Most wireless APs come set to work on a particular channel from the factory, and you can change it if other networks in the area are using that channel, but be aware that no particular channel is any more secure than another. Wireless stations do *not* use channel numbers as the criteria when seeking a connection. They only pay attention to SSIDs!

WEP/WPA   Although it isn't a requirement per se, I definitely recommend enabling security right from the start as soon as you turn on the AP. Commercial APs typically come configured as an open network so that it's easy to log in, whereas enterprise APs come unconfigured and don't work until they are configured. WEP and Wi-Fi Protected Access (WPA) allow data to be encrypted before it's sent over the wireless connection, and all configuring entails is to enable it and pick a key to be used for the connections. Simple, easy-to-configure security is certainly worth your time!

So here's what you do: First, you'll be asked to enter one or more human-readable passphrases called *shared keys*—secret passwords that won't ever be sent over the wire. After entering each one, you'll generally click a button to initiate a one-way hash to produce a WEP key of a size related to the number of bits of WEP encryption you want. Entering the same passphrase on a wireless client causes the hash (not the passphrase) to be sent from the wireless client to the AP during a connection attempt. Most configuration utilities allow you to create multiple keys in case you want to grant someone temporary access to the network, but you still want to keep the primary passphrase a secret. You can just delete the key you enabled to permit temporary access after you don't need it anymore without affecting access by any primary LAN participants.

Here's an example of connecting to a Linksys access point (not a Linksys wireless router, which is a different device):

1. The first screen shows that I've connected using HTTP to configure the device. The IP address of the Linksys AP is 192.168.1.245. If it was a Linksys wireless router instead—the typical home DSL/cable modem wireless connection device around today—then the address would be 192.168.1.1.

2. As you can see, there's no username required, and the password is just *admin*. Again, be sure not to leave this login configuration as the default! Once I click OK, I get taken to a screen where I can change my IP address.

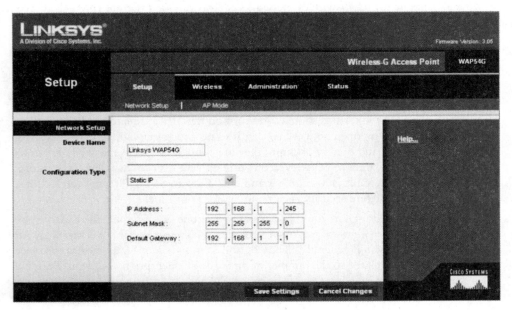

3. It isn't vital for an AP to have an IP address, but it comes in handy for management purposes. You can change the IP address as well as the device name from this screen if you want. I clicked the Wireless tab on top, and this screen appeared.

4. From here, you can set the device to run b/g, only g, or ideally the newer technologies, but if all you have is g, that will work too. You can also change the SSID from Linksys to another name, and I *highly* recommend doing this. The AP channel can also be changed, and you can turn off the AP beacons as well, which is also recommended, but understand that if you do this, you'll have to set the new SSID name in each of your clients! Last thing—you can see that by default, there's no encryption. Click the Wireless Security tab, and you'll get this screen.

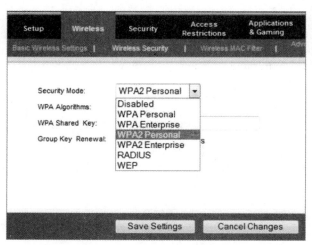

5.   From the pull-down menu, you get to choose from various wireless security options if you want.

I'll talk more about security after I hammer on about site surveys for a bit—they really are that important!

EXERCISE 12.1

Examining Wireless Settings

Most of the time, we set up our home wireless and never reexamine the settings. In this exercise, you will examine your home wireless settings and compare them to what you have learned. Since every consumer wireless access point is different, you should be able to answer the following questions:

1.   Open a web browser and place the IP address of your wireless access point in the address bar. If you are not sure of the address, you can use the default gateway of the wireless access point, if you are connected wirelessly.

2.   Examine and identify the wireless standard configured on the equipment.

3.   Examine the SSID configured along with the PSK (if possible).

4.   Try to identify the channel that SSID is being broadcast on.

Are the settings what you expect? These settings should be put in a safe location. This is done so that if you upgrade your equipment in the future, you can transition the settings to the new equipment without disruption to the clients.

Site Survey

I want to be sure you're completely clear about where I stand regarding site surveys. They are absolutely and vitally imperative to bringing a premium-quality—even just a reasonably viable—WLAN into this world! You should carry out a predeployment survey and a postdeployment survey, but keep in mind that your predeployment survey isn't actually your first step to begin this key process.

So, because you positively must know how to formulate and implement a solid site survey, I'm going to walk you through executing the three major steps to doing that effectively. And just to be really thorough, I'm also going to cover some issues commonly encountered as we progress through these steps.

Information Gathering   This is actually your first step, and during this stage, you must determine three key factors:

▪   The scope of the network, including all applications that will be used, data types that will be present, and how sensitive these data types are to delay

- The areas that must be covered and the expected capacity at each location
- The types of wireless devices that will need to be supported, such as, for example, laptops, tablets, smartphones, IP phones, and barcode readers

During this phase, a key goal of mine would be to create a coverage model that maps to all areas that need coverage, along with those that don't, and have my client sign off in agreement to this document before I do anything else. You definitely want to do this too—just trust me!

Predeployment Site Survey   In this phase, I use live APs to verify the optimal distances between their prospective locations. I base this placement on the expected speed at the edge of the cell, the anticipated number of devices, and other information gathered. Usually, after I get one AP positioned, I'll place the next one based on the distance from the first, with special consideration given to any sources of interference I've found.

Postdeployment Site Survey   I utilize the postdeployment survey phase to confirm and verify that the original design and placements are happily humming along, problem-free, when all stations are using the network. This pretty much never happens, so at this point, it's likely changes will need to be made—sometimes, significant ones—in order to optimize the performance of a WLAN operating under full capacity.

EXERCISE 12.2

Performing a Simple Site Survey

When you first set up your wireless in your house, you probably didn't perform a site survey. After it was set up, you probably made some adjustments for coverage. However, this type of deployment method in a corporate environment can result in big costs. So, a site survey is performed before and after the deployment. In this exercise, you will perform a postdeployment site survey. Typically, you need specialized equipment to measure noise and signal strength, but for your house, a simple strength meter will work.

1. Draw a picture of your house as a two-dimensional floor plan with doors, windows, and walls.

2. Open a command prompt and type in **netsh wlan show interface**. The output will give you signal percentage and channel number.

3. Move to each corner of the room in your house and display the command. Make a note of the output on the picture you have drawn.

4. After you are done with the basic survey in your house, take a reading from outside your house.

You will find that the survey will present a good representation of your coverage. If you do move your access point(s), perform the survey again to see if coverage got better.

Providing Capacity

Now here's a big issue that frequently rears its ugly head: providing enough capacity in areas where many wireless stations will be competing for the airwaves. Remember that stations share access to the RF environment with all other stations in the BSS, as well as with the AP, so really, the only way to increase capacity is by increasing the number of APs in an area requiring serious density.

This can get complicated, but basically it comes down to placing APs on non-overlapping channels while still sharing the same SSID. Take a look at Figure 12.17 for an example of this scenario.

FIGURE 12.17 Basic coverage

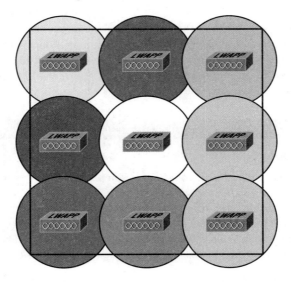

In Figure 12.17, nine APs have been configured in the same area using the three non-overlapping channels in the 2.4 GHz frequency (1, 6, and 11). Each shade represents a different channel. Even though the APs on the same channel have been positioned far enough away from one another so that they don't overlap much and/or cause interference, surprisingly, it's actually better if there is some overlap. But bear in mind that the channels should be used in a way that no APs on the same channel overlap in a detrimental way. Another thing I want to point out that's not so ideal about this arrangement is that all the APs would have to run at full power. This isn't a good way to go because it doesn't give you much fault tolerance at all!

So, we've got two problems with our design: lack of overlap and lack of fault tolerance. To address both issues, you need more APs using 802.11ac or later, which would get you more channels and provide better throughput, as shown in Figure 12.18.

FIGURE 12.18   Enterprise design

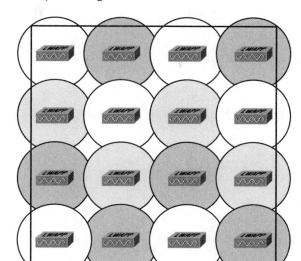

A key benefit to this design is it would also gain the critical ability to run the APs at less than full power. This allows the controller to strategically boost the power of specific APs in the event of an AP outage in a given area.

When you know exactly the type of applications and activity a WLAN will need to support, you can then determine the data rate that must be attained in a particular area. Since the received signal strength indicator (RSSI), signal-to-noise ratio (SNR), and data rate are correlated, the required data rate will tell you what the required RSSI or SNR should be as seen at the AP from the stations. Keep in mind that stations located at the edge of the cell will automatically drop the data rate and that the data rate will increase as a station moves toward the AP.

Multiple Floors

Another special challenge is a multistory building where WLANs are located on all floors. In these conditions, you've got to think about channel usage in a three-dimensional way, and you'll have to play nicely with the other WLANs' administrators to make this work! Facing this scenario, your channel spacing should be deployed as shown in Figure 12.19.

To prevent bleed from one floor to another, use semi-directional or patch antennas to control radiation patterns.

FIGURE 12.19 A multifloor installation

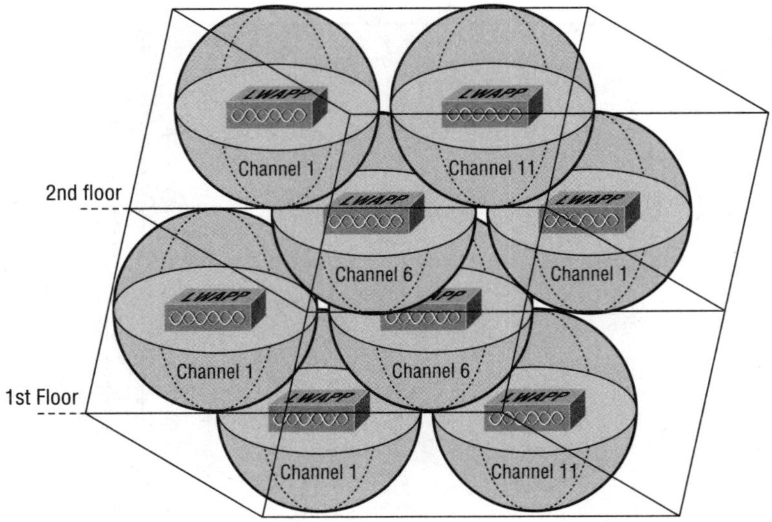

Location-Based WLAN

When using a location device such as the Cisco 2710, your restrictions get even tighter. The additional requirements for the location device to operate properly are as follows:

- APs should be placed at the edge even when they're not needed there for normal coverage purposes so that devices at the edge can be located.

- The density of APs must be higher. Each AP should be 50 to 70 feet apart—much closer than is normally required.

- Some APs will need to be set in monitor or scanner mode so that they won't transmit and interfere with other APs.

All of this means that the final placement will be denser and a bit more symmetrical than usual.

Site Survey Tools

As I touched upon at the beginning of our site survey section, there are some highly specialized, very cool site survey tools that can majorly help you achieve your goals. The AirMagnet Survey and Ekahau Site Survey tools make it possible to do a client walk-through with the unit running, and you can click each location on the map.

These tools will gather RSSI and SNR from each AP in the range, and at the end of your tour, global heat map coverage will be magically displayed, as shown in Figure 12.20.

FIGURE 12.20   A heat map of a building

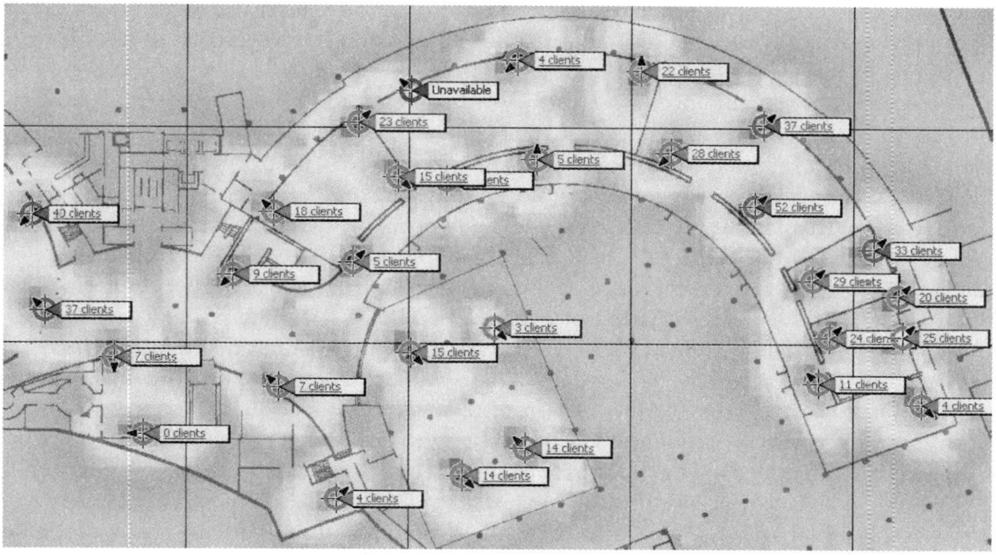

Wireless Security

So, wireless security is basically nonexistent on access points and clients. The original 802.11 committee just didn't imagine that wireless hosts would one day outnumber bounded media hosts, but that's actually where we're headed now. Also, unfortunately, just as with the IPv4 routed protocol, engineers and scientists didn't include security standards that are robust enough to work in a corporate environment. So we're left with proprietary solution add-ons to aid us in our quest to create a secure wireless network. And no—I'm not sitting here bashing the standards committees, because the security problems we're experiencing were also created by the US government because of export issues with its own security standards. Our world is a complicated place, so it follows that our security solutions would have to be as well.

Wireless Threats

Key threats happen in the authentication processes and data, but there are other wireless security perils lurking out there as well. We'll dive deeper into the processes and procedures designed to mitigate these dangers in Chapter 14, "Using Statistics and Sensors to Ensure Network Availability," but I want to briefly discuss them here.

Rogue APs

First, there's the evil we call rogue APs. These are APs that have been connected to your wired infrastructure without your knowledge. The rogue may have been placed there by a determined hacker who snuck into your facility and put it in an out-of-the-way location or, more innocently, by an employee who just wants wireless access and doesn't get just how dangerous doing this is. Either way, it's just like placing an open Ethernet port out in the parking lot with a sign that says "Corporate LAN access here—no password required!"

Clearly, the worst type of rogue AP is the one some hacker has cleverly slipped into your network. It's particularly nasty because the bad guy probably didn't do it to simply gain access to your network. Nope—the hacker likely did it to entice your wireless clients to disastrously associate with their rogue AP instead! This ugly trick is achieved by placing their AP on a different channel from your legitimate APs and then setting its SSID in accordance with your SSID. Wireless clients identify the network by the SSID, not the MAC address of the AP or the IP address of the AP, so jamming the channel that your AP is on will cause your stations to roam to the bad guy's AP instead. With the proper DHCP software installed on the AP, the hacker can issue the client an address, and once that's been done, the bad guy has basically "kidnapped" your client over to their network and can freely perform a peer-to-peer attack. Believe it or not, this can all be achieved from a laptop while Mr. Hacker simply sits in your parking lot, because there are many types of AP software that will run on a laptop—yikes!

Mitigation

But you're not helpless—one way to keep rogue APs out of the wireless network is to employ a wireless LAN controller (WLC) to manage your APs. This is a nice mitigation technique because APs and controllers communicate using Lightweight Access Point Protocol (LWAPP) or the newer CAPWAP, and it just so happens that one of the message types they share is called Radio Resource Management (RRM). Basically, your APs monitor all channels by momentarily switching from their configured channel and by collecting packets to check for rogue activity. If an AP is detected that isn't usually managed by the controller, it's classified as a rogue, and if a wireless control system is in use, that rogue can be plotted on a floor plan and located. Another great benefit to this mitigation approach is that it enables your APs to also prevent workstations from associating with the newly exposed rogue.

Ad Hoc Networks

As you already know, ad hoc networks are created peer to peer or directly between stations and not through an AP. This can be a dangerous configuration because there's no corporate security in place, and since these networks are often created by unsophisticated users, you end up with the scenario I just described that's primed for, and wide open to, a peer-to-peer attack. Even uglier, if the laptop happens to connect to the corporate LAN through an Ethernet connection at the same time the ad hoc network is created, the two connections could be bridged by a hacker to gain them access straight up into the wired LAN itself!

Mitigation

When you've got a Cisco Unified Wireless Network (CUWN) in operation, ad hoc networks can be identified over the air by the kind of frames they send, which are different from those belonging to an infrastructure network. When these frames are identified, the CUWN can prevent harmful intrusions by sending out something known as deauthentication frames to keep your stations from associating via ad hoc mode.

Denial of Service

Not all attacks are aimed at the goal of stealing information. Sometimes the hacker just wants to cause some major network grief, like jamming the frequency where your WLAN lives to cause a complete interruption of service until you manage to ferret out the jamming signal and disable it. This type of assault is known as a denial-of-service (DoS) attack.

Mitigation

And this is how we deal with them. First, if someone is jamming the frequency, there isn't much, if anything, you can do. However, many DoS, on-path (formerly known as man-in-the-middle), and penetration attacks operate by deauthenticating, or disassociating, stations from their networks. Some DoS attacks take the form of simply flooding the wireless network with probe requests or association frames, which effectively makes the overwhelmed network unavailable for normal transmissions. These types of management frames are sent unauthenticated and unencrypted. Since deauthentication and disassociation frames are classified as management frames, the Management Frame Protection (MFP) mechanism can be used to prevent the deluge. There are two types of MFP you can use, referred to as infrastructure and client. Let's take a look at each of them now.

Infrastructure Mode

This sweet strategy doesn't require configuration on the station—only the AP. Controllers generate a specific signature for each WLAN, which is added to each management frame it sends, and any attempt to alter this is detected by the message integrity check (MIC) in the frame. Therefore, when an AP receives a management frame from an unknown SSID, it reports the event to the controller and an alarm is generated.

When an AP receives an MFP protected frame from an unknown SSID, it queries the controller for the key. If the BSSID isn't recognized by the controller, it will return an "unknown BSSID" message, which causes the AP to drop the frame.

Client Mode

Often rogue APs attempt to impersonate the company AP. With client MFP, all management frames between the AP and the station are protected because clients can detect and drop spoofed or invalid management frames.

Passive Attacks

So far, the attacks I've talked about are in a category referred to as active attacks because, in deploying them, the hacker is interacting with stations, the AP, and the network in real time. But beware—there are other ways into the fort!

Passive attacks are most often used to gather information to be used in an active attack a hacker is planning to execute later, and they usually involve wireless sniffing. During a passive attack, the hacker captures large amounts of raw frames to analyze online with sniffing software used to discover a key and decrypt it "on the fly." Or the data will be analyzed offline, which simply means the bad guy will take the data away and analyze it later.

Mitigation

In addition to the tools already described, you can use an intrusion detection system (IDS) or an intrusion protection system (IPS) to guard against passive attacks:

IDS   An intrusion detection system (IDS) is used to detect several types of malicious behaviors that can compromise the security and trust of your system. These malicious behaviors include network attacks against vulnerable services; data-driven attacks on applications; host-based attacks like privilege escalation; unauthorized logins; access to sensitive files; and malware like viruses, Trojan horses, and worms.

IPS   An intrusion prevention system (IPS) is a computer security device that monitors network and/or system activities for malicious or unwanted behavior and can react, in real time, to block or prevent those activities. For example, a network-based IPS will operate inline to monitor all network traffic for malicious code or attacks. When either is detected, it can drop the offending packets while still allowing all other traffic to pass.

Which approach you'll opt to go with depends on the size of your wireless network and how tight your security needs to be. The goal of a security mechanism is to provide three features:

- Confidentiality of the data
- Data integrity
- An assured identification process

When faced with decisions about security, you need to consider these three things:

- The safety of the authentication process
- The strength of the encryption mechanism
- Its ability to protect the integrity of the data

Real World Scenario

War Driving

It's a fact—wireless networks are pretty much everywhere these days. You can get your hands on a wireless access point for less than $100, and they're flying off the shelves. You can find APs in public places like shopping malls, coffee shops, airports, and hotels, and in some cities, you can just hang out in a downtown area and zero in on a veritable menu of APs operating in almost every nearby business.

Predictably, this proliferation of APs has led to a new hobby for those with enough skill: It's called *war driving*. Not for the technologically challenged, war driving involves driving around in a car with a laptop, a wireless NIC, and a high-gain antenna, trying to locate open APs. If one with high-speed Internet access is found, it's like hitting the jackpot. People do this aided by various software programs and Global Positioning Systems (GPSs) to make their game even easier. But it's not always innocent—war drivers can be a serious security threat because they can potentially access anything on your wireless LAN as well as anything it's attached to! Even though they're not a sinister threat most of the time, realize that, in the very least, they're consuming precious resources from your network. So, if you happen to notice unusually slow-moving vehicles outside your home or business—especially those with computer equipment inside—know that you're the potential target of a war driver.

A good place to start discussing Wi-Fi security is by talking about the basic security that was incorporated into the original 802.11 standards and why those standards are still way too flimsy and incomplete to help us create a secure wireless network relevant to today's challenges.

Open Access

All Wi-Fi Certified small-office, home-office (SOHO) wireless LAN products are shipped in "open-access" mode, with their security features turned off. Although open access or no security may be appropriate and acceptable for public hot spots such as coffee shops, college campuses, and maybe airports, it's definitely not an option for an enterprise organization, and it's probably not even adequate for your private home network.

With what I've told you so far, I'm sure you agree that security needs to be enabled on wireless devices during their installation in enterprise environments. Yet surprisingly, many companies actually don't enable any WLAN security features. Obviously, the companies that don't enable security features are exposing their networks to tremendous risk.

The reason that the products are shipped with open access is so that any person who knows absolutely nothing about computers can just buy an access point, plug it into their cable or DSL modem, and *voilà*—they're up and running. It's marketing, plain and simple, and simplicity sells.

Service Set Identifiers, Wired Equivalent Privacy, and Media Access Control Address Authentication

What the original designers of 802.11 did to create basic security was to include the use of SSIDs, open or shared-key authentication, static WEP, and optional *Media Access Control (MAC) authentication/MAC filtering*. That sounds like a lot, but none of these really offers any type of serious security solution—all they may be close to adequate for is use on a common home network. But we'll go over them anyway.

An SSID is a common network name for the devices in a WLAN system that create the wireless LAN. An SSID prevents access by any client device that doesn't have the SSID. The thing is, by default, an access point broadcasts its SSID in its beacon many times a second. And even if SSID broadcasting is turned off, a bad guy can discover the SSID by monitoring the network and just waiting for a client response to the access point. Why? Because, believe it or not, that information, as regulated in the original 802.11 specifications, must be sent in the clear—how secure!

 If you cannot see an AP when trying to perform a site survey, verify that the AP has SSID beaconing enabled.

Two types of authentication were specified by the IEEE 802.11 committee: open authentication and shared-key authentication. Open authentication involves little more than supplying the correct SSID—but it's the most common method in use today. With shared-key authentication, the access point sends the client device a challenge-text packet that the client must then encrypt with the correct WEP key and return to the access point. Without the correct key, authentication will fail, and the client won't be allowed to associate with the access point. But shared-key authentication is still not considered secure because all an intruder has to do to get around this is to detect both the clear-text challenge and the same challenge encrypted with a WEP key and then decipher the WEP key. Surprise—shared-key authentication isn't used in today's WLANs because of clear-text challenge.

With open authentication, even if a client can complete authentication and associate with an access point, the use of WEP prevents the client from sending and receiving data from the access point unless the client has the correct WEP key. A WEP key is composed of either 40 or 128 bits, and in its basic form, it's usually statically defined by the network administrator on the access point and all clients that communicate with that access point. When static WEP keys are used, a network administrator must perform the time-consuming task of entering the same keys on every device in the WLAN. Obviously, we now have fixes for this because tackling this would be administratively impossible in today's huge corporate wireless networks!

Last, client MAC addresses can be statically typed into each access point, allowing MAC filtering, and any frames that show up to the AP without a known MAC address in the filter table will be denied access. Sounds good, but of course all MAC layer information must be sent in the clear—anyone equipped with a free wireless sniffer can just read the client packets sent to the access point and spoof their MAC address. If you have a small number of wireless clients and you don't want to deploy an encryption-based access method, MAC address filters may be sufficient.

If you cannot connect to an AP and you've verified that your DHCP configuration and WEP key are correct, check the MAC address filtering on the AP.

WEP can actually work if administered correctly. But basic static WEP keys are no longer a viable option in today's corporate networks without some of the proprietary fixes that run on top of WEP.

Geofencing

Geofencing is the process of defining the area in which an operation can be performed by using global positioning (GPS) or radio frequency identification (RFID) to define a geographic boundary. An example of usage involves a location-aware device of a location-based service (LBS) user entering or exiting a geo-fence. This activity could trigger an alert to the device's user as well as messaging to the geo-fence operator.

Remote Authentication Dial-In User Service (802.1X)

Remote Authentication Dial-In User Service (RADIUS) is a networking protocol that offers us several security benefits: authorization, centralized access, and accounting supervision regarding the users and/or computers that connect to and access our networks' services. Once RADIUS has authenticated the user, it allows us to specify the type of rights a user or workstation has, plus control what it, or they, can do within the network. It also creates a record of all access attempts and actions. The provision of authentication, authorization, and accounting is called AAA, which is pronounced just like the automobile insurance company, "triple A," and it's part of the IEEE 802.1X security standard.

RADIUS has risen to stardom because of its AAA features and is often employed by ISPs, web servers, wireless networks, and APs as well as network ports—basically, by anybody who wants or needs an AAA server. And these servers are becoming only more critically important in large corporate environments, and that's because they offer security for wireless networks. From the Linksys security screen shown earlier, you can see that RADIUS is an available option. If you choose it, you'll be asked for the IP address of the RADIUS server so the AP can send authentication packets.

Figure 12.21 shows how the AP becomes an authenticator when you choose the RADIUS authentication method.

FIGURE 12.21   RADIUS authentication server

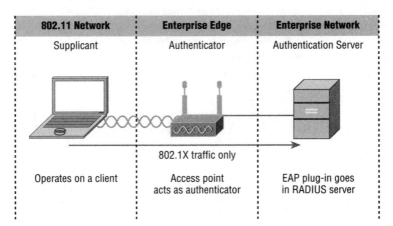

Now packets must pass through the AP until the user and/or host gets authenticated by the RADIUS server.

Temporal Key Integrity Protocol

Put up a fence, and it's only a matter of time until bad guys find a way over, around, and through it. And true to form, they indeed found ways to get through WEP's defenses, leaving our Wi-Fi networks vulnerable—stripped of their Data Link layer security! So someone had to come to the rescue. In this case, it happened to be the IEEE 802.11i task group and the Wi-Fi Alliance, joining forces for the cause. They came up with a solution called Temporal Key Integrity Protocol (TKIP). The Wi-Fi Alliance unveiled it back in late 2002 and introduced it as *Wi-Fi Protected Access (WPA)*. This little beauty even saved us lots of money because TKIP—say this like "tee kip"—didn't make us upgrade all our legacy hardware equipment in order to use it. Then, in the summer of 2004, the IEEE put its seal of approval on the final version and added even more defensive muscle with goodies like 802.1X and AES-CCMP (AES-Counter Mode CBC-MAC Protocol) upon publishing IEEE 802.11i-2004. The Wi-Fi Alliance responded positively by embracing the now-complete specification and dubbing it WPA2 for marketing purposes.

A big reason that TKIP doesn't require buying new hardware to run is that it really just kind of wraps around the preexisting WEP encryption key (which was way too short) and upgrades it a whole lot to much more impenetrable 128-bit encryption. Another reason for TKIP's innate compatibility is that both its encryption mechanism and the RC4 algorithm used to power and define WEP, respectively, remained the same.

But there are still significant differences that help make it the seriously tough shield it is, one of them being that it actually changes each packet's key. Let me explain: Packet keys are made up of three things: a base key, the transmitting device's MAC address, and the packet's serial number. It's an elegant design because, although it doesn't place a ton of stress on workstations and APs, it serves up some truly formidable cryptographic force. Here's how it works: Remember the packet serial number part of the transmission key? Well, it's not just your average serial number; it's special—very special.

TKIP-governed transmission ensures that each packet gets its very own 48-bit serial number, which is augmented with a sequence number whenever a new packet gets sent out, and not only serves as part of the key but also acts as the initialization vector. And the good news doesn't end there—because each packet is now uniquely identified, the collision attacks that used to happen using WEP are also history. Plus, the fact that part of the packet's serial number is also the initialization vector prevents something called *replay attacks*. It takes an ice age for a 48-bit value to repeat, so replaying packets from some past wireless connection is just not going to happen; those "recycled" packets won't be in sequence, but they will be identified, thus preventing the attack.

Now for what may be the truly coolest thing about TKIP keys: the base key. Because each base key that TKIP creates is unique, no one can recycle a commonly known key over and over again to gain access to a formerly vulnerable WEP wireless LAN. This is because TKIP throws the base key into the mix when it assembles each packet's unique key, meaning that even if a device has connected to a particular access point a bunch of times, it won't be permitted access again unless it has a completely new key granting it permission.

Even the base key itself is a fusion of something called *nonces*—an assortment of random numbers gleaned from the workstation, the access point, and each of these devices' MAC addresses, so this should also be referred to as a *session secret*. So basically, if you've got IEEE 802.1X authentication working for you, rest assured that a session secret absolutely will be transmitted securely to each machine every time it initiates a connection to the wireless LAN by the authentication server—unless you're using preshared keys, that is, because if you happen to be using them, that important session secret always remains the same. Using TKIP with preshared keys is kind of like closing an automatically locking security door but not enabling its security settings and alarm—anyone who knows where the secret latch is can get right in!

Wi-Fi Protected Access or WPA2 Pre-Shared Key

These are both essentially another form of basic security that's really just an add-on to the specifications. Even though you can totally lock the vault, as I mentioned in the previous section, WPA/WPA2 Pre-Shared Key (PSK) is a better form of wireless security than any other basic wireless security method I've talked about so far. And note that I did say basic! But if you are using only MAC address filters and/or WEP and you find that interlopers are still using your network and dragging down the performance, adding this layer of security should help tremendously since it's a better form of access control than either of those measures.

Wi-Fi Protected Access (WPA) is a standard developed by the Wi-Fi Alliance, formerly known as the Wireless Ethernet Compatibility Alliance (WECA). WPA provides a standard for authentication and encryption of WLANs that's intended to solve known security problems. The standard takes into account the well-publicized AirSnort and on-path (man-in-the-middle) WLAN attacks. So of course we use WPA2 to help us with today's security issues.

The PSK verifies users via a password or identifying code (also called a *passphrase*) on both the client machine and the access point. A client gains access to the network only if its password matches the access point's password. The PSK also provides keying material that TKIP or Advanced Encryption Standard (AES) uses to generate an encryption key for each packet of transmitted data.

Although more secure than static WEP, PSK still has a lot in common with static WEP in that the PSK is stored on the client station and can be compromised if the client station is lost or stolen (even though finding this key isn't all that easy to do). It's a definite recommendation to use a strong PSK passphrase that includes a mixture of letters, numbers, and non-alphanumeric characters. With WPA, it's still actually possible to specify the use of dynamic encryption keys that change each time a client establishes a connection.

The benefit of WPA over a static WEP key is that WPA can change dynamically while the system is used.

WPA is a step toward the IEEE 802.11i standard and uses many of the same components, with the exception of encryption—802.11i (WPA2) uses AES-CCMP encryption. The IEEE 802.11i standard replaced WEP with a specific mode of AES known as the CCMP, as mentioned earlier. This allows AES-CCMP to provide both data confidentiality (encryption) and data integrity.

The highest level of wireless encryption you can run is WPA3-SAE.

The following screen shows that if you choose WPA2 Personal on the Linksys AP, you can then enter your passphrase—it's really called WPA2 Pre-Shared Key, but whatever.

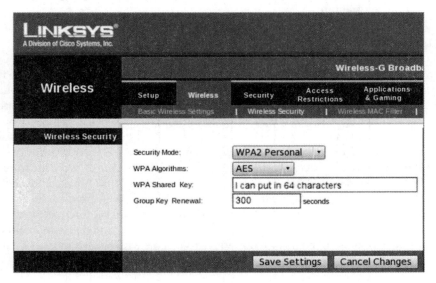

You have a choice of TKIP or AES as the encryption, and by the way, you can choose up to a 64-character key—pretty tight!

WPA's mechanisms are designed to be implementable by current hardware vendors, meaning that users should be able to implement WPA on their systems with only a firmware/ software modification.

> The IEEE 802.11i standard has been sanctioned by WPA and is called WPA version 2.

Certificates and PKI

WPA2 can use the Extensible Authentication Protocol (EAP) method for authentication.

EAP isn't a single method but a framework that enhances the existing 802.1X framework. The EAP framework describes a basic set of actions that will take place, and each EAP type differs in the specifics of how it operates within the framework. These variables include things like whether they use passwords or certificates as well as the ultimate level of security provided. Some of the EAP methods require that certificates be used as the credential during authentication. This means that to implement those methods, you must have a Public Key Infrastructure (PKI) in your network. A PKI requires a certificate server that issues certificates to your users and/or devices. These certificates, which consist of a public/private key pair, must be securely installed on the devices and renewed at regular intervals.

In symmetric encryption, the two encryption keys are the same, just as they are with WEP keys, but in asymmetric encryption, the key used to encrypt is different from the key used to decrypt. In PKI, asymmetric keys are used, and the keys are called a public/private key pair. Certificates are binding regulations of a public/private key pair generated by a certificate server to a user or computer. As long as two parties trust the same certificate source, called the trusted certificate authority (CA), they can trust the certificate they're presented with for authentication. These keys can also be used for encryption and as digital signatures.

Despite the other uses of public/private keys, our focus here is the use of the certificates as a form of authentication and authorization. And as a means of identifying the device or the user, this is considered the highest form of authentication and authorization when compared to names and passwords. What all this means is that as long as the AP or controller and the station or user trust the CA that issued the certificates, the certificate is trusted as a means of identification as well.

EAP   Extensible Authentication Protocol (EAP) is not a single protocol but a framework for port-based access control that uses the same three components that are used in RADIUS. A wide variety of these include certificates, a PKI, or even simple passwords.

PEAP   Protected Extensible Authentication Protocol, also known as Protected EAP or simply PEAP, is a protocol that encapsulates the Extensible Authentication Protocol (EAP) within an encrypted and authenticated Transport Layer Security (TLS) tunnel.

It requires only a server-side PKI certificate to create a secure TLS tunnel to protect user authentication.

EAP-FAST   EAP-FAST works in two stages. In the first stage, a TLS tunnel is established. Unlike PEAP, however, EAP-FAST's first stage is established by using a pre-shared key called a Protected Authentication Credential (PAC). In the second stage, a series of type/length/value (TLV)-encoded data is used to carry a user authentication.

EAP-TLS   EAP Transport Layer Security (EAP-TLS) is the most secure method, but it's also the most difficult to configure and maintain. To use EAP-TLS, you must install a certificate on both the authentication server and the client. An authentication server pair of keys and a client pair of keys need to be generated first, signed using a PKI, and installed on the devices. On the station side, the keys can be issued for the machine itself and/or for the user.

In the authentication stage, the station, along with the authentication server (RADIUS, etc.), exchange certificates and identify each other. Mutual authentication is a solid beneficial feature, which ensures that the station it's communicating with is the proper authentication server. After this process is completed, random session keys are created for encryption.

Preshared Key   Finally, a preshared key can be used to secure wireless transmissions. This is most labor intensive as it requires that all devices use the same key as the AP and that the keys be changed frequently to provide adequate security.

 Tunneled Transport Layer Security (TTLS) provides authentication as strong as EAP-TLS, but it doesn't require each user to be issued a certificate. Instead, only the servers are issued certificates.

Summary

Like rock 'n' roll, wireless technologies are here to stay. And for those of us who have come to depend on wireless technologies, it's actually pretty hard to imagine a world without wireless networks—what did we do before cell phones?

So we began this chapter by exploring the essentials and fundamentals of how wireless networks function. Springing off that foundation, I then introduced you to the basics of wireless radio frequencies (RFs) and the IEEE standards. We discussed 802.11 from its inception through its evolution to current and near-future standards and talked about the subcommittees that create these standards.

All of this led into a discussion of wireless security—or rather, nonsecurity for the most part—which we went over in detail.

We finished the chapter by bringing you up to speed on TKIP and WPA/WPA2 security solutions, which are important tools used to protect the wireless LANs of today.

Exam Essentials

Understand the IEEE 802.11a specification.   802.11a runs in the 5 GHz spectrum, and if you use the 802.11h extensions, you have 23 non-overlapping channels. 802.11a can run up to 54 Mbps, but only if you are less than 50 feet from an access point.

Understand the IEEE 802.11b specification.   IEEE 802.11b runs in the 2.4 GHz range and has three non-overlapping channels. It can handle long distances but with a maximum data rate of up to 11 Mbps.

Understand the IEEE 802.11g specification.   IEEE 802.11g is 802.11b's big brother and runs in the same 2.4 GHz range, but it has a higher data rate of 54 Mbps if you are less than 100 feet from an access point.

Understand the IEEE 802.11n specification.   IEEE 802.11n operates in the 2.4 GHz and 5 GHz range. Support for 5 GHz bands is optional. Its net data rate ranges from 54 Mbit/s to 600 Mbit/s. The standard also added support for multiple-input, multiple-output (MIMO) antennas.

Understand the IEEE 802.11ac specification.   IEEE 802.11ac-2013 is an amendment that builds on 802.11n. Changes include wider channels (80 or 160 MHz versus 40 MHz) in the 5 GHz band and more spatial streams (up to eight versus four). Wave 2 products include additional features like MU-MIMO, 160 MHz channel width support, support for more 5 GHz channels, and four spatial streams with four antennas.

Understand the IEEE 802.11ax specification.   IEEE 802.11ax is the successor to 802.11ac. It's marketed as Wi-Fi 6 (2.4 GHz and 5 GHz) and Wi-Fi 6E (6 GHz). It is also known as High Efficiency Wi-Fi, for the overall improvements to Wi-Fi 6. Data rates against the predecessor (802.11ac) are only 39%. For comparison, this improvement was nearly 500% for the other predecessors.

Understand the different Wi-Fi standards, frequencies, and ranges.   Wi-Fi standards are 802.11a/b/g/n/ac/ax using 2.4 GHz and 5 GHz. 802.11ac is also known as Wi-Fi 5, and 802.11ax is also known as Wi-Fi 6.

Remember the various service set identifiers (SSIDs).   SSIDs can use a basic service set, an extended service set, an independent service set (ad hoc), and a roaming service set.

Remember the antenna types.   Wi-Fi antennas can be Omni directional or directional.

Remember the encryption standards.   Encryption standards include Wi-Fi Protected Access (WPA), WPA2 Personal (Advanced Encryption Standard-AES), Temporal Key Integrity Protocol (TKIP), and WPA/WPA2 Enterprise (AES/TKIP).

Remember the cellular technologies.   Technologies used in cellular communications include code division multiple access(CDMA), global System Mobile (GSM), Long-Term Evolution (LTE), and 3g, 4g, and 5g.

Understand MIMO/MU-MIMO.   MIMO is multiple-input, multiple output, which is widely used in 802.11n and 802.11zc. MU-MIMO is multiuser multiple input, multiple output, which is used in the new 802.11ax protocol.

Remember the wireless LAN modulation techniques.   Direct-sequence spread spectrum (DSSS) is the most widely used modulation technique, but it has speeds only to 11 Mbps. However, the old and pretty much no-longer used frequency-hopping spread spectrum (FHSS), although it is still used in old wireless devices like Bluetooth, isn't the technique of choice for either vendors or the 802.11 working group. To get the higher speeds needed in today's WLANs, we use orthogonal frequency-division multiplexing (OFDM) in 802.11g/a/n and 802.11ac/ax networks.

Understand how WPA works in a WLAN.   Wi-Fi Protected Access (WPA) is the security of choice in today's home and corporate networks. It provides both authentication and encryption (either TKIP or AES).

Written Lab

You can find the answers to the written labs in Appendix A. Fill in the blank with the term that best fits the statement.

1. 5G cellular provides up to _____ speeds to subscribers.
2. The IEEE 802.11a standard operates on the _____ frequency band.
3. The IEEE _____ standard operates at speeds up to 10 Gbps.
4. The IEEE 802.11g standard operates on the _____ frequency band.
5. The IEEE 802.11 standard operates with the contention mechanism of _____.
6. The MIMO mechanism to increase data throughput was first introduced in the IEEE _____ standard.
7. A _____ antenna is a directional antenna.
8. ____ _____ mode is also called an independent basic service set (IBSS).
9. A ____ _____ should be performed before and after deployment of wireless equipment.
10. _____ wireless attacks are used to gather information.

Review Questions

You can find the answers to the review questions in Appendix B.

1. Which wireless standard first introduced channel bonding?
   - **A.** 802.11n
   - **B.** 802.11ac
   - **C.** 802.11g
   - **D.** 802.11a

2. Which three wireless channels on 2.4 GHz wireless are nonoverlapping?
   - **A.** 1, 3, and 9
   - **B.** 1, 9, and 11
   - **C.** 1, 6, and 11
   - **D.** 1, 6, and 12

3. You are setting up a wireless network for a client. Their requirements are to minimize the infrastructure and support the highest security. Which wireless encryption standard should be configured to satisfy the requirements?
   - **A.** WPA-Enterprise
   - **B.** WPA2-Personal
   - **C.** WPA3-Enterprise
   - **D.** WPA-Personal

4. You are configuring a WPA2 WLAN. Which security configuration should you use for the highest level of security?
   - **A.** WPA-AES
   - **B.** WPA2-TKIP
   - **C.** WPA2-RC4
   - **D.** WPA2-AES

5. How many pre-shared keys can be configured for a specific WPA2 WLAN?
   - **A.** One PSK (one hex or one ASCII)
   - **B.** Two PSKs (one hex and one ASCII)
   - **C.** Four PSKs (two hex and two ASCII)
   - **D.** Unlimited number of PSKs

6. After configuring a WLAN, your users complain that they do not see the SSID. What could be wrong?

    A. SSID beaconing is enabled.

    B. Multicast support is disabled.

    C. Radio Policy is configured to all.

    D. SSID beaconing is disabled.

7. What is the mechanism that allows for authentication using a symmetrical key with WPA2?

    A. PSK

    B. AES

    C. Certificates

    D. TKIP

8. When configuring WPA2, you want to ensure that it does not fall back to the older WPA specification. What parameter should you disable?

    A. 802.1X

    B. AES

    C. TKIP

    D. MAC filtering

9. Which mode of encryption does 802.11i (WPA2) introduce?

    A. RC4

    B. MD5

    C. AES-CCMP

    D. SHA1

10. Which statement is correct about WPA?

    A. WPA was released at the same time as WEP.

    B. WPA was released as a fix for poor coverage.

    C. WPA was released as a fix for poor encryption.

    D. The Wi-Fi Alliance wanted to rebrand WEP with WPA.

11. Matilda is interested in securing her SOHO wireless network. What should she do to be assured that only her devices can join her wireless network?

    A. Enable WPA2

    B. Enable MAC filtering

    C. Enable port security

    D. Disable SSID broadcasts

12. Which device is the supplicant during the 802.1X authentication process?

    A. The device requesting access

    B. The server that is providing authentication

    C. The device that is controlling access via 802.1X

    D. The device connecting the layer 3 network

13. What is the access point called in an 802.1X configuration?

    A. Authenticator

    B. Supplicant

    C. AAA server

    D. RADIUS server

14. You need to install wireless Internet access in an open warehouse environment. After installing the equipment, the technician notices varying signal strengths throughout the warehouse. How do you make sure there is full coverage?

    A. Turn on broadcast key rotation.

    B. Change the encryption method used on all the APs.

    C. Change the antenna placement.

    D. Use channel bonding.

    E. Use traffic shaping.

15. What is the frequency range of the IEEE 802.11g standard?

    A. 2.4 Gbps

    B. 5 Gbps

    C. 2.4 GHz

    D. 5 GHz

16. Which devices can interfere with the operation of a wireless network because they operate on similar frequencies? (Choose two.)

    A. Copier

    B. Microwave oven

    C. Toaster

    D. Cordless phone

    E. IP phone

    F. AM radio

17. Which wireless standard allows you to channel-bond to increase bandwidth and uses both the 2.4 GHz and 5 GHz frequencies?

   A. 802.11b

   B. 802.11g

   C. 802.11a

   D. 802.11n

   E. 802.11ac

18. You have installed a point-to-point connection using wireless bridges and Omni directional antennas between two buildings. The throughput is low. What can you do to improve the link?

   A. Replace the bridges with APs.

   B. Replace the Omni directional antennas with Yagis.

   C. Configure 802.11a on the links.

   D. Install amps to boost the signal.

19. Which wireless LAN design ensures that a mobile wireless client will not lose connectivity when moving from one access point to another (roaming)?

   A. Using adapters and access points manufactured by the same company

   B. Overlapping the wireless cell coverage by at least 10 percent

   C. Configuring all access points to use the same channel

   D. Utilizing MAC address filtering to allow the client MAC address to authenticate with the surrounding APs

20. Which spread-spectrum technology does the 802.11b standard define for operation?

   A. IR

   B. DSSS

   C. FHSS

   D. DSSS and FHSS

   E. IR, FHSS, and DSSS

Chapter

13

Remote Network Access

THE FOLLOWING COMPTIA NETWORK+ EXAM OBJECTIVES ARE COVERED IN THIS CHAPTER:

✓ **Domain 3.0 Network Operations**

✓ **3.5 Compare and contrast network access and management methods.**

- Site-to-site VPN
- Client-to-site VPN
    - Clientless
    - Split tunnel vs. full tunnel
- Connection methods
    - SSH
    - Graphical user interface (GUI)
    - API
    - Console
- Jump box/host
- In-band vs. out-of-band management

Think of remote access as a telecommuting tool because companies use it to allow remote employees to connect to the internal network and access resources in the office. Remote access is great for users who work from home or travel frequently, but clearly, to a stalking hacker, using an unsecured remote access connection is like stealing candy from a baby.

Using remote access requires a server configured to accept incoming calls and also requires remote access software to be installed on the client. Microsoft Windows operating systems, since Windows 95, have had remote access client software built in, and there are many third-party remote access clients available as well. Several different methods exist to create remote access connections. In this chapter, we'll look at remote access and the VPN types that make it secure.

To find Todd Lammle CompTIA videos and practice questions, please see www.lammle.com.

Site-to-Site VPN

Site-to-site VPNs, or intranet VPNs, allow a company to connect its remote sites to the corporate backbone securely over an insecure public medium like the Internet instead of requiring more expensive wide area network (WAN) connections like Frame Relay. This is the best solution for connecting a remote office to a main company office because all traffic between the offices will be encrypted with no effort on the part of the users.

In this scenario, all office traffic will go through the VPN tunnel. Figure 13.1 shows a site-to-site VPN, along with a remote access called a *client-to-site VPN* covered in the next section.

This solution requires a remote access client on the user device.

FIGURE 13.1   Site-to-site and client-to-site VPN

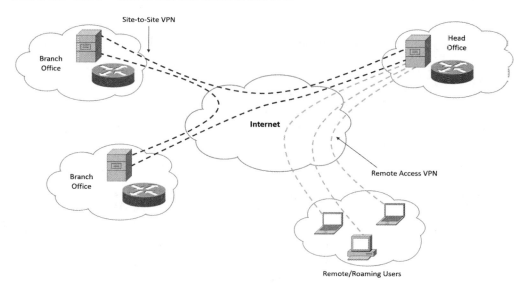

Client-to-Site VPN

Remote access VPNs or client-to-site VPNs (shown in Figure 13.1) allow remote users like telecommuters to securely access the corporate network wherever and whenever they need to. It is typical that users can connect to the Internet but not to the office via their VPN client because they don't have the correct VPN address and password. This is the most common problem and one you should always check first.

In this scenario, only the user and office traffic will go through the VPN tunnel. This solution requires a remote access client on the user's device.

Clientless VPN

A *clientless* VPN enables end users to securely access resources on the corporate network from anywhere using an SSL/TLS-enabled web browser. They need no remote access client to do this, only a browser that can perform SSL or the more secure TLS. Figure 13.2 shows a clientless VPN.

Split Tunnel vs. Full Tunnel

When a client-to-site VPN is created, it is possible to do so in two ways, split tunnel and full tunnel. The difference is whether the user uses the VPN for connecting to the Internet as well as for connecting to the office.

FIGURE 13.2   Clientless VPN

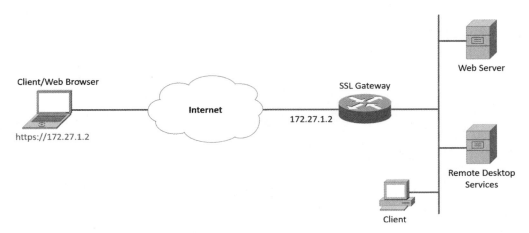

Split tunneling works by using two connections at the same time: the secure VPN connection and an open connection to the Internet. So in split tunneling, *only* traffic to the office goes through the VPN. Internet traffic does not. The security issue with this is that while the user is connected to the VPN, they are also connected to the most untrusted network, the Internet.

Figure 13.3 shows the split and full tunnels.

FIGURE 13.3   Split and full tunnels

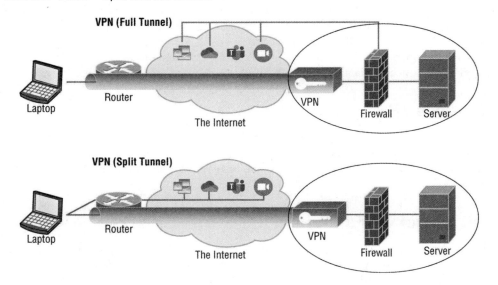

With a full tunnel, all traffic goes through the VPN, which means the user is accessing the Internet through the connection of the office, and so all traffic will be examined by the office security.

Remote Desktop Connection

There are times when you need to make a remote connection to a machine to perform troubleshooting but you are miles away. Connectivity software is designed to allow you to make a connection to a machine, see the desktop, and perform any action you could perform if you were sitting in front of it.

Microsoft has made what it calls Remote Desktop software available for free with Windows products since Windows NT. When this software is installed (installed by default in later versions) on both source and destination computers, a remote desktop connection can be made.

Microsoft allows one remote user connection or a local connection on desktop operating systems via Remote Desktop Protocol (RDP), but not both. On server operating systems, Microsoft allows two administrative connections that can be a combination of local or remote access, but not to exceed two connections.

RDP can also be used to deliver applications to the end users via Microsoft *RemoteApp* on terminal services. When RemoteApp is used, the server still requires a terminal services license. However, just the application is delivered to the user host rather than the entire desktop.

Commercial tools are also available that (of course) claim to have more functionality, and they probably do have a few extra bells and whistles. These include LogMeIn.com, GoToMyPC, and others.

The advantages of these connectivity tools are obvious. With these tools, you can do anything you need to on the machine as long as you can connect. They also allow you to see what a user is actually doing when they encounter a problem rather than having to rely on what they tell you they are doing. You can even show a user what they are doing wrong. Most of these tools allow for chat sessions and for either end of the connection to take control of the machine. You can also transfer files to them if required (maybe a dynamic-link library got deleted, for example).

Remote Desktop Protocol

Remote Desktop Protocol is a proprietary protocol developed by Microsoft. It allows you to connect to another computer and run programs. RDP operates somewhat like Telnet, except instead of getting a command-line prompt as you do with Telnet, you get the actual graphical user interface (GUI) of the remote computer. Clients exist for most versions of Windows, and macOS now comes with a preinstalled RDP client.

Microsoft currently calls its official RDP server software Remote Desktop Services; it was called Terminal Services for awhile. Microsoft's official client software is currently referred to as Remote Desktop Connection (RDC), which was called Terminal Services Client in the past.

RDP is an excellent tool for remote clients, allowing them to connect to their work computer from home, for example, and get their email or perform work on other applications without running or installing any of the software on their home computer.

RDP allows users to connect to a computer running Microsoft's Remote Desktop Services, but a remote computer must have the right kind of client software installed for this to happen. Most Windows-based operating systems include an RDP client, and so do most other major operating systems, like Linux and macOS. Microsoft began calling all terminal services products Remote Desktop with Windows Server 2008 R2. RDP uses the TCP protocol and port 3389.

After establishing a connection, the user sees a terminal window that's basically a preconfigured window that looks like a Windows desktop or another operating system's desktop. From there, the user on the client computer can access applications and files available to them by using the remote desktop.

When logged in using RDP, clients are able to access local files and printers from the remote desktop just as if they were logged into the network.

EXERCISE 13.1

Experimenting with RDP

This exercise is best if you have two stand-alone Windows computers on the same network. In this exercise, you will experiment and explore the setting for Microsoft Remote Desktop Protocol:

1. Select Start ≻ Settings ≻ System ≻ Remote Desktop to open the Windows Settings for Remote Desktop.

2. Flip the Enable Remote Desktop switch to on.

3. Click Confirm on the Enable Remote Desktop? dialog box.

4. Click Advanced Settings to investigate the various settings for Remote Desktop.

   If you have a second computer, continue with the following steps.

5. On the same computer, find the IP address by opening a command prompt and typing **ipconfig**.

6. On a second computer, click the Start menu, begin typing the word **Remote**, and select the Remote Desktop Connection result.

7. Click Show Options on the Remote Desktop App.

8. Explore the tabs and various options.

9. Click the General tab and enter the IP address from step 5.

10. Click Connect on the Remote Desktop App.

RDP Gateway

The Remote Desktop Protocol Gateway is a Microsoft server role that allows centralized access to remote desktops, such as remote desktop workstations or remote desktop servers. The gateway usually sits between the users and the remote desktops and controls the access to the remote desktops. Although the term Remote Desktop Gateway is a Microsoft Server role, every vendor for Remote Desktop Protocol Services has a similar server or virtual appliance. The Remote Desktop Gateway is mainly responsible for brokering clients to their respective remote desktops.

The Remote Desktop Gateway is typically installed on the edge of the network, where it will border the external network it serves, such as the Internet. Because the gateway is installed on the edge of the network, it is also responsible for the security or the remote desktop sessions and users. The gateway provides TLS encryption via certificates, authentication for clients via Active Directory, and the authorization to the internal resources. The Remote Desktop Gateway operates on port 443 and protocol TCP.

During the setup of the Remote Desktop Gateway, two policies must be configured for controlling authorization. The Connection Authorization Policy (CAP) specifies which group of users can access the Remote Desktop Gateway. The Resource Authorization Policy (RAP) then specifies which remote desktop or servers are allowed for each group of users. Between the CAP and RAP authentication policies, the Remote Desktop Gateway can be configured with granular security for both users and the remote hosts.

It is more secure than allowing RDP to be published directly to the public over the Internet in the following ways:

- No VPN needed. Using the SSL channel, the RDP Gateway can tunnel directly to the remote server to increase the security of RDS.

- No pass through a third-party website or service.

- Native Windows Server service.

- Can be combined with Network Access Protection (NAP).

- Can be used along with Microsoft Internet Security and Acceleration (ISA), the Microsoft implementation of RADIUS.

Virtual Network Computing

Virtual Network Computing (VNC) is a remote control tool for sharing desktops. The VNC client normally operates on TCP port 5900. VNC is similar to Microsoft RDP, with the exception that VNC is an open-source protocol and allows only one console session on a Microsoft operating system. It supports encryption via plug-ins but is not encrypted by default.

VNC operates in a client and server model. The server install for the host enables remote control of the host, and the client install allows for means to connect to the VNC server.

It is normally configured with a simple shared password, but it can also be configured with Windows groups. Several clients can be used such as RealVNC, TightVNC, and many others, but all of the clients perform in a similar way.

VNC includes the following components:

- **VNC server:** Software that runs on the machine sharing its screen
- **VNC client (or viewer):** Software on the machine that is remotely receiving the shared screen
- **VNC protocol:** The protocol

One big difference between VNC and RDP is that VNC sends raw pixel data (which does make it work on any desktop type), while RDP uses graphic primitives or higher-level commands for the screen transfer process.

Virtual Desktop

Using operating system images for desktop computers is not a new concept. Nor is delivering these desktop images to users from a virtual environment when they start their computer. This allows for the user desktop to require less computing power, especially if the applications are also delivered virtually and those applications are running in a virtual machine (VM) in the cloud rather than in the local desktop eating up local resources. Another benefit of using virtual desktops is the ability to maintain a consistent user environment (same desktop, applications, etc.), which can enhance user support.

Connection Methods

This section will cover various connection methods for accessing hosts, servers, and network devices. We already covered RDP in this chapter, so let's talk about the following:

- Secure Shell (SSH)
- Graphical user interface (GUI)
- Application programming interface (API)
- Console

Secure Shell

Secure Shell is a network protocol that is designed as a secure alternative to command-based utilities such as Telnet that transmit requests and responses in clear text. It creates a secure channel between the devices and provides confidentiality and integrity of the data transmission. The SSH protocol uses the TCP protocol and port 22.

It uses public-key cryptography to authenticate the remote computer and allow the remote computer to authenticate the user, if necessary. This public key is placed on any computer that must allow access to the owner of a matching private key (the owner keeps the private key in secret). The private key is never transferred through the network during authentication.

Don't use Telnet! Telnet is insecure because it sends all data in crystal-clear text—including your name and password. And I'm pretty sure you know that's a terrible thing these days. If Microsoft doesn't even enable it on its latest OSs, then you know it really must be insecure.

Figure 13.4 shows how an encrypted session might look between a host and a network device.

FIGURE 13.4 Clientless VPN

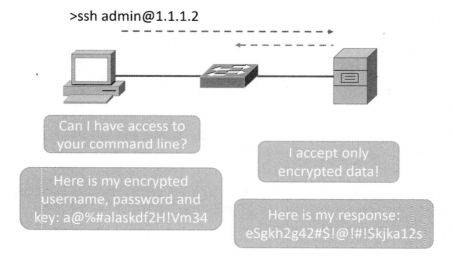

Some configuration is usually necessary if you want things to work as they really should, and yes, sometimes it's a little painful to get everything running smoothly, but it's all worth it in the long run. Personally, I disable Telnet on all my routers and use SSH exclusively. No lie—I never use Telnet anymore if I can help it. Even so, you should still understand Telnet and get some practice with it in case you do ever need it.

Graphical User Interface

As mentioned earlier, Remote Desktop Services is a great GUI to connect to remote devices, get a GUI window, and then use it to administer the device, server, and/or network devices on the connected zone. Very useful. You'll learn about a jump host in the next section, which can be used similarly.

Application Programming Interface

An application programming interface allows you to quickly access an application resource without mapping out the application and manually reverse engineering your functionality.

For example, if you wanted to create an application that suggests restaurants near a user, you would need access to map information to know what restaurants are nearby.

To get map information on your own, you would have to either get your own map data or develop your own way of accessing Google Maps through your own interface. Neither one of these is a practical option. Fortunately, Google offers many APIs that, like you, consume their map information in your application.

One of the most common ways of accessing APIs is through Representational State Transfer (REST). REST is a resource-based API, which means that URIs should be:

- Things, not actions
- Nouns, not verbs

If we break the words in Representational State Transfer apart, we have the following:

Representational   A resource state is transferred between a client and server.

State Transfer   Each request has all the information it needs to complete the operation.

Lastly, REST has six constraints it needs to follow to be considered a RESTful API.

- **Client-server:** Connections are always initiated by a client requesting something from a server.
- **Stateless:** The server doesn't store any information from previous requests.
- **Cacheable:** The server response includes a version number so the client can decide if it can use the cached information or if it needs a new request.
- **Uniform interface:** This defines the interface between the client and the server. This is divided into four subsections.
  - **Resource identification:** Each resource must have its own unique URI.
  - **Resource representation:** This is how the resource will return data to the client; this is usually JSON or XML.
  - **Self-descriptive messages:** Each message sent must have enough information in it to determine how to process the message.
  - **Hypermedia as the engine of application state (HATEOAS):** This is a bit of a mouthful but basically means you should be able to easily discover other functionalities of the API. For example, suppose you are looking at a Cisco router API to view an interface. In that case, you should be able to view other items without too much documentation.
- **Layered system:** You can add layers between the API and the server data, such as a firewall or a load balancer, without impacting operations.
- **Code on demand:** This optional constraint allows REST to send executable code responses back to the client.

Console/Rolled Serial Cable

Although *rolled cable* isn't used to connect any Ethernet connections together, you can use a rolled Ethernet cable to connect a host EIA-TIA 232 interface to a router console serial communication (COM) port.

If you have a Cisco router or switch, you would use this cable to connect your PC, your Mac, or a device like an iPad to the Cisco hardware. Eight wires are used in this cable to connect serial devices, although not all eight are used to send information, just as in Ethernet networking. Figure 13.5 shows the eight wires used in a rolled cable.

FIGURE 13.5   Rolled Ethernet cable

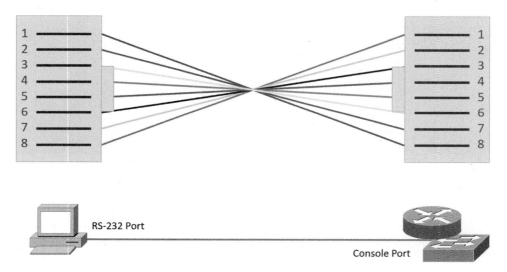

These are probably the easiest cables to make because you just cut the end off on one side of a straight-through cable, turn it over, and put it back on—with a new connector, of course!

Once you have the correct cable connected from your PC to the Cisco router or switch console port, you can start your emulation program such as PuTTY or SecureCRT to create a console connection and configure the device. Set the configuration as shown in Figure 13.6.

Notice that Baud Rate is set to 9600, Data Bits to 8, Parity to None, and no Flow Control options are set. At this point, you can click Connect and press the Enter key, and you should be connected to your Cisco device console port.

Figure 13.7 shows a nice Cisco switch with two console ports.

Notice there are two console connections on this new switch—a typical original RJ45 connection and the newer mini type-B USB console.

FIGURE 13.6 Configuring your console emulation program

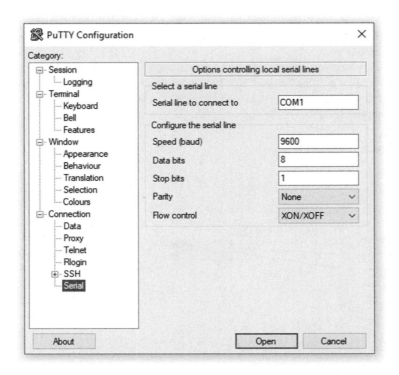

FIGURE 13.7 A Cisco 2960 console connections

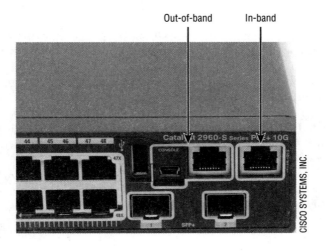

Remember that the new USB port supersedes the RJ45 port if you happen to plug into both at the same time, and the USB port can have speeds up to 115,200 Kbps, which is awesome if you have to use Xmodem to update an IOS. I've even seen some cables that work on iPhones and iPads, allowing them to connect to these mini-USB ports!

Jump Box/Host

Referred to as a jump server, jump host, or jump box, this can be a very useful device. A jump box is defined as a system on a private network that will allow you to remotely access and manage devices in a separate security zone. This host is a very hardened device that connects two or more security zones, allowing authenticated and controlled access between chosen zones.

Created in the early 1990s to provide secure access to remote networks and multiple security zones, this was initially used with proxy services, which were all the rage by the mid-1990s, and then provided a connection from a local desktop. However, once SSH became popular and replaced Telnet, SSH became the standard access method instead of proxies for the jump box. Alternatively, I am using a jump box in my data center. I have set it up so I can RDP into the GUI interface and get to all my network devices in the DC I use daily.

Similarly, and created around this same time, a *bastion* host was created. Named bastion because it means or is defined as "Military Fortification" and considered a critical strong point of network security, it was typically designed and configured to stop multiple attacks by only running the needed application, and all other ports are disabled. Another reason to use a bastion is the network interfaces were designed to look for and stop high-bandwidth attacks. Pretty amazing.

Jumping back to the jump box (see what I did there?), it's vital that you set up a VPN termination point in the location where the host is located. In my DC, I use a Cisco ASA—it's old but sturdy—and can handle all my terminations with an easy-to-use CLI.

Where Should You Implement a Jump Box/Host?

Jump servers are often placed between a secure zone and a screened subnet (also known as DMZ) to provide easy management of devices in the screened subnet once a management session has been set up and configured.

Figure 13.8 shows where a typical jump host could be placed in a network. Notice my firewall termination point for my VPN.

This allows for an administrator to log into the jump server to gain access to the screened subnet, servers, and other assets, and all access and configuration can be logged for audit.

FIGURE 13.8   Where a jump box is implemented

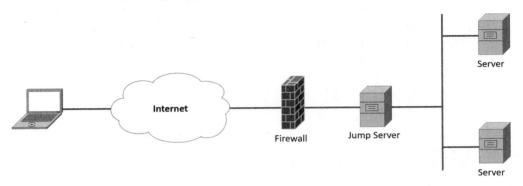

In-Band vs. Out-of-Band Management

Out-of-band management is any method of managing a server or network device that does not use or go through the network. You'd use a console cable to attach directly to the device to do this.

However, many newer network devices have separate Ethernet ports that are configured with a different subnet than the management IP of the local zone and is considered out-of-band because it is not connecting through the production network.

In-band refers to managing a network, server, or network device through the network using tools like RDP or SSH, for example.

Summary

In this chapter, you learned the importance of providing remote network access. You learned about VPN architectures. These include site-to-site VPNs, client-to-site VPN, clientless VPN, split tunnel versus full, and SSH VPN.

We also looked at SSL and TLS, including common applications with respect to VPNs. Finally, we identified other remote access solutions, such as VNC, RDP, Remote Desktop Gateway, remote desktop connections, and virtual connections.

Exam Essentials

Explain VPN architectures.   These include site-to-site VPNs, client-to-site VPN, clientless VPN, split tunnel versus full, and SSH VPN.

Describe SSL and TLS.   This includes the differences between the two and the advantages of TLS. It also includes common applications with respect to VPNs.

Identify other remote access solutions.   These include VNC, RDP, Remote Desktop Gateway, remote desktop connections, and virtual connections.

Understand in-band and out-of-band management.   In-band management is access via the network over SSH, Telnet, or some other network protocol. Out-of-band management is access via a method not connected to the network, such as a serial connection.

Written Lab

Complete the table by filling in the appropriate term for each definition.
    You can find the answers in Appendix A.

Definition	Term
Only traffic to the office goes through the VPN. Internet traffic does not.	
Only the traffic between the user and the office will go through the tunnel.	
All traffic goes through the VPN, including Internet traffic.	
All traffic goes through the VPN tunnel.	
Requires only a browser that can perform SSL/TLS.	

Review Questions

You can find the answers to the review questions in Appendix B.

1. A serial console cable is an example of which of the following technologies?
   A. Captive portal
   B. Out-of-band management
   C. Clientless VPN
   D. AAA

2. You need to implement a secure connection for your users to access sensitive sites internally for your organization. Which technology should you select?
   A. Captive portal
   B. Clientless VPN
   C. LDAP
   D. RDP

3. Which of the following is an operating system image delivered over the network at each startup?
   A. VNC
   B. Virtual desktop
   C. Remote desktop
   D. RDP

4. Which of the following is *not* a component of Virtual Network Computing (VNC)?
   A. VNC server
   B. VNC client
   C. VNC desktop
   D. VNC protocol

5. Which of the following is a network protocol that is designed as an alternative to command-based utilities such as Telnet?
   A. SSL
   B. SSH
   C. STP
   D. STFP

6. Which of the following allows you to tunnel directly to the remote server with no VPN?
   A. Split tunnel
   B. RDP Gateway
   C. Full tunnel
   D. VNC

7. Which of the following was formerly called Terminal Services Client?

   A. Virtual desktop

   B. Remote Desktop Connection

   C. VNC

   D. RDP Gateway

8. Which of the following operates somewhat like Telnet, except instead of getting a command-line prompt as you do with Telnet, you get the actual graphical user interface (GUI) of the remote computer?

   A. RBAC

   B. SSH

   C. RDP

   D. SSL

9. Which of the following is *not* an example of a remote desktop connection?

   A. RDP

   B. LogMeIn

   C. GoToMyPC

   D. SSH

10. Split tunnel and full tunnel are examples of which type of VPN?

   A. Client-to-site

   B. Site-to-site

   C. RDP VPN

   D. Clientless VPN

11. You have several remote offices that you need to connect securely over the Internet. Which technology would best suit the connectivity for this requirement?

   A. GRE tunnel

   B. Wireless WAN

   C. Client-to-site VPN

   D. Site-to-site VPN

12. Why should Telnet be replaced with SSH?

   A. Telnet has weak encryption.

   B. SSH allows for file copy.

   C. SSH makes it easier to create ACLs for access.

   D. SSH is encrypted.

13. What type of encryption does a clientless VPN use?

   A. SSH

   B. SSL/TLS

   C. RDP

   D. ACLs

14. What are the terminal parameters that are the most common for serial configuration of a Cisco router or switch?

   A. 9600 baud, 8 data bits, parity none, no stop bits

   B. 9600 baud, 8 parity bits, no data bits, 1 stop bit

   C. 9600 baud, 7 data bits, parity none, 1 stop bit

   D. 9600 baud, 8 data bits, parity none, 1 stop bit

15. You are connecting to a network switch with the SSH protocol. Which type of connection is this considered?

   A. Out-of-band management

   B. In-band management

   C. GUI-based management

   D. API-based management

16. Which of the following is an operating system image delivered over the network?

   A. VNC

   B. Virtual desktop

   C. VPN

   D. RDP

17. Which port and protocol does the VNC protocol operate on?

   A. 443/TCP

   B. 5900/TCP

   C. 5900/UDP

   D. 3389/TCP

18. What is the most common way to access resource-based APIs?

   A. RDP

   B. Terminal-based

   C. REST

   D. GUI-based

19. Which out-of-band management connectivity method provides for up to 115,200 Kbps?

   A. USB

   B. EIA-TIA 232

   C. COM

   D. SSH

20. Which port and protocol are used for the Remote Desktop Gateway connection?

   A. 3389/TCP

   B. 5900/TCP

   C. 443/TCP

   D. 80/TCP

Chapter

14

Using Statistics and Sensors to Ensure Network Availability

THE FOLLOWING COMPTIA NETWORK+ EXAM OBJECTIVES ARE COVERED IN THIS CHAPTER:

✓ **Domain 3.0 Network Operations**

✓ **3.2 Given a scenario, use network monitoring technologies.**

- Methods
    - SNMP
        - Traps
        - Management information base (MIB)
        - Versions: v2c, v3
        - Community strings
        - Authentication
    - Flow data
    - Packet capture
    - Baseline metrics
        - Anomaly alerting/notification
    - Log aggregation
        - Syslog collector
        - Security information and event management (SIEM)
    - Application programming interface (API) integration
    - Port mirroring

- Solutions
  - Network discovery
    - Ad hoc
    - Scheduled
  - Traffic analysis
  - Performance monitoring
  - Availability monitoring
  - Configuration monitoring

All organizations detest downtime. It costs money, and it damages their brand and reputation. So, they spend millions trying to solve the issue. One of the keys to stopping downtime is to listen to what the devices may be telling you about their current state of health. Doing so forms a sort of early warning system that lets you know before a system goes down so there is time to avoid it. In this chapter, you'll learn what sort of data you should be monitoring and some of the ways to do so.

To find Todd Lammle CompTIA videos and practice questions, p ease see www.lammle.com.

Performance Monitoring/ Metrics/Sensors

Let's imagine you were just brought from the 1800s to the present by a time machine and in your first trip in a car you examine the dashboard. Speed, temperature, tire inflation, tachometer. . .what does all that stuff mean? It would be meaningless to you and useless for monitoring the state of the car's health. Likewise, you cannot monitor the health of a device or a network unless you understand the metrics. In these opening sections, you will learn what these are and how to use them.

Device/Chassis

There are certain basic items to monitor about physical computing devices, regardless of whether it's a computer, router, or switch. While not the only thing to monitor, these items would be on the dashboard if they had dashboards.

Temperature

Heat and computers do not mix well. Many computer systems require both temperature and humidity control for reliable service. The larger servers, communications equipment, and drive arrays generate considerable amounts of heat; this is especially true of mainframe and older minicomputers. An environmental system for this type of equipment is a significant expense beyond the actual computer system costs. Fortunately, newer systems operate in a wider temperature range. Most new systems are designed to operate in an office environment.

Overheating is also a big cause of reboots. When CPUs get overheated, a cycle of reboots can ensue. Make sure the fan is working on the heat sink and the system fan is also working. If required, vacuum the dust from around the vents.

Under normal conditions, the PC cools itself by pulling in air. That air is used to dissipate the heat created by the processor (and absorbed by the heat sink). When airflow is restricted by clogged ports, a bad fan, and so forth, heat can build up inside the unit and cause problems. Chip creep—the unseating of components—is one of the more common byproducts of a cycle of overheating and cooling of the inside of the system.

Since the air is being pulled into the machine, excessive heat can originate from outside the PC as well because of a hot working environment. The heat can be pulled in and cause the same problems. Take care to keep the ambient air within normal ranges (approximately 60 to 90 degrees Fahrenheit) and at a constant temperature.

Replacing slot covers is vital. Computers are designed to circulate air with slot covers in place or cards plugged into the ports. Leaving slots on the back of the computer open alters the air circulation and causes more dust to be pulled into the system.

Finally, note whether the fan is working; if it stops, that is a major cause of overheating.

Central Processing Unit Usage

When monitoring the central processing unit (CPU), the specific counters you use depend on the server role. Consult the vendor's documentation for information about those counters and what they mean to the performance of the service or application. The following counters are commonly monitored:

- **Processor\% Processor Time:** The percentage of time the CPU spends executing a non-idle thread. This should not be more than 85% on a sustained basis.

- **Processor\% User Time:** Represents the percentage of time the CPU spends in user mode, which means it is doing work for an application. If this value is higher than the baseline you captured during normal operation, the service or application is dominating the CPU.

- **Processor\% Interrupt Time:** The percentage of time the CPU receives and services hardware interrupts during specific sample intervals. If this is more than 15%, there could be a hardware issue.

- **System\Processor Queue Length:** The number of threads (which are smaller pieces of an overall operation) in the processor queue. If this value is more than two times the number of CPUs, the server is not keeping up with the workload.

Memory

Different system roles place different demands on the memory, so there may be specific counters of interest you can learn by consulting the documentation provided by the vendor of the specific service. Some of the most common counters monitored by server administrators are listed here:

- **Memory\% Committed Bytes in Use:** The amount of virtual memory in use. If this is more than 80%, you need more memory.

- **Memory\Available Mbytes:** The amount of physical memory, in megabytes, currently available. If this is less than 5%, you need more memory.

- **Memory\Free System Page Table Entries:** Number of entries in the page table not currently in use by the system. If the number is less than 5,000, there may well be a memory leak.

- **Memory\Pool Non-Paged Bytes:** The size, in bytes, of the non-paged pool, which contains objects that cannot be paged to the disk. If the value is greater than 175 MB, you may have a memory leak (an application is not releasing its allocated memory when it is done).

- **Memory\Pool Paged Bytes:** The size, in bytes, of the paged pool, which contains objects that *can* be paged to disk. (If this value is greater than 250 MB, there may be a memory leak.)

- **Memory\Pages per Second:** The rate at which pages are written to and read from the disk during paging. If the value is greater than 1,000, as a result of excessive paging, there may be a memory leak.

Network Metrics

The health of the operation of a network can also be monitored and should be to maintain its performance at peak efficiency. Just as you can avoid a problem issue with a workstation or server, you can react to network conditions before they cause an issue by monitoring these items.

Bandwidth

In a perfect world, there would be unlimited bandwidth, but in reality, you're more likely to find Bigfoot. So, it's helpful to have some great strategies up your sleeve.

If you look at what computers are used for today, there's a huge difference between the files we transfer now versus those transferred even three to five years ago. Now we do things like watch movies online without them stalling, and we can send huge email attachments. Video teleconferencing is almost more common than Starbucks locations. The point is that the files we transfer today are really large compared to what we sent back and forth just a few years ago. And although bandwidth has increased to allow us to do what we do, there are still limitations that cause network performance to suffer miserably.

Bandwidth can be measured in two different ways; the first is available bandwidth, and the second is bandwidth utilization or throughput. Simply put, the bandwidth is the connections capacity, and throughput is the utilized bandwidth. When we talk about bandwidth utilization or throughput, we simply refer to it as utilization. The bandwidth of a connection is often referred to as a connection's speed, and it is measured in bits per second (bps). The throughput can never exceed the bandwidth for a given connection.

Throughput measurement is often performed on a connection such as the Internet. We will collect the metric by measuring the path to a given host on the Internet. It's not a perfect measurement because a host can sometimes be down or overwhelmed with other traffic. However, most of the time the destination host has a much bigger connection than the Internet connection you are connected with.

The following are metrics to follow for bandwidth on a system:

- **Network Interface\Bytes Total/Sec:** The percentage of bandwidth the NIC is capable of that is currently being used. If this value is more than 70% of the bandwidth of the interface, the interface is saturated or not keeping up.

- **Network Interface\Output Queue Length:** The number of packets in the output queue. If this value is over 2, the NIC is not keeping up with the workload.

Latency

Latency is the delay typically incurred in the processing of network data. A low-latency network connection is one that generally experiences short delay times, while a high-latency connection generally suffers from long delays. Many security solutions may negatively affect latency. For example, routers take a certain amount of time to process and forward any communication. Configuring additional rules on a router generally increases latency, thereby resulting in longer delays. An organization may decide not to deploy certain security solutions because of the negative effects they will have on network latency.

Auditing is a great example of a security solution that affects latency and performance.

When auditing is configured, it records certain actions as they occur. The recording of these actions may affect the latency and performance.

Measuring latency is typically done using a metric called round-trip time (RTT). It is calculated using Ping, a command-line tool that bounces a user request off a server and calculates how long it takes to return to the user device.

Jitter

Jitter occurs when the data flow in a connection is not consistent; that is, it increases and decreases in no discernable pattern. Jitter results from network congestion, timing drift, and route changes. Jitter is especially problematic in real-time communications like IP telephony and videoconferencing.

Loss

Loss occurs when packets are dropped or otherwise lost! Loss should never occur on an organization's internal network. However, it is somewhat common on public networks like the Internet. Network problems can occur outside of the organization's control and cause packet loss from end to end. The packet loss then requires retransmission of data and slow downs for applications. Just a fraction of a percent can affect real-time application performance, such as VoIP, where data lost is never retransmitted.

Additional Monitoring Solutions

While monitoring for acceptable performance is certainly important, there are other monitoring techniques that provide benefits and can help to keep the network and its systems operating correctly. In this section, we'll look at some of these.

Network Discovery

Even if you think you know the topology of your network, you may be surprised to find that it has changed over time. Network discovery is a process that scans the network and identifies all devices and systems and their network relationship to one another. There are a number of tools designed to do just this, including Discovery Profile in OpManager. There are two different approaches to conducting network discovery, covered in the next sections.

Ad Hoc

An ad hoc scan is simply one that is performed on demand as a one-time event. The issue with ad hoc scans is that someone must initiate the process each time and the network can change significantly without notice between these manual scans.

Scheduled

Scheduled scans that are automated are possible with network discovery tools and provide the benefit of reminding the humans that this needs to be done. Alerts trigger when unexpected devices are detected on networks, signaling rogue devices or misconfigurations.

Baseline Metrics

When collecting performance information, there must be a standard against which the data can be measured. This is called a *baseline*. Baseline metrics should represent the normal and expected functioning of the network or of the device being measured. Therefore, when gathering the data that will represent this baseline, it should be done during normal operation and not during periods of unusual stress to the system or network.

Anomaly Alerting/Notification

Once a baseline has been established, it becomes possible to identify when performance falls below the baseline. Anomaly detection and alerting monitor the incoming performance data and create a notification via email or text message to the team to alert them of the issue. This frees the team from constantly pouring over the log files for performance issues.

Traffic Analysis

The most common use of network traffic analysis is to identify root causes of performance issues. For example, it can help determine that there is a bottleneck on one router or switch.

It can also identify systems and users who are creating the most traffic. Armed with this information, technicians can take steps to alter the flow of traffic to eliminate bottlenecks or, in the case of a user who is creating excessive traffic, block their access to that gaming site they use all day!

While traffic analysis can focus on network performance, it also entails determining what type of traffic there is on the network. Why is that important? Some types of traffic may indicate that malware is present on the network. Other types of traffic may indicate the use of services that are against policy. It also may show that encryption is not in use when policy requires it for certain operations.

Performance Monitoring

Performance problems are the toughest and often take a great deal of time to resolve. When you experience a performance problem, the first question to come to mind is "How was it performing before?" This is where a performance baseline comes in handy. The performance baseline should be captured over a period of time that involves normal activity. An example of normal activity is Monday through Sunday during hours of business and normal times of inactivity.

The best scenario is to constantly monitor and record the performance of selected network services. There are several tools you can use to monitor performance and compile baselines of the performance of the network. Microsoft includes a tool called Performance Monitor that is built into the operating system. Other performance monitoring tools are Multi Router Traffic Grapher (MRTG) and Paessler AG's PRTG, which use the Simple Network Management Protocol, which you will learn about later in this chapter. There are also many different applications that you can purchase that can monitor performance—too many to mention.

Availability Monitoring

Some organizations have systems that must be available 24/7. Consider an e-commerce server that processes an average of $5,000 of transactions per hour. If the team is not made aware that the server is down, the loss is $5,000 an hour, not to mention the damage done to the confidence of users concerning the security and functionality of your site.

A function of a network management system/station is to calculate uptime and downtime for the network; uptime/downtime is also called the availability. The network as a whole is made up of many different services on the various servers. The uptime calculated by the network management system is the total time all network services are up and responding to requests. The downtime is how long the network services were down and not responding to requests. The network management system will check each service and keep a running tally of down services, as shown in Figure 14.1. It will then calculate the outages and display the total uptime of the network.

FIGURE 14.1   Network management system/station availability

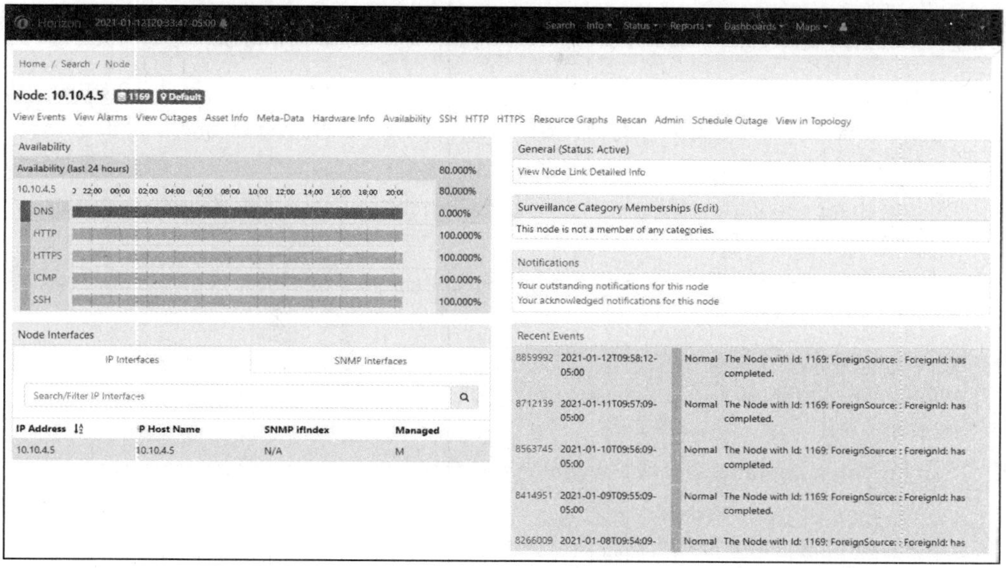

Configuration Monitoring

When multiple technicians are manually implementing system configurations and making changes to them, it becomes easy for systems to fall out of compliance with the intended configuration. While some incorrect settings will become immediately noticeable (incorrect IP address, etc.), others can take some time to show their effects.

Configuration monitoring is the process of either manually checking settings on a schedule or using a monitoring tool to check configurations. Altera is just one example of a network monitoring tool that can verify that a system conforms to the appropriate configuration.

EXERCISE 14.1

Working with Performance Monitor

In this exercise, you will use a built-in tool in the Windows operating system to view performance. The Performance Monitor exists in every version of Windows and can be used to establish performance metrics for monitoring and establishing baselines.

1. Select Start, type **perfmon,** and then select Performance Monitor from the search results.

2. Choose the Performance Monitor section under Monitoring Tools.

3. Click the plus sign [+] or right-click in the graphical display area and select Add Counters.

4. Expand the Processor section, and then select the %ProcessorTime object.

5. Click Add >> and then OK.

6. Open Windows File Explorer, click the C: drive, type * into the search box, and then press Enter.

7. Quickly change to Performance Monitor and watch the impact of this search on the processor.

   This action is time-consuming and therefore will help you notice the changes that take place in Performance Monitor.

8. Run the same operation again. This time, however, change your view within Performance Monitor to a Histogram bar by clicking the button directly to the left of the plus sign [+].

9. Run the same operation again, changing your view within Performance Monitor to Report.

10. Exit Performance Monitor.

SNMP

The Simple Network Management Protocol (SNMP) allows the collection of metrics, also known as counters. SNMP can also be used for reporting events from a device back to a centralized *network management station (NMS)*. Although the expansion of the acronym SNMP includes the word *simple*, it is not a simple protocol because there are many components, as shown in Figure 14.2. But don't worry; I will discuss each component in detail in the following sections. As always, you might feel like you need to know everything about this subject before you can understand a specific topic about this subject. For that reason, I recommend reading the following sections twice.

Agent

The SNMP agent is a small piece of software that resides on the device or operating system to be monitored. The agent is responsible for answering requests from a network management station, or the agent will send messages to the NMS. The agent is configured with a specific set of counters (metrics) called object identifiers (OIDs) for which it is responsible. It will be responsible for collecting the values for these counters and presenting them upon request. The agent can also be set up to transmit to an NMS if a counter crosses a threshold value.

FIGURE 14.2 SNMP components

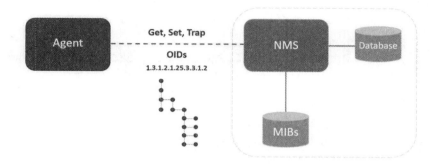

NMS

OpenNMS and PRTG Network Monitor are two examples of network management systems. An NMS is responsible for collecting statistics such as bandwidth, memory, and CPU from devices and operating systems. An NMS can also be configured to store these counters in a database, so you have the ability to review past performance. When a service goes down or stops responding to NMS queries, an NMS can send an alert or notification for network administrator intervention. We can also set thresholds for specific counters, and when a counter crosses the threshold, alerts and notifications are sent to the administrator from the NMS. For instance, if we are collecting the metric of temperature and the value crosses a threshold we set in the NMS, an email can be sent to the administrator with a warning.

Network management systems are generally used for the ongoing collection of statistics from network devices and operating systems. This constant recording of statistics creates baselines for comparison over time. It also helps us identify trends and problematic periods of time. As shown in Figure 14.3, at around 17:00 hours bandwidth spiked up to 9.2 Mbps. Looking at the weekly graph, these spikes seem normal for brief periods of time.

Commands

Network management stations can operate with two basic command methods: the SNMP get command and the SNMP trap command, as shown in Figure 14.4. An SNMP get command is a solicited request to the OS or network device for an *object ID (OID)* value; SNMP get commands are considered polling requests since they happen at a set interval. An SNMP trap command is unsolicited information from the OS or network device. An SNMP trap command is sent when the threshold on the device has been exceeded, such as a bandwidth setting or disk space, or in the event an interface goes down. These SNMP trap commands can be configured on the SNMP monitor to create alerts and notifications for the administrator.

FIGURE 14.3 SNMP monitor graph

`Daily' Graph (5 Minute Average)

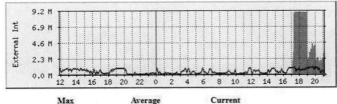

	Max	Average	Current
In	8914.4 kb/s (89.1%)	621.1 kb/s (6.2%)	2996.9 kb/s (30.0%)
Out	1047.7 kb/s (10.5%)	393.4 kb/s (3.9%)	594.2 kb/s (5.9%)

`Weekly' Graph (30 Minute Average)

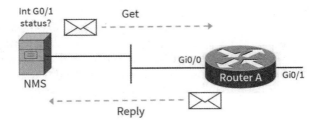

	Max	Average	Current
In	8914.4 kb/s (89.1%)	533.2 kb/s (5.3%)	1658.6 kb/s (16.6%)
Out	1115.5 kb/s (11.2%)	509.7 kb/s (5.1%)	335.2 kb/s (3.4%)

FIGURE 14.4 SNMP get and trap methods

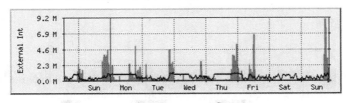

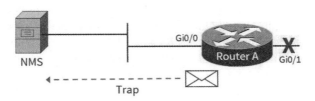

There is a third command method called the SNMP set command, but it is not normally used by the NMS. It allows a variable to be set on the device or operating system. It functions similarly to an SNMP get command, with the exception you are setting a value. The SNMP set command is normally initiated by a technician or script when setting a value, such as a password on a group of network devices.

SNMP operates on two different ports, 161 and 162, depending on if you are sending an SNMP get command to retrieve a value for a counter or a device is reporting an event. All SNMP get and set commands (polling type commands) are sent via UDP port 161. SNMP trap commands are sent from the agent to the NMS on UDP port 162. By default, SNMP uses UDP since the messages sent are simple commands that require simple responses. However, TCP can be configured for moving data in an environment where data delivery is not always assured, such as across the Internet.

Community Name

The community name is a shared passphrase authentication for SNMP versions 1 and 2c. SNMPv3 uses community names, but it is not the main authentication method, as you will learn later. The SNMP community name allows an NMS or technician to send SNMP commands to an SNMP instance running on a device or operating system. The default community name for read-only (get commands) is public. The default community name for read-write (set commands) is private. So, we often refer to the community name as public and private regardless of the actual community name. Obviously if someone obtains the community name, they can read sensitive information such as configuration information and possibly write new configurations if they obtain a read-write community name.

Versions

SNMP version 1, known as SNMPv1, is obviously the first version of SNMP, and it is the oldest. SNMPv1 was defined in RFC 1155 and 1157 back in 1990. It is old and should no longer be used; it is covered for historical purposes only. SNMPv2 expanded on SNMPv1 by adding support for 64-bit counters for handling large counter numbers. SNMPv2c added support for proxy agents. Both version 1 and version 2c lack any kind of encryption or authentication outside of the community name string. They should both be avoided when setting up SNMP, but many vendors still promote setting up SNMPv2c.

SNMPv3 was released in 2002 and added the much-needed encryption and authentication that prior versions lacked. User accounts can be set up along with a type of access control called an SNMP view. The SNMP view is a way of scoping access down to a specific OID or group of OIDs. SNMPv3 is a lot more difficult to set up, but it is a lot more secure than prior versions. My personal recommendation is to use it over SNMPv1 and v2c, but every situation has its considerations. SNMPv3 is defined in RFCs 3413 to 3415.

Here's a summary of the three versions of SNMP:

- **SNMPv1:** Supports plaintext authentication with community strings and uses only UDP.

- **SNMPv2c:** Supports plaintext authentication with MD5 or SHA with no encryption but provides GET BULK, which is a way to gather many types of information at once and minimize the number of GET requests. It offers a more detailed error message reporting method, but it's not more secure than v1. It uses UDP even though it can be configured to use TCP.

- **SNMPv3:** Supports strong authentication with MD5 or SHA, providing confidentiality (encryption) and data integrity of messages via DES or DES-256 encryption between agents and managers. GET BULK is a supported feature of SNMPv3, and this version also uses TCP. (Note: MD5 and DES are no longer considered secure.)

OIDs and the MIB

Object identifiers (OIDs) are uniquely managed objects on a device or operating system that can be queried or configured. The OIDs are organized into a hierarchal tree and are noted in dotted decimal notation, such as `.1.3.6.1.2.1.2.2`. Each number represents a portion of the hierarchy, from least significant on the left to most significant on the right. For example, the OID `.1.3.6.1.2.1.2.2` is broken down to `iso(1) identified-organization(3) dod(6) internet(1) mgmt(2) mib-2(1) interface(2) ifTable(2)`. So, if this OID is queried, a value will be returned for each interface on the system. From there, you can choose which interface you want to query and the specific attribute. To query interface 3, the OID would look like `.1.3.6.1.2.1.2.2.3`, adding a 3 on the rightmost OID string. The attributes would then follow, such as `.1.3.6.1.2.1.2.2.3.5` for `ifSpeed`. This might look like dark magic, but it is all very well documented in the *management information base (MIB)*.

The guide of attributes is always contained in the MIB, which is a database of OIDs published by the vendor of the OS or network device. The MIB defines the OID counters along with the type of data the OID offers for collection. Otherwise, the value you get back is just an arbitrary value. The MIB gives definition to the value, such as an interface error rate, bandwidth, or many other attributes of an interface. The NMS will require a specific MIB for the device or OS in order to collect statistics for the counter. Without a proper MIB installed, the SNMP process on the NMS cannot be configured to retrieve the values.

Authentication

Imagine the following scenario: One day, you receive an alarming email from your security team, notifying you of a potential breach in your network. Panic sets in as you realize that confidential information could be compromised, jeopardizing your business and its reputation. This is where SNMP authentication comes into play. By implementing authentication measures, you can ensure that only authorized devices and users can access your network.

SNMP authentication is crucial for securing your network and protecting sensitive data from unauthorized access. There are various authentication methods for SNMP, including community strings and additional authentication methods that were added in SNMPv3. Implementing SNMP authentication involves configuring SNMP agents and managers to ensure secure network communication. Securing SNMP in a network environment is important to protect against vulnerabilities and ensure reliable network management.

Authentication is essential for verifying the identity and integrity of SNMP entities, preventing unauthorized access, and ensuring secure communication.

SNMPv1 and SNMPv2c provide limited security features, relying on community strings for access control. SNMPv3 introduced enhanced authentication and security features to address the vulnerabilities of previous versions including authentication and encryption. The SNMPv3 version introduced the user security model (USM) as a replacement for the community string method. The user-based security model supports no-authentication, authentication, and privacy security levels. It supports authentication protocols such as MD5. It ensures that only authorized users can access and manage SNMP agents.

SNMPv3 can also employ encryption protocols like DES and AES to ensure confidential transmission of SNMP messages. The use of SNMPv3 adds an extra layer of authenticity and confidentiality to SNMP communications. SNMP authentication methods should be used in conjunction with other security measures, such as access control lists (ACLs) and firewall rules, to strengthen network security.

As mentioned, SNMP is not a simple protocol as its name states, mainly because it has many different components. For the exam, you should know the various components and not their intricacies, as an entire book could be devoted to those topics. That being said, if you would like to learn more about the MIB file referenced in this section, visit www .net-snmp.org/docs/mibs/IF-MIB.txt and browse the file. Net-SNMP is the de facto standard used by many devices and operating systems. The website at www.net-snmp.org is a great source for documentation on the subject.

Application Programming Interface Integration

An alternative to using SNMP to extract data from systems is to use application programming interfaces (APIs), also called webhooks. An API is a way for two or more computer programs to communicate with each other. Utilizing APIs makes automating network tasks much more accessible than using SNMP. By utilizing an API, network engineers can create repeatable code blocks that can be interconnected and operate automatically based on certain conditions.

Protocol Analyzer/Packet Capture

Packet sniffers are software-based tools for capturing network traffic, also known as packet capturing. Packet sniffers can be used with wireless and wired network connections to capture packets. An example of a packet sniffer is the open-source Wireshark packet sniffer and analyzer.

The packet sniffer's ability to capture network traffic is also directly dependent on the NIC. The NIC must support promiscuous mode, which allows the capture of frames with any destination MAC address. Although newer NICs will allow promiscuous mode, the feature should be checked for the model of NIC with the vendor's specifications.

Protocol analyzers decipher frames of data that have been captured with a packet sniffer. Protocol analyzers such as Wireshark and Microsoft Message Analyzer also provide packet-sniffing capabilities. The protocol analyzer allows the network administrator to see the details of the data being transmitted or received. This allows the administrator to confirm that the data is being transmitted or received correctly or enables the administrator to focus on the problem area.

The protocol analyzer comes preloaded with parsers that help decipher the captured data. The parser is nothing more than a list of protocol numbers that define what protocols are being used from layer 2 through layer 7. Once the protocol is known, the data contained in the rest of the layer can be deciphered and displayed in a readable format.

For example, if a frame is captured with a Type field of 0x0806, then the frame is an ARP request, and the rest of the data contained within is parsed according to an ARP frame layout. If the Type field is 0x0800, then the frame is an IPv4 frame, and the data is parsed according to an IPv4 header layout. The data can be parsed further for the Transport and Application layers. In effect, the protocol analyzer de-encapsulates the data captured so it is readable, as shown in Figure 14.5.

Port Mirroring

When you need to use a sniffer or protocol analyzer to capture packets traversing the network, you face a challenge when connecting to one of your switchports. Switches create a separate collision domain for each switchport, which is great for performance but not so good when you are capturing traffic.

A consequence of creating a separate collision domain for each port is that *only* traffic destined for the port to which you have the sniffer connected will be captured. To capture *all* traffic, you must send a copy of all traffic from the other ports to the port to which you have connected the sniffer. This is called port mirroring.

Cisco calls this Switched Port Analyzer (SPAN). You can even send packets to the sniffer port from other switches, a process Cisco called Remote SPAN (RSPAN) when the switches are in the same subnet and Encapsulated Remote Switched Port Analyzer (ERSPAN) when the switches are not in the same subnet.

FIGURE 14.5   Protocol analyzer of a TCP packet

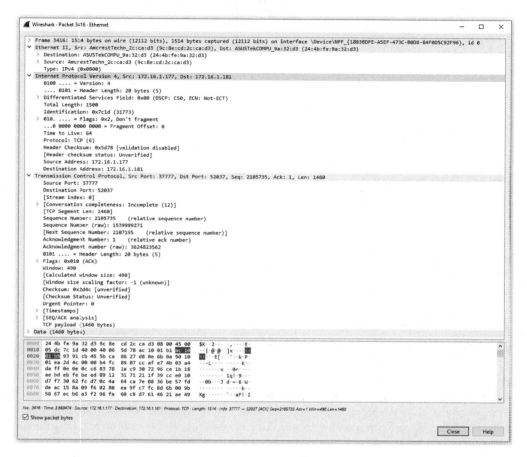

Flow Data

While SNMP is used to extract data from systems, tools that create flow data, such as NetFlow, capture conversations between systems. A flow is a unidirectional sequence of packets that all share seven values that define a unique key for the flow:

- Ingress interface
- Source IP address
- Destination IP address
- IP protocol number
- Source port for UDP or TCP, 0 for other protocols

- Destination port for UDP or TCP, type and code for ICMP, or 0 for other protocols
- IP type of service

Routers and switches that support NetFlow can collect flows on all interfaces where NetFlow is enabled and later export those flows toward at least one NetFlow collector—typically a server that does the actual traffic analysis.

> The NetFlow protocol is a Cisco proprietary protocol used to collect IP traffic information and the monitoring of network flows of data.

Log Aggregation

All the systems in the network have log files that record all system events. Monitoring these logs individually wherever they exist is a monumental task. One of the techniques that have been developed is to aggregate those logs in one place to make these tasks easier. The most common tool used for this is Syslog, which is a system to which all log files are directed. You will learn more about Syslog in this section.

Network Device Logs

While SMTP should be in your toolbox when monitoring the network, there is also a wealth of information to be found in the logs on the network devices. You will now learn about the main log types and methods to manage the volume of data that exists in these logs.

In networking, a baseline can refer to the standard level of performance of a certain device or to the normal operating capacity for your whole network. For instance, a specific server's baseline describes norms for factors such as how busy its processors are, how much of the memory it uses, and how much data usually goes through the NIC at a given time.

A network baseline delimits the amount of bandwidth available and when. For networks and networked devices, baselines include information about these four key components:

- Processor
- Memory
- Hard-disk (or other storage) subsystem
- Wired/wireless utilization

After everything is up and running, it's a good idea to establish performance baselines on all vital devices and your network in general. To do this, measure things such as network usage at three different strategic times to get an accurate assessment. For instance, peak usage usually happens around 8 a.m. Monday through Friday, or whenever most people log in to the network in the morning. After hours or on weekends is often when usage is the lowest. Knowing these values can help you troubleshoot bottlenecks or determine why certain system resources are more limited than they should be. Knowing what your baseline is can even tell you if someone's complaints about the network running like a slug are really valid—nice!

It's good to know that you can use network-monitoring software to establish baselines. Even some server operating systems come with software to help with network monitoring, which can help find baselines, perform log management, and even do network graphing as well so you can compare the logs and graphs at a later period of time on your network.

In my experience, it's wise to re-baseline network performance at least once a year. And always pinpoint new performance baselines after any major upgrade to your network's infrastructure.

Log Reviews

High-quality documentation should include a baseline for network performance because you and your client need to know what "normal" looks like to detect problems before they develop into disasters.

Don't forget to verify that the network conforms to all internal and external regulations and that you've developed and itemized solid management procedures and security policies for future network administrators to refer to and follow.

Traffic Logs

Some of your infrastructure devices will have logs that record the network traffic that has traversed the device. Examples include firewalls and intrusion detection and prevention devices.

Many organizations choose to direct the traffic logs from these devices to a Syslog server or to security information and event management (SIEM) systems (both covered later in this section).

Audit Logs

Audit logs are those that record the activities of the users. Windows Server 2022 (and most other Windows operating systems) comes with a tool called Event Viewer that provides you with several logs containing vital information about events happening on your computer. Other server operating systems have similar logs, and many connectivity devices like routers and switches also have graphical logs that gather statistics on what's happening to them. These logs can go by various names, like history logs, general logs, or server logs. Figure 14.6 shows an Event Viewer Security log display from a Windows Server 2022 machine.

On Windows servers and client systems, a minimum of three separate logs hold different types of information:

- **Application Log:** Contains events triggered by applications or programs determined by their programmers. Example applications include LiveUpdate, the Microsoft Office suite, and SQL and Exchange servers.

FIGURE 14.6 Event Viewer Security log

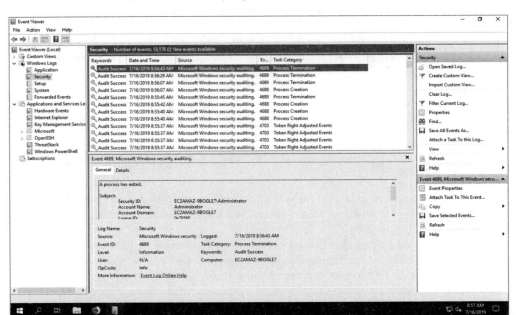

- **Security Log:** Contains security events like valid or invalid logon attempts and potential security problems.
- **System Log:** Contains events generated by Windows system components, including drivers and services that started or failed to start.

The basic "big three" can give us lots of juicy information about who's logging on, who's accessing the computer, and which services are running properly (or not). If you want to find out whether your Dynamic Host Configuration Protocol (DHCP) server started up its DHCP service properly, just check out its System log.

Syslog

Syslog is a client-server protocol that allows just about any device on the network to send logs as they happen. The protocol operates on UDP port 514, and it's considered a "fire-and-forget" type protocol. This means that the device sending the message never receives an acknowledgment that the message was received. So, you really need to make sure that the logs are being collected at the Syslog server, also known as the Syslog collector.

It is also important to note that by default network devices and Linux/UNIX operating systems will write a file called Syslog because it contains local events for the device. This comes in handy when troubleshooting, but it also causes challenges if the device completely fails. Therefore, it's always best to ship the logs off the network device or operating system with the Syslog protocol pointed to a Syslog collector.

Syslog Collector

The Syslog server is also called the Syslog collector. This is the server to which all log files are sent from the various servers, router, switches, and other devices that send the logs. Figure 14.7 shows the data flow.

FIGURE 14.7   Syslog collector

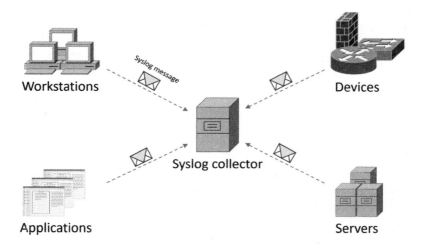

Network devices can be configured to generate a Syslog message and forward it to various destinations. These four examples are popular ways to gather messages from Cisco devices:

- Logging buffer (on by default)
- Console line (on by default)
- Terminal lines (using the terminal monitor command)
- Syslog server

Syslog Messages

The Syslog message format is standardized, as shown in Figure 14.8. The message will start with a timestamp so you know when it was created. On some network devices, sequence numbers can be used in lieu of timestamps. Sequence numbers are useful because some events can happen simultaneously and the sequence number helps sort out which happened first. The next field, called the Device-id, is optional. By default, for most network devices, the Device-id is not sent. However, it's useful to send it if you are sending these messages to a centralized syslog server. The Device-id can be a hostname, an IP address, or any string that identifies the device. The next field actually comprises three different parts: the facility, severity, and mnemonic. The facility is the internal system inside the device that has generated the log message. The severity is standardized based upon a 0–7 severity level that we will cover in the next section. The mnemonic is nothing more than the action the facility took, and the value is a simple string. The last section of a Syslog message is the message text itself. This is what exactly happened to generate the syslog message.

FIGURE 14.8 Anatomy of a Syslog message

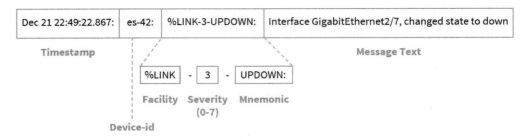

Logging Levels/Severity Levels

Most services like DNS and DHCP have some sort of debug feature to help you diagnose problems. The debug feature will produce some form of logs, either on the screen or to a file. Keep in mind that when logs are produced, you will end up with a certain level of noise from normal events. So, some services allow you to specify a logging level in an effort to reduce the noise or dive deeper into the problem. This of course all depends on what you specify, your mode of diagnostic, and your tolerance for the noise in the log file.

The Syslog protocol/service is used solely for logging events on network devices and operating systems. Therefore, it has a built-in logging level called a severity level. These severity levels range from the most critical level of 0 (emergency) to the least critical of 7 (debug). This gives you a total of eight levels to choose from, as shown in Table 14.1.

TABLE 14.1 Syslog severity levels

Level	Severity	Description
0	Emergency	System is unusable.
1	Alert	Action must be taken immediately.
2	Critical	Critical conditions.
3	Error	Error conditions.
4	Warning	Warning conditions.

Level	Severity	Description
5	Notice	Normal, but significant conditions.
6	Informational	Informational messages.
7	Debug	Debug-level messages.

A level can be throttled back and forth depending on what you are trying to capture. The severity level is also inclusive of lower levels. This means that if you choose a level of 3, it will include the logging that would be produced at level 2 and level 1. For example, if you configure the severity level to the lowest value of 0, you will receive only the emergency messages. However, if you configure the severity level to 4, you will receive all of the warning (4), error (3), critical (2), alert (1), and emergency (0) messages.

SIEM

Security information and event management (SIEM) is a term for software products and services combining security information management (SIM) and security event management (SEM). SIEM technology provides real-time analysis of security alerts generated by network hardware and applications. You can get this as a software solution or a hardware appliance, and some businesses sell managed services using SIEM. Any one of these solutions provides log security data and can generate reports for compliance purposes.

The acronyms SEM, SIM, and SIEM are used interchangeably; however, SEM is typically used to describe the management that deals with real-time monitoring and correlation of events, notifications, and console views.

The term SIM is used to describe long-term storage, analysis, and reporting of log data.

Recently, the term voice security information and event management (vSIEM) was introduced to provide voice data visibility.

SIEM can collect useful data about the following items:

- Data aggregation
- Correlation
- Alerting
- Dashboards
- Compliance
- Retention
- Forensic analysis

Notifications

SIEM systems not only assess the aggregated logs in real time but also generate alerts or notifications when an issue is discovered. This allows for continuous monitoring of the environment in a way not possible with other log centralization approaches such as Syslog.

Summary

In this chapter, you learned that one of the keys to stopping downtime is to listen to what the devices may be telling you about their current state of health. You learned how to use performance metrics to monitor the health of a device's CPU, memory, and NIC. You learned about metrics that are used to monitor network interface performance and about settings that may impact that performance.

Finally, you were introduced to the use of SNMP and NetFlow to monitor both device health and network traffic from a central location, and you learned how to send log files either to a Syslog server or to a SIEM system.

Exam Essentials

Understand how to use performance metrics.   These include device metrics such as temperature, central processing unit (CPU) usage, and memory and network metrics, such as bandwidth, latency, jitter, and packet loss.

Describe the operation of SNMP.   Identify the roles that traps, object identifiers (OIDs), and management information bases (MIBs) play in monitoring the network with SNMP.

Know the various versions of SNMP.   The two versions covered on the Network+ exam are v2c and v3. Version 3 allows for better authentication and encryption of messages.

Utilize network device logs in addressing system issues.   Locate relevant information by reviewing logs such as traffic logs and audit logs. Describe the use of Syslog in centralizing these logs.

Written Lab

Complete the table by filling in the appropriate term for the description provided. You can find the answers in Appendix A.

Description	Term
The percentage of time the CPU spends executing a non-idle thread.	
The amount of physical memory, in megabytes, currently available.	
The percentage of bandwidth the NIC is capable of that is currently being used.	
The delay typically incurred in the processing of network data.	
Occurs when the data flow in a connection is not consistent; that is, it increases and decreases in no discernable pattern.	
Supports plaintext authentication with MD5 or SHA with no encryption but provides GET BULK.	
Sent by SNMP agents to the NMS if a problem occurs.	
Identifier mechanism standardized by the International Telecommunications Union (ITU) and ISO/IEC for naming any object, concept, or "thing" with a globally unambiguous persistent name.	
Hierarchical structure into which SNMP OIDs are organized.	
Refers to the standard level of performance of a certain device or to the normal operating capacity for your whole network.	
Centralizes and stores log messages and can even time-stamp and sequence them.	
Provides real-time analysis of security alerts generated by network hardware and applications.	
Errors that mean packets have been damaged.	

Review Questions

You can find the answers to the review questions in Appendix B.

1. Which measurement describes the delay a packet incurs from source to destination?
   A. Bandwidth
   B. Latency
   C. Jitter
   D. Loss

2. You are using a network management station (NMS) to collect data for network devices. What must be loaded before you can capture data from the network devices via the Simple Network Management Protocol (SNMP)?
   A. OID
   B. MIB
   C. Traps
   D. Gets

3. Which service can identify major users of the network, meaning top talkers?
   A. Syslog
   B. SIEM
   C. NetFlow
   D. SNMP

4. Which of the following refers to the standard level of performance of a certain device or to the normal operating capacity for your whole network?
   A. Baseline
   B. Target
   C. Normal
   D. Utilization

5. Which version of SNMP supports authentication and encryption?
   A. SNMP version 1
   B. SNMP version 2e
   C. SNMP version 2c
   D. SNMP version 3

6. Which component receives information from an SNMP agent?
   A. Syslog
   B. Network management station
   C. Object identifier
   D. Management information base

7. Which metric is the variation from the delay between the source and destination?

   A. Latency

   B. Jitter

   C. Bandwidth

   D. Throughput

8. Which SNMP component is used to address a performance counter?

   A. Syslog

   B. Network management station

   C. Object identifier

   D. Management information base

9. What type of SNMP message is sent to a network management station when an interface goes down?

   A. Get-request message

   B. Get-response message

   C. Set-request message

   D. Trap message

10. Which security method does SNMP version 2c employ?

   A. Encryption

   B. User authentication

   C. Community strings

   D. Message integrity

11. What is the database of variables that SNMP uses to allow for collection of data?

   A. Object identifiers (OIDs)

   B. Management information base

   C. SNMP agent

   D. SNMP community string

12. Which of the following can be used in conjunction with an SNMP agent configuration for added security?

   A. Encrypted communities

   B. Access control lists

   C. SNMP callback security

   D. SHA-256

13. Which protocol and port number does SNMP use for trap and inform messages to the NMS?

   A. UDP/161

   B. TCP/162

   C. UDP/162

   D. UDP/514

14. Which syslog severity level is used to convey a failure of a component?

    A. Level 3

    B. Level 4

    C. Level 0

    D. Level 7

15. Which SNMP component is installed on a network device that will respond to NMS queries?

    A. Object identifiers (OIDs)

    B. Management information base

    C. SNMP agent

    D. SNMP community string

16. What type of SNMP message is sent from a network management station to an agent for retrieving information?

    A. Get-request message

    B. Get-response message

    C. Set-request message

    D. Trap message

17. Which of the following is *not* a commonly used NetFlow identifier?

    A. Source IP

    B. Destination port number

    C. Layer 2 protocol field

    D. Input logical interface

18. Which provides the ability to mirror port traffic on a switch?

    A. Syslog

    B. SNMP

    C. NetFlow

    D. SPAN

19. Which device components should never be allowed to reach full capacity? (Choose two.)

    A. Memory

    B. Voltage

    C. CPU

    D. Delay

20. Which network metric will describe the utilization for a connection?

    A. Latency

    B. Jitter

    C. Throughput

    D. Bandwidth

Chapter 15

Organizational Documents and Policies

THE FOLLOWING COMPTIA NETWORK+ EXAM OBJECTIVES ARE COVERED IN THIS CHAPTER:

✓ **Domain 2.0 Network Implementations**

✓ **2.4 Explain important factors of physical installations.**

- Important installation implications
    - Locations
    - Intermediate distribution frame (IDF)
    - Main distribution frame (MDF)
- Rack size
- Port-side exhaust/intake
- Cabling
    - Patch panel
    - Fiber distribution panel
- Lockable

✓ **Domain 3.0 Network Operations**

✓ **3.1 Explain the purpose of organizational processes and procedures.**

- Documentation
    - Physical vs. logical diagrams
    - Rack diagrams
    - Cable maps and diagrams
    - Network diagrams

- Layer 1
- Layer 2
- Layer 3
- Asset inventory
  - Hardware
  - Software
  - Licensing
  - Warranty support
- IP address management (IPAM)
- Service-level agreement (SLA)
- Wireless survey/heat map
- Life-cycle management
  - End-of-life (EOL)
  - End-of-support (EOS)
  - Software management
    - Patches and bug fixes
    - Operating system (OS)
    - Firmware
  - Decommissioning
- Change management
  - Request process tracking/service request
- Configuration management
  - Production configuration
  - Backup configuration
  - Baseline/golden configuration

It's up to us, individually and corporately, to nail down exactly what solid guidelines there should be for policies and procedures for network installation and operation. Some organizations are bound by regulations that also affect how they conduct their business, and that kind of thing clearly needs to be involved in their choices.

Of note, one of the most important aspects of any policy or procedure is that it's given high-level management support. This is because neither will be very effective if there aren't any consequences for not following the rules!

 To find Todd Lammle CompTIA videos and practice questions, please see www.lammle.com.

Plans and Procedures

Let me take a minute to make sure you understand the difference between policies and procedures.

Policies govern how the network is configured and operated as well as how people are expected to behave on it. They're in place to direct things like how users access resources and which employees and groups get various types of network access and/or privileges. Basically, policies give people guidelines as to what they are expected to do. Procedures are precise descriptions of the appropriate steps to follow in a given situation, such as what to do when an employee is terminated or what to do in the event of a natural disaster. They often dictate precisely how to execute policies as well.

- Procedures are the actions to be taken in specific situations:
  - Disciplinary action to be taken if a policy is broken
  - What to do during an audit
  - How issues are reported to management
  - What to do when someone has locked themselves out of their account
  - How to properly install or remove software on servers
  - What to do if files on the servers suddenly appear to be "missing" or altered

- How to respond when a network computer has a virus
- Actions to take if it appears that a hacker has broken into the network
- Actions to take if there is a physical emergency like a fire or flood

So you get the idea, right? For every policy on your network, there should be a credible related procedure that clearly dictates the steps to take in order to fulfill it. And you know that policies and procedures are as unique as the wide array of companies and organizations that create and employ them. But all this doesn't mean you can't borrow good ideas and plans from others and tweak them a bit to meet your requirements.

 An example of a network access policy is a time-of-day restriction on logging into the network.

Change Management

Change should be introduced in a managed fashion. For this to occur, an organization must have a formal change management process in place. The purpose of this process is to ensure that all changes are approved by the proper personnel and are implemented in a safe and logical manner. Let's look at some of the key items that should be included in these procedures.

Document Reason for a Change

Clearly, every change should be made for a reason, and before the change is even discussed, that reason should be documented. During all stages of the approval process (discussed later), this information should be clearly communicated and attached to the change under consideration.

Change Request

A change should start its life as a change request. This request will move through various stages of the approval process and should include certain pieces of information that will guide those tasked with approving or denying it.

Configuration Procedures

The exact steps required to implement the change and the exact devices involved should be clearly detailed. Complete documentation should be produced and submitted with a formal report to the change management board.

Rollback Process

Changes always carry a risk. Before any changes are implemented, plans for reversing changes and recovering from any adverse effects from them should be identified. Those making the changes should be completely briefed in these rollback procedures, and they should exhibit a clear understanding of them prior to implementing the changes.

Potential Impact

While unexpected adverse effects of a change can't always be anticipated, a good-faith effort should be made to identity all possible systems that could be impacted by the change. One of the benefits of performing this exercise is that it can identify systems that may need to be more closely monitored for their reaction to the change as the change is being implemented.

Notification

When all systems and departments that may be impacted by the change are identified, system owners and department heads should be notified of all changes that could potentially affect them. One of the associated benefits of this is that it creates additional monitors for problems during the change process.

Approval Process

Requests for changes should be fully vetted by a cross section of users, IT personnel, management, and security experts. In many cases, it's wise to form a change control board to complete the following tasks:

- Assure that changes made are approved, tested, documented, and implemented correctly.
- Meet periodically to discuss change status accounting reports.
- Maintain responsibility for assuring that changes made do not jeopardize the soundness of the verification system.

Maintenance Window

A maintenance window is an amount of time a system will be down or unavailable during the implementation of changes. Before this window of time is specified, all affected systems should be examined with respect to their criticality in supporting mission-critical operations. It may be that the time required to make the change may exceed the allowable downtime a system can suffer during normal business hours, and the change may need to be implemented during a weekend or in the evening.

Authorized Downtime

Once the time required to make the change has been compared to the maximum allowable downtime a system can suffer and the optimum time for the change is identified, the authorized downtime can be specified. This amounts to a final decision on when the change will be made.

Notification of Change

When the change has been successfully completed and a sufficient amount of time has elapsed for issues to manifest themselves, all stakeholders should be notified that the change is complete. At that time, these stakeholders (those possibly affected by the change) can continue to monitor the situation for any residual problems.

Documentation

The job isn't complete until the paperwork is complete. In this case, the following should be updated to reflect the changed state of the network:

- Network configurations
- Additions to network
- Physical location changes

Incident Response Plan

Often when an attack or security breach occurs in the network, valuable time and information are lost in the critical first minutes and hours after the incident occurs. In some cases, evidence is inadvertently destroyed, making prosecution of the offending party impossible. In other cases, attacks that could have been interrupted and prevented before damage occurs are allowed to continue.

An incident response plan or policy is designed to prevent this by establishing in advance the procedures that should be followed when an attack occurs. It may categorize incidents in such a way that certain event types (such as an active port scan) may require a response (such as disabling certain services) within 10 minutes, while other events (such as an attempt to access a file without proper credentials) may require only a notation and follow-up in the next few days. The point is to establish these rules ahead of time to ensure that events are handled in a way that minimizes damage and preserves evidence.

Disaster Recovery Plan

A disaster is an emergency that goes beyond the normal response of resources. The causes of disasters are categorized into three main areas according to origin:

- Technological disasters (device failures)
- Manmade disasters (arson, terrorism, sabotage)
- Natural disasters (hurricanes, floods, earthquakes)

The severity of financial and reputational damage to an organization is largely determined by the amount of time it takes the organization to recover from the disaster. A properly designed disaster recovery plan (DRP) minimizes the effect of a disaster. The DRP is implemented when the emergency occurs and includes the steps to restore systems so the organization can resume normal operations. The goal of a DRP is to minimize or prevent property damage and prevent loss of life.

Business Continuity Plan

One of the parts of a DRP is a plan to keep the business operational while the organization recovers from the disaster; this is known as a business continuity plan (BCP). Continuity planning deals with identifying the impact of any disaster and ensuring that a viable recovery plan for each function and system is implemented. By prioritizing each process and its supporting technologies, the company can ensure that mission-critical systems are recovered first and systems that are considered luxuries can be recovered as time allows.

One document that should be created to drive this prioritization is the business impact analysis (BIA). In this document, the impact each system has on the ability of the organization to stay operational is determined. The results list the critical and necessary business functions, their resource dependencies, and their level of criticality to the overall organization.

Inventory Management

Inventory management for IT assets has two specific purposes. The first is the tracing of assets valued by the company. The second is allowing IT to internally account for replacement and upgrades.

Every company has *fixed tangible assets*, such as land, furniture, and equipment. The management of the network equipment is the obvious responsibility of the IT department. When equipment is initially purchased, the accounting department will record it an asset of the company's general ledger.

However, over time the asset will lose its initial value. The accounting department will depreciate the value of assets based on their perceived lifespan. The IT department should work directly with the accounting department when assets are destroyed or no longer function since they will no longer be considered an asset.

These assets don't always need to be hardware assets; an asset can be anything worth value. Examples of assets are software packages purchased, licensing for activation of products that have been purchased, and even the warranty support on a product.

All network equipment should be tracked from the cradle to the grave by the IT department. When equipment enters the company, it should be labeled with an asset tag. This *asset tag* should then be entered into the inventory management software. The inventory management software is often a module of the accounting package used by the company.

The IT department also uses inventory management to assess upgrades and the replacement of assets. Inventory management is used when a patch or update to firmware needs to be installed. An inventory management system will create a report of how many systems are affected. Another example is a report of all client systems and the amount of RAM for the evaluation of a software upgrade. This type of inventory management is more detailed than a purchasing record. These applications are often internal IT systems that collect data from the operating system through the use of an agent.

System Life Cycle

The life cycle for IT systems is cyclical and differs slightly depending on the assets. The typical life cycle for IT systems consists of purchasing, deploying, managing, and retiring. When an asset is purchased, it becomes an asset to the organization and is depreciated over its useful life in the organization. Once the asset is purchased, it is deployed. The deployment phase could involve plugging the equipment into the network and turning it on. Or the deployment phase could involve imaging, configuring, or installing software for the IT system. The management of the system is usually performed directly by the IT department once the system is deployed. However, the management of the system can also involve the end users—for example, in the case of an accounting software package.

Eventually all IT systems near the end of their useful life and are retired. IT systems will have two important dates to keep in mind when resource planning. The first date is the end-of-life (EOL); this is the date that the vendor will no longer sell the product. The second date is the end-of-support (EOS); this is the date that the vendor will no longer provide support for the product. The EOL and EOS can coincide with each other, but often they are two separate dates. In either case, planning to replace the product should be prompted by the EOL. The retirement of the old product should be done once the vendor ends support (EOS).

The retirement of IT systems can be done several different ways depending on the type of equipment. End-user computing equipment might be sold for scrap costs, or they could be appropriated elsewhere in the organization. In the case of server and SAN equipment, these systems are usually moved to less critical workloads, such as development or development testing. An organization will commonly have generations of equipment, retiring the prior generation of equipment to another part of the organization. It is also important to note that the retirement process dovetails with the planning and repurchasing process that begins the life cycle again.

The last phase of the equipment life cycle is asset disposal. There are two responsibilities of the IT department and the organization pertaining to asset disposal. The first responsibility is to prevent data loss when equipment is disposed of. A procedure should be in place to wipe organization data from systems that are disposed of. The second responsibility is an ethical and legal responsibility to properly dispose of equipment. There are several environmental issues that can arise from trashing electronic equipment. Often electronics end up in landfills, and depending on the equipment and the local laws, the organization can be liable for fines. When selling equipment for scrap value, the buyer should be able to provide documentation to shield the company from legal ramifications if equipment is dumped.

Standard Operating Procedures

Once your business is launched, each department leader will need to develop practical methods to implement their assigned tasks using the specific part of the business model's blueprint that relates to their branch. These practical methods, or protocols, must be compiled into a standard operating procedures manual and followed closely. The procedures in your manual will have been included for different reasons and have varying degrees of importance and implementation. If you form a partnership or acquire another company, it will be crucial for its business protocols to either match or be compatible with yours.

EXERCISE 15.1

Creating Standard Operating Procedures

This exercise will help you understand standard operating procedures, by creating your first SOP.

1. Think of a particular procedure that you perform on a daily basis.

2. Make a list of all of the major steps.

3. Go back and fill in the details at all of the major steps.

4. Review the SOP and make sure that if you gave it to someone else, they could follow it without any direction.

Bonus: Have someone else follow your procedure without any direction from yourself.

Hardening and Security Policies

One of the ongoing goals of operations security is to ensure that all systems have been hardened to the extent that is possible and still provide functionality. The hardening can be accomplished on both a physical and logical basis. From a logical perspective:

- Remove unnecessary applications.

- Disable unnecessary services.

- Block unrequired ports.

- Tightly control the connections of external storage devices and media if they're allowed at all.

But hardening is only part of the picture. There needs to be a set of security policies that are enforced through the use of security profiles, sometimes also called baselines. Let's look at some of the more important policies that should be implemented.

Acceptable Use Policy

Acceptable use policies (AUPs) should be as comprehensive as possible and should outline every action that is allowed in addition to those that are not allowed. They should also specify which devices are allowed, which websites are allowed, and the proper use of company equipment.

🌐 Real World Scenario

Implement the appropriate policies or procedures.

You operate a midsize network for Acme Inc. Recently a rogue access point was discovered in the network, which constituted a security breach. While the original fear was that it was installed as an evil twin, further investigation revealed it was placed there by an employee so his department could have wireless access. It has now been removed.

Question: What two actions do you need to take, and what security policy document do you need to access?

Answer: Remind/inform the employee of the security policy prohibiting this activity and discipline the employee. This will require access to an acceptable use policy (AUP), specifically the one that the employee signed when hired/onboarded.

To prevent this in the future, you should schedule a training session for employees that reinforces the rules contained in the AUP and explains the motivation behind each.

Password Policy

The password policy defines the requirements for all passwords, including length, complexity, and age. Password management considerations include, but may not be limited to, the following:

- **Password life:** How long a password will be valid. For most organizations, passwords are valid for 60 to 90 days.

- **Password history:** How long before a password can be reused. Password policies usually remember a certain number of previously used passwords.

- **Authentication period:** How long a user can remain logged in. If a user remains logged in for the specified period without activity, the user will be automatically logged out.

- **Password complexity:** How the password will be structured. Most organizations require upper- and lowercase letters, numbers, and special characters.

  The following are some recommendations:

  - Passwords shouldn't contain the username or parts of the user's full name, such as their first name.

  - Passwords should use at least three of the four available character types: lowercase letters, uppercase letters, numbers, and symbols.

- **Password length:** How long the password must be. Most organizations require 8 to 12 characters.

Bring Your Own Device Policy

Increasingly, users are doing work on their mobile devices that they once performed on laptops and desktop computers. Moreover, they are demanding that they be able to use their personal devices to work on the company network. This presents a huge security issue for the IT department because they have to secure these devices while simultaneously exercising much less control over them.

The security team must have a way to prevent these personal devices from introducing malware and other security issues to the network. Bring your own device (BYOD) initiatives can be successful if implemented correctly. The key is to implement control over personal devices that leave the safety of your network and return later after potentially being exposed to environments that are out of your control.

Educating users on the risks related to mobile devices and ensuring that they implement appropriate security measures can help protect against threats involved with these devices. Some of the guidelines that should be provided to mobile device users include implementing a device locking PIN, using device encryption, implementing GPS location services, and implementing remote wipe. Also, users should be cautioned on downloading apps without ensuring that they are coming from a reputable source. In recent years, mobile device management (MDM) and mobile application management (MAM) systems have become popular in enterprises. They are implemented to ensure that an organization can control mobile device settings, applications, and other parameters when those devices are attached to the enterprise.

Remote Access Policy

Remote access policies define the requirements for all remote access connections to the enterprise. This may cover VPN, dial-up, and wireless access methods. One method of securing remote access connections is using Network Access Control (NAC). Remote access was covered in Chapter 13, "Remote Network Access."

Onboarding and Offboarding Policy

Every new user that is hired undergoes what is called an onboarding process that should be guided by a consistent onboarding policy. Thus, policy prescribes the way in which users are assigned accounts and access to resources as well as the issuance of equipment to them. The following items should be defined and standardized by this policy:

- Required training
- Account creation
- Resource access

Also, several documents should be executed and signed prior to the start of work:

- Acceptable use agreement
- Nondisclosure agreement

There should also be an offboarding policy that defines what actions take place when a user leaves the organization. Special items of concern are as follows:

- Proper recovery of all equipment
- Secure removal of all resource access
- Deletion or disablement of account

Patch Management

As a general rule, updates fix a lot of things, and patches fix a few; multiple patches are rolled together into updates. Updates typically contain bug-fixes to the operating system or applications. You can't always afford to wait for updates to be released and need to install patches—particularly security-related patches—when they are released. Bear in mind that if all the security patches are not installed during the installation of the operating system, attackers can exploit the weaknesses and gain access to information.

A number of tools are available to help with patch management, although the intentions of some are better than others. For example, rather than probe a service remotely and attempt to find a vulnerability, the Nessus vulnerability scanner (`www.tenable.com/downloads/nessus`) will query the local host to see if a patch for a given vulnerability has been applied. This type of query is far more accurate (and safer) than running a remote check. Since remote checks actually send the exploit in order to check to see if it is applicable, this can sometimes crash a service or process.

Patch management is important to security, and installing the latest patches/updates often means the difference between a threat actor entering your network, and you being able to repel them. For this reason, many vendors have incorporated patch management into their products. You should always set up patch management so that the latest security patches are installed.

Driver/Firmware Updates

With any operating system, it is essential to keep the drivers and *firmware* updated. Always remember to back up your configurations (such as with routers) before making any significant changes—in particular, a firmware upgrade—to provide a fallback in case something goes awry.

Many network devices contain firmware with which you interact during configuration. For security purposes, you must authenticate to make configuration changes and do so initially by using the default account(s). Make sure that the default password is changed after the installation on any network device; otherwise, you are leaving that device open for anyone recognizing the hardware to access it using the known factory password.

Security Policy

So what, exactly, is a security policy? Ideally, it should precisely define how security is to be implemented within an organization and include physical security, document security, and network security. Plus, you have to make sure these forms of security are implemented completely and solidly because if they aren't, your security policy will be a lot like a block of Swiss cheese—some areas are covered, but others are full of holes.

Before a network can be truly secure, the network support staff should post the part of the security policy that applies to employee conduct on bulletin boards and social media. It should, for example, forbid posting any company and/or employee information that's not absolutely necessary—like, believe it or not, putting sticky notes with usernames and passwords on computer screens. Really clean desks, audits, recordings of email communications, and, in some cases, phone calls should also be requirements. And don't forget to also post the consequences of not complying with the security policy.

Security Audit

Let me take a minute to explain all this a little more, beginning with security audits. A *security audit* is a thorough examination of your network that includes testing all its components to make sure everything is secure. You can do this internally, but you can also contract an audit with a third party if you want the level of security to be certified. A valid and verified consultant's audit is a good follow-up to an internal audit. One reason for having your network's security certified like this is that government agencies usually require it before they'll grant you contract work, especially if that work is considered confidential, secret, or top secret.

Clean-Desk Policy

That clean-desk policy doesn't just end with "get rid of the crumbs from your last snack." It means requiring that all potentially important documents like books, schematics, confidential letters, notes to self, and so on aren't left out in the open when someone is away from their desk. Instead, they're locked away, securely out of sight. And make sure it's clear that this rule applies to users' PC desktops too. Policies like this apply to offices, laboratories, and workbenches as well as desks, and it's really important for employees who share workspaces and/or workstations.

It's super easy to nick something off someone's desk or screen. Because most security problems involve people on the inside, implementing and enforcing a clean-desk policy is a simple way to guard against security breaches.

It might sound really nitpicky, but for a clean-desk policy to be effective, users have to clean up their desks every time they walk away from them—without exception. The day someone doesn't will be the very day when some prospective tenant is being shown the building's layout and a sensitive document suddenly disappears. You should make sure workstations are locked to desks and do random spot checks once in a while to help enforce the policy. For obvious reasons, before company picnics and parties and before "bring your child to work day" are good times to do this.

Recording Equipment

Recording equipment—such as tape recorders, cell phones, and small memory devices like USB flash memory keychains—can contain sensitive, confidential information, so a good security policy should prohibit their unauthorized presence and use.

Just walk into almost any large technology company and you'll be immediately confronted with signs. A really common one is a camera with a circle surrounding it and a slash through the center of the circle. Read the text below the sign and you'll be informed that you can't bring any recording devices onto the premises.

Here's a good example. The Federal Communications Commission (FCC) implemented regulations with the Secure Equipment Act to prohibit the import of certain Chinese-made surveillance products. The surveillance products had been flagged as a national security risk because the vendors of the equipment are potentially linked to the Chinese government. This means that if the equipment is used by the US government, the Chinese government could use the equipment as a spy tool.

Other Common Security Policies

So you get the idea—security policies can cover literally hundreds of items. Here are some common ones:

Notification   Security policies aren't much good if no one knows about them, right? So, make sure you give users a copy of the security policy when you give them their usernames and passwords. It's also a good idea to have computers display a summarized version of the policy when any user attempts to connect. Here's an example: "Unauthorized access is prohibited and will be prosecuted to the fullest extent of the law." Remember, your goal is to close loopholes. One hacker actually argued that because a computer didn't tell him otherwise, anyone was free to connect to and use the system!

Equipment Access   Disable all unused network ports so that any nonemployees who happen to be in the building can't connect a laptop to an unused port and gain access to the network. And don't forget to place all network equipment under lock and key.

Wiring   Your network's wires should never run along the floor where they can be easily accessed (or tripped over, getting you sued). Routers, switches, and concentrators should live in locked closets or rooms, with access to those rooms controlled by anything ranging from a good lock to a biometric access system, depending on the level of security your specific network and data require.

Door Locks/Swipe Mechanisms   Be sure that only authorized people know the combination to the cipher lock on your data-center doors or that only the appropriate people have badges that allow access to the data center. Change lock combinations often, and never leave server room doors open or unlocked.

Badges   Require everyone to wear an RFID badge, including contractors and visitors, and assign appropriate access levels to everyone.

Tracking   Require badge access to all entrances to buildings and internal computer rooms. Track and record all entry to and exits from these rooms.

Passwords   Reset passwords at least every month. Train everyone on how to create strong passwords. Set BIOS/UEFI passwords on every client and server computer to prevent BIOS/UEFI changes.

Monitor Viewing   Place computer monitors strategically so that visitors or people looking through windows can't see them, and make sure unauthorized users/persons can't see security-guard stations and server monitors. Use monitor privacy screens if necessary.

Accounts   Each user should have their own, unique user account, and employees should never share user accounts. Even temporary employees should have their own account. Otherwise, you won't be able to isolate a security breach.

Testing   Review and audit your network security at least once a year.

Background Checks   Do background checks on all network support staff. This may include calling their previous employers, verifying their college degrees, requiring a drug test, and checking for a criminal background.

Firewalls   Use a firewall to protect all Internet connections, and use the appropriate proxies and dynamic-packet-filtering equipment to control access to the network. Your firewall should provide as much security as your company requires and your budget allows.

Intrusion Detection   Use intrusion detection and logging software to discover security breaches, and be sure you're logging the events you want to monitor.

Cameras   Cameras should cover all entrances to the building and the entire parking lot. Be sure that cameras are in weatherproof and tamper-proof housings, and review the output at a security-monitoring office. Record everything on extended-length tape recorders.

Mail Servers   Provide each person with their own email mailbox, and attach an individual network account to each mailbox. If several people need to access a mailbox, don't give all of them the password to a single network account. Instead, assign individual privileges to each person's network account so you can track activity down to a single person, even with a generic address like info@mycompany.com.

DMZ   Use a screened subnet, also known as a demilitarized zone (DMZ), for all publicly viewable servers, including web servers, FTP servers, and email relay servers. Figure 15.1 shows a common DMZ setup.

It is not advisable to put a screened subnet outside the firewall because any servers outside your firewall defeat the whole purpose of having one. However, it is possible that you may see a screened subnet outside the firewall in some networks.

Mail Relay   Mail servers relay to other email servers by design. When the email server relays from any server that requests it, it is called *open relay*. Hackers use this feature to forward spam. Modern email systems allow you to control which servers your email server will relay for, which helps to prevent this.

Patches   Make sure the latest security updates are installed after being properly tested on a nonproduction computer.

Backups   Store backup tape cartridges and other media securely, not on a shelf or table within reach of someone working at the server. Lock tapes in a waterproof, fireproof safe, and keep at least some of your backups off-site.

FIGURE 15.1 A common screened subnet configuration

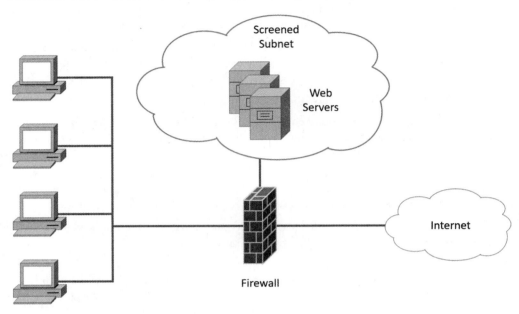

Private Network

Hotspots Do not ever allow hotspots because they can be used to get to the Internet without your knowledge. Restrict hotspot access within your organization, unless you need them for remote access.

Guards If you need security guards, they shouldn't patrol the same station all the time. As people become familiar with an environment and situation, they tend to become less observant about that environment, so rotating guards to keep their concentration at the highest possible level makes a lot of sense. Clearly, guards are people who need breaks to ensure alertness, but make sure that all patrol areas are covered during shift changes, rotations, and breaks. Guards should also receive periodic training and testing to make sure they can recognize a threat and take appropriate action.

WARNING

Believe it or not, covering all these bases still won't guarantee that your network or facility is secure. All of this is really just a starting point that's meant to point you in the right direction.

Breaking Policy

You know that for your policy to be effective it's got to be enforced consistently and completely. Nobody is so special that they don't have to adhere to it. And people have to understand the consequences of breaking policy too. Your network users need to have a clearly written document, called a *security policy*, that fully identifies and explains what's expected of them and what they can and can't do. Plus, people must be made completely aware of the consequences of breaking the rules, and penalties have to match the severity of the offense and be carried out quickly, if not immediately, to be effective.

Let's take a minute and talk about those penalties. As far back as the mid-1980s, employees were immediately terminated for major technology policy infractions. For example, one guy from a large computer company immediately got his pink slip when pornography was found on his computer's hard drive. The situation was handled decisively—his manager informed him that he was being immediately terminated and that he had one hour to vacate the premises. A security guard stood watch while he cleaned out his desk to make sure the employee touched only personal items—no computer equipment, including storage media—and when he had finished gathering his personal things, the guard then escorted him from the building.

Downloading and installing software from the Internet to your PC at work is not as major (depending on where you work), but from the things we've been over so far, you know that doing that can compromise security. Beta products, new software, and patches/updates need to be tested by the IT department before anyone can use them, period! Here's an example: After an employee installed the untested beta release of a web browser and rebooted their PC, the production Windows server at a national telephone company crashed. The resulting action was to revoke that employee's Internet FTP privileges for three months.

Data Loss Prevention

The data loss prevention (DLP) policy defines all procedures for preventing the egress of sensitive data from the network and may include references to the use DLP software.

Data leakage occurs when sensitive data is disclosed to unauthorized personnel either intentionally or inadvertently. DLP software attempts to prevent data leakage. It does this by maintaining awareness of actions that can and cannot be taken with respect to a document. For example, it might allow printing of a document but only at the company office. It might also disallow sending the document through email. DLP software uses ingress and egress filters to identify sensitive data that is leaving the organization and can prevent such leakage.

Another scenario might be the release of product plans that should be available only to the Sales group. A security professional could set a policy like the following for that document:

- It cannot be emailed to anyone other than Sales group members.
- It cannot be printed.
- It cannot be copied.

There are two locations where DLP can be implemented:

- **Network DLP:** Installed at network egress points near the perimeter, network DLP analyzes network traffic.
- **Endpoint DLP:** Endpoint DLP runs on end-user workstations or servers in the organization.

Common Documentation

Ending up with a great network requires some really solid planning before you buy even one device for it. And planning includes thoroughly analyzing your design for potential flaws and optimizing configurations everywhere you can to maximize the network's future throughput and performance. If you blow it in this phase, trust me—you'll pay dearly later in bottom-line costs and countless hours consumed troubleshooting and putting out the fires of faulty design.

Start planning by creating an outline that precisely delimits all goals and business requirements for the network, and refer to it often to ensure that you don't deliver a network that falls short of your client's present needs or fails to offer the scalability to grow with those needs. Drawing out your design and jotting down all the relevant information really helps in spotting weaknesses and faults. If you have a team, make sure everyone on it gets to examine the design and evaluate it, and keep that network plan up throughout the installation phase. Hang on to it after implementation has been completed as well because having it is like having the keys to the kingdom—it will enable you to efficiently troubleshoot any issues that could arise after everything is in place and up and running.

High-quality documentation should include a baseline for network performance because you and your client need to know what "normal" looks like in order to detect problems before they develop into disasters. Don't forget to verify that the network conforms to all internal and external regulations and that you've developed and itemized solid management procedures and security policies for future network administrators to refer to and follow.

Physical Network Diagram

A physical network diagram contains all the physical devices and connectivity paths on your network and should accurately picture how your network physically fits together in glorious detail. Again, I know it seems like overkill, but ideally, your network diagram should list and map everything you would need to completely rebuild your network from scratch if you had to. This is actually what this type of diagram is designed for. But there's still another physical network diagram variety that includes the firmware revision on all the switches and access points in your network. Remember, besides having your physical network accurately detailed, you must also clearly understand the connections, types of hardware, and their firmware revisions. I'm going to say it again—you will be so happy you have this documentation when troubleshooting! It will prevent much suffering and enable you to fix whatever the problem is so much faster!

Real World Scenario

Avoiding Confusion

Naming your network devices is no big deal, but for some reason, coming up with systems for naming devices and numbering connections can really stress people out.

Let me ease the pain. Let's say your network has two racks of switches, creatively named Block A and Block B. (Sounds like a prison, I know, but it's just to keep things simple for this example. In the real world, you can come up with whatever naming system works for you.)

Anyway, I'm going to use the letters *FETH* for Fast Ethernet; and because each rack has six switches, I'm going to number them (surprise!) 1 through 6. Because we read from left to right, it's intuitive to number the ports on each switch that way too.

Having a solid naming system makes thing so much more efficient—even if it's a bit of a hassle to create. For instance, if you were the system administrator in this example and suddenly all computers connected to FETHB-3 couldn't access any network resources, you would have a pretty good idea of where to look first, right?

If you can't diagram everything, at least make sure all network devices are listed. As I said, physical network diagrams can run from simple, hand-drawn models to insanely complex monsters created by software packages like SmartDraw, Visio, and Auto-CAD. Figure 15.2 shows a simple diagram that most of us could draw by hand.

FIGURE 15.2 Simple network physical diagram

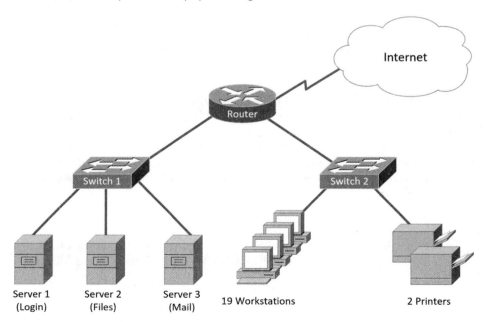

For the artistically impaired, or if you want a flashier version, Figure 15.3 exhibits a more complex physical diagram. This is an actual sample of what SmartDraw can do for you, and you can get it at www.smartdraw.com. Personally, I like OmniGraffle for my Mac; it works very well but has a more complex learning cycle. In addition, Microsoft Visio provides many or possibly more of these same functions.

FIGURE 15.3   Network diagram with firewalls from SmartDraw

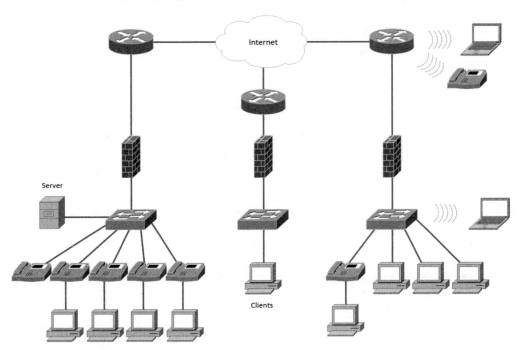

Please don't throw anything at me, but I need to bring up one last thing: Never forget to mirror any changes you make to your actual network in the network's diagram. Think of it like an updated snapshot.

If you give the authorities your college buddy's baby picture after he goes missing, will that really help people recognize him? Not without the help of some high-tech, age-progression software, that's for sure—and they don't make that for networks, so it's better to keep things up-to-date.

Floor Plan

The floor plan (see Figure 15.4) is a physical drawing that is often overlooked and under-estimated in its potential. In large environments, it helps the IT worker locate network assets. This drawing might depict the location of a computer in an office building or a piece of networking equipment on a factory floor, for example. The floor plan also allows new employees to get acclimated with an organization's network equipment.

FIGURE 15.4   A floor plan drawing

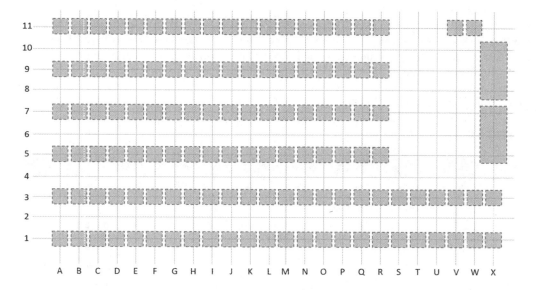

The floor plan in a data center is really important for two reasons: planning and locating equipment. The planning aspect is critical in a data center because of environmental factors such as temperature, humidity, electricity, and network connections. Locating equipment is equally important, since one rack of equipment can look like the next in the data center.

The *American National Standards Institute (ANSI)* and *Telecommunications Industry Association (TIA)* have standardized a generic naming convention for the location of network equipment in the ANSI/TIA-606-B standard. As shown in Figure 15.4, the floor space is divided into quadrants. These quadrants are then identified on one axis with letters and on the other axis with numbers. So, grid coordinate K9 defines a specific floor space in an office or server room. It is a common practice to label server racks with this naming scheme on the server room floor. The rack location should coincide with the rack diagrams, so you know exactly what equipment is in rack K9 or any other rack in the grid.

Rack Diagram

Rack diagrams help us to document the configuration of our server racks for three purposes. The first purpose is obvious: being able to locate the servers in the rack. The second purpose is the planning of new server locations. The third purpose is creating a physical diagram to detail how the racks are wired.

A typical server rack is 42 rack units (42U) high, and each rack unit is approximately 1.75 inches, or 44.45 millimeters, for an overall height of about 73.5 inches. The typical rack numbering starts at the bottom of the rack with number 1 and the top of the rack with 42. In data centers, it's all about density. Therefore, it's also common to see rack units that are 48 units high for a total height of 84 inches.

Microsoft Excel can be used to document and detail each rack unit in the server racks with the server equipment that occupies the rack unit(s), as shown in Figure 15.5. This allows for quick changes when equipment is decommissioned or added and ensures that all administrators can update the documentation. This documentation also helps with planning when a new piece of equipment is ordered and you need to move servers and equipment around.

FIGURE 15.5 A rack diagram

Rack K9		Rack L9		Rack M9	
Rack Unit	Equipment	Rack Unit	Equipment	Rack Unit	Equipment
48	TOR Switch TOR-K9	48	TOR Switch TOR-L9	48	TOR Switch TOR-M9
47		47		47	
46	Empty	46		46	
45	Empty	45		45	
44	Storage JBOD Research	44	Disk-to-Disk Backup D2D-SAN1	44	Storage JBOD General
43		43		43	
42		42		42	
41		41		41	
40	SAN Processor A Research	40	Tape Library Unit TLU-A	40	SAN Processor A General
39		39		39	
38	SAN Processor B Research	38		38	SAN Processor B General
37		37		37	
36	Reseach Dept File Server	36	ESXi-General-SRV8	36	Reserved for VDI Expansion
35		35		35	
34	ESXi-RD-SRV1	34	ESXi-General-SRV7	34	
33		33		33	
32	ESXi-RD-SRV2	32	ESXi-General-SRV6	32	VDI-General-SRV5
31		31		31	
30	ESXi-RD-SRV3	30	ESXi-General-SRV5	30	VDI-General-SRV4
29		29		29	
28	Empty	28	ESXi-General-SRV4	28	VDI-General-SRV3
27	Empty	27		27	
26	Empty	26	ESXi-General-SRV3	26	VDI-General-SRV2
25	Empty	25		25	
24	Empty	24	ESXi-General-SRV2	24	VDI-General-SRV1
23	Empty	23		23	
22	Empty	22	ESXi-General-SRV1	22	Empty
21	Empty				
20					
19					

Many vendors offer Microsoft Visio templates for the ongoing management of server racks. These templates allow for a finished diagram of network-server racks in the Visio application. I often use these templates when I am working as a contractor because it provides a finished look at the work being performed or pitched to the customer.

Intermediate Distribution Frame/Main Distribution Frame Documentation

Intermediate distribution frame (IDF) and *main distribution frame (MDF)* were terms originally used by telephone providers to describe the distribution of communications. Today, they are used to describe the wiring distribution points of our internal networks.

The main distribution frame (MDF) connects equipment (inside plant) to cables and subscriber carrier equipment (outside plant). It also terminates cables that run to intermediate distribution frames distributed throughout the facility.

An intermediate distribution frame (IDF) serves as a distribution point for cables from the MDF to individual cables connected to equipment in areas remote from these frames. Figure 15.6 shows the relationship between the IDFs and the MDF. This should also be clearly documented and continually updated.

FIGURE 15.6   MDF and IDFs

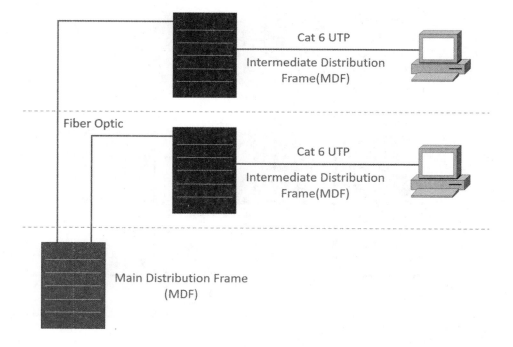

 Often, these numbers do not match the actual room numbers because rooms get renumbered and reconfigured over the years. A document detailing the translation of these room and patch numbers should be kept up-to-date and available at the IDF locations for network technicians.

Logical Network Diagram

Physical diagrams depict how data physically flows from one area of your network to the next, but a logical network diagram includes things such as protocols, configurations, addressing schemes, access lists, firewalls, types of applications, and so on—all things that apply logically to your network. Figure 15.7 shows what a logical network diagram could look like.

And just as you mirror any physical changes you make to the network (like adding devices or even just a cable) on your physical diagram, you map logical changes (like creating a new subnet, VLAN, or security zone) on your logical network diagram. It is important that you keep this oh-so-important document up-to-date.

FIGURE 15.7 Logical network diagram

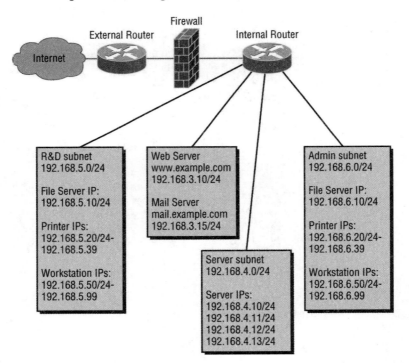

Wiring Diagram

Wireless is definitely the wave of the future, but for now even the most extensive wireless networks have a wired backbone they rely on to connect them to the rest of humanity.

That skeleton is made up of cabled physical media like coax, fiber, and twisted pair. Surprisingly, it is the latter—specifically, unshielded twisted-pair (UTP)—that screams to be pictured in a diagram.

When you're troubleshooting a network, having a diagram is golden. Let's say you discover a connectivity problem between two hosts. Because you've got the map, you know the cable running between them is brand new and custom made. This should tell you to go directly to that new cable because it's likely it was poorly made and is therefore causing the snag.

Another reason it's so important to diagram all things wiring is that all wires have to plug into something somewhere, and it's really good to know what and where that is. Whether it's into a hub, a switch, a router, a workstation, or the wall, you positively need to know the who, what, where, when, and how of the way the wiring is attached.

NOTE   After adding a new cable segment on your network, you need to update the wiring schematics.

Cable Maps

Cable maps are a type of wiring diagram that is essential when troubleshooting equipment of any type that the IT department is responsible for maintaining. The cable map can help the technician quickly locate the connection so that a test can be performed or the connection can simply be plugged back in. In Figure 15.8, you will see a cable map for audiovisual equipment. The cable map details the type of cabling and the label on the cabling so a technician can quickly diagnose a problem. Cable maps diagrams are sometimes called as-built diagrams because the drawings represent wiring that was revised as the system was built.

FIGURE 15.8   Typical wiring diagram

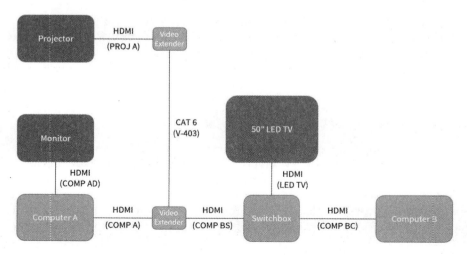

Layered Network Diagram

Network technicians focus on three main layers of the network: Physical, Data Link, and Network layers. When troubleshooting network issues, it is important to have documentation for all three of these layers.

The network technician should know how devices are connected at a physical level, by looking at the wiring diagrams or physical diagrams. The technician should also know how devices are logically connected to the network at layer 2. For example, the logical network diagrams should detail the VLAN, servers, clients, and network equipment are configured in. Lastly, network diagrams should be prepared that detail the IP addressing and routing of the VLANs. The diagrams should also detail any special ACLs that might be applied to IP subnets.

EXERCISE 15.2

Documenting Your Network

This exercise will help you understand network documentation, by having you document your own home network. You will use paper and pencil first, because it is a lot easier without the struggle of learning a new tool.

1. Grab a piece of paper and a pencil.

2. Sketch out your network from a physical perspective, and detail all of the connections and their specific physical ports.

3. Sketch out your network from a logical perspective, and detail all of the logical flow of information.

4. Use a graphical documenting program to transfer your scratch drawing to a finished document.

Note: Step 4 is probably the hardest, since there will be a learning curve to the new graphical documenting program. You can use a tool like Microsoft Visio if you have access to it, or simply use the online free version of SmartDraw.

Site Survey Report

The site survey report is a special document that pertains to wireless coverage, and it is often called a heat map. A site survey is typically performed before wireless equipment is purchased so that proper coverage can be attained and a build of materials (BOM) can be compiled. A site survey should also be performed after the wireless equipment is installed. The site survey report will then guide any adjustments to the wireless parameters, as well as document the as-built wireless network. Figure 15.9 shows an example of a site survey heat map.

FIGURE 15.9   Typical site survey report

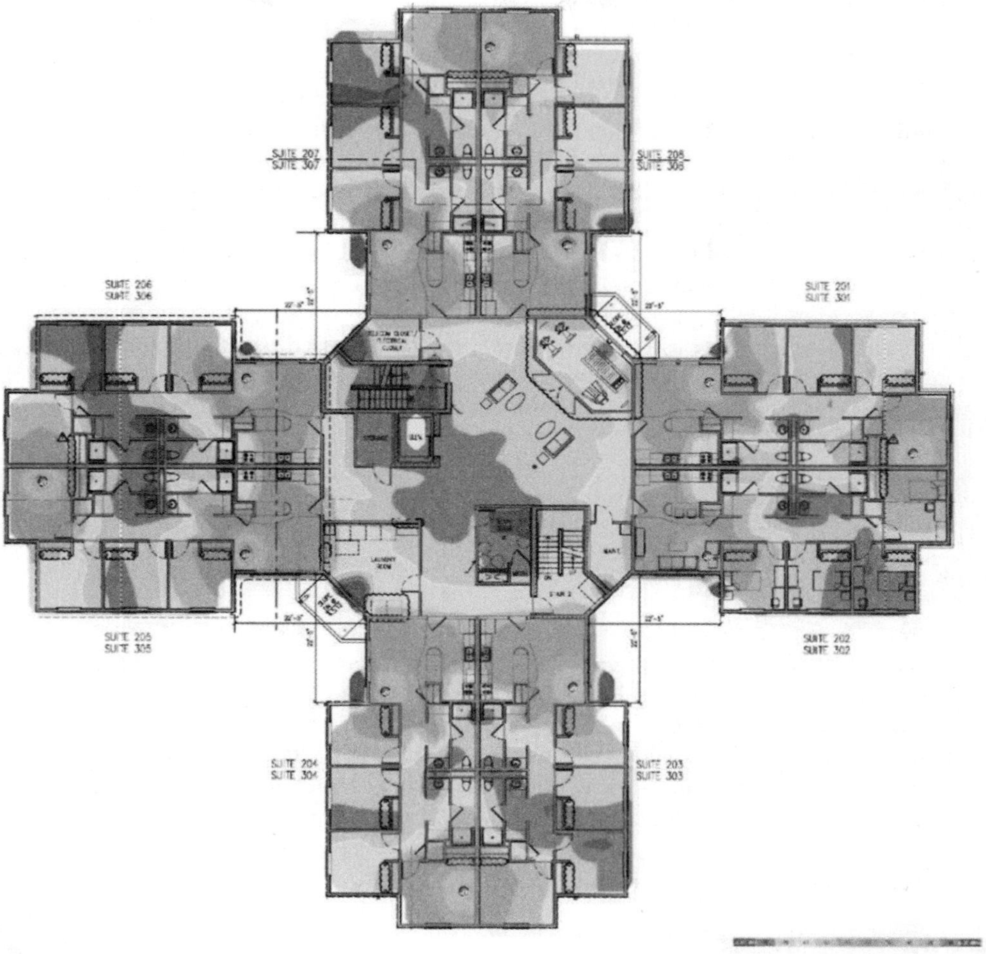

Wireless site surveys were covered in great detail in Chapter 12, "Wireless Networking."

Audit and Assessment Report

When audits and assessments are performed, there should be reports created that organize the collected information in a format that can be understood by those who are charged with making security decisions based on the reports. The language should be clear, and all terms used should be defined. Avoid using technical jargon. Keep in mind that decision-makers do not always have the same security skills as those they manage.

Security Audit

Let me take a minute to explain all this a little more, beginning with security audits. A security audit is a thorough examination of your network that includes testing all its components to make sure everything is secure. You can do this internally, but you can also contract an audit with a third party if you want the level of security to be certified. A valid and verified consultant's audit is a good follow-up to an internal audit. One reason for having your network's security certified like this is that government agencies usually require it before they'll grant you contract work, especially if that work is considered confidential, secret, or top secret.

Results of these audits or assessments should be kept and used to perform gap analysis. The results of the latest audit are compared with those of the previous audit to determine if issues have been corrected or if there are still "gaps" to close.

 Real World Scenario

Walk Your Beat

A great way to begin a basic security audit to get a feel for any potential threats to your network is to simply take a walk through the company's halls and offices. I've done this a lot, and it always pays off because invariably I happen upon some new and different way that people are trying to "beat the system" regarding security. This doesn't necessarily indicate that a given user is trying to cause damage on purpose; it's just that following the rules can be a little inconvenient—especially when it comes to adhering to strict password policies. Your average user just doesn't get how important their role is in maintaining the security of the network (maybe even their job security as well) by sticking to the network's security policy, so you have to make sure they do.

Think about it. If you can easily discover user passwords just by taking a little tour of the premises, so can a bad guy, and once someone has a username and a password, it's pretty easy to hack into resources. I wasn't kidding about people slapping sticky notes with their usernames and/or passwords right on their monitors—this happens a lot more than you would think. Some users, thinking they're actually being really careful, glue them to the back of their keyboards instead, but you don't have to be James Bond to think about looking there either, right? People wouldn't think of leaving their cars unlocked with the windows down and the keys in the ignition, but that's exactly what they're doing by leaving sensitive info anywhere on or near their workstations.

Even though it might not make you Mr. or Ms. Popularity when you search workspaces or even inside desks for notes with interesting or odd words written on them, do it anyway.

People will try to hide these goodies anywhere. Or sometimes, not so much. I kid you not—I had a user who actually wrote his password on the border of his monitor with a Sharpie, and when his password expired, he just crossed it off and wrote the new one underneath it. Sheer genius! But my personal favorite was when I glanced at this one guy's keyboard and noticed that some of the letter keys had numbers written on them. All you had to do was follow the numbers that (surprise!) led straight to his password. Oh sure—he'd followed policy to the, ahem, letter by choosing random letters and numbers, but a lot of good that did—he had to draw himself a little map in plain sight on his keyboard to remember the password.

So, like it or not, you have to walk your beat to find out if users are managing their accounts properly. If you find someone doing things the right way, praise them for it openly. If not, it's time for more training—or maybe worse, termination.

Baseline Configurations

High-quality documentation should include a baseline for network performance because you and your client need to know what "normal" looks like in order to detect problems before they develop into disasters. Don't forget to verify that the network conforms to all internal and external regulations and that you've developed and itemized solid management procedures and security policies for future network administrators to refer to and follow.

In networking, *baseline* can refer to the standard level of performance of a certain device or to the normal operating capacity for your whole network. For instance, a specific server's baseline describes norms for factors like how busy its processors are, how much of the memory it uses, and how much data usually goes through the NIC at a given time. A network baseline delimits the amount of bandwidth available and when. For networks and networked devices, baselines include information about four key components:

- Processor
- Memory
- Hard-disk (or other storage) subsystem
- Wired/wireless utilization

After everything is up and running, it's a good idea to establish performance baselines on all vital devices and your network in general. To do this, measure things like network usage at three different strategic times to get an accurate assessment. For instance, peak usage usually happens around 8 a.m. Monday through Friday, or whenever most people log into the network in the morning. After hours or on weekends is often when usage is the lowest. Knowing these values can help you troubleshoot bottlenecks or determine why certain system resources are more limited than they should be. Knowing what your baseline is can even tell you if someone's complaints about the network running like a slug are really valid—nice!

It's good to know that you can use network-monitoring software to establish baselines. Even some server operating systems come with software to help with network monitoring, which can help find baselines, perform log management, and even do network graphing as well so you can compare the logs and graphs at a later period of time on your network.

In my experience, it's wise to re-baseline network performance at least once a year. And always pinpoint new performance baselines after any major upgrade to your network's infrastructure.

Golden Configuration

A baseline is a snapshot of your network's performance when it is running optimally. The performance of your network is tied directly to the configuration. The baseline configuration is also called the golden configuration. In addition to collecting a performance baseline, the golden configuration should be captured along with it. This will allow you to assess the performance along with the configuration. If the configuration changes, then the performance might be impacted.

IP Address Management

IP address management (IPAM) is important in any size environment. Without a good understanding of an organization's IP address usage, an organization will have problems scaling up. Luckily, IPAM can come to the rescue. IPAM can be performed manually with spreadsheets detailing which IP address is assigned to which servers or system. In larger environments, you might even employ a software package to perform the IP address management.

Common Agreements

In the course of supporting mergers and acquisitions, and in providing support to departments within the organization, it's always important to keep the details of agreements in writing to reduce the risk of misunderstandings. In the following sections, I'll discuss standard documents that are used in these situations. You should be familiar with the purpose of these documents.

Nondisclosure Agreement

A nondisclosure agreement (NDA) is an agreement between two parties that defines what information is considered confidential and cannot be shared outside the two parties. An organization may implement NDAs with personnel regarding the intellectual property of the organization. NDAs can also be used when two organizations work together to develop a new product. Because certain information must be shared to make the partnership successful, NDAs are signed to ensure that each partner's data is protected.

While an NDA cannot ensure that confidential data is not shared, it usually provides details on the repercussions for the offending party, including but not limited to fines, jail time, and forfeiture of rights. For example, an organization should decide to implement an NDA when it wants to legally ensure that no sensitive information is compromised through a project with a third party or in a cloud-computing environment.

Service-Level Agreement

The *service-level agreement (SLA)* is an expected level of service that the service provider will adhere to for uptime. The SLA is detailed in the service contract as a percentage of uptime per year; it is often called "the nines." When a service provider exceeds the percentage of uptime defined in the SLA, the provider is in breach of the contract. The contract will often identify what is considered in the SLA requirement as well as the terms if they breach the SLA requirement.

You should be careful with SLAs because being up 99% of the time means the service provider can be down 3 days and 15 hours over the course of a year before breaching the contract. A service provider with 5 nines (99.999%) can be down 5 minutes and 15 seconds over the course of a year before breaching the contract. Table 15.1 details the different nines of an SLA for uptime.

TABLE 15.1 Uptime for nines of an SLA

SLA %	Downtime per Year	Downtime per Month	Downtime per Day
99% (two nines)	3.65 days	7.2 hours	14.4 minutes
99.9% (three nines)	8.76 hours	43.8 minutes	1.44 minutes
99.99% (four nines)	52.56 minutes	4.38 minutes	8.64 seconds
99.999% (five nines)	5.26 minutes	25.9 seconds	864.3 milliseconds
99.9999% (six nines)	31.5 seconds	2.59 seconds	86.4 milliseconds

Memorandum of Understanding

The memorandum of understanding (MOU) is a mutual agreement between two or more parties. The MOU is not a legal contract, but the terms, conditions, and deliverables stated in the MOU can be legally binding. It is drafted when the parties do not want to interfere with an established agreement or slow the process down by creating a new formal legal agreement. The MOU is often used in situations where a union and the organization are currently contracted. The MOU then serves as an amendment to an already established agreement. Therefore, the MOU is commonly agreed upon before it is drafted in a formal contract.

Summary

In this chapter, you learned that plans and procedures should be developed to manage operational issues such as change management, incident response, disaster recovery, business continuity, and the system life cycle. You also learned that standard operating procedures should be developed to guide each of these processes.

We also discussed the hardening of systems and the use of security policies that help mitigate security issues such as acceptable use, password, bring your own device (BYOD), remote access, and onboarding and offboarding policies.

Finally, you learned about the importance of critical network documentation such as physical network diagrams, floor plans, rack diagrams, intermediate distribution frame (IDF)/main distribution frame (MDF) documentation, logical network diagrams, and wiring diagrams. We also covered common agreements such as nondisclosure agreements (NDA), service-level agreements (SLA), and memorandums of understanding (MOUs).

Exam Essentials

Understand the importance of plans and procedures.   These include change management, incident response, disaster recovery, business continuity, and the system life cycle.

Describe hardening and security policies.   Among these are acceptable use, password, bring your own device (BYOD), remote access, and onboarding and offboarding policies.

Utilize common documentation.   These include physical network diagrams, floor plans, rack diagrams, intermediate distribution frame (IDF)/main distribution frame (MDF) documentation, logical network diagrams, wiring diagrams and site survey reports.

Identify common business agreements.   These agreements include nondisclosure agreements (NDA), service-level agreements (SLA), and memorandums of understanding (MOUs).

Written Lab

Complete the table by filling in the appropriate plan of which the given step is a part. Choose from the following list:

- Change management plan
- Incident response plan
- Disaster recovery plan
- Business continuity plan
- System life-cycle plan

You can find the answers in Appendix A.

Step	Plan
Utilization of three network interfaces on the DNS server	
Phased introductions of security patches	
Degaussing of all discarded hard drives	
Security issue escalation list	
System recovery priority chart	

Review Questions

You can find the answers to the review questions in Appendix B.

1. The way to properly install or remove software on the servers is an example of which of the following?

   A. Plan

   B. Policy

   C. Procedure

   D. Code

2. Which of the following is a plan for reversing changes and recovering from any adverse effects from the changes?

   A. Backup

   B. Secondary

   C. Rollback

   D. Failover

3. Which of the following is the amount of time a system will be down or unavailable during the implementation of changes?

   A. Downtime

   B. Maintenance window

   C. MTBF

   D. Work factor

4. Which of the following is *not* a device hardening technique?

   A. Remove unnecessary applications.

   B. Deploy an access control vestibule.

   C. Block unrequired ports.

   D. Disable unnecessary services.

5. Which policy automatically logs a user out after a specified period without activity?

   A. Password complexity

   B. Password history

   C. Password length

   D. Authentication period

6. BYOD policies apply to what type of device?

   A. Mobile

   B. Router

   C. Server

   D. Firewall

7. Which tool can prevent the emailing of a document to anyone other than Sales group members?

A. BYOD

B. Password policy

C. DLP

D. AUP

8. Which of the following connects equipment (inside plant) to cables and subscriber carrier equipment (outside plant)?

A. IDF

B. MDF

C. Hardware rack

D. Access control vestibule

9. Which of the following is *not* part of the information gathering step of a site survey?

A. Determine the scope of the network with respect to applications in use.

B. Verify optimal distances between prospective AP locations.

C. Identify areas that must be covered.

D. Assess types of wireless devices that will need to be supported.

10. Device baselines include information about all but which of the following components?

A. CPU

B. Memory

C. Hard disk

D. Display

11. You just finished repairing a network connection, and in the process, you traced several network connections. Which type of documentation should you create so that another technician does not need to repeat the task of tracing connections?

A. Logical diagram

B. Knowledge base article

C. Change management document

D. Physical diagram

12. You just had an outage of Internet connectivity due to a denial-of-service attack. Which document should you follow during the outage?

A. Change management plan

B. Knowledge base article

C. Acceptable use policy

D. Incident response plan

13. You are currently troubleshooting a network issue. Which type of diagram allows you to view the flow of information from a high-level overview? (Choose the best answer.)

   A. Logical diagram

   B. Physical diagram

   C. Symbol diagram

   D. Knowledge base article

14. End users are abusing the email system by selling personal items. Which policy would detail the proper use of the email system for business purposes?

   A. BYOD

   B. Password policy

   C. AUP

   D. Incident response plan

15. Why should performance baselines be captured over a long period of time?

   A. To define normal operations and activity

   B. To define a historical representation of activity

   C. To help validate when a problem is solved

   D. All of the above

16. Which policy would you create to define the minimum specification if an employee wanted to use their own device for email?

   A. MDM

   B. AUP

   C. BYOD

   D. NDA

17. You are contracting with a new service provider and are reviewing their service level agreement (SLA). The SLA states that their commitment to uptime is 99.99%. What is the expected downtime per year?

   A. 3.65 days

   B. 8.76 hours

   C. 52.56 minutes

   D. 5.29 minutes

18. You have been informed that all material must be removed from your desk before you leave for the day. What type of policy is this?

   A. NDA

   B. Clean-desk policy

   C. Password policy

   D. BYOD

19. Which type of document will contain heat maps of wireless equipment after installation?

    A. Logical network diagram

    B. Physical network diagram

    C. Site survey report

    D. Baseline

20. You have been tasked with planning the IP addressing in your organization. Which tool should you employ to help you with this task?

    A. IPAM

    B. SLA

    C. MOU

    D. NDA

Chapter

16

High Availability and Disaster Recovery

THE FOLLOWING COMPTIA NETWORK+ EXAM OBJECTIVES ARE COVERED IN THIS CHAPTER:

✓ **Domain 2.0 Network Implementations**

✓ **2.4 Explain important factors of physical installations.**

✓ **Power**

- Uninterruptible power supply(UPS)
- Power distribution unit (PDU)
- Power load
- Voltage

✓ **Environmental factors**

- Humidity
- Fire suppression

✓ **Temperature**

✓ **Domain 3.0 Network Operations**

✓ **3.3 Explain disaster recovery (DR) concepts.**

✓ **DR metrics**

- Recovery point objective (RPO)
- Recovery time objective (RTO)
- Mean time to repair (MTTR)
- Mean time between failures (MTBF)

✓ **DR sites**

- Cold site
- Warm site
- Hot site

✓ **High-availability approaches**

- Active-active
- Active-passive

✓ **Testing**

- Tabletop exercises
- Validation tests

High availability is a system-design protocol that guarantees a certain amount of operational uptime during a given period. The design attempts to minimize unplanned downtime—the time users are unable to access resources. In almost all cases, high availability is provided through the implementation of duplicate equipment (multiple servers, multiple NICs, etc.). Organizations that serve critical functions obviously need this; after all, you really don't want to blaze your way to a hospital ER only to find that they can't treat you because their network is down!

Fault tolerance means that even if one component fails, you won't lose access to the resource it provides. To implement fault tolerance, you need to employ multiple devices or connections that all provide a way to access the same resource(s).

A familiar form of fault tolerance is configuring an additional hard drive to be a mirror image of the original so that if either fails, there's still a copy of the data available. In networking, fault tolerance means that you have multiple paths from one point to another. What's cool is that fault-tolerant connections can be configured to be available either on a standby basis only or all the time if you intend to use them as part of a load-balancing system.

In this chapter, you will learn about redundancy concepts, fault tolerance, and the disaster recovery process.

To find Todd Lammle CompTIA videos and practice questions, please see www.lammle.com/network+.

Load Balancing

Load balancing is a technique to spread work out to multiple computers, network links, or other devices.

Using load balancing, you can provide an active/passive server cluster in which only one server is active and handling requests. For example, your favorite Internet site might consist of 20 servers that all appear to be the same site because its owner wants to ensure that its users always experience quick access. You can accomplish this on a network by installing multiple redundant links to ensure network traffic is spread across several paths and maximize the bandwidth on each link.

Think of this as similar to having two or more different freeways that will both get you to your destination equally well—if one is really busy, take the other one.

Multipathing

Multipathing is the process of configuring multiple network connections between a system and its storage device. The idea behind multipathing is to provide a backup path in case the preferred connection goes down. For example, a SCSI hard disk drive may connect to two SCSI controllers on the same computer, or a disk may connect to two Fibre Channel ports.

The ease with which multipathing can be set up in a virtual environment is one if the advantages a virtual environment provides. Figure 16.1 shows a multipath configuration.

FIGURE 16.1   Multipathing

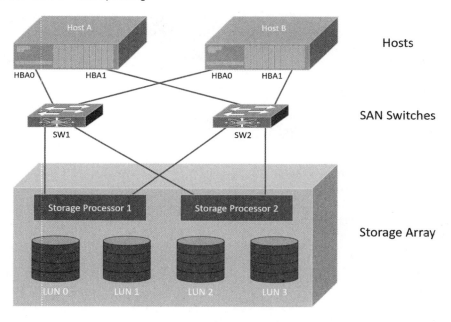

Both Host A and Host B have multiple host bus adapters (NICs) and multiple connections through multiple switches and are mapped to multiple storage processors as well. This is a highly fault-tolerant arrangement that can survive an HBA failure, a path failure, a switch failure, and a storage processor failure.

Network Interface Card (NIC) Teaming

NIC teaming allows multiple network interfaces to be placed into a team for the purposes of bandwidth aggregation and/or traffic failover to prevent connectivity loss in the event of a network component failure. The cards can be set to active/active state, where both cards are load balancing, or active/passive, where one card is on standby in case the primary card fails. Most of the time, the NIC team will use a multicast address to send and receive data, but it can also use a broadcast address so all cards receive the data at the same time.

It can be done with a single switch or multiple switches. Figure 16.2 shows what is called static teaming, where a single switch is in use. This would provide failover only for the connection and would not protect against a switch failure.

FIGURE 16.2   Static teaming

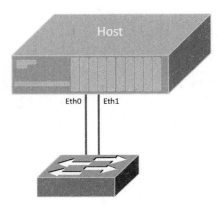

Figure 16.3 shows a more redundant arrangement, where a switch-independent setup is in use. This provides fault tolerance for both switches and connections.

FIGURE 16.3   Switch-independent setup

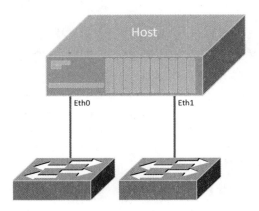

Redundant Hardware/Clusters

By now it must be clear that redundancy is a good thing. While this concept can be applied to network connections, it can also be applied to hardware components and even complete servers. In the following sections, you'll learn how this concept is applied to servers and infrastructure devices.

Switches

As you saw in the previous section, multiple switches can be deployed to provide for failover if a switch fails. When this is done, it sometimes creates what is called a switching loop. Luckily, as you learned in Chapter 11, "Switching and Virtual LANs," Spanning Tree Protocol (STP) can prevent these loops from forming. There are two forms of switch redundancy: switch stacking and switch clusters.

Switch Stacking

Switch stacking is the process of connecting multiple switches (usually in a stack) and managing them as a single switch. Figure 16.4 shows a typical configuration.

FIGURE 16.4   Switch stacking

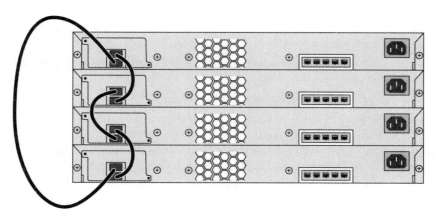

The stack members work together as a unified system. Layer 2 and layer 3 protocols present the entire switch stack as a single entity to the network.

A switch stack always has one active switch and one standby switch. If the active switch becomes unavailable, the standby switch assumes the role of the active switch and continues to keep the stack operational.

The active switch controls the operation of the switch stack and is the single point of stack-wide management.

A typical access closet contains one or more access switches placed next to each other in the same rack and uses high-speed redundant links with copper, or more typically fiber, to the distribution layer switches.

Here are three big drawbacks to a typical switch topology:

- There is management overhead.

- STP will block half of the uplinks.

- There is no direct communication between switches.

Cisco StackWise technology connects switches that are mounted in the same rack together so they basically become one larger switch. By doing this, you clearly get more access ports for each closet while avoiding the cost of upgrading to a bigger switch. So you're adding ports as you grow your company instead of front loading the investment into a pricier, larger switch all at once. And since these stacks are managed as a single unit, it reduces the management in your network.

All switches in a stack share configuration and routing information so you can easily add or remove switches at any time without disrupting your network or affecting its performance. Figure 16.4 shows a typical switch stack.

To create a StackWise unit, you combine switches into a single, logical unit using special stack interconnect cables, as shown in Figure 16.4. This creates a bidirectional closed-loop path in the stack.

Here are some other features of StackWise:

- Any changes to the network topology or routing information are updated continuously through the stack interconnect.

- A master switch manages the stack as a single unit. The master switch is elected from one of the stack member switches.

- You can join up to nine separate switches in a stack.

- Each stack of switches has only a single IP address, and the stack is managed as a single object. You'll use this single IP address for all the management of the stack, including fault detection, VLAN database updates, security, and QoS controls. Each stack has only one configuration file, which is distributed to each switch in StackWise.

- Using Cisco StackWise will produce some management overhead, but at the same time, multiple switches in a stack can create an EtherChannel connection, eliminating the need for STP.

Here's a list of the benefits to using StackWise technology:

- StackWise provides a method to join multiple physical switches into a single logical switching unit.

- Switches are united by special interconnect cables.

- The master switch is elected.

- The stack is managed as a single object and has a single management IP address.
- It reduces management overhead.
- STP is no longer needed if you use EtherChannel.
- Up to nine switches can be in a StackWise unit.

One more very cool thing: When you add a new switch to the stack, the master switch automatically configures the unit with the currently running IOS image as well as the configuration of the stack. So you don't have to do anything to bring up the switch before it's ready to operate. Nice!

Switch Clustering

A switch cluster is another option. This is a set of connected and cluster-capable switches that are managed as a single entity without interconnecting stack cables. This is possible by using Cluster Management Protocol (CMP). The switches in the cluster use the switch clustering technology so that you can configure and troubleshoot a group of different switch platforms through a single IP address. In those switches, one switch plays the role of cluster command switch, and the other switches are cluster member switches that are managed by the command switch.

Figure 16.5 shows a switch cluster.

FIGURE 16.5   Switch cluster

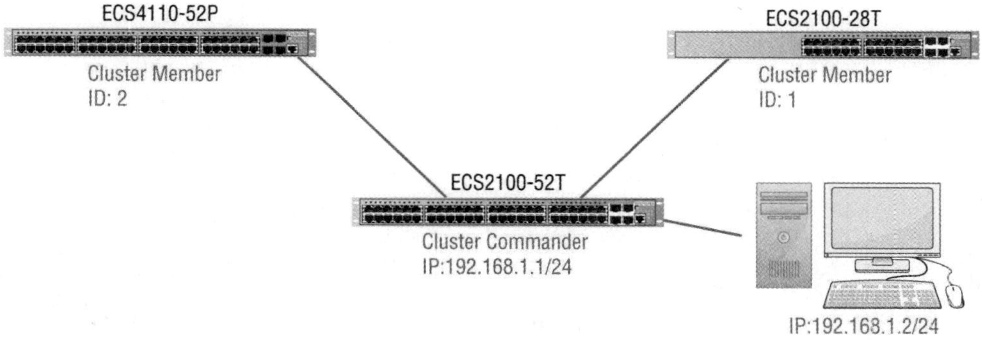

Notice that the cluster is managed by using the CMP address of the cluster commander.

Routers

Routers can also be set up in a redundant fashion. When we provide router redundancy, we call it providing first-hop redundancy since the router will be the first hop from any system to get to a destination. Accomplishing first-hop redundancy requires an FHRP protocol.

First-hop redundancy protocols (FHRPs) work by giving you a way to configure more than one physical router to appear as if they were only a single logical one. This makes client configuration and communication easier because you can configure a single default gateway, and the host machine can use its standard protocols to communicate.

First hop is a reference to the default router being the first router, or first router hop, through which a packet must pass.

So, how does a redundancy protocol accomplish this? The protocols I'm going to describe to you do this basically by presenting a virtual router to all of the clients. The virtual router has its own IP and MAC addresses. The virtual IP address is the address that's configured on each of the host machines as the default gateway. The virtual MAC address is the address that will be returned when an ARP request is sent by a host. The hosts don't know or care which physical router is actually forwarding the traffic, as you can see in Figure 16.6.

FIGURE 16.6   FHRPs use a virtual router with a virtual IP address and virtual MAC address.

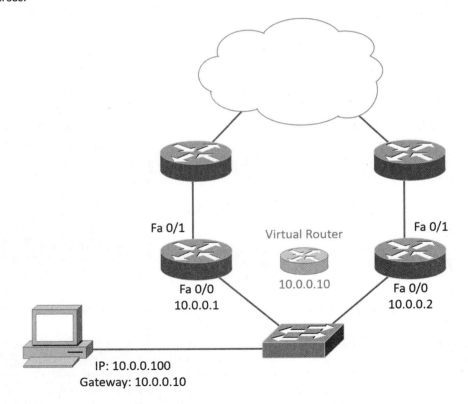

It's the responsibility of the redundancy protocol to decide which physical router will actively forward traffic and which one will be placed in standby in case the active router fails. Even if the active router fails, the transition to the standby router will be transparent to the hosts because the virtual router, identified by the virtual IP and MAC addresses, is now used by the standby router. The hosts never change default gateway information, so traffic keeps flowing.

Fault-tolerant solutions provide continued operation in the event of a device failure, and load-balancing solutions distribute the workload over multiple devices. Later in this chapter you will learn about the two most common FHRPs.

Firewalls

Firewalls can also be clustered, and some can also use FHRPs. A firewall cluster is a group of firewall nodes that work as a single logical entity to share the load of traffic processing and provide redundancy. Clustering guarantees the availability of network services to the users.

Cisco Adaptive Security Appliance (ASA) and Cisco Firepower next-generation firewall (NGFW) clustering allow you to group multiple ASA nodes as a single logical device to provide high availability and scalability. The two main clustering options discussed in this chapter are active/standby and active/active. In both cases, the firewall cluster looks like a single logical device (a single MAC/IP address) to the network.

Later in this chapter, you will learn more about active/active and active/standby operations.

Servers

Fault tolerance is the ability of a system to remain running after a component failure. Redundancy is the key to fault tolerance. When systems are built with redundancy, a component can suffer a failure and an identical component will resume its functionality. Systems should be designed with fault tolerance from the ground up.

Power Supply Redundancy

If a power supply in a piece of network equipment malfunctions, the equipment is dead. With the best support contracts, you could wait up to 4 hours before a new power supply arrives and you are back up and running again. Therefore, dual-power supplies are a requirement if high availability is desired. Fortunately, most networking equipment can be purchased with an optional second power supply. Dual-power supplies operate in a few different ways:

- *Active/passive* dual-power supplies allow only one power supply to supply power at a time. When a power fault occurs, the entire load of the device is shifted to the passive power supply, and then it becomes the active power supply. One problem with active-passive dual-power supplies is that only one power supply operates at a time. If the passive power supply is worn with age and the load is transferred, it has a higher chance of not functioning properly.

- *Load balancing* dual-power supplies allow both power supplies to operate in an active-active configuration. Both power supplies will supply a portion of the power to balance out the load. Load balancing dual-power supplies have a similar problem as active-passive dual-power supplies, because one will eventually have to carry the entire load.

- *Load-shifting* dual-power supplies are found in servers and data center equipment. As power is supplied by one power supply, the load, or a portion of the load, is slowly transferred to the other power supply and then back again. This method allows for testing of both power supplies, so problems are identified before an actual power outage.

Storage Redundancy

When installing the operating system on a hard drive or *Secure Digital (SD) card*, you should mirror the operating system onto an identical device, as shown in Figure 16.7. Redundant Array of Independent Disks *(RAID-1)* is also called mirroring, which supports the fault tolerance of the operating system in the event of a drive or card failure.

FIGURE 16.7 RAID-1 (mirroring)

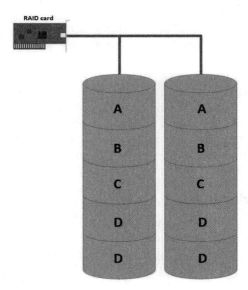

The data drives should be placed on a RAID level as well, but mirroring is too expensive since it requires each drive to be mirrored to an equal size drive. Striping with parity, also called *RAID-5*, is often used for data drives. RAID-5 requires three or more drives and operates by slicing the data being written into blocks, as shown in Figure 16.8. The first two drives receive the first two sequential blocks of data, but the third is a parity calculation of the first two blocks of data. The parity information and data blocks will alternate on the drives so that each drive has an equal amount of parity blocks. In the event of failure, a parity block and data block can create the missing block of data. Read performance is enhanced because several blocks (drives) are read at once. However, write performance is decreased because the parity information must be calculated. The calculated overhead of RAID-5 is 1/N: If three drives are used, one-third of the capacity is used for parity; if four drives are used, one-fourth of the capacity is used for parity; and so on.

FIGURE 16.8   RAID-5 (striping with parity)

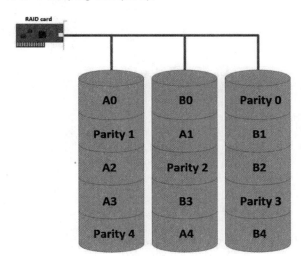

RAID-5 has its disadvantages. Because of the larger data sets, when a drive fails, the other drives must work longer to rebuild the missing drive. This puts the other drives under a severe stress level. If another drive fails during this process, you are at risk of losing your data completely.

Luckily, *RAID-6* helps ease the burden of large data sets. As shown in Figure 16.9, RAID-6 achieves this by striping two blocks of parity information with two independent parity schemes, but this requires at least four drives. RAID-6 allows you to lose a maximum of two drives and not suffer a total loss of data. The first parity block and another block can rebuild the missing block of data. If under a severe load of rebuilding a drive fails, a separate copy of parity has been calculated and can achieve the same goal of rebuilding. The overhead of RAID-6 is 2/N: If four drives are used, two-fourths, or one-half, the capacity is for parity; if five drives are used, two-fifths the capacity is used for parity; and so on.

Server hardware can manage faults related to a CPU and the motherboard and will switch processing to the second CPU, in the event of failure. Memory faults can also be predicted and managed so that information is not lost in the event of memory failure. All of these redundant systems can operate, and the only noticeable event will be an amber warning light on the server to notify the administrator the system requires attention.

FIGURE 16.9   RAID-6 (striping with two parity schemes)

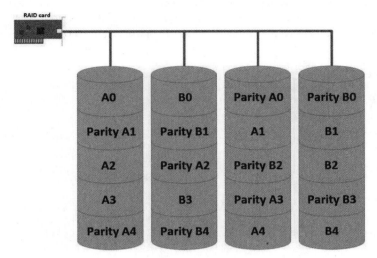

Clusters

Today's servers can be purchased with full redundancy so they maintain functionality in the event of any component failure. However, component redundancy does not address periods in which you need to take the system down for maintenance, nor does it address the load of processes that require several servers processing together.

Clusters are redundant groupings of servers that can balance the load of processes and allow maintenance or complete failure on a node without consequence to overall operation. The Microsoft Server 2019 product contains a feature called Failover Clustering that allows applications to run in a high availability mode. If one server fails or is put into maintenance mode, then the application will fail to another server. The application must be written for failover clustering, and although it was popular 5 to 10 years ago, today it has been upstaged by virtualization clusters.

Mean Time to Repair

One of the metrics that's used in planning both SLAs and IT operations in general is mean time to repair (MTTR). This value describes the average length of time it takes a vendor to repair a device or component. By building these into SLAs, IT can assure that the time taken to repair a component or device will not be a factor that causes them to violate the SLAs' requirements. Sometimes MTTR is considered to be from the point at which the failure is first discovered until the point at which the equipment returns to operation. In other cases it is a measure of the elapsed time between the point where repairs actually begin until the point at which the equipment returns to operation. It is important that there is a clear understanding by all parties with regard to when the clock starts and ends when calculating MTTR.

Mean Time Between Failure

Another valuable metric typically provided is the mean time between failures (MTBF), which describes the amount of time that elapses between one failure and the next. Mathematically, this is the sum of mean time to failure (MTTF) and MTTR, which is the total time required to get the device fixed and back online.

Planned Downtime

There's a difference between planned downtime and unplanned downtime. Planned downtime is good—it's occasionally scheduled for system maintenance and routine upgrades. Unplanned downtime is bad—it's a lack of access due to system failure, which is exactly the issue high availability resolves.

Facilities and Infrastructure Support

When infrastructure equipment is purchased and deployed, the ultimate success of the deployment can depend on selecting the proper equipment, determining its proper location in the facility, and installing it correctly. Let's look at some common data center and server room equipment and a few best practices for managing these facilities.

Uninterruptible Power Supply

One risk that all organizations should prepare for is the loss of power. All infrastructure systems should be connected to uninterruptible power supplies (UPSs). These devices can immediately supply power from a battery backup when a loss of power is detected. You should keep in mind, however, that these devices are not designed as a long-term solution. They are designed to provide power long enough for you to either shut the system down gracefully or turn on a power generator. In scenarios where long-term backup power is called for, a gas-powered generator should be installed.

There are several types of UPS systems that you may encounter. The main types are as follows:

- A *standby UPS* is the most common UPS, the kind you find under a desk protecting a personal computer. It operates by transferring the load from the AC line to the battery-supplied inverter, and capacitors in the unit help to keep the power sag to a minimum. These units work well, but they are not generally found in server rooms.

- A *line interactive UPS* is commonly used for small server rooms and racks of networking equipment. It operates by supplying power from the AC line to the inverter. When a power failure occurs, the line signals the inverter to draw power from the batteries. This might seem similar to a standby UPS, but the difference is that the load is not shifted. In a standby UPS, the load must shift from AC to a completely different circuit (the inverter), whereas on a line interactive UPS, the inverter is always wired to the load, but only during the power outage is the inverter running on batteries. This shift in power allows for a much smoother transition of power.

- An *online UPS* is the standard for data centers. It operates by supplying AC power to a rectifier/charging circuit that maintains a charge for the batteries. The batteries then supply the inverter with a constant DC power source. The inverter converts the DC power source back into an AC power circuit that supplies the load. The benefit of an online UPS is that the power is constantly supplied from the batteries. When there is a power loss, the unit maintains a constant supply of power to the load. The other benefit is that the online UPS always supplies a perfect AC signal.

Power Distribution Units

Power distribution units (PDUs) simply provide a means of distributing power from the input to a plurality of outlets. Intelligent PDUs normally have an intelligence module that allows for remote management of power metering information, power outlet on/off control, and/or alarms. Some advanced PDUs allow users to manage external sensors such as temperature, humidity, and airflow.

While these can be as simple as a power strip, larger PDUs are needed in data centers to power multiple server cabinets. Each server cabinet or row of cabinets may require multiple high-current circuits, possibly from different phases of incoming power or different UPSs. Stand-alone cabinet PDUs are self-contained units that include main circuit breakers, individual circuit breakers, and power monitoring panels.

Figure 16.10 shows a standard rack mount PDU.

Generator

Power generators supply power during a power outage. They consist of three major components: fuel, an engine, and a generator. The engine burns the fuel to turn the generator and create power. The three common sources of fuel are natural gas, gasoline, and diesel.

FIGURE 16.10   Rack-mounted PDU

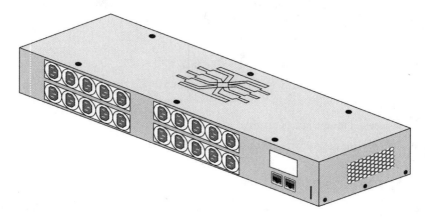

Diesel-fueled generators are the most common type of generator supplying data centers around the world.

As mentioned earlier, generators require a startup period before they can supply a constant source of electricity. In addition to the startup period, there is also a switchover lag. When a power outage occurs, the transfer switch moves the load from the street power to the generator circuit. UPSs help bridge both the lag and sag in electricity supply during the switchover and startup periods.

HVAC

Like any device with a CPU, infrastructure devices such as routers, switches, and specialty appliances must have a cool area to operate. When temperatures rise, servers start rebooting, and appliance CPUs start overworking as well.

The room(s) where these devices are located should be provided with heavy-duty heating, ventilation, and air conditioning (HVAC) systems and ample ventilation. It is advisable to dedicate a suite for this purpose and put the entire system on a UPS with a backup generator in the case of a loss of power.

The heating and air-conditioning systems must support the massive amounts of computing equipment most enterprises deploy. Computing equipment and infrastructure devices like routers and switches do not like the following conditions:

- **Heat:** Excessive heat causes reboots and crashes.
- **High humidity:** It causes corrosion problems with connections.
- **Low humidity:** Dry conditions encourage static electricity, which can damage equipment.

The American Society of Heating, Refrigerating and Air-Conditioning Engineers (ASHRAE) publishes standards for indoor air quality and humidity. Their latest recommendations are as follows:

- A class A1 data center
- Can range in temperature from 59°F to 89.6°F
- Can range in relative humidity from 20 percent to 80 percent.

Also keep in mind:

- At 175 degrees, damage starts occurring to computers and peripherals.
- At 350 degrees, damage starts occurring to paper products.

Fire Suppression

While fire extinguishers are important and should be placed throughout a facility, when large numbers of computing devices are present, it is worth the money to protect them with a fire-suppression system. There are five basic types of fire suppression you may find in a facility:

Wet Pipe System This is the most common fire suppression system found in facilities such as office complexes and even residential buildings. The wet pipe system is constantly charged with water from a holding tank or the city water supply. The sprinkler head contains a small glass capsule that holds a glycerin-based liquid that keeps the valve shut. When the glass capsule is heated between 135°F to 165°F, the liquid expands, breaking the glass and opening the value. Gallons of water will dump in that area until either the fire is extinguished or another head opens from excessive heat.

Dry Pipe System Although the name is deceiving, a dry pipe system uses water, similar to a wet pipe system. The difference is that a dry pipe system does not initially contain water. The pipes in a dry pipe system are charged with air or nitrogen. When a pressure drop occurs because a sprinkler head is heated between 135°F to 165°F, the air escapes out of the sprinkler head. The water is then released behind the initial air charge and the system will operate similarly to a wet pipe system.

Preaction Systems The preaction system is identical to the dry pipe system in operations. The preaction system employs an additional mechanism of an independent thermal link that pre-charges the system with water. The system will not dump water unless the sprinkler head is heated between 135°F to 165°F and the thermal link is tripped by smoke or fire. This is an additional factor of safety for the equipment, so a sprinkler head is not tripped by an accident such as a ladder banging into it.

Deluge Systems The deluge systems are some of the simplest systems, and they are often used in factory settings. They do not contain a valve in the sprinkler head, just a deflector for the water. When a fire breaks out, the entire system dumps water from all of the sprinkler heads.

Clean Agent   There are many different clean agents available on the market today. These systems are deployed in data centers worldwide because they do not damage equipment in the event of a fire. The principle of operation is simple: The system displaces oxygen in the air below 15% to contain the fire. The clean agent is always a gas, and these systems are often mislabeled as halon systems. At one time, fire suppression systems used halon gas, which works well by suppressing combustion through a chemical reaction. However, the US Environmental Protection Agency (EPA) banned halon manufacturing in 1994 as it has been found to damage the ozone layer.

The EPA has approved the following replacements for halon:

- Water
- Argon
- NAF-S-III
- FM-200
- Or mixture of gases

EXERCISE 16.1

Designing Facilities and Infrastructure

In this exercise, you will design a mock facility with all of the items you learned about in this section and explain their various functions and why you chose the items.

You need to support a dedicated data center of server. There are three racks of server in the data center. In the event of a power failure, the data center needs to remain in operation. And in the event there is a fire, the equipment must remain unharmed.

After you have made your list of items that you would recommend building the data center with, go back through this section and check if each one was appropriate.

Redundancy and High Availability Concepts

All organizations should identify and analyze the risks they face. This is called risk management. In the following sections, you'll find a survey of topics that all relate in some way to addressing risks that can be mitigated with redundancy and high availability techniques.

Disaster Recovery Sites

Although a secondary site that is identical in every way to the main site with data kept synchronized up to the minute would be ideal, the cost cannot be justified for most organizations. Cost-benefit analysis must be applied to every business issue, even disaster recovery. Thankfully, not all secondary sites are created equally. They can vary in functionality and cost. We're going to explore four types of sites: cold sites, warm sites, hot sites, and cloud sites.

Cold Site

A cold site is a leased facility that contains only electrical and communications wiring, air conditioning, plumbing, and raised flooring. No communications equipment, networking hardware, or computers are installed at a cold site until it is necessary to bring the site to full operation. For this reason, a cold site takes much longer to restore than a hot or warm site.

A cold site provides the slowest recovery, but it is the least expensive to maintain. It is also the most difficult to test.

Warm Site

The restoration time and cost of a warm site is somewhere between that of a hot site and a cold site. It is the most widely implemented alternate leased location. Although it is easier to test a warm site than a cold site, a warm site requires much more effort for testing than a hot site.

A warm site is a leased facility that contains electrical and communications wiring, full utilities, and networking equipment. In most cases, the only thing that needs to be restored is the software and the data. A warm site takes longer to restore than a hot site but less than a cold site.

Hot Site

A hot site is a leased facility that contains all the resources needed for full operation. This environment includes computers, raised flooring, full utilities, electrical and communications wiring, networking equipment, and uninterruptible power supplies. The only resource that must be restored at a hot site is the organization's data, usually only partially. It should take only a few minutes to bring a hot site to full operation.

Although a hot site provides the quickest recovery, it is the most expensive to maintain. In addition, it can be administratively hard to manage if the organization requires proprietary hardware or software. A hot site requires the same security controls as the primary facility and full redundancy, including hardware, software, and communication wiring.

Cloud Site

A cloud recovery site is an extension of the cloud backup services that have developed over the years. These are sites that, while mimicking your on-premises network, are totally virtual, as shown in Figure 16.11.

FIGURE 16.11   Cloud recovery site

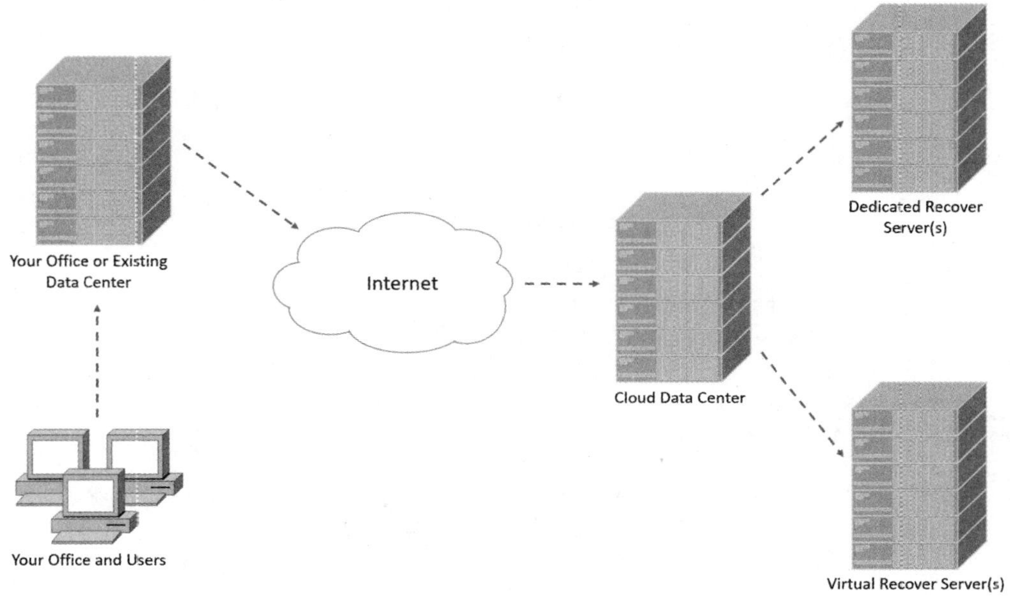

Your Office or Existing Data Center

Internet

Cloud Data Center

Dedicated Recover Server(s)

Virtual Recover Server(s)

Your Office and Users

Organizations that lack the expertise to develop even a cold site may benefit from engaging with a cloud vendor of these services.

Active/Active vs. Active/Passive

When systems are arranged for fault tolerance or high availability, they can be set up in either an active/active arrangement or an active/passive configuration. Earlier in this chapter you learned that when set to active/active state, both or all devices (servers, routers, switches, etc.) are performing work, and when set to active/passive, at least one device is on standby in case a working device fails. Active/active increases availability by providing more systems for work, while active/passive provides fault tolerance by holding at least one system in reserve in case of a system failure.

Multiple Internet Service Providers/Diverse Paths

Redundancy may also be beneficial when it comes to your Internet connection. There are two types of redundancy that can be implemented.

Path redundancy is accomplished by configuring paths to the Internet service provider (ISP), as shown in Figure 16.12. There is a single ISP with two paths extending to the ISP from two different routers.

FIGURE 16.12   Path redundancy

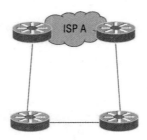

That's great, but what if the ISP suffers a failure (it does happen)? To protect against that you could engage two different ISPs with a path to each from a single router, as shown in Figure 16.13.

FIGURE 16.13   ISP redundancy

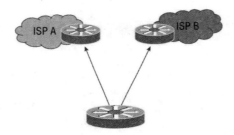

For complete protection you could combine the two by using a separate router connection to each ISP, thus protecting against an issue with a single router or path in your network, as shown in Figure 16.14.

FIGURE 16.14   Path and ISP redundancy

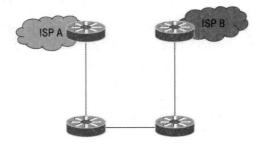

First-Hop Redundancy Protocol

Earlier in this chapter I mentioned First-Hop Redundancy Protocol (FHRP) and said we would come back to it. Now is the time. There are two first-hop redundancy protocols: Hot Standby Router Protocol (HSRP) and Virtual Router Redundancy Protocol (VRRP). HSRP is a Cisco proprietary protocol, while VRRP is a standards-based protocol. Let's look at them.

Hot Standby Router Protocol

Hot Standby Router Protocol is a Cisco proprietary protocol that can be run on most, but not all, of Cisco's router and multilayer switch models. It defines a standby group, and each standby group that you define includes the following routers:

- Active router
- Standby router
- Virtual router
- Any other routers that may be attached to the subnet

The problem with HSRP is that, with it, only one router is active, and two or more routers just sit there in standby mode and won't be used unless a failure occurs—not very cost effective or efficient! Figure 16.15 shows how only one router is used at a time in an HSRP group.

FIGURE 16.15   HSRP active and standby routers

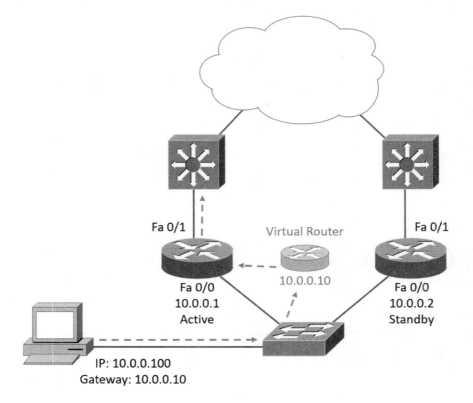

The standby group will always have at least two routers participating in it. The primary players in the group are the one active router and one standby router that communicate to each other using multicast Hello messages. The Hello messages provide all of the required communication for the routers. The Hellos contain the information required to accomplish the election that determines the active and standby router positions. They also hold the key to the failover process. If the standby router stops receiving Hello packets from the active router, it then takes over the active router role, as shown in Figure 16.16.

FIGURE 16.16   HSRP active and standby routers

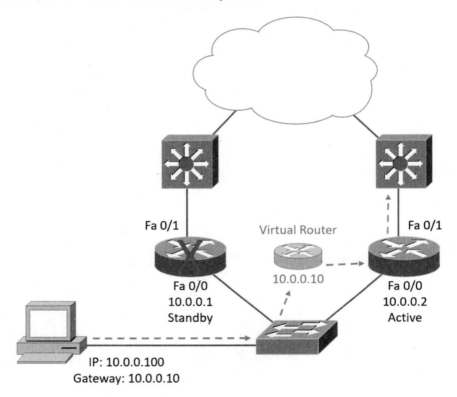

As soon as the active router stops responding to Hellos, the standby router automatically becomes the active router and starts responding to host requests.

VIRTUAL MAC ADDRESS

A virtual router in an HSRP group has a virtual IP address and a virtual MAC address. So where does that virtual MAC address come from? The virtual IP address isn't that hard to figure out; it just has to be a unique IP address on the same subnet as the hosts defined in the configuration. But MAC addresses are a little different, right? Or are they? The answer is yes—sort of. With HSRP, you create a totally new, made-up MAC address in addition to the IP address.

The HSRP MAC address has only one variable piece in it. The first 24 bits still identify the vendor that manufactured the device (the organizationally unique identifier, or OUI). The next 16 bits in the address tells us that the MAC address is a well-known HSRP MAC address. Finally, the last 8 bits of the address are the hexadecimal representation of the HSRP group number.

Let me clarify all this with an example of what an HSRP MAC address would look like:

0000.0c07.ac0a

Here's how it breaks down:

- The first 24 bits (0000.0c) are the vendor ID of the address; in the case of HSRP being a Cisco protocol, the ID is assigned to Cisco.

- The next 16 bits (07.ac) are the well-known HSRP ID. This part of the address was assigned by Cisco in the protocol, so it's always easy to recognize that this address is for use with HSRP.

- The last 8 bits (0a) are the only variable bits and represent the HSRP group number that you assign. In this case, the group number is 10 and converted to hexadecimal when placed in the MAC address, where it becomes the 0a that you see.

You can see this MAC address added to the ARP cache of every router in the HSRP group. There will be the translation from the IP address to the MAC address as well as the interface on which it's located.

HSRP TIMERS

Before we get deeper into the roles that each of the routers can have in an HSRP group, I want to define the HSRP timers. The timers are very important to HSRP function because they ensure communication between the routers, and if something goes wrong, they allow the standby router to take over. The HSRP timers include hello, hold, active, and standby.

- **Hello timer:** The hello timer is the defined interval during which each of the routers sends out Hello messages. Their default interval is 3 seconds, and they identify the state that each router is in. This is important because the particular state determines the specific role of each router and, as a result, the actions each will take within the group. Figure 16.17 shows the Hello messages being sent, and the router uses the hello timer to keep network traffic flowing in case of a failure.

  This timer can be changed, and people used to avoid doing so because it was *thought* that lowering the hello value would place an unnecessary load on the routers. That isn't true with most of the routers today; in fact, you can configure the timers in milliseconds, meaning the failover time can be in milliseconds! Still, keep in mind that increasing the value will cause the standby router to wait longer before taking over for the active router when it fails or can't communicate.

FIGURE 16.17 HSRP active and standby routers

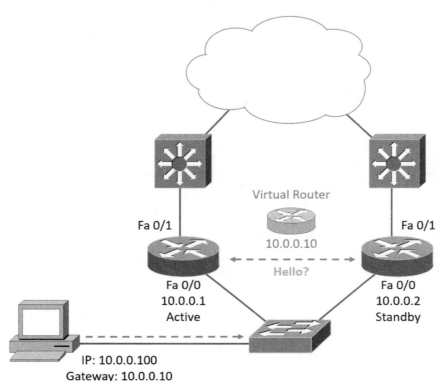

- **Hold timer:** The hold timer specifies the interval the standby router uses to determine whether the active router is offline or out of communication. By default, the hold timer is 10 seconds, roughly three times the default for the hello timer. If one timer is changed for some reason, I recommend using this multiplier to adjust the other timers too. By setting the hold timer at three times the hello timer, you ensure that the standby router doesn't take over the active role every time there's a short break in communication.

- **Active timer:** The active timer monitors the state of the active router. The timer resets each time a router in the standby group receives a Hello packet from the active router. This timer expires based on the hold time value that's set in the corresponding field of the HSRP Hello message.

- **Standby timer:** The standby timer is used to monitor the state of the standby router. The timer resets anytime a router in the standby group receives a Hello packet from the standby router and expires based on the hold time value that's set in the respective Hello packet.

⊕ **Real World Scenario**

Large Enterprise Network Outages with FHRPs

Years ago when HSRP was all the rage, and before VRRP, enterprises used hundreds of HSRP groups. With the hello timer set to 3 seconds and a hold time of 10 seconds, these timers worked just fine, and we had great redundancy with our core routers.

However, as we've seen in the last few years, and will certainly see in the future, 10 seconds is now a lifetime! Some of my customers have been complaining about the failover time and loss of connectivity to their virtual server farms.

So lately I've been changing the timers to well below the defaults. Cisco had changed the timers so you could use subsecond times for failover. Because these are multicast packets, the overhead that is seen on a current high-speed network is almost nothing.

The hello timer is typically set to 200 milliseconds (msec), and the hold time is 700 msec. The command is as follows:

```
(config-if)#Standby 1 timers msec 200 msec 700
```

This almost ensures that not even a single packet is lost when there is an outage.

Virtual Router Redundancy Protocol

Like HSRP, Virtual Router Redundancy Protocol allows a group of routers to form a single virtual router. In an HSRP or VRRP group, one router is elected to handle all requests sent to the virtual IP address. With HSRP, this is the active router. An HSRP group has only one active router, at least one standby router, and many listening routers. A VRRP group has one master router and one or more backup routers and is the open standard implementation of HSRP.

COMPARING VRRP AND HSRP

The LAN workstations are configured with the address of the virtual router as their default gateway, just as they are with HSRP, but VRRP differs from HSRP in these important ways:

- VRRP is an IEEE standard (RFC 2338) for router redundancy; HSRP is a Cisco proprietary protocol.

- The virtual router that represents a group of routers is known as a VRRP group.

- The active router is referred to as the master virtual router.

- The master virtual router may have the same IP address as the virtual router group.

- Multiple routers can function as backup routers.

- VRRP is supported on Ethernet, Fast Ethernet, and Gigabit Ethernet interfaces as well as on Multiprotocol Label Switching (MPLS), virtual private networks (VPNs), and VLANs.

VRRP REDUNDANCY CHARACTERISTICS

VRRP has some unique features:

- VRRP provides redundancy for the real IP address of a router or for a virtual IP address shared among the VRRP group members.

- If a real IP address is used, the router with that address becomes the master.

- If a virtual IP address is used, the master is the router with the highest priority.

- A VRRP group has one master router and one or more backup routers.

- The master router uses VRRP messages to inform group members.

Backups

Backups are not just there for disasters. For example, you may need a backup simply because of mistakes on the part of a user deleting files. However, backups are typically used for larger problems such as malicious data loss or failures of disk subsystems.

Administrators will adopt a rotation schedule for long-term archiving of data. The most popular backup rotation is *grandfather, father, son (GFS)*. The GFS rotation specifies that the daily backup will be rotated on a *first-in, first-out (FIFO)* basis. One of the daily backups will become the weekly backup. And last, one of the weekly backups will become the month-end backup. Policies should be created such as retaining 6 daily backups, retaining 4 weekly backups, and retaining 12 monthly backups. As you progress further away from the first six days, the RPO jumps to a weekly basis and then to a monthly basis. However, the benefit is that you can retain data over a longer period of time with the same number of tapes.

Three types of media are commonly used for backups:

- *Disk-to-tape* backups have evolved quite a bit throughout the years. Today, *Linear Tape-Open (LTO)* technology has become the successor for backups. LTO can provide 6 TB of raw capacity per tape, with plans for 48 TB per tape in the near future. Tapes are portable enough to rotate off-site for safekeeping. However, time is required to record the data, resulting in lengthy backup windows. Restores also require time to tension the tape, locate the data, and restore the data, making the RTO a lengthy process.

- *Disk-to-disk* backups have become standard in data centers as well because of the short RTO. They can record the data quicker, thus shortening backup windows. They also do not require tensioning and do not require seeking for the data as tape media requires. However, the capacity of a disk is much smaller than tapes because the drives remain in the backup unit. Data deduplication can provide a nominal 10:1 compression ratio, depending on the data. This means that 10 TB of data can be compressed on 1 TB of disk storage. So a 10 TB storage unit can potentially back up 100 TB of data; this depends on the types of files you are backing up.

- *Disk-to-cloud* is another popular and emerging backup technology. It is often used with disk-to-disk backups to provide an off-site storage location for end-of-week backups or monthly backups. The two disadvantages of disk-to-cloud is the ongoing cost and the lengthy RTO. The advantage is that expensive backup equipment does not need to be purchased along with the ongoing purchase of tapes.

Network Device Backup/Restore

Files are not the only thing that should be backed up on the network. Network devices should be backed up as well, since their configuration is usually completely unique. Configurations such as the various port configurations on a network switch can be a nightmare to reconfigure. Configurations can be lost because they were erased by accident or overwritten or due to just plain failure of the equipment. There are automated appliances and software that can automatically back up configuration of switches on a daily basis. Many vendors also have mechanisms so that the equipment can back itself up to a TFTP, FTP, SFTP server, or even a flash card.

In the case of a cluster host or virtualization host, configuration is not the only thing you will need to back up in the event of failure. The overall state of the device should be saved as well, in the event the device needs to be completely replaced. The software installed on the device expects MAC addresses and disk configuration to be the same when it is moved to new hardware. Otherwise, the software could need to be completely reinstalled. Thankfully, many vendors allow for state to be saved. This allows a complete forklift of the operating system and data without reinstalling.

Recovery

The concept of the *recovery point objective (RPO)* defines the point in time that you can restore to in the event of a disaster. The RPO is often the night before, since backup windows are often scheduled at night. The concept of *recovery time objective (RTO)* defines how fast you can restore the data. In this section I discuss backup methods, some of which can speed up the process. However, the disadvantage is that these methods will increase the recovery time, as I will explain.

Recovery Point Objective   An RPO is a measurement of time from the failure, disaster, or comparable loss-causing event. RPOs measure back in time to when your data was preserved in a usable format, usually to the most recent backup.

Recovery Time Objective   This is the shortest time period after a disaster or disruptive event within which a resource or function must be restored in order to avoid unacceptable consequences. RTO assumes that an acceptable period of downtime exists.

Testing

When discussing testing, you must understand that your network plan needs testing. To do that, the industry uses what is called tabletop exercises.

Tabletop exercises are cost-effective to test and validate your plan, procedure, network, and security policies. This can also be called walk-throughs or table-top exercises (TTXs).

This exercise is a discussion-based event where staff or personnel with roles and responsibilities in a particular IT plan meet in a classroom setting or breakout groups to discuss their roles during an emergency and their responses to a particular emergency.

These are meant to be a very informal environment, with an open discussion, guided by an administrator, through a discussion designed to meet predefined objectives.

These can be a cost-effective tool to validate the plans of IT, such as backups, contingency plans, and incident response plans. This ensures the plan content is viable and implementable in an emergency.

Tabletop Exercises

TTXs exercises, also called play, are a great way to test processes and plans. By communicating with the group members, you can stress test all the procedures and other processes.

You can use a TTX play to perform a tabletop exercise, verify the existing integration plane, and identify areas that would break if you were to implement the plans.

Tabletop exercises can do the following:

- Help assess plans, policies, and procedures.
- Identify gaps and challenges.
- Clarify roles and responsibilities.
- Identify additional mitigation and preparedness needs.
- Provide hands-on training.
- Highlight flaws in incident response planning.

Validation Tests

Once your plan is in place, next comes the validation.

Validation of the plan comes from listening or reading all group and group participants' feedback. These sessions allow for the plan, procedures, and policies to be revised.

Before you design and execute any exercise, you must clearly understand what you want to achieve and plan your testing methods.

Consider these questions: What are the specific goals and outcomes? What are the potential threats and risks that could disrupt your operations? How will you measure and evaluate your performance and improvement? You can focus your exercise on the most relevant and essential aspects by identifying your objectives first.

Here is a list to use well-validating and tabletop tests:

Set Up the Initial Meeting   Gather all cross-functional leads and domain experts and lay out the scenario. Provide all the facts regarding the deal for evaluation and input for the next meeting.

Listen to Feedback   In this second meeting, listen to the cross-functional teams. They will be able to provide good insights into how the integration will affect their respective function. If it's too complicated, a third meeting might be required.

Conclusion   Come up with conclusions on the things that are possible. Everyone should be clear on what can be safely integrated, the risks that come with it, and mitigation plans.

Document the Process   A new practice, process, or function should be generated at the end of these exercises. Document them for future reference.

Summary

In this chapter, you learned the importance of providing both fault tolerance and high availability. You also learned about disaster recovery concepts.

We discussed ensuring continued access to resources with load balancing, multipathing, and NIC teaming. Expanding on that concept, we looked at setting up clusters of routers, switches, and firewalls. Finally, we took up facilities redundancy with techniques such as UPS systems, PDUs, and generators and environmental issues such as HVAC systems and fire suppression systems.

In disaster recovery you learned about hot, cold, warm, and cloud sites and how they fit into a disaster recovery plan. You also learned terms critical to planning for disaster recovery, such as MTTR, MTBF, RTO, and RPO.

Finally, we covered backup operations for both configurations and system state and planning and validating a tabletop test.

Exam Essentials

Understand the importance of fault tolerance and high availability techniques.   These include load balancing, multipathing, NIC teaming, and router, switch, and firewall clusters.

Describe facilities and infrastructure redundancy techniques.   Among these are uninterruptible power supplies (UPSs), power distribution units (PDUs), generators, HVAC systems, fire suppression, and multiple Internet service providers (ISPs)/diverse paths.

Utilize disaster recovery techniques.   These include physical cold sites, warm sites, hot sites, and cloud sites. It also requires an understanding of RPO, MTTR, MTBF, and RTO.

Identify applications of active/active and active/passive configurations. These include switch clusters, VRRP and HSRP, and firewall clusters.

Written Lab

Complete the table by filling in the appropriate term for each definition.

You can find the answers in Appendix A.

Definition	Term
Technique used to spread work out to multiple computers, network links, or other devices	
Allows multiple network interfaces to be placed into a team for the purposes of bandwidth aggregation	
Devices that can immediately supply power from a battery backup when a loss of power is detected	
A leased facility that contains all the resources needed for full operation	
A Cisco proprietary FHRP	

Review Questions

You can find the answers to the review questions in Appendix B.

1. You have a high demand of normal requests on the company's web server. Which strategy should be implemented to avoid issues if demand becomes too high? (Choose the best answer.)

   A. Clustering

   B. Port aggregation

   C. Fault tolerance

   D. Load balancing

2. Which of the following is a measure back in time to when your data was preserved in a usable format, usually to the most recent backup?

   A. RTO

   B. MTBF

   C. RPO

   D. MTTR

3. Which of the following is an IEEE standard (RFC 2338) for router redundancy?

   A. HSRP

   B. VRRP

   C. HDLC

   D. MLPS

4. Which of the following is the defined interval during which each of the routers send out Hello messages in HSRP?

   A. Hold timer

   B. Hello timer

   C. Active timer

   D. Standby timer

5. What is the HSRP group number of the group with the following HSRP MAC address?

   0000.0c07.ac0a

   A. 10

   B. 17

   C. 20

   D. 25

6. Which of the following provides only fault tolerance?

A. Two servers in an active/active configuration

B. Three servers in an active/passive configuration with one on standby

C. Three servers in an active/passive configuration with two on standby

D. Three servers in an active/active configuration

7. Which site type mimics your on-premises network yet is totally virtual?

A. Cold site

B. Cloud site

C. Warm site

D. Hot site

8. Which of the following fire suppression systems is not a good choice where computing equipment will be located?

A. Deluge

B. CO2

C. Argon

D. NAF-S-III

9. Which of the following protocols gives you a way to configure more than one physical router to appear as if they were only a single logical one?

A. FHRP

B. NAT

C. NIC teaming

D. STP

10. Which of the following provides a method to join multiple physical switches into a single logical switching unit?

A. Stacking

B. Daisy chaining

C. Segmenting

D. Federating

11. Which type of recovery is the least expensive to maintain over time?

A. Cold site recovery

B. Warm site recovery

C. Hot site recovery

D. Cloud site recovery

12. A recovery from tape will take 4 hours; what is this an example of?

   A. The recovery point objective (RPO)

   B. The recovery time objective (RTO)

   C. GFS rotation

   D. Backup window

13. You need to purchase a power backup system for a mission critical data center. Which backup systems will ensure long-term power that has a flawless AC signal? (Choose two.)

   A. Standby UPS

   B. Line interactive UPS

   C. Online UPS

   D. Generator

14. Which allows for the feedback and revision of plans, procedures, and policies?

   A. Tabletop exercises

   B. SOP

   C. RTO

   D. Validation tests

15. Which fire suppression system is normally found in data centers?

   A. Deluge

   B. Clean agent

   C. Preaction

   D. Dry pipe

16. Which environmental factor can cause the potential for electrostatic discharge?

   A. Temperature

   B. Electrical

   C. Humidity

   D. Flooding

17. Which type of uninterruptable power supplies (UPS), often found in data centers, provides constant power from the battery-powered inverter circuit?

   A. Line interactive UPS

   B. Standby UPS

   C. Online UPS

   D. Failover UPS

18. You need to choose a vendor based on their speed in fixing issues. Which metric should you evaluate?

A. MTTR

B. VRRP

C. HSRP

D. MTBF

19. You need to supply power for a rack of servers. Which device should you use?

A. Inverter

B. HVAC

C. UPS

D. PDU

20. You have a server in a data center that has two interfaces. What should you employ to make sure that a switch failure will not impede network function of the server?

A. HSRP

B. VRRP

C. NIC teaming

D. STP

Chapter

17

Data Center Architecture and Cloud Concepts

THE FOLLOWING COMPTIA NETWORK+ EXAM OBJECTIVES ARE COVERED IN THIS CHAPTER:

✓ **Domain 1.0 Networking Concepts**

✓ **1.3 Summarize cloud concepts and connectivity options.**

- Network functions virtualization (NFV)
- Virtual private cloud (VPC)
- Network security groups
- Network security lists
- Cloud gateways
  - Internet gateway
  - Network address translation (NAT) gateway
- Cloud connectivity options
  - VPN
  - Direct Connect
- Deployment models
  - Public
  - Private
  - Hybrid
- Service models
  - Software as a service (SaaS)
  - Infrastructure as a service (IaaS)
  - Platform as a service (PaaS)

- Scalability
- Elasticity
- Multitenancy

✓ **1.8 Summarize evolving use cases for modern network environments.**

- Software-defined network (SDN) and software-defined wide area network (SD-WAN)
  - Application-aware
  - Zero-touch provisioning
  - Transport agnostic
  - Central policy management
- Virtual Extensible Local Area Network (VXLAN)
  - Data Center Interconnect (DCI)
  - Layer 2 encapsulation
- Zero trust architecture (ZTA)
  - Policy-based authentication
  - Authorization
  - Least privilege access
- Secure Access Secure Edge (SASE)/Security Service Edge (SSE)
- Infrastructure as code (IaC)
  - Automation
    - Playbooks/templates/reusable tasks
    - Configuration drift/compliance
    - Upgrades
    - Dynamic inventories
  - Source control
    - Version control
    - Central repository
    - Conflict identification
    - Branching

The traditional compute model was based on a one-to-one relation of application to server. However, most applications use only a fraction of the compute resources during idle periods, and all applications collectively seldom use all of the compute resources at the same time.

Virtualization allows us to partition compute resources for each guest operating system (OS) supporting an application running on the host hardware. The hypervisor allows the partitioning of compute resources. The partitioning of virtualization allows each OS to operate as if it had exclusive control of the host hardware. Compute resources consist of the central processing unit (CPU), memory, and devices related to a physical server.

Cloud services allow us to pool the resources together for each host server providing virtualization. When the resources of computer, network, and storage are pooled together, the cloud gains fault tolerance and scale. This allows us to lose a host and still maintain the ability to compute the workload of the guest operating systems supporting our applications. It also allows us to add resources of compute, network, and storage to scale the cloud out for additional workloads. The scale of workloads is referred to as elasticity.

The cloud model is based on a many-to-many model where the exact location of the resources doesn't matter to the end user. We can create an application by allocating available resources to a guest OS from a pool of resources. The guest OS will then gain the fault tolerance of the cloud along with the added benefit of elasticity of the cloud.

In this chapter, you will learn about the data center where your private cloud would be located, as well as the public cloud.

To find Todd Lammle CompTIA videos and practice questions, please see www.lammle.com.

Cloud Computing

Cloud computing is by far one of the hottest topics in today's IT world. Basically, cloud computing can provide virtualized processing, storage, and computing resources to users remotely, making the resources transparently available regardless of the user connection. To put it simply, some people just refer to the cloud as "someone else's hard drive." This is true, of course, but the cloud is much more than just storage.

The history of the consolidation and virtualization of our servers tells us that this has become the de facto way of implementing servers because of basic resource efficiency. Two physical servers will use twice the amount of electricity as one server, but through virtualization, one physical server can host two (or more) virtual machines, which is the reason for the main thrust toward virtualization. With it, network components can simply be shared more efficiently.

Users connecting to a cloud provider's network, whether it be for storage or applications, really don't care about the underlying infrastructure because as computing becomes a service rather than a product, it's then considered an on-demand resource.

Centralization/consolidation of resources, automation of services, virtualization, and standardization are just a few of the big benefits cloud services offer.

Cloud computing has several advantages over the traditional use of computer resources. The following are the advantages to a cloud service builder or provider:

- Cost reduction, standardization, and automation
- High utilization through virtualized, shared resources
- Easier administration
- Fall-in-place operations model

The following are the advantages to cloud users:

- On-demand, self-service resource provisioning
- Fast deployment cycles
- Cost effective
- Centralized appearance of resources
- Highly available, horizontally scaled application architectures
- No local backups

Having centralized resources is critical for today's workforce. For example, if you have your documents stored locally on your laptop and your laptop gets stolen, you're pretty much screwed unless you're doing constant local backups. That is so 2005!

After I lost my laptop and all the files for the book I was writing at the time, I swore (yes, I did that too) to never have my files stored locally again. I started using only Google Drive, OneDrive, and Dropbox for all my files, and they became my best backup friends. If I lose my laptop now, I just need to log in from any computer from anywhere to my service provider's logical drives, and presto, I have all my files again. This is clearly a simple example of using cloud computing, specifically SaaS (which is discussed next), and it's wonderful!

So, cloud computing provides for the sharing of resources, lower cost operations passed to the cloud consumer, computing scaling, and the ability to dynamically add new servers without going through the procurement and deployment process.

Characteristics of a Cloud

The National Institute of Standards and Technology (NIST) defines cloud computing with five distinct characteristics: on-demand self-service, broad network access, resource pooling, rapid elasticity, and measured service. Any service that contains these characteristics can be considered a cloud-based service or application.

On-Demand Self-Service   A customer can provision computer capabilities and resources, such as CPU, memory, storage, the network, instances of a virtual machine, or any other component of the service, including the service itself, without any human interaction.

Broad Network Access   The capabilities are accessible over a network and are not a contrived system like the old mainframe systems, where you needed a proprietary connection. Broad access includes the device as well, such as mobile devices, laptops, and desktop computers, just to name a few.

Resource Pooling   The intent of cloud computing is to time-share a pool of resources over many several virtual instances. If it is a public cloud, the resource pools can be allotted by customer or organization. If it is a private cloud, then chances are the resource pool will be allotted to virtual instances in the same organization.

Rapid Elasticity   Computer capabilities can be elastically provisioned based on the customer's requirements at the time, such as load. The same capabilities can be released when the customer's requirement requires less resources. An example of rapid elasticity is a web-based company that requires additional capacity during a peak busy time. The resources can be allocated during the peak and deallocated when the traffic reaches a nominal level.

Measured Service   Any cloud service should have the capability to meter the resources of CPU, network, storage, and accounts, just to name a few. In addition, most cloud services charge based on any or all of these resources. Resources usage should be monitored, reported, and ultimately controlled without the consumer ever realizing that any of these are being applied.

The five characteristics of cloud computing can be found in the NIST publication SP 800-145. This document is titled "The NIST Definition of Cloud Computing" and it sets the guidelines for cloud computing. The document can be accessed at https://csrc.nist.gov/publications/detail/sp/800-145/final.

Cloud Delivery Models

When we discuss the cloud, names like Amazon AWS and Microsoft Azure come to mind. However, anyone can own their own cloud as long as the resources meet the criteria of the NIST standard for cloud computing. We can classify the ownership of these models within the four main categories of public, private, hybrid, and community.

I often find that companies will begin entering into the cloud via a public cloud provider. Using these public clouds is like renting compute power. The costs are charged to an operational expense budget because there is no equity in the service, much like renting a house. Once companies realize the savings of virtualization, they often purchase the equipment to transform into a private cloud. The purchase of the equipment is a capital investment because we have equity in the equipment, much like owning a house.

Private

The private cloud model is defined as cloud infrastructure that is provisioned for exclusive use by a single organization, as shown in Figure 17.1. It can be owned, managed, and operated by the organization, a third party, or a combination of both. The infrastructure can also be located on- or off-premises. This makes the cloud resources exclusive to the owner.

FIGURE 17.1   A private cloud

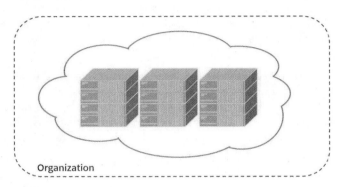

Organization

There are several reasons to move to a private cloud deployment, such as regulations, privacy, monetary and budgetary impact, and overall control. Private clouds give the owner ultimate control of the cloud and its design. Sometimes the public cloud may not offer certain features or hardware that a private cloud can be built to support. The creation of the private cloud might not be for purposes of new technology; it could be designed to support legacy systems that may not be compatible with public cloud offerings.

The private cloud model has the advantage of ultimate control, with a price that is not immediately evident. When equipment is purchased such as compute, network, and storage, the company must forecast growth over a nominal five- to seven-year period. In a public cloud, resources can be purchased on demand and relinquished when not needed, but in the private cloud model, we must acquire these additional resources and are burdened with the ownership.

Obsolescence of the equipment must also be considered, because the average expected life of compute, network, and storage resources is usually five to seven years. Private clouds often need hardware refreshes every five to seven years because of newer features or end-of-life warranties.

Public

The public cloud model is defined as infrastructure that is provisioned for open use by the general public. It can be owned, managed, and operated by a business entity, government organization, or a combination thereof. However, the infrastructure exists on the premises of the cloud provider, as shown in Figure 17.2.

FIGURE 17.2 A public cloud

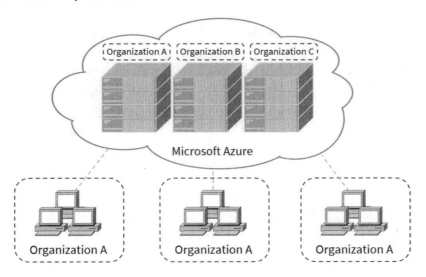

The public cloud is often a public marketplace for compute, network, and storage in which you can rent or lease compute time. This compute time, of course, is segregated from other customers, so there is a level of isolation between customers on the same infrastructure. Examples of public cloud providers are Amazon Web Services (AWS), Microsoft Azure, and Google Cloud; these are just a few providers, and the list grows every day.

A benefit of the public cloud is the pay-as-you-go utility model. You can purchase the compute power you need for a period of time. You are charged only for the compute time that you use or purchase, and there is no initial capital investment on the part of the customer.

Another benefit to the public cloud is the elasticity of compute, network, and storage resources. If a customer is an online retailer and needs extra compute power for the holiday season, the customer can purchase more scale-out, and when the busy period is over, they can relinquish the resources.

A disadvantage to the public cloud is the lack of control and hardware configuration. If custom hardware is required, then the public cloud is not an option. Heavily regulated industries might not be able to use the public cloud because of restrictions on where data can be stored and who can access it.

Hybrid

The hybrid cloud model is a combination of both the private and public cloud models. It is the most popular model because many businesses leverage public cloud providers while maintaining their own infrastructure, as shown in Figure 17.3.

FIGURE 17.3   A hybrid cloud

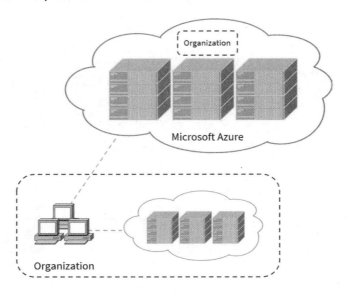

Many cloud providers now offer integration for private cloud software, such as Microsoft Hyper-V and VMware vSphere. This integration allows private clouds to gain the on-demand elasticity of the public cloud. When a private cloud uses the public cloud for elasticity of resources or additional capacity, it is called cloud bursting.

Types of Services

The term *cloud* has become a ubiquitous buzzword in IT, applied to anything involving hosted services. However, the *National Institute of Standards and Technology (NIST)* has defined three service types for cloud computing: software as a service (SaaS), platform as a service (PaaS), and infrastructure as a service (IaaS).

There are many more service types than the three mentioned, but they are not defined by the NIST standards for cloud computing. That doesn't mean they are just buzzwords; it just means that NIST believes they fit into one of the three categories already. An example of this is a cloud provider that offers disaster recovery as a service (DRaaS); this service would fit into the IaaS service type. In addition to the NIST standard model, I will cover an immerging aaS (as a service) model called desktop as a service (DaaS), which is quickly becoming an offering that is popular among providers.

SaaS

Software as a service is one of the oldest models of cloud computing, existing before the term was created. It dates back to the dial-up services of the 1980s and 1990s like CompuServe,

AOL, and the Dow Jones stock service. Today, SaaS providers are accessed through a web browser, such as the services of Twitter, Facebook, and Gmail.

SaaS is any application that you use but do not own or maintain. The application is the provided service and is maintained by the service provider on its cloud. Facebook and Gmail are popular examples; you use their services and never have to worry about the underlying infrastructure.

Social media and email are not the only examples of SaaS. There are many others that you might not even think of, such as Webex by Cisco and GitHub. The provider extends these services to you as either a pay-as-you-go, contract, or free service.

PaaS

Platform as a service is another model of cloud computing. PaaS allows a customer to generate code on the provider's platform that can be executed. Web hosting providers like GoDaddy and A Small Orange are examples of PaaS. You can purchase web hosting from these providers and set up a WordPress or custom web application using PHP or ASP.NET.

Web hosting is not the only example of PaaS. Google App Engine is a platform that allows an application to be coded in Java, Python, or PHP. The application then is executed on Google's PaaS cloud; web hosts can even provide storage like SQL.

SaaS applications can be produced on a PaaS platform. Evernote is hosted as of this writing on Google's cloud platform. Evernote is a SaaS application that allows the collecting and sharing of ideas across various mobile and desktop devices.

Google App Engine is not the only PaaS provider—there are countless other providers. Amazon Web Services and Microsoft Azure are other examples, and countless other providers have begun to offer PaaS as well.

Applications are isolated between customers. The processes are allotted resources by the customer and can scale out for demand. PaaS providers generally charge the customer according to CPU cycles used.

IaaS

Infrastructure as a service is the established model of computing that we generally associate with cloud computing. Amazon Web Services, Microsoft Azure, and Rackspace are just a few providers. Customer are allowed to use the provider's infrastructure of compute, network, and storage.

When the customer needs IaaS, it is as simple as purchasing an instance of compute resources and then choosing an operating system and region of the world for the instance and connecting to it. The customer will not know the exact host server, network equipment, or storage the guest VM is running upon. All of the worries of the infrastructure are left up to the provider.

Computing resources are not the only services that you can purchase from a cloud provider. For example, Amazon Web Services and Microsoft Azure offer backup services. You can purchase space on the provider's cloud and back up straight to it.

Any infrastructure that you would normally purchase as a capital expense (lease or own) can be converted into an operational expense (rent) via services from the provider. Whenever

I am looking to purchase physical infrastructure, I incorporate IaaS into my cost analysis. However, you must also weigh the nonmonetary saving such as infrastructure maintenance and overall administration of the infrastructure. You must ask yourself, is it better to own this infrastructure or rent this infrastructure long term?

DaaS

Desktop as a service is the latest offering by cloud providers, such as Microsoft and VMware, just to name a couple. In a normal compute model, the end-user computer, also known as the edge device, processes the data. This also means that the edge device can retain a copy of the data and that data can be copied off onto a USB drive. The edge device can be stolen, and depending on the data, it might mean that your company has to report it as a data loss. Another emerging threat is for the end-user computer to get infected and ransom the data. These scenarios can cost a company a lot of money to remediate.

DaaS doesn't solve all the problems, but it does give the administrator a lot more control by pushing the processing of data to the cloud. Because the edge device is no longer responsible for processing the data, it can be a repurposed computer, tablet, Chromebook, or any other device. These devices are called thin clients because the only software they need to support is the client for DaaS. In many cases all that a person needs is a web browser to access the desktop in the cloud. This allows for mobility and flexibility in provisioning desktops for workers. You can even scale up or down depending on usage. Coupled with a bring your own device (BYOD) policy, a company could save some real money.

Administrators gain the greatest amount of control when an organization decides to switch to DaaS. Data can be tightly controlled by turning off clipboard sharing between the thin client and the virtual desktop. USB access can be controlled, and printing can be controlled; these are just a few examples. Security patches can be centrally controlled and quickly installed as they are released. Antivirus and antimalware can be managed and monitored to thwart ransomware attempts. The best part is that, with the right mix of policies, the data remains in the cloud and never makes it to the edge device. So, there is no chance of data loss and costly proceedings can be avoided.

Network Function Virtualization

Network functions such as firewalls and routing can all be virtualized inside the hypervisor. They operate just like their physical versions, but we don't have to worry about power supplies failing, CPUs going bad, or anything else that can cause a physical network device to fail. We do have to worry about the host that runs the virtual network functions; however, redundancy is built into many hypervisors. Personally, I prefer to virtualize as many functions as I can possibly virtualize.

The following are the most common network function virtualization (NFV) types you will encounter, but the list grows every day. If you need it for your on-premises infrastructure, then it can be virtualized and put in the cloud.

Virtual Firewall

A *virtual firewall* is similar to a physical firewall. It can be a firewall appliance installed as a virtual machine or a kernel mode process in the hypervisor. When installed as a firewall appliance, it performs the same functions as a traditional firewall. In fact, many of the traditional firewalls today are offered as virtual appliances. When virtualizing a firewall, you gain the fault tolerance of the entire virtualization cluster for the firewall—compared to a physical firewall, where your only option for fault tolerance may be to purchase another unit and cluster it together. As an added benefit, when a firewall is installed as a virtual machine, it can be backed up like any other VM and treated like any other VM.

A virtual firewall can also be used as a hypervisor virtual kernel module. These modules have become popular from the expansion software-defined networking. Firewall rules can be configured for layer 2 MAC addresses or protocol along with traditional layer 3 and layer 4 rules. Virtual firewall kernel modules use policies to apply to all hosts in the cluster. The important difference between virtual firewall appliances and virtual firewall kernel modules is that the traffic never leaves the host when a kernel module is used. Compared to using a virtual firewall appliance, the traffic might need to leave the current host to go to the host that is actively running the virtual firewall appliance.

Virtual Router

The virtual router is identical to a physical router in just about every respect. It is commonly loaded as a VM appliance to facilitate layer 3 routing. Many companies that sell network hardware have come up with unique features that run on their virtual routing appliances; these features include VPN services, BGP routing, and bandwidth management, among others. The Cisco Cloud Services Router (CSR) 1000v is a virtual router that is sold and supported by cloud providers such as Amazon and Microsoft Azure. Juniper also offers a virtual router called the vMX router, and Juniper advertises it as a carrier-grade virtual router.

Virtual Switch

A *virtual switch (vSwitch)* is similar to a physical switch, but it is a built-in component in your hypervisor. It differs in a few respects; the first is the number of ports. On a physical switch, you have a defined number of ports. If you need more ports, you must upgrade the switch or replace it entirely. A virtual switch is scalable compared to its physical counterpart; you can just simply add more ports.

Virtual Private Cloud

A virtual private cloud (VPC) is a cloud environment that uses all virtual functions. It is private in the sense that it is available only to the tenant, although it might be located within a public cloud. By means of authentication and encryption, the remote access of the organization to its VPC resources is secured from other tenants.

Connectivity Options

By default, traffic into and out of your public cloud traverses the Internet. This is a good solution in many cases, but if you require additional security when accessing your cloud resources and exchanging your data, there are two common solutions that we will discuss. The first is a virtual private network (VPN) that sends data securely over the Internet or dedicated connections. The second solution is to install a private non-Internet connection, and then a direct connection can be configured.

Virtual Private Network

Cloud providers offer site-to-site VPN options that allow you to establish a secure and protected network connection across the public Internet. The VPN connection verifies that both ends of the connection are legitimate and then establishes encrypted tunnels to route traffic from your data center to your cloud resources. If a bad actor intercepts the data, they will not be able to read it due to the encryption of the traffic.

VPNs can be configured with redundant links to back up each other or to load-balance the traffic for higher-speed interconnections.

Another type of VPN allows desktops, laptops, tablets, and other devices to establish individual secure connections into your cloud deployment.

Private Direct Connection

A dedicated circuit can be ordered and installed between your data center and an interconnection provider or directly to the cloud company. This provides a secure, low-latency connection with predictable performance.

Direct connection speeds usually range from 1 Gbps to 10 Gbps and can be aggregated together. For example, four 10 Gbps circuits can be installed from your data center to the cloud company for a total aggregate bandwidth of 40 Gbps.

It is also a common practice to establish a VPN connection over the private link for encryption of data in transit.

There are often many options when connecting to the cloud provider that allow you to specify which geographic regions to connect to as well as which areas inside of each region, such as storage systems or your private virtual cloud.

Internet exchange providers maintain dedicated high-speed connections to multiple cloud providers and will connect a dedicated circuit from your facility to the cloud providers as you specify.

There are several ways to connect to a virtual server that is in a cloud environment:

- **Remote Desktop:** While the VPN connection connects you to the virtual network, an RDP connection can be directly to a server. If the server is a Windows server, then you will use the Remote Desktop Connection (RDC) client. If it is a Linux server, then the connection will most likely be an SSH connection to the command line.

- **File Transfer Protocol (FTP) and Secure File Transfer Protocol (SFTP):** The FTP/FTPS server will need to be enabled on the Windows/Linux server, and then you can use the

FTP/FTPS client or work at the command line. This is best when performing bulk data downloads.

- **VMware Remote Console:** This allows you to mount a local DVD, hard drive, or USB drive to the virtual server. This is handy for uploading ISO or installation media to the cloud server.

Cloud Gateways

A gateway, either physical or virtual, arbitrates access to a set of resources, and in the case of a cloud gateway, it connects local applications to cloud-based storage. In some cases, it also enables a legacy application that cannot speak the same language as the public cloud to interact by translating between the traditional storage-area network (SAN) or network-attached storage (NAS). This section provides additional examples of gateways and the functions they can perform.

Internet Gateway

An Internet gateway is a physical or virtual system that stands between a LAN and the Internet. While in a home situation this is provided by the Internet service provider (ISP), in an enterprise network, the organizational IT team will probably configure this device.

One of the options is to implement a proxy server, to which all Internet traffic is directed. The proxy server makes the connection to the web server on behalf of the source device and then returns results to the source device. From a security standpoint, this is beneficial in that it will appear to the outside world that all traffic is coming from the proxy server and not the original device.

Network Address Translation Gateway

Network address translation (NAT) is a feature found in firewalls and many router platforms that allows for the translation of private IP addresses to public IP addresses at the network edge. While one of the driving forces beginning the development of NAT was the conservation of the public IPv4 address space, it also has a security component in that the process helps to hide the interior addressing scheme.

There are three types of NAT that can be implemented. In static NAT, each private IP address is mapped to a public IP address. While this does not save any of the public IPv4 address space, it does have the benefit of hiding your internal network address scheme from the outside world.

In dynamic NAT, a pool of public IP addresses is obtained that is at least equal to the number of private IP addresses that require translation. However, rather than mapping the private IP addresses to the public IP addresses, the NAT device maps the public IP addresses from the pool on a dynamic basis much like a DHCP server does when assigning IP addresses.

Finally, port address translation (PAT) is a form of NAT in which all private IP addresses are mapped to a single public IP address. This provides both benefits of saving the IPv4 address space and hiding the network address scheme. This system is called port address translation because the ephemeral port numbers that devices choose as the source port for a connection (which are chosen randomly from the upper ranges of the port numbers) are used to identify each source computer in the network. This is required since all devices are mapped to the same public IP address.

Multitenancy

The term *tenant* is used to describe a group of users or devices that share a common pool of resources or common access with specific privileges. A popular example of a tenant is the Microsoft 365 platform. When you sign up your organization and associate it with Microsoft 365, each user or device you add is grouped to your tenant. You can then manage the privileges for your users across your entire organization. Another classic example of a tenant is when you create a private virtualization cloud in your organization with Hyper-V or VMware vSphere. You have a single tenant that can share the pool of resources, and you can define policies for all of the VMs across your organization.

Now that we have a broad definition of a tenant, let's get into what a multitenant is. Simply put, it's a platform that supports multiple tenants at the same time. Microsoft 365 is a great example of this. When your organization is created, it is scaled over many different servers. These servers also have other organizations (tenants) processing on them, so they are considered multitenant.

Another example of a multitenant is a virtualization cloud. It is possible to have two organizations defined on the same set of hardware. Using resource pool policies, the multiple tenants could be configured so they would not affect each other. This is common practice with ISPs that offer a hosted virtualization service. There is often middleware that allows the users to create and modify VMs without directly accessing the hypervisor platform.

Elasticity

Elasticity is one of the five essential characteristics of cloud computing, and it is defined here, as per the NIST publication SP 800-145:

> A consumer can unilaterally provision computing capabilities, such as server time and network storage, as needed automatically without requiring human interaction with each service provider.

Cloud providers offer configuration of virtual CPU, virtual RAM, network bandwidth down and up, storage, and many other resources for a virtual machine or virtual service. When that service needs more resources, elasticity allows the consumer to add or remove the resources without any human interaction from the hosting provider. The customer of course has to pay for these resources, but in traditional circumstances of real hardware, your only option would be to purchase new hardware or add upgrades to existing hardware. Elastic upgrades can normally be performed through a GUI, a command line, or an API for automation and orchestration. They can sometimes even be added without a reboot or disruption of service.

Scalability

Scalability follows along the same lines as elasticity. Both elasticity and scalability technically increase resources for an application or service. Elasticity is considered to be tactical in its approach, and scalability is considered to be strategic in its approach. As an example, if you see a rise in CPU utilization for a virtual machine, you can simply increase the virtual CPU count and decrease its virtual CPU when the load has subsided.

What if your company has a website in a US data center where 80% of your business is and your company wanted to expand to an overseas location? Strategically, you should place the web server across both data centers. This is where a scale-out cluster comes in handy. With the use of a load balancer, you could scale your website over several data centers all over the world.

The previous example is a classic geographic scale-out scenario. There are many other examples like this, but the concept remains pretty much the same: they are all strategic in nature. Keep in mind that the application needs to support scalability, and some applications are written as to be optimized for scalability. Your organization needs to take a strategic approach from the design of the application to deployment of the application to make it scalable.

Network Security Groups

One of the ways in which access to a VPC can be secured is through the use of network security groups. For example, a Microsoft Azure network security group can be used to filter network traffic to and from Azure resources in an Azure virtual network. You can use a rule to specify allowed traffic by destination, port number, or protocol number and then apply that rule to a network security group. This group can specify membership by subnet or by network interface on a virtual machine.

Network Security Lists

A networking security list is a set of ingress and egress security rules that apply to all virtual network interfaces in any subnet with which the security list is associated. It acts as a virtual firewall by confining all incoming and outgoing traffic to that allowed by the security list.

Security Implications/Considerations

While an entire book could be written on the security implications of the cloud, there are some concerns that stand above the others. Among them are these:

- While clouds increasingly contain valuable data, they are just as susceptible to attacks as on-premises environments. Cases such as the Salesforce.com incident in which a technician fell for a phishing attack that compromised customer passwords remind us of this.

- Customers are failing to ensure that the provider keeps their data safe in multitenant environments. They are failing to ensure that passwords are assigned, protected, and changed with the same attention to detail they might desire.

- No specific standard has been developed to guide providers with respect to data privacy.

- Data security varies greatly from country to country, and customers have no idea where their data is located at any point in time.

Relationship Between Local and Cloud Resources

When comparing the advantages of local and cloud environments and the resources that reside in each, several things stand out:

- A cloud environment requires very little infrastructure investment on the part of the customer, while a local environment requires an investment in both the equipment and the personnel to set it up and manage it.

- A cloud environment can be extremely scalable and at a moment's notice, while scaling a local environment either up or out requires an investment in both equipment and personnel.

- Investments in cloud environments involve monthly fees rather that capital expenditures as would be required in a local environment.

- While a local environment provides total control for the organization, a cloud takes some of that control away.

- While you always know where your data is in a local environment, that may not be the case in a cloud, and the location may change rapidly.

EXERCISE 17.1

Exploring Cloud Services

In this exercise, you explore the cloud service offering for Microsoft Azure.

1. Set up an Azure account a free account on the Azure portal via `https://portal.azure.com`.

2. After you have signed into the portal, click the menu in the upper-left corner of the web page and select All Services.

3. Explore the Compute, Networking, and Storage categories.

This exercise simply gives you a glimpse of the enormous cloud offering for Microsoft Azure. Other providers have equal portfolios of services.

For extra credit, research some of the services to get a better understanding of what they represent. As an example, virtual networks, firewalls, and NAT gateways are all network virtual functions. How many others are there in that category?

Infrastructure as Code

With the new hyperscale cloud data centers, it is no longer practical to configure each device in the network individually. Also, configuration changes happen so frequently it would be impossible for a team of engineers to keep up with the manual configuration tasks. Infrastructure as code (IaC) is the managing and provisioning of infrastructure through code instead of through manual processes.

The concept of infrastructure as code allows all configurations for the cloud devices and networks to be abstracted into machine-readable definition files instead of physical hardware configurations. IaC manages the provisioning through code so manually making configuration changes is no longer required.

These configuration files contain the infrastructure requirements and specifications. They can be stored for repeatable use, distributed to other groups, and versioned as you make changes. Faster deployment speeds, fewer errors, and consistency are advantages of infrastructure as code over the older, manual process.

Deploying your infrastructure as code allows you to divide your infrastructure into modular components that can be combined in different ways using automation. Code formats include JSON and YAML, and they are used by tools such as Ansible, Salt, Chef, Puppet, Terraform, and AWS CloudFormation.

Automation/Orchestration

Automation and orchestration define configuration, management, and the coordination of cloud operations. Automation involves individual tasks that do not require human intervention and are used to create workflows that are referred to as orchestration. This allows you to easily manage very complex and large tasks using code instead of a manual process.

Automation is a single task that orchestration uses to create the workflow. By using orchestration in the cloud, you can create a complete virtual data center that includes all compute, storage, database, networking, security, management, and any other required services. Very complex tasks can be defined in code and used to create your environment.

Common automation tools used today include Puppet. Puppet, Docker, Jenkins, Terraform, Ansible, Kubernetes, CloudBees, CloudFormation, Chef, and Vagrant.

Playbooks/Templates/Reusable Tasks

Automation requires creating all the details of a task that are scheduled to occur automatically. These details can be contained in playbooks or templates. A playbook is somewhat like a batch file in that it lists all tasks or commands to be executed, and then the tasks or commands are run when the playbook is scheduled to run. Automation tools such as Ansible use these playbooks to guide their actions.

Templates are preconfigured playbooks that vendors of automation tools provide for common tasks. These reusable tasks can be deployed whenever desired without the need to create a new playbook.

There are two approaches to orchestrate the tasks of automation: imperative and declarative. Both come with advantages and disadvantages.

Imperative   An imperative approach is probably the route most of us would take. It's a classic approach of listing all of the steps to get to the desired state. For example, an imperative approach might look like the following pseudocode. You might think that the pitfall is configuring specifics like hostname or IP, but those can be turned into variables. The pitfall is actually the fact that the install of PHP is dependent on the Apache web server getting installed properly. If this were more complex and step 234 errored, we would need to debug the other 233 lines to see what changed.

```
Install Ubuntu 20.04
Configure hostname:ServerA
Configure IP:192.168.1.10
Install Apache 2.4.24
Set home directory
Install PHP 7.4.13
Enable PHP module
Install MySQL 5.7.23
Set MySQL password:Password20!
Configure firewall:open TCP 80
```

Declarative   A declarative approach is a desired state that you want to reach in the end. Basically, we know that when we are done we want to have an Ubuntu 20.04 server with Apache, PHP, and MySQL installed. How we get there is really irrelevant to the script or the developer. The same defaults need to be set, such as the hostname, IP address, MySQL password, and so on. The following pseudocode represents a declarative approach. The orchestration software would contain the specifics on how to install the appropriate pieces.

```
Ubuntu::install { '20.04':
  hostname => 'ServerA',
  ip       => '192.168.1.10',

}
apache:package install { 'dev.wiley.com':
  port    => '80',
  docroot => '/var/www/',
  module  => 'php'
  open_fw => 'true'
}
mysql:package install { 'db_app':
  password => 'Password20!'
}
```

Configuration Drift/Compliance

When configurations are handled manually, over time systems may fall out of compliance with policy because they have not been updated to reflect the new policy. This is called configuration drift. Many automation tools such as Puppet can automate the process of identifying and correcting policy compliance issues.

Upgrades

Another area where automation is used is in the application of upgrades to operating system and applications. One of the earliest versions of this was Windows Server Update Services (WSUS), a service that downloaded updates and hot fixes over the Internet and then applied them automatically to systems over the LAN. Newer automation tools can also do this as well.

Dynamic Inventories

Maintaining a proper inventory of organizational assets can be difficult especially for large organizations. Some tools, such as Ansible, can perform what are called dynamic inventories, which use plugins to extract information from the source of inventory information. Dynamic inventory updates can be scheduled or run at the beginning of a job to get the most up-to-date information.

Source Control

When using infrastructure as code, source control of the code is important. Let's survey some of the issues and techniques involved in source control.

Version Control

A version control system is designed to track changes in source code and other text files during the development of a piece of software. This allows the user to retrieve any of the previous versions of the original source code and the changes that are stored. It is important that the latest versions are in use in all instances.

Central Repository

It is important for all code to be housed in a central repository. This model is utilized to create a single source of truth, providing significant benefits to visibility, collaboration, and consistency within data management

Conflict Identification

Code conflicts occur when two or more developers make incompatible changes to the same file or codebase, resulting in errors, bugs, or merge failures. Conflict resolution tools can identify and resolve code conflicts when they occur. They can identify differences between conflicting files or codebases, and allow you to choose or edit the correct version. Some of the most common conflict resolution tools are Git, GitHub, and Bitbucket.

Branching

Code branching enables development teams to work on different parts of a project without impacting each other. The codebase is often referred to as the trunk, baseline, master, or mainline. Developers create branches—originating either directly or indirectly from the mainline—to experiment in isolation. This keeps the overall product stable.

Software-Defined Networking

As modern networks grew in complexity and size, it has become increasingly difficult to configure, manage, and control them. There has traditionally been no centralized control plane, which means to make even the simplest of changes many switches had to be individually accessed and configured.

With the introduction of software-defined networking, a centralized controller is implemented, and all of the networking devices are managed as a complete set and not individually. This greatly reduced the number of configuration tasks required to make changes to the network and allows the network to be monitored as a single entity instead of many different independent switches and routers.

Benefits of Software-Defined Networking

Software-defined networking has a number of benefits over traditional physical networking. Let's look at some of these benefits.

Application-Aware

Any system including a software-defined network (SDN) that has built-in information or "awareness" about individual applications is said to be application-aware. Application awareness enables the system to better interact with these applications. Application-aware networks can take network queries from individual applications and, in some cases, can facilitate easier transaction channels. It can also improve efficiency of network administration and maintenance.

Zero-Touch Provisioning

Zero-touch provisioning provides the ability to configure and remotely deploy multiple network devices without the need to touch each individually. It not only saves time but eliminates the human errors that can occur when done manually. Many SDN controllers, such as the Omada Cloud-Based Controller by TP-Link, use zero-touch provisioning for more efficient deployments.

Transport Agnostic

SDN systems typically can work with different types of transport mechanisms without being dependent on any one of them. Systems such as these that are not confined to a particular transport medium are said to be transport agnostic. When discussing a transport-agnostic SDN, we are usually referring to a transport-agnostic overlay network. This is a network architecture that abstracts the underlying physical network infrastructure and creates a virtual network overlay on top of it. This approach can replace a plethora of legacy and proprietary branch network and security equipment to simplify operations, lower costs, and provide greater control of the orchestration, monitoring, and visibility of the infrastructure.

Central Policy Management

Most SDN systems provide central policy management, which means IT, cloud, and security teams can gain clear, holistic visibility across all network environments—on-premises and private and public clouds—enabling unified management of all on-premises firewalls and cloud-security controls. Security policies can be applied consistently from a single pane of glass using a uniform set of commands and syntax without requiring disparate management tools for different deployments.

Components of Software-Defined Networking

The functions of software-defined networking operate on several layers. Figure 17.4 details a schematic of a common SDN controller. Let's look at these layers and what operations occur on the various layers.

Application Layer

The application layer contains the standard network applications or functions such as intrusion detection/prevention appliances, load balancers, proxy servers, and firewalls that either explicitly and programmatically communicate their desired network behavior or network requirements to the SDN controller.

Control Layer

The control layer, or management plane, translates the instructions or requirements received from the application layer devices, proceeds the requests, and configures the SDN-controlled devices in the infrastructure layer.

The control layer also pushes to the application layer devices information received from the networking devices.

The SDN controller sits in the control layer and processes configuration, monitoring and any other application-specific information between the application layer and infrastructure layer.

FIGURE 17.4   SDN controller schematic

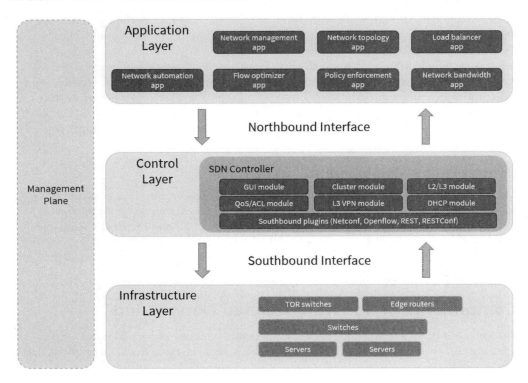

The northbound interface is the connection between the controller and applications, while the southbound interface is the connection between the controller and the infrastructure layer.

Infrastructure Layer

The infrastructure layer, or forwarding plane, consists of the actual networking hardware devices that control the forwarding and processing for the network. This is where the spine/leaf switches sit and are connected to the SDN controller for configuration and operation commands.

The spine and leaf switches handle packet forwarding based on the rules provided by the SDN controller.

The infrastructure layer is also responsible for collecting network health and statistics such as traffic, topology, usage, logging, errors, and analytics and sending this information to the control layer.

SDN Planes

SDN architectures are often broken into three main functions: the management plane, the control plane, and the data plane, also known as the forwarding plane.

Management Plane   The management plane is the configuration interface to the SDN controllers and is used to configure and manage the network. The protocols commonly used are HTTP/HTTPS for web browser access, Secure Shell (SSH) for command-line programs, and application programming interfaces (APIs) for machine-to-machine communications.

The management plane is responsible for monitoring, configuring, and maintaining the data center switch fabric. It is used to configure the forwarding plane. The management plane is considered to be a subset of the control plane

Control Plane   The control plane includes the routing and switching functions and protocols used to select the path used to send the packets or frames as well as a basic configuration of the network.

Data Plane   The data plane refers to all the functions and processes that forward packets/frames from one interface to another; it moves the bits across the fabric.

Application Programming Interfaces

Software-defined networking removes the control plane intelligence from the network devices by having a central controller manage the network instead of having a full operating system (Cisco IOS, for example) on the devices. In turn, the controller manages the network by separating the control and data (forwarding) planes, which automates configuration and the remediation of all devices.

So instead of the network devices each having individual control planes, we now have a centralized control plane, which consolidates all network operations in the SDN controller. APIs allow for applications to control and configure the network without human intervention. The APIs are another type of configuration interface just like the CLI, SNMP, or GUI interfaces, which facilitate machine-to-machine operations.

Southbound APIs

Logical southbound interface (SBI) APIs (or device-to-control-plane interfaces) are used for communication between the controllers and network devices. They allow the two devices to communicate so that the controller can program the data plane forwarding tables of your routers and switches.

Since all the network drawings had the network gear below the controller, the APIs that talked to the devices became known as southbound, meaning, "out the southbound interface of the controller." And don't forget that with software-defined networking, the term *interface* is no longer referring to a physical interface!

Unlike northbound APIs, southbound APIs have many standards. Let's talk about them now:

OpenFlow   Describes an industry-standard API, which the ONF (`opennetworking.org`) defines. It configures white label switches, meaning that they are nonproprietary, and as a result defines the flow path through the network. All the configuration is done through NETCONF.

NETCONF Although not all devices support NETCONF yet, what this provides is a network management protocol standardized by the IETF. Using RPC, you can install, manipulate, and delete the configuration of network devices using XML.

> NETCONF is a protocol that allows you to modify the configuration of a networking device, but if you want to modify the device's forwarding table, then the OpenFlow protocol is the way to go.

onePK A Cisco proprietary SBI that allows you to inspect or modify the network element configuration without hardware upgrades. This makes life easier for developers by providing software development kits for Java, C, and Python.

OpFlex The name of the southbound API in the Cisco ACI world is OpFlex, an open-standard, distributed control system. Understand that OpFlex first sends detailed and complex instructions to the control plane of the network elements in order to implement a new application policy—something called an imperative SDN model. On the other hand, OpFlex uses a declarative SDN model because the controller, which Cisco calls the APIC, sends a more abstract, "summary policy" to the network elements. The summary policy makes the controller believe that the network elements will implement the required changes using their own control planes, since the devices will use a partially centralized control plane.

Northbound APIs

To communicate from the SDN controller and the applications running over the network, you'll use northbound interfaces (NBIs).

By setting up a framework that allows the application to demand the network setup with the configuration that it needs, the NBIs allow your applications to manage and control the network. This is priceless for saving time because you no longer need to adjust and tweak your network to get a service or application running correctly.

The NBI applications include a wide variety of automated network services, from network virtualization and dynamic virtual network provisioning to more granular firewall monitoring, user identity management, and access policy control. This allows for cloud orchestration applications that tie together for server provisioning, storage, and networking that enables a complete rollout of new cloud services in minutes instead of weeks!

Sadly, as of this writing, there is no single northbound interface that you can use for communication between the controller and all applications. So instead, you use various and sundry northbound APIs, with each one working only with a specific set of applications.

Most of the time, applications used by NBIs will be on the same system as the APIC controller, so the APIs don't need to send messages over the network since both programs run on the same system. However, if they don't reside on the same system, Representational State Transfer (REST) comes into play; it uses HTTP messages to transfer data over the API for applications that sit on different hosts.

Virtual Extensible Local Area Network

Virtual eXtensible Local Area Network (VXLAN) is a tunneling protocol that tunnels Ethernet (layer 2) traffic over an IP (layer 3) network. It can be used to address the scalability issues found in large cloud environments.

Using a VXLAN enables us to move data in the data center for a VLAN over the fastest path using layer 3. The VXLAN accomplishes this by encapsulating the frame within an IP packet, which allows the frame to traverse data centers and retain VLAN information. It also allows for the integration of virtual infrastructure without compromise of the virtual network traffic.

Layer 2 Encapsulation Limitations Addressed by VXLAN

VLANs provide a limited number of layer 2 VLANs (typically using 12-bit VLAN ID). VXLAN increases scalability up to 16 million logical networks (with 24-bit VNID) and allows for layer 2 adjacency across IP networks.

Physical pods in the data center may not have layer 2 connectivity. VLAN extends layer 2 segments over the underlying network infrastructure so that tenant workload can be placed across the DC to these pods.

The Spanning Tree protocol (STP) causes issues with layer 2 communication by blocking some potential delivery paths to prevent switching loops. VXLAN improves network utilization as VXLAN packets are transferred through the underlying network based on its layer 3 header and can take complete advantage of layer 3 routing and link aggregation protocols to use all available paths.

Data Center Interconnect

While VXLAN provides the ability to seamlessly get layer 2 traffic across a layer 3 network, Data Center Interconnect (DCI) provides the ability to get data seamlessly from one data center to another. Typically, DCI is achieved by connecting data centers through a VPN, leased lines, or the Internet. Overlay networks such as VXLAN can be built on top of an existing physical network, enabling the creation of scalable and flexible inter-data-center connections. Overlay networks can simplify the process of connecting and managing different data centers.

Zero Trust Architecture

Zero trust architecture (ZTA), also called perimeter-less network security, is a concept that when applied to connectivity options means no user or device is trusted even if they have been previously authenticated. Every request to access data needs to be authenticated dynamically to ensure least privileged access to resources. Let's look at some of the concepts and techniques used to support ZTA.

Policy-Based Authentication

Policy-based authentication is an authentication system that uses rules sets called policies to manage authentication processes. Some implementations call this attribute-based access control (ABAC). Attributes are requirements placed on characteristics of the request that must be met for successful authentication. The following are some examples of attributes:

- Time of day when request was made
- Device from which the request was sourced

By combining multiple attributes, a policy can be created that controls all requests according to configured attributes.

Authorization

While authentication identifies the user or device, authorization determines what they can do (for example, read a document, manage a printer, etc.). Policy-based authorization can also be configured. For example, between 9 and 5, Joe may be able to edit a document, but between 5 and 9, he may only be able read it.

Least Privilege Access

Whenever an administrator grants a user the right to do something normally done by the administrator, such as manage a printer or change permissions, it is referred to as privileged access. The granting of all rights and permissions, especially privileged access, should be guided by a principle called least privilege access, which prescribes that only the minimum rights or permissions needed to do the job should be granted. This helps support a ZTA.

Secure Access Secure Edge/Security Service Edge

Techniques that support ZTA include Secure Access Secure Edge (SASE) and Security Service Edge (SSE). Let's look at these two connectivity options for cloud-based design.

SASE

Secure Access Secure Edge is a security framework that adheres to ZTA and supports ZTA and software-defined networking. It departs from the centralized corporate data center secured by on-premises network perimeter design and creates a converged cloud-delivered platform that securely connects users, systems, endpoints, and remote networks to apps and resources. The following are some of its traits:

- Access is granted based on the identity of users and devices.

- Both infrastructure and security solutions are cloud-delivered.

- Every physical, digital, and logical edge is protected.

- Users are secured no matter where they work.

SSE

Security Service Edge uses integrated, cloud-centric security capabilities to facilitate safe access to websites, SaaS applications, and private applications. You might think of it as a subset of SASE. SSE provides the security service elements of a comprehensive SASE. Some examples of its fundamental security capabilities include the following:

- Zero trust architecture (discussed earlier in this chapter).

- Secure web gateway (SWG) protects users from web-based threats by connecting to a website on behalf of a user, while using filtering, malicious content inspection, and other security measures.

- Cloud Access Security Broker (CASB) enforces an organization's security, governance, and compliance policies while allowing authorized users to access and consume cloud resources.

- Firewall as a service (FWaaS) provides consistent application and security enforcement of policies across all locations and users.

Summary

In this chapter, we went into great detail on cloud computing because it continues to evolve and take on more and more of IT workloads. You learned about the most common services models, including infrastructure as a service, platform as a service, and software as a service. You learned about the various types of clouds, such as private, public, and hybrid clouds.

Next, you learned about infrastructure as code (IaC). You learned how you can automate the installation of network services through automation and orchestration tools, such as Ansible, Salt, Chef, and Puppet, to name a few.

Next, you learned about software-defined networking and how software-defined networking is used to centrally configure large networks. We discussed the components of a software-defined network, including the management and forwarding planes, the use of application programming interfaces, and north- and southbound configuration flows.

Finally, we ended with learning about Virtual eXtensible Local Area Network (VXLAN), zero trust architecture (ZTA), and Secure Access Secure Edge (SASE)/Security Service Edge (SSE).

Exam Essentials

Know and understand the various type of cloud services.   Software as a service (SaaS) allows us to use an application provided and maintained by the service provider. Platform as a service (PaaS) is a platform for designing applications that are compiled and executed in the cloud. Infrastructure as a service (IaaS) allows the customer to rent the infrastructure of compute, network, and storage from the cloud provider.

Know and understand the various cloud delivery models.   In a private cloud, resources are owned by the organization and exclusively used by the organization. In a public cloud, resources at the provider are provisioned and used by the general public. A hybrid model is a blend of both the public cloud and private cloud within an organization.

Understand the basic operations of infrastructure as code (IaC).   Infrastructure as code allows an administrator to provision servers with code-based automation and orchestration tools, in lieu of manual provisioning. IaC is performed through the methods of automation and source control.

Know the basic concepts of software-defined networking.   SDN controllers are centralized management plane systems that use application programming interfaces (APIs) to configure the data network as a whole, which eliminates the need to log in and make changes individually to a large number of individual networking devices. Infrastructure as code allows you to divide your infrastructure into modular components that can be combined in different ways using automation.

Written Lab

You can find the answers to the written labs in Appendix A. In this section, write the answers to the following management questions:

1. _____ clouds are owned and managed by an organization.

2. AWS, Microsoft Azure, and Rackspace are examples of _____.

3. _____ and orchestration define configuration, management, and the coordination of cloud operations.

4. _____ are used to create repeatable tasks.

5. _____ allows you to add cloud services such as storage and compute on demand, often in seconds or minutes.

6. _____ is a platform that supports multiple tenants at the same time.

7. _____ is a method of encapsulating layer 2 traffic inside an IP packet for data center scalability.

8. _____ is another name for using virtualization to provide services.

9. _____ assumes that no user or device is trusted, even if they have previously authenticated.

10. _____ is the managing and provisioning of resources through software instead of through manual processes.

Review Questions

You can find the answers to the review questions in Appendix B.

1. Amazon Web Services (AWS) and Microsoft Azure are examples of what?

    A. Public cloud providers

    B. Private cloud providers

    C. Hybrid cloud providers

    D. Dynamic cloud providers

2. A hosted medical records service is an example of which cloud model?

    A. PaaS

    B. IaaS

    C. SaaS

    D. BaaS

3. Which is not a NIST criterion for cloud computing?

    A. Resource pooling

    B. Rapid elasticity

    C. Automated billing

    D. Measured service

4. Which term describes the type of cloud an internal IT department hosting virtualization for a company would host?

    A. Public cloud

    B. Elastic cloud

    C. Private cloud

    D. Internal cloud

5. Hosting a disaster recovery (DR) site on Microsoft Azure is an example of which National Institute of Standards and Technology (NIST) type of cloud service?

    A. IaaS

    B. DRaaS

    C. PaaS

    D. SaaS

6. A hosted environment that allows you to write and run programs is an example of which cloud model?

    A. PaaS

    B. IaaS

    C. SaaS

    D. BaaS

7. You purchase a VM on a public cloud and plan to create a VPN tunnel to the cloud provider. Your IP network is 172.16.0.0/12, and the provider has assigned an IP address in the 10.0.0.0/8 network. What virtual network function (VNF) will you need from the provider to communicate with the VM?

   A. Virtual switch

   B. Virtual firewall

   C. Virtual router

   D. Another IP scheme at the provider

8. Where does the SDN controller interface with the switching fabric?

   A. Spine

   B. Control plane

   C. Forwarding plane

   D. Core

9. You are running several web servers in a cloud with a server load balancer. As demand increases, you add web servers. According to the NIST standard of cloud computing, which feature can you use to increase your compute capability for demand?

   A. Resource pooling

   B. Measured services

   C. Broad network access

   D. Rapid elasticity

10. Abstracting the cloud hardware into software objects for automated configuration is referred to as which of the following?

    A. Application programming interface

    B. Elasticity

    C. Infrastructure as code

    D. Software-defined networking

11. Which network plane is used by SSH for command-line configuration?

    A. Data plane

    B. Control plane

    C. Management plane

    D. Switch plane

12. Which is used for communicating directly to the SDN devices in the network?

    A. The northbound interface (NBI)

    B. The southbound interface (SBI)

    C. The core of the controller

    D. Applications hosted on the controller

13. When the vendor provides the hardware platform or data center and the company installs and manages its own operating systems and application systems, which service type is being used?

A. Software as a service

B. Infrastructure as a service

C. Platform as a service

D. Desktop as a service

14. When an application communicates with an SDN controller, which mechanism does it use to communicate?

A. The southbound interface (SBI)

B. The core of the controller

C. The northbound interface (NBI)

D. Simple Network Management Protocol (SNMP)

15. What are machine-to-machine configuration interfaces called?

A. Northbound interfaces

B. Southbound interfaces

C. APIs

D. SDN

16. Public clouds are divided into logical groupings that allow many different customers to access a section as if it were their own private data center. What is this known as?

A. Scalability

B. Elasticity

C. Multitenancy

D. Platform as a service

17. Which of the following are methods used to connect a private cloud to a public cloud? (Choose all that apply.)

A. Internet

B. SDN

C. VPN

D. Direct Connect

E. Virtual switches

18. Which protocol allows for the tunneling of layer 2 traffic over a layer 3 network?

A. GRE

B. VLAN

C. VXLAN

D. STP

19. Which function does Ansible, Chef, and Puppet perform in the network?

    A. Network management station

    B. Automation and orchestration

    C. Software-defined networking

    D. Centralized logging

20. Which concept assumes a user or device is not trusted, regardless of whether it was previously authenticated?

    A. ZTA

    B. SDN

    C. IaC

    D. IaaS

Chapter 18

Network Troubleshooting Methodology

THE FOLLOWING COMPTIA NETWORK+ EXAM OBJECTIVES ARE COVERED IN THIS CHAPTER:

✓ **Domain 5.0 Network Troubleshooting**

✓ **5.1 Explain the troubleshooting methodology.**

- Identify the problem

    - Gather information

    - Question users

    - Identify symptoms

    - Determine if anything has changed

    - Duplicate the problem, if possible

    - Approach multiple problems individually

- Establish a theory of probable cause

    - Question the obvious

    - Consider multiple approaches

        - Top-to-bottom/bottom-to-top OSI model

        - Divide and conquer

- Test the theory to determine the cause

    - If the theory is confirmed, determine the next steps to resolve the problem

    - If the theory is not confirmed, reestablish a new theory or escalate

    - Establish a plan of action to resolve the problem and identify potential effects

- Implement the solution or escalate as necessary

- Verify full system functionality and, implement preventive measures if applicable

- Document findings, actions, and outcomes and lessons learned throughout the process

✓ **5.2 Given a scenario, troubleshoot common cabling and physical interface issues.**

- Cable issues

  - Incorrect cable

    - Single mode vs. multimode

    - Shielded twisted pair (STP) vs. unshielded twisted pair (UTP)

  - Signal degradation

    - Crosstalk

    - Interference

    - Attenuation

  - Improper termination

  - Transmitter (TX)/Receiver (RX) transposed

- Interface issues

  - Increasing interface counters

    - Cyclic redundancy check (CRC)

    - Runts

    - Giants

    - Drops

  - Port status

    - Error disabled

    - Administratively down

    - Suspended

- Hardware issues

  - Power over Ethernet (PoE)

    - Power budget exceeded

    - Incorrect standard

- Transceivers
  - Mismatch
  - Signal strength

✓ **5.3 Given a scenario, troubleshoot common issues with network services.**

- Switching issues
  - Incorrect VLAN assignment
  - ACLs
- Route selection
  - Routing table
- Incorrect default gateway
- Incorrect IP address
  - Duplicate IP address
- Incorrect subnet mask

✓ **5.4 Given a scenario, troubleshoot common performance issues.**

- Congestion/contention
- Bottlenecking
- Bandwidth
  - Throughput capacity
- Latency
- Packet loss
- Jitter
- Wireless
  - Interference
    - Channel overlap
- Signal degradation or loss
- Insufficient wireless coverage
- Client disassociation issues
- Roaming misconfiguration

There is no way around it. Troubleshooting computers and networks is a combination of art and science, and the only way to get really good at it is by doing it—a lot! So it's practice, practice, and practice with the basic yet vitally important skills you'll attain in this chapter. Of course, I'm going to cover all the troubleshooting topics you'll need to sail through the Network+ exam, but I'm also going to add some juicy bits of knowledge that will really help you to tackle the task of troubleshooting successfully in the real world.

First, you'll learn to check quickly for problems in the "super simple stuff" category, and then we'll move into a hearty discussion about a common troubleshooting model that you can use like a checklist to go through and solve a surprising number of network problems. We'll finish the chapter with a good briefing about some common troubleshooting resources, tools, tips, and tricks to keep up your sleeve and equip you even further.

I won't be covering any new networking information in this chapter because you've gotten all the foundational background material you need for troubleshooting in the previous chapters. But no worries. I'll go through each of the issues described in this chapter's objectives, one at a time, in detail, so that even if you've still got a bit of that previous material to nail down yet, you'll be good to get going and fix some networks anyway.

 To find Todd Lammle CompTIA videos and practice questions, please see www.lammle.com.

Narrowing Down the Problem

When initially faced with a network problem in its entirety, it's easy to get totally overwhelmed. That's why it's a great strategy to start by narrowing things down to the source of the problem. To help you achieve that goal, it's always wise to ask the right questions. You can begin doing just that with this list of questions to ask yourself:

- Did you check the super simple stuff (SSS)?
- Is hardware or software causing the problem?
- Is it a workstation or server problem?
- Which segments of the network are affected?
- Are there any cabling issues?

Did You Check the Super Simple Stuff?

Yes—it sounds like a snake's hiss (appropriate for a problem, right?), but exactly what's on the SSS list that you should be checking first, and why? Well, as the saying goes, "All things being equal, the simplest explanation is probably the correct one," so you probably won't be stunned and amazed when I tell you that I've had people call me in and act like the sky is falling when all they needed to do was check to make sure their workstation was plugged in or powered on. (I didn't say "super simple stuff" for nothing!) Your SSS list really does include things that are this obvious—sometimes so obvious no one thinks to check for them. Even though anyone experienced in networking has their own favorite "DUH" events to tell about, almost everyone can agree on a few things that should definitely be on the SSS list:

- Check to verify login procedures and rights.
- Look for link lights and collision lights.
- Check all power switches, cords, and adapters.
- Look for user errors.

The Correct Login Procedure and Rights

You know by now that if you've set up everything correctly, your network's users absolutely have to follow the proper login procedure to the letter (or number, or symbol) to successfully gain access to the network resources they're after. If they don't do that, they will be denied access, and considering that there are truly tons of opportunities to blow it, it's a miracle, or at least very special, that anyone manages to log into the network correctly at all.

Think about it. First, a user must enter their username and password flawlessly. Sounds easy, but as they say, "in a perfect world. . . ." In this one, people mess up, don't realize it, and freak out at you about the "broken network" or the imaginary IT demon that changed their password on them while they went to lunch and now they can't log in. (The latter could be true—you may have done exactly that. If you did, just gently remind them about that memo you sent about the upcoming password-change date and time that they must have spaced about due to the tremendous demands on them.)

Anyway, it's true. By far the most common problem is bad typing—people accidentally enter the wrong username or password, and they do that a lot. With some operating systems, a slight brush of the Caps Lock key is all it takes: The user's username and password are case sensitive, and suddenly, they're trying to log in with what's now all in uppercase instead—oops.

Plus, if you happen to be running one of the shiny new operating systems around today, you can also restrict the times and conditions under which users can log in, right? So, if your user spent an unusual amount of time in the bathroom upon returning from lunch or if they got distracted and tried to log in from their BFF's workstation instead of their own, the network's operating system would've rejected their login request even though they still can type impressively well after two martinis.

Remember, you can also restrict how many times a user can log in to the network simultaneously. If you've set that up and your user tries to establish more connections than you've allowed, access will again be denied. Just know that most of the time, if a user is denied access to the network and/or its resources, they're probably going to interpret that as a network problem even though the network operating system is doing what it should.

 Real World Scenario

Can the Problem Be Reproduced?

The first question to ask anyone who reports a network or computer problem is, "Can you show me what 'not working' looks like?" This is because if you can reproduce the problem, you can identify when it happens, which may give you all the information you need to determine the source of the problem and maybe even solve it in a snap. The hardest problems to solve are those of the random variety that occur intermittently and can't be easily reproduced.

Let's pause for a minute to outline the steps to take during any user-oriented network problem-solving process:

1. Make sure the username and password are being entered correctly.

2. Check that Caps Lock key.

3. Try to log in yourself from another workstation, assuming that doing this doesn't violate the security policy. If it works, go back to the user-oriented login problems, and go through them again.

4. If none of this solves the problem, check the network documentation to find out whether any of the aforementioned kinds of restrictions are in place; if so, find out whether the user has violated any of them.

 Remember, if intruder detection is enabled on your network, a user will get locked out of their account after a specific number of unsuccessful login attempts. If this happens, either they'll have to wait until a predetermined time period has elapsed before their account will unlock and give them another chance or you'll have to go in and manually unlock it for them.

Network Connection LED Status Indicators

The link light is that little light-emitting diode (LED) found on both the network interface card (NIC) and the switch. It's typically green and labeled Link or some abbreviation of that. If you're running 100/1000BaseT, a link light indicates that the NIC and switch are making a logical (Data Link layer) connection. If the link lights are lit up on both the workstation's NIC and the switch port to which the workstation is connected, it's usually safe to assume that the workstation and switch are communicating just fine.

 The link lights on some NICs don't activate until the driver is loaded. So, if the link light isn't on when the system is first turned on, you'll have to wait until the operating system loads the NIC driver. But don't wait forever!

The *collision light* is also a small LED, but it's typically amber in color, and it can usually be found on both Ethernet NICs and hubs. When lit, it indicates that an Ethernet collision has occurred. If you've got a busy Ethernet network on which collisions are somewhat common, understand that this light is likely to blink occasionally; if it stays on continuously, though, it could mean that there are way too many collisions happening for legitimate network traffic to get through. Don't assume this is really what's happening without first checking that the NIC or other network device is working properly because one or both could simply be malfunctioning.

 Don't confuse the collision light with the network-activity or network-traffic light (which is usually green) because the latter indicates that a device is transmitting. This particular light *should* be blinking on and off continually as the device transmits and receives data on the network.

The Power Switch

Clearly, to function properly, all computer and network components must be turned on and powered up first. Obvious, yes, but if I had a buck for each time I've heard, "My computer is on, but my monitor is all dark," I'd be rolling in money by now.

When this kind of thing happens, just keep your cool and politely ask, "Is the monitor turned on?" After a little pause, the person calling for help will usually say, "Ohhh . . . ummmm . . . thanks," and then hang up ASAP. The reason I said to be nice is that, embarrassing as it is, this, or something like it, will probably happen to you, too, eventually.

Most systems include a power indicator (a Power or PWR light). The power switch typically has an On indicator, but the system or device could still be powerless if all the relevant power cables aren't actually plugged in—including the power strip.

 Remember that every cable has two ends, and both must be plugged into something. If you're thinking something like, "Sheesh—a four-year-old knows that," you're probably right. But again, I can't count the times this has turned out to be the root cause of a "major system failure."

The best way to go about troubleshooting power problems is to start with the most obvious device and work your way back to the power-service panel. There could be a number of power issues between the device and the service panel, including a bad power cable, bad outlet, bad electrical wire, tripped circuit breaker, or blown fuse, and any of these things could be the actual cause of the problem that appears to be device-death instead.

Operator Error

Or, the problem may be that you've got a user who simply doesn't know how to be one. Maybe you're dealing with someone who doesn't have the tiniest clue about the equipment they're using or about how to perform a certain task correctly—in other words, the problem may be due to something known as *operator error (OE)*. Here's a short list of the most common types of OEs and their associated acronyms:

- Equipment exceeds operator capability (EEOC)
- Problem exists between chair and keyboard (PEBCAK)
- ID Ten T error (an ID10T)

A word of caution here, though—assuming that all your problems are user-related can quickly make an ID10T error out of you.

Although it can be really tempting to take the easy way out and blow things off, remember that the network's well-being and security are ultimately your responsibility. So, before you jump to the operator-error conclusion, ask the user in question to reproduce the problem in your presence, and pay close attention to what they do. Understand that doing this can require a great deal of patience, but it's worth your time and effort if you can prevent someone who doesn't know what they're doing from causing serious harm to pricey devices or leaving a gaping hole in your security. You might even save the help-desk crew's sanity from the relentless calls of a user with the bad habit of flipping off the power switch without following proper shutdown procedures. You just wouldn't know they always do that if you didn't see it for yourself, right?

And what about finding out that that pesky user was, in fact, trained really badly by someone and that they aren't the only one? This is exactly the kind of thing that can turn the best security policy to dust and leave your network and its resources as vulnerable to attack as that goat in *Jurassic Park*.

The moral here is, always check out the problem thoroughly. If the problem and its solution aren't immediately clear to you, try the procedure yourself, or ask someone else at another workstation to do so. Don't just leave the issue unsettled or make the assumption that it is user error or a chance abnormality because that's exactly what the bad guys out there are hoping you'll do.

This is only a partial list of super simple stuff. No worries. Rest assured you'll come up with your own expanded version over time.

Is Hardware or Software Causing the Problem?

A hardware problem often rears its ugly head when some device in your computer skips a beat and/or dies. This one is pretty easy to discern because when you try to do something requiring that particular piece of hardware, you can't do it and instead get an error telling you that you can't do it. Even if your hard disk fails, you'll probably get warning signs before it actually kicks, like a Disk I/O error or something similar.

Other problems drop out of the sky and hit you like something from the wrong end of a seagull. No warning at all—just splat! Components that were humming along fine a second ago can and do suddenly fail, usually at the worst possible time, leaving you with a mess of lost data, files, everything—you get the idea.

Solutions to hardware problems usually involve one of three things:

- Changing hardware settings
- Updating device drivers
- Replacing dead hardware

If your hardware has truly failed, it's time to get out your tools and start replacing components. If this isn't one of your skills, you can either send the device out for repair or replace it. Your mantra here is "back up, back up, back up," because in either case, a system could be down for a while—anywhere from an hour to several days—so it's always good to keep backup hardware around. And I know everyone and your momma has told you this, but here it is one more time: Back up all data, files, hard drive, everything, and do so on a regular basis.

Software problems are muddier waters. Sometimes you'll get General Protection Fault messages, which indicate a Windows or Windows program (or other platform) error of some type, and other times the program you're working in will suddenly stop responding and hang. At their worst, they'll cause your machine to randomly lock up on you. When this type of thing happens, I'd recommend visiting the manufacturer's support website to get software updates and patches or searching for the answer in a knowledge base.

Sometimes you get lucky and the ailing software will tell the truth by giving you a precise message about the source of the problem. Messages saying the software is missing a file or a file has become corrupt are great because you can usually get your problem fixed fast by providing that missing file or by reinstalling the software. Neither solution takes very long, but the downside is that whatever you were doing before the program hosed will probably be at least partially lost; so again, back up your stuff, and save your data often.

It's time for you to learn how to troubleshoot your workstations and servers.

Is It a Workstation or a Server Problem?

The first thing you've got to determine when troubleshooting this kind of problem is whether it's only one person or a whole group that's been affected. If the answer is only one person (think, a single workstation), solving the issue will be pretty straightforward. More than that and your problem probably involves a chunk of the network, like a segment.

A clue that the source of your grief is the latter case is if there's a whole bunch of users complaining that they can't discover neighboring devices/nodes.

So either way, what do you do about it? Well, if it's the single-user situation, your first line of defense is to try to log in from another workstation within the same group of users. If you can do that, the problem is definitely the user's workstation, so look for things like cabling faults, a bad NIC, power issues, and OSs.

But if a whole department can't access a specific server, take a good, hard look at that particular server, and start by checking all user connections to it. If everyone is logged in correctly, the problem may have something to do with individual rights or permissions. If no one can log in to that server, including you, the server probably has a communication problem with the rest of the network. And if the server has totally crashed, either you'll see messages telling you all about it on the server's monitor or you'll find its screen completely blank—screaming indicators that the server is no longer running. And keep in mind that these symptoms do vary among network operating systems.

Which Segments of the Network Are Affected?

Figuring this one out can be a little tough. If multiple segments are affected, you may be dealing with a network-address conflict. If you're running Transmission Control Protocol/Internet Protocol (TCP/IP), remember that IP addresses must be unique across an entire network. So, if two of your segments have the same static IP subnet addresses assigned, you'll end up with duplicate IP errors—an ugly situation that can be a real bear to troubleshoot and can make it tough to find the source of the problem.

If all of your network's users are experiencing the problem, it could be a server everyone accesses. Thank the powers that be if you nail it down to that because if not, other network devices like your main router or hub may be down, making network transmissions impossible and usually meaning a lot more work on your part to fix.

Adding wide area network (WAN) connections to the mix can complicate matters exponentially, and you don't want to go there if you can avoid it, so start by finding out if stations on both sides of a WAN link can communicate. If so, get the champagne—your problem isn't related to the WAN—woo hoo! But if those stations can't communicate, it's not a happy thing: You've got to check everything between the sending station and the receiving one, including the WAN hardware, to find the culprit. The good news is that most of the time, WAN devices have built-in diagnostics that tell you whether a WAN link is working okay, which really helps you determine if the failure has something to do with the WAN link itself or with the hardware involved instead.

Is It Bad Cabling?

Back to hooking up correctly. . . . Once you've figured out whether your plight is related to one workstation, a network segment, or the whole tamale (network), you must then examine the relevant cabling. Are the cables properly connected to the correct port? More than once,

I've seen a Digital Subscriber Line (DSL) modem connection to the wall cabled all wrong—it's an easy mistake to make and an easy one to fix.

And you know that nothing lasts forever, so check those patch cables running between a workstation and a wall jack. Just because they don't come with expiration dates written on them doesn't mean they don't expire. They do go bad, especially if they get moved, trampled on, or tripped over a lot. (I did tell you that it's a bad idea to run cabling across the office floor, didn't I?) Connection problems are the tell here—if you check the NIC and there is no link light blinking, you may have a bad patch cable to blame.

It gets murkier if your cable in the walls or ceiling is toast or hasn't been installed correctly. Maybe you've got a user or two telling you the place is haunted because they only have problems with their workstations after dark when the lights go on. Haunted? No . . . some genius probably ran a network cable over a fluorescent light, which is something that just happens to produce lots of electromagnetic interference (EMI), which can really mess up communications in that cable.

Next on your list is to check the medium dependent interface/medium dependent interface-crossover (MDI/MDI-X) port setting on small, workgroup hubs and switches. This is a potential source of trouble that's often overlooked, but it's important because this port is the one that's used to uplink to a switch on the network's backbone.

First, understand that the port setting has to be set to either MDI or MDI-X depending on the type of cable used for your hub-to-hub or switch-to-switch connection. For instance, the crossover cables I talked about way back in Chapter 3, "Networking Connectors and Wiring Standards," require that the port be set to MDI, and a standard network patch cable requires that the port be set to MDI-X. You can usually adjust the setting via a regular switch or a dual inline package (DIP) switch, but to be sure, if you're still using hubs, check out the hub's documentation. (You did keep that, right?)

Cable Considerations

Cable installs should fall within the specifications for a successful installation, such as for speed and distance. However, the type of installation should also be considered when planning an installation of cabling. The cabling might require flexibility or strength running up a wall. If the cable is run in a ventilated space, there may also be fire code considerations. The following sections will discuss the common considerations for cable installation.

Shielded and Unshielded

Unshielded twisted-pair (UTP) is the most common cabling for Ethernet networks today due to its cost and ease of installation. However, it is unshielded from electromagnetic interference (EMI), which is why its use can be problematic in areas where EMI exists. Therefore, UTP should be avoided in close proximity to heavy industrial equipment that can emit EMI. *Shielded twisted-pair (STP)* is not as common for Ethernet cabling as UTP, due to its cost and difficult installation. However, it is shielded for EMI, and therefore it should be used in industrial settings where EMI is present. It is important to note that there are several different types of STP cable. Some STP cabling has a foil shielding around all four pairs of wires, some is foil shielded around each pair of wires with an overall foil shielding, and some cabling is shielded with a wire mesh. The consideration is more shielding, and a heavier shield increases the cost and lowers the chance that EMI will affect data transfer.

When installing cable in an industrial setting such as a factory where cabling is exposed to vibrations, chemicals, temperature, and EMI, the MICE (Mechanical, Ingress, Climatic, Chemical, and Electromagnetic) classification should be followed. The standard is defined in an ISO/IEC (International Organization for Standardization/International Electrotechnical Commission) publication. It is best to engage an engineer to define the type of cabling to use when in doubt for an industrial setting because safety can be compromised.

Plenum and Riser-Rated

Riser-rated cable is used when cable is run between floors in a non-plenum area. The cable is made with a polyvinyl chloride (PVC) plastic–jacketed sheathing. However, if the PVC cabling catches fire, it emits a toxic black smoke and hydrochloric acid that irritates the lungs and eyes. Therefore, when installing cabling in circulated airspace such as HVAC ducting and air returns, also called plenum areas, the type of cabling should be considered. *Plenum cable* is made with Teflon-jacketed cable or fire retardant–jacketed cable. It does not emit toxic vapors when burned or heated, and it is more expensive than PVC cables. It is specified in the National Electric Code (NEC) that is published by the National Fire Protection Association (NFPA). Because a circulated airspace is highly subjective, when in doubt use plenum cabling. You will not want to be responsible for failing a code inspection because a code inspector defines a cabling passage as an airspace.

Cable Application

Cables can be used for many different applications. The most common is obviously Ethernet host connectivity. However, a network cable can be used for several other purposes, as I will describe.

Rollover Cable/Console Cable

A rollover cable is typically flat stock cable that contains eight wires. A rollover cable is unmistakably different than an Ethernet cable, mainly because it is flat, and each wire is a different color. A rollover cable is crimped with an RJ-45 end with pin 1 matched with wire 1 on one side. The other side is also crimped with an RJ-45; however, pin 1 is matched with wire 8. So pin 2 is connected to pin 7 on the other side, pin 3 is connected to pin 6, pin 4 is connected to pin 5, and so on.

Eventually, pin 8 will be connected with pin 1 on the other side, as shown in Table 18.1.

TABLE 18.1   Rollover cable pinouts

Side A	Side B
Pin 1	Pin 8
Pin 2	Pin 7
Pin 3	Pin 6
Pin 4	Pin 5
Pin 5	Pin 4
Pin 6	Pin 3
Pin 7	Pin 2
Pin 8	Pin 1

Rollover cables are used with an EIA/TIA adapters that convert a DB-9 serial port to an RJ-45 end. The opposite end will plug directly into the router or switch for console access, as shown in Figure 18.1.

FIGURE 18.1   A router/switch console connection

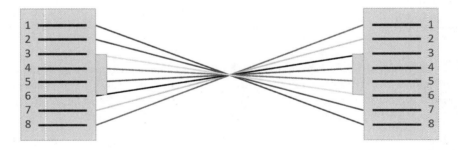

Over the years I've seen variations on the cable used for a console connection. The EIA/TIA adapter can also be wired to use a standard Ethernet cable, so it is always best to read the manual before making any connections. It is also becoming very popular for routers and switches to furnish a mini-USB connection so that when they are plugged into a laptop or computer, the operating system detects as a USB serial COM port.

Crossover Cable

When connecting a switch to a switch, a router to a router, or a host to a host, the cabling often needs to be crossed over. This means that the transmit pairs are crossed over to the receive pairs on the other side of the cable and vice versa. This is easily achieved with a crossover cable, which has the EIA/TIA 586A wiring specification crimped on one end and the EIA/TIA 568B wiring specification on the other end.

Table 18.2 lists the EIA/TIA 568A and 568B wiring specifications.

TABLE 18.2   EIA/TIA 568 crossover cabling

RJ-45 Pins	568A	568B
Pin 1	White/green	White/orange
Pin 2	Green	Orange
Pin 3	White/orange	White/green
Pin 4	Blue	Blue
Pin 5	White/blue	White/blue
Pin 6	Orange	Green
Pin 7	White/brown	White/brown
Pin 8	Brown	Brown

Problems can arise when a straight-through cable connects a switch to a switch, a router to a router, or a host to a host. You simply won't get a link light. However, most newer routers and switches have medium dependent interface crossover (MDI-X) ports that sense a similar device is being plugged in and automatically cross the signals over.

A valuable tool to have in your toolbox is a small length of cable that acts as a crossover cable and a female-to-female RJ-45 adapter. If there is doubt that the connection requires a crossover cable, you can pop this small crossover cable onto the existing cable and verify that the link light comes on.

Other Important Cable Issues Causing Performance Issues

They may be basic, but they're still vital—an understanding of the physical issues that can happen on a network when a user is connected via cable (usually Ethernet) is critical information to have in your troubleshooting repertoire.

Because many of today's networks still consist of large amounts of copper cable, they suffer from the same physical issues that have plagued networking since the very beginning and have throughput capacity issues and signal degradation. Newer technologies and protocols have helped to a degree, but they haven't made these issues a thing of the past yet. Some physical issues that still affect networks are listed and defined next:

Incorrect Pinout/TX/RX Reverse/Damaged Cable   The first things to check when working on cabling are the cable connectors to make sure they haven't gone bad. After that, look to make sure the wiring is correct on both ends by physically checking the cable pinouts. Important to remember is that if you have two switches, you need a crossover cable where you cross pins 1 and 2 with 3 and 6. On the other hand, if you have a PC going into a switch, you need a straight-through cable where pins 1 and 2 correspondingly connect to pins 1 and 2 on each side—the same with 3 and 6. Finally, make sure the termination pins on both ends are the correct type for the kind of cable you're using.

Bad Port   In some cases, the issue is not the cable but the port into which the cable is connected. On many devices, ports have LEDs that can alert you to a bad port. For example, a Cisco router or switch will have an LED for each port, and the color of the LED will indicate its current state. In most cases, a lack of any light whatsoever indicates an issue with the port. Loopback plugs can be used to test the functionality of a port. These devices send a signal out and then back in the port to test it.

Transceiver Mismatch   Interfaces that send and receive are called transceivers. When a NIC is connected to a port, the two transceivers must have the same certain settings or issues will occur. These settings are the duplex and the speed settings. If the speed settings do not match, there will be no communication. If the duplex settings are incorrect, there may be functionality, but the performance will be poor. An incorrect standard mismatch can cause signal strength issues.

Crosstalk   Again, looking back to Chapter 3, remember that crosstalk is what happens when there's signal bleed between two adjacent wires that are carrying a current. Network designers minimize crosstalk inside network cables by twisting the wire pairs together, putting them at a 90-degree angle to each other. The tighter the wires are twisted, the less crosstalk you have, and newer cables like Cat 6 cable really make a difference. But like I said, not completely—crosstalk still exists and affects communications, especially in high-speed networks. This is often caused by using the wrong category of cable or by mismatching the member of one pair with a member of another when terminating a cable.

Near-End/Far-End Crosstalk   Near-end crosstalk is a specific type of crosstalk measurement that has to do with the EMI bled from a wire to adjoining wires where the current originates. This particular point has the strongest potential to create crosstalk issues because the crosstalk signal itself degrades as it moves down the wire. If you have a problem with it, it's probably going to show up in the first part of the wire where it's connected to a switch or a NIC. Far-end crosstalk is the interference between two pairs of a cable measured at the far end of the cable with respect to the interfering transmitter.

This condition is often caused by improperly terminating a cable. For example, it's important to maintain the twist right up to the punch-down or crimp connector. In the case of crimp connectors, it's critical to select the correct grade of connector even though one grade may look identical to another.

Attenuation/dB Loss/Distance Limitation   As a signal moves through any medium, the medium itself will degrade the signal—a phenomenon known as *attenuation* that's common in all kinds of networks. True, signals traversing fiber-optic cable don't attenuate as fast as those on copper cable, but they still do eventually. You know that all copper twisted-pair cables have a maximum segment distance of 100 meters before they'll need to be amplified, or *repeated*, by a hub or a switch, but single-mode fiber-optic cables can sometimes carry signals for miles before they begin to attenuate (degrade). If you need to go far, use fiber, not copper. Although there is attenuation/dB loss in fiber, it can go much farther distances than copper cabling can before being affected by attenuation.

Latency   Latency is the delay typically incurred in the processing of network data. A low-latency network connection is one that generally experiences short delay times, while a high-latency connection generally suffers from long delays. Many security solutions may negatively affect latency. For example, routers take a certain amount of time to process and forward any communication. Configuring additional rules on a router generally increases latency, thereby resulting in longer delays. An organization may decide not to deploy certain security solutions because of the negative effects they will have on network latency.

Auditing is a great example of a security solution that affects latency and performance. When auditing is configured, it records certain actions as they occur. The recording of these actions may affect the latency and performance.

Packet Loss   Protocol Data Units (PDUs) define "data" encapsulation or de-encapsulation at each layer of the OSI and/or DoD model. At the Network or Internet layer, this defines a "packet," which are small units of the data stream transmitted on a network from a source to a destination. You'll see packet loss when a network packet fails to reach the destination, resulting in loss. This is caused by wireless low signal strength, interference, excessive noise, software corruption, or high CPUs on hosts. All of this can cause network congestion.

Jitter   Jitter occurs when the data flow in a connection is inconsistent; that is, it increases and decreases in no discernable pattern. Jitter results from network congestion, timing drift, and route changes. Jitter is especially problematic in real-time communications like IP telephony and videoconferencing.

Collisions   A network *collision* happens when two devices try to communicate on the same physical segment simultaneously. Collisions like this were a big problem in the early Ethernet networks, and a tool known as *carrier sense multiple access with collision detection (CSMA/CD)* was used to detect and respond to them in Ethernet_II. Nowadays, we use switches in place of hubs because they can separate the network into multiple collision domains, learn the Media Access Control (MAC) addresses of the devices attached to them, create a type of permanent virtual circuit between all network devices, and prevent collisions.

Shorts   Basically, a *short circuit*, or *short*, happens when the current flows through a different path within a circuit than it's supposed to; in networks, they're usually caused by some physical fault in the cable. You can find shorts with circuit-testing equipment, but because sooner is better when it comes to getting a network back up and running, replacing the ailing cable until it can be fixed (if it can be) is your best option.

Open Impedance Mismatch (echo)   Open impedance on cable-testing equipment tells you that the cable or wires connect into another cable, and there is an impedance mismatch. When that happens, some of the signal will bounce back in the direction it came from, degrading the strength of the signal, which ultimately causes the link to fail.

Interference/Cable Placement   EMI and *radio frequency interference (RFI)* occur when signals interfere with the normal operation of electronic circuits. Computers happen to be really sensitive to sources of this, such as TV and radio transmitters, which create a specific radio frequency as part of their transmission process. Two other common culprits are two-way radios and cellular phones.

Your only way around this is to use shielded network cables like shielded twisted-pair (STP) and coaxial cable (rare today) or to run EMI/RFI-immune but pricey fiber-optic cable throughout your entire network.

Split Pairs   A split pair is a wiring error where two connections that are supposed to be connected using the two wires of a twisted pair are instead connected using two wires from different pairs. Such wiring causes errors in high-rate data lines. If you buy your cables precut, you won't have this problem.

TX/RX Transposed   Just like the first item discussed in this section, incorrect pinout, when connecting from a PC-type device into a switch, for the PC use pins 1 and 2 to transmit and 3 and 6 for receiving a digital signal. This means that the pins must be reversed on the switch, using pins 1 and 2 for receiving and 3 and 6 for transmitting the digital signal. If your connection isn't working, check the cable end pinouts.

Bent Pins   Many of the connectors you will encounter have small pins on the end that must go into specific holes on the interface to which they plug. If these pins get bent, either they won't go into the correct hole or they won't go into a hole at all. When this occurs, the cable either will not work at all or will not work correctly. Not bending these fragile pins when working with these cable types will prevent this issue from occurring.

Bottlenecks/Bottlenecking   Bottlenecks are areas of the network where the physical infrastructure cannot handle the traffic. In some cases, this is a temporary issue caused by an unusual burst of traffic. In other scenarios, upgrading the infrastructure or reorganizing the network to alleviate the bottleneck is a wake-up call. The apparent result of a bottleneck is poor performance.

Fiber Cable Issues

Fiber is definitely the best kind of wiring to use for long-distance runs because it has the least attenuation at long distances compared to copper. The bad news is that it's also the hardest to troubleshoot. First, let's understand the difference between the different fiber modes and then go onto troubleshooting.

There are two major types of fiber optics: single-mode and multimode. Figure 18.2 shows the differences between multimode and single-mode fibers.

FIGURE 18.2 Multimode and single-mode fibers

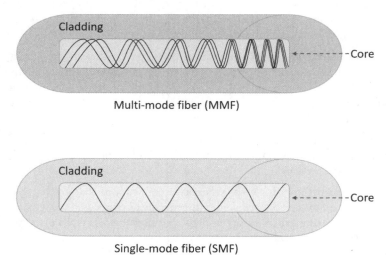

Single mode is more expensive, has tighter cladding, and can go much farther distances than multimode. The difference comes in the tightness of the cladding, which makes a smaller core, meaning that only one mode of light will propagate down the fiber. Multimode is looser and has a larger core so it allows multiple light particles to travel down the glass. These particles must be put back together at the receiving end so the distance is less than that with single-mode fiber, which allows only very few light particles to travel down the fiber.

Here are some common fiber issues to be aware of:

SFP/GBIC (Cable Mismatch) The small form-factor pluggable (SFP) is a compact, hot-pluggable transceiver used for networking and other types of equipment. It interfaces a network device motherboard for a switch, router, media converter, or similar device to a fiber-optic or copper networking cable. Due to its smaller size, SFP obsolesces the formerly ubiquitous gigabit interface converter (GBIC), so SFP is sometimes referred to as a mini-GBIC. Always make sure you have the right cable for each type of connector type and that they are not mismatched.

Bad SFP/GBIC (Cable or Transceiver)   If your link is down, verify that your cable or transceiver hasn't gone bad. Also, if the termination end is GBIC or SFP based, many network systems have console commands that output statistics on the status of the device. You can also swap out the SFP/GBIC to verify if it is faulty or not.

Wavelength Mismatch   One of the more confusing terms used regarding fiber networks is *wavelength*. Though it sounds very complicated and scientific, it's actually just the term used to define what we think of as the color of light. Wavelength mismatch occurs when two different fiber transmitters at each end of the cable are using either a longer or shorter wavelength. This means you've got to make sure your transmitters match on both ends of the cable.

Fiber Type Mismatch   Fiber type mismatches, at each of the transceivers, can cause wavelength issues, massive attenuation, and dB loss.

Dirty Connectors   It's important to verify your connectors to make sure no dirt or dust has corrupted the cable end. You need to polish your cable ends with a soft cloth, but do not look into the cable if the other end is transmitting—it could damage your eyes!

Connector Mismatch   Just because it fits doesn't mean it works. Make sure you have precisely the right connectors for each type of cable end or transceiver.

Bend Radius Limitations   Fiber, whether it is made of glass or plastic, can break. You need to make sure you understand the bend radius limitations of each type of fiber you purchase and that you don't exceed the specifications when installing fiber in your rack.

Distance Limitations   The pros of fiber are that it's completely immune to EMI and RFI and that it can transmit up to 40 kilometers—about 25 miles! Add some repeater stations and you can go between continents. But all fiber types aren't created equally. For example, single mode can perform at much greater distances than multimode can. And again, make sure you have the right cable for the distance you'll require to run your fiber!

Unbounded Media Issues (Wireless)

Now let's say your problem-ridden user is telling you they use only a wireless connection. Well, you can definitely take crosstalk and shorts off the list of suspects, but don't get excited, because with wireless, you've got a whole new bunch of possible Physical layer problems to sort through.

Wireless networks are really convenient for the user but not so much for administrators. They can require a lot more configuration; with wireless networks, you don't just get to substitute one set of challenges for another—you pretty much add all those fresh new issues on top of the wired challenges you already have on your plate.

The following are some of those new wireless challenges:

Interference   Because wireless networks rely on radio waves to transmit signals, they're more subject to interference, even from other wireless devices like Bluetooth keyboards, mice, or cell phones that are all close in frequency ranges. Any of these—even microwave ovens!—can cause signal bleed that can slow down or prevent wireless communications.

Factors like the distance between a client and a wireless access point (WAP) and the stuff between the two can also affect signal strength and even intensify the interference from other signals. So, careful placement of that WAP is a must.

Device Saturation/Bandwidth Saturation Limits the Throughput Capacity   Clearly, it's important to design and implement your wireless network correctly. Be sure to understand the number of hosts connecting to each AP you'll be installing. If you have too much device saturation on an AP, it will result in low available bandwidth. Just think about when you're in a hotel and how slow the wireless is because of throughput issues. This is directly due to device/bandwidth saturation for each AP. And more Aps don't always solve the problem— you need to design correctly!

Simultaneous Wired/Wireless Connections   It's not unusual to find that a laptop today will have a wired and wireless connection simultaneously. Typically this doesn't create a problem, but don't think you get more bandwidth or better results because of it. It's possible that the configurations can cause a problem, although that's rare today. For instance, if each provides a DNS server with a different address, it can cause name resolution issues, or even default gateway issues. Most of the time, it just causes confusion in your laptop, making it work harder to determine the correct DNS or default gateway address to use. And the laptop can give up and stop communicating completely! Because of this, you need to remind the user to turn off their wireless when they take it into their office and connect it to their dock.

Configurations   Mistakes in the configuration of the wireless access point or wireless router or inconsistencies between the settings on the AP and the stations can also be the source of problems. The following list describes some of the main sources of configuration problems.

Incorrect Encryption/Security Type Mismatch   You know that wireless networks can use encryption to secure their communications and that different encryption flavors are used for wireless networks, like Wired Equivalent Privacy (WEP) and WI-FI Protected Access 3 (WPA3) with Advanced Encryption Standard (AES). WPA3 is the latest standard, and it is common now. To ensure the tightest security, configure your wireless networks with the highest encryption protocol that both the WAP and the clients can support. Oh, and make sure the AP and its clients are configured with the same type of encryption. This is why it's a good idea to disable security before troubleshooting client problems, because if the client can connect once you've done that, you know you're dealing with a security configuration error.

Incorrect, Overlapping, or Mismatched Channels   Wireless networks use many different frequencies within the 2.4 GHz or 5 GHz band, and I'll bet you didn't know that these frequencies are sometimes combined to provide greater bandwidth for the user. You actually do know about this—has anyone heard of something called a *channel*? Well, that's exactly what a channel is, and it's also the reason some radio stations come in better than others—they have more bandwidth because their channel has more combined frequencies. You also know what happens when the AP and the client aren't quite matching up. Have you ever hit the scan button on your car's radio and only kind of gotten a station's static-ridden broadcast? That's because the AP (radio station) and the client (your car's radio) aren't quite on the same channel. Most of the time, wireless networks use channel 1, 6, or 11, and because clients auto-configure themselves to any channel the AP is broadcasting on, it's not usually a configuration issue unless someone has forced a client onto an incorrect channel. Also, be sure not to use the same channel on APs within the same area. Overlapping channels cause your signal-to-noise ratio to drop because you'll get a ton of interference and signal loss!

Incorrect Frequency/Incompatibilities   So, setting the channel sets the frequency or frequencies that wireless devices will use. But some devices, such as an AP running 802.11ac and ax, allow you to tweak those settings and choose a specific frequency such as 2.4 GHz or 5 GHz. As with any relationship, it works best if things are mutual. So if you do this on one device, you've got to configure the same setting on all the devices with which you want to communicate, or they won't—they'll argue, and you don't want that. Incorrect-channel and frequency-setting problems on a client are rare, but if you have multiple APs and they're in close proximity, you need to make sure they're on different channels/frequencies to avoid potential interference problems.

Wrong Passphrase   When a passphrase is used as an authentication method, the correct passphrase must be entered when authenticating to the AP or to the controller. When an incorrect passphrase is provided, access will be denied. This is another issue that will impair functionality.

SSID Mismatch   When a wireless device comes up, it scans for service set identifiers (SSIDs) in its immediate area. These can be basic service set identifiers (BSSIDs) that identify an individual access point or extended service set identifiers (ESSIDs) that identify a set of APs. In your own wireless LAN, you clearly want the devices to find the ESSID that you're broadcasting, which isn't usually a problem: Your broadcast is closer than the neighbor's, so it should be stronger—unless you're in an office building or apartment complex that has lots of different APs assigned to lots of different ESSIDs because they belong to lots of different tenants in the building. This can definitely give you some grief because it's possible that your neighbor's ESSID broadcast is stronger than yours, depending on where the clients are in the building. So if a user reports that they're connected to an AP but still can't access the resources they need or authenticate to the network, you should verify that they are, in fact, connected to your ESSID and not your neighbor's. This is very typical in an open security wireless network. You can generally just look at the information tool tip on the wireless software icon to find this out. However, you can easily solve this problem today by making the office SSID the preferred network in the client software.

Wireless Standard Mismatch   As you found out in Chapter 12, "Wireless Networking," wireless networks have many standards that have evolved over time, like 802.11a, 802.11b, 802.11g, and 802.11n, and 802.11ac and ax. Standards continue to develop that make wireless networks even faster and more powerful. The catch is that some of these standards are backward compatible and others aren't. For instance, most devices you buy today can be set to all standards, which means they can be used to communicate with other devices of all four standards. So, make sure the standards on the AP match the standards on the client or that they're at least backward compatible. It's either that or tell all your users to buy new cards for their machines. Be sure to understand the throughput, frequency, distance capabilities, and available channels for each standard you use.

Untested Updates   It's really important to push updates to the APs in your wireless network, but not before you test them. Just like waiting for an update from Microsoft or Apple to become available for weeks or months before you update, you need to wait for the OS or patch updates for your AP. Then, you need to test the updates thoroughly on your bench before pushing them to your live network.

Distance/Signal Strength/Power Levels Causing Signal Degradation or Loss   Location, location, location. You've got only two worries with this one: Your clients are either not far enough away or too far from the AP. Suppose your AP doesn't seem to have enough power to provide a connectivity point for your clients. In that case, you can move it closer to them, increase the distance that the AP can transmit by changing the type of antenna it uses, or use multiple APs connected to the same switch or set of switches to solve the problem. If the power level or signal is too strong, and it reaches out into the parking area or farther out to other buildings and businesses, place the AP as close as possible to the center of the area it's providing service for. And don't forget to verify that you've got the latest security features in place to keep bad guys from authenticating to and using your network.

Client Disassociation Issues   Wireless clients randomly disassociating with an AP can be a difficult item to troubleshoot, especially if it's random or intermittent. It's frustrating for users, and they'll take it out on the engineer. There are a couple of reasons that I have found that caused this, although this may not be the answer for all the issues you see. Disabling the 802.11b client access actually prevented a customer from having them intermittently disconnect and then reconnect. Most clients are 802.11a or g or higher, so when the AP encoding goes down to 802.11b, then all other clients may run that same encoding, which disconnects them. By not allowing 802.11b clients, this solved this customer issue. Another client had a Meraki AP with automatic channel planning set to on. This caused the channels to randomly change, which disconnects the clients, so we had to disable this feature.

Roaming Misconfiguration   When you walk through a building and lose connection on your AP, it's common to initially blame signal coverage and assume a dead spot. As you know, this is referred to as roaming between APs, and there are several reasons why devices can have problems transitioning from one access point to the next. Here are a few of the causes I have found causing roaming issues:

- Excessive coverage
- Poor Signal coverage
- Re-authentication
- Mismatching configuration
- Hidden SSIDs

Latency and Overcapacity   When wireless users complain that the network is slow (latency) or that they are losing their connection to applications during a session, it is usually a capacity or distance issue. Remember, 802.11 is a shared medium, and as more users connect, all user throughput goes down. Suppose this becomes a constant problem as opposed to the occasional issue where 20 guys with laptops gather for a meeting every six months in the conference room. In that case, it may be time to consider placing a second AP in the area. When you do this, place the second AP on a different non-overlapping channel from the first and make sure the second AP uses the same SSID as the first. In the 2.4 GHz frequency, the three non-overlapping channels are 1, 6, and 11. Now the traffic can be divided between them, and users will get better performance. It is also worth noting that when clients move away from the AP, the data rate drops until at some point it is insufficient to maintain the connection.

Bounce   For a wireless network spanning large geographical distances, you can install repeaters and reflectors to bounce a signal and boost it to cover about a mile. This can be a good thing, but if you don't tightly control signal bounce, you could end up with a much bigger network than you wanted. To determine exactly how far and wide the signal will bounce, make sure you conduct a thorough wireless site survey. However, bounce can also refer to multipath issues, where the signal reflects off objects and arrives at the client degraded because it is arriving out of phase. The solution is pretty simple. APs use two antennas, both of which sample the signal and use the strongest signal and ignore the out-of-phase signal. However, 802.11ac and ax takes advantage of multipath and can combine the out-of-phase signals to increase the distance hosts can be from the AP.

Incorrect Antenna Type or Switch Placement Can Cause Insufficient Wireless Coverage   Most of the time, the best place to put an AP and/or its antenna is as close to the center of your wireless network as possible. But you can position some antennas a distance from the AP and connect to it with a cable—a method used for a lot of the outdoor installations around today. If you want to use multiple APs, you've also got to be a little more sophisticated about deciding where to put them all; you can use third-party tools like the packet sniffers Wireshark and AirMagnet on a laptop to survey the site and establish how far your APs are actually transmitting. You can also hire a consultant to do this for you—there are many companies that specialize in assisting organizations with their wireless networks and the placement of antennas and APs. This is important because poor placement can lead to interference and poor performance, or even no performance at all.

Environmental Factors   It's vital to understand your environmental factors when designing and deploying your wireless network. Do you have concrete walls, window film, or metal studs in the walls? All of these will cause a degradation of dB or power level and result in connectivity issues. Again, plan your wireless network carefully!

Reflection   When a wave hits a smooth object that is larger than the wave itself, depending on the media the wave may bounce in another direction. This behavior is categorized as reflection.

Reflection can be the cause of serious performance problems in a WLAN. As a wave radiates from an antenna, it broadens and disperses. If portions of this wave are reflected, new wave fronts will appear from the reflection points. If these multiple waves all reach the receiver, the multiple reflected signals cause an effect called multipath.

Multipath can degrade the strength and quality of the received signal or even cause data corruption or canceled signals. APs mitigate this behavior by using multiple antennas and constantly sampling the signal to avoid a degraded signal.

Refraction   Refraction is the bending of an RF signal as it passes through a medium with a different density, thus causing the direction of the wave to change. RF refraction most commonly occurs as a result of atmospheric conditions.

In long-distance outdoor wireless bridge links, refraction can be an issue. An RF signal may also refract through certain types of glass and other materials that are found in an indoor environment.

Absorption   Some materials will absorb a signal and reduce its strength. While there is not much that can be done about this, this behavior should be noted during a site survey, and measures such as additional APs or additional antenna types may be called for.

Signal-to-Noise Ratio   Signal-to-noise ratio (SNR) is the difference in decibels between the received signal and the background noise level (noise floor).

If the amplitude of the noise floor is too close to the amplitude of the received signal, data corruption will occur and result in layer 2 retransmissions, negatively affecting both throughput and latency. An SNR of 25 dB or greater is considered good signal quality, and an SNR of 10 dB or lower is considered very poor signal quality.

Now that you know all about the possible physical network horrors that can befall you on a typical network, it's a good time for you to memorize the troubleshooting steps that you've got to know to ace the CompTIA Network+ exam.

Troubleshooting Steps

In the Network+ troubleshooting model, there are seven steps you've got to have dialed in:

1. Identify the problem.
2. Establish a theory of probable cause.
3. Test the theory to determine cause.
4. Establish a plan of action to resolve the problem and identify potential effects.
5. Implement the solution or escalate as necessary.
6. Verify full system functionality and implement preventative measures if applicable.
7. Document findings, actions, outcomes, and lessons learned throughout the process.

To get things off to a running start, let's assume that the user has called you yet again, but now they're almost in tears because they can't connect to the server on the intranet and they also can't get to the Internet. (By the way, this happens a lot, so pay attention—it's only a matter of time before it happens to you!)

Absolutely, positively make sure you memorize this seven-step trouble-shooting process/methodology in the right order when studying for the Network+ exam!

Step 1: Identify the Problem

Before you can solve the problem, you've got to figure out what it is, right? Again, asking the right questions can get you far along this path and really help clarify the situation. Identifying the problem involves steps that together constitute *information gathering*.

Gather Information by Questioning Users

A good way to start is by asking the user the following questions:

- Exactly which part of the Internet can't you access? A particular website? A certain address? A type of website? None of it at all?
- Can you use your web browser?
- Is it possible to duplicate the problem?
- If the hitch has to do with an internal server to the company, ask the user if they can ping the server and talk them through doing that.
- Ask the user to try to SSH/telnet or SFTP/FTP to an internal server to verify local network connectivity; if they don't know how, talk them through it.
- If there are multiple complaints of problems occurring, look for the big stuff first and then isolate and approach each problem individually.

Here's another really common trouble ticket that just happens to build on the last scenario: Now let's say you've got a user who's called you at the help desk. By asking the previous questions, you found out that this user can't access the corporate intranet or get out to any sites on the Internet. You also established that the user can use their web browser to access the corporate FTP site, but only by IP address, not by the FTP server name. This information tells you two important things: that you can rule out the host and the web browser (application) as the source of the problem and that the physical network is working.

Duplicate the Problem, If Possible

When a user reports an issue, you should attempt to duplicate the issue. When this is possible, it will aid in discovering the problem. When you cannot duplicate the issue, your challenge becomes harder because you are dealing with an intermittent problem. These issues are difficult to solve because they don't happen consistently.

Determine If Anything Has Changed

Moving right along, if you can reproduce the problem, your next step is to verify what has changed and how. Drawing on your knowledge of networking, you ask yourself and your user questions like these:

Were you ever able to do this?   If not, then maybe it just isn't something the hardware or software is designed to do. You should then tell the user exactly that, as well as advise them that they may need additional hardware or software to pull off what they're trying do.

If so, when did you become unable to do it?   If, once upon a time, the computer was able to do the job and then suddenly could not, whatever conditions surrounded and were involved in this turn of events become extremely important. You have a really good shot at unearthing the root of the problem if you know what happened right before things changed. Just know that there's a high level of probability that the cause of the problem is directly related to the conditions surrounding the change when it occurred.

Has anything changed since the last time you could do this?   This question can lead you right to the problem's cause. Seriously—the thing that changed right before the problem began happening is almost always what caused it. It's so important that if you ask it and your user tells you, "Nothing changed. . .it just happened," you should rephrase the question and say something like, "Did anyone add anything to your computer?" or "Are you doing anything differently from the way you usually do it?"

Were any error messages displayed?   These are basically arrows that point directly at the problem's origin; error messages are designed by programmers for the purpose of pointing them to exactly what it is that isn't working properly in computer systems. Sometimes error messages are crystal clear, like Disk Full, or they can be cryptically annoying little puzzles in and of themselves. If you pulled the short straw and got the latter variety, it's probably best to hit the software or hardware vendor's support site, where you can usually score a translation from the "programmerese" in which the error message is written into plain English so you can get back to solving your riddle.

Are other people experiencing this problem?   You've got to ask this one because the answer will definitely help you target the cause of the problem. First, try to duplicate the problem from your own workstation because if you can't, it's likely that the issue is related to only one user or group of users—possibly their workstations. (A solid hint that this is the case is if you're being inundated with calls from a bunch of people from the same workgroup.)

Is the problem always the same?   It's good to know that when problems crop up, they're almost always the same each time they occur. But their symptoms can change slightly as the conditions surrounding them change. A related question would be, "If you do x, does the problem get better or worse?" For example, ask a user, "If you use a different file, does the problem get better or worse?" If the symptoms lighten up, it's an indication that the problem is related to the original file that's being used. It's important to try to duplicate the problem to find the source of the issue as soon as possible!

Understand that these are just a few of the questions you can use to get to the source of a problem.

Okay, so let's get back to our sample scenario. So far, you've determined that the problem is unique to one user, which tells you that the problem is specific to this one host. Confirming that is the fact that you haven't received any other calls from other users on the network.

And when watching the user attempt to reproduce the problem, you note that they're typing the address correctly. Plus, you've got an error message that leads you to believe that the problem has something to do with Domain Name System (DNS) lookups on the user's host. Time to go deeper. . .

Identify Symptoms

I probably don't need to tell you that computers and networks can be really fickle—they can hum along fine for months, suddenly crash, and then continue to work fine again without ever seizing in that way again. That's why it's so important to be able to reproduce the problem and identify the affected area to narrow things down so you can cut to the chase and fix the issue fast. This really helps—when something isn't working, try it again, and write down exactly what is and is not happening.

Most users' knee-jerk reaction is to straight up call the help desk the minute they have a problem. This is not only annoying but also inefficient, because you're going to ask them exactly what they were doing when the problem occurred and most users have no idea what they were doing with the computer at the time because they were focused on doing their jobs instead. This is why if you train users to reproduce the problem and jot down some notes about it *before* calling you, they'll be much better prepared to give you the information you need to start troubleshooting it and help them.

So, with that, here we go. The problem you've identified results in coughing out an error message to your user when they try to access the corporate intranet. It looks like Figure 18.3.

And when this user tries to ping the server using its hierarchical web name, it also fails (see Figure 18.4).

You're going to respond by checking to see whether the server is up by pinging the server by its IP address (see Figure 18.5).

Nice—that worked, so the server is up, but you could still have a server problem. Just because you can ping a host, it doesn't mean that host is 100% up and running, but in this case, it's a good start.

And you're in luck because you've been able to re-create this problem from this user's host machine. By doing that, you now know that the URL name is not being resolved from Internet Explorer, and you can't ping it by the name either. But you can ping the server IP address from your limping host, and when you try this same connection to the `internal .lammle.com` server from another host nearby, it works fine, meaning the server is working fine. So, you've succeeded in isolating the problem to this specific host!

FIGURE 18.3 Cannot connect

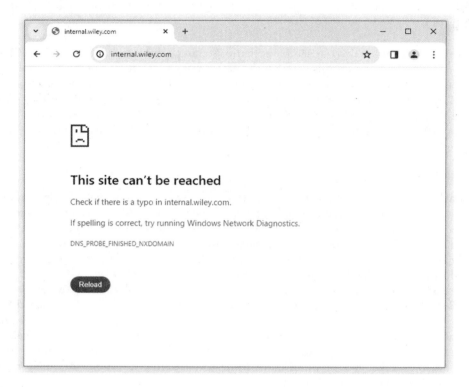

FIGURE 18.4 Host could not be found.

```
Microsoft Windows [Version 10.0.19045.3803]
(c) Microsoft Corporation. All rights reserved.

C:\Users\User>ping internal.wiley.com
Ping request could not find host internal.wiley.com. Please check the
name and try again.

C:\Users\User>|
```

It is a huge advantage if you can watch the user try to reproduce the problem themselves because then you know for sure whether the user is performing the operation correctly. It's a really bad idea to assume the user is typing in what they say they are.

FIGURE 18.5   Successful ping

```
Microsoft Windows [Version 10.0.19045.3803]
(c) Microsoft Corporation. All rights reserved.

C:\Users\User>ping 104.237.128.65

Pinging 104.237.128.65 with 32 bytes of data:
Reply from 104.237.128.65: bytes=32 time=59ms TTL=40
Reply from 104.237.128.65: bytes=32 time=52ms TTL=40
Reply from 104.237.128.65: bytes=32 time=53ms TTL=40
Reply from 104.237.128.65: bytes=32 time=57ms TTL=40

Ping statistics for 104.237.128.65:
    Packets: Sent = 4, Received = 4, Lost = 0 (0% loss),
Approximate round trip times in milli-seconds:
    Minimum = 52ms, Maximum = 59ms, Average = 55ms

C:\Users\User>
```

Approach Multiple Problems Individually

You should never mix possible solutions when troubleshooting. When multiple changes are made, interactions can occur that muddy the results. Always attack one issue at a time and make only a single change at a time. When a change does not have a beneficial effect, reverse the change before making another change.

You've now nailed down the problem. This leads us to step 2.

Step 2: Establish a Theory of Probable Cause

After you observe the problem and identify the symptoms, next on the list is to establish its most probable cause. (If you're stressing about it now, don't, because though you may feel overwhelmed by all this, it truly does get a lot easier with time and experience.)

You must come up with at least one possible cause, even though it may not be completely on the money. And you don't always have to come up with it yourself. Someone else in the group may have the answer. Also, don't forget to check online sources and vendor documentation.

Again, let's get back to our scenario, in which you've determined the cause is probably an improperly configured DNS lookup on the workstation. The next thing to do is to verify the configuration (and probably reconfigure DNS on the workstation; we'll get to this solution later, in step 4).

Understand that there are legions of problems that can occur on a network—and I'm sorry to tell you this, but they're typically not as simple as the example we've been using. They can be, but I just don't want you to expect them to be. Always consider the physical aspects of a network, but look beyond them into the realm of logical factors like the DNS lookup issue we've been using.

Question the Obvious

The probable causes that you've got to thoroughly understand to meet the Network+ objectives are as follows:

- Port speed
- Port duplex mismatch
- Mismatched MTU
- Incorrect virtual local area network (VLAN)
- Interface shutdown/disabled/suspended
- Interface issues/increasing counters
- Incorrect IP address/duplicate IP address
- Wrong gateway
- Wrong DNS
- Incorrect subnet mask
- Incorrect interface/interface misconfiguration
- Duplicate MAC addresses
- Expired IP address
- Rogue DHCP server
- Untrusted SSL certificate
- Incorrect time
- DHCP address pool exhaustion
- Blocked TCP/UDP ports
- Incorrect host-based firewall settings
- Incorrect ACL settings
- Unresponsive service
- Multicast flooding
- Asymmetrical routing
- Low optical link budget
- Network Time Protocol issues
- Hardware issues with Power over Ethernet (PoE)
- Bring your own device challenges
- Licensed features
- Network performance issues

Let's talk about these logical issues, which can cause an abundance of network problems. Most of these happen because a device has been improperly configured.

Port Speed   Because networks have been evolving for many years, there are various levels of speed and sophistication mixed into them—often within the same network. Most of the newest NICs can be used at 10 Mbps, 100 Mbps, and 1000 Mbps. Most switches can support at least 10 Mbps and 100 Mbps, and an increasing number of switches can also support 1G or 25/40/100 Gbps. Plus, many switches can also autosense the speed of the NIC that's connected and use different speeds on various ports. As long as the switches are allowed to autosense the port speed, it's rare to have a problem develop that results in a complete lack of communication. But if you decide to set the port speed manually, make positively sure to set the same speed on both sides of a link.

Port Duplex Mismatch   There are generally three duplex settings on each port of a network switch: full, half, and auto. For two devices to connect effectively, the duplex setting has to match on both sides of the connection. If one side of a connection is set to full and the other is set to half, they're mismatched. More elusively, if both sides are set to auto but the devices are different, you can also end up with a mismatch because the device on one side defaults to full and the other one defaults to half.

Duplex mismatches can cause lots of network and interface errors, and even a lack of a network connection. This is partially because setting the interfaces to full duplex disables the CSMA/CD protocol. This is definitely not a problem in a network that has no hubs (and therefore no shared segments in which there could be collisions), but it can make things really ugly in a network where hubs are still being used. This means the settings you choose are based on the type of devices you have populating your network. If you have all switches and no hubs, feel free to set all interfaces to full duplex, but if you've got hubs in the mix, you have shared networks, so you're forced to keep the settings at half duplex. With all new switches produced today, leaving the speed and duplex setting to auto (the default on both switches and hosts) is the recommended way to go.

Mismatched MTU   Ethernet LANs enforce what is called a maximum transmission unit (MTU). This is the largest size packet that is allowed across a segment. In most cases, this is 1500 bytes. Left alone this is usually not a problem, but it is possible to set the MTU on a router interface, which means it is possible for a mismatch to be present between two router interfaces. This can cause problems with communications between the routers, resulting in the link failing to pass traffic. To check the MTU on an interface, execute the command `show interface`.

Incorrect VLAN   Switches can have multiple VLANs each, and they can be connected to other switches using trunk links. As you now know, VLANs are often used to represent departments or the occupations of a group of users. This makes the configurations of security policies and network access lists much easier to manage and control. On the other hand, if a port is accidentally assigned to the wrong VLAN in a switch, it's as if that client was magically transported to another place in the network. If that happens, the security policies that should apply to the client won't anymore, and other policies will be applied to the client that never should have been. The correct VLAN port assignment of a client is as important as air; when I'm troubleshooting a single-host problem, this is the first place I look.

It's pretty easy to tell if you have a port configured with a wrong VLAN assignment. If this is the case, it won't be long before you'll get a call from some user screaming something at you that makes the building shake, like, "I can get to the Internet, but I can't get to the Sales server, and I'm about to lose a huge sale. DO SOMETHING!" When you check the switch, you will invariably see that this user's port has a membership in another VLAN, like Marketing, which has no access to the Sales server.

Interface Shutdown/Disabled/Suspended   You can check a switch and router interface port status with the show interfaces command. You can administratively disable a switch or router port with the shutdown command.

```
Switch(config)#int f0/1
Switch(config-if)#shutdown
%LINK-5-CHANGED: Interface FastEthernet0/1, changed state to
administratively down
```

Understand that on switches you can configure what is called the Port-security command, which can help you administrate, mostly to stop people from plugging multiple devices into the same port. But how do we actually prevent someone from simply plugging a host into one of our switch ports—or worse, adding a hub, switch, or access point into the Ethernet jack in their office? By default, MAC addresses will dynamically appear in your MAC forward/filter database, but you can stop them in their tracks by using port security!

Figure 18.6 shows two hosts connected to the single switch port Fa0/3 via either a hub or access point (AP).

Port Fa0/3 is configured to observe and allow only certain MAC addresses to associate with the specific port. So in this example, Host A is denied access, but Host B is allowed to associate with the port.

You can configure the device to take one of the following actions when a security violation occurs by using the switchport port-security command:

```
Switch(config)#int f0/3
Switch(config-if)#switchport port-security violation ?
protect Security violation protect mode
restrict Security violation restrict mode
shutdown Security violation shutdown mode
```

These are the three options for port security:

- Protect: The protect violation mode drops packets with unknown source addresses until you remove enough secure MAC addresses to drop below the maximum value.

FIGURE 18.6   Port Security on a switch port restricts port access by MAC address.

interface fastethernet 0/3
  switchport mode access
  switchport port-security
  switchport port-security mac-address bb:bb:bb:22:22:22

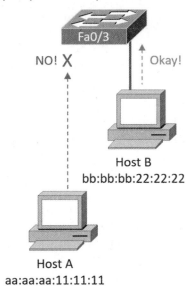

- **Restrict:** The restrict violation mode also drops packets with unknown source addresses until you remove enough secure MAC addresses to drop below the maximum value.

- **Shutdown:** Shutdown is the default violation mode. The shutdown violation mode puts the interface into an *error-disabled* state immediately.

Interface Issues/Increasing Counters   Let's zoom in on an interface Fa0/0 and talk about what to expect if there were errors on this interface that cause increasing counters:

```
R2#sh int fa0/0
FastEthernet0/0 is up, line protocol is up
[output cut]
  Full-duplex, 100Mb/s, 100BaseTX/FX
  ARP type: ARPA, ARP Timeout 04:00:00
  Last input 00:00:05, output 00:00:01, output hang never
  Last clearing of "show interface" counters never
  Input queue: 0/75/0/0 (size/max/drops/flushes); Total output drops: 0
  Queueing strategy: fifo
```

```
Output queue: 0/40 (size/max)
5 minute input rate 0 bits/sec, 0 packets/sec
5 minute output rate 0 bits/sec, 0 packets/sec
    1325 packets input, 157823 bytes
    Received 1157 broadcasts (0 IP multicasts)
    0 runts, 0 giants, 0 throttles
    0 input errors, 0 CRC, 0 frame, 0 overrun, 0 ignored
    0 watchdog
    0 input packets with dribble condition detected
    2294 packets output, 244630 bytes, 0 underruns
    0 output errors, 0 collisions, 3 interface resets
    347 unknown protocol drops
    0 babbles, 0 late collision, 0 deferred
    4 lost carrier, 0 no carrier
    0 output buffer failures, 0 output buffers swapped out
```

CRC Errors   Cyclic redundancy check (CRC) errors happen when the last 4 bytes of the frame (FCS) fail to verify the incoming frame. As you can see in the following example, this interface has both input errors and CRC errors. Input errors are any error encountered on the interface, whereas CRC errors are exclusively failed FCS checks. Both of these counters are accumulative and need to be manually cleared with the clear counters command, specifying the interface name and number, such as gigabitEthernet 4/27.

```
es-29#show interface gigabitEthernet 4/27
GigabitEthernet4/27 is up, line protocol is up (connected)
```

```
[ Output Cut]
    Received 72917 broadcasts (99 multicasts)
    232 runts, 0 giants, 0 throttles
    112085 input errors, 111853 CRC, 0 frame, 0 overrun, 0 ignored
    0 input packets with dribble condition detected
    161829497 packets output, 20291962434 bytes, 0 underruns
    0 output errors, 0 collisions, 3 interface resets
```

```
[ Output Cut ]
```

It important to understand that you can view only incoming CRC errors. Outgoing frames are the responsibility of the other side of the connection, to be checked against the FCS. Common causes of CRC errors usually involve wiring, but having the wrong duplex manually configured on both sides can also cause CRC errors.

Giants   Giant frames are just what their name suggests; they are large frames. When the interface receives an incoming frame larger than the configured maximum transmission unit (MTU) for an interface or VLAN, the giant frame counter will increment. The giants counters can be found in the output of the show interface command, as shown in the following example. The default MTU for Ethernet is 1500 bytes. It is very common to see this counter increment if the connected host is sending jumbo frames with an MTU of 9000 bytes.

```
es-29#show interface gigabitEthernet 4/27
GigabitEthernet4/27 is up, line protocol is up (connected)

[ Output Cut]
    Received 72917 broadcasts (99 multicasts)
    232 runts, 0 giants, 0 throttles
    112085 input errors, 111853 CRC, 0 frame, 0 overrun, 0 ignored
    0 input packets with dribble condition detected
    161829497 packets output, 20291962434 bytes, 0 underruns
    0 output errors, 0 collisions, 3 interface resets

[ Output Cut ]
```

Runs   If giant frames are large frames, then logically, runts are small frames. When an interface receives an incoming frame smaller than 64 bytes, the frame is considered a runt. This commonly happens when there are collisions, but it can also happen if you have a faulty connection. In the following example, the interface has received a number of runt frames, but no collisions were detected. However, the interface has received a number of CRC errors, so this is probably a bad physical connection.

```
es-29#show interface gigabitEthernet 4/27
GigabitEthernet4/27 is up, line protocol is up (connected)

[ Output Cut]
    Received 72917 broadcasts (99 multicasts)
    232 runts, 0 giants, 0 throttles
    112085 input errors, 111853 CRC, 0 frame, 0 overrun, 0 ignored
    0 input packets with dribble condition detected
    161829497 packets output, 20291962434 bytes, 0 underruns
    0 output errors, 0 collisions, 3 interface resets

[ Output Cut ]
```

Drops   The number of drops is caused when the output queue is full. For example, when you receive traffic on a 1000Mb interface and forward through a 100Mb interface, you'll see congestion, which causes packet loss and high delay.

Input Queue Drops   If the input queue drops counter increments, this signifies that more traffic is being delivered to the router that it can process. If this is consistently high, try to determine exactly when these counters are increasing and how the events relate to CPU usage. You'll see the ignored and throttle counters increment as well.

Output Queue Drops   This counter indicates that packets were dropped due to interface congestion, leading to packet drops and queuing delays. When this occurs, applications like VoIP will experience performance issues. If you observe this constantly incrementing, consider QoS.

Input Errors   Input errors often indicate high errors such as CRCs. This can point to cabling problems, hardware issues, or duplex mismatches.

Output Errors   This is the total number of frames that the port tried to transmit when an issue such as a collision occurred.

You've got to be able to analyze interface statistics to find problems if they exist, so let's pick out the important factors relevant to meeting that challenge effectively now.

Speed and Duplex Settings   It's good to know that the most common cause of interface errors is a mismatched duplex mode between two ends of an Ethernet link. This is why it's so important to make sure that the switch and its hosts (PCs, router interfaces, etc.) have the same speed setting. If not, they just won't connect. And if they have mismatched duplex settings, you'll receive a legion of errors, which cause nasty performance issues, intermittent connectivity—even total loss of communication!

Using autonegotiation for speed and duplex is a very common practice, and it's enabled by default. But if this fails for some reason, you'll have to set the configuration manually like this:

```
Switch(config)#int gi0/1
Switch(config-if)#speed ?
  10    Force 10 Mbps operation
  100   Force 100 Mbps operation
  1000  Force 1000 Mbps operation
  auto  Enable AUTO speed configuration
Switch(config-if)#speed 1000
Switch(config-if)#duplex  ?
  auto  Enable AUTO duplex configuration
  full  Force full duplex operation
  half  Force half-duplex operation
Switch(config-if)#duplex  full
```

If you have a duplex mismatch, a telling sign is that the late collision counter will increment.

Incorrect IP Address/Duplicate IP Address   The most common addressing protocol in use today is IPv4, which provides a unique IP address for each host on a network. Client computers usually get their addresses from Dynamic Host Configuration Protocol (DHCP) servers. But sometimes, especially in smaller networks, IP addresses for servers and router interfaces are statically assigned by the network's administrator. An incorrect or duplicate IP address on a client will keep that client from being able to communicate and may even cause a conflict with another client on the network, and a bad address on a server or router interface can be disastrous and affect a multitude of users. This is exactly why you need to be super careful to set up DHCP servers correctly and also when configuring the static IP addresses assigned to servers and router interfaces.

Wrong Gateway A *gateway*, sometimes called a *default gateway* or an *IP default gateway*, is a router interface's address that's configured to forward traffic with a destination IP address that's not in the same subnet as the device itself. Let me clarify that one for you: If a device compares where a packet wants to go with the network it's currently on and finds that the packet needs to go to a remote network, the device will send that packet to the gateway to be forwarded to the remote network. Because every device needs a valid gateway to obtain communication outside its own network, it's going to require some careful planning when considering the gateway configuration of devices in your network.

 If you're configuring a static IP address and default gateway, you need to verify the router's address. Not doing so is a really common "wrong gateway" problem that I see all the time.

Wrong DNS DNS servers are used by networks and their clients to resolve a computer's hostname to its IP addresses and to enable clients to find the server they need to provide the resources they require, like a domain controller during the login and authentication process. Most of the time, DNS addresses are automatically configured by a DHCP server, but sometimes these addresses are statically configured instead. Because lots of applications rely on hostname resolution, a botched DNS configuration usually causes a computer's network applications to fail just like the user's applications in our example scenario.

 If you can ping a host using its IP address but not its name, you probably have some type of name-resolution issue. It's probably lurking somewhere within a DNS configuration.

Incorrect Subnet Mask When network devices look at an IP address configuration, they see a combination of the IP address and the subnet mask. The device uses the subnet mask to establish which part of the address represents the network address and which part represents the host address. So clearly, a subnet mask that is configured wrong has the same nasty effect as a wrong IP address configuration does on communications. Again, a subnet mask is generally configured by the DHCP server; if you're going to enter it manually, make sure the subnet mask is tight or you'll end up tangling with the fallout caused by the entire address's misconfiguration.

Incorrect Interface/Interface Misconfiguration If a host is plugged into a misconfigured switch port or if it's plugged into the wrong switch port that's configured for the wrong VLAN, the host won't function correctly. Make sure the speed, duplex, and correct Ethernet cable is used. Get any of that wrong and either you'll get interface errors on the host and switch port or, worse, things just won't work at all!

Duplicate MAC Addresses There should never be duplicate MAC addresses in your environment. Each interface vendor is issued an organizationally unique identifier (OUI), which will match on all interfaces produced by that vendor, and then the vendor is responsible for ensuring unique MAC addresses. That means duplicate MAC addresses usually indicate a MAC spoofing attack, in which some malicious individual changes their MAC address, which can be done quite easily in the properties of the NIC.

Expired IP Address   In almost all cases, when DHCP is used to allocate IP configurations to devices, the configuration is supplied to the DHCP client on a temporary basis. The lease period is configurable, and when the lease period and a grace period transpire, the lease is expired. The effect of an expired lease is the next time that client computer starts, it must enter the initialization state and obtain new TCP/IP configuration information from a DHCP server. There is nothing, however, to prevent the client from obtaining a new lease for the same IP address.

Rogue DHCP Server   Dynamic Host Configuration Protocol (DHCP) is used to automate the process of assigning IP configurations to hosts. When configured properly, it reduces administrative overload, reduces the human error inherent in manual assignment, and enhances device mobility. But it introduces a vulnerability that when leveraged by a malicious individual can result in an inability of hosts to communicate (constituting a DoS attack) and peer-to-peer attacks.

When an illegitimate DHCP server (called a rogue DHCP server) is introduced to the network, unsuspecting hosts may accept DHCP Offer packets from the illegitimate DHCP server rather than the legitimate DHCP server. When this occurs, the rogue DHCP server will not only issue the host an incorrect IP address, subnet mask, and default gateway address (which makes a peer-to-peer attack possible), it can also issue an incorrect DNS server address, which will lead to the host relying on the attacker's DNS server for the IP addresses of websites (such as major banks) that lead to phishing attacks.

Figure 18.7 shows an example of how this can occur.

In Figure 18.7, after receiving an incorrect IP address, subnet mask, default gateway, and DNS server address from the rogue DHCP server, the DHCP client uses the attacker's DNS server to obtain the IP address of his bank. This leads the client to unwittingly connect to the attacker's copy of the bank's website. When the client enters his credentials to log in, the attacker now has the client's bank credentials and can proceed to empty out his account.

Untrusted SSL Certificate   Reception of an untrusted SSL certificate error message can be for several reasons. Figure 18.8 shows the possible reasons for the warning message.

The first reason, "A trusted certificate authority did not issue the Security certificate presented by this website," means the CA that issued the certificate is not trusted by the local machine. This will occur if the certificate of the CA that issued the certificate is not found in the Trusted Root Certification Authorities Folder on the local machine.

The second reason this might occur is that the certificate is not valid. The certificate may have been presented before the validity period begins, or it may have expired, meaning the validity period is over.

FIGURE 18.7 Rogue DHCP

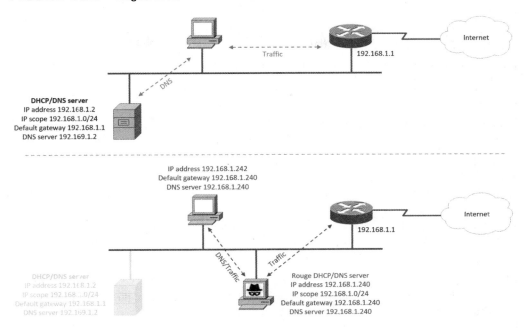

FIGURE 18.8 Certificate error

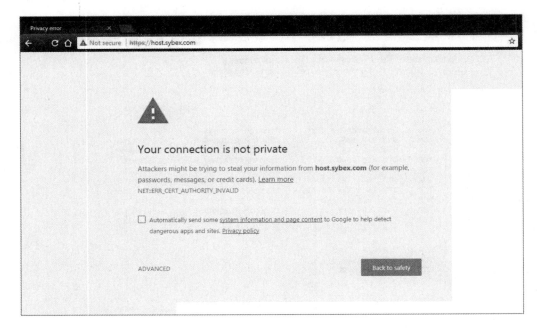

The third reason is that the name on the certificate does not match the name listed on the certificate.

Incorrect Time   Incorrect time on a device can be the cause of several issues. First, in a Windows environment using Active Directory, a clock skew of more than 5 minutes between a client and server will prevent communication between the two.

Second, proper time synchronization is critical for successful operation when certificates are in use.

Finally, when system logs are sent to a central server such as a syslog server, proper time synchronization is critical to understand the order of events.

DHCP Address Pool Exhaustion   When a DHCP server is implemented, it is configured with a limited number of IP addresses. When the IP addresses in a scope are exhausted, any new DHCP clients will be unable to obtain an IP address and will be unable to function on the network.

DHCP servers can be set up to provide backup to another DHCP server for a scope. When this is done, it is important to ensure that while the two DHCP servers service the same scope, they do not have any duplicate IP addresses.

Blocked TCP/UDP Ports   When the ports used by common services and applications are blocked, either on the network firewall or on the personal firewall of a device, it will be impossible to make use of the service or application. One easy way to verify the open ports on a device is to execute the `netstat` command.

Figure 18.9 shows an example of the output.

FIGURE 18.9   Netstat –a output

```
Microsoft Windows [Version 10.0.19045.3803]
(c) Microsoft Corporation. All rights reserved.

C:\Users\User>netstat -a

Active Connections

  Proto  Local Address          Foreign Address        State
  TCP    0.0.0.0:135            DESKTOP-CI2QP04:0       LISTENING
  TCP    0.0.0.0:445            DESKTOP-CI2QP04:0       LISTENING
  TCP    0.0.0.0:5040           DESKTOP-CI2QP04:0       LISTENING
  TCP    0.0.0.0:49664          DESKTOP-CI2QP04:0       LISTENING
  TCP    172.16.1.167:139       DESKTOP-CI2QP04:0       LISTENING
  TCP    172.16.1.167:58789     52.123.189.107:https    ESTABLISHED
  TCP    172.16.1.167:58799     52.123.189.107:https    ESTABLISHED
  TCP    [::]:135               DESKTOP-CI2QP04:0       LISTENING
  TCP    [::]:445               DESKTOP-CI2QP04:0       LISTENING
  UDP    0.0.0.0:5050           *:*
  UDP    0.0.0.0:5353           *:*
  UDP    0.0.0.0:52083          *:*
  UDP    0.0.0.0:53916          *:*
  UDP    0.0.0.0:64082          *:*


C:\Users\User>
```

Incorrect Host-Based Firewall Settings   As you saw in the explanation of blocked TCP/UDP ports, incorrect host-based firewall settings can either prevent transmissions or allow unwanted communications. Neither of these outcomes is desirable. One of the best ways to ensure that firewall settings are consistent and correct all the time is to control these settings with a group policy. When you do this, the settings will be checked and reset at every policy refresh interval.

Incorrect ACL Settings   Access control lists (ACLs) are used to control which traffic types can enter and exit ports on the router. When mistakes are made either in the construction of the ACLs or in their application, many devices may be affected. The creation and application of these tools should be done only by those who have been trained in their syntax and in the logic ACLs use in their operation.

Unresponsive Service   Services can fail for several reasons. Many services depend on other services for their operation. Therefore, the failure of one service sometimes causes a domino effect, taking down other services that depend on it. You can use the Services snap-in inside the Computer Management Microsoft Management Console (MMC) to identify these dependencies as well as start and stop services. To identify the services upon which a particular service depends, use the Dependencies tab on the Services snap-in, as shown in Figure 18.10.

FIGURE 18.10   Service dependencies

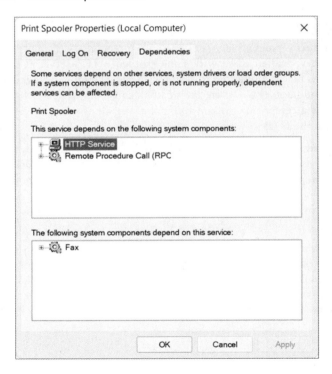

In Figure 18.10, the spooler service is selected and the Dependencies tab is displayed. Here we see that the spooler service depends on the HTTP and RPC services. Therefore, if the spooler service will not start, we may need to restart one of these two services first.

Multicast Flooding   Multicasting is used for network devices to communicate with each other and to save network capacity by having only one sender but many listeners. This is handy for video because the content server does not have to generate an individual stream for every subscribed listener. However, multicast can flood a network with packets as they are sent to every networking device and potentially out every port, even if there are no listeners on the switch port. To resolve these issues, you must enable the multicast features on modern switches and routers that are designed to lessen the impact of multicast flooding.

Asymmetrical Routing   Asymmetrical routing is when a session takes different paths through a network. Generally a routed network will have only one path for both send and receive traffic from a client to a server and vice versa. However, conditions can exist where a router sends traffic out and it comes back using another path. Check that you are not running multiple routing protocols inside your network or that your ISP is not retuning traffic via another path than what you are sending out.

Low Optical Link Budget   When you're troubleshooting fiber-optic links, a test set should be used to make sure the received light level is not too low as to be detected. If there is too much loss over a fiber link due to too many interconnects where additional loss is added, if the distance is greater than the standard dictates, or if there are dirty connections, a link may not be able to be established.

Network Time Protocol Issues   Networks and computers have the ability to sync their time clock to a central server called a Network Time Protocol (NTP) server. If communications are lost, or NTP was never configured to begin with, time stamps for logging, application synchronizations and licenses based on dates can all cause major headaches. It is always a good practice to use a center time source and make sure all of your devices get their data and time data from the NTP servers.

Hardware issues with PoE   As the networking world evolved and it became common to attach devices such as IP phones and remote WI-FI access points to the network, the requirement to supply power to these devises arose. Many IP phones could be powered from a central access Ethernet switch to save having to find a power outlet at every desk. With Wi-Fi access ports, many are located in office ceilings or remote locations where local power may not be available or may be costly to install.

The network switch manufacturers responded with a PoE option for these use cases. PoE allows for both the power and data to be transmitted on a standard Ethernet connection. This technology is what allows VoIP phones, WAPs, video cameras, clocks, and a number of other devices to be powered from the switching equipment without the need for power adapters.

The IEEE has created a standard for PoE called 802.3af. For PoE+ it's referred to as 802.3at. These standards describe precisely how a powered device is detected and also define two methods of delivering Power over Ethernet to a given powered device. Keep in mind that the PoE+ standard, 802.3at, delivers more power than 802.3af, which is compatible with Gigabit Ethernet with four-wire pairs at 30w.

This process happens one of two ways: either by receiving the power from an Ethernet port on a switch (or other capable device) or via a power injector. And you can't use both approaches to get the job done. And be careful here because doing this wrong can lead to serious trouble! Be sure before connecting.

A common problem with PoE is that the switch won't support the power required by the device. For example, you have a PoE+ device, but the switch only supports normal PoE (802.3af). In this circumstance, you will need to upgrade the switch.

Another common problem is exceeding the power budget of the device. This is usually caused by not using *Link Layer Discovery Protocol (LLDP)* or *Cisco Discovery Protocol (CDP)* to communicate power requirements to the switch. These power requirements conveyed to the switch to lower the supply wattage of PoE and PoE+ at the switch. This allows for more efficient power usage of the end devices.

Bring Your Own Devices (BYOD) Challenges   It has become more and more common for workers to want to bring their own smartphones, tablets, and laptops to work and connect them to the corporate network. This can raise a whole host of security issues for a company. There are several approaches to this dilemma. First, a device can be scanned for patches, virus software, and configuration parameters that meet corporate policy. This can be very complex to set up and administer.

A more common approach is to set up a separate WI-FI or LAN network for the BYOD devices that has little or no internal network connectivity but allows a connection out to the Internet. When troubleshooting network problems where a user can connect to some services but not others, it is a good idea to see what device they are using and if they are limited by design.

Licensed Features   If you are troubleshooting a device or application that is missing areas in its configuration, the issue could very well be that the feature has never been enabled. It is common for software to come with a basic feature set and then licenses must be purchased to enable enhanced features. Always take the time in your troubleshooting to investigate if the feature requires a license and if the license is active.

Network Performance Issues   If there is a problem with the network itself, trouble calls will arrive from many affected users. It is important to isolate the problem to see if it is local to a computer or more widespread. This can be a single switch or a whole building. Take the steps outlined in this chapter to really understand the problem and how widespread it is. By isolating it to network segments, you can focus your troubleshooting to determine the cause of the problem.

Consider Multiple Approaches

There are two standard approaches that you can use to establish a theory of probable cause. Let's take a look at them next:

Top-to-Bottom/Bottom-to-Top OSI Model   As its name implies, when you apply a *top-down* approach to troubleshooting a networking problem, you start with the user application and work your way down the layers of the OSI model. If a layer is *not* in good working condition, you inspect the layer below it. When you know that the current layer is not in working condition and you discover that a lower layer works, you can conclude that the problem is within the layer above the lower working layer. Once you've determined which layer is the lowest layer with problems, you can begin identifying the cause of them from within that layer.

The *bottom-up* approach to troubleshooting a networking problem starts with the physical components of the network and works its way up the layers of the OSI model. If you conclude that all the elements associated with a particular layer are in good working order, move on to inspect the elements associated with the next layer up until the cause(s) of the problem is/are identified. The downside to the bottom-up approach is that it requires you to check every device, interface, and so on. In other words, regardless of the nature of the problem, the bottom-up approach starts with an exhaustive check of all the elements of each layer, starting with the physical layer and working its way up from there.

Divide and Conquer   Unlike when opting for the top-down and bottom-up troubleshooting strategies, the *divide-and-conquer* approach to network troubleshooting doesn't always begin the investigation at a particular OSI layer. When using the divide-and-conquer approach, you select a layer and test its health, and based on the results, you can move up or down through the model from the layer you began scrutinizing.

With all that in mind, let's move on with our troubleshooting steps.

Step 3: Test the Theory to Determine the Cause

Once you've gathered information and established a plausible theory, you have to determine the next steps to resolve your problem. If you can't confirm your theory during this step, you must formulate a new theory or escalate the problem.

Let's return to our troubleshooting example by first checking the IP configuration of the host that just happens to include DNS information. You use the `ipconfig /all` command to show the IP configuration. The `/all` switch will give you the DNS information you need, as shown in Figure 18.11.

Check out the DNS entries: 1.1.1.1 and 2.2.2.2. Is this right? What are they supposed to be? You can find this out by checking the addresses on a working host, but let's check the settings on your troubled host's adapter first. Click Start, then Settings, then Network And Internet, and then Ethernet or Wireless (depending on your connection), which will take you to the screen shown in Figure 18.12.

FIGURE 18.11   Output from `ipconfig /all`

```
Ethernet adapter Ethernet0:

   Connection-specific DNS Suffix  . : wiley.local
   Description . . . . . . . . . . . : Intel(R) 82574L Gigabit Network Connection
   Physical Address. . . . . . . . . : 00-0C-29-C6-30-8B
   DHCP Enabled. . . . . . . . . . . : Yes
   Autoconfiguration Enabled . . . . : Yes
   Link-local IPv6 Address . . . . . : fe80::973:7887:9f70:6af8%5(Preferred)
   IPv4 Address. . . . . . . . . . . : 172.16.1.167(Preferred)
   Subnet Mask . . . . . . . . . . . : 255.240.0.0
   Lease Obtained. . . . . . . . . . : Saturday, January 6, 2024 2:27:27 PM
   Lease Expires . . . . . . . . . . : Saturday, January 6, 2024 5:29:52 PM
   Default Gateway . . . . . . . . . : 172.16.1.1
   DHCP Server . . . . . . . . . . . : 172.16.1.1
   DHCPv6 IAID . . . . . . . . . . . : 83889193
   DHCPv6 Client DUID. . . . . . . . : 00-01-00-01-22-CF-6B-86-00-0C-29-C6-30-8B
   DNS Servers . . . . . . . . . . . : 1.1.1.1
                                       2.2.2.2
   NetBIOS over Tcpip. . . . . . . . : Enabled
```

FIGURE 18.12   Ethernet connection

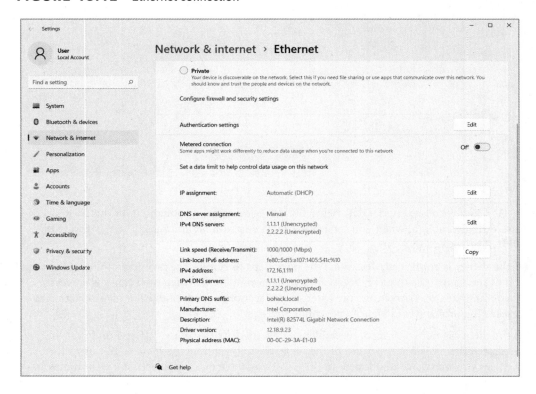

Now, click the Edit on the DNS settings. You receive this screen, shown in Figure 18.13. Do you see what may be causing the problem?

FIGURE 18.13   DNS properties

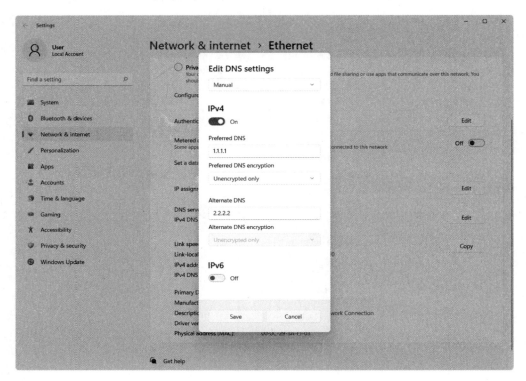

As I said, you're using DHCP, right? But DNS is statically configured on this host. Interestingly enough, when you set a static DNS entry on an interface, it will override the DHCP-provided DNS entry.

If the theory is confirmed, determine the next steps to resolve the problem.   When the testing of the theory is complete, you will have determined if the suggested cause is correct. If you find you are correct, the next steps (next section) are to establish a plan of action to resolve the problem and identify potential effects.

If the theory is not confirmed, reestablish a new theory or escalate.   If you find that the suggested theory is not the cause of the issue, then you should move on to test any other theories you may have developed. In the event you have exhausted all theories you may have developed, it is advisable to escalate the issue to a more senior technician or, when it involves a system with which you are unfamiliar, the system owner or manager.

Step 4: Establish a Plan of Action to Resolve the Problem and Identify Potential Effects

Now that you've identified some possible changes, you've got to follow through and test your solution to see if you really solved the problem. In this case, you ask the user to try to access the intranet server (because that's what they called about). Basically, you just ask the user to try doing whatever it was they couldn't do when they called you in the first place. If it works, sweet—problem solved. If not, try the operation yourself.

Now you can test the proposed solution on the computer of the user who is still waiting for a solution. To do that, you need to check the DNS configuration on your host. But first, let me point out something about the neglected user's network. All hosts are using DHCP, so it's really weird that a single user is having a DNS resolution issue.

So, to fix the problem and get your user back in the game, just click the switch for IPv4 (to turn off the override), then select Automatic for the DNS settings (see Figure 18.14), and finally click Save. *Voilà!*

FIGURE 18.14   Obtaining a DNS server address automatically

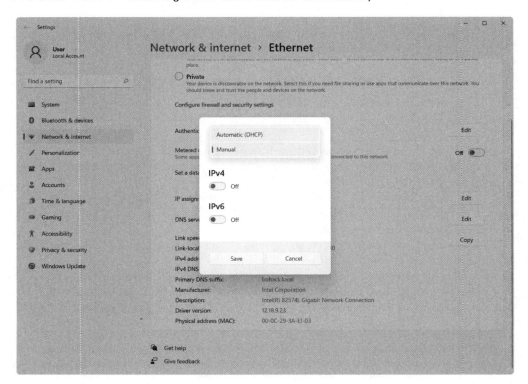

Let's take a look at the output of `ipconfig /all` in Figure 18.15 and see if you received new DNS server addresses.

FIGURE 18.15 `ipconfig /all` output

```
Windows IP Configuration

   Host Name . . . . . . . . . . . . : DESKTOP-RJSJ2Q2
   Primary Dns Suffix  . . . . . . . :
   Node Type . . . . . . . . . . . . : Hybrid
   IP Routing Enabled. . . . . . . . : No
   WINS Proxy Enabled. . . . . . . . : No
   DNS Suffix Search List. . . . . . : wiley.local

Ethernet adapter Ethernet0:

   Connection-specific DNS Suffix  . : wiley.local
   Description . . . . . . . . . . . : Intel(R) 82574L Gigabit Network Connection
   Physical Address. . . . . . . . . : 00-0C-29-3A-E1-03
   DHCP Enabled. . . . . . . . . . . : Yes
   Autoconfiguration Enabled . . . . : Yes
   Link-local IPv6 Address . . . . . : fe80::5d15:a107:1405:541c%10(Preferred)
   IPv4 Address. . . . . . . . . . . : 172.16.1.111(Preferred)
   Subnet Mask . . . . . . . . . . . : 255.240.0.0
   Lease Obtained. . . . . . . . . . : Saturday, January 6, 2024 7:39:10 PM
   Lease Expires . . . . . . . . . . : Saturday, January 6, 2024 9:39:09 PM
   Default Gateway . . . . . . . . . : 172.16.1.1
   DHCP Server . . . . . . . . . . . : 172.16.1.1
   DHCPv6 IAID . . . . . . . . . . . : 100666409
   DHCPv6 Client DUID. . . . . . . . : 00-01-00-01-2D-2B-AA-78-00-0C-29-3A-E1-03
   DNS Servers . . . . . . . . . . . : 172.16.1.1
   NetBIOS over Tcpip. . . . . . . . : Enabled
```

All good; you did it. And you can test the host by trying to use HTTP/HTTPS to connect to a web page on the intranet server and even pinging by hostname. Congratulations on solving your first trouble ticket!

If things hadn't worked out so well, you would go back to step 2, select a new possible cause, and redo step 3. If this happens, keep track of what worked and what didn't so you don't make the same mistakes twice.

It's pretty much common sense that you should change settings like this only when you fully understand the effect your changes will have or when you're asked to by someone who does. The incorrect configuration of these settings will disable the normal operation of your workstation, and, well, it seems that someone (the user, maybe?) did something they shouldn't have or you wouldn't have had the pleasure of solving this problem.

 You have to be super careful when changing settings and always check out a troubled host's network settings. Don't just assume that because they're using DHCP, someone has screwed up the static configuration.

Step 5: Implement the Solution or Escalate as Necessary

Although it's true that CompTIA doesn't expect you to fix every single network problem that could possibly happen in the universe, they actually do expect you to get pretty close to determining exactly what the problem is. And if you can't fix it, you'll be expected to know how to escalate it and to whom. You are only as good as your resources—be they your own skill set, a book like this one, other more reference-oriented technical books, the Internet, or even a guru at a call center.

I know it seems like I talked to death physical and logical issues that cause problems in a network, but trust me, with what I've taught you, you're just getting started. There's a galaxy of networking evils that we have not even touched on because they're far beyond the objectives for Network+ certification and, therefore, the scope of this book. But out there in the real world, you'll get calls about them anyway, and because you're not yet equipped to handle them yourself, you need to escalate these nasties to a senior network engineer who has the additional experience and knowledge required to resolve the problems.

Some of the calamities that you should escalate are as follows:

- Switching loops
- Missing routes
- Routing loops
- Routing problems
- MTU black hole
- Bad modules
- Proxy Address Resolution Protocol (ARP)
- Broadcast storms
- NIC teaming misconfiguration
- Power failures/power anomalies

 If you can't implement a solution and instead have to escalate the problem, there is no need for you to go on with steps 6 and 7 of the seven-step troubleshooting methodology model. You now need to meet with the emergency response team to determine the next step.

And just as with other problems, you have to be able to identify these events because if you can't do that, how else will you know that you need to escalate them?

Switching Loops   Today's networks often connect switches with redundant links to provide for fault tolerance and load balancing. Protocols such as Spanning Tree Protocol (STP) prevent switching loops and simultaneously maintain fault tolerance. If STP fails, it takes some expertise to reconfigure and repair the network, so you just need to be concerned with being able to identify the problem so you can escalate it. Remember, when you hear users complaining that the network works fine for a while, then unexpectedly goes down for about a minute, and then goes back to being fine, it's definitely an STP convergence issue that's pretty tough to find and fix. Escalate this problem ASAP!

Missing Routes   Routers must have routes either configured or learned to function. There are a number of issues that can prevent a router from learning the routes that it needs. To determine if a router has the route to the network in question, execute the show ip route command and view the routing table. This can save a lot of additional troubleshooting if you can narrow the problem to a missing route.

Routing Loops   Routing protocols are often used on networks to control traffic efficiently while preventing routing loops that happen when a routing protocol hasn't been configured properly or network changes didn't get the attention they deserved. Routing loops can also happen if you or the network admin blew the static configuration and created conflicting routes through the network. This evil event affects the traffic flow for all users, and because it's pretty complicated to fix, again, it's up, up, and away with this one. You can expect routing loops to occur if your network is running old routing protocols like Routing Information Protocol (RIP) and RIPv2. Just upgrading your routing protocol to Enhanced Interior Gateway Routing Protocol (EIGRP), Open Shortest Path First (OSPF), or Intermediate System-to-Intermediate System (IS-IS) will usually take care of the problem once and for all. Anyway, escalate this problem to the router group—which ideally is soon to be you.

Routing Problems   Routing packets through the many subnets of a large enterprise while still maintaining security can be a tremendous challenge. A router's configuration can include all kinds of stuff like access lists, network address translation (NAT), port address translation (PAT), and even authentication protocols like Remote Authentication Dial-In User Service (RADIUS) and Terminal Access Controller Access-Control System Plus (TACACS+). Particularly diabolical, errant configuration changes can trigger a domino effect that can derail traffic down the wrong path or even cause it to come to a grinding halt and stop traversing the network completely. To identify routing problems, check to see if someone has simply set a wrong default route on a router. This can easily create routing loops. I see it all the time. These configurations can be highly complex and specific to a particular device, so they need to be escalated to the top dogs—get the problem to the best sys admin in the router group.

MTU Black Hole   On a WAN connection, communication routes may fail if an intermediate network segment has an MTU that is smaller than the maximum packet size of the communicating hosts—and if the router does not send an appropriate Internet Control Message Protocol (ICMP) response to this condition. If ICMP traffic is allowed, the routers will take care of this problem using ICMP messages. However, as ICMP traffic is increasingly being blocked, this can create what is called a black hole. This will probably be an issue you will escalate.

Bad Modules   Some multilayer switches and routers have slots available to add new features. The hardware that fits in these slots is called a module. These modules can host fiber connections, wireless connections, and other types as well. A common example is the Cisco Small Form-Factor Pluggable (SFP) Gigabit Interface Ethernet Converter (GBIC). This is an input-output device that plugs into an existing Gigabit Ethernet port or slot, providing a variety of additional capabilities to the device hosting the slot or port. Conversions can happen in all types of cables, from Ethernet to fiber, for example. Like any piece of hardware made by humans, the modules can fail. It is always worth checking if there are no other reasons a link is not functioning.

Proxy ARP   Address Resolution Protocol (ARP) is a service that resolves IP addresses to MAC addresses. Proxy ARP is just wrong to use in today's networks, but hosts and routers still have it on by default. The idea of Proxy ARP was to solve the problem of a host being able to have only one configured default gateway. To allow redundancy, Proxy ARP running on a router will respond to an ARP broadcast from a host that's sending a packet to a remote network—but the host doesn't have a default gateway set. So the router responds by being the proxy for the remote host, which in turn makes the local host think the remote host is really local; as a result, the local host sends the packets to the router, which then forwards the packets to the remote host. Most of the time, in today's networks, this does not work well, if at all. Disable Proxy ARP on your routers, and make sure you have default gateways set on all your hosts. If you need router redundancy, there are much better solutions available than Proxy ARP! This is another job for the routing group.

Broadcast Storms   When a switch receives a broadcast, it will normally flood the broadcast out all the ports except for the one the broadcast came in on. If STP fails between switches or is disabled by an administrator, it's possible that the traffic could continue to be flooded repeatedly throughout the switch topology. When this happens, the network can get so busy that normal traffic can't traverse it—an event referred to as a *broadcast storm*. As you can imagine, this is a particularly gruesome thing to have to troubleshoot and fix because you need to find the one bad link that is causing the mess while the network is probably still up and running—but at a heavily congested crawl. Escalate ASAP to experts!

NIC Teaming Misconfiguration   NIC teaming, also known as load balancing/failover (LBFO), allows multiple network interfaces to be placed into a team for the purposes of bandwidth aggregation and/or traffic failover to prevent connectivity loss in the event of a network component failure. The cards can be set to active-active state, where both cards are load-balancing, or active-passive, where one card is on standby in case the primary card fails. Most of the time, the NIC team will use a multicast address to send and receive data, but it can also use a broadcast address so all cards receive the data at the same time. If these are not configured correctly, either they will operate at a severely diminished capacity or, worse, neither card will work at all!

Power Failures/Power Anomalies   When you have power issues, whether it's a full-blown power outage or intermittent power surges, it can cause some serious issues with your network devices. Your servers and core network devices require a fully functional UPS system.

Step 6: Verify Full System Functionality and Implement Preventative Measures if Applicable

A trap that any network technician can fall into is solving one problem and thinking it's all fixed without stopping to consider the possible consequences of their solution. The cure can be worse than the disease, and it's possible that your solution falls into this category. So before you fully implement the solution to a problem, make sure you totally understand the ramifications of doing so—clearly, if it causes more problems than it fixes, you should toss it and find a different solution that does no harm.

Many people update a router's operating system or firmware just because a new version of code is released from the manufacturer. Do not do this on your production routers—just say no! Always test any new code before upgrading your production routers: Like a bad solution, sometimes the new code provides new features but creates more problems, and the cons outweigh the pros.

Step 7: Document Findings, Actions, Outcomes, and Lessons Learned Throughout the Process

I can't stress enough how vital network documentation is. Always document problems and solutions so that you have the information at hand when a similar problem arises in the future. With documented solutions to documented problems, you can assemble your own database of information that you can use to troubleshoot other problems. Be sure to include information like the following:

- A description of the conditions surrounding the problem
- The OS version, the software version, the type of computer, and the type of NIC
- Whether you were able to reproduce the problem
- The solutions you tried
- The ultimate solution
- The lessons you learned to achieve great success in the future

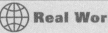

Real World Scenario

Network Documentation

I don't know how many times I've gone into a place and asked where their documentation was only to be met with a blank stare. I was recently at a small business that was experiencing network problems. The first question I asked was, "Do you have any kind of network documentation?" I got the blank stare. So, we proceeded to search through lots of receipts and other paperwork—anything we could find to help us understand the network layout and figure out exactly what was on the network. It turned out they had recently bought a WAP, and it was having trouble connecting—something that would've taken me five minutes to fix instead of searching through a mess for a couple hours!

Documentation doesn't have to look like a sleek owner's manual—it can consist of a simple three-ring binder with an up-to-date network map; receipts for network equipment; a pocket for owner's manuals; and a stack of loose-leaf paper to record services, changes, network-addressing assignments, access lists, and so on. Just this little bit of documentation can save lots of time and money and prevent grief, especially in the critical first few months of a new network install.

Troubleshooting Tips

Now that you've got the basics of network troubleshooting down pat, I'm going to go over a few really handy troubleshooting tips for you to arm yourself with even further in the quest to conquer the world's networking evils.

Don't Overlook the Small Stuff

The super simple stuff I referred to at the beginning of this chapter should never be overlooked—ever! Here's a quick review: Just remember that problems are often caused by little things like a bad power switch; a power switch in the wrong position; a card or port that's not working, indicated by a link light that's not lit; or simply operator error (OE). Even the most experienced system administrator has forgotten to turn on the power, left a cable unplugged, or mistyped a username and password—not me, of course, but others . . .

And make sure that users get solid training for the systems they use. An ounce of prevention is worth a pound of cure, and you'll experience dramatically fewer ID10T errors this way.

Prioritize Your Problems

Being a network administrator or technician of even a fairly small network can keep you hopping, and it's pretty rare that you'll get calls for help one at a time and never be interrupted by more coming in. Closer to reality is receiving yet another call when you already have three people waiting for service. So, you've got to prioritize.

You start this process by again asking some basic questions to determine the severity of the problem being reported. Clearly, if the new call is about something little and you already have a huge issue to deal with, you should put the new call on hold or get their info and get back to them later. If you establish a good set of priorities, you'll make much better use of your time. Here's an example of the rank you probably want to give to networking problems, from highest priority to lowest:

- Total network failure (affects everyone)

- Partial network failure (affects small groups of users)

- Small network failure (affects a small, single group of users)

- Total workstation failure (single user can't work at all)

- Partial workstation failure (single user can't do most tasks)

- Minor issue (single user has problems that crop up now and then)

Mitigating circumstances can, of course, change the order of this list. For example, if the president of the company can't retrieve email, you'd take the express elevator to their office as soon as you got the call, right? And even a minor issue can move up the ladder if it's persistent enough.

Don't fall prey to thinking that simple problems are easier to deal with because even though you may be able to bring up a crashed server in minutes, a user who doesn't know how to make columns line up in Microsoft Word could take a chunk out of your day. You'd want to put the latter problem toward the bottom of the list because of the time involved—it's a lot more efficient to solve problems for a big group of people than to fix this one user's problem immediately.

Some network administrators list all network-service requests on a chalkboard or a whiteboard. They then prioritize them based on the previously discussed criteria. Some larger companies have written support-call tracking software whose only function is to track and prioritize all network and computer problems. Use whatever method makes you comfortable, but prioritize your calls.

Check the Software Configuration

Often, network problems can be traced to software configuration, like our DNS configuration scenario; so when you're checking for software problems, don't forget to check these types of configurations:

- DNS configuration/misconfiguration

- DHCP configuration/misconfiguration

- WINS configuration

- Hosts file

- The Registry

Software-configuration settings love to hide in places like these and can be notoriously hard to find (especially in the Registry).

Also, look for lines that have been commented out either intentionally or accidentally in text-configuration files—another place for clues. A command such as REM or REMARK, or asterisk or semicolon characters, indicates comment lines in a file.

EXERCISE 18.1

Examining IP Configuration

In this exercise, you will examine the output of the `ipconfig` output to identify issues.

1. Open the command prompt by clicking Start, typing **cmd**, right-clicking the Command Prompt result, selecting Run As Administrator, and pressing Enter.

2. Type **ipconfig**, and press Enter.

3. Check if the field for DHCP Enabled is set to Yes.

4. If the prior field is set to Yes, then make note of the DHCP Server IP address. Is it the correct address?

5. Make note of the DNS Servers addresses. Are they correct?

In this exercise, you should have been able to identify if the host is DHCP enabled, which DHCP server provided your IP address, and your DNS servers. With this knowledge, you can troubleshoot basic DHCP problems.

    In the hosts file, a pound sign (#) is used to indicate a comment line.

Don't Overlook Physical Conditions

You want to make sure that from a network-design standpoint, the physical environment for a server is optimized for placement, temperature, and humidity. When troubleshooting an obscure network problem, don't forget to check the physical conditions under which the network device is operating. Check for problems like these:

- Excessive heat
- Excessive humidity (condensation)
- Low humidity (leads to electrostatic discharge [ESD] problems)
- EMI/RFI problems
- ESD problems
- Power problems
- Unplugged cables

Don't Overlook Cable Problems

Cables, generally speaking, work fine once they are installed properly. If the patch cable isn't the problem, use a cable tester (not a tone generator and locator) to find the source of the problem.

One of the easiest mistakes to make, especially if cables are not labeled, is to use a crossover cable where a straight-through cable should be used, or vice versa. In either case, when you do this it causes TX/RX reversal. What's that? That's when the transmit wire is connected to Transmit and the receive wire to Receive. That sounds good, but it needs to be Transmit to Receive. See more about straight-through and crossover cables in Chapter 3.

Wires that are moved can be prone to breaking or shorting, and a short can happen when the wire conductor comes in contact with another conductive surface, changing the path of the electrical signal. The signal will go someplace else instead of to the intended recipient. You can use cable testers to test for many types of problems:

- Broken cables

- Incorrect connections

- Interference levels

- Total cable length (for length restrictions)

- Cable shorts

- Connector problems

- Testing the cable at all possible data rates

 As a matter of fact, cable testers are so sophisticated that they can even indicate the exact location of a cable break, accurate to within 6 inches or better.

Check for Viruses

People overlook scanning for viruses because they assume that the network's virus-checking software has already picked them off. But to be effective, the software must be kept up-to-date, and updates are made available pretty much daily. You've got to run the virus-definition update utility to keep the virus-definition file current.

If you are having strange, unusual, irreproducible problems with a workstation, try scanning it with an up-to-date virus-scan or antimalware utility. You'd be surprised how many times people have spent hours and hours troubleshooting a strange problem only to run a virus-scan utility, find and clean out one or more viruses, and have the problem disappear like magic.

Summary

In this chapter, you learned about all things troubleshooting, and you now know how to sleuth out and solve a lot of network problems. You learned to first check all the SSS and about how to approach problem resolution by eliminating what the problem is *not*. You learned how to narrow the problem down to its basics and define it.

Next, you learned a systematic approach using a seven-step troubleshooting model to troubleshoot most of the problems you'll run into in networking. And you also learned about some resources you can use to help you during the troubleshooting process. In addition, you learned how important documentation is to the health of your network.

Finally, I gave you a bunch of cool tips to further equip you, tips about prioritizing issues, checking for configuration issues, considering environmental factors, and even hunting down viruses. As you venture out into the real world, keep these tips in mind; along with your own personal experience, they'll really help make you an expert troubleshooter.

Exam Essentials

Know the seven troubleshooting steps, in order.   The steps, in order, are as follows:

1. Identify the problem.
2. Establish a theory of probable cause.
3. Test the theory to determine a cause.
4. Establish a plan of action to resolve the problem and identify potential effects.
5. Implement the solution or escalate as necessary.
6. Verify full system functionality and implement preventative measures if applicable.
7. Document findings, actions, outcomes, and lessons learned throughout the process.

Be able to identify a link light.   A link light is the small, usually green LED on the back of a network card. This LED is typically found next to the media connector on a NIC and is usually labeled Link.

Understand how proper network use procedures can affect the operation of a network.   If a user is not following a network use procedure properly (for example, not logging in correctly), that user may report a problem where none exists. A good network troubleshooter should know how to differentiate between a network hardware/software problem and a "lack of user training" problem.

Know how to narrow down a problem to one specific area or cause.   Most problems can be traced to one specific area or cause. You must be able to determine if a problem is specific to one user or a bunch of users, specific to one computer or a bunch of computers, and related to hardware or software. The answers to these questions will give you a very specific problem focus.

Know how to detect cabling-related problems.   Generally speaking, most cabling-related problems can be traced by plugging the suspect workstation into a known, working network port. If the problem disappears (or at the very least changes significantly), it is related to the cabling for that workstation.

Written Lab

In this section, write the answers to the following questions. You can find the answers in Appendix A.

1. What is step 3 of the seven-step troubleshooting model?

2. What is step 7 of the seven-step troubleshooting model?

3. How is crosstalk minimized in twisted-pair cabling?

4. If you plug a host into a switch port and the user cannot get to the server or other services they need to access despite a working link light, what could the problem be?

5. What is it called when a cable has two wires of a twisted pair connected to two wires from a different pair?

6. When a signal moves through any medium, the medium itself will degrade the signal. What is this called?

7. What is step 4 of the seven-step troubleshooting model?

8. What is step 5 of the seven-step troubleshooting model?

9. What are some of the problems that, if determined, should be escalated?

10. What cable issues should you know and understand for network troubleshooting?

Review Questions

You can find the answers to the review questions in Appendix B.

1. Which of the following are not specific steps in the Network+ troubleshooting methodology model? (Choose all that apply.)

   A. Reboot the servers.

   B. Identify the problem.

   C. Test the theory to determine the cause.

   D. Implement the solution or escalate as necessary.

   E. Document findings, actions, outcomes, and lessons learned

   F. Reboot all the routers.

2. You have a user who cannot connect to the network. What is the first thing you could check to determine the source of the problem?

   A. Workstation configuration

   B. Connectivity

   C. Patch cable

   D. Server configuration

3. When wireless users complain that they are losing their connection to applications during a session, what is the source of the problem?

   A. Incorrect SSID

   B. Latency

   C. Incorrect encryption

   D. MAC address filter

4. Several users can't log in to the server. Which action would help you to narrow the problem down to the workstations, network, or server?

   A. Run `tracert` from a workstation.

   B. Check the server console for user connections.

   C. Run `netstat` on all workstations.

   D. Check the network diagnostics.

5. A user can't log into the network. She can't even connect to the Internet over the LAN. Other users in the same area aren't experiencing any problems. You attempt to log in as this user from your workstation with her username and password and don't experience any problems. However, you cannot log in with either her username or yours from her workstation. What is a likely cause of the problem?

   A. Insufficient rights to access the server

   B. A bad patch cable

   C. Server down

   D. Wrong username and password

6. A user is experiencing problems logging into a Linux server. He can connect to the Internet over the LAN. Other users in the same area aren't experiencing any problems. You attempt logging in as this user from your workstation with his username and password and don't experience any problems. However, you cannot log in with either his username or yours from his workstation. What is a likely cause of the problem?

   A. The Caps Lock key is pressed.

   B. The network hub is malfunctioning.

   C. You have a downed server.

   D. You have a jabbering NIC.

7. You receive a call from a user who is having issues connecting to a new VPN. Which is the first step you should take?

   A. Test a theory.

   B. Reboot the workstation.

   C. Document the solution.

   D. Identify the symptoms and potential causes.

8. A workstation presents an error message to a user. The message states that a duplicate IP address has been detected on the network. After establishing what has changed in the network, what should be the next step using the standard troubleshooting model?

   A. Test the result.

   B. Select the most probable cause.

   C. Create an action plan.

   D. Identify the results and effects of the solution.

9. You have gathered information on a network issue and determined the affected areas of the network. What is your next step in resolving this issue?

   A. You should implement the best solution for the issue.

   B. You should test the best solution for the issue.

   C. You should check to see if there have been any recent changes to this affected part of the network.

   D. You should consider any negative impact to the network that might be caused by a solution.

10. A user calls you, reporting a problem logging in to the corporate intranet. You can access the website without problems using the user's username and password. At your request, the user has tried logging in from other workstations but has been unsuccessful. What is the most likely cause of the problem?

   A. The user is logging in incorrectly.

   B. The network is down.

   C. The intranet server is locked up.

   D. The server is not routing packets correctly to that user's workstation.

11. You have just implemented a solution, and you want to celebrate your success. But what should you do next before you start your celebration?

    A.   Gather more information about the issue.

    B.   Document the issue and the solution that was implemented.

    C.   Test the solution and identify other effects it may have.

    D.   Escalate the issue.

12. You can ping the local router and web server that a local user is trying to reach, but you cannot reach the web page that resides on that server. From step 2 of the troubleshooting model, what is a possible problem that would lead to this situation?

    A.   Your network cable is unplugged.

    B.   There is a problem with your browser.

    C.   Your NIC has failed.

    D.   The web server is unplugged.

13. When troubleshooting an obscure network problem, what physical conditions should be reviewed to make sure the network device is operating correctly? (Choose all that apply.)

    A.   Excessive heat

    B.   Low/excessive humidity

    C.   ESD problems

    D.   Time of day

14. Which of the following is not a basic physical issue that can occur on a network when a user is connected via cable?

    A.   Crosstalk

    B.   Shorts

    C.   Open impedance mismatch

    D.   DNS configurations

15. You are troubleshooting a LAN switch and have identified the problem is complex. What is the next step you should take?

    A.   Escalate the issue.

    B.   Create an action plan.

    C.   Implement the solution.

    D.   Determine the scope of the problem.

16. A user calls you complaining that he can't access the corporate intranet web server. You try the same address, and you receive a Host Not Found error. Several minutes later, another user reports the same problem. You can still send email and transfer files to another server. What is the most likely cause of the problem?

    A.   The hub is unplugged.

    B.   The server is not routing protocols to your workstation.

    C.   The user's workstation is not connected to the network.

    D.   The web server is down.

17. You have implemented and tested a solution and identified any other effects the solution may have. What is your next step?

  A.   Create an action plan.

  B.   Close the case and head home for the day.

  C.   Reboot the Windows server.

  D.   Document the solution.

18. Users are reporting that they can access the Internet but not the internal company website. Which of the following is the most likely problem?

  A.   The DNS entry for the server is non-authoritative.

  B.   The intranet server is down.

  C.   The DNS address handed out by DHCP is incorrect.

  D.   The default gateway is incorrect.

19. Several users have complained about the server's poor performance as of late. You know that the memory installed in the server is sufficient. What could you use to determine the source of the problem?

  A.   Server's NIC link light

  B.   Protocol analyzer

  C.   Performance-monitoring tools

  D.   Server's system log file

20. You lose power to your computer room, and the switches in your network do not come back up when everything is brought online. After you have identified the affected areas, established the cause, and escalated this problem, what do you do next?

  A.   Start to implement a solution to get those users back online ASAP.

  B.   Create an action plan and solution.

  C.   Meet with the emergency response team to determine the next step.

  D.   Copy all the working routers' configurations to the nonworking switches.

Chapter

19

Network Software Tools and Commands

THE FOLLOWING COMPTIA NETWORK+ EXAM OBJECTIVES ARE COVERED IN THIS CHAPTER:

✓ **5.5 Given a scenario, use the appropriate tool or protocol to solve networking issues.**

✓ **Software tools**

- Protocol analyzer
- Command line
  - ping
  - traceroute/tracert
  - nslookup
  - tcpdump
  - dig
  - netstat
  - ip/ifconfig/ipconfig
  - arp
  - Nmap
  - Link Layer Discovery Protocol (LLDP)/Cisco Discovery Protocol (CDP)
  - Speed tester

✓ **Hardware tools**

- Toner
- Cable tester
- Taps
- Wi-Fi analyzer
- Visual fault locator

✓ **Basic networking device commands**

- show mac-address-table
- show route
- show interface
- show config
- show arp
- show vlan
- show power

Specialized tasks require specialized tools, and installing network components is no exception. We use some of these tools, like network scanners, on an everyday basis, but most of the software tools I'll be covering in this chapter are used mainly in the telecommunications industry.

Still, to meet the CompTIA Network+ Exam objectives, and also because you're likely to run across them in today's networking environments, you must be familiar with them.

To find Todd Lammle CompTIA videos and practice questions, please see www.lammle.com.

Software Tools

To effectively test and troubleshoot networks, it is important to be aware of, and know how to operate, the many different types of tools available for you to use.

We will start the chapter by going over many of the software applications designed for network testing and troubleshooting. Knowledge on how to use these tools allows you to locate, troubleshoot, and resolve any networking issues you may come across.

Protocol Analyzer/Packet Capture

Protocol analyzers, also called sniffers or network monitors, are used to capture packets in their raw format as they cross the network. Windows desktop operating systems before Windows Vista came with a built-in protocol analyzer called Network Monitor, but that is no longer the case, although you can download one for free that will work with the newer operating systems.

The Network Monitor tool that comes with these operating systems will capture only packets that are sourced from or destined to the computer on which the tool is running. Commercial sniffers like Wireshark and Omnipeek can capture any packets because they set the NIC to operate in promiscuous mode, which means the NIC processes all packets that it sees.

Protocol analyzers can be used to determine the type of traffic that you have in your network, and depending on the product and the bells and whistles contained therein, you may be able to sort the results based on port numbers, protocols, and so on. Another use of a sniffer is to examine the traffic that should be occurring on the network when something is not working to aid in troubleshooting. These devices can capture and display all packets involved in the connection setup, including, for example, request and response headers to a web server.

Let's review the series of four packet types that must occur for a DHCP client to receive an IP configuration from the server. As a review, those packets are as follows:

- DHCP Discover
- DHCP Offer
- DHCP Request
- DHCP ACK

If you turned on the analyzer and then executed the `ipconfig/release` and `ipconfig/ renew` commands on the client system (more on those commands later in this chapter), you should see these four packets in the analyzer's capture file. The packets would be interspersed with the hundreds and perhaps thousands of other packet types that would be captured, but by using the display filtering options in the software, you can easily segregate out the DHCP traffic. Figure 19.1 shows an example of the DHCP process, as seen in a capture.

FIGURE 19.1 DHCP capture

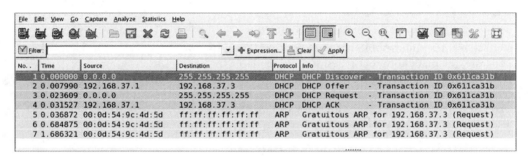

If all you saw in the capture were the DHCP Discover packets with no DHCP Offer packets, you could reasonably assert that the DHCP server is not receiving the DHCP Discover packets (perhaps it is located in another broadcast domain or perhaps it is not on). Additionally, you could examine fields in the DHCP Offer packets that may tell you that the DHCP server is out of addresses. The point is that the tool can be used to troubleshoot the issue.

Bandwidth Speed Testers

Users of a network often complain about the speed of the network. Network "speed" is in some ways a personal perception because some people have more patience than others. To determine when a network slowdown is real as opposed to perceived, you need to actually measure the throughput. That's what throughput testers are used for.

These devices, typically software-based, work much like a protocol analyzer in that they measure the traffic seen on the network and can also classify the types of traffic that are eating up your bandwidth (which is probably what you really need to know). Figure 19.2 shows one version of this software by TamoSoft.

FIGURE 19.2   Throughput

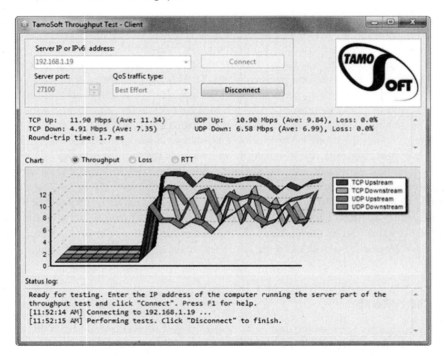

This software is installed on a server and also on a client. In the figure, the software is measuring traffic between the client and a server. It shows the throughput for traffic in real time and in this shot is breaking that traffic up by unicast (TCP) and broadcast (UDP) types and by direction.

Earlier in this book, I discussed the importance of baselines, and this is another area where they are important. Network throughput figures mean little without a baseline with which comparisons can be made. How do you know what is abnormal when you don't know what normal is? Baselines should be taken when the network is operating well, but they should also be taken when the traffic load is normal.

IPerf is an open-source software tool that measures network throughput and is very handy for testing and creating baselines of your network. The software runs as a server on one end and a client on the other.

IPerf can run on both Linux and Windows operating systems. It is highly customizable, allowing you to specify if you want to use TCP or UDP and what port numbers and packet size.

After the test is run, reports are generated that give you throughput, the parameters used, and a timestamp.

Port Scanners

A *port scanner* is a software tool designed to search a host for open ports. Those of us administering our networks use port scanners to ensure their security, but bad guys use them to find a network's vulnerabilities and compromise them. To *port scan* means to scan for TCP and UDP open ports on a single target host either to legitimately connect to and use its services for business and/or personal reasons or to find and connect to those ports and subsequently attack the host and steal or manipulate it for nefarious reasons.

In contrast, *port sweeping* means scanning multiple hosts on a network for a specific listening TCP or UDP port, like SQL. (SQL injection attacks are super common today.) This just happens to be a favorite approach used by hackers when trying to invade your network. They port sweep in a broad manner, and then, if they find something—in this case, SQL—they can port scan the particular host they've discovered with the desired service available to exploit and get what they're after. This is why it's a really good idea to turn off any unused services on your servers and routers and to run only the minimum services required on every host machine in your network. Do yourself a big favor and make sure this is in your security policy.

NetFlow Analyzers

The NetFlow protocol allows for viewing and analyzing application-level traffic across an interface. NetFlow is a step above SNMP in that it looks at the actual conversations taking place on your network and, based on that information, allows you to gain deep visibility of what traffic is moving across your network.

NetFlow collects information on each unique traffic flow into and out of a network device interface. NetFlow collects source and destination addresses, application information, and quality of service (QoS) data and is very helpful in troubleshooting causes of networking problems.

A flow exporter is a network device such as a router that monitors traffic flowing in and out of an interface and exports not the complete packet but a summary of its contents to a flow collector. A flow collector is a server on the network that receives the flows from multiple exporters and consolidates the NetFlow data in a centralized storage location.

A NetFlow application then analyzes the data and creates reports, charts, graphs, and sometimes analytics on the received information.

Trivial File Transfer Protocol Server

When the time comes to upgrade the software on a piece of networking equipment such as a switch or router, the code is downloaded from the vendor site to your laptop or a management server. Then steps are taken to transfer the code to the actual device. One of the most common methods is to use the Trivial File Transfer Protocol (TFTP) as it is supported by all vendors.

A TFTP server is a small application that is available from a wide variety of developers as freeware for Windows and Linux computers. All that is needed is to run the TFTP server on your local machine and point its source directory to where the file to upload resides. Then from the network device, specify the IP address of the TFTP server and the name of the file you want to upload. TFTP is designed to be a simple, effective, and fast method to upload code to a network device.

Connectivity Software

There are times when you need to make a remote connection to a machine to perform troubleshooting but you are miles away. Connectivity software is designed to allow you to make a connection to the machine, see the desktop, and perform any action you could perform if you were sitting in front of it.

The Microsoft operating system has had software called Remote Desktop installed since Windows NT. The Remote Desktop software enables GUI-based remote access, as you learned in Chapter 13, "Remote Network Access." The Remote Desktop software operates via the Remote Desktop Protocol (RDP) via the TCP protocol port 3389. Since that time, Microsoft has introduced a number of other remote assistance software packages, such as Quick Assist, as shown in Figure 19.3.

Commercial tools are also available that (of course) claim to have more functionality, and they probably do have a few extra bells and whistles. These include LogMeIn.com, GoTo-MyPC, and others.

The advantages of these connectivity tools are obvious. With these tools, you can do anything you need to on the machine as long as you can connect. They also allow you to see what a user is actually doing when they encounter a problem rather than having to rely on what they tell you they are doing. You can even show a user what they are doing wrong. Most of these tools allow for chat sessions and for either end of the connection to take control of the machine. You can also transfer files to them if required (maybe a file got deleted, for example).

For networking, it is common to access the devices command-line interface remotely. This will require you use terminal emulation software. Today the Telnet protocol is rarely used because it has no security and all data is sent unencrypted. Secure Shell (SSH) is the preferred method of accessing a remote device command line from across a network. There are many free and commercial terminal emulation packages for you to use. The most common open-source emulator is PuTTY, and it supports Telnet, SSH, and serial interfaces. PuTTY is widely used and found in almost every networking shop. As for commercial packages, SecureCRT is popular and has an extensive feature set.

FIGURE 19.3   Quick Assist

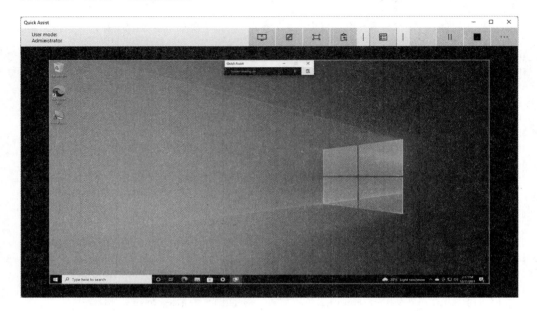

IP Scanner

It is often very helpful to know what is running on a server or networking device. Scanners can tell you what IP addresses are active and what they are "listening for." All IP applications have an associated port number that is open for incoming connections, such as port 80 for HTTP and 443 for HTTPS. An IP scanner can be run on your local computer and will scan for open ports on each IP host. However, be very careful doing this on live production networks because security appliances such as intrusion and firewall systems may generate an alarm when they detect scans as it may be an indication of fingerprinting your network by hackers.

Scanners can be used for network mapping by listing all of the active IP addresses in each subnet and what applications are running on them. There are many commercial and open-source scanners available on the market. Many have advanced features such as listing bugs and vulnerabilities of a scanned device and providing information on remediation.

Using *traceroute*

Most of us are running Transmission Control Protocol/Internet Protocol (TCP/IP) version 4 on our networks these days, so we absolutely need a way to test IP connectivity. But we also need to be able to test and verify IPv6 networks. The reason for this is that even though

Microsoft makes the majority of client platforms, a lot of the commands used to test IP connectivity are really platform independent, and most of the platforms can now use both IPv4 and IPv6. Even so, keep in mind that the Network+ exam focuses on the basic concepts of the function and use of the TCP/IP utilities that come with Windows.

You can use several utilities, both command line and GUI, to verify TCP/IP function on Windows workstations, and most of them are listed in the chapter objectives. Here's a list of all the utilities I'll discuss:

- `traceroute` (`tracert` in Microsoft)
- `ipconfig` (`ifconfig` in Linux/UNIX)
- `ping`
- `arp`
- `nslookup` (`dig` in Linux/UNIX)
- `Resolving Names`
- `Mtr` (pathping)
- `Nmap`
- `route`
- `netstat`
- `tcpdump`
- `ftp`

By the way, it's important that you don't just blow through the output that I've supplied for each command. Instead, pay serious attention to it because to meet the Network+ objectives, you'll be required to correctly identify each command's output.

So, let's cut right to the chase and take a look at some of these commands and their output. Oh, and do try and have fun with it!

For starters, let's pose these questions: Where do all those packets really go when we send them over the Internet? And, how do all the packets actually get to their destinations? Well, we can use the TCP/IP `traceroute` (`tracert` with Windows) command-line utility to help us answer both questions because its output will show us every router interface a TCP/IP packet passes through on the way to its destination.

`traceroute` (trace for short) displays the path a packet takes to get to a remote device in all its glory by using something we call IP packet time to live (TTL) timeouts and Internet Control Message Protocol (ICMP) error messages. And it's also a handy tool for troubleshooting an internetwork because we can use it to figure out which router along a path through that internetwork happens to be causing a network failure when a certain destination machine or network is, or suddenly becomes, unreachable.

To use `tracert`, at a Windows command prompt, type **tracert**, a space, and the Domain Name System (DNS) name or IP address of the host machine to which you want to find the route. The `tracert` utility will respond with a list of all the DNS names and IP addresses of the routers that the packet is passing through on its way. Plus, `tracert` uses TTL to indicate the time it takes for each attempt.

The following is the `tracert` output from my workstation in Boulder, Colorado, to my Lammle.com server in Dallas, Texas:

```
C:\Users\tlammle>tracert www.lammle.com

Tracing route to lammle.com [206.123.114.186]
over a maximum of 30 hops:
  1      1 ms     <1 ms     <1 ms   dslmodem.domain.actdsltmp [192.168.0.1]
  2     53 ms     52 ms     52 ms   hlrn-dsl-gw36-228.hlrn.qwest.net
[207.225.112.228]
  3     52 ms     53 ms     52 ms   hlrn-agw1.inet.qwest.net [71.217.189.25]
  4     75 ms     75 ms     74 ms   dal-core-01.inet.qwest.net [67.14.2.53]
  5     76 ms     76 ms     76 ms   dap-brdr-01.inet.qwest.net [205.171.225.49]
  6     76 ms     76 ms     76 ms   205.171.1.110
  7     75 ms     76 ms    106 ms   xe-0-0-0.er2.dfw2.us.above.net [64.125.26.206]
  8     76 ms     76 ms     76 ms   209.249.119.74.available.above.net
[209.249.119.74]
  9     76 ms     76 ms     76 ms   65.99.248.250
 10     76 ms     76 ms     76 ms   pageuppro.pageuppro.com [206.123.114.186]
Trace complete.
```

 With the adoption of IPv6 on the Internet, you could see IPv6 addresses in the results. Also, your `tracert` output will be obviously different than the previous example.

Were you able to see that the packet bounces through several routers before arriving at its destination? Good! This utility is useful if you are having problems reaching a web server on the Internet and you want to know if a wide area network (WAN) link is down or if the server just isn't responding. What this means to you is that, basically, wherever the trace stops is a great place to start troubleshooting. No worries here, though—the previous output shows that every router is up and responding. Last, notice in the output the ms. This is the latency of each hop, meaning the delay. `tracert` (or `traceroute`) is a great trouble-shooting tool you can use to find out where your network bottlenecks are.

If you use `traceroute` or `tracert` and receive an asterisk, this indicates that the attempt to reach that router took longer than the default timeout value. This is good to know because it can mean that either the router is extremely busy or a particular link is slow. Another reason for getting an asterisk could be that the administrator has disabled ICMP on the router that the packet is trying to hop through.

Why would someone want to do that? For security reasons, that's why. It happens to be a typical strategic move done on the routers that interface to the ISP to conceal their actual location so bad guys can't hack into them and therefore into your internetwork. It's a good idea, and I highly recommend doing it.

> If you are running traceroute and see repeating addresses and TTL timeouts, you probably have a routing loop.

In addition to `traceroute` and `tracert`, you can use `pathping`, which is a lot like traceroute:

```
C:\Users\Todd Lammle>pathping lammle.com
Tracing route to lammle.com [184.172.53.52]
over a maximum of 30 hops:
  0  WIN-Q14VTD8DH0G.localdomain [192.168.133.147]
  1  192.168.133.2
  2     *         *          *
Computing statistics for 25 seconds...
            Source to Here   This Node/Link
Hop  RTT    Lost/Sent = Pct  Lost/Sent = Pct  Address
  0                          WIN-Q14VTD8DH0G.localdomain [192.168.133.147]
                                0/ 100 =  0%   |
  1    0ms   0/ 100 =  0%      0/ 100 =  0%  192.168.133.2

Trace complete.

C:\Users\Todd Lammle>
```

This provides excellent feedback at the end of the output.

> In addition to `traceroute` and `tracert`, which show the path of an IPv4 packet, you can use `tracert -6` for a Windows trace, `traceroute6` for macOS and Linux/UNIX, and `traceroute -6` for Cisco routers to trace an IPv6 packet through an internetwork.

Using *ipconfig, ifconfig,* and *ip*

The utilities known as `ipconfig` (in Windows) and `ifconfig`/`ip` (in UNIX/Linux/macOS) will display the current configuration of TCP/IP on a given workstation—including the current IP address, DNS configuration, configuration, and default gateway. In the following sections, I will show you how to use both.

Using the *ipconfig* Utility

With the new macOS, Windows 10/11, and Windows Server 2019/2022 operating systems, you can now see the IPv6 configuration because IPv6 is enabled by default. The output of the ipconfig command provides the basic routed protocol information on your machine. From a DOS prompt, type **ipconfig**, and you'll see something like this:

```
C:\Users\tlammle>ipconfig
Windows IP Configuration
Ethernet adapter Local Area Connection:
   Connection-specific DNS Suffix  . : domain.actdsltmp
   Link-local IPv6 Address . . . . . : fe80::2836:c43e:274b:f08c%11
   IPv4 Address. . . . . . . . . . . : 192.168.0.6
   Subnet Mask . . . . . . . . . . . : 255.255.255.0
   Default Gateway . . . . . . . . . : 192.168.0.1

Wireless LAN adapter Wireless Network Connection:
   Connection-specific DNS Suffix  . : qwest.net
   Link-local IPv6 Address . . . . . : fe80::20e7:7fb8:8a00:832b%10
   IPv4 Address. . . . . . . . . . . : 10.0.1.198
   Subnet Mask . . . . . . . . . . . : 255.255.255.0
   Default Gateway . . . . . . . . . : fe80::21b:63ff:fef3:3694%10
                                       10.0.1.1

Tunnel adapter Local Area Connection* 6:
   Media State . . . . . . . . . . . : Media disconnected
   Connection-specific DNS Suffix  . :

Tunnel adapter Local Area Connection* 7:
   Media State . . . . . . . . . . . : Media disconnected
   Connection-specific DNS Suffix  . :
 [output cut for brevity]
```

Wow, there sure are a lot of options in this output compared to the output for earlier versions of Windows! First, what's up with all these interfaces showing? I have only two—one Ethernet and one wireless. You can see that my Ethernet adapter shows up first, and it has an IP address, a mask, and a default gateway plus an IPv6 address and a DNS suffix. The next configured interface is the wireless local area network (LAN) adapter, which has an IP address, a mask, a default gateway, an IPv6 address, and the IPv6 default gateway as well. This IPv6 default gateway address is simply my router advertising that it runs IPv6 and saying, "I am the way out of the local LAN!"

The next adapters are disconnected because they are logical interfaces and I'm not using them—my machine actually shows eight, but I cut the output because it provides no new information. They're automatically inserted because IPv6 is installed and running on my machine, and these adapters allow me to run IPv6 over an IPv4-only network.

But just in case the ipconfig command doesn't provide enough information for you, try the ipconfig /all command—talk about details. Here's the beginning of that output:

```
C:\Users\tlammle>ipconfig /all
Windows IP Configuration
     Host Name . . . . . . . . . . . . : globalnet-todd
     Primary Dns Suffix  . . . . . . . : globalnet.local
     Node Type . . . . . . . . . . . . : Hybrid
     IP Routing Enabled. . . . . . . . : No
     WINS Proxy Enabled. . . . . . . . : No
     DNS Suffix Search List. . . . . . : globalnet.local
                                         domain.actdsltmp
                                         qwest.net

Ethernet adapter Local Area Connection:
     Connection-specific DNS Suffix  . : domain.actdsltmp
     Description . . . . . . . . . . . : Intel(R) 82566MM Gigabit
Network Connection
     Physical Address. . . . . . . . . : 00-1E-37-D0-E9-35
     DHCP Enabled. . . . . . . . . . . : Yes
     Autoconfiguration Enabled . . . . : Yes
     Link-local IPv6 Address . . . . . : fe80::2836:c43e:274b:f08c%11(Preferred)
     IPv4 Address. . . . . . . . . . . : 192.168.0.6(Preferred)
     Subnet Mask . . . . . . . . . . . : 255.255.255.0
     Lease Obtained. . . . . . . . . . : Monday, October 20, 2008 9:08:36 AM
     Lease Expires . . . . . . . . . . : Tuesday, October 21, 2008 9:08:39 AM
     Default Gateway . . . . . . . . . : 192.168.0.1
     DHCP Server . . . . . . . . . . . : 192.168.0.1
     DNS Servers . . . . . . . . . . . : 192.168.0.1
                                         205.171.3.65
     NetBIOS over Tcpip. . . . . . . . : Enabled

Wireless LAN adapter Wireless Network Connection:
     Connection-specific DNS Suffix  . : qwest.net
     Description . . . . . . . . . . . : Intel(R) Wireless WiFi Link 4965AGN
     Physical Address. . . . . . . . . : 00-1F-3B-3F-4A-D9
     DHCP Enabled. . . . . . . . . . . : Yes
     Autoconfiguration Enabled . . . . : Yes
     Link-local IPv6 Address . . . . . : fe80::20e7:7fb8:8a00:832b%10(Preferred)
     IPv4 Address. . . . . . . . . . . : 10.0.1.198(Preferred)
```

```
    Subnet Mask . . . . . . . . . . . : 255.255.255.0
    Lease Obtained. . . . . . . . . : Monday, October 20, 2008 10:43:53 AM
    Lease Expires . . . . . . . . . : Monday, October 20, 2008 2:43:53 PM
    Default Gateway . . . . . . . . : fe80::21b:63ff:fef3:3694%10
                                      10.0.1.1
    DHCP Server . . . . . . . . . . : 10.0.1.1
    DNS Servers . . . . . . . . . . : 10.0.1.1
    NetBIOS over Tcpip. . . . . . . : Enabled

Tunnel adapter Local Area Connection* 6:
    Media State . . . . . . . . . . : Media disconnected
    Connection-specific DNS Suffix  . :
    Description . . . . . . . . . . : isatap.globalnet.local
    Physical Address. . . . . . . . : 00-00-00-00-00-00-00-E0
    DHCP Enabled. . . . . . . . . . : No
    Autoconfiguration Enabled . . . . : Yes

Tunnel adapter Local Area Connection* 7:
    Media State . . . . . . . . . . : Media disconnected
    Connection-specific DNS Suffix  . :
    Description . . . . . . . . . . : isatap.{9572A79F-3A58-4E9B-
9BD0-8F6FF2F058FC}
    Physical Address. . . . . . . . : 00-00-00-00-00-00-00-E0
    DHCP Enabled. . . . . . . . . . : No
    Autoconfiguration Enabled . . . . : Yes
[output cut]
```

As you can see, it's more of the same—a whole lot more. The most important thing I want you to notice is that I've received the hardware information about each interface, including the Media Access Control (MAC) address. Also significant is that I can see the Dynamic Host Configuration Protocol (DHCP) lease times and DNS addresses now.

But why stop here? There are two more valuable options you need to use with the ipconfig command. They are /release and /renew.

When you change networks, you need to get the IP address of that subnet and/or virtual LAN (VLAN). Windows 10/11 works most of the time without doing anything, but sometimes I do have to renew the IP configuration when changing networks. But that's easy—just type **ipconfig /renew** from a command prompt, and if you're connected to a DHCP server that's available, you'll then magically receive an IP address.

Now, if it still doesn't work, you'll need to release and renew your TCP/IP settings. To release your current DHCP TCP/IP information, you must elevate (run as administrator) your command prompt or you'll get this warning:

```
C:\Users\tlammle>ipconfig /release
The requested operation requires elevation.
C:\Users\tlammle>
```

Should this happen to you, left-click in the search box in the lower-left menu bar, type in **command prompt,** right-click the command prompt icon, and choose Run As Administrator. (Of course, you'll have to enter your name and password to do this if you are using Windows 10/11. But we love Windows 10/11, right? Okay, maybe not always.) Figure 19.4 shows how I did this.

FIGURE 19.4   Elevating your command prompt

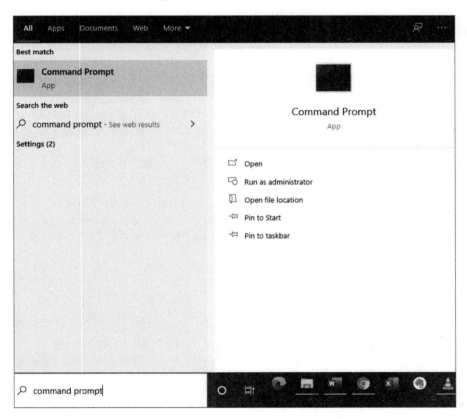

Once your command prompt has been duly elevated, you can use the `ipconfig /release` command and then the `ipconfig /renew` command to get new TCP/IP information for your host.

Using the *ifconfig* Utility

There is a utility in Linux/UNIX/macOS that will give you information similar to what ipconfig shows. It's called ifconfig (short for *interface configuration*). Although ipconfig and ifconfig show similar information, there are major differences between these two utilities. The ipconfig utility is mainly used to view the TCP/IP configuration for a computer. You can use ifconfig to do the same thing, but ifconfig can also be used to configure a protocol or a particular network interface.

The general syntax of the ifconfig command is as follows:

```
ifconfig interface [address [parameters]]
```

The interface parameter equals the Linux/UNIX name of the interface, such as eth0. If the optional address parameter is specified, the ifconfig command sets the IP address for the interface to the address you've specified. When the ifconfig command is used by itself with no parameters, all configured interfaces will be reported on. But if only the interface name is specified, you'll get output that looks like this:

```
# ifconfig eth0
eth0  Link encap 10Mbps Ethernet  HWaddr 00:00:C0:90:B3:42
inetaddr 172.16.0.2 Bcast 172.16.0.255 Mask 255.255.255.0 UP
BROADCAST RUNNING  MTU 1500  Metric 0
   RX packets 3136 errors 217 dropped 7 overrun 26
   TX packets 1752 errors 25 dropped 0 overrun 0
```

Looking at this, we can see that the eth0 interface is a 10 Mbps Ethernet interface. The interface's MAC and IP address information is displayed in this output as well. And, although not shown in the output, the ifconfig tool can show you the DNS information configured on the host.

Using the *ip* Utility

Newer versions of the Linux operating system have added the ip utility to replace the ifconfig command. This command serves the same purpose as ifconfig and is used to assign an address to a network interface and/or configure network interface parameters on Linux operating systems.

The ip command allows us to find out what interfaces are configured on the computer, view and configure their IP values, take an interface up or down, configure routing, display network status information, view and configure multicast values, view the ARP table, add or remove static routes, and view the host's routing table.

For example, to add the IP address of 192.168.1.1 to interface Ethenrnet0, use the following command:

`#`**ip a add 192.168.1.1/255.255.255.0 dev eth0Using the *iptables* utility**

Using the *iptables* Utility

While iptables is not part of the exam objectives, it is added here as it is an important Linux networking utility and good to be aware of. The iptables firewall utility is built for the Linux operating system. It is a command-line utility that uses *chains* to allow or disallow traffic. When traffic arrives, iptables looks for a rule that addresses that traffic type, and if none exists, it will enforce the default rule. There are three different chain types:

- **Input:** Controls behavior for incoming connections
- **Forward:** Used for incoming connections that aren't being delivered locally (like a router would receive)
- **Output:** Used for outgoing connections

You can set the default action to accept, drop, or reject, with the difference between reject and drop being that reject sends an error message back to the source.

Examples of *iptables*

To block a connection from the device at 192.168.10.1, use this command:

```
iptables -A INPUT -s 192.168.10.1 -j DROP
```

To block all connections from all devices in the 172.16.0.0/16 network, use this command:

```
iptables -A INPUT -s 172.16.0.0/16 -j DROP
```

Here is the command to block SSH connections from 10.110.61.5:

```
iptables -A INPUT -p tcp --dport ssh -s 10.110.61.5 -j DROP
```

Use this command to block SSH connections from any IP address:

```
iptables -A INPUT -p tcp --dport ssh -j DROP
```

The following command is used to save the changes in Ubuntu (a Linux distribution):

```
sudo /sbin/iptables-save
```

In Red Hat–based systems, use either of the following commands:

```
/sbin/service iptables save
/etc/init.d/iptables save
```

Using the *ping* Utility

The ping utility is the most basic TCP/IP utility, and it's included with most TCP/IP stacks for most platforms. Windows, again, is no exception. In most cases, ping is a command-line utility, although there are many GUI implementations available. You use the ping utility for two primary purposes:

- To find out if a host is responding
- To find out if you can reach a host

Here's the syntax (you can use either command):

```
ping hostname
ping IP address
```

If you ping any station that has an IP address, the ICMP that's part of that particular host's TCP/IP stack will respond to the request. The ICMP test and response looks something like this:

```
ping 204.153.163.2

Pinging 204.153.163.2 with 32 bytes of data:

Reply from 204.153.163.2: bytes=32 time<10ms TTL=128
Reply from 204.153.163.2: bytes=32 time=1ms TTL=128
Reply from 204.153.163.2: bytes=32 time<10ms TTL=128
Reply from 204.153.163.2: bytes=32 time<10ms TTL=128
```

Because I've received a reply from the destination station (204.153.163.2, in this case), I know that I can reach the host and that it's responding to basic IP requests. Don't forget that you can use name resolution and ping to a name, such as ping www.sybex.com, and as long as that name can be resolved, you're golden.

Most versions of ping work the same way, but there are some switches you can use to specify certain information, like the number of packets to send, how big a packet to send, and so on. And if you're running the Windows command-line version of ping, just use the /? or -? switch to display a list of the available options like this:

```
C:\Users\tlammle>ping /?

Usage: ping [-t] [-a] [-n count] [-l size] [-f] [-i TTL] [-v TOS]
            [-r count] [-s count] [[-j host-list] | [-k host-list]]
            [-w timeout] [-R] [-S srcaddr] [-4] [-6] target_name
```

The command will also output a table showing what each of the options does, presented in Table 19.1.

TABLE 19.1 Options for ping switches

Option	Description
-t	Pings the specified host until stopped. To see statistics and continue, press Ctrl+Break; to stop, press Ctrl+C.
-a	Resolves addresses to hostnames.
-n *count*	Specifies the number of echo requests to send.
-l *size*	Sends the buffer size.
-f	Sets the Don't Fragment flag in the packet (IPv4 only).
-i *TTL*	Specifies the time to live of the packet.
-v *TOS*	Specifies the type of service (IPv4 only).
-r *count*	Records the route for count hops (IPv4 only).
-s *count*	Specifies the timestamp for count hops (IPv4 only).
-j *host-list*	Uses a loose source route along the host list (IPv4 only).
-k *host-list*	Uses a strict source route along the host list (IPv4 only).
-w *timeout*	Specifies the time-out to wait for each reply in milliseconds.
-R	Uses the routing header to test the reverse route also (IPv6 only).
-S *srcaddr*	Specifies the source address to use.
-4	Forces using IPv4.
-6	Forces using IPv6.

You can ping your local TCP/IP interface by typing **ping 127.0.0.1** or **ping localhost**. Understand that both addresses represent the local interface. Really, you can use any address in the 127.0.0.0 network range to provide a loopback test.

As you can see, there's a plethora of options you can use with the ping command from a Windows DOS prompt. But I really want you to focus on a few from the previous output. (I'm going to go over only a few of them, but you can get on your host machine and play with all the options.)

The -a switch is very cool because if you have name resolution (such as a DNS server), you can see the name of the destination host even if you know only its IP address. The -n switch sets the number of echo requests to send, where four is the default, and the -w switch allows you to adjust the timeout in milliseconds. The default ping time-out is 1 second (1,000 ms).

The -6 is also nice if you want to ping an IPv6 host. By the way, unless you really love typing 128-bit addresses, this is a wonderful example of how important name resolution is. And then there's -t, which keeps the ping running. Here's an example of a ping to an IPv6 address:

```
C:\Users\tlammle>ping -6 fe80::1063:16af:3f57:fff9

Pinging fe80::1063:16af:3f57:fff9 from fe80::1063:16af:3f57:fff9%25
with 32 bytes of data:
Reply from fe80::1063:16af:3f57:fff9: time<1ms
Reply from fe80::1063:16af:3f57:fff9: time<1ms
Reply from fe80::1063:16af:3f57:fff9: time<1ms
Reply from fe80::1063:16af:3f57:fff9: time<1ms

Ping statistics for fe80::1063:16af:3f57:fff9:
Packets: Sent = 4, Received = 4, Lost = 0 (0% loss),
Approximate round trip times in milli-seconds:
Minimum = 0ms, Maximum = 0ms, Average = 0ms
C:\Users\tlammle>
```

From a Mac, you can use the ping6 command. Here are the options:

```
$ ping6
usage: ping6 [-DdfHmnNoqrRtvwW] [-a addrtype] [-b bufsiz] [-B boundif]
[-c count][-g gateway] [-h hoplimit] [-I interface] [-i wait] [-l preload]
[-p pattern] [-S sourceaddr] [-s packetsize] [-z tclass]
[hops ...] host
```

And if I want to have a continuous ping, I just use that -t option like this:

```
C:\Users\tlammle>ping -t 192.168.0.1

Pinging 192.168.0.1 with 32 bytes of data:
Reply from 192.168.0.1: bytes=32 time=7ms TTL=255
Reply from 192.168.0.1: bytes=32 time=1ms TTL=255
Reply from 192.168.0.1: bytes=32 time=1ms TTL=255
```

```
Reply from 192.168.0.1: bytes=32 time=1ms TTL=255
Reply from 192.168.0.1: bytes=32 time=1ms TTL=255
Reply from 192.168.0.1: bytes=32 time=1ms TTL=255

Ping statistics for 192.168.0.1:
Packets: Sent = 6, Received = 6, Lost = 0 (0% loss),
Approximate round trip times in milli-seconds:
Minimum = 1ms, Maximum = 7ms, Average = 2ms
Control-C
^C
C:\Users\tlammle>
```

This ping will just keep going and going like the Energizer Bunny until you press Ctrl+C. By the way, it's an awesome tool for troubleshooting links.

The Address Resolution Protocol

The *Address Resolution Protocol (ARP)* is part of the TCP/IP protocol stack. It's used to translate TCP/IP addresses to MAC addresses using broadcasts. When a machine running TCP/IP wants to know which machine on an Ethernet network is using a certain IP address, it will send an ARP broadcast that says, in effect, "Hey. . .exactly who is IP address xxx .xxx.xxx.xxx?" The machine that owns the specific address will respond with its own MAC address, supplying the answer. The machine that made the inquiry will respond by adding the newly gained information to its own ARP table.

In addition to the normal usage, the ARP designation refers to a utility in Windows that you can use to manipulate and view the local workstation's ARP table.

The Windows ARP Table

The *ARP table* in Windows includes a list of TCP/IP addresses and their associated physical (MAC) addresses. This table is cached in memory so that Windows doesn't have to perform ARP lookups for frequently accessed TCP/IP addresses like those of servers and default gateways. Each entry contains an IP address and a MAC address plus a value for TTL that determines how long each entry will remain in the ARP table.

Remember that the ARP table contains two kinds of entries:

- Dynamic
- Static

Dynamic ARP table entries are created whenever the Windows TCP/IP stack performs an ARP lookup but the MAC address isn't found in the ARP table. When the MAC address of the requested IP address is finally found, or *resolved*, that information is then added into the ARP table as a dynamic entry. Whenever a request to send a packet to the host is sent to the Data Link layer, the ARP cache is checked first before an ARP broadcast is sent out. Remember, the ARP request is broadcast on the local segment—it does not go through a router.

 The ARP table is cleared of dynamic entries whose TTL has expired to ensure that the entries are current.

Static ARP table entries serve the same function as dynamic entries but are made manually using the arp utility.

Using the *arp* Utility

You now know that ARP is a protocol included in the TCP/IP suite. You also understand that ARP is used by IP to determine the MAC address of a device that exists on the same subnet as the requesting device. When a TCP/IP device needs to forward a packet to a device on the local subnet, it first looks in its own table, called an *ARP cache* or *MAC address lookup table*, for an association between the known IP address of the destination device on the local subnet and that same device's MAC address. The cache is called that because the contents are periodically weeded out.

If no association that includes the destination IP address can be found, the device will then send out an ARP broadcast that includes its own MAC and IP information as well as the IP address of the target device and a blank MAC address field. Filling in that blank is the object of the whole operation—it's the unknown value that the source device is requesting to be returned to it in the form of an ARP reply. Windows includes a utility called arp that allows us to check out the operating system's ARP cache. To view this, from a Windows DOS prompt, use the arp command like this:

```
C:\Users\tlammle>arp

Displays and modifies the IP-to-Physical address translation tables used
by address resolution protocol (ARP).

ARP -s inet_addr eth_addr [if_addr]
ARP -d inet_addr [if_addr]
ARP -a [inet_addr] [-N if_addr] [-v]
```

Table 19.2 describes the various options that you can use with the arp command.

TABLE 19.2   arp options

Option	Description
-a	Displays current ARP entries by interrogating the current protocol data. If inet_addr is specified, the IP and physical addresses for only the specified computer are displayed. If more than one network interface uses ARP, entries for each ARP table are displayed.
-g	Same as -a.
-v	Displays current ARP entries in verbose mode. All invalid entries and entries on the loopback interface will be shown.
inet_addr	Specifies an Internet address.
-N	Displays the ARP entries for the network interface specified by if_addr.
-d	Deletes the host specified by inet_addr. inet_addr may be wildcarded with * to delete all hosts.
-s	Adds the host, and associates the Internet address inet_addr with the physical address eth_addr. The physical address is given as six hexadecimal bytes separated by hyphens. The entry is permanent.
eth_addr	Specifies a physical address.
if_addr	If present, specifies the Internet address of the interface whose address translation table should be modified. If not present, the first applicable interface will be used.

Sheesh. Looking at that output really makes me wish we were all just running IPv6 because, as you already should know, IPv6 doesn't need ARP as well as many other annoying features and protocols required when running IPv4.

Of note, the Windows arp utility is primarily useful for resolving duplicate IP addresses. For example, let's say your workstation receives its IP address from a DHCP server, but it accidentally receives the same address that some other workstation gets. And so, when you try to ping it, you get no response. Your workstation is basically confused—it's trying to determine the MAC address, and it can't because two machines are reporting that they have the same IP address. To solve this little snag, you can use the arp utility to view your local ARP table and see which TCP/IP address is resolved to which MAC address.

To display the entire current ARP table, use the `arp` command with the –a switch like so to show you the MAC address lookup table:

```
C:\Users\tlammle>arp -a

Interface: 192.168.0.6 --- 0xb
Internet Address      Physical Address      Type
192.168.0.1           00-15-05-06-31-b0     dynamic
192.168.0.255         ff-ff-ff-ff-ff-ff     static
224.0.0.22            01-00-5e-00-00-16     static
224.0.0.252           01-00-5e-00-00-fc     static
239.255.255.250       01-00-5e-7f-ff-fa     static
255.255.255.255       ff-ff-ff-ff-ff-ff     static

Interface: 10.100.10.54 --- 0x10
Internet Address      Physical Address      Type
10.100.10.1           00-15-05-06-31-b0     dynamic
10.100.10.255         ff-ff-ff-ff-ff-ff     static
224.0.0.22            01-00-5e-00-00-16     static
224.0.0.252           01-00-5e-00-00-fc     static
239.255.255.250       01-00-5e-7f-ff-fa     static
```

By the way, the –g switch will produce the same result.

Now, from this output, you can tell which MAC address is assigned to which IP address. Then, for static assignments, you can tell which workstation has a specific IP address and if it's indeed supposed to have that address by examining your network documentation—you do have that record, right?

For DHCP-assigned addresses, you can begin to uncover problems stemming from multiple DHCP scopes or servers doling out identical addresses and other common configuration issues. And remember that under normal circumstances, you shouldn't see IP addresses in the ARP table that isn't a member of the same IP subnet as the interface.

If the machine has more than one network card (as may happen in Windows servers and on laptops with both Ethernet and wireless cards), each interface will be listed separately.

It's good to know that in addition to displaying the ARP table, you can use the `arp` utility to manipulate the table itself. To add static entries to the ARP table, you use the `arp` command with the –s switch. These static entries will stay in the ARP table until the machine is rebooted. A static entry essentially hardwires a specific IP address to a specific MAC address so that when a packet needs to be sent to that IP address, it will automatically be sent to that MAC address. Here's the syntax:

```
arp -s [IP Address] [MAC Address]
```

Simply replace the [*IP Address*] and [*MAC Address*] sections with the appropriate entries, like so:

```
arp -s 204.153.163.5 00-a0-c0-ab-c3-11
```

Now, take a look at your new ARP table by using the arp -a command. You should see something like this:

```
Internet Address        Physical Address        Type
204.153.163.5           00-a0-c0-ab-c3-11       static
```

Finally, if you want to delete entries from the ARP table, you can either wait until the dynamic entries time out or use the –d switch with the IP address of the static entry you'd like to delete, like this:

```
arp -d 204.153.163.5
```

Doing so effectively deletes the entry from the ARP table in memory.

The arp utility doesn't confirm successful additions or deletions (use arp –a or arp –g for that), but it will give you an error message if you use incorrect syntax.

Using the *nslookup* Utility

Whenever you're configuring a server or a workstation to connect to the Internet, you've got to start by configuring DNS if you want name resolution to happen (that is, if you want to be able to type **www.sybex.com** instead of an IP address). When configuring DNS, it's a very good thing to be able to test what IP address DNS is returning to ensure that it's working properly. The nslookup utility allows you to query a name server and quickly find out which name resolves to which IP address.

The Linux/UNIX dig (short for *domain information groper*) utility does the same thing as nslookup. It's primarily a command-line utility that allows you to perform a single DNS lookup for a specific entity, but it can also be employed in batch mode for a series of lookups. Detailed information on this command is beyond the scope of this study guide, but you can find more information on the web by searching for "UNIX/Linux dig."

The nslookup utility comes with Windows as well as most versions of UNIX and Linux. You can run it from a Windows command prompt. At the command prompt, you can start the nslookup utility by typing **nslookup** and pressing Enter. When you're inside this utility, the command prompt will change from something similar to a C:\> sign to a shorter > sign. It will also display the name and IP address of the default DNS server you will be querying (you can change it, if necessary). Then you can start using nslookup. The following output gives you a sample of the display after the nslookup command has been entered at the C:\> prompt:

```
C:\Users\tlammle>nslookup
Default Server:  gnt-corpdc1.globalnet.local
Address:  10.100.36.12

>
```

The primary job of nslookup is to tell you the many different features of a particular domain name, the names of the servers that serve it, and how they're configured. To get that, just type in a domain name at the > prompt, and the nslookup utility will then return this information:

```
> lammle.com
Server:  dslmodem.domain.actdsltmp
Address:  192.168.0.1
```

The non-authoritative answer is as follows:

```
Name:      lammle.com
Address:  206.123.114.186
```

What this tells you is that the server that returned the information is not responsible (authoritative) for the zone information of the domain for which you requested an address and that the name server for the domain lammle.com is located at the IP address 206.123.114.186.

You can also ask nslookup for other information by setting a different option within nslookup. Just type **set *option*** at the > prompt and replace option with the actual option you want to use—for example, use >set type=mx to determine the IP address of your email server. If you can't decide which one you want, use the question mark (?) at the greater than sign (>) to see all available options.

If you type in **nslookup** and receive this reply

```
NS request timed out.
    timeout was 2 seconds.
***Can't find server name for address 206.123.114.186: Timed out
Default Server:  UnKnown
Address:  fec0:0:0:ffff::1
```

then you know your DNS servers are not answering. You need to get over to the DNS server, stat!

Examining DNS with *nslookup*

In this exercise, you will examine how to use the `nslookup` command.

1. Open the command prompt by clicking Start and then typing **cmd**. Right-click the command prompt result, select Run As Administrator, and press Enter.

2. Type **nslookup -type=A wiley.com**, press Enter, and note the results.

3. Type **nslookup -type=MX wiley.com**, press Enter, and note the results.

Reflecting back on Chapter 5, "Networking Devices," remember the various resource records. An A record is a host record, and an MX record is a mail exchanger record. Try other records with `wiley.com` and other domains.

Resolving Names with the Hosts File

The hosts file is really a lot like DNS, except its entries are static for each and every host and server. Within the Hosts table, you'll find a collection of hostnames that devices reference for name-resolution purposes. And even though it works in both IPv4 and IPv6 environments, it's unlikely you will use it these days because the hosts file is a way-ancient relic left over from old UNIX machines.

But just because it's museum quality doesn't mean you won't run into it now and then, which is the main reason I'm showing it to you. You can find the Hosts table in `C:\Windows\System32\drivers\etc`. Just double-click the file, and then choose to open the file in Notepad or another text editor. Here's the default information—it's really nothing more than an explanation of how to use it and the local hosts for both IP and IPv6:

```
# Copyright (c) 1993-2006 Microsoft Corp.
#
# This is a sample HOSTS file used by Microsoft TCP/IP for Windows.
#
# This file contains the mappings of IP addresses to host names. Each
# entry should be kept on an individual line. The IP address should
# be placed in the first column followed by the corresponding host name.
# The IP address and the host name should be separated by at least one
# space.
#
# Additionally, comments (such as these) may be inserted on individual
# lines or following the machine name denoted by a '#' symbol.
```

```
#
# For example:
#
#      102.54.94.97      rhino.acme.com          # source server
#       38.25.63.10      x.acme.com              # x client host

127.0.0.1        localhost
::1              localhost
```

> Any information entered to the right of a pound sign (#) in a hosts file is ignored, so you can use this space for comments.

Because it's a plain ASCII text file, you add the IP address under the local hosts and then the name to which you want to resolve the IP address. It's a pretty simple configuration and, again, one I don't recommend using because you have to type in the names of every host on every machine in your network. DNS is definitely the name resolution of choice for networks today.

> Do not get the hosts file confused with the hostname command. The hostname command doesn't do much but display the name of your host, as shown here:

```
C:\Users\tlammle>hostname /?

Prints the name of the current host.

hostname

C:\Users\tlammle>hostname
globalnet-todd
```

Using the *mtr* Command *(pathping)*

The mtr, or My traceroute command, is a computer program that combines the functions of the traceroute and ping utilities in a single network diagnostic tool. It also adds round-trip time and packet loss to the output—very cool.

The mtr command probes routers on the route path by limiting the number of hops individual packets are allowed to traverse and listening to news of their termination. It will regularly repeat this process (usually once per second) and keep track of the response times of the hops along the path.

The mtr command is great if you have Linux or UNIX, but by default, it's not installed on Windows devices. Third-party applications of mtr are available to install on Windows, but Microsoft did respond with its own version of mtr—it's called pathping, and it provides the same functions as mtr. Here's a look at the output and the options:

```
C:\Users\tlammle>pathping

Usage: pathping [-g host-list] [-h maximum_hops] [-i address] [-n]
                [-p period] [-q num_queries] [-w timeout]
                [-4] [-6] target_name
```

Table 19.3 lists the options of the Windows pathping command.

TABLE 19.3 pathping options

Option	Description
-g *host-list*	Uses a loose source route along the host list
-h *maximum_hops*	Specifies the maximum number of hops to search for the target
-i *address*	Uses the specified source address
-n	Does not resolve addresses to hostnames
-p *period*	Waits *period* milliseconds between pings
-q *num_queries*	Specifies the number of queries per hop
-w *timeout*	Waits *timeout* milliseconds for each reply
-4	Forces using IPv4
-6	Forces using IPv6

The mtr utility is basically the same as traceroute and ping, but it does give you some additional output that can help you troubleshoot your network.

Using the Nmap Utility

Nmap is one of the most popular port scanning tools used today. After performing scans with certain flags set in the scan packets, security analysts (and hackers) can make certain assumptions based on the responses received. These flags are used to control the TCP connection process and so are present only in TCP packets. Figure 19.5 shows a TCP header with the important flags circled. Normally flags are "turned on" because of the normal TCP process, but hackers can craft packets to check the flags they want to check.

Figure 19.5 shows these flags, among others:

FIGURE 19.5   TCP flags

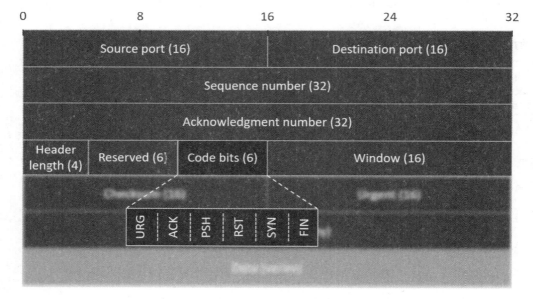

- **URG:** Urgent pointer field significant
- **ACK:** Acknowledgment field significant
- **PSH:** Push function
- **RST:** Reset the connection
- **SYN:** Synchronize sequence numbers
- **FIN:** No more data from sender

While application of a scan and interpretation of the responses are beyond the scope of this book, security analysts and hackers alike can perform scans with these flags set in the scan packets to get responses that allow them to determine the following information:

- If a port is open on a device
- If the port is blocked by a firewall before it gets to the device

Nmap can also be used as follows:

- To determine the live hosts on a network
- To create a logical "map" of the network

Using the *route* Command

I went over static routing in Chapter 9, "Introduction to IP Routing," so you know that Windows devices like routers perform routing. Most of the time, it's a good idea to leave Windows alone, but it's still good to know how to add and delete routes on your Windows machines.

Probably the biggest reason for manipulating the routing table on a Windows server is to create a firewall. For instance, let's say we're running an Application layer firewall on a Windows server located between a screen subnet, formerly known as a demilitarized zone (DMZ), and the internal network. This scenario would mean the routing that's happening on the server or hosts located in the DMZ wouldn't be able to reach the internal network's hosts and vice versa.

To circumvent this problem, we would need to employ both static and default routing because while Windows 10/11 and Windows Server versions support some routing protocols, running routing protocols on hosts and servers wouldn't be a good solution for today's networks, and Microsoft knows that.

To view the routing table on a Windows device, use the route print command, as shown in Figure 19.6.

In this output, you can see that each of the routes were added automatically when the system booted up. (This is all based on the configuration of your IP stack.) To see all the options available with the route command, type the route command and then press Enter. To add a route to your routing table, use the following syntax:

```
route [-f] [-p] [Command [Destination] [mask Netmask] [Gateway]
[metric Metric]] [if Interface]]
```

FIGURE 19.6   route print output

```
C:\Users\Wiley>route print
===========================================================================
Interface List
 10...........................NordLynx Tunnel
 19...........................Wintun Userspace Tunnel
  3...24 4b fe 9a 32 d3 ......Realtek Gaming GbE Family Controller
  5...00 ff 2f 7d 84 66 ......TAP-Windows Adapter V9
 24...04 7f 0e 64 fd f0 ......Bluetooth Device (Personal Area Network) #2
  1...........................Software Loopback Interface 1
===========================================================================

IPv4 Route Table
===========================================================================
Active Routes:
Network Destination        Netmask          Gateway       Interface  Metric
          0.0.0.0          0.0.0.0       172.16.1.1     172.16.1.181     25
        127.0.0.0        255.0.0.0         On-link         127.0.0.1    331
        127.0.0.1  255.255.255.255         On-link         127.0.0.1    331
  127.255.255.255  255.255.255.255         On-link         127.0.0.1    331
       172.16.0.0      255.240.0.0         On-link      172.16.1.181    281
     172.16.1.181  255.255.255.255         On-link      172.16.1.181    281
   172.31.255.255  255.255.255.255         On-link      172.16.1.181    281
        224.0.0.0        240.0.0.0         On-link         127.0.0.1    331
        224.0.0.0        240.0.0.0         On-link      172.16.1.181    281
  255.255.255.255  255.255.255.255         On-link         127.0.0.1    331
  255.255.255.255  255.255.255.255         On-link      172.16.1.181    281
===========================================================================
Persistent Routes:
  None

IPv6 Route Table
===========================================================================
Active Routes:
 If Metric Network Destination      Gateway
  1    331 ::1/128                   On-link
  3    281 fe80::/64                 On-link
  3    281 fe80::1b58:d0d9:8d3c:861c/128
                                     On-link
  1    331 ff00::/8                  On-link
  3    281 ff00::/8                  On-link
===========================================================================
Persistent Routes:
  None

C:\Users\Wiley>|
```

Using the *route* Command Options

Let's start with the switches you can use:

-f   Using this switch with any of the options like add, change, or delete will clear the routing table of all entries that aren't host routes (routes with the subnet mask 255.255.255.255), the loopback network route or routes (routes with a destination of 127.0.0.0 and the subnet mask 255.0.0.0), and any multicast routes (those with a destination of 224.0.0.0 and the subnet mask 240.0.0.0).

-p   If you use this with the add command, the individual route will be added to the Registry and then used to initialize the IP routing table whenever TCP/IP is started. It's important to remember that by default the routes you've statically added won't remain in the routing table the next time TCP/IP boots. And if you use -p with the print command, you'll get shown a list of the persistent routes that are stored in the Registry location of HKEY_LOCAL_MACHINE\SYSTEM\CurrentControlSet\Services\Tcpip\Parameters\ PersistentRoutes.

Now, let's take a look at how and when you would use the route command. Table 19.4 shows the command options available and what they do when you are using the route command with them.

TABLE 19.4   route command options

Command	Purpose
Add	Adds a route
Change	Modifies an existing route
Delete	Deletes a route (or routes)
Print	Prints a route (or routes)

Here's a description of some other tasks you can accomplish via the rest of the command's options:

Destination   This will give you the network destination of a given route. If the host bits of the network address are set to 0, it will be depicted with the destination's IP network address, an IP address for a specific host route, or the default route of 0.0.0.0.

mask *netmask*   This will provide you with the *netmask*—often referred to as the *subnet mask*—that's associated with the destination network. The default destination subnet mask is 0.0.0.0, and typically you'll see 255.255.255.255 representing a host route. It's really important to remember that the destination address can't be more specific than its corresponding subnet mask. What I'm saying is that there absolutely can't be a bit set to 1 in the destination address if the equivalent bit in the subnet mask is a 0.

Gateway   The gateway also depends on the network address and subnet mask, but it's even more specific and delimits what's called the *next-hop IP address*. For routes located on a local subnet, the gateway address maps directly to a particular interface. If the destination is on a remote network, the gateway IP address will direct packets to the neighboring router.

metric *metric*   *Metric* refers to the cost of a given route from the sending to the receiving device, and it's a value between 1 and 9999. Devices use this value to choose the best, or most efficient, routes among those in their routing table—the route with the lowest value wins. This decision can also include factors like the number of hops and the speed, reliability, and available bandwidth of the path being considered plus the various administrative aspects associated with it.

if *interface*   This tool depends on information from the gateway address and determines the interface index for the specific interface that needs to receive the data. You can get a list of interfaces along with their relevant interface indexes by typing the `route print` command.

/?   Using this will allow you to view help at the command prompt.

Some Examples of the *route* Command

Even though the finer points of the `route` command demand that you use caution when deploying some of the options, I'll still list the basics of the `route` command because it can be really useful. I highly recommend that you spend some time practicing them on a non-production server, though—especially at first.

- To display the entire IP routing table, type **route print**.
- To add a default route with the default gateway address 192.168.10.1, type **route add 0.0.0.0 mask 0.0.0.0 192.168.10.1**.
- To add a route to the destination 10.1.1.0 with the subnet mask 255.255.255.0 and the next-hop address 10.2.2.2, type **route add 10.1.1.0 mask 255.255.255.0 10.2.2.2**.
- If you want to, let's say, add a persistent route to the destination 10.100.0.0 with the subnet mask 255.255.0.0 and the next-hop address 10.2.0.1, type **route -p add 10.100.0.0 mask 255.255.0.0 10.2.0.1**. If you want to delete the route to the destination 10.100.0.0 with the subnet mask 255.255.0.0, enter **route delete 10.100.0.0 mask 255.255.0.0**.
- Finally, if you want to change the next-hop address of a route with the destination 10.100.0.0 and the subnet mask 255.255.0.0 from 10.2.0.1 to 10.7.0.5, type **route change 10.100.0.0 mask 255.255.0.0 10.7.0.5**.

Let's move on to some other important Windows utilities.

Using the *netstat* Utility

Using `netstat` is a great way to check out the inbound and outbound TCP/IP connections on your machine. You can also use it to view packet statistics like how many packets have been sent and received, the number of errors, and so on.

When used without any options, `netstat` produces output similar to the following, which shows all the outbound TCP/IP connections. This utility is a great tool to use to determine the status of outbound web connections. Take a look:

```
C:\Users\tlammle>netstat
```

```
Active Connections

  Proto  Local Address         Foreign Address         State
  TCP    10.100.10.54:49545    gnt-exchange:epmap      TIME_WAIT
  TCP    10.100.10.54:49548    gnt-exchange:epmap      TIME_WAIT
  TCP    10.100.10.54:49551    gnt-exchange:1151       ESTABLISHED
  TCP    10.100.10.54:49557    gnt-exchange:1026       ESTABLISHED
  TCP    10.100.10.54:49590    gnt-exchange:epmap      TIME_WAIT
  TCP    127.0.0.1:49174       globalnet-todd:62214    ESTABLISHED
  TCP    127.0.0.1:62514       globalnet-todd:49174    ESTABLISHED
  TCP    192.168.0.6:2492      blugro2relay:2492       ESTABLISHED
  TCP    192.168.0.6:2492      blugro3relay:2492       ESTABLISHED
  TCP    192.168.0.6:49170     64.12.25.26:5190        ESTABLISHED
  TCP    192.168.0.6:49171     oam-d05c:5190           ESTABLISHED
  TCP    192.168.0.6:49473     205.128.92.124:http     CLOSE_WAIT
  TCP    192.168.0.6:49625     64-190-251-21:ftp       ESTABLISHED
  TCP    192.168.0.6:49628     210-11:http             ESTABLISHED
  TCP    192.168.0.6:49629     varp1:http              ESTABLISHED
  TCP    192.168.0.6:49630     varp1:http              ESTABLISHED
  TCP    192.168.0.6:49631     varp1:http              ESTABLISHED
  TCP    192.168.0.6:49632     varp1:http              ESTABLISHED
  TCP    192.168.0.6:49635     199.93.62.125:http      ESTABLISHED
  TCP    192.168.0.6:49636     m1:http                 ESTABLISHED
  TCP    192.168.0.6:49638     spe:http                ESTABLISHED
```

The Proto column lists the protocol being used. You can see that I'm connected to my Exchange server and an FTP server and that I have some HTTP sessions open; by the way, all of them use TCP at the Transport layer.

The Local Address column lists the source address and the source port (source socket). The Foreign Address column lists the address of the destination machine (the hostname if it's been resolved). If the destination port is known, it will show up as the well-known port. In the previous output, you see `http` instead of port 80 and `ftp` instead of port 21.

The State column indicates the status of each connection. This column shows statistics only for TCP connections because User Datagram Protocol (UDP) establishes no virtual circuit to the remote device. Usually, this column indicates ESTABLISHED when a TCP connection between your computer and the destination computer has been established. All sessions eventually time out and then close, and you can see that I have all of these listed in my netstat output.

 If the address of either your computer or the destination computer can be found in the hosts file on your computer, the destination computer's name, rather than the IP address, will show up in either the Local Address or Foreign Address column.

The output of the netstat utility depends on the switch. By using the netstat /? command, we can see the options available to us.

C:\Users\tlammle>**netstat /?**

Table 19.5 lists all of the netstat switch options.

TABLE 19.5   netstat options

Option	Description
-a	Displays all connections and listening ports.
-b	Displays the executable involved in creating each connection or listening port. In some cases, well-known executables host multiple independent components, and in these cases the sequence of components involved in creating the connection or listening port is displayed. Note that this option can be time consuming and will fail unless you have sufficient permissions.
-e	Displays Ethernet statistics. This may be combined with the -s option.
-f	Displays fully qualified domain names (FQDNs) for foreign addresses.
-n	Displays addresses and port numbers in numerical form.
-o	Displays the owning process ID associated with each connection.
-p proto	Shows connections for the protocol specified by proto; proto may be TCP, UDP, TCPv6, or UDPv6. If used with the -s option to display per-protocol statistics, proto may be IP, IPv6, ICMP, ICMPv6, TCP, TCPv6, UDP, or UDPv6.
-r	Displays the routing table.
-s	Displays per-protocol statistics. By default, statistics are shown for IP, IPv6, ICMP, ICMPv6, TCP, TCPv6, UDP, and UDPv6; the -p option may be used to specify a subset of the default.
-t	Displays the current connection offload state. Redisplays selected statistics, pausing interval seconds between each display. Press Ctrl+C to stop redisplaying statistics. If -t is omitted, netstat will print the current configuration information once.

Simply type **netstat** followed by a space and then the particular switch you want to use. Some switches have options, but no matter what, the syntax is basically the same.

 Note that with UNIX/Linux-type switches, the hyphen absolutely must be included. This is common in Microsoft operating systems for TCP/IP utilities that originate from UNIX systems. I'm not going to exhaustively go over each and every switch, but make sure you practice all of these on your own Windows machine.

The –a Switch When you use the –a switch, the netstat utility displays all TCP/IP connections and all UDP connections. Figure 19.7 shows sample output produced by the netstat –a command.

FIGURE 19.7 Sample output of the netstat –a command

```
C:\Windows\system32>netstat -a

Active Connections

  Proto  Local Address          Foreign Address         State
  TCP    172.16.1.181:54563     e2:https                ESTABLISHED
  TCP    172.16.1.181:54566     52.107.251.23:https     TIME_WAIT
  TCP    172.16.1.181:54567     52.109.92.7:https       TIME_WAIT
  TCP    172.16.1.181:54568     52.109.92.7:https       TIME_WAIT
  TCP    172.16.1.181:54573     162.159.137.232:https   ESTABLISHED
  TCP    172.16.1.181:54587     13.107.138.10:https     TIME_WAIT
  TCP    172.16.1.181:54588     Ceres:37777             ESTABLISHED
  TCP    [::]:135               Ceres:0                 LISTENING
  TCP    [::]:445               Ceres:0                 LISTENING
  TCP    [::]:554               Ceres:0                 LISTENING
  UDP    0.0.0.0:3702           *:*
  UDP    0.0.0.0:3702           *:*
  UDP    0.0.0.0:5050           *:*
  UDP    0.0.0.0:5353           *:*
  UDP    0.0.0.0:5353           *:*
  UDP    0.0.0.0:5353           *:*
  UDP    0.0.0.0:5353           *:*
  UDP    0.0.0.0:5353           *:*

C:\Windows\system32>
```

The last two entries in Figure 19.7 show that the protocol is UDP and give the source-port nicknames nbname and nbdatagram. These are the well-known port numbers of 137 and 138, respectively. These port numbers are commonly seen on networks that broadcast the NetBIOS name of a workstation on the TCP/IP network. You can tell that this is a broadcast because the destination address is listed as *:* (meaning "any address, any port").

> The State column in Figure 19.7 has no entry for the UDP rows because UDP is not a connection-oriented protocol and, therefore, has no connection state.

The most common use for the –a switch is to check the status of a TCP/IP connection that appears to be hung. You can determine if the connection is simply busy or is actually hung and no longer responding.

The –e Switch

The –e switch displays a summary of all the packets that have been sent over the network interface card (NIC) as of an instance. The Received and Sent columns show packets coming in as well as being sent:

```
C:\Users\tlammle>netstat -e
Interface Statistics

                           Received              Sent

Bytes                       7426841           7226953
Unicast packets               25784             35006
Non-unicast packets            1115             12548
Discards                          0                 0
Errors                            0                71
Unknown protocols                 0
```

You can use the –e switch to display the following categories of statistics:

Bytes   The number of bytes transmitted or received since the computer was turned on. This statistic is useful for finding out if data is actually being transmitted and received or if the network interface isn't doing anything at all.

Unicast Packets   The number of packets sent from or received at this computer. To register in one of these columns, the packet must be addressed directly from one computer to another and the computer's address must be in either the source or destination address section of the packet.

Non-Unicast Packets   The number of packets that weren't directly sent from one workstation to another. For example, a broadcast packet is a non-unicast packet. The number of non-unicast packets should be smaller than the number of unicast packets. If the number of non-unicast packets is as high as or higher than that of unicast packets, too many broadcast packets are being sent over your network. Definitely find the source of these packets and make any necessary adjustments to optimize performance.

Discards   The number of packets that were discarded by the NIC during either transmission or reception because they weren't assembled correctly.

Errors   The number of errors that occurred during transmission or reception. (These numbers may indicate problems with the network card.)

Unknown Protocols   The number of received packets that the Windows networking stack couldn't interpret. This statistic shows up only in the Received column because if the computer sent them, they wouldn't be unknown, right?

Unfortunately, statistics don't mean much unless they can be colored with time information. For example, if the Errors row shows 71 errors, is that a problem? It might be if the computer has been on for only a few minutes. But 71 errors could be par for the course if the computer has been operating for several days. Unfortunately, the `netstat` utility doesn't have a way of indicating how much time has elapsed for these statistics.

The *–r* Switch

You use the `-r` switch to display the current route table for a workstation so that you can see exactly how TCP/IP information is being routed. This will give you the same output as the `route print` command that we covered earlier in this chapter.

The *–s* Switch

Using the `-s` switch displays a variety of TCP, UDP, IP, and ICMP protocol statistics. But be warned—the output you'll get is really long, which may or may not be okay for you. For this book, it's way too long for me to insert. With that in mind, we can add another modifier called the -p switch.

The *–p* Switch

Like the `-n` switch, the -p switch is a modifier that's usually used with the `-s` switch to specify which protocol statistics to list in the output (IP, TCP, UDP, or ICMP). For example, if you want to view only ICMP statistics, you use the -p switch like so:

```
netstat -s -p ICMP
```

The `netstat` utility then displays the ICMP statistics instead of the entire gamut of TCP/IP statistics that the -s switch will typically flood you with. For a different example, let's use the `-s` and `-p` switches to retrieve some IPv6 information:

```
C:\Users\tlammle>netstat -s -p IPV6

IPv6 Statistics

    Packets Received            = 1400
    Received Header Errors      = 0
    Received Address Errors     = 6
```

```
Datagrams Forwarded                 = 0
Unknown Protocols Received          = 0
Received Packets Discarded          = 451
Received Packets Delivered          = 10441
Output Requests                     = 24349
Routing Discards                    = 0
Discarded Output Packets            = 3575
Output Packet No Route              = 41
Reassembly Required                 = 0
Reassembly Successful               = 0
Reassembly Failures                 = 0
Datagrams Successfully Fragmented   = 0
Datagrams Failing Fragmentation     = 0
Fragments Created                   = 0
```

C:\Users\tlammle>

Nice! Gets right to the point. Now, let's see the TCP connections my host has:

C:\Users\tlammle>**netstat -s -p tcp**

```
TCP Statistics for IPv4

Active Opens                = 7832
Passive Opens               = 833
Failed Connection Attempts  = 1807
Reset Connections           = 2428
Current Connections         = 11
Segments Received           = 1391678
Segments Sent               = 1340994
Segments Retransmitted      = 6246

Active Connections

Proto  Local Address            Foreign Address          State
TCP    10.100.10.54:54737       gnt-exchange:1151        ESTABLISHED
TCP    10.100.10.54:54955       gnt-exchange:1026        ESTABLISHED
TCP    10.100.10.54:55218       gnt-exchange:epmap       TIME_WAIT
TCP    127.0.0.1:2492           globalnet-todd:54840     ESTABLISHED
TCP    127.0.0.1:54516          globalnet-todd:62514     ESTABLISHED
TCP    127.0.0.1:54840          globalnet-todd:2492      ESTABLISHED
TCP    127.0.0.1:62514          globalnet-todd:54516     ESTABLISHED
```

```
TCP    192.168.0.6:2492      blugro2relay:2492     ESTABLISHED
TCP    192.168.0.6:2492      blugro3relay:2492     ESTABLISHED
TCP    192.168.0.6:54527     64.12.25.26:5190      ESTABLISHED
TCP    192.168.0.6:54531     oam-d05c:5190         ESTABLISHED
TCP    192.168.0.6:55163     207.123.44.123:http   CLOSE_WAIT
```

C:\Users\tlammle>

This kind of efficiency is exactly why it's good to use the -p modifier with the -s switch.

> Because the Network+ exam doesn't cover them, we won't go into detail about what all these statistics mean for most of these commands. You can probably figure out most of them—for instance, Packets Received. For more details, go to Microsoft's support website at https://support.microsoft.com/en-us.

The *–n* Switch

The −n switch is a modifier for the other switches. When used with them, it reverses the natural tendency of netstat to use names instead of network addresses. In other words, when you use the −n switch, the output always displays network addresses instead of their associated network names. The following is output from the netstat command used with the netstat −n command. It's showing the same information but with IP addresses instead of names.

C:\Users\tlammle>**netstat**

Active Connections

```
  Proto  Local Address          Foreign Address         State
  TCP    10.100.10.54:54737     gnt-exchange:1151       ESTABLISHED
  TCP    10.100.10.54:54955     gnt-exchange:1026       ESTABLISHED
  TCP    127.0.0.1:2492         globalnet-todd:54840    ESTABLISHED
  TCP    127.0.0.1:54516        globalnet-todd:62514    ESTABLISHED
  TCP    127.0.0.1:54840        globalnet-todd:2492     ESTABLISHED
  TCP    127.0.0.1:62514        globalnet-todd:54516    ESTABLISHED
  TCP    192.168.0.6:2492       blugro2relay:2492       ESTABLISHED
  TCP    192.168.0.6:2492       blugro3relay:2492       ESTABLISHED
  TCP    192.168.0.6:54527      64.12.25.26:5190        ESTABLISHED
  TCP    192.168.0.6:54531      oam-d05c:5190           ESTABLISHED
```

```
   TCP     192.168.0.6:55163        207.123.44.123:http    CLOSE_WAIT

C:\Users\tlammle>netstat -n

Active Connections

   Proto  Local Address            Foreign Address          State
   TCP    10.100.10.54:54737       10.100.36.13:1151        ESTABLISHED
   TCP    10.100.10.54:54955       10.100.36.13:1026        ESTABLISHED
   TCP    127.0.0.1:2492           127.0.0.1:54840          ESTABLISHED
   TCP    127.0.0.1:54516          127.0.0.1:62514          ESTABLISHED
   TCP    127.0.0.1:54840          127.0.0.1:2492           ESTABLISHED
   TCP    127.0.0.1:62514          127.0.0.1:54516          ESTABLISHED
   TCP    192.168.0.6:2492         65.55.239.100:2492       ESTABLISHED
   TCP    192.168.0.6:2492         65.55.248.110:2492       ESTABLISHED
   TCP    192.168.0.6:54527        64.12.25.26:5190         ESTABLISHED
   TCP    192.168.0.6:54531        205.188.248.163:5190     ESTABLISHED
   TCP    192.168.0.6:55163        207.123.44.123:80        CLOSE_WAIT

C:\Users\tlammle>
```

 Real World Scenario

Uses for *netstat*

You might be saying to yourself, "Fine. I can use lots of cool switches with netstat, but really, what for?" I'm always finding uses for netstat. For instance, once I found a particularly nasty worm on my PC using netstat. I just happened to run netstat for giggles one day and noticed a very large number of outbound connections to various places on the Internet. My PC was sending out SYN packets to a large number of hosts (an indication that my computer was involved—unknowingly—in a large-scale denial-of-service attack). Upon further examination, I noticed that this activity would start shortly after bootup.

I tried running netstat after bootup and noticed that the first outbound connection was to TCP port 6667, some Internet Relay Chat (IRC) server I'd never heard of—I didn't even have an IRC client on my machine at the time. The worm was particularly nasty to try to get rid of while active, so I turned off port 6667 on my firewall. That prevented the initial connection to the IRC server and, as I found out later, nicely prevented the worm from getting its instructions from the IRC server. I was then able to simply remap without netstat. Even my antivirus program missed it.

EXERCISE 19.2

Examining Connections with *netstat*

In this exercise, you will examine how to use the `netstat` command to identify TCP connections.

1. Open the command prompt by clicking Start and then typing **cmd**. Right-click the command prompt result, select Run As Administrator, and press Enter.

2. Type **netstat -n** and wait for the output.

3. Examine the foreign addresses and the state of the connections.

4. Open a web browser, type **http://1.2.3.4:1234**, and press Enter.

Note: The web browser will eventually time out; you are just creating traffic for the next step.

5. Type **netstat -n** and wait for the output.

6. Examine the foreign addresses and the state of the connections.

Notice that the output will show 1.2.3.4:1234 with a state of SYN. Remember from Chapter 6, "Introduction to the Internet Protocol," that the TCP protocol requires a three-way handshake. Since this host does not exist, only the first part of the three-way handshake (SYN) will be displayed in the output of the command.

Using *tcpdump*

The `tcpdump` utility is used to read either packets captured live from a network or packets that have been saved to a file. Although there is a Windows version called `windump`, `tcpdump` works only on UNIX-like operating systems.

Examples of Using *tcpdump*

Use this command to capture traffic on all interfaces:

```
# tcpdump -i any
```

Here is the command to capture traffic on a particular interface:

```
# tcpdump -i eth0
```

To filter traffic by IP, whether it's the source or the destination, use this command:

```
# tcpdump host 192.168.5.5
```

Basic Networking Device Commands

In this section, I'll run through some basic and common router and switch commands. Let's get started with the common CLI command, show running-config.

show running-config (Show Run)

To verify the configuration in dynamic RAM (DRAM), use the show running-config command (sh run for short), which provides the current configuration the device is using:

```
Router#show running-config
Building configuration...
Current configuration : 877 bytes
!
version 15.0
```

Next, you should check the configuration stored in non-volatile RAM (NVRAM), which is basically RAM that is not deleted when the device is either turned off or rebooted. To see this, use the show startup-config command (sh start for short):

```
Router#sh start
Using 877 out of 724288 bytes
!
! Last configuration change at 04:49:14 UTC Fri Mar 7 2024
!
version 15.0
```

As shown in the following output, by copying running-config to NVRAM as a backup, you ensure that your running-config file will always be reloaded if the router gets rebooted. Starting in the 12.0 IOS, you'll be prompted for the filename you want to use.

```
Router#copy running-config startup-config
Destination filename [startup-config]?[enter]
Building configuration...
[OK]
```

To delete the startup-config file on a Cisco router or switch, use the command erase startup-config:

```
Todc#erase startup-config
Erasing the nvram filesystem will remove all configuration files!
Continue? [confirm][enter]
[OK]
Erase of nvram: complete
*Mar 7 17:55:20.405: %SYS-7-NV_BLOCK_INIT: Initialized the geometry of nvram
```

```
Todd#reload
System configuration has been modified. Save? [yes/no]:n
Proceed with reload? [confirm][enter]
*Mar 7 17:55:31.079: %SYS-5-RELOAD: Reload requested by console.
Reload Reason: Reload Command.
```

This command deletes the contents of NVRAM on the switch and router. If you type **reload** while in privileged mode and say no to saving changes, the switch or router will reload and come up into setup mode since you no longer have a configuration on the device.

show config

The show config command displays all the configuration settings for the device that have been changed from the default settings on many various industry devices. See the earlier show running-config command output for an example of a Cisco configuration.

Cisco Discovery Protocol

The Cisco Discovery Protocol (CDP) is a Cisco proprietary Data Link layer protocol used for gathering information. CDP broadcasts every 120 seconds advertising the details of the Cisco device to include IP address, version information, and capabilities.

Even though the CDP doesn't technically provide management access, it's really useful if you're working on Cisco networks and need to figure out how the various Cisco devices are connected.

show cdp neighbors

The show cdp neighbors command (sh cdp nei for short) delivers information about directly connected devices. It's important to remember that CDP packets aren't passed through a Cisco switch and that you see only what's directly attached. This means that if your router is connected to a switch, you won't see any other Cisco devices connected to that switch!

The following output shows the show cdp neighbors command:

```
SW-3#sh cdp neighbors
Capability Codes: R - Router, T - Trans Bridge, B - Source Route Bridge
S - Switch, H - Host, I - IGMP, r - Repeater, P - Phone,
D - Remote, C - CVTA, M - Two-port Mac Relay Device ID Local Intrfce Holdtme
Capability Platform Port ID
SW-1 Fas 0/1 150 S I WS-C3560- Fas 0/15
SW-1 Fas 0/2 150 S I WS-C3560- Fas 0/16
SW-2 Fas 0/5 162 S I WS-C3560- Fas 0/5
SW-2 Fas 0/6 162 S I WS-C3560- Fas 0/6
```

The previous output shows that SW-3 is directly connected with a console cable to the SW-3 switch and that SW-3 is directly connected to two other switches. CDP lets me see who my directly connected neighbors are and gather information about them.

From the SW-3 switch, you can see that there are two connections to SW-1 and two connections to SW-2. SW-3 connects to SW-1 with ports Fas 0/1 and Fas 0/2, and there are connections to SW-2 with local interfaces Fas 0/5 and Fas 0/6. Both the SW-1 and SW-2 switches are 3650 switches. SW-1 is using ports Fas 0/15 and Fas 0/16 to connect to SW-3. SW-2 is using ports Fas 0/5 and Fas 0/6.

To summarize, the device ID shows the configured hostname of the connected device, that the local interface is our interface, and that the port ID is the remote device's directly connected interface. Remember that all you get to view are directly connected devices!

Table 19.6 summarizes the information displayed by the show cdp neighbors command for each device.

TABLE 19.6   Output of the show cdp neighbors command

Field	Description
Device ID	The hostname of the device directly connected.
Local Interface	The port or interface that CDP packets are received on.
Holdtime	The amount of time the router will hold the information before discarding it if no more CDP packets are received.
Capability	The capability of the neighbor—the router, switch, or repeater. The capability codes are listed at the top of the command output.
Platform	The type of Cisco device directly connected. In the previous output, the SW-3 shows that it's directly connected to two 3560 switches.
Port ID	The neighbor device's port or interface that CDP packets are multicast from.

Another command that will deliver the goods on neighbor information is the show cdp neighbors detail command (show cdp nei de for short).

The show cdp neighbors detail command can be run on both routers and switches. It displays detailed information about each device connected to the device you're running the command on. Check out the router output:

```
SW-3#sh cdp neighbors detail
-------------------------
Device ID: SW-1
Device ID: SW-1
```

```
Entry address(es):
  IP address: 10.100.128.10
Platform: cisco WS-C3560-24TS,  Capabilities: Switch IGMP
Interface: FastEthernet0/1,  Port ID (outgoing port): FastEthernet0/15
Holdtime : 135 sec

Version :
Cisco IOS Software, C3560 Software (C3560-IPSERVICESK9-M), Version 12.2(55)SE5,
RELEASE SOFTWARE (fc1)
Technical Support: http://www.cisco.com/techsupport
Copyright (c) 1986-2013 by Cisco Systems, Inc.
Compiled Mon 28-Jan-13 10:10 by prod_rel_team

advertisement version: 2
Protocol Hello:  OUI=0x00000C, Protocol ID=0x0112; payload len=25,
value=00000000FFFFFFFF010221FF000000000000001C555EC880Fc00f000
VTP Management Domain: 'NULL'
Native VLAN: 1
Duplex: full
Power Available TLV:

    Power request id: 0, Power management id: 1, Power available: 0, Power
management level: -1
Management address(es):
  IP address: 10.100.128.10
-------------------------

[output cut]

-------------------------
Device ID: SW-2
Entry address(es):
  IP address: 10.100.128.9
Platform: cisco WS-C3560-8PC,  Capabilities: Switch IGMP
Interface: FastEthernet0/5,  Port ID (outgoing port): FastEthernet0/5
Holdtime : 129 sec

Version :
Cisco IOS Software, C3560 Software (C3560-IPBASE-M), Version 12.2(35)SE5,
RELEASE SOFTWARE (fc1)
Copyright (c) 1986-2005 by Cisco Systems, Inc.
```

```
Compiled Thu 19-Jul-05 18:15 by nachen

advertisement version: 2
Protocol Hello:  OUI=0x00000C, Protocol ID=0x0112; payload len=25,
value=00000000FFFFFFFF010221FF000000000000B41489D91880Fc00f000
VTP Management Domain: 'NULL'
Native VLAN: 1
Duplex: full
Power Available TLV:

    Power request id: 0, Power management id: 1, Power available: 0, Power
management level: -1
Management address(es):
  IP address: 10.100.128.9
[output cut]
```

What do we see here? We've been given the hostname and IP address of all directly connected devices. In addition to the same information displayed by the show cdp neighbors command, the show cdp neighbors detail command tells us the IOS version and IP address of the neighbor device. Nice!

Link Layer Discovery Protocol

Before moving away from CDP, I need to discuss a nonproprietary discovery protocol that provides much of the same information as CDP but works in multivendor networks.

The IEEE created a new standardized discovery protocol called 802.1AB for Station and Media Access Control Connectivity Discovery. We'll just call it the Link Layer Discovery Protocol (LLDP).

LLDP defines basic discovery capabilities, but it was also enhanced to specifically address the voice application, and this version is called LLDP- Media Endpoint Discovery (MED). LLDP and LLDP-MED are not compatible.

show ip route (route Command in Windows)

By using the command show ip route on a router, you can see the routing table (map of the internetwork) that the following router output used to make its forwarding decisions:

```
Lab_A#sh ip route
Codes: L - local, C - connected, S - static,
[output cut]
10.0.0.0/8 is variably subnetted, 6 subnets, 4 masks
C 10.0.0.0/8 is directly connected, FastEthernet0/3
L 10.0.0.1/32 is directly connected, FastEthernet0/3
C 10.10.0.0/16 is directly connected, FastEthernet0/2
L 10.10.0.1/32 is directly connected, FastEthernet0/2
C 10.10.10.0/24 is directly connected, FastEthernet0/1
L 10.10.10.1/32 is directly connected, FastEthernet0/1
S* 0.0.0.0/0 is directly connected, FastEthernet0/0
```

The C in the routing table output means that the networks listed are directly connected. Until you add a dynamic routing protocol like RIPv2, OSPF, etc. to the routers in your internetwork, or enter static routes, only directly connected networks will show up in our routing table.

show version

You can see the current value of the configuration register by using the show version command (sh version or show ver for short), as follows:

```
Router#show version
[output cut]
System returned to ROM by power-on
System image file is "flash:c2600nm-advsecurityk9-mz.151-4.M6.bin"
[output cut]
Cisco 2611 (revision 1.0) with 249656K/12266K bytes of memory.
Processor board ID FTX1049A1AB
2 FastEthernet interfaces
2 Serial(sync/async) interfaces
1 Virtual Private Network (VPN) Module
DRAM configuration is 64 bits wide with parity enabled.
239K bytes of non-volatile configuration memory.
62820K bytes of ATA CompactFlash (Read/Write)
Configuration register is 0x2102
```

Notice that the show version command provides the IOS version. In the preceding example, it shows the IOS version as 15.1(4)M6. This output also shows the RAM, NVRAM, and flash size.

The last information given from this command is the value of the configuration register. In this example, the value is 0x2102—the default setting. The configuration register setting of 0x2102 tells the router to look in NVRAM for the boot sequence.

The show version command displays system hardware configuration information, the software version, and the names of the boot images on a router.

To change the configuration register, use the config-register command from global configuration mode:

```
Router(config)#config-register 0x2142
Router(config)#do sh ver
[output cut]
Configuration register is 0x2102 (will be 0x2142 at next reload)
```

Be careful when setting the configuration register!

show inventory

The show inventory command displays a list of the specified components in the chassis. If no components are specified when you run the command, all components are listed.

This command also retrieves and displays inventory information about each Cisco product in the form of a universal device identifier (UDI). The UDI is a combination of three separate data elements: a product identifier (PID), a version identifier (VID), and the serial number (SN).

The PID is the name by which the product can be ordered; it has been historically called the *Product Name* or *Part Number*. This is the number that you would use to order a replacement part.

Here is the show inventory command run on a Cisco Firepower 1010 series device. The command provides useful information about that device, such as the number and types of ports and the serial number of the device:

```
firepower# show inventory
Name: "module 0", DESCR: "Firepower 1010 Appliance, Desktop, 8 GE, 1 MGMT"
PID: FPR-1010        , VID: V01     , SN: JMX2539X06S
```

Here is the same command on the Cisco 12008 switch. It shows the cards in each slot, their capability, and the S/N.

```
Router# show inventory
NAME: "Chassis", DESCR: "12008/GRP chassis"
PID: GSR8/40          ,  VID: V01,  SN: 63915640

NAME: "slot 0", DESCR: "GRP"
PID: GRP-B            ,  VID: V01,  SN: CAB021300R5

NAME: "slot 1", DESCR: "4 port ATM OC3 multimode"
PID: 4OC3/ATM-MM-SC   ,  VID: V01,  SN: CAB04036GT1

NAME: "slot 3", DESCR: "4 port 0C3 POS multimode"
PID: LC-4OC3/POS-MM   ,  VID: V01,  SN: CAB014900GU

NAME: "slot 5", DESCR: "1 port Gigabit Ethernet"
PID: GE-GBIC-SC-B     ,  VID: V01,  SN: CAB034251NX

NAME: "slot 7", DESCR: "GRP"
PID: GRP-B            ,  VID: V01,  SN: CAB0428AN40
```

show switch

A typical access closet contains one of more access switches placed next to each other in the same rack and uses high-speed redundant links with copper, or more typically fiber, to the distribution layer switches.

Here are three big drawbacks to a typical switch topology:

- There is an overhead of management.
- STP will block half of the uplinks.
- There is no direct communication between switches.

Cisco StackWise technology connects switches that are mounted in the same rack so that they basically become one larger switch. By doing this, you can add more access ports for each closet while avoiding the cost of upgrading to a bigger switch.

So, you're adding ports as you grow your company, instead of front-loading the investment into a pricier, larger switch all at once. And since these stacks are managed as a single unit, it reduces the management of your network.

All switches in a stack share configuration and routing information, so you can easily add or remove switches at any time without disrupting your network or affecting its performance.

The show switch command provides information about switch stacks. The following options are available with the show switch command:

```
3560-New#show switch ?
  <1-8>        Switch Number
  detail       show detailed information about the stack ring
  hstack-ports show the status of the horizontal stack ports
  neighbors    show each switch's neighbors
  stack-ports  show the status of the stack ports
  stack-ring   show stack ring
  |            Output modifiers
  <cr>
```

I ran the command on my Master switch. The following output shows the base MAC address, the priority to become Master, the version, and the state of the switch:

```
3560-New#show switch
Switch/Stack Mac Address : 4ca6.4d28.2380
                                        H/W   Current
Switch#  Role   Mac Address     Priority Version State
--------------------------------------------------------
*1       Master 4ca6.4d28.2380     1       4     Ready
```

show mac-address-table

When a frame arrives at a switch interface, the destination hardware address is compared to the forward/filter MAC database. If the destination hardware address is known and listed in the database, the frame is sent only out of the appropriate exit interface. The switch won't transmit the frame out any interface except for the destination interface, which preserves bandwidth on the other network segments. This process is called *frame filtering*.

But if the destination hardware address isn't listed in the MAC database, also known as the content addressable memory (CAM) table, then the frame will be flooded out all active interfaces except the interface it was received on. If a device answers the flooded frame, the MAC database is then updated with the device's location—its correct interface.

If a host or server sends a broadcast on the LAN, by default, the switch will flood the frame out all active ports except the source port. Remember, the switch creates smaller collision domains, but it's always still one large broadcast domain by default.

Now let's take a look at the output that results from using a show mac address-table command:

```
Switch#sh mac address-table
Vlan Mac Address Type Ports]]>
---- ----------- -------- -----
1 0005.dccb.d74b DYNAMIC Fa0/1
1 000a.f467.9e80 DYNAMIC Fa0/3
1 000a.f467.9e8b DYNAMIC Fa0/4
1 000a.f467.9e8c DYNAMIC Fa0/3
1 0010.7b7f.c2b0 DYNAMIC Fa0/3
1 0030.80dc.460b DYNAMIC Fa0/3
1 0030.9492.a5dd DYNAMIC Fa0/1
1 00d0.58ad.05f4 DYNAMIC Fa0/1
```

Let's say the preceding switch received a frame with the following MAC addresses:

Source MAC: 0005.dccb.d74b

Destination MAC: 000a.f467.9e8c

How will the switch handle this frame? The right answer is that the destination MAC address will be found in the MAC address table and the frame will be forwarded only out Fa0/3. Never forget that if the destination MAC address isn't found in the forward/filter table, the frame will be forwarded out all of the switch's ports except for the one on which it was originally received in an attempt to locate the destination device.

show interface

The command show interface x reveals the hardware address, logical address, and encapsulation method as well as statistics on collisions, as shown here:

```
Router#sh int f0/0
FastEthernet0/0 is up, line protocol is up
  Hardware is MV96340 Ethernet, address is 001a.2f55.c9e8 (bia 001a.2f55.c9e8)
  Internet address is 192.168.1.33/27
MTU 1500 bytes, BW 100000 Kbit, DLY 100 usec,
     reliability 255/255, txload 1/255, rxload 1/255
  Encapsulation ARPA, loopback not set
  Keepalive set (10 sec)
  Auto-duplex, Auto Speed, 100BaseTX/FX
  ARP type: ARPA, ARP Timeout 04:00:00
  Last input never, output 00:02:07, output hang never
  Last clearing of "show interface" counters never
  Input queue: 0/75/0/0 (size/max/drops/flushes); Total output drops: 0
  Queueing strategy: fifo
  Output queue: 0/40 (size/max)
  5 minute input rate 0 bits/sec, 0 packets/sec
  5 minute output rate 0 bits/sec, 0 packets/sec
```

The show interfaces command, plural, displays the configurable parameters and statistics of all interfaces on a router.

The preceding interface is working and looks to be in good shape. The show interfaces command will show you if you're receiving errors on the interface, and it will also show you the maximum transmission unit (MTU). MTU is the maximum packet size allowed to transmit on that interface, bandwidth (BW) is for use with routing protocols, and 255/255 means that reliability is perfect! The load is 1/255, meaning no load.

Continuing through the output, can you figure out the bandwidth of the interface? Well, other than the easy giveaway of the interface being called a "FastEthernet" interface, you can see that the bandwidth is 100,000 Kbit, which is 100,000,000. Kbit means to add three zeros, which is 100 Mbits per second, or Fast Ethernet. Gigabit would be 1,000,000 Kbits per second.

Be sure that you don't miss the output errors and collisions, which show 0 in my output. If these numbers are increasing, then you have some sort of Physical or Data Link layer issue. Check your duplex! If you have one side as half-duplex and one as full-duplex, your interface will work, albeit really slow, and those numbers will be increasing fast!

The most important statistic of the show interface command is the output of the line and Data Link protocol status.

If the output reveals that FastEthernet 0/0 is up and the line protocol is up, then the interface is up and running at layers 1 and 2:

```
Router#sh int fa0/0
FastEthernet0/0 is up, line protocol is up
```

Troubleshooting with the *show interfaces* Command

Let's take a look at the output of the show interfaces command one more time, as there are some important statistics in this output:

```
275496 packets input, 35226811 bytes, 0 no buffer
   Received 69748 broadcasts (58822 multicasts)
   0 runts, 0 giants, 0 throttles
   0 input errors, 0 CRC, 0 frame, 0 overrun, 0 ignored
   0 watchdog, 58822 multicast, 0 pause input
   0 input packets with dribble condition detected
   2392529 packets output, 337933522 bytes, 0 underruns
   0 output errors, 0 collisions, 1 interface resets
   0 babbles, 0 late collision, 0 deferred
   0 lost carrier, 0 no carrier, 0 PAUSE output
   0 output buffer failures, 0 output buffers swapped out
```

Knowing where to start when troubleshooting an interface can be difficult, but you should look right away for the number of input errors and CRCs. Typically, you would see those statistics increase with a duplex error, but it could be another Physical layer issue such as the cable might be receiving excessive interference or the network interface cards might have a failure. Typically, you can tell if it is interference when the CRC and input errors output grow but the collision counters do not.

Let's take a look at some of the output:

No Buffer   This isn't a number you want to see incrementing. This means you don't have any buffer room left for incoming packets. Any packets received once the buffers are full are discarded. You can see how many packets are dropped with the ignored output.

Ignored   If the packet buffers are full, packets will be dropped. You see this increment along with the no buffer output. Typically, if the no buffer and ignored outputs are incrementing, you have some sort of broadcast storm on your LAN. This can be caused by a bad NIC or even a bad network design.

Runts   Runts are frames that did not meet the minimum frame size requirement of 64 bytes. Typically caused by collisions.

Giants   Giants are frames received that are larger than 1,518 bytes.

Input Errors   This is the total of many counters: runts, giants, no buffer, CRC, frame, overrun, and ignored counts.

CRC   At the end of each frame is a frame check sequence (FCS) field that holds the answer to a cyclic redundancy check (CRC). If the receiving host's answer to the CRC does not match the sending host's answer, then a CRC error will occur.

Frame   This output increments when the frames received are of an illegal format or not complete. Typically, the output is incremented when a collision occurs.

Packets Output   This is the total number of packets (frames) forwarded out the interface.

Output Errors   This is the total number of packets (frames) that the switch port tried to transmit but for which some problem occurred.

Collisions   When transmitting a frame in half-duplex, the NIC listens on the receiving pair of the cable for another signal. If a signal is transmitted from another host, a collision has occurred. This output should not increment if you are running full-duplex.

Late Collisions   If all Ethernet specifications are followed during the cable installation, all collisions should occur by the 64th byte of the frame. If a collision occurs after 64 bytes, the late collisions counter increments. This counter will increment on a duplex mismatched interface.

show ip interface brief

The show ip interface brief command is probably one of the best commands that you can ever use on a Cisco router or switch. This command provides a quick overview of the device's interfaces, including the logical address and interface status at layers 1 and 2:

```
Router#sh ip int brief
Interface          IP-Address      OK? Method Status                Protocol
FastEthernet0/0    unassigned      YES unset  up                    up
FastEthernet0/1    unassigned      YES unset  up                    up
Serial0/0/0        unassigned      YES unset  up                    down
Serial0/0/1        unassigned      YES unset  administratively down down
Serial0/1/0        unassigned      YES unset  administratively down down
Serial0/2/0        unassigned      YES unset  administratively down down
```

Remember, *administratively down* means that you need to type **no shutdown** to enable the interface. Notice that Serial0/0/0 is up/down, which means that the Physical layer is good and carrier detect is sensed but no keepalives are being received from the remote end. In a nonproduction network, like the one I am working with, this tells us the clock rate hasn't been set.

Verifying with the *show ip interface* Command

The show ip interface command provides you with information regarding the layer 3 configurations of a router's interfaces:

```
Router#sh ip interface
FastEthernet0/0 is up, line protocol is up
  Internet address is 1.1.1.1/24
  Broadcast address is 255.255.255.255
  Address determined by setup command
  MTU is 1500 bytes
  Helper address is not set
```

```
 Directed broadcast forwarding is disabled
 Outgoing access list is not set
 Inbound  access list is not set
 Proxy ARP is enabled
 Security level is default
 Split horizon is enabled
[output cut]
```

The status of the interface, the IP address and mask, information on whether an access list is set on the interface, and basic IP information are all included in this output.

show arp

Using this command displays the forward filter table, also called a content-addressable memory (CAM) table. Here's the output from the S1 switch:

```
S3#sh mac address-table
Mac Address Table]]>
-----------------------------------------
Vlan Mac Address Type Ports]]>
---- ----------- -------- -----
All 0100.0ccc.cccc STATIC CPU
[output cut]
1 000e.83b2.e34b DYNAMIC Fa0/1
1 0011.1191.556f DYNAMIC Fa0/1
1 0011.3206.25cb DYNAMIC Fa0/1
1 001a.2f55.c9e8 DYNAMIC Fa0/1
1 001a.4d55.2f7e DYNAMIC Fa0/1
1 001c.575e.c891 DYNAMIC Fa0/1
1 b414.89c9.1886 DYNAMIC Fa0/5
1 b414.89c9.1887 DYNAMIC Fa0/6
```

The switches use things called base MAC addresses, which are assigned to the CPU. The first one listed is the base MAC address of the switch. From the preceding output, you can see that we have six MAC addresses dynamically assigned to Fa0/1, meaning that port Fa0/1 is connected to another switch. Ports Fa0/5 and Fa0/6 have only one MAC address assigned, and all ports are assigned to VLAN 1.

show vlan

You configure a port to belong to a VLAN by assigning a membership mode that specifies the kind of traffic the port carries plus the number of VLANs it can belong to. You can also configure each port on a switch to be in a specific VLAN (access port) by using the interface `switchport` command. You can even configure multiple ports at the same time with the `interface range` command.

In the next example, I'll configure interface Fa0/3 to VLAN 3. This is the connection from the S3 switch to the host device:

```
S3#config t
S3(config)#int fa0/3
S3(config-if)#switchport mode ?
access Set trunking mode to ACCESS unconditionally
dot1q-tunnel set trunking mode to TUNNEL unconditionally
dynamic Set trunking mode to dynamically negotiate access or trunk mode
private-vlan Set private-vlan mode
trunk Set trunking mode to TRUNK unconditionally
S3(config-if)#switchport mode access
S3(config-if)#switchport access vlan 3
S3(config-if)#switchport voice vlan 5
```

By starting with the `switchport mode access` command, you're telling the switch that this is a nontrunking layer 2 port. You can then assign a VLAN to the port with the `switchport access` command, as well as configure the same port to be a member of a different type of VLAN, called the voice VLAN.

Let's take a look at our VLANs now:

```
S3#show vlan
VLAN Name Status Ports
---- ----------------------- --------- -------------------------------
1 default active Fa0/4, Fa0/5, Fa0/6, Fa0/7
Fa0/8, Fa0/9, Fa0/10, Fa0/11,
Fa0/12, Fa0/13, Fa0/14, Fa0/19,
Fa0/20, Fa0/21, Fa0/22, Fa0/23,
Gi0/1 ,Gi0/2
2 Sales active
3 Marketing active Fa0/3
5 Voice active Fa0/3
```

Notice that port Fa0/3 is now a member of VLAN 3 and VLAN 5—two different types of VLANs. But, can you tell me where ports 1 and 2 are? And why aren't they showing up in the output of `show vlan`? That's right, because they are trunk ports!

We can also see this with the `show interfaces` *interface* `switchport` command:

```
S3#sh int fa0/3 switchport
Name: Fa0/3
Switchport: Enabled
Administrative Mode: static access
Operational Mode: static access
```

```
Administrative Trunking Encapsulation: negotiate
Negotiation of Trunking: Off
Access Mode VLAN: 3 (Marketing) Trunking Native Mode VLAN: 1 (default)
Administrative Native VLAN tagging: enabled Voice VLAN: 5 (Voice)
```

The output shows that Fa0/3 is an access port and a member of VLAN 3 (Marketing), as well as a member of the Voice VLAN 5.

That's it. Well, sort of. If you plug devices into each VLAN port, they can talk only to other devices in the same VLAN. But as soon as you learn more about trunking, we will enable inter-VLAN communication!

show power

The `show power` command displays the current power status of system components:

```
Router#show power
system power redundancy mode = combined
system power redundancy operationally = combined(2+0)
system power total = 5699.72 Watts (109.61 Amps @ 52V)
system power used = 3930.16 Watts (75.58 Amps @ 52V)
system power available = 1769.56 Watts (34.03 Amps @ 52V)
```

The `show power inline` displays PoE status for a switch or a switch stack for the specified interface or can use a `module/port number` at the end of the command for a specific stack member.

```
Switch#show power inline
Available:780.0(w) Used:0.0(w) Remaining:780.0(w)

Interface Admin Oper Power Device Class Max
(Watts)
```

Hardware Tools

In this section, we'll discuss the following:

- Toner
- Cable tester
- Taps
- Wi-Fi analyzer
- Visual fault locator

Toner/Toner Probe

A *toner probe*, also called a tone generator, is a simple copper cable tester that is simple to use and can be used to trace a wire in a wall. It is a two-piece unit that's basically a tone generator and probe, sometimes called a "fox and hound" wire tracer. This type of device consists of one part that you connect to a cable with a standard jack—or to an individual wire with alligator clips that transmit a signal over the cable or wire—and another part that's a penlike probe that emits an audible tone when it touches the other end of the cable, the wire, or even its insulating sheath.

Most often, you will use a toner probe to locate a specific connection in a punch-down block because (annoyingly) some installers run all the cables for a network to the central punch-down block without labeling them. They (or you, if you're unlucky enough) then have to use a tone generator to identify which block is connected to which wall plate and label the punch-down block accordingly. This tool can identify a particular cable at any point between the two ends, and because the probe can detect the cable containing the tone signal through its sheath, it can help you to locate one specific cable out of a massive cable-spaghetti bundle in a ceiling conduit or other type of raceway.

Just connect the tone generator to one end and touch the probe to each cable in the bundle until you hear the tone. Figure 19.8 shows a picture of my toner and the probe I use to find the tone on the other end of the cable.

FIGURE 19.8   A toner probe

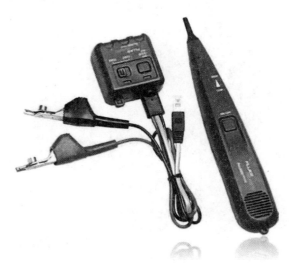

Also, by testing the continuity of individual wires using alligator clips, you can use a tone generator and probe to find opens, shorts, and miswires. An open wire won't produce a tone at the other end, a short will produce a tone on two or more wires at the other end, and an improperly connected wire will produce a tone on the wrong pin at the other end.

Sound like fun to you? Well, not so much—it takes a really long time, and it's super tedious. Worse, the whole process is almost as prone to errors as the cable installation itself. You have to either continually travel from one end of the cable to the other to move the tone generator unit or use a partner to test each connection, keeping in close contact using radios or some other means of communication to avoid confusion. So, considering the time and effort involved, investing in a wire-map tester is just a much more practical solution unless you're numbingly bored or really easily amused.

Cable Tester

The best way to deal with a faulty cable installation is to avoid the problem in the first place by purchasing high-quality components and installing them carefully. Still, this isn't a perfect world—no matter how careful you are, problems are bound to arise anyway. The tools that I'm going to cover can be used to test cables at the time of their installation and afterward, if and when you need to troubleshoot cabling problems. Cable-testing tools can range from simple, inexpensive mechanical devices to elaborate electronic testers that automatically supply you with a litany of test results in an easy-to-read pass/fail format. Figure 19.9 shows an example of an inexpensive cable tester for twisted-pair wiring testing.

FIGURE 19.9   An inexpensive cable tester

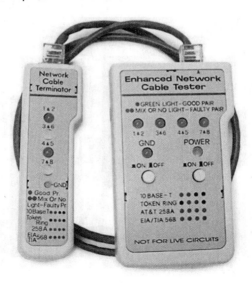

This little box can verify the connection through the cable and tell you if the cable is straight-through or crossover. It can also identify problems such as grounding issues. Sometimes the problem is not a complete lack of connectivity. Sometimes performance is slow, which can also be a cabling issue that a cable tester can identify. This tool is as cheap as they come.

Let's focus on the types of tools available for both copper and fiber-optic cable testing. This is not to say that you need all of the tools listed here. In fact, I'll try to steer you away from certain types of tools. Sometimes you'll get lucky and have the luxury of choosing between high-tech and low-tech devices that perform roughly the same function. You can choose which ones you prefer according to the requirements of your network, your operational budget, and even your temperament and time constraints. Some of the tools are extremely complicated and require extensive training to use effectively, whereas others can be used by pretty much anybody equipped with a functioning brain.

Other important considerations to keep in mind when selecting the types of tools that you need are based on the descriptions of cable tests given earlier in this chapter, the test results required by the standards you're using to certify your network, and the capabilities of the people who will be doing the actual work. And don't forget the potentially painful cost of some of them.

Taps

A tap is a network hardware device that lets you passively insert test equipment in the traffic flow between two devices. This allows you to connect a network traffic analyzer to a third port of a tap that also has two ports that are connected between the two communicating devices.

Taps can be used to monitor for intrusions and for packet captures during troubleshooting. Taps are used only for monitoring the data flow in a cable; they are receive only and cannot be used to insert frames into the stream.

Wi-Fi Analyzers

When deploying and troubleshooting wireless networks, you must have some way to determine signal levels, noise readings, SSIDs, and interference. To resolve these problems, most WI- FI analyzers can look into the air and gather valuable information so you can see what is healthy and what is not. Using Wi-Fi analyzers, you can see the Wi-Fi coverage in an area and use that information for optimal access-point placement to get complete coverage and avoid dead spots.

Many vendors now have Wi-Fi analyzers built into access points and client software running on your laptop. Wireless controllers that manage multiple access points can also act as an analyzer and gather data from many access points in your network to give you a consolidated view of coverage, interference, and signal receive levels.

Visual Fault Locator

A visual fault locator cable continuity tester can locate fiber, find faults, and verify continuity as well as polarity. These can be inexpensive and well worth the time to find and purchase one.

A visual fault locator can do all of the following, depending on the model you choose:

- Locates visual faults including tight bends, breaks, and bad connectors

- Accelerates end-to-end fiber checks

- Easily verifies polarity and identifies fibers

- Features continuous and flashing modes

Figure 19.10 shows a visual fault locator.

FIGURE 19.10 An inexpensive visual fault locator

Summary

In this chapter, you learned about many of the utilities for using and troubleshooting TCP/IP. These utilities include GUI tools like protocol analyzers, throughput testers, and connectivity software like Remote Desktop, and they include command-line utilities like `tracert`, `ping`, `arp`, `netstat`, `ipconfig`, `ifconfig`, and `nslookup`.

We discussed many of the tools that are used for troubleshooting wireless, wired copper and optical networks. The commonly used command-line tools for both the Windows and Linux operating systems were introduced, including `ping`, `ipconfig/ifconfig/ip`, `nslookup/dig`, `traceroute/tracert`, `arp`, `netstat`, `hostname`, `route`, `telnet/SSH`, `tcpdump par`, and `nmap`.

You also learned how these utilities are used, including their various options and switches and how they all affect the use of the utilities. Finally, you learned about how these utilities work within the TCP/IP suite such as NetFlow analyzers, terminal emulators, and IP network scanners.

Exam Essentials

Describe some of the GUI tools available to assist in testing and troubleshooting. These include protocol analyzers, bandwidth speed testers, and connectivity software. Understand each product's purpose and how to use it.

Know how to describe and use the troubleshooting information and statistics that `arp` and `netstat` provide for you. The `arp` utility shows whether an IP address is being resolved to your MAC address (or someone else's, in case of conflicts). The `netstat` utility produces TCP/IP statistics.

Know how to diagnose a network by using TCP/IP's troubleshooting commands. The `ping` command echoes back if a machine is alive and active on a network. The `tracert` command shows the path that the ping packets take from source to target. And `telnet` enables a user to participate in a remote text-based session.

Know what the `tracert` utility does. The `tracert` utility finds the route from your computer to any computer on a network.

Know what the `ping` utility does. The `ping` utility determines whether a particular IP host is responding.

Know what the `ftp` utility does. The `ftp` utility allows you to reliably download and upload files from and to an FTP server across the Internet.

Know what the `ipconfig` and `ifconfig` utilities do. The `ipconfig` utility displays TCP/IP configuration information for Windows NT and later operating systems. The `ifconfig` utility performs a similar function in Linux/UNIX environments, in addition to performing certain interface-configuration tasks.

Know what the `nslookup` and `dig` utilities do. The `nslookup` and `dig` utilities allow you to look up DNS resolution information.

Identify `nmap` and `tcpdump`. While `tcpdump` is a command-line packet capture utility for Linux, `nmap` is a network reconnaissance tool that can identify live hosts, open ports, and the operating systems of devices.

Describe the use of the `iptables` utility. `iptables` is a firewall utility built for the Linux operating system. It is a command-line utility that uses what are called chains to allow or disallow traffic. When traffic arrives, `iptables` looks for a rule that addresses that traffic type, and if none exists, it will enforce the default rule.

Understand what network scanners are and how to use each one.   Packet sniffers, IDS/IPS software, and port scanners are all network scanners. These devices can help you both troubleshoot and fix your network as well as find and stop hackers in their tracks.

Remember the basic purpose of a packet sniffer.   The basic purpose of packet sniffers or network analyzers is to collect and analyze each individual packet that is captured on a specific network segment to determine if problems are happening.

Written Lab

You can find the answers to the written labs in Appendix A. Write the answers to the following questions about command-line tools:

1. What command can you type from a command prompt to see the hops a packet takes to get to a destination host?

2. What tool would you use to verify a complaint about a slow network?

3. You need your IP address, subnet mask, default gateway, and DNS information. What command will you type from a Windows command prompt?

4. You need to log in as a dumb terminal to a server or UNIX host and run programs. What application will you use?

5. You need to add a route to your Windows server's routing table. What command will you use?

6. You want to log into a server and transfer files. What application will you use?

7. You need to check your name-resolution information on your host. What command will you type from the command prompt?

8. You want to use `netstat`, but you want to see only the IP address, not the names of the hosts. Which modifier will you use?

9. You want the IP configuration on a UNIX host. What command will you type at the command prompt?

10. Which Windows command will show you the routing table of your host or server?

Review Questions

You will find the answers to the review questions in Appendix B.

1. Which TCP/IP utility is most often used to test whether an IP host is up and functional?

   A. `ftp`

   B. `telnet`

   C. `ping`

   D. `netstat`

2. Which TCP/IP utility will produce the following result?

```
Interface: 199.102.30.152
Internet Address    Physical Address    Type
199.102.30.152      A0-ee-00-5b-0e-ac   dynamic
```

   A. `arp`

   B. `netstat`

   C. `tracert`

   D. `tcpdump`

3. Which Windows utility can you use to connect to a machine 50 miles away to troubleshoot?

   A. Remote Desktop

   B. `netstat`

   C. `arp`

   D. Wireshark

4. Which TCP/IP utility might produce the following output?

```
Reply from 204.153.163.2: bytes=32 time=1ms TTL=128
Reply from 204.153.163.2: bytes=32 time=1ms TTL=128
Reply from 204.153.163.2: bytes=32 time=1ms TTL=128
Reply from 204.153.163.2: bytes=32 time<10ms TTL=128
```

   A. `tracert`

   B. `ping`

   C. `arp`

   D. `ipconfig`

5. Which utility can you use to find the MAC and TCP/IP addresses of your Windows workstation?

    A. `ping`

    B. `ipconfig`

    C. `ipconfig /all`

    D. `tracert`

6. Which `ping` commands will verify that your local TCP/IP interface is working? (Choose all that apply.)

    A. `ping 204.153.163.2`

    B. `ping 127.0.0.1`

    C. `ping localif`

    D. `ping localhost`

    E. `ping iphost`

7. Which newer Linux command was added recently to configure IP and interface parameters?

    A. `netstat`

    B. `ipconfig`

    C. `ip`

    D. `ifconfig`

8. You need to find a NIC's specific MAC address and IP address. Which command-line tool can you use to find this information without physically going to the computer?

    A. `ping`

    B. `ipconfig`

    C. `arp`

    D. `netstat`

    E. `ftp`

9. Which `netstat` utility switch displays all connections and listening ports?

    A. `-a`

    B. `-f`

    C. `-p`

    D. `-t`

10. Wireshark is an example of which of the following?

    A. Throughput tester

    B. Protocol analyzer

    C. Remote connection tool

    D. IDS

11. Which utility produces output similar to the following?

```
1   110 ms   96 ms   107 ms fgo1.corpcomm.net [209.74.93.10]
2   96 ms    126 ms  95 ms someone.corpcomm.net [209.74.93.1]
3   113 ms   119 ms  112 ms Serial5-1-1.GW2.MSP1.alter.net       [157.130.100.185]
4   133 ms   123 ms  126 ms 152.ATM3-0.XR2.CHI6.ALTER.NET        [146.188.209.126]
5   176 ms   133 ms  129 ms 290.ATM2-0.TR2.CHI4.ALTER.NET      [146.188.209.10]
6   196 ms   184 ms  218 ms 106.ATM7-0.TR2.SCL1.ALTER.NET      [146.188.136.162]
7   182 ms   187 ms  187 ms 298.ATM7-0.XR2.SJC1.ALTER.NET      [146.188.146.61]
8   204 ms   176 ms  186 ms 192.ATM3-0-0.SAN-JOSE9- GW.ALTER.NET
[146.188.144.133]
9   202 ms   198 ms  212 ms atm3-0-622M.cr1.sjc.globalcenter.net [206.57.16.17]
10  209 ms   202 ms  195 ms pos3-1-155M.br4.SJC.globalcenter.net [206.132.150.98]
11  190 ms    *       191 ms pos0-0-0-155M.hr3.SNV.globalcenter.net [206.221.5.93]
12  195 ms   188 ms  188 ms pos4-1-0-    155M.hr2.SNV.globalcenter.net
[206.132.150.206]
13  198 ms   202 ms  197 ms www10.yahoo.com [204.71.200.75]
```

A. arp

B. tracert

C. tcpdump

D. netstat

12. You are the network administrator. A user calls you complaining that the performance of the intranet web server is sluggish. When you try to ping the server, it takes several seconds for the server to respond. You suspect that the problem is related to a router that is seriously overloaded. Which workstation utility could you use to find out which router is causing this problem?

A. netstat

B. tracert

C. ping

D. arp

13. Which ipconfig switch will display the most complete listing of IP configuration information for a station?

A. /all

B. /renew

C. /release

D. /?

14. Which utility will display a list of all the routers that a packet passes through on the way to an IP destination?

    A. `netstat`

    B. `tracert`

    C. `ping`

    D. `arp`

15. You are inspecting traffic to and from your workstation. When you issue the `netstat` command, you don't see any UDP entries. What could be the reason for a lack of UDP entries?

    A. UDP is connectionless.

    B. UDP is connection-based.

    C. There are no UDP ports listening.

    D. There is no UDP traffic.

16. Which `arp` command can you use to display the currently cached ARP entries?

    A. `arp`

    B. `arp -all`

    C. `arp -a`

    D. `ipconfig -arp`

    E. `arp -ipconfig`

17. Which command-line tool would best be used to verify DNS functionality in Linux?

    A. `netstat`

    B. `dig`

    C. `icmp`

    D. `arp`

18. Which of the following `arp` utility switches perform the same function? (Choose all that apply.)

    A. `-g`

    B. `-A`

    C. `-d`

    D. `-a`

19. Which of the following is *not* a chain type used by `iptables`?

    A. Forward

    B. Backward

    C. Input

    D. Output

20. Which command captures traffic on all interfaces?

    A. `tcpdump -i any`

    B. `tcpdump -i eth0`

    C. `tcpdump host 192.168.5.5`

    D. `tcpdump host all`

Chapter 20

Network Security Concepts

THE FOLLOWING COMPTIA NETWORK+ OBJECTIVES ARE COVERED IN THIS CHAPTER:

✓ **Domain 4.0 Network Security**

✓ **4.1 Explain the importance of basic network security concepts.**

- Logical security
  - Encryption
    - Data in transit
    - Data at rest
  - Certificates
    - Public key infrastructure (PKI)
    - Self-signed
  - Identity and access management (IAM)
    - Authentication
      - Multifactor authentication (MFA)
      - Single sign-on (SSO)
      - Remote Authentication Dial-in User Service (RADIUS)
      - LDAP
      - Security Assertion Markup Language (SAML)
      - Terminal Access Controller Access Control System Plus (TACACS+)
      - Time-based authentication

- Authorization
  - Least privilege
  - Role-based access control
- Risk
- Vulnerability
- Exploit
- Threat
- Confidentiality, Integrity, and Availability (CIA) triad
- Audits and regulatory compliance
  - Data locality
  - Payment Card Industry Data Security Standards (PCI DSS)
  - General Data Protection Regulation (GDPR)

An administrator's life was so much simpler in the days before every user had access to the Internet and the Internet had the ability to access organizational data. It was much simpler when an administrator only had to maintain a number of dumb terminals connected to a mainframe. If you didn't have physical access, you simply didn't have a means to access the organization's data. A lot of the headaches for the administrator have come with the inherent security risks of the data availability as networks expand. As our world—and our networks—have become more connected, the need to secure data and keep it away from the eyes of those who can do harm has increased exponentially.

Realizing this increasing risk, CompTIA added the domain of Network Security to the Network+ exam a number of years ago. Network security is now a topic in which every Network+ candidate must be proficient in order to pass the exam. A Network+ candidate must understand the basic security concepts, security concerns, and how to mitigate various security concerns.

This chapter is one of two chapters that focus primarily on security. This particular chapter will cover a myriad of security concepts that we will build upon. In this chapter, we will cover basic security terminology, and then we will explore the AAA security framework for authentication, authorizing, and auditing users.

Network+ is not the only IT certification that CompTIA offers. Security+ is one of the more popular choices. The topics found in this chapter are a subset of what you need to know for that certification.

Common Security Terminology

Security can be intimidating for the average administrator, because the advanced topics can be confusing and carry a tremendous consequence if not fully understood. An administrator could have a rude awakening if their network security is insufficient; they could even end up in the unemployment line. Fortunately, just like networking concepts, there are common security concepts that build off each other. In the following sections, I will cover some common security terminology that can help in understanding more advanced topics of security as we progress through this chapter.

Threats and Risk

A threat is a perceived danger to the organization, and a risk is the potential that the threat will come to fruition and disrupt the organization. The concept of threat and risk are two concepts that are intertwined together when talking about any potential for disruption. You can also find these terms as the basis of risk assessment for organizations, analyzing everything from simple changes in practice to major changes. When we think of threats, we tend to think of just cyberattack threats, where a bad actor uses the network to carry out an attack. However, threats can also be physical, such as weather or other environmental factors that have a potential to be disruptive to the organization.

As an oversimplified example, let's use the trip to the grocery store to set the stage in understanding threats. If we purchase groceries and place them in the car, there are all kinds of potential dangers (threats) to our groceries. We could get into an accident on the way home, they could be stolen, or our ice cream could melt. For each threat, there is a certain amount of risk. Risk is the likelihood it could or will happen. If you are a good driver, then the risk of an accident is low. If you live in a relatively safe neighborhood, then the risk that the groceries will be stolen is low. However, if it's a really hot day, there is a high risk of the ice cream melting.

Unfortunately, an organization's network is a lot more complicated than a grocery store visit. In most organizations there are two types of threats: external and internal.

External Threats

External threats are almost always carried out by an attacker with malicious intent. The definition of an external threat is that it is a threat that you cannot control. The risk or potential of these threats is usually our connection to the outside world, such as the Internet, email, and our Internet-facing servers, as well as our proactiveness in mitigating the threats. If you mitigate the external threat, then the threat is less likely to occur and the risk is lower.

Examples of external threats are denial-of-service (DoS) attacks, ransomware, and viruses, just to name a few. There are many ways of leveraging the risks associated with the aforementioned threats. For example, DoS attacks can be leveraged with firewall rules, ransomware can be leveraged with backups, and viruses can be leveraged with antimalware software. All of these leverages lower the potential risk for the perceived threats.

External threats do not need to be exclusive to security threats; they can also be the threat of availability of information. For example, say you served information from your organization, had only one connection to the Internet for the server, and the link went down. This would be an example of an external threat outside of your direct control. Mitigating the threat might be obtaining a second link to the Internet as failover. External nonsecurity threats and risks is a much broader subject and lends itself better to a discussion on risk assessment, which is outside the scope of this chapter.

Internal Threats

Internal threats, also known as threats from within or internal or insider threats, are potentially carried out by an employee. The various motivations behind attacks are monetary gain, ideology, and revenge, just to name a few. A disgruntled employee can compromise your organization's network by intentionally leaking the organization's data or intentionally running malicious code.

Internal threats can be much more dangerous than external threats because employees often know exactly how systems are configured and how to circumvent controls. However, because these threats emanate from within our organization, we can mitigate or control a lot of the potential threats. Later in this chapter, we will explore some ways to mitigate insider threats.

Unintentional Threats

An unintentional threat is a threat that is not malicious in its intent, such as a leaked password or misconfigured antimalware software. The number of unintentional threats to an organization can be expansive. As network administrators we should be focused on the threats we can directly mitigate to effectively lower our risk. For most unintentional threats we can use system policies, human resource policies, and training, or a combination to mitigate the potential threat.

Vulnerability

Vulnerabilities introduce weakness to the security of our organization. Therefore, vulnerabilities can contribute to the threats an organization could fall victim to. These weaknesses in security can be physical and network-based. An example of physical vulnerabilities are often doors that are not locked to sensitive areas where data is accessible. Network vulnerabilities are typically found in applications, operating systems, and network products.

Vulnerabilities are the reason we need to constantly patch/update applications and network operating systems. However, even with constant patching, we can never be assured that we have eliminated all vulnerabilities. Some vulnerabilities will always exist and sometimes never be known by the owners of the system or the threat actors attempting access to these systems. Patching does, however, lower our risk or potential for an attack through known vulnerabilities.

Common Vulnerabilities and Exposures

Common Vulnerabilities and Exposures (CVE) is a system that provides a reference-method for publicly known vulnerabilities and exposures. The CVE system was originally created in 1999 by a working group based upon a white paper published by David E. Mann and Steven M. Christey of the MITRE Corporation. The purpose of the CVE system is to create a common naming scheme for vulnerabilities while reducing any overlaps in documentation from varying agencies documenting the same vulnerability.

A typical CVE will look similar to this common nomenclature of CVE-2020-17084. This particular CVE details a buffer overflow in Microsoft Exchange Server that was discovered in 2020. By investigating this CVE on the Internet, you can see that regardless of who hosts the information, it pertains to the same vulnerability. For example, Microsoft references the same vulnerability the National Institute of Standards and Technology (NIST) references using this CVE number. All sources have the same relative information about the vulnerability, such as affected versions, a score that explains the associated risk, the impact, and references.

Keep in mind that the CVE is not a database. It is a numbering system for tracking vulnerabilities. The numbering and characterization of a CVE is up to the CVE Numbering Authority (can). As in the previous example, Microsoft is CNA and therefore created the initial CVE-2020-17084 document that all other CVE repositories must reference similarly. There are CNAs all around the world, and most of them are software manufacturers such as IBM, Microsoft, and VMware. However, some of the CNAs are security organizations. The underlying theme is not who creates the CVE, but that once it is created, the CVE should be consistent across all references.

EXERCISE 20.1

Identifying Vulnerabilities

This exercise will help you identify vulnerabilities of applications installed on your operating system. It is not a complete assessment of all vulnerabilities, but it will help you understand the application vulnerabilities that exist and how they can be mitigated.

1. On your operating system navigate to your installed applications list. This is typically done by opening your Settings app and clicking Installed Apps.

2. Navigate to `https://cve.mitre.org` and select Search CVE List.

3. Start researching each application by submitting a search for each application.

4. Review each CVE result and compare the affected version to the installed version.

5. Research how to mitigate the security vulnerability.

You will find that not every vulnerability is patchable by upgrading to the latest software. You will also find that the steps to mitigate the vulnerability are often found on the software publisher's site. The CVE is simply to let you know that there is a security concern.

Many different antimalware software packages will scan your computer for malware, and as an added benefit, they will also identify vulnerable software installed. Typically, these antimalware software packages are tailored for the end user and do not detail the CVEs associated with each product. You will find that more complex systems for the organization, such as the Microsoft 365 E5/A5 Security add-on, will report to the administrator vulnerabilities across the entire organization. The administrator can then plan to mitigate vulnerabilities and threats across the entire organization. You can read more about the Microsoft product at `https://learn.microsoft.com/en-us/microsoft-365/security/defender-vulnerability-management/defender-vulnerability-management?view=o365-worldwide`.

Zero-Day

Typically, all publicly known vulnerabilities usually have either a workaround or a patch, and at the very least they are known vulnerabilities. However, some vulnerabilities are discovered before a patch or workaround can be made available. These vulnerabilities are known as zero-day vulnerabilities, and they carry high risk because there is no way to defend from an attack. Sometimes, you might not even be made aware that a vulnerability even exists!

A zero-day vulnerability doesn't mean that the attack is imminent; some zero-day vulnerabilities are remediated the very next day. However, it does mean that until a patch or workaround is devised, you are vulnerable.

The term *zero-day* can be applied to both a vulnerability and an exploit. A zero-day vulnerability means that a weakness is known before the vendor has time to acknowledge a workaround or patch. A zero-day exploit is much more serious, since there is an automated method created to exploit a weakness not yet documented. You may come across the term *zero-day* used in either of these two contexts.

Exploit

A vulnerability is a weakness in security, as you have learned. An exploit is a method that acts on a weakness (vulnerability). I will use a luggage lock as an example, mainly because they are notoriously weak security solutions. A simple paper clip bent appropriately could be used to exploit the weakness and open the lock. It would be nice if all problems were as simple as getting a better lock, but networks are complicated systems that can have many complex vulnerabilities, as well as known exploits.

When we talk about exploits, we generally refer to scripts, software, or sequences of commands that exploit a known vulnerability. The CVE published against a vulnerability can be used to patch or block the exploit, but it all depends on the vulnerability. Just like zero-day vulnerabilities, where there is a weakness that is not documented yet, there exists zero-day exploits, in which an attack is carried out without understanding the vulnerability it is carried out upon.

The Stuxnet malware was used to sabotage Iranian centrifuges in a nuclear facility in 2010. The Stuxnet malware exploited a vulnerability that existed in the Microsoft Print Spooler service. The malware infected computers and altered programmable logic controllers (PLCs) code that ran the centrifuges. No one knew of the vulnerability or the crafted exploit until after the attack was launched, and a significant amount of equipment was damaged. This vulnerability is about the most famous zero-day vulnerability to date, mainly because it was never disclosed and remained in the wild until it was found. More information can be found on Stuxnet at https://spectrum.ieee.org/the-real-story-of-stuxnet.

Confidentiality, Integrity, and Availability

One of the most important and basic security concepts is the CIA triad, shown in Figure 20.1. Although the Central Intelligence Agency (CIA) has the same acronym as the CIA triad, the two have nothing to do with each other, other than that the CIA organization adheres to the CIA triad for its own information security, but I digress.

FIGURE 20.1   The CIA triad

The CIA triad stands for confidentiality, integrity, and availability, and these concepts apply to the information security and the storage of information. It defines how we protect the confidentiality, integrity, and availability of information for an organization.

Confidentiality   The confidentiality of information focuses on limiting access to only the individuals allowed to access the information while denying access for those individuals who are restricted from accessing the information. Confidentiality can be achieved with physical locks (such as locked doors), file cabinets, safes, and, in extreme cases, security guards. Confidentiality can also be achieved electronically with authentication, encryption, and firewalls. Essentially, you need to decide how secure the information needs to be, and that will dictate the level and method of protecting the data's confidentiality.

Integrity   The integrity of information focuses on its accuracy and how susceptible it is to being altered by an unauthorized individual. Integrity of data must be protected both at rest and in transit. The integrity of data at rest can be protected with file hashes to detect unauthorized altering of the data. Unauthorized altering of information can also be prevented with the use of access control lists (ACLs). The integrity of data in transit can be protected with the use of digital signatures and checksums, such as the use of the Authentication Header (AH) protocol. This ensures that the data is not altered as it is being transmitted across the network.

Availability   The availability of the information pertains to the uptime of the systems serving the information. The availability of the data can be heightened by using redundant systems or redundant components to create highly available information systems. Information can also be backed up, which also raises the availability of the information because you are creating a point-in-time snapshot of the data. The restoration of information must be considered from two perspectives: the point in time from which you can restore the data and the time it takes to restore the data to that point.

When designing systems that will store and serve data, all three of these concepts must be applied to support the security of the information. Confidentiality alone cannot ensure that data is not taken offline or altered. The integrity alone cannot ensure that the information is not accessed by an unauthorized individual or taken offline. Finally, if the information is taken offline, the data is definitely secure and can't be tampered with, but it is useless to the authorized users because it is unavailable. Therefore, it is the combination of all three of these concepts that must be equally applied to the information.

Encryption

In an effort to maintain confidentiality and integrity, data encryption should be employed. Data encryption ensures that data loss to an unauthorized user will not occur. Although the term data loss might be construed as the actual loss of data in the form of availability, the term actually means that you have lost control of the data. Without encryption, a threat actor can obtain a copy of the data, the data could be sent unintentionally to an unauthorized user, or it could be modified in an unauthorized manner.

Consider an example of a laptop with sensitive patient record information stored on it. If the laptop were to be stolen, the threat actor could use a number of utilities that could provide unauthorized access to the patient records. However, with encryption (such as BitLocker) enabled, both the operating system and the data would remain encrypted and inaccessible to unauthorized users.

There are three concepts associated with data encryption: data in transit, data at rest, and data in use, as shown in Figure 20.2.

FIGURE 20.2   Data and encryption

Data in Transit   Encryption of data in transit refers to information traversing the network and should always be encrypted so that it is not intercepted. Over the past decade, just about every website and application has adopted some form of encryption, so there is no reason not to use encryption in transit.

Data at Rest   Data at rest refers to data that is written out to disk. This concept is a point of contention, because it is believed that once the data hits the server, it's safe. However, the data is more vulnerable because it's in one spot. If a drive needed to be replaced because it went bad, outside of physical destruction, there is no way to assure the data is inaccessible. When backup tapes are used, it is not only a good idea but should be a requirement.

Data in Use   Encryption of data in use refers to data that is in an inconsistent state, and or currently resident in memory. Most of the time, you don't need to be too concerned with data in memory, since that is normally a function of the operating system. However, when data is written to virtual memory such as the pagefile or swap file, it is considered data in use, and therefore it could be intercepted.

The use of encryption is not just a good idea; in a lot of information sectors, the use of encryption is a regulatory requirement. Most regulatory requirements only define that data must be transmitted and stored with strong encryption. Data in use encryption is not typically defined, simply because network administrators use off-the-shelf products like Windows, Linux, and SQL, just to name a few. These products typically adhere to standards that make them secure for data that resides in memory. However, some regulatory requirements might require you to crank the security down (so to speak) on the operating system or application. One such regulatory requirement is the Federal Information Processing Standard (FIPS), but there are many others.

When securing information with encryption, there are two basic methods that will encrypt the information: symmetrical encryption and asymmetrical encryption. Figure 20.3 shows a side-by-side comparison of the two types of encryption methods.

FIGURE 20.3   Symmetrical and asymmetrical encryption

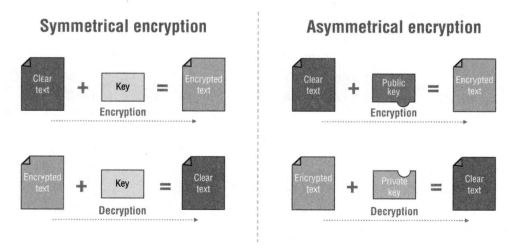

Symmetrical

Symmetrical encryption operates by using the same key to encrypt the information, as is used to decrypt the information. Symmetrical encryption is the oldest type of encryption used, dating thousands of years ago. It is still useful today for securing various types of information that require a shared key. One of the issues with symmetrical encryption is it uses a shared key to encrypt and decrypt data. If the key is stolen or leaked, then the data can easily be decrypted by a threat actor. Since the same key used to encrypt the data is required to decrypt the data, the likelihood of the key being leaked is high.

Asymmetrical

Asymmetrical encryption operates by using a different key to encrypt the data, as is used to decrypt the data. These two keys are called the public and private keys, and they are created using a complex mathematical algorithm called Rivest-Shamir-Adleman (RSA), named after the original creators of the algorithm. The RSA algorithm creates two large prime numbers that can be factored to the same number. These two large prime numbers are called the key pair, one being the public key and the other being the private key. This explanation of the RSA process is oversimplified, and the actual algorithm is very complex, but we need only a surface understanding for day-to-day use, as well as for the exam.

Certificates

The common use of certificates became popular in the mid-1990s, at around the time the Internet became a household word. Certificate services were created for two main purposes: to encrypt/decrypt entities and to digitally verify entities. Keep in mind that in the 1990s when the Internet became mainstream, there was a tremendous drive for Internet commerce, and this drove the need for certificate services. Today certificate services are an integral part of the Internet, our daily lives, and the world's commerce.

Certificate services were taken for granted by the public, but in June 2013, all of that changed with an ex-government employee named Edward Snowden. Edward Snowden released reports that the government was actively listening to Internet conversations for years. This report validated why privacy and the use of encryption were important for the average person. After the report was released, nobody made a transaction or visited a website without checking for the lock symbol in the address bar. Today, in modern web browsers, encryption is assumed, and if the page isn't encrypted, the browser will alert you. Google Chrome even actively blocks any element that is not encrypted, such as a picture, audio, or video, just to name a few.

Certificates are typically used for securing data transfers to and from the web browsers for the security of day-to-day operations. We use our web browsers for accessing sensitive information at work, doing our personal banking, accessing social media, and the list goes on. So, securing data in transit is a primary concern to manage the risk of eavesdropping from threat agents. The Hypertext Transfer Protocol over Secure Sockets Layer (SSL), also known as HTTPS, is a method for securing web data communications. SSL is a cryptographic suite of protocols that use public key infrastructure (PKI) to provide secure data transfer.

> Although the S in HTTPS stands for secure, SSL is the protocol suite used for securing communications. The SSL suite is a suite of protocols that includes the current standard of Transport Layer Security (TLS) 1.3. TLS 1.3 is used for securing websites, as of this writing.

Public Key Infrastructure

Public key infrastructure (PKI), also referred to as certificate services, supports many different operations, such as securing websites, client authentication, and code signing, just to name a few. PKI operates on two key concepts of mutual trust and encryption. The concepts seem simple, but don't let that fool you; there are a lot of different configurations for PKI, and it can get complex quickly. Thankfully, we just need to understand the basics, and once you have the basics, your knowledge can be expanded to more advanced configurations.

Before we start to learn how PKI works, let's learn some terminology that we can build from:

Certificate Authority (CA)   The certificate authority is responsible for enrolling the clients and issuing the key pairs. In addition, the CA stores the public key and serves it to anyone who requests the public key.

Authority Information Access (AIA)   The location of the public keys is stored in the Authority Information Access (AIA). The AIA typically defines a path to a file share, or URL to access the public keys.

Enrollment Policy   The enrollment policy contains the requirements the client must fulfill to enroll and obtain a key pair. The enrollment policy might require specific credentials, a monetary fee, or even manual verification, just to name a few. The enrollment process will depend on the organization's needs. Windows allows for auto-enrollment of clients based upon Windows group membership. A digital notary might require a physical verification that you are the person receiving the certificate.

Key Pair   The public and private key pair provides asymmetrical encryption for PKI. After issuance, the client will receive the private key of the key pair. The private key is stored safely in the client's private key store. The public key of the key pair is stored in the public key store located on the CA for everyone to access. The AIA defines the location where the public key can be attained. By default, the certificate authority will never store the client's private key.

Root CA   This CA is the root of all trust for the PKI model being deployed. Both the client and the device using the key pair for encryption of signing must mutually trust the root CA. The root CA servers can be found in the Certificate MMC on Windows under Trusted Root Certification Authorities. Every operating system will have a similar method for trusting the root CA servers.

Issuing CA   The CA that issues the key pair is the issuing CA. Each issuing CA can be set up with different enrollment policies, to issue a specific type of key pair. For example, some issuing CAs can be set up to only issue key pairs for people, while others can be set up to issue key pairs for computers, or even code signing, just to name a few. For the certificate to be accepted, the issuing CA must be trusted by the client or entity using the certificate.

Certificate Revocation List (CRL)   The CRL is a list of certificates (key pairs) that have been revoked for various reasons. Typically, the trusting party will download the CRL and compare the certificate in question against the list before trusting the certificate. However, this behavior can be optional depending on the use of the certificate.

Expiration Date   Each certificate has an expiration date, and from time to time, certificates expire, so they must constantly be renewed or they will not be valid after the expiration.

Now that we have a better understanding of the terminology associated with public key infrastructure, let's review the two basic ways a key pair can be used for encryption and validating the sender message, also known as signing.

Encryption   In Figure 20.4, the sender needs to send an encrypted document to the receiver. We will assume the receiver already fulfilled the enrollment policy requirements, was subsequently enrolled by the issuing CA, and received its private key. The sender will retrieve the receiver's public key from the public key store located on the CA, via the AIA. The sender will then encrypt the document with the receiver's public key and transmit it to the receiver. When the receiver obtains the encrypted document, the receiver's private key will be used to decrypt the document.

FIGURE 20.4   Encryption with PKI

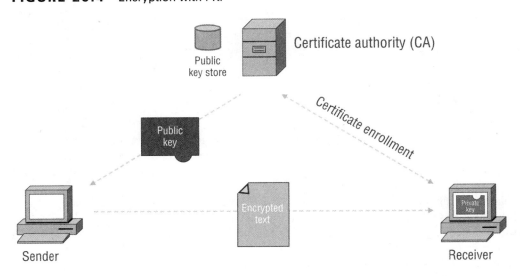

Signing   In Figure 20.5, the sender needs to sign a document to assure the sender's identity for the receiver, as well as integrity of the document. If the document is altered in the process of transfer, the signature will be invalidated. Again, we will assume the sender (in this case) already fulfilled the enrollment policy requirements, was subsequently enrolled by the issuing CA, and received its private key. The sender will use its private key located in the key store to encrypt the document and send it to the receiver. When the receiver obtains the document, it will be decrypted with the sender's public key obtained from the public key store via the AIA. Because only the sender's public key can decrypt the document encrypted by the sender's private key, the document is considered irrefutable.

FIGURE 20.5   Singing with PKI

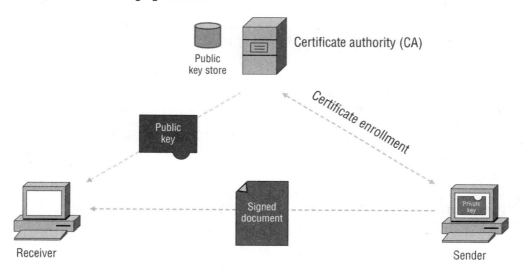

Public vs. Private CA

It is often misunderstood that all public key infrastructure implementations require a third-party vendor, such as GoDaddy, DigiCert, or GlobalSign, to name a few, to issue a certificate. This is untrue; you can implement a private CA to save costs and have great flexibility.

Public vendors are a great option, if you need the root trust pre-established in the browser or application. When you purchase a certificate from one of the big vendors, you can be guaranteed that their root trust is in 99.9% of all web browsers and operating systems. In fact, the list of trusted root certificate authorities must be updated now and then. The Microsoft Windows platform does this with routine Windows Updates, but browsers may update their own list with updates of their own. When creating a public web server, using a public vendor is a requirement for both compatibility and ease of use.

Private CAs are an option if you plan to establish root trust, prior to using the certificates. The root trust can be created via Group Policy Object (GPO), Microsoft Intune, or preinstalling the root certificate, to name a few. When you use a private CA, you have the most control and flexibility, but all the work is on you to keep everything up-to-date. Using a private CA is the best option if using a public vendor is too costly.

Self-Signed

One of the key concepts to PKI is mutual trust. The parties participating in PKI must mutually trust the root CA. In public settings, we can use public vendors, and in corporate environments, we can use private CAs. However, sometimes we just need an individual device to perform some cryptographic function, such as the web page for an appliance or your local computer's encryption of files, to name a few. For these instances, self-signed certificates are an option.

A self-signed certificate is a certificate that is issued to and issued by the same entity. For example, if the firewall you are working on requires encryption of the web interface, it will require a certificate. You can install a self-signed certificate issued to the firewall by the firewall. Using a self-signed certificate negates the need to create a PKI infrastructure for one or two devices. It does, however, mean that you will need to explicitly trust the issuer by placing the self-signed certificate in your Trusted Root Certification Authorities certificate store.

EXERCISE 20.2

Examining Self-Signed Certificates

This exercise will help you understand how self-signed certificates are used by the Windows operating system.

1. Open the Start menu, enter **mmc.exe**, and select Run As Administrator.

2. Select Yes in the User Account Control dialog box.

3. Select File ➤ Add/Remove Snap-In.

4. Find and select Certificates on the Ad Or Remove Snap-ins dialog box, and then click Add.

5. Select My User Account from the option in the Certificates Snap-In dialog box, and then click Finish.

6. Click OK in the Add Or Remove Snap-ins dialog box.

7. Open the chevron next to Certificates - Current User ➤ Personal ➤ Certificates in the navigation pane.

8. Examine the certificates issued in the results pane of the Microsoft Management Console (MMC).

You will find any certificates issued to your account in the results pane. Don't worry if you don't see any certificates issued. If you do have certificates issued, look for the existence of the certificate with the Intended Purpose of Encrypting File System. If you find the cert, skip to step 13.

9. Minimize the MMC application.

10. Create a new text file on the Desktop and then right-click it and select Properties.

11. Click Advance in the properties dialog box, check the box Encrypt Contents To Secure Data, click OK, and then click OK again in the Properties dialog box.

12. Maximize the MMC application and refresh the results pane.

13. Double-click the certificate with the Intended Purpose of Encrypting File System.

14. Examine the Issue To, Issue By, and Validity From fields.

The Windows Encrypting File System (EFS) system uses a self-signed certificate to protect the encryption key used to encrypt files. When you encrypt your first file, a self-signed certificate is created on your behalf. Do not delete this certificate or you will lose access to your decryption key, and subsequently you will not be able to decrypt your files.

AAA Model

The majority of an administrator's day-to-day job is managing users and managing and monitoring access to resources. These day-to-day tasks can be summarized with the AAA model. The AAA model is a security framework that defines the administration of authentication, authorization, and accounting. You will find the AAA model referenced when configuring network switches, routers, or RADIUS servers, just to name a few. The AAA model is referenced anywhere you need to authenticate users, authorize access, and account for the authorized or unauthorized access. In the following sections, you will learn the basic concepts of the AAA model.

Authentication

When a user wants to access a resource, they must first prove their identity with the act of *authentication* that states they are who they say they are. As shown in Figure 20.6, a user provides their authentication credentials to the identity store where the credentials are validated. A user can provide authentication credentials using several different factors. The most common authentication factors are something you know (passwords), something you have (smartcard), and something you are (biometrics). Besides the various factors of authentication, there are several protocols that can be used to transmit credentials or aid in the authentication of a user. In the following sections, I will cover in detail all of the various protocols as well as the various factors of authentication that can be used to authenticate a user or computer.

FIGURE 20.6 Authentication components

Multifactor Authentication

All authentication is based on something that you know, have, are, or do, or your location. A common factor of authentication is a password, but passwords can be guessed, stolen, or cracked. No one factor is secure by itself, because by themselves they can be compromised easily. A fingerprint can be lifted with tape, a key can be stolen, or a location can be spoofed.

Multifactor authentication (MFA) helps solve the problem of a compromised single-factor authentication method by combining the authentication methods. With multifactor authentication, a single factor will no longer authenticate a user; two or more of the factors discussed in this section are required for authentication. This makes the credentials of the user more complex to compromise.

One of the most common examples where MFA is used in everyday life is at an ATM. To withdraw money, a user must provide a card (one factor) and a PIN (a second factor). If you know the PIN but do not have the card, you cannot get money from the machine. If you have the card but do not have the PIN, you cannot get money from the machine.

In this section we will cover the most common two-factor (2FA)/ MFA methods used by protected applications. The following methods are generally used in conjunction with a traditional user and password combination. It should be assumed that when we talk about 2FA, it provides the same functionality as MFA. MFA just has more than two factors of authentication. For the rest of this section, we will use the term MFA.

Something You Know   Computing has used the factor of something a person knows since computer security began. This is commonly in the form of a username and password. We can make passwords more complex by requiring uppercase, lowercase, numeric, and symbol combinations. We can also mandate the length of passwords and the frequency in which they are changed. However, the username/password combination is among the most common type of credential to be stolen because they can be phished or sniffed with a keylogger.

Something You Have   Authentication based on something a person has relates to physical security. When we use a key fob, RFID tag, or magnetic card to enter a building, we are using something we have. An identification badge is something we have, although technically it is also something we are if it has a picture of us on it. Credit cards have long since been something we have to authenticate a transaction. Within the past two decades, it has also become the most stolen credentials. Recently, credit cards have implemented a new authentication method called Europay, MasterCard, and Visa (EMV). EMV will make it harder to steal and duplicate cards. However, if a card is lost, it can still be used by an unscrupulous person because it is something you physically have.

Something You Are   A decade or so ago, authenticating a user based on something they are was science fiction. We now have biometric readers built into our phones for our convenience! All we need to do is place our finger on the reader, speak into the phone, or allow the phone to recognize our face and we are instantly logged in. Computers can be outfitted with fingerprint readers to allow logon of users based on their fingerprint as well. When this technology entered the market, there were various ways to get around it, such as tape-lifting a print, playing back someone's voice, or displaying a picture of a person for the camera. These systems have gotten better since they have entered the market by storing more points of the fingerprint, listening to other aspects of a user's voice, and looking for natural motion in the camera.

Somewhere You Are   A relatively new factor of authentication is based on somewhere you are. With the proliferation of Global Positioning System (GPS) chips, your current location can authenticate you for a system. This is performed by creating authentication rules on the location. GPS sensors are not the only method of obtaining your current location. Geographic IP information queried from Geo-IP services can also be used for the authentication process. We can restrict login to a specific IP or geographic location based on the IP address provided.

Something You Do   Another relatively new factor of authentication for network systems is based on something you do. Although it has been used for hundreds of years for documents and contracts, a signature is something you do, and you don't even think about how you do it. It is unique to you and only you because there is a specific way you sign your name. Typing your name into the computer is something you do and don't think about, but there is a slight hesitation that you make without knowing it. Algorithms pick up on this and use the keystrokes as a form of authentication. Arguably, it can be considered biometrics because it is something your brain does without you consciously thinking about it.

Multifactor Authentication Methods

Now that you understand the various factors of authentication, let's examine the various methods to employ MFA. Depending on the application, you may see any number of these methods being used for MFA. In the example shown in Figure 20.7, the MFA method can be replaced with any of the following methods to provide MFA for the application.

FIGURE 20.7   Authentication methods

Email   Some applications will use email as an MFA method. However, using email as an MFA option is probably the least secure method. This is mainly because people reuse passwords. For example, if your banking website username and password is compromised (something you know) and you reuse the same credentials on email, it provides no protection. As the threat actor will quickly log into your email and use it as a factor of authentication. Ideally the email account is protected with MFA in a way that it requires something you have.

Email is useful as a notification method when someone logs into a secure login. However, keep in mind the threat agents know this as well. If your email account is compromised, a threat agent will often create a rule in your email box to dump these notifications directly to the trash. They have also been known to create forwarding rules to redirect communications directly to their own disposable email account.

Short Message Service   Some applications will allow the use of short message service (SMS) text messages as the MFA method. When this method is used, a simple text message is sent to the user's phone number. The message will contain a random 5-to-8-digit code that the user will use to satisfy the MFA requirement. When you first set up this MFA method, the protected application will request the code before turning on MFA. This is done to verify that the phone number is correct and that you can receive text messages, before the security is applied to your account.

Voice Call   Some applications that are protected by MFA will allow voice calls to be initiated to the end user. This is usually done if the person does not have a phone that accepts text messages. The voice call will recite a five- to eight-digit code that the user will use to satisfy the MFA requirement. This process is similar to SMS, with the difference being it is an automated voice call.

Time-Based Hardware and Software Tokens   *Time-based hardware tokens* are devices that enable the user to generate a one-time password (OTP) to authenticate their identity. SecurID from RSA is one of the best-known examples of a physical hardware token, as shown in Figure 20.8.

FIGURE 20.8   An RSA security key fob

Time-based hardware tokens operate by rotating a code every 60 seconds. The token typically uses the time-based one-time password (TOTP) or HMAC-based one-time password (HOTP) algorithm to calculate the rotating code. This rotating code is combined with a user's PIN or password for authentication. A time-based hardware token is considered multifactor authentication because it is something you have (hardware token) along with something you know, such as your PIN or password.

A new type of time-based hardware token is becoming the new standard, and it can be considered a time-based software token or soft token. It operates the same as a hardware token, but it is an application on your cell phone that provides the code. Google Authenticator is one example of these types of applications. Microsoft also has an authenticator application similar to Google Authenticator.

When configuring MFA on an application, you have two ways of adding an account to the authenticator application. You can take a picture of a quick response (QR) code, or you can enter a security code into the authenticator application. If you choose to use a QR code, then the application turning the MFA on will present a QR code that can be scanned by the authenticator application. If you choose to use a setup key, the application turning on the MFA will provide a key. There is generally a second step before the application is protected by MFA, where you will be required to enter a code from the authenticator application to the protected application. A lengthy one-time-use backup key is also generated, in case you need to turn MFA off in the event your device is lost or stolen.

Single Sign-On

One of the big problems larger networks must deal with is the need for users to access multiple systems or applications. This may require users to remember multiple accounts and passwords. An alternative to this is that the application must support Active Directory authentication, but that creates other considerations.

Single sign-on is a great benefit to cloud applications and can help aid in implementing *zero-trust* model. The zero-trust model is a security strategy that assumes that no one or nothing can be trusted to access the resource. The resource will require authentication each time it is accessed, to provide the greatest level of security. With typical authentication, this would require the user to log in repeatedly. Single sign-on helps by allowing the user to pass a token (cookie) each time the user accesses the resource; this process is totally unbeknownst to the user.

Single sign-on (SSO) is an aspect of authentication and not a protocol. SSO assists the user log on by allowing the user to authenticate to the first application and then reusing the credentials for other applications. This way, the user no longer has to enter the same username and password for each application they access. Single sign-on is often used with cloud-based resources.

The principle behind SSO is that the resource, also known as the service provider, will trust that the user has already been authenticated by the authentication server, also known as the identity provider (IdP). The IdP will send a claim on behalf of the user, as shown in Figure 20.9. This claim can contain any number of Active Directory user attributes, such as first name, last name, email, and username. It is important to understand that at no time during the authentication process are the username and password sent to the service provider that is requesting authentication. The service provider must trust that the user has already been authenticated and accept the claim at face value.

FIGURE 20.9   Claims-based authentication

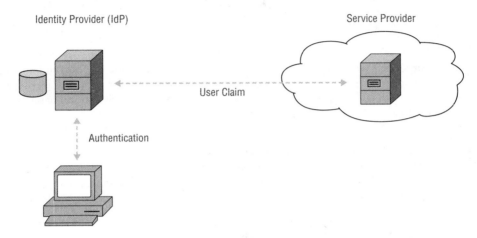

The *Security Assertion Markup Language (SAML)* protocol is used to initially authenticate the user to the IdP and authenticate the user to the service provider. The SAML protocol is based on Extensible Markup Language (XML) and provides a universal method for obtaining the claims for the user. The SAML protocol also supports signing and encryption of claims so that the claims being passed can be trusted as originating from the IdP.

Setting up SSO with SAML can be challenging because you must coordinate the accepted claims sent by your IdP, and the claims must match the service provider's expectations. Other settings such as the mutual use of signing certificates and encryption must match as well. Some of the best deployments of SSO happen when both the IdP admin (typically you) and the service provider admin can get on a conference call to set up, test, and adjust settings. If you do your homework up front, you are guaranteed to get everything up and running within about 15 minutes, as opposed to days or weeks without proper communication and feedback from the service provider.

Remote Authentication Dial-In User Service

Remote Authentication Dial-In User Service (RADIUS) was originally proposed as an Internet Engineering Task Force (IETF) standard. It has become a widely adopted industry standard for authenticating users and computers for network systems. RADIUS creates a common authentication system, which allows for centralized authentication and accounting.

The origins of RADIUS are from the original Internet service provider (ISP) dial-up days, as its acronym describes. Today, RADIUS is commonly used for authentication of virtual private networks (VPNs), wireless systems, and any network system that requires a common authentication system. RADIUS operates as a client-server protocol. The RADIUS server controls authentication, authorization, and accounting (AAA). The RADIUS client can be wireless access points, a VPN, or wired switches.

The RADIUS client will communicate with the RADIUS server via UDP port 1812 for authentication and UDP port 1813 for accounting. RADIUS is synonymous with the AAA security framework, since it provides authentication, authorization, and accounting for users and computers.

Authentication The main purpose of the RADIUS server is to provide centralized authentication of users or computers. This can be performed by means of username and password, or authentication can be extended with MFA. We can even authorize computers based upon their attributes, such as their MAC address. All of these authentication methods are dependent on the RADIUS installation.

Authorization Authorization of a user on a computer to allow a connection to a resource, is based upon the attributes returned after successful authorization. The returned attributes can be used by the authenticating application to configure the user account or computer with a VLAN, configure a connection type, or even enforce restrictions, just to name a few.

Accounting Accounting is performed by recording each transaction to the data store configured with the RADIUS server. The key takeaway is that the RADIUS server accepts the RADIUS accounting packet and then stores the data.

The RADIUS server can be installed on many different operating systems, such as Linux and Windows. Microsoft Windows Server includes an installable feature, called the Network Policy Server (NPS), that provides RADIUS functionality. The authentication of users and computers is based upon Active Directory. The authorization is based upon the settings in the NPS. The accounting is directed to a logfile in the file system, but an account can also be configured for a Microsoft SQL database.

Terminal Access Controller Access Control System Plus

The *Terminal Access Controller Access-Control System Plus (TACACS+)* protocol is also an AAA method and an alternative to RADIUS. Like RADIUS, it is capable of performing authentication on behalf of multiple wireless APs, RRAS servers, or even LAN switches that are 802.1X capable. Based on its name, you would think it's an extension of the TACACS protocol (and in some ways it is), but the two definitely are not compatible.

Here are two major differences between TACACS+ and RADIUS:

- RADIUS combines user authentication and authorization into one profile, but TACACS+ separates the two.

- TACACS+ utilizes the connection-based TCP port 49, but RADIUS uses UDP instead.

Even though both are commonly used today, because of these two reasons TACACS+ is considered more stable and secure than RADIUS.

Figure 20.10 shows how TACACS+ works.

FIGURE 20.10   TACACS+ login and logout sequence

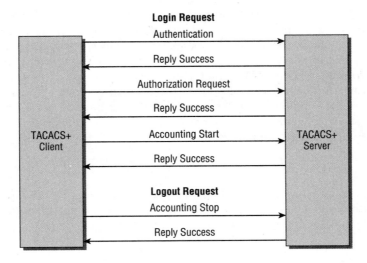

When a TACACS+ session is closed, the information in the following list is logged, or accounted for. This isn't a complete list; it's just meant to give you an idea of the type of accounting information TACACS+ gathers:

- Connection start time and stop time
- The number of bytes sent and received by the user
- The number of packets sent and received by the user
- The reason for the disconnection

LDAP

Lightweight Directory Access Protocol (LDAP) is an open standard directory service protocol originally defined by the IETF. LDAP is based on the earlier standard of X.500 that uses Directory Access Protocol (DAP), but LDAP is more efficient and requires less code; therefore, it is considered lightweight in its implementation.

LDAP operates as a client-server protocol used for looking up objects in a directory service and their respective attributes. LDAP was adopted by Microsoft for Active Directory (AD) lookups of objects on domain controllers. It was released with Windows 2000 Server to compete with Novell Directory Services (NDS). Active Directory is a highly scalable directory service that can contain many different objects, including users, computers, and printers, just to name a few.

Today, LDAP is an integral part of Active Directory for quick lookups of objects. It is also important to understand the components of Active Directory. Active Directory itself is *not* the authentication mechanism; Active Directory is only the directory for storing objects. LDAP assists in the lookup of objects stored inside of Active Directory. Kerberos is the authentication mechanism that is used with Active Directory to actually authenticate the user or computer, as well as its subsequent authentication to other servers and services.

An LDAP client queries requests to an LDAP server with a specifically formatted uniform resource identifier (URI). The URI will contain the object to search for and the attributes to be retrieved. In addition, filters can be supplied so that only specific objects are searched. LDAP uses a default protocol and port of TCP/389. When SSL is used with LDAP called LDAPS, the protocol and port of TCP/636 is used.

The following LDAP query will query an LDAP data store for the object with a user ID of `rick.sanchez` and return the `givenName`, `sn`, and canonical name, `cn`, attributes. The directory searched will be `contoso.com` located on the LDAP server (DC) of `dc1.contoso.com` listening on port 389.

```
ldap://dc1.contoso.com:389/dc=contoso,dc=com?givenName,sn,cn? (uid=rick
.sanchez)
```

As you can see, forming your own LDAP query is intimidating, and searching for a user in a directory such as AD is simpler with a right-click. However, it is important to understand what happens under the covers (so to speak).

> Typically, when configuring LDAP as an authentication method, you will be working with Microsoft Active Directory. Other operating systems can be configured with LDAP, but Microsoft is the dominant consumer of the technology.

Authorization

In this section, we'll discuss how authorization is needed when using the following:

- Identity and Access Management
- Least Privilege
- Role-Based Access Control
- Geofencing

Identity and Access Management

Identity and access management (IAM) is a security framework used for the authentication and authorization of users. The IAM model has been adopted by service providers as a means of managing users with their application. The IAM framework allows a service provider to define the authentication of users by means of a username and password, certificate key pair , or even SSO, just to name a few methods.

The framework also defines the authorization of user access for a resource within the service provider. Many service providers have adopted a model of security in which the object and accompanying permission is defined. This allows a granular control of what can be accessed by the user and what can be done with the service or object by the user. For example, if a database is created on a service provider, the specific database can be security so that a particular user has access only to read objects within the database. However, administrators might have a higher level of permissions to alter information.

Least Privilege

The principle of least privilege is a common security concept that states a user should be restricted to the least amount of privileges that they need to do their job. By leveraging the principle of least privilege, you can limit internal and external threats. For example, if a front-line worker has administrative access on their computer, they have the ability to circumvent security; this is an example of an internal threat. Along the same lines, if a worker has administrative access on their computer and received a malicious email, a bad actor could now have administrative access to the computer; this is an example of an external threat. Therefore, only the required permissions to perform their tasks should be granted to users, thus providing least privilege.

Security is not the only benefit to following the principle of least privilege, although it does reduce your surface area of attack because users have less access to sensitive data that can be leaked. When you limit workers to the least privilege they need on their computer or the network, fewer intentional or accidental misconfigurations will happen that can lead to downtime or help-desk calls. Some regulatory standards require following the principle of least privilege. By following the principle of least privilege, an organization can improve upon compliance audits by regulatory bodies.

Role-Based Access Control

As administrators, we are accustomed to file-based access controls and the granularity that accompany these access control models. However, with today's emerging cloud-based systems, we often do not need the granularity of individual permissions. Role-based access control (RBAC) helps remove the complex granularity by creating roles for users who accumulate specific rights. The user is then given a role or multiple roles in which specific rights have been established for the resource, as shown in Figure 20.11.

FIGURE 20.11   Role-based access

As an example, Microsoft Teams has roles for a Teams meeting. You can be an attendee, presenter, or organizer. The attendee can attend a Teams meeting and share their video and audio feed. The presenter can do that plus they can share a presentation, mute participants, and perform several other presentation key functions. The organizer can do everything the presenter can do plus they can create breakout rooms and view attendance. By changing someone's role in the meeting, from attendee to presenter, for example, we can allow them to share a document with the meeting's other attendees. If we had to find the specific permission to allow that person to perform the function, it would take a lot longer and would be prone to error.

Role-based access doesn't stop with just cloud-based applications. We can use role-based access controls in our day-to-day operations by standardizing permissions based upon specific roles in our organization. When a marketing person is hired, the standardized role of marketing can be applied. This can be performed with Active Directory groups and the permission groups we include.

Geofencing

Geofencing is the process of defining the area in which an operation can be performed by using GPS or radio frequency identification (RFID) to define a geographic boundary. An example of usage involves a location-aware device of a location-based service (LBS) user entering or exiting a geofence. This activity could trigger an alert to the device's user as well as messaging to the geofence operator.

Accounting

Accounting is the last A in the AAA model, and after learning about authentication and authorization, this section is where we can see it all together. Ironically, let's use the analogy of a transaction in a physical bank. In Figure 20.12, the customer (user) appears on the far left, and their money (resource) is shown on the far right. As an example, I will use the analogy of a bank transaction in which a customer will withdraw money.

FIGURE 20.12   AAA bank analogy

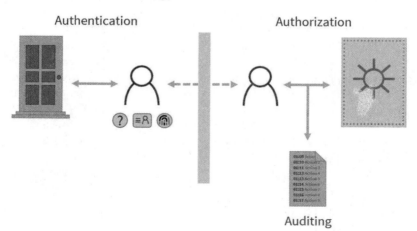

A customer (user) will provide their *authentication* via their account number (something they know) and identification (something they are). The bank teller can then authenticate that they are the person they say they are.

Once the teller has authenticated the customer (user), *authorization* will be checked. With the analogy of a bank, authorization might be how much money is in your bank account. However, a better example is who in the bank is allowed to enter the vault and touch the money! I'm sure even if my bank authenticates me, they won't authorize me to count and withdraw my own money. I'm pretty sure that if I tried, I would go to jail and not collect my $200. The teller is authorized to touch the money and hand it to you. It is important to note that, in this example, the teller is also authenticated when they come into work, though this authentication process is less rigorous than your authentication process.

Now that you have been authenticated and authorized to receive your money, an audit trail is created. If you had $400 and withdrew $200, your account would be debited $200. The audit trail in this example is the *accounting* process of the AAA system. Accounting allows us to trust, but audit.

In a network system, when a user logs on, they will commonly authenticate with a username and password. When the user tries to access the resource, their authorization to the resource will be checked. If they are authorized to access the resource, the accounting of access will be recorded. It is important to note that accounting can record denied access to a resource as well.

Although the analogy of a bank has to deal with money and the word *accounting* is synonymous with money, the word *accounting* in the IT world has nothing to do with money. Accounting in the IT world has to do with the audit trail that users and computers leave when they authenticate and access information. The only time the accounting feature has anything to do with money is if your service provider is charging you based on the amount of time you've spent logged in or for the amount of data sent and received.

Regulatory Compliance

Regulations are rules imposed on your organization by an outside agency, like a certifying board or a government entity, and they're usually totally rigid and immutable. The list of possible regulations that your organization could be subjected to is so exhaustively long, there's no way I can include them all in this book. Different regulations exist for different types of organizations, depending on whether they're corporate, nonprofit, scientific, educational, legal, governmental, and so on, and they also vary by where the organization is located.

For instance, US governmental regulations vary by county and state, federal regulations are piled on top of those, and many other countries have multiple regulatory bodies as well. The Sarbanes-Oxley Act of 2002 (SOX) is an example of a regulation system imposed on all publicly traded companies in the United States. Its main goal was to ensure corporate responsibility and sound accounting practices, and although that may not sound like it would have much of an effect on your IT department, it does because a lot of the provisions in this act target the retention and protection of data. Believe me, something as innocent sounding as deleting old emails could get you in trouble—if any of them could've remotely had a material impact on the organization's financial disclosures, deleting them could actually be breaking the law. So, be aware, and be careful!

One of the most commonly applied regulations is the ISO/IEC 27002 standard for information security, previously known as ISO 17799, renamed in 2007 and updated in 2013. It was developed by the International Organization for Standardization (ISO) and the International Electrotechnical Commission (IEC), and it is based on British Standard (BS) 7799-1:1999.

The official title of ISO/IEC 27002 is *Information technology - Security techniques - Code of practice for information security controls*. Although it's beyond our scope to get into the details of this standard, know that the following items are among the topics it covers:

- Risk assessment
- Security policy
- Organization of information security
- Asset management
- Human-resources security
- Physical and environmental security
- Communications and operations management
- Access control
- Information systems acquisition, development, and maintenance
- Information security incident management
- Business-continuity management
- Compliance

The following are various regulations you may encounter while working in the IT field. They are in no way a complete list of regulations, just the most common.

Data Locality   With the adoption of cloud computing by private and government entities, it has created new challenges for collecting, processing, and storing information about citizens or residents. Data locality, also known as data localization laws, requires data of a citizen to be collected, processed, and stored within the same country, before being transferred to other countries. This ensures that local laws for privacy can be applied to the information of the country's citizens. In certain situations, specific data about a citizen might even need to be removed from the data set before it can be transferred. Once these requirements are met, then the governed data can be moved outside of the country.

Family Educational Rights and Privacy Act   The *Family Educational Rights and Privacy Act (FERPA)* affects education providers and organizations that process student records. FERPA regulates the handling of student records, such as grades, report cards, and disciplinary records. It was created to protect the rights of both students and parents for educational privacy. The Department of Education enforces FERPA compliance.

Gramm–Leach–Bliley Act   The *Gramm–Leach–Bliley Act (GLBA)* affects providers of financial services. GLBA requires financial institutions that offer products and services, such as loans, investment advice, or insurance, to safeguard customer information and detail the practices for sharing consumer information. It was created to protect consumer information and avoid the loss of consumer information. The Federal Trade Commission (FTC) enforces GLBA compliance.

General Data Protection Regulation   The *General Data Protection Regulation (GDPR)* is a European Union (EU) law governing how consumer data can be used and protected. The GDPR was created primarily to protect citizens of the European Union. It applies to anyone involved in the processing of data based upon the citizens of the European Union, regardless of where the organization is located.

The GDPR recommends that organizations hire a *data protection officer (DPO)*. This person is the point of contact for all compliance for GDPR, as well as any other compliances your organization fall under. The underlying goal is to achieve consent from the end user of your product or service. Consent to collect information must be proven by an organization beyond a shadow of doubt. This means that if someone visits your website from the European Union, you must receive consent in clear language to even place a cookie in their web browser. The DPO is responsible for coordinating this language, as well as the life cycle of any data that is collected.

Health Insurance Portability and Accountability Act   The *Health Insurance Portability and Accountability Act (HIPAA)* affects healthcare providers and providers that process health records. It regulates how a patient's information is secured and processed during the patient's care. HIPAA regulations are imposed on healthcare providers to ensure patient privacy. The Department of Health & Human Services (HHS) enforces HIPAA compliance.

Payment Card Industry Data Security Standards   Payment Card Industry Data Security Standards (PCI DSS) is a standard of processes and procedures used to handle data related to transactions using payment cards. A *payment card* is any card that allows the transfer of money for goods or services. Types of payment cards include credit cards, debit cards, or even store gift cards.

PCI DSS compliance is not enforced by government entities. PCI DSS compliance is actually enforced by banks and creditors. Merchants must comply with the PCI DSS standard to maintain payment card services. If a merchant does not comply with PCI DSS standards and a breach occurs, the merchant can be fined by the banks. Once a breach of PCI data occurs, then local, state, and federal laws can apply to the merchant. For example, some laws require the merchant to pay for credit-monitoring services for victims after a breach.

Sarbanes–Oxley Act   The *Sarbanes–Oxley Act (SOX)* affects publicly traded companies. It regulates how companies maintain financial records and how they protect sensitive financial data. The Securities and Exchange Commission (SEC) enforces SOX compliance.

Policies, Processes, and Procedures

Your organization must comply with the various regulations, or you could risk fines or, in some cases, even jail time. Your organization can comply with regulations by creating internal policies. These policies will have a major influence on processes and ultimately procedures that your business unit in the organization will need to follow, as shown in Figure 20.13. So, to answer the question of why you need to follow a procedure, it's often the result of regulations imposed on your organization.

FIGURE 20.13 Regulations, compliance, and policies

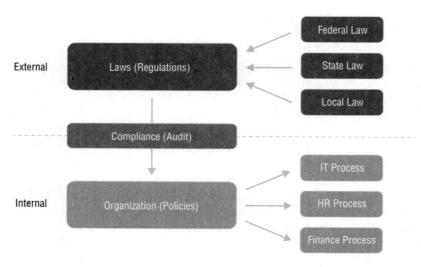

The overall execution of policies, processes, and procedures when driven by regulations is known as compliance. Ensuring compliance to regulations is often the responsibility of the compliance officer in the organization. This person is responsible for reading the regulations (laws) and interpreting how they affect the organization and business units in the organization. The compliance officer will then work with the business unit directors to create a policy to internally enforce these regulations so that an organization is compliant.

Once the policy is created, the process can then be defined or modified. A process consists of numerous procedures or direct instructions for employees to follow. Figure 20.14 shows a typical policy for disposing of hazardous waste.

The process of decommissioning network equipment might be one of the processes affected by the policy. Procedures are steps within a process, and these, too, are affected (indirectly) by the policy. As the example shows, a regulation might have been created that affects the handling of hazardous waste. To adhere to compliance, a hazardous waste policy was created. The process of decommissioning equipment was affected by the policy. As a result, the procedures (steps) to decommission equipment have been affected as well.

FIGURE 20.14 Policy for disposing of hazardous waste

Audit

You can internally ensure that your organization adheres to regulatory compliance, by creating policies, processes, and procedures based around the regulations imposed on your organization. However, over time, policies, processes, and procedures mature and change to fit the environment and business requirements. Therefore, periodically we must ensure that these changes in policies, processes, and procedures keep our organization in a state of compliance with the imposed regulations.

An audit process is typically created so that an organization can verify they still comply with regulations. Internal audits are typically performed by the managers of each department, since they know their policies, processes, and procedures best. The compliance officer will oversee the audit and will generate a report stating the compliance of the organization. These internal audits can be ongoing, quarterly, bi-annually, or annual, depending on the requirements and consequences of the regulations. It really all comes down to time versus money in the end.

Audits can also be performed externally by a group of auditors. An external audit is performed for several reasons, but it is typically required by the regulation that you must comply with. Audits that require organizations to comply with financial regulations often require external audits. Some regulations might even require a different group of auditors each year; this prevents complacency or collusion. The frequency of external audits is typically annually, but again it depends on the regulations your organization must comply with.

Where compliance is not a concern, security is always a concern, and we should apply the mantra of trust, but audit. As an administrator you should continually audit your logs for suspicious or irregular activity.

Summary

In this chapter, you learned the basic concepts, terms, and principles that all network professionals should understand to secure an enterprise network. We covered concepts such as the CIA triad, internal and external threats, and how vulnerabilities can be classified using the CVE database.

You then learned about the two common encryption methods used to protect information. We then focused on how encryption can be used with public key infrastructure (PKI) to protect documents for integrity and confidentiality. You learned a few ways to deploy PKI for public and private infrastructure, as well as self-signed certificates that do not require any infrastructure.

We then focused on the AAA security model and covered the various authentication factors. You also learned that including more than one method for authentication can strengthen security and is called multifactor authentication (MFA). We then focused on technologies that authorize user access. Lastly, you learned how accounting could be used to review user access.

Finally, you learned about the various regulatory compliances that various organizations must adhere to be compliant. You learned that policies, processes, and procedures are created to assure compliance. Audits can be performed to ensure compliance, over a period of time, so an organization stays compliant.

Exam Essentials

Know the CIA triad and how it applies to information security. The CIA triad consists of the three concepts of confidentiality, integrity, and availability. Confidentiality defines how data is secured. Integrity defines how data is protected from unauthorized altering. Availability defines how data in systems is kept available to users and outages are avoided.

Understand the various security concepts. A threat can be internal or external to your organization. A threat is the opportunity for a security event. Risk is the potential that a threat can occur. A vulnerability is a weakness in security. The Common, Vulnerabilities, and Exposures (CVE) is a standardized cataloging system for vulnerabilities across all vendors. Exploits are code or techniques that can be carried out upon a vulnerability.

Know the two basic types of encryptions. Symmetric encryption uses the same key as used to decrypt the information. Asymmetrical encryption uses a key pair: One key is used to encrypt, and the other is used to decrypt.

Understand how PKI is used to protect information. PKI uses asymmetrical key encryption to protect information by signing documents for integrity. PKI can also be used to encrypt documents for the purpose of confidentiality.

Identify common authentication methods. These include multifactor methods, Terminal Access Controller Access-Control System Plus (TACACS+), single sign-on (SSO), Remote Authentication Dial-In User Service (RADIUS), and LDAP.

Understand the various authorization concepts. Identity and access management (IAM) is a security framework. The principle of least privilege defines that an employee is given only the access required to perform their duties. Role-based access is the technique of combining privileges together for common roles in an organization.

Written Lab

You can find the answers to the written labs in Appendix A. Fill in in the blank with the term that best fits the statement.

1. A _____ is a perceived danger to an organization.

2. _____ is the term used to describe the potential damage to occur.

3. _____ encryption uses the same key to encrypt, as to decrypt.

4. PKI uses _____ encryption to sign and encrypt information.

5. _____ uses claims to authenticate a user to a service provider.

6. _____ certificates require no initial setup of PKI infrastructure.

7. The concept of only giving permissions to perform a function is considered the principle of _____ _____.

8. _____ is a security framework adopted by service providers to secure resources.

9. Windows Active Directory uses the _____ protocol to provide queries for objects.

10. _____ is a European Union (EU) law governing how consumer data can be used and protected.

Review Questions

You can find the answers to the review questions in Appendix B.

1. Which element of the CIA triad ensures that information can always be accessed?

   A. Accessibility

   B. Integrity

   C. Confidentiality

   D. Availability

2. You are implementing an encryption key for backups to tape. Which encryption concept is being exercised?

   A. Data in use

   B. Data in transit

   C. Data at rest

   D. Data on tape

3. Which of the following is not an external threat?

   A. Ransomware via a threat actor

   B. Denial of service

   C. Virus via an unknown USB drive

   D. Exploitation of a web server

4. The system used to create a common naming scheme for vulnerabilities is called?

   A. CVE

   B. Zero day

   C. IAM

   D. MFA

5. Which security concept dictates that a user be given only the permission to perform their job?

   A. Zero trust

   B. Role-based access

   C. Least privilege

   D. Defense in depth

6. Which principle describes the process of verification of a user's identity?

   A. Authentication

   B. Authorization

   C. Accounting

   D. Auditing

7. Which authentication system is an open standard originally proposed by the Internet Engineering Task Force (IETF)?

    A. RADIUS

    B. TACACS+

    C. Kerberos

    D. LDAP

8. Which protocol is used with single sign-on (SSO) to exchange credentials in the form of a claim?

    A. LDAP

    B. SAML

    C. AD

    D. Kerberos

9. Which principle describes the process of verifying a user's permissions?

    A. Authentication

    B. Authorization

    C. Accounting

    D. Auditing

10. What protocol and port number does LDAP use for directory lookups?

    A. TCP/389

    B. TCP/1812

    C. UDP/389

    D. UDP/1812

11. Which option accurately describes an exploit?

    A. A known weakness in the operating system

    B. A configuration that weakens the security of the operating system

    C. A known operating system security flaw

    D. A technique used to gain unauthorized access

12. Which of the following occurs when a threat agent takes advantage of a weakness and uses it to advance an attack?

    A. Threat

    B. Risk

    C. Vulnerability

    D. Exploit

13. You are seeing a large number of packets for UDP port 1813 on the network. What is this traffic likely to be for?

   A. RADIUS authentication

   B. RADIUS accounting

   C. TACACS+ authentication

   D. LDAP queries

14. You receive an SSL error when you visit a network appliance that has a self-signed certificate in use. What can you do to fix the issue?

   A. Add the network appliance public certificate to the root CA CRL.

   B. Add the network appliance public certificate to the root CA AIA.

   C. Add the network appliance public certificate to the trusted root CA certificate store.

   D. Add the network appliance private certificate to the trusted root CA certificate store.

15. Which factor of authentication requires you to present something that is unique to you and can't be copied?

   A. Password

   B. Signature

   C. Fingerprint

   D. Location

16. Which European law protects consumers?

   A. SOX

   B. HIPAA

   C. GLBA

   D. GDPR

17. You are asked to secure records and prevent them from being viewed off-site. Which authorization method would prevent someone from viewing records off-site?

   A. Least privilege

   B. Geofencing

   C. RBAC

   D. IAM

18. Which PKI element is used to check to see if a certificate has been revoked?

   A. CRL

   B. Root CA

   C. AIA

   D. Private key

19. You are designing a security strategy for a cloud-based application. You want to make it simple for other administrators to grant permissions without complexity. Which security strategy should you implement?

    A. TACACS+

    B. PKI

    C. RBAC

    D. RADIUS

20. Which protocol uses public/private keys for encryption?

    A. AIA

    B. TLS

    C. CRL

    D. IAM

Chapter 21

Common Types of Attacks

THE FOLLOWING COMPTIA NETWORK+ EXAM OBJECTIVES ARE COVERED IN THIS CHAPTER:

✓ **Domain 4.0 Network Security**

✓ **4.1 Explain the importance of basic network security concepts.**

- Physical security
  - Camera
  - Locks
- Deception technologies
  - Honeypot
  - Honeynet
- Network segmentation enforcement
  - Internet of Things (IoT) and Industrial Internet of Things (IIoT)
  - Supervisory control and data acquisition (SCADA), industrial control System (ICS), operational technology (OT)
  - Guest
  - Bring your own device (BYOD)

✓ **4.2 Summarize various types of attacks and their impact to the network.**

- Denial-of-service (DoS)/distributed denial-of-service (DDoS)
- VLAN hopping
- Media Access Control (MAC)

- Flooding
- Address Resolution Protocol
- (ARP) poisoning
- ARP spoofing
- DNS poisoning
- DNS spoofing
- Rogue devices and services
  - DHCP
  - AP
- Evil twin
- On-path attack
- Social engineering
  - Phishing
  - Dumpster diving
  - Shoulder surfing
  - Tailgating
- Malware

✓ **4.3 Given a scenario, apply network security features, defense techniques, and solutions.**

- Device hardening
  - Disable unused ports and services
  - Change default passwords
- Network access control (NAC)
  - Port security
  - 802.1X
  - MAC filtering
- Key management

- Security rules
  - Access control list (ACL)
  - Uniform Resource Locator (URL) filtering
  - Content filtering
- Zones
  - Trusted vs. untrusted
  - Screened subnet

It's true. . .you're not paranoid if they really are out to get you. Although "they" probably aren't after you personally, your network—no matter the size—is seriously vulnerable, so it's wise to be very concerned about keeping it secure. Unfortunately, it's also true that no matter how secure you think your network is, it's a good bet that there are still some very real threats out there that could breach its security and totally cripple your infrastructure!

I'm not trying to scare you; it's just that networks, by their very nature, are not secure environments. Think about it—the whole point of having a network is to make resources available to people who aren't at the same physical location as the network's resources.

Because of this, it follows that you've got to open access to those resources to users you may not be able to identify. One network administrator I know referred to a server running a much-maligned network operating system as "a perfectly secure server until you install the NIC." You can see the dilemma here, right?

With all this doom and gloom, what's a network administrator to do? Well, the first line of defense is to know about the types of threats out there because you can't do anything to protect yourself from something you don't know about. But once you understand the threats, you can begin to design defenses to combat bad guys lurking in the depths of cyberspace just waiting for an opportunity to strike.

I'm going to introduce you to some of the more common security threats and teach you about the ways to mitigate them. I'll be honest—the information I'll be giving you in this chapter is definitely not exhaustive. Securing computers and networks is a huge task, and there are hundreds of books on this subject alone. To operate securely in a network environment, one must understand how to speak the language of security. As in any field, there is specific terminology.

In this chapter, you will learn the common types of attacks that all network professionals should understand to secure an enterprise network.

To find Todd Lammle CompTIA videos and practice questions, please see www.lammle.com.

Technology-Based Attacks

All attacks upon an organization are either technology-based or physically-based. A technology-based attack is one in which the network and operating systems are used against the organization in a negative way. Physical attacks use human interaction or physical access, which I will cover later. I will now cover several different types of technology-based attacks that are commonly used against networks and organizations.

Denial of Service/Distributed Denial of Service

A *denial of service (DoS)* is an attack launched to disrupt the service or services a company receives or provides via the Internet. A DoS attack is executed with an extremely large number of false requests, resulting in the servers not being able to fulfill valid requests for clients and employees. As shown in Figure 21.1, a bad actor sends many false requests for information to a server. Then when the valid requests are sent to the server, the resources, such as memory and CPU, are exhausted, and the server cannot fulfill the valid requests. There are several different types of DoS attacks.

FIGURE 21.1   Typical DoS attack

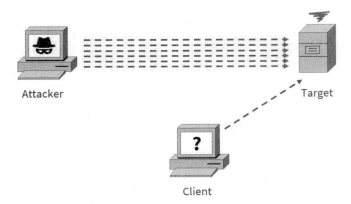

Reflective   A reflective DoS attack is not a direct attack; it requires a third party that will inadvertently execute the attack. The attacker will send a request to a third-party server and forge the source address of the packet with the victim's IP address. When the third party responds, it responds to the victim. There are two victims in this type of DoS attack; the first is the victim the attack is aimed at, and the second is the third-party server used to carry out the attack, as shown in Figure 21.2.

FIGURE 21.2   Typical reflective attack

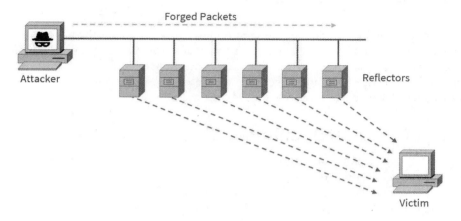

Amplified   An amplified DoS attack is a variant of a reflective DoS attack. It is carried out by making a small request to the third-party server that yields a larger response to the victim. The most common third-party servers used to carry out this type of attack are DNS and NTP. For example, an attacker will request a DNS query for a single hostname that contains 20 aliases while forging the source IP address. The victim is then barraged with the 20 answers from the query, as shown in Figure 21.3.

FIGURE 21.3   Typical amplified attack

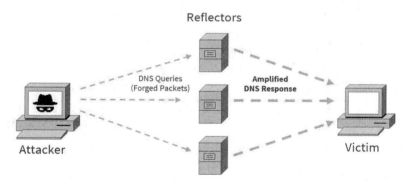

Distributed   A *distributed denial of service (DDoS)* has become the most common type of DoS, because the source of the DoS is varied. A DDoS employs many bots to create a botnet. A botnet is a series of compromised servers or hosts that are under a bad actor's control. It is common for botnets to launch DDoS attacks on organizations. When a single host is used to create a DoS, it can simply be blocked. However, when traffic is coming from millions of different hosts, it is impossible to isolate the DoS and firewall the source. A bad actor will leverage a key server called a command-and-control server to deliver commands to each bot in the botnet, as shown in Figure 21.4. The command-and-control server is often a compromised server as well; it just happens to be where the bad actor has set up shop (so to speak).

FIGURE 21.4   Components of a DDoS attack

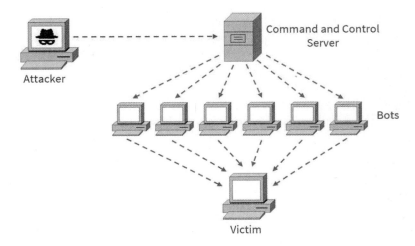

Friendly/Unintentional DoS

An unintentional DoS attack (also referred to as attack from "friendly fire") is not one that is not caused by malicious individuals; instead, it's a spike in activity to a website or resource that overpowers its ability to respond. In many cases, it is the result of a relatively unknown URL suddenly being shared in a larger medium such as a popular TV or news show.

Physical DoS

Physical DoS attacks are those that cause hardware damage to a device. These attacks can be mitigated, but not eliminated, by preventing physical access to the device. Routers, switches, firewalls, servers, and other infrastructure devices should be locked away and protected by strong access controls. Otherwise, you may be confronted with a permanent DoS, covered in the next section.

Permanent DoS

A permanent DoS attack is one in which the device is damaged and must be replaced. It requires physical access to the device, or does it? Actually, it doesn't! An attack called a phlashing denial of service (PDoS) attacks the firmware located in many systems. Using tools that fuzz (introduce errors) the firmware, attackers cause the device to be unusable. Another approach is to introduce a firmware image containing a Trojan or other type of malware.

On-Path Attack (Previously Known as Man-in-the-Middle Attack)

Many of the attacks we're discussing can be used in conjunction with an on-path attack, which was previously known as a *man-in-the-middle (MitM)* attack. For example, the evil twin attack, discussed later, allows the attacker to position themselves between the compromised user and the destination server. The attacker can then eavesdrop on a conversation and possibly change information contained in the conversation. Conventional on-path attacks allow the attacker to impersonate both parties involved in a network conversation. This allows the attacker to eavesdrop and manipulate the conversation without either party knowing. The attacker can then relay requests to the server as the originating host attempts to communicate on the intended path, as shown in Figure 21.5.

FIGURE 21.5   On-path attack

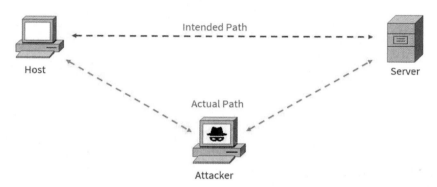

DNS Poisoning/Spoofing

DNS clients send requests for name to IP address resolution (called queries) to a DNS server. The search for the IP address that goes with a computer or domain name usually starts with a local DNS server that is not authoritative for the DNS domain in which the requested computer or website resides. When this occurs, the local DNS server makes a request of the DNS server that does hold the record in question. After the local DNS server receives the answer, it returns it to the local DNS client. After this, the local DNS server maintains that record in its DNS cache for a period called the time to live (TTL), which is usually an hour but can vary.

In a DNS cache poisoning attack, the attacker attempts to refresh or update that record when it expires with a different address than the correct address. If the attacker can convince the DNS server to accept this refresh, the local DNS server will then respond to client requests for that computer with the address inserted by the attacker. Typically, the address they now receive is for a fake website that appears to look in every way like the site the client is requesting. The hacker can then harvest all the name and password combinations entered on his fake site.

The DNS servers should be limited in the updates they accept to prevent this type of attack. In most DNS software, you can restrict the DNS servers from which a server will accept updates. This can help prevent the server from accepting these false updates.

DNS spoofing is slightly different than DNS poisoning. DNS spoofing, also called DNS cache poisoning, is an attack created by manipulating DNS records to redirect users toward a fraudulent, malicious website that looks like the destination host or web page.

VLAN Hopping

VLANs, or virtual LANs, are layer 2 subdivisions of the ports in a single switch. A VLAN may also span multiple switches. When devices are segregated into VLANs, access control lists can be used in a router to control access between VLANs in the same way it is done between real LANs. When VLANs span switches, the connection between the switches is called a trunk link, and it carries the traffic of multiple VLANs. Trunk links are also used for the connection from the switch to the router.

A VLAN hopping attack results in traffic from one VLAN being sent to the wrong VLAN (see Figure 21.6). Normally, this is prevented by the trunking protocol placing a VLAN tag in the packet to identify the VLAN to which the traffic belongs. The attacker can circumvent this by a process called double tagging, which is placing a fake VLAN tag into the packet along with the real tag. When the frame goes through multiple switches, the real tag is taken off by the first switch, leaving the fake tag. When the frame reaches the second switch, the fake tag is read and the frame is sent to the VLAN to which the hacker intended the frame to go. This process typically occurs to launch an attack on the native VLAN.

FIGURE 21.6   VLAN hopping

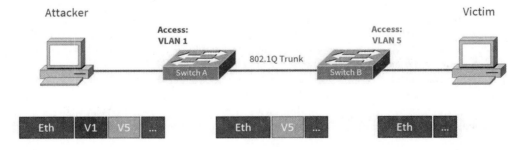

ARP Spoofing/Poisoning

ARP spoofing is the process of adopting another system's MAC address for the purpose of receiving data meant for that system. It usually also entails ARP cache poisoning. ARP cache poisoning is usually a part of an on-path/man-in-the middle attack. The ARP cache contains IP address to MAC address mappings that a device has learned through the ARP process.

One of the ways this cache can be poisoned is by pinging a device with a spoofed IP address. In this way, an attacker can force the victim to insert an incorrect IP address to MAC address mapping into its ARP cache. If the attacker can accomplish this with two computers having a conversation, they can effectively be placed in the middle of the transmission. After the ARP cache is poisoned on both machines, they will be sending data packets to the attacker, all the while thinking they are sending them to the other member of the conversation.

Rogue Devices and Services

Rogue devices and services consist of any physical device or logical services that are not commissioned by the organization. These devices and services are typically malicious in intent, but they can also be triggered by an employee plugging in a device. This introduction of a rogue device can consequently have the potential for distruption. The following are some of the most common rogue devices and services you may encounter.

Rogue DHCP

Dynamic Host Configuration Protocol (DHCP) is used to automate the process of assigning IP configurations to hosts. When configured properly, it reduces administrative overload, reduces the human error inherent in manual assignment, and enhances device mobility. But it introduces a vulnerability that when leveraged by a malicious individual can result in an inability of hosts to communicate (constituting a DoS attack) and peer-to-peer attacks.

When an illegitimate DHCP server (called a rogue DHCP server) is introduced to the network, unsuspecting hosts may accept DHCP Offer packets from the illegitimate DHCP server rather than the legitimate DHCP server. When this occurs, not only will the rogue DHCP server issue the host an incorrect IP address, subnet mask, and default gateway address (which makes a peer-to-peer attack possible), but it can also issue an incorrect DNS server address, which will lead to the host relying on the attacker's DNS server for the IP addresses of websites (such as those resembling major banks' websites) that lead to phishing attacks. Figure 21.7 shows an example of the effect of a Rogue DHCP server.

In Figure 21.7, after receiving an incorrect IP address, subnet mask, and default gateway from the rogue DHCP server, the DHCP client unwittingly uses the attacker as the gateway. The attacker can then launch an on-path attack without the client ever knowing what happened.

Rogue Access Point

Rogue access points (APs) are APs that have been connected to your wired infrastructure without your knowledge. The rogue may have been placed there by a determined hacker who snuck into your facility and put it in an out-of-the-way location or, more innocently, by an employee who just wants wireless access and doesn't get just how dangerous doing this is. Either way, it's just like placing an open Ethernet port out in the parking lot with a sign that says "Corporate LAN access here—no password required!"

FIGURE 21.7   Effects of a rogue DHCP

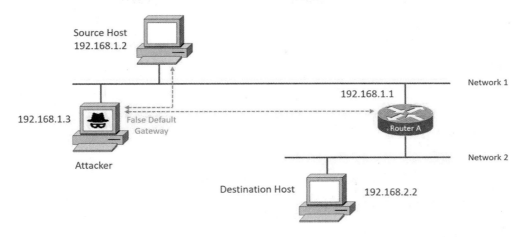

Clearly, the worst type of rogue AP is the one some hacker has cleverly slipped into your network. It's particularly nasty because the bad guy probably didn't do it to simply gain access to your network. Nope—the hacker likely did it to entice your wireless clients to disastrously associate with their rogue AP instead! This ugly trick is achieved by placing their AP on a different channel from your legitimate APs and then setting its SSID in accordance with your SSID. Wireless clients identify the network by the SSID, not the MAC address of the AP or the IP address of the AP, so jamming the channel that your AP is on will cause your stations to roam to the bad guy's AP instead. With the proper DHCP software installed on the AP, the hacker can issue the client an address, and once that's been done, the bad guy has basically "kidnapped" your client over to their network and can freely perform a peer-to-peer attack. Believe it or not, this can all be achieved from a laptop while Mr. Hacker simply sits in your parking lot, because there are many types of AP software that will run on a laptop—yikes!

Evil Twin

An evil twin is an AP that is not under your control but is used to perform a hijacking attack. A hijacking attack is one in which the hacker connects one or more of your users' computers to their network for the purpose of a peer-to-peer attack.

The attack begins with the introduction of an access point that is under the hacker's control. This access point will be set to use the same network name or SSID your network uses, and it will be set to require no authentication (creating what is called an open network).

Moreover, this access point will be set to use a different channel than the access point under your control.

To understand how the attack works, you must understand how wireless stations (laptops, tablets, and so on) choose an access point with which to connect. It is done by SSID and not by channel. The hacker will "jam" the channel on which your access point is transmitting. When a station gets disconnected from an access point, it scans the area for another access point with the same SSID. The stations will find the hacker's access point and will connect to it, as shown in Figure 21.8.

FIGURE 21.8   An evil twin attack

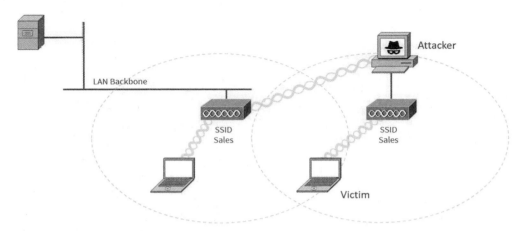

Once the station is connected to the hacker's access point, it will receive an IP address from a DHCP server running on the access point, and the user will now be located on the same network as the hacker. At this point, the hacker is free to commence a peer-to-peer attack.

Deauthentication

The 802.11 wireless protocol contains a method for deauthentication of clients via a deauthentication frame. An attacker can send a deauthentication frame on behalf of the user, which disconnects them from the access point. Attackers will use this method in conjunction with an evil twin attack to deauthenticate the user from a valid access point so they can try to reconnect to the evil twin access point. The deauthetication attack can also be used to generate association traffic for purposes of cracking a wireless passphrase.

Password Attacks

When an attacker attempts to guess a password for a known username, it is considered a password attack. Usernames such as admin, administrator, and root should always be avoided since these are considered privileged accounts. You should always use passwords that are at least 10 characters or longer. Complexity should also be used when formulating a password, such as using lowercase, uppercase, symbols, and numbers. An attacker will perform a password attack with two primary tactics of a dictionary attack and brute-force attack.

Dictionary Attacks   A dictionary attack is just how it sounds; the attack is carried out by using a database of common words called a dictionary. These dictionary files can be kilobytes to gigabytes in size, and they contain commonly used passwords. The obvious dictionary words are *password*, *privilege*, and variations of *password* using numbers, such as *passw0rd*. Password complexity and length settings are often implemented to mitigate password dictionary attacks.

Brute-Force Attacks   Brute force is a last-ditch effort to crack a passphrase or password. A brute-force application will try every combination of a password until access is granted. These combinations will include uppercase letters, lowercase letters, symbols, and numbers. The number of combinations is exponential with every character added to a password, so long passwords of 10 characters or more are best. There are two brute-force attack methods: the online method and offline method, as shown in Figure 21.9.

FIGURE 21.9   Brute-force password attacks

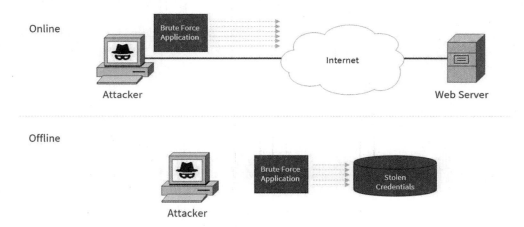

Both methods use a brute-force application to try each permutation of the password. The online method accesses the application directly and attempts to crack the password. However, the weakness to an online brute-force attack is the use of automatic lockouts after so many failed attempts, and it slows the attacker down considerably. The offline method requires the theft of the credentials file, and the brute-force attack is attempted directly on the offline credentials file. Passwords are never stored in clear text; they are commonly hashed. So, theft of the credential file requires hashing password combinations in an attempt to match the hash. With the use of a high-end graphics card, an attacker can try millions of password hashes a minute or even in seconds. An attacker can also employ a database of password-to-hash combinations, called rainbow tables. Rainbow tables can be terabytes in size.

MAC Spoofing

MAC spoofing is the assumption of another system's MAC address for the following purposes:

- To pass through a MAC address filter
- To receive data intended for another system
- To impersonate a gateway (router interface) for the purpose of receiving all data leaving a subnet

MAC spoofing is the reason we don't rely solely on security at layer 2 (MAC address filters), while best practices call for basing access on user accounts rather than device properties such as IP addresses or MAC addresses.

IP Spoofing

Spoofing is performed by an attacker so they can impersonate an IP address of an organization's assets. Spoofing allows the attacker to bypass access control systems and gain access to protected resources on the network. Spoofing is often used in DoS attacks to hide the attacker's IP address. The attacker forges a packet with the pawn's IP address as the source IP address and proceeds to attack the victim at the destination IP address. IP spoofing can be used in more elaborate attacks involving MAC spoofing to carry on a two-way conversation. Access control lists are an effective way to mitigate spoofing of internal IPs from outside the trusted network.

MAC Flooding

MAC flooding is a cyberattack targeting switches on a local area network (LAN). It involves sending multiple packets with fake MAC addresses to overflow the switch's address table, causing the buffer to overflow and making the switch unable to process any legitimate traffic.

Malware

Malware is a broad term describing any software with malicious intent. Although we use the terms *malware* and *virus* interchangeably, distinct differences exist between them. The lines have blurred because the delivery mechanism of malware and viruses is sometimes indistinguishable.

A virus is a specific type of malware, the purpose of which is to multiply, infect, and do harm. A virus distinguishes itself from other malware because it is self-replicating code that often injects its payload into documents and executables. This is done in an attempt to infect more users and systems. Viruses are so efficient in replicating that their code is often programmed to deactivate after a period of time, or they are programmed to only be active in a certain region of the world.

Malware can be found in a variety of other forms, such as covert cryptomining, web search redirection, adware, spyware, and even ransomware, and these are just a few. Today the largest threat of malware is ransomware because it's lucrative for criminals.

Ransomware

Ransomware is a type of malware that is becoming popular because of anonymous currency, such as Bitcoin. Ransomware is software that is often delivered through an unsuspecting random download. It takes control of a system and demands that a third party be paid. The "control" can be accomplished by encrypting the hard drive, by changing user password information, or via any of a number of other creative ways. Users are usually assured that by paying the extortion amount (the ransom), they will be given the code needed to revert their systems back to normal operations. CryptoLocker was one of the first ransomware threats that made headlines across the world (see Figure 21.10). You can protect yourself from ransomware by having antivirus/antimalware software with up-to-date definitions and by keeping current on patches.

FIGURE 21.10 CryptoLocker

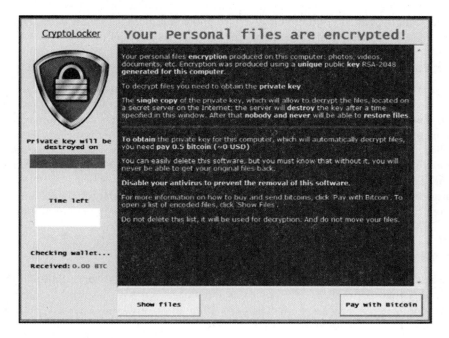

Trojans

Trojan horses are programs that enter a system or network under the guise of another program. A Trojan horse may be included as an attachment or as part of an installation program. The Trojan horse can create a backdoor or replace a valid program during installation. It then accomplishes its mission under the guise of another program. Trojan horses can be used to compromise the security of your system, and they can exist on a system for years before they're detected.

The best preventive measure for Trojan horses is to not allow them entry into your system. Immediately before and after you install a new software program or operating system, back it up! If you suspect a Trojan horse, you can reinstall the original program(s), which should delete the Trojan horse. A port scan may also reveal a Trojan horse on your system. If an application opens a TCP or UDP port that isn't supported in your network, you can track it down and determine which port is being used.

Keyloggers

A *keylogger* is normally a piece of software that records an unsuspecting victim's keystrokes. Keyloggers can stay loaded in memory and wait until you log into a website or other authentication system. They will then capture and relay the information to an awaiting host on the Internet.

Keyloggers don't always have to be in the form of software. Some keyloggers are hardware dongles that sit between the keyboard and computer. These must be retrieved, and the data must be downloaded manually, so they are not very common.

Rootkits

Rootkits are software programs that have the ability to hide certain things from the operating system. They do so by obtaining (and retaining) administrative-level access. With a rootkit, there may be a number of processes running on a system that don't show up in Task Manager, or connections that don't appear in a Netstat display of active network connections that may be established or available. The rootkit masks the presence of these items by manipulating function calls to the operating system and filtering out information that would normally appear.

Unfortunately, many rootkits are written to get around antivirus/antimalware and anti-spyware programs that aren't kept up-to-date. The best defense you have is to monitor what your system is doing and catch the rootkit in the process of installation.

Spyware

Spyware differs from other malware in that it works—often actively—on behalf of a third party. Rather than self-replicating, like viruses and worms, spyware is spread to machines by users who inadvertently ask for it. The users often don't know they have asked for it but have done so by downloading other programs, visiting infected sites, and so on.

The spyware program monitors the user's activity and responds by offering unsolicited pop-up advertisements (sometimes known as *adware*), gathers information about the user to pass on to marketers, or intercepts personal data, such as credit card numbers.

Cryptominers

With the rise of Bitcoin, so came the rise of cryptominers. A cryptominer is typically a purpose-built device that grinds out cryptographic computations. When the computation is balanced, a cryptocoin is created and equates to real money, such as Bitcoin, Ethereum, and Dogecoin, just to name a few. A cryptominer does not always have to be a dedicated purpose-built device; it can also be a distributed group of computers called a cryptopool.

Malware in the form of cryptominers became very popular, because it is a very lucrative way for threat agents to make money. The problem is that the threat agents use your computer to grind out the computations. The most common way a threat agent will run a cryptominer remotely is with JavaScript embedded on a malicious web page. Threat agents have also been known to create viruses in which the payload (cryptominer) uses your video card to grind out the computations. However, the JavaScript variant is more common to find in the wild.

Viruses

Viruses can be classified as polymorphic, stealth, retrovirus, multipartite, armored, companion, phage, and macro viruses. Each type of virus has a different attack strategy and different consequences.

EXERCISE 21.1

Testing Your Antimalware

1. Navigate to the Eicar antimalware test file site at www.eicar.org/download-anti-malware-testfile.

2. Scroll down to the download section.

3. Download a few of the Eicar test files and notice how your antivirus detects the malware.

4. Examine the alerts your antimalware software uses to report the malware.

The Eicar website contains a totally benign piece of malware that triggers your antimalware engine. Any search for Eicar will produce similar results and the contents are benign.

Human and Environmental

While some vulnerabilities come from technical challenges such as attacks on cryptography and network protocols, many are a result of environmental issues within the facility or of human error and poor network practices by the users (we call these self-inflicted wounds). In the following sections, you'll learn about human and environmental vulnerabilities.

Social Engineering

Hackers are more sophisticated today than they were 10 years ago, but then again, so are network administrators. Because most of today's sys admins have secured their networks well enough to make it pretty tough for an outsider to gain access, hackers decided to try an easier route to gain information: They just asked the network's users for it.

Social engineering attacks occur when attackers use believable language and user gullibility to obtain user credentials or some other confidential information. The best countermeasure against social engineering threats is to provide user security awareness training. This training should be required and must occur on a regular basis because social engineering techniques evolve constantly.

Phishing

Phishing is a social engineering attack in which attackers try to learn personal information, including credit card information and financial data. This type of attack is usually carried out by implementing a fake website that is nearly identical to a legitimate website. Users are led there by fake emails that appear to come from a trusted source. Users enter data, including credentials, on the fake website, allowing the attackers to capture any information entered. Spear phishing is a phishing attack carried out against a specific target by learning about the target's habits and likes. The best defense is security awareness training for the users.

Environmental

Some attacks become possible because of the security environment we have allowed to develop. The following are issues that are created by user behavior.

Tailgating

Tailgating is the term used for someone being so close to you when you enter a building that they are able to come in right behind you without needing to use a key, a card, or any other security device. Many social-engineering intruders who need physical access to a site will use this method of gaining entry. Educate users to beware of this and other social-engineering ploys and prevent them from happening.

 Access control vestibules (mantraps) are a great way to stop tailgating. An access control vestibule (mantrap) is a series of two doors with a small room between them that helps prevent unauthorized people from entering a building.

Piggybacking

Piggybacking and tailgating are similar but not the same. Piggybacking is done with the authorization of the person with access. Tailgating is done when the attacker sneaks inside without the person with access knowing. This is why access control vestibules (mantraps) and turnstiles deter tailgating, and live guards and security training deter piggybacking.

Dumpster Diving

Dumpster diving is a way for attackers to gain information that they use to establish trust from data or sensitive documents that you discarded in one way or another.

Law enforcement, journalists, and hackers who don't mind getting dirty—any of them could use this technique.

Shoulder Surfing

Shoulder surfing involves nothing more than watching someone when they enter their sensitive data. They can see you entering a password, typing in a credit card number, or entering any other pertinent information. The best defense against this type of attack is to survey your environment before entering personal data. Privacy filters can be used that make the screen difficult to read unless you are directly in front of it.

EXERCISE 21.2

Experimenting with Social Engineering

1. Call the receptionist from an outside line when the sales manager is at lunch. Tell the receptionist that you're a new salesperson, that you didn't write down the username and password the sales manager gave you last week, and that you need to get a file from the email system for a presentation tomorrow. Does the receptionist direct you to the appropriate person or attempt to help you retrieve the file?

2. Call the human resources department from an outside line. Don't give your real name but instead say that you're a vendor who has been working with this company for years. You'd like a copy of the employee phone list to be emailed to you, if possible. Do they agree to send you the list, which would contain information that could be used to try to guess usernames and passwords?

3. Pick a user at random. Call them and identify yourself as someone who works with the company. Tell them that you're supposed to have some new software ready for them by next week and that you need to know their password to finish configuring it. Do they do the right thing?

The best defense against any social engineering attack is education. Make certain that the employees of your company know how to react to the requests presented here. Social engineering works on the premise that people try to help when they are vested in your efforts, such as a co-worker or if you are trying to help them.

Hardening Security

There are many different hardening techniques we can employ to secure our networks from compromise. When evaluating the techniques to be employed in your network, you should keep a few things in mind: Evaluate your risk, evaluate the overhead the hardening introduces, and prioritize your list of hardening techniques to be implemented. Many of these hardening techniques are "low-hanging fruit" and should be employed, such as changing default passwords on network appliances and operating systems. Just make sure you have a system in place so complex passwords are not forgotten and are kept safe. Other techniques might require much more effort, such as patch management and firmware changes. In the following sections, I will introduce you to a myriad of hardening techniques that can be used to secure your organization.

Device Gardening

Device hardening is the action of changing the network device or operating system's defaults to make it more secure. When we install a new device, the first thing we do is change the default passwords and patch the device. This effectively hardens the device from attacks. Other common hardening techniques consist of disabling services and network ports we don't need for the use of the device or operating system.

Changing Default Credentials

When installing a network device, the very first thing you must do is log into the device. There is often a standardized default username and password for each vendor or vendor's product line. Most devices make you change the default password upon login to the device.

Changing the default password to a complex password is a good start to hardening the device. However, changing the username will also ensure that a brute-force attack cannot be performed against the default username. There are many different websites dedicated to listing the default credentials for network devices, so it doesn't take tremendous skill to obtain the default username and password of the device.

Avoiding Common Passwords

Avoiding common passwords is another simple measure to harden the device or operating system. There are several dictionaries that you can find on the Internet that will include common passwords. Some dictionaries are even collections of compromised passwords that have been made public.

When creating a password, it is always best practice to make the password at least 12 to 18 characters, based on the sensitivity of its use. You should always include symbols, numbers, and uppercase and lowercase alpha characters. You should also resist substituting characters for symbols that look like the character. This substitution is often called "leet speak," and it is in every dictionary downloadable on the Internet. An example of a "leet speak" password is *p@$$word*. Another common pitfall in creating passwords is the use of words; passwords should be random and complex. An example of a complex password is *GLtNjXu#W6*qkqGkS$*. You can find random password generators on the Internet, such as https://passwordsgenerator.net.

Disabling Unnecessary Services

When services are enabled that are unneeded, it expands the surface area of attack. The surface area of attack is the range of possible exploitable services on an operating system or network device. If an operating system was a house, the entry points would be the doors, windows, and chimney. If we disable services, we remove entry points that can be exploited by attackers.

One of the major design changes to the Microsoft Server operating system was introduced with Windows Server 2008. Starting with Windows 2008, Microsoft disabled all services out of the box, and the firewall was turned on by default. This dramatically reduced the surface area of attack for the operating system compared to prior versions such as Windows Server 2003 R2.

Linux and UNIX have long since used this minimalistic approach to installation. When the Linux/UNIX operating systems are installed, no services are installed by default. All functionality must be added via the repository tools such as apt for Ubuntu and Debian and yum for Red Hat–based systems.

Operating systems are not the only network system that contains services; many network devices have services. Network devices are not immune to exploit; therefore, the surface area of attack should be reduced by disabling nonessential services. A typical example is a network printer; printers will often have several protocols enabled for printing, such as Server Message Block (SMB), Internet Printing Protocol (IPP), and File Transfer Protocol (FTP). Unnecessary protocols and services should be disabled since each one could potentially have a vulnerability.

Using Secure Protocols

Secure protocols are protocols that provide encryption. Many of the protocols used today by network devices do not provide any encryption. Secure protocols should be used to thwart eavesdropping and manipulation of the network device from an unauthenticated source.

A typical protocol used to manage network devices for firmware upgrades is Trivial File Transfer Protocol (TFTP). TFTP is unencrypted and easily exploitable by way of an on-path attack, because it uses the UDP protocol. Protocols such as Secure Copy Protocol (SCP) should be used in lieu of older outdated protocols if the device supports it. SCP provides both encryption and authentication.

Telnet is insecure as well and a worse choice because login credentials are sent in clear text! Telnet is a console-based maintenance protocol that is frequently used by network devices because of its small code footprint. Protocols such as Secure Shell (SSH) should be used if the device supports it. SSH provides both encryption and authentications just like SCP, since SCP is an extension of SSH.

Console-based management protocols such as TFTP and Telnet are not the only protocols immune to insecurity. Hypertext Transfer Protocol (HTTP) is sent in clear text as well. Hypertext Transfer Protocol Secure (HTTPS) should be enabled and used for management of network devices. HTTPS requires a certificate to be installed, but most network devices allow the use of self-signed certificates that are locally managed. HTTPS provides encryption and a minimal layer of authentication for the management endpoint but will thwart an on-path attack.

Disabling Unused Ports

A port is considered any interface that serves to connect two host systems. The port can be an IP port related to TCP or UDP, or it can be a physical port such as a serial or USB port. If the interface allows data to be transferred, then it is considered a port and is a risk to security. In this section, I will cover the most common ports that should be disabled if not needed for hardening of systems.

IP Ports

The term *port* is often associated with TCP/IP ports. Throughout this book you will find protocols that operate on TCP or UDP; these ports are considered well-known ports. A list of the registered ports can be found at www.iana.org/assignments/service-names-port-numbers/service-names-port-numbers.txt. However, this is not a full list because application designers are not required to register the ports the application runs on.

After a system has been installed, it is best practice to disable any TCP/IP port that is not being used for the primary purpose of the network system. This is achieved via host-based firewalls. Microsoft operating systems are proficient at securing the operating system, because starting with Windows Server 2008 the firewall is on by default. Linux systems are also being packaged with firewalls that are enabled by default. Only ports necessary for operations are allowed through the host firewall. When we disable TCP/IP ports, we reduce the surface area of attack of a network system.

Device Ports (Physical and Virtual)

When we disable and/or firewall TCP/IP ports on a network operating system, we prevent remote exploits. However, physical ports are just as susceptible to exploitation. If a network device has a serial port, also known as a console port, an attacker could plug in and manipulate the system. Any unused ports on network devices should be either disabled or password protected.

Virtual ports are also susceptible to attacks. Many virtual machine technologies allow for serial ports to be extended to a remote workstation over TCP/IP. These ports generally are just as exploitable as their physical counterparts. If virtual console ports are not required, they should be disabled.

Key Management

Both the Secure Shell and Hypertext Transfer Protocol Secure protocols require public private key pairs. The key pairs are often generated when the protocols are first enabled. The *modulus* is the length in bits of the encryption key pair. A 512-bit modulus can be cracked within a relatively short period of time. A 2048-bit modulus can take much longer, if it is even possible. The expiry time on the key pairs is directly related to the modulus length. A low-bit modulus key pair will expire sooner than a high-bit modulus key pair, but all key pairs expire at some point. The generation of new keys is required by the network operating system at some point because of the expiration date set on the key pair. Some network operating systems generate the key pair automatically; others require manual intervention.

A generation of new key pairs can also be required if they are compromised. As the administrator, you should rekey the system if it is compromised, but the operating system will not care and continue to function as normal.

It is important to note that SSH clients will detect a new key pair upon initial connection after generating new keys. The SSH client by default will prompt the user to accept this new key pair. All SSH clients cache the key pairs previously shown in a key chain that is used for future authentication of connections.

Access Control Lists

Access control lists (ACLs) are used to control traffic and applications on a network. Every network vendor supports a type of ACL method; for the remainder of this section, I will focus on Cisco ACLs.

An ACL method consists of multiple access control entries (ACEs) that are condition actions. Each entry is used to specify the traffic to be controlled. Every vendor will have a different type of control logic. However, understanding the control logic of the ACL system allows you to apply it to any vendor and be able to effectively configure an ACL. The control logic is defined with these simple questions:

- How are the conditions of an ACL evaluated?

- What is the default action if a condition is not met?

- How is the ACL applied to traffic?

- How are conditions edited for an ACL?

Let's explore the control logic for a typical Cisco layer 3 switch or router. The conditions of the ACL are evaluated from top to bottom. If a specific condition is not met for the ACL, the default action is to deny the traffic. Only one ACL can be configured per interface, per protocol, and per direction. When you are editing a traditional standard or extended ACL, the entire ACL must be negated and reentered with the new entry. With traditional ACLs, there is no way to edit a specific ACL on the fly. When editing a named access list, each condition is given a line number that can be referenced so that the specific entry can be edited. For the remainder of this section, I will use named access lists to illustrate an applied access list for controlling traffic.

In Figure 21.11 you can see a typical corporate network. There are two different types of workers: HR workers and generic workers. We want to protect the HR web server from access by generic workers.

FIGURE 21.11   A typical corporate network

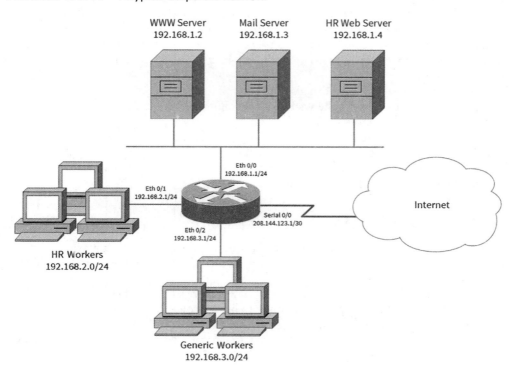

We can protect the HR server by applying an ACL to outgoing traffic for Eth 0/0 and describing the source traffic and destination to be denied. We can also apply an ACL to the incoming interface of Eth 0/2 describing the destination traffic to be denied. For this example, we will build an access list for incoming traffic to Eth 0/2, blocking the destination of the HR server.

```
Router(config)# ip access-list extended block-hrserver
Router(config-ext-nacl)# deny ip any host 192.168.1.4
Router(config-ext-nacl)# permit ip any any
Router(config-ext-nacl)# exit
Router(config)# interface ethernet 0/2
Router(config-if)# ip access-group block-hrserver in
```

This ACL, called block-hrserver, contains two condition action statements. The first denies any source address to the specific destination address of 192.168.1.4. The second allows any source address to any destination address. We then enter the interface of Eth 0/2 and apply the ACL to the inbound direction of the router interface. The rule will protect the HR server from generic worker access while allowing the generic workers to access all other resources and the Internet.

It is important to note that the focus of this section is to understand how ACLs are used to protect resources. It is not important to understand how to build specific ACLs since commands will be different from vendor system to vendor system.

Content Filtering

Content filters are useful in networks to restrict users from viewing material that is non-work-related, questionable, or malware. Content filtering is usually dictated by organization policy and management. The content filter operates by watching content and requests from web browsers and other applications. The content filter functions in two ways: The first is content-based; when images and text are requested from a website, the content filter can use heuristic rules to filter the content according to administrator-set policies. The second method is URL-based, which is much more common since many websites now use SSL/TLS (encryption) and the traffic is encrypted. Content filters are typically purchased with a subscription that provides updates to the categories of material administrators block. Content filters can be hardware solutions or software solutions, although it is common to find them installed as software solutions.

Implementing Network Segmentation

One of the biggest reasons for implementing segmentation is for security purposes. At layer 1, this means complete physical separation. However, if you don't want to go with complete segmentation, you can also segment at layer 2 on switches by implementing VLANs and port security. This can prevent connections between systems that are connected to the same switch. They can also be used to organize users into common networks regardless of their physical location.

If segmentation at layer 3 is required, it's achieved using access control lists on routers to control access from one subnet to another or from one VLAN to another. Firewalls can implement these types of access lists as well.

Finally, network segmentation may be required to comply with an industry regulation. For example, while it's not strictly required, the Payment Card Industry Data Security Standard (PCI DSS) strongly recommends that a credit card network should be segmented from the regular network. If you choose not to do this, your entire network must be compliant with all sections of the standard.

Network Segmentation Enforcement

When a network is flat with no segmentation, it is impossible to secure because an intruder has potential access to all hosts and devices once the initial network is compromised. Fortunately, there are a number of methods to implement segmentation in the network. We can use physical routers, separate switches, and firewalls. However, the easiest method is to implement virtual local area networks (VLANs) in the network. When VLANs are implemented, each VLAN has a distinct network ID. The VLANs become routable networks because they create segments in the network. This concept can then be taken one step further by implementing ACLs between these segments to increase security.

If you are implementing a firewall to create network segmentation, the various networks are given a label, and a value of trust is associated with them. The labels are also commonly called zones. As an example, the Internet is often labeled as the public zone and carries the least amount of trust. Internal networks are often labeled as private zones and carry a higher amount of trust. Rules can then be enforced that dictate that a public zone cannot communicate to a private zone, unless the private zone has initiated the connection.

Segmentation can be taken even further, by segmenting internal private networks within the organization, such as production, research, and sales, with each zone carrying a different level of trust. Enforcement rules can then be put into place to protect each segment.

Screened Subnet

The *screened subnet* is also known as the demilitarized zone (DMZ). The DMZ gets its name from the segmentation that is created between the exterior and the interior of the network. This is similar to where borders of two opposing countries meet with military presence on both sides. Between the two sides, there is a neutral segment called the DMZ. As it pertains to a network, hosts that serve Internet clients are placed in the DMZ subnet. As shown in Figure 21.12, a network segment called the screened subnet (formerly called DMZ) sits between an external firewall and the internal firewall. The external firewall contains ACLs to restrict Internet hosts from accessing nonessential services on the server in the DMZ. The internal firewall restricts which hosts can talk to internal servers. A typical rule on the external firewall would allow HTTP access for a web server in the DMZ and would restrict all other ports. A typical rule on the internal firewall would allow only the web server to communicate with the SQL backend database in the internal network.

FIGURE 21.12   A typical DMZ with two firewalls

External Network   External Firewall   DMZ   Internal Firewall   Internal Network

Although the concept of the DMZ is still used today in network design, a screened subnet can be created between any two segments in the network. The subnets don't necessarily need to be external and internal in relation to the network. Routers containing ACLs can be implemented in lieu of firewalls to filter traffic to the screened subnet, as shown in Figure 21.13. In the figure, a network called Network A is segmented from the screened subnet by a router with ACLs filtering traffic. On the other side of the screened subnet is another network called Network B, and it too is segmented by a router with ACLs filtering traffic. Each of these two networks has equal access to the hosts in the screened subnet. These two networks, Network A and Network B, could potentially be a wireless network and the wired network, respectively.

FIGURE 21.13   A typical screened subnet with two routers

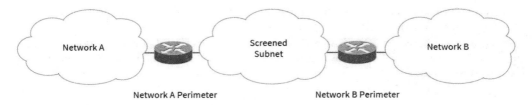

Some screened subnets are just another interface on a single firewall, as shown in Figure 21.14. In this example, the rules for both the Network A subnet and the Network B subnet would be on the same firewall. The benefit of a single firewall is centralized administration of firewall rules. Each interface is placed into a trust zone, and the firewall rules allow incoming and outgoing connections.

FIGURE 21.14   A typical screened subnet with one firewall

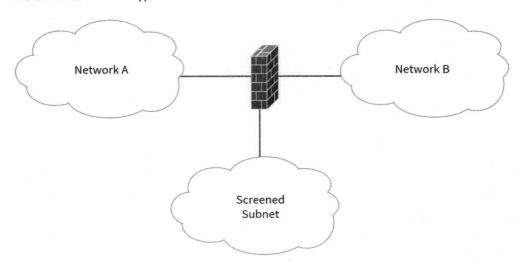

802.1X

The *802.1X* protocol is used to control access on the internal network, as shown in Figure 21.15. 802.1X commonly uses RADIUS as the authentication server. However, other AAA authentication servers can be used, such as LDAP and TACACS+. 802.1X is used for both wired and wireless network access. When you are using 802.1X with a wired connection, the physical port allows communications of 802.1X credentials. The port will not allow user traffic to be switched until the AAA process is completed and the user or computer is verified. The user's device is called the supplicant, and the port it is plugged into is called the control port, because it controls access to the organization's LAN or resources. The switch that is set up for 802.1X is called the authenticator.

802.1X works with wireless connections, but in lieu of a physical connection an association occurs. When 802.1X is used with wireless, the control port is the port leading back to the network. All 802.1X authentication between the supplicant and the authenticator occurs over the associated connection.

FIGURE 12.15   802.1X switch control

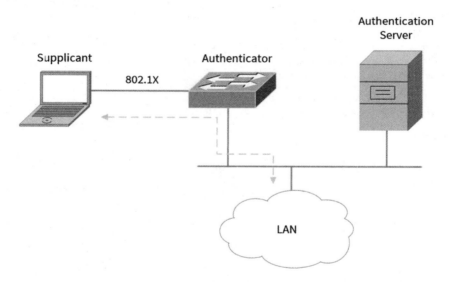

NAC

Although 802.1X can be used by itself for AAA, it is often used in conjunction with a *network access control (NAC)* system. It is often referred to as port-based network access control (PNAC).

As shown in Figure 21.16, NAC agents check the reported health and integrity of the client before allowing it on the network. The NAC agent can check the current patch level of the client, antivirus signature date, and firewall status. The NAC policy is defined by the network administrator. If the client passes the checks, the client is allowed on the network. If the client fails the checks, the client is placed into a remediation network, where the user must remediate the client. It is important to mention that although the figure details a separate NAC server, the NAC and 802.1X are usually the same server.

FIGURE 21.16   NAC and 802.1X

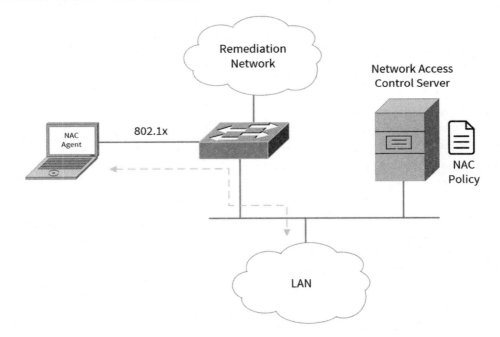

MAC Filtering

MAC address filtering is used to secure wireless by providing only an allowed list of MAC addresses access to the wireless system. This is also sometimes referred to as whitelisting MAC addresses. It is extremely effective because an attacker will not have knowledge of which MAC addresses are allowed. There is an administrative burden in entering the MAC addresses to be whitelisted if your installation has a few clients or static clients that do not change frequently. MAC filtering is more commonly used with wireless LAN controllers (WLCs) to control specific clients by their MAC address. When it is used in conjunction with an 802.1X/NAC solution, the devices can be controlled globally from the authentication server. MAC filtering is a very effective method of security because of the difficulty an attacker has identifying the MAC addresses that are specifically allowed to be forwarded by the switch or WAP. Switches can be configured to filter specific MAC addresses as well. Port security is considered a form of MAC filtering for switching.

Port Security

Port security is a method of restricting specific MAC addresses or a specific number of MAC addresses on a physical access mode switch port. Port security is supported on many different vendor switches, but I will focus on the Cisco switching platform for this section; all switches support similar port security function. Port security is commonly implemented by the network administrator to mitigate the threat of end users plugging in hub, switches, or wireless access ports (WAPs) to extend switching of a single port.

When a switch powers on, a blank table is created in memory called the switching table. When a frame is received on the switch port, the switch records the source MAC address of the frame with the switch port the frame is received on. Each MAC address receives an entry in the switching table for future forward filter decisions. We can restrict how many entries each switch port can record with the following commands on a Cisco switch. In the example, port security is configured, and a maximum of one MAC address will be allowed.

```
switch(config)# interface gigabitethernet 0/1
switch(config-if)# switchport port-security
switch(config-if)# switchport port-security maximum 1
```

By using `switchport port-security mac-address sticky`, we can configure the switch to record the first MAC address and limit the port to only that MAC address indefinitely or until an administrator clears it. By default, with only the previous commands, the MAC address learned will be cleared after a period of inactivity.

```
switch(config)# interface gigabitethernet 0/1
switch(config-if)# switchport port-security
switch(config-if)# switchport port-security maximum 1
switch(config-if)# switchport port-security mac-address sticky
```

We can also constrain the switch port to a specific MAC address statically. In lieu of the `switchport port-security mac-address sticky` command, we can specify the specific MAC address to limit the switch port to. When we configure the following command, the MAC address will be locked to 0678.e2b3.0a02 for the switch port:

```
switch(config)# interface gigabitethernet 0/1
switch(config-if)# switchport port-security
switch(config-if)# switchport port-security maximum 1
switch(config-if)# switchport port-security mac-address 0678.e2b3.0a02
```

Internet of Things

Over the past 20 years, IP-based technology has become cheaper, and the availability of technology has improved. The Internet of Things (IoT) and Industrial Internet of Things (IIoT) are a direct result of this expanse in IP-based technology. Wireless technology further propelled IoT to become a standard in our homes today. The following are some common IoT/IIoT devices you will find in home and industrial networks today:

Refrigerator   The refrigerator has been the hub for every family. The refrigerator door displays our bills, our photos, our messages, and the shopping list for the week, among other things. The smart refrigerator operates pretty much the same way a traditional refrigerator does. The only difference is a smart refrigerator has a touchscreen on the door that resembles a giant smart phone, and everything you displayed on the refrigerator is now an app.

Smart Speakers   The smart speaker is more than just a speaker; it is an audible way to use the Internet, control other smart devices in your home, and have a digital assistant at your beck and call. By saying "Hey, Google," "Alexa," or "Hey, Siri," you can prompt the smart speaker to listen. You can then follow up with a task, such as asking what time it is, setting a reminder, checking the weather, controlling the lights, or even playing some music.

Smart Thermostats   The old round mechanical thermostat was a foolproof mechanism that has heated and cooled houses for decades. However, with the modern technology of electronics and the Internet, the smart thermostat has forever changed the way our home is made comfortable. Smart thermostats don't just cycle heating when it's cold and cooling when it's hot, they perform in an economical way. Since everyone has a cell phone and no one leaves the house without it, the thermostat can track when you are home and when you aren't. The thermostat will turn the cooling or heating cycle off when you are not home, and it can even turn them back on when you are expected to be home. The smart thermostat learns your habits and adjusts the heating and cooling cycles.

Smart Doorbells   With the rise of eBay, Amazon, and many other online retailers, it is ever so common to have packages dropped off at your door. It has also become common to have these packages stolen. The thieves even have the nickname "porch pirates." Now you can secure your home and packages with a simple smart doorbell. The smart doorbell communicates with the Internet and an app on your cellphone. When someone walks up to the door, it will sense motion and instantly send an alert to your cell phone with video and the ability to talk back to the person.

Although this section is focused on IoT home devices, IoT is much bigger than home gadgets. The smart devices we use in our homes are the by-product of big data and machine learning. These applications of big data and machine learning can also be applied to industry, such as agriculture, manufacturing, and research, just to name a few. IIoT devices are cheap and expendable units, so a couple dozen might be deployed in a crop field to monitor soil dampness. IIoT devices might also be used to monitor heat in factory devices to signal a foreseeable failure. The solutions are limitless; if you can monitor it and forecast the outcome, you can use IIoT to achieve better results.

Industrial Control Systems/Supervisory Control and Data Acquisition

Industrial control systems (ICS) are the systems that are used in manufacturing processes. Products come into the process on an assembly or production line and exit as a final product. Supervisory control and data acquisition (SCADA) is an automated system used to control and monitor products such as energy production, water, electric distribution, and oil and gas, just to name a few. Figure 21.17 shows an example of what an industrial control system/SCADA system looks like. Although industrial control systems are typically used in manufacturing, and SCADA systems are used to create and distribute resources, they both share common components, and the two are sometimes indistinguishable.

FIGURE 21.17 SCADA systems

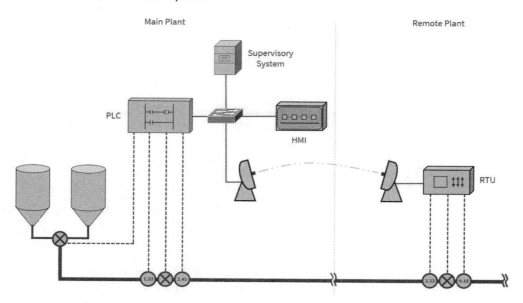

Supervisory System

All plant operations require a supervisory system to measure, monitor, and control plant production. They are often redundant systems because if a server fails, it could mean the entire production line stops. Supervisory systems also have a database where production metrics are stored for quality control and customer usage in the case of utilities. The supervisory system is usually located in the server farm at the main plant and not in the cloud because it needs to be as low latency as possible.

Operational Technology

Operational technology (OT) components of ICS/SCADA control the delivery of information from the ICS/SCADA systems. The following are a few OT devices that you will find in ICS/SCADA systems. You can see some of these devices in Figure 21.17.

Programmable Logic Controller (PLC)   A PLC is nothing more than a bunch of logic circuits performing a task. On PLCs there are often inputs and outputs. The inputs might be wired to buttons, switches, or position sensors, just to name a few. The outputs may be wired to solenoids or motors or may even be robotic, and again, these are just a few things a PLC may control. It is up to the manufacturing engineer to design and program the PLC to perform a task. The programming language a PLC uses is actually not a language. The programming resembles a type of logic circuit. It is called ladder logic and is quite popular. A specialized program is usually required for programming PLCs; it is used to develop and program the ladder logic into the controller. Once the ladder logic is programmed into the PLC, the controller will run the program until it is powered off or programmed to stop.

Human Machine Interface (HMI)   The HMI is used by plant operators so an overview of the production line can be observed. The HMI might have an oversimplified drawing of the production line with metrics displayed so a plant operator can adjust processes. In the event of a failure on the production line, it is used to identify where the fault exists. Just like PLCs, the HMI is programmed with specialized software. Once programmed, they will continue to operate until turned off and the programming software is no longer required, unless a major change is needed. The HMI can interface with the PLC and the supervisory system, depending on the requirements of the plant and operators.

Remote Terminal Unit (RTU)   An RTU is extremely similar to a PLC. Just like the PLC, it can run autonomously and manage production. However, the RTU also has an independent microprocessor, so it can be installed at a remote facility and programmed for remote control capabilities. The supervisory system would oversee all the field RTUs, and in the event something needs to be controlled, an operator can intervene. RTUs can use a multitude of communications methods to communicate back to the main plant. You can find these units everywhere from oil rigs in the middle of the ocean to power substations. They are basically ruggedized computers that can withstand harsh temperature and humidity. The language they are programmed in will differ from proprietary languages, Visual Basic, C#, C++, and even ladder logic.

Communications Infrastructure

The communications infrastructure is unique for industrial controls because everything must be low latency. Keep in mind these networks need to maintain production lines. If a canning line is processing five cans a second, you have a 200 ms window for problems if latency is experienced, and that is cutting it close! There are a number of protocols and wiring you will find in industrial control systems, such as Modbus, Profibus, Hart, EtherNet/IP (Rockwell), and RS-485, and these are just a few of them. Every PLC and RTU will use a set of standardized protocols that will work with the various components like the HMI, sensors, and actuators. Some of these protocols are compatible with Ethernet, and some are completely proprietary to industrial controls. The PLCs and RTUs will normally support Ethernet and IP-based connectivity back to the supervisor systems. However, the production network is often logically or physically separated from the operational network, so the two do not interfere with each other. Lessons have been learned from the 2010 Stuxnet infection that targeted PLCs and used the production network as an entry point. It is important to isolate a problem on the operations network, so production is not affected.

Separate Private/Public Networks

Public IP addressing isn't typically used in a modern network. Instead, private IP addresses are used and network address translation (NAT) services are employed to convert traffic to a public IP address when the traffic enters the Internet. While this is one of the strategies used to conserve the public IP address space, it also serves to segment the private network from the public network (Internet). Hiding the actual IP address (private) of the hosts inside the network makes it very difficult to make an unsolicited connection to a system on the inside of the network from the outside.

Honeypot/Honeynet

Another segmentation tactic is to create honeypots and honeynets. Honeypots are systems strategically configured to be attractive to hackers and to lure them into spending enough time attacking them to allow information to be gathered about the attack. In some cases, entire networks called honeynets are attractively configured for this purpose.

You need to make sure that either of these types of systems do not provide direct connections to any important systems. Their ultimate purpose is to divert attention from valuable resources and to gather as much information about an attack as possible. A tarpit is a type of honeypot designed to provide a very slow connection to the hacker so that the attack takes enough time to be properly analyzed.

Bring Your Own Device

The traditional workforce is very quickly becoming a mobile workforce, with employees working from home, on the go, and in the office. Mobile devices such as laptops, tablets, and smartphones are used by employees to connect to the organization's cloud resources.

Bring your own device (BYOD) has been embraced as a strategy by organizations to alleviate the capital expense of equipment by allowing employees to use devices they already own.

The various devices that employees bring into the network are often outside of the organization's control. These devices can pose a severe risk to the network. For this reason, the BYOD network should be segmented from the operational network.

Guest Network Isolation

Most guests in your network never need to connect to the organization's servers and internal systems. When guests connect to your wireless network, it is usually just to get connectivity to the Internet. Therefore, a guest service set identifier (SSID) should be created that isolates guest traffic from production traffic. These guest network SSIDs are usually created by default on consumer wireless devices. On enterprise wireless LAN controllers, the guest network typically needs to be created.

Some considerations for the guest network are what is open to guests, how long they have access, how much bandwidth, SSID name. . .the list goes on depending on your organization. Guest networks usually don't give totally unrestricted Internet access; certain sensitive ports like TCP 25 SMTP are normally blocked. The length of time they have access is another concern. Generally, a guest is just that, a guest. So, 4 hours, 8 hours, or 24 hours of access seem responsible. This needs to be thought through as too short a time will create administrative overhead and too long a window of access allows for abuse of service.

Captive Portal

A *captive portal* is a method of redirecting users who connect to wireless or wired systems to a portal for login or agreement to the acceptable use policy (AUP). Using a captive portal is common for guest networks. More than likely, if you have stayed in a hotel that offers wireless, you have been redirected to the captive portal to accept the terms. Some hotels require you to purchase the wireless service; this type of service would also redirect you to the portal for login or payment. Captive portals are not exclusively used for hotels; they are also used for corporate access to an organization's wireless system.

Physical Security Concepts

Physical security is the most overlooked element of security in a network. A simple lock can keep out the most curious prying eyes from a network closet or server room. A more layered approach can be implemented for higher security installations. However, the simple fact is that not a lot of time is spent on physically securing the network. In the following sections, we will cover the CompTIA objectives related to physical security of networks.

Video Surveillance

Video surveillance is the backbone of physical security. It is the only detection method that allows an investigator to identify what happened, when it happened, and, most important, who made it happened. Two types of cameras can be deployed: fixed and *pan-tilt-zoom (PTZ)*. Fixed cameras are the best choice when recording for surveillance activities.

Pan-tilt-zoom (PTZ) cameras allow for 360-degree operations and zooming in on an area. PTZs are most commonly used for intervention, such as covering an area outside during an accident or medical emergency. PTZ cameras are usually deployed for the wrong reasons, mainly because they are cool! PTZs are often put into patrol mode to cover a larger area than a fixed camera can. However, when an incident occurs, they are never pointed in the area you need them! It is always best to use a fixed camera or multiple fixed cameras, unless you need a PTZ for a really good reason. They are usually more expensive and require more maintenance than fixed cameras.

Video surveillance can be deployed using two common media types: coaxial cable and Ethernet. Coaxial cable is used typically in areas where preexisting coaxial lines are in place or distances are too far for typical Ethernet. These systems are called closed-circuit television (CCTV). Coaxial camera systems generally use appliance-like devices for recording video. These CCTV recorders generally have a finite number of ports for cameras and a finite amount of storage in the form of direct-attached storage (DAS).

 Most video installations for CCTV are coaxial cable and Ethernet, as previously described. However, wireless is popular for consumer applications, such as doorbells and home surveillance cameras. These devices generally use cloud storage and require an Internet connection.

Ethernet (otherwise known as IP) surveillance is becoming the standard for new installations. Anywhere an Ethernet connection can be installed, a camera can be mounted. Power over Ethernet (PoE) allows power to be supplied to the camera, so the additional power supplies used with coaxial cameras are not needed. Ethernet also provides the flexibility of virtual local area networks (VLANs) for added security so that the camera network is isolated from operational traffic. IP surveillance uses network video recorder (NVR) software to record cameras. Because NVRs are server applications, you can use traditional storage such as network area storage (NAS) or storage area network (SAN) storage. This allows you to treat the video recordings like traditional data.

Coaxial camera networks can be converted to IP surveillance networks with the use of a device called a *media converter*. These devices look similar to a CCTV recorder. They have a limited number of ports for the coaxial cameras and are generally smaller than the CCTV recorder. This is because they do not have any DAS. The sole purpose of the media converter is to convert the coaxial camera to an Ethernet feed to the NVR.

The use of IP video surveillance allows for a number of higher-end features such as camera-based motion detection, license plate recognition (LPR), and motion fencing. Advanced NVR software allows cameras to send video only when motion is detected at the camera; this saves on storage for periods of nonactivity. LPR is a method of detecting and capturing license plates in which the software converts the plate to a searchable attribute for the event. With motion fencing, an electronic fence can be drawn on the image so that any activity within this region will trigger an alert. Among the many other features are facial recognition and object recognition.

Planning Video Surveillance

In this exercise, you will plan video surveillance for the exterior of your home.

1. Draw a simple map of your property.

2. Draw your home on the property map.

3. Identify important areas to cover with video surveillance, such as entryways.

4. Plan cameras and angles to be covered.

5. Detail how the cameras will be wired and powered.

6. Detail the storage for the cameras.

7. Make detailed notes as to why you chose a certain camera location.

Door Locks

The most common physical prevention tactic is the use of locks on doors and equipment. This might mean the installation of a tumbler-style lock or an elaborate electronic combination lock for the switching closet. If a tumbler-style lock is installed, then the appropriate authorized individuals who require access will need a physical key. Using physical keys can become a problem, because you may not have the key with you when you need it the most, or you can lose the key. The key can also be copied and used by unauthorized individuals. Combination locks, also called cipher locks, can be reprogrammed and do not require physical keys, as shown in Figure 21.18. Combination locks for doors can be purchased as mechanical or electronic.

FIGURE 21.18   A typical combination door lock

When physical locks use keys, the factor of authentication is considered something that you have—because you must have the key. When physical locks use ciphers, the authentication is considered something you know—because you must know the cipher.

Equipment Locks

There are many different types of *equipment locks* that can secure the information and the device that holds the information. Simply thwarting the theft of equipment containing data and restricting the use of USB thumb drives can secure information. In the following sections, we will cover several topics that are directly related to the physical aspects of information security.

Cable Locks

Cable locks are used to secure laptops and any device with a universal security slot (USS), as shown in Figure 21.19. A cable lock is just that—a cable with a lock at one end. The lock can be a tumbler or a combination, as shown in Figure 21.20. The basic principle is that the end of the lock fits into the USS. When the cable is locked, the protruding slot of metal turns into a cross that cannot be removed. This provides security for expensive equipment that can be stolen due to its portability or size.

FIGURE 21.19   A USS

FIGURE 21.20   A standard cable lock

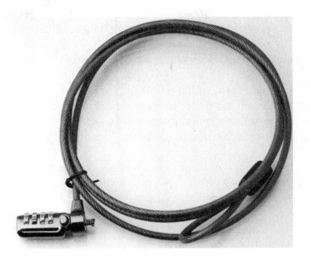

Server Locks

Most servers come with a latch-style lock that prevents someone from opening the server, but the tumbler-style lock is trivial to open. Anyone with a paper clip can open these locks if they have forgotten the keys. Other types of server locks are holes for padlocks that latch through the top cover and the body of the server. However, over the past 10 years, a declining number of servers come with this feature. This is mainly because servers can be better secured behind a locked rack-mounted enclosure. Rack-mounted enclosures generally come with a tumbler-style lock that can protect all the servers and network equipment installed in the cabinet, while still providing airflow.

USB Locks

Universal serial bus (USB) locks can be put into place to physically lock out USB ports on a workstation or server from use. These devices are extremely rare to find, because most equipment and operating systems allow for the USB ports to be deactivated. USB locks work by inserting a small plastic spacer into the USB port. Once inserted, the spacer latches to the USB detent with plastic teeth. A tool is required to remove the USB spacer.

Summary

In this chapter, you learned about common attack types that one might expect on an enterprise network. These attack types can be categorized into technology-based attacks and those that are the result of human failure or of the network environment that exists.

Technology-based attacks include denial-of-service (DoS)/distributed denial-of-service (DDoS) attacks, on-path attacks, DNS poisoning, VLAN hopping, ARP spoofing, rogue DHCP and rogue access point (AP) attacks, evil twin attacks, ransomware, and password attacks.

Human and environmental attacks include social engineering, phishing, tailgating, piggybacking, and shoulder surfing.

An entire book can be dedicated to hardening security. However, the key objectives for the CompTIA Network+ exam are device hardening, key management, access control lists, and content filtering. One of the best ways to protect a network asset is to isolate it from other network assets. This tactic is called network segmentation, which is covered in this chapter as well.

The last topic that we covered in this chapter was a topic that is often overlooked or not associated with network security, which is physical security. Topics covered for the CompTIA Network+ exam are video surveillance and the various locks you can use for physical security.

Exam Essentials

Explain common technology-based attacks. These include denial-of-service (DoS)/distributed denial-of-service (DDoS) attacks, on-path attacks, DNS poisoning, VLAN hopping, ARP spoofing, rogue DHCP and rogue access point (AP) attacks, evil twin attacks, ransomware, and password attacks.

Identify human and environmental attacks. These include social engineering, phishing, tailgating, piggybacking, and shoulder surfing.

Understand the various methods of hardening network systems. Changing default credentials for network systems will thwart brute-force attacks against default usernames. Disabling unused services on a network system reduces the area of attack by reducing the number of services that are potentially vulnerable. Access control lists (ACLs) consist of conditions and actions to control traffic for applications.

Know the various techniques of implementing network segmentations. Screened subnets, 802.1X, NAC, and port security are just a few of the many tactics used for network segmentation covered in this chapter. You should review the various techniques listed in this chapter.

Know the various tactics used for physical security. Video surveillance can be deployed as a coaxial network called closed-circuit television (CCTV) or Ethernet. Using locks prevent equipment from being affected by malicious intent, mistakenly being affected, or stolen. Locking doors and cabinets safeguards against snooping employees or attackers looking for files or equipment.

Written Lab

Complete the table by filling in the appropriate term for each attack method.
You can find the answers in Appendix A.

Disruption of service by an attacker

An indirect DoS attack

A DoS attack that is carried out making a small request to a third party

Disruption of service by many attackers

Disruption of service because of theft of equipment

Disruption of service due to a deliberate modification of firmware

An attack in which the threat actor eavesdrops and manipulates the conversation

A threat actor sends a malicious reply back for a DNS query

Access to a VLAN is attempted by double tagging the frame

Client receives a malicious DNS entry along with their IP and subnet mask

A threat actor duplicates an SSID to intercept wireless traffic

Review Questions

You can find the answers to the review questions in Appendix B.

1. Which of the following is *not* a technology-based attack?
   - **A.** DoS
   - **B.** Rogue DHCP
   - **C.** Shoulder surfing
   - **D.** Malware

2. A command-and-control server is a part of which of the following attacks?
   - **A.** DDoS
   - **B.** Password attacks
   - **C.** Shoulder surfing
   - **D.** Malware

3. Which attack involves the attacker impersonating both sides of a conversation between two hosts?
   - **A.** On-path attack
   - **B.** Deauthentication
   - **C.** DoS
   - **D.** Spoofing

4. Which type of attack will attempt to configure hosts with a malicious default gateway?
   - **A.** DoS
   - **B.** VLAN hopping
   - **C.** Deauthentication
   - **D.** Rogue DHCP

5. In which of the following does the attacker (and his bots) send a UDP packet to vulnerable NTP servers that requests that a large amount of data (megabytes worth of traffic) be sent to the DDoS's target IP address?
   - **A.** Distributed
   - **B.** NTP amplification
   - **C.** Reflective
   - **D.** DNS amplification

6. Which of the following was previously known as a man-in-the-middle attack?
   - **A.** VLAN hopping
   - **B.** On-path attack
   - **C.** DoS attack
   - **D.** Deauthentication attack

7. Double tagging is a part of which of the following attacks?

   A. VLAN hopping

   B. On-path attack

   C. DDoS

   D. Malware

8. Which of the following is the process of adopting another system's MAC address for the purpose of receiving data meant for that system?

   A. Rogue DHCP

   B. ARP spoofing

   C. IP spoofing

   D. DNS spoofing

9. Which of the following is connected to your wired infrastructure without your knowledge?

   A. Rogue AP

   B. Command-and-control server

   C. Malware

   D. Botnet

10. Which of the following uses the same SSID as your AP?

   A. Rogue AP

   B. Rogue DHCP

   C. Evil twin

   D. DNS poisoning

11. What attack vector can be used for an on-path attack?

   A. DHCP

   B. DNS

   C. Wireless

   D. All of the above

12. Which attack can be used on a native VLAN?

   A. Double tagging

   B. VLAN traversal

   C. Trunk popping

   D. Denial of service

13. Which form of social engineering is nothing more than looking over someone's shoulder while they enter or view sensitive information?

   A. Shoulder surfing

   B. Phishing

   C. Tailgating

   D. Whaling

14. You need to protect your users from Trojans, viruses, and phishing emails. What should you implement?

   A. Multifactor authentication

   B. Software firewalls

   C. Antimalware

   D. Antivirus

15. What can you use to protect against spoofing of internal IP addresses on the perimeter of your network?

   A. Access control lists

   B. Intrusion detection systems

   C. Transport Layer Security

   D. Host intrusion detection systems

16. You are implementing a public guest wireless network and require that users accept an acceptable use policy (AUP). What should you implement to accomplish the goal?

   A. ACLs

   B. MAC filtering

   C. Captive portal

   D. 802.1X

17. You are implementing a wireless network and need to make sure that only hosts that have up-to-date antivirus protection can join. Which technology should you implement?

   A. NAC

   B. 802.1X

   C. EAP-TLS

   D. ACLs

18. Which statement is correct about applying ACLs to an interface?

   A. An access control list can be applied in only one direction.

   B. An access control list can be applied only to a single protocol.

   C. An access control list can be applied only to a single port.

   D. All of the above.

19. As part of your training program, you're trying to educate users on the importance of security. You explain to them that not every attack depends on implementing advanced technological methods. Some attacks, you explain, take advantage of human shortcomings to gain access that should otherwise be denied. Which term do you use to describe attacks of this type?

    A. Social engineering

    B. IDS

    C. Perimeter security

    D. Biometrics

20. You've discovered that credentials to a specific application have been stolen. The application is accessed from only one computer on the network. Which type of attack is this most likely to be?

    A. On-path attack

    B. Zero day

    C. Denial of service (DoS)

    D. ARP spoofing

Appendix
A

Answers to Written Labs

Chapter 1: Introduction to Networks

Answers:

1. Local area network (LAN)
2. Wide area network (WAN)
3. Star topology
4. Demarc or demarcation point
5. Collapsed-core
6. Virtual NIC (vNIC)
7. Storage area network (SAN)
8. Network segment
9. Multiprotocol Label Switching (MPLS)
10. Spine leaf

Chapter 2: The Open Systems Interconnection (OSI) Reference Model

Answers:

7. Application
6. Presentation
5. Session
4. Transport
3. Network
2. Data Link
1. Physical

Chapter 3: Networking Connectors and Wiring Standards

Answers:

EIA/TIA 568A

Pin 1	White/Green
Pin 2	Green
Pin 3	White/Orange
Pin 4	Blue

Pin 1	White/Green
Pin 5	White/Blue
Pin 6	Orange
Pin 7	White/Brown
Pin 8	Brown

EIA/TIA 568B

Pin 1	White/Orange
Pin 2	Orange
Pin 3	White/Green
Pin 4	Blue
Pin 5	White/Blue
Pin 6	Green
Pin 7	White/Brown
Pin 8	Brown

Chapter 4: The Current Ethernet Specifications

Answers:
1. 16
2. 0101
3. 0xE
4. 7
5. 00011100
6. 0xF
7. 0011
8. 1101
9. 10110001
10. 0xD0

Chapter 5: Networking Devices

Answers:

Description	Device or OSI Layer
This device sends and receives information about the Network layer.	Router
This layer creates a virtual circuit before transmitting between two end stations.	Transport
A layer 3 switch or multilayer switch.	Router
This device uses hardware addresses to filter a network.	Bridge or switch
Ethernet is defined at these layers.	Data Link and Physical
This layer supports flow control and sequencing.	Transport
This device can measure the distance to a remote network.	Router
Logical addressing is used at this layer.	Network
Hardware addresses are defined at this layer.	Data Link (MAC sublayer)
This device creates one big collision domain and one large broadcast domain.	Hub
This device creates many smaller collision domains, but the network is still one large broadcast domain.	Switch or bridge
This device can never run full-duplex.	Hub
This device breaks up collision domains and broadcast domains.	Router

Chapter 6: Introduction to the Internet Protocol

Answers:

Service Protocol	Transport Protocol	Port Number
SFTP	TCP	22
Telnet	TCP	23

Service Protocol	Transport Protocol	Port Number
SMTP	TCP	25
NTP	UDP	123
LDAP	TCP	389
TFTP	UDP	69
RDP	TCP	3389
Syslog	UDP	514
SMB	TCP	445
IMAP	TCP	143
HTTP	TCP	80
HTTPS	TCP	443
LDAPS	TCP	636
SMTPS	TCP	587
SSH	TCP	22
SQL	TCP	1433

Chapter 7: IP Addressing

Lab 7.1 Answers:

1. The class C private range is 192.168.0.0 through 192.168.255.255.
2. IPv6 has the following characteristics, among others, that make it preferable to IPv4: more available addresses, simpler header, options for authentication, and other security.
3. Automatic Private IP Addressing (APIPA) is the technology that results in hosts automatically configuring themselves with addresses that begin with 169.254.
4. An IP address assigned to an interface, considered a one-to-one communication.
5. One-to-many address.
6. A MAC address, sometimes called a hardware address or even a burned-in address.
7. IPv6 has 128-bit (16-octet) addresses, compared to IPv4's 32-bit (4-octet) addresses, so 96 more bits than IPv4.
8. 172.16.0.0 through 172.31.255.255.

9. 192–223, 110xxxxx.

10. Loopback or diagnostics. Actually, the full range of 127.0.0.1 through 127.255.255.254 is referred to as the loopback address.

Lab 7.2 Answers:

1. Unicast

2. Global unicast

3. Link-local

4. Unique local (used to be called site-local)

5. Multicast

6. Anycast

7. Anycast

8. ::1

9. FE80::/10

10. FC00::/7

Chapter 8: IP Subnetting, Troubleshooting IP, and Introduction to NAT

Answers:

CIDR	Subnet Mask
/13	255.248.0.0
/8	255.0.0.0
/15	255.254.0.0
/30	255.255.255.252
/22	255.255.252.0
/26	255.255.255.192
/28	255.255.255.240
/4	240.0.0.0
/18	255.255.192.0
/27	255.255.255.224
/29	255.255.255.248

CIDR	Subnet Mask
/21	255.255.248.0
/11	255.224.0.0
/25	255.255.255.128
/10	255.192.0.0

Chapter 9: Introduction to IP Routing

Answers:

Destination Network	Exit Interface
172.16.10.0/24	Interface E0
172.16.20.0/24	Interface E1
172.16.30.0/24	Interface E2

1. Interface E0
2. Host_D
3. E2, Host_D
4. 172.16.10.2, 172.16.30.2
5. E1, Host_B

Chapter 10: Routing Protocols

Answers:

Lab_A

Network ID	Exit Interface	Metric
10.0.10.0/24	E0	0
10.0.20.0/24	E0	1
10.0.30.0/24	E0	1
10.0.40.0/24	E0	2
10.0.50.0/24	E0	2
10.0.60.0/24	E0	3

Lab_B

Network ID	Exit Interface	Metric
10.0.10.0/24	E0	0
10.0.30.0/24	E1	0
10.0.20.0/24	E0	1
10.0.40.0/24	E0	2
10.0.50.0/24	E0	2
10.0.60.0/24	E0	3

Lab_C

Network ID	Exit Interface	Metric
10.0.10.0/24	E0	0
10.0.30.0/24	S0	0
10.0.20.0/24	E0	1
10.0.40.0/24	S0	1
10.0.50.0/24	S0	1
10.0.60.0/24	S0	2

Lab_D

Network ID	Exit Interface	Metric
10.0.30.0/24	S0	0
10.0.40.0/24	E0	0
10.0.50.0/24	S1	0
10.0.10.0/24	S0	1
10.0.20.0/24	S0	2
10.0.30.0/24	S1	1

Lab_E

Network ID	Exit Interface	Metric
10.0.50.0/24	S0	0
10.0.60.0/24	E0	0
10.0.40.0/24	S0	1
10.0.30.0/24	S0	1
10.0.10.0/24	S0	2
10.0.20.0/24	S0	3

Chapter 11: Switching and Virtual LANs

Answers:

1. Destination
2. Source
3. Spanning Tree Protocol
4. 802.1Q
5. 802.3at
6. Access
7. Blocking
8. 50 seconds
9. Forward/filter
10. QoS

Chapter 12: Wireless Networking

Answers:

1. 10 Gbps
2. 5 GHz
3. 802.11ax
4. GHz
5. CSMA/CA
6. 802.11n

7. Yagi antenna
8. Ad hoc
9. Site survey
10. Passive

Chapter 13: Remote Network Access

Answers:

Definition	Term
Only traffic to the office goes through the VPN. Internet traffic does not.	Client-to-site VPN
Only the traffic between the user and the office will go through the tunnel.	Split tunnel
All traffic goes through the VPN, including Internet traffic.	Full tunnel
All traffic goes through the VPN tunnel.	Site-to-site VPN
Requires only a browser that can perform SSL/TLS.	Clientless VPN

Chapter 14: Using Statistics and Sensors to Ensure Network Availability

Answers:

Description	Term
The percentage of time the CPU spends executing a non-idle thread.	Processor\% Processor Time
The amount of physical memory, in megabytes, currently available.	Memory\Available Mbytes
The percentage of bandwidth the NIC is capable of that is currently being used.	Network Interface\Bytes Total/Sec

Description	Term
The delay typically incurred in the processing of network data.	Latency
Occurs when the data flow in a connection is not consistent; that is, it increases and decreases in no discernable pattern.	Jitter
Supports plaintext authentication with MD5 or SHA with no encryption but provides GET BULK.	SNMPv2
Sent by SNMP agents to the NMS if a problem occurs.	SNMP trap
Identifier mechanism standardized by the International Telecommunications Union (ITU) and ISO/IEC for naming any object, concept, or "thing" with a globally unambiguous persistent name.	Object identifiers (OIDs)
Hierarchical structure into which SNMP OIDs are organized.	Management information bases (MIBs)
Refers to the standard level of performance of a certain device or to the normal operating capacity for your whole network.	Baseline
Centralizes and stores log messages and can even time-stamp and sequence them.	Syslog
Provides real-time analysis of security alerts generated by network hardware and applications.	SIEM
Errors that mean packets have been damaged.	CRC errors

Chapter 15: Organizational Documents and Policies

Answers:

Step	Plan
Utilization of three network interfaces on the DNS server	Business continuity plan
Phased introductions of security patches	Change management plan

Step	Plan
Degaussing of all discarded hard drives	System life cycle plan
Security issue escalation list	Incident response plan
System recovery priority chart	Disaster recovery plan

Chapter 16: High Availability and Disaster Recovery

Answers:

Definition	Term
Technique used to spread work out to multiple computers, network links, or other devices	Load balancing
Allows multiple network interfaces to be placed into a team for the purposes of bandwidth aggregation	NIC teaming
Devices that can immediately supply power from a battery backup when a loss of power is detected	UPS
A leased facility that contains all the resources needed for full operation	Hot site
A Cisco proprietary FHRP	HSRP

Chapter 17: Data Center Architecture and Cloud Concepts

Answers:

1. Private
2. Infrastructure as a service (IaaS)
3. Automation
4. Playbooks
5. Elasticity
6. Multitenancy
7. VXLAN

8. Cloud computing

9. Zero trust architecture (ZTA)

10. Infrastructure as code (IaC)

Chapter 18: Network Troubleshooting Methodology

Answers:

1. Test the theory to determine a cause.

2. Document findings, actions, outcomes, and lessons learned.

3. By twisting the wire pairs together.

4. IP addressing.

5. Crossover.

6. Attenuation.

7. Establish a plan of action to resolve the problem and identify potential effects.

8. Implement the solution or escalate as necessary.

9. Routing problems.

10. Incorrect pinout, transceiver mismatch, crosstalk, and attenuation.

Chapter 19: Network Software Tools and Commands

Answers:

1. `traceroute or tracert`

2. Throughput tester/bandwidth speed tester

3. `ipconfig /all`

4. Telnet

5. `route`

6. FTP

7. `nslookup`

8. `netstat -n`

9. `ifconfig`

10. `route print`

Chapter 20: Network Security Concepts

Answers:

1. Threat
2. Risk
3. Symmetrical
4. Asymmetrical
5. Single-sign on
6. Self-signed
7. Least privilege
8. IAM
9. LDAP
10. GDPR

Chapter 21: Common Types of Attacks

Answers:

Disruption of service by an attacker.	DoS
An indirect DoS attack.	Reflective
A DoS attack that is carried out making a small request to a third party.	Amplified
Disruption of service by many attackers.	DDoS
Disruption of service because of theft of equipment.	Physical DoS
Disruption of service due to a deliberate modification of firmware.	Permanent DoS
An attack in which the threat actor eavesdrops and manipulates the conversation.	On-path attack
A threat actor sends a malicious reply back for a DNS query.	DNS spoofing
Access to a VLAN is attempted by double tagging the frame.	VLAN hopping
Client receives a malicious DNS entry along with their IP and subnet mask.	Rogue DHCP
A threat actor duplicates an SSID to intercept wireless traffic.	Evil Twin

Appendix B

Answers to Review Questions

Chapter 1: Introduction to Networks

1. B. A campus area network (CAN) is a connectivity method that is locally owned and managed by an organization to connect multiple LANs together. A metropolitan area network (MAN) is a connectivity method used in a metropolitan area, but it is owned and managed by someone other than the organization. A wide area network (WAN) is a connectivity method that is used for connectivity in a wide area, and it is owned and managed by someone other than the organization. A personal area network (PAN) is a network that connects personal devices within an extremely close vicinity.

2. A. A star topology, also known as hub-and-spoke topology, has a centralized switch connecting all of the devices outward like a star. A full mesh topology allows for a decentralized switching design, where any link failure will not affect switching. A partial mesh topology is normally performed between the layers of core, distribution, and access to allow for a single link failure while maintaining switching services. A hybrid topology is where several different topologies are employed, such as star and mesh.

3. A. Bluetooth is a common networking protocol found inside a personal area network (PAN) connecting personal devices. Multiprotocol label switching (MPLS) is a technology that uses labels to switch packets. A software-defined wide area network (SDWAN) is a virtual WAN architecture that uses software to manage connectivity, devices, and services. A virtual NIC (vNIC) is used to connect a virtual machine (VM) to a virtual switch (vSwitch).

4. D. A workgroup is a logical grouping of computers on a local area network (LAN) based upon a department's function. A backbone is the connectivity method that connects multiple network segments together. A campus area network (CAN) is a network that connects multiple buildings together in close proximity. A personal area network (PAN) is a network that connects personal devices together in close proximity often using Bluetooth technology.

5. C. A benefit to the star topology is that it is easy to troubleshoot since each host has its own connection. Equal access is typically a benefit of ring topologies. Bus topologies are typically the simplest network in terms of design, whereas star networks can have redundancy, loops, and many other complex design considerations. Redundancy is not found in star topologies; it is typically in mesh networks.

6. D. A circuit is the logical connection that MPLS creates to connect networks together. A peer-to-peer connection is a bidirectional logical connection for sharing files and accessing files. A client-server connection is another logical connection created for accessing information in one direction from client to server. East-west is a term used to describe traffic within the same network or data center.

7. B. A storage area network (SAN) is a network that is used exclusively for storage traffic. A campus area network (CAN) is a network that connects buildings together in close proximity. A metropolitan area network (MAN) is a network that connects clients within a metropolitan area, such as a city, together. A local area network (LAN) is a network within a building or residence that connects hosts together.

8. A. North-south traffic flow describes the flow of information from an internal network to the Internet or other routed destination. East-west traffic is kept within the internal network or data center and not routed. Wide area network (WAN) and metropolitan area (MAN) network describe a general network type, not traffic flow or a specific connection.

9. D. A mesh topology incorporates redundancy in the form of switches and redundant connections to provide complete fault tolerance to the network design. When a mesh topology is combined with the star (hub-and-spoke) topology, it creates a hybrid topology that allows for fault-tolerant design at a lower cost than a full mesh topology. Ring and bus topology are susceptible to total network failure if there is a failure anywhere in the network.

10. B. A point-to-multipoint topology should be selected if a central office needs to connect with several branch offices. Popular point-to-multipoint connection technologies are frame relay and MPLS, to name a few. A point-to-point connection is typically used to connect two offices together. Mesh and bus topologies are not used for WAN connectivity.

11. A. Peer-to-peer is a network architecture that allows the same host to both access and share resources in a network. Client-server network architecture strictly defines the client that will access the information and the server that shares the information. Local area network (LAN) is a network type and not related to sharing information. Hybrid topology describes a topology that incorporates two or more topologies.

12. B. The major advantage to a client-server network architecture is the ability to have centralized management. Distributed security is not applicable to client-server network architecture and is found in a peer-to-peer network architecture. The client-server relationship is rigid and not very flexible. Equal access is an attribute of peer-to-peer network architecture.

13. D. A mesh topology is used for redundancy and protects a network in the event of a switch or link failure. Bus and ring topologies are very susceptible to failure and require a fully functioning network. A star topology by itself does not offer redundancy in the event of failure.

14. B. Distribution layer switches are fully meshed for redundancy. The core layer is normally implemented with a star topology. The access layer is normally implemented with a partial mesh topology or hybrid topology. *Routing layer* is not a valid term in the three-tier design model.

15. A. A metropolitan area network (MAN) is a network type used in a metropolitan area to connect an organization together. A local area network (LAN) is a connectivity method that connects the immediate network together. A storage area network (SAN) is used exclusively for storage connectivity. A personal area network (PAN) is a network that connects personal devices within an extremely close vicinity.

16. B. A virtual switch (vSwitch) is used to connect multiple VMs together. A hypervisor is software that allows the sharing of the compute, network, and storage of a physical host or group of hosts that have direct access to these resources. A load balancer is used to distribute the load for a network service. A network function virtualization (NFV) is a function that is virtualized, such as a router or firewall, to name a few.

17. D. A personal area network (PAN) is a network that connects personal devices within an extremely close vicinity, such as a cell phone to a laptop. A storage area network (SAN) is used exclusively for storage connectivity. A metropolitan area network (MAN) is a network type used in a metropolitan area to connect an organization together. A campus area network (CAN) is a connectivity method that connects several LANs together in a small geographic area.

18. A. A backbone is the connectivity method that connects multiple network segments at high speed. A wide area network (WAN) is typically used for Internet connectivity. A personal area network (PAN) is a network that connects personal devices in close proximity. A workgroup is a logical grouping of computers on a local area network (LAN) based upon a department's function.

19. A. The demarc, also known as the demarcation point, is a term used to describe a smart jack for a service provider. A network function virtualization (NFV) is a function that is virtualized, such as a router or firewall, to name a few. A load balancer is used to distribute the load for a network service. A router will typically connect to the smart jack for WAN connectivity.

20. A. Multipoint Generic Routing Encapsulation (mGRE) is used in conjunction with dynamic multipoint VPN to facilitate connections. Multiprotocol Label Switching (MPLS) is a technology that uses labels to switch packets and is an alternative to dynamic multipoint VPN. Software-defined wide area network (SDWAN) is a virtual WAN architecture that uses software to manage connectivity, devices, and services. A virtual NIC (vNIC) is used to connect a virtual machine to a virtual switch (vSwitch).

Chapter 2: The Open Systems Interconnection (OSI) Reference Model

1. A. The Transport layer is responsible for flow control via the TCP/IP protocols of TCP and UDP. The Network layer is responsible for the logical addressing of network nodes. The Data Link layer is responsible for the framing of data and the physical addressing of local nodes. The Session layer is responsible for setting up the dialogue between two hosts.

2. A. A three-way handshake is required between the sender and receiver before TCP can begin sending segments. During this three-way handshake, the sender's window buffer size is synchronized with the receiver's window buffer size. Ports are not agreed upon; they are used to address traffic at the Transport layer. The sequencing and acknowledgment of segments are functions of the TCP protocol.

3. C. The Session layer is responsible for offsetting up the dialogue between two hosts. The Application layer is responsible for API access and beginning the network communication process. The Physical layer is responsible for transmitting data over light, electricity, and air waves. The Network layer is responsible for the logical addressing of IP addresses.

4. D. The Presentation layer is responsible for compression and decompression, as well as encryption and decryption. The Application layer is responsible for API access and beginning the network communication process. The Physical layer is responsible for transmitting data over light, electricity, and air waves. The Session layer is responsible for setting up the dialogue between two hosts.

5. B. The Network layer is responsible for logical addressing. Routers use logical addressing to determine the path to remote networks. The Transport layer is responsible for flow control and creating virtual circuits. The Application layer is responsible for API access and beginning the network communication process. The Data Link layer is responsible for the framing of data and the physical addressing of local nodes.

6. C. As information travels down the network stack from the Application later to the Physical layer, the information is encapsulated by each layer. The information at the upper layers is referred to as datagrams. The terminology of each type of data as it pertains to the OSI layers is protocol data units (PDUs). Decapsulation is the action of removing the encapsulated information as it goes up the network stack from the Physical layer to the Application layer.

7. B. The logical link control (LLC) sublayer is responsible for managing access to Network layer protocols. The media access control (MAC) sublayer is responsible for physical addressing and framing data for the transmission media. The Data Link layer is responsible for framing data and contains the LLC and MAC sublayers. The Session layer is responsible for dialogue control.

8. D. The OSI reference model will not aid in allowing software to run at network speeds; this will be up to the developer. The OSI reference standardized model will allow for multivendor development. The OSI reference model will prevent a change in one layer from affecting other layers. The OSI reference model will also allow various network hardware and software to communicate.

9. A. The Application, Presentation, and Session layers operate together to process datagrams. All other answers are incorrect.

10. A. The IEEE 802.2 working group defines the Logic Link Control (LLC) sublayer of the Data Link layer. The IEEE 802.3 and 802.11 working groups define the Media Access Control (MAC) sublayer of the Data Link layer. The IEEE 802.15 working group defines wireless personal area networks (WPANs).

11. C. The concept of transmitting multiple segments before the receiving host acknowledges the data is windowing. Sequencing is done with each segment so they can be combined back together at the Transport layer. Compression and encryption are found at the Presentation layer, and neither is the correct answer.

12. A. By default, a router will stop broadcasts from propagating the network. A switch, hub, and wireless access point (WAP) will not stop broadcasts from propagating the network.

13. D. The route table is checked for a destination packet, but the metric associated with the destination network is how the best path is determined. Acknowledgments are used by the receiving computer to acknowledge the receipt of segments. The network address is the logical addressing of hosts. The interface is the physical connection to the network.

14. B. The PDU that describes data at the Physical layer is bits. The PDU of datagrams is used to describe data at the upper layers. The PDU of frames is used to describe data at the Data Link layer. The PDU of segments is used to describe data at the Transport layer.

15. B. The Data Link and Physical layers are responsible for framing data and transmitting it on the media. The LLC is a sublayer that is responsible for encapsulating Network layer protocols. All other answer are incorrect.

16. C. The Transport layer is responsible for flow control and creating virtual circuits. The Presentation layer is responsible for compression/decompression and encryption/decryption. The Session layer is responsible for dialogue control. The Network layer is responsible for logical addressing.

17. D. Both TCP and UDP reside at the Transport layer. All other answers are incorrect.

18. A. The correct order for data encapsulation is datagram, segment, packet, frame, bits. All other answers are incorrect.

19. D. The Network layer is responsible for routing network packets. The Physical layer is responsible for physical connectivity and transmitting bits. The Data Link layer is responsible for framing bits. The Transport layer is responsible for creating virtual circuits and flow control.

20. B. The IEEE standard of 802.3 specifies the carrier sense multiple access/collision detection (CSMA/CD) contention method. The IEEE standard of 802.2 specifies how the network layer should be encapsulated for multiprotocol operation. The IEEE standard for 802.5 details the disbanded Token Ring specification. The 802.11 details the wireless specifications.

Chapter 3: Networking Connectors and Wiring Standards

1. A. A single-mode fiber (SMF) cable can carry signals up to 80 km before the signal needs to be repeated. Multimode fiber (MMF) has a maximum distance of 3,000 feet. A main distribution frame (MDF) is a wiring point that's generally used as a main reference point for telephone lines. An intermediate distribution frame (IDF) is a remote point of reference typically located in an equipment or telecommunications room.

2.   C. A crossover cable is the proper cable to connect a switch to a switch. A straight-through cable is not the proper cable to connect a switch to a switch and is typically used to connect hosts to a switch. A rolled cable is used for serial connectivity to the switch. A T1 crossover cable is used to connect a router to a router via T1 serial lines.

3.   D. Fiber-optic cable should be used to eliminate electromagnetic interference (EMI) and radio frequency interference (RFI). Category 5e is a type of unshielded twisted-pair (UTP); it will not prevent EMI. Twinaxial cable is a type of coaxial cable used to connect network equipment at high speeds for short distances.

4.   A. An RJ-45, also known as a registered jack 45, is used for terminating networking cabling, such as Category 5/6/7/8 cable. An RJ-11 registered jack is used to terminate phone cabling. A Bayonet Neill–Concelman (BNC) connector is used to terminate coaxial cable. An angled physical contact (APC) is used to terminate fiber-optic cable.

5.   B. When making a crossover cable for any network cable, the 568B wiring standard should be used on one end, and the 568A wiring standard should be used on the other end. A straight-through cable is created when you crimp the 568A-to-568A or 568B-to-568B wiring standard on both ends of a network cable. The terms *angled physical contact (APC)* and *ultra physical contact (UPC)* are used to describe the finish on a fiber-optic cable end.

6.   D. You should always use plenum-rated cable in office spaces to avoid toxic vapors released in the event of a fire. Polyvinyl chloride (PVC) and fluoroethylene propylene (FEP) are plastics that can create poisonous vapers in the event of a fire. Non-plenum rated cables are typically made from plastics.

7.   B. A Universal Serial Bus (USB) connection method is typically used for connecting peripherals to a PC. A DB-9 connector is typically used to connect serial connections for router or switch configuration. A Category 3 cable is a network cable specification. A rolled cable is used to connect a router or switch to a PC for configuration.

8.   D. Category 6A (augmented) will handle speeds of 10 Gbps at a distance of 100 meters. Category 5 is capable of speeds of 100 Mbps at a distance of 100 meters. Category 5e is capable of 1 Gbps at a distance of 100 meters. Category 6 is capable of 10 Gbps up to a maximum distance of 55 meters.

9.   C. A smart jack cannot report trouble in a circuit. The smart jack is typically the demarcation point for a provider. A smart jack can remotely be put into a loopback mode to verify operations. A smart jack is also known as a network interface device (NID) or network interface unit (NIU).

10.   A. The signal on a cable will attenuate as the distance of the cable lengthens. Duplex refers to the path of signaling on a network cable. Demarcation or demarc refers to the point of responsibility for a network provider. Electromagnetic interference (EMI) is interference that is induced into a network cable from an external source.

11.   B. Unshielded twisted-pair (UTP), as its name implies, is unshielded cabling. Shielded twisted-pair (STP), coaxial, and twinaxial have metallic shielding around the outside of the cabling.

12. D. An F-type or BNC connector is typically found on the end of a coaxial cable. RJ-45 connectors are typically found on the ends of network cable. RJ-11 connectors are typically used for phone connection. A subscriber (or square) connector (SC) is used with fiber-optic cables.

13. A. The straight tip (ST) connector uses a BNC style mechanism to lock the fiber-optic cable in place. The subscriber (or square) connector (SC) is a square plastic connector. The local connector (LC) is a square style connector that is made for high-density applications. The mechanical transfer registered jack (MT-RJ or MTRJ) is another small form factor connector.

14. A. The Telecommunications Industry Association/Electronic Industries Alliance (TIA/EIA) T-568A/B wiring standard is used to prevent crosstalk. The use of shield twisted-pair (STP) cabling will prevent electromagnetic interference (EMI). A rolled cable is a type of wiring used with console ports on switches and routers for configuration; it does not prevent crosstalk. Short distance installations will not prevent crosstalk on cables.

15. C. The quad small form-factor pluggable+ (QSFP+) transceiver will support 4x10 Gbps for a total of 40 Gbps. The enhanced small form-factor pluggable (SFP+) transceiver will support up to 16 Gbps. The QSFP transceiver will support up 4x1 Gbps for a total of 4 Gbps. The QSFP28 will support 4x28 Gbps for a total of 100 Gbps.

16. B. An RJ-45 connector also known as a registered jack 45 is used for terminating a rolled cable that is used to connect to a switch or router for configuration. An RJ-11 connector is used to terminate phone cabling. A Bayonet Neill–Concelman (BNC) connector is used to terminate coaxial cable. The subscriber (or square) connector (SC) is a square plastic fiber-optic connector.

17. B. The main difference between single-mode fibers and multimode fibers is in the number of light rays (and thus the number of signals) they can carry. Fiber-optic cables carry light waves and not electrical signals. Category ratings are used for copper Ethernet Twisted-pair cables. Single-mode fiber can run very far distances up to 80 kilometers.

18. C. The local connector (LC) is a small form factor (SFF) connector used for high-density installations. The subscriber (or square) connector (SC) is a square plastic connector. The straight tip (ST) connector uses a BNC-style mechanism to lock the fiber-optic cable in place. Fibre Channel (FC) is a SAN technology that can use any of fiber-optic connector, but typically the connector is an LC connector for high-density installation.

19. D. A media converter that converts single-mode fiber (SMF) to multimode fiber (MMF) is required to create a solid connection. The angled physical contact (APC) cable end is slightly angled to reduce decibel loss. The ultra physical contact (UPC) cable end is domed to reduce decibel loss. The enhanced small form-factor pluggable (SFP+) transceiver supports data rates up to 16 Gbps.

20. A. A straight-through cable is used to patch hosts to a network switch; therefore, it is known as a patch cable. A rolled cable is used for serial connectivity to the switch. A crossover cable is typically used to connect a switch to a switch. Shielded twisted-pair (STP) cable is a type of cable that has metallic shielding to resist electromagnetic interference (EMI) and radio frequency interference (RFI).

Chapter 4: The Current Ethernet Specifications

1. **A.** Ethernet uses carrier sense multiple access with collision detection (CSMA/CD) as the main contention method for collisions with half-duplex communications. Carrier sense multiple access with collision avoidance (CSMA/CA) is used with 802.11 wireless communications as the main contention method for collisions. Half-duplex mode requires a contention method since the same pair is used for transmitting and receiving bits. Full-duplex mode does not require a contention method for collisions since there is a dedicated pair of wires for transmitting and a dedicated pair of wire for receiving bits.

2. **D.** The frame checking sequence (FCS) is a cyclical redundancy check (CRC) calculation used to check the integrity of the frame. The start of frame (SOF) delimiter is a one-byte field of alternating 1s and 0s that signifies the start of the frame. The preamble allows the other physical connection to synchronize its clocks for the data that follows. The destination address (DA) is the destination MAC address the frame is destined for.

3. **C.** The preamble allows for the source computer to sync its timing of the physical media–independent interface with the destination computer. It achieves this via an alternating 1 and 0 pattern at a specific frequency depending on data transfer speed. The SFD has an extra bit to let the destination computer know anything that follows is data.

4. **A.** The 6-byte destination MAC address is after the preamble/SFD so that it can be read by the switch for forwarding. All other answers are incorrect.

5. **C.** The organizationally unique identifier (OUI) is 24 bits or the first 3 bytes of the MAC address.

6. **C.** When the I/G bit is set, it means that the MAC address is intended to be a broadcast or multicast for a group of recipients. All other answers are incorrect.

7. **B.** When the L/G bit (sometimes referred to as the U/L bit) is set, it means the MAC address is locally governed. This means the user has manually set the MAC address. All other answers are incorrect.

8. **C.** MAC addresses are physical addresses that are burnt into every NIC card and network device. It is unique at the data link layer from direct communication purposes. All other answers are incorrect.

9. **B.** The Ethernet type field is 2 bytes, and it identifies at layer 2 which upper-layer protocol to send the data to. When IPv4 is used, the type field is 0x0800. When IPv6 is used, the type field is 0x86dd. All other answers are incorrect.

10. **C.** The preamble is 7 bytes of alternating 1s and 0s at a frequency that matches the bandwidth of the link. It is important to note that the 1s and 0s pattern starts with a 1 and ends with a 0 for 7 bytes (10101010). The SFD has an extra lower bit signaling the end of timing and the start of data (10101011). All other answers are incorrect.

11. B. There are 4 bits in a nibble. A single bit is the lowest value in the binary system, with a potential value of 0 or 1. There are 8 bits in a byte or octet, depending on the base value. 16 bits is a double byte, also called a word.

12. C. There are 48 bits that compose a MAC address. 24 bits are assigned by the Electrical and Electronics Engineers (IEEE) to the organization. The other 24 bits are assigned by the organization for uniqueness. All other answers are incorrect.

13. C. 10GBaseSR will support 10 Gb/s for a maximum distance of 300 meters. 10GBaseLR will support 10 Gb/s up to 10 kilometers and will provide ample connectivity between buildings. 10GBaseER will operate at 10 Gb/s for a total of 40 kilometers. 10GBaseT will support 10 Gb/s over copper UTP cables for a maximum distance of 100 meters. Although 10GBaseER and 10GBaseLR can accomplish the task, these technologies are much more expensive than 10GBaseSR.

14. A. Broadband over Power Line (BPL) called IEEE 1901 is a technology that provides Internet connectivity over power lines. Multimedia over Coax (MoCA) is a technology that provides network connectivity over coaxial lines. HDMI Ethernet Channel technology consolidates video, audio, and data streams into a single HDMI cable. HomePlug is a technology that allows you to run local area network (LAN) traffic in your home, over your home's power line.

15. B. When a collision occurs, a jam signal is sent to all hosts on the segment to notify them of the collision. A random backoff algorithm will take effect, after which all hosts will have equal priority to transmit again. All other answers are incorrect.

16. D. The hexadecimal value of 0x0020 contains 16 bits. Each digit is a hexadecimal value, and there are 4 digits that trail the 0x hex identifier. Each digit has 4 bits and 4 digits × 4 bits = 16 bits. All other answers are incorrect.

17. C. The last 3 bytes, E4-F4-42, of the Media Access Control (MAC) address designate the unique station identifier. The first 3 bytes, F3-B2-CD, are the organizationally unique identifier (OUI). All other answers are incorrect.

18. C. Address Resolution Protocol (ARP) is used to find the MAC address of another host on the same LAN. On an Ethernet network, the MAC address (hardware address) is used for one host to communicate with another. The Transmission Control Protocol (TCP) and User Datagram Protocol (UDP) are both Transport layer protocols used to transmit segments. The Domain Name System (DNS) protocol is used for name resolution.

19. C. The Ethernet specification of 10GBaseT is 10 Gb/s with a maximum distance of 100 meters over copper. All other answers are incorrect.

20. A. 1000BaseTX uses two pairs of wires, one pair for transmitting and one pair for receiving. All other answers are incorrect.

Chapter 5: Networking Devices

1.   A. The alias, or A, record that matches the MX record configured for the mail server should be changed. If you were to change the MX record, a new alias record would need to be created as well, since every MX record contains the FQDN that maps to an alias record. A PTR record is used for reverse DNS and will not solve the problem. A TXT record is used to resolve plaintext and does not solve the problem.

2.   A. Centralized provisioning of lightweight wireless access points (LWAPs) is a valid reason to implement a WLAN controller. Although a wireless LAN controller makes it easier to implement multiple SSIDs and VLANs, this task can be performed with autonomous WAPs, each performing its own authentication. The use of autonomous WAPs negates the reasons you would use a WLAN controller because each WAP would be independently managed and no coordination would exist between the autonomous WAPs. The use of multiple SSIDs can be achieved with an autonomous WAP without a WLAN controller. Multiple VLANs can also be used with an autonomous WAP without a WLAN controller.

3.   B. Network segmentation increases the number of broadcast domains. This effectively decreases the number of broadcasts seen on a network segment and effectively increases bandwidth. All other answers are incorrect.

4.   A. The DHCP server waits for connection from clients on UDP/67; the clients will send the requests from UDP/68. Therefore, the inbound host-based firewall should be configured to accept traffic from UDP/67.

5.   C. An IDS, or intrusion detection system, will detect unauthorized access. However, it will not prevent unauthorized access. It is a form of audit control in a network. A firewall will protect your network from attack by placing rules defining how people can connect as well as which traffic can pass. An intrusion protection system (IPS) will detect the presence of an intrusion and alert an administrator. A honeypot will attract a malicious user so that their tactics can be observed. It performs this function by diverting the malicious user from production systems to the honeypot, which is a sacrificial system.

6.   C. A load balancer will direct a user's request to the next free web server. A router will only route traffic to a destination network. A firewall would not accomplish the requirement of distribution of the load. A proxy is something that might fetch the web page on the web server, but it will not provide load balancing.

7.   D. Autonomous WAPs do not have any coordination between them for roaming clients. When a client roams from one WAP to another, they must reauthenticate, and this causes a drop. Implementing a wireless LAN controller will coordinate roaming clients and not require reauthentication.

8.   C. A DHCP reservation will allow for the printer to obtain the same IP address every time it is turned on. The DHCP server will serve the same IP address to the printer based on the printer's MAC address in the reservation. Configuring an A record will not achieve the goal. Configuring a DHCP exclusion for the printer would work only if you had already set it to a static IP address and didn't want that IP address assigned to another host. Configuring an PTR record will not achieve the goal.

9. C. The PTR, or pointer record, is used to look up IP addresses and return FQDNs that are mapped to them. This is helpful to identify an IP address, and in the case of SSH, it is used to positively identify the host you are connecting to. The A record is used to look up an IP address for a given hostname. The CName record is used to look up the alias for a given hostname. The AAAA record is used to look up an IPv6 address for a given hostname.

10. A. A hub will act as a multiport repeater by repeating the physical bits on an incoming port to all the other connected ports. A switch or bridge will forward the frame only to the port it is destined for. Even when broadcasts are received, the frame is still processed and not blindly repeated. A WAP acts similarly to a switch and will forward frames only to the connected wireless or wired network.

11. A. The replacement of hubs with switches increases collision domains and effectively increases bandwidth. The replacement of switches with hubs can decrease the number of collision domains, creating a much larger collision domain. The replacement of hubs with switches has no effect on broadcast domains. Broadcast domains would be affected only if a router was introduced.

12. C. The demilitarized zone (DMZ) or screen subnet is where Internet-facing servers/services are placed. The outside zone is where the public Internet connection is connected, and it is the least trusted. The enterprise network zone is considered the inside zone. The inside zone is considered to be the highest trusted network because it is the internal network that you control.

13. B. Firewalls are not commonly deployed to provide protection from internal attacks on internal resources. They are designed to protect networks from external attacks or attacks emanating from the outside or directed toward the Internet. Firewalls normally provide stateful packet inspection. Firewalls can also control application traffic by port number and higher-layer attributes.

14. B. A reverse lookup is when the fully qualified domain name (FQDN) is resolved from an IP address. This is useful when you want to identify an IP address. From the IP address, you can derive the FQDN. A reverse lookup is not when the request needs to be reversed to another DNS server. A reverse lookup is not when the DNS queried can answer the request without asking another DNS server. A reverse lookup is not the resolution of an FQDN to an IP address; it is the resolution of an IP address to an FQDN.

15. A. The configured DNS suffix is appended to the hostname query. As an example, if you query a hostname of hosta and the configured domain name is network.local, the DNS server will see a query for hosta.network.local. The DNS zone is the database of records contained in DNS. *Host header* is a term used with web servers and therefore not relevant to DNS resolution. The hostname PTR record is the reverse DNS record for a given IP address.

16. A. The A record is the DNS record that is queried when you want to resolve a hostname to an IP address. The CName record is used to look up the alias for a given hostname. The PTR, or pointer record, is used to look up IP addresses and return FQDNs that are mapped to them. The AAAA record is used to look up an IPv6 address for a given hostname.

17. C. A multilayer switch can provide both routing and switching capabilities since it operates on layers 2 and 3. A hub is a device that operates only on layer 1. A switch or bridge is a layer 2 device that segments the network.

18. D. An advantage to DHCP in a network environment is that it automatically assigns IP addresses to hosts. There is minimal difficulty to administrate DHCP, and this is not considered a benefit. Static IP addressing is used in lieu of a DHCP. DHCP does not send an operating system to a PC, but it can direct it to do so with DHCP options.

19. A. Web caching is a tremendous benefit to employing a proxy server. Commonly accessed web pages will be cached, and subsequent requests will be returned locally from the proxy server. The throughput for the network will not increase. DHCP services will not be provided with a proxy server, only the proxying of web pages. Support for user authentication is not a benefit of employing a proxy server.

20. A. Domain Name System (DNS) direct queries are performed over the UDP protocol to port 53. The queries do not require the TCP setup and teardown because the queries are simple request and reply messages, so UDP is used for direct queries. TCP port 53 is used for DNS zone transfers between DNS servers. UDP port 55 is not used for any popular protocols. UDP port 68 is used with the Dynamic Host Configuration Protocol (DHCP).

Chapter 6: Introduction to the Internet Protocol

1. D. TCP is a connection-based protocol via the three-way handshake. It is not faster than UDP. However, it allows for the retransmission of lost segments because of sequences and acknowledgments. TCP does not allow or account for error correction, only the detection of errors and lost or missing segments.

2. D. TCP guarantees delivery of segments with sequence and acknowledgment numbers. At the Transport layer, each segment is given a sequence number that is acknowledged by the receiver. The source and destination ports are used for the delivery of segments, but they do not guarantee delivery. TCP checksums are used to detect errors in segments but do not guarantee delivery. Window size is used to adjust buffer size on the sending and receiving hosts.

3. A. When a programmer decides to use UDP, it is normally because the programmer is sequencing and acknowledging datagrams already. The redundancy of acknowledgments at the Transport layer is not needed. Guaranteed delivery of segments is not a function of UDP. UDP does not provide windowing flow control because acknowledgment is not a function of UDP. A virtual circuit can be created only with a setup and teardown of communications, such as TCP offers.

4.   B. Port numbers allow the Transport layer to communicate with the Session layer. An example is a web server binding to the port number of TCP/80. A port is communicated in the header of TCP and UDP segments, but the header does not listen for requests or bind. MAC addresses are physical locations on a local area network (LAN) that are used to transmit framed data. Checksums are used to verify that data are not erroneously modified in transit.

5.   C. DNS requests are usually small and do not require the overhead of sequence and acknowledgment of TCP. If a segment is dropped, the DNS protocol will ask again. Acknowledgment of data is not a function of UDP. Flow control is not a function of UDP since UDP does not offer flow control of data other than a stop/go action. UDP does not build temporary virtual circuits; this is a function of TCP.

6.   C. User Datagram Protocol (UDP) does not guarantee segments are delivered. Therefore, the programmer must account for segments that are never received or out of order. Secure Sockets Layer (SSL) is a protocol used to encrypt a network transmission. SSL is the predecessor to the modern TLS encryption used today. Transmission allows for the network to automatically deal with lost segments because TCP guarantees segments are delivered. *Network management station (NMS)* is a term used with Simple Network Management Protocol (SNMP) to describe the collecting host for SNMP messages.

7.   A. Generic Routing Encapsulation (GRE) is a tunneling protocol that can encapsulate many protocols inside an IP tunnel. Reverse Address Resolution Protocol (RARP) is used to obtain an IP address from a MAC address. Address Resolution Protocol (ARP) is used by the Network layer to obtain a MAC address from an IP address. Internet Control Message Protocol (ICMP) is used by the Network layer to communicate network information such as Ping, Traceroute, and many other information services.

8.   B. Encapsulating Security Payload (ESP) is used by IP Security Protocol (IPSec) for the confidentiality of the payload. The AH protocol provides authentication for the data and the IP header of a packet using a one-way hash for packet authentication. Generic Routing Encapsulation (GRE) is a tunneling protocol that can encapsulate many protocols inside an IP tunnel. The protocol data unit (PDU) is a way to describe the data at each layer of the OSI model.

9.   C. Telnet is used for configuration access to network appliances, but it is not encrypted. Secure Shell (SSH) has become the successor of Telnet, since it is encrypted and provides configuration access. Hypertext Transfer Protocol Secure (HTTPS) is a secure method to transfer web pages. The Remote Desktop Protocol (RDP) is a Microsoft protocol that provides a secure method to access a server desktop.

10.   D. The User Datagram Protocol (UDP) is a Transport layer protocol that provides applications with low overhead. The Transmission Control Protocol (TCP) is a connection-oriented protocol and has higher overhead. The Internet Protocol (IP) is a Network layer protocol. The Address Resolution Protocol (ARP) is Network layer helper protocol that resolves MAC addresses from a known IP address.

11. B. The Host-to-Host DoD layer is directly related to the Transport layer of the OSI model. The Process/Application DoD layer is related to the Application, Presentation, and Session layers of the OSI model. The Internet DoD layer is related to the Network layer of the OSI model. The Network Access DoD layer is related to the Data Link and Physical layers of the OSI model.

12. D. Port numbers are used to create a virtual circuit with TCP. The port numbers are open and in use during the entire TCP conversation. Sequence and acknowledgment numbers are used to assure data is delivered. Protocol numbers are used to direct communications to the next respective upper layer.

13. B. The Network Time Protocol (NTP) operates on the UDP protocol, port 123. The Trivial File Transfer Protocol operates on the UDP protocol, port 69. The Hypertext Transfer Protocol Secure (HTTPS) operates on the TCP protocol, port 443. The Domain Name Service protocol operates on UDP or TCP, port 53.

14. C. The Internet DoD layer is directly related to the Network layer in the OSI model, which is responsible for the logical addressing of hosts. The Process/Application layer is where most networked applications will operate on the Application, Presentation, and Session layers in the OSI model. The Host-to-Host DoD layer is directly related to the Transport layer in the OSI model, which is responsible for segmenting data and transporting it. The Network Access DoD layer is directly related to the Data Link and Physical OSI layers.

15. B. Data decapsulation is the process of moving data up the OSI model back up to the receiving application. Data encapsulation is the process of moving data down the OSI model to be transmitted on the network. The Frame Checking Sequence (FCS) is a cyclical redundancy check (CRC0) that is processed on the data at the Data Link layer to validate a frame of data. The protocol data unit (PDU) is the reference to the type of data as it passes up and down the OSI layers.

16. D. The Reverse Address Resolution Protocol (RARP) provides an IP address from a physical MAC address. Internet Control Message Protocol (ICMP) works at the Network layer and is used by IP for many different services. The Transmission Control Protocol (TCP) is a Transport layer protocol for segmenting and transporting data. The Address Resolution Protocol (ARP) provides a MAC address from an IP address.

17. B. Internet Control Message Protocol (ICMP) is used for diagnostics (`ping` and `traceroute`) and for sending error messages through the network. The Transmission Control Protocol (TCP) is a Transport layer protocol for segmenting and transporting data. The Address Resolution Protocol (ARP) provides a MAC address from an IP address. The User Datagram Protocol (UDP) is a Transport layer protocol used to send segments of data.

18. A. The Dynamic Host Configuration Protocol (DHCP) operates on UDP port 67 and UDP port 68. The Simple Mail Transport Protocol (SMTP) operates on TCP port 25. The File Transport Protocol (FTP) operates on TCP ports 20 and 21. The Hypertext Transfer Protocol (HTTP) operates on TCP port 80.

19. C. The Network Time Protocol (NTP) helps synchronize your computer clock over the Internet with the help of an NTP server. The File Transfer Protocol (FTP) allows you to transfer files across the network. The Secure File Transfer Protocol (SFTP) is used when transferring files over an encrypted connection. The Secure Shell (SSH) protocol sets up a secure console session over a standard TCP/IP connection.

20. A. Through the use of port numbers, TCP and UDP can establish multiple sessions between the same two hosts without creating any confusion. The sessions can be between the same or different applications, such as multiple web-browsing sessions or a web-browsing session and an FTP session. The IP address that the request originates from does not distinguish among different simultaneous requests. Servers are able to accept multiple simultaneous sessions from the same host. The sequence and acknowledgment numbers do not distinguish among different simultaneous requests from the same host.

Chapter 7: IP Addressing

1. D. The addresses in the range 172.16.0.0 through 172.31.255.255 are all considered private, based on RFC 1918. Use of these addresses on the Internet is prohibited so that they can be used simultaneously in different administrative domains without concern for conflict. These addresses are not and should not be routable on the public Internet.

2. B. The Automatic Private IP Addressing (APIPA) uses the link-local private address range of 169.254.0.0 through 169.254.255.255 and a subnet mask of 255.255.0.0. APIPA addresses are used by DHCP clients that cannot contact a DHCP server and have no static alternate configuration. These addresses are not Internet routable and cannot, by default, be used across routers on an internetwork.

3. C. Private IP addresses are not routable over the Internet, as either source or destination addresses. Therefore, any entity that wants to use such addresses internally can do so without causing conflicts with other entities and without asking permission of any registrar or service provider. Despite not being allowed on the Internet, private IP addresses are fully routable on private intranets.

4. D. The Class A range is 1 through 126 for the first octet/byte. The Class B range is 127 through 191 for the first octet/byte. Class C range is 192 through 223 for the first octet/byte.

5. C. The Class B range is 128 through 191 in the first octet/byte. The Class A range is 1 through 126 for the first octet/byte. Class C range is 192 through 223 for the first octet/byte.

6. B. If you turned on all host bits (all of the host bits are 1s), this would be a broadcast address for that network. Turning all the network bits to 1s would define a different network address. Turning all the network bits to 0s would make the network address invalid. Turning all the host bits to 0s would make the address invalid, as well, since this is how the network is defined.

7. B. A layer 2 broadcast is also referred to as a MAC address broadcast, which is in hexa-decimal and is FF.FF.FF.FF.FF.FF. A layer 3 broadcast would have a destination address of 255.255.255.255.

8. C. A default Class C subnet mask is 255.255.255.0, which means that the first three octets, or first 24 bits, are the network number.

9. A. Packets addressed to a unicast address are delivered to a single interface. For load balancing, multiple interfaces can use the same address.

10. C. I wonder how many of you picked APIPA address as your answer? An APIPA address is 169.254.x.x. The host address in this question is a public address. This was somewhat of a tricky question if you did not read carefully.

11. B. An IPv6 address is 128 bits in size.

12. B. Packets addressed to a multicast address are delivered to all interfaces identified by the multicast address, the same as in IPv4. A multicast address is also called a one-to-many address. You can tell multicast addresses in IPv6 because they always start with FF.

13. C. Anycast addresses identify multiple interfaces, which is the same as multicast; however, the big difference is that the anycast packet is delivered to only one address: the first one it finds defined in terms of routing distance. This address can also be called one-to-one-of-many or one-to-nearest.

14. A, C. The loopback address with IPv4 is 127.0.0.1. With IPv6, that address is ::1.

15. B, D. To shorten the written length of an IPv6 address, successive fields of zeros may be replaced by double colons. In trying to shorten the address further, leading zeros may also be removed. Just as with IPv4, a single device's interface can have more than one address; with IPv6, there are more types of addresses, and the same rule applies. There can be link-local, global unicast, and multicast addresses all assigned to the same interface.

16. C, D. IPv4 addresses are 32 bits long and are represented in decimal format. IPv6 addresses are 128 bits long and represented in hexadecimal format.

17. D. Only option D is in the Class C range of 192 through 224. It might look wrong because there is a 255 in the address, but this is not wrong—you can have a 255 in a network address, just not in the first octet.

18. C, E. The Class A private address range is 10.0.0.0 through 10.255.255.255. The Class B private address range is 172.16.0.0 through 172.31.255.255, and the Class C private address range is 192.168.0.0 through 192.168.255.255.

19. B. This can be a hard question if you don't remember to invert the 7th bit! Always look for the 7th bit when studying for the exam. The EUI-64 autoconfiguration inserts an FF:FE in the middle of the 48-bit MAC address to create a unique IPv6 address.

20. C. The IP address of 224.0.0.1 is a multicast address and cannot be used to address hosts. The IP address of 10.0.0.1 is a valid IP address for a private host. The IP address of 128.0.0.1 is a valid IP address for a public host. The IP address of 172.0.01 is a valid IP address for a public host.

Chapter 8: IP Subnetting, Troubleshooting IP, and Introduction to NAT

1. B. The IP address 135.20.255.255 is a Class B broadcast address. It is not a Class A address, nor is it the default gateway address. The default mask of a Class B address is 255.255.0.0.

2. A. The mask you will need to use is 255.255.255.252. This will allow for two hosts per network for a total of 64 networks. The formula for solving for hosts is $2^x - 2$ is equal to or greater than 2(hosts), which in this case is $(2^2 - 2) = (4 - 2) = 2$. So 2 bits are used for the host side, leaving 6 bits for the subnet side. 6 bits + 24 bits (original subnet mask) = /30, or 255.255.255.252. All of the other answer options are incorrect.

3. C. The subnet mask of 255.255.255.240 will allow for 14 hosts per subnet and a maximum of 16 subnets. No other answer options are correct.

4. B. The network ID granted to your organization is a Class B address, in which the last 16 bits can be subnetted. Using the formula of 2 to the power of 2 gives you a perfect result of 4. Using 2 bits for the subnet mask would make the subnet mask 255.255.192.0 (128 + 64 = 192). This would leave you with 14 bits for further subnetting or host IDs.

5. B. The CIDR notation for 255.255.240.0 is /20. The first two subnets are 8 bits (8 × 2 = 16), and the 240 is 4 more bits (16 + 4 = 20). All of the other options are incorrect.

6. D. The mask you will need to use is 255.255.255.224. This will allow for 30 hosts per network for a total of 8 networks. The formula for solving for hosts is $2^x - 2$ is equal to or greater than 2 hosts, which in this case is $(2^5 - 2) = (32 - 2) = 30$. So 5 bits are used for the host side, leaving 3 bits for the subnet side. 3 bits + 24 bits (original subnet mask) = /27, or 255.255.255.224. All of the other answer options are incorrect.

7. A. The valid IP address range for the 192.168.32.0/26 network is 192.168.32.1 to 192.168.32.62, 192.168.32.65 to 192.168.32.126, etc. Therefore, 192.168.32.59 is within the valid IP range of 192.168.32.61/26. 192.168.32.63 is the broadcast address for the 192.168.32.0/26 network. 192.168.32.64 is the network ID for the 192.168.32.64/26 network. 192.168.32.72 is a valid IP address in the 192.168.32.64/26 network.

8. B. The subnet mask will be 255.255.240.0. Since you need to solve for the number of networks, the equation is as follows: 2^x is equal to or greater than 15 networks. $2^4 = 16$ completed the equation; the 4 bits represent the subnet side; you add the 4 bits to the 16 bits of the class B subnet mandated by the IETF. 16 + 4 = /20 = 255.255.240.0. All of the other answer options are incorrect.

9. C. The valid IP address range for 209.183.160.45/30 is 209.183.160.45–209.183.160.46. Both IP addresses are part of the 209.183.160.44/30 network. The IP address 209.183.160.47/30 is the broadcast address for the 209.182.160.44/30 network. The IP address 209.183.160.43/30 is the broadcast IP address for the 209.183.160.40/30 network.

10. C. The default gateway address for Computer A is 192.168.1.63. The IP address on the router (default gateway) is the broadcast address for the 192.168.1.0/26 network and cannot be used as that network's gateway. If you were to change Computer A's IP address, it would still not be able to communicate with Computer B because of the incorrect gateway address. Computer B's IP address and default gateway are fine, and both will function properly.

11. A. Computer A needs to have its IP address changed to align with the network that its gateway is in. Computer A is in the 192.168.1.32/27 network, while its gateway address is in the 192.168.1.0/27 network. Although changing the gateway address would work, the solution needs to be the one with the least amount of effort. Changing the gateway address, which is a valid IP address, would create more work for other clients. Computer B's IP address and default gateway are fine, and both will function properly.

12. B. The /21 subnet mask has subnets in multiples of 8. So the networks would be 131.50.8.0/21, 131.50.16.0/21, 131.50.24.0/21, 131.50.32.0/21, and 131.50.40.0/21. The IP address of 131.50.39.23/21 would belong to the 131.50.32.0/21 network with a valid range of 131.50.32.1 to 131.50.39.254. Therefore, the network 131.50.39.0/21 cannot be a network ID because it belongs to the 131.50.32.0/21 network. Both the 131.50.16.0/21 and 131.50.8.0/21 network IDs are outside of the range for the host used in this question.

13. D. The network for the computer with an IP address of 145.50.23.1/22 is 145.50.20.0/22. Its valid range is 145.50.20.1 to 145.50.23.254; the broadcast address for the range is 145.50.23.255. All of the other answer options are incorrect.

14. C. Network address translation (NAT) was created to slow the depletion of Internet addresses. It does this by translating RFC 1918 privatized addresses to one or many public IP addresses. It allows the packets to masquerade as the public IP address on the Internet until it is translated back to the private IP address. Classless Inter-Domain Routing (CIDR) is a notation used to express the network for a host. Classful addressing is the original addressing scheme for the Internet. Virtual private networks (VPNs) are used for remote access.

15. A. The inside local address is the address local to the enterprise (private), and the address is inside the enterprise. The inside local address will almost always be an RCF 1918 address, unless NAT is being used for purposes other than enterprise Internet access. If NAT is used for Internet access, then the inside local address is any host address destined for the Internet through NAT. 192.168.1.1 is the router's interface address used to communicate with inside local hosts during the NAT process. 179.43.44.1 is the inside global address for the NAT process. 198.23.53.3 is the outside global address for the NAT process.

16. C. The inside global address is the address public to the enterprise. The address is inside of or controlled by the enterprise. The inside global address in this case is the public side of the NAT, which is Router A's S0/0 IP address. 192.168.1.2 is the inside local address of the host computer. 192.168.1.1 is the router's interface address used to communicate with inside local hosts during the NAT process. 198.23.53.3 is the outside global address for the NAT process.

17. D. The outside global address is the address public to the enterprise. The address is outside of the enterprise or outside of its control. When using NAT for Internet access, the outside global address is the destination host on the Internet. The outside global address in this exhibit is the web server. 192.168.1.2 is the inside local address of the host computer. 192.168.1.1 is the router's interface address used to communicate with inside local hosts during the NAT process. 179.43.44.1 is the inside global address for the NAT process.

18. A. A /29 (255.255.255.248) is 5 bits for the network mask and 3 bits for the hosts. This provides 32 subnets, each with 6 hosts. Does it matter if this mask is used with a Class A, B, or C network address? Not at all. The number of host bits would never change.

19. D. A /30, regardless of the class of address, has a 252 in the fourth octet. This means we have a block size of 4, and our subnets are 0, 4, 8, 12, 16, and so on. Address 14 is obviously in the 12 subnet.

20. C. Devices with layer 3 awareness, such as routers and firewalls, are the only ones that can manipulate the IP header in support of NAT. A hub operates at the physical layer and cannot perform NAT. Ethernet switches and bridges operate at the Data Link layer and cannot perform NAT.

Chapter 9: Introduction to IP Routing

1. C. Routing decisions are based upon the route table contained in the router's memory and knowledge of the destination network of a packet. The originating network of a packet is not needed throughout the entire routing process. The return path of the network packet is not needed on its journey but will be needed when a packet is sent back from the destination host. The destination of the specific host is not required as long as the destination network is known; routing is typically done by network.

2. A. The command show ip route will display the route table contained in the router's memory. All other commands are incorrect.

3. D. All routes must be manually configured when you use static routes. Routes are not automatically updated because they are statically assigned. The learning of new routes and updating of existing routes is a function of dynamic routing protocols. Static routes are not the best for network traffic since a packet will always take the same route regardless of network status.

4. C. The C in the route statement means that the network is directly connected on the interface because it is configured on the interface. The gateway of last resort is the default gateway and has no influence on the individual route statement. If the route was statically configured, the letter would be an S. A network that is a continuation of another network is called a summary route and not depicted as another route entry.

5. B. When the destination IP address of a packet is not in the same network as the host, the host will set the destination MAC address to the default gateway. The destination IP address will never change throughout the IP routing process. The source IP address and MAC address have no influence over the routing process.

6. D. The command `show ip arp` can be used on a Cisco router to view the ARP cache. The commands `show arp` and `show arp-cache` are invalid commands. The command `arp -g` can be used on a Windows computer to view the ARP cache.

7. B. The route table is the term used to describe the map of the internetwork inside a router. The route table is used to make routing decisions based upon the destination network address of the packet. A route map is not a valid answer for this question. A dynamic route is a route derived from a dynamic routing protocol. A static route is a route that has been explicitly configured.

8. A. Address Resolution Protocol (ARP) is used to derive the MAC address of the default gateway, in the event that a packet must be routed. The Internet Control Message Protocol (ICMP) is used to convey messages about layer 3 connectivity. Reverse Address Resolution Protocol (RARP) is used to derive an IP address from a known MAC address, similar to DHCP.

9. C. The Ether-Type field will always be set to 0x800 for the IPv4 protocol. When data is destined for the ARP protocol, the Ether-Type field will contain 0x806. These are the two common Ether-Types you will commonly see. All other answers are incorrect.

10. B. Dynamic routing will ensure that routing in the network is automated as new locations are added to the network. Static routing will require manual intervention by the administrator updating all routing tables. Dynamic Host Configuration Protocol (DHCP) will automate the serving of IP addresses to hosts, but it will not update route tables. Reverse Address Resolution Protocol (RARP) is like DHCP in its utility, but it will not update routing tables.

11. C, D. If a route is not present for the destination network, the packet will be dropped. An Internet Control Message Protocol (ICMP) destination unreachable packet will be sent back to the sender to notify them the route is unreachable. The original packet is never sent back to the sender; it is just dropped. Packet logging happens only when it is appropriately configured. Routers will not request dynamic routing updates upon an unknown destination network.

12. D. The frame checking sequence (FCS) is a cyclical redundancy check (CRC) at the end of the frame that is 4 bytes long. The FCS allows the destination to verify that the frame has been received intact. The source MAC address, destination MAC address, and Ether-Type have no significance to the validity of the frame other than they are included in the CRC when it is calculated.

13. A. When an ICMP ping packet or any packet is lost along its route, the result will be "Request timed out." A ping or tracert to the destination will return the message, where normal application will just result in a timeout. The request timeout is an unknown error, but the message "Unknown error" will not be returned for the ping command. "Destination unreachable" will be returned as an error if a router does not have the route in its route table. "Problem occurred" is not an error message returned.

14. C. The destination IP address of 172.16.20.94 is within the 172.16.20.64/27 network; the exit interface will be FastEthernet 0/2. All other answers are incorrect.

15. C. In dynamic routing, routers update each other about all the networks they know about and place this information into the routing table. This is possible because a protocol on one router communicates with the same protocol running on neighbor routers. If changes occur in the network, a dynamic routing protocol automatically informs all routers about the event. The network and host IDs do not need to be manually entered unless you are static routing. Dynamic routing is not the default for all routers; static routing is the default.

16. B. MAC addresses are always local to the LAN, since they are used for physical addressing. IP addresses are routed through the router and not MAC addresses. During the routing process the MAC address is changed to the next physical address of the next device accepting the frame. The default gateway MAC address will always be unique on all the interfaces. Route decisions are made based only upon the destination IP address.

17. D. Convergence is the term used to describe the result of all routes updated in a routing table via a dynamic routing protocol. The fastest convergence is always desirable to keep packets routing properly. Convergence is achieved by dynamic route updates from other routers. DNS resolution is not a component of routing.

18. D. The command arp -a will show the ARP cache on your host. The command show ip route will display the route table on a router. The command show ip arp will display the ARP cache on a router or switch. The command show protocols will display all the configured layer 3 protocols on the router.

19. C. A frame changes at each hop, but the packet is never changed in any way until it reaches the destination host. Once it reaches the destination host, the packet is moved up the network stack and to the respective application. This is where the packet is modified and sent back to the originating host.

20. A. An autonomous system is the term used to describe a collection of networks or subnets that are in the same administrative domain. An interior gateway protocol (IGP) is a dynamic routing protocol that is used inside of a network. The administrative distance (AD) is used to decide the most trusted route when two or more routes to the same network exist. An exterior gateway protocol (EGP) is a dynamic routing protocol used outside of the network.

Chapter 10: Routing Protocols

1. **D.** Virtual Router Redundancy Protocol (VRRP) is an open standard protocol that is used for high availability of default gateways. Network Load Balancing (NLB) is a Windows service that allows for load balancing of network services. Hot Standby Router Protocol (HSRP) is a Cisco proprietary high availability protocol. Open Shortest Path First (OSPF) is a dynamic routing protocol.

2. **A.** Routers are grouped into the same autonomous system (AS). When they are within the same AS, they can exchange information such as routes to destination networks and converge their routing tables. Routing protocols are not normally redistributed between ASs because the network is usually managed as one AS. All routers do not necessarily use the same routing protocols; many different portions of the network can use different protocols. All network IDs are not advertised with the same autonomous system number. Routers are normally grouped into one AS logically, such as an organization. Inside that organization (AS), many different autonomous system numbers can be used.

3. **A.** The maximum hop count for RIP is 15. A hop count over 15 hops is considered non-routable or unreachable, so the other options are incorrect.

4. **C.** By default, RIPv2 multicasts the full routing table on all active interfaces every 30 seconds. RIPv2 does not allow for neighborship through hello packets, such as link-state and hybrid dynamic routing protocols. RIPv2 uses multicasts, not broadcasts. RIPv2 multicasts the full routing table every 30 seconds, not every 60 seconds.

5. **B.** RIPv2 uses the multicast address 224.0.0.9 to advertise routes. The multicast address 224.0.0.5 is used by OSPF for hello messages. The multicast address 224.0.0.6 is also used by OSPF for hello messages for designated routers (DRs) and backup designated routers (BDRs). The multicast address 224.0.0.2 is a special multicast group for all routers, and it is not used by any particular routing protocol.

6. **B.** Routing Information Protocol (RIP) does not contain a topology table. RIP compiles its table from multiple broadcasts or multicasts in the network from which it learns routes. However, it never has a full topological diagram of the network like OSPF, EIGRP, and BGP.

7. **A.** Static routes are highly trusted routes, since an administrator created them. Therefore, they have the lowest administrative distance (AD) with a number of 1. The administrative of 0 is used for connected interfaces. The administrative distance of 2 is a wrong answer and does not map to a route source. The administrative distance of 255 is reserved for unknown sources and is entered into the route process.

8. **B.** Administrative distance (AD) is an order of reliability between dynamic routing protocols and static routes. Administrative distances do not define protocol standards; they only reference them. Administrative distances do not allow for the shortest distance between routers; they allow the router to choose the best path to the destination network. Although administrative distances are programmed into route statements by administrators, they do not calculate path selection.

9. D. Cisco uses a metric for OSPF that is calculated as 10 to the power of 8/bandwidth. This cost value is of 100 Mbps (reference bandwidth) divided by the interface bandwidth. Delay, bandwidth, reliability, and load are used as a composite metric with EIGRP. K metrics are used to weight the calculation of the composite metric used with EIGRP. Link is not used as a metric; if the link is not present, the route will not populate.

10. A. Since both routes are default routes, the route with the lowest administrative distance (AD) will be selected. The route with the highest administrative distance will never be selected first. The route with the lowest metric will be used only if two routes exist to the same destination network and have equal administrative distances. The RIP routing protocol has an administrative distance of 120; therefore, it has a higher administrative distance over a statically defined default route and will not be selected.

11. B. The Routing Information Protocol (RIP) is a distance-vector protocol. Open Shortest Path First (OSPF) is a link-state protocol. Enhanced Interior Gateway Routing Protocol is a hybrid protocol that more closely resembles a link-state protocol. Border Gate-way Protocol (BGP) is a path-vector protocol used for Internet routing.

12. B. A routing loop occurs when packets are routed between two or more routers and never make it to their destination. Routing loops can occur with more than two routers; it is in effect making the packet travel in a loop till its TTL expires. When packets are routed out one interface and come back in on a different interface, this is considered asynchronous routing and not typical of a routing loop. Packets reaching the expiry TTL could mean that there are too many hops to the destination network, but not that a routing loop is occurring. Packets being routed via an inefficient path is not a symptom of a routing loop.

13. D. The administrative distance of the Routing Information Protocol (RIP) is 120. The administrative distance of 90 is used for internal Enhanced Interior Gateway Routing Protocol (EIGRP). The administrative distance of 100 is used for Interior Gateway Routing Protocol (IGR). The administrative distance of 110 is used for Open Shortest.

14. A. Open Shortest Path First (OSPF) is a link-state protocol. A link-state protocol tracks the state of a link between two routers and chooses the most efficient routes based upon the shortest path. Routing Information Protocol (RIP) is a distance-vector protocol. Enhanced Interior Gateway Routing Protocol (EIGRP) is considered a hybrid protocol. Interior Gateway Routing Protocol (IGRP) is a distance-vector protocol.

15. A. Dynamic routing does not require any administrator intervention when routes go down. This is because dynamic routes send route notifications and recalculate the routing tables of all participating routers. Directly connected routes will require administrator intervention if the admin is relying upon the connected route as the route source and an interface goes down. Default routing requires administrator intervention if the default route goes down; the admin will need to pick a new default route and configure it. Static routing always requires an amount of administrator intervention for setup and maintenance of the routes since they are all done manually.

16. A. The benefit of a dynamic routing protocol is that it creates resiliency when routes become unavailable. It does this by recalculating the best route in the network around the outage. When using dynamic routing protocols, there is a higher RAM usage because of the route tables collected. CPU usage is also higher with dynamic routing protocols because of calculations. Bandwidth usage is also higher with dynamic routing protocols because of the traffic involved learning the various routes.

17. A. The Routing Information Protocol version 1 (RIPv1) broadcasts updates for routing tables. Open Shortest Path First (OSPF) exclusively uses multicast to send updates. EIGRP uses multicast to send updates as well and has a backup of direct unicast. BGP uses unicast to retrieve updates on network paths.

18. B. Optimized route selection is a direct advantage of using dynamic routing protocols. A protocol such as OSPF uses the shortest path first algorithm for route selection. Routing tables will not be centralized since all routers participating in dynamic routing will contain their own routing tables. Dynamic routing is not easier to configure due to the up-front planning and configuration. A portion of the available bandwidth will also be consumed for the dynamic routing protocol.

19. C. The Enhanced Interior Gateway Routing Protocol (EIGRP) is a hybrid protocol. It has features of a vector-based protocol and a link-state protocol; hence, it is considered a hybrid protocol. RIP is a distance-vector routing protocol that is used for small networks. OSPF is an extremely scalable link-state protocol. Border Gateway Protocol (BGP) is the routing protocol that is used to route packets on the Internet, and it is considered a path-vector protocol.

20. B. Protocols such as Routing Information Protocol (RIP) re-advertise routes learned. This can be problematic since it is the equivalent of gossiping about what they have heard. Routes learned through this method are never tracked for status or double-checked for validity. Distance-vector protocols do not keep a topology database; they just feed routes to the route table. Distance-vector protocols never check the routes they learn because of the method of routing through rumor.

Chapter 11: Switching and Virtual LANs

1. B. Switches provide the lowest latency with the use of application-specific integrated circuits (ASICs). Hubs are multiport repeaters and diminish usable bandwidth. Bridges are software-based switches and provide higher latency than switches. Routers introduce latency because of decapsulation, routing, and encapsulation of the packets.

2. D. Switches learn MAC addresses based upon incoming ports and examination of the source MAC address. It will build a MAC address table for future lookups. It then determines forwarding interfaces based upon the destination MAC address contained in the frame. Forwarding of data is based upon physical addresses "burned" into the network interface card (NIC) called MAC addresses. Repeating electrical signals to all ports describes how a dumb hub would operate. MAC addresses are learned by the source MAC address on incoming frames to the switch, not the destination frames.

3.   D. The Class of Service (CoS) marking is a 3-bit field in the 802.1Q trunk frame. This 3-bit field contains eight possible queues for QoS at layer 2. Although the 802.1Q protocol supports quality of service (QoS) via the CoS field, 802.1Q is a trunking protocol. Type of Services (ToS) and Diffserv are layer 3 methods for QoS.

4.   C. The 802.1Q protocol is an open standard trunking protocol. Inter-Switch Link (ISL) is another trunking protocol, but it can be used only on Cisco devices. Because your switches are from two different vendors, they are not both Cisco devices; therefore, 802.1Q must be used. The 802.1D protocol is Spanning Tree Protocol (STP), used to prevent loops in networks. The 802.1w protocol is Rapid Spanning Tree Protocol (RSTP), which is also used to prevent loops in networks.

5.   D. When calculating Spanning Tree Protocol (STP), the switch with the lowest MAC address will become the root bridge if all of the priorities are set to the default. However, if the priority on a particular switch is lower than the others, it will always become the root bridge. All other answers are incorrect.

6.   D. Port security can restrict a switch port to a specific number of ports configured by the administrator. The specific MAC addresses can be preconfigured or learned dynamically. The use of jumbo frames will allow 9000 bytes to be framed, in lieu of 1500 bytes normally in a frame. The use of 802.1X will restrict users from communicating on a switch, but it does not limit the number of devices communicating on a switchport. Access control lists are used to restrict traffic based upon IP address and destination port, among other attributes.

7.   C. The flexibility of design for workgroups of clients, servers, services, etc., and the ongoing management of moving and adding people is a benefit of a routed VLAN-enabled network. Migrating from a flat layer 2 network to a routed layer 3 network will not increase collision domains for increased bandwidth. When you add a layer 3 routed infrastructure to your flat layer 2 network, the network complexity of design and operation will increase. You will increase the number of broadcast domains for increased bandwidth when you add multiple routed VLANs.

8.   D. Frames with MAC addresses that are not in the MAC address table are flooded only to the ports in the respective VLAN. Broadcast frames will not be sent outside of the VLAN they originate from because they cannot traverse a router. Unicast frames are not flooded to all ports in all VLANs; they are only flooded to all ports in the VLAN the frame has originated from. The ports that link switches together are usually trunk links so that multiple VLANs can traverse the connection.

9.   C. Static VLANs are VLANs that have been manually configured versus dynamic VLANs, which are configured via a VLAN Membership Policy Server (VMPS). A node will not know which VLAN it is assigned to when it is statically set via the command `switchport access vlan 3`. Nodes use a VLAN Membership Policy Server (VMPS) if the VLAN is dynamically configured. Nodes are not assigned VLANs based on their MAC addresses when they are statically configured. All nodes are not necessarily in the same VLAN when static VLANs are being used.

10. B. When adding VLANs, you immediately increase the number of broadcast domains. At the same time, you increase collision domains. If a switch had 12 ports and they all negotiated at 100 Mb/s half-duplex (one collision domain), when a VLAN is added, you will automatically create two collision domains while adding an additional broadcast domain.

11. C. Dynamic VLANs are deprecated, but you may still see them in operations. A switch configured with dynamic VLANs checks a VLAN Management Policy Server (VMPS) when clients plug in. The VMPS has a list of MAC addresses to their respective VLANs. It is now recommended that dynamic VLAN installations are converted to 802.1X. The access port cannot be controlled with a VMPS based upon user credentials. The access port is also not switched into the respective VLAN based upon the computer's IP address, because the IP address is normally associated based upon the VLAN. The access port cannot be switched into a respective VLAN based upon ACLs since ACLs are used to restrict layer 3 traffic and not layer 2 traffic.

12. A. All VLAN tagging is removed from the frame before it egresses an access port to the end device. Trunk ports carry the VLAN tagging from end to end. Voice ports tag packets only when the CoS value is modified from the default. Native ports are used when frames arrive on a trunk and do not contain any tagging information.

13. A. When you are configuring port security on an interface, the switch port should have a mode of access configured. This will also protect the switch from transitioning into a trunk if another switch is connected. There is no such mode as dynamic mode. If the interface is configured in trunk mode, port security will not be effective since many different MAC addresses can traverse the link. Voice mode is not a mode; it is a function of an access port that tags traffic when a CoS value is detected.

14. D. All switches are configured by default with all interfaces in VLAN 1. This simplifies configuration if the switch is to be used as a direct replacement for a hub since nothing needs to be configured. All of the other options are incorrect.

15. A. Creating the new VLAN will logically segment this work group. Creating a Switched Virtual Interface (SVI) will allow routing on the layer 3 switch. The ACLs should be applied only to VLAN interfaces. Although the other solutions achieve a similar goal, they do not provide flexibility. Extended ACLs cannot be applied to the R&D switch ports since they are layer 2 ports and extended ACLs are layer 3 entries. Creating a new VLAN for R&D and placing the R&D server in the VLAN will not accomplish the goal of restricting the server. Creating a new VLAN and using a trunk to connect the production and R&D network will not accomplish the task.

16. C. 802.1Q inserts a field containing the 16-bit Tag Protocol ID of 0x8100, a 3-bit COS field, a 1-bit drop-eligible indicator (used with COS), and the 12-bit VLAN ID, which equals 32 bits, or 4 bytes. All of the other options are incorrect.

17. C. The client computer connected to an access port cannot see any VLAN tagging information. It is removed before the frame egresses the interface. An access port cannot carry VLAN tagging information because it is stripped. The client computer cannot request the VLAN that it wants to operate in. The administrator must manually configure the VLAN. A client computer cannot see the VLAN tagging information because it is stripped out as it egresses an access port.

18. C. VLANs 1 and 1002 through 1005 are protected by the IOS and cannot be changed, renamed, or deleted. VLAN 1 cannot be deleted, regardless of whether it is still configured on a port. The VLAN that serves as the switch's main management IP can be changed to any other VLAN; it only defaults to VLAN 1 from the factory. VLAN 1 cannot be deleted regardless of whether it is configured as a native VLAN on a trunk.

19. C. Native VLANs are used only for traffic that is not tagged, in which untagged frames are placed on a trunk link. A common use for native VLANs is management traffic between switches, before both sides are configured as a trunk. Traffic that is tagged will traverse the trunk link and not use the native VLAN. Native VLANs are not used for disallowed VLANs on a trunk link. Any traffic that is tagged with ISL on an 802.1Q trunk will not be distinguishable on either side since the frame will be mismatched.

20. B. VLAN Trunking Protocol, or VTP, propagates the VLAN database from an initial master copy on the "server" to all of the "clients." VTP does not help facilitate the dynamic trunking between links. VTP does not detect trunk encapsulation and negotiate trunks. VTP allows for the propagation of the VLAN database, not the trunking database.

Chapter 12: Wireless Networking

1. A. The 802.11n wireless standard introduced channel bonding. The 802.11n standard allows for the bonding of up to two channels to provide a 40 MHz channel. All other answers are incorrect.

2. C. The 2.4 GHz wireless band has three nonoverlapping channels: 1, 6, and 11. Although they overlap with other channels, these three channels do not overlap between themselves. All other answers are incorrect.

3. B. To satisfy the requirements of the client, WPA2-Personal should be configured for the wireless network. WPA2-Personal will allow for 128-bit AES-CCMP encryption and work with a pre-shared key (PSK) to minimize infrastructure. WPA-Enterprise and WPA3-Enterprise require certificate services and an AAA server. WPA-Personal is weaker encryption than WPA2-Personal.

4. D. The Wi-Fi Protected Access 2 (WPA2) protocol can be configured with Advanced Encryption Standard (AES) encryption to provide the highest level of security. Wi-Fi Protected Access (WPA) cannot be configured with AES encryption; therefore, this is a wrong answer. WPA2 cannot be configured with Temporal Key Integrity Protocol (TKIP); only WPA uses the RC4 encryption algorithm and TKIP.

5. A. A single pre-shared key (PSK) is configured for a WPA2 WLAN. The PSK can be either one hex or one ASCII key, but it cannot be both. If you need multiple keys, then WPA2-Enterprise should be used. Keep in mind that a PSK is symmetrical encryption, whereas WPA2-Enterprise uses certificates and asymmetrical encryption. All of the other options are incorrect.

6. D. SSID beaconing is enabled by default; if it were disabled, the clients would not see the SSID. Multicast support is used for multimedia applications and would not prevent the SSID from being seen by clients. The Radio Policy could possibly restrict clients from seeing the SSID depending on what it is set to. However, when it is set to all, there are no restrictions.

7. A. A pre-shared key (PSK) is the mechanism used for configuring authentication with WPA2 using a symmetrical key. Advanced Encryption Standard (AES) is an encryption protocol that is used in conjunction with WPA2. AES is not used for authentication of hosts. Certificates are used with WPA2-Enterprise; they are asymmetrical keys used for authentication. The Temporal Key Integrity Protocol (TKIP) is used alongside the RC4 protocol to provide encryption for WPA; it is not used for authentication.

8. C. You should disable the Temporal Key Integrity Protocol (TKIP) when configuring WPA. Since WPA relies on TKIP and WPA2 requires AES-Counter Mode CBC-MAC Protocol (AES-CCMP). This will ensure that the WAP and client do not fall back to the older WPA protocol. 802.1X will operate independently from the WPA2 and WPA fallback mechanism. Advanced Encryption Standard (AES) is an encryption protocol that is used in conjunction with WPA2; therefore, it should not be disabled. MAC filtering is not related to WPA or WPA2 and works independently as a security mechanism.

9. C. The 802.11i (WPA2) specification introduced a specific mode of Advanced Encryption Standard (AES) encryption called Counter Mode with Cipher Block Chaining Message Authentication Code Protocol (CCMP). The Rivest Cipher 4 (RC4) algorithm is used by Wired Equivalent Privacy (WEP) and Wi-Fi Protected Access (WPA) as an encryption protocol. Message-Digest algorithm 5 (MD5) and Secure Hash Algorithm 1 (SHA1) are popular hashing algorithms but not related to wireless communications.

10. C. After the weaknesses in WEP encryption were discovered, the Wi-Fi Alliance rushed the release of the WPA security protocol. The WPA security protocol incorporated the 802.11i standard of TKIP, which allowed for better integrity of 802.11 transmissions. The WPA security protocol was released after the WEP security protocol. The WPA security protocol did not address any problems related to coverage. It was not a rebranding of the WEP security protocol; it was intended to be a replacement.

11. B. Enabling MAC filtering on the access point will allow the devices that she specifies. Enabling WPA2 encryption will not prevent unauthorized access to the SOHO network. Port security is enabled on wired network switches to prevent unauthorized access. Disabling the SSID from broadcasting will not prevent unauthorized access.

12. A. The device requesting access is the supplicant. The supplicant is built into the operating system in which it is authenticating. The server that is providing authentication is the authentication server, which is commonly the AAA RADIUS server. The device that is controlling the access via the 802.1X protocol is the authenticator. The device connecting the layer 3 network is normally a router or layer 3 switch.

13. A. The access point is responsible for communicating with the supplicant and sending information to the authenticating server. This device is called the authenticator. The end device that sends credentials is called the supplicant. The supplicant is a piece of software in the operating system that supplies the credentials for AAA authentication. The AAA server is normally a RADIUS server or TACACS+ server that is configured for 802.1X.

14. C. It is imperative that a good site survey is completed before you install your wireless network. Trying various types of antennas and their placements is the key to covering the whole wireless area. Turning on broadcast key rotation is a security-related setting and will not affect signal strength. Changing the encryption method used at all the APs will change only the level of encryption and not signal strength. The use of channel bonding and traffic shaping will help increase throughput, but not signal strength.

15. C. The IEEE 802.11b and IEEE 802.11g both run in the 2.4 GHz RF range. 2.4 Gbps and 5 Gbps describe a bandwidth speed and not a frequency range. 5 GHz is a wrong answer.

16. B, D. If you are running 802.11b/g frequency, then you can receive interference from microwave ovens and cordless phones. Copiers, toasters, and IP phones will not interfere with wireless because they are typically wired. An AM radio receives radio waves and will not interfere with wireless.

17. D. 802.11n uses channel bonding of both the 2.4 GHz range and the 5 GHz range to get increased bandwidth of over 100 Mbps. All other answers are incorrect.

18. B. You need to use directional antennas, like a Yagi, to get the best signal between antennas. Replacing bridges with APs will have no difference on a point-to-point connection. Configuring 802.11a on the links will require more power than 2.4GHz. Installing amps to boost the signal could violate wireless regulations.

19. B. If you are running an extended service set (meaning more than one AP with the same SSID), you need to overlap the cell coverage by 10% or more so clients will not drop out while roaming. Using adapters and access points manufactured by the same vendor is not required, since the adapters and APs are manufactured with standards. Configuring all access points to use the same channel is not recommended when using multiple access points. Utilizing MAC address filtering is a security method and is not attributed to coverage.

20. B. The IEEE 802.11b standard uses direct-sequence spread spectrum (DSSS). If you are running 802.11g, it uses orthogonal frequency-division multiplexing (OFDM). All other answers are incorrect.

Chapter 13: Remote Network Access

1. B. Out-of-band management refers to any method of managing the server that does use the network. An example of out-of-band management is the use of a console port to configure a switch or router. A captive portal is used to verify credentials or assert a policy, before access is given to the network for a client. A clientless VPN is a VPN connection that does not require a client, only a web browser, for a secure connection. An AAA server is used to authenticate, authorize, and account for connections.

2. B. A clientless VPN allows users to access internal sensitive sites via a secure tunnel. A captive portal is used to verify credentials or assert a policy, before access is given to the network for a client. The Lightweight Directory Access Protocol (LDAP) is used by Active Directory to look up objects. The Remote Directory Protocol (RDP) is used by Microsoft for remote access.

3. B. A virtual desktop requires less computing power, especially if the applications are also delivered virtually and those applications are running in a VM in the cloud rather than in the local desktop eating up local resources. Virtual Network Computing (VNC) is a protocol used for remote access. Remote desktop is a method of remote access, and it is provided by the Remote Desktop Protocol (RDP).

4. C. VNC includes the following components: VNC server, VNC client (or viewer), and VNC protocol. The VNC server allows the VNC client to connect and provide the VNC desktop over the VNC protocol.

5. B. Secure Shell (SSH) creates a secure channel between the devices and provides confidentiality and integrity of the data transmission. It uses public-key cryptography to authenticate the remote computer and allow the remote computer to authenticate the user, if necessary. Secure Sockets Layer (SSL) is a suite of encryption protocols that includes Transport Layer Security (TLS). Spanning Tree Protocol (STP) is a protocol used to prevent loops in networks with redundant links. Secure File Transfer Protocol (SFTP) is a file transfer protocol that uses encryption.

6. B. Using a TLS channel, the RDP Gateway can tunnel directly to the remote server to increase the security of Remote Desktop Services (RDS). Split tunnel is a type of VPN connection that allows Internet traffic to flow around the VPN connection. A full tunnel is a type of VPN connection, in which all traffic is sent through the VPN connection. Virtual Network Computing (VNC) is an open-source protocol that supports a remote desktop connection.

7. B. Microsoft began calling all terminal services products Remote Desktop Connection with Windows Server 2008 R2. Virtual desktop is a type of remote access. Virtual Network Computing (VNC) is an open-source protocol that supports a remote desktop connection. The RDP Gateway provides secure access for an RDP client to allow access to RDP applications and desktops.

8. C. The Remote Desktop Protocol (RDP) is a proprietary protocol developed by Microsoft. It allows you to connect to another computer and run programs. RDP operates somewhat like Telnet, except instead of getting a command-line prompt as you do with Telnet, you get the actual graphical user interface (GUI) of the remote computer. Role-based access control (RBAC) is a method of assigning permissions to users based upon their role. Secure Shell Protocol (SSH) is an encrypted alternative to the insecure Telnet protocol. Secure Sockets Layer (SSL) is a suite of encryption protocols that includes Transport Layer Security (TLS).

9. D. Secure Shell (SSH) is a terminal-based remote access method. Remote Desktop Protocol (RDP) is a Microsoft protocol used for remote desktop connections. LogMeIn and GoToMyPC are proprietary third-party remote desktop assistance tools.

10. A. When a client-to-site VPN is created, it is possible to do so in two ways, split tunnel and full tunnel. The difference is whether the user uses the VPN for connecting to the Internet as well as for connecting to the office. A site-to-site VPN is used to connect branch offices together over an encrypted tunnel via the Internet. There is no such thing as a Remote Desktop Protocol (RDP) VPN. A clientless VPN allows access to specific services behind the VPN server.

11. D. Site-to-site VPN connections are intended for connecting sites or remote offices to each other via an encrypted tunnel over the Internet. A GRE tunnel is unencrypted and will not provide any security. A wireless WAN can be used to connect VPN clients to the Internet. A client-to-site VPN allows remote workers to telecommute securely over the Internet.

12. D. SSH is encrypted, and Telnet is in clear text. To keep passwords and configuration safe, SSH should always be used. Telnet contains no encryption whatsoever, and all usernames, passwords, and commands are sent in clear text. SSH allows for file copy if it is turned on in the IOS, but it is not a main reason to replace Telnet. Telnet and SSH make it equally easy to create ACLs for access.

13. B. Secure Sockets Layer/Transport Layer Security (SSL/TLS) encryption is used for encryption of clientless VPNs. Secure Shell (SSH) is a type of remote access that provides encrypted terminal-based access. Remote Desktop Protocol (RDP) is a Microsoft GUI-based remote access technology. Access control lists (ACLs) are permissions rules that protect network and file access.

14. D. Most network equipment that uses serial connection, such as Cisco routers and switches, will connect with 9600 baud, 8 data bits, no parity, and 1 stop bit. All other answers are incorrect.

15. B. Connecting to a network switch with the Secure Shell (SSH) protocol is an example of in-band management. An example of out-of-band management is connecting to a router or switch with a serial connection. An example of GUI-based management is Remote Desktop Protocol (RDP). An example of API-based management is configuration through the REST protocol.

16. B. A virtual desktop requires less computing power, especially if the applications are also delivered virtually and those applications are running in a VM in the cloud rather than in the local desktop eating up local resources. Virtual Network Computing (VNC) is a protocol that is used for remote desktop access. A VPN is used to create an encrypted tunnel over the insecure public Internet. Remote Desktop Protocol (RDP) is a Microsoft protocol used for remote desktop access.

17. B. The VNC protocol operates on 5900/TCP. Port 443 protocol TCP is used for HTTPS communications. Port 5900 protocol UDP is a wrong answer. Port 3389 protocol TCP is used for Remote Desktop Protocol (RDP).

18. C. Representational State Transfer (REST) is the most common way to access resource-based APIs. Remote Desktop Protocol (RDP) is a Microsoft protocol used to deliver remote access to desktops and applications. Terminal-based access is used by terminal emulation programs to access routers and switches. GUI-based remote access allows remote control of servers and workstation.

19. A. A USB connection is an out-of-band management connectivity method that provides for up to 115,200 Kbps speeds. EIA-TIA 232 connections are typically low-speed connections. COM is short for the communications port that the EIA-TIA 232 connection would connect to. Secure Shell (SSH) is an in-band management protocol used to connect to routers and switches over the network.

20. C. The Remote Desktop Gateway provides security via TLS and operates on port 443 with protocol TCP. Port 3389 and TCP are used for the Remote Desktop Protocol (RDP). Port 5900 and TCP are used for the Virtual Network Computing (VNC) protocol. Port 80 and TCP are used for HTTP communications.

Chapter 14: Using Statistics and Sensors to Ensure Network Availability

1. B. Latency is the delay typically incurred in the processing of network data from source to destination. Bandwidth is the measured maximum of throughput for a connection. Jitter is the difference between the delay of packets. Loss is the measurement of packets lost in the transfer of data.

2. B. Before an NMS can collect SNMP statistics, the management information base (MIB) from the manufacturer must be loaded. The object ID (OID) is the hierarchal notation of the counter. An SNMP trap command is a message from the SNMP agent to the NMS when a threshold for a counter is exceeded. A SNMP get command is a request message from the NMS to the SNMP agent for the value of a counter.

3. C. NetFlow statistics can analyze the traffic on your network by showing the major users of the network, meaning top talkers, top listeners, top protocols, and so on. Syslog can identify problems or be used for post-mortem analysis. Security information and event management (SIEM) is used to capture security events for further analysis. The Simple Network Management Protocol (SNMP) is a protocol used to capture performance statistics of servers, applications, and network devices.

4. A. In networking, a baseline can refer to the standard level of performance of a certain device or to the normal operating capacity for your whole network. All other answers are incorrect.

5. D. SNMP version 3 introduced message integrity, authentication, and encryption to the SNMP suite. SNMP version 1 was the first release of SNMP, and it is considered deprecated. SNMP version 2e is not a valid version of SNMP. SNMP version 2c is an amendment of SNMP version 2 that added the set command and other improvements.

6. B. The network management station (NMS) is a server to which SNMP is polled back or in which SNMP information is trapped (sent to). The NMS can escalate problems via email, text message, or even visual indicators. Examples of NMS systems are SolarWinds Orion and OpenNMS. The Syslog is a logging file where system messages are sent. The object identifier (OID) is used to describe the SNMP counter being requested. The management information base (MIB) is a sort of database of counters that SNMP can use for a specific device.

7. B. Jitter is the variation of latency (delay) between the source and destination, and it is measured in milliseconds. Latency is the time it takes for a packet or frame to travel from source to destination. Bandwidth is the speed of a connection, and throughput is the utilization of the connection.

8. C. The object identifier (OID) is used to describe the SNMP counter being requested. The Syslog is a logging file where system messages are sent. The network management station (NMS) is a server to which SNMP is polled back or in which SNMP information is trapped. The NMS can escalate problems via email, text message, or even visual indicators. The management information base (MIB) is a sort of database of counters that SNMP can use for a specific device.

9. D. Trap messages are sent from the network device to the SNMP network management station when an event has triggered over a set threshold on the device. An example of an event to be trapped is an interface going down or a restriction by port security. The get-request message is used by an NMS to request information from an SNMP agent. The get-response message is the message sent back from the client to the NMS after a get-request message is received. The set-request message is sent by the NMS to the SNMP client requesting a specific writable counter be set to the specified value.

10. C. SNMP version 2c is identical to SNMP version 1 with respect to security. Both transmit information in clear text and use the security of community strings to authenticate users for access to information. SNMP version 2c does not employ encryption. SNMP version 2c does not employ user authentication. SNMP version 2c does not employ message integrity.

11. B. The management information base (MIB) is a database of variables in which SNMP allows retrieval of information. The attributes in the MIB are the description, variable type, and read-write status. Object identifiers (OIDs) are the addressable counters that are arranged in a hierarchical fashion. The SNMP agent is the software on the client that allows SNMP to collect or pass information. The SNMP community string is used to restrict communications to only the clients or servers that have a matching SNMP community string.

12. B. Standard access control lists (ACLs) can be used in conjunction with the SNMP agent configuration. There is no such thing as encrypted communities. There is no such thing as SNMP callback security; callback security is related to PPP. SNMP does not employ SHA-256 as its encryption protocol.

13. C. SNMP uses UDP port 162 for communication from an SNMP agent to the network management station (NMS) for trap and inform messages. SNMP agents listen on UDP/161. SNMP does not use TCP for messaging. UDP/514 is used for Syslog messaging.

14. C. The severity levels are from 0 to 7, where 0 is an emergency and 7 is debugging. A component failure would be categorized as a level 0 (emergency). All other answers are incorrect.

15. C. The SNMP agent is the software on the client (network device) that allows SNMP to collect, respond, or pass information to the network management station (NMS). Object identifiers (OIDs) are the addressable counters that are arranged in a hierarchical fashion. The management information base (MIB) is a database of variables in which SNMP allows retrieval of information. The SNMP community string is used to restrict communications to only the clients or servers that have a matching SNMP community string.

16. A. The get-request message is used by a network management station (NMS) to request information from an SNMP agent. The get-response message is the message sent back from the client to the NMS, after a get-request message is received. The set-request message is sent by the NMS to the SNMP client requesting a specific writable counter be set to the specified value. Trap messages are sent from the network device to the SNMP network management station when an event has triggered over a set threshold on the device.

17. C. Commonly used NetFlow flows include the following identifiers: source IP address, destination IP address, source port number, destination port number, layer 3 protocol field, Type of Service (ToS) marking, and input logical interface.

18. D. Switched Port Analyzer (SPAN) is a Cisco proprietary method used to mirror port traffic on a switch. Simple Network Management Protocol (SNMP) is a protocol used to capture performance statistics of servers, applications, and network devices. The NetFlow protocol provides session information including the source and destination addresses, applications, and traffic volume. Syslog is a method of collecting system messages to identify problems, or it can be used for post-mortem analysis.

19. A, C. When a system uses all available memory or CPU resources, it may become very unstable and fail. Devices must have available memory and CPU capacity available to be able to function. Voltage is not typically measured as a metric and should always remain at a certain voltage level. Delay is related to network functionality and not part of a component.

20. C. Throughput is the utilization for a given connection. Latency is the measurement of the time it takes for a packet or frame to traverse the network. Jitter is the variance of latency for packets and frames. Bandwidth is the total speed of a connection.

Chapter 15: Organizational Documents and Policies

1. C. For every policy on your network, there should be a credible related procedure that clearly dictates the steps to take in order to fulfill it. All other answers are incorrect.

2. C. Those making the changes should be completely briefed in these rollback procedures, and they should exhibit a clear understanding of them prior to implementing the changes. All other answers are incorrect.

3. B. A maintenance window is an amount of time a system will be down or unavailable during the implementation of changes.

4. B. An access control vestibule is a physical access control solution, not a device hardening technique. Removing unnecessary applications, blocking unrequired ports, and disabling unnecessary services are all device hardening techniques.

5. D. Authentication period controls how long a user can remain logged in. If a user remains logged in for the specified period without activity, the user will be automatically logged out. The password complexity policy specifies how complex a password is required to be. A password history policy specifies how many passwords should be kept in cache, so the user does not reuse the password. The password length policy specifies how long a password is required to be in length.

6. A. Bring your own device (BYOD) initiatives can be successful if implemented correctly. The key is to implement control over these personal mobile devices that leave the safety of your network and return later after potentially being exposed to environments that are out of your control. BYOD initiatives do not apply to routers, servers, and firewalls.

7. C. Data loss prevention (DLP) software attempts to prevent data leakage. It does this by maintaining awareness of actions that can and cannot be taken with respect to a document. A bring your own device (BYOD) policy defines how personal devices can be used in the organization. A password policy defines the life, history, and complexity of passwords in the organization. An acceptable use policy (AUP) defines the acceptable use of organizational resources.

8. B. The main distribution frame (MDF) connects equipment (inside plant) to cables and subscriber carrier equipment (outside plant). It also terminates cables that run to intermediate distribution frames (IDFs) distributed throughout the facility. The hardware rack houses equipment such as servers and equipment. An access control vestibule is used for physical security.

9. B. Verifying optimal distances between prospective AP locations is part of the Predeployment Site Survey step.

10. D. For networks and networked devices, baselines include information about four key components: processor, memory, hard-disk (or other storage) subsystem, and wired/wireless utilization.

11. D. A physical network diagram details all connections so that the next technician does not need to trace connections. A logical network diagram shows the flow of information. A knowledge base article documents a symptom and solution for a problem but not the connections. A change management document is used to evaluate a potential change to a network.

12. D. The incident response plan should be followed during the event since the event is a security incident. A change management plan is used for proposed changes to the network. Knowledge base articles are used to document symptoms and solutions. An acceptable use policy (AUP) is used to protect an organization's resources from user abuse.

13. A. A logical diagram is a high-level overview of a system so that you can see the flow of information. A physical diagram shows specifics, and although it can be used to trace the flow of information, it is not used as a high-level overview. A symbol diagram is not a type of diagram. A knowledge base article details a solution for symptoms and is not used to view the flow of information.

14. C. The acceptable use policy (AUP) details the acceptable use of the email system for business purposes. The bring your own device (BYOD) policy defines the use of personal devices for organization business. A password policy details the appropriate handling and management of passwords. An incident response plan is how a network or security incident is handled.

15. D. Performance baselines gathered over time help create a historical representation of activity and normal operations. When a server is performing poorly, the baseline can validate both the problem and implemented solution.

16. C. A bring your own device (BYOD) policy defines the minimum specifications for an employee's device used for work-related access. The mobile device management (MDM) software would usually dictate these specifications. The acceptable use policy (AUP) defines acceptable usage on the network. The network disclosure agreement (NDA) is an agreement that includes specifics that are not disclosed outside of an organization.

17. C. An SLA of 4 nines is 52.56 minutes per year of expected downtime. This equates to 4.38 minutes per month that the service can be down. All other answers are incorrect.

18. B. A clean-desk policy requires all materials to be removed from your desk before you leave for the day. A nondisclosure agreement (NDA) defines the confidentiality of the organization and what can't be disclosed. The password policy defines the length, complexity, history, and validity time of a user's password. A bring your own device (BYOD) policy defines the use of personal devices for organizational use.

19. C. The site survey report is the document that is prepared before equipment is purchased and deployed. The site survey is then used post-deployment to verify coverage and any adjustments for coverage, and will contain heat maps. Logical network diagrams define the flow of network traffic. Physical network diagrams define how everything is connected for the flow of information. A baseline is captured to establish normal operations, so it can be contrasted upon times of trouble to define the issue.

20. A. The tool you should employ is IP address management (IPAM). This tool will help you plan the allocation of IP addressing for your organization. A service level agreement (SLA) is used to establish a level of service expected from a provider. A memorandum of understanding (MOU) is a mutual agreement between two or more parties. A nondisclosure agreement (NDA) is an agreement in which you agree not to disclose organizational information.

Chapter 16: High Availability and Disaster Recovery

1. D. Load balancing should be implemented with two or more web servers to scale out the servers and lower demand on any one single web server. Clustering creates high availability for an application or operating system. Port aggregation combines two or more connections to aggregate their combined bandwidth. Fault tolerance is the ability of a system to remain running after a component failure.

2. C. The recovery point objective (RPO) is a measurement of time from a failure, disaster, or comparable loss-causing event. RPOs measure back in time to when your data was preserved in a usable format, usually to the most recent backup. The recovery time objective (RTO) is how long it takes to recover your data back to the RPO. The mean time between failures (MTBF) is an average time between failures. The mean time to repair (MTTR) is the average time it takes for a vendor to repair a failure.

3. B. Virtual Router Redundancy Protocol (VRRP) is an IEEE standard (RFC 2338) for router redundancy; Hot Standby Router Protocol (HSRP) is a Cisco proprietary protocol. All other answers are incorrect.

4. B. The Hello timer is the defined interval during which each of the routers sends out Hello messages. Their default interval is 3 seconds, and they identify the state that each router is in. The Hold timer is the amount of time before the Active router is considered offline. The Active timer monitors the state of the Active router and resets each time a Hello packet is seen from the active router. The Standby timer is used to monitor the state of the Standby router and resets each time a Hello packet is seen from the Standby router.

5. A. The last 8 bits (0a) are the only variable bits and represent the HSRP group number that you assign. In this case, the group number is 10 and converted to hexadecimal when placed in the MAC address, where it becomes the 0a that you see. All other answers are incorrect.

6. C. With three servers in an active/passive configuration with two on standby, only one is doing work. Therefore, it does not provide load balancing, only fault tolerance. Having two servers in an active/active configuration provides a scale-out of services. Having three servers in an active/passive configuration with one in standby does not provide fault tolerance because it requires two in standby to match the active count. Having three servers in an active/active configuration does not allow for any failure.

7. B. A cloud recovery site is an extension of the cloud backup services that have developed over the years. These are sites that while mimicking your on-premises network are totally virtual. Cold sites require equipment to be installed and configured. Warm sites are between cold and hot sites and require some intervention. Hot sites typically do not require any intervention, except for organizational data restoration.

8. A. Deluge systems allow large amounts of water to be released into the room, which obviously makes this not a good choice where computing equipment will be located. CO_2, argon, and NAF-S-III systems use heavy gases to extinguish a fire.

9. A. First-hop redundancy protocols (FHRPs) work by giving you a way to configure more than one physical router to appear as if they were only a single logical one. This makes client configuration and communication easier because you can simply configure a single default gateway, and the host machine can use its standard protocols to communicate. Network address translation (NAT) is used to route packets from a private network through the Internet. NIC teaming is not a protocol; it is a method of combining two or more network cards for load balancing or fault tolerance. Spanning Tree Protocol (STP) is switching the protocol used to prevent switching loops for redundant links.

10. A. Switch stacking is the process of connecting multiple switches together (usually in a stack) that are managed as a single switch. All other answers are incorrect.

11. A. A cold site is the least expensive to maintain over time because very little or no hardware is at the site. If a disaster occurs, it will take time to acquire hardware and configure it. A warm site contains equipment but requires intervention to bring it online. A host site or cloud site contains a replica of the organization's servers and is probably the most expensive. The difference between a hot and cloud site is where the servers are running.

12. B. The recovery time objective (RTO) is a measurement of how quickly you can recover from data loss using backup. The recovery point objective (RPO) is the point in time to which you can recover in the event of a disaster. The grandfather, father, son (GFS) rotation is a systematic way to archive backup media. The backup window is the window of time in which a backup can be performed.

13. C, D. An online UPS will supply a flawless AC signal since the DC power source is fed into the rectifier and the AC power only charges the DC batteries. A generator will supply long-term AC power to charge the DC batteries in the event of a power failure. A line interactive and standby UPS does not supply flawless power because the load is shifted during a power outage.

14. D. During the validation tests, the team has the opportunity to give feedback and revise the plans, procedures, and policies. The tabletop exercise is when you should follow the plans, procedures, and policies for your organization. The standard operating procedures (SOPs) are defined by your organization as step-by-step directions. The recovery time objective (RTO) is how long it takes to recover from the failure or deletion of files.

15. B. Clean agent systems are normally found in data centers because the suppression agent is in the form of a gas and will not hurt electronics. A deluge system dumps water out of all the fire suppression nozzles. A preaction system requires a detector to pre-charge the system before water is released. A dry pipe system doesn't contain water in the pipes. When the pressure drops, the water will be released from the nozzles.

16. C. When humidity falls below 20%, there is a huge potential for electrostatic discharge (ESD). Although lower temperatures create lower humidity levels, they do not directly attribute to ESD. Electrical factors are related to power surges, sags, and spikes. Flooding will not cause electrostatic discard, but it will cause electrical shorts.

17. C. An online UPS uses the AC power for the rectifier/charging circuit that maintains a charge for the batteries. The batteries then supply the inverter with a constant DC power source. The inverter converts the DC power source back into an AC power circuit again that supplies the load. A line interactive UPS starts inverting power when the power is lost. A standby UPS shifts the load to a separate inverter circuit. There is no such thing as a failover UPS.

18. A. The mean time to repair (MTTR) is the average time it takes to repair a component and get the system running. Virtual Router Redundancy Protocol (VRRP) is an open standard first hop redundancy protocol (FHRP). Host Standby Router Protocol (HSRP) is a Cisco proprietary FHRP. The mean time between failures (MTBF) is the average time between failures for a device.

19. D. A power distribution unit (PDU) is a device used to supply power for servers and devices; it is similar to a power strip. An inverter is a component of an uninterruptable power supply (UPS). Heating, ventilation, and air conditioning (HVAC) units are used to cool data centers and office spaces. An uninterruptable power supply (UPS) is used to supply short-term power during a power outage.

20. C. NIC teaming will allow you to use both network interfaces connected to independent switches. If one switch fails, the NIC team will allow failure of the NIC to the functioning switch. Hot Standby Router Protocol (HSRP) and Virtual Router Redundancy Protocol (VRRP) are First Hop Redundancy Protocols (FHRPs) used for redundancy of upstream routers. Spanning Tree Protocol (STP) is used to prevent loops in switching networks with redundant paths.

Chapter 17: Data Center Architecture and Cloud Concepts

1. A. AWS and Microsoft Azure are examples of public cloud providers. Private clouds are internally created, and hybrid clouds are a combination of services between your private cloud and the public cloud. Private clouds are purchased and maintained by a private entity and not available for public use, usually on your internal network. Hybrid clouds are a mixture of private and public clouds, usually where your infrastructure exists partially in the public cloud and partially in your private cloud. There is no such thing as dynamic cloud providers since all cloud providers must have a level of elasticity for their clients.

2. C. A hosted medical records service is an example of the SaaS, or software as a service, model. The customer cannot choose variables such as vCPU or RAM. The cloud provider is responsible for the delivery of the software, maintenance of the OS, and maintenance of the hardware. An example of platform as a service (PaaS) would be Google App Engine or Microsoft Azure, where code could be executed on a virtual stack of equipment (programming platform).

3. C. Automated billing is not a NIST criterion for cloud computing. It is essential for the cloud computing vendor but is not relevant if you are hosting your own private cloud. The five NIST criteria for cloud computing are on-demand self-service, broad network access, resource pooling, rapid elasticity, and measured service.

4. C. When an internal IT department hosts the virtualization for a company, it is hosting a private cloud. A public cloud is virtualization infrastructure that is open to the public. An elastic cloud is a cloud that has elasticity. Rapid elasticity is one of the five characteristics that NIST defines as a characteristic of cloud computing. *Internal cloud* is not a term that describes virtualization; therefore, it is an invalid answer.

5. A. The National Institute of Standards and Technology (NIST) defines three cloud types: platform as a service (PaaS), software as a service (SaaS), and infrastructure as a service (IaaS). A DR site hosting at a cloud provider is an example of IaaS. Although DRaaS can be used as a term to advertise a type of cloud service, it is not defined by NIST as a type of service.

6. A. A hosted service that allows you to develop upon it is an example of the platform as a service (PaaS) model. The cloud provider is responsible for delivering APIs that developers can use to create programs. An example of infrastructure as a service (IaaS) is Amazon Web Services (AWS), where a VM can be started up with virtual network services with only a credit card and you are billed periodically. An example of software as a service (SaaS) is your email provider or a customer relation management (CRM) company such as Salesforce. An example of backup as a service is Microsoft Azure cloud backup or Google Drive, just to name a couple.

7. C. You will need a virtual router running static NAT to translate the two different IP networks. This type of service is called a virtual network function (VNF). A virtual switch is built into just about every virtualization platform, since layer 2 communications are normally required. A virtual firewall is a piece of software that allows you to protect your virtualization infrastructure, just like their hardware counterparts. Another IP scheme at the provider could help, but a router would still be required for connectivity.

8. B. The software-defined networking controller provides the control plane for an SDN-based switching fabric.

9. D. Rapid elasticity is the ability to add and remove compute capability in the cloud. As demand increases, compute power can be increased by adding more CPUs or servers. As demand for compute power decreases, CPUs or servers can be removed. Resource pooling is the concept that all of the physical hosts the provider has are pooled together to provide a customer with resources. Measured services is the concept that the provider can determine the amount of computing, network, or storage a customer has used so that they can be billed or a report can be created. Broad network access is the concept that the resources can be accessed from anywhere on the Internet.

10. C. The practice of creating infrastructure definitions in software is called infrastructure as code (IaC).

11. C. The management plane is any mechanism that helps in the management of a router or switch. Some of the common mechanisms are SSH and Telnet. The control plane refers to any mechanism that controls the data plane. The data plane is responsible for switching and routing data. Any data that is destined for endpoints is switched or routed on the data plane. *Switch plane* is not a term normally used to describe data types; therefore, option D is an invalid answer.

12. B. The southbound interface (SBI) directly communicates with the SDN devices. This control is done via several different types of SBI protocols, such as OpenFlow, OpFlex, and CLI (Telnet/SSH). The northbound interface (NBI) is responsible for allowing communication between applications and the core of the controller. The core of the controller is the mechanism that connects the NBI to the SBI. Applications hosted on the controller interface with the NBI.

13. B. There are many different service type offerings from the cloud providers. IaaS, or infrastructure as a service, is when the cloud vendor provides the hardware platform and the company installs and manages its own operating systems. An example of software as a service is an email provider or CRM application. An example of platform as a service is any platform in which you can develop and not maintain the underlying infrastructure. An example of desktop as a service is a platform that offers a virtual desktop login over the Internet.

14. C. The northbound interface (NBI) is responsible for allowing communication between applications and the core of the controller. Applications therefore directly communicate with the core through the northbound interface. The southbound interface (SBI) directly communicates with the SDN devices. The core of the controller is the mechanism that connects the NBI to the SBI. The Simple Network Management Protocol (SNMP) is used for the monitoring and collection of device metrics.

15. C. Machine-to-machine configuration interfaces are called application programming interfaces (APIs) and are used to communicate with each other instead of human-based interfaces such as a GUI or the command line. The northbound interface (NBI) is responsible for allowing communication between applications and the core of the controller. The southbound interface (SBI) directly communicates with the SDN devices. A software-defined network (SDN) is a network that is managed and controlled by a network controller.

16. C. Multitenancy or multitenant clouds offer isolated space in the data centers to run services such as compute, storage, and databases. Scalability is the strategic ability to scale network operations. Elasticity is the tactical ability to scale network operations by adding resources. Platform as a service (PaaS) is a cloud service development environment that allows code to be executed on.

17. A, C, D. Common cloud interconnect methods include Internet, VPN, and Direct Connect. A software-defined network (SDN) is a network that is managed and controlled by a network controller. A virtual switch is a network virtual function (NVF).

18. C. The Virtual eXtensible LAN (VXLAN) protocol is used to create layer 2 tunnels over a layer 3 network. The VXLAN protocol functions by encapsulating layer 2 traffic inside of a layer 3 packet. Generic Router Encapsulation (GRE) is a protocol for encapsulation IP packets inside other IP packets. Virtual local area network (VLAN) is a switching technology that creates network segmentation by creating logical networks in a physical switch. Spanning Tree Protocol (STP) prevents loops in networks with redundant switch links.

19. B. Ansible, Chef, and Puppet are configuration management tools that perform automation and orchestration. A network management station (NMS) is typically used with the Simple Network Management Protocol (SNMP) to centralize polling of SNMP counters and allow for devices to send alerts. Software-defined networking is a method of centralizing the control and management planes of a network so that the network device can focus on the data plane. Centralized logging is used with Syslog so that all logs can be sent to a centralized area for analysis.

20. A. Zero trust architecture (ZTA) assumes a user or device is not trusted, regardless of whether it was previously authenticated. Software-defined networking is a method of centralizing the control and management planes of a network so that the network device can focus on the data plane. Infrastructure as code (IaC) is a method of provisioning and configuring network resources via code. Infrastructure as a service (IaaS) is a cloud type that provides the underlying infrastructure to virtualize a network.

Chapter 18: Network Troubleshooting Methodology

1. A, F. Rebooting servers and rebooting routers are not specifically part of the troubleshooting methodology model. All other answers are incorrect.

2. B. You need to check basic connectivity. The link light indicates that the network card is making a basic-level connection to the rest of the network. It is a very easy item to check, and if the link light is not lit, it is usually a very simple fix (like plugging in an unplugged cable). All other answers are incorrect.

3. B. When wireless users complain that the network is slow (latency) or that they are losing their connection to applications during a session, it is usually latency arising from a capacity issue. An incorrect SSID, encryption, or MAC address filter would prevent the user from ever connecting to the wireless network.

4. B. Although all of these are good tests for network connectivity, checking the server console for user connections will tell you whether other users are able to log into the server. If they can, the problem is most likely related to one of those users' workstations. If they can't, the problem is either the server or network connection. This helps narrow down the problem.

5. B. Because of all the tests given and their results, you can narrow the problem down to the network connectivity of that workstation. And because no other users in this user's area are having the same problem, it can't be the hub or server. You can log in as the user from your workstation, so you know it isn't a rights issue or username/password issue. The only possible answer listed is a bad patch cable.

6. A. Because other users in the same area aren't having a problem, it can't be a downed server, network hub, or jabbering NIC. And because both you and the user can't log in, more than likely it's a problem specific to that workstation. The only one that would affect your ability to log in from that station is the Caps Lock key being pressed. That will cause the password to be in all uppercase (which most server operating systems treat as a different password), and thus it will probably be rejected.

7. D. Since this is a new connection, you need to start by troubleshooting and identify the symptoms and potential causes. Testing a theory is done after you have established a theory and identified the symptoms and potential causes. Rebooting the workstation will probably not fix the issue. Documenting the solution is the last step.

8. B. According to the Network+ troubleshooting model, the next step would be step 2, establishing the most probable cause.

9. C. After determining the affected area, you need to find out if any changes have taken place. All other answers are incorrect.

10. A. Because the user can't log in correctly from any machine, more than likely he is using the wrong procedure for logging in. Because no one else is having that problem (including yourself), the problem must be related to that user.

11. C. After you have implemented a solution, you need to test if the solution works and identify other effects it may have. Gathering information about the issue is one of the first steps. Documenting the issue and the solution that was implemented is the very last step. Escalating the issue is usually done in the middle of troubleshooting when knowledge is exhausted or a fast answer can be derived.

12. B. Because you cannot reach the web page that resides on the server, the problem is most likely related to your browser. If your cable was unplugged or your NIC had failed, you would not get a ping back from the network. If the web server was unplugged, you would not get a ping back from the web server.

13. A, B, C. From a design standpoint, the physical environment for a server should be optimized for items such as placement, temperature, and humidity. When troubleshooting, don't forget to check the physical conditions under which the network device is operating. Check for problems such as those mentioned here as well as EMI/RFI problems, power problems, and unplugged cables. The time of day typically does not have any effect on the problem or solution.

14. D. Because most of today's networks still consist of large amounts of copper cable, networks can suffer from the physical issues that have plagued all networks since the very beginning of networking (and the answers here are not a complete list). Newer technologies and protocols have lessened these issues but have not resolved them completely. Crosstalk, shorts, and open impedance mismatch are all basic physical issues that can occur.

15. A. Once you have determined that the switch or the configuration of the switch is complex, you should escalate the issue. Creating an action plan and implementing a solution should be done after a possible solution is derived. Determining the scope of the problem is one of the first steps that should be accomplished.

16. D. Because other people are experiencing the problem, most likely it is either network-or server-related. Because you can transfer files to and from another server, it can't be the network. Thus, the problem is related to the web server.

17. D. After investigating the problem thoroughly and successfully testing and resolving an issue, you need to document the solution. All other answers are incorrect.

18. B. Since users can get to the Internet, this means the DNS server is working, and they have the correct default gateway. The intranet server is probably down.

19. C. Performance-monitoring tools can give you an idea of how busy the server and the rest of the network are. These tools use graphs to indicate how much traffic is going through the server. The server's NIC link light will only verify the physical connection. A protocol analyzer will allow you to diagnose applications problems at a very finite level. The server's system log file will only detail failures.

20. C. Once you escalate the problem, you are done with the seven-step troubleshooting model. Meet with the escalation team to determine the next step. All other answers are incorrect.

Chapter 19: Network Software Tools and Commands

1. C. The program Packet Internet Groper (ping) is used to find out if a host has the IP stack initialized. File Transfer Protocol (FTP) is a protocol used to transfer files. Telnet is an unencrypted terminal-based emulator that operates across TCP/IP. The netstat command will detail all of the connections to the operating system.

2. A. The arp utility is used to display the contents of the ARP cache, which tracks the resolution of IP addresses to physical (MAC) addresses and will produce the displayed output. The netstat command will detail all of the connections to the operating system. The tracert command will display the path a packet will take through the network to the destination. The tcpdump command will display all packets that are seen by the network interface card (NIC).

3.   A. The Microsoft operating system has a Remote Desktop software built in called Remote Desktop. Connections can be made from anywhere in the world, permitting that it is enabled on the destination computer. The `netstat` command will detail all of the connections to the operating system. The `arp` utility is used to display the contents of the ARP cache, which tracks the resolution of IP addresses to physical (MAC) addresses and will produce the displayed output. Wireshark is a packet capture and analyzer tool used to determine issues.

4.   B. The purpose of the `ping` utility is to test the communications between two IP hosts as well as how long it takes the packets to get from one host to another. The `tracert` command will display the path a packet will take through the network to the destination. The `arp` utility is used to display the contents of the ARP cache, which tracks the resolution of IP addresses to physical (MAC) addresses and will produce the displayed output. The `ipconfig` command is used on Microsoft operating systems to display the IP address configuration.

5.   C. The `ipconfig /all` utility will display the current configuration of TCP/IP on a given workstation—including the current IP address, DNS configuration, and default gateway. The purpose of the `ping` utility is to test the communications between two IP hosts as well as how long it takes the packets to get from one host to another. The `ipconfig` command alone will display basic IP configuration information, such as IP address, subnet mask, and default gateway. The `tracert` command will display the path a packet will take through the network to the destination.

6.   B, D. The address 127.0.0.1 is the special IP address designated for the local TCP/IP interface. The hostname localhost is the hostname given to the local interface. Therefore, pinging either the IP address or the hostname for the local interface will tell you whether the local interface is working. All other answers are incorrect.

7.   C. The command `ip` was added to most Linux distributions and is replacing the depreciated `ifconfig` command. The `netstat` command will detail all of the connections to the operating system. The `ipconfig` command is a Microsoft command-line tool that will display basic IP configuration information.

8.   C. The `arp` utility will show you the resolved MAC to IP address of all hosts on your network segment. Remember, this will work for only local hosts, not remote hosts. The `ping` command tests connectivity and round-trip time between two hosts. The `ipconfig` command is a Microsoft command-line tool that will display basic IP configuration information. The `netstat` command will detail all of the connections to the operating system. The `ftp` command will transfer files between two hosts.

9.   A. The `netstat -a` command will display all connections and listening ports on the host computer. Remember that the `-a` must be lowercase and that it will not work correctly without the hyphen before it. The lowercase `-p` switch selects the protocol for the output of the `netstat` command. The `-f` and `-t` are not valid switches for the `netstat` command.

10.   B. Commercial sniffers like Wireshark and Omnipeek can capture any packets because they set the NIC to operate in promiscuous mode, which means the NIC processes all packets that it sees. All other answers are incorrect.

11. B. The `tracert` utility will give you that output. The `tracert` command (or `trace` for short) traces the route from the source IP host to the destination host. The `arp` utility is used to display the contents of the ARP cache, which tracks the resolution of IP addresses to physical (MAC) addresses and will produce the displayed output. The `tcpdump` command will display all packets that are seen by the network interface card (NIC).

12. B. The `tracert` utility will tell you which router is having the performance problem and how long it takes to move between each host. The `tracert` command can be used to locate problem areas in a network. The `netstat` command will detail all of the connections to the operating system. The purpose of the `ping` utility is to test the communications between two IP hosts as well as how long it takes the packets to get from one host to another. The `arp` utility is used to display the contents of the ARP cache, which tracks the resolution of IP addresses to physical (MAC) addresses and will produce the displayed output.

13. A. The `ipconfig /all` switch will display the most complete listing of TCP/IP configuration information, also displaying the MAC address, DHCP lease times, and the DNS addresses. The `/renew` switch will renew the current DHCP lease. The `/release` switch will release the current DHCP lease. The `/?` switch will display the help for the `ipconfig` command.

14. B. The `tracert` utility returns the names and addresses of all routers through which a packet passes on its way to a destination host. The `netstat` command will detail all of the connections to the operating system. The purpose of the `ping` utility is to test the communications between two IP hosts as well as how long it takes the packets to get from one host to another. The `arp` utility is used to display the contents of the ARP cache, which tracks the resolution of IP addresses to physical (MAC) addresses and will produce the displayed output.

15. D. Although UDP traffic is connectionless and a state will not be shown in the `netstat` command output, traffic will still show if there is traffic. When you issue the command `netstat` without any switches, listening ports will not be shown. Only when you issue the command `netstat -n` will you see listening ports.

16. C. The `arp -a` command will display the current contents of the ARP cache on the local workstation. All other answers are incorrect.

17. B. The `dig` command is a UNIX/Linux command that will show you DNS server information. The `netstat` command will detail all of the connections to the operating system. ICMP is the protocol that `ping` and `tracert` operate on. The `arp -a` command will display the current contents of the ARP cache on the local workstation.

18. A, D. The `arp` command's –a and –g switches perform the same function. They both show the current ARP cache. All other answers are incorrect.

19. B. There are three different chain types:

Input: Controls behavior for incoming connections

Forward: Used for incoming connections that aren't being delivered locally (like a router would receive)

Output: Used for outgoing connections

20. A. To capture traffic on all interfaces, use the any keyword with the −i (interface) switch. All other answers are incorrect.

Chapter 20: Network Security Concepts

1. D. The availability element of the CIA triad ensures that information can be accessible. The integrity element ensures that information is not tampered with. The confidentiality element ensures that information is kept confidential and can't be viewed by others, only its intended audience. Accessibility is not an element of the CIA triad.

2. C. Data at rest is the encryption concept being exercised when you implement an encryption key for backup to tape. The data is at rest on its storage device. Data in use is protection for data in memory. Data in transit is protection for data being transmitted. Data on tape is not an encryption concept and falls under data at rest.

3. C. The introduction of a virus with an unknown USB drive is an inadvertent insider threat. It could be controlled with education and vigilance. Ransomware via a threat actor, a DoS, and the exploitation of a web server would all be considered external threats, out of your control.

4. A. The common vulnerabilities and exposures (CVE) system is used by all major software vendors to create a common naming scheme for vulnerabilities. A zero day is an exploit in which no patch is available for. Identity and access management (IAM) is a security framework adopted by service providers. Multifactor authentication (MFA) is the use of multiple factors to authenticate a user.

5. C. The principle of least privilege dictates that a user be given the least permission to perform their job. Zero trust is a method of requiring the user to authenticate for each resource they access, regardless of where the asset is located. Role-based access is a method of granting permissions based upon a role in the organization. The defense-in-depth security concept is a layered approach to security, where several layers are used to protect the organization.

6. A. Authentication is the process of verifying a user's identify. It can be performed with various factors such as something you know, something you are, or something you have, in addition to other factors. Authorization is the process of checking the permission of the authenticated user for the resource. Accounting is the principle that describes the process of recording a user's action based upon the AAA security model of authentication, authorization, and accounting. Auditing is typically performed for compliance or review of log files.

7. A. Remote Authentication Dial-In User Service (RADIUS) was originally proposed by the IETF and became an open standard for authentication, often used with wireless. TACACS+ is a Cisco technology that became an open standard. Kerberos is exclusively used by Microsoft for the authentication of users. Lightweight Directory Access Protocol (LDAP) is a protocol that is also exclusively used by Microsoft for looking up objects in Active Directory.

8. B. Security Assertion Markup Language (SAML) is an open-standard XML-based framework used for transmitting authentication and authorization information of users and computers. Lightweight Directory Access Protocol (LDAP) is a protocol that is exclusively used by Microsoft for looking up objects in Active Directory. Active Directory (AD) is Microsoft's directory services product. Kerberos is exclusively used by Microsoft for authenticating users with Active Directory.

9. B. Authorization is the process of verifying whether a user has permission for a specific action; it is followed by the authentication of the user. Authentication is the process of verifying the user's identify. It can be performed with various factors such as something you know, are, or have, in addition to other factors. Accounting is the principle that describes the process of recording a user's action based upon the AAA security model of authentication, authorization, and accounting. Auditing is typically performed for the compliance or review of log files.

10. A. The protocol TCP and port number of 389 are used for LDAP lookups. All of the other answers are incorrect.

11. D. An exploit is a script, code, application, or technique used to gain unauthorized access to an operating system through a vulnerability. A weakness in the operating system and a known operating system security flaw are considered vulnerabilities. A configuration that weakens the security of the operating system is considered a threat.

12. D. An exploit is an attack against a weakness, also known as a vulnerability. The threat is the potential for an exploit to be carried out. The risk is the potential for the threat to become exploited. The vulnerability is the weakness in the system.

13. B. The protocol is most likely for RADIUS accounting, which uses UDP port 1813. RADIUS authentication uses UDP port 1812. TACACS+ authentication uses TCP port 49. LDAP queries Active Directory on TCP port 389.

14. C. To fix the issue, you will need to add the network appliance public certificate to the trusted root CA certificate store on your computer. This will allow your computer to trust the self-signed certificate and validate the signing. Adding the public certificate for the network appliance to the root CA certificate revocation list (CRL) is incorrect. Adding the network appliance public certificate to the root CA AIA is incorrect. Adding the network appliance private certificate to the trusted root CA certificate store will not fix the issue.

15. C. Your fingerprint is an example of something that you are, because it is unique to you. A password is something that you know. A signature is something that you do, as it is unique to how you sign and can be forged. A location is somewhere you are, according to your GPS location.

16. D. The General Data Protection Regulation (GDPR) is a European law that protects consumers and regulates how their data can be used. The Sarbanes–Oxley Act (SOX) is a federal law and regulates how financial records are kept. The Health Insurance Portability and Accountability Act is a law that regulates how patient information is protected. The Gramm–Leach–Bliley Act (GLBA) is a Federal Trade Commission (FTC) regulation that protects US consumers.

17. B. Geofencing is a technique to protect data, so it is viewed only within a geographic location. The principle of least privilege is a concept where you only grant the necessary permissions to do a task. Role-based access control (RBAC) is a system in which people are given roles and the roles contain the permissions to complete a task. Identity and access management (IAM) is a security framework for creating users and granting permissions.

18. A. The certificate revocation list (CRL), which is located in the public certificate, is checked to make sure that a certificate has not been revoked. The root certificate authority (CA) is the root of all trust for an issued certificate. The Authority Information Access (AIA) defines how the client can obtain the public certificate for a presented certificate. The private key is used to sign and decrypt.

19. C. Role-based access control (RBAC) is a strategy where you grant roles to users that contain the various permissions. Another admin simply needs to place the user into the role to grant permissions. Terminal Access Controller Access-Control System + (TACACS+) and Remote Authentication Dial-In User Service (RADIUS) are authentication/authorization servers used for wired and wireless access. Public key infrastructure (PKI) is a system that is used for encryption and signing.

20. B. The Transport Layer Security (TLS) protocol uses public/private key pairs for encryption. The Authority Information Access (AIA) defines how the client can obtain the public certificate for a presented certificate. The certificate revocation list (CRL) contains a location to check to make sure that a certificate has not been revoked. Identity and access management (IAM) is a security framework for creating users and granting permissions.

Chapter 21: Common Types of Attacks

1. C. Shoulder surfing is not a technology-based attack. It is a social engineering attack. Denial of service (DoS), rogue DHCP, and malware are all technology-based attacks.

2. A. The command-and-control server is used to control a botnet, which is part of a distributed denial-of-service (DDoS) attack. All other answers are incorrect.

3. A. An on-path attack, also known as a man-in-the-middle (MiTM) attack, allows the attacker to impersonate both parties involved in a network conversation. A deauthentication attack is a method of deauthenticating all of the wireless users in an attempt to hijack the access point. A denial-of-service (DoS) attack attempts to run a service out of resources, thereby denying valid service requests. Spoofing is the act of impersonating a user or computer.

4. D. A rogue DHCP is an attack in which another DHCP serves out IP addresses along with a malicious default gateway. User traffic is then redirected through the malicious gateway in an attempt to steal information. A denial-of-service (DoS) attack is an attempt to deny legitimate service requests, by overutilizing resources. VLAN hopping is an attack in which malicious traffic is double-tagged in an attempt to hop to another VLAN. Deauthentication is an attack that attempts to deauthenticate 802.11 traffic and hijack a wireless SSID.

5. B. An NTP amplification attack is carried out by sending a small UDP packet to a vulnerable NTP server. The server then sends a large amount of data to the victim, amplifying the attack. A distributed denial-of-service (DDoS) attack happens when many hosts attack a central host. A reflective attack happens when the threat actor requests data from a third party with a return address to the victim. DNS amplification attacks are similar in design to NTP amplification attacks, except they use a different protocol.

6. B. A man-in-the-middle attack (also known as an on-path attack) happens when someone intercepts packets intended for one computer and reads the data. A VLAN hopping attack happens when frames are double tagged in an effort to hop VLANs. A denial-of-service (DoS) attack happens when a threat actor denies service to other users by attacking the intended victim. A deauthentication attack is carried out by sending deauthentication frames to wireless clients to disassociate them with the SSID they are connected to.

7. A. The threat actor can attack a VLAN they are not permitted to by a process called double tagging; this attack is called VLAN hopping. A man-in-the-middle attack (also known as an on-path attack) happens when someone intercepts packets intended for one computer and reads the data. A distributed denial-of-service (DDoS) attack is comprised of many hosts that attack a central victim. Malware is a generic term used to describe a number of infections, such as ransomware, Trojans, and key loggers, just to mention a few.

8. B. ARP spoofing is the process of adopting another system's MAC address for the purpose of receiving data meant for that system. A rogue DHCP attack happens when a threat actor introduces a DHCP server to the network that populates the threat actor's IP address. IP spoofing is an attack when a threat actor imposters a legitimate IP address. DNS spoofing is an attack when the DNS answers are spoofed coming from the threat actor.

9. A. Rogue access points are access points (APs) that have been connected to your wired infrastructure without your knowledge. The rogue may have been placed there by a determined hacker who snuck into your facility and put it in an out-of-the-way location or, more innocently, by an employee who just wants wireless access and doesn't get just how dangerous doing this is. Command-and-control servers are used to control botnets. Malware is an infection that has malicious intent of the network or user. A botnet is a group of computers controlled by a command-and-control server for malicious purposes.

10. C. This ugly trick is achieved by placing their AP on a different channel from your legitimate APs and then setting its SSID in accordance with your SSID. A rogue access point (AP) is wireless equipment that is connected to your network without your permission or knowledge. A rogue DHCP is used by a threat actor to populate malicious IP addresses to DHCP clients. DNS poisoning is an attack in which the victim's DNS cache is attacked with malicious answers.

11. D. Any service that allows the user to create a connection or access to information can be used as an attack vector. In the case of DHCP, the attacker will set the gateway to their IP address. In the case of DNS, the attacker could spoof a request to redirect the traffic. In the case of wireless, the attacker can spoof the secure set identifier (SSID).

12. A. Double tagging is an attack that can be used against the native VLAN. The attacker will tag the native VLAN on a frame and then tag another inside that frame for the VLAN that the attacker intends to compromise. When the switch receives the first frame, it removes the default VLAN tag and forwards it to other switches via a trunk port. When the other switch receives the frame with the second VLAN tag, it forwards it to the VLAN upon which the attacker is targeting the attack. VLAN traversal is not an attack; it is a term to describe a VLAN traversing a trunk link between two switches. Trunk popping is not a valid attack; it is not a term used in networking, and therefore, it is an invalid answer. A denial-of-service (DoS) attack is an attack in which an attempt to exhaust a service's resources is launched to knock the service offline.

13. A. Shoulder surfing involves looking over someone's shoulder as they enter information. Phishing is the act of attempting to steal credentials by sending an email that takes the recipient to a fraudulent login. Tailgating is the act of following a person through an access control point using their credentials. Whaling is a form of phishing that targets high-profile individuals.

14. C. Antimalware covers a wide array of security threats to users, including Trojans, viruses, and phishing emails. Multifactor authentication combines two or more single-factor authentication methods to create very secure authentication for users. Software firewalls will not prevent threats such as Trojans, viruses, and phishing emails. Antivirus software protects you only from viruses and Trojans, not phishing emails.

15. A. Access control lists (ACLs) are an effective way to mitigate spoofing of internal IPs from outside the trusted network. ACLs are used to control traffic by allowing, denying, or logging traffic depending on specific conditions. An intrusion detection system (IDS) can be used to notify you if it detects an attack, but it will not prevent an attack. Transport Layer Security (TLS) communications offer both encryption and authentication of the data via certificate signing. This would prevent tampering of the data end to end, but it will not prevent spoofing. A host intrusion detection system (HIDS) is an application that runs on a host to detect intrusions. An HIDS is similar to an IDS, but it is all software-based and resides on the host it is to protect.

16. C. A captive portal will capture the users' first web page request and redirect them to either a login page or an AUP. Access control lists (ACLs) and MAC filtering restrict specific traffic. The 802.1X protocol is used to authenticate users and devices to control a layer 2 switchport.

17. A. Network access control (NAC) is used in conjunction with 802.1X and can restrict clients if specific security policies are not met, such as current antivirus and software updates. The 802.1X protocol is used to authenticate users and devices to control a layer 2 switchport. EAP-TLS is a protocol used to authenticate users and computers. Access control lists (ACLs) are used to restrict specific traffic.

18. D. Access lists can be applied to a port, to a protocol, and in a direction. For example, you could apply only one ACL to the interface Fa0/1 to the protocol IP in the inbound direction.

19. A. Social engineering uses the inherent trust in the human species, as opposed to technology, to gain access to your environment. IDSs are network-based systems that detect intrusions. Perimeter security describes physical security. Biometrics describes an authentication method based on human physical traits.

20. A. An on-path attack intercepts data and then sends the information to the server as if nothing were wrong while collecting the information. Zero-day attacks are attacks in which a developer has not properly patched a hole yet and is unaware of the hole. A denial-of-service (DoS) attack is used to disrupt legitimate requests from being answered. An ARP spoofing attack occurs when the threat actor spoofs a legitimate MAC address.

Appendix C

Subnetting Class A

Class A subnetting is not performed any differently than subnetting with Classes B and C, but there are 24 bits to play with instead of the 16 in a Class B address and the 8 in a Class C address.

Let's start by listing all the Class A masks:

```
255.0.0.0      (/8)
255.128.0.0    (/9)          255.255.240.0    (/20)
255.192.0.0    (/10)         255.255.248.0    (/21)
255.224.0.0    (/11)         255.255.252.0    (/22)
255.240.0.0    (/12)         255.255.254.0    (/23)
255.248.0.0    (/13)         255.255.255.0    (/24)
255.252.0.0    (/14)         255.255.255.128  (/25)
255.254.0.0    (/15)         255.255.255.192  (/26)
255.255.0.0    (/16)         255.255.255.224  (/27)
255.255.128.0  (/17)         255.255.255.240  (/28)
255.255.192.0  (/18)         255.255.255.248  (/29)
255.255.224.0  (/19)         255.255.255.252  (/30)
```

That's it. You must leave at least 2 bits for defining hosts. I hope you can see the pattern by now. Remember, we're going to do this the same way as a Class B or C subnet. It's just that, again, we simply have more host bits, and we use the same subnet numbers we used with Class B and Class C, but we start using these numbers in the second octet.

Subnetting Practice Examples: Class A Addresses

When you look at an IP address and a subnet mask, you must be able to distinguish the bits used for subnets from the bits used for determining hosts. This is imperative. If you're still struggling with this concept, please reread Chapter 6, "Introduction to the Internet Protocol." It shows you how to determine the difference between the subnet and host bits and should help clear things up.

Practice Example #1A: 255.255.0.0 (/16)

Class A addresses use a default mask of 255.0.0.0, which leaves 22 bits for subnetting since you must leave 2 bits for host addressing. The 255.255.0.0 mask with a Class A address is using 8 subnet bits.

- *Subnets?* $2^8 = 256$.
- *Hosts?* $2^{16} - 2 = 65,534$.
- *Valid subnets?* What is the interesting octet? $256 - 255 = 1$. 0, 1, 2, 3, etc. (all in the second octet). The subnets would be 10.0.0.0, 10.1.0.0, 10.2.0.0, 10.3.0.0, etc., up to 10.255.0.0.
- *Broadcast address for each subnet?*
- *Valid hosts?*

The following table shows the first two and last two subnets, valid host range, and broadcast addresses for the private Class A 10.0.0.0 network:

Subnet	10.0.0.0	10.1.0.0	...	10.254.0.0	10.255.0.0
First host	10.0.0.1	10.1.0.1	...	10.254.0.1	10.255.0.1
Last host	10.0.255.254	10.1.255.254	...	10.254.255.254	10.255.255.254
Broadcast	10.0.255.255	10.1.255.255	...	10.254.255.255	10.255.255.255

Practice Example #2A: 255.255.240.0 (/20)

255.255.240.0 gives us 12 bits of subnetting and leaves us 12 bits for host addressing.

- *Subnets?* $2^{12} = 4096$.
- *Hosts?* $2^{12} - 2 = 4094$.
- *Valid subnets?* What is your interesting octet? $256 - 240 = 16$. The subnets in the second octet are a block size of 1 and the subnets in the third octet are 0, 16, 32, etc.
- *Broadcast address for each subnet?*
- *Valid hosts?*

The following table shows some examples of the host ranges—the first three and the last subnets:

Subnet	10.0.0.0	10.0.16.0	10.0.32.0	...	10.255.240.0
First host	10.0.0.1	10.0.16.1	10.0.32.1	...	10.255.240.1
Last host	10.0.15.254	10.0.31.254	10.0.47.254	...	10.255.255.254
Broadcast	10.0.15.255	10.0.31.255	10.0.47.255	...	10.255.255.255

Practice Example #3A: 255.255.255.192 (/26)

Let's do one more example using the second, third, and fourth octets for subnetting.

- *Subnets?* $2^{18} = 262,144$.
- *Hosts?* $2^6 - 2 = 62$.
- *Valid subnets?* In the second and third octet, the block size is 1, and in the fourth octet, the block size is 64.
- *Broadcast address for each subnet?*
- *Valid hosts?*

The following table shows the first four subnets and their valid hosts and broadcast addresses in the Class A 255.255.255.192 mask:

Subnet	10.0.0.0	10.0.0.64	10.0.0.128	10.0.0.192
First host	10.0.0.1	10.0.0.65	10.0.0.129	10.0.0.193
Last host	10.0.0.62	10.0.0.126	10.0.0.190	10.0.0.254
Broadcast	10.0.0.63	10.0.0.127	10.0.0.191	10.0.0.255

The following table shows the last four subnets and their valid hosts and broadcast addresses:

Subnet	10.255.255.0	10.255.255.64	10.255.255.128	10.255.255.192
First host	10.255.255.1	10.255.255.65	10.255.255.129	10.255.255.193
Last host	10.255.255.62	10.255.255.126	10.255.255.190	10.255.255.254
Broadcast	10.255.255.63	10.255.255.127	10.255.255.191	10.255.255.255

Subnetting in Your Head: Class A Addresses

This sounds hard, but as with Class C and Class B, the numbers are the same; we just start in the second octet. What makes this easy? You only need to worry about the octet that has the largest block size (typically called the interesting octet; one that is something other than 0 or 255)—for example, 255.255.240.0 (/20) with a Class A network. The second octet has a block size of 1, so any number listed in that octet is a subnet. The third octet is a 240 mask, which means we have a block size of 16 in the third octet. If your host ID is 10.20.80.30, what is your subnet, broadcast address, and valid host range?

The subnet in the second octet is 20 with a block size of 1, but the third octet is in block sizes of 16, so we'll just count them out: 0, 16, 32, 48, 64, 80, 96. . .*voilà*! (By the way, you can count by 16s by now, right?) This makes our subnet 10.20.80.0, with a broadcast of 10.20.95.255 because the next subnet is 10.20.96.0. The valid host range is 10.20.80.1 through 10.20.95.254. And yes, no lie! You really can do this in your head if you just get your block sizes nailed!

Let's practice on one more, just for fun!

Host IP: 10.1.3.65/23

First, you can't answer this question if you don't know what a /23 is. It's 255.255.254.0. The interesting octet here is the third one: 256 − 254 = 2. Our subnets in the third octet are 0, 2, 4, 6, etc. The host in this question is in subnet 2.0, and the next subnet is 4.0, so that makes the broadcast address 3.255. And any address between 10.1.2.1 and 10.1.3.254 is considered a valid host.

Written Lab C.1

Given a Class A network and the net bits identified (CIDR), complete the following table to identify the subnet mask and the number of host addresses possible for each mask:

Classful Address	Subnet Mask	Number of Hosts per Subnet (2x − 2)
/16		
/17		
/18		
/19		
/20		
/21		
/22		
/23		
/24		
/25		
/26		
/27		
/28		
/29		
/30		

Written Lab C.2

Given the decimal IP address, write in the address class, number of subnet and host bits, number of subnets, and number of hosts for each IP address.

Decimal IP Address	Address Class	Number of Subnet and Host Bits	Number of Subnets (2x)	Number of Hosts (2x – 2)
10.25.66.154/23				
172.31.254.12/24				
192.168.20.123/28				
63.24.89.21/18				
128.1.1.254/20				
208.100.54.209/30				

Answers to Written Lab C.1

Classful Address	Subnet Mask	Number of Hosts per Subnet (2x – 2)
/16	255.255.0.0	65,534
/17	255.255.128.0	32,766
/18	255.255.192.0	16,382
/19	255.255.224.0	8,190
/20	255.255.240.0	4,094
/21	255.255.248.0	2,046
/22	255.255.252.0	1,022
/23	255.255.254.0	510
/24	255.255.255.0	254
/25	255.255.255.128	126
/26	255.255.255.192	62
/27	255.255.255.224	30

Classful Address	Subnet Mask	Number of Hosts per Subnet $(2x - 2)$
/28	255.255.255.240	14
/29	255.255.255.248	6
/30	255.255.255.252	2

Answers to Written Lab C.2

Decimal IP Address	Address Class	Number of Subnet and Host Bits	Number of Subnets $(2x)$	Number of Hosts $(2x - 2)$
10.25.66.154/23	A	15/9	32768	510
172.31.254.12/24	B	8/8	256	254
192.168.20.123/28	C	4/4	16	14
63.24.89.21/18	A	10/14	1,024	16,382
128.1.1.254/20	B	4/12	16	4094
208.100.54.209/30	C	6/2	64	2

Index

A

A record (address record), 159, 160
-a switch, 724, 728, 741, 742
AAA model
    about, 790
    accounting, 800–801
    authentication, 790–798
    authorization, 798–800
AAAA record (quad-A record), 159, 160
ABAC (attribute-based access control), 634
absorption, unbounded media and, 666
acceptable-use policy (AUP), 545–546
access control lists (ACLs)
    about, 835–837
    incorrect settings, 683
access control vestibules (mantraps), 830
access layer, 27
access link, 403, 405
access point (AP)
    about, 135, 146
    configuring, 462–466
    rogue, 472, 822–824
Access Point mode, 463
access ports, 403–404
accounting, 800–801
accounts, security and, 551
acknowledgements, Transport layer and, 46–47
ACLs. See access control lists (ACLs)
Active Directory, 174
Active Timer (HSRP), 598
active/active, 593–600
active/passive, 583, 593–600
ad hoc mode, 451–452
ad hoc networks, 472–473
ad hoc scan, 515
Adaptive Security Appliance (ASA), 583
add command, 736
address learning, 387–389
address record (A record), 159, 160
Address Resolution Protocol (ARP)
    about, 220, 225–226, 252, 324
    inspection, 415
    spoofing, 821–822
    table, 725–726
    using, 725–726
administrative distances (AD), 344–346
Advanced Research Projects Agency (Department
        of Defense), 195
agencies, wireless, 434

aggregate rate, 108
AH (Authentication Header), 228
AIA (Authority Information Access), 786
alias record, 161
American National Standards Institute (ANSI), 557
American Society of Heating, Refrigerating and
        Air-Conditioning Engineers (ASHRAE), 590
amplified/reflected attacks, 818
analog modem, 157, 169–170
analog modulation, 55
angled physical contact (APC), 76
anomaly alerting/notification, 515
anonymous username, 198
ANSI (American National Standards Institute),
        557
ANT+, 460
antennas, unbounded media and, 665
anycast, 255
AP. See access point (AP)
APC (angled physical contact), 76
API (application programming interface),
        498
APIDS (application protocol based IDS), 145
APIPA (Automatic Private IP Addressing),
        204, 250–251
APIs. See application programming
        interfaces (APIs)
application awareness, as a benefit of SDN, 628
Application layer. See also Process/
        Application layer
    about, 40–41, 629
    DHCP as Application layer protocol, 155, 164
    features of, 39
    proxy server as operating on, 167
    some firewalls as operating up to, 144
application log, 527
application programming interfaces (APIs)
    about, 498, 631
    integration, 523
    northbound, 632
    southbound, 631–632
application protocol based IDS (APIDS), 145
application server, 6
applications, cable, 654–656
application-specific integrated circuit (ASIC)
    about, 385–386
    hardware, 157, 183
architecture, network, 12–13
ARP. See Address Resolution Protocol (ARP)
arp -a, 299

arp utility, 726–729
ARPAnet, 195
AS (autonomous system), 332, 343
ASA (Adaptive Security Appliance), 583
ASBR (autonomous system border router), 359
ASHRAE (American Society of Heating,
   Refrigerating and Air-Conditioning
   Engineers), 590
ASIC. *See* application-specific integrated
   circuit (ASIC)
assets, fixed tangible, 543
asymmetrical encryption, 785
asymmetrical routing, 684
AT&T, 456–457
Attachment Unit Interface (AUI) connectors, 118
attacks
   about, 816
   ARP spoofing, 821–822
   deauthentication, 824
   denial-of-service (DoS), 473, 817–820
   distributed denial-of-service (DDoS), 817–820
   DNS poisoning, 820–821
   environmental, 829–831
   evil twin, 823–824
   exam essentials, 852
   human, 829–831
   MAC flooding, 826
   MAC spoofing, 825–826
   malware, 826–829
   on-path (man-in-the-middle), 820
   password, 824–825
   phishing, 830
   ransomware, 826–827
   review questions, 854–857, 922–925
   rogue access point (AP), 822–824
   rogue DHCP, 822
   social engineering, 829–830
   technology-based, 817–829
   VLAN hopping, 821
   written lab, 853, 872
attenuation, 82, 658
attribute-based access control (ABAC), 634
audit and assessment report, 563–565
audit logs, 527–528
audits, 805
AUI (Attachment Unit Interface) connectors, 118
AUP (acceptable-use policy), 545–546
authentication
   about, 522–523, 790–791
   Lightweight Directory Access Protocol
      (LDAP), 797–798
   multifactor, 791–794
   Remote Authentication Dial-In User Service
      (RADIUS), 795–796

single sign-on, 794–795
   Terminal Access Controller Access Control
      System Plus (TACACS+), 796–797
authentication and authorization
   about, 634, 798
   authentication, authorization, and accounting
      (AAA), 790–801
   802.1X, 840
   Extensible Authentication Protocol
      (EAP), 481–482
   geofencing, 800
   identity and access management
      (IAM), 798–799
   least privilege, 799
   Lightweight Directory Access Protocol
      (LDAP), 797–798
   multifactor authentication (MFA), 791–794
   Remote Authentication Dial-In User Service
      (RADIUS), 795–796
   role-based access control (RBAC), 799–800
   single sign-on (SSO), 794–795
   Terminal Access Controller Access Control
      System Plus (TACACS+), 796–797
Authentication Header (AH), 228
Authority Information Access (AIA), 786
authorization. *See* authentication and authorization
auto-detect mechanism, 109
Automatic Private IP Addressing (APIPA),
   204, 250–251
automation, 625–627
autonomous system (AS), 332, 343
autonomous system border router (ASBR), 359
availability
   about, 576, 603
   backups, 600–601
   in CIA triad, 782–783
   exam essentials, 603–604
   facilities and infrastructure support, 587–591
   load balancing, 576–577
   mean time between failure (MTBF), 587
   mean time to repair (MTTR), 586–587
   multipathing, 577
   network device backup/restore, 601
   network device logs, 526–527
   network interface card (NIC)
      teaming, 578
   recovery point objective (RPO), 601
   recovery time objective (RTO), 601
   redundancy and, 591–600
   redundant hardware/clusters, 579–587
   review questions, 605–608, 910–912
   testing, 602–603
   written lab, 604, 870
availability monitoring, 516–517

B

backbone
  collapsed, 382
  network, 24–25
background checks, 551
backups
  about, 600–601
  network device backup/restore, 601
  recovery, 601
  security and, 551
badges, security and, 550
bandwidth metric, 513–514
bandwidth speed testers, 708–710
barriers, signal degradation and, 457
baseband, 55, 106–107
baseline metrics, 515
baselines
  about, 207
  configurations, 565–566
basic firewall, 135. *See also* firewalls
basic router, 135. *See also* routers
basic service area (BSA), 452–453
basic service set (BSS), 452–453
basic switch, 135, 139–140. *See also* switches
baud rate, 107
Baudot, Jean-Maurice-Émile, 107
BCP (business continuity plan), 543
bend radius limitations, 661
bent pins, 659
Berkeley Software Distribution (BSD) series, 196
BGP (Border Gateway Protocol),
  332, 343, 355–356
bidirectional communication, 77
binary code, 2
binary conversion, 110–114
binary IP address method, 244
binding, 37
bit rate, 107
BIX block, 94
BLE (Bluetooth Low Energy), 459
block acknowledgement, 443
blocked port, 394
Bluetooth, 458–459, 460
Bluetooth Low Energy (BLE), 459
BNC connectors, 6
bonding ports, 417–418
Bootstrap Protocol (BootP), 202–204
Border Gateway Protocol (BGP), 332,
  343, 355–356
bottlenecks, 659
bounce, 665
BPDUs (Bridge Protocol Data Units), 393, 416
BPL (Broadband over Power Line), 124–125

branching, 628
breaking policy, 552–553
Bridge Protocol Data Units (BPDUs), 393, 416
bridges, 135, 138–139, 179, 183–184, 383
bridging
  about, 179
  LAN switching *vs.*, 386–387
Bridging mode, 463
Bring Your Own Device (BYOD) policy, 547,
  685, 846
broadband, 106–107
Broadband over Power Line (BPL),
  124–125
broadcast, use of term, 251–252
broadcast domain, 104–105, 138, 144, 155, 176,
  178–181, 184, 252, 274, 398
broadcast storms, 693
brute-force attacks, 825
BSA (basic service area), 452–453
BSD (Berkeley Software Distribution) series, 196
BSS (basic service set), 452–453
buffer, 44
bus topology, 15
business continuity plan (BCP), 543
BYOD (Bring Your Own Device) policy, 547,
  685, 846
bytes, 110–111, 742

C

CA (Certificate Authority), 786
CAA (Certificate Authority Authorization)
  record, 161
cable connectivity
  applications, 654–656
  common issues, 657–666
  considerations, 653–654
  specifications and limitations, 658
  tap, 765
cable locks, 850–851
cable maps, 561
cable modem, 136, 173, 1537
cable testers, 764–765
cables
  categories of, 67–69, 118–121
  coaxial, 64–66
  copper, 76–77
  crossover, 86, 87–88
  DB-25, 81
  distance of, 82
  duplex of, 83
  Ethernet, 67–69, 121–122
  feeder, 93

fiber-optic, 71
frequency of, 83–84
multimode fiber-optic (MMF), 72
network, 23
noise immunity of, 83
patch, 86
plain old telephone service (POTS), 67
plenum-rated coating of, 64
properties of, 82–84
public switched telephone network (PSTN), 67
Recommended Standard 232 (RS-232), 80–81
rolled/rollover, 89, 499–501
serial, 80–82
shielded twisted-pair (STP), 66
single-mode fiber-optic (SMF), 71–72
straight-through, 86–87
T1 crossover, 89–90
Thin Ethernet (thinnet), 64
tips for, 70–71
transmission speeds of, 82
troubleshooting, 652–666, 698
25-pair, 93
twinaxial, 66–67
twisted-pair, 66
Universal Serial Bus (USB), 81–82
unshielded twisted-pair (UTP), 66, 67–70,
    88–89, 118
caching proxy server, 168
call setup, 213
cameras, 136, 174, 551
campus area network (CAN), 10
canonical name (CNAME) record, 161–162
captive portal, 456, 847
CAPWAP (Control and Provisioning of Wireless
    Access Points), 455, 472
Carrier Sense Multiple Access with Collision
    Avoidance (CSMA/CA), 148–149, 440, 658
Carrier Sense Multiple Access with Collision
    Detection (CSMA/CD), 105–106,
    138, 149–150
Carrier Sense Multiple Access with Collision
    Detection (CSMA/CS), 658–659
carrier signal, 54
CASB (Cloud Access Security Broker), 635
C&C (command and control), 818–819
CCTV (closed-circuit television), 848
CDMA (code division multiple access), 436
CDP (Cisco Discovery Protocol), 685, 749–752
cellular technologies, 436–437
central policy management, as a benefit of
    SDN, 629
Central Processing Unit (CPU), metrics for, 512
central repository, 627
centralized WAN, 9

Certificate Authority (CA), 786
Certificate Authority Authorization (CAA)
    record, 161
Certificate Revocation List (CRL), 787
certificates, 785–790
certificates, security and, 481–482
change command, 736
change management, 540–542
change request, 540
channel service unit/data service unit (CSU/
    DSU), 52–53
channels, overlapping/mismatched, 662–663
chip creep, 512
Chrome, Application layer and, 40
CIA triad, 782–783
CIDR (Classless Inter-Domain Routing),
    253–254, 276–278
Cisco
    about, 383, 418, 455, 580
    Hot Standby Router Protocol (HSRP), 362
    routers, 176
    switch, 140, 141–142
Cisco Cloud Services Router (CSR), 619
Cisco Discovery Protocol (CDP), 685, 749–752
Cisco Unified Wireless Network (CUWN), for
    mitigating ad hoc networks, 473
cladding, 72
Class A
    addresses, 246–247, 250
    network, 245–246
    subnetting, 928–933
Class B
    addresses, 247–248, 250, 289–296
    network, 245–246
Class C
    addresses, 248, 250, 279–289
    network, 245–246
Class D addresses, 249, 252–253
Class E addresses, 249
classful routing, 349, 350
Classless Inter-Domain Routing (CIDR),
    253–254, 276–278
classless routing, 286, 349, 350, 355, 357
clean-desk policy, 549
Client mode, 410–411, 473
clientless VPN, 491
clients, 167. See workstations
client-server networks, 13
client-to-site VPN, 491–493
CLNS (Connectionless Network Service), 361
closed-circuit television (CCTV), 848
Cloud Access Security Broker (CASB), 635
cloud computing
    about, 611–612

characteristics of, 612–613
cloud gateways, 621–622
connectivity options, 620–621
delivery models, 613–616
elasticity, 622
multitenancy, 622
network function virtualization
(NFV), 618–619
network security groups, 623
network security lists, 623–624
resources for, 624
scalability, 623
security implications/considerations, 623–624
service models, 616–618
virtual private cloud (VPC), 619
cloud gateways, 621–622
cloud sites, 592–593
Cluster Management Protocol (CMP), 581
clusters, redundancy and, 579–587
CMSA/CD (carrier sense multiple access with
collision detection), 658–659
CNAME (canonical name) record, 161–162
coaxial cable, 64–66
code division multiple access (CDMA), 436
cold sites, 592
collapsed backbone, 382
collision domain, 104, 138–139, 143, 146, 157,
176, 178–184
collision event, 104
collision light, 649
collisions, 19, 658–659
command and control (C&C), 818–819
Common Vulnerabilities and Exposures
(CVE), 779–780
Common Vulnerability Scoring System
(CVSS), 779–780
communication
bidirectional, 77
connection-oriented, 42–43
full-duplex, 83
half-duplex, 83
infrastructure for, 845–846
local area network (LAN), 102–104
Session layer and, 41
Compaq, 392
compliance, 627
Confidentiality, in CIA triad, 782
configuration drift, 627
configuration monitoring, 517
conflict identification, 627
Connectionless Network Service (CLNS), 361
connection-oriented communication, 42–43
connectivity
for cloud computing, 620–621

common devices for, 135–157
software for, 711–712
specialized devices, 157–173
connectors
about, 94
BNC, 6
D series, 81
dirty, 661
exam essentials, 95
fiber-optic, 73–75
F-type, 64, 66
local connector (LC), 74
mechanical transfer registered jack
(MT-RJ), 74–75
registered jack (RJ), 69–70, 118
review questions, 97–100, 878–880
small form factor (SFF), 73–75
square, 73
straight tip (ST), 72
subscriber, 73
written lab, 95–96, 861
console serial communication port, 499–501
content filters, 168–169, 837
contention methods, 136, 148–150
Control and Provisioning of Wireless Access Points
(CAPWAP), 455, 472
control layer, 629–630
control plane, 631
convergence, STP, 395–396
copper cable, 76–77
core layer, 27
CPU. *See* Central Processing Unit (CPU)
CRC (cyclic redundancy check), 115, 215, 222,
231, 234, 324–328, 676
credentials, changing default, 832
CRL (Certificate Revocation List), 787
crossover cable, 86, 87–88, 656
crosstalk, 67, 118, 657–658
cryptominers, 828–829
CSMA/CA (Carrier Sense Multiple Access with
Collision Avoidance), 148–149, 440, 658
CSMA/CD (Carrier Sense Multiple Access with
Collision Detection), 105–106, 138, 149–150
CSU/DSU (channel service unit/data service
unit), 52–53
CUWN (Cisco Unified Wireless Network), for
mitigating ad hoc networks, 473
CVE (Common Vulnerabilities and
Exposures), 779–780
CVSS (Common Vulnerability Scoring
System), 779–780
cyclic redundancy check (CRC), 115, 215, 222,
231, 234, 324–328, 676

D

DA (destination address), 115
DaaS (Desktop as a Service), 618
DAI (dynamic ARP inspection), 415
DARPA, 195
data at rest, 784
data center architecture
    about, 611, 635–636
    application layer, 629
    application programming interfaces
        (APIs), 631–632
    backbone, 24–25
    cloud computing, 611–624
    control layer, 629–630
    exam essentials, 636
    infrastructure as code (IaC), 625–628
    infrastructure layer, 630
    management plans, 630–631
    network monitoring, 707–708
    review questions, 638–641, 912–915
    Secure Access Secure Edge (SASE), 634–635
    Security Service Edge (SSE), 635
    software-defined networking, 628–632
    spine-leaf-based two-tier networks, 630
    Virtual eXtensible Local Area Network
        (VXLAN), 633
    written lab, 636–637, 870–871
    zero trust architecture, 633–634
Data Center Interconnect (DCI), 633
data communication equipment (DCE), 52–53
data encapsulation, 230–234
data frame, 50
data in transit, 783
data in use, 784
Data Link layer
    about, 50–52
    in data encapsulation, 231, 234
    Ethernet and, 110–117
    features of, 39
    frames within, 114–116
    in IP routing, 324, 326, 327
    Logical Link Control (LCC) within, 51
    MAC address as residing on, 136
    Media Access Control (MAC) within, 51
    switches and bridges at, 183–184
data locality, 802
data loss prevention (DLP), 553
Data Over Cable Service Interface Specifications
    (DOCSIS) standard, 173
data packets, 48
data (forwarding) plane, 631
data protection officer (DPO), 803
data terminal equipment (DTE), 52–53

datagrams, in data encapsulation, 231
dB (decibel) loss, 658
DB-25 cable, 81
DCE (data communication equipment), 52–53
DCI (Data Center Interconnect), 633
DDoS (distributed denial of service)
    attacks, 817–820
deauthentication, 824
DEC (Digital Equipment Corporation), 392
decibel (dB) loss, 658
decimal conversion, 110–114
declarative approach, 626
de-encapsulation, 231
delete command, 736
delivery models, 613–616
demarcation point (demarc), 25, 94
demilitarized zone (DMZ), 144, 145, 165,
    551, 838–839
denial of service (DoS) attacks, 473,
    817–820
Desktop as a Service (DaaS), 618
destination address (DA), 115
Device Hardening, 418
device logs, 526–527
device ports, 834
device saturation, with unbounded media
    (wireless), 662
devices
    about, 186
    exam essentials, 186–187
    hardening, 832–834
    before Layer 2 switching, 381–384
    performance metrics/sensors for, 511–513
    review questions, 189–192, 883–885
    written lab, 187–188, 862
DFS (Dynamic Frequency Selection), 442
DHCP. *See* Dynamic Host Configuration
    Protocol (DHCP)
DHCP server. *See* Dynamic Host Configuration
    Protocol (DHCP) server
dictionary attacks, 824
Diffusing Update Algorithm (DUAL), 354
Digital Equipment Corporation (DEC), 392
digital modulation, 55
Digital Subscriber Line (DSL), 25
Digital Subscriber Line (DSL) modem, 136,
    173, 1537
Dijkstra algorithm, 357
dipole antennas, 449
directional antennas, 448
direct-sequence spread spectrum (DSSS), 441
dirty connectors, 661
disabled port, 394
disaster recovery plan (DRP), 542. *See also* high
    availability (HA)

discards, 742
discontinuous networks, 350–353
disk-to-cloud backups, 601
disk-to-disk backups, 600–601
disk-to-tape backups, 600
distance
    limitation for cables, 82, 658, 661
    signal degradation and, 457
    unbounded media and, 664
distance-vector (DV) routing protocols, 332–333,
    346, 347–356
distributed denial of service (DDoS)
    attacks, 817–820
distributed switching, 392
distributed WAN, 9
distribution layer, 27
distribution system (DS), 452
distributions, wiring, 92–94
divide-and-conquer approach, 686
DLP (data loss prevention), 553
DMZ (demilitarized zone), 144, 145, 165,
    551, 838–839
DNAT (dynamic NAT), 306
DNS. See Domain Name Service (DNS)
DNS amplification attack, 818
DNS over HTTPS (DoH), 166
DNS over TLS (DoT), 166
DNS poisoning, 820–821
DNS (Domain Name Service) server, 152,
    157–165, 201–202
DNSSEC (Domain Name System Security
    Extensions), 165–166
DOCSIS (Data Over Cable Service Interface
    Specifications) standard, 173
documents and policies
    about, 539, 568
    audit and assessment report, 563–565
    baseline configurations, 565–566
    business continuity plan (BCP), 543
    change management, 540–542
    common, 554–566
    disaster recovery plan (DRP), 542
    exam essentials, 568
    hardening and security policies, 545–553
    incident response plan, 542
    inventory management, 543
    IP address management, 566
    layered network diagram, 562
    logical network diagram, 560
    memorandum of understanding (MOU), 567
    nondisclosure agreement (NDA), 566–567
    physical network diagram, 554–559
    plans and procedures, 539–545
    review questions, 570–573, 907–909
    service-level agreement (SLA), 567

site survey report, 562–563
standard operating procedures, 544–545
system life cycle, 544
wiring diagram, 560–561
written lab, 568–569, 870
DoD model, layers of, 196–198
DoH (DNS over HTTPS), 166
Domain Name Service (DNS)
    incorrect, 679
    name resolutions and, 103
Domain Name Service (DNS) server, 152,
    157–165, 201–202
Domain Name System Security Extensions
    (DNSSEC), 165–166
domains
    broadcast domain (See broadcast domain)
    collision domain (See collision domain)
    hierarchical tree structure of, 158
    root domains, 158
    top-level domains, 158
door locks, 550, 849–850
doorbells, smart, 136, 843
DORA process, 204
DoS (denial of service) attacks, 473, 817–820
DoT (DNS over TLS), 166
dotted-decimal IP address method, 244
downtime
    authorized, 541
    planned, 576
downtime, planned, 587
DPO (data protection officer), 803
driver updates, 548
drops, 677
DRP (disaster recovery plan), 542. See also high
    availability (HA)
DS (distribution system), 452
DSL (Digital Subscriber Line), 25
DSL (Digital Subscriber Line) modem, 136,
    173, 1537
DSSS (direct-sequence spread spectrum), 441
DTE (data terminal equipment) (Physical
    layer), 52–53
DTP (Dynamic Trunking Protocol), 403
DUAL (Diffusing Update Algorithm), 354
dual stacking, 261, 369–370
dumb terminals, 8
dumpster diving, 830–831
duplex
    of cables, 83
    mismatch, 673
DV (distance-vector) routing protocols, 332–333,
    346, 347–356
dynamic ARP inspection (DAI), 415
dynamic ARP table entries, 725–726
dynamic assignment, 164

Dynamic Frequency Selection (DFS), 442
Dynamic Host Configuration Protocol (DHCP)
    as compared to Bootstrap Protocol
        (BootP), 202–204
    DHCPv6, 260
    exhausted scope, 682
    snooping, 415
Dynamic Host Configuration Protocol
    (DHCP) server
    about, 150–156
    as common network connectivity device, 136
    DHCP relay, 155–156
    dynamic DNS, 164
    internal and external DNS, 165
    rogue, 680, 681, 822
    third-party/cloud-hosted DNS, 165
dynamic inventories, 627
dynamic NAT (DNAT), 306
dynamic routing, 321, 331–334
Dynamic Trunking Protocol (DTP), 403
dynamic VLANs, 403

E

–e switch, 742–743
EAP (Extensible Authentication Protocol), 481–482
EAP-FAST (Extensible Authentication Protocol -
    Fast), 482
EAP-TLS (Extensible Authentication Protocol -
    Transport Layer Security), 482
east-west traffic flow, 28
EDNS (Extension Mechanisms for DNS), 165
EGPs (exterior gateway protocols), 332, 343
EIA/TIA (Electronic Industries Association/
    Telecommunications Industry Alliance)
    standards, 118
802.1X standards, 840. *See also* Remote
    Authentication Dial-In User Service (RADIUS)
802.3 standards, 118–121
802.11 standards
    about, 438–439, 460
    comparing, 445–446
    5 GHz (802.11a), 441–442
    5 GHz (802.11ac), 444
    5 GHz (802.11h), 442–443
    2.4 GHz (802.11b), 439–440
    2.4 GHz (802.11g), 440–441
    2.4 GHz/5 GHz (802.11n), 443–444
    WiFi 6 (802.11ax), 444–445
EIGRP (Enhanced Interior Gateway Routing
    Protocol), 345, 353–355, 371

EIGRPv6, 371
elasticity
    as a characteristic of cloud computing, 613
    cloud computing and, 622
Electronic Industries Association/
    Telecommunications Industry Alliance (EIA/
    TIA) standards, 118
email, for multifactor authentication, 793
Encapsulating Security Payload (ESP), 229
encapsulation
    defined, 36
    introduction to, 53–54
encryption
    about, 783–785
    of certificates, 787
    devices for, 157, 168–169
encryption/security type mismatch, 662
end-of-life (EOL), 544
end-of-support (EOS), 544
Enhanced Interior Gateway Routing Protocol
    (EIGRP), 345, 353–355, 371
enhanced small form-factor pluggable (SFP+)
    transceiver, 78
enrollment policy, 786
environmental attacks, 829–831
environmental factors/sensors, 665
EOL (end-of-life), 544
EOS (end-of-support), 544
EPA (US Environmental Protection Agency), 591
equipment access, security and, 550
equipment locks, 850–851
Ericsson, 458
errors
    displaying, 743
    operator, 650
ESP (Encapsulating Security Payload), 229
EtherChannel, 418
Ethernet
    about, 104–109, 127
    addressing within, 114
    baseband, 106–107
    baud rate of, 107
    bit rate of, 107
    broadband, 106–107
    broadcast domain within, 104–105
    carrier sense multiple access with collision
        detection (CSMA/CD), 105–106
    collision domain within, 104
    Data Link layer (OSI reference model)
        and, 110–117
    defined, 104
    exam essentials, 127

Fast, 119
frames of, 114–116
full-duplex, 107–109
half-duplex, 107–109
number conversions within, 110–114
over Broadband over Power Line
    (BPL), 124–125
over HDMI, 125–126
over Power Line Communication
    (PLC), 124–125
Physical layer (OSI reference model)
    and, 117–123
review questions, 129–132, 881–882
specifications for, 118–120
wavelength of, 107
written lab, 127–128, 861–862
Ethernet cables, 67–69
European Telecommunications Standards Institute
    (ETSi), 434
evil twin, 823–824
exam essentials
    attacks, 852
    connectors, 95
    data center architecture, 636
    documents and policies, 568
    Ethernet, 127
    high availability, 603–604
    Internet Protocol (IP), 235
    IP address, 264, 309–310
    IP routing, 334
    Layer 2 switching, 424–425
    Network Address Translation (NAT), 309–310
    networking devices, 186–187
    networks, 29–30
    Open Systems Interconnection (OSI) model, 56
    performance metrics/sensors, 532
    remote access security, 502–503
    routing, 372
    security, 806, 852
    software tools and commands, 767–768
    subnetting, 309–310
    troubleshooting, 699–700
    virtual local area network (VLAN), 424–425
    wireless networking, 483–484
exclusion ranges, 151
expiration date, 787
exploits, 781
Extensible Authentication Protocol (EAP), 481–482
Extensible Authentication Protocol - Fast (EAP-
    FAST), 482
Extensible Authentication Protocol - Transport
    Layer Security (EAP-TLS), 482

Extension Mechanisms for DNS (EDNS), 165
exterior gateway protocols (EGPs), 332, 343
external threats, 778

F

-f option (route command), 736
facilities support, 587–591
Family Educational Rights and Privacy Act
    (FERPA), 802–803
far-end crosstalk, 657–658
Fast Ethernet standards, 119
fault tolerance, 15
fax server, 6
FCC (Federal Communications Commission), 434
FCS (Frame Check Sequence) field,
    116, 231, 234, 324, 325, 326, 327
FDM (frequency-division multiplexing), 55
FDMA (frequency-division multiple access), 436
FDPs (fiber distribution panels), 77
feasible successor, 355
Federal Communications Commission (FCC), 434
feeder cable, 93
FERPA (Family Educational Rights and Privacy
    Act), 802–803
FHRP (first-hop redundancy protocol), 362–363,
    582–583, 595–600
fiber cable, 660–661
fiber distribution panels (FDPs), 77
fiber to coaxial converter, 79
fiber type mismatch, 661
fiber-optic cables
    about, 71
    connectors for, 72–76
fiber-optic transceivers, 77
file server, 6
File Transfer Protocol (FTP), 198–199, 620–621
fire suppression, 590–591
Firefox, Application layer and, 40
Firewall as a Service (FWaaS), 635
firewalls
    defined, 144
    demilitarized zone (DMZ) of, 144
    incorrect host-based settings, 683
    next-generation firewall (NGFW), 173
    private side of, 144
    public side of, 144
    redundancy and, 583
    security and, 551
    typical design of, 144
    virtual, 619

firmware updates, 548
first hop, 362
first-hop redundancy protocol (FHRP), 362–363,
    582–583, 595–600
5 GHz (802.11a), 441–442
5 GHz (802.11ac), 444
5 GHz (802.11h), 442–443
5G, 437
fixed tangible assets, 543
flat network, 398
flood guard, 415–416
flooding, 684, 826
floor plan, 556–557
flow control, Transport layer and, 43–45
flow data, 525–526
40 MHz channels, 443
forward/filter decision, 389–390
forward/filter table, 387
forwarding port, 394
4G, 437
FQDN (fully qualified domain name), 201
frame, in data encapsulation, 231, 234
Frame Check Sequence (FCS) field, 116, 231, 234,
    324, 325, 326, 327
frames
    within the Data Link layer (OSI reference
        model), 114–116
    filtering, 389
    jumbo, 424
frequency
    of cables, 83–84
    incorrect, 663
frequency-division multiple access (FDMA), 436
frequency-division multiplexing (FDM), 55
friendly/unintentional DoS, 819
FTP. *See* File Transfer Protocol (FTP)
F-type connector, 64, 66
full tunneling, 491–493
full-duplex communication, 83
full-duplex Ethernet, 107–109
full-duplex mode, 41
fully qualified domain name (FQDN), 201
FWaaS (Firewall as a Service), 635

G

gateways
    defined, 8
    incorrect, 679
General Data Protection Regulation (GDPR), 803
generators, 588–589

Generic Routing Encapsulation (GRE), 220,
    227–228, 363–364
geofencing, 477, 800
giants, 676–677
Gigabit Media Independent Interface (GMII), 119
gigabit wiring, 88–89
GLBA (Gramm-Leach-Bliley Act), 803
global addresses, 306
global positioning (GPS), 477
Global System Mobile (GSM), 436
GMII (Gigabit Media Independent Interface), 119
golden configuration, 566
GPS (global positioning), 477
Gramm-Leach-Bliley Act (GLBA), 803
graphical user interface (GUI), 497
GRE (Generic Routing Encapsulation), 220,
    227–228, 363–364
GSM (Global System Mobile), 436
guards, security and, 552
guest network isolation, 847
guest networks, 455
GUI (graphical user interface), 497

H

H.323 protocol, 212
HA. *See* high availability (HA)
half-duplex communication, 83, 433
half-duplex Ethernet, 107–109
half-duplex mode, 41
handshake
    defined, 42
    three-way, 42–43
hardening
    about, 831–832
    access control lists (ACLs), 835–837
    content filters, 837
    devices, 832–834
    key management, 834–835
    security policies and, 545–553
hardware
    addressing of, 50
    redundancy and, 579–587
    tools, 762–766
    troubleshooting, 651
hardware address, 103, 110, 220–221
HDMI, Ethernet over, 125–126
Health Insurance Portability and Accountability
    Act (HIPAA), 803
heating, ventilation, and air conditioning (HVAC)
    sensors, 136, 174, 589–590

Hello Timer (HSRP), 597–598
hexadecimal conversion, 110–114
hexadecimal IP address method, 244
HIDS (host-based IDS), 135, 145
hierarchical addressing, 244–251
high availability (HA)
    about, 576, 603
    backups, 600–601
    exam essentials, 603–604
    facilities and infrastructure support,
      587–591
    load balancing, 576–577
    mean time between failure (MTBF), 587
    mean time to repair (MTTR),
      586–587
    multipathing, 577
    network device backup/restore, 601
    network interface card (NIC) teaming,
      578
    recovery point objective (RPO), 601
    recovery time objective (RTO), 601
    redundancy and, 591–600
    redundant hardware/clusters, 579–587
    review questions, 605–608, 910–912
    testing, 602–603
    written lab, 604, 870
high throughput (HT), 444
HIPAA (Health Insurance Portability and
    Accountability Act), 803
HMI (Human Machine Interface), 845
Hold Timer (HSRP), 598
honeypot/honeynet, 846
hop count, 49, 344, 347, 348, 349, 350, 357,
    358, 370
host address, 245
host-based IDS (HIDS), 135, 145
hosts. *See* workstations
Hosts file, resolving names with, 731–732
Host-to-Host layer
    of DoD model, 197
    protocols of, 213–220
    Transport layer also known as, 197, 202
hot sites, 592
Hot Standby Router Protocol (HSRP),
    362, 595–600
hotspots, security and, 552
HT (high throughput), 444
HTTP (Hypertext Transfer Protocol), 206
HTTPS (Hypertext Transfer Protocol Secure), 209
hub-and-spoke topology. *See* star topology
hubs
    access point (AP) as, 146

as common network connectivity device,
    135, 138
considering replacing of with switches, 181–182
defined, 3
hub-and-spoke topology, 228
as older technology, 179
at Physical layer of SOHO network, 184–185
switches as compared to, 139, 181–182
switches as replacing, 177
use of as contributing to congestion, 179
human attacks, 829–831
Human Machine Interface (HMI), 845
HVAC (heating, ventilation, and air conditioning)
    sensors, 136, 174, 589–590
hybrid cloud model, 615–616
hybrid mesh topology, 18–19
hybrid protocol, 333–334, 345, 347, 349, 353, 355
hybrid topology, 22
Hypertext Transfer Protocol (HTTP), 206
Hypertext Transfer Protocol Secure (HTTPS), 209
hypervisor, 26

I

IaaS (Infrastructure as a Service), 617–618
IAM (identity and access management), 798–799
IBSS (independent basic service set), 451–452
ICMP (Internet Control Message Protocol), 220,
    223–225, 323
ICS (industrial control system), 175, 844–846
identity and access management (IAM), 798–799
IDF (intermediate distribution frame), 92, 559
IDSs (intrusion detection systems), 135, 145,
    474, 551
IEEE. *See* Institute of Electrical and Electronics
    Engineers (IEEE)
IEEE 802.1D, 392
IEEE 802.1Q, 406–407
IEEE 802.1X, 403
IEEE 802.3ad standard, 418
IEEE 802.11, 476
IETF (Internet Engineering Task Force),
    165–166, 195
ifconfig utility, 720
I/G (Individual/Group) address, 114
IGMP (Internet Group Management Protocol), 213
IGPs (interior gateway protocols), 332, 343, 360
IGRP (Interior Gateway Routing Protocol),
    333, 346
IKE (Internet Key Exchange), 229–230
IMAP (Internet Message Access Protocol), 207, 211

imperative approach, 626
in-band management, 411, 502
incident response policies, 542
independent basic service set (IBSS), 451–452
Individual/Group (I/G) address, 114
industrial control system (ICS), 175, 844–846
information gathering, during site survey, 466–467
infrared (IR), 460
Infrastructure as a Service (IaaS), 617–618
infrastructure as code (IaC), 625–628
infrastructure layer, 630
infrastructure mode, 452–453, 473
infrastructure support, 587–591
inherent attenuation, 118
input errors, 678
input queue drops, 677
inside global address, 307
inside local address, 307
Institute of Electrical and Electronics
        Engineers (IEEE)
    about, 434
    Data Link layer specifications of, 51–52
    802.3 Committee, 117, 118–120
    1905.1-2013, 123–126
    organizationally unique identifier (OUI) by, 114
    Project 802, 51–52
Integrity, in CIA triad, 782
interface
    about, 49
    configurations, 141–144
    incorrect, 674–676, 679
    misconfiguration, 674–676
    misconfigured, 679
interference
    cables and, 659
    signal degradation and, 458
    with unbounded media (wireless), 661–662
interior gateway protocols (IGPs), 332, 343, 360
Interior Gateway Routing Protocol (IGRP),
        333, 346
intermediate distribution frame (IDF), 92, 559
Intermediate System-to-Intermediate System (IS-IS),
        333, 345, 346, 357, 360–361
internal threats, 778–779
Internet Control Message Protocol (ICMP), 220,
        223–225, 323
Internet Engineering Task Force (IETF),
        165–166, 195
Internet gateways, 621
Internet Group Management Protocol (IGMP), 213
Internet Key Exchange (IKE), 229–230
Internet layer

as describing same thing as Network layer, 197
    of DoD model, 197
    protocols of, 220–230
    TCP as preparing data stream for, 214
Internet Message Access Protocol (IMAP), 207, 211
Internet of Things (IoT), 136, 175, 460, 843
Internet Protocol (IP)
    about, 220–223, 234–235
    defined, 48
    exam essentials, 235
    review questions, 237–249, 885–888
    as routed protocol, 320
    routing process, 323–328
    terminology of, 243–244
    troubleshooting IP addressing, 296–304
    version 4 (IPv4) (See IPv4)
    version 6 (IPv6) (See IPv6)
    written lab, 236, 863
Internet Protocol Security (IPSec), 220, 228–230
Internet Service Providers (ISPs), 593–594
internetwork, 140, 178, 179, 180, 183
internetworking models
    about, 36
    router within, 49–50
Inter-Switch Link (ISL), 405–406
inter-VLAN communication, 401
intranet, 9
Intra-Site Automatic Tunnel Addressing Protocol
        (ISATAP) tunneling,
        368–369
intrusion detection systems (IDSs), 135, 145,
        474, 551
intrusion prevention systems (IPSs), 135, 145, 474
inventory management, 543
IoT (Internet of Things), 136, 175, 460, 843
IP. See Internet Protocol (IP)
IP address
    about, 263, 309
    AP, 463
    determining problems with, 299–304
    duplicate, 678–679
    exam essentials, 264, 309–310
    expired, 680
    hierarchical scheme for, 244–251
    incorrect, 678–679
    IP address management (IPAM), 156
    network addressing, 245–249
    review questions, 267–270, 311–314, 888–892
    VLAN Trunking Protocol (VTP) and, 411–413
    written labs, 265–266, 310, 863–865
IP address management (IPAM), 156, 566
IP exclusions, 151

IP ports, 834
IP routing
    about, 334
    exam essentials, 334
    process of, 323–328
    review questions, 336–339, 892–894
    testing your understanding of, 329–331
    written lab, 335, 865
IP scanner, 712
IP spoofing, 826
ip utility, 720–721
IPAM (IP address management),
        156, 566
ipconfig utility, 299, 715–719
IPSec (Internet Protocol Security), 220, 228–230
IPSs (intrusion prevention systems), 135, 145, 474
iptables utility, 721
IPv4 (Internet Protocol version 4)
    address types, 251–253
    address-exhaustion crisis of, 253
    header, 222, 255, 261
    loopback address, 297
    popularity of, 281
    prolific use of broadcasts in, 255
    use of with dual stacking, 261, 369–370
IPv6 (Internet Protocol version 6)
    about, 48
    address types in, 257–258
    addressing and expressions in, 255–256
    advanced concepts of, 363–370
    benefits of and uses for, 253–254
    DHCPv6, 260
    dual stacking, 261
    introduction, 253
    migrating to, 260–261
    Neighbor Discovery Protocol (NDP), 365–366
    as routed protocol, 320
    router advertisement, 363–365
    routing protocols of, 370–371
    shortened expression in, 256–257
    6to4 tunneling, 261–262
    special addresses in, 258
    stateless address autoconfiguration
        (SLAAC), 259–260
    why we need it, 253–254
IR (infrared), 460
ISATAP (Intra-Site Automatic Tunnel Addressing
        Protocol) tunneling,
        368–369
IS-IS (Intermediate System-to-Intermediate System),
        333, 345, 346, 357, 360–361
ISL (Inter-Switch Link), 405–406

ISO/IEC 27002, *Information technology - Security
        techniques - Code of practice
        for information security controls,* 802
isotropic antennas, 449
issuing CA, 787

J

jitter
    about, 514
    cables and, 658
jumbo frames, 424
jump box/hosts, 501–502

K

Kardach, Jim, 458
key management, 834–835
key pair, 786
keyloggers, 828
Krone block, 93

L

Lammle, Todd (author), 63
LAN. *See* local area network (LAN)
latency
    about, 183, 514
    cables and, 658
    unbounded media and, 664–665
Layer 1 device
    analog modem as, 169–170
    hub as, 138
    media converter as, 172
Layer 2
    access point (AP) as operating at, 146
    broadcasts, 184, 202, 252
    DORA components as operating at, 155
    encapsulation, 633
Layer 2 device
    bridge as, 139
    NIC as, 136
    as propagating layer 2 broadcast storms, 184
    switch as, 139, 140, 141, 183
Layer 2 switching. *See also* virtual local area
        network (VLAN)
    about, 144, 178, 183, 381, 424
    exam essentials, 424–425
    limitations of, 386
    networking before, 381–384

port mirroring/spanning (SPAN/
    RSPAN), 421–423
Power over Ethernet (PoE/PoE+),
    419–421
review questions, 426–429, 897–900
services for, 385–392
Spanning Tree Protocol (STP), 392–397
switch functions at, 387–392
written lab, 425, 867
Layer 3
    broadcasts, 202, 252
    design, 141, 144
    Network layer as, 178
    protocol, 228
    switch, 140, 157, 178
Layer 3 device
    as all about location, 183
    multilayer switch as, 141, 157
    router as, 140, 141, 183, 184, 221
Layer 7 firewall, 157, 173
layered approach, 37
layered architecture, 37
layered network diagram, 562
layers
    defined, 37
    of OSI reference model, 39
LBFO (load balancing/failover), 693
LC (local connector), 74
LCAP (Link Aggregation Control Protocol), 418
LCC (Logical Link Control) (Data Link layer), 51
LDAP (Lightweight Directory Access Protocol),
    208–209, 211, 797–798
learning port, 394
lease time, 154
leased line, 25
least privilege, 799
least privilege access, 634
LEDs. See Light-Emitting Diodes (LEDs)
Length field, 116
L/G (Local/Global) bit, 114
licensed features, 685
light source
    of fiber-optic cables, 83
    of multimode fiber-optic (MMF), 72
    of single-mode fiber-optic (SMF) cables, 71–72
Light-Emitting Diodes (LEDs)
    in network interface cards (NICs), 137
    Status Indicators, 657
Lightweight Access Point Protocol (LWAPP),
    455, 472
Lightweight Directory Access Protocol (LDAP),
    208–209, 211, 797–798

line interactive UPS, 588
Linear Tape-Open (LTO) technology, 600
Link Aggregation Control Protocol (LCAP), 418
Link Layer Discovery Protocol (LLDP),
    685, 752–757
link-local address, 364
link-state advertisements or packets
    (LSAs or LSPs), 357
link-state (LS) routing protocol, 332–333,
    346–347, 357–361
listening port, 394
LLDP (Link Layer Discovery Protocol),
    685, 752–757
load balancing, 136, 147–148, 344, 576–577, 584
load balancing/failover (LBFO), 693
load-shifting, power supply redundancy and, 584
local addresses, 306–307
local area network (LAN)
    about, 3–5
    baseband of, 107
    bridging vs. switching, 386–387
    communication within, 102–104
    Ethernet media within, 118–120
    traffic congestion, 176
local connector (LC), 74
Local/Global (L/G) bit, 114
location-based WLAN, 470
log reviews, 527–528
logical address, 220–221
Logical Link Control (LCC) (Data Link layer), 51
logical network diagrams, 560
login procedure/rights, troubleshooting, 647–648
Long-Term Evolution (LTE), 437
loop avoidance, 390–392
LS (link-state) routing protocol, 332–333,
    346–347, 357–361
LSAs/LSPs (link-state advertisements or
    packets), 357
LTE (Long-Term Evolution), 437
LWAPP (Lightweight Access Point Protocol),
    455, 472

M

MAC. See Media Access Control (MAC)
MAC address. See Media Access Control
    (MAC) address
MAC filtering, 841–842
MAC flooding, 826
magnetic flux, 83
mail exchanger (MX) record, 159–160, 161

mail relay, security and, 551
mail servers
    about, 6
    security and, 551
main distribution frame (MDF), 92, 559
mainframes, 8
maintenance window, 541
malware (malicious software), 826–829
MAM (mobile application management), 547
MAN (metropolitan area network), 8
managed switches, 140, 412
Management Frame Protection (MFP), 473
Management Information Base (MIB), 208, 522
management plane, 630–631
man-in-the-middle attack (on-path attack), 820
mantraps (access control vestibules), 830
maximum transmission unit (MTU), 673, 692
MDF (main distribution frame), 92, 559
MDI/MDI-X (medium dependent interface/medium
    dependent interface-crossover), 653
MDM (mobile device management), 547
mean time between failure (MTBF), 587
mean time to repair (MTTR), 586–587
measured service, as a characteristic of cloud
    computing, 613
Mechanical, Ingress, Climatic, Chemical, and
    Electromagnetic (MICE) standard, 654
mechanical transfer registered jack (MT-RJ)
    connector, 74–75
media, physical, 63–82
Media Access Control (MAC)
    about, 51
    defined, 110
    efficiency, 443
    Ethernet addressing and, 114
    frame format, 115
    spoofing, 825–826
Media Access Control (MAC) address
    about, 136, 139–140, 148, 153, 156, 226, 252,
        256, 259–260, 324, 328, 362, 387–389
    authentication/MAC filtering, 476–477
    duplicate, 679–680
    virtual, 596–597
media converters, 78–80, 157, 172
Media Gateway Control Protocol (MGCP), 212
Media Independent Interface (MII), 119
medium dependent interface/medium dependent
    interface-crossover (MDI/MDI-X), 653
memberships, VLAN, 402
Memorandum of Understanding (MOU), 567
memory
    buffer within, 44

metrics for, 512–513
mesh topology, 18–19
metrics, 49. *See also* performance metrics/sensors
metropolitan area network (MAN), 8
MFA (multifactor authentication), 791–794
MFP (Management Frame Protection), 473
MGCP (Media Gateway Control Protocol), 212
mGRE (Multipoint Generic Routing
    Encapsulation), 11
MIB (Management Information Base), 208, 522
MICE (Mechanical, Ingress, Climatic, Chemical,
    and Electromagnetic) standard, 654
Microsoft
    Active Directory, 174
    SQL Server, 211
Microsoft Word, Application layer and, 41
MII (Media Independent Interface), 119
Mills, David, 206
MILNET, 195
MIMO (multiple-input, multiple-output), 444
mirroring, 584–586
missing routes, 692
mitigation
    ad hoc networks, 473
    denial of service (DoS), 473
    passive attacks, 474–475
    rogue APs, 472
MLS (multilayer switch), 141, 157
MMF (multimode fiber-optic) cable, 72
mobile application management (MAM), 547
mobile device management (MDM), 547
mobile hot spots, 456–457
modems
    analog modem, 157, 169–170
    cable modem, 136, 173, 1537
    DSL modem, 136, 173, 1537
modulation techniques, 54–55, 441
modulator, 55
modules, bad, 692–693
monitors, security and viewing, 551
MOU (Memorandum of Understanding), 567
MPLS (Multiprotocol Label Switching), 10–11
MTBF (mean time between failure), 587
Mtr utility (pathping), 732–733
MT-RJ (mechanical transfer registered jack)
    connector, 74–75
MTTR (mean time to repair), 586–587
MTU (maximum transmission unit), 673, 692
multicast addresses, 252–253
multicast flooding, 684
multifactor authentication (MFA), 791–794
multilayer switch (MLS), 141, 157

multimode fiber to Ethernet converter, 78–79
multimode fiber-optic (MMF) cable, 72
multipathing, 577
multiple-input, multiple-output (MIMO), 444
Multipoint Generic Routing Encapsulation (mGRE), 11
Multiprotocol Label Switching (MPLS), 10–11
multitenancy, 622
Multiuser Multiple-Input, Multiple-Output (MU-MIMO), 444
MX (mail exchanger) record, 159–160, 161
MySQL, 211

N

–n switch, 745–746
NAC (network access control) system, 547, 840–841
name resolution, 158, 731–732
name server (NS) record, 161
NAT. *See* Network Address Translation (NAT)
National Electric Code (NEC), 654
National Fire Protection Association (NFPA), 64, 654
NAT/PAT. *See* network address translation (NAT); port address translation (PAT)
NBIs (northbound interface) APIs, 632
nbstat utility, 738–747
NCP (Network Control Protocol), 195
NDA (nondisclosure agreement), 566–567
NDP (Neighbor Discovery Protocol), 365–366
near-end crosstalk, 657–658
near-end/far-end crosstalk, 657–658
near-field communication (NFC), 460
NEC (National Electric Code), 654
Neighbor Discovery Protocol (NDP), 365–366
neighbor table, 354, 357
Nessus vulnerability scanner, 548
Net8, 211
NetBIOS (Network Basic Input/Output System), 213
NETCONF, 632
NetFlow analyzers, 710
NetFlow protocol, 526
netmask, 737
netstat utility, 738–747
NetWare services, 383
network access, as a characteristic of cloud computing, 613

network access control (NAC) system, 547, 840–841
Network Access layer, of DoD model, 197
Network Address Translation (NAT)
    about, 309, 621–622
    defined, 249
    exam essentials, 309–310
    how it works, 307–309
    introduction, 304–309
    names in, 306–307
    review questions, 311–314, 890–892
    types of, 306
    WAPs and, 447–448
    written labs, 310, 864–865
network addresses
    about, 49
    Class A addresses, 246–247, 250
    Class B addresses, 247–248, 250, 289–296
    Class C addresses, 248, 250, 279–289
    Class D addresses, 249, 252–253
    Class E addresses, 249
    defined, 245
    special purposes of, 249
Network Basic Input/Output System (NetBIOS), 213
network connection LED status indicators, 648–649
Network Control Protocol (NCP), 195
network device backup/restore, 601
network device commands
    Cisco Discovery Protocol (CDP), 749–752
    Link Layer Discovery Protocol (LLDP), 752–757
    show arp, 760
    show cdp neighbors, 749–752
    show interface, 756–759
    show inventory, 754
    show ip interface, 759–760
    show ip route, 752–753
    show mac-address-table, 756
    show power, 762
    show switch, 755
    show version, 753
    show vlan, 760–762
network device logs, 526–527
network discovery, 515
network function virtualization (NFV), 26, 618–619
network interface card (NIC)

about, 135, 136–137, 448
configuring, 461–462
teaming, 578, 693
network interface device (NID), 94
network interface unit (NIU), 94
Network layer
about, 48–50
in data encapsulation, 231–232
data packets within, 48
as describing same thing as Internet layer, 197
features of, 39
ICMP as working at, 223
IGMP as working at, 213
interface within, 49
as layer 3, 178
metric within, 49
network addresses within, 49
responsibilities of, 234, 325
routers as using logical address in header of, 182
route-update packets within, 48
as working with Transport layer, 222, 231–232
Network Management System (NMS), 208, 519
Network Monitor tool, 707–708
network security groups, 623
network security lists, 623–624
network segmentation
about, 837
bring your own device (BYOD), 846
captive portal, 847
defined, 176
802.1X protocol, 840
enforcement of, 837–838
guest network isolation, 847
honeypot/honeynet, 846
industrial control systems (ICS), 844–846
Internet of Things (IoT), 843
MAC filtering, 841–842
network access control (NAC) system, 840–841
planning and implementing a basic SOHO network using, 175–185
port security, 842
private/public networks, 846
screened subnet, 838–839
Supervisory Control and Data Acquisition (SCADA), 844–846
network stack, 40
Network Time Protocol (NTP), 157, 166–167, 206–207, 684
Network Time Security (NTS), 167
network-activity light, 649

networked devices, 174–175
networking
network function virtualization (NVF), 26
spine and leaf switching, 27–28
three-tiered model, 26–27
traffic flow, 28–29
networking device commands
show config, 749
show running-config, 748–749
networks
about, 2–3, 29, 102–104
architecture, 12–13
backbone, 24–25
cables, 23
campus area network (CAN), 10
client-server, 13
components of, 5–8
device logs, 526–527
exam essentials, 29–30
hosts, 7–8
implementing segmentation, 837–838
local area network (LAN), 3–5
metrics for, 513–514
metropolitan area network (MAN), 8
Multipoint Generic Routing Encapsulation (mGRE), 11
Multiprotocol Label Switching (MPLS), 10–11
peer-to-peer, 12–13
performance issues, 685
personal area network (PAN), 9–10
physical topologies, 14–22
review questions, 31–34, 874–876
segments, 25
selecting topologies, 23–24
servers, 6–7
software-defined wide area network (SDWAN), 10
storage area network (SAN), 10
virtual networking, 25–26
wide area network (WAN), 8–9
workstations, 5–6
written lab, 30, 860
network-traffic light, 649
next-generation firewall (NGFW), 157, 173, 583
next-hop IP address, 737
NFC (near-field communication), 460
NFPA (National Fire Protection Association), 64, 654
NFV (network function virtualization), 26, 618–619
NGFW (next-generation firewall), 157, 173, 583

nibble, 110
NIC. *See* network interface card (NIC)
NID (network interface device), 94
1905.1-2013 (IEEE) standards, 123–126
NIST SP 800-145, "The NIST Definition of Cloud
      Computing," 613
NIU (network interface unit), 94
Nmap utility, 734–735
NMS (Network Management System), 208, 519
noise immunity, of cables, 83
nondisclosure agreement (NDA), 566–567
non-unicast packets, 742
northbound interface (NBIs) APIs, 632
north-south traffic flow, 28
notifications
      security and, 550
      security information and event management
            (SIEM), 532
Novell, 383
NS (name server) record, 161
nslookup utility, 729–731
NTP (Network Time Protocol), 157, 166–167,
      206–207, 684
NTS (Network Time Security), 167

O

Object Identifiers (OIDs), 519, 522
octet, 110–111
OE (operator error), 650
offboarding, policy for, 547–548
OIDs (Object Identifiers), 519, 522
omni directional antennas, 448
onboarding, policy for, 547–548
on-demand self-service, as a characteristic of cloud
      computing, 613
110 block, 93
onePK, 632
one-time password (OTP), 793–794
one-to-many, 251
online UPS, 588
on-path attack (man-in-the-middle attack), 820
open access, 475–476
Open Impedance Mismatch (echo), 659
open relay, 551
Open Shortest Path First (OSPF)
      as link-state protocol, 346–347, 357–360
      OSPFv3, 371
      use of, 345
Open Systems Interconnection (OSI)
      reference model

about, 55–56, 195, 197
      advantages of, 38
      Application layer of, 40–41
      Data Link layer of, 39, 50–52
      exam essentials, 56
      as hierarchical, 37
      layer functions of, 39
      Network layer of, 39
      origin of, 36
      Physical layer of, 39, 52–53
      Presentation layer of, 39, 41
      protocols of, 41
      review questions, 57–60, 876–878
      Session layer of, 39, 41
      Transport layer of, 39, 41–47
      written lab, 56, 860
OpenFlow, 631
operating mode, 463
operational technology (OT), 845
operator error (OE), 650
OpFlex, 632
optical link budget, 684
Oracle, 211
orchestration, 625–627
organizationally unique identifier (OUI), 114
OSFP. *See* Open Shortest Path First (OSPF)
OSI. *See* Open Systems Interconnection (OSI)
      reference model
OSPFv3, 371
OT (operational technology), 845
OTP (one-time password), 793–794
OUI (organizationally unique identifier), 114
out-of-band management, 412, 502
output errors, 678
output queue drops, 677–678
outside global address, 307
outside local address, 307
overcapacity, unbounded media and,
      664–665
overhead, 43
overlapping channels, 662–663
overloading, 306, 307

P

-p option (`route` command), 737
-p switch, 743–745
PaaS (Platform as a Service), 617
packet, in data encapsulation, 231–232, 233
packet capture, 524–525
Packet InterNet Groper (ping), 299

packet loss, 658
packet shaper, 157, 170–171
packet switching, 178
PAgP (Port Aggregation Protocol), 418
PAN (personal area network), 9–10
Pan/Tilt/Zoom (PTZ) camera feature,
    174, 847–848
passive attacks, 474–475
passphrase, 480, 663
password attacks, 824–825
password policy, 546
passwords
    avoiding common, 832
    for network interface card (NIC), 463
    security and, 550
PAT (port address translation), 306, 307
patch cable, 86
patch management, 548
patches, security and, 551
paths, diversity of, 593–594
Payment Card Industry Data Security Standards
    (PCI DSS), 803
PBX (private branch exchange), 172
PCI DSS (Payment Card Industry Data Security
    Standards), 803
PDUs (power distribution units), 588
PDUs (protocol data units), 53, 230
PEAP (Protected Extensible Authentication
    Protocol), 481–482
peer-to-peer networks, 12–13
performance metrics/sensors
    about, 511, 532
    baselines, 515
    device/chassis, 511–513
    environmental factors/sensors, 665
    exam essentials, 532
    interface errors/alerts, 674–676
    NetFlow data, 526, 710
    network, 513–514
    network device logs, 526–527
    review questions, 534–536, 905–907
    Simple Network Management Protocol
        (SNMP), 518–523
    written lab, 532–533, 869
performance monitoring, 516
permanent DoS, 819
personal area network (PAN), 9–10
phishing, 830
physical access control devices, 136, 174
physical attack, 819
physical carrier sense, 148
physical conditions, 697

Physical layer
    about, 52–53
    data communication equipment (DCE)
        within, 52–53
    data terminal equipment (DTE) within, 52–53
    Ethernet and, 117–123
    features of, 39
    hubs at, of SOHO network, 184–185
    responsibilities of, 231, 234, 324, 325, 326, 327
physical media, 63–82
physical network diagrams, 554–559
physical security
    about, 847
    door locks, 849–850
    equipment locks, 850–851
    video surveillance, 847–849
physical star network, 184–185
physical topologies
    about, 14
    bus topology, 15
    hybrid topology, 22
    mesh topology, 18–19
    point-to-multipoint topology, 20–21
    point-to-point topology, 19–20
    ring topology, 17–18
    selecting, 23–24
    star topology, 16–17
PIDS (protocol based IDS), 145
piggybacking, 830
ping utility, 722–725
pinouts, 657
PKI (Public Key Infrastructure), 481–482,
    786–788
plain old telephone service (POTS) cable, 67
planned downtime, 587
plans, 539–545
Platform as a Service (PaaS), 617
playbooks, 625–626
PLC (Power Line Communication), 124–125
PLC (Programmable Logic Controller), 175, 845
plenum cables, 64, 654
plenum-rated coating, 64
PoE (Power over Ethernet), 419–421, 684–685
pointer record (PTR), 159, 161
point-to-multipoint topology, 20–21
point-to-point link, 17
point-to-point topology, 19–20
policy-based authentication, 634
POP (Post Office Protocol), 206, 211
port address translation (PAT), 306, 307
Port Aggregation Protocol (PAgP), 418
port channeling/bonding, 418

port mirroring/spanning (SPAN/RSPAN), 421–423, 524–525
port numbers, 218–220
port scanners, 710
port sweeping, 710
port tagging, 406–407
ports
  ARP inspection, 415
  bad, 657
  bonding, 417–418
  BPDU guard, 416
  DHCP snooping, 415
  disabling unused, 834
  duplex mismatch, 673
  flood guard, 415–416
  root guard, 416–417
  security, 414, 842
  speed of, 673
  STP and, 394–395
positive acknowledgement with retransmission, 46
Post Office Protocol (POP), 206, 211
postdeployment site survey, 467
POTS (plain old telephone service) cable, 67
power distribution units (PDUs), 588
power failures/anomalies, 693
power levels, 664
Power Line Communication (PLC), 124–125
Power over Ethernet (PoE, PoE+/802.3af, 802.3at), 419–421
power supply redundancy, 583–584
power switch, 649–650
preamble, 115
predeployment site survey, 467
prefix routing, 349
Presentation layer, 39, 41
preshared keys (PSKs), 482
print command, 737
print server, 6
printer, 136, 174
private branch exchange (PBX), 172
private CA, 788–789
private cloud model, 614
private direct connection, 620–621
private IP addresses, 249–251
private networks, 846
procedures, 539–545
Process/Application layer
  of DoD model, 197
  protocols of, 198–220
Programmable Logic Controller (PLC), 175, 845
Project 802 (IEEE), 51–52
Protected Extensible Authentication Protocol (PEAP), 481–482

protocol analyzers/packet capture, 524–525, 707–708
protocol based IDS (PIDS), 145
protocol data units (PDUs), 53, 230
protocols. *See also specific protocols*
  distance-vector (DV) routing protocols, 332–333, 346, 347–356
  exterior gateway protocols (EGPs), 332, 343
  first-hop redundancy protocols (FHRPs), 362–363
  of Host-to-Host layer, 213–220
  interior gateway protocols (IGPs), 332, 343, 360
  of Internet layer, 220–230
  of IPv6, 370–371
  of Process/Application layer, 198–220
  routing protocols, 320, 343–347
  security of, 833–834
  shortest path first protocols, 346–347
  signal degradation and, 457–458
proxy ARP, 693
proxy server, 6, 136, 157, 167–168
PSKs (preshared keys), 482
PSTN (public switched telephone network), 173
PSTN (public switched telephone network) cable, 67
PTR (pointer record), 159, 161
PTZ (Pan/Tilt/Zoom) camera feature, 174, 847–848
public CA, 788–789
public cloud model, 614–615
Public Key Infrastructure (PKI), 481–482, 786–788
public networks, 846
public switched telephone network (PSTN), 173
public switched telephone network (PSTN) cable, 67
PuTTY, 712

Q

QoS (quality of service), 174, 401–402
quad small form-factor pluggable (QSFP), 78
quad-A record (AAAA record), 159, 160
quality of service (QoS), 174, 401–402

R

-r switch, 743
rack diagram, 557–558
radio frequency identification (RFID), 460, 477, 659

radio frequency interference (RFI), 659
Radio Resource Management (RRM), for
    mitigating rogue APs, 472
RADIUS (Remote Authentication Dial-In User
    Service), 403, 477–478, 795–796
range, 802.11 standards and, 446
ransomware, 826–827
Rapid Spanning Tree Protocol (RSTP), 396–397
RARP (Reverse Address Resolution Protocol),
    220, 226–227
rate shifting, 440
RBAC. *See* role-based access control (RBAC)
RDC (Remote Desktop Connection), 620
RDP (Remote Desktop Protocol), 212, 493–494
RDP Gateway, 495
Real-time Transport Protocol (RTP), 212
Recommended Standard 232 (RS-232)
    cable, 80–81
recording equipment, 549–550
records, types of found on DNS servers, 160–161.
    See also specific records
recovery point objective (RPO), 601
recovery sites, 592–593
recovery time objective (RTO), 601
redundancy
    hardware/clusters, 579–587
    high availability and, 591–600
    protocol for, 362–363
Redundant Array of Independent Disks
    (RAID), 584–586
reference model, 3–40
reflected/amplified attacks, 818
reflection, unbounded media and,
    665–666
refraction, unbounded media and, 666
refrigerator, 136
registered jack (RJ) connector
    for Ethernet, 118
    use of, 69–70
regulatory compliance
    about, 801–803
    audits, 805
    policies, processes, and procedures, 804–805
reliable networking, 42
remote access policy, 547
remote access security
    about, 490, 502
    client-to-site VPN, 491–493
    connection methods, 496–501
    exam essentials, 502–503
    in-band management, 502
    jump box/host, 501–502
    out-of-band management, 502
    Remote Desktop Connection, 493–495

Remote Desktop Gateway, 495
review questions, 504–507, 902–905
site-to-site VPN, 490–491
virtual desktop, 496
Virtual Network Computing (VNC), 495–496
written lab, 503, 868
Remote Authentication Dial-In User Service
    (RADIUS), 403, 477–478, 795–796
Remote Desktop Connection (RDC), 493–495, 620
Remote Desktop Protocol (RDP), 212, 493–494
Remote Terminal Unit (RTU), 845
repeater, 136, 185
replay attacks, 479
Representational State Transfer (REST), 498
Request for Comments (RFCs)
    in Class B network, 248
    in Class C network, 248
    RFC 791, 221
    RFC 1487, 209
    RFC 1518, 278
    RFC 1777, 209
    RFC 1918, 249
    RFC 3232, 218
    RFC 3377, 209
    very first ones, 195
Request to Send, Clear to Send (RTS/CTS), 440
resource pooling, as a characteristic of cloud
    computing, 613
resources, for cloud computing, 624
REST (Representational State Transfer), 498
reusable tasks, 625–626
Reverse Address Resolution Protocol (RARP),
    220, 226–227
reverse lookup zone (or table), 162
review questions
    attacks, 854–857, 922–925
    connectors, 97–100, 878–880
    data center architecture, 638–641, 912–915
    documents and policies, 570–573, 907–909
    Ethernet, 129–132, 881–882
    high availability, 605–608, 910–912
    Internet Protocol (IP), 237–249, 885–888
    IP address, 267–270, 311–314, 888–892
    IP routing, 336–339, 892–894
    Layer 2 switching, 426–429, 897–900
    Network Address Translation (NAT),
        311–314, 890–892
    networking devices, 189–192, 883–885
    networks, 31–34, 874–876
    Open Systems Interconnection (OSI) model,
        57–60, 876–878
    performance metrics/sensors,
        534–536, 905–907
    remote access security, 504–507, 902–905

routing, 375–378, 895–897
security, 808–811, 854–857, 920–925
software tools and commands,
    769–773, 917–920
subnetting, 311–314, 890–892
troubleshooting, 701–704, 915–917
virtual local area network (VLAN),
    426–429, 897–900
wireless networking, 485–488, 900–902
RFI (radio frequency interference), 659
RFID (radio frequency identification), 460,
    477, 659
RIB (Routing Information Base), 356
ring topology, 17–18
RIP. See Routing Information
    Protocol (RIP)
RIPng, 370
riser-related cables, 654
RJ. See registered jack (RJ) connector
rogue access point (AP), 822–824
rogue APs, 472
rogue DHCP, 822
role-based access control (RBAC), 799–800
rollback, 540–541
rolled/rollover cable, 89, 499–501, 654–655
root CA, 786
root domains, 158
root guard, 416–417
rootkits, 828
round-robin load balancing, 347
route command, 735–738
route redistribution, 355
routed protocols, 48, 320
router advertisement, 363–365
router interface, 143
routers
    about, 48–50
    advantage of using in network, 178
    defined, 9
    described, 140–141
    purpose of, 178, 182–183
    redundancy and, 581–583
    virtual, 619
route-update packets (Network layer), 48
routing
    about, 371
    asymmetrical, 684
    basics of, 320–323
    exam essentials, 372
    issues with, 692
    protocols of, 320, 343–347
    review questions, 375–378, 895–897

by rumor, 347
written lab, 372–374, 866–867
Routing Information Base (RIB), 356
Routing Information Protocol (RIP).
    See also RIPng
    about, 345, 346, 349, 350, 358, 370
    hop count within, 49
    Version 2 (RIPv2), 349–350, 358
routing loops, 692
routing protocols
    administrative distances (AD),
        344–346
    basics of, 343–347
    classes of, 346–347
    defined, 320
routing table, 178, 321, 354–355
RPO (recovery point objective), 601
RRM (Radio Resource Management), for
    mitigating rogue APs, 472
RS-232 (Recommended Standard 232)
    cable, 80–81
RSTP (Rapid Spanning Tree Protocol), 396–397
RTO (recovery time objective), 601
RTP (Real-time Transport Protocol), 212
RTS/CTS (Request to Send, Clear to Send), 440
RTU (Remote Terminal Unit), 845
runts, 677

S

-s switch, 743
SA (source address), 116
SaaS (Software as a Service), 616–617
SAML (Security Assertion Markup Language), 795
SANs (storage area networks), 10
Sarbanes-Oxley Act (SOX), 801–802, 803
SASE (Secure Access Secure Edge), 634–635
SBI (southbound interface) APIs, 631–632
SC (square (subscriber) connector), 73
SCADA (Supervisory Control and Data
    Acquisition), 175, 844–846
scalability, of cloud computing, 623
scheduled scans, 515
scope options, 152
screened subnet (demilitarized zone), 145, 165
SDN. See software-defined networking (SDN)
SDWAN (software-defined wide area network), 10
Secure Access Secure Edge (SASE), 634–635
Secure Digital (SD) card, 584
Secure File Transfer Protocol (SFTP), 620–621
Secure File Transfer Protocol (TCP 22), 199

Secure Shell (SSH) protocol, 199, 496
Secure Sockets Layer (SSL), 209, 211
secure web gateway (SWG), 635
SecureCRT, 712
security
    AAA model, 790–801
    about, 805–806, 851–852
    certificates, 785–790
    CIA triad, 782–783
    encryption, 783–785
    exam essentials, 806, 852
    hardening, 545–553, 831–837
    implications and considerations for, 623–624
    Media Access Control (MAC) authentication/
        MAC filtering, 476–477
    network segmentation, 837–847
    open access, 475–476
    physical, 847–851
    ports, 414
    of protocols, 833–834
    Public Key Infrastructure (PKI), 481–482
    regulatory compliance, 801–805
    Remote Authentication Dial-In User Service
        (RADIUS), 477–478
    review questions, 808–811, 854–857, 920–925
    segmentation and, 837–838
    service set identifier (SSID), 476–477
    Temporal Key Integrity Protocol
        (TKIP), 478–479
    terminology, 777–789
    threats, 778–779
    vulnerabilities, 779–781
    Wi-Fi Protected Access (WPA),
        479–482
    wired equivalent privacy (WEP),
        476–477
    wireless, 471–482
    WPA2 pre-shared key, 479–482
    written lab, 807, 853, 872
Security Assertion Markup Language (SAML), 795
security audits, 549, 564–565
security information and event management
    (SIEM), 531–532
security log, 528
security policies, 548–553
Security Service Edge (SSE), 635
segments/segmentation
    in data encapsulation, 231–232
    network, 25
    troubleshooting, 652
self-signed certificates, 789–790
serial cables, 80–82

server locks, 851
Server Message Block (SMB), 209
Server mode (VTP), 410
servers
    about, 167
    network, 6–7
    redundancy and, 583–586
    troubleshooting, 651–652
service models, 616–618
service provider links, 25
service set identifier (SSID), 463, 476–477, 663
Service-Level Agreement (SLA), 567
service-related entry points, 25
services
    disabling unnecessary, 833
    unresponsive, 683–684
Session Initiation Protocol (SIP), 212
Session layer (OSI reference model),
    39, 41
session secret, 479
severity levels, 530–531
SFF (small form factor) connector,
    73–75
SFP (small form-factor pluggable) transceiver, 78
SFP+ (enhanced small form-factor pluggable)
    transceiver, 78
SFP/GBIC (cable mismatch), 660–661
SFTP (Secure File Transfer Protocol), 620–621
shared keys, 463–464
shielded twisted-pair (STP) cable, 66, 653–654
short circuit, 659
Short Message Service (SMS), for multifactor
    authentication, 793
Shortest Path Bridging (SPB), 371
shortest path first protocols, 346–347
shoulder surfing, 831
show arp command, 760
show cdp neighbors command, 749–752
show config, 749
show interface command, 756–759
show inventory command, 754
show ip interface command, 759–760
show ip route command, 752–753
show mac-address-table command, 756
show power command, 762
show running-config, 748–749
show switch command, 755
show version command, 753
show vlan command, 760–762
signal degradation, 457–459
signal strength, unbounded media and, 664
signal-to-noise ratio, unbounded media and, 666

signing certificates, 788
Simple Mail Transfer Protocol (SMTP), 200, 210
Simple Network Management Protocol (SNMP)
    about, 207–208, 518
    authentication, 522–523
    community name, 521
    Management Information Bases (MIBs), 522
    Object Identifiers (OIDs), 519, 522
    traps, 519–521
    versions, 521–522
simplex mode, 41
simultaneous wired/wireless connections, with
    unbounded media (wireless), 662
single sign-on (SSO), 794–795
single-mode fiber to Ethernet converter, 78
single-mode fiber-optic (SMF) cable, 71–72
single-mode to multimode fiber converter, 79–80
SIP (Session Initiation Protocol), 212
site survey
    about, 466–467
    capacity, 468–469
    location-based WLAN, 470
    multiple floors, 469–470
    report for, 562–563
    tools for, 470–471
site-to-site VPN, 490–491
6to4 tunneling, 261–262, 367–368
66 block, 93
SLA (Service-Level Agreement), 567
SLAAC (stateless address
    autoconfiguration), 259–260
small form factor (SFF) connector, 73–75
small form-factor pluggable (SFP) transceiver, 78
small office, home office (SOHO) network
    about, 475
    determining requirements of, 176–184
    environmental considerations of, 185
    hubs at Physical layer of, 184–185
    planning and implementing of basic on using
        network segmentation, 175–185
    switches and bridges at Data Link layer
        of, 183–184
small office, home office (SOHO) router, 140, 142
smart antennas, 443
smart doorbells, 136, 843
smart jack, 25, 94
smart speakers, 136, 843
smart thermostats, 136, 843
SMB (Server Message Block), 209
SMF (single-mode fiber-optic) cable, 71–72
SMTP (Simple Mail Transfer Protocol), 200, 210
SNAT (static NAT), 306, 307–309

SNMP. *See* Simple Network Management
    Protocol (SNMP)
Snowden, Edward, 785
SOA (start of authority) record, 161
social engineering attacks, 829–830
software
    checking configurations, 696–697
    troubleshooting, 651
software address, 220–221
Software as a Service (SaaS), 616–617
software tools and commands
    about, 707, 766–767
    Address Resolution Protocol (ARP), 725–726
    `arp` utility, 726–729
    bandwidth speed testers, 708–710
    connectivity software, 711–712
    exam essentials, 767–768
    hardware tools, 762–766
    `ifconfig` utility, 720
    IP scanner, 712
    `ip` utility, 720–721
    `ipconfig` utility, 715–719
    `iptables` utility, 721
    `Mtr` utility (`pathping`), 732–733
    `nbstat` utility, 738–747
    NetFlow analyzers, 710
    `netstat` utility, 738–747
    networking device commands, 748–752
    Nmap utility, 734–735
    `nslookup` utility, 729–731
    `ping` utility, 722–725
    port scanners, 710
    protocol analyzers/packet capture,
        524–525, 707–708
    resolving names with Hosts file, 731–732
    review questions, 769–773, 917–920
    `route` command, 735–738
    `tcpdump` utility, 747
    `traceroute`/`tracert`, 712–715
    Trivial File Transfer Protocol (TFTP) server, 711
    written lab, 768, 871
software-defined networking (SDN)
    application layer, 629
    benefits of, 628–629
    components of, 629–632
    control layer, 629–630
    infrastructure layer, 630
    management plane, 630–631
    spine-leaf-based two-tier networks, 630
software-defined wide area network (SDWAN), 10
SOHO (small office, home office) router, 140, 142
source address (SA), 116

source control, 627–628
southbound interface (SBI) APIs, 631–632
SOX (Sarbanes-Oxley Act), 801–802, 803
Spanning Tree Algorithm (STA), 393
Spanning Tree Protocol (STP)
    about, 392–394, 633, 691–692
    convergence, 395–396
    port states, 394–395
    Rapid Spanning Tree Protocol (RSTP), 396–397
SPAN/RSPAN (port mirroring/spanning), 421–423
SPB (Shortest Path Bridging), 371
speakers, smart, 843
speakers, smart speakers, 136
speed
    802.11 standards and, 446
    of ports, 673
spine and leaf switching, 27–28
spine-leaf-based two-tier networks, 630
split MAC, 454–455
split pairs, 659
split tunneling, 491–493
spyware, 828
SQL (Structured Query Language) Server, 211
SQLnet, 211
SQL*Net, 211
square (subscriber) connector (SC), 73
SRV record, 161
SSE (Security Service Edge), 635
SSH (Secure Shell) protocol, 199, 496
SSID (service set identifier), 463, 476–477, 663
SSL (Secure Sockets Layer), 209, 211
SSL certificate, untrusted, 680–682
SSO (single sign-on), 794–795
ST (straight tip) connector, 72
STA (Spanning Tree Algorithm), 393
StackWise technology, 580–581
standard operating procedures, 544–545
Standby Timer (HSRP), 598
standby UPS, 588
star topology, 16–17
start of authority (SOA) record, 161
Start of Frame Delimiter (SOF)/Synch, 115
state transitions, 52
state/configuration, 601
stateless address autoconfiguration
    (SLAAC), 259–260
static assignment, 150
static IP addressing, 204
static NAT (SNAT), 306, 307–309
static routing, 321, 331–334
static VLANs, 402–403
storage area networks (SANs), 10

storage redundancy, 584–586
STP. *See* Spanning Tree Protocol (STP)
STP (shielded twisted-pair) cable, 66, 653–654
straight tip (ST) connector, 72
straight-through cable, 86–87
stratum levels, 167
Structured Query Language (SQL)
    Server, 211
subnet mask, 679, 736–738
subnetting
    about, 309
    basics of, 273–296
    benefits of, 274
    Class A, 928–933
    Class B addresses, 289–296
    Class C addresses, 279–289
    Classless Inter-Domain Routing
        (CIDR), 276–278
    exam essentials, 309–310
    how to create, 274–275
    review questions, 311–314, 890–892
    subnet masks, 276
    written lab, 310, 864–865, 931–933
subscriber (square) connector (SC), 73
successor route, 355
Supervisory Control and Data Acquisition
    (SCADA), 175, 844–846
SWG (secure web gateway), 635
Switch Port Analyzer (SPAN) and Remote
    SPAN, 421–423
switch stacking, 579–581
switches. *See also specific switches*
    about, 139–140, 178, 181–182, 183–184
    clustering, 581
    defined, 3
    placement of, 665
    redundancy and, 579–581
    virtual, 619
switching loops, 691–692
switching services, 385–392
symmetrical encryption, 785
syslog, 209–210, 528–531
system life cycle, 544
system log, 528

T

T1 crossover cable, 89–90
T568A wiring standard, 85–86
T568B wiring standard, 85–86
tabletop exercises, 602

TACACS+ (Terminal Access Controller Access Control System Plus), 796–797
tailgating, 830
tap, 765
tapping the wire, 83
TCP. *See* Transmission Control Protocol (TCP)
TCP 23 (Telnet), 200, 497
TCP segment format, 214–216
tcpdump utility, 747
TCP/IP. *See* Transmission Control Protocol/Internet Protocol (TCP/IP)
TCP/UDP ports, blocked, 682
TDM (time-division multiplexing), 55
TDMA (time-division multiple access), 436
technology-based attacks, 817–829
Telecommunications Industry Association (TIA), 557
telephony server, 6
Telnet (TCP 23), 200, 497
temperature, as an environmental concern, 511–512
templates, 625–626
Temporal Key Integrity Protocol (TKIP), 478–479
10Base2, 118
10Base5, 118
10BaseT, 119
Teredo, 369
Terminal Access Controller Access Control System Plus (TACACS+), 796–797
testing
    about, 602
    tabletop exercises, 602
    validation tests, 602–603
testing, security and, 551
TFTP (Trivial File Transfer Protocol), 204–205, 833–834
TFTP (Trivial File Transfer Protocol) server, 711
thermostats, smart, 843
thermostats, smart thermostats, 136
thicknet, 118
Thin Ethernet (thinnet), 64
thin protocol, 216
thinnet, 118
threats
    categories of, 778–779
    wireless, 471–475
3G, 436, 437
three-tiered model, 26–27
three-way handshake, 42–43, 213
TIA (Telecommunications Industry Association), 557

time, incorrect, 682
time to live (TTL) value, 162, 820
time-based hardware/software tokens, for multifactor authentication, 793–794
time-based one-time password (TOTP), 794
time-division multiple access (TDMA), 436
time-division multiplexing (TDM), 55
TKIP (Temporal Key Integrity Protocol), 478–479
TLS (Transport Layer Security), 209
TNS (Transparent Network Substrate), 211
tone generator, 763–764
toner probe, 763–764
tools, hardware, 762–766
top-level domains, 158
topology table, 354–355, 357
Top-to-Bottom/Bottom-to-Top OSI model, 686
TOTP (time-based one-time password), 794
TPC (Transmit Power Control), 442
Traceroute, 299
traceroute/tracert, 712–715
Tracert, 299
tracking, security and, 550
traffic analysis, 515–516
traffic flow, 28–29
traffic logs, 57
transceivers
    about, 77–78
    incorrect, 657
    mismatch, 657
Transmission Control Protocol (TCP)
    connection-oriented communication, 42–43
    as Host-to-Host layer protocol, 213–216
    key concepts of, 217–228
    segment format, 214–216
    Transport layer and, 41–42
Transmission Control Protocol/Internet Protocol (TCP/IP)
    about, 7, 652
    brief history of, 195–196
    creation of, 195
    and DoD model, 196–198
    pinging, 722
    traceroute/tracert and, 712–715
transmission speeds, of cables, 82
Transmit and Received (TX/RX) Reversed, 659
Transmit Power Control (TPC), 442
transparent bridge, 138, 184
Transparent mode (VTP), 409, 411
Transparent Network Substrate (TNS), 211
transport agnostic, as a benefit of SDN, 629

Transport Control Protocol (TCP), 163
Transport layer
    about, 41–42
    acknowledgements within, 46–47
    connection-oriented communication
        within, 42–43
    in data encapsulation, 230–234
    features of, 39
    flow control within, 43–45
    Host-to-Host layer also known as, 197, 202
    port numbers for, 218, 223, 307–309
    separation of data at, 330
    use of UDP at, 163, 202
    windowing within, 45–46
    as working with Network layer, 222, 231–232
Transport Layer Security (TLS), 209
traps, 519–521
Trivial File Transfer Protocol (TFTP),
        204–205, 833–834
Trivial File Transfer Protocol (TFTP) server, 711
Trojan horses, 827–828
troubleshooting
    about, 646–647, 698
    cables, 652–666
    exam essentials, 699–700
    hardware vs. software, 651
    login procedure/rights, 647–648
    network connection LED status
        indicators, 648–649
    network segments, 652
    operator error, 650
    power switch, 649–650
    review questions, 701–704, 915–917
    steps for, 666–695
    tips for, 695–698
    unbounded media (wireless),
        661–666
    workstation vs. server, 651–652
    written lab, 700, 871
trunk ports, 404–405
TTL (time to live) value, 162, 820
Tunneled Transport Layer Security (TTLS), 482
tunneling, 366–369
25-pair cable, 93
twinaxial cable, 66–67
twisted-pair cable, 66
2.4 GHz (802.11b), 439–440
2.4 GHz (802.11g), 440–441
2.4 GHz/5 GHz (802.11n), 443–444
2G, 436–437
TX/RX (Transmit and Received) Reversed, 659

TXT (DKIM) record, 160
TXT (SPF) record, 160
Type field, 116

U

UDP (User Datagram Protocol), 41–42, 163,
        214, 216–217
ultra physical contact (UPC), 76
unbounded media issues (wireless), 661–666
unicast addresses, 252
unicast packets, 742
unified threat management (UTM) devices, 173
unintentional/friendly DoS, 819
uninterruptible power supply (UPS),
        587–588
Universal Serial Bus (USB), 81–82
Unix, BSD version of, 196
unknown protocols, 743
unknown unicast flood blocking (UUFB), 415–416
unknown unicast flood rate-limiting
        (UUFRL), 415–416
unmanaged switches, 140, 412
unreliable protocol, 216
unshielded twisted-pair (UTP) cable
    about, 653–654
    categories of, 67–69
    connecting, 69–70
    defined, 66
    for Ethernet, 118
    gigabit wiring of, 88–89
untested updates, 664
UPC (ultra physical contact), 76
updates
    driver, 548
    firmware, 548
upgrades, 627
UPS (uninterruptible power supply),
        587–588
US Environmental Protection Agency (EPA), 591
USB (Universal Serial Bus), 81–82
USB locks, 851
User Datagram Protocol (UDP), 41–42, 163,
        214, 216–217
UTM (unified threat management) devices, 173
UTP. See unshielded twisted-pair (UTP)
        cable
UUFB (unknown unicast flood blocking), 415–416
UUFRL (unknown unicast flood
        rate-limiting), 415–416

V

validation tests, 602–603
variable-length subnet mask (VLSM), 253–254, 276, 350–353
version control, 627
versions, SNMP, 521–522
very high throughput (VHT), 444
video surveillance, 847–849
virtual circuit, 42
virtual desktops, 496
Virtual eXtensible Local Area Network (VXLAN), 633
virtual firewall, 619
virtual IP address, 250
virtual LANs (VLANs)
    about, 180–181
    hopping, 821
    incorrect, 673
virtual local area network (VLAN). *See also* Layer 2 switching
    about, 180–181, 397–409, 424
    dynamic, 403
    exam essentials, 424–425
    hopping, 821
    identifying, 403–405
    incorrect, 673
    memberships, 402
    quality of service (QoS), 401–402
    review questions, 426–429, 897–900
    static, 402–403
    trunking protocol, 409–418
    written lab, 425, 867
virtual MAC address, 362, 596–597
Virtual Network Computing (VNC), 495–496
virtual network interface card (vNIC), 26
virtual networking, 25–26
virtual private cloud (VPC), 619
Virtual Private Network (VPN)
    about, 620
    clientless, 491
    client-to-site, 491–493
    site-to-site, 490–491
virtual router, 619
Virtual Router Redundancy Protocol (VRRP), 362, 595–600
virtual switch (vSwitch), 25–26, 619
virtual terminals, 411
viruses
    about, 829
    checking for, 698

visual fault locator, 766
VLAN. *See* virtual local area network (VLAN)
VLAN Management Policy Server (VMPS), 403
VLAN Trunking Protocol (VTP)
    about, 409–410
    IP addresses and, 411–413
    modes of operation, 410–411
VLSM (variable-length subnet mask), 253–254, 276, 350–353
VMPS (VLAN Management Policy Server), 403
VMware Remote Console, 621
VNC (Virtual Network Computing), 495–496
vNIC (virtual network interface card), 26
voice access ports, 404
voice calls, for multifactor authentication, 793
voice gateway, 136
voice security information and event management (vSIEM), 531
VoIP endpoint, 157, 172
VoIP gateway, 157, 173
VoIP PBX, 157, 172
VoIP phone, 136, 174
VPC (virtual private cloud), 619
VPN. *See* Virtual Private Network (VPN)
VPN concentrator headend, 157, 171
VPN headend, 136
VRRP (Virtual Router Redundancy Protocol), 362, 595–600
vSIEM (voice security information and event management), 531
vSwitch (virtual switch), 25–26
VTP. *See* VLAN Trunking Protocol (VTP)
vulnerabilities, categories of, 779–781
VXLAN (Virtual eXtensible Local Area Network), 633

W

walls, signal degradation and, 457
WAN. *See* wide area network (WAN)
WAP (wireless access point), 447–448
war driving, 475
warm sites, 592
waveform, 55
wavelength
    about, 107
    mismatch, 661
web proxy server, 168
web server, 6
well-known port numbers, 218
WEP (wired equivalent privacy), 463, 476–477

wide area network (WAN)
    about, 8–9
    troubleshooting, 652
wide local area network (WLAN)
    installing and configuring hardware, 460–466
    location-based, 470
WiFi 6 (802.11ax), 444–445
Wi-Fi Alliance, 434, 443
Wi-Fi Analyzers, 765
Wi-Fi Protected Access (WPA), 463, 478, 479–482
windowing, Transport layer and, 45–46
wire tapping, 83
wired equivalent privacy (WEP), 463, 476–477
wireless access point (WAP), 447–448
wireless antennas, 448–450
wireless channel, for network interface card
    (NIC), 463
wireless controllers, 453–456
wireless LAN controller (WLC), 147, 472
wireless network interface card (NIC), 448
wireless networking
    about, 433–436, 482
    cellular technologies, 436–437
    components, 447–450
    802.11 standards, 438–446
    exam essentials, 483–484
    installing, 450–466
    review questions, 485–488, 900–902
    security, 471–482
    site survey, 466–471
    written lab, 484, 868
wireless range extender, 136, 147
wireless standard, 663–664
wireless threats, 471–475
wiring
    diagrams for, 560–561
    installing distributions, 92–94
    security and, 550
    standards for, 84–92
WLAN. *See* wide local area network (WLAN)
WLAN Association (WLANA), 434
WLC (wireless LAN controller), 147, 472
Word (Microsoft), Application layer and, 41
workgroup, 3
workstations
    auto-detecting by, 109
    carrier sense multiple access with collision
        detection (CSMA/CD) and, 105–106

network, 5–6, 7–8
    troubleshooting, 651–652
WPA (Wi-Fi Protected Access), 463, 478, 479–482
WPA2 pre-shared key, 479–482
WPA3-SAE encryption, 480
written lab
    attacks, 853, 872
    connectors, 95–96, 860
    data center architecture, 636–637, 870–871
    documents and policies, 568–569, 869
    Ethernet, 127–128, 861–862
    high availability, 604, 870
    Internet Protocol (IP), 236, 862
    IP address, 265–266, 310, 863–865
    IP routing, 335, 865
    Layer 2 switching, 425, 867
    Network Address Translation (NAT),
        310, 864–865
    networking devices, 187–188, 862
    networks, 30, 860
    Open Systems Interconnection (OSI)
        model, 56, 860
    performance metrics/sensors, 532–533, 869
    remote access security, 503, 868
    routing, 372–374, 866–867
    security, 807, 853, 872
    software tools and commands, 768, 871
    subnetting, 310, 864–865, 931–933
    troubleshooting, 700, 871
    virtual local area network (VLAN), 425, 867

    wireless networking, 484, 868

Y

Yagis, 449

Z

zero trust architecture (ZTA), 633–634
zero-day attacks, 781
zero-touch provisioning, as a benefit of SDN, 628
zone updates, 163
ZTA (zero trust architecture), 633–634
Z-Wave, 460

Online Test Bank

To help you study for your CompTIA Network+ certification exam, register to gain one year of FREE access after activation to the online interactive test bank—included with your purchase of this book! All of the chapter review questions and the practice tests in this book are included in the online test bank so you can practice in a timed and graded setting.

Register and Access the Online Test Bank

To register your book and get access to the online test bank, follow these steps:

1. Go to www.wiley.com/go/sybextestprep. You'll see the **"How to Register Your Book for Online Access"** instructions.
2. Click "here to register" and then select your book from the list.
3. Complete the required registration information, including answering the security verification to prove book ownership. You will be emailed a pin code.
4. Follow the directions in the email or go to www.wiley.com/go/sybextestprep.
5. Find your book on that page and click the "Register or Login" link with it. Then enter the pin code you received and click the "Activate PIN" button.
6. On the Create an Account or Login page, enter your username and password, and click Login or, if you don't have an account already, create a new account.
7. At this point, you should be in the test bank site with your new test bank listed at the top of the page. If you do not see it there, please refresh the page or log out and log back in.